REPORTS OF CASES IN THE COURT OF EXCHEQUER IN THE TIME OF KING GEORGE I

(1714 TO 1727)

Volume II:

Cases 403 to 675

403

Rex v. Mann

(Ex. 1723–1727)

A writ of execution, including a prerogative writ of extent, cannot be antedated so as to defeat the priorities of the creditors of a bankrupt.

An irregularity in a writ of execution should be challenged upon a simple motion rather than upon a plea.

Harvard Law School MS. 1082, vol. 1, p. 165, pl. 2

[May 1723.]

Mann was assignee of the commissioners of bankruptcy against the two Norcotts. The two Norcotts were bound for Jay and Douce, receivers of the County of Huntingdon.

On 4th October, the commissioners against Norcotts make an assignment dated 4th of October 7 [Geo.]. The *fiat* for extents against Norcott [was dated] 5th of October. But two of them bear *teste* the 6th of July and two the 6th of October.

Mr. *Foley* [said] that these two extents dated 6th of July are void being antedated. Stat. 33 Hen. VIII, cap. 39.[1] Authority is given by that Act to this court to issue this process upon a certificate, which the course of the court has explained to be an affidavit. No [writ of] extent can issue until there had been an award for such extents. Here is no warrant for these extents on the 6th of July, the *fiat* being subsequent to them. As a court of revenue, it is always open, and, so, as a court of equity. And the adjournment at the end of the term does not extend to the court in this consideration. And the reason why executions in vacation are tested as of the preceding term in other courts is out of necessity because they are adjourned. It may be attended with very ill consequence of this method of antedating, for, Cro. Car. 149,[2] goods are bound from the *teste* of the extent.

Sir Constantine Phipps, pro eodem: The bond to account is only the 2nd of July, which is only four days before the *teste* of the extents. Upon the affidavits, it appears to be only an extent in aid of Jay and Douce, and, therefore, process should have first gone upon the extent against Jay and Douce. See 6th Rule 15 Car. I. The extent ought by the course of the court to bear *teste* the day of the *fiat* or after, but not before. All is of consequence for that it will overreach all fair traders etc. in the meantime.

---

[1] Stat. 33 Hen. VIII, c. 39, s. 37 (*SR*, III, 886–887).

[2] *Audley v. Halsey* (1629), Croke Car. 148, 79 E.R. 731, also W. Jones 202, 82 E.R. 107.

[To the] objection of Quash's Case,[1] [he] responded, because it was antedated, *per totam curiam*, that extents were set aside.

[To the] objection of the case of a [writ of] *fieri facias*, [he] responded, at common law, it is so out of necessary, but, now, by the Statute of Frauds,[2] it only binds from the delivery to the sheriff, which seems to be done to prevent the inconveniences. Here, the extent may be tested in vacation. And, therefore, it ought not to bind but from the warrant.

Mr. *Fazakerly*: A *fiat* is necessary, but there can issue no more than one extent upon one *fiat*. Query. Note this is the usual course. If no extent can issue without a warrant by a *fiat*, then it cannot appear in this case there was any warrant. It is contradictory to the writ itself, which says it issues by virtue of a *fiat*. If original writs may be antedated, the Statute of Limitations will be of no effect. And they may be antedated as well as extents. In common law courts, the executions bear *teste* in term out of necessity, which is not in this case, which may be in a vacation time. The reason of the legislature in respect of creditors by making a *fieri facias* bind the property only from the delivery etc. will equally extend to this case. Mann would not have been at the extreme in suing out of a commission of bankruptcy if he had known of this extent thus made prior.

Mr. *Ward*, *pro eodem*: No extent can issue in vacation time but by warrant from one of the barons. If an application had been made to a baron the 6th of July, which was only four days after the bond, could any affidavit have been made that the crown debt was in danger? The *fiat* is that which gives life to the extent.

[To the] objection this court has a right of forming a new process by 33 Hen. VIII, [he] responded but that must be *secundum sanam discretionem*. The Case of Quash was in 1713. Co., lib. 11, Sir Gerard Fleetwood's Case.[3] As to the lien, he admitted that the crown is not within the Statute of Frauds and Perjuries. Whatever inconvenience may have arisen to the crown arises upon their own act by making scriveners etc. security contrary to the rule. Faringdon v. Eliot, Trinity 1722; Bowdage's Case;[4] an extent was renewed there by a special order, the first not being completely served by the fraud of the party.

Mr. *Raby*, for the king: The bond binds the lands from the time it is entered into. Here, the case is between the subject and the crown. In the Case of Quash,

[1] *Regina v. Quash* (1713), Parker 281, 145 E.R. 780, Dodd 365.

[2] Stat. 29 Car. II, c. 3, s. 15 (*SR*, V, 841).

[3] *Regina v. Quash* (1713), *ut supra*; *Fleetwood's Case* (1610), 8 Coke Rep. 171, 77 E.R. 731.

[4] *Rex v. Bowdage* (Ex. 1717), see above, Case No. 32, note also *Attorney General v. Bowdage* (1709), Parker 277, 145 E.R. 779, Dodd 218, Lincoln's Inn MS. Misc. 535, f. [214], Georgetown Univ. Law Sch. MS. B88–9, f. 340v (Edward Ward's Reports), Public Record Office, E.127/26, f. 70, Public Record Office, E.127/27, f. 33, Public Record Office, E.126/19, ff. 166, 192v.

it was between the crown and the crown. Secondly, there was no warrant to issue the writ in that case.

[To the] objection it was irregular, being tested before the warrant, [he] responded a [writ of] *certiorari* must be by *fiat* in vacation time and is tested [as] of the precedent term, so must all judicial processes; Lutwyche 333, Aldworth; Lestrange v. Keys College, Trinity 5 Geo. R., rot. 1676, in the Common Bench; see former book; Bayley v. Burneing, 1 Levinz, 1 Siderfin.[1] An immediate assignment may now be made, which is a reason that this method of antedating ought to be encouraged.

Mr. *Bootle*: There being an inquisition taken and returned, query whether they ought not to plead this matter and not come by way of motion. King v. Ashly. It is proper in this case to have an immediate extent, and there is no necessity to have an extent and inquisition first against Jay and Douce, for the Norcotts are jointly bound to the crown. And, in the case of receivers, it is not necessary to mention in the affidavit that they are indebted or that the debt is in danger whoever receives the crown's money. The crown's money may follow that in whosoever's hands it is.

[To the] objection of the antedate, [he] responded the crown had far greater advantages even at common law than the subject before the Stat. 33 Hen. VIII. Dyer 224; Sir William Herbert, Lib. 3; Plowden.[2] And if the crown shall not be allowed this privilege, as is contended for, now, it will be in a worse case than the subject.

[To the] objection that it is preposterous that an extent should be precedent to a *fiat*, [he] responded this is only to be considered as a judicial process and not to be compared to the case of an original. The *fiat* is only a mere warrant from one baron, but the writ is *per barones*, and this proves it to be the act of the court. And the *fiat* is only to prevent the objection in court to issuing these writs *ad libitum*. When the writ is once issued, it is to be considered as the judicial act of the court and, therefore, to be pleaded. If an extent may be dated as of the term before, then the *fiat* is not so material. Hardres 125.[3]

N.B. in the case of judgments, it may, but not upon bonds.

Sir Constantine Phipps replies: [To the] objection it is proper to plead, [he] responded, in the Case of Ashley, it was proper on motion, and that is to come on again.

---

[1] *Aldworth v. Hutchinson* (1688), 1 Lutwyche 329, 125 E.R. 173; *Baily v. Bunning* (1665), 1 Levinz 173, 83 E.R. 355, 1 Siderfin 271, 82 E.R. 1100, also 1 Keble 638, 930, 932, 83 E.R. 1157, 1326, 1327, 2 Keble 32, 84 E.R. 21.

[2] *Seyntloo's Case* (1563), 2 Dyer 224, 73 E.R. 497, also Jenkins 226, 145 E.R. 157; *Harbert's Case* (1584), 3 Coke Rep. 11, 76 E.R. 647, also Moore K.B. 169, 72 E.R. 510; *Davy v. Pepys* (1573), 2 Plowden 438, 75 E.R. 658.

[3] *Attorney General, ex rel. Ceely v. Bagg* (1658), Hardres 125, 145 E.R. 413.

An extent upon a *fiat* will go into several counties, but, into the same county, it cannot unless there is some fraud. Upon a judgment, the king's prerogative was as mentioned, but, upon a bond, no extent could issue but by the Stat. 33 Hen. VIII.

[To the] objection a trial is not necessary, [he] responded, by that Statute, it is necessary. Upon a judgment for the crown, [there is] no occasion for a *fiat* at common law, but it is otherwise upon a statute.

Lord Chief Baron [MONTAGU]: This is an execution, as said, of what? What is to be executed on? Why the *mandatum* of the baron? Can there be an execution if the mandate is before the mandate is made? In the cases of *fieri facias*, it is the execution of the judgment and it is to bear *teste* accordingly.

[To the] objection, at common law, the king might take body, lands, and goods, [he] responded but not altogether, but one after another. The king has [. . .] the same powers upon judgments obtained by the crown, but not upon bonds, but only according to 33 Hen. VIII.

Baron GILBERT: Before the Statute of Frauds and Perjuries, the crown would be in a worse case than the subject if it could not antedate their extents. But then, there ought to be precedents searched if there were any antedating before that Statute. Otherwise, it would be hard to establish such a prerogative.

Baron PAGE: Before the Stat. 33 Hen. VIII, the king might antedate an extent which was at common law, and it is not a new process. The Stat. 33 Hen. VIII has made all bonds to the crown in the nature of a statute staple. The process is not upon the warrant, but upon the condition, which is a statute staple. I think this warrant is only for a check upon the clerks. It is a writ issued by the court, and it is an issuing out of their own process, and, if it is, [it is] discretionary.

Baron PRICE: I believe there is no precedent of extents upon bonds issuing without fiats. But the mischief here in this case was not foreseen. There is no receiver now but does employ a trader, and yet it is against the Rules of 15 Car. II. I do not think the *fiat* so essential a part of an extent but that it may be good without. And we shall only punish the clerk for issuing it without a *fiat*.

[The case is] to be spoken to again.

Taussig MS. 311, vol. 1, p. 494

Easter term 1723.

[There is] no instance of any [writ of] extent tested before the *fiat* except in Quash's Case, where it was set aside on solemn argument for that very reason. This case is not like to a *fieri facias*, first, because there was no application to the court to take out a [writ of] *fieri facias*, otherwise in the case of an extent; second, a *fieri facias* must bear *teste* on the last day of the term, but an extent may bear *teste* in vacation.

Fazakerly: If a *fiat* be necessary, then the power to issue an extent is executed by one extent and one cannot take out 1000.

Second, it is improper to antedate, for no writ of this sort can issue without a *fiat*, but this writ, as all others, is said to issue at the time it bears *teste* and so it must be pleaded. Therefore, it issued and was depending before the *fiat*.

The common law bound goods from the *teste* of the writ. But the Statute of Frauds and Perjuries altered this for the inconvenience arising thereby and made the property bound only from the time of the delivery of that writ to the sheriff.

He insists very strongly on the inconveniences of overreaching honest creditors.

The *teste* of common law process is from necessity, but here is no necessity. Antedating deeds is severely punished by the courts of justice, but with what face can they do this while they are antedating process themselves.

This case came on upon the Master's report. This extent bears *teste* four days after the very bond was entered into. Trinity 1713, Quash's Case. There must be an affidavit to warrant the *fiat*. And this affidavit could not have been made at the time this extent bears date for, at that time, the Norcotts were in full credit, though they did fail in October after.

Raby, e contra: The bond was dated 2 July, the extent issued 6 July, and so the bond was not forfeited. This may be pleaded if there is any hope in this point. Quash's Case is only a single instance. That case differs, for there was only a controversy between two different sets of the crown officers. This is a controversy between the crown and a subject. In all cases where the writs do issue by a warrant, they are antedated, as affidavits to have the writ quashed by the judge for special bail. So in cases of *certiorari* to remove causes, which must be warranted by a *fiat*, they bear date *ultimo die termini* though the *fiat* be signed in the middle of the vacation. Lutw. 333;[1] Lestrange's Case, Trinity 5 George, roll 1676, in the Common Bench; he gives a warrant of attornment to confess judgment on 18 August, he died 19, the judgment was signed 20, execution was *teste* of the precedent term. And this was held well.

The Statute of Frauds and Perjuries does not bind the crown so that the law remains in the case of the crown as it was in the case of a subject before the Statute of Frauds and Perjuries.

If the king has a prerogative to *teste* his writ in vacation time, which a subject cannot do, it is a strange way of arguing that he may not do what the subject may, since he may do more. 1 Syd., Bailey and Bunning's Case. If this may not be done, the crown will never be satisfied, for the subject will have the first notice. In the case of a judgment for the king, the writ may be tested back to the last day of the term. Why not in this case?

Bootle: This question may come on and be taken advantage of in pleading. Everyday's experience is to take out several extents on one *fiat*. In the case of a receiver, it is not necessary that the affidavit should mention that the money was due to the crown. Hardres 125.[2]

---

[1] *Aldworth v. Hutchinson* (1688), *ut supra*.

[2] *Attorney General, ex rel. Ceely v. Bagg* (1658), Hardres 125, 145 E.R. 413.

Sir Constantine Phipps: It is improper for a motion. As to several extents, it is certain several extents [may go] into several counties but not into the same county unless in the case of some fraudulent opposition to the execution of the first writ.

Chief Baron [Montagu]: This is agreed to be an execution. But of what? Why of nothing but a *mandatum* of the barons? Therefore, it cannot be prior to the *mandatum*. Before the Stat. 33 Hen. VIII, body, lands, and goods were subject, but only one after another, not all together, but this is by the Statute only. Plowd., Davis's Case.[1]

In Doctor Woodward's Case,[2] the warrant was expressly to confess a judgment of Hilary term or any subsequent term; he dies, and then judgment is entered. And this is justifiable by the express words of the Act. The prerogative as to the antedating must be learned from precedents and not from mere reasoning. Therefore, one must look back and see whether there are any such precedents. If there are any such, there is a prerogative; if not, no man can say there is such a prerogative.

Page: The Statute makes the bond a statute staple. The king may as well antedate upon a statute as upon a judgment. And the extent issues upon the statute staple not upon the warrant. So we will construe the Statute of 33 Hen. VIII according to the old rule before the Statute, *viz.* so as he might have antedated an extent before the Statute, so he may do now, for, if an old process be given in a new case, the manner of issuing that process shall be directed as in prior cases before the Statute. So in cases of taking fines, we take them in a circuit by a *dedimus* that is not actually issued at that time. The Lord Chancellor may antedate a writing original. Why may not we? Where there is a reason, the court may do it. And so it is proved by the case cited by Mr. Ward. The question is only whether here is a good reason.

Price: I am very glad to see My Lord Chief Baron so closely attached to the ancient practice. I believe there is no precedent for this sort of antedating. But I believe, if the legislature had had any view of this matter, then they would not have tied up the crown. The practice was formerly for a trial for a *quo minus.*

Adjornatur pro ultimo argumento.

Taussig MS. 311, vol. 1, p. 517, pl. 1

Trinity term 1723.

The business of antedating the extent was again mentioned.

And Mr. Attorney General [*Raymond*] did admit that he was informed upon an inquiry into the practice of Chancery that the execution made out upon the

[1] *Davy v. Pepys* (1573), 2 Plowden 438, 75 E.R. 658.

[2] *Oades v. Woodward* (1702), 7 Modern 93, 87 E.R. 1116, Holt K.B. 401, 90 E.R. 1121, 1 Salkeld 87, 91 E.R. 82, 3 Salkeld 116, 91 E.R. 725, 2 Lord Raymond 766, 849, 92 E.R. 12, 67.

statutes staple was never tested before the certificate from the Clerk of the Statutes, but always subsequent to it.

Harvard Law School MS. 1082, vol. 1, p. 202, pl. 2

Easter term 1724.

The warrant for an extent was in October, and it was tested the 6th July preceding to overreach a commission of bankruptcy.

Chief Baron [Eyre] seemed to think that this court was always open, so there is no such necessity of antedating as in the King's Bench.

Gilbert: If this matter cannot be pleaded, then we ought to hear it by way of motion. And if you can satisfy me that it cannot be by pleading, I am for hearing you.

Chief Baron [Eyre] cited Baily v. Bunning, *scire facias*, in 3 Levinz, 1 Siderfin 273; Pilsoe v. Johnson, in Raymond's reports.[1]

Price: The Stat. 5 Ann., about bankruptcy,[2] was not to prejudice the crown.

Fazakerly, for the defendant, said that it cannot be pleaded because you cannot aver against a record. Lutwyche 332.[3]

Chief Baron: Where the time of issuing the writ is material, there, it ought to be pleaded.

Page: It is not doubted but it may be pleaded.

Gilbert desired a reason to know why it could not be pleaded.

Ward, for the defendant: The defendant loses the advantage of the course of the court to set aside such an irregularity by motion.

Fazakerly, for the defendant: If this court should be of opinion that we can aver against a record and another court should be of a different opinion upon a writ of error, then we lose this advantage of moving it.

Ward, for the defendant, cited Rex v. Williamson, Hardres 226; Rex v. Quash, in the Exchequer, 1713.[4]

Price cited Rex v. Tanner Arnold,[5] upon a demurrer.

Chief Baron [Eyre] seemed to think than an extent so antedated was of bad consequence.

Foley, for the defendant, cited Rex v. Powell, 1717.

Gilbert: Whether this extent irregularly issued is a solemn point between the king and the subject, and though, by motion, the determination would be more speedy, yet it ought to be settled in a solemn manner, and, therefore, it

---

[1] *Baily v. Bunning* (1665), *ut supra*; *Bilton v. Johnson* (1667), T. Raymond 161, 83 E.R. 85, also 2 Keble 173, 198, 84 E.R. 108, 124.

[2] Stat. 4 & 5 Ann., c. 4 (*SR*, VIII, 461–465).

[3] *Aldworth v. Hutchinson* (1688), *ut supra*.

[4] *Rex v. Williamson* (1662), Hardres 226, 145 E.R. 465; *Regina v. Quash* (Ex. 1713), Parker 281, 145 E.R. 780, Dodd 365.

[5] *Regina v. Arnold* (Ex. 1710), Dodd 356.

ought to be pleaded. And you may aver that it is *erronice emanavit* notwithstanding the record.

So it was agreed that it should be pleaded, *per* TOTAM CURIAM.

Taussig MS. 311, vol. 2, p. 653

Easter term 1724.

This case was now appointed to be argued upon the former foot as a motion to supersede the writ *quia erronice*. But the court thought that, it being a matter of very great consequence, it should come before them upon a pleading to the extent and, if they erred in judgment, a writ of error would lie. And so they ordered that the party injured by this antedating of the extent should plead it, *viz.* that *in revera* the extent was taken out such a day *absque hoc* that it issued on the day of the date and, [upon a] demurrer to such a plea, the question would be whether such an antedating would bind the property of the goods.

N.B. This seemed to me to be very extraordinary, for, though I do not doubt but that such plea would be good and bring that question before the court, yet I think it was very hard to put the party to this expense and trouble when he was already in a right method and, as I think, in a much more proper one, for now, upon a motion, the practice of the court would be the first point in question, i.e. whether there was any one precedent to justify this antedating and, if there was not, I think the writ ought to have been quashed for that reason only. And I do not see how the party can have any advantage of the practice of the court, though it continued without any alteration for near 180 years upon the pleadings. And to be sure, it was thought by those who antedated the writ that the writ would bind from the *teste*, else what use could the antedating answer. And, if so, the altering of the method the cause was now in was depriving the party supposed to be injured by this new invention of the best and most likely mean to set it aside.

N.B. In the speaking to this case, PRICE asserted that, in the Case of Tanner Arnold, the court held that simple contract debts might be found on an extent in aid without a previous motion in court for that purpose notwithstanding the rule of court made in the year [*blank*]. *Quaere de ceo.*

Bunbury 164, 145 E.R. 633

Jay and Dowse are receivers general of the County of Huntingdon. The two Norcotts, bankers, were securities for them in a bond to the crown. The king's money was returned up by Jay and Dowse to the Norcotts to be paid by them into the Exchequer. The two Norcotts, afterwards, became bankrupts. And, upon the 4th of October 7 Geo. [1720], a commission of bankrupt issued against them. And, upon the same day, Mann was chosen assignee, and an assignment was made to him by the commissioners of the estate and effects of the Norcotts.

The receivers, Jay and Dowse, on the 5th of October 7 Geo. [1720], obtained a *fiat* dated that day for an extent against the two Norcotts, their own securities, which was tested the 6th of October, which was irregular in that it should have been only to find debts. And finding that the assignment of the commissioners was prior in time to the *teste* of their extent, they procured a new extent, which was tested before the assignment, *viz.* the 6th of July before.

Whether this extent thus antedated before the *fiat* was not void was, by way of motion, twice argued before by several counsel on both sides, *viz.* 18 November 1720 and 22 May 1723, when the barons were equally divided.

And this day, 12 May 1724, this matter came on again before the court, when the question was whether the antedating of this extent should not be taken advantage of by pleading, and not determined upon a motion. It was objected to pleading that it would be averring against the *fiat* and that this was matter of irregularity, and not erroneous.

But *per* CURIAM, it was ordered to be pleaded to.

Mr. Attorney General [Yorke] demurred to the plea. And, afterwards, in Hilary term 1726, it came on again to be argued by Mr. Bootle, for the king, and Mr. Strange, for the defendant.

And then the court, as I think, seemed against antedating the extents, but adjourned the matter without giving any judgment, only they all now said this was a matter of irregularity, and not of error, and ought to have been determined on motion.

The plaintiff, seeing the court incline against antedating of the extent, submitted, *ut audivi*.

Gilbert Rep. 220, 25 E.R. 153

28 January 1726[/27]. Mr. *Strange*'s argument in the Exchequer for the defendants.

My Lord, it is truly said that this is a matter that very much concerns the crown in point of revenue and that Your Lordships will at all times and upon all occasions take a particular care of the prerogative of the crown. But I humbly hope I may be admitted to observe at the same time that this is a case too wherein the property of all the subjects of England is very highly affected, for I am bold to say that, if the practice which is now contended for be allowed to prevail, no man can be safe in transacting with another who has anything to do with the money of the crown.

My Lord, the case has been fairly opened by Mr. Bootle as it stands upon the record. And, as to the objection that we are improper to take advantage of antedating the extent upon a plea, as averring against the record, which imports it to have issued on the 6th of July, I must own I am a little surprised to find that matter so strongly insisted on after what has already passed in this cause.

It is in the memory of everybody who attends this court how much we pressed to have this writ superseded as a writ that had irregularly issued. And we then offered the distinction between an erroneous and an irregular proceeding that the one may be taken advantage of by a writ of error or by plea and that the other depended upon the practice of the court and was proper to be redressed at my motion. But the court being of opinion that we might have advantage of this matter on a plea, we acquiesced accordingly. And having now pleaded it in consequence of that opinion, it is very extraordinary now to see how the argument is turned upon us. On the other side, when we moved on the irregularity, we were told by them it was a matter we might have the advantage of by plea, and, now, we have pleaded it, they object against it for that very reason.

My Lord, in Lutwytch 332; 1 Levinz 173, 1 Siderfin 273, there are instances of these averments, that writs did not issue until a day subsequent to the *teste*. I cannot say the judgment of the court is either way upon these cases. But since, in this case, the court have already given their opinion that this was a matter pleadable, I do not think myself any otherwise concerned to answer this objection.

If I rightly apprehend, the design of the court in refusing to relieve us on a motion was in order for a more solemn determination of a point of this prodigious consequence. And since this was a method not invented by us, but prescribed by the court in order to bring that point upon the stage, I little expected to hear a matter of form insisted on when I apprehended we should be confined to the merits of the question, and, as it was brought before the court upon record with that only view, we must rely upon the justice of the court that we shall suffer no prejudice by the putting this question into the one or the other method of determination.

Taking it too for granted that we are properly before the court on this plea, I shall beg leave to offer that, Mr. Attorney [General Yorke] having demurred to the plea, he has thereby admitted all the facts contained in our plea, *viz.* that, in reality, the extent did not issue until the 5th of October, before which there had been a regular commission of bankruptcy and assignment. And that this is a bar to the extent appears from Capel's Case, 2 Shower 480,[1] where a prior commission of bankruptcy and assignment was held a good plea to the extent. So 2 Rolle, *Abridgment*, 158, G.2,[2] where a subject extended lands and goods and, after seizure, but before a *liberate*, there came a prerogative writ and which had place because there was not an actual *liberate*. But in that case, it is not pretended it would have avoided the subject's extent in case there had been a complete execution, as in Dyer 61.[3]

That these writs issued tested in the vacation is a fact nobody will deny. Your Lordship's records afford us a thousand instances of that nature, and none of them bear *teste* before the *fiat*, except in only one instance, which I shall account for by and by. That in Capel's Case was tested the 24th of December, which must necessarily be out of term.

---

[1] *Attorney General v. Capell* (1686), 2 Shower K.B. 480, 89 E.R. 1053.

[2] *Stringefellow v. Brownesoppe* (1549), 1 Dyer 67, 73 E.R. 142, 2 Rolle, Abr., *Prerogative le Roy*, pl. G, 2, p. 158.

[3] *Executors of Skewys v. Chamond* (1454), 1 Dyer 59, 61, 73 E.R. 131, 134, 109 Selden Soc. 3.

But then, it is objected that the subject's execution bears *teste* the last day of the preceding term and that, at common law, the goods were bound from that time. And why then, say they, should the crown be in a worse condition than the subject, especially, since it must be admitted that the crown is not bound by the Statute of Frauds and Perjuries?[1]

To this I answer that there is a very material difference between the case of the crown and that of the subject. The subject, it is true, has his writ tested the last day of the preceding term because he has run through the whole course of a judicial proceeding and his cause was ripe for execution at that time, and he can have no process tested out of the term, whereas the king, by his prerogative, may have execution awarded out of term and that in the first instance. And, if he has an immediate execution upon that award, he is not in a worse condition than the subject, nay, he is in a much better, for the subject must stay until the next term if his cause was not ripe for execution.

And this differs it from the case of a [writ of] *certiorari* made out in vacation tested the last day of the preceding term, when there is a necessity to test it in term time, it not being a prerogative writ. And, besides, it is of no consequence in the case of a *certiorari*, which removes all orders, though after the *teste*, so as they be before the return.

And I take the true reason why this is not provided against by the Statute of Frauds is that it was not a practice so much as thought of at that time. It was certainly a case within equal mischief, no doubt, but there have been many occasions to antedate extents before this. And the never doing it until now is, according to Littleton, a strong argument against the legality of doing it at all. Capel's Case, cited before, was 2 Jac. II [1686], and even then, there was no thought that it might have been tested backwards so as to overreach the assignment, though everybody knows matters of prerogative went very high at that time. And as this is a novelty in law and practice, I beg leave, in the next place, to consider a little what will be the consequence of it.

The goods will, without question, in the case of the crown, be bound from the award of the execution, according to Sir Gerard Fleetwood's Case, 8 Coke 171.[2] Now, the award of execution is in point of time the *teste* of the writ, so that all transactions by the bankrupt, all sales *bona fide* for a valuable consideration, and all payments by them made in the way of trade between the 6th of July and the 3d of December will be avoided, which will introduce great confusion.

By law, the king's execution relates, as to land, to the time of becoming in debt to the king, and, as to goods, from the award of execution. But by this means, it must, as to goods, be made to relate to a time precedent, even to the being in debt, for a debt may be contracted in the vacation, so that the execution, according to this new practice, shall issue before any debt, whereas the process is

1 Stat. 29 Car. II, c. 3 (*SR*, V, 839–842).

2 *Fleetwood's Case* (1610), 8 Coke Rep. 171, 77 E.R. 731.

to be awarded for the debt and must recite the bond entered into to the crown. In this case, indeed, it was four days old at the *teste* of the writ. But what an absurdity will it be if it should happen to bear date after the term, which may be the case. It has been thought a little hard to make it relate, as to lands, to the being in debt, which debt could not appear to a purchaser. But it will be much harder if it be suffered to relate to a time before the being in debt.

My Lord, the practice of every court is the law of that court; and it has been so strictly adhered to that, in the Case of Bewdly,[1] a practice of seven years only was allowed to prevail against the express words of an Act of Parliament.

I would too consider this writ, in the next place, upon the practice and the Stat. 33 Hen. VIII, c. 39, s. 35.[2] That Act says that the king's process shall be preferred and he first shall have execution. So [it is] always that the king's said suit be taken and commenced or process awarded for the said debt at the suit of the king before judgment [is] given for the said other person.

Upon this Act, I take it the suit must be said to be then taken and commenced when the first step is made towards the proceeding to execution. Now, the first step to be taken is to procure the *fiat* of a baron, and, then, it is in fact that the process is awarded. So, upon the foot of the Act of Parliament, this was not a suit taken or commenced or a process awarded until the assignment of the defendant had taken place. The court will, I apprehend, take notice of its own practice. And, therefore, since it appears upon the record that there was no *fiat* until the 5th of October, the court will take notice that such a writ as this could not issue according to the course of the court. And then, whether we can be admitted to say that, in fact, it issued at a day subsequent to the *teste* will not be material since it appears to the court to be so without our averment.

My Lord, I did mention before that there had been one instance of antedating an extent, and that it was the case of the Attorney General and Quash, in 1713.[3] There, the *fiat* was the 24th of February, and the writ taken out upon it was tested the last day of the preceding term, which was the 12th of February, and, after great consideration and search of precedents, that writ was set aside on account of the novelty and consequences of such a practice.

So that as to precedents, Your Lordship will consider how the case stands with regard to them. Here is a new sort of writ taken out, and the only instance of such a writ is an instance wherein it was set aside. They who would introduce this practice are to justify it by precedents. And we say there are none on that side, but that every extent which bears *teste* in vacation is a strong precedent in our favor, since, if it might have been tested in the precedent term, it is impossible to think

[1] *Regina v. Bewdley Corporation* (1712–1713), 1 Peere Williams 207, 24 E.R. 357, 10 Modern 151, 88 E.R. 670.

[2] Stat. 33 Hen. VIII, c. 39, s. 36 (*SR*, III, 886).

[3] *Regina v. Quash* (Ex. 1713), Parker 281, 145 E.R. 780, Dodd 365.

so great an advantage would not be taken by such learned and eminent men as are employed for the crown.

If this be a prerogative, it is, like all others, to be proved by usage. And that there is no pretence of usage to support it is clear. If the crown has engaged by Magna Charta[1] not to run upon the subject, *nisi per legem terrae*, let them show us the *lex terrae*, by which this extraordinary proceeding is to be warranted.

My Lord, there having been so great an alteration in this court since the time of the motion, it may not be improper to mention what seemed to be the opinion of the court as to the merits of this question. The Lord Chief Barons Bury and Montagu were both of opinion the writ was illegal and would have suspended it; Price and Page indeed were for having it pleaded. But I did not observe that the opinion of either of them was that the writ was right.

My Lord, I humbly apprehend Your Lordship will consider this extent on the foot it stood on the 6th of July, when the bond was but four days old. And, if, at that time, there was no ground for this proceeding, surely it is not to be supported by matter *ex post facto*, by a mere relation or fiction of law without precedent to divest a right which has been once legally vested.

For this purpose, I beg leave to mention a case that was in the King's Bench, Trinity 4 Geo. I [1718], Waring v. Dewberry.[2] There, a landlord, who had rent due to him, died intestate, after which the plaintiff in action sued out execution against the defendant, who was tenant, and levied the debt upon him; after this, administration was committed to J.S. who, thereupon, came into the court and moved for a rule on the sheriff to pay him a year's rent out of the levied monies, pursuant to the [Statute] 8 Ann., c. 17,[3] urging that, though he was no administrator at the time of serving the execution, yet, as soon as the administration was committed, it had relation to the death of the intestate and he might bring [an action of] trover for goods taken between the death of the intestate and the commission of the administration. But the court held that relations, which are but fictions of law, should never divest any right legally vested in another between the death of the intestate and the commission of administration, and the plaintiff in the action, having duly served his execution before the administrator had a right to demand his rent, it was not reasonable the plaintiff should be defeated by any relation whatsoever. They did not, in that case, deny the authorities which give the administrator [an action of] trover by relation, but they went on a distinction that will govern this case, between relations that are to defeat lawful acts and such as are to punish those that are unlawful.

An objection was taken that we should not have *oyer* of the first writ. But if Your Lordship pleases to cast your eye upon the writ itself, you will find it is indorsed upon it and made part of the record in the case. It is marked at the bottom

1 Stat. 25 Edw. I, Magna Carta, c. 29 (*SR*, I, 117).

2 *Waring v. Duberry* (1718), Fortescue 360, 92 E.R. 891, 1 Strange 97, 93 E.R. 408.

3 Stat. 8 Ann., c. 18 (*SR*, IX, 247–248).

of the writ. But they were so sensible of the absurdity of the *fiat* in October for a writ that issued in July that, in this particular instance, they have deviated from the common form and have modestly indorsed it upon the back of the writ.

The traverse is objected to that it is to put the matter of law in issue. But surely that is no new thing where matter of fact and matter of law are intermixed. It was necessary to put the matter of bankruptcy and the assignment in issue. And, as we pleaded to the inquisition, we must traverse that which is the point of it.

Upon the whole, too, it is certain that His Majesty has many great and valuable privileges and prerogatives, and may he live long to enjoy them to their full extent; our own experience of the happiness of his government may assure us that he himself designs only to make the law of the land the measure of his actions. And it is a pleasure to observe that this single attempt to stretch his prerogative beyond its bounds proceeds only from a private dispute between two co-obligors in the same bond to the crown and wherein it was necessary to make use of His Majesty's name, though he is not concerned in interest. It is one article of the Bill of Rights,[1] that the late King James had, under pretence of prerogative, levied money on his subjects in other manner than was warranted by the laws of the land, and, yet, it does not appear that the practice now set up was attempted even in that reign. And I am sure that we now live in times so much happier than those that it will be sufficient to confute this doctrine if we only show, as I have already done, that this is an unprecedented attempt to stretch the prerogative of the crown to the subversion of the liberties and properties of the subject.

2 Strange 749, 93 E.R. 826

Upon 5 October 7 Geo. [1720], Mr. Baron Price granted his *fiat* for an extent against Daniel Norcott and Joseph Norcott, whereupon an extent was taken out into London, *teste* 6 July *anno* 6 Geo., which was the last day of the Trinity term preceding. And it was subscribed at the bottom of the writ *fact' per warrantum* Baron Price, *dat' 5 die Octobris anno 7 regni regis*. Upon this extent, an inquisition is taken, and several goods and debts are found. And then, the defendant Mann comes in and claims property in the debts and effects. And to make it out, he first prays *oyer* of the bond entered into by the Norcotts to the crown, which appears by the condition to be a security for Jeay and Dowse as receivers general of the County of Huntington. Then, he prays *oyer* of the extent and the *fiat, quibus lectis*, he pleads that, by the course of the Exchequer, these writs have time out of mind issued out of term by virtue of a baron's *fiat*, and not otherwise, that the *fiat* in this case was granted 5 October, and not before, and that the writ of extent *in rei veritate* issued the said 5 October, and not before, that the several persons named in the inquisition to be debtors to the Norcotts were so indebted long before the extent and at the time of the act of bankruptcy after mentioned,

[1] Stat. 1 Will. & Mar., sess. 2, c. 2, pr. (*SR*, VI, 142).

and that the Norcotts before and at the time of the said bankruptcy were possessed of the effects found by the inquisition, and, being so possessed of those debts and effects and the Norcotts having for several years been goldsmiths and partners, they became indebted to the defendant Mann and others in £500 and 3 October 7 Geo. [1720] withdrew from their house for fear of being arrested for just debts and with intent to defraud their creditors and, thereby, committed an act of bankruptcy, that, upon the same 3 October, a petition was exhibited by the creditors and a commission of bankruptcy issued against the Norcotts, *teste* 3 October, *anno* 7 Geo., upon which the commissioners met the next day and found them to be bankrupts, and that, they being possessed of the effects and entitled to the debts mentioned in the inquisition, the commissioners the same 4 October assigned to the defendant all the goods, chattels, debts, and effects of the Norcotts, in trust for himself and the other creditors, by virtue whereof the defendant was possessed and so continued until the sheriff seized on the extent. And then, he traverses that, at the time of the inquisition, the persons therein named were debtors to the Norcotts or that the Norcotts were entitled to the goods mentioned in the inquisition, wherefore he prays an *amoveas manus.* To this plea the Attorney General demurs and shows for cause that the defendant ought not to have had *oyer* of the *fiat* and that the traverse is double. And the defendant joins in demurrer.

Bootle, pro rege, argued that this was an ill plea, both in form and substance, and as to the form:

1. That the traverse was immaterial, the former matter set forth in the plea confessing and avoiding the crown's title, upon any part of which matter the crown might take issue. Dyer 366; Moore 551.[1] Or if a traverse was necessary, yet the first traverse covers the whole, and there was no occasion for the second.

2. The *fiat* is not material, and it is what the defendant ought not to have *oyer* of. 7 Edw. IV, 8; 10 Hen. VII, 18.[2]

3. It is improper to plead that a writ issued at a time which is contrary to what the writ itself imports. 1 Siderfin 271.[3] The *fiat* is only to control the clerks, but has no operation as to the *teste* of the writ. The emanation of it is the act of the court, and not of a single baron. And if a writ issued without any *fiat*, yet it would fall within the rule *fieri non debet, factum valet* like the case of an execution whereon the sheriff breaks open doors, the execution is well executed, though the sheriff has done more than he can warrant.

As to the substance of the plea, I do insist that the court may antedate an extent, and this extent bearing *teste* 6 July will bind the goods from that time,

---

[1] *Fowler v. Clayton* (1579), 3 Dyer 366, 73 E.R. 821, also Benloe 319, 123 E.R. 224; *Helyer v. Whiteacre* (1598), Moore K.B. 551, 72 E.R. 752, also Croke Eliz. 650, 78 E.R. 889, 6 Coke Rep. 24, 77 E.R. 290.

[2] YB Mich. 7 Edw. IV, f. 18, pl. 14 (1467); YB Pas. 10 Hen. VII, f. 18, pl. 3 (1495).

[3] *Baily v. Bunning* (1665), *ut supra.*

8 Coke 171,[1] and then it overreaches the bankruptcy and assignment. This is no more than what is done every day in the case of the subject, who takes out his execution *teste* the last day of the preceding term and which had the same effect at common law, to bind the goods from the *teste*, as the execution of the crown has now. The king's prerogative is *ab origine legis*. Godbolt 250.[2] And he might take the body of his debtor, though the subject could not, until the writ of *capias ad satisfaciendum* was given by Statute.[3] He might break open a house on his execution, which could not be done upon an execution at the suit of a subject. 5 Coke 91; Sir T. Jones 234.[4] He might grant a protection against any subject's demands upon the king's debtor until the debt of the crown was satisfied. F.N.B. 28; Register 281.[5] And if, in this case, he might have granted the Norcotts a protection, the other creditors are not in a worse condition upon this extent. The Court of Exchequer is a court of revenue, and it must issue such process and of such *teste* as the nature of the case requires. 41 Edw. III, Fitzherbert, Ex., 38; Dyer 197; 45 Edw. III, Fitzherbert, *Abridgment*, 'Decies Tantum', 12; Godbolt 290.[6] In Dyer 67,[7] an extent came before a *liberate*, and the sheriff was directed to prefer the king. Before the Statute of Frauds and Perjuries, the subject had the same right, which the crown, as not being bound by the Statute of Frauds, retains to this day, Cro. El. 174; 1 Leonard 304; Cro. El. 440; Moore 21, 873, and should overreach any sale, though for a valuable consideration; 1 Siderfin 271.[8] Or even though the party was dead. 1 Modern 188; 1 Leonard 245; Trinity 11 Will. III, King's Bench, Oats v. Dr. Woodward; Trinity 9 Will. III, King's Bench, Pennoir v. Brace.[9] Are not the inconveniences in those cases as great as in this?

---

[1] *Fleetwood's Case* (1610), *ut supra*.

[2] *Coke's Case* (1623), Godbolt 289, 290, 78 E.R. 169, also Benloe 108, 117, 73 E.R. 976, 983.

[3] Stat. 25 Edw. III, stat. 5, c. 17 (*SR*, I, 322).

[4] *Semayne v. Gresham* (1604), 5 Coke Rep. 91, 77 E.R. 194, also Moore K.B. 668, 72 E.R. 828, Croke Eliz. 908, 78 E.R. 1131, Yelverton 29, 80 E.R. 21; *Anonymous* (1683), T. Jones 233, 234, 84 E.R. 1233.

[5] A. Fitzherbert, *Natura Brevium*; *Registrum Brevium*.

[6] Pas. 41 Edw. III, Fitzherbert, Abr., *Execucion*, pl. 38 (1367); *Lord Dacre v. Lassells* (1561), 2 Dyer 197, 73 E.R. 435; Hil. 45 Edw. III, Fitzherbert, Abr., *Decies tantum*, pl. 12 (1371); *Coke's Case* (1623), *ut supra*.

[7] *Stringfellow v. Brownesoppe* (1549), 1 Dyer 67, 73 E.R. 142.

[8] *Anonymous* (1590), Croke Eliz. 174, 78 E.R. 431; *Wangford and Sexton's Case* (1580), 1 Leonard 304, 74 E.R. 277; *Boucher v. Wiseman* (1595), Croke Eliz. 440, 78 E.R. 680, also Noy 51, 74 E.R. 1020; *Anonymous* (1560), Moore K.B. 21, 72 E.R. 413; *Comyn v. Brandlyn* (1614), Moore K.B. 873, 72 E.R. 965; *Baily v. Bunning* (1665), *ut supra*.

[9] *Farrer v. Brooks* (1674), 1 Modern 188, 86 E.R. 819; *Oades v. Woodward* (1702), *ut supra*; *Penoyer v. Brace* (1722), Carthew 404, 90 E.R. 834, Holt K.B. 640, 90 E.R. 1254, 1 Lord Raymond 244, 91 E.R. 1059, 1 Salkeld 319, 91 E.R. 282, 8 Modern 108, 88 E.R. 85, Comberbach 441, 90 E.R. 579, 5 Modern 338, 87 E.R. 692, 12 Modern 130, 88 E.R. 1214.

But it should be doubted whether this writ could be thus issued at common law. Yet, I apprehend that, by the Statute 33 Hen. VIII, c. 39, § 7, 8, 25, the court have this power. It is left to them to issue process for the king's debt according to their discretion. The words, after giving instances, are 'or otherwise at their discretion'. This is a case wherein to exercise that discretion. It appears the crown is to be overreached by these hasty proceedings upon the commission, which will have this consequence, to sweep away the effects and totally exclude the king, who cannot come in and prove his debt upon the commission. And the only fence we had against those quick proceedings was by testing our writ backward. A debtor might be protected for two years. Register 281. We only carry it back for three months. In Hardres 125,[1] a *diem clausit extremum* was made *teste* the last day of the precedent term, and it was held right. And in July 1712, Regina v. Ellins and Farringdon, an extent was ordered to be made out *teste* 8 November 1711.

This, in its nature, is a case of great consequence to the crown and will, in many instances, be of dangerous tendency if the crown cannot have the liberty of fencing against these expeditious proceedings upon commissions, which are taken out without notice, by making the process in such a manner as shall secure the debt of the crown.

Therefore, the plea being ill, both in form and substance, I pray judgment for the king.

Strange, contra: It is truly said that this is a matter which very much concerns the crown in point of revenue and that Your Lordship will at all times and upon all occasions take particular care of the prerogative. But I may be admitted at the same time to observe that this is a case too wherein the property of all the subjects of England is very highly affected, for, if the practice which is now contended for be allowed to prevail, no man can be safe in transacting with another, who has anything to do with the money of the crown.

The case has been fairly opened by Mr. Bootle as it stands upon the record. And, as to the objection that we are improper to take advantage of the antedating the extent upon a plea, as averring against the record which imports it to have issued on the 6th of July, I must own I am a little surprised to find that matter so strongly insisted upon after what has already passed in this cause. It is in the memory of everybody who attends this court how much we pressed to have this writ superseded as a writ that had irregularly issued. And we, then, offered the distinction between an erroneous and an irregular proceeding, that one might be taken advantage of by writ of error or by a plea and that the other, which depended upon the practice of the court, was proper to be redressed by a motion. But the court being of opinion that we might have advantage of this matter upon a plea, we acquiesced. And having now pleaded it in consequence of that opinion,

[1] *Attorney General, ex rel. Ceely v. Bagg* (1658), Hardres 125, 145 E.R. 413.

it is very extraordinary to see how the argument is turned upon us by the other is side. When we moved on the irregularity, we were told by them it was a matter we might have advantage of by plea. And now [that] we have pleaded it, they object against it for that reason.

In Lutwytch 322; 1 Levinz 173, 1 Siderfin 273, there are instances of these averments that writs did not issue until a day subsequent to the *teste*. I cannot say the judgment of the court is either way upon those cases. But, since, in this case, the court have already given their opinion, that this was a matter pleadable, I do not think myself any otherwise concerned to answer this objection.

If I rightly apprehend the design of the court in refusing to relieve us upon a motion, it was in order for the most solemn determination of a point of this prodigious consequence. And since this was a method not invented by us, but prescribed by the court in order to bring that point before them in judgment, I little expected to hear a matter of form insisted on, when I apprehended we should be confined to the merits of the question. And as it was brought before the court upon record with that only view, we must rely upon the justice of the court that we shall suffer no prejudice by putting this question into one or other method of determination.

Taking it, therefore, for granted that we are properly before the court upon this plea, I shall beg leave to observe, that Mr. Attorney [General Yorke], having demurred to the plea, has thereby admitted all the facts contained in our plea, *viz.* that, in reality, the extent did not issue until 5 October, before which there had been a regular commission of bankruptcy and assignment. And that this is a bar to the extent appears from Capel's Case, 2 Shower 480, where a prior commission of bankruptcy and assignment was held a good plea to an extent; so 2 Rolle, *Abridgment*, 158, G.2,[1] where a subject extended lands and goods and, after seizure, but before a *liberate*, there came a prerogative writ, which had place, because there was not an actual execution of the *liberate*, as there was not likewise in the case cited out of Dyer. But, in that case, it is not pretended it would have avoided the subject's extent, in case there had been a complete execution.

That these writs issue tested in vacation is a fact nobody will deny. Your Lordship's records afford a thousand instances of that nature, and none of them bear *teste* before the *fiat*, except in one instance, which I shall account for by and by. That in Capel's case was *teste* 24th December, which must necessarily be out of term.

But then, it is objected that the subject's execution bears *teste* the last day of the preceding term and that, at common law, the goods were bound from that time. And why, then, say they, should the crown be in a worse condition than the subject, especially since it must be admitted that the crown is not bound by the Statute of Frauds and Perjuries?

---

[1] *Attorney General v. Capell* (1686), *ut supra*; *Stringefellow v. Brownesoppe* (1549), *ut supra*.

To this, I answer that there is a very material difference between the case of the crown and that of the subject. The subject, it is true, has his writ *teste* the last day of the preceding term because he has run through the whole course of a judicial proceeding and his cause was ripe for execution at that time and he can have no process *teste* out of term, whereas the king, by his prerogative, may have execution awarded out of term, and that in the first instance. And if he has an immediate execution upon that award, he is not in a worse condition than the subject. Nay, he is in a much better, for the subject must stay until the next term if his cause was not ripe for execution.

And this differs it from the case of a *certiorari* made out in vacation *teste* the last day of the preceding term, where there is a necessity to *teste* in term time, it not being a prerogative writ. And besides, it is of no consequence in the case of a *certiorari*, which removes all orders, though after the *teste*, so as they be before the return.

And I take the true reason why this is not provided against by the Statute of Frauds is that it was not a practice so much as thought of at that time. It was certainly a case within equal mischief. [There is] no doubt but there have been many occasions to antedate extents before this. And the never doing it until now is, according to Littleton, a strong argument against the legality of doing it at all. Capel's Case, cited before, was 2 Jac. II, and even then there was no thought that it might have been tested backwards so as to overreach the assignment, though everybody knows matters of prerogative went very high at that time.

And as this is a novelty in law and practice, I beg leave, in the next place, to consider a little what will be the consequence of it. The goods, without question, will, in the case of the crown, be bound from the award of execution, according to Sir Gerard Fleetwood's Case, 8 Coke 171. Now, the award of execution is, in point of time, the *teste* of the writ, so that all transactions by the bankrupts, all sales *bona fide* for a valuable consideration, and all payments by them made in the way of trade between 6 July and 3 October will be avoided, which will introduce great confusion.

By the law, the king's execution relates, as to land, from the date of the bond given to the king and, as to goods, from the award of execution. But, by this means, it may be made to relate to a time precedent even to the being in debt, for a debt may be contracted in vacation, and the execution, according to his new practice, shall issue before any debt. The process must be awarded for the debt and must recite the bond entered into to the crown. In this case, indeed, it was four days old at the *teste* of the writ. But what an absurdity will it be if it should happen to bear date after the term, which may be the case. It has been thought a little hard to make it relate, as to lands, to the date of the bond, which could not appear to a purchaser. But it will be much harder if it be suffered to relate to a time before the being in debt.

The practice of every court is the law of that court. And it has been so strictly adhered to that, in the Case of Bewdley, a practice of seven years only was allowed to prevail against the express words of an Act of Parliament.

I would, therefore, in the next place, consider this writ upon the practice, and the Stat. 33 Hen. VIII, c. 39, § 35. That Act says that 'the king's process shall be preferred and he shall first have execution, so always that the king's said suit be taken and commenced or process awarded for the said debt at the suit of the king before judgment given for the said other person.'

Upon this Act, I take it the suit must be said to be then taken and commenced when the first step is made towards proceeding to execution. The first step to be taken is to procure the *fiat* of a baron, and then it is that, in fact, the process is awarded, so that, upon the foot of the Act of Parliament, this was not a suit taken or commenced or a process awarded until the assignment of the defendant had taken place. It is said that the court has a discretionary power by the Statute 33 Hen. VIII, but that is only to act according to law. The Statute does not leave it to Your Lordship's discretion to act contrary to law, which is what is contended for by the other side. This court will take notice of its own practice. And, therefore, since it appears upon the record that there was no *fiat* until 5 October, you will take notice that such a writ as this could not issue according to the course of the court, and, then, whether we can be admitted to say that, in fact, it issued at a day subsequent to the *teste* will not be material, since it appears to the court to be so without our averment.

I did mention before that there had been one instance of antedating an extent and that was the case of The Attorney General v. Quash, in 1713. There, the *fiat* was the 24th February and the writ taken out upon it was *teste* the last day of the preceding term, which was 12th February, and, after great consideration and search of precedents, that writ was set aside upon account of the novelty and consequence of such a practice. So that, as to precedents, Your Lordship will consider how the case stands. Here is a new sort of writ taken out, and the only instance of such a writ is an instance wherein it was set aside. They, who would introduce this practice, are to justify it by precedents. And we say there are none on that side, but that every extent which bears *teste* in vacation is a strong precedent in our favor, since, if it might have been tested in the precedent term, it is impossible to think so great an advantage would not have been taken.

As to the precedents cited by Mr. Bootle, that of a *diem clausit extremum* is nothing to the purpose, for there was a necessity to *teste* it in term, it not being a prerogative writ. And as to the case of The Queen v. Ellins, that was no more than ordering a new writ to be made out of the same *teste* and return of a former that had been lost and for which there was a regular *fiat*.

If this be a prerogative, it is, like all others, to be proved by usage, and yet there is no pretence of usage to support it. If the crown has engaged by Magna Charta not to run upon the subject *nisi per legem terrae*, let them show us the *lex terrae* by which this extraordinary proceeding is to be warranted.

And as to the argument drawn from other prerogatives that the king has other prerogatives which may be as inconvenient to the subject as this, and, therefore, why should he not have this, surely that is the most absurd way of reasoning in the world. We are upon a single question, whether he has this prerogative or not. And if it cannot be shown he has, it is to no purpose to talk of protections or other legal prerogatives, which are not disputed.

There having been so great an alteration in this court since the time of the motion, it may not be improper to mention what seemed to be the opinion of the court as to the merits of this question. Lord Chief Baron Bury and [Baron] Montagu were both of opinion the writ was illegal and would have superseded it; Mr. Baron Price and Mr. Baron Page, indeed, were for having it pleaded, but I did not observe that the opinion of either of them was that the writ was right.

Your Lordship will consider this extent upon the foot it stood on 6 July, when the bond was but four days old. And if, at that time, there was no ground for this proceeding, it is not to be supported by matter *ex post facto* by a mere relation and fiction of law, which ought to divest no right that has been once legally vested. For this purpose, I beg leave to mention a case that was in the King's Bench, Trinity 4 Geo., Waring v. Dewberry; there, a landlord, who had rent due to him, died intestate, after which the plaintiff in the action sued out execution against the defendant, who was the tenant, and levied the debt upon it; after this, administration was committed to J.S., who, thereupon, came into court and moved for a rule on the sheriff to pay him a year's rent out of the money levied, pursuant to Stat. 8 Ann., c. 17, urging that, though he was not administrator at the time of serving the execution, yet, as soon as the administration was committed, it had relation to the death of the intestate, and he might bring [an action of] trover for goods taken between the death of the intestate and the commission of administration. But the court held that relations, which are but fictions of law, should never divest any right legally vested in another mesne between the death of the intestate and the commission of administration and that the plaintiff in the action, having duly served his execution before the administrator, had a right to demand his rent; it was not reasonable the plaintiff should be defeated by any relation whatsoever. They did not in that case deny the authorities which give the administrator trover by relation, but went upon a distinction that will govern this case, between relations that are to defeat lawful acts and such as are to punish those which are unlawful.

An objection was taken, and indeed it is mentioned in the demurrer, that we should not have had *oyer* of the *fiat*. But if Your Lordship casts your eye upon the writ itself, you will find that is indorsed upon it and made part of the record and appears in their setting out the extent. In the common case, it is marked at the bottom of the writ, but they were so sensible of the absurdity of a *fiat* in October for a writ that had issued in July that, in this particular instance, they have deviated from the common form and have modestly indorsed it upon the back of the writ.

The traverse is objected to. But surely that is very proper, and the crown may take issue either on the inducement or the traverse. It was necessary to put the matter of the bankruptcy and the assignment in issue. And as we plead to the inquisition, we must traverse that which is the point of it. And it is not a double traverse, but two distinct matters, the first covers the debts and the second the effects found by the inquisition.

Upon the whole, therefore, it is certain that His Majesty has many great and valuable prerogatives; and may he long live to enjoy them in their full extent. Our own experience of the happiness of his government may assure us that he desires only to make the law of the land the measure of his actions. And it is some pleasure to observe that this single attempt to stretch the prerogative beyond its due bounds proceeds only from a private dispute between two co-obligors in the same bond to the crown and wherein it was necessary to make use of His Majesty's name, though he is not at all concerned in point of interest. It is one article of the Bill of Rights that the late king had under pretence of prerogative levied money on his subjects in other manner than was warranted by the laws of the land. And yet it does not appear that this practice now set up was attempted even in that reign. And we live in times so much happier than those that it will be sufficient to confute this doctrine if we only show, as I have done already, that it is an unprecedented attempt to stretch the prerogative of the crown to the subversion of the liberty and property of the subject.

Pengelly, Chief Baron: This is a matter of very great consequence to the revenue, to the method of proceeding, and to the subject. I take it to be our duty on all these considerations to maintain the prerogatives of the crown, but not to raise any new ones. Every prerogative that is not affected by the interposition of an Act of Parliament must depend upon prescription only. And we must have the same evidence of a prerogative that we have of all other prescriptions.

I should have thought this a matter far more proper to be determined upon a motion than by special pleading, for, as has been observed, this is more a matter of irregularity than error. And I apprehend it never was the intent of the court to deprive the defendant of any legal benefit by putting him into this method. If, therefore, this is improper for a plea, I shall be of opinion still to turn it into a motion again and set aside the extent as irregularly issued.

As to the *oyer* of the *fiat*, that cannot be bad. But then, it being set out in the very writ, it is before us. And we must take notice of it.

I am afraid we shall be under great difficulty how to do the defendant justice upon this record. We cannot give judgment for him unless he makes out a title, which, if the matter pleaded be improper for a plea, he can never do.

I think the traverses are not double, and, being a plea to the title of the crown, which the defendant was bound to answer, it was proper to add the traverse, which is for the benefit of the crown by giving them an opportunity of taking issue on the traverse or any part of the title before set forth. This is the usual way of pleading upon outlawries.

As to the principal question, whether this extent can be antedated or not, I must observe that they issue from the equity side of the court, which is always open. If the usage has been to have a *fiat* and *teste* the writ the day the *fiat* is granted, I should think the *fiat* was in the nature of an award of the court, which formerly sat longer than it does now. And now, when it is not sitting, a *fiat* is to be had at a baron's chamber. And that is an evidence that the writ and *fiat* ought to tally with one another.

I think the usage must determine in this case. There is no instance of antedating, where it has been allowed, for, as to the case cited by Mr. Bootle, that was only the continuance of a writ that had regularly issued. On the other side, there is the consideration that such a thing was never attempted before, and there is Quash's Case, which is a judicial authority. That was in a manner given up at the bar by Sir Edward Northey, who was the Attorney General and who was known to be enough tenacious of the rights of the crown; and the court, in their judgment, treated the extent as a writ that had issued without any *fiat* or authority.

If this be a novelty, it is not to be supported. At present, it seems to me to be so, but it is proper to be farther considered.

Baron HALE: If this is to go against the defendant upon a point of pleading, it would be exceeding hard. But rather than so, I think the court is bound in honor to interpose and turn it again into a motion. I think this is a very extravagant attempt and have wondered ever since I heard of it upon what foundation it could be supported. I do not now find anything offered to that purpose, and I think there is no such prerogative as has been exercised in this case. The crown is in a very good condition by having this extent as their first process. It is hard enough upon the subject, and we ought not to enlarge the prerogative.

Baron CARTER: No such writ can regularly issue before a *fiat*, which ought to be the direction in making the *teste*. It is impossible to foresee the ill consequence of allowing those writs to be antedated. And it is considerable that, in all the time this court has sat, it never was attempted before.

Baron COMYNS: Surely this is much more proper for a motion than a plea, and it can never be determined according to justice upon the record. The *teste* is matter of record, and I think we are obliged to take it to have issued at the time of the *teste*. And there can be no averment against it. As to the Statute 33 Hen. VIII, I think that does not leave it to our discretion to alter the course and nature of proceedings or to do a thing that was never done before and may have such mischievous consequence.

Per CURIAM, *ulterius concilium.*

Afterwards, in Trinity term following, I [*Strange*] moved to set aside the extents upon the point of irregularity, and Mr. Attorney General [*Yorke*] consented, so nothing further was done upon the pleadings.

Harvard Law School MS. 1082, vol. 2, p. 17

Hilary term 1726/27.

This comes upon a demurrer to the plaintiff's [complaint] upon an extent and inquisition against the two Northcotes. The inquisition finds several persons indebted. And the defendant craves *oyer* of the extent and inquisition and of the warrant for the extent, which was tested 5 October 7 Geo. [1720], but the writ of extent was tested 6 July before.

The defendant pleads that the extent issued 5 October and not before and that, upon 3 October, the Northcotes absconded and they became bankrupts and commissioners assigned [their] effects to the defendant. And, therefore, he traverses whether the several persons in the inquisition mentioned were then indebted to the Northcotes or not.

Attorney General [*Yorke*] demurs, and he assigns two causes of demurrer: first, for that the defendant ought not to have craved *oyer* of the warrant; and, secondly, that it is a double traverse.

Bootle, for the king: The extent will take place from the *teste*. Sir G. Fleetwood's Case, 8 Rept. The plea is insufficient because it is an immaterial traverse. There is no occasion to traverse that the persons were indebted. Dyer 366, pl. 36; Moore 551. There is no occasion to pray *oyer* of the warrant. 7 Edw. IV, fo. 18; 20 Edw. IV, fo. 8, pl. 10; 10 Hen. VII, fo. 18, pl. 3.[1] An extent must be taken to be when it is tested, and the endorsement will not alter the case. 1 Siderfin 271, Baily v. [*blank*].

The *fiat* is only to control the clerks of the office and to hinder them from issuing such writs as they thought proper, but, when issued, it is well executed though without a warrant though *fieri non debet factum valet*. 5 Rep. 93; 6 Rept. 53, Rutland's Case.[2]

The power of courts is in general of antedating extents for subjects, and surely, in the case of the crown, it is much stronger. Before the Stat. 33 Hen. VIII, the common law for the benefit of the crown takes the body and lands. 5 Rept. 9; 3 Rept., Herbert's Case; Godbolt 290; Sir Thomas Jones 34.[3]

The Court of Exchequer, as a court of revenue, ought to take care of the crown revenue. And by the prerogative, until the crown is satisfied, no common

---

[1] *Fowler v. Clayton* (1579), *ut supra*; *Helyer v. Whiteacre* (1598), *ut supra*; YB Mich. 7 Edw. IV, f. 18, pl. 14 (1467); YB Trin. 20 Edw. IV, f. 8, pl. 10 (1480); YB Pas. 10 Hen. VII, f. 18, pl. 3 (1495).

[2] *Semayne v. Gresham* (1604), *ut supra*; *Attorney General v. Stevenson* (1605), 6 Coke Rep. 52, 77 E.R. 332, also Moore K.B. 765, 72 E.R. 892.

[3] *Brudnel v. Skidmore* (1592), 5 Coke Rep. 9, 77 E.R. 61; *Harbert's Case* (1584), *ut supra*; *Coke's Case* (1623), Godbolt 289, 290, 78 E.R. 169, also Benloe 108, 117, 73 E.R. 976, 983; *Anonymous* (1683), T. Jones 233, 234, 84 E.R. 1233.

person can have an advantage. Dyer 197, Lord Darcy's Case; 45 Edw. III, pl. 12; Godbolt 290; Dyer 67, Stringfellow's Case.[1]

The crown, surely had always as good a remedy as the subject by the common law. And, before the Statute of Frauds, the [. . .] entries took place as of precedent terms. Moore 21; Cro. Eliz. 440, 174; 1 Leonard 304; Moore 873, Cummin v. [*blank*]; 1 Siderfin 271, Baily v. Bunnings.[2] And in the case of a common person, though the party was dead, yet execution has been taken. 1 Modern 188; 1 Leonard 145; Odes v. Dr. Woodward; P[enn]ie v. Brace.

If the argument *ex inconvenienti* is to prevail, then surely it cannot be called a greater inconvenience in the case of the crown. And the Statute of Frauds does not affect the crown. Writs original are formed by statute. 2 Inst. 407; Cro. Car. 527.[3] Judicial writs may be formed as the court shall direct. And the writ of extent is a judicial writ. And this will extend to the Exchequer as well as Chancery and included within it as upon the Statute of Frauds, 14 Car. II, sec. 24, which only mentions the Court of Chancery. And so, by the same rule upon the Statute of Westminster II, it extends to this court. I think the Stat. 33 Hen. VIII is material, sec. 2, 7, 8. the crown is still preferred. The Court of Exchequer has a discretionary power to issue out process to recover the king's debts. And in this case, the crown will be defeated of this debt, for the crown cannot be a creditor under the commission of bankrupts. And from the necessity, it is proper for the Court of Exchequer to use this discretionary power, and the rather because the king might have given protection for a year or two to a bankrupt for the service of the crown.

Perhaps it may be said and objected that judicial writs cannot issue but from term to term and that the Court of Exchequer is always open, so there is no occasion to *teste* the extents as of the preceding term. In the long vacation in the case of a judgment, the subject will antedate to overreach an act of bankruptcy. Yet the crown cannot have the same benefit though esteemed to have such a privilege. Process may be antedated. Hardres 125; July 1712, Queen v. Ellins and Farringdon; Rex v. Quash. Here are precedents for antedating extents. Therefore, he prayed judgment for the king.

Strange, for the defendant: By the practice of the Court of Exchequer, extents are tested in vacation. And the property of the subject is very material in

---

[1] *Lord Dacre v. Lassells* (1561), 2 Dyer 197, 73 E.R. 435; Hil. 45 Edw. III, Fitzherbert, Abr., *Decies tantum*, pl. 12 (1371); *Coke's Case* (1623), *ut supra*; *Stringfellow v. Brownesoppe* (1549), *ut supra*.

[2] *Anonymous* (1560), Moore K.B. 21, 72 E.R. 413; *Boucher v. Wiseman* (1595), *ut supra*; *Anonymous* (1590), Croke Eliz. 174, 78 E.R. 431; *Wangford and Sexton's Case* (1580), 1 Leonard 304, 74 E.R. 277; *Comyn v. Brandlyn* (1614), Moore K.B. 873, 72 E.R. 965; *Baily v. Bunning* (1665), *ut supra*.

[3] E. Coke, *Second Institute* (1642), p. 407; *Lord Mounson v. Bourn* (1638–1639), Croke Car. 518, 527, 79 E.R. 1049, 1056, also W. Jones 417, 82 E.R. 219.

this case. It is not improper in the plea, and no form is to be insisted on. Lutwyche 332; 1 Siderfin 273.

The Attorney General having demurred to the plea, the facts are admitted. The warrant is granted 5 October to give authority to a writ to issue 6 July preceding. The commissioner's of bankrupts assignment is the 3rd October. 2 Shower 280, Capel's Case; Rolle, *Abridgment*, 158.

[To the] objection that the execution for a party is antedated, [he] responded the subject has that right because he runs through the whole course of the law, but an extent is a judgment and execution at once without any previous notice.

This case differs from a [writ of] *certiorari*, which must be tested as of the preceding term.

I admit inconvenience from the rule of relation. And there is no instance of ever antedating an extent. And the award of execution is from the *teste* of the extent. And it would be of the greatest mischief to set aside all proceedings between 6 July and 5 October. And all payments [would be] void if it is to be made to have relation even before the party became indebted, even upon entering into the bond.

The practice of the court is the law of the court. And though there may be a discretionary power lodged in the court by Stat. 33 Hen. VIII, yet that ought to be bound by the rules of law. In this case of the King v. Quash, cited, the writ was set aside. And [in] the King v. Ellins and Farringdon, there was a regular *fiat*. Writs of extent issue in vacation, and if any such prerogative usage ought to have confirmed it, there being no such usage, it is an argument there is no such prerogative.

Bootle replies: The question is what may be lawfully done. And therefore, Mr. Strange's argument that it never was done will have no weight. The Stat. 25 Edw. III is to be considered. He insisted on the crown's right of protection. The Stat. 33 Hen. VIII was not answered, wherein a discretionary power is given to the court for taking care of the revenue. I say and concede that everything that is well pleaded is admitted, but not that which is ill. And so is Lord Hobart. There is no answer to the objection in relation to the traverse. And whatever is traversed and avoided cannot be traversed again. Sir James Bagg's Case of *diem clausit extremum* in Hardres[1] is not answered. This is a public question for the benefit of the crown. And he prayed for judgment for the king.

Chief Baron [PENGELLY]: It is a case of great consequence. And I cannot enter into a new prerogative for the crown. And this matter will depend upon usage, as in the Case of Mines, in Plowden.[2]

I admit the manner of obtaining commissions of bankrupts has been of bad consequence. But we ought not to go farther than the rules of law will admit. If a question does arise whether process of the court does well issue, I think it more proper by a motion than by a record and pleading, for it is difficult to have an advantage by pleading to such a process, and the party defendant may not have

[1] *Attorney General, ex rel. Ceely v. Bagg* (1658), Hardres 125, 145 E.R. 413.

[2] *Attorney General v. Earl of Northumberland* (1568), 1 Plowden 310, 75 E.R. 472.

the advantage by pleading as by a motion where the whole matter will come in question. And upon the Deputy [Remembrancer's] report, the court might give judgment.

You cannot in pleading pray *oyer* of the endorsement. And it is no part of it. And it being set out upon the record itself by the king and [the court] takes notice of it in that manner. And that may let the court into some consideration of the trial whether the process issued properly.

Upon the form of pleading, the objections are strong. Here are two traverses, but not a double traverse. It may be necessary to traverse in this case, for the crown has taken notice of it.

Whatever power the court has as a court of revenue or equity to form new writs, yet they ought to have the qualifications of the writs at law. And they issue as well in vacation time as others. If these writs of extent, by the course of the court, only issued in term time, the court would not order them to issue in vacation. This *fiat* by a baron in vacation is the judgment of the court. And this is the constant course of the common law.

The Stat. 33 Hen. VIII was for new instances and not to alter the ancient and usual proceedings of this court. No precedent was showed of such a case. An extent is an award of execution. [In] Rex v. Quash, the writ was quashed. [In] Rex v. Ellins and Farringdon, the first writ was well executed and a fraud was used to obstruct it, 3 Levinz, against Baily and Bunning's Case.

The writ of *diem clausit extremum* is only in the nature of an enquiry, and those only bear *teste* in term time. And so is Sir James Bagg's Case, Hardres.

It is in the power of the court to issue out writs, but only at such time as they are tested, not to antedate them. And I doubt I have no such power.

CARTER: This is more properly to be considered by way of a motion. And there could be no writ without a warrant. I shall not make a new law.

COMYNS: This is more proper by way of a motion, for it puts a difficulty upon the defendant because the writ is supposed to issue at the time it is tested. The judgment is the warrant for execution. But here is an execution without a warrant. To take a step upon the Stat. 33 Hen. VIII may be dangerous.

Parker 130, 145 E.R. 735

In the case of The King and Mann, Hilary [term] 1726[/27], in this court, it was expressly laid down by Lord Chief Baron PENGELLY that whoever pleads to the title of the crown, found by an inquisition, is obliged to traverse that title so found, and not to put the crown to traverse the title set up by the defendant or to force the crown to take a traverse, though the crown has an election to traverse the inducement or title set out by the defendant.

404

Rex v. Hollingsby

(Ex. 1723)

Where goods are seized for non-payment of customs duties, the horse and wagon used to carry them are forfeited only where the goods are being transported initially from the waterside, but not a common carrier that later receives the goods without notice.

Taussig MS. 311, vol. 1, p. 500

Easter term 1723.

A carrier takes in a cask of brandy at Southwark to carry to Basingstoke in Hampshire. A Custom House officer seizes the brandy and wagon at Alverstoke and gives an information before two justices at Winchester, which was twenty miles distant from Alverstoke where the seizure was made.

And *Sir Constantine Phipps* moved to set aside the proceedings before the said two justices for three reasons: first, for that the information was given *coram* justices of peace twenty miles distant, whereas the Act[1] says justices residing near the place where the seizure [was made]; second, because the Act only subjects the brandy to forfeiture and not the wagon; third, there was no summons to the person, as the Act directs.

Chief Baron [MONTAGU]: I question whether this matter is proper for a motion. The proper way would be to suggest, as in other cases for prohibitions, and move for a [writ of] prohibition.

PRICE: I think the officer should show cause why a writ of delivery should not be granted for the wagon.

PAGE: Residing near the place is not so strong as next justices, which is the direction of the Act of Bastardy.[2] And yet it is known any justices in a county may proceed. And whether there is a summons or no, if they have jurisdiction, perhaps it is not material.

But by PRICE and PAGE: [There is] no color to say they have any jurisdiction as to the wagon or horses.

The rule was at last pronounced by three barons that the officer should show cause and all things to stay in the meantime, MONTAGU doubting and rather inclining to a prohibition.

Harvard Law School MS. 1082, vol. 1, p. 168

23 May 1723.

Sir Constantine Phipps moved to stay proceedings before two justices of peace. The defendant is a common wagoner, and some brandy was put into his wagon

[1] Stat. 8 Geo. I, c. 18, s. 16.

[2] Stat. 18 Eliz. I, c. 3, s. 1 (*SR*, IV, 610).

to carry from Southwark to Alverstoke. At Alverstoke, officers seized the brandy and were proceeding before two justices, who lived twenty miles from the place of the seizure, to condemn the wagon.

He objected that the wagon is not forfeited by Stat. 6 Geo., fo. 403;[1] secondly, to what by the Statute the complaint ought to be before two justices near residing to the place of seizure; thirdly, that the summons was not to the party but was left with a bookkeeper at the Excise Office at Alverstoke.

Note: The Statute extends only to the brandy and casks. In a case of coming from the waterside, the wagon and horses may be forfeited, but not in this.

Lord Chief Baron [Montagu] thought this was not proper to be done upon motion, but, by way of suggestion, move for a [writ of] prohibition.

Baron Price [was] for the wagoner: They have no jurisdiction in this case. And we may grant a writ of delivery. By [the Rules of] 15 Car. II, summonses may be left at the house of the party, but in no other case. By this Statute, the justices have jurisdiction, even upon importation, where the quantity of brandy does not exceed sixty-three gallons.

Baron Page: The justices have no jurisdiction of the wagon any more than if the Statute had not been made.

An order was made to the officer who seized to show cause why a writ of delivery should not go for the wagon.

Bunbury 130, 145 E.R. 621

23 May 1723.

Sir Constantine Phipps moved to stay proceedings before two justices upon a seizure of brandy and the wagon which it was put into. As to the brandy, the justices have jurisdiction by the Stat. 6 Geo., cap. [*blank*], and so they would have as to the wagon and horses if they had been running goods from the waterside. But, here, the brandy was taken in at Southwark to be carried to Alverstoke. And, therefore, the officer who seized was ordered to show cause why there should not be a writ of delivery for the wagon.

405

Strong v. Duchess of Marlborough

(Ex. 1723)

A request by counsel for a rehearing will be granted as a matter of course.

Taussig MS. 311, vol. 1, p. 502

Easter term 1723.

---

[1] Stat. 6 Geo. I, c. 2.

This cause came on upon the Master's report on Thursday the [*blank*] in this term. And so the court confirmed the Master's report. And the truth of the case was that the cause was set down to be heard the 7th; that day, and some of the preceding causes being agreed, this cause was called and the counsel for the defendant would not open the exceptions, alleging they were not ready. And so the report was confirmed.

And this day upon a petition of the defendant to rehear signed by *Reeves* and *Ward* suggesting the aforesaid matter and also assigning some particular error in the decree, [it was said] by MONTAGU and all the other barons the counsel's not being ready is no cause for a rehearing.

And by Chief Baron [MONTAGU]: I think the court may refuse a rehearing if they do not think the error assigned to be sufficient.

But by PRICE *et al.*: We look upon a rehearing to be matter of course if signed by counsel, and it is upon their credit. So the rehearing was granted by three barons. But the court made the defendant's attorney strike out of the petition the excuse for not being ready.

Query, what costs for this rehearing?

[For earlier proceedings in this litigation, see Strong v. Duke of Marlborough (Ex. 1721), above, Case No. 193.]

[On appeal: 1 Brown P.C. 175, 1 E.R. 496, 4 Brown P.C. 539, 2 E.R. 367, 2 Eq. Cas. Abr. 531, 22 E.R. 448.]

406

Robinson v. Thornycroft

(Ex. 1723)

A delay in a trial in London or in Middlesex is the same as a delay at the assizes.

Taussig MS. 311, vol. 1, p. 503

Easter term 1723.

The Master reported in this case that there was a special *quo minus* in debt upon a bond as well as in case and, secondly, that the delaying the plaintiff a trial in London or Middlesex was of the like consequence as delaying him a trial at the assizes.

407

Bassett v. Parsons

(Ex. 1723)

A demurrer to a bill of complaint cannot be filed to the prayer for discovery on the ground that the relief prayed for is below the dignity of the court.

Taussig MS. 311, vol. 1, p. 504, pl. 1

Easter term 1723.

The plaintiff, as executor of A., exhibits his bill against the defendant suggesting that his testator lent the defendant £5, and he prays a discovery thereof and relief. The defendant demurs as to both, *viz.* as well to the discovery as the relief. And for the cause of the demurrer, he assigns that it was below the dignity of the court to hold suit for so small a sum.

Sed per CURIAM: The demurrer is naught being to the discovery as well as the relief whereas it should have been only to the relief.

408

Mosse v. Weeks

(Ex. 1723)

A retailer of imported goods may be required to prove that the customs duties were duly paid.

Taussig MS. 311, vol. 1, p. 510

Easter term 1723.

At *nisi prius coram* MONTAGU on the 28th May 1722 on an information of seizure for cocoa nuts, the evidence was that seven bags of cocoa nuts were seized on the road between Blandford and Salisbury at 12 o'clock at night. The defense was that the defendant was a retailer and, therefore, not obliged to prove payment of duties. They proved that the defendant lived at Winfred, about twelve miles from Blandford, about two or three miles from the sea and kept a warehouse, *viz.* a room up one pair of stairs where he stowed such sort of goods in a country village and sold sometimes one pound, sometimes one-half a pound, of tea, and that he bought such sort of goods from the East India House and sometimes from the Exchequer.

But by Chief Baron [MONTAGU], Attorney and Solicitor General [*Raymond* and *Yorke*]: This is not of a retailer, for a retailer is only a person that keeps an open and visible shop for such sort of wares, and, besides, there may be many instances where a retailer may be obliged to prove duties, as where a parcel of goods come into a shop in a suspicious manner and are freshly pursued. There, the retailer ought either to discover the person he bought these goods from or prove the duties were paid.

The *onus probandi* is on the claimer as importer upon the Act of Navigation by 13 Car. II, ca. 11, an act for preventing frauds and regulating abuses in His Majesty's customs, § 28, fol. 1223.[1]

Proof of duties paid is to lie on the claimer as importer thereof of vinegar and wines imported, negatively, not on the king, by 1 Jac., ca. 3, § 9, fol. 1497.[2]

The *onus probandi* of duties paid for tobacco or sugar is to lie on the claimer generally and, negatively, not on His Majesty, by 1 Jac. II, ca. 4, § 12, *ad finem* page 1500.[3]

The *onus probandi* that the goods were not of the growth of France is to lie on the importer, claimer, seller, and retailer. 1 Will. & Mar., ca. 34, § 4, fo. 1550.[4] 1 Will. & Mar., ca. 6, § 4, page 1557, the clause on which the information is grounded.

Proof where goods were manufactured is to lie on the owner, 12 Will., ca. 10, § 4, page 2100, East India Act, claimed by any person or persons as importer thereof.

409

Scott, *qui tam* v. Caukwell

(Ex. 1723)

The question in this case was whether, in a qui tam *action for smuggling, the master of the vessel involved must be alleged to have been aware of it.*

Taussig MS. 311, vol. 1, p. 512

Easter term 1723. John Scott, *qui tam* v. Caukwell.

An information [was exhibited] upon the seizure of a keel for being employed in running goods. And the evidence was that brandy was put on board the keel, but [there was] no evidence that the master of the keel was either present in the keel at the time of the putting the brandy on board or was any way privy to it. See 8 Queen Anne, ca. 7, § [*blank*], page 122.[5] And the information did not set forth so much that the master was cognizant of this fact, but, however, for fear of any conclusion of a verdict, the information being *contra formam statuti*, the Chief Baron [Montagu] gave way to saving this point to the defendant.

So there was a verdict for the king, subject to the Chief Baron [Montagu]'s opinion.

Query what became of this case.

---

[1] Stat. 14 Car. II, c. 11 (*SR*, V, 393–400).

[2] Stat. 1 Jac. II, c. 3, s. 8 (*SR*, VI, 3).

[3] Stat. 1 Jac. II, c. 4, s. 14 (*SR*, VI, 7).

[4] Stat. 1 Will. & Mar., c. 34, s. 2 (*SR*, VI, 100).

[5] Stat. 8 Ann., c. 14, s. 1 (*SR*, IX, 233–234).

410

Snow, *qui tam* v. Marshall

(Ex. 1723)

The question in this case was whether, in a suit for non-payment of import duties, the defendant can give evidence of a condemnation of the goods in issue.

Harvard Law School MS. 1082, vol. 1, p. 169

25 May 1723.

An information of seizure was brought for non-payment of duties etc. Upon the trial, the defendant produced a condemnation in evidence. And the same point was now spoken to again, as in the case of Carter v. Saywell, *vide ante*,[1] whether this condemnation ought not to be pleaded and they could not give it in evidence. This condemnation is a judgment of the court. Whoever offers to give this in evidence admits the goods were once forfeited, which is the very point of the information, and this being a confession and an evidence of the charge, it cannot be given in evidence. 2 Rolle, *Abridgment*, [Triall, p.] 682.

[To the] objection, upon the general issue, the defendant may give everything in evidence that proves the plaintiff has no cause of action, [he] responded this rule is too general, but it ought to be confined to that which shows there never was any cause of action. A good deal of inconvenience has arisen by the admission of infancy or coverture being given in evidence upon [a plea of] *non assumpsit*, but, even in those cases, that shows that there never was a cause of action.

[To the] objection the condemnation extinguishes the liableness there was of the goods for the payment of duties, [he] responded that is only by way of special discharge and does not show that they were originally not liable. Duties paid is admitted in evidence [upon a plea of] *non importata modo et forma*, but that is the very point of the information so that the defendant is a relator is admitted in evidence because it goes to prove that the duties have been paid. Inconveniences if this evidence be admitted are: first, matter of fact and law and matter of record are put in issue to the jury; second, if the condemnation had been pleaded, the Attorney General might here have replied *per fraudem*, which he cannot be prepared to do in evidence, so the Attorney General might to the plea have admitted the condemnation, but taken issue upon the identity of the goods.

Mr. *Ward*, for the defendant: [To the] objection whatever confesses and avoids etc. is not to be given in evidence, [he] responded courts are not so thick now in pleadings as they have been, and, therefore, in civil actions, parties are admitted to give matters of discharge upon the general issue, as in *assumpsit* usury, which admits the promise, but avoids it. Infancy and coverture upon *non*

[1] *Carter v. Saywell* (Ex. 1719), see above, Case No. 108; *Saywell, qui tam v. Carter* (Ex. 1720–1722), see above, Case No. 155.

assumpsit is admitted. That condemnation is a good defense and it is consistent with the issue joined upon this information, which charges that the goods were liable to payment of customs and did not pay customs, the law puts the *onus probandi* upon the defendant, and the plaintiff goes no farther on these informations than to prove the seizure. And, therefore, the defendant has a right to show everything which proves the plaintiff had no cause of seizure. Condemnation does purge the payment of duties. Syms v. Reynoldson, 1709; Doe v. Hobbs.

[To the] objection condemnation admits the goods were once imported, [he] responded no, for they might be prohibited, as they might be condemned for want of a claim. Condemnation cannot admit that, at the time of the seizure by the plaintiff, the goods were liable to the payment of duties, but the contrary. The practice and usage of the court is the law of the court, and there is no instance of any condemnation pleaded.

[To the] objection of inconveniences of the part of the crown if the cond[emnation] be given in evidence, [he] responded, when law is blended with fact, it is proper to be determined by a jury under the direction of the judge. Upon evidence, the Attorney General may show the condemnation was by fraud; so he may controvert the identity of the goods. [As to] inconvenience of the defendant's side, it would discourage bidders that they must take out and plead these long records and at this vast expense, upon informations *non importatis* it is common to show the ship came in involuntarily and by stress of weather, yet this admits the importation but avoids it. Payment of duties is admitted in evidence. The evidence of his being a retailer is admitted and it is not an evidence that the duties were paid. And it would be hard that a fair purchaser should not be as much favored as a common retailer.

[To the] objection that *non importata* is not the general issue in this case, 2 Keble, fo. 859,[1] [he] responded this is totally unintelligible; the Stat. 21 Jac. I, cap. 4, par. 4, see the paragraph.[2]

Chief Baron [MONTAGU]: *Non importata* is not the general issue within the Act of Parliament. Mr. Ward is taking the two clauses together. It is plain informations of seizure are within the clause of the Act.

[To the] objection it is not an information brought against any parties, [he] responded the defendant comes in, prays oyer, claims and *gravite vexato forae* etc. A claimer is always looked upon as a defendant to the information within the Statute and may take advantage of it. See Stat. 6 Geo. *Rex*.

Solicitor General [*Yorke*]: Usury upon a promissory note may be given in evidence because the contract is void, but it cannot upon a bond. The time when the goods were imported is not material, but if they are fixed at any time upon lands, the duties not being paid, they are liable to forfeiture.

---

[1] *Burleigh v. Child* (1672), 2 Keble 859, 84 E.R. 544.

[2] Stat. 21 Jac. I, c. 4, s. 4 (*SR*, IV, 1215).

[To the] objection that everybody is to take notice of the rules of law, [he] responded that is the very point now in debate. Inconvenience to the crown is real; to the defendant, only imaginary, for the Attorney General cannot possibly know this matter before it is produced.

[To the] objection of discouragement to bidders, [he] responded they must defend their property as other persons do.

[To the] objection of great expense, [he] responded the same is when he gives it in evidence.

[To the] objection of importation by the stress of weather, [he] responded there is a great difference between an issue of excuse and a matter of discharge. A man's being a retailer is accepted as evidence that the goods in his ship have paid duties.

But note this is by reason of the impossibility the retailer would be under to prove the payment of the duties. The Stat. 21 Jac. I only extends to personal informations, but not to real informations. *Non importata* is not a general issue in these informations. And this is not the only instance where there is no general issue, for, in the case of informations on *quo warranto*, there is no general issue.

Lord Chief Baron MONTAGU seemed clear of opinion this could not be given in evidence.

Baron PRICE: If this ever had been pleaded, the record must be produced, but no such is to be found.

Baron GILBERT: Confessing and avoiding must be pleaded, but what tends to the direct proof of the issue may be given in evidence.

This is a traverse of the offense in the information; it is a denial, and the question is whether this is evidence of the denial.

[The case is] to be spoken to again.

Taussig MS. 311, vol. 1, p. 504, pl. 2

Easter term 1723.

Solicitor General [*Yorke*] exhibited an information of seizure of coffee for non-payment of duties.

[There was] a plea that they were not imported and laid upon land *contra formam statuti*. For the defendant, it was insisted that this coffee was condemned in this court.

But it was objected that this was not to be given in evidence, but it ought to have been pleaded. The information charges that these goods were between 1 June 1721 and May 1722 brought and imported and laid on land, duties not paid or agreed for. Either pleading or giving in evidence a condemnation admits an unlawful importation. Therefore, it is not evidence on this issue because the issue is a negative. 2 Rolle's *Abr.*, 682, pl. 2, a confession and avoidance is not to be given in evidence; ditto, pl. 3; ditto, pl. 11, that a license to buy up is not evidence upon *non culpabilis* for engrossing. So, if there is a former recovery for the same penalty, it must be pleaded; so *autrefois acquit ou convict* must be pleaded.

These cases prove that a confession and avoidance is not evidence. The rule that a defendant may give in evidence whatever shows that the plaintiff has no cause of action is not the right rule, but whatever proves that the plaintiff never had a cause of action. [In an action of] debt for rent, eviction is evidence because the rent was due; therefore, there is no cause of action; so infancy or coverture on [a plea of] *non assumpsit*.

Condemnation has extinguished their liableness to duties. [He] answered it is true, but the question is whether it is to be given in evidence or is pleadable only.

Payment of duties may be given in evidence because it is evidence going to the very point of the information. And this is the reason why a man's being a retailer is given in evidence because it is evidence of duties paid and so comes up to the former case.

If upon this issue, such is evidence, then matter of fact and matter of record is put in issue. This is inconvenient.

The second inconvenience is that it deprives the Attorney General of replying that the condemnation was by fraud or he might have joined issue on the identity of the goods; so neither in point of law nor reason is this evidence admissible.

Ward, contra: Answers to a general proposition are not so strict now as formerly in points of pleadings. And, therefore, it is now admitted in [an action of] *assumpsit* to give usury in evidence; so infancy and coverture on the same issue, and yet those matters are matters of discharge.

Mr. Solicitor [General] admits a condemnation to be a good defense. And I shall prove it. The information charges that the goods were liable to pay duties. And this is evidence of a condemnation, no admission of this point. And, besides, it is stronger in the case of an information than in other cases because the *onus probandi* lies on the defendant. And all informations allege that goods are liable to pay duties.

Mr. Solicitor [General] says that the condemnation admits the goods were once imported without payment of duties. [He] answered the goods might have been condemned as being prohibited or for want of a claim. Secondly, the liableness of the goods to pay duty must be applied to the time of the seizure. And that is very far from being admitted by this sort of evidence. But the practice of this court, which is the law of the court, is always to give this matter in evidence. During Ward, Dodd, and Bury's time, this was always given in evidence.

As to the inconvenience of fraud, the Attorney General may show fraud in evidence as well as reply to it.

Secondly, if the identity of the goods is not proved, then the condemnation is not proved. But the inconvenience is great on the other side because it is a great expense to plead this and it would make records tedious and prolix.

That a ship came in but involuntary is always admitted on the general issue; so payment of duties; so being a retailer. Retailer is not evidence of duties paid, but that he need not show payment of them. Surely a bidder is much more to be favored than a retailer.

2 Keble 859 has been cited to prove *non importata* was not the general issue. But the case is unintelligible.

Chief Baron [Montagu]: The Act of King James only extends to personal informations. And the meaning of Lord Chief Baron Hale in the case in Keble is that *non importata fuerunt* was not the general issue within that Statute.

Sed per Ward: The proviso in the Statute shows that the Statute was not only intended with relation to personal informations. 6 Geo.; exception of goods condemned shows it may be given in evidence.

Mr. Solicitor [General *Yorke*] replies: [To the] objection that this was the constant rule, the solution [is] I do not hear any one case cited for this point.

[To the] objection that rules of pleading are not so strictly held to as formerly, the solution [is] it is true, but I think this is rather an argument against going further than for it. The *onus probandi* lies upon every defendant who is to show a discharge. The time in the information is not material. And, therefore, the question is whether, at any time, these goods were imported, duties not paid.

Matter of excuse is very different from matter of discharge. And that is the case of importation by stress of weather; that is not an importation *contra formam statuti*.

The Statute confines evidence to the very two identical general issues of *non culpabilis* or *nil debet*. Both these issues are issues in personal informations, and that shows that the Statute extended no further. [There is] no general issue in *quo warranto*, and, therefore, no such wonderful thing that there should be cases where there is no general issue. And, indeed, these informations *in rem* upon a seizure are like to informations in the nature of a *quo warranto*.

Chief Baron: Trials here are very long. And this sort of evidence would make them much longer. He insists that no instances have been cited of this practice. And, during the time he was Attorney General, he never remembered any such case.

411

Wright v. Grove

(Ex. 1723)

A supersedeas *upon a writ of error in the House of Lords survives a prorogation of Parliament.*

Taussig MS. 311, vol. 1, p. 515

Friday, the first day of [Trinity] term [1723]. Grove v. Wright.

Sir Constantine Phipps moved for liberty to take out execution, the writ of error in Parliament being determined by the prorogation of Parliament.

N.B. The defendant in error gave notice that they would move to have liberty to take out execution.

The motion was opposed by counsel. And 2 Lev. 75[1] was cited as an express authority in point that the prorogation of Parliament is no determination of the writ of error. Raymond 383; to the same effect in 1 Ventr. 236.[2]

But the court would make no rule.

Sir Constantine Phipps: [*blank*] and Roberts, in Trinity 7 George;[3] it was determined that error was not a *supersedeas* after a prorogation. In this case, the record was not transcribed.

Chief Baron [Montagu]: The defendant in error is under this dilemma, if it is a *supersedeas*, then we cannot grant you liberty to take out execution, if it is not, you have no reason to apply to us.

The court denied to do anything in it.

And by Page: I believe the law is and has been since settled, as in Levinz.

Then the plaintiff's counsel moved for costs of the motion.

But the court rejected it with anger. And the Chief Baron said that counsel should not move an extraordinary thing because they had a lord for their client.

Bunbury 131, 145 E.R. 621

14 June 1723.

A writ of error was brought upon a judgment in [an action of] trespass into the House of Lords. The House being prorogued, the writ of error, as was alleged, was expired.

And, therefore, it was now moved by *Sir Constantine Phipps*, for leave to take out [a writ of] execution, the record also having never been transcribed, it was said, the Lords could do nothing upon it.

But *per* curiam (*absente* Price, baron), if the prorogation is a *supersedeas*, you may take out execution without applying to the court. If it is not, we cannot grant the motion. What the Lords do in their judicial capacity goes over from session to session, as matters below do from term to term.

And the motion was denied, being opposed by Mr. *Kettleby* and Mr. *Raby*.

Harvard Law School MS. 1082, vol. 1, p. 172, pl. 1

[Trinity term 1723.]

Sir Constantine Phipps moved for liberty to take out execution upon a judgment in [an action of] trespass, there being a writ of error brought into the House

---

[1] *Pibus v. Mitford* (1673–1674), 2 Levinz 75, 83 E.R. 456, also 3 Keble 239, 316, 338, 84 E.R. 697, 741, 754, 1 Ventris 372, 86 E.R. 239, 3 Salkeld 337, 91 E.R. 859, T. Raymond 228, 83 E.R. 119, 1 Modern 98, 121, 159, 86 E.R. 761, 780, 800, 1 Freeman 351, 369, 89 E.R. 262, 275, Lincoln's Inn MS. Misc. 500, ff. 214v, 224, 236 (Edward Ward's reports).

[2] *Rex v. Earl of Castlemain* (1680), T. Raymond 379, 383, 83 E.R. 198, 200, 3 State Trials 36 (Hargrave, ed., 1776); *Anonymous* (1673), 1 Ventris 236, 86 E.R. 158.

[3] *White v. Roberts* (Ex. 1720), see above, Case No. 140.

of Lords and the House being prorogued, 2 Levinz 93,[1] the writ of error, as was alleged, was expired.

But this was opposed by Mr. *Kettleby*, who quoted the case above to prove the prorogation is not a discharge of the writ of error.

Mr. *Raby*, of the same side: It is not a motion of course. Raymond 383, 4; Lord Statton; 2 Cro., Bishop of Ossery's Case; Orders of the Lords, 19 June 1673; 1 Ventris 266.[2]

Sir Constantine Phipps replies: White v. Roberts, Trinity 7 Geo. *Rex*. The record was never transcribed, and, therefore, there never was anything before the House of Lords that they cannot do anything upon.

Lord Chief Baron MONTAGU: This is not a motion of course. If the prorogation is a *supersedeas*, you may take out an execution without applying to the court. If it is not a *supersedeas*, then, we cannot grant the motion. What the Lords do in their judicial capacity goes over from session to session, as matters before us do from term to term.

Per TOTAM CURIAM (*absente* Price), the motion was denied.

412

Rodd v. Lord Coningsby

(Ex. 1723)

Ancient demesne is not a good plea to a personal action in the Court of Exchequer for money damages only.

Where a plea to the jurisdiction of a court in overruled, the defendant can plead further.

Harvard Law School MS. 1082, vol. 1, p. 172, pl. 3

19 June 1723.

An action of trespass was brought for entering his house. The defendant pleads that the house was part of the manor of the Manden and that it was ancient demesne and all lands in ancient demesne etc. ought to be tried *in manerii* etc. The plaintiff demurs.

Mr. *Wills*, for the plaintiff: This plea is not sufficient to oust this court of jurisdiction. Courts of ancient demesne have no jurisdiction in personal actions, especially in trespass. 4 Inst. 269, 270, 224; Lib. 5, 150, Aldsworth, Cro. El. 826,

[1] *Goston v. Sedgwick* (1673), 2 Levinz 93, 83 E.R. 465.

[2] *Rex v. Earl of Castlemain* (1680), *ut supra*; *Bishop of Ossory's Case* (1619), Croke Jac. 534, 79 E.R. 458, Palmer 22, 81 E.R. 959; *Lord Eure v. Turton* (1675), 1 Ventris 266, 86 E.R. 178, also 2 Levinz 120, 83 E.R. 478, 3 Keble 416, 84 E.R. 797.

Arden; Hobart 47, Fox v. [*blank*].[1] The reason given why the court of ancient demesne has not jurisdiction in personal actions is because the title does not come in question. 1 Rolle's *Abridgment*, 322.[2] But only the wrong is in question.

Mr. *Raby* for the defendant: In an action where the title may come in question, jurisdiction of ancient demesne courts is admitted, then the title may come in question here, which is a *clausum fregit*.

This action of account is grounded on 21 Edw. III, fo. 10,[3] because the tenure might be drawn in question. 4 Edw. III, fo. 47.[4]

Replevin being the avower's, it might be that it was damage feasant in the freehold. This plea is allowed [so] that the title in this action might come in question. Dyer 23, 183.[5]

It was objected by Baron Page that this could not be pleaded after a full defense.

He responded upon looking into the record, it was only *venit et defendit vim et injuriam etc.* without *quando etc.* And he said also that this would have been only a matter of form.

Mr. *Wills* replies: Though the freehold might come in question in trespass, yet that is only accidentally and it does not naturally attend to bring the title in question and no judgment in this action can bind the freehold, but only damages are given. The case of account was against a guardian and the question was whether he was a guardian in socage or chivalry.

Replevins were formerly (before the use of ejectments came up) the common method of trying titles.

Lord Chief Baron Montagu: Nothing can be recovered in this action but damages, which affect the person only. And, therefore, this plea cannot be good. There can be no other tenure in ancient demesnes than only socage tenure. Whenever damages only can be recovered, ancient demesne is no plea.

Baron Price: Whenever an action is *contra pacem* or *vi et armis*, even though the title comes in question, the court of ancient demesnes has no jurisdiction and consequently is not pleadable. The house ought to be ancient demesne as well as the manor. In an action against a lord of a manor, he shall not insist upon his own jurisdiction in his own court so as to be judge in his own cause. But now, it did not appear upon the record that the defendant was lord of the manor.

---

1 E. Coke, *Fourth Institute* (1644), pp. 269–270, 224; *Smith v. Alden* (1601), 5 Coke Rep. 105, 77 E.R. 217, Croke Eliz. 826, 78 E.R. 1053, also 2 Anderson 178, 123 E.R. 609; *Cox v. Barnsly* (1613), Hobart 47, 80 E.R. 197, also Moore K.B. 211, 72 E.R. 537.

2 1 Rolle, Abr., *Auntient demeasne*, pl. E, 11, 12, p. 322.

3 YB Hil. 21 Edw. III, f. 10, pl. 30 (1347).

4 YB Mich. 4 Edw. III, f. 47, pl. 34 (1330).

5 *Anonymous* (1538), 1 Dyer 23, 73 E.R. 49; *Anonymous* (1560), 2 Dyer 183, 73 E.R. 403.

Baron PAGE: Ejectment is *vi et armis*, but the term is to be recovered there where the title is impeached so that it was *in rem*. The court of ancient demesne may have jurisdiction, but if it affects the person only, they have not.

And so *per opinionem* TOTIUS CURIAE (*absente* Gilbert, Baron), judgment was given for the plaintiff.

And judgment was given in another case of the same nature at the same time. Wherever a party pleads to the jurisdiction of the court, the judgment is only *respondeat ouster indilate*.

Taussig MS. 311, vol. 1, p. 517, pl. 2

Trinity term 1723.

Thomas Rodd brings [an action of] trespass against Lord Coningsby *et alios* for entering into his house in Marden and keeping possession thereof *a tali die usque talem diem*.

The defendants plead that the house was *infra manerii de* Marden, which manor was ancient demesne. The plaintiff demurs.

Pro querente: This is no plea to an action of trespass *quare clausum fregit*. 4 Inst., ca. 42, page [*blank*]; ditto, ca. 58, page 269, 270; 5 Rep. 105, Alden's Case, in ejectment it was held a good [plea], but in trespass *quare clausum fregit*, it is not a good plea; 44 Edw. III, 38; 46 Edw. III, 1; Cro. Eliz. 826, Case of Alden; Hob. 47; 2 Hen. VII, 17; *Doctrina Placitandi*, page 51, 52; Bro., *Abr.*, title Ancient Demesne; 1 Rolle's *Abr.*, 322.[1]

Raby admitted that, in real actions and in actions where title may come in question, it is a good plea. But this is such an action as the title may come in question upon. Alden's Case goes no further in judgment than that it is good in [an action of] ejectment. Only 46 Edw. III, 1, is that it is not good in [an action of] trespass, but that is a trespass *de bonis asportatis*. And the books of 21 Edw. III, fo. 10, in [an action of] account against a guardian in socage, and 4 Edw. III, 47, in [an action of] replevin are stronger than the case in question. So that the rule is where the right may possibly be brought into question. Dier 23 [is] to show that the title may come in question on this action *quare clausum fregit*. Dier 183.

PAGE: Here is a full defense *vim et injuriam quando* etc., but that happened by mistake, for the defense went no further than *vim et injuriam*.

Mr. *Wills* replies: The case in 46 Edw. III is a *clausum fregit*, as in this very case.

Chief Baron [MONTAGU]: [It is] not a good plea because damages only are recoverable in this action. And that is the true distinction. Tenants in ancient demesne are taxable *de alto et basso*, and they are not chargeable towards a knight's fee for the county and not bound thereby, which is the reason of 21 Edw. III, [an

[1] E. Coke, *Fourth Institute* (1644), pp. 224, 269–270; *Smith v. Alden* (1601), *ut supra*; YB Mich. 44 Edw. III, ff. 37, 38, pl. 30 (1370); YB Hil. 46 Edw. III, f. 1, pl. 2 (1372); *Cox v. Barnsly* (1613), Hobart 47, 80 E.R. 197, also Moore K.B. 211, 72 E.R. 537; YB Trin. 2 Hen. VII, f. 17, pl. 1 (1487); 1 Rolle, Abr., *Auntient demeasne*, pl. E, 11, 12, p. 322.

action of] account against a guardian in socage. And [an action of] replevin is for profits of the land and so *in rem.*

PRICE: Your plea is wrong on another account, for you do not allege that the house is ancient demesne, but only that it is held of an ancient demesne manor and, notwithstanding that, it may be a frank fee. But where this action is brought against a lord of such a manor, he cannot plead it.

But note that it did not appear by the record that the defendant was lord of the manor.

PAGE: The plea is only good where the possession is affected by the judgment in the action.

And so judgment was *quod respondeat ouster pro omnes.*

Per CHIEF BARON: Ancient demesne [. . .] plea in waste because the Statute only gives the place wasted.

Per PAGE: Wherever judgment is given upon a plea to the jurisdiction, the judgment is *respondeat ouster indilate.*

Bunbury 132, 145 E.R. 621

19 June 1723.

An action of trespass was brought for entering the plaintiff's house. The defendant pleads the house was held of his manor of Marden and that it was ancient demesne and all actions etc. ought to be tried *in curia manerii.* The plaintiff demurs.

Per TOTAM CURIAM: Judgment for the plaintiff, for whatever damages only are to be recovered and [where] an action is *contra pacem* or [*vi*] *et armis*, though the title may come in question, ancient demesne is not pleadable.

Mr. *Wills* [was] for the plaintiff; Mr. *Raby* [was] for the defendant.

413

Edwards v. Hughes

(Ex. 1723–1726)

In this case, the amercement in issue by the custom of the manor without affeering was void.

A custom can be well pleaded without mentioning the exceptions thereto.

Taussig MS. 311, vol. 1, p. 531

Trinity term 1723.

[An action of] trespass [was brought] for taking two oxen. The justification was it was for an amercement for non-appearance.

Comyns, serjeant, *pro querente*: *Quilibet tenens de quolibet libero tenemento non residant infra [. . .]*.[1] Co. Lit. 68b; 2 Inst. 121.[2] All ecclesiastical persons having cure of souls are excused by the common law. F.N.B. 160; 52 Hen. III, ca. 10, Stat. Marlebridge.[3]

And so it was always used to be pleaded. And this Act is in the negative. And so there can be no prescription against it. (Unintelligible.[4]) He is to appear at one of the three courts *semel in anno*. And, if he does not appear *ad duas alias curias*, he shall pay to the steward an essoin penny, and, if he did not appear *ad aliam curiam*, he should be amerced 7s.

3. The amercement by the steward is 7s. By Magna Carta, an amercement is to be affeered. F.N.B. 75; 1 Rolle 542, Hob. 129; Greisley's Case, 8 Rep. 41; Keilway 65; 1 Lev. 19; Cro. Car. 275, 1 Jones 300; 3 Lev. 206; Shore 61, Salkeld [*blank*]; 3 Lev. 48.[5] An amercement is called *misericordia*.

4. They do not pursue their own custom as set forth, for they amerce him more than by the custom as set forth.

5. How far the levying by distress is good.

6. *De injuria sua propria*, if not good in this case, as Crogate's Case,[6] yet it is only a matter of form. Hob. 76; 1 Rolle's *Abr.*, 200; Raymond 60; Raymond 50; 3 Lev. 49.[7] [Stat.] 4 & 5 *Reginae* aids all matters of form.[8]

---

[1] any tenant of any free tenement not residing within [. . .].

[2] E. Coke, *First Institute* (1628), f. 68b; E. Coke, *Second Institute* (1642), p. 121.

[3] A. Fitzherbert, *Natura Brevium*; Stat. 52 Hen. III, c. 10 (*SR*, I, 22).

[4] Sic in MS.

[5] Stat. 25 Edw. I, Magna Carta, c. 14 (*SR*, I, 116); A. Fitzherbert, *Natura Brevium*; *Wilton v. Hardingham* (1616), 1 Rolle, Abr., *Court*, pl. Y, 5, p. 542, Hobart 129, 80 E.R. 278; *Griesley's Case* (1588), 8 Coke Rep. 38, 77 E.R. 530, also Savile 93, 123 E.R. 1031; *Anonymous* (1505), Keilwey 65, 72 E.R. 225, 116 Selden Soc. 457; *Conyers v. Franke* (1681), 3 Levinz 19, 83 E.R. 555; *Griffith v. Biddle* (1632), Croke Car. 275, 79 E.R. 840, W. Jones 300, 82 E.R. 158; *Evelin v. Davies* (1685), 3 Levinz 206, 83 E.R. 653; *Matthews v. Cary* (1689), 1 Shower K.B. 61, 89 E.R. 449, 1 Salkeld 107, 91 E.R. 98, 3 Salkeld 52, 91 E.R. 686, also 3 Modern 137, 87 E.R. 88, Comberbach 76, 90 E.R. 353, Carthew 73, 90 E.R. 646, Holt K.B. 408, 90 E.R. 1125; *Wells v. Cotterell* (1682), 3 Levinz 48, 83 E.R. 571.

[6] *Crogate v. Marys* (1608), 8 Coke Rep. 66, 77 E.R. 574, *sub nom. Crogate v. Morris*, 1 Brownlow & Goldesborough 197, 123 E.R. 751, 2 Brownlow & Goldesborough 55, 146, 123 E.R. 812, 864.

[7] *Banks v. Parker*, Hobart 76, 80 E.R. 226; *Nois v. Jackman* (1609), 1 Rolle, Abr., *Amendment*, pl. B, 28, p. 200; *Herbert v. Walters* (1695), 1 Lord Raymond 59, 91 E.R. 935, also Comberbach 344, 90 E.R. 518, 12 Modern 85, 88 E.R. 1181, 5 Modern 118, 87 E.R. 556, Carthew 362, 90 E.R. 811, 1 Salkeld 205, 91 E.R. 183, Skinner 595, 90 E.R. 267, Holt K.B. 191, 90 E.R. 1004; *Collins v. Walker* (1661), T. Raymond 50, 83 E.R. 28, also 1 Keble 164, 83 E.R. 876; *Wells v. Cotterell* (1682), 3 Levinz 48, 83 E.R. 571.

[8] Stat. 4 & 5 Ann., c. 3, s. 22 (*SR*, VIII, 460).

Bootle, contra: The replication is naught and the demurrer to the replication [is good]. Crogate's Case shows plainly it is substance and not form. This is a court leet held by custom. And that appears by Magna Carta, which confines keeping courts leets to twice *per annum.*[1]

As to the power of a steward, [*blank*] Case of 11 Hen. VI, fo. 12,[2] the difference between a fine and an amercement.

None of the statutes extend to particular customs. West., ca. 18; 2 Inst. 196, fine and amercement used promiscuously; 10 Hen. VI, 7; Bro., Amercement, pl. 50, *quilibet tenens.*[3] 2 Hen. IV, 15;[4] a traveler may be summoned into the leet. And the Statute only intended to excuse lords going through a leet in journeys and not to excuse them if tenants. The answer to not affeering the amercements is that this is a leet held according to customs and not according to the common law. Customs are allowed contrary to the common law. 12 Hen. IV, fol. 8, Bro., Amercements, 19; Cro. Car. 551, William Jones 349.[5]

The argument was put off.

Taussig MS. 311, vol. 1, p. 561

Michaelmas term 1723.

Bootle: The replication *de injuria sua propria* generally is not good because there is matter of right and title in the justification, and it is certain by Crogate's Case it is not good. And by the case in 3 Lev. 65,[6] it is not good upon a general demurrer, though it may be helped after a verdict. Hob. 76; Raymond 50; 3 Lev. 49.

[To the] objection the custom is *quilibet tenens* and so too large and does not take in the exceptions of the Statute of Marlebridge, [he] answered this is a special custom and so not affected by the Statute of Magna Carta referred to by the Statute of Marlebridge, for there is in that Statute a saving of custom. 2 Sanders 290[7] is that a leet may be held otherwise; 2 Hen. IV, 15,[8] by the common law, even travelers are bound to attend a leet.

---

1 Stat. 25 Edw. I, Magna Carta, c. 35 (*SR*, I, 118).

2 *Prior of Montague's Case* (1428), YB Mich. 7 Hen. VI, f. 12, pl. 17.

3 Stat. 3 Edw. I, Westminster I, c. 18 (*SR*, I, 31–32); E. Coke, *Second Institute* (1642), p. 196; YB Mich. 10 Hen. VI, f. 7, pl. 22, Brooke, Abr., *Amerciament*, pl. 50 (1431).

4 YB Mich. 7 Hen. VI, ff. 12, 13, pl. 17 (1428).

5 YYB Mich. 12 Hen. IV, f. 8, pl. 15 (1410), Brooke, Abr., *Amerciament*, pl. 19; *Evelin's Case* (1639), Croke Car. 551, 79 E.R. 1075, W. Jones 439, 82 E.R. 230.

6 *Fursdon v. Weeks* (1682), 3 Levinz 61, 83 E.R. 577.

7 *Dakin's Case* (1671), 2 Williams Saunders 290, 85 E.R. 1077, also 1 Ventris 107, 86 E.R. 74, 2 Keble 731, 84 E.R. 462.

8 YB Mich. 7 Hen. VI, ff. 12, 13, pl. 17 (1428).

[To the] objection the alleging the custom is uncertain, [he] answered it is stated that there are three courts in every year, *viz.* the Mondays after Christmas, Easter, and [*blank*], and if he appears not at any, he is to pay 7s.

[To the] objection that the amercement is not affeered, [he] answered this is not an amercement set by a jury. Those amercements must be affeered. Hob. 129. But this being set by the steward, there is no need of affeering. 11 Hen. VI, fol. 12; the authority of a steward is equal with that of a justice that is within his jurisdiction. If, indeed, this had been a fine, then, according to Greisley's Case, it must have been affeered, and, though these are taken sometimes to be different, yet amercement and fine are sometimes used as synonymous terms, as in Westminster I, ca. 18; 2 Inst. 196.

Secondly, this is already certain. And the very end of affeering is only *in certitudinem pro onere* as by Lord Coke; Fitz. N.B. 75, the writ *de moderata misericordia*; Greisley's Case; 38 Hen. III [*blank*] 7 *in dorso*, cited in Greisley's Case; Bro. *Amercements* 50; 10 Hen. VI, 7, is express that amercements by a steward need no affeering.[1] But, however, if amercements set by a steward ought generally to be affeered, yet here is a custom directly contrary, and a custom will prevail against the common law.

Cases to show that a custom prevails against the common law [are] Cro. Car. 551, Jones 439; Cro. Jac. 532; 1 Lutw. [*blank*], Mayor of Bedford and Fox; 12 Hen. IV, 8, by custom, a lord may amerce a man for a trespass to himself.[2]

[It was] objected the amercement does not pursue the custom; it does.

[To the] objection it cannot justify a sale, [he] answered, by a custom, he may. 11 Rep. 44, in Godfrey's Case.

Serjeant *Comyns* replies: In 1 Lev. 65, it was held a good plea upon a general demurrer. As to custom, a woman is a tenant of the freehold; so is a parson. But they owe no service at a court leet. And the Statute is in the negative and not to be prescribed against.

The saving in Magna Carta only extends to the time of keeping courts, not to the persons who are to attend it.

Secondly, the plea is *ad unam praedictam curiam* not *ad aliquam praedictam curiam*. [There was] no allegation that the tenant was summoned at any time or by any person in certain.

Amercements. There is less necessity to affeer an amercement set by the homage than where set by the steward. And there is no one instance that ever it was adjudged that an amercement ought not to be affeered. A fine is for an offense done in court. An amercement is for an offense done out of court, though

[1] A. Fitzherbert, *New Natura Brevium*; *Griesley's Case* (1588), *ut supra*; YB Mich. 10 Hen. VI, f. 7, pl. 22, Brooke, Abr., *Amerciament*, pl. 50 (1431).

[2] *Evelin's Case* (1639), *ut supra*; *Mayor of Bedford v. Fox* (1698), 1 Lutwyche 562, 125 E.R. 295; YB Mich. 12 Hen. IV, f. 8, pl. 15 (1410).

it is true that, sometimes, the words are promiscuously used. And he agrees the steward's fine is not to be affeered because he is a judge of record.

10 Hen. VI was for a contempt in going out of court, and the book takes notice of the other distinction. A writ of *moderata misericordia* does not prove that there was no other redress of the grievance. Dean [*blank*], Shores 61, Salkeld [*blank*], *per* Holt, an amercement not affeered is not good.[1] Every prescription is contrary or variant from the common law. But no prescription can be good against a negative Act of Parliament.

Gilbert: Whether ecclesiastical persons must be always excepted in such prescription [*blank*].

Price: In setting forth the custom, one need not set forth the exceptions that must come on the other side. The replication seems to be [*blank*], but all the books hold it to be a matter of form. And so, perhaps, it is aided by the Statute for Amendment of Law.[2]

Page: I take the prescription of *quilibet liber tenens* to be an entire prescription.

Adjornatur for another argument.

Fitz., title Leet 7, Avowry 11; a steward only has power to fine for offenses in court.[3]

Harvard Law School MS. 1082, vol. 1, p. 184, pl. 3

Michaelmas term 1723.

This was a case concerning the steward's amercing and levying those amercements and upon the replevin and whether a general demurrer on the part of the plaintiff was good.

Bootle, for the defendant, [said] that it was good and cited 8 Rept., Gresley; Hobart 76; Raymond 50; 3 Levinz 49; 3 Levinz 65, express resolution.[4]

[To the] objection that *quilibet tenens* is not good because there is no exception of persons that are not obliged to come to the leet, as clergymen and noblemen, see 2 Inst. 121,[5] [he] answered it does not affect this case, it being a special custom. 2 Saun. 290; Stat. of Mar., cap. 9; 2 Hen. IV, 15.[6]

---

1 *Matthews v. Cary* (1689), *ut supra*.

2 Stat. 4 & 5 Ann., c. 3, s. 22 (*SR*, VIII, 460).

3 YB Pas. 13 Edw. III, Rolls Ser. 31b, vol. 2, p. 215, pl. 22 (1339), Fitzherbert, Abr., *Leete et Hundred*, pl. 7; YB Mich. 20 Hen. VI, f. 6, pl. 16 (1441), Fitzherbert, Abr., *Avowrie*, pl. 11.

4 *Griesley's Case* (1588), *ut supra*; *Banks v. Parker*, *ut supra*; *Collins v. Walker* (1661), *ut supra*; *Wells v. Cotterell* (1683), *ut supra*; *Fursdon v. Weeks* (1682), *ut supra*.

5 E. Coke, *Second Institute* (1642), p. 121.

6 *Dakin's Case* (1671), *ut supra*; Stat. 52 Hen. III, c. 10 (*SR*, I, 22); *Parson of Yuel's Case* (1401), YB Hil. 2 Hen. IV, f. 15, pl. 19.

[To the] second objection, that it was uncertain in alleging the custom, [he] answered it is alleged that there were three customary limits, *viz.* after Easter, Michaelmas, and Christmas every Monday.

[To the] third objection, that this amercement does not appear to be affeered, [he] answered I do agree that, generally, amercements ought to be affeered, and so is Hobart 29; 542; 3 Levinz 19.[1] Here, the jury set the amercements, and so I compare it to a fine. 11 Hen. VI, fo. 12; Stat. Westminster, cap. 18; Gresley's Case, 8 Rept.; 2 Inst. 196.[2] The import of the word affeered is only to reduce it to a certainty. Lord Coke in Gresley's Case, 8 Rept.; Fitzherbert, *Natura Brevium*, 40, 751; 38 Hen. III; 10 Hen. VI, Brooke, *Abridgment*, tit. Am., 50.[3]

Customs may be good contrary to the common law, as to choose a churchwarden. 11 Hen. VII, 14; 21 Hen. VII, 40, pl. 61, Brooke, pres., 40; 21 Edw. III, 46b; 1 Lutwyche 562, Mayor of Bedford v. Fox; 12 Hen. IV.[4]

By custom, the steward may fine or amerce at a sum certain, yet the custom aids and assists it, though contrary to the canon or common law. So the justification is good on the part of the defendant.

[To the] fourth objection, that this amercement does not pursue the custom, [he] answered I think it does, that the person was duly summoned but did not appear on the jury in contempt of the court so that John Edwards was according to the custom amerced.

[To the] fifth objection, that this is bad because the officer has justified not only the distress, but the sale of the goods, [he] answered this is alleged to be by custom, though not perhaps good by [common] law, 11 Rept. 44, Godsal's Case,[5] so being alleged to be by custom so, *pari ratione*, it is good. The case before cited in Lutwyche comes up to this point.

Therefore, for these reasons, I apprehend that the justification is good.

Serjeant *Comyns*, for the plaintiff, [said] that the justification is not good [to the] objection of 3 Levinz 65,[6] that 'every tenant' is too large laid by the custom; [there is] no instance of a prescription laid so large, but the right and usual method is that every person that owes suit and service to the court, and not so

---

1 *Wilton v. Hardingham* (1616), *ut supra*; *Conyers v. Franke* (1681), *ut supra*.

2 *Prior of Montague's Case* (1428), *ut supra*; Stat. 3 Edw. I, Westminster I, c. 18 (*SR*, I, 31–32); *Griesley's Case* (1588), *ut supra*; E. Coke, *Second Institute* (1642), p. 196.

3 *Griesley's Case* (1588), *ut supra*; A. Fitzherbert, *New Natura Brevium*; YB Mich. 10 Hen. VI, f. 7, pl. 22, Brooke, Abr., *Amerciament*, pl. 50 (1431).

4 YB Hil. 11 Hen. VII, ff. 13, 14, pl. 8 (1496); YB Mich. 21 Hen. VII, f. 40, pl. 61 (1505), Brooke, Abr., *Prescription*, pl. 40; *Master of Merton College v. Prior of St. Austin's* (1347), YB Hil. 21 Edw. III, f. 46, pl. 65; *Mayor of Bedford v. Fox* (1698), *ut supra*; YB Mich. 12 Hen. IV, f. 8, pl. 15 (1410).

5 *Bullen v. Godfrey* (1614), 11 Coke Rep. 42, 77 E.R. 1199, also 1 Rolle Rep. 32, 73, 81 E.R. 306, 337.

6 *Fursdon v. Weeks* (1682), *ut supra*.

general as '*quilibet tenens de quolibet tenemento*'. And it is repugnant to the Statute of Marlebridge, for ecclesiastics, married women, infants, and noblemen are excused by that Statute.

The custom as alleged is unintelligible. If he does not appear *ad unam curiam*, I take the natural construction to be that, if he does not appear at each of the courts, then [he is] to forfeit 7s. It is not alleged when the party was summoned or said to be duly summoned so as to take issue upon it. And I think that it is a fatal objection that it is not said that the amercement was affeered. Where the amercement is set by the jury, the better opinion is that it ought to be affeered, but [it is] much stronger when set by the steward. So is Magna Carta, which intended a remedy that no amercement shall be but where affeered and not leave such an arbitrary judgment in the steward, and [it was] never allowed without affeering.

[To the] objection of 10 Hen. VI, I do not dispute that the fines may be set by the steward, and the law directs how it shall be reasonable. And though called an amercement in that book, yet there is a difference between an amercement and a fine, for a fine can only be in the court and the amercement is where it is out of the court. A steward is a judge of record; so he may fine, and there is no occasion for affeering it. Shore Rept. 61, Mathews v. Cary, Salkeld.[1]

No time can corroborate anything against an act of Parliament. A presumption is good against the common law, but it cannot be resembled to this because this custom or prescription is against an act of Parliament. And therefore, it is not like the case of the churchwardens, and there is no parity between them, for the canon cannot take away the custom. Canons may bind as received by virtue of acts of Parliament, and there is no instance of a custom prevailing against an act of Parliament.

GILBERT said that the custom is laid so in the precedents and the difference is as Serjeant Comyns stated it.

PAGE thought the custom good. It is not necessary in laying the custom to set forth the exceptions, and it ought to be construed only such that ought to attend. It is bad on a general demurrer. 3 Levinz 65. And I think that it ought to be assigned particularly.

[The case was] adjourned for a further argument.

Harvard Law School MS. 1082, vol. 1, p. 209, pl. 2

Trinity term 1724.

This was [an action] in replevin. The defendant justified the taking as bailiff under Mr. Morgan, lord of the manor of Brecon, and he sets forth the customs of the court of the said manor *quod quilibet tenens, residens, et inhabitans* in the said

[1] *Matthews v. Cary* (1689), *ut supra*.

manor should appear once in every year, 7s. amerced for that default three times, 1d. for an essoin.

Serjeant *Pengelly*, for the plaintiff, [said] that these amercements not being affeered, it was contrary to Magna Carta and the Statute of Marlbridge. The custom is too general *quod quilibet tenens* and no exception to the persons, for infants are not obliged to appear. 2 Inst. 120, 121; 1 Inst. 28; Statute of Marlebridge, cap. 10.

Amercements imposed contrary to Magna Carta are void. Reg. 175; Coke's explanation of the Statute of Marlbridge, *Coke upon Littleton* 115; 2 Rolle, *Abridgment*, 266; Sir Wm. Jones 270, 290; 2 Inst. 27.

Affeering is *taxare.* 1 Rolle, *Abridgment*, 211; Fitzherbert, *Natura Brevium* 75.[1]

No pretense of any custom is alleged to set 7s. for non-payment of the essoin, and there cannot be a double amercement for the same fault and at the same court. And the absence is only one single default, and it exceeds the custom. And this amercement is not justified which ought not to be for more than the defaulting at three courts. And if a distress is bad for part, it is so for the whole. 1 Saunders 27; Cro. Eliz. 434.

Mr. *Reeves*, for the defendant: [To the] first objection, that the custom is too general and contrary to the acts of Parliament, [he] answered this is a good custom. And though there are exemptions, yet [one is] not obliged to set forth that exemption, but it must come on the other side to show that he is exempt, for this is *lex loci*, as if there is a custom that nobody not free shall exercise a trade within that borough and if the party is a soldier whereby he is exempt and is at liberty to set up in the town, yet the custom is laid generally and it must come on the soldier's part to show he was so. And there is no occasion to set forth the exemptions because it would occasion prolixity. 1 Siderfin 17, Hill v. Bury.[2]

[To the] second objection, [it was a] void custom to amerce at a certain sum and that no amercement ought to be without affeerment, [he] answered this Statute of Magna Carta is in affirmance of the common law and there may be a general custom laid against that Statute. 1 Inst. 115a; Plowden, Commentaries, 465; 2 Inst.; 8 Coke Rept. 48, Gresley's Case.

This amercement is a customary fine, and a steward of a leet is a judge of record. And a fine need not be affeered, as in Gresley's Case, 8 Rept.; 16 Hen. VI, 7; Brooke, tit. Am., 50.

The sum, by the custom, is reduced to a certainty and so there is no occasion for affeering. A custom to sell a distress is good. 11 Hen. VII, 14; 21 Hen. VII, 40, pl. 61.[3]

---

[1] 1 Rolle, Abr., *Amercement*, pl. E, 3, p. 211; A. Fitzherbert, *New Natura Brevium.*

[2] *Hill v. Bunning* (1661), 1 Siderfin 17, 82 E.R. 943.

[3] YB Hil. 11 Hen. VII, ff. 13, 14, pl. 8 (1496); YB Mich. 21 Hen. VII, f. 40, pl. 61 (1505).

[To the] objection that it is not alleged so particularly that for non-payment of the essoin penny, [he] answered but the amercement is not for that but for want of appearing, being duly summoned on the jury.

[To the] objection [it was a] double amercement for the same fault, [he] answered it is not the same fault, though at the same court for not appearing and making defaults at two other courts. If the person takes more rent than he ought, yet he is no trespasser. Godfrey's Case, 11 Rept.

Serjeant *Pengelly* replies for the plaintiff: Where the exemption [was] by the common law, there, laying it generally it will do, but not where it is directed by an act of Parliament, as in this case; so for a toll; where there is an exemption, it ought to be mentioned. The amercement remains as it was introduced by Magna Carta. So great a sum as 7s. must be originally more than a man could be supposed to be worth.

It cannot be a fine because it is not an offense done before the steward in court, yet if a fine is imposed contrary to law, it is void. Godfrey's Case, 11 Rept. 42. In a case of trespass where the justification is entire and if bad in part, it is so for the whole. And so is 2 Ventris.

So he prayed judgment for the plaintiff.

Chief Baron Eyre: It has been objected that the custom is too general to oblige all the inhabitants. It is agreed that, if the exemption is only what arises at common law, that the exemption need not be alleged. And I take this custom to be that all residents within the leet not otherwise exempt are obliged to attend, and there is not one case cited since the Statute of Marlebridge but it is laid as here. 8 Rept., Gresley's Case. And if we should adjudge otherwise, it would set aside all former judgments.

As to 7s. being an amercement, such amercements are in the nature of fines, so there is no occasion for affeering but where the sum is uncertain and left to the discretion of the steward. But this is a sum certain according to the custom and, therefore, in the nature of a fine which we set in the courts [?]. So there is nothing in that objection.

Another objection is 7s. imposed for not appearing or paying the essoin penny; [he] answered, if this is maintainable for either, it is good; there was a sufficient ground for the amercements, 7s. for not appearing and not being of the jury and one default for two offenses and if the party is under two obligations to appear. And, therefore, he was for overruling that objection. I cannot say that that is too much. And I do not see but that it is a good custom.

Price: The custom may be well laid if the custom is justified by the union of England with Wales, for the Statute of 27 Hen. VIII[1] takes away the customs in Wales. And there is no custom subsisting but those returned and of record in the Court of Chancery. And as a custom, it is not good whether it is an amercement

[1] Stat. 27 Hen. VIII, c. 26 (*SR*, III, 563–569).

or a fine. But it is a certain sum, and so there is no occasion for affeering it. And I think that it is not well laid in the plea, for though summoned to appear, yet the question is whether there is such a custom laid for the payment of the essoin penny. And I think it is an extravagant fine to pay 7s. for a default at each court. And, therefore, I think the custom is bad *in toto*, for, if part is bad, the custom being laid together, it must all fall to the ground. So I differ from My Lord Chief Baron.

PAGE: I can get over the first exception as to the custom being laid so generally, and there is no occasion for setting forth the particular exemption. A question has arisen whether it is a fine or amercement. But I take it to be rather a fine, so there is no occasion for affeering it.

If any part was wrong and if too much has been levied, then the whole will be bad. I think that we are bound to judge whether 7s. at each court is a reasonable fine. And I think it too high and it could not have a reasonable commencement, and three times 7s. for a tenant to pay [for] each court every year is more than his inheritance was worth, for the difference of money is very great since the discovery of the East Indies. It seems to me too great. And, therefore, I would consider of it.

GILBERT: I have not considered of the reasonableness of the custom as to the value of 7s. I think that the Statute of Marlbridge was not to destroy *legem loci*, and the presumption must remain in the same manner. So there is nothing in the exception that the custom is laid too generally. I am not so clear in my opinion that this amercement should not be affeered, for Magna Carta has ordered it so to be. The difference between a fine and an amercement is *viz.* that a fine is a ransom from imprisonment and confined to breaches of the peace and contempt in court, and a *capiatur* is awarded for the fine, but, for the amercement, it is always *in misericordia*. The orders of the House of Lords have ascertained amercements. And I question whether a court leet can set a fine. And the Statute of Magna Carta settled that these amercements should be fixed *per pares*, for there might not be the same fault. Dalton 400; Fitzherbert, *Abridgment*, 11.

Per CURIAM, it was ordered this case to be considered further.

Taussig MS. 311, vol. 2, p. 679

Saturday, 13 June 1724.

Serjeant *Pengelly* states the record.

[It was] objected that amercements have not been affeered and a custom to amerce without affeering is void. And likewise there is no exception of any person whatsoever, whereas, at common law, infants are excused. 2 Inst. 121b; 1 Inst. 168. And ecclesiastical persons are excused. Stat. Marlbridge, ca. 10. And a writ of excuse lies upon this Statute for them *prout*. 2 Inst. 120, 121; Reg. 175a; 1 Inst. 115; Jones 270, 290; Rolle's *Abr.*, 2d part, 106, pl. 1, title *Prescription*.

As to affeering the amercements (2 Inst. 27), they must be affeered either by jurors or other affeerors. 1 Rolle's *Abr.*, 211; F.N.B. 75. The Act of Parliament is in the negative. [There is] no practice that there is a custom for the sheriff to impose an amercement for not paying the essoin penny.

[It was] objected there is also a double amercement for one and the same default, and this amercement exceeds the custom laid, for he is only to pay an essoin penny when he appears at one court and makes default at the two others, whereas he is amerced for not appearing at any and for not paying his essoin penny too. 1 Sanders 27, 28; Cro. Eliz. 434, the justification ill in part is ill for the whole.

Reeves: As to the objection of the universality of the custom with respect to persons, the exception ought to come and be pleaded by the party who is to take advantage thereby. And, therefore, the custom may be alleged generally as a custom in a corporation not to exercise a trade within the corporation not being free thereof, whereas the Act of Parliament for Disbanding the Army[1] gives soldiers a liberty to set up a trade in any corporation. Hill and Bunning, 1 Syd. 17; a custom was laid to distrain everything brought on the manor.

[To the] second objection of no affeerment, the solution is, notwithstanding this Statute, there may be a custom to amerce to a certain sum because Magna Carta is in affirmance of the common law and, therefore, though such Statute is in the negative, there may be a prescription against it. 1 Inst. 115; Plowd. 465.

Peers are within the Statute as well as commoners. 2 Inst. 28. An amercement upon peers is by custom reduced to a certainty; so is Greisly's Case; 8 Rep. 39. If an amercement may be reduced to a certainty against peers, why may it not by a particular custom of a place be ascertained against commoners?

This is in the nature of a fine, and a fine need not be affeered. 8 Rep. 39; 10 Hen. VI, 7; Bro., Amercement, 50, where the sum is reduced to a certainty, [there is] no occasion for affeerance if the quantum is reasonable [and] certain; if unreasonable, then the custom is void. 11 Hen. VII, 14; 21 Hen. VII, 40, pl. 61, a custom to pay £3 for a pound breach or making an affray where blood is drawn. A custom will warrant the sale of the distress. 21 Hen. VII, 40, pl. 61.

As to the other objections, they are answered by reading the record. And so there is no occasion to enter into a debate whether the justification may not be good in part. 11 Rep., Godfrey's Case.

Reply: Where an exemption is at common law, there is no need to show it; otherwise, where, by act of Parliament, it is introductive of new law. The custom is to amerce, not that he shall pay 7s. So a custom to amerce must imply affeerment because affeerment belongs to an amercement and the Statute only introduces an oath in affeerment.

Secondly, an amercement was outrageous at common law if considered as a fine. But this is not a fine, for that must be done for an offense in court, whereas this amercement is for not appearing in court. Godfrey's Case, 11 Rep. 42, 43; if a fine be unreasonable, the party may avoid it by a plea.

---

[1] Stat. 12 Ann., c. 14 (*SR*, IX, 791–793).

Chief Baron [Eyre]: Clergymen, having *curam animarum*, and women are exempted at common law; so are infants under twelve and those above sixty. There is no instance of any prescription. Where any exception or exemption is mentioned, there could have been some reason for mentioning the exemptions unless the exemptions are part of the custom. So he thinks this is no objection of weight, for, if it was, it would overturn all the judgments that have been ever given.

Amercements in the nature of fines need not be affeered. And so is Coke's opinion and authority in Greisly's Case.

This is a contempt of court, and we fine gentlemen every assizes for not appearing on the grand jury. Besides, there is no need to affeer any amercement but where the amercement is discretionary, which it is not in this case, for the amercement is fixed to a certain sum. So this objection is of no weight.

Nor can I see what can set aside this custom because the penalty of 7s. is too great.

As to the objection that here are two fines for the same offense, [he] answered that is not so, for the one non-appearance is a double breach of his duty and so may well infer a double penalty.

As to the plea's being ill because there is an amercement for not appearing and not paying the essoin penny, if one 7s. is due, the distress and taking is good.

Price: 27 Hen. VIII takes away all customs in Wales unless returned upon a commission. But he thinks it is too hard to fine him for not appearing as a juryman and a resident too. And he thinks 7s. an outrageous fine or amercement.

Page thinks there is no weight in the first objection. It seems rather to be a fine, but if a custom be to amerce to a sum certain, then there cannot be any other sort of amercement. The court must judge of the reasonableness of the custom. And the judgment must be exercised on the custom at the time of commencement, and this seems to be much too large.

Gilbert accords as to the first objection. He doubts as to the second about affeerment. A fine is out of the Statute, but an amercement is within the Statute. As to amercements of peers, they have been ascertained by the House of Lords. This not appearing is a new feasance, and I doubt whether a fine can be assessed for it. Dalton 400; Fitzherbert, *Abridgment*, Leet 11, Avowry 194. The difference between a fine and an amercement is that a fine is a redemption and a [writ of] *capias* [lies] for it; it is otherwise for an amercement. And the affeering of amercements was to difference freemen from villeins, who were fineable *de alto et basso*.

Taussig MS. 311, vol. 2, p. 722

Michaelmas term 1724.

Fazakerly: The first exception is now waived.

The second exception was that the amercement is not affeered. But, by him, this is a fine. Greisly's Case, 8 Rep.; a fine ought not to be affeered. Keilway 65, that all fines in an act ought to be by the steward. Bro., Amerciament, pl. 50.

The third exception, one cannot sell a distress. Easter 7 *Reginae*, Allenn and Jarvis, in the King's Bench; it was expressly held that, where there is a custom to sell, such custom, Bro., Execution, 80, will justify a sale. But this was waived.

The fourth exception, double amercement, two fines for two offenses and but one non-appearance; so he is punished for non-appearance on two several occasions. So he may, it being *diversis expectibus*.

The fifth objection is the fine is unreasonable. He answered the court is of great jurisdiction and things there of great consequence enquirable as of great use to the public, and, therefore, the punishment ought to be for considerable in order to enforce a compliance. 1 Rolle, *Abr.*, 506, for refusal to appear, he forfeits his estate, pl. 2, 5, 6; 1 Leonard 104. And these are stronger instances than a pecuniary fine.

Wearg, Solicitor General: At common law and by the Statute of Magna Carta, all amercements must be affeered. This has been endeavored to be distinguished: first, because this is a certain sum; second, because there is a custom.

In judicial proceedings, he must not call it, an amercement, a fine or a fine an amercement. There is no such thing as a customary fine. Cro. Eliz. 241; a steward cannot fine for not doing suit of court. Nor is there any one authority in law to show that a steward of a leet may fine for any contempt but such as are done in court and in his presence.

If you take it as an amercement, it must be affeered by the express words of Magna Carta. And that Statute extends to all amercements certain as well as others. And, if there was any such thing as an amercement certain, it is taken away by that Statute, the Statute being designed to let every person who was liable to an amercement into the benefit of having such amercement affeered and mitigated by his peers so that he should not be subject to an arbitrary power of any nature whatsoever.

Gilbert Rep. 209, 25 E.R. 146

This is an action of trespass for taking away two steers. To this, the defendants pleaded that William Morgan was seised of the manor of Brecon in his demesne as of fee and that the said William Morgan, and all those whose estate he had, had, time out mind, within the said manor, a court leet or view of frankpledge three times a year, *viz.* on Monday next after the Close of Easter, on Monday next after the Feast of St. Michael, and on Monday next after St. Hilary, that, in the manor, there was a custom that every tenant of every freehold tenement within the said manor used and ought to appear personally, without any notice or summons, once in every year at one of the said three courts of view of frankpledge so to be held and, if he did not appear at the two other courts, then, he was to pay the steward for the use of the lord of the manor an essoin penny for each of the two said courts for his default and that every such tenant not appearing at either of the said three courts was to be amerced by the steward for his default 7s. for each of the said three courts and that every tenant being lawfully summoned to appear and inquire and present upon oath all such matters as ought to be inquired into and presented and, therein making default, was to be amerced by the steward for his contempt at 7s. and that the bailiffs of the said manor, by the warrant of the steward, should levy these amercements by distress and sale of the goods and chattels of the defaulter.

And the defendants farther say that John Edwards, then and for three years before, was a tenant of a freehold tenement and resident and inhabiting within the said manor and that there was a court held on Monday next after the Close of Easter, *viz.* upon the 25th of April in the 6th of the king [1720], and that the plaintiff was lawfully summoned to appear and to be put upon the jury to present all things presentable within the said manor and that the plaintiff did not appear, for which he was amerced by the steward at 7s., and that, at the second court held on Monday after Michaelmas, *viz.* the 3d of October in the 7th of the king [1720], the plaintiff was summoned to appear and be on the jury, but did not, and for that default was amerced another 7s., and that the third court was held the Monday after Hilary, *viz.* the 16th of January in the 7th of the king [1721], and that the plaintiff was lawfully summoned to the said court to be on the jury and made default, for which the steward amerced him another 7s. And because he did not appear and pay his essoin penny for his non-appearance according to custom, for this default, the steward amerced him another 7s.

And for not paying his several amercements, Hughes, the steward, directed his precept to John Pritchard, Thomas Lloyd, John Meredith, and John Powell, which was delivered to them, by virtue of which they took the two steers, in the declaration mentioned, as a distress and levied on the said steers the several sums amounting to £1 8s. to the use of William Morgan, the said lord of the manor, and sold them to certain persons, to them unknown, for £5, as they lawfully might, and paid the said £1 8s. to the lord of the manor and were ready and offered to pay the overplus to the plaintiff, which he refused to receive, which is the same transgression of which the plaintiff complains.

The plaintiff replies *de injuria sua propria*; to this the defendant demurs.

The question in this case is whether the custom is good.

And we are of opinion that this custom is not good for many reasons, first, because this amercement is not affeered.

By the Statute of Magna Carta, cap. 14, it is directed expressly that *nulla praedictarum misericordiarum ponatur nisi per sacramentum proborum et legalium hominum de vicineto.*[1] And by 27 Hen. VIII, c. 26,[2] all laws and statutes in England are to run in Wales. And so, if this custom be against Magna Carta, it is as much abolished in Wales as it is in England.

---

[1] None of the said amercements shall be assessed but by the oath of honest and lawful men of the vicinage.

[2] Stat. 27 Hen. VIII, c. 26 (*SR*, III, 563–569).

The Statute of Magna Carta was intended to take away all fines and amercements at the will and pleasure of the lord and his steward and, likewise, all excessive fines and amercements if they were never so certain, for, before this Charter of Liberties, the lords used to set such excessive and grievous amercements on their tenants that, under pretence of such amercements, they used to seize the whole profit of the tenement which they had granted. To hinder this oppression, Magna Carta appoints that every amercement should be affeered.

This has been so understood that, though a court may award that the party shall be amerced, yet the quantity of the amercement is to be settled by the affeerors and they are particularly sworn to that purpose. And they are called affeerors because they do affeer, or bring in, the quantity of the amercement.

In a court baron, where the suitors are judges, the homage may present the defaults on small trespasses within the manor, but the amercements must be afterwards particularly affeered by the affeerors. Hobart 129.[1] And Kitchen 153[2] says that the office of the homage and that of the affeerors are not to be confounded. The homage are to present the little offenses and trespasses within the manor, as Kitchen says; but the affeerors are in the nature of trustees to settle the quantity of the amercement.

Indeed, Hobart goes so far as to say that the homage may set a sum upon the offence; but the affeerors are then to mitigate it so that the quantity of the amercement is totally to be settled by the affeerors. And so, in the courts above, where amercements were ordered either against plaintiff or defendant, they were carried down to the coroner to be settled and affeered.

In a court leet, which was a court of record, if an amercement was imposed, if it were affeered even by the jury and not sworn by affeerors appointed for that purpose, it was a void amercement, and the lord of the leet could not maintain his action for it. 3 Levinz 206.[3]

It is very reasonable there should be such an affeerment, for, in this very case, it is very possible the tenant might not have been summoned and that this might come to the knowledge of the affeerors and that would be an excuse for this default.

Objection: This is an amercement in the nature of a fine, and a fine may be set by the court without any affeerment.

Answer: It is true a fine may be set without affeerment because it is out of the Statute of Magna Carta, for the Statute of Magna Carta does not comprehend the cases where a court of justice may imprison and, where the fine is set by way of mercy as a ransom and purgation of the offence, for the Statute was designed in mercy to the offenders and not to hinder them from mercy and so did not extend to offenses that might be punished by imprisonment.

---

[1] *Wilton v. Hardingham* (1616), Hobart 129, 80 E.R. 278.

[2] J. Kitchin, *Le Court Leete et Court Baron*.

[3] *Evelin v. Davies* (1685), 3 Levinz 206, 83 E.R. 653.

So in all breaches of the peace, the court may set a fine; and so for all contempts because the court may imprison. So a steward of a court leet may impose a reasonable fine for a disturbance committed *in facie curiae*, which is Griesley's Case, 8 Coke 39.[1] And so he may if a suitor will not be sworn on the homage because, in those cases, the steward may imprison, as is expressly resolved in Fitzherbert, *Abridgment*, tit. Leet, n. 4; Dalton, *Sheriffs*, 400.[2] And when such a fine is imposed, it becomes a debt to the lord, for which an action of debt lies. Croke Eliz. 581.[3]

Nobody can say that a default for not appearing in a court leet is such a default upon which a steward may imprison the party and so cannot set a fine as a ransom from imprisonment. But it is said that this may be good by custom. Now, as to the custom, that is in the very teeth of Magna Carta, for it is a custom to amerce without affeerment and this Statute was made to abrogate and abolish such customs.

Secondly, another reason against this custom is that the amercement is too excessive; it is not *salvo contenemento*.

Now, if the amercement was so great as to sweep away the whole profits of the freehold of the offender, it was too great, as if he were a socman and it extended to take away the beasts of his plow; if he were a military man and it extended to take away his arms; if he was a merchant if it extended to take away his merchandize; if he were a villein if it took away his cart or wainage. All these amercements were too grievous and against the Statute of Magna Carta, which says *Liber homo non amercietur pro parvo delicto nisi secundum modum illius delicti et pro magno delicto secundum magnitudinem delicti salvo sibi contenemento suo et mercator eodem modo salva merchandiza sua et villanus ulterius quam noster eodem modo amercietur salvo homagio suo et si amercietur sit in misericordia nostra.*[4]

And this makes an essential difference between a fine and an amercement, for the amercement is to be set as that he may sustain his station as feudatory to his lord. But the case of a fine has no relation thereunto, for, where the offender is imprisoned, he cannot sustain that station.

This case is among the *minora delicta*, and, as such, there should be only an amercement, and that [should be] reasonable.

---

[1] *Griesley's Case* (1588), *ut supra*.

[2] YB Trin. 8 Hen. VII, ff. 1, 3, pl. 1 (1493), Fitzherbert, Abr., *Leete et Hundred*, pl. 4; M. Dalton, *Officium Vicecomitum*.

[3] *Earl of Lincoln v. Fisher* (1595), Croke Eliz. 581, 78 E.R. 824, also Moore K.B. 470, 72 E.R. 702.

[4] A freeman shall not be amerced for a small fault but according to the manner of that fault and, for a great fault, according to the greatness of the fault, saving to him his contenement and a merchant likewise saving to him his merchandise and another's villein than ours shall be likewise amerced saving his homage, and, if he shall be amerced, he shall be in our mercy.

But, according to the custom, it may happen that the amercement may sweep away the whole profit of the tenement, for a man that has but a rood of land or a tenement of 5s. *per annum* must be obliged to pay £1 8s. for his default.

Lord Coke, in 2 Inst., fo. 28,[1] expounds the words of the Statute in such a manner that the amercement must not destroy the livelihood of the offender. But such amercements as these, in ancient times, would certainly have been thought very exorbitant before the quantity of money was so very much increased. And, even at this day, the fine would swallow the annual profit of a small tenement.

Thirdly, another reason against the amercement here is that it admits of no essoin to excuse the default. Now, there are several essoins that excuse even an appearance at the king's courts upon demand, as the essoin *de malo lecti, de malo veniendi, de servitio regis, etc.*

But here, at this court, if a man were summoned and were taken ill the day before the leet or were sent for into the service of the king, this was to be no excuse, but, immediately, the amercement was to run upon him. Now, this is perfectly against reason because these essoins excuse these defaults; but, here, by this custom, he is to be amerced, even where the law excuses his non-appearance.

Fourthly, it is not *secundum modum delicti* because the non-attendance of a poor man or day laborer is a less fault than of a rich man that has his time to command. And the Statute was made on purpose to proportion punishments to the default. But this custom runs alike upon all defaults, small and great. This is contrary to that known rule, i.e. *regula peccatis quae poenas irrogat aequas.*[2]

Objection: But though they say that this cannot be maintained as an amercement, yet it might begin by tenure and the lord might settle what sum he pleased on making default at his leet and, then, such sum ought not to be reckoned excessive and subject to affeerment because it was settled in the original settlement of the tenure.

Answer: First, this is pleaded as an amercement for a default and not as a sum due by tenure, and we must take it as it was pleaded, and not by any imagination out of the plea.

Secondly, if it were due by tenure, it must be laid upon the lands and tenements in certain, and not personally upon the tenant, because, upon the contingency, it will be a sum issuing out of the lands.

Thirdly, this could never grow into a custom because, upon any alienation of part of the lands or any division of the same upon descent, the sum must be divided and could not remain the same entire and uniform sum.

This was the opinion of the court delivered by Lord Chief Baron Gilbert.

---

1 E. Coke, *Second Institute* (1642), pp. 27–28.

2 Horace, *Satires*, 1, 3, 118; Use a scale which assigns penalties according to the crime. J. Fuchs, trans., *Horace's Satires and Epistles* (1977), p. 8.

8 Modern 296, 88 E.R. 211

Trinity term 10 Geo. I [1724].

In trespass for taking his cattle etc., the defendant justified as servant to one Morgan, setting forth that Morgan was seised of the manor of D. in fee, to which a court leet did belong etc. and that, time out of mind, there had been a custom that *quilibet tenens* of a freehold tenement and who was a resident and an inhabitant within that manor ought upon notice or summons to appear personally at the said court leet three times in every year, *viz.* at the feasts of St. Michael and St. Hilary and at Easter, and, for default of appearance at the said courts, to pay to the steward of the said leet to the use of the lord 7s. for every default, and that, if he did not appear at two of the said courts, but did appear at the third, then to pay an essoin penny only and, farther, that, if any such tenant, being summoned to be of the grand jury, should not appear that, then, he should be amerced 7s. by the steward and that the bailiff of the manor, by warrant from the steward, might distrain for such amercements and sell the distress etc. Then, he sets forth that the plaintiff was summoned to appear at two several courts and made default and that he was likewise summoned to be of the grand jury etc. but did not appear at that court, for which defaults, he was amerced 28s. and, because it was not paid, Richard Hughes, steward of the said leet, made his warrant directed to the defendant to levy the same by distress and sale of the plaintiffs goods, *virtute cuius*, he distrained the cattle etc. and sold them and paid 28s. to the steward for the use of the lord of the said manor, *quae est eadem transgressio etc.*

And upon a demurrer to this plea, several exceptions were taken to it: first, that the custom was void because it was laid too generally; secondly, that it was void because it is for the steward to amerce without any affeerment; thirdly, that here was a double amercement for one and the same default at one court, *viz.* in not being of the homage and not appearing at that court.

As to the first exception, this custom is void because it is laid too generally, *viz.* that *quilibet tenens etc.* used and ought to appear without exception of the quality, degree, or sex of persons, whereas several are exempted from appearing and attending at the leet, both by the common law and statutes of this realm, as infants under the age of twelve years, and this is by the common law, and ecclesiastical persons are exempted by the Statute of Marlbridge,[1] *viz.* archbishops, bishops, etc. are not to appear at the sheriffs tourns, and consequently not at leets, which were derived out of the tourns; and, if they should be distrained for any amercements etc. for not appearing in the leet, they have a writ upon the Statute by way of privilege, for, as they are not obliged by law to appear at leets, so they are not amerciable for not appearing. Therefore, this custom, being general and not setting forth these exemptions, is void and cannot subsist against the Statute

[1] Stat. 52 Hen. III, c. 10 (*SR*, I, 22).

of Marlbridge, which is introductory of a new law and destroys all customs and prescriptions against it.

Secondly, this custom is void because it is laid for the steward to amerce without an affeerment. And this is directly against Magna Carta,[1] by which it is enacted, 'that amercements shall be assessed by . . . lawful men of the vicinage', i.e. shall be affeered by those lawful men appointed in courts leet, upon oath, to settle and moderate the amercements of such who have committed faults arbitrarily punishable and have no express penalty expressed by any law or statute, so that to affeer is properly to tax or to reduce a thing to a certainty by persons on their oaths, and it ought to be *per pares*. But this is a certain amercement imposed by the steward without any affeerment and is therefore void.

Thirdly, this is a double amercement for one and the same default at the last court, for the plea sets forth that the plaintiff, being summoned to be of the grand jury, did not appear, for which he was amerced 7s., and he was amerced 7s. more for not appearing at that court, which is double and exceeds the custom.

To which it was answered, as to the first exception, thus. The custom is good and well pleaded, though the exemptions are not set forth in the plea, for that the defendant is not obliged by law so to do, but the person distrained is to show that he is exempted from such distress if he be really entitled to any such exemption, for the custom is *lex loci*. And, if there was any exemption by virtue of the custom, the plaintiff ought to have shown it. Now, to instance a parallel case, upon disbanding the army, an Act of Parliament was made, giving privilege to the soldiers to exercise their trades anywhere in England. Now, supposing that there is a custom in the borough of H. that no person shall exercise a trade therein unless he is free of that borough and an action should be brought against a soldier upon a by-law founded on this custom, certainly, the custom may be laid in general and the exemption must come on the soldier's side, for it is not required, either by the statute or common law, that exemptions should be set out in pleading of customs, but the party who is to have the benefit of an exemption must set it forth and show that he is not within the custom by reason of the exemption. So, where a custom was alleged to distrain anything within such an honor, it was objected to be too general, because several things are not distrainable, but are privileged and exempted from distresses, *viz. averia carucae*, and goods taken in execution by the sheriff, and workmen's tools, etc. And the book tells it is not necessary to set forth such exemptions because it is immaterial and would make the pleadings too long. Therefore, the person exempted must show it and that he is not within the custom by reason of his exemption.

As to the second point, it was argued that this custom is good to amerce without an affeerment, for, though it has been objected that it is contrary to Magna Carta and that the general rule of pleading in such cases is to set forth

[1] Stat. 25 Edw. I, Magna Carta, c. 14 (*SR*, I, 116).

an amercement and that it was affeered; yet, notwithstanding Magna Carta and that rule of pleading, there may be an amercement by custom to a certain sum, for this Statute was made in affirmance of the common law and, therefore, though it is in the negative, *viz.* that no freeman shall be amerced, yet there may be a prescription or custom against it. This was the Lord Coke's opinion in his *First Institute*,[1] *viz.*, where a statute in the negative is in affirmance of the common law, a man may prescribe against it, as, for instance, by the Statute of Magna Carta, it is provided,[2] that leets shall be held twice a year only, *viz.* after Easter and Michaelmas, yet a man may prescribe to hold them oftener and at other times because that Statute is but an affirmance of the common law. Besides, peers of the realm are within this Statute as well as commoners. And the amercement of peers is not used at this day because it is reduced to a certainty by custom, *viz.* a duke to £10 and others to £5, and such custom is good. By the same reason, an amercement may be reduced to a certainty by custom. And, if such custom be good, then there cannot be any occasion to affeer an amercement because to affeer is only a taxation reducing that to a certainty which was uncertain before. But it is absurd to say that a thing shall be reduced to a certainty which was certain in itself before the affeerment, so that the reason of affeering fails in this case if the sum be reasonable, but, if it be unreasonable, then the custom is void and cannot stand.

It appears by the old books[3] that customs to have particular sums are good, as a custom that the lord of a manor shall have £3 for every pound-breach; this is good against the tenants, though not against strangers. So, in the principal case, the sum is reduced to a certainty and the custom charges the tenants, but not strangers. A man may prescribe to have a certain sum of money from any person found guilty of an affray in a leet, and such prescription is good. This punishment is here called an amercement, but it is not properly so, but a fine imposed by the court, whereas amercements are always by the jury. Now, Magna Carta mentioning amercements, for that reason, they are to be affeered, for the judgment in an amercement is general, *viz. quod sit in misericordia*, and, afterwards, upon estreats directed to the coroner, they are affeered. But a fine is not to be affeered because not mentioned in that Statute, which is the foundation of all affeerments. And there are authorities in point[4] that an amercement imposed by a steward of a leet which is in the nature of a customary fine need not be affeered, though the custom had not ascertained the sum. Therefore, there can be no need of an affeerment where the sum is made certain by the custom.

---

[1] E. Coke, *First Institute* (1628), f. 115a.

[2] Stat. 25 Edw. I, Magna Carta, c. 35 (*SR*, I, 118).

[3] YB Hil. 11 Hen. VII, ff. 13, 14, pl. 8 (1496); YB Mich. 21 Hen. VII, f. 40, pl. 61 (1505).

[4] YB Mich. 10 Hen. VI, f. 7, pl. 22, Brooke, Abr., *Amerciament*, pl. 50 (1431).

As to the third exception, that the plaintiff is doubly amerced for one and the same fault, it is not so. And this appears by setting forth the custom, *viz.* that every tenant who shall not appear etc., being summoned to be of the homage, shall pay 7s., and, if he do not appear at two of the said courts and appear at the third, he shall pay an essoin penny, but, if he do not appear at the third and pay the essoin penny, he shall then pay 7s. for each of those defaults. But the custom is not laid to amerce for non-payment of the essoin penny, for that was not to be paid but where the party neglected to appear at two courts and appeared at the third, but here was a total neglect, for the defendant did not appear when he was summoned to be of the homage, nor at two other courts, nor at the third court. The custom being that, if he did not appear at that court and pay the essoin penny, then, for every default, he should pay 7s. must be understood for every default in not appearing etc., and not for non-payment of the essoin penny, so that this is not a double amercement for the same default, but several amercements for several defaults in not appearing etc.

THE COURT. It is agreed that this custom would have been well laid if the exemptions had been set forth and not so generally that *quilibet tenens* should appear etc. But it is certain that such exemptions which are by the common law, as of infants under twelve years and women etc. were never yet set forth in pleading of customs.

But it has been objected that, by the Statute of Marlbridge, clergymen are exempted and that this custom cannot prevail against that Statute, which is very true. But this does not alter the method of laying a prescription or custom in pleading, which, ever since the Statute was made, have been laid without mentioning any exemptions, but generally as in this case. It is true, if any persons had been exempted by the custom itself, such exemption must have been set forth in pleading because the custom is entire. But it is not necessary to set forth any other exemptions. Therefore, this custom is well laid. The Statute of Marlbridge never intended by those exemptions of ecclesiastical persons to destroy *leges loci*. But those laws still remain as they did before, and persons who will have any advantage of them must plead them, for it is the nature of exemptions to be exceptions out of the general rule. And it would be not only informal, but unreasonable, to set them all forth in pleading. So, as to the first point, the court were all of opinion that the custom was well pleaded.

As to the second point, it was agreed that amercements are to be affeered unless they are in the nature of a fine and that there is no occasion for an affeerment but where the amercement is discretionary, which is not this case, for, here, the sum is ascertained by custom and the steward cannot increase or diminish it, and, therefore, this amercement ought not to be affeered: first, because it is in the nature of a fine for a contempt; secondly, because the custom has ascertained it and it is not discretionary, and, of this opinion, were the Chief Baron [GILBERT] and two more.

But the other baron differed, for he was of opinion that, if the custom be abrogated by Magna Carta, then this amercement must be affeered and that the custom was abrogated by that Statute, by which it is enacted, 'that all amercements shall be affeered *per pares*'. It is true fines are not within this Statute, but amercements are. And a fine is a ransom from imprisonment. And wherever a leet may imprison, it may assess a fine as a price to redeem the party from an imprisonment, and a commitment always follows a fine. And, therefore, a *capiatur* lies for fineable offenses. But, in amercements, where the judgment is that the party shall be *in misericordia*, as it is in this case, there they are to be affeered. It is true the amercement of peers is made to a certain sum, but it is by order of the House of Lords, and this was to prevent the frequent application to the House when a peer was to be amerced. But the principal case being only a nonfeasance and no breach of the peace or contempt of the court, the steward cannot set a fine for it. And, if so, then, it falls back to an amercement and must be affeered *per judicium parium*.

As to the third point, that here is a double amercement for one default, the Chief Baron [GILBERT] was of another opinion, for amercement was in two instances, *viz.* for a default in not being of the grand jury and for a default in not appearing at that court. And where a man is bound to appear in two respects and does not appear, those are several defaults.

And another baron was of the same opinion, *viz.* that it is not a double amercement for the same default, for, if an officer who ought to attend the court by virtue of his office and likewise as a grandjuryman should make default, he is to be fined in both respects. And in one, there is no consideration to be had of the other. Therefore, notwithstanding this objection, the plea is good.

But two of the barons were of opinion that this custom was void for the reasons following, *viz.* every custom must have a reasonable commencement, which this custom had not, for it being in time immemorial, 7s. is too great a sum to pay for such a default; besides, it is unreasonable because it involves every person in it, when some persons may have a reasonable excuse to be absent, as for instance, a sheriff may be called to attend on the king's person etc.

Adjornatur.

The court took time to consider of this case; and in Hilary term, 12 Geo. 1 [1726], GILBERT, Chief Baron, delivered the opinion of himself and the other barons that this custom was not good for the reasons assigned.

Taussig MS. 311, vol. 2, p. 924

Trinity term 1726.

Serjeant *Whitaker*, for the defendant: First, there ought to be several distresses. 2 Lev. 243; Levinz, *Entries*, 176–181; 27 Hen. VIII, ca. 26, § 2, annexing the principality of Wales.[1] The steward of a court leet may impose a fine, but cannot amerce without an affeerance. Cro. Eliz. 581, Moor 470, Earl of Lincoln v. Fisher; F.N.B. 75 B. This amercement is very extravagant. 3 Lev. 206; debt for an amercement, by all the justices, it ought to be affeered. Keilway 66a; an amercement for a nuisance. He pleads an affeerance, but he does not name the affeerors. And, therefore, it is naught.

Bootle, contra: Here is a special custom alleged for holding this court.

[To the] first objection that the distresses ought to be several, the solution is the authorities cited only prove that the distresses may be several, not that they must, nor is there any authority in law they must be several.

[To the] second objection that the pleader does not show whether the distress is for non-appearance or for refusing to be sworn, the solution is reading the record answers this.

The third objection is want of affeerment; the solution is, as to amercements, a [writ of] *moderata misericordia* will lie, as the serjeant admits, and this makes against him, for then there is no such necessity for an affeerment. There is no doubt but amercements must be affeered speaking generally.

But here is a particular sum fixed by the custom. 11 Hen. VI, fo. 12; a steward of a leet has equal power with justices. Fines and amercements are used often as synonymous terms. Stat. Will. I, ca. 18; 2 Inst. 196. Common fine and amercement are convertible terms. 38 Hen. III, a manuscript of Lord Chief Baron Hale; 10 Hen. VI, 7, Bro., *Amercements*, 50. However, the custom will warrant this case whatever be the case of common amercements. 2 Inst. 120, 116, relating to keeping these courts, saves customs and prescriptions. Laken's Case, in 2 Sanders; 11 Rep. 44, in Godfrey's Case; distress *pro certo laetae* is good by custom.

So a distress for an amercement in a court baron is naught but by custom. Cro. Car. 551; Sir W. Jones 439; 2 Rolle's *Abr.*, 234, pl. 1; Cro. Jac. 532. Custom will prevail against canons. 11 Hen. VII, 14; 21 Hen. VII, 40, pl. 1; Bro., Prescription, 40, a custom to have £3 for a pound breach. 21 Edw. III, 46b; if seised for forty weeks, one shall not be ousted by an entry, but only an action. 1 Lutwich 561; a custom to exclude setting up a trade. So it is that custom has great force. But this case might rest wholly upon the tenure and be part thereof.

Whitaker replies: A writ of *moderata misericordia* lies after an affeerment. There were no justices in eyre after Henry VI. The amercements in the courts of Westminster Hall are affeered by the coroners. In common parlance, fine and amercement are synonymous, but not in legal proceedings in pleadings. There must be a separate avowry for several distresses. So he leaves it to the court.

The court will give judgment next term.

[1] Stat. 27 Hen. VIII, c. 26 (*SR*, III, 563–569).

Taussig MS. 311, vol. 2, p. 948

Trinity term 1726.

Lord Chief Baron [GILBERT] gives judgment. He opens the record. The single doubt is upon the plea [that] it is not a good custom, first, for all amercements ought to be affeered and this is by the express words of Magna Carta, ca. [*blank*]. This Statute was made to prevent excessive fines in relief of the tenants of the manors. The difference between the homage and the affeerors is the homage present [and] the affeerors settle the quantum. Hob. 129; Kitchin 153; and 3 Lev. 206. As this is true in courts baron, so it holds true even to amercements in the courts above, which are affeered by the coroners.

[To the] objection this is in the nature of a fine and fines and amercements are sometimes used as synonyms, the solution is there is an essential difference between a fine and an amercement because a fine is a redemption from imprisonment; so courts which can imprison may fine. A steward of a leet may fine. Bro., [*Abr.*], Amercement, pl. 50; Fitz., *Abr.*, Leet, 11; Dalton's *Sheriffs* 400. But courts which cannot imprison cannot fine. No man can say that, for non-appearance, the steward can imprison.

[To the] objection this may be made good by a custom, the solution is this cannot be because it was the very end of the Statute to destroy such unreasonable and arbitrary customs.

Second, another reason against this custom is that it is excessive *non salvo contenemento*. And, therefore, a fine which affected the livelihood of the tenant is forbidden by [*blank*]. If, in this case, the man holds but one acre of land, he is subject to this custom and is consequently liable to absolute ruin.

Third, this amercement admits of no essoin neither *de malo lecti* nor *de servitio regis*.

Fourth, it is not *secundum modum delicti*, for this custom affects the rich and poor alike.

[To the] objection, if it is not good by way of custom, yet it may be good by way of tenure, the solution is, first, it is not pleaded as a tenure; secondly, if it were a tenure, it must be annexed to a certain and definite tenancy or portion of land and is not chargeable on residents; third, a descent to coparceners would give occasion to many alterations as to apportionments.

So all of us are of the opinion that the custom is void as directly in the teeth of Magna Carta.

414

Shirley v. Dacosta

(Ex. 1723)

Where a seller contracts to deliver, the buyer need not accept a delivery from a third party.

In this case, a court of equity granted an injunction against a final judgment at common law on the ground that the contract was incorrectly construed by the jury.

Harvard Law School MS. 1082, vol. 1, p. 176

[Trinity term 1723.]

Before the Act, a man might agree to sell stocks at the time of agreement if he has it by the time of transferring. A man may covenant to make a feoffment at a future day of lands he has not the time of the contract.

Lord Chief Baron MONTAGU: This bill is to set aside this verdict. It is now too late to say a court of equity cannot relieve against a verdict if it appears wrong was done by it. See the case of Rhodes v. Lovell.[1] It does not appear the defendant had the stock ready to transfer on the day, but only that he procured Evans to settle the transfer, which is not sufficient. Note the contract is to sell ten shares which the defendant had not. We are all of opinion that a contractor is not obliged to take stock from anybody but the person with whom the contract itself [was made]. This was the ground of his opinion, that he thought it not material what was said of the Act of Parliament, but he thought that, being *ex post facto*, it should not extend to that case. But upon the other reason, he was decreeing for the plaintiff [Lady Betty Shirley].

Baron PRICE: I think the Stat. 7 Geo. does not reach this case, the judgment having altered the nature of the contract. But he founded his opinion for the plaintiff upon the contract to sell upon the latter words ordered the n[ote] in the contract.[2] He thought the plaintiff can lose no more then the £200. And he decreed for the plaintiff on his paying the £200.

Baron PAGE was of the same opinion that the £200 was to be forfeited only. But the question is where the default is to be different from the case of Rhodes v. Lovel. A sale can be no more than a contract to transfer because there is no other way of selling stock than by transferring in the company books. The plaintiff by accepting the shares from Evans makes it a good transfer, which differs it from Rhodes v. Lovel. If he had refused, it would bear another construction. He doubted whether the evidence made it out that he accepted it. But he seemed to think that he did not agree to accept it. But the plaintiff was the occasion of misleading the defendant. And, therefore, he was of opinion the plaintiff should be relieved, only paying the £200 forfeiture.

Baron GILBERT: If this be a verdict against conscience, we may relieve. All the damages given over the deposit is too much, for I think the parties have mutually agreed in the deposit and the defendant cannot in conscience be entitled to any more. He thought the Statute would operate in this contract notwithstanding the judgment. And he decreed that the plaintiff should be relieved paying the £200.

[1] *Rhodes v. Lovit* (Ex. 1721), see above, Case No. 165.

[2] Sic in MS.

415

Reynolds v. Vincent

(Ex. 1723)

The tithe in kind of lambs is not payable until they are old enough to live alone.

Taussig MS. 311, vol. 1, p. 538

Sittings after [Trinity] term 1723.

The plaintiff, parson of Old Stoke Charity in the County of Southampton, exhibits his bill for [tithes of] milk, honey, [and] lambs, As to milk, a *modus* of 3½d. for a cow [was pleaded]. But no day was fixed for the time of payment. As to lambs, they set forth a custom to tithe them at St. Mark's Day.

Pro querente: Lambs are tithable when they can live without their dams. And this custom of tithing at St. Mark's Day has been twice adjudged ill, *viz*. Easter 32 Car. II, Crofts v. Blake, a Hampshire cause, book of decrees, fol. 217, and Trinity 24 Car. II, Heaton v. Rigghal, a Lincolnshire cause, fo. 101.[1]

And of this opinion was the court. And they decreed an account.

Bunbury 133, 145 E.R. 622,
1 Rayner 192, 1 Eagle & Younge 790

At Serjeants' Inn, 11 July 1723.

A bill was brought for tithe, *inter alia*, of lamb. The defendant insists that it was customary to tithe their lambs at St. Mark's day, 25th of April. But, for the plaintiff, it was said that, by the defendant's own proofs, it appears they generally then are but three weeks old and cannot live without the dam, but it is usual to tithe them not until August, and, sometimes, not until Michaelmas, but the general rule is to tithe them when they are capable of living without the dam.

And PER CURIAM, the custom insisted upon by the defendant is unreasonable. And they decreed for the plaintiff.

416

Vernon v. Heaford

(Ex. 1723)

Whether land is sterile and unprofitable or not for the purposes of tithes is not within the jurisdiction of an ecclesiastical court.

Taussig MS. 311, vol. 1, p. 530

---

[1] *Croft v. Blake* (1680), 2 Gwillim 530, 1 Eagle & Younge 527, see also *Croft's Case* (1721), above, Case No. 238; *Heaton v. Regal* (Ex. 1721), see above, Case No. 266.

Trinity term 1723.

Upon a suit in the ecclesiastical court for tithes upon a libel general, the defendant alleges there that he had come to an agreement for the tithe in question. And he suggests for [a writ of] prohibition that a particular close whereof tithes were demanded was *sterilis sua parte natura* and the seven years were not expired from the improvement of it.[1] And a rule was [made] to show cause.

Fazakerly: This suggestion is contrary to the party's own plea. And so it ought not to be admitted. Secondly, the fact whether *sterilis* may be tried in an ecclesiastical court, as they have incontrovertibly a jurisdiction of the original cause.

And the court made no doubt of either point, but granted a prohibition.

417

Cutts v. Shaw

(Ex. 1723)

A court of equity will not order specific performance of a contract where the plaintiff has not performed precisely his part of the bargain.

Taussig MS. 311, vol. 1, p. 533

Trinity term 1723.

GILBERT: Lord Somers[2] always used to lay down for a rule that the bargain ought to be equal in order to entitle the party to demand the execution of it in equity. And for this very reason, he was for dismissing the bill.

PAGE: This is a mere action at law. And, in such cases, the court will dismiss though the defendant does not take advantage by a demurrer for want of equity, but does join in the commission and examination of witnesses, as in the case of the City of Exeter v. Bond. Secondly, wherever a man comes into equity for a performance of an agreement wherein he has himself omitted a circumstance, he must put the party into the same condition in all respects as if he had not omitted such circumstance. But, in this case, it cannot be done, for we cannot put the defendant into as good circumstances as if the plaintiff had transferred to him the stock on the day appointed by the contract.

PRICE: If the agreement be honest and fair at the time of creation, yet if, by accident, it becomes exceeding hard afterwards, I think a court of equity ought [not] to execute it. Besides, this matter is only or at least most proper for a jury, and they can best assess the damages for non-performance of the contract.

Chief Baron [MONTAGU]: I do not understand the rule laid down by my brothers that a court of equity cannot compel the execution of a bargain which, by accident, [has become] a hard bargain. And I think this way of reasoning is not

---

1 Stat. 2 & 3 Edw. VI, c. 13, s. 5 (*SR*, IV, 56).

2 John Somers, lord Somers, was lord chancellor from 1693 to 1700.

consistent with what has been already done in this court. In the case of Stukely and Cain,[1] we were all of us of a different opinion and decreed a specific performance of that contract. And, in the case of Harcourt and Thompson,[2] though the other barons differed from me in my opinion upon the whole of the case, yet they did not differ from me as to this point, but only as to the quantum of stock Mr. Thompson had. And, for that stock which they agreed Mr. Thompson had, they made Mr. Harcourt pay £920 percent, as unconscionable a price as it was.

And as to what My Brother Price says, that a jury are the proper judges of damages, he nor any of us were of that opinion in the case of Shenton and Jordan,[3] for we set aside that verdict purely because they assessed damages by a wrong measure.

I think the rule for dismissing because proper at law is as has been laid down by Brother Stevens, *scil.* upon a demurrer or by the defendant's insisting thereon in his answer. But he must not sit by and acquiesce in the suit and examine witnesses and put the plaintiff to the whole charge and trouble of going through the cause and then object to the jurisdiction of the court. This is unconscionable. And for other particular reasons, he thought the subject matter of the bill was proper for equity.

But the three others being of a contrary opinion, the bill was dismissed.

418

Farwell v. Medcalfe

(Ex. 1723)

The question in this case was whether the seizer of forfeited goods can sue an officer of the Custom House for his share of the proceeds of the sale.

Taussig MS. 311, vol. 1, p. 536

Trinity term 1723.

At *nisi prius coram* Montagu, Chief Baron, at the Guildhall, Farwell brings [an action of] *indebitatus assumpsit* against Medcalfe for money received to his own use. And the case as opened by the plaintiff's counsel was this. Farwell had been a Custom House officer and had seized some wines, which were appraised at £700, and upon a claim entered, the information was tried. And the judgment was that the goods were forfeited, that Farwell *oneratur versus regem pro £350, una medietate bonorum praedictum* and that, *quoad alteram medietatem*, Farwell should have them to his own use, the goods remaining all this while in the king's warehouse. The Commissioners of the Customs, on the pretense that Farwell

[1] *Stukely v. Cain* (Ex. 1722), see above, Case No. 277.

[2] *Harcourt v. Thompson* (Ex. 1721–1723), see above, Case No. 236.

[3] *Shenton v. Jordan* (Ex. 1723), see above, Case No. 385.

had waived the benefit of his seizure and had put the crown to the whole expense of prosecuting this information, order one Dobson, their warehouse keeper, to sell the wines, which he accordingly did for £506 5s. And he received the money. And, then by like order of the Commissioners, Dobson paid the money into the hands of Mr. Medcalfe, Solicitor of the Custom House. And for a moiety of this money paid to Medcalfe, the action was brought.

And by the opinion of Chief Baron [MONTAGU], the plaintiff was nonsuited, not having brought either a proper action or against a proper person.

Query by me as to the action itself whether it is not in the election of the plaintiff to charge a wrongdoer either as for a tort or as upon an implied contract for the produce of the goods, both actions sounding in damages.

N.B. On the reading the aforesaid case, Bunbury told me the following, which he heard *coram* Holt between Garret and Cullum. Garret was a merchant in Ireland and sends over goods to one A., who was his factor. The factor sells the goods to B., and, then, the factor becomes bankrupt. And B., supposing the money he owed the factor was due to the factor as for the factor's own goods, pays the money to an assignee of the commissioner of bankruptcy. And Garret brings his action of *indebitatus assumpsit* against the assignee for money had and received to Garret's use, and, by Holt, Chief Justice, the action well lies.

419

Motteaux v. Appleby

(Ex. 1723)

What is a reasonable period of time within which to demand payment of a bill of exchange is a question of fact to be determined by a jury.

Taussig MS. 311, vol. 1, p. 540, pl. 2

Trinity term 1723.

A bill of exchange of £100 drawn on Appleby is sent to Motteaux. Appleby accepts it on 18 September. The bill became payable the 18th, being a Sunday. On Saturday the 17th about or before 12 o'clock, Motteaux goes to Appleby. Appleby's servant pays £25 and gives a note of Cox and Cleaves for £75, and a receipt was given on the bill of exchange. And Cox and Cleave failed and stopped payment about 5 o'clock in the afternoon on Monday. And on Tuesday morning, the £75 note was carried to Cox and Cleaves. And then, the plaintiff found they were broken, and he applied to the defendant for payment.

And, for the plaintiff, the case of Selwin and Lancaster was cited as a case in point. The receipt endorsed on the bill of exchange was 'received the contents' [*blank*]. Salkeld 132; Ward and Evans, 442; Mainwaring and Harrison.[1]

Chief Baron [MONTAGU]: Holt held there was no precise time, but a reasonable time must be allowed and what is a reasonable time must depend on the circumstances of the case. Here seems a manifest laches in the plaintiff, for here was a considerable time on Saturday, especially the plaintiff's being so near, but, however, there was no pretense of an excuse for not coming on Monday.

PRICE: I think this point is proper to be tried, for a jury are better judges than we are.

PAGE was also for a trial. He never demanded payment of his own money, as appears in the cause. He could not have had payment all Monday, for he failed in the afternoon.

GILBERT: If a credit is given to the party from whom the note be due, this is payment. But here are no laches of an entire complete day. So he was for a trial at law.

CHIEF BARON: The laches of the plaintiff is shown in not going at all on Monday, though the party failed on Monday.

And so it went on to a trial. And the cause was adjourned to wait the event of the trial.

420

Mansel v. Clavel

(Ex. 1723)

The question in this case whether there was evidence of a discharge of certain lands from the payment of tithes.

Taussig MS. 311, vol. 1, p. 542

Trinity term 1723. Concerning the discharge of monastery lands belonging to the Cistercian Order.

In this case, PRICE and PAGE, the Chief Baron [MONTAGU] and GILBERT not contradicting, held that a surrender of the Abbey of Bindon in 30 Hen. VIII was an evidence of the Abbey's having been continued by letters patent to that time and so that it might be capable of discharge within the exception in 27 Hen. VIII,[2] which seems strange to me because I should think no evidence of this

[1] *Hill v. Lewis* (1694), 1 Salkeld 132, 91 E.R. 124, also Skinner 410, 90 E.R. 182, Holt K.B. 116, 90 E.R. 962; *Ward v. Evans* (1704), 2 Salkeld 442, 91 E.R. 383, also 3 Salkeld 118, 91 E.R. 726, 2 Lord Raymond 928, 92 E.R. 120, 1 Comyns 138, 92 E.R. 1002, Holt K.B. 120, 90 E.R. 965, 6 Modern 36, 87 E.R. 799, 12 Modern 521, 88 E.R. 1492; *Manwaring v. Harrison* (1722), 1 Strange 508, 93 E.R. 666.

[2] Stat. 27 Hen. VIII, c. 28, s. 10 (*SR*, III, 577).

could be admitted but the letters patent themselves. And it is certain that it has been determined that all the lesser abbeys must be supposed to have come to the crown by 27 Hen. VIII, though in fact many of them were not surrendered until long after. *Ideo quaere.*

421

Anonymous

(Ex. 1723)

Where one of several plaintiffs resides within the jurisdiction of the court, the posting of security for court costs will not be required.

Taussig MS. 311, vol. 1, p. 547, pl. 1

Saturday, 9th November 1723. PRICE, PAGE, GILBERT *praesentibus.*

Mr. [*blank*] moved that the plaintiffs should give security for costs, they living in Ireland, as appeared by the bill itself. But it also appearing that one plaintiff lived in England, the court would not grant the motion.

422

Case of Pygram, Harris, and Bayley

(Ex. 1723)

A person who has made a bid for forfeited goods must pay the price bid even though the goods have diminished in value in the meantime.

Taussig MS. 311, vol. 1, p. 560

Michaelmas term 1723.

There was a seizure and appraisement of brandy in Easter term and bidding thereupon, but no prosecution. And at the later end of Trinity term following, Harris comes in and enters a claim and moves for a writ of delivery for the goods. But he never uses his writ, but, in the beginning of this term, he drops his claim, the brandies being now much sunk in value. And then, Pygram comes in this term and prays that, since the claim was dropped and there was now a judgment of condemnation, Bayley, the bidder, might take the brandies and pay in his bidding money.

And, on the other side, it was insisted that, since there has been so long a delay and that by a contrivance between Pygram and Harris to prejudice the bidder, the bidder should be discharged.

But the court thought the contrivance was on the other side and so would not discharge the bidding.

423

Rex v. Enderupp

(Ex. 1723)

An accountant to the crown can have a writ of extent in aid against his own debtors in order to collect his private debts.

Taussig MS. 311, vol. 1, p. 549

Trinity term 1723.

A motion was made by Serjeant *Stevens* to set aside a [writ of] extent in aid as irregularly issued. [There was a] bond by Lonsdale and [*blank*] to the crown conditioned for Mr. Lonsdale's accounting for £30,000 impressed to him from the Ordnance Office. Endroup was bound in a bond to Lonsdale for £1600 payable in two months time. And the serjeant insisted that the impresting money does not make a man such an accountant as is entitled to an immediate extent.

2. This extent has issued against the body of Endroup, which it ought not nor has used to do.

3. The affidavit does not mention that Endroup had absconded from his house, but only that he has sold a ship.

4. The allegations in the affidavit are false. Extents in aid have been always discountenanced, being only to prefer one subject to another.

5. The affidavit ought to be that the money was the king's money. And I believe further that it was paid to the party to be paid into the Exchequer. And he cited a case *coram* Ward, Chief Baron, for that purpose.

Bunbury: Our affidavit satisfies theirs. (1) Though the affidavit alleges him to be a foreigner, he was naturalized sixteen years ago. (2) He was in good circumstances.

1. There is a difference between debts originally due to the crown and debts immediately due. *Scire facias* ought to issue first upon debts found due to the king's debtor. But I do agree that, upon a motion in court, such extents have been granted, but always with an exception to the body.

2. Mr. Lansdale is only an Under-Treasurer to the Board of Ordnance and so not an officer for whom [a writ of] extent should issue.

[3.] 15 Car. I, Rule 6, the debt must be in manifest jeopardy.

4. It must be crown money, but this is only a debt to Lansdale.

31 Car. II, Rule [*blank*], is that the affidavit ought to be express that the party absconded. 15 Car. II, Rule 9, no deputy shall be a tradesman. Rule 3, [there is] no further inquisition than to inquire into lands and goods, so it ought not to affect the person. Rule 6, no immediate extent lies but in cases of extremity. So it ought not to issue in cases where it was not the crown's money and the

original crown debtor is solvent. Hardres 404;[1] the Rules of 15 Car. I only extend to crown debts. Rex v. Newman.[2]

Attorney General [*Raymond*]: 8 February 1719, Lansdale's bond to the crown bears date. 1 November 1721, the bond from Endroup to Lansdale [*blank*].

Mr. Lansdale is an accountant for the money as immediately impressed to him by the Lords of the Treasury under the sign manual of the king so that he is immediately accountant at this time. The Treasurer of the Ordnance was dead, and Lansdale executed his office.

The Rules of 15 Car. II have not been so regularly observed, for tradesmen every day are made receivers.

2. A baron at his chambers may as well grant an extent against the body as in court, business having now taken another course than formerly. And that business is now usually done in chambers which was formerly done always in court.

3. This is a case of extremity, for the affidavit swears that Endroup often said and declared that he was not able to pay the debt to Lansdale or to give him any other security for it.

He insists upon an agreement which Endroup entered into subsequent to his being taken into custody, by which Lansdale accepted [*blank*] less than was originally due, i.e. instead of [*blank*].

1 March 1721, Endroup was taken. 3 March 1721 was the agreement. 8 March 1721, the commission of bankruptcy was sued out against Endroup. In April 1722 following, notice was given to discharge the extent. But instead of moving, they get a certificate of discharge. And they now come to set aside the extent so that, by this proceeding, Mr. Lansdale is tricked of his debt, having been deprived of coming in as a creditor on the commission. And if the extent is set aside, he is totally without a remedy. And, therefore, no court of justice can interpose in a case of this nature, for the whole of this transaction has been carried on by the defendant's own attorney.

Serjeant *Stevens*: This agreement subsequent will never support the extent if, at the time of the issuing thereof, it went out irregularly.

PRICE: This extent is not irregular, but, if it is irregular, the acquiescence under it and all the proceedings upon it, *viz.* the agreement subsequent to it, which is in part executed, must prevent our setting it aside.

1. Lansdale was Under-Treasurer. A sum of £30,000 was impressed to him. And, surely, he is accountable to the crown, and more fully so when the Treasurer was dead at that time.

Doctor Fouquier was not a deputy receiver and so was not entitled, but that case did not determine that a deputy receiver is not entitled to an extent in aid.

2. The affidavit is sufficient.

---

[1] *Attorney General v. Poultney* (1665), Hardres 403, 404, 145 E.R. 519.

[2] *Rex v. Taylor* (Ex. 1723), see above, Case No. 394.

3. The alteration of affairs since have made us recede[1] from the letter of the Rules of 15 Car.

4. Many proceedings are now done at a baron's chambers which formerly were done in court, as proclamations, recognizances.

5. It is not the danger of losing the king's debt, but the danger of losing the debt due to the king's debtor.

PAGE: 'Precise.' No precise form is necessary in an affidavit. This has the substance. What is done by a baron is, as it were, done by the court, but it may be set aside if [. . .] if the baron is either surprised by misinformation or otherwise mistaken. And it is not necessary to be the king's money in order to have an immediate extent. If money be due to the crown's debtor, it is sufficient. He thinks the extent was regular, but if it had not been so, yet the proceedings since would have determined him not to set it aside.

GILBERT: The court has a discretionary power over its rules. The crown's prerogative is not to be made to get in private debts, but wherever there is a fair accountant, as here, where the money is impressed to a man to lay out for the crown's occasions, such a man is fairly entitled to an extent in aid against his debtors. And this sort of process is part of the security the crown has for the well payment of its revenues and debts.

A baron is obliged *ex officio* to grant such an extent on an affidavit, which is not to be tied up to any precise form of words, but to satisfy the baron that the debt is in danger to be lost unless speedy process [issues].

And, in this case, if the process of extent had been ill conducted, the party against whom it issued should have complained to the baron, who would have set it aside, and should not have acquiesced in it and made an agreement in pursuance thereof and when, by such agreement, he has prevented the king's debtor from taking hold of any other remedy to recover his debt, then come to the court to set aside the extent, by which only it can be now secured.

Sed quaere per me: What Baron Gilbert meant by saying that a baron was bound *ex officio* to grant such immediate extent, I suppose, by *ex officio*, he meant *ex debito justitiae. Et quaere* also how a baron in his chambers can set aside the execution of an extent when it is once executed. The truth is the court spoke to this case offhand and seemed to have a pretty deal of resentment against the defendant and his attorney for endeavoring to set aside their own agreement, which they made when under execution of the extent.

And so by all the barons aforesaid, the serjeant is to take nothing by his motion.

---

[1] accede *MS.*

Bunbury 134, 145 E.R. 622

Lansdell was Under-Treasurer of the Board of Ordnance, to whom money had been impressed for the king's use. Enderupp was a merchant, and he became indebted to Lansdell by bond for £1600 on private account. Lansdell, apprehending that Enderupp was declining in his circumstances, got an extent against himself, and, upon the inquisition taken thereon, this bond from Enderupp to him was found. Upon that, he applied (making an affidavit before Baron Price at his chambers that Enderupp was likely to become insolvent, having told him he could not pay the debt nor give security and was selling off his effects in order to withdraw himself etc., much according to the common form, but did not say he absconded) for an immediate extent in aid against Enderupp, which was granted 1 March 1721. Now, this day, being the 12th of November 1723, it was moved to discharge this extent:

First, because Lansdell was not an officer within any of the rules to entitle him to this extent.

To this, it was answered *per* CURIAM that money has been impressed to him and he is an accountant before the court.

Secondly, the affidavit is not in the common form.

To this, it was answered *per* CURIAM there is no certain form of words prescribed in affidavits for extents.

Thirdly, it is not according to the rules of the court of the 15th year of Car. I, nor of the 35th of Car. II.

To this, it was answered *per* CURIAM that an extent in aid, being a prerogative process, is always under the care of the court, and they have a discretionary power over their own rules. They will not indeed let the prerogative be made an handle to get in a private debt.

And fourthly, it was objected that a *scire facias* ought to have gone. But this seemed to have no weight, later practice being otherwise.

So PRICE, PAGE, and GILBERT, barons, only in court, denied the motion, for that the extent was regularly sued out, but, if not, they would not have set it aside in this case because Enderupp had come to an agreement with Lansdell the day after he was in custody and also by reason of the long acquiescence after the extent.

424

Cappur v. Harris

(Ex. 1723)

A court of equity will not specifically enforce a harsh contract, but it will not set aside a harsh bargain that has been fully performed on both sides.

Harvard Law School MS. 1082, vol. 1, p. 179

Michaelmas term 1723.

This was a bill brought to have £400 and £200 repaid to the plaintiff on account of a third subscription because he never had it. There was an agreement between the plaintiff and defendant touching a third subscription of South Sea [stock], for the defendant apprehended that he should have £500 in director Joy's list, and, thereupon, the plaintiff Capper agreed to give the defendant a £200 premium and to pay down the money into South Sea [shares]. And this agreement was 14 June 1720. And at last, it came out that the defendant had only £400 and then, subscriptions rising, the defendant refused to stand to the agreement. But on 29 June 1720, the agreement was perfected between the plaintiff and the defendant, and, thereby, the defendant, by writing, acknowledged the receipt of £200 and promised to give receipt when the same issued and, in return, the plaintiff promised to pay £200 more if subscriptions continued at that price. And so, upon the whole, the plaintiff would now have it taken that, since subscriptions were fallen, that the defendant had waived the agreements by his shuffling and, therefore, the plaintiff was entitled to the £400 and £200.

And, upon this, it was heard and resolved by the court as follows.

Price: I cannot decree the £400 and £200 back again to the plaintiff, though each party might have waived the first agreement of the 14 June 1720. But the contract was perfected the 29 June 1720 and is still subsisting. And a mutual agreement 'for upon delivering receipts', those words do not make a condition precedent, for the legislature has fully settled that affair. And, after an agreement thus executed, I cannot decree a repayment of this money as if there was no agreement. But I think that the plaintiff ought to have the stock allowed in lieu of the subscription. And since the defendant did shuffle a little, it shall be without costs on either side.

Baron Page, *contra*: There must be a decree for the plaintiff in all events. And though the contract of 14 June 1720 did not bind at law, yet it did in conscience. And, at that time, the defendant offered to pay the principal and interest of the whole money, and so I shall decree it. And though I admit what has been allotted by the legislature shall amount to a receipt, but I think that the defendant has not fully performed his part. Stukely v. Kirn, in the House of Lords,[1] because all the deeds were not produced by Michaelmas, which were the terms of the agreement, and, therefore, the House of Lords would not order a specific performance. Where a bill is brought for money, there, an equivalent may be given, but not for a specific performance. I am of opinion that it is proper for the plaintiff to have the note up and to have a decree for the £400 [and] £200 and interest.

---

[1] *Keen v. Stuckely* (1722), Gilbert Rep. 155, 25 E.R. 109, 2 Eq. Cas. Abr. 19, 22 E.R. 16; see also *Stukely v. Cain* (Ex. 1722), above, Case No. 277.

Baron GILBERT: I take it that, when these contracts have been executed, that the court will not set them aside, but only where they are executory. Sometimes, where the performance is prayed for a hard bargain, there, perhaps, a court of equity will not help or give any assistance to such hard bargain and so not decree an execution of such agreement. The case in question must be esteemed a contract executed, and the bargain is closed. And it cannot be rescinded but by mutual agreement. And on 29 June 1720, all was closed. And though the defendant Harris kept off, yet the note was not to unravel anything, but only to pay £200 if it continued at such a price. And the discourse of waiving the agreement will not do without the positive consent of both parties, and that does not appear. And, therefore, I entirely agree with my brother Price that the stock allowed in lieu of the subscription should be transferred to the plaintiff with the dividends and profits without costs, but no return of the £400 or £200.

Bunbury 135, 145 E.R. 623

In this case, these rules were laid down by Baron GILBERT in relation to contracts for South Sea stock or subscriptions: first, that, if a contract be executed, a court of equity will not unravel or break into it; secondly, if it be only executory and a man comes to have it carried into execution, there, a court of equity will not aid the plaintiff, but leave him to such remedy as he can have by law.

425

Smee v. Martin

(Ex. 1723)

Parents are responsible for the maintenance and education of their children, and they cannot use a child's legacy for those purposes without a court order.

Taussig MS. 311, vol. 1, p. 545

Thursday, 31 October, *coram* PAGE and GILBERT, by English bill.

Probatum Londini coram venerabili viro Gulielmo Strahan, legum doctore, surrogato, etc. tertio die mensis Augusti anno Domini 1717 juramento Henrici Spakman executoris etc. cui etc. de bene etc. jurato. On another part was written *'Augusti 3, 1717, juratus fuit Henricus Spackman executor nitus*[1] *nominatus coram me Gulielmo Strahan, surrogato.'*

Edward Martin makes his will and dies. By his will, he makes his wife Elizabeth Martin executrix and devises £100 to his son Edward Martin to be paid at 21 and, if he did not attain 21, then not to be paid. Edward Martin is fitted out by his mother to sea while under age and dies at Fort St. George. But, before he

[1] Sic in MS.

died, he attained his age and made his will and devised his legacy to the plaintiff. And he made Spackman, another defendant, executor. And now, the plaintiff exhibited her bill against Elizabeth Martin and this Spackman for this legacy.

Elizabeth Martin admits the will of her husband, admits the legacy and assets, but puts the proof of Edward Martin junior's will on the plaintiff. And the only proof the plaintiff made of this will was by producing the original will with the two endorsements, before, which the defendants' counsel insisted was not sufficient, but she ought either to have produced the probate under the seal of the ordinary or, at least, ought to have had the Register's hand to the endorsement, for any person might write this on the back of the will.

Against the paying of the legacy, the mother insisted that the money she had paid for fitting him out to sea should be set against the legacy.

E contra et per CURIAM: There is no color for this in the case of a mother; it is otherwise in the case of a stranger, but especially in this case where there is an express devise of £5 *per annum* for education during his infancy. A mother and grandmother are bound by law to provide for children, and they shall never break into a legacy unless where they are necessitous and cannot provide otherwise for their children, and that must be by the direction of a court of equity.

They decreed payment of the legacy with interest from the time of the second will, by which the legacy was vested in the plaintiff.

Bunbury 136, 145 E.R. 623

W. Martin, in April 1700, by will, devises to his son Edward £100 not to be paid until he came of age and, in the meantime, £5 *per annum* to be allowed out of the produce of the personal estate for his maintenance. And he made his wife, the defendant Elizabeth, sole executrix and died. Edward, when he was an infant, went to the East Indies, where he came of age in the year 1709, and he made his will in the year 1712 and then died there. By his will, he gave the plaintiff Abigail this £100, and he made the defendant Spakeman sole executor, who proved the will according to the method in the East Indies, and, at the charge of the defendant Elizabeth, he proved it again in the prerogative court here. And now, the plaintiffs preferred their bill here for this £100 legacy.

The defendant Elizabeth in her answer insisted that she had, when her son Edward was an infant, laid out in binding him apprentice and in fitting and setting him out for the East Indies and in other necessaries for him more than the £100.

But by PAGE and GILBERT, barons, only in court, no deduction ought to be made for this, for the mother, by nature, ought to provide for the maintenance and education of her own son. 2 Ventris 346.[1] Besides, it appears plainly the intention of the testator that this £100 should not be touched until Edward came

[1] *Anonymous* (1679), 2 Ventris 346, 86 E.R. 478.

of age, for there was an yearly allowance in the meantime of £5 and it was at her peril that she exceeded that. And the plaintiff had a decree for this £100 with interest from the date of Edward's will.

Harvard Law School MS. 1082, vol. 1, p. 181, pl. 1

Michaelmas term 1723.

A bill was brought for a legacy of £100 left by William Martin, husband of the defendant [Elizabeth] Martin, which was devised to Edward Martin, his son, and £5 *per annum* in the meantime. And William dies. And Edward proving extravagant, the defendant Elizabeth, his mother, at his own desire put him out an apprentice and laid out several sums for him amounting to more than the legacy of £100 and interest. Edward Martin dies and devises this legacy of £100 to the plaintiff's wife. And Edward dies in 1712. And so the plaintiffs bring this bill for their legacy of £100 devised to Edward Martin.

The defendant insists on the several allowances of apprenticeship and other necessaries laid out. And no probate of Edward's will was produced, but only the original will in Doctors' Commons, where it was marked *probatum*.

I was counsel for the defendant and insisted that, no probate being produced, that the original will was no evidence as to personal estate, or, if it was, yet that the allowances ought to be made for the apprenticeship and necessaries to the defendant, the executrix, who was the mother.

But the court was of opinion that producing the original will where *probatum* was endorsed was sufficient without producing it under seal and the rather since the probate was in the custody of the defendant executrix and that no allowances ought to be made to the defendant in respect of the apprenticeship or other necessaries, for, as she was the mother, she had the allowance of £5 *per annum* and ought to take care of her child. If it had been that the executrix had been a stranger, there perhaps, an allowance ought to have been made. So they decreed for the plaintiffs the legacy of £100 and interest from 1712, from the death of Edward, though the bill was not filed or the money demanded but a year before.

426

Lucy v. Gardener

(Ex. 1723)

In this case, the court ordered a jointure to be paid out of a freehold estate so that a leasehold could be used to pay a legacy.

Bunbury 136, 145 E.R. 623

11 November 1723.

A bill [was brought] for a legacy of £1500 given to the plaintiff Sarah by the will of her father, who made the defendant, his son and heir, executor; the defendant insists there are not assets sufficient to answer the whole. And, to make out the deficiency, he says that the testator, upon his marriage with his last wife, conveyed a freehold estate and also a term for years in the Sun Tavern in Holborn to trustees to raise £1500 for his wife in full [satisfaction] of any demand she might otherwise have and that he the defendant had sold the term for years and thereby raised the £1500, and paid the same to the wife; and therefore the residue of the personal estate was not sufficient to answer the whole £1500 legacy now demanded.

But it was decreed *per* CURIAM, PRICE, PAGE, and GILBERT, barons, that the executor should not apply this term to the payment of the widow's £1500; but the same should go, in case of a deficiency of other personal assets, towards payment of the debts and other legacies, and the £1500 given to the widow, but now paid, should remain a charge on the freehold estate.

Harvard Law School MS. 1082, vol. 1, p. 180, pl. 1

Michaelmas term 1723.

A bill was brought for a portion of £1500 given by the will of the plaintiff's father, who, upon his marriage with his wife, charged his real estate and likewise a term for years with the payment of £1500 to his wife and made the defendant, his son, his executor, who, by his answer, insists that he had sold the term for years in order to satisfy his wife the £1500, and therefore, there is a deficiency of assets. And the question was whether the executor had such a power to sell the personal estate, *viz.* the leasehold estate to make a deficiency of assets in order to deprive the plaintiff of her portion.

Solicitor General [*Yorke*], for the defendant: This is a devise to the son and an executory devise over. And it is not pretended to charge anything further. And there is no color to charge the real estate with these legacies by any words in the will.

PAGE was of opinion that it would be hard to make such a construction as is contended for to deprive the plaintiff of her portion. But he thought that the first £1500 ought to be on the real estate and the leasehold estate decreed liable to pay the portion to the plaintiff and that it was not in the power to charge the leasehold estate with the payment of £1500.

And so it was agreed by the whole court.

427

Lambert v. Cumming

(Ex. 1723)

In this case, a parishioner proved that part of his land and a common were discharged from the payment of tithes.

Taussig MS. 311, vol. 1, p. 566

Michaelmas term 1723.

A bill was exhibited by the plaintiff as lessee of the Dean and Chapter of Worcester, impropriators of the rectory of Wharton in the County of Lancaster, for all sorts of tithes.

The defendant, as to some lands called Hilderton, insists they were part of Cockersand Abbey, which was one of the greater monasteries and came to the crown by 31 Hen. VIII[1] and was surrendered by the 30th Hen. VIII [1539]. This Abbey was of the Order of the Premonstratensians, who were discharged *quamdiu propriis manibus*, [and was] granted from the king in 36 Hen. VIII [1545].

Pengelly, pro defendente: The plaintiff has shown no possession of the tithes [and] no pretense of any payment. However, notwithstanding this objection, he went over to prove this to be one of the greater abbeys etc.

Browne insists that a lay impropriator must prove possession.

The surrender of 29th January 30 Hen. VIII [1539] was read, by which it is recited to be *ordinis Premonstratensis*, [and] ministers' accounts while in the king's hands in 35 Hen. VIII, which was a year before the grant, the account from 34 to 35 Hen. VIII, *viz. pro uno anno integro*, the total [was] £220 *ultra reprisas*. There was a grant 36 Hen. VIII 23 March [1545] from the king to John Braddyl; under this grant, the defendant claimed. Depositions of witnesses were read to prove that Hilderton and the commons and mosses in the rectory of Wharton were reputed to be part of the dissolved Abbey of Cockersand and that the lands were occupied by the defendants as owners thereof and that no tithes had been paid.

Ward, e contra: The ministerial accounts here do not show it to be above £200. (2) The defendants insist by their answer on a grant of 23 May 36 Hen. VIII, whereas they produce in evidence a grant of 23 March 36 Hen. VIII. (3) They do not show that the lands granted to Braddyl were the same lands as they now pretend an exemption to. (4) The defendant does not show that he is owner of the lands. (5) The objection of [being a] lay impropriator does not here conclude because the dean and chapter are grantees of the rectory and the dean and chapter are not able to discharge or extinguish tithes, as a mere layman may do.

Bootle: The minister's accounts do not prove that the parish of Warton was parcel of the Abbey of Cockersand. (2) He should have produced the certificate of the value sent into the Exchequer. (3) He does not show that the lands were in the hands of the abbot *tempore dissolutionis*, but only shows that, five years after the dissolution, the crown granted these lands to Braddyl.

[1] Stat. 31 Hen. VIII, c. 13 (*SR*, III, 733-739).

PRICE: The defendant has made a very good defense. We do not admit non-payment solely to be evidence, but non-payment with this evidence is the strongest proof. The surrender in 30 Hen. VIII seems to show that it was one of the greater monasteries, for else if it was vested by 27 Hen. VIII, what need [is there of] a surrender in 30 Hen. VIII. (2) The value is pretty clearly proved in the minister's account and that together with the former presumption leaves no room to doubt the fact that it was one of the greater monasteries. (3) The witnesses prove these lands to have been in the possession of this family for fifty years last and also prove that no tithes have been paid. And I think there is no need to produce deeds to prove a title after this evidence. (4) Yeeland Common belonging to Elderton, it is part of Hilderton and the exemption goes along with the land to which the common belongs. Common and the land to which it belongs must go together because the farm is not of value without the common.

And so *per* CURIAM, the plaintiff's bill was dismissed with costs as to Hilderton Farm etc. and [it is] to go to an account for the rest.

Bunbury 138, 145 E.R. 624,
1 Rayner 196, 2 Gwillim 647, 1 Eagle & Younge 790

21 November 1723.

A bill was brought for tithes in the parish of Warton in the County of Lancaster. The defendant insists upon an exemption for his estate called Hilderston and for his right of common without number in Yealand, which estate was parcel of the Abbey of Cockersand, one of the greater abbeys, which exemption was proved. But it was objected for the plaintiff that the common is only a profit *a prendre* out of other land and an exemption cannot arise for an appendancy or an appurtenancy.

But *per* CURIAM: We will make no distinction between the common and the estate. And they decreed for the defendant.

3 Gwillim 1016

Josiah Lambert, gent., lessee of the dean and chapter of Worcester, brought his bill against Edward Cummin and others for tithes in Warton in Lancashire. The defendant Cummin, by his answer, alleged that King Henry VIII, on 23 March *anno* 36 [1545], granted the lands in the answer mentioned to John Bradyll in fee, under whom the defendants claimed. He said that no impropriator or lessee thereof ever took or received any tithe in kind or anything in lieu thereof on the said lands. He insisted that the said lands were parcel of the dissolved Abbey of Cockersand, which was one of the greater abbeys and came to the crown by the Statute 31 Hen. VIII, and were held and enjoyed always and, at the time of the dissolution, by the said abbot and convent discharged of tithes, and they had been so enjoyed ever since the dissolution, that the plaintiff, or any former lessee, never demanded tithes of the said estate, and he was advised such exemption was not lost by the dissolution of the abbey, but the privilege continued by virtue of the said Statute, and that he, as owner and occupier, ought to have the advantage of such discharge, that he and his predecessors had enjoyed the said estate above 100 years free of tithes.

Now, on the hearing, upon reading the surrender of the said abbey in the [*blank*] year of Hen. VIII and the letters patent to John Braddyll and the minister's accounts of 35 Hen. VIII, whereby it appears that the said Abbey of Cockersand was one of the greater abbeys, the court declared the said estate to be discharged of tithes and dismissed the bill with costs.

N.B. This was a decree made by the three barons, PRICE, PAGE, and GILBERT.

[Order of 21 November 1723: 2 Wood 215, 1 Eagle & Younge 790.]

428

Gregory, *qui tam* v. Packer

(Ex. 1723)

Both the Court of Exchequer and the local justices of the peace have jurisdiction over forfeitures of horses and carts used to carry away smuggled goods.

Harvard Law School MS. 1082, vol. 1, p. 178, pl. 1

Michaelmas term 1723.

The defendant moved for a writ of appraisement and delivery for carts and horses, which, by the Stat. 8 Geo.,[1] the justices have a jurisdiction. And an order was obtained *nisi*.

The Attorney General [*Raymond*] showed cause against this order and insisted that the justices of peace have the jurisdiction.

Baron PRICE said that he was sorry for that law, but, since there was such an Act, he could not repeal it.

PAGE: After the order for a writ of appraisement and delivery, the summons before the justices was taken out and the crown has an election to proceed in the Court of Exchequer or before the justices. And so he concluded to discharge the former order.

GILBERT: If the officer proceeds in a reasonable time, the order was well made, but, since it appears that the officer has not delayed, he may proceed where he pleases.

Attorney General v. Hollingsby, Easter 1723,[2] was cited.

Taussig MS. 311, vol. 1, p. 571

Michaelmas term 1723.

---

[1] Stat. 8 Geo. I, c. 18, s. 16.

[2] *Rex v. Hollingsby* (Ex. 1723), see above, Case No. 404.

Gregory seizes coffee etc. under a load of hay at Hoddesdon and seizes the cart and horses on the 7 [*blank*]. On the 15th, the owner of the cart and horses applies to this court for a writ of appraisement and delivery. On the same day, after a rule to show cause, the officer takes out a summons to appear on the 19th before a justice of peace.

And now, the Attorney General [*Raymond*] showed cause, *viz.* that the Act of Parliament had given authority to the justices and this court, though its jurisdiction is not taken away by this Statute, yet it cannot prohibit or prevent the justices from proceeding.

And the court held they might interpose where there is a delay of prosecution, but, if there is no delay, then the justices may certainly proceed. And because the court thought there had been no delay in this case sufficient to justify their interposing, they discharged the rule and took no notice of the priority of their own possession of the cause.

Quod mirum mihi videbatur since they acknowledged their jurisdiction was not taken away. This motion was founded on the [Stat.] 8th of the present king, entitled an Act to Prevent Clandestine Running of Goods, pa. 285 etc. See before, the case of Rex v. Hollingsby.

429

Gregory, *qui tam* v. Hunt

(Ex. 1723)

Both the Court of Exchequer and the local justices of the peace have jurisdiction to determine forfeitures of carts and horses used to carry away smuggled goods.

Bunbury 139, 145 E.R. 624

22 November 1723.

Upon a motion for a writ of appraisement and delivery for a cart and horses seized for carrying tea and coffee, the customs not being paid, there being a proceeding against them before two justices pursuant to the Stat. 8 Geo. I, cap. 18, which refers to the 6 Geo., cap. [*blank*], and also to two statutes 8 Anne.[1]

Per CURIAM: Though the statutes, having no negative words, do not take away the jurisdiction of this court, yet the party has his election to proceed here, or before the justices. And that being now attached in the justices and there not appearing to have been any great delay, they denied the motion.

[1] Stat. 8 Geo. I, c. 18, s. 16; Stat. 6 Geo. I, c. 2; Stat. 8 Ann., c. 12, s. 17 (*SR*, IX, 221); Stat. 8 Ann., c. 14, s. 20 (*SR*, IX, 238).

430

Rex v. Astell

(Ex. 1723-1724)

A recognizance can be discharged upon a plea, but not upon a simple motion in court.

Harvard Law School MS. 1082, vol. 1, p. 178, pl. 2

Michaelmas term 1723.

A motion was made for discharging the recognizances of the late South Sea [Company] directors, who had entered into them in the penalty of £40,000 each with their sureties that they would not depart the kingdom within a year. And an affidavit was made by themselves and a servant that they had not been out of the kingdom. And so [it was] moved for a discharge.

Baron PRICE: Though this motion does concern four millions and a half, yet I think that we have an ample jurisdiction to discharge these recognizances. And I think that they ought not to hang over their heads forever. And so let the rule be *nisi* sitting.

PAGE: I am not fully satisfied. It does not appear that the South Sea directors have had notice, and they are proper persons, for the forfeitures are for the use of the Company.

GILBERT: I think that the matters of this great concern ought to appear judicially upon record before they are discharged and that it ought to be pleaded. And, therefore, he inclined against Price.

And, afterwards, the court being full and the Chief Baron EYRE being come up sometime afterward, it was ordered by the whole court that the defendants, the directors and sureties, should plead to these recognizances. And if the Attorney General did not proceed in three terms, then the plea to be taken *pro confesso*.

Taussig MS. 311, vol. 1, p. 586

Hilary term 1723/24.

Mr. *Aris* moved upon the affidavit of Astell and others, his friends, that he had not been abroad, to have his recognizance discharged. And the question was whether it was proper to do this upon a motion or whether there was any way to do it upon a plea to the recognizance.

EYRE, Chief Baron: I do not know there is any way to get rid of this recognizance by way of a plea. How can this be done? How is the cognizor to come into court and plead without process against him?

PRICE: A person may come in officiously upon a recognizance and suggest that he has not been abroad. And, if, upon three terms' notice, the Attorney [General] does not reply, the court will give judgment of discharge, for, in this court, there may be suits without a plaintiff or a defendant. But I think we may do it by motion and that, if we make a rule that, if no cause be shown to the contrary before the end of the term, we may well do it this way.

PAGE and GILBERT: This is a recognizance by an Act of Parliament subsequent to our commission by a privy seal. And, therefore, it is better and safer to put it upon the defendant to come into court and make his suggestion and so give the Attorney General liberty to reply and put the fact in issue.

CHIEF BARON: If there is such a method as all the barons agree there is, then I concur with this method. But I desire before I confine the cognizor to this method to see precedents whether ever recognizances have been discharged by the aforementioned method.

Adjornatur.

Taussig MS. 311, vol. 1, p. 638

Hilary term 1723/24.

The case of the South Sea directors was again stirred. And now, the court, having looked into the precedents, declared that they could not find one instance of a recognizance or port bond discharged by an order, but it was always upon a judgment. And so they ordered them to plead.

431

Boys v. Ellis

(Ex. 1723)

It is not a fraud on the right to receive tithes of lambs for the parishioner in the usual course of husbandry to take the sheep into another parish at the time of the year that lambs are usually born.

Harvard Law School MS. 1082, vol. 1, p. 182

Michaelmas term 1723.

This was a bill for tithes. And the question did arise upon a removing the sheep from one parish into another for the conveniency of pasturage and not by fraud.

Mr. *Fazakerly*, for the plaintiff, insisted that it was fraud apparent by the removing them out of one parish into another. And he cited Moore 913; 1 Rolle, *Abridgment*, 652; Lane 16, 17; Popham 197; 2 Keble 293, Weemes v. Aymondsham.[1]

Ward, for the defendant: The sheep were removed into the parish of Skerne from Michaelmas to Lady Day. Tithes are due generally where they fall; if not, it would introduce great confusion. And where is the fraud in this case when the

[1] *Stebs v. Goodock* (1588), Moore K.B. 913, 72 E.R. 992, 1 Gwillim 158, 1 Eagle & Younge 93; *Anonymous* (1619), 1 Rolle, Abr., *Dismes*, pl. G, 1, p. 652; *Huddleston v. Hills*, Lane 16, 145 E.R. 262; *Anonymous* (1626), Popham 197, 79 E.R. 1289, 1 Eagle & Younge 356; *Weems v. Amersom* (1667), 2 Keble 293, 84 E.R. 183, 1 Eagle & Younge 457.

removal is according to the course of husbandry and tithes are paid to the parish of Skerne? And though it is objected that there is only a *modus* there due in lieu of tithes in kind, rate tithe is not receivable by common law and the demand of a rate tithe is not stated by the bill. And the parson of the other parish is no party. The notion of a rate tithe is taken from the canon law, and [it is] not received here. And Dr. Gibson, in his *Codex*,[1] complains that it is not received. And I desire to know what defense could the defendant set up against the parson of Skerne, and if that parson has exhibited his bill.

I humbly insist that fraud is not to be presumed.

Confusion would arise by the apportionment, and it would be impossible to ascertain how much wool in one parish and how much in another. And I do agree that, if the removal had been some few days or a short time before the shearing, there, it would be fraud apparent.

Fazakerly replies: Not one case against the plaintiff's demand and not one single instance was cited.

[To the] objection that no fraud is proved, [he] answered it appears by the circumstances to be fraud apparent, for it is admitted that, if [they were] removed about a fortnight before, there, it would be fraud, and, in this case, the falling of lambs continues for three months.

Mr. *Bootle* replies [to the] objection no demand is proper for a rateable or proportionable tithe because the other parson is not a party, [he] answered [there was] no occasion for the parson of Skerne to be a party because he is not affected by this question, for the parson of Skerne has his *modus*. This will amount to a *non decimando* as to lambs. The satisfaction given for the tithes of wool and lambs was only for what happened in Griffin.

Price: I think that the bill must be dismissed for everything except the tithe of lambs. The bill suggests a fraud, and no rate tithe is mentioned in the bill. But whether this is a fraud is now the question. I do not deny but that, generally, tithe of lambs is due where the lambs fall. And if a party comes for a rateable tithe, ought it not to be particularly alleged in the bill, which is not in this case. Is here fraud apparent or circumstances to make it? I cannot call it fraud apparent or that fraud is proved. I remember in a case in this court that the person declared that he would cheat the parson, yet I cannot call it fraud and [there is] no badge of it, for the removal of the sheep for three months before cannot be called so. So the bill must be entirely dismissed.

Page: This is a case of some concern, for the rule is too generally laid down that tithes are always due where they fall, for, if so, the parsons would be deprived of their right. The payment of wool is nothing in comparison to the lambs. If such sheep are removed to lands that are tithe free or under a composition, it is fraud. And in the proof in this cause, the answer is contradicted as to the

[1] E. Gibson, *Codex Juris Ecclesiastici Anglicani*.

necessity of the removal of them. Tithe wool is divisible, but tithe of lambs cannot be. But whether [it is] fraud or not, it ought to be tried.

GILBERT: I allow the principle laid down that tithe of lambs is due where they fall, but lambs are indivisible, though wool is not. But the question is whether there is any fraud in this case, and, if so, the defendant must be decreed to pay the tithes in kind. And the circumstances of the case must be considered. And, in this case, there is a *modus* at Skerne, which covers everything. And if these sheep were carried some little time before lambing, then I should construe it a fraud. But where the occupier does it only but in the way and course of husbandry and as is usually practiced in the country, then I cannot call it a fraud. And the intention must be considered. And if the course of husbandry is changed by this renewal, there, I should call it a fraud. And so he concluded and agreed with Price. And the bill was dismissed.

Bunbury 139, 145 E.R. 624,
1 Rayner 197, 2 Gwillim 647, 1 Eagle & Younge 793

25 November 1723.

In a bill for tithes, a question arose whether there was fraud in tithing lambs, on this case. The ewes were kept by the defendant in the parish of Driffield in the County of York, where the demand lay, all the year until Christmas, when they were ready to drop their lambs, and then they were removed into the parish of Skern, where there was a small *modus* only for lambs, and there kept until Lady Day [25 March] for convenience of forage, as insisted upon by the defendant, and at Lady Day they were brought back to Driffield.

Note: There was no demand of tithe *pro rata*, and query if there had, if it could be decreed, for the tithe of lamb must be paid where they fall and is not a divisible thing as wool is.

Note: The land in Skern was the defendant's own.

Per CURIAM: Here is not a sufficient proof of fraud, and the plaintiff's bill was dismissed.

But PAGE and GILBERT, barons, thought at first it might be proper to send it to an issue to try whether fraud or not fraud and whether this had been the usual method of the defendant's course of husbandry. But, afterwards, they concurred with Baron PRICE.

432

Martin v. Freelove

(Ex. 1723)

A bill in equity lies for an account of the assets of a decedent's estate that are liable for the payment of a note.

Harvard Law School MS. 1082, vol. 1, p. 181, pl. 2

Michaelmas term 1723.

A bill was brought for an account of assets in order to be paid two promissory notes given by the defendant's intestate, for that the plaintiff had before brought an action and *plene administravit* was pleaded and, therefore, the plaintiff was obliged to bring a bill. And though the plaintiff denied assets, yet assets were proved. And though it was objected that, after an answer, the party might go to law, yet it was answered and decreed that it was proper in a court of equity and the rather since there was a concealment in the defendant by denying assets and this court is as proper, if not more proper, to take an account of assets than a court of law. And so they decreed the defendant to account, according to the cases of Dupuis v. Duke of Kingston, Trinity 1718; Thomas v. Williams, Michaelmas 1718.[1]

433

Godfrey v. Eyles

(Ex. 1723)

In this case, the defendants were not in privity with the wrongdoer for the purposes of service of process or for liability.

Taussig MS. 311, vol. 1, p. 557

Godfrey v. Sir John Eyles et al., trustees under the Act of Parliament of the [*blank*].

Godfrey applies to Knight for £2000 of the fourth subscription and told him at the same time that he had not money to pay for it. But Knight told him the [South Sea] Company would lend him £4000 on his stock, he having £1000 stock in the Company and, accordingly, gave him a permit to assign his stock. And Godfrey, thereupon, gave him a promissory note for £4000 in expectation of the £2000 subscription. Godfrey goes to borrow the money, but he was then told the Company did not lend it. So he had it not, nor had he the £2000 of the fourth subscription given him. The trustees sue him at law upon his £4000 note. Godfrey exhibits his bill against Knight and the trustees setting forth this matter. And he verifies his bill by an affidavit. And he had an order that serving the trustees with process to answer should be deemed service on Mr. Knight.

But upon motion, the court set aside the order because Knight was now to be looked upon as dead and could not answer. And the trustees, as the court said, were perfect strangers to Knight and had no power over or privity with him.

[1] *Thomas v. Williams* (Ex. 1718), see above, Case No. 59.

Harvard Law School MS. 1082, vol. 1, p. 184, pl. 2

Michaelmas term 1723.

Mr. Godfrey, the plaintiff, having given a note to Mr. Knight, whose estate was forfeited by Act of Parliament and vested in the defendants [the commissioners or trustees for the sale of the South Sea estates], brought his bill against the defendants to be relieved against this note and suggested good equity upon it. And, thereupon, the plaintiff moved that, as the defendants stood in the place of Knight, that they might answer for him, who was abroad. And this case was compared to that of assignees of bankrupts, that stood in the place of the bankrupt.

But the court denied the motion and said that there was no sufficient privity between the trustees and Knight, *quod vide*.

434

Newins v. Worth

(Ex. 1723)

A case can be removed out of an ecclesiastical court where that court has no jurisdiction.

Taussig MS. 311, vol. 1, p. 572

Thursday, 28 November 1723.

2 Inst. 602;[1] a [writ of] prohibition is not too late, where the court has not jurisdiction, after a sentence. Suggestions [for writs of prohibition] may be amended at any time before the declaration and, sometimes, even after the declaration. There is no need of a plea where the nullity of the jurisdiction appears upon the proceedings themselves.

Query whether, after a sentence in the ecclesiastical court for calling [one a] whore in London, the court can prohibit. In this case, it did not appear by the libel or otherwise that the words were spoken in the City of London, excepting only by the depositions in the cause wherein the witnesses swear the words to have been spoken in the kitchen of the Three Tun Tavern in Newgate Street, London. Cro. Eliz. 178;[2] this case was answered before because one may amend a suggestion before the declaration.

Price: This prohibition now prayed is certainly wrong because the prohibition prayed is to the consistory court of a peculiar, whereas there is now no cause in that peculiar, for it is removed now to the [Court of] Arches. Secondly, the libel alleges the words spoken in Middlesex; therefore, the defendant should have come in and showed this and prohibited before the sentence, but, after the sentence, it is too late.

---

[1] E. Coke, *Second Institute* (1642), p. 602.

[2] *Transam's Case* (1590), Croke Eliz. 178, 78 E.R. 434.

PAGE: It is never too late, but in a case of citing out of the diocese. So he was of opinion that the prohibition should stand.

GILBERT: A [writ of] prohibition ought to go because of no jurisdiction. An action lies for calling [one] a whore in London because whoring is cartable in London and so is a temporal offense in London and, therefore, the ecclesiastical court is ousted of any conusance of this crime. And it is enough that the fact appears by the *probata* though not by the *allegata* because, if it appears by the *probata*, it appears before the sentence and the sentence is a nullity.

And prohibition went.

435

White v. Hatters

(Ex. 1723)

The ecclesiastical courts have jurisdiction over cases of calling a woman a prostitute.

Harvard Law School MS. 1082, vol. 1, p. 187, pl. 1

Michaelmas term 1723.

Bootle moved for a [writ of] prohibition to the court at Aylesbury for proceeding there for calling a woman a whore. Brown v. Tanner, in Salkeld, Hilary 1713; Goldsborough 65; 2 Rolle, *Abridgment*, 256, sec. 14, 15.[1]

PRICE: [They were] idle words. Yet I take it that the ecclesiastical court has a jurisdiction of this matter. And in London, a prohibition is granted because it is actionable by the custom.

PAGE agreed.

GILBERT: The ecclesiastical court has jurisdiction of this matter *pro reformatione morum*. And there is no remedy but in the ecclesiastical court.

So a [writ of] prohibition was denied.

436

Mercer v. Tutt

(Ex. 1723)

The Court of Exchequer can grant a writ of ne exeat regno.

Harvard Law School MS. 1082, vol. 1, p. 187, pl. 2

Sittings after Michaelmas term 1723.

---

[1] *Brown v. Tanner* (1703), 3 Salkeld 288, 91 E.R. 830; 2 Rolle, Abr., *Prohibition*, p. 296.

The plaintiff moved that the defendant should give security before he went abroad, which the plaintiff admitted to be a [writ of] *ne exeat regno*. And it was opposed by the defendant. And he cited Sir Edward Bettison v. Long,[1] where the Chief Baron Montagu said that the writ was only grantable by having the custody of the great seal and not as a court of equity, so he would not order security to be given.

GILBERT: I do not know but that this court may grant such a writ, which may be granted to every person where it is the king's debtor. But I think that there is no occasion for giving security.

PRICE said that he did not know why this court should not grant such a writ as well as the Court of Chancery.

Taussig MS. 311, vol. 1, p. 577

Friday, the 6 December, sittings after Michaelmas term 1723.

The plaintiff moved that the defendant, who was going abroad to the East Indies before the hearing of the cause, should give security for the payment of costs.

PRICE: If it did appear plainly that there was a debt due to the plaintiff, I should make no scruple to make the defendant give security. But in this case, it rather appears that the contrary is true, *viz.* that there is a debt due to defendant.

GILBERT: I do not see why this court should not grant a *ne exeat regno*.

And PRICE seemed to think so too. But this point was not determined. However, both agreed if they could not grant a *ne exeat regno*, they could force the party to give security. But both agreeing there was no occasion for it in this case, they only obliged the defendant to consent to hear the cause *gratis*.

[On appeal: 2 Brown P.C. 563, 1 E.R. 1134.]

437

Fuller, *qui tam* v. Jackson

(Ex. 1723)

The master of a ship that is liable to forfeiture for smuggling is not competent because of interest to testify as a witness in a proceeding for the forfeiture of the goods that were imported in his ship without paying the customs duties.

Harvard Law School MS. 1082, vol. 1, p. 187, pl. 3

Sittings after Michaelmas term 1723.

This was an information for importing goods contrary to the Act of Navigation.[2] And Bryan, the master [of the ship], was produced as a witness for the

---

[1] *Bettison v. Long* (Ex. 1722-1723), see above, Case No. 338.

[2] Stat. 12 Car. II, c. 18, s. 4 (*SR*, V, 247).

defendant, who, upon a *voir dire*, said that he was not concerned in interest, either in the goods or the ship, and had no share therein. And so the question arose whether he was a proper witness or not.

PAGE and GILBERT said that the master might be concerned in consequence and for that he swears to excuse himself against an action which might be commenced against him by his owner, for he is liable thereto if he has been guilty of any miscarriage.

And, therefore, the court set aside the master and would not allow him to be an evidence.

Quod mirum est, for, where he has no share in the ship, it is too remote a consequence for to take off his testimony.

Taussig MS. 311, vol. 1, p. 576

Michaelmas term 1723.

An information [was exhibited] against the defendant upon the Statute of Navigation for importing tea and sussies from Ostend into Great Britain. The defendant called the master of the ship, who being examined upon *voir dire*, swore he was not concerned in interest. But by the course of the evidence, it appeared that he was the master of the ship.

Mr. Attorney General [*Raymond*] said that, though this information was not for the ship, yet, by the Statute, the ship was forfeited. And, therefore, he is no good witness because he will be answerable over to his owners for bringing the ship into port whereby it was forfeited. Therefore, it is his interest to swear that the ship was not within the limits of the port in order to avoid the consequences of such an action.

The objection was allowed *per* PAGE and GILBERT at the sittings in Middlesex November 29th, 1723.

Bunbury 140, 145 E.R. 625

Upon a trial upon an information for importing teas etc. from Ostend, not being the place of their growth etc. contrary to the Act of Navigation, the master of the ship was produced as evidence for the defendant. But it was objected to him that the ship etc. being forfeited by the Act as well as the goods by the fault of the master, he thereby is become responsible to the owners and, therefore, swears to discharge himself in consequence.

And this objection was allowed by PAGE and GILBERT, barons, before whom it was tried at the sittings after Michaelmas term 1723 at Westminster.

But note: This objection had never been allowed before, especially if there had been no information against the ship etc. And at these very sittings, the same objection was made to the master of a cart, which, by the Stat. 6 & 7 Geo.,[1] is forfeited for running goods, and was not allowed.

438

Bishop of London v. Nicholls

(Ex. 1723)

A bishop can sequester a parish during the incapacity of the rector.

Where a parish has been sequestered because of the incapacity of the rector, the rector must nevertheless be a party plaintiff in a suit for the payment of tithes.

Harvard Law School MS. 1082, vol. 1, p. 188

Sittings after Michaelmas term 1723.

This was a bill setting forth that Barefoot was rector of Birchanger in the County of Essex. But he becoming incapacitated, the bishop of London, by letters, granted a sequestration to the plaintiff Beaumont. And so the bill was brought for tithes by the sequestrator and the ordinary [the bishop of London], to which bill, the defendant demurred for that, the plaintiff Beaumont being only a sequestrator, he ought to take his remedy in the ecclesiastical court.

And we that were for the defendant insisted that, by the Statute 28 Hen. VIII,[2] the succeeding minister has the tithes. And what defense could the present occupier make against the succeeding minister that this was of mere spiritual cognizance as offerings and there is no suit here for offerings only. And the sequestrator is only as a collector, and the accounts are to be passed in the ecclesiastical court. And Barefoot, the rector, is not before the court, which he ought to be.

But it was insisted for the plaintiff that, the ordinary and the sequestrator being joined together, it made a good title. And they cited Bishop of Norwich and Eachard v. Bulley and Butler, Trinity 1713.[3] The bishop as ordinary has the *curam animarum*. J. Selden, *History*, 251, *instituo ad meam et tuam curam*; Banks v. Rye, 1686.[4]

Price: This demurrer is good. And I think that it appears that Barefoot has a right, which is not dropped. There is a difference between a discharge for tithes and setting forth a tithe. But I think, in all events, that Barefoot ought to have been a party, which might have been by a guardian. And I do not think that this

---

1 Stat. 6 Geo. I, c. 2.

2 Stat. 28 Hen. VIII, c. 11 (*SR*, III, 666-667).

3 *Bishop of Norwich v. Bucklea* (1713), Dodd 231, 2 Gwillim 610, 1 Eagle & Younge 705.

4 J. Selden, *History of Tithes* (1618); *Bankes v. Rye* (1686), Eq. Cases Exch. 247, 1 Rayner 65.

suit is well instituted if Barefoot was [not] a party, being of spiritual cognizance. And I should doubt in this case if the bill was proper if it was in the case of a vacancy.

PAGE: If the rector had been a party, the bill would have been proper. And the execution is good upon a sequestration. If the bishop's sequestrator does not give a title, then sequestration will be ineffectual and the writ directed to the bishop of no effect. And as the bishop must do it by the writ, so it would be extraordinary to find fault with it. If it can be done at all, it ought to be in this case. And it is the office of the bishop to take care of the church and that it is duly supplied.

It would be extraordinary to say that the occupier should keep the tithes until the rector becomes sensible. And the bishop, during the vacancy or the incapacity of the rector, ought to take care of the church. And the next incumbent must take the tithes subject to the sequestration and no hurt is done. But yet I think the rector ought to be a party. So it not being particularly assigned but only generally, then the demurrer must be allowed for want of parties without costs.

GILBERT: The written demurrer is not good, but that *ore tenus* for want of parties is good. There was no proper establishment of tithes until the Council of Lateran, though there were canons before that preserved some parochial rights. In case of lunacy, age, or infirmity, the bishop ought to take care of the church. And the defendant is obliged to pay tithes. But the rector ought to be before the court. So he allowed the demurrer *ore tenus* without costs.

Taussig MS. 311, vol. 1, p. 578

Saturday, 7th December 1723. Bishop of London and Beaumont, sequestrator v. Nicholls.

A bill [was exhibited] by the plaintiffs for tithe wood during the incapacity of the incumbent by indisposition by reason of sickness. And there was a demurrer for this cause, *scil.* that the sequestrator and the bishop had not a right to sue for tithes. And for the demurrer were cited the case of Banks and Rye and that the incumbent should have been made a party.

Contra Selden's *History of Tithes*, page 251, and Michaelmas 3 Will. [1691], Herriot v. Maidstone, that payment to a sequestrator is a bar against the incumbent, and the case of the Bishop of Norwich and Buckler.

PRICE: The demurrer is good; neither the sequestrator not the bishop singly has any right, nor jointly, especially, as this case is, where there is an incumbent not made a party. But if payment be made to a sequestrator, that may perhaps be a discharge. But there is a difference between pleading in discharge and making a demand.

PAGE: If the rector had been a party, I should have thought the bill was right. How can execution be against a parson *non habens laicum feodum* if the bishop cannot sequester? I think the bishop's power to sequester is not capable of being disputed. And that the power to do so in this case ought to be allowed and encouraged if in any because no man can tell what is to become of the tithes, for the parishioners are not obliged to keep them until the incumbent is recovered. But I think the incumbent ought to have been made a party.

GILBERT: The incumbent ought to have been a party. But I think that the written cause of the demurrer is not good, but that the bishop and sequestrator may sue, for the parishioner is bound in conscience to pay the tithes to a person who is a safe hand to receive them. And if the paying them to the bishop's sequestrator will be a discharge of the parishioner from paying them again to the next incumbent, then he ought to pay them to such sequestrator. But since the incumbent is alive in this case, I think he should be made a party. And, therefore, though the written cause of demurrer, which is that the bishop and sequestrator have no title to the tithes is not good, yet it is as much as want of parties is a good cause of demurrer. And upon quitting, the costs may be assigned *ore tenus*. Therefore, we must allow the demurrer.

And the demurrer was accordingly allowed without costs.

Bunbury 141, 145 E.R. 625,
1 Rayner 198, 2 Gwillim 648, 1 Eagle & Younge 793

A bill was brought by the bishop of London and Beaumont, as sequestrator during the incapacity of mind of Barefoot, the present incumbent, for tithe wood in the parish of Birchanger in the County of Essex. The defendant demurs, for that it does not appear that either of the plaintiffs had any title. And it was insisted upon by the counsel for the defendant that, now, since the division of parishes, the whole right to tithe was vested in the rector and the bishop had nothing to do with the right, even since the Stat. Hen. VIII, which relates to a vacancy, but only to take care that the cure be supplied and the profits sequestered for that purpose. And the other plaintiff was only a sequestrator, who, as it appears by the form of the sequestration and by his own showing in the bill, was only an agent or collector; besides, the incumbent, Barefoot, should have been made a party, for possibly, at this time, he may have recovered his right senses. And if he should exhibit his bill, a recovery now could not be pleaded in bar of his demand.

Baron PRICE was of opinion that no decree could have been for the plaintiff if it had been a sequestration during the vacancy, nor can there be in this case.

But PAGE and GILBERT, barons, were of opinion the bill had been well enough if Barefoot had been a party, either in person or by his committee. And the bill was dismissed, but without costs, the want of parties not being expressly assigned as cause of demurrer.

And note: The words 'and for divers other causes' etc. were not in the demurrer, as they should have been.

439

Anonymous

(Ex. 1723)

Where there has been a great delay in a prosecution of a condemnation of goods, the Court of Exchequer can discharge the bidders for the goods from their bids.

Taussig MS. 311, vol. 1, p. 580

Michaelmas term 1723.

At the setting down of causes, the barons discharged two bidders from their biddings on account of the long delay of prosecuting the information to a condemnation, one *ex motione* Cox, the other *ex motione* Foley. And in this last, Mr. *Stevens*, Solicitor of Customs, said he would not oppose the court's discharging the bidder because there had been a long delay in prosecuting the seizure, which arose from the Attorney [General] and Solicitor [General] taking time to consider in what manner the seizure should be prosecuted. The seizure was made in Scotland, and the goods were sent up and proclaimed here. And then, they doubted whether they could prosecute a seizure in Scotland here, and so the information had not been proceeded upon.

440

Periam v. Dawson

(Ex. 1723)

An executor or administrator de son tort *cannot retain.*

Harvard Law School MS. 1082, vol. 1, p. 189

Sittings after Michaelmas term 1723. Periam, executor of Colthurst v. Dawson.

The question in this case was whether an executor *de son tort* could retain. And in this case, the defendant's letters of administration were repealed.

Mr. *Wynn*, for the administrator *de son tort*, [said] that, by law, the administrator *de son tort* before notice might retain, for all acts done by him during that time were good.

But the court declared that the administrator could not retain and that, upon the repeal of the letters patent, all were void *ab initio*; so it is if a person takes out administration where there is a will, all is void *ab initio*.

441

Devallar v. Herring

(Ex. 1723-1725)

The question in this case was whether a bona fide *purchaser for value without notice of a stolen security had a superior right to the true owner.*

In this case, the ownership of the security in issue did not pass because the assignee of it did not properly register the transfer.

9 Modern 44, 88 E.R. 305

One Smith, who was proprietor of an annuity ticket in one of the public funds, sold it to White, who sold it to Devallar, a single man, who made the plaintiffs his executors, and died.

The plaintiffs, coming to his house after his death, found one of his scrutoires opened, which they suspected to be done by one Powell,[1] his manservant, by the contrivance of the servant maid, they being the only persons in the house and are since intermarried.

Upon examining the books of account, the plaintiffs found an entry made of an annuity ticket bought of White on such a day, which was a little before his death. And that ticket being now lost, the plaintiffs advertised it in the public papers with a promise of a reward to any person who should produce it and to stop it before it passed the office. But this advertisement being not made until about two months after the testator's death, the ticket was sold before that time in Exchange Alley and passed through several hands until it came to the defendant Herring, who purchased it for a valuable consideration and had it transferred at the office to himself as from Smith, the first proprietor, whose name was endorsed. And a blank space was left over it to fill up the indorsement as usual, all which was done before the advertisement.

The plaintiffs, the executors, knowing this ticket to be in the possession of the defendant Herring, brought an action of trover against him.

At the trial, they were nonsuited, because the defendant having a transfer from Smith, the first proprietor, and it being counter-signed in the office, he had thereby a propriety, and no other person could have a legal right to it, for the Statute 11 & 12 Ann., c. 9,[2] by which these annuity tickets were created, or the fund for the same, expressly provides, 'that every transfer of these tickets shall be filled up and counter-signed at the office, and an entry kept of every assignment, or transfer, with the names of the parties contracting for the same'.

---

1 Note *Rex v. Powell* (1716), 1 Strange 8, 93 E.R. 350.

2 Stat. 12 Ann., c. 11 (*SR*, IX, 771-781).

And it being a question at this trial, whether any evidence ought to be admitted of the right to this ticket claimed by any person who had not complied with this Statute against the right of him who had complied.

It was ruled by the Court that it ought not. And, thereupon, the plaintiffs were nonsuited.

Afterwards, the executors exhibited a bill in the Exchequer, in which they set forth the death of the testator, the entry of this ticket in his books, and all the aforesaid matter, and that such tickets are constantly sold in Exchange Alley without indorsing any transfer, but only the name of the first proprietor, and that such which have not transfers indorsed sell better than those which have many such indorsements, and that it is the common practice never to make any indorsement over the first proprietor's name whilst these tickets are in agitation, nor until they come into the hands of such persons who intend to keep them, for, if every transfer should be indorsed, the tickets would be so full of them that they could be no longer transferable.

Therefore, it was insisted that the not indorsing the transfer should not, in equity, prejudice the plaintiffs, it being the constant method of assigning such tickets not to indorse the transfer as aforesaid.

The defendant, by his counsel, insisted that he purchased this ticket at a market rate and *bona fide* for a valuable consideration in Exchange Alley without any covin or fraud and that he had complied with the Statute and filled up an indorsement, which was proved by one Mackoy, a broker, of whom he bought this ticket. And, therefore, it was insisted that this bill might be dismissed with costs, as having no equity against the defendant and for that the plaintiffs had already been defeated at law.

It being objected against reading the depositions of Mackoy, for, though he is a broker and, as such, might be a witness, yet it appears by his own deposition that, in this case, he did not act as a broker, but sold the ticket in his own right. And because the defendant may have some demand against him if the plaintiffs should prevail in this suit, therefore, he ought not to be an evidence for the defendant, for that, in consequence, it might be to discharge himself.

But the Court was of opinion that his depositions should be read, for, though his evidence might not be admitted before a jury of freeholders, for the reason before mentioned, yet this Court are proper judges what stress or weight ought to be laid on it.

And after reading the answer and Mackoy's evidence confirming it in everything, the Chief Baron [Montagu] and Baron Gilbert were of opinion that the bill ought to be dismissed, for that every purchaser of such tickets who keeps them open after the purchase without filling them up with an indorsement and transfer according to the Statute keeps them at his own risk or peril. And, if they come afterwards into the hands of a stranger *bona fide* and for a valuable consideration, who gets a transfer indorsed as directed by the Statute, he has an absolute right to them, both in law and in equity.

And Baron GILBERT held that, whatever the Court might do, if the cause was open and came before them without a trial at law, yet there could be no equity now to set aside the nonsuit because that would be an admittance that the defendant had a legal right.

The CHIEF BARON was likewise for dismissing the bill. It is true, if the testator Devallar, when he purchased this ticket, had procured a transfer to himself and thereby had a legal right to it, in such case, if, after his death, the defendant had purchased it of a stranger without acquainting his executors, the plaintiffs, therewith, they might have some equity on their side because the name of their testator was indorsed on the ticket and, by that means, the defendant might have been sure who was the owner of it and who had the power to transfer it to him, yet, as this case is, there could be no negligence in the purchaser, for he bought it for a valuable consideration and had done everything necessary to establish his right and could not know that the plaintiffs' testator had any right to this ticket because there was no transfer indorsed to him. Therefore, by keeping it open without any transfer, he kept it at his own risk for any man to fill up who came to the possession honestly and without fraud so that this bill ought to be dismissed.

Baron PRICE differed in opinion. And he argued from the hardship of the case and that the defendant should have taken care when he bought this ticket of whom he bought it, especially since Mackoy, the seller, had no transfer to himself, but only the bare possession. And since the name of Smith, the first proprietor, was indorsed, he might have been informed whose ticket it was he then bought, that it was a hard case on both sides, it was hard for the plaintiffs, the executors, that they should lose their right because they did not know it soon enough to advertise it, and it is hard for the defendant to lose the benefit of his purchase. He put the case of a promissory note, which, if indorsed and afterwards lost and passed in way of trade to a third person for a valuable consideration, yet the indorsee might bring an action of trover for the note against the third person, which the other barons did not deny.

Thereupon, it was proposed by Baron PRICE that this ticket should be divided between the contending parties, but that was not agreed to.

And, at last, the Court took time farther to consider until next Michaelmas term.

Taussig MS. 311, vol. 2, p. 770

Thursday, 5th February 1724/25.

Samuel Davila, as administrator of David Davila, exhibits his bill against the defendant John Herring for a lottery order, No. 62 in 34 course of payment for £50 and sets forth that David Davila's scrutoire and trunks were sealed up by the direction of David with the consent of the plaintiff and Elizabeth Davila. But the scrutoire was broken open by two servants, *viz.* Elizabeth Shepheard and Powell, the coachman. And this order, among others, was taken out and, at last, came to the hands of the defendant Herring. And he charges a confederacy among them.

Herring, by his answer, says he purchased this order in Exchange Alley of an exchange broker for a valuable consideration, that the plaintiff brought an action of trover against him in the King's Bench and was nonsuited; so he hopes a court of equity will not take it away from him.

The order was taken out in Ainsworth's name. He assigned it to Smith, who sold it to David Davila. Shepheard and Powell give Haward power to sell it, and he sells it to Key, and Key sells it to Herring. The order was endorsed in blank by Ainsworth.

The first point was whether Herring paid anything for it; second, whether, under these circumstances, the property is altered. At common law [*blank*] supposing Herring paid [*blank*], this is not in the nature of money for the delivery of money does transfer property because there is no earmark. Salkeld 283, Ford and Hopkins, lottery tickets.[1] Holt's opinion was that the true proprietor may maintain [an action of] trover for lottery tickets though payable to J.S. or bearer. Ram and Chevalier, *coram* Holt.

Secondly, by the Statute 12 Anne, [there is] no other sort of assignment. Sir Peter Vandeputt's Case, before Sir Peter King, in the Common Bench, about three years ago, an annuity order; 1715, in this court, between Roberts and Crull; 2 Inst. 714; Moor 624, Sir Gervase Clifton's Case.[2]

It was not pretended that Key was a sworn broker, and yet there is an Act of Parliament[3] that none but sworn brokers should act.

If the assignment is yet to be registered, this court must direct in whose favor the assignment must be registered.

[On] 14 December, Mr. Davila bought it; Davila dies in March following; in June following, Herring bought it.

Probyn, e contra: They have not proved that this order was in David's possession at the time of his death, and, if not, the administrator can have no title to it.

Secondly, the plaintiff has not proved that Smith paid any money to Ainsworth or that Davila paid any money to Smith so that Ainsworth is no trustee for them. But the defendant has proved that he has actually paid £46 to Key for it and Key sold it in Exchange Alley. Key commonly deals as a broker and in the usual manner of selling such orders.

Salkeld 156; Letchmore and Bostock, *coram* King, South Sea bonds three years ago were sold in a tavern and the sale was held good.

---

[1] *Ford v. Hopkins* (1701), 1 Salkeld 283, 91 E.R. 250, also Holt K.B. 119, 90 E.R. 964.

[2] E. Coke, *Second Institute* (1642), p. 714; *Clifton v. Chancellor* (1600), Moore K.B. 624, 72 E.R. 800.

[3] Stat. 8 & 9 Will. III, c. 32 (*SR*, VII, 285-287).

EYRE, Chief Baron: The plaintiff has no title at law because property is not vested until the assignment be entered and registered. And, though the words of the Act of Parliament are affirmative, yet they imply a negative that the property is not otherwise changed. So other acts of Parliament have had the same construction where new offenses were created and the method of punishment was particularly appointed.

Ainsworth has done all he could. The assignee must fill up. Supposing the assignee loses it out of his pocket, he must come to a court of equity.

Davila was guilty of a neglect in not entering and registering the assignment, and this defect has occasioned the defendant's buying it, which he would not otherwise have done. And the plaintiff shall not take advantage of the intestate's neglect.

This is like the case of a banker and goldsmith's note received in payment. It is a loss to the receiver if he neglects to receive the money in time.

The defendant has purchased this thing fairly, though I do not think that the law of market overt extends to this case, for a market overt is only for a sale of goods and merchandises, which these things are not, but only in the nature of money.

PRICE and PAGE were of the same opinion.

And so the plaintiff's bill was dismissed with costs.

442

St. Eloy v. Pryor

(Ex. 1724)

A modus decimandi *in lieu of tithes in kind must be payable on a certain day.*

Harvard Law School MS. 1082, vol. 1, p. 191

Hilary term 1723[/24].

The plaintiff, as rector of Marston Morton in the County of Bedford, exhibited his bill for tithes. And the defendant insisted that a *modus* or rate of 1s. in the pound was yearly paid to the rector of the said parish for the time being for all the pasture and sward ground within the said parish as the pasture ground had formerly been valued, which included all tithe hay, calves, milk, pigs, and all small tithes arising on such pasture ground and in discharge of all tithes whatsoever arising out of the same excepting some particular lands in the answer mentioned. And he says further in his answer that the close was valued at £40 *per annum* and that he had offered 40s. *per annum* and 10s. *per annum* for Horsecroft and he offered by his answer 45s. for four years and a half due at Lady Day [25 March] before and £9 for four years and a half tithes due at Lady Day last.

It was objected to us that were counsel for the defendant that the *modus* was uncertain and no time of payment was mentioned and that it was too fluctuating for a *modus*, it being 1s. in the pound as the same has been formerly valued at, which is too uncertain, and likewise that the *modus* was too high. And [there was] cited for these particular purposes Whitehall v. Offley, Easter 1720; Michaelmas 5 Geo., Jones v. Calvert, that 6d. per lamb was too high; Franklin v. Aubry, Trinity 1716; Cotterell v. Athol, 36 Car. II; Burnaby v. Bletsoe; Mason v. Holton,[1] where one part of the tithes was given for another and this related to an execution taken by the plaintiff for pasture or sward ground.

And [it was said] that there is no declaration upon a [writ of] prohibition, but the time for payment of a *modus* is fixed, except one case in Lutwyche.

We that were for the defendant answered that this might have a good commencement and that, as all *modus*es spring from compositions, that this was good and that 2s. in the pound was a good *modus* according to Dr. Grant's Case, 11 Rept.,[2] and yearly payable, that was upon request; that it was not too high, Bishop v. Arundel, Easter 1706.[3]

Chief Baron Eyre [said] that this was a void *modus* because no certain time of payment is laid and from and to what time and it is not supplied by the answer.

And so it was agreed by the whole court, and it was decreed for the defendant to account.

Taussig MS. 311, vol. 1, p. 592

Hilary term 1723/24. St. Eloy, rector of Marston Morton in the County of Bedford v. Prior.

[To a] bill for tithes, the defendant pleads a *modus* of 10s. for a close called Horse Craft and of 1s. in the pound for all pastureland within the parish except some particular lands.

Edlin: 1s. in the pound for every close of pasture according to what each pasture ground was anciently valued at or rated in lieu of tithes of hay, calves, and all small tithes, this is uncertain because it is not set forth what is meant by valuation or rating.

Secondly, what are small tithes? 2 Inst. 649;[4] there have been divers notions about this matter, and the first distinction is as to place, as gardens and fields. The second is as to the species of the tithes themselves. Rolle, 643; saffron are small tithes, after[wards they were] adjudged great tithes. Ventr. 61. Wood has been twice adjudged small tithes. Hutton 77. The third distinction is taken from

---

[1] *Offley v. Whitehall* (Ex. 1717), see above, Case No. 28; *Cotterell v. Athrop* (1684), 1 Wood 235, 1 Eagle & Younge 548; *Mason v. Holton* (Ex. 1722), see above, Case No. 346.

[2] *Graunt's Case* (1613), 11 Coke Rep. 15, 77 E.R. 1165, 1 Gwillim 259, 1 Eagle & Younge 222.

[3] *Bishop v. Arundel* (1704), Dodd 205, 1 Rayner 98, 1 Eagle & Younge 664, 2 Gwillim 585, 1 Wood 459.

[4] E. Coke, *Second Institute* (1642), p. 649.

the general course of the husbandry in the parish. And this is the opinion of Lord Holt in Wharton and Lille's Case.[1]

The second objection to the *modus* is that 1s. in the pound is but half the value and so it cannot be supposed ever to have been made. Mason v. Holton, Trinity term last in this court; the court set aside a *modus* of a close of four acres in lieu of a great meadow of 120 acres; Michaelmas 36 Car. II, Cotterell v. Athorp, a *modus* of £60 *per annum* for three farms of £300 *per annum*; Hilary 9 William, Layfield and Denton, the *modus* was too big; Bishop v. Arundell, 5 Geo., Jones v. [*blank*] 6d. for a calf is too high; and in Trinity 7 George, Frankland v. Master and Brethren of St. Cross,[2] 6d. for calf was also set aside.

Thirdly, here is no day of payment set forth, which is necessary, for, without it, no man knows when the year is to end or when to begin, so, consequently, it cannot be known to whom shall the tithes belong.

Tithes severed go to the executor of the incumbent, and the tithes not severed [go] to the successor. And there is no decree since the Restoration [1660] in this court where this court has declared a *modus* good without a day, nor is there any of the printed suggestions in the books of a *modus* without a day, except one in Lutwich.

Bootle: The *modus* is uncertain in this, that the word 'formerly' refers to no time in particular, whether one or 200 or 60 years ago. A pound rate has been allowed because a pound rate goes along with the land and always bears the same proportion to the rent or value in being.

Secondly, pasture ground and sward ground are different. And, if so, here is a *modus* of pasture ground in satisfaction of sward ground.

Thirdly, there is no rule to go by in the valuation of the land.

Serjeant *Selby, contra*: In Doctor Atterbury's Case,[3] 16d. in the pound was decreed to be a good *modus*. And, as to pasture and sward ground, they are the same. As to want of the day, it is said we offered 10s. for a year and a half at Lady Day, so then Michaelmas is the day.

This *modus* is confined to the yearly value so it is not like to the case of Harrison and Sharp.[4]

As to the uncertainty of the expression 'formerly valued', if the counsel had not stopped short, they would have found that we have expressly said that 40s. *per annum* was [time] out of mind the rate which has been paid for the close.

---

[1] *Wharton v. Lisle* (1693), 4 Modern 183, 87 E.R. 337, 3 Levinz 365, 83 E.R. 733, Comberbach 201, 209, 90 E.R. 428, 433, Carthew 263, 90 E.R. 756, Skinner 341, 356, 90 E.R. 152, 158, 3 Salkeld 349, 91 E.R. 865, 12 Modern 41, 88 E.R. 1152, 1 Eagle & Younge 579.

[2] *Franklyn v. Jenkins* (Ex. 1721), see above, Case No. 204.

[3] *Atterbury v. Turner* (1684), 1 Wood 227, 1 Eagle & Younge 543, *sub nom. Atterbury v. Stafford*, Eq. Cases Exch. 209.

[4] *Harrison v. Sharp* (Ex. 1724), see below, Case No. 490.

Thirdly, as to the day, there will be the same difficulty where there is a certain day as where not, for, if the incumbent dies a day or two before the certain day, who must have the *modus*, whether the executor or the successor?

Edlin replies: The tender does not supply the day. It ought to have been laid in the *modus*. *Modus*es per pound rate have never been established in this court.

As to the greatness of a *modus* of a certain sum in gross, it is an objection to it. But this is a pound *modus*, which always bears the same proportion.

If a parson dies before the day, the *modus* belongs to the successor. Whitehall and Offley, in prohibition, three years ago. And the court was unanimously of opinion that a certain day ought to be alleged.

Lord Chief Baron [Eyre]: The defendant must account for want of a day certain on which the *modus* is payable. And this cannot be supplied out of the tender. And there is no occasion to give any opinion as to the other points.

And the other barons agreeing with him, the defendants were decreed to account upon this single point.

N.B. This seems a little strange when the court, in the case of Harrison and Sharpe, had made this a point to be argued and now determined it in the intermediate time.

[Order of 3 February 1723[/24]: 2 Wood 217.]

443

Egerton v. Bromhall

(Ex. 1724)

A modus decimandi *in lieu of tithes in kind must be payable in certain by certain persons so that the rector can have a remedy in court for it.*

Harvard Law School MS. 1082, vol. 1, p. 192

Hilary term 1723[/24].

A bill was brought by the plaintiff as rector of Whitchurch in the County of Salop for tithe hay, clover cinque foine, depasturing of cattle, and potatoes. All the defendants in bar to this demand set forth in their answer that this parish consists of several townships and that, time out of mind, the owners and occupiers of land had paid a *modus* for tithe hay and each township in the parish paid yearly at All Saints Day [1 November] a sum of money, which was formerly to prevent trouble, collected by the constable and by him paid to the rector in one sum and, afterwards, to prevent trouble to the constable, some of them paying but a small sum, one person of each township undertook the collection and paid that in one entire sum to the rector. And they insisted that, by the usage, custom, and prescription in the parish of Whitchurch, that the inhabitants, owners, and occupiers in the several townships of the parish had, time out of mind, paid a yearly customary rent to the rector for tithe hay according to the proportions particularly set forth in the answer and that this had been confirmed by Bishop Fowler and that clover when cut is included within the tithe of hay and apprehend the *modus* in lieu of depasturing cattle as well as tithe hay.

We that were for the defendant insisted that the *modus* for hay would include clover and cited Lutwyche 1071, Durrant v. Booty; 3 Keble 479; Hale v. Babb, Trinity 1683; Franklin v. Jenkins, Trinity 1721,[1] that payments by these townships were good and certain enough in payment, for the parson may bring and have his remedy easier against fewer persons. Though it mentioned owners and occupiers, yet the *modus* is annexed to the land so that, if the owner is the occupier, he shall pay. *Modus*es did arise from the agreement of the parties, and this might have a good commencement, and, though the parson sues one, yet the party sued might have contribution over.

But [it was] said for the plaintiff that the *modus* was not good. The 'owners and occupiers' is bad for, unless the occupier be owner and the owner occupier, nothing is paid to the parson and the plaintiff has no remedy, for he cannot come against the township and all the occupiers must be parties.

If the *modus* was good, it was not denied but that it would include tithe clover as well as hay.

Ward, for the plaintiff, cited 1 Keble 602[2] and compared this *modus* to that. In all *modus*es, there ought to be something certain with respect to the persons, the time of payment, and the thing given in lieu of it. And he cited St. Eloy v. Pryor, before,[3] where the time of payment would not be taken by construction. We do not demand tithe herbage fed in after pasture.

Serjeant *Chesshyre*, for the plaintiff, insisted peremptorily that there was no remedy for the plaintiff in respect of this *modus*, for it cannot be demanded unless every occupier of the township is made a party.

Chief Baron EYRE: I agree that, if the *modus* was good, it would include tithe clover as well as hay. I do not see that this *modus* is good because the plaintiff cannot have a remedy for it. And unless the parson has a proper remedy for the *modus*, I cannot establish it and the party against whom the remedy might be taken should be mentioned. Keble 280[4] is expressly in point. So he decreed against the *modus*.

---

[1] *Durrant v. Booty* (1701), 2 Lutwyche 1071, 125 E.R. 595, 2 Gwillim 578, 1 Eagle & Younge 639; *Darrel v. Withers* (1675), 3 Keble 479, 514, 535, 728, 84 E.R. 833, 852, 864, 977, 1 Eagle & Younge 505; *Hall v. Babb* (1683), 1 Wood 220, 1 Eagle & Younge 541; *Franklyn v. Jenkins* (Ex. 1721), see above, Case No. 204.

[2] *Baudry v. Bushel* (1663), 1 Keble 602, 83 E.R. 1136, also 1 Levinz 116, 83 E.R. 325, 1 Eagle & Younge 440.

[3] *St. Eloy v. Pryor* (Ex. 1724), see above, Case No. 442.

[4] *Anonymous* (1667), 2 Keble 280, 84 E.R. 174, 1 Eagle & Younge 457.

PRICE: I agree with My Lord Chief Baron. 'Owners and occupiers' is bad. And this *modus* is inconsistent and incoherent. And constant usage is no agreement. And it was not said by whom paid. And the want of a remedy is a great objection. So he decreed the defendants to account.

PAGE: I think that this *modus* might be made good if a hundred consists of one particular farm which is let to several persons, yet, though there are never so many, the whole is liable to the demand. And the *modus* is entire. Pensions out of hundreds are suable.

It is laid too uncertain by 'owners and occupiers'. So he decreed for the plaintiff for that reason only.

GILBERT: Here seems to be no remedy for the parson, so I decree against the *modus*.

Upon the whole, all the defendants were decreed to account [for tithes in kind].

444

Egerton v. Laiton

(Ex. 1724)

A modus decimandi *in lieu of tithes in kind must be payable in certain by certain persons so that the rector can have a remedy in court for it.*

Taussig MS. 311, vol. 1, p. 611

Hilary term 1723[/24]. The Honorable Henry Egerton, clerk, doctor of laws, plaintiff v. Owen Laiton, Thomas Povah, George Payne, Margaret Hauton, George Smith, and several others, defendants.

The plaintiff, as rector of Whitchurch in the County of Salop, exhibited his bill against the defendants, occupiers of lands within that parish, for the tithes of agistment, clover, hay, and potatoes from the death of his predecessor Peter Leigh, late rector of the said parish.

The defendants, by their answers, as to the tithe hay, insist that there was an ancient usage, custom, and prescription used time out of mind that the owners and occupiers of lands did pay a certain yearly *modus* to the rector of the said parish in lieu of all tithe hay and that each township within the said parish paid yearly on All Saints Day [1 November] a certain sum of money as such *modus*, which, formerly, to prevent trouble, was collected by the constables of each township in the said parish from the said several owners and occupiers of lands therein and, by him, paid to the rector of the same parish in one sum on the said feast day and, afterwards, to prevent that trouble, some one person in each respective township in or that lived in the said parish undertook the collection of each respective township and paid that in one entire payment to the rector of the said parish on the aforesaid feast day, that the same was an ancient *modus* and that, by an instrument of the 20th July 1683, executed by Doctor Matthew Fowler, the rector of the said parish, reciting that there was an ancient prescription, that the inhabitants, owners, and occupiers of the lands in the said several townships of the parish of Whitchurch had time out of mind paid a certain customary rent to the rector for the tithe hay yearly growing within the said township according to the proportion following, *viz*:

The inhabitants, owners, and occupiers of lands in the township of Whitchurch and Bubury are to pay to the rector on All Saints Day yearly forever in full satisfaction of all tithe hay yearly growing in the said townships, £2 0s. 1d.

The inhabitants, owners, and occupiers of lands in the township of Doddington for the like, £1 16s. 10d.

The inhabitants etc. of Woodhouse for the like, £0 6s. 11d.

The inhabitants etc. of Hollyhurst and Chincell for the like, £0 6s. 10d.

The inhabitants etc. of New Woodhouses for the like, £0 19s. 6d.

Of Worsewall and Bradley Green for the like, £1 6s. 2d.

Of Alkington for the like, £1 2s. 9d.

Of Edgly for the like, 7s. 0d.

Of Burghall for the like, 18s. 1d.

Of Hinton for the like, 14s. 0d.

Of Little Ash for the like, 13s. 4d.

Of Black Park for the like, £1 0s. 3d.

Of Tilstock for the like, 17s. 11½d.

Of Great Ash for the like, 5s. 8d.

That the said Doctor Fowler, by the said writing, ratified and confirmed the said custom and prescription to be good and binding to himself and his successors forever and referred to the said instrument. And they say that the particular sums mentioned in the said instrument to be paid by the several townships have not only constantly been paid yearly on the said feast to the rector since the execution of the said instrument, but they were the particular sums paid immemorially to the said rector as a *modus* in lieu of all tithe hay within the said parish and that the said instrument was no new agreement, but a declaration of an ancient custom or *modus* and so understood by all the parties at the execution thereof, wherefore they insist upon the said *modus* and that no tithe is payable in kind within the said parish. And they say they are all of them inhabitants of some of the townships mentioned in the said instrument and that, as long as they have been so, they or their landlords have paid their proportions of the said *modus* until the complainant refused to accept thereof. They insist that the clover when mowed and made is hay and included in the aforesaid *modus*. And, as to the agistment tithes and potatoes, they insist in effect upon a *non decimando*.

And now upon hearing the cause, it was insisted for and on behalf of the defendants, first, that no tithes are due for after-pasture of land mowed, 2 Inst. 621, 652; Yelv. 86, 87; 2 Rolle's Rep. 191; 1 Rolle's *Abr.*, 641, pl. 17; Poph. 142, and that a sum of money may go in discharge of many different tithes arising upon the same lands. C. *Entries* 464; Cro. Eliz. 136; Hob. 30.[1] And the Case of Frankland v. the Masters of St. Cross, Trinity term 1721, was cited to prove that clover is included in hay.[2] And the Case of Underwood and Gibbon, in Hilary 1716, was cited to show that saddle horses pay no tithe.[3] The use of which authorities and positions, as far as I understood the defendants' counsel, was to incline the court to believe that the *modus* by them set up was in lieu and satisfaction as well of tithe hay as of the tithe of agistment.

Per CURIAM: The plaintiff's demand by his bill is not for tithe hay generally, but is confined to hay from clover grass only. And the instrument signed by Doctor Fowler bearing date 20 July 1683 to the purpose aforesaid was read.

Serjeant *Chesshyre*, for the plaintiff, objected to the *modus*, first, that there was no remedy for the parson against the township for that every occupier of land was a debtor to the parson and the parson could not go against any one occupier for the whole, for this case is not like the case of rent where every terre tenant is liable to the whole rent. But no occupier is liable for more than the tithable matters in his own occupation. Secondly, he said that the defendants did not lay the *modus* for tithe hay and agistment, but only some of them did conclude that they hoped that the *modus* might be extended to agistment as well as hay. He cited the case in 4 Mod. 336, *viz.* the Case of Hicks v. Woodeson, and the Case of Doctor Smith and Johnson, in Trinity 1709, that a custom not to pay tithe for agistment is void.[4]

And by Serjeant *Stevens*: If a parishioner sets out his after-pasture to a foreigner, such foreigner shall pay an agistment tithe to the parson, as was determined in this court in the year 1685, in a case between Hall and Babb, a

---

1 E. Coke, *Second Institute* (1642), pp. 621, 651-652; *Grene v. Austin* (1606), Yelverton 86, also Croke Jac. 116, 79 E.R. 100, 80 E.R. 59, 1 Eagle & Younge 164; *Johnson v. Parker* (1620), 2 Rolle Rep. 191, 81 E.R. 743, also Croke Jac. 575, 79 E.R. 492, 1 Eagle & Younge 321; 1 Rolle, Abr., *Dismes*, pl. Q, 17, p. 641; *Richardson v. Cabell* (1617), Popham 142, 79 E.R. 1243, 1 Eagle & Younge 296; *Skilling's Case* (1567), E. Coke, *A Booke of Entries* (1614), 'Prohibition', pl. 10, f. 464; *Coteford v. Pease* (1589), Croke Eliz. 136, 78 E.R. 392, also 1 Leonard 128, 74 E.R. 119, 1 Eagle & Younge 93; *Botham v. Lady Gresham* (1589), Croke Eliz. 136, 78 E.R. 393, also 3 Leonard 203, 74 E.R. 634, 1 Eagle & Younge 94.

2 *Franklyn v. Jenkins* (Ex. 1721), see above, Case No. 204.

3 *Underwood v. Gibbon* (Ex. 1716), see above, Case No. 7.

4 *Hicks v. Woodson* (1694), 4 Modern 324, 336, 87 E.R. 422, 429, also 2 Salkeld 655, 91 E.R. 558, 1 Eagle & Younge 592, 2 Gwillim 550, 3 Lord Raymond 116, 92 E.R. 595, 1 Lord Raymond 137, 91 E.R. 987, 12 Modern 111, 88 E.R. 1200, Skinner 560, 90 E.R. 252, Comberbach 403, 90 E.R. 555, Carthew 392, 90 E.R. 827, Holt K.B. 671, 90 E.R. 1271, Dodd 171; *Smith v. Johnson* (1709), Eq. Cases Exch. 606, Dodd 221, Bunbury 1, 145 E.R. 574, 1 Rayner 121, 2 Gwillim 606, 1 Eagle & Younge 692, 705, PRO E.126/19, ff. 118v, 144, 1 Wood 514.

Wiltshire cause.[1] And it was said for the plaintiff that the case in 2 Keble Rep. 280[2] is an express case in point, it being there determined that all the occupiers of land within a vill should pay 2s. 6d. in full [satisfaction] of all the tithes of the vill is not good, there being no remedy to compel any who refuse to contribute, which is the very case now before the court. And the case in 1 Keble 602[3] was also cited against the *modus*. Besides, it is said the *modus* is to be paid by owners and occupiers, and yet these are very different sorts of persons and they have very different interests.

Serjeant *Pengelly*, for the defendants, observed that the demand of the tithe of agistment is for the very same land as for the tithe hay whereof the *modus* is alleged and that it appeared upon the face of the answers that the money was to be paid whether the lands were grazed or mowed or plowed. And so, by him, it is a certain payment for the land itself. He likewise insisted that there was a certain payment for every township and the parson might as well bring his bill against several occupiers in every township as against several occupiers in the parish at large. And by him, every occupier in the township is liable to pay the whole, as well in this case as in the case of repairing a county bridge or upon the Statute of Hue and Cry.[4]

As to the case in Keble, he said the *modus* there alleged was inconsistent, but it is not so here. And besides, it is alleged here that the quota of the township is collected for the parson, which is in the case of the parson. As to the uncertainty of owners and occupiers, it must be understood when in possession and, when the owners are not so, then by the occupiers. Courts of equity are not so nice in form as common law courts if the substance is sufficient.

Chesshyre: If the *modus* is not good at law, it is not good here. And uncertainty is as great an objection to a *modus* as can be. Even uncertainty of time of payment makes the whole *modus* void, as was ruled in the case of Whitehall and Offley[5] and has been held ever since.

EYRE, Chief Baron: The great question is about the validity of the *modus*. And the objection to it is from its uncertainty. And to be sure, every *modus* must be certain. The uncertainty here objected is this, whether it must be demanded from and paid by all the land-holders in the vill or whether the parson may have it from one occupier only.

If a day of payment is omitted in setting forth a *modus* by the parishioners, it may perhaps be supplied by the bill of the parson. But it is the business of the parishioners to ascertain what the *modus* is, and not of the parson. If this *modus*

---

1 *Hall v. Babb* (1683), 1 Wood 220, 1 Eagle & Younge 541.

2 *Anonymous* (1667), 2 Keble 280, 84 E.R. 174, 1 Eagle & Younge 457.

3 *Baudry v. Bushel* (1663), 1 Keble 602, 83 E.R. 1136, also 1 Levinz 116, 83 E.R. 325, 1 Eagle & Younge 440.

4 Stat. 27 Eliz. I, c. 13 (*SR*, IV, 720-722).

5 See *Offley v. Whitehall* (Ex. 1717), above, Case No. 28.

here insisted on by the defendants be looked upon as an agreement between the parson and his parishioners, it is defective for want of ascertaining the proportions which the parishioners are to pay. And the case cited out of Keble 280 is express in point. And though I do not look upon the book as of very great authority, yet there is no case cited to the contrary on the other side. And, therefore, he concluded that the *modus* was void.

Price, baron: I do not think Doctor Fowler's book is any evidence against his successors. The *modus* here insisted on is inconsistent and, therefore, void. All *modus*es which are pretended only are time out of mind. And yet we set them aside every day in this court. And these sort of compositions or agreements are, in my opinion, only compliments from his patron. So he agreed with the Chief Baron.

Page, baron: Suppose a man has a farm for which a certain sum is payable. The dividing it into parcels and portioning it out into several hands will not destroy the *modus*. And, therefore, I cannot see why a vill may not pay a certain sum for the tithes arising within it. And the parson's remedy for such sum will be the same as for the *modus* of the farm in the case before put or, as in the case of a pension, the remedy at common law for tithes was only in the ecclesiastical court and the like of pensions. And, though you cannot now form an action at law for the recovery of tithes or a pension, yet it is easy to be done either in the ecclesiastical court or in a court of equity. But as to the form of laying this *modus* or prescription, I think it is faulty, for, in the instruments written by Doctor Fowler, it is laid upon 'inhabitants, owners, and occupiers' so that everyone who is chargeable with this *modus* must be an inhabitant and an owner as well as an occupier of lands in the [vill] and, if he is not every one of these, he is not chargeable by this custom. So he thinks the *modus* is wrong upon this account.

Gilbert, baron: We are not only to distinguish between the good and bad *modus*es, for every *modus* that is good is as much to be countenanced as tithes in kind, some *modus*es, that is such as are pretended to be so, do in their very nature show that they could not be *modus*es in law, *viz.* such as are too rank and such as do not carry along with them any remedy for them. I take it the inhabitants, anciently, might have made an agreement. But we cannot presume an agreement that has had no remedy for it or [one] so very difficult as to be next to none. If the parson could have charged every occupier and so have made it *lex loci*, it would have been good.

And upon the whole, the court decreed that the defendants should go to an account for the tithe of the clover hay during the time demanded by the bill.

445

Pugh v. Rossington

(Ex. 1724)

Where a witness refuses to give his testimony, the proper remedy for the aggrieved litigant is the statutory one, not arrest for contempt of court.

Bunbury 142, 145 E.R. 625

R., an officer of the Navy Office, was served with a subpoena to attend as a witness on the behalf of the plaintiff. He attended two hours and then went away before he was examined, by reason whereof the plaintiff was nonsuited. Wherefore, it was now moved that an attachment of contempt might go against him. But this was opposed because there is a proper remedy given in this case by the Stat. 5 Eliz., cap. 9.[1]

And *per* CURIAM, the motion was denied.

446

Allinson v. Aland

(Ex. 1724)

The question in this case was whether a witness can be arrested for contempt of court for failing to appear and give his evidence.

Harvard Law School MS. 1082, vol. 1, p. 195, pl. 1

Hilary term 1723/24.

It was moved for an attachment for not attending with the book. And he cited Pugh v. Rossington.[2]

Chief Baron EYRE: I am not satisfied to grant an attachment because there is a proper remedy at law. And unless there appears something else of a contempt and, then, perhaps, I might incline to do it.

Taussig MS. 311, vol. 1, p. 583

Hilary term 1723/24. Dalison v. Aland.

Upon Mr. Girdler's motion, the court last term granted a rule to show cause why an attachment should not go against Rossington, who was subpoenaed to give evidence for the plea in this cause, which was an action on the case for a seaman's wages. And he was subpoenaed to attend with the book wherein the wages were entered. And he went away out of the court just before the cause was called on. And so the plaintiff was nonsuited.

Per EYRE, Chief Baron: I am not satisfied of the practice of granting attachments in such cases, though perhaps there may be some extraordinary instances wherein such a power may be exercised.

---

[1] Stat. 5 Eliz. I, c. 9, s. 6 (*SR*, IV, 438).

[2] *Pugh v. Rossington* (Ex. 1724), see above, Case No. 445.

Girdler cited a case in the King's Bench, Hilary 8 George, between Steward and Hamond.[1]

And in this case now before the court, the court discharged the rule because the affidavit for the attachment was not full and the party against whom it was prayed came and by affidavit contradicted the facts in that affidavit and so purged himself of the contempt.

But that an attachment may be granted against a witness for contempt in not giving evidence, see Lite's Case, who was summoned to be a witness upon a [writ of] extent in aid against Wood before the Secondary of London, and he refused to discover debts, though he acknowledged he knew them, whereby the extent was lost and the debts were assigned by the commissioners of bankruptcy. And, upon an attachment and examination of the party, the contempt appeared, and he was committed to the Fleet [Prison] for this contempt. And the first attachment was awarded upon a certificate of the Secondary and an affidavit of the truth thereof. Mss. P, lib. K, fol. 155.[2]

447

Crossley v. Shadforth

(Ex. 1724)

The question in this case was whether there can be a rehearing before the decree is entered in the order book.

Taussig MS. 311, vol. 1, p. 584

Monday, 27th January 1723/24.

The court determined that they would not permit a rehearing before the decree was drawn up unless where it was recent in the memory of the court, as in the next term. And, therefore, they ordered in this case that the decree should be renewed. And they reserved the consideration of the costs of the bringing the cause to a hearing on this petition for a rehearing on the minutes to the hearing of the cause afterwards.

Bunbury 142, 145 E.R. 626

27 January 1724.

This cause came on upon a rehearing. But the petition was for a rehearing upon the minutes and the decretal order was never drawn up, for which reason, the court would not permit the plaintiff to proceed, but ordered the plaintiff to draw up the decree, and they would rehear upon that.

But note there have been often petitions for a rehearing on the minutes only.

---

[1] *Hammond v. Stewart* (1722), 1 Strange 510, 93 E.R. 667.

[2] *Lite's Case* (1697), Lincoln's Inn MS. Misc. 557, f. 155.

448

Rex v. Norton

(Ex. 1724)

Where a person is committed to jail upon an accusation of smuggling, his remedy is to obtain a writ of habeas corpus, not to file a motion in the Court of Exchequer.

Taussig MS. 311, vol. 1, p. 585

28 January 1723[/24].

Mr. *Bunbury* moved to discharge one Norton out of Lincoln Gaol, who was committed there by William Marshall, a Justice of the Peace, for being an assistant in the running of tape and thread and, as the *mittimus* expressed it, for refusing to find security for his good behavior and the *mittimus* to the jailer was to keep him until discharged by the Lords of the Treasury or the barons of the Exchequer or due course of law. And upon showing the copy of the commitment and an affidavit that he was not concerned in running the said goods and that he offered bail but the Justice refused to take the bail, this motion was grounded.

But the court refused so to do, but ordered that Norton should bring his [writ of] *habeas corpus* and that notice should be given to the Justice of the Peace and to the prosecutor if any.

Bunbury 143, 145 E.R. 626

28 January 1724.

Norton was committed to Lincoln Gaol by a justice of the peace for aiding and assisting in the running of goods. It was now moved to discharge him out of jail upon an affidavit that he was not concerned in the running the goods and that he offered good bail.

But the Court denied to discharge him without giving notice to the justice of peace and also bringing his [writ of] *habeas corpus*.

449

Lasco v. Moys

(Ex. 1724)

Where a defendant answers and afterwards one of the plaintiffs dies and the suit abates, the court will not allow the defendant to withdraw his answer.

Taussig MS. 311, vol. 1, p. 591

Hilary term 1723/24. Lascow v. Moise.

Two plaintiffs exhibit their bill and take out a subpoena. And, before the return of the subpoena, one plaintiff dies. And the return of the subpoena being out, the surviving plaintiff takes out an attachment. Hereupon, the defendant puts in an answer, and now he moves that his own answer might be taken off from the file because there is no cause in court.

Sed per CURIAM: We cannot grant any such motion. Either the interest survives to the co-plaintiff or else the bill is abated. If an interest survives, the answer ought to stand. If not, the defendant may take advantage of the abatement of the suit. But we cannot take the answer from the file.

Bunbury 144, 145 E.R. 626

After the bill was filed and the subpoena taken out and served, but before the return thereof, one of the plaintiffs dies. The other plaintiff, without reviving, takes out an attachment. And, it being in the vacation time, the defendant could not apply to the court, but he was forced to put in his answer. It was now moved on the behalf of the defendant that the answer obtained from him in this manner might be taken off the file, for there must be a bill of revivor unless it appears that all the matter in demand by the bill survives, which it did not in this case.

But the court would not do it, for, they said, if the plaintiff is irregular and the suit is abated, the defendant will have the benefit of it at the hearing.

450

Goole v. Jordan

(Ex. 1724)

A vicar need not prove actual possession of every individual species of small tithes which he demands by his bill.

Taussig MS. 311, vol. 1, p. 601

6 February 1723[/24]. Gould, vicar of Eynsham in the County of Oxford v. Jordan.

In this case, the court seemed fully of opinion that a vicar need not prove an actual possession of the small tithes of any particular close or parcel of land or of any particular species of small tithes if he has had possession of small tithes in general in other parts of the parish or of all other sorts of small tithes besides those that he particularly demands by his bill unless there be evidence that such small tithes, either of a particular close or particular species of small tithes, are payable to the rector and this notwithstanding the case of Powell and Powell, which was heard at the sittings after Michaelmas term 1720 or 1721,[1] which was cited by Mr. *Browne* to prove that a vicar must prove possession of every sort of tithe which he demands, as having no common right to any.

[1] *Powell v. Powell* (Ex. 1721), see above, Case No. 172.

But PAGE, baron, said the question in that case of Powell and Powell was this, whether the vicar who claimed the tithe of clover grass ought not to show either a special endowment or possession of tithe hay in general and the court were of opinion he ought because tithe hay is a great tithe and so *de communi jure* belongs to the impropriator and, if clover grass be made into hay, it must go to the rector as all other common grass does.

And by EYRE, Chief Baron, clover seed is a small tithe. Therefore, in that case, had the vicar demanded tithe of clover seed and the court had ruled it that he ought to show possession of that particular specie of small tithe as well as of all other small tithes throughout or in any particular place of the parish, then that case would have been an authority for the defendant in this, *viz.* it would have proved that the vicar must in all cases have proved actual possession of every individual species of small tithes which he demands by his bill.

Harvard Law School MS. 1082, vol. 1, p. 194, pl. 1

Hilary term 1723/24.

The plaintiff, as vicar of Ensham in the County of Oxford, brought his bill against the defendants for vicarial tithes in a close called Amberry, *alias* Almery, Close. The defendants insisted on a *non decimando* for this close. And they further insisted that they hoped to prove that the said close was parcel of the manor and ancient demesne of Ensham and part of the Abbey of Ensham and was held discharged of tithes by 31 Hen. VIII.[1]

We that were counsel for the defendants insisted that a vicar was entitled to nothing of common right and that a *non decimando* might be insisted on against a vicar and, even if a *modus* was insisted on, yet the vicar was put to prove his title to the tithes.

And I cited Powell v. Powell, sittings after Hilary 1720/21; Town of Warwick v. Lucas, 1710; Wright v. Elderton, December 1710; Bateman v. Nun.[2]

Yet the court decreed the defendants to account though there was no proof that any tithes were ever paid for this close, yet upon the general proof that the plaintiff was entitled to all vicarial tithes, the defendants were decreed as aforesaid.

Quod mirum est; see the case of Powell v. Powell.

---

[1] Stat. 31 Hen. VIII, c. 13 (*SR*, III, 733-739).

[2] *Powell v. Powell* (Ex. 1721), see above, Case No. 172; see *Corporation of Warwick v. Lucas* (1711), Eq. Cases Exch. 671, Public Record Office, E.126/19, ff. 191, 221; *Wright v. Elderton* (Ex. 1710), Dodd 224, Eq. Cases Exch. 659, 1 Rayner 119, 1 Eagle & Younge 694, 2 Gwillim 607, Public Record Office, E.126/19, ff. 149, 250, 1 Wood 518; *Bateman v. Nunn* (Ex. 1722), see above, Case No. 312.

Bunbury 144, 145 E.R. 626,
1 Rayner 199, 2 Gwillim 648, 1 Eagle & Younge 793

6 February.

A bill was brought by the vicar of Eynsham in the County of Oxford for six years tithe herbage and furze of a close called Amberry, *alias* Hanborough, Close in the parish of Eynsham. The defendants insisted that they did not know that the vicar was entitled to these tithes, that they were informed no tithes thereof ought to be paid to the vicar, but that the great tithes, herbage, and furze, if any was due, belonged to the impropriator. And then, they say that it was part of the dissolved abbey of Eynsham and exempted by the Stat. 31 Hen. VIII. The plaintiff made out by his proof that the vicar was entitled to all small tithes within the parish, that the great tithes were constantly paid to the impropriator. And they gave one instance within thirty years of a composition with the vicar for the agistment tithe of this close. The defendants' proof was negative, that they never knew tithe paid for this close.

And, although it was objected that a vicar should have made out a fuller title to the small tithes, yet the court were of opinion it was sufficient. And they decreed the defendant to account.

[Order of 6 February 1724: 2 Wood 218.]

451

Bland v. Pearson

(Ex. 1724)

Accord and satisfaction is a good defense to an action of assault.

Harvard Law School MS. 1082, vol. 1, p. 194, pl. 2

Hilary term 1723/24.

To an action of assault, the defendant pleads a concord. The plaintiff replies [that there was] no such concord, and issue is joined. And the defendant moves to set it aside as an immaterial issue.

Bootle for the plaintiff cited Dyer 365; Yelverton 195; 2 Saunders 206; 2 Cro. 99; 4 Hen. VII, 9; Brooke, tit. Traverse, 179.[1]

Chief Baron [Eyre]: The issue is proper, and it answers the whole. So he denied the motion.

[1] *Leke's Case* (1579), 3 Dyer 365, 73 E.R. 819; *Tatem v. Perient* (1610), Yelverton 195, 80 E.R. 128; *Goram v. Sweeting* (1670), 2 Williams Saunders 200, 85 E.R. 964, also 2 Keble 717, 722, 84 E.R. 453, 456; *Alden v. Blague* (1605), Croke Jac. 99, 79 E.R. 85; YB Trin. 4 Hen. VII, f. 9, pl. 2 (1489); Brooke, Abr., *Travers per sauns ceo*, pl. 179.

452

City of London v. Thompson

(Ex. 1724)

Municipal books and by-laws that are public records can be inspected by litigants before trial.

Taussig MS. 311, vol. 1, p. 588

Hilary term 1723/24.

Upon a controversy whether the City had a right to a duty upon the exportation of corn, a bill was exhibited by the City to assert and establish this right, laying a prescription for it. And the defendants denied it by their answer. And a trial at the bar was directed for to try the point.

And now a motion was made for the defendants that they might inspect the books kept in the Cocket Office, which was an office relating to this duty, and they might also inspect the by-laws of the City. And they likened it to the case of copyhold tenants, who have a right to inspect the court rolls.

Sed e contra: This is obliging the plaintiff to show his evidence to the defendants beforehand. And it is not like to the case of a copyholder, for, in such case, the copyholder affirms the lord's title, but here the very right of the City is controverted and the city's right is disaffirmed.

Eyre, Chief Baron: The defendants have a right to inspect the books of the Cocket Office and to take copies of them at their own costs. And as to the by-laws, I think there is no difference between a citizen's right to inspect and one that is not a citizen. And I have known the books of a corporation inspected where the being of the corporation was in question.

Price: I think this notice to inspect all books and all by-laws is too large. But they have a right to inspect the books of the Cocket Office because it is a public office if any office at all. It is a question whether the books in this office are evidence or no. I believe, unless they are very old, they will not. But to be sure, if they are evidence at all, they are evidence for both.

Page concurs with the Chief Baron, especially because this trial was directed by the court of equity to inform the conscience of the court and so they have the right to direct that all evidence shall be laid before them and cannot confine the defendants to any particular books or by-laws.

Gilbert: Where the evidence is of a public nature, this evidence may be inspected beforehand, but it is otherwise where private, for, there, it being his own property, the court cannot free it out of his hands.

And the rule was that they might inspect all the books and by-laws.

Harvard Law School MS. 1082, vol. 1, p. 195, pl. 2

Hilary term 1723/24.

A motion was made for the producing of books. And it was made by the defendant for the plaintiffs to produce. And Philip Brown v. Ryland was cited in the King's Bench, where the question was concerning the select vestry and the books concerning that vestry were ordered to be produced.

And the court ordered a sight of such books as were of a public nature.

453

Williams v. Jones

(Ex. 1724)

A county court is properly described as the sheriff's court.

An under sheriff can be fined for improperly delaying an election and making a false return to Parliament.

Harvard Law School MS. 1082, vol. 1, p. 195, pl. 4

Hilary term 1723/24.

This was an action brought by the plaintiff [Sir Nicholas Williams] against the defendant [Jones, under sheriff of Carmarthen] for a false return and refusing to proceed regularly in the election of the county, whereby the defendant forfeited £500 according to the Act of Parliament 7 & 8 Will. III.[1] And a verdict was found for the plaintiff. And now several exceptions were taken in arrest of judgment.

And now, to answer those objections, Serjeant *Pengelly*, for the plaintiff, said this action was grounded on the Act of Parliament, and it is laid against the defendant for making several unnecessary adjournments whereby the election was delayed and protracted contrary to the Statute of 7 & 8 Will. III.

[To the] first objection, that the county court is alleged to be held before the sheriff of the county whereas it ought to be before the suitors, and 4 Inst. 66[2] was cited, [he] answered I admit the general rule; in any suit between party and party there, the suitors are judges, but not in this case; the sheriff presides and [it is] founded on the king's writ and Act of Parliament, and the sheriff is to collect and take the votes. The suitors are only voters and the authority remains in the sheriff, for he is the person that adjourns the court and the writ commands the sheriff to act. 4 Hen. VII, cap. 5; 3 Hen. VI, cap. 15.[3] In redisseisin, the sheriff is judge. See the Statute of Merton; 4 Inst. 266; Plowden 119, Buckley v. Thomas; Rastall, *Entries*, 186, 187, 447, 74; Robinson, *Entries*, 417; Crompton, *Of Courts*, 207.[4]

---

[1] Stat. 7 & 8 Will. III, c. 7 (*SR*, VII, 64).

[2] E. Coke, *Fourth Institute* (1644), p. 266.

[3] Stat. 11 Hen. VII, c. 15 (*SR*, II, 579-580); Stat. 23 Hen. VI, c. 14 (*SR*, II, 340-342).

[4] Stat. 20 Hen. III, Merton, c. 3 (*SR*, I, 2); E. Coke, *Fourth Institute* (1644), p. 266;

[To the] second objection, it is not alleged that the adjournment was unnecessary and that all the freeholders had not [been] polled, [he] answered this is answered by reading the record, for, there, the defendant is charged for protracting and delaying the poll so that, if there were no freeholders to poll, then the poll had been ended, and so it could not be said to protract the poll.

[To the] third objection, because there are several adjournments and only one £500 claimed. [He] answered we ought to be thanked for not laying more offenses, but this which we complain of was at one and the same election. The Act of Parliament[1] that prohibits a man from selling wine in glass bottles and, though each was an offense, yet it was held good for one, though several offenses were laid in the declaration.

[To the] fourth objection, because it appears that the high sheriff began the poll, and this has relation to the first Act, and, therefore, the action should have been brought against the high sheriff and not the under sheriff, [he] answered this Act lays the penalty in each person, and, on the under sheriff by name, that is sufficient. See Stat. 7 & 8 Will. III, sec. 4. In the absence of the high sheriff, the under sheriff will act, and this is alleged in the absence of the high sheriff, and the under sheriff is liable for his own tort. 1 Rolle, *Abridgment*, 94, pl. 5; 1 Rolle Rept. 78; *Doctor and Student* 190.[2]

And so he concluded with praying judgment for the plaintiff.

Serjeant *Probyn*, for the plaintiff: The suitors cannot be judges of their own acts. When the writ is directed to the sheriff, then it is a court of record for that purpose. Jentelman's Case, 6 Rept.[3] As to the adjournments' being unnecessary or not, that is a fact which the jury has found.

Fazakerly, for the plaintiff, cited [M.] Dalton, [*Office and Authority of Sheriffs*], 406; 4 Inst. 266. The court is the sheriff's court in all writs of execution. 3 Levinz 203; Fitzherbert, *Natura Brevium*, 18, 69, 80.[4] After verdict, every [. . .] is supplied. 1 Modern 173.[5] This case of a county court is like a court baron, where it is *coram sectatoribus*, yet the steward is judge. 4 Inst. 267; 2 Jones 23, 24; 1 Leonard 316; 2 Lutwyche 1211; Wynch, *Entries*, 1014.[6]

Buckley v. Thomas (1554), 1 Plowden 118, 75 E.R. 182, also 2 Dyer 113, 73 E.R. 249; W. Rastell, *Collection of Entries*; T. Robinson, *Book of Special Entries* (1684); R. Crompton, *Authority and Jurisdiction of Courts*.

[1] Stat. 2 Will. & Mar., sess. 2, c. 14, s. 2 (*SR*, VI, 247).

[2] *Bell v. Catesby* (1614), 1 Rolle, Abr., *Action sur Case*, pl. R, 5, p. 94; 1 Rolle Rep. 78, 81 E.R. 341; C. St. German, *Doctor and Student* (T. F. T. Plucknett and J. L. Barton, edd., 1974), 91 Selden Soc. 268.

[3] *Crosby v. Jentleman* (1583), 6 Coke Rep. 11, 77 E.R. 269.

[4] *Cannon v. Smallwood* (1674), 3 Levinz 194, 83 E.R. 646; A. Fitzherbert, *New Natura Brevium*.

[5] *Anonymous* (1673), 1 Modern 170, 86 E.R. 807.

[6] E. Coke, *Fourth Institute* (1644), p. 267; *Eure v. Wells*, T. Jones 22, 23, 84 E.R.

Solicitor General [*Wearg*] for the defendant: This does not alter the court, neither does it erect a new court. And this court is *coram sectatoribus*. If the clerk of the crown was ordered by act of Parliament to do a particular act, yet that would not alter the style of the Court of King's Bench.

Upon the whole, the court overruled all the objections in arrest of judgment, and so gave judgment for the plaintiff.

Taussig MS. 311, vol. 1, p. 597

Hilary term 1723/24.

An action of debt was brought upon 7 & 8 William, ca. 26, for unnecessary adjournments of the poll at an election for knights of the shire.

Serjeant *Pengelly*: Objection: County courts are alleged to be held *coram* the sheriff, whereas it is not the sheriff's court, *prout* 4 Inst. 66.

Second objection: That it does not appear that adjournments were unnecessary not showing that freeholders present had not been polled.

Third objection: That there are several adjournments and a penalty is due by the Act for every adjournment.

Fourth objection: That the beginning of the poll was [*blank*].

Answer to the first objection: In causes between party and party in the county court, the sheriff is not the judge, but, for this purpose, he is judge. And it is his court, and all the management of the election is his and under his direction. The sheriff is the person who adjourns, and he may adjourn without consent. And this he does by virtue of the king's writ. 7 Hen. IV, ca. 1, calls it *electionem tuam in comitatu*; 23 Hen. VI, ca. 15, says the election [*blank*]; William [*blank*] says the sheriff shall elect at his next county court. And, therefore, the court is well alleged to be held *coram vicecomitis*. And in a writ of redisseisin, the sheriff is judge. 266, Jentleman's Case, 6 Rep.; Plowden 119; Rastall's *Entries* 447; 74 Robinson 417; Brown [*blank*] 463; so in Ashby and White;[1] Crompton, *Of Courts*; *eligi feci* and takes *manucaptores* upon the return of this writ.

Second objection: It is expressly set forth that the adjournments were made before the poll finished.

1128; *Anonymous* (1588), 1 Leonard 316, 74 E.R. 288; *Tonkin v. Crocker* (1694), 2 Lutwyche 1211, 125 E.R. 672, also Holt K.B. 452, 90 E.R. 1149, 2 Lord Raymond 860, 92 E.R. 74, 3 Lord Raymond 224, 92 E.R. 656, 2 Salkeld 604, 91 E.R. 512; *White v. Moore* (1615), H. Winch, *Le Beau-Pledeur* (1680), 'Replevin', p. 1013.

[1] *Ashby v. White* (1703), 6 Modern 45, 87 E.R. 808, Holt K.B. 524, 90 E.R. 1188, 1 Salkeld 19, 91 E.R. 19, 3 Salkeld 17, 91 E.R. 665, 2 Lord Raymond 938, 92 E.R. 126, 3 Lord Raymond 320, 92 E.R. 710, 1 Brown P.C. 62, 1 E.R. 417, 8 State Trials 89 (F. Hargrave, ed., 1778).

Secondly. The plaintiff could not have had a verdict if adjournments were not unnecessary. And if not so precisely alleged, all the statutes of jeofails[1] extend to this case, it being an action for the party.

Third. The offense is protracting and delaying the election and the several adjournments are only evidence or proof thereof.

Fourth. The action is given against the under sheriff, for the Act imposes the penalty on the party committing the offense or misdemeanor and the under sheriff succeeds in the absence of the high sheriff. 1 Rolle's *Abr.* [*blank*]; 1 Rolle's Rep.; *Doctor and Student.*

Per Probyn: First exception: The suitors cannot be judges, for they are pollers and cannot be judges of their own actions.

Second exception: The adjournments being necessary or unnecessary is determined by the verdict, and it is expressly alleged that the adjournment was made before the poll finished.

The third objection is answered as to the serjeant. The penalty is annexed to the species of the offense and not to the repetition of the same sort of offense.

The fourth objection is answered as the serjeant. And we cannot bring the action against anybody else.

Fazakerly, on the same side:

First objection: The saying it was held *coram vicecomitis* does not affirm the sheriff to be a judge. Dalton 406.

Second: It cannot be held without him.

Third: He is a judge in many cases, as redisseisin and in all crown causes, *prout* Dalton.

Fourth: The Act calls it his court in writs of execution, 3 Levinz 203, writs of *pone*, *recordari*, etc. F.N.B. 18, 69, 70, directed to the sheriff.[2]

Fifth: This is after a verdict, and, therefore, if it can be held in any court before the sheriff, it is now aided. And 1 Modern 173[3] is express that this court may be held *coram vicecomitis* by custom.

4 Inst. 267; a hundred court is *coram seneschallo*; 268 a court baron is *coram seneschallo*; and so Lord Coke says. 2 Jones 22, 13; a court baron is *coram seneschallo* though the suitors are judges; 1 Leon. 316; Lutw. 1211, the jury find the court held by prescription *coram seneschallo.* Coke's *Entries,* 570, *coram deputato seneschalli*; Winche's *Entries,* 1014.[4]

Wearg, Solicitor General: The Act directs the election to be at an old court, the style whereof is well known to be *coram sectatoribus.* And, therefore, though

---

[1] Stat. 4 Hen. VI, c. 3 (*SR*, II, 230); Stat. 18 Eliz. I, c. 14 (*SR*, IV, 625); Stat. 21 Jac. I, c. 13 (*SR*, IV, 1221).

[2] *Cannon v. Smallwood* (1674), *ut supra*; A. Fitzherbert, *Natura Brevium.*

[3] *Anonymous* (1673), 1 Modern 170, 86 E.R. 807.

[4] *Joyner v. Skype* (1594), E. Coke, *A Booke of Entries* (1614), 'Replevin & Avowrie', pl. 1, f. 570; *White v. Moore* (1615), *ut supra.*

the sheriff prescribes, yet it must be at this court, as suppose that the Clerk of the Crown should have power to do anything in the Court of King's Bench, this would not warrant the calling it his court, but the old style must still be made use of.

Secondly, I agree that it is said that the adjournment was made during the continuance of the poll, but it is not said that any freeholders were present at the court at any of the times when the court was actually adjourned.

Adjornatur.

Taussig MS. 311, vol. 1, p. 603

Friday, 7th February, 1723[/24]. Sir Nicholas Williams v. Jones.

See Robinson's *Entries*, title 'Faux Judgment', fo. 317, where it is assigned *inter alia* for error on a judgment in the county court *quod per recordum apparet quod curia comitatu praedictae tenta fuit coram vicecomiti praedicti tanta ubi teneri debuisset coram vicecomiti et sectatoribus ejusdem curia sieque loquela levat' fuit coram non judice*. But the entry goes no[1] further than the assignment of errors, so that it does not appear whether this error was allowed.

Kettleby: The several adjournments are so many several offenses.

Bootle: The sheriff's court is held *coram sectatoribus*, and the suitors ought to be named or at least two of them. 4 Inst. 266; Keylway 71.[2]

EYRE, Chief Baron: 4 Inst. is not to that purpose, nor can I find any one precedent where the county court is expressly mentioned to be held *coram sectatoribus*. But there are precedents where it is entered to be *coram vicecomiti*. And I think *in pleno comitatu suo* is sufficient without saying *coram sectatoribus*. F.N.B. 85, 86, 109, 151, 184, pl. 119; Rastall, 186, 447; Dy. 113, 114; Bernardiston and Somes, see 2nd book of arguments; 3 Keble, Do and Permitter, fo. 117; Co. *Entries* 314b.[3]

In the court baron, the steward is not a judge, even with the suitors. But, in the county court, the sheriff is a judge with the suitors. And Jentlemen's Case is only that the sheriff is not the sole judge.

The second objection is answered by a view of the record.

The third objection is the offense is protracting the election. And the several adjournments, therefore, make but one offense. Cro. Eliz. 486.

---

[1] on *MS.*

[2] E. Coke, *Fourth Institute* (1644), p. 266; *Anonymous* (1505), Keilwey 71, 72 E.R. 231, 116 Selden Soc. 473.

[3] A. Fitzherbert, *Natura Brevium*; *Bulkeley v. Thomas* (1556), 2 Dyer 113, 73 E.R. 249, also 1 Plowden 118, 75 E.R. 182; *Barnardiston v. Soame* (1674), Pollexfen 470, 86 E.R. 615, 1 Freeman 380, 387, 390, 430, 89 E.R. 283, 287, 290, 321, 3 Keble 365, 389, 419, 428, 439, 442, 586, 84 E.R. 769, 783, 798, 804, 810, 812, 894, 2 Levinz 114, 83 E.R. 475; *Do v. Permiter* (1673), 3 Keble 117, 126, 84 E.R. 627, 632; *Denny v. Clerke* (1606), E. Coke, *A Booke of Entries* (1614), 'False judgement', pl. 5, f. 314.

The fourth objection is the Statute is express that the under sheriff is liable, and the declaration expressly mentions that the sheriff was absent, so there is no weight in the objections and the plaintiff must have his judgment. F.N.B. 17, *nullus comitatus* signifies the county court. And it is so understood by Lord Coke in his exposition upon the Statute.

454

Porter v. Hornby

(Ex. 1724)

An equity of redemption is a devisable chattel real and not a chose in action.

Harvard Law School MS. 1082, vol. 1, p. 197, pl. 2

Sittings after Hilary term 1723/24.

This was a bill in equity upon this short case, *viz*. Patience Minster was entitled to the sixteenth part of a lighthouse. And having mortgaged the same, she devised the equity of redemption to Mary Hall, who left her husband [*blank*] Hall, to whom the plaintiff is executor. The query [was] whether this was a real chattel, and, if so, the husband of Mary Hall ought to have taken an administration to her, so in all choses in action, and whether an equity of redemption is not a real chattel.

Bootle said that it was a mortgage forfeited and, after a long series of time, it shall be taken to be a real interest; so, in the case of a trust, the husband surviving must take out letters of administration.

Chief Baron [Eyre]: The mortgagor is only trustee for the mortgagee[1] and there was an interest well vested in the wife of Hall, and so in the husband without taking letters of administration.

Gilbert: Mary had it in her own right and not *in auter droit*.

So they decreed for the plaintiff.

Taussig MS. 311, vol. 1, p. 641

Hilary term 1723/24.

Patience Minster was entitled to a sixteenth part of a lighthouse at Harwich. She mortgages it and, being entitled to the equity of redemption thereof, devises it to Mary Hall, her daughter, who was the wife of [*blank*] Hall. She dies, and then Hall, the husband, dies. And he makes Porter his executor.

And *per* Chief Baron [Eyre]: This equity of redemption was actually vested in Mary, the wife. And so it survived to her husband. And it is well disposed of by his will, for an equity of redemption is not like a chose in action.

---

[1] Sic in MS.

Baron Gilbert agrees. And so the defendant was decreed to account with the plaintiff for the receipt of the profits of the lighthouse.

455

Bathurst v. Lady Shovel

(Ex. 1724)

A bill in equity lies for an account of the arrears of a rent.

Taussig MS. 311, vol. 1, p. 629, pl. 1

Hilary term 1723/24.

A bill was exhibited by the plaintiff as executor of a lord of a manor, deceased, for £38 arrears of £40 quit rent (not a fee farm rent) as issuing out of and payable for a certain farm called sometimes Walstead and sometimes Battens.

Et per CURIAM: It is very proper to exhibit a bill for this purpose though, perhaps, there is a remedy at law by distress or an action of debt because the law proceedings in such cases are nice and hazardous. And, in such a bill as this, there is no need to make the reversioner of the land out of which a party because no proof or decree in this case can affect the reversioner.

N.B. The last time rent was paid was in the year 1702, after Sir Cloudsley Shovell's purchase.

Harvard Law School MS. 1082, vol. 1, p. 200

Sittings after Hilary term 1723/24.

A bill was brought to have an account of a rent issuing out of a farm and lands suggesting that the lands were not known, so the bill prays a commission to ascertain the lands.

Chief Baron [Eyre] thought the bill proper in a court of equity.

Price [was] *contra* [and] for dismissing it.

Page agreed with the Chief Baron and was for retaining the bill. And he compared it to an account of assets.

Gilbert inclined to retain the bill.

And so the court retained it, *quod mirum est.*

456

Butler v. Gastrell

(Ex. 1724)

A man may not lawfully marry his deceased wife's aunt.

Bunbury 145, 145 E.R. 627

John Butler and Elizabeth, his wife, against Peregrine Gastrell, Esq., Bachelor of Laws, Judge of the Consistory Court of Chester. 8 February [1724].

John Butler was libelled in the spiritual court of Chester for incest, in marrying Elizabeth Lounds, who is the sister of the mother of Hannah Butler, *alias* Berrington, deceased, who was the late wife of the same John Butler, who in Michaelmas term 6 Geo. [1719] came and suggested for a [writ of] prohibition that his marriage with Elizabeth, his first wife's mother's sister, was lawful, *ac per legem Leviticalem minime prohibitum*, and was lawful and good by the Statute[1] and that, although he had pleaded this matter and offered to prove the same, yet the defendant refused to admit that plea and endeavors to dissolve the marriage *contra divinam sententiam, in regis contemptum et exhaeredationem et contra formam statuti*. And upon hearing counsel on both sides, the court ordered the plaintiffs to declare in prohibition, that it might come judicially before the court and be determined in a solemn manner.

And it was argued by Mr. *Bunbury*, on the side of the defendant, that a [writ of] consultation ought to be granted. The question that arises upon this record is whether the marriage of the plaintiff John with Elizabeth, who is his first wife's mother's sister, *matitera*, i.e. aunt, be a marriage within the Levitical degrees,[2] for that is the rule the temporal courts will govern themselves by. If it be *extra gradus Leviticales*, now, since the Stat. 32 Hen. VIII, c. 38, they will prohibit where there is any proceeding in the spiritual court to impeach any such marriage. But before that Statute, no prohibitions were ever granted, but causes matrimonial were entirely left to the jurisdiction of the spiritual court, even after the statutes of the 25 Hen. VIII, cap. 22, the 28 Hen. VIII, cap. 7, and the 28 Hen. VIII, cap. 16.[3] The first of which statutes enacts that a separation by definitive sentence in the spiritual court shall be without prohibition or appeal. But this is repealed by the 28 Hen. VIII, cap. 7, which is still in force, and adds, in the cases mentioned in the former Statute, 'if carnally known' etc. The 28 Hen. VIII, cap. 16, makes good all marriages not prohibited by God's law where there was no divorce before the third day of November, *anno* 26 Hen. VIII.

And even since the Statute 32 Hen. VIII, the judges of the temporal courts have very unwillingly granted prohibitions in causes matrimonial, the reason of which seems to be because marriages were originally of spiritual cognizance, and that, if it was now *res integra*, they would not do it, but leave them to the decision of the spiritual courts, and so it appears in the case of Harrison v. Dr.

1 Stat. 32 Hen. VIII, c. 38 (*SR*, III, 792).

2 Leviticus, chap. 18, verse 14.

3 Stat. 25 Hen. VIII, c. 22, s. 2 (*SR*, III, 472); Stat. 28 Hen. VIII, c. 7, s. 7 (*SR*, III, 658); Stat. 28 Hen. VIII, c. 16 (*SR*, III, 672-673).

Burwell, as reported by Lord Vaughan and Ventris,[1] and in the case of Good v. Hill, Vaughan 304.[2]

But as there have been several instances of prohibitions granted in matrimonial causes since the Stat. 32 Hen. VIII, that practice is now to be altered, for it must be admitted that that Statute has made the temporal courts judges of the Levitical degrees in consequence of these words, 'that no reservation or prohibition (God's law except) shall disturb or impeach any marriage without the Levitical degrees', and that no persons shall be admitted to any allegation or plea in any spiritual court, contrary to that Act of Parliament, so that the temporal courts must take cognizance of what the Levitical degrees are before they can know whether the plea or allegation in the spiritual court be without the Levitical degrees or contrary to the Act of Parliament.

But still this leaves it as it was before the Statute as to all marriages within the Levitical degrees. And, therefore, the jurisdiction of the spiritual court as to them still subsists. And the temporal courts, whenever they find that the proceedings in the spiritual court are in relation to a marriage within the Levitical degrees, never interpose, but leave them to that jurisdiction they had before the Stat. 30 Hen. VIII, so that it brings it to what was before said is the question in this case, *viz.* whether this is a marriage within the Levitical degrees or not?

This proposition may be laid down that will not be controverted, that divers marriages which are not expressly specified either in the 18th or 20th chapters of Leviticus or in the Stat. of the 32 [Hen. VIII] or any other of the Stat. of Hen. VIII, mentioned before, yet are most certainly prohibited by the Levitical law and consequently by the Statute because they come within the same degree and consequently fall under the same reason as those expressly prohibited.

Of this, many instances may be given. (1) For the son to marry the mother is within the express prohibition. But for the father to marry the daughter is not expressly prohibited, but is in consequence as being within the degree prohibited. (2) The marriage of the nephew with the aunt is within the express prohibition. But the marriage of the uncle with the niece is only implied, as being within the same degree. And many more might be put, all which fall under this rule of prohibition in 2 Inst. 684, *Quia eandem habent rationem propinquitatis cum eis qui nominatim prohibentur.*[3]

Taking it, therefore, for granted that marriages within the degree of the express prohibition are prohibited by the Levitical law and that the Statute makes no marriages good which are within the Levitical degrees, it remains next to be considered which rule in the Levitical law extends to this case.

---

[1] *Harrison v. Burwell* (1670), Vaughan 206, 124 E.R. 1039, 2 Ventris 9, 86 E.R. 278, also Lincoln's Inn MS. Misc. 500, f. 96v (Edward Ward's reports).

[2] *Hill v. Good* (1673), Vaughan 302, 124 E.R. 1085, also 1 Freeman 73, 107, 141, 152, 167, 89 E.R. 54, 80, 102, 111, 120, 3 Keble 166, 84 E.R. 656.

[3] E. Coke, *Second Institute* (1642), p. 684.

And it is this prohibition in the 18th chapter of Leviticus, verse 14, 'Thou shalt not uncover the nakedness of thy father's brother, thou shalt not approach to his wife; she is thine aunt.'[1] That reason extends fully to this case. The wife of a father's brother is an aunt, not in consanguinity, but in affinity only.

The first wife's mother's sister is also an aunt in affinity. The degrees are equally distant, whether we compute by the method of the civil, canon, or common law. And Lord Vaughan says in the case of Hill v. Good, fo. 308, that the near of kin to the wife's near of kin are prohibited by a second general law deduced from this verse of Leviticus. It will not be disputed, but the mother's sister is near of kin to the daughter, who was the first wife.

The next consideration is how far the judges of the courts of law have extended the rules laid down in the Levitical law as to the comprehending of cases not expressly prohibited therein. And here, it must be owned that the case now before the court is not to be found expressly determined. What this is to be imputed to is not very clear, since it is a case which must have frequently happened before, unless that, when prohibitions have been moved for, they have been denied. And then, there is no entry made of such motions. And, if this supposition is true, then it may be argued, according to what is said in Hardres 457,[2] that want of precedents where a thing may frequently happen is an argument that the thing is not allowable.

But however this be and though there be no express resolution of the case in question, yet it has been fully settled by resolutions which extend to the reason of this case and, therefore, comes under that known maxim, *ubi eadem est ratio, idem est jus*, as in the case of the marriage with the first wife's sister's daughter. In Mann's Case, as reported by Moore, fo. 907, a prohibition was granted, but, by Croke Eliz. 228,[3] a consultation was granted; and Lord Vaughan, fo. 322,[4] says a consultation was granted in that case, and, therefore, he conceived that marriage with his wife's sister's daughter to be within the Levitical degrees, though not specified to be prohibited in the 18th chapter of Leviticus. 4 Leonard 16, same case.[5]

There was a case of one Peirson, against whom a libel was exhibited in the spiritual court for marrying his first wife's sister's daughter. And it was said by Lord Coke *on Littleton* 235a,[6] that a prohibition was granted in that case. But that was plainly a mistake, for Lord Vaughan, fo. 322, examined the record of

[1] Leviticus, chap. 18, verse 14.

[2] *Attorney General v. Meller* (1667), Hardres 451, 457, 145 E.R. 542, 546, also Lincoln's Inn MS. Misc. 499, p. 405 (Edward Ward's reports).

[3] *Mann's Case* (1591), Moore K.B. 907, 72 E.R. 987, Croke Eliz. 228, 78 E.R. 484, also 4 Leonard 16, 74 E.R. 697.

[4] *Hill v. Good* (1673), *ut supra.*

[5] *Mann's Case* (1591), *ut supra.*

[6] E. Coke, *First Institute* (1628), f. 235.

that case, whereby it appears that a consultation was awarded. And in all the editions of *Coke upon Littleton* since the first, that case is omitted. And in the case of Worthly v. Watkinson, 3 Keble 660,[1] it is said that, by order of the king and council, that case was expunged.

In the case of Howard v. Barlett, Hobart 181,[2] the case of one Kennington is cited, who married his first wife's niece, for which he was questioned as for an incestuous marriage and put to penance by the High Commission Court and bound from her company, and then he died. The widow came into court and prayed her widow's estate. And it was resolved her widow's estate was due to her inasmuch as she was never divorced *a vinculo matrimonii*, though there was cause, by which it appears they should have been divorced *a vinculo matrimonii*, for the omission of which only she had her dower.

Lord Vaughan, in his observation on these cases, fo. 322, says that the marriage with the wife's niece is prohibited within the Levitical degrees for nearness of kin to the wife, which reason fully takes in the case now before the court, the wife's mother's sister being full as near of kin as the wife's sister's daughter.

This point of the illegality of the marriage with the wife's sister's daughter has been established by several resolutions subsequent to those already mentioned, which, as they in a great measure govern the case in question, it may be necessary to take notice of.

In the case of Wortley v. Watkinson, 2 Levinz 254, 31 Car. II,[3] a prohibition was prayed to the court of York, where there was a suit for a marriage with the wife's sister's daughter. The court ordered the plaintiff to declare in prohibition that the matter might come judicially before the court. Upon the argument of that case, Mr. Wallop, who was for the prohibition, gave up the point of the marriage of the nephew with the aunt, and a consultation was granted, *ut audivi*, says Levinz. But as it is reported in Sir Tho. Jones 118, it appears a consultation was granted.

Raymond 464, Watkinson v. Mergatron;[4] there, a prohibition was denied *per totam curiam* in the same case to the court of York. And query if this is not the same case with that in Levinz.

This point of marrying the wife's sister's daughter came again to be debated in the case of Snowling v. Nursey, Lutwyche 1075, Mich. 13 Will. III, rot. 361,[5] but the judgment is in 1 Anne. That was upon a general demurrer to a declaration in prohibition, where the only question was as to the validity of that marriage.

---

[1] *Wortly v. Watkinson* (1676-1679), 3 Keble 660, 84 E.R. 938, also 2 Levinz 254, 83 E.R. 544, T. Jones 118, 84 E.R. 1175, 2 Shower K.B. 70, 89 E.R. 800.

[2] *Howard v. Bartlet*, Hobart 181, 80 E.R. 328.

[3] *Wortly v. Watkinson* (1676-1679), *ut supra*.

[4] *Watkinson v. Mergatron* (1682), T. Raymond 464, 83 E.R. 243, also Skinner 37, 90 E.R. 19, T. Jones 191, 84 E.R. 1211.

[5] *Snowling v. Nursey* (1701), 2 Lutwyche 1075, 125 E.R. 598.

And, after three several arguments, Lord Chief Justice Trevor gave the opinion of the whole court that this was a marriage within the Levitical degrees, and a consultation was granted.

So that it may be concluded, this point is fully established by the repeated resolutions of the courts of law, and that the case in question is not to be distinguished from it, either in reason or in the distance of the degree, the mother's sister is certainly as near of kin to the mother's daughter, as the niece is to the mother's sister. If the husband cannot marry the wife's sister's daughter because he is her uncle, neither can he, as in this case, marry the first wife's mother's sister because she is his aunt. If John Butler, the plaintiff, had married his last wife first and then married her who was his first wife, she then would have been his first wife's sister's daughter, which is the determined case. The marrying the aunt first or the niece first can make no alteration in the degree or in the reason of the thing. If these cases are not to be distinguished, then it may be fairly concluded that the cases above are, though not express, yet in the reason of them, a full determination of the case now before the court.

It may be argued *a fortiori*, if the marriage with the niece is unlawful, that the marriage with the wife's aunt is more so, for, by the civil law, uncles and aunts are taken to be *in loco parentum*. And one of the reasons given why marriages with the near of kin are prohibited is because that subjection which by nature is due to a parent would by the marriage of a man with his aunt be subverted, and she, who, before, was entitled to some degree of subjection by virtue of her parental right, would, by such intermarriage, become subject herself, which seems incongruous and *contra naturae ordinem*.

If this case now in question was to be determined by the canons, there would be no room left for dispute, for, by the 99th Canon,[1] none shall marry within the degrees mentioned in a table for that purpose. And, in that table, the marriage of a man with his first wife's mother's sister is expressly prohibited.

These canons were made *anno* 1603, 1 Jac. I, and were confirmed and ratified under the great seal according to the Stat. 25 Hen. VIII, cap. 19,[2] and have always been received here. As to the authority of these canons and how far they are binding upon the subject is Moore 78, Trinity 4 Jac., Smith v. Bird;[3] in one point of that case, it was resolved that the canons of the church made by the Convocation and king without Parliament shall bind in all matters ecclesiastical as well as an act of Parliament. The case of matrimony is properly a matter ecclesiastical and of which their courts had originally the sole cognizance, and it is to be observed that this resolution in Smith v. Bird was but a year or two after the making of the canons.

---

[1] G. Bray, ed., *The Anglican Canons 1529-1947* (1998), p. 399.

[2] Stat. 25 Hen. VIII, c. 19 (*SR*, III, 460-461).

[3] *Bird v. Smith* (1606), Moore K.B. 781, 72 E.R. 902.

In the case of Corey v. Pepper, 2 Levinz 222,[1] it is said that the canons made in 1571, and those 2 Jac. I, being confirmed by the queen and king, are good by the Stat. 25 Hen. VIII, so long as they do not impugn the common law or prerogative of the crown. They cannot be said to impugn the common law, for the common law did not interfere in causes matrimonial, but left them to the jurisdiction of the spiritual courts; nor to impugn the Stat. 32 Hen. VIII, which has given cognizance to the temporal courts only in cases *extra gradus Leviticales*; nor the prerogative of the crown, no branch of which is effected or encroached upon by this canon, which received its sanction from the crown itself, being ratified under the great seal.

Lord Vaughan, in the case of Harrison v. Dr. Burwell, and so it is reported also in 2 Ventris 20, argues that this canon is so penned that it must be understood that all the degrees are expressed there, within which marriage was intended to be prohibited. And he concludes that Harrison's marriage, which was with the wife of the great uncle, was not prohibited because not mentioned there.

And in the case of Hill v. Good, 327, he again argues from the parochial tables, and he concludes Hill's marriage, which was with the first wife's sister, to be illegal because expressly mentioned there, and he says, by a lawful canon, which is enough, and not only so, but by a canon warranted by act of Parliament, the marriage of Hill is declared to be prohibited by God's law. Therefore, we must admit it to be so. From this reasoning, it is apparent that it was his opinion and that of the whole court, whose opinion he gave, that these canons so ratified were binding upon all subjects, as well ecclesiastical as lay.

Lastly, an objection was taken to the declaration, that there is no express averment that the marriage was *extra gradus Leviticales*, for these words in the first part of the declaration, before the libel, '*cumque matrimonium praedictum inter praedictum Johannem et Elizabetham fuit et est matrimonium extra Leviticales gradus*',[2] are only by way of recital and do not amount to an averment.

But notwithstanding this objection, the court this day gave judgment upon the merits of the question before them that this was a marriage within the Levitical degrees.

Lord Chief Baron Eyre said, if a man cannot marry his own aunt, he cannot marry his wife's aunt; and if there be aunt and niece and a man marries one of them, he cannot afterwards marry the other. Let him marry which he will first, it makes no difference. And he thought the case of marrying the first wife's mother's sister a much stronger case, and he said the case of Snowling v. Nursey was a proper foundation for the court's present determination. But he seemed to think that the parochial tables were not binding upon the laity.

---

[1] *Cory v. Pepper* (1678), 2 Levinz 222, 83 E.R. 528.

[2] whatever aforesaid marriage between the aforesaid John and Elizabeth was and is a marriage outside the Levitical degrees.

Baron Price: I am of the same opinion that this is a marriage within the Levitical degrees and that this case is not to be distinguished from the marriage with the first wife's niece.

Baron Page: I am of the same opinion. And there is no difference whether you marry the aunt first or the niece first.

Baron Gilbert: I am of the same opinion. The Statute has set the bounds to the spiritual court, which are the Levitical degrees. The Levitical computation is the same as the civil law computation. By the law of God, a marriage in the third degree is incestuous, and all marriages within the third degree have been construed to be within and prohibited by the Statute. And the canon goes so far as to show the sense of the Church of England as to the exposition of the Levitical law.

And *per* totam curiam, a consultation was awarded 8 February 1723/24.

Taussig MS. 311, vol. 1, p. 608

Hilary term 1723[/24]. John Butler *et ux.*, plaintiffs v. Gastrell, defendant.

A declaration in prohibition sets forth that all pleas relating to marriage belong to temporal courts. Then, it sets forth the Statute of 32 Hen. VIII and the libel, one article whereof is that whoever marries his wife's mother's sister is guilty of incest [and] that Butler did so. And so the question was whether this was a lawful matrimony.

There was a general demurrer.

Bunbury, *pro defendente*, in prohibition: No reservation by prohibition goes except it shall impeach etc. There was no prohibition in causes matrimonial before 32 Hen. VIII, either upon the Statute of 28 Hen. VIII or [*blank*]. So the spiritual court had certainly original jurisdiction in causes matrimonial. 2 Inst. 488; Bracton, L. 2, ca. 20, fo. 7; 1 Inst. 235, 2 edit. 1629.[1] But the words in the Statute do give jurisdiction to temporal courts. And he agrees that the court must determine according to the Levitical law.

18 or 20 Leviticus does not indeed expressly prohibit this marriage, but many marriages are prohibited *a pari* with the cases which are there expressly prohibited. 18 Leviticus, v. 6; 'none of you shall approach' etc. Vinnius, edit. Amsterdam 1665, fo. 61 and fo. 50, in 2d column, near of kin, extends to affinity as well as to consanguinity. Vaughan 308, 314.[2] It must be agreed that this case has not been expressly judged, but there is a want of precedents. Hardres 457, in a case frequently happening, proves the case never to have been doubted, but to be very plain, the point following, *viz.* of the first wife's sister's daughter. Moor, fol. 907, Cro. Eliz. 628; Vaughan 322, is within the degrees; 4 Leon. 16; Hob.

1 E. Coke, *Second Institute* (1642), p. 488; E. Coke, *First Institute* (1628), f. 235.

2 *Hill v. Good* (1673), *ut supra*.

180, 181; 3 Keble 660, that the comment in Co. Lit. 235 was expunged by order of the Council.

A wife's mother's sister is parallel to the wife's sister's daughter. 2 Lev. 254, Jones 118; Raymond 464; Lutw. 1075; all these cases relate to the wife's sister's daughter. Uncles and aunts are *in loco parentis* in the notion and account of the civil law. 99th Canon of 1603.

That these can bind the laity, [see] Moor 731; 2 Ventr. 44; 2 Lev. 222, good by 25 Hen. VIII. These cases were cited to confirm the authority of the parochial tables to which the 99th Canon refers.

[It was] objected to the plea that there was no averment that this marriage was within the Levitical degrees, and the averment is only that it is not within the prohibition of the Levitical law.

Bootle: [As to the] first wife's aunt, [see] 1 Inst. 235; God's law and the Levitical degrees are the same thing. This is not within the prohibition, express nor implied, Vaughan 242,[1] for uncles do not at all contribute to the natural being of the nephew. [As to where the] first wife's aunt marries her nephew, [see] Grotius, lib. 2, ca. 5, § 13, fol. 247; 1 Inst. 235; Mann's Case; 1 Mod. 25; 1 Syd. 434; 3 Lev. 364.[2]

Chief Baron [EYRE] and PRICE were clear of opinion that [a writ of] consultation should go as being rather a stronger case than the case of marrying one's wife's sister's daughter because the niece continues subject still, whereas, in this case, the aunt becomes subject to her nephew, though, before, she was *in loco parentis* to him. And there is no pretense to shake the authority of the cases in Jones and Lutwitch.

PAGE and GILBERT agreed.

457

Boughton v. Wright

(Ex. 1724-1725)

A custom of setting out tithes for the parson without giving him an opportunity to see if they were a true tenth is invalid.

Tithes are due for pollards and furze.

Harvard Law School MS. 1082, vol. 1, p. 198, pl. 2

Sittings after Hilary term 1723/24.

[1] *Harrison v. Burwell* (1670), *ut supra*.

[2] E. Coke, *First Institute* (1628), f. 235; *Mann's Case* (1591), *ut supra*; *Howard v. Chancellor of Salisbury* (1669), 1 Modern 25, 86 E.R. 704; *Heyward v. Foine* (1670), 1 Siderfin 434, 82 E.R. 1202; *Honour v. Bradshaw* (1693), 3 Levinz 364, 83 E.R. 732.

A bill was brought for tithes. The defendant insisted on several things, *viz.* setting out of tithes without the view of the plaintiff and setting out tithe grass in windrows and a *non decimando* as to furze and for a milk cow 4d. and a *non decimando* as to agistment.

Ward, for the plaintiff, [said] that the defendant insists on a custom to bring a cart and load without setting out the tithes, that this is contrary to the Statute of Edw. VI,[1] which orders tithes to be fairly set out. Hobart 107, 359.[2] The setting out of tithe hay in windrows is not good because it is liable to fraud and it is impossible to collect it or take it and the parson has a right to make the hay on the ground, which is impossible if setting out in windrows is allowed. Without a hearth penny, tithe wood spent in the house is due. Pollards being above twenty years growth are not excused from payment of tithes, for the exemption only extends to timber, which pollard trees cannot be. [For] pigeons sold, tithes are due.

Edlin, for the plaintiff: [For] a prescription to be discharged of the tithe of tares where eaten by cattle for the plow and pail, it ought to be shown that there was not sufficient pasture in the parish. Cro. Eliz. 139, 2 Leonard 27.[3] No hearth penny was insisted on; therefore, tithe of wood spent in the house is due of common right. Bates v. Sprackling.[4] And though a hundred may prescribe in *non decimando*, yet a parish cannot. [It is] not distinguished whether [it is] timber or not. Colley v. Jordan, Easter 1720; Trinity 2 Jac., Gaton v. Molesworth; Trinity 6 Will. III, Budd v. Martin; Hilary 4 Queen Anne, Greenway v. Earl of Kent; 1 Levinz 189, Hawes v. [*blank*].[5]

Solicitor General *Wearg*, for the defendants: The plaintiff's own witnesses prove this custom of tithing. The tithes are fairly set out and are not liable to fraud. But he admitted tithes are due for furze sold. There was no occasion to set forth a hearth penny to excuse the payment of wood used in the farm because it is to ameliorate the farm. The present minister has received the tithes according to this method. And, therefore, the plaintiff cannot object to it.

Serjeant *Chesshyre*, for the defendants: The parson is obliged to take the tenth as it is set out by the occupier without having notice to view the same.

---

1 Stat. 2 & 3 Edw. VI, c. 13 (*SR*, IV, 55-58).

2 *Wilson v. Bishop of Carlisle* (1615), Hobart 107, 80 E.R. 256, 1 Gwillim 279, 1 Eagle & Younge 250.

3 *Perry v. Soam* (1589), Croke Eliz. 138, 78 E.R. 395, 2 Leonard 27, 74 E.R. 330, 1 Eagle & Younge 96.

4 *Bate v. Sprackling* (Ex. 1718), see above, Case No. 37.

5 *Jordan v. Colley* (Ex. 1720); see above, Case No. 130; *Greenway v. Earl of Kent* (Ex. 1706), Bunbury 98, 145 E.R. 609, 1 Rayner 161, 1 Wood 479, 1 Eagle & Younge 677, Eq. Cases Exch. 546, 644; *Hawes v. Cornwall* (1666), 1 Levinz 189, 83 E.R. 362, also 1 Siderfin 300, 82 E.R. 1118, 2 Keble 1, 90, 833, 84 E.R. 1, 56, 527, 1 Eagle & Younge 450.

Pigeons used in the family are exempt from tithes. And so are trees above twenty years growth. 1 Rolle, *Abridgment*, 640; 3 Cro. 477; Plowden, *Commentaries*, 470; March 58; 1 Rolle, *Abridgment*, 646; Watson 435.[1]

Mr. *Cox*: The bill is a general demand and is not confined by the replication. Tithe of furze is not due. Moore 909; 2 Inst. 655.[2]

Lord Chief Baron [Eyre]: It seems to me to be reasonable to set out hay in cocks in this manner, but I cannot think that the flinging out the corn in this manner is right, for it ought to be set out as the rector may have an opportunity of seeing what is done, and this method is liable to fraud. And therefore, I cannot countenance this method. And I shall not consider or have a regard to a custom that is void in law. The toppings and loppings of trees are pollards and ought to be accounted for because [there is] no excuse unless they be timber. And so likewise [he] decreed an account for furze.

And he said that no tithes were due for tares because they were eaten by the cattle that were employed for the plow and pail.

Price: I agree with My Lord Chief Baron as to the tithe of corn and that it is irregularly set out, and the custom is void. And though the Statute of Edw. VI does refer to a custom, yet it ought to be consistent with the law. And this custom is illegal. As to grass and hay, I think that it is irregularly set out where there is a great quantity together as to setting out in small parcels.

But afterwards, he retracted his opinion as to hay and he seemed to agree that the tithe was well set out.

Loppings and toppings of pollards are tithable and [. . .] I would waive the consideration of green tares.

Page: We all agree that tithe hay is regularly set out. And I think that the tithe of corn is regularly set out. The parson has a view here, as much as if the whole was set out. And I insist that there is no occasion to give the parson notice.

Gilbert agreed that tithe hay was well set out, but he decreed the defendant to account for toppings and loppings of pollards, and so for furze. And I think that the custom of setting out tithe corn is well supported and that it is well set out. If this was liable to fraud, I should not establish it. But I do not think it is. And here, by the custom, notice is to be given, which, by the law, there is no occasion to do; so that notice is sufficient to recompense. The flinging out of corn in this manner, this usage obtains the force of a law and, in several places, the corn is taken away as soon as reaped.

---

[1] 1 Rolle, Abr., *Dismes*, pl. Q, 1-3, p. 640; *Soby v. Molins* (1574), 2 Plowden 468, 75 E.R. 700, 1 Gwillim 133, 1 Eagle & Younge 60; *Porter v. Skinner* (1639), March 58, 82 E.R. 410; W. Watson, *Clergy-Man's Law*.

[2] *Austin v. Lucas* (1598), Moore K.B. 909, 72 E.R. 990, also Croke Eliz. 609, 78 E.R. 852, 1 Rolle, Abr., *Dismes*, pl. Z, 3, p. 644, 1 Eagle & Younge 145; E. Coke, *Second Institute* (1642), p. 655.

Chief Baron [Eyre] again insisted that, by law, the occupier cannot carry away the corn until it is set out, but, since the custom has prevailed over the whole country, I would consider of it.

So they adjourned the consideration as to setting out tithe of corn.

Taussig MS. 311, vol. 2, p. 760

Monday, 25 January 1724[/25].

The defendants were now decreed to go to an account because they had not expressly insisted in their answers on the *modus extra ponendi decimas*, which they and the plaintiff himself had examined to in their depositions, which seemed strange to me because, if the whole truth appears in equity and no inconvenience or prejudice to either party, this want of formality, if it was one, should not have prevented the hearing of the cause upon the merits, especially after a case had been made and signed by counsel by the direction of the court to be argued, in which the only point was whether the *modus extra ponendi decimas* insisted on by the defendants was a valid *modus*.

And it seems to me there is a difference between a *modus extra ponendi* and a *modus* which goes in bar of the tithes themselves, for the latter must be pleaded or insisted on, particularly in order to give the plaintiff aim what to examine to. But the former admits tithes in kind, but only differs in this manner and form of paying them. And the answer did say they were paid according to the usage and custom of the parish and the usage and custom was, as is before mentioned, examined to on both sides so that this could be no other than a defect in mere formality. *Et quaere* how the court could decree an account of tithes in the common way if satisfied from the depositions on both sides that there was a particular method of tithing here which was not inconsistent with the rules of law.

Harvard Law School MS. 1082, vol. 1, p. 227, pl. 1

Hilary term 1724/25.

The plaintiff, as rector of Barrow in Suffolk, brought his bill for tithes. The defendants [Wright and Payman] say that they set out their tithes in such a manner as was customary within the parish. But they do not set forth the particular method, but only insist generally. And the defendants prove a particular custom of setting it forth upon giving notice to the parson. But the court would not give them leave to prove a particular custom upon such a general pleading in their answer without specifying such and such particular method. So they decreed the defendants to account without prejudice.

Bunbury 186, 145 E.R. 641,
1 Rayner 201, 2 Gwillim 658, 1 Eagle & Younge 803

26 January 1724[/25].

A bill was brought by the rector of Barrow in the County of Suffolk for the tithes of corn etc. The defendant insisted that he set out the tenth sheaf of wheat and rye and the tenth shock of barley, according to the custom of the parish. The custom he would have proved was that the defendant's cart was brought into the field and he threw nine sheaves into the cart and left the tenth for the plaintiff.

The question was whether this customary method of tithing the corn was good, for it was insisted upon on behalf of the plaintiff that nine sheaves ought to be set out on the ground and the tenth left out and marked with a green bough for the plaintiff and that they ought not to bring the cart into the field and throw the nine sheaves into the cart before the whole ten are set out, for the plaintiff ought to be able to view and judge whether he has a fair and just tenth part.

And the court would not let the defendant in to prove the particular custom upon this general allegation; so he was decreed to account, for they thought the whole ten ought first to be set out before the nine are thrown into the cart.

458

Janson v. Bury

(Ex. 1724)

Where a person dies intestate without leaving children, his brothers and sisters having predeceased him, all his nieces and nephews of the whole blood and of the half blood take per capita.

Bunbury 157, 145 E.R. 631

Sittings after Hilary term 1723[/24].

The late Lord Chief Baron Bury had several brothers and sisters, some of the half, and some of the whole blood, who all died in his lifetime, all leaving several children. And now, upon a bill exhibited for the distribution of his estate, it was decreed *per* TOTAM CURIAM that the distribution should be *per capita*, and not *per stirpes*, for, now, they do not take by representation, but as next of kin to the intestate, by virtue of the Stat. 22 & 23 Car. II.[1] But, if one of the brothers or sisters of the chief baron had survived him, the children of the rest must have taken only by representation, that is to say *per stirpes*. And the case in this court between Wall and Theedham[2] was cited, which was 28th June 1711; Dr. Wall, the intestate, had two sisters, Susanna Sumpter of the half blood, who left Samuel, and Elizabeth of the whole blood, who left John, Mary, and Dorothy. Both the sisters died in the lifetime of Dr. Wall. His wife, as administratrix, preferred a bill for direction in the distribution. And the court decreed one moiety of the intestate's estate to the wife, the other moiety to be divided into four parts, one part for the issue of Susanna and three for the issue of Elizabeth. And no distinction was made between the whole and the half blood.

1 Stat. 22 & 23 Car. II, c. 10 (*SR*, V, 719-720).

2 *Wall v. Theedam* (1711), Dodd 227.

459

Banks v. Corden

(Ex. 1724)

The question in this case was whether a parishioner can assert the Statute of Limitations or a prescriptive discharge of the payment of tithes against a lay owner of the tithes.

Harvard Law School MS. 1082, vol. 1, p. 201

Sittings after Hilary term 1723/24.

This was a bill for tithes brought by a lay impropriator.

Baron Page: In the case of a glebe, the Statute of Limitations[1] bars as well as in any other case. And I think in the case of non-payment, it may be presumed that the tithes were sold.

Price: I was always of opinion that a lay impropriator was not entitled to tithes of common right. And see the case of ejectment brought for a glebe. Must not the parson show he was in possession within twenty years, though this case does not come up to Bateman v. Nun[2] because tithes of corn and grain had been paid here.

Gilbert: I always thought that there was a difference between a lay impropriator and an ecclesiastical person. And the reason that you cannot prescribe in *non decimando* [is] because the parson, patron, and ordinary would not betray the Church.

Before the Dissolution, the [monastic] house might have sold the tithes for a solid sum. And there is no difference between this and a lay fee. A presumption is where a deed or writing is supposed to be [lost], and so is the case of a lay impropriator. Query whether he may prescribe in *non decimando.*

The defendant claims under a grant of Queen Elizabeth, and this was the rectory of Leek. But in this case, the defendant insists that this is part of the Monastery of De Lacres and he insisted upon it, so I think that the defendant ought to make out his defense [by] saying no tithes were ever paid. That is only laid as general words and part of the exemption, but he seemed to deny the case of prescribing in *non decimando* against a lay impropriator.

And upon the proof in this case, it appeared that a composition had been made. And therefore, there was no occasion for the former question. But the court decreed the defendant to account for tithes in kind.

Taussig MS. 311, vol. 1, p. 637

Friday, 21 February 1723[/24].

---

1 Stat. 21 Jac. I, c. 16 (*SR*, IV, 1222-1223).

2 *Bateman v. Nunn* (Ex. 1722), see above, Case No. 312.

The plaintiff, a lay impropriator of tithes under a grant of Queen Elizabeth of 2 *regni suae* [1559 x 1560], brought his bill against the defendant who was the occupier of certain lands and closes in the parish. And, by the defendant's answer, he insisted that, as to the land sowed with corn, tithe was paid. As to agistment of pasture and hay, he insisted on a *non decimando*, and, secondly, he insisted that the land was parcel of the dissolved monastery of Abbey De L'Acres, one of the greater monasteries and so was discharged from the payment of tithes.

The defendant's counsel insisted that they need not prove payment of tithes because the lands were pretended to be discharged by virtue of their being lands of the monastery, which the defendant ought to show.

And of this opinion was PRICE.

Sed PAGE and GILBERT: The defendant may insist on several defenses. And here, he insists on a *non decimando*, which is good against a lay impropriator.

And *per* GILBERT: I think a *non decimando* may be admitted against all appropriated rectories because the abbot etc. had a right without the patron and ordinary to alienate the tithes *in solido*, which a rector could not do.

Chief Baron [EYRE] came in after the cause was opened and said nothing.

But they read a witness or two to prove the payment of the tithe. And the defendant was, therefore, decreed to account.

But PRICE said he thought, now, as he had done, that *non decimando* might be admitted against a lay impropriator, but, if any particular discharge was set up, then there was an end of the *non decimando*.

460

Barefoot v. Fry

(Ex. 1724)

A bill in equity lies to quiet a landowner in his possession and title against bad faith litigation at common law.

Bunbury 158, 145 E.R. 631

At Serjeants' Inn, 20 February 1723[/24].

This was a bill preferred for a perpetual injunction to quiet the plaintiff in his possession, the defendant Fry having brought five ejectments and been nonsuited upon full evidence in three of them, and he had verdicts against him in the other two, and having also brought two bills against the plaintiff, one in Chancery and the other in this court, which were both dismissed. And the case of The Earl of Bath v. Sherwin,[1] *coram* Lord Cowper, in 1709, upon an appeal to the House of Lords, wherein a perpetual injunction was decreed, was cited.

[1] *Earl of Bath v. Sherwin* (1706-1710), 10 Modern 1, 88 E.R. 596, Precedents in Chancery 261, 24 E.R. 126, Gilbert Rep. 2, 25 E.R. 2, 2 Eq. Cas. Abr. 171, 243, 522, 22

Mr. *Ward*, of counsel for the defendant, said that this was the first instance of attempting to obtain a perpetual injunction upon ejectments brought at law and that courts of equity have never decreed it but upon an issue directed, and not upon ejectments.

Lord Chief Baron EYRE: At law, a man could not bring the same real action twice for the same thing. But now, ejectments being introduced in the place of real actions, he may bring as many of them as he pleases at law. And this is a reason why a court of equity should settle and quiet the rights of people and, after so many trials, grant a perpetual injunction.

And *per* TOTAM CURIAM, a perpetual injunction was decreed.

And Baron PRICE said that, since the decree in the House of Lords in the case of The Earl of Bath v. Sherwin, it had been usual to grant injunctions perpetual under such circumstances as are in the case now before the court.

Baron PAGE said that, in the case of Sherwin, he claimed under a voluntary deed, which occasioned some doubt before the decree by the Lords. But the plaintiff in the present case, it appears, is a purchaser for a valuable consideration, so there is no doubt at all but that a perpetual injunction ought to be decreed in the present case.

Taussig MS. 311, vol. 1, p. 629, pl. 2

Thursday, 20th February 1723[/24].

A bill was exhibited by the plaintiff to quiet his possession and title to a copyhold tenement which had been found for him upon four several trials at law on so many ejectments and two bills in equity for discovery of deeds or relief [had been] dismissed.

Et per EYRE, Chief Baron, PRICE, PAGE, and GILBERT, a perpetual injunction was decreed. And though my Lord Cowper in the case of the Earl of Bath and Sherwin dismissed the plaintiff's bill which was exhibited in Chancery in that case to quiet the title after three or four ejectments, yet, upon an appeal, the Lords reversed his decree and decreed a perpetual injunction, which is a sufficient authority for courts of equity to proceed upon in like cases for the future. And this jurisdiction or power of courts of equity is highly reasonable, and exerting it is in aid of the common law and in favor of the old method of proceeding before ejectments were invented where there could not be above two trials as to the right of the title. But, since real actions have been laid aside and ejectments have been brought, there would be no need of vexation.[1] [If] courts of equity could not interpose and thereby prevent an unconscionable use of this new method of trial of titles in [actions of] ejectment, which, by their too frequent repetition, not only render a man's possessions of little value but, in cases of small concern or value, of

E.R. 147, 206, 440; 4 Brown P.C. 373, 2 E.R. 253.

[1] Sic in MS.

no use or indeed rather a burden to the owner, for he had better have no property than a property liable to perpetual and endless suits of law.

N.B. The defendant in this case was a pauper.

461

Proctor v. Henzell

(Ex. 1724)

An offeree does not have a cause of action if he has not accepted the offer.

Taussig MS. 311, vol. 1, p. 620

Hilary term 1723[/24]. [An action] in debt.

Henzell covenants to serve for seven years and covenants to give notice to Proctor within six months of the end of that term and offer to serve the said Proctor and his assigns for the term of seven years more and, if accepted, that he would serve accordingly. And the breach assigned is that he did not give notice and offer to serve nor did he serve.

The defendant pleads that he did give notice and offer to serve. But he does not say that he did serve or that the plaintiff refused to accept of his proffered service. The plaintiff demurs to the plea. And it was objected that the plea is naught for that reason. The solution is a breach is only assigned that he did not give notice and offer his service and serve, but it does not show the plaintiff accepted. Ughtred's Case, 7 Rep., fo. 10;[1] acceptance of the offer is a condition precedent and, therefore, the plaintiff ought to have shown his acceptance of the offer to serve.

Chief Baron [Eyre]: The first part of the covenant is to be done by the defendant, *viz.* to give notice and offer, and the other is to be done by the plaintiff, *viz.* to accept. And, if the defendant has given notice and offered, then he has done all on his part, and the plaintiff, if that is true, must accept in order to entitle himself to his action for not serving, for the defendant could not serve without the plaintiff's acceptance of his offer to serve.

Price doubts.

Page concurs with the Chief Baron.

Gilbert: The covenant to offer to serve and to serve are two distinct and independent covenants in law. The assigning a breach on the covenant to serve is contradictory or, at least impertinent, when it is assigned as a breach that he did not give notice or offer.

The plaintiff discontinued on the payment of costs, the three barons being very clear for the defendant.

[1] *Ughtred v. Marquess of Winchester* (1591), 7 Coke Rep. 9, 77 E.R. 425, also Jenkins 260, 145 E.R. 186.

462

Anonymous, *qui tam* v. Potts

(Ex. 1724)

Upon a seizure of clothes made of India silk, the seizer need only prove that the clothes were worn after the date prohibited by the Statute.

Taussig MS. 311, vol. 1, p. 625

Saturday, 15 February 1723[/24].

An information was exhibited upon 11 & 12 Will., ca. 10,[1] against the defendant for having in her custody an Indian silk gown and petticoat not made up into any garment or furniture before the 29 September 1701. And the information charged that this India silk had been imported since the 29th September 1701. And the case was this. The gown and petticoat were seized in the defendant's house and appeared to have been made up by her and worn about ten or twelve years ago. And the question was whether the informer should be obliged to prove this silk was actually imported since 29th September 1701.

Et per Chief Baron [EYRE]: No, for the Act extends to prohibit the wearing of India silks imported before the 29th September 1701 as well as silks imported after if such silks were not made into furniture [before the] 29th September 1701. And so the time of importing is not material. And, consequently, it need not be proved by the informer. And I think this is the plain construction of the Statute upon the reading of it. See the form of the information in the *Book of Precedents*, fo. 7.

Sed quaere whether the information charging that these goods were imported *post* 29th September 1701 had not made this a part of the description of the goods seized and so necessary to be proved, though, upon the Statute, it was not material whether imported before or after that day if not made up into apparel or furniture before that day. This objection was not started by the counsel for the defendant.

463

Finch v. Masters

(Ex. 1724)

In this case, the defendants proved a modus decimandi *in lieu of tithes in kind of hay, but they were ordered to pay tithes of agistment of cattle.*

Taussig MS. 311, vol. 1, p. 627

Wednesday, 19 February [1723/24], at the setting down of causes.

[1] Stat. 11 Will. III, c. 10 (*SR*, VII, 598-599).

A bill was exhibited for the tithes of agistment and hay from 30th March 1722 to the filing of the bill. But the bill was marked 28th September and was filed as a bill of Trinity term preceding this, not including the tithe of hay for that year. And the defendant's pleading a *modus* for hay, the plaintiff now moved upon an affidavit of the fact that there was no direction for drawing the bill before September so that the words 'to the time of the bill' were intended to take in the hay of that year.

And it making no difference in the defendant's answer, the court gave way to it and ordered it should be taken off from the file of the bills of Trinity term and should be put on the file of the bills of Michaelmas term following.

Taussig MS. 311, vol. 2, p. 644

Easter term 1724.

The plaintiff, as rector of Winwick in the County of Lancaster, exhibits his bill for tithe hay and agistment within that parish against Sir William Gerrard, baronet, Legh Masters, esquire, Richard Barker, and Christopher Green, yeoman.

The defendant Legh Masters, by answer, insisted that he was owner of an ancient messuage called Newhall and arable meadow and pasturelands thereto belonging, containing by admeasurements sixty-eight acres lying in Ashton *in parochia praedicta* and that all the owners of the said messuage and lands, their tenants, and farmers have time immemorial yearly at the feast of Easter or so soon after as the same has been demanded paid or ought to pay to or to the use of the rector for the time being 1d. as a certain *modus* or compensation and in lieu and satisfaction for the tithe of all and all manner of hay arising yearly upon the said lands, which for the time aforesaid has been received and accepted accordingly by the said rectors for the time being.

The defendant Sir William Gerrard, by his answer, insisted that he was owner of two ancient messuages called Garwood and Brynnshall and arable meadow and pasturelands thereto belonging, containing by estimation 625 acres lying in Ashton in Mackersfield in the said parish and that he and all those whose estate he has of and in the said messuages and lands have time immemorially yearly at the feast of Easter or so soon after as the same has been demanded paid and ought to pay unto or to the use of the rector of the said parish for the time being £1 6s. 8d. as a certain *modus* or compensation for and in lieu and satisfaction for the tithes of hay, small and privy tithes, and Easter dues and offerings arising yearly on or payable for or in respect of the same premises, which for the time aforesaid has been received and accepted accordingly by the said rectors for the time being. The said defendant insisted also upon a *modus* for certain lands called Callands containing fourteen acres, *viz.* 1d. for the hay thereof, and the *modus* was set forth as the *modus* for New Hall.

The defendant Baker insisted on the like *modus* of 1d. for hay of an ancient messuage and certain arable mead and pasture containing sixteen acres and lying in Newton in the said parish.

Green insisted on the like *modus* of 1d. for an ancient messuage and certain arable meadow and pasturelands containing by estimation twenty acres lying in Risley within Culsheth in the said parish of Winwick.

N.B. The plaintiff, by his proofs, in the cause did not contradict the actual payment of the *modus*es, but endeavored to show that there were divers pretended *modus*es within the parish in relation to hay, most of them different one from another and not consistent with the rules of law. But the defendants having applied their proofs to the *modus*es pleaded, the court, [being] satisfied with the proof, rejected all the plaintiff's evidence concerning the several other pretended *modus*es as not applicable to the matter in issue on this bill. And so they dismissed the plaintiff's bill as to the demand of tithe hay arising on the aforesaid farms and as to the demand of agistment tithe with relation to Garwood and Byrnnshall. But the defendants were decreed to account for agistment tithes in other parts of the parish.

N.B. Tithe hay and agistment is scarce anywhere paid in Lancashire. But whether this proceeds from the old notion that no agistment is due for barren cattle or from what other reason *non constat*. In Doctor Turton's Case, who was rector of Standish,[1] there was a *modus* of 3d. by every parishioner for hay, house, hen, and yard insisted on and overruled by this court. And, upon the success of that cause, the present suit was instituted and the plaintiff's proofs mentioned such like *modus*es as insisted on in this parish being applied to certain farms and so good.

Bunbury 161, 145 E.R. 632,
1 Rayner 205, 2 Gwillim 652, 1 Eagle & Younge 799

7 April 1724.

A bill was brought by the rector of Winwick in the County of Lancaster for tithe grass cut and made into hay. One defendant insists that he and all those etc. in an ancient messuage called Newhall and the demesne lands thereunto belonging, containing sixty-eight acres, two roods, and eighteen perches in Ashton within the said parish have immemorially paid a *modus* of 1d. at Easter annually in lieu of the tithe hay growing on the premises.

Another defendant insisted upon a *modus* of 26s. 8d. for hay, small tithes, and Easter offerings for an ancient tenement called Brynn and Graswood, containing 625 acres.

It was objected for the plaintiff that it appearing by the proof in the cause that this payment was for hay, as a small tithe, therefore, hay made from grass being in its nature a great tithe, it must be intended that this hay penny was for something else. And the ancient import of the word hay or haw was an hedge or some small inclosure belonging to an house. It was also objected to this and the other *modus* that they were uncertain, could not be supposed to have a reasonable

[1] *Turton v. Clayton* (1721), see above, Case No. 211.

commencement, and, thirdly, were liable to fraud, for, if all the land was turned into meadow, it would pay but 1d.

But notwithstanding these objections, both these *modus*es were allowed *per* CURIAM.

Harvard Law School MS. 1082, vol. 1, p. 207

Easter term 1724.

The plaintiff brought his bill as rector of Winwick for tithe hay and agistment of cattle. Some of the defendants [Gerrard and Masters] insisted on particular *modus*es for their farms, and others insisted that a hay penny was in lieu of hay and all small tithes and a *non decimando* as to agistment of cattle.

It was insisted on by the plaintiff's counsel that this hay penny could only be in lieu of small tithes and not for tithe hay but only hay was an old word taken for hedge or enclosure and it could have no good commencement and if one person should hold all of these ancient messuages and lands, then he would pay but 1d. for the whole. [He] cited for the plaintiff Turton v. Clayton *et al.*

Chief Baron [EYRE] and the court decreed the defendants to account for agistment of cattle, but they allowed the *modus* of a hay penny to be good. See Turton v. Clayton *et al.*

[Order of 27 April 1724: 2 Wood 222.]

464

Birch v. Stone

(Ex. 1724)

A modus decimandi *in lieu of tithes in kind that is uncertain is void.*

Taussig MS. 311, vol. 1, p. 628

Hilary term 1723/24.

The defendant to a tithe bill insisted that no tithes in kind were ever paid in the parish. And by one answer, they insisted that the parson enjoyed a meadow called the Parson's Mead and some beast gates or £16 *per annum* or otherwise in lieu of tithes within the parish. But others, by their answer, insisted that the mead before and some beast gates in a certain place were in lieu of tithes.

Sed per CURIAM: Some beast gates without saying how many is uncertain. And, though it was said that the proof in the cause ascertained the number to five and that, if the *modus* as to this point was not certain, yet being certain as to the meadow, there was a *modus* and the being of any *modus* is a bar to tithes in kind and so the plaintiff was not entitled to an account, as, in [a petition for a writ of] prohibition, if any *modus* is proved, no [writ of] consultation[1] shall go, as by Moor 911, Cro. Eliz. 736.[2]

Sed CURIA *contra*, and they would not so much as direct any issue. But if they made out a better case another time, they might then consider it.

2 Gwillim 649

To a bill for tithes, the defendants said that there is a meadow in the said parish called the Parson's Meadow and that the plaintiff and his predecessors had, time out of mind, enjoyed the said meadow and also several beast grasses in the said parish in lieu of the tithes within the said parish.

The court, upon mature deliberation had thereon, declared that the *moduses* laid in the answer, by reason of their uncertainty, are not good. And, thereupon, they ordered the defendants to account for their several tithable matters and things.

[Order of 19 February 1724: 2 Wood 219, 1 Eagle & Younge 797.]

465

Lady Clarges v. Williams

(Ex. 1724)

A court of equity will set aside a contract entered into through fraud in the inducement.

Taussig MS. 311, vol. 1, p. 631

Hilary term 1723/24.

There was an agreement between the plaintiff and defendant about a £1000 subscription in the third subscription of the South Sea Company. And the agreement was in writing and not under seal. And by that agreement, Lady Clarges was to give the defendant Williams a £200 premium for the benefit of this subscription when the Company should deliver out the same. Afterwards, the subscription rising, Lady Clarges generously agreed to advance the premium to £400, and, by way of kindness to the defendant, she advanced the money beforehand. Then, the agreement was to be drawn up in form, which was done by Williams and sent to her and after[wards] engrossed. And, when it came to be executed, Lady Clarges objected that it was not inserted in the deed that the money, that is the £400, was to be repaid to her in case the receipts were not delivered out by the Company. But Williams told her this would be of course, as it was indeed at that time the general notion of people. But Lady Clarges said it was better it

[1] construction *MS.*

[2] *Austin v. Pigot* (1600), Moore K.B. 911, 72 E.R. 991, Croke Eliz. 736, 78 E.R. 968, 1 Eagle & Younge 151.

should be expressed and proposed an endorsement, which the defendant avoided doing by assuring her the deed imported as much. And so she and he executed the deed. And it was witnessed by two of her servants, who, being sworn in the cause, deposed to the same effect as above, and the substance of their depositions seemed to be confessed by the defendant in his answer.

And the court unanimously relieved her and decreed Williams to repay the £400 to her with interest.

N.B. The only objection that seemed of any weight in this case was this, that, here, the operation and effect of the deed was avoided by parol evidence and so was said to be evidence against the deed and not to be admitted because it might give a great inlet to perjury.

Sed per CURIAM: The inducing her to sign this deed under the aforesaid circumstances and by such persuasions was a fraud fit to be relieved against in a court of equity and, by this way of arguing, the Statute against Frauds and Perjuries[1] would become a means to encourage fraud.

466

Sherwood v. Ward

(Ex. 1724)

In this case, a parishioner was ordered to pay tithes.

Taussig MS. 311, vol. 1, p. 639

Hilary term 1723/24.

In this case, Mr. *Edlin* said that he had seen many endowments of vicarages wherein the impropriators have endowed the vicar of all small tithes throughout the rectory excepting such small tithes as should arise on their own proper land or demesne lands within the said rectory. Therefore, he submitted it that non-payment of tithes for lands proved to have belonged to the religious house was good evidence against a vicar, which notion I think is right. But in the case before the court, there was evidence of a yearly payment of money, *viz.* £8 *per annum* for the tithes of those very lands for which he would now claim a discharge by the former way of reasoning.

And the court decreed the defendant to account.

467

Beardmore v. Gilbert

(Ex. 1724)

[1] Stat. 29 Car. II, c. 3 (*SR*, V, 839-842).

Woodland put into agricultural production is not barren ground that has been improved and thus is not exempt from the payment of tithes for seven years thereafter.

Bunbury 159, 145 E.R. 632,
1 Rayner 200, 2 Gwillim 649, 1 Eagle & Younge 794

21 February 1723[/24].

This was a bill brought by the impropriator for the tithe of Forley and Oakmore in the parish of Alford in the County of Stafford. The defendant, in his answer, insists that the ground for which the tithe is demanded is heath and barren ground and exempted by the Stat. Edw. VI[1] for seven years. But he admits by his answer that it was wood ground which had been grubbed up. And, therefore, the plaintiff's counsel insisted it had yielded profit before and was not barren ground within the meaning of the Stat. of Edw. VI. This came on upon bill and answer, and, it appearing from the defendant's own admission that it was wood ground grubbed up, *per* CURIAM, the defendant was decreed to account.

468

Note

(Ex. 1724)

Proceedings at common law will not be stayed if the defendant agrees to abide by the final order of the court and pays the disputed funds into court pendente lite.

Taussig MS. 311, vol. 2, p. 642

Saturday, 25 [April 1724].

The court declared that, for the future, they would not stay proceedings at law upon an attorney's bill upon the defendant's submitting to pay the bill and costs when taxed, but would expect that the client should bring the money into court, as was done in the other courts of law.

Note this rule is not to extend to equity proceedings.

469

Roupe v. Atkinson

(Ex. 1724)

Where the beneficiary of a trust sells the corpus of the trust, a court of equity will enforce the sale.

[1] Stat. 2 & 3 Edw. VI, c. 13, s. 5 (*SR*, IV, 56).

Bunbury 162, 145 E.R. 633

4 May 1724.

A lease for a term of years was assigned to trustees before marriage in trust that they should make leases for the benefit of the husband and wife. After the marriage, the husband and wife assign to Sparke in consideration of building the premises. Sparke assigns to Atkinson for a valuable consideration.

The husband being dead, Mary Roupe, his widow, brings a bill against Sparke and Atkinson to be relieved against this lease made during the coverture, no fine having been levied.

And note this bill must have been dismissed as being proper at law but that the defendants had filed a cross-bill to be quieted and for an injunction.

It was insisted upon for the defendant in the original bill, first, that this lease being assigned by the husband and wife, who were *cestuis que trust*, should bind in equity as much as if it had been by the trustees.

Per CURIAM: If the trustees had been parties, they should have been decreed to have executed the trust to the defendants pursuant to the assignment of the *cestuis que trust.*

Secondly, it appeared that the plaintiff was present often during the rebuilding and took no notice of her interest; but this appeared to be only during the coverture.

Thirdly, it was said that the plaintiff, after her husband's death, had affirmed the lease by accepting the rent; but this was not made out in the proof.

For the plaintiff, it was insisted that she had both the law and equity on her side, which ought to prevail against equity alone, for the defendants do not pretend to law. But to this, it was answered that the trustees are trustees for the defendants, who have the equitable interest.

Upon the whole, *per* CURIAM, the original bill was dismissed, and an injunction was decreed upon the cross-bill.

And it was said by Lord Chief Baron EYRE that Sparke is a purchaser for a valuable consideration by building, nor does it appear he ever had notice; but if he had, I should have been of the same opinion.

470

Chambers v. Robinson

(Ex. 1724)

Court costs upon a referral of a pleading for scandal can include damages for the defamation.

Harvard Law School MS. 1082, vol. 1, p. 202, pl. 1

Easter term 1724.

A bill was reported as scandalous, and £60 were allowed for costs by the Deputy [Remembrancer].

Chief Baron [Eyre] thought it too much.

Price said that it was the course of a court of equity to consider damages in costs in these cases. And, therefore, he did not think it too much. And he mentioned the case of Culpeper v. Sir Thomas Taylour, in the Exchequer.

Page cited Sir Cecil Bishop v. Parry in the Court of Chancery. Damages were included in costs, and Sir William Whitlock as counsel was obliged to pay £100 for signing a scandalous bill.

Gilbert: In taxing costs, some regard is to be had to the scandal, and it is relatory to the record. And when the party is scandalized upon the record, the party ought to have a recompense. And I do not take the articles of the bill of costs to be material.

Price: I would desire to know, if this came before a jury, whether £60 damages would be too high. And I think not.

So £60 was allowed. But Chambers agreed not to bring any action for the scandal.

Taussig MS. 311, vol. 2, p. 652

Easter term 1724.

Chambers exhibited a bill in this court against Robinson, who put in an answer to it and therein inserted several very scandalous and impertinent expressions. And it was referred to the Deputy [Remembrancer] to expunge the passages and tax costs for the same. Upon this occasion, he brought in a bill of costs amounting to a very great sum, wherein £120 was charged for counsel's fees, which items were purely fictitious. And the Master in taxing the bill did not proceed item by item, but lumped the whole together and moderated the bill to £60.

And now Mr. *Aris* moved that it should be referred back to the Master to re-tax the bill and that, in so doing, he should proceed item by item, thereby intending to cut off the fees charged to counsel which were not paid.

But this was opposed because the Court of Chancery upon such occasions do give the party costs by way of damages and do not admeasure the costs or proportion of the real expense the party has been at.

And, upon this reasoning, the court refused to refer the bill to be re-taxed.

Friday, 8th May 1724.

The court now declared that, upon reconsideration of the former matter, though they would not send the bill to be re-taxed, yet they thought the Master's allowance was too great and, therefore, they moderated the costs to £40.

Bunbury 164, 145 E.R. 633

6 May 1724.

The defendant's answer was referred for scandal. And it was reported by the Master to be scandalous, and the plaintiff's costs were ordered to be taxed. The plaintiff, in the taxation of costs, had allowed to him several items, of £21 6s., and £3, as fees given to counsel, although he did not pretend that such sums had been really given. But it was alleged, and so admitted now, that it was the constant method in Chancery to allow costs in this manner by way of damages and satisfaction to the party for the scandal. The whole in this case that was thus itemed to counsel amounted to £60, which, this day, the court would not alter, but, upon the 8th of May, they thought it too extravagant and reduced it to £40.

Bunbury 169, 145 E.R. 635

6 June 1724.

Where a defendant submits to exceptions or exceptions on arguing are allowed, the plaintiff has a right, of course, to amend his bill without costs, he amending the defendant's copy.

471

Williams v. Ord

(Ex. 1724)

Neither an attorney nor an agent can delegate his duty to another without an express authority to delegate.

Taussig MS. 311, vol. 2, p. 656, pl. 1

At *nisi prius coram* EYRE, Chief Baron, 13 May 1724 at Westminster.

It was ruled that, though where a letter of attorney was given to A. to make a demand of a sum of money due to B. and to receive it and give an acquittance for it, A. cannot make another person his attorney to do it because an attorney or deputy cannot make another attorney or deputy. Yet if the original letter of attorney to A. authorizes A. to demand or to depute another person to make the demand, such deputy may make a demand. And the Chief Baron [EYRE] said this was the plain and express intention of the party giving the letter of attorney and he knew no authority in law to the contrary.

472

Palliser v. Ord

(Ex. 1724)

A plaintiff must prove the exact same sum to be due as it was pleaded.

Neither an attorney nor an agent can delegate his duty to another without an express authority to delegate.

Bunbury 166, 145 E.R. 634

At the sittings in Middlesex. 13 May 1724.

An action of debt was brought upon the certificate of the Commissioners for Stating the Debts Due to the Army pursuant to the Stat. 6 Geo.[1] for £105 18s. 7d. qa., certified to be due to the plaintiff, for which the Statute gave an action of debt upon a demand made and refusal. In proving the demand, it was of £105 18s. 6d. qa., instead of 7d. qa., which varied from the sum certified.

Lord Chief Baron EYRE, before whom this cause was tried, was of opinion that this certificate was in the nature of a judgment, that, it being a debt thereby reduced to a certainty and the demand being of a different sum, it was fatal. And, thereupon, the plaintiff was nonsuited.

Note: The plaintiff gave an authority to Moore, his attorney, to make the demand or to authorize any other person to do it, who, accordingly, executed a letter of attorney to another to do it; so it was objected for the defendant that a naked authority could not be delegated.

But the CHIEF BARON was of opinion it might, by express authority for that purpose, otherwise not.

Taussig MS. 311, vol. 2, p. 656, pl. 2

At the same sittings [at *nisi prius coram* EYRE, Chief Baron, 13 May 1724 at Westminster].

[An action of] debt [was brought] upon a certificate of the Commissioners for Stating the Debts of the Army upon 7 Geo., ca. 18.[2] The certificate under the Commissioners' hands was for £105 18s. 7¼d. and so was the declaration. But the Act requiring a demand before an action be brought, the witness called upon to prove the demand swore he demanded the sum of £105 8s. 6¼d.; so the demand varied 1d. from the sum due. And the plaintiff was nonsuited.

By the opinion of the Chief Baron [EYRE], who said at the same time that, if the plaintiff's counsel doubted his opinion, he would direct the jury to find for the plaintiff and they might move the court upon it upon the peril of costs.

473

Note

(Ex. 1724)

[1] Stat. 6 Geo. I, c. 3.

[2] Stat. 7 Geo. I, cc. 6, 30.

After a port has been officially designated as such, it cannot be afterwards discharged from being an official port.

British Library MS. Hargrave 70, f. 32, pl. 156,
Harvard Law School MS. 1162, p. 53, pl. 302

Note: Sir James Montagu's opinion upon the clause in the Stat. 14 Car. II, cap. [*blank*], sec. 14,[1] which gives the crown power to appoint lawful ports and quays for the shipping and unloading of goods etc. was that, where a port and quay has been once appointed by virtue of a commission out of the Exchequer, that port, etc. cannot afterwards be discharged.

474

Mitchell v. Soaper

(Ex. 1724)

In an action of trespass, where the trial judge does not certify that court costs are warranted, a prevailing plaintiff cannot receive court costs that are greater than the damages awarded.

Harvard Law School MS. 1082, vol. 1, p. 203

Easter term 1724.

This was an action of trespass. And the word *divulsit* was in the declaration. And [the jury] found for the plaintiff, and 1d. damages [were] given.

Serjeant *Chapple* moved for the defendant that there might be no costs, the judge having not certified. Stat. 22 & 23 Car. II; 8 & 9 Will. III.[2]

Serjeant *Shepherd*, for the plaintiff, [said] that there should be full costs because *divulsit* amounts to an *asportavit*, which will always entitle the plaintiff to costs though the damages are never so small. *Asportatio* and *divulsio* are synonymous terms and show a voluntary trespass. *Prostravit* has been adjudged to carry costs. Raymond 487.[3] And there is no occasion for the certificate of the judge where there is sufficient [matter] upon the record.

Serjeant *Chapple* replied [and] said that case in Raymond was before the Statute of 8 & 9 Will. III.[4]

Chief Baron [Eyre] was for no costs.

Price inclined for no costs, but for adjourning it.

---

[1] Stat. 14 Car. II, c. 11, s. 15 (*SR*, V, 397).

[2] Stat. 22 & 23 Car. II, c. 9, s. 9 (*SR*, V, 719); Stat. 8 & 9 Will. III, c. 11, s. 4 (*SR*, VII, 202).

[3] *Smith v. Batterton* (1683), T. Raymond 487, 83 E.R. 255, also 2 Shower K.B. 258, 89 E.R. 927.

[4] Stat. 8 & 9 Will. III, c. 11, s. 4 (*SR*, VII, 202).

PAGE and GILBERT: No costs.

Bunbury 167, 145 E.R. 634

18 May 1724.

In an action of trespass, there was a verdict for the plaintiff, *quoad transgressione cum averiis et sepium et fensurarum fractionem, prostrationem, et divulsionem,*[1] that the defendant was guilty and 1d. damages. The judge who tried the cause had not certified as the statutes 22 & 23 Car. II, c. 9, s. 136, and 8 & 9 Will. III, c. 10, s. 4, direct.

And now, it was moved that the defendant should have no more costs than damages, here being no word which amounts to an asportation, nor any voluntary trespass certified, and *divulsionem* did not in itself import either

And of that opinion were the court. And the plaintiff had but 1d. costs.

Taussig MS. 311, vol. 2, p. 659

Easter term 1724.

In an action of trespass *quare clausum fregit et 10 particat. sepium prostravit et divulsit*, there was no certificate from the judge. And it was insisted that the word '*divulsit*' would carry costs, as it is allowed an *asportavit* will do. And 2 Ventr. 215[2] and 2 Mod. [*blank*] were cited.

But the court seemed strongly that no more costs could be had in this case than damages, there being no certificate.

475

De Bank v. Gregg

(Ex. 1724)

An action of escape not being local in its nature, any escape or being at large in any county is sufficient venue to maintain a declaration.

A debt on a bond or on a judgment is located where the bond or judgment is located. If such a debt be bona notabilia, *administration of the decedent's estate must be granted in that diocese where the debt was located at the time of the death or in the prerogative court of the archbishop.*

In this case, the letters of administration to the plaintiff were invalid and, therefore, the plaintiff was not a proper party to bring the action and the judgment was arrested.

---

[1] as to a trespass with cattle and hedges and fences broken, thrown down, and torn down.

[2] *Anonymous* (1690), 2 Ventris 215, 86 E.R. 401.

Taussig MS. 311, vol. 1, p. 605

Hilary term 1723[/24].

The action was in Stafford, and the escape was laid there, but the escape in Lancashire was only given in evidence.

If there are two causes of action, the plaintiff has his election in which he will bring his action. 7 Rep., Bulwar's Case; Hob. 209; 1 Mod. 198; Syd. 364; Dier 38, Dier 40; 30 Hen. VI, 6; Bro., Lieu, 82; Fitz., Debt [*blank*]; Plow. 37; Cro. Eliz. 271.[1] If a party may have an action in any county where an escape was, then he ought to take his action in the county where he can prove the escape. 1 Lev. 114; Cro. Eliz. 625.[2]

Solicitor General [*Wearg*]: This is no local action, that is such as is confined to the place. When once escaped, he may go all over England, and that is no particular fault of the sheriff. Style's Rep. 341;[3] an escape in B. is an escape all the world over. 1 Ric. II, ca. 12,[4] is the foundation of this action of debt. And every action of debt is transitory. Plowden 36, 37,[5] proves the debt is founded on that Statute. The Statute of Jac. I [*blank*] confines actions against officers to places, but a sheriff is not included in that Act.

Wilbraham: This action arises *ex delicto*. Dier 40, pl. 21.[6]

Chief Baron [Eyre]: There is no color for changing venues but in transitory actions, so I do not understand the case in Styles. However, we will look upon the books. But I am of opinion at present that evidence may be given of an escape in any county. Rolle's *Abr.*, 602.[7]

Price was doubtful.

Page and Gilbert: If it is not confined to the county where he first escaped, why should it be confined to any other county? There is no distinction between the

---

[1] *Bulwer v. Smith* (1583), 7 Coke Rep. 1, 77 E.R. 411, also 4 Leonard 52, 74 E.R. 724; *Parkhurst v. Powell* (1617), Hobart 209, 80 E.R. 356, also Croke Jac. 532, 79 E.R. 456, 1 Brownlow & Goldesborough 12, 123 E.R. 634; *Naylor v. Sharply* (1675), 1 Modern 198, 86 E.R. 826, also 2 Modern 23, 86 E.R. 919, 1 Freeman 191, 89 E.R. 136; *Hopping v. Holmy* (1668), 1 Siderfin 364, 82 E.R. 1159, also 2 Keble 340, 350, 84 E.R. 212, 219; *Gawen v. Hussee* (1537), 1 Dyer 38, 73 E.R. 84; YB Trin. 30 Hen. VI, f. 6, pl. 5 (1452); Brooke, Abr., *Lieu & countie ou action sera port*, pl. 82; Fitzherbert, Abr., *Dett*; *Platt v. Lock* (1550), 1 Plowden 35, 75 E.R. 57; *Richbell v. Goddard* (1592), Croke Eliz. 271, 78 E.R. 526.

[2] *Gilbert v. Martin* (1663), 1 Levinz 114, 83 E.R. 324, 325, also 1 Siderfin 157, 82 E.R. 1030, 1 Keble 575, 601, 83 E.R. 1120, 1135; *Bennion v. Watson* (1598), Croke Eliz. 625, 78 E.R. 865.

[3] *Anonymous* (1652), Style 341, 82 E.R. 761.

[4] Stat. 1 Ric. II, c. 12 (*SR*, II, 4).

[5] *Platt v. Lock* (1550), 1 Plowden 35, 75 E.R. 57.

[6] *Gawen v. Hussee* (1537), *ut supra*.

[7] *Carewe v. Broughton* (1610), 1 Rolle, Abr., *Dett*, pl. P, 1, p. 602.

locality of a debt arising *ex delicto* or arising *ex contractu*. But the truth of this case is this, that, here, a debt arising *ex contractu* is transferred upon another *ex delicto.*

Taussig MS. 311, vol. 2, p. 648

Tuesday, 5th May 1724.

The court declared their opinion that the action of escape not being local in its nature, any escape or being at large in any county was sufficient evidence to maintain the declaration though the declaration laid the escape to be in a particular county.

Taussig MS. 311, vol. 2, p. 660

Easter term 1724.

The plaintiff, as administrator of S.D., *de bonis non* administrator for J.D., who was the executor of the said S.D., brought an action of escape against the sheriff of [*blank*] for suffering [to escape] J.S., against whom J.D., as executor of S.D., had recovered a judgment and was in execution thereupon. And the plaintiff counted of an administration committed to him by the bishop of Lichfield and Coventry. And the judgment was for £40.

And it was now moved in arrest of judgment that this action, being founded on the judgment which was of record in Middlesex and so [was] assets there, could not be maintained by virtue of an administration in the diocese of Lichfield.

To prove that the action of escape must be founded on and brought by him or in his right only who recovered the judgment, 1 Rolle's Rep. 276[1] was cited and that an administration out of a peculiar would not entitle to an action of debt or a *scire facias* upon a judgment at Westminster. Salkeld 40, 6 Mod. 134; 1 Lutw. 399;[2] and York v. Pike, Michaelmas 1 Ann., King's Bench, were cited.

E contra: It was said that, at the time of the death of the first testator, this was or, at least, did not appear to be other than a simple contract debt and so due to the testator at the place of his residence or in any place and so, consequently, in the diocese of Lichfield as well as in any other place, that the executor suing for it and recovering it did not enter the locality of it so as to prejudice the legality of the administration, for the administration relates to the death of the testator at which time the debt was *bona notabilia* in the diocese of Lichfield.

The Chief Baron [Eyre] doubted and was rather inclined to think the administration was not good. Price ditto and Gilbert. But Page seemed of a contrary opinion.

---

[1] *Slingsby v. Lambert* (1615), 1 Rolle Rep. 276, 81 E.R. 486, also 3 Bulstrode 112, 81 E.R. 96, Croke Jac. 394, 79 E.R. 337, Godbolt 262, 78 E.R. 153.

[2] *Adams v. Savage's Tenants* (1704), 1 Salkeld 40, 91 E.R. 41, also 2 Salkeld 601, 679, 91 E.R. 510, 577, 3 Salkeld 321, 91 E.R. 848, 6 Modern 133, 134, 199, 226, 87 E.R. 890, 892, 954, 977, 2 Lord Raymond 854, 1253, 92 E.R. 71, 326, Holt K.B. 179, 90 E.R. 997; *Kegg v. Horton* (1687), 1 Lutwyche 399, 125 E.R. 209.

Et adjornatur.

Harvard Law School MS. 1082, vol. 1, p. 204

Easter term 1724.

This was an action for an escape brought by an administrator *de bonis non* granted by a peculiar, *viz.* the bishop of Lichfield and Coventry, which escape happened in the executor's time. And the debt was grounded on a judgment obtained in Middlesex. In this action, you must recite the judgment and where recovered. Saunders 38; Noy 15.[1]

It was said for the defendant here was no title shown by the plaintiff because the escape was grounded on a judgment in Middlesex and the administration granted by a peculiar will not affect it. Adams v. Terre Tenants of Savage, Hilary, 1 Ann., Easter 3 Ann., Salkeld 40,[2] that the administration as to this judgment was totally void.

Mr. *Wilbraham*, for the defendant, cited York v. Pyke, Michaelmas, 1 Ann.; 6 Modern 134; fully reported Lutwyche 199.

Mr. *Wills*, for the plaintiff: This is not an action grounded on the judgment, but on the escape, which is grounded on the Statute of Ric. II. In the cases there cited, judgment was obtained in the executor's time, which made it local. But he denied in the principal case that judgment was obtained in the executor's time and that, at the death of Simon De Bank, the intestate, it was only a debt upon a simple contract, which is transitory. And such are *bona notabilia* anywhere.

Bootle, for the defendant, replies: This escape is grounded in the judgment. And if the foundation fails, the whole must fall. 1 Rolle Rept. 176, Shagsby's Case. The case of York v. Pyke is an authority in point. So he prayed judgment to be arrested.

Wilbraham, for the defendant, said that, if the debt was grounded on a bond, it made it local.

Chief Baron [Eyre]: I am not satisfied that the administration is well granted. The debt is altered by the judgment and it only relates to the time of that judgment. Perhaps it is proper to be considered.

Price: I desire to consider of it. But I think than an administrator so obtained *de bonis non* could not have brought an action on a judgment obtained at Westminster, which is only *bona notabilia* here. A prerogative administration is only voidable, but a peculiar administration, if not good, is totally void. And by the Stat. 18 Car. II, cap. 18,[3] the administrator *de bonis non* is entitled to execution.

---

[1] *Jones v. Pope* (1666), 1 Williams Saunders 37, 85 E.R. 49, also 1 Siderfin 305, 82 E.R. 1122, 2 Keble 93, 84 E.R. 59, 1 Levinz 191, 83 E.R. 363; *Barnehurst v. Yelverton* (1606), Noy 15, 74 E.R. 986, also Yelverton 83, 80 E.R. 57, 1 Brownlow & Goldesborough 91, 123 E.R. 685.

[2] *Adams v. Savage's Tenants* (1704), *ut supra.*

[3] Stat. 17 Car. II, c. 8, s. 2 (*SR*, V, 580).

Page: I am very doubtful whether this administration so granted is void if the testator had no other *bona notabilia* elsewhere than in the diocese of Lichfield etc. And I think that this ought to have relation to the debt as it was and in the same manner as in the intestate's lifetime. And the administrator only stands in the place of the first executor. I desire to consider of it.

Gilbert: It must be considered whether turning this debt into a judgment at Westminster does not require a prerogative administration. And it seems to me that the bishop of Lichfield could not grant an administration of this debt because [it is] above the value as well as the other objection for its being obtained at Westminster. If an obligation is *bona notabilia* where the bond is given, [it is] much stronger in the case of a judgment. And so I am for arresting the judgment.

But the court would consider of it.

Harvard Law School MS. 1082, vol. 1, p. 220

Michaelmas term 1724.

Mr. *Reeves*, for the defendant, [made a] motion in arrest of judgment. This was an action against the sheriff of Lancashire for that Mary De Bank was executrix of Simon De Bank, who did bring an action against Gold, obtained judgment and that Mary died intestate, and administration of the goods not administered by Mary was committed to the plaintiff, that Gold was delivered over in execution to the defendant, who suffered him to escape in the lifetime of Mary De Bank. The administration granted to the plaintiff was by the bishop of Lichfield and Coventry. So he insisted for the defendant that the plaintiff had no right to bring this action, for that the administration granted by the peculiar, *viz.* the bishop of Lichfield and Coventry, was void. If administration is granted by a peculiar where there are *bona notabilia* in several dioceses, there, it ought to be a prerogative administration. 5 Rept., Prince's Case.[1] The judgment obtained by the executrix is assets of the first testator, Simon De Bank. The judgment must be construed *bona notabilia* where it was obtained and so made it local by its being so here at Westminster. And that takes away the jurisdiction of the inferior diocese.

During the lifetime of Mary De Bank, the testator, Simon De Bank, could not be said to be intestate, and he is only so esteemed since the death of Mary De Bank. If Mary had appointed an executrix, then such executrix would have been so to the first testator. 9 Coke 40, Henshaw's Case.[2] If Mary had made an executor and left goods that were the first testator's in several dioceses, I think that the metropolitan ought to have granted such a probate.

This case must be considered how the ordinary's authority does arise upon intestate's goods. See Stat. 51 (or 31) Edw. III[3] and what was the power of the

---

1 *Prince v. Simpson* (1599), 5 Coke Rep. 29, 77 E.R. 96, also Croke Eliz. 718, 78 E.R. 953, 2 Anderson 132, 123 E.R. 584, 3 Leonard 278, 74 E.R. 682.

2 *Hensloe v. Gage* (1600), 9 Coke Rep. 36, 77 E.R. 784.

3 Stat. 31 Edw. III, stat. 1, c. 11 (*SR*, I, 351).

ordinary before that Statute. And he had only power over the goods in his own diocese. Dyer 255b; 9 Rept. 39, Henshaw's Case.[1]

This case must depend upon the reason of it, for there [is] no case in point. And if this appears upon the face of the record, it is sufficient to move in arrest of judgment after verdict. See Easter 3 Anne, Savage v. Tenants of Adams; see Salkeld.

Mr. *Philip Ward*, for the plaintiff: I do admit the cases of a peculiar and of a prerogative administration in our law, though it is not so by the civil law. The judgment for Mary De Bank is assets of her testator. The Stat. 31 Edw. III is out of the case, and I may admit the case in Salkeld.

But the question in this case is concerning the escape which is collateral to the judgment, and the escape is the ground and jet of the action against the sheriff. This is an action grounded on the personal tort of the sheriff, and it is not grounded on the judgment. Plowden, *Commentaries*, 36.[2]

[To the] objection of Richards v. Speke, Hobart 206,[3] [he] answered that is not like this case; there, the money was levied. Dyer 322; Cro. Car. 540.[4]

Prerogative administration and the time of ascertaining the right of administration commences from the death of the party. Coke, *Entries*, 128; 8 Rept. 135; Dyer 305, concerning the locality of a bond.[5]

This was a good administration at the time of the death of Simon De Bank, for, then, it was within the jurisdiction of the bishop of Lichfield and Coventry. But the right of bringing the action for the escape is collateral.

Mr. *Reeves* replies: It is admitted that the judgment is *bona notabilia*. If so, then, it must be where that was obtained, which was at Westminster. But [it was] objected that it is collateral, to which I answer that the party is wrong as to the administration, which is consequential. And it entirely depends upon the judgment, for in an action for an escape, the judgment must be set forth. And so is 1 Saunders 38.[6]

Mr. *Philip Ward* spoke again. And he said that an action of escape would lie for an administrator *de bonis non*. 16 Modern, Clarke v. Withers;[7] 1 Siderfin 290.

---

[1] *Anonymous* (1566), 3 Dyer 255, 73 E.R. 567; *Hensloe v. Gage* (1600), *ut supra*.

[2] *Platt v. Lock* (1550), 1 Plowden 35, 75 E.R. 57.

[3] *Speake v. Richards* (1617), Hobart 206, 80 E.R. 353, also Moore K.B. 886, 72 E.R. 974, 2 Shower K.B. 281, 89 E.R. 940, Hutton 11, 123 E.R. 1065, 1 Brownlow & Goldesborough 51, 123 E.R. 659, Noy 22, 74 E.R. 992.

[4] *Whitacres v. Onsley* (1573), 3 Dyer 322, 73 E.R. 729; *Perkinson v. Gilford* (1639), Croke Car. 539, 79 E.R. 1064, also W. Jones 430, 82 E.R. 226, March 13, 82 E.R. 389.

[5] *Parker v. Clere* (1605), E. Coke, *A Booke of Entries* (1614), 'Det', pl. 12, f. 128; *Post v. Nedham* (1610), 8 Coke Rep. 135, 77 E.R. 678; *Daniel v. Luker* (1571), 3 Dyer 305, 73 E.R. 687.

[6] *Jones v. Pope* (1666), *ut supra*.

[7] *Clerk v. Withers* (1704), 6 Modern 290, 87 E.R. 1030, also 11 Modern 34, 88

Chief Baron [Eyre]: The question may be whether, in personal actions, there is such a privity as for the administrator to be entitled to the action. Cleave v. Vere, in Cro. Car. and Jones.[1] This is an action grounded upon a judgment, and it is a debt and transfers this action, and an action of debt will lie, but, then, the judgment must be set forth, and so in an action of escape grounded on the judgment. Adams v. Terre Tenants of Savage.

The court, *ex officio*, will take notice of the jurisdiction of the ordinary. If a bond is a specialty, it is much stronger in the case of a judgment. And, therefore, I cannot think that this administration is well granted.

An administrator *de bonis non* cannot bring a *scire facias* because he is not privy to the first intestate. An administrator could not bring an action grounded on a judgment until the Stat. 17 Car. II, and it cannot go further than the Statute declares. It will be difficult to maintain the action. First, there is no privity if grounded on the judgment. And secondly, there does not appear to be a proper administration.

Price: The action will not lie, and judgment ought to be arrested on both points.

Page agreed.

Gilbert: I have no doubt. I allow that, when the judgment is executed, it will go to the administrator *de bonis non,* but not otherwise, though I am a little doubtful whether the judgment does entitle the party to a prerogative administration.

But the judgment was arrested.

Taussig MS. 311, vol. 2, p. 730

Michaelmas term 1724.

See the paper book and the argument in the case of this term. The judgment was arrested, and the court seemed unanimous in arresting.

8 Modern 244, 88 E.R. 174

In an action of debt against the sheriff, the case was thus. A., by his last will and testament, made B. his executor and died. The executor proved the will before the commissary of the bishop of Lichfield, and, as executor of A., brought an action against C. and obtained a verdict and judgment. And, thereupon, C. was taken in execution upon a *capias ad satisfaciendum* and committed, and, afterwards, he escaped. Then, B., the executor, died intestate, and D. took out administration *cum testamento annexo de bonis non* of A. in the diocese of Lichfield. And he brought this action of debt against the sheriff for this escape.

E.R. 866, Holt K.B. 303, 646, 90 E.R. 1067, 1257, 1 Salkeld 322, 91 E.R. 286, 2 Lord Raymond 1072, 92 E.R. 211.

[1] *Cleve v. Veer* (1636), Croke Car. 450, 456, 79 E.R. 992, 996, W. Jones 385, 82 E.R. 201.

The defendant demurred, for that the judgment being the foundation of this action and that being entered in Middlesex, the plaintiff could have no right to it by virtue of an administration taken in the diocese of Lichfield, which, as to this demand, was void, for he ought to have a prerogative administration.

But the counsel for the plaintiff insisted that this action would lie for two reasons: first, because the escape, which was in the diocese of Lichfield, was the principal and immediate cause of the action and the judgment set forth in the declaration was only an inducement to it; secondly, that it was not in the power of the executor to alter the condition of his testator, so as to put the administrator to take out a prerogative administration, for he took it *cum testamento annexo*, so he should have it in the same condition it was in at the death of the testator; and one of the barons was of that opinion.

But three of the barons, of which Eyre, Chief Baron, was one, were of opinion that the plaintiff could not maintain this action without taking out a prerogative administration or an administration where the judgment was entered and that was in the diocese of London, that it was absolutely necessary he must take out administration somewhere, and that there could be no inconveniency in taking out administration above, according to the case of Byron v. Byron,[1] where it was held that a man dying in one diocese and having a bond in another diocese, in such case, there must be a prerogative administration, because the debt does not follow the person, but it is a debt where the bond is at the time of the decease of the intestate. So, in the case of Adams v. Savage,[2] it was held that administration granted by the archdeacon of Dorset could be no title to a judgment in any of the courts at Westminster. It is true a will of a personal estate which lies in a foreign country, and none in England, may be proved in that country where the estate is,[3] and need not be proved here.

476

Dummer v. Chomley

(Ex. 1724)

A contract to sell real estate must be made in writing and must be signed by the parties thereto.

Taussig MS. 311, vol. 2, p. 647

Saturday, 2nd May 1724.

The bill suggests that Ramsey and Chomley, being jointly seised in their own right or in the right of their wives, did, by the consent of their wives, authorize

[1] *Byron v. Byron* (1596), Croke Eliz. 472, 78 E.R. 709.

[2] *Adams v. Savage's Tenants* (1704), *ut supra*.

[3] *Jauncy v. Sealey* (1686), 1 Vernon 397, 23 E.R. 541.

one A.B. to contract with the plaintiff for selling the estate in question. The defendants plead the Statute of Frauds and Perjuries[1] that no agreement in writing was signed by the wives or [with] their consent to authorize any person to contract with the plaintiff.

The court overruled the plea because here was a writing. But whether it was sufficient to bind the wives is quite another question, but there being a writing such which brings the case out of the Statute.

477

Floyer v. Sydenham

(Ex. 1724)

A court will not compel a party to produce deeds and writings that do not go to prove the requesting party's title.

Taussig MS. 311, vol. 2, p. 649

Easter term 1724.

The plaintiff exhibited his bill in this court and thereby alleged that he was co-heir with the defendant to Sir John St. Barbe. And he showed how and alleged that, by some settlement made in the family by some of the St. Barbes, the lands were so settled as to come to him and the defendant as co-heirs and consequently that the devise of the lands by the late Sir John St. Barbe to the defendant was void. And he likewise impeached the said will as being procured by fraud, imposition, and artifice. And he prayed a discovery of the deeds and that the defendant might produce them as likewise all papers relating to any will.

The defendant admitted the pedigree and co-heirship and that he had many writings, some in his own custody, which he had perused, some in the hands of a gentleman at the bar, who refused to deliver them, and some were in the hands of A.B., who was in reality the defendant's steward in the country, though not said to be so in his answer. And, by his answer, he admitted a settlement made upon the marriage of the late Sir John's father and set forth part thereof, but not to the effect as the plaintiff desired it. And, as to the deeds and writings in the hands of A.B., he said that A.B. had informed him that he had looked them over, but could find no such settlement as the plaintiff inquired after. And further, he said he believed there never was any such.

And now the plaintiff moved the court that the defendant should produce and bring before the Deputy [Remembrancer] all his deeds and writings and that he the plaintiff might have liberty to inspect them as also the writings and papers relating to the will. And it was insisted that this motion was usually granted in Chancery, and two precedents were produced, one in the Case of the Lord

[1] Stat. 29 Car. II, c. 3 (*SR*, V, 839-842).

Ferrers, who claimed as heir in tail, and the other in the Case of Lord Suffolk, where, upon a like motion, the family deeds were by the order of the court brought before a master and the plaintiffs had liberty to inspect them, the Chancellor saying that the plaintiff had a right to see with his own eyes whether he was barred or defeated.

But PRICE said he thought those precedents were very extraordinary and he should not have consented to them and that there never was anything of the like nature done in this court. And, therefore, he was against it.

PAGE thought the plaintiff was too early in his motion and that he should have excepted in the first place to the defendant's answer, it being in his opinion defective and insufficient.

GILBERT said he thought the court would never compel a defendant to produce family deeds and writings, but in such cases where it did appear that the plaintiff and defendant's title to the deeds stood upon an equal foot, as, in this case, it did, considering them as co-heirs. But the defendant insisting now on another title as devisee, which was different from the plaintiff's, the court ought not to compel the defendant to produce them.

And the Chief Baron [EYRE], who said nothing to the point at first, it being a matter of practice, as he said, concurred with them in rejecting the motion.

N.B. I was of counsel with the plaintiff.

478

Stephens, *qui tam* v. Vivian

(Ex. 1724)

As to unlawfully imported goods, the testimony of the master of the ship in which they were carried is inadmissible.

Taussig MS. 311, vol. 2, p. 657

Easter term 1724.

An information [was exhibited] upon 8 Geo., fol. 287,[1] for landing foreign goods coming coastwise without the presence of a Custom House officer. The Attorney General [*Yorke*], in order to prove the goods were brought coastwise, asked the witness what the master of the ship declared concerning these goods.

But the Chief Baron [EYRE] said that what the master had declared was not evidence against the owner of the goods. And the Attorney [General *Yorke*] saying that it had been often admitted as evidence in this court upon such occasions, the CHIEF BARON appealed to the practicers who sat by and were not concerned in the cause. And my brother [*Edward Ward, Jr.*] saying that he had never heard it allowed, the CHIEF BARON refused to admit the evidence. 8 Geo., ca. 18.

[1] Stat. 8 Geo. I, c. 18.

479

Lesley, *qui tam* v. Gray

(Ex. 1724)

The testimony of the master of a ship in which goods were unlawfully imported is admissible in evidence.

Taussig MS. 311, vol. 2, p. 658

Easter term 1724.

An information [was exhibited] upon 9 Geo., fol. 599,[1] upon a seizure of tobacco pretended to be brought from Scotland, but in truth taken into the ship out of another at sea. The defendants [Gray and Corbett] had examined their witnesses by consent before a baron, and so their depositions were read at the trial. And among the witnesses for the defendants, the master of the ship was examined to prove the goods were not taken in at sea, to which the Attorney [General *Yorke*] objected because the Act says the master of the ship shall forfeit the value of the goods so taken in and, therefore, he has a strong bias on him to swear the negative.

But it being said that this point had been sometimes ruled one way and sometimes another, the Chief Baron [Eyre] permitted the deposition to be read.

See Lib. 3, fo. 176, Fuller, *qui tam* v. Jackson.[2] This objection was allowed by Page and Gilbert.

480

Curtis v. Browne

(Ex. 1724)

A modus decimandi *in lieu of tithes in kind must be certain.*

Harvard Law School MS. 1082, vol. 1, p. 205

Easter term 1724.

This was a bill brought for tithes. The plaintiff was rector of Shenley in the County of Buckingham. The defendant insisted on 2d. for every cow running in certain closes at Shenley Croke End, two of which closes were particularly described, the other two not only lying at Shenley Croke End, and that this 2d. was in lieu of the tithes of each such cow so running as aforesaid, and that such payment was reputed to be payable at or about Martinmas [11 November] yearly by the owners and occupiers. In this case, likewise, there was another joint occupier with the defendant, who was dead.

---

1 Stat. 9 Geo. I, c. 21.

2 *Fuller, qui tam v. Jackson* (Ex. 1723), see above, Case No. 437.

Chief Baron [Eyre] was of opinion that the interest survived, but the other three judges were of a contrary opinion and that, if the plaintiff went for what concerned the other occupier, the executor or administrator of such person ought to be a party.

Mr. *Ward*, for the plaintiff: As to the *modus* itself, that it was void and uncertain as to how long these cows were to run in the closes and as to the time of payment, for reputing it to be payable is not sufficient, and that the closes were not particularly described, which makes another uncertainty. And as to the time of going, if they went half an hour in these closes, it would occasion to set up this *modus* or exemption but come to set out tithes *absque visu et tactu* is void. See Hobart.

Bunbury, for the defendant: [To the] objection of uncertainty as to place, *viz.* the closes' time of payment and for how long going, [he] answered the particular parcels are mentioned and two closes containing eleven acres at Shenley Croke End is so sufficient for the place, and, as to how long, yearly going, it must be taken the whole year or for such time as they go there. And 'at or about Martinmas' is sufficient, for it must be reduced to a certainty by the proof.

Bootle, for the defendant: *Modus*es are not to be taken so strictly in equity where the party is to swear to it and the 2d. is to be paid if only going a week on those closes. And so he insisted that it was certain enough.

Chief Baron [Eyre]: It is agreed to be the rule in this court that a *modus* is the same in equity as at law. And you cannot by construction make a *modus* good. So was St. Eloy v. Pryor, last term.[1] I think, as to the description of the *locus in quo*, it is well enough. But it is a bad prescription for not ascertaining the time how long they were to go, and [it is] likewise bad as to the reputing to be payable about Martinmas.

Price: I think that the rule is the same in equity as it is at law as to a *modus*, and it ought to be as strictly laid. I cannot think this *modus*, as laid, is bad as to what time going and as to the time of payment reputed to be payable at or about Martinmas.

Page: At this distance of time, *modus*es should not be taken too strictly. [If] it said that four closes [were] in satisfaction, that would be sufficient. *Modus*es are perhaps the same in equity as at law, but I will construe everything in favor of constant usage, and greater latitude is always allowed in proceedings in equity. And I think the *modus* good throughout. 'Payable about Martinmas' is sufficient. And it is as much as the defendant can swear. And if the defendant was to swear to a *modus* at law, it would be impossible to do it. And I cannot think that, by this *modus*, the cow is to run the whole year. And, upon this *modus*, the parson has a proper remedy for it.

Gilbert: The occupier has the same right to the *modus* as the parson has to the tithe. And it must be proved an immemorial custom. And I do not stand upon a particular form of words. And if it appears upon the whole to be a good

[1] *St. Eloy v. Pryor* (1724), see above, Case No. 442.

modus, it is sufficient. And these payments ought to be certain. And the question is only whether it is substantially set forth. And the closes in this case are sufficiently described, and the cows must pay tithe of milk if fed in other places. And the *modus* only covers the cows whilst fed or going on the closes. Deemed and reputed payable at Martinmas is sufficient. And it is substantially good. The particular form is not required in an answer, for *allegata* and *probata* are to be taken together, for, in equity, strictness in precise matters is rejected. And this is certain enough for the minister's maintenance. The canon[1] recommended that a composition should be accepted in lieu of tithe milk.

Chief Baron [EYRE]: I apprehended from the case of St. Eloy v. Pryor that the *modus* ought to be ascertained. And if a *modus* is to be collected from the whole body of the answer, that may alter this case. Let the consideration of this case be adjourned for further consideration. See St. Eloy v. Pryor, last term.

481

Glover v. Young

(Ex. 1724)

A married woman should file an answer by her husband or by a guardian ad litem *unless her husband has absconded and her friends refuse to be her guardian.*

Bunbury 167, 145 E.R. 635

At Serjeants' Inn in Chancery Lane. 21 May 1724.

Although the rule is that a *feme covert*, in the absence of her husband, must answer by her guardian that there may be somebody answerable for the costs, yet, upon an affidavit made that her husband, since he entered his appearance, was run away and could not be found, that she had applied to all her friends and acquaintances to be her guardian, but that all had refused because she could not give security to indemnify them against the costs, in this case of necessity, the court gave leave to file her answer without a guardian.

482

Granslade v. Baker

(Ex. 1724)

Property sequestered for not performing a final decree can be ordered to be sold for the benefit of the judgment creditor.

Where a sequestration of property is obstructed, the court can grant a writ of assistance.

---

[1] W. Lyndwood, *Provinciale* (1929), p. 78.

Bunbury 168, 145 E.R. 635

4 June 1724.

It was ordered *per* CURIAM, upon the motion of Mr. *Foley*, that the sequestrators nominated for not performing a decree might sell so much of the estate as appeared by their certificate they had sequestered and also that they should have a writ of assistance to sequester the rest, it appearing by their affidavit and certificate that they were opposed in such sequestration.

It was moved by Mr. *Edlin*, in behalf of two persons, that part of the estate sequestered belonged to them, and a lease was offered to be produced.

But *per* CURIAM: We will not enter into the title upon motion, but they must go before the Master upon perils of costs.

483

Coulston v. Richardson

(Ex. 1724)

Where exceptions to an answer are allowed and the plaintiff is given leave to file an amended bill of complaint, after an amended answer is filed, the plaintiff can except to the second answer.

Bunbury 168, 145 E.R. 635

Eodem die [4 June 1724].

Upon arguing exceptions, they were allowed, whereupon the plaintiff obtained an order to amend his bill without costs, he amending the defendant's copy. The defendant, without waiting for the amendment, put in a further answer and then moved to dissolve the injunction upon the coming in of his second answer. But it was moved for the plaintiff that this answer came irregularly before he had amended his bill. And it appeared, although delay on the plaintiffs side was suggested, that the plaintiff offered to amend his, the defendant's, copy. And the court thought the most proper method in this case was for the plaintiff to take exceptions to the second answer and to turn the whole amendments into exceptions. And the order for showing cause why the injunction should not be dissolved was enlarged.

Taussig MS. 311, vol. 2, p. 677, pl. 1

Friday, 12 June 1724. Cole v. Richardson.

A bill is exhibited; an answer [is made] thereto, and exceptions are taken to the answer. And the defendant submitted to answer again and put in a second answer. And then, the plaintiff amended his bill and put down the former exceptions to the second answer and also filed new exceptions as to the amendments in the bill.

And *per* CURIAM, the amending the bill does not waive the liberty of excepting to the second answer as on the foot of the original bill so that they might still be argued.

484

Shorter v. Scortin

(Ex. 1724)

Witnesses can be compelled to give evidence before a master of the court upon a decree of reference.

Taussig MS. 311, vol. 2, p. 668, pl. 1

Friday, 5th June 1724, being the first day of Trinity term; EYRE, Chief Baron, PRICE, PAGE, GILBERT, barons *praesentibus*.

The court now declared that they had spoken with the other judges and that they were all of opinion that, where a reference was made to the Master to examine facts contested between the parties and either of the parties had witnesses who would not appear before the Master to be examined, the court would compel them by a rule to be examined.

And this is to be a rule for the future.

Bunbury 169, 145 E.R. 635

5 June 1724.

Per CURIAM: Where a matter is referred to the Master to make his report thereupon, we will compel the witnesses, though they are strangers, to attend by rule, as they do in the Common Pleas.

485

Hassell v. Wilkes

(Ex. 1724)

A court of equity will not grant an injunction to stay proceedings at common law where the plaintiff can apply to the common law court itself for relief there.

Taussig MS. 311, vol. 2, p. 668, pl. 2

Trinity term 1724.

An action of trespass is brought for an illegal and irregular distress against Gutter and the constables and two appraisers. And this distress was by the command and by the order of one Gutter. Upon the trial of the cause at the assizes, it was referred to the three first men of the jury to make an award in the premises and that the award should be final and judgment should be for the plaintiff for £63 to stand for security for abiding by the award and no [suit in] equity to be brought. The arbitrators award that Gutter should pay £23 and all costs and, upon payment thereof, the plaintiff at law, i.e. Wilks, should release the others. Gutter pays not the money according to the award, whereupon Wilks sues execution on the judgment against the others. And they bring their bill here against Wilks and Gutter, and it prays an injunction against execution and that Gutter should pay the £23 and costs and they be discharged.

And upon the defendants' answer setting forth the award as above, it was moved for an injunction against execution of the judgment because it was unconscionable to take out execution for the whole judgment when only £23 was awarded due and, besides, it was hard to make the bailiffs and constable pay the money, who only acted by the command of Gutter.

But the court refused an injunction because the remedy for the parties' submitting to the award upon any unjust and inequitable proceeding is by applying to the court at law, which had the entire jurisdiction in these matters by virtue of the Statute. And the court thought that the plaintiffs here might be laid by the heels for bringing this bill, it being expressly mentioned in the rule that the parties should not go into equity.

And the Chief Baron [EYRE] thought there was no occasion to go to hearing. *Sed per alios* and by him afterwards, the cause must come to a hearing as against Gutter, against whom the plaintiffs have certainly good equity.

486

Gumley v. Burt

(Ex. 1724)

The tithes of pease and beans grown in fields, rather than in gardens, are great tithes payable to the rector or impropriator.

Taussig MS. 311, vol. 2, p. 672

Thursday, 11 June 1724.

The plaintiff Gumley, as lessee of the vicar of Isleworth, exhibited his bill in this court against Burt, lessee of the Dean and Chapter of Windsor, who were the impropriators of the rectory, and others, parishioners within the said rectory, setting forth the vicar to be entitled to all small vicarial tithes arising within the parish and that he was the lessee of the same and so demanded tithes of pease and beans which were set and sowed in rows in the open fields and were drilled, hoed, and hand-weeded in a garden-like manner, as belonging to the vicar of the said parish. And he also demanded small tithes arising upon the rector's glebe and upon certain lands, parts of Sion Lands. And there was also a demand in the bill of tithe of carrots growing in two gardens.

And for the plaintiff, it was said by Serjeant *Chesshyre*, of counsel with the plaintiff, that pease and beans in gardens were small tithes and that it had been twice determined in this court that pease and beans set in a garden-like manner, though in the open fields, were small tithes and did belong to the vicar. And for this, he cited the case of Stephens and Martin, 20 February 7 Will. III, and Nicholas and Elliot, 28 June 1711.[1] And it was insisted that it was admitted by the answer that the vicar was entitled to all small vicarial tithes in this parish, and though the admission was restrained to such manner as his predecessors, yet that made no alteration in this case, for, if these were small tithes, his right to them was fairly admitted.

On the other side, for the defendants, it was insisted by Serjeant *Stevens* and Mr. *Ward* that, as to the demand of tithes out of the rector's glebe, the case in Cro. Eliz. 578 and Moor 910[2] was a flat refutation to any such pretense. And there had been much more color for the impropriator to have demanded tithes from the glebe of the vicar than for the vicar to do it from the rector's glebe. Secondly, that, as to the demand of the tithes of pease and beans in the open fields, though it was pretty plain that the person who advised the bill took his aim from the two before-mentioned cases, which had been read to the court in this cause, yet those cases were very different from the present, for the first case appears to be a demand by the vicar of pease and beans founded on a composition or endowment between the impropriator and himself.

And, as to the second case, it was this, the vicar, by ancient usage, was entitled to the tithes of pease and beans managed by the plow and spade and the impropriator to the tithes of such as were managed by the plow only. There was an engine or instrument invented which was fixed to the plow and made the plow do the service and answer the end of a plow and spade too. And it was determined in that case that the parishioners' managing their husbandry by this new engine or invention should not deprive the vicar of his right to pease and beans. But in both those cases, there was a right proved in the vicar to the tithes of pease and beans either by endowment or usage, whereas, in the case before the court, there is not the least syllable of proof that the vicar ever had any tithes of pease or beans within the parish, and the vicar has no common right to any sort of tithes. His right to everything he demands must be supported either by an express endowment or by usage which supports an endowment. And, therefore, it is by no means a true proposition that the vicar is entitled of course to all sorts of small tithes. And to call small tithes by the name or title of vicarial tithes is a very inac-

[1] *Stevens v. Martin* (1696), Eq. Cases Exch. 362, Dodd 157, 1 Eagle & Younge 616, 1 Rayner 82, 2 Gwillim 549, 1 Wood 357, *Lords' Journal*, vol. 16, pp. 104-105; *Nicholas v. Elliot* (1711), Dodd 227, 4 Gwillim 1581, 1 Eagle & Younge 698, 1 Rayner 119, 1 Wood 523, Bunbury 19, 145 E.R. 580.

[2] *Blinco v. Backsdale* (1597), Croke Eliz. 578, 78 E.R. 821, Moore K.B. 910, 72 E.R. 990, 1 Gwillim 197, 1 Eagle & Younge 134.

curate expression, at least for properly speaking, there is no such thing as vicarial tithes. But because, by the generality of endowments, all the small tithes have been usually allotted to the vicars, by the process of time, they have gained the name of vicarial tithes.

And to this way of reasoning, the whole court consented. And, therefore, they unanimously dismissed the plaintiff's bill with costs as to the said demands.

And by EYRE, Chief Baron, and GILBERT, baron: Pease and beans are in their nature great tithes, and the setting of them in greater or lesser quantities in gardens or fields does not alter their nature or denomination. And they thought the vicar by the endowment of small tithes was not entitled to pease or beans in gardens.

PRICE, baron, said that the endowment seldom went farther than of pease and beans in the garden or home close.

As to the demand of carrots etc. in two gardens, the defendants had made no defense, so, as to these, there was a decree to account. But the bill was dismissed as to the other matters, for, as to Sion Lands, there was in the lease under which the plaintiff claimed an express exception of all tithes arising on those lands.

N.B. Notwithstanding the Case of Blinco in Cro. Eliz. 578 and Moor 910, above cited, it does not seem to be so clear a point that the lessee of a vicar may not have the small tithes arising upon the glebe of the rectory when the rector's glebe is leased out, for it is expressly asserted by Coke that, if the rector lets his glebe, the rector shall have the great tithes and the vicar the small tithes arising from the glebe. *Sed quaere.*

Bunbury 169, 145 E.R. 636,
1 Rayner 206, 2 Gwillim 656, 1 Eagle & Younge 799

11 June 1724.

A bill was brought by the plaintiff, as lessee of the vicar of Thistleworth, for tithe of peas and beans set and sowed in rows, drilled, hoed, and hand-weeded in a garden-like manner against the lessee of the impropriator, the dean and chapter of Windsor, as being a small tithe. The defendant insists that a great part of the parish is converted into this method of cultivation and that this tithe was never paid to the vicar, but always to the impropriator.

Two cases were quoted by Mr. *Amyrant*, for the plaintiff; first, Stephens v. Martin, Hilary 7 Will. III, which was affirmed upon an appeal to the House of Lords; second, Nicholas v. Elliot, to which it was answered by Serjeant *Stevens* and Mr. *Ward*, for the defendant, as to the first, that it did not appear in that case that the impropriator contested it, nor what the endowment was. And, as to the second, there was a proof of usage by the vicar for forty or fifty years receiving tithe peas and beans, where plow and spade were used; but where the plow only was used, the impropriator received them.

And *per* CURIAM, there being no endowment produced, nor usage proved in the present case, the bill was dismissed as to the demand of peas and beans.

[Order of 11 June 1724 *sub nom.* Gumley v. Birt and Fountleroy: 2 Wood 231.]

[Note also above, Gumley v. Fontleroy (1720-1721), Case No. 127.]

487

Davies v. Williams

(Ex. 1724)

An ecclesiastical court does not have the jurisdiction to try a case based upon a contract for legal services, even if the services are to be performed in the ecclesiastical court itself.

Except for tithes cases, wherever there is a remedy available at common law, the parties may not sue in an ecclesiastical court.

Bunbury 170, 145 E.R. 636

Eodem die [11 June 1724].

There was a libel in the spiritual court for proctor's fees.

Mr. *Bootle* moved for a writ of prohibition, which was granted, for, *per* CURIAM, where there is remedy at law, the spiritual court ought not to proceed, and this case depends upon a contract and retainer, which is triable at law.

The cases cited for the prohibition were 2 Rolle, *Abridgment*, 285, p. 37; 3 Keble 441; Hyde v. Partridge, Salkeld; 2 Keble 810, 845.[1]

Mr. *Weldon*, against the prohibition, cited Register 53; 2 Rolle Rep. 59; 1 Modern 67; 3 Keble 203; 4 Modern 255; 1 Ventris 165; March 45; 5 Modern 238.[2]

Harvard Law School MS. 1082, vol. 1, p. 212

Trinity term 1724.

A suit was brought in the spiritual court for fees, and this Court [of Exchequer] granted a writ of prohibition *nisi causa*.

Mr. *Weldon* showed cause against that rule that the spiritual court was the best judge of their own fees and their attendance is necessary in those courts.

---

[1] *Skinner v. Mingey* (1611), 2 Rolle, Abr., *Prohibition*, pl. 37, p. 285; *Rex v. Hastings* (1675), 3 Keble 441, 84 E.R. 812; *Hyde v. Partridge* (1705), 2 Salkeld 424, 91 E.R. 369, 3 Salkeld 227, 91 E.R. 792, also 2 Lord Raymond 1204, 92 E.R. 295; *Doyly v. Dod* (1671), 2 Keble 810, 845, 84 E.R. 512, 534.

[2] *Registrum Omnium Brevium*; *Anonymous* (1618), 2 Rolle Rep. 59, 81 E.R. 659; *Haughton v. Wilson* (1673), 1 Modern 167, 86 E.R. 805, 3 Keble 203, 84 E.R. 677, also 1 Freeman 113, 122, 129, 89 E.R. 83, 90, 94; *Johnson v. Oxendon* (1694), 4 Modern 254, 87 E.R. 380, also Comberbach 237, 90 E.R. 451; *Anonymous* (1671), 1 Ventris 165, 86 E.R. 112; *Saint John's Case* (1639), March 44, 82 E.R. 404; *Johnson v. Lee* (1696), 5 Modern 238, 87 E.R. 631, also Skinner 589, 90 E.R. 264, Holt K.B. 656, 90 E.R. 1262, 1 Comyns 18, 92 E.R. 937.

And, therefore, they are not to be troubled to follow their suits elsewhere. Reg. 253; 3 Keble 203; 2 Rolle 59; 1 Modern 167; 5 Modern 238, Johnson v. Lee, March 45; 1 Ventris 165; 4 Modern 254.

Mr. *Bootle*, for a prohibition: It appears by the libel that there was a retainer, and, where there is a retainer, there is a contract which makes it properly triable at law. It is custom, and not provincial constitutions, that gives fees. 4 Modern 255. A retainer for money laid out in expenses is not triable in the ecclesiastical court; because the business is done in the ecclesiastical court, that does not give a jurisdiction. And I think a bill in equity is very improper for fees, though the business was done in equity. The case in 1 Modern is where there is a contract, that is properly triable at law, and so [it is] against what Mr. Weldon cited it for. 2 Rolle, *Abridgment*, 285. If they are permitted to proceed in an ecclesiastical court, it will repeal the Statute of Limitations,[1] which does not operate there. 6 Modern, Hyde v. Partridge, 2 Anne.[2]

Weldon replies: It is only a common expression used in libels and not an actual retainer. And the cases are that you may sue in both courts. 1 Rolle 420; Sir Wm. Jones 230.[3]

[To the] objection of 3 Keble 441, I admit that the validity of grants is properly triable at law.

Chief Baron EYRE: Wherever there is a proper remedy at common law, there, they shall not sue in the ecclesiastical court, except for tithes. This depends on a contract and retainer, which is properly triable at law. That case of 2 Rolle 59 is no authority. 3 Keble 203; 2 Keble 810, 845. In Johnson v. Lee, a writ of prohibition was granted, 5 Will. III. And I am for a prohibition.

PRICE: I am for a prohibition. And I do not understand 1 Ventris 165.

GILBERT: I would grant a prohibition, but I would have it declared upon. If fees are founded on provincial constitutions, then an ecclesiastical court has jurisdiction, but, if on the custom, it is triable at law. I am doubtful whether a Christian bishop under the penalty of damnation can settle this matter between the proctor and his client. And so he concluded for a prohibition.

Taussig MS. 311, vol. 2, p. 677, pl. 2

Trinity term 1724.

[There was a] rule to show cause why a [writ of] prohibition should not be granted to the ecclesiastical court in a suit there by a proctor for fees in carrying

---

1 Stat. 21 Jac. I, c. 16 (*SR*, IV, 1222-1223).

2 *Hyde v. Partridge* (1705), Holt K.B. 428, 90 E.R. 1135, 2 Salkeld 424, 91 E.R. 369, 3 Salkeld 227, 91 E.R. 792, 2 Lord Raymond 1204, 92 E.R. 295, 11 Modern 43, 88 E.R. 872.

3 *Reynolds v. Newberry* (1616), 1 Rolle Rep. 420, 81 E.R. 578, 1 Eagle & Younge 259; *Halsey v. Halsey* (1631), W. Jones 230, 82 E.R. 121, 2 Gwillim 468, 1 Eagle & Younge 371.

on a suit in that court. And the libel expressly suggested a retainer and set forth several disbursements by the proctor in the cause made by him at the request and special instance of Davis.

Mr. *Weldon* showed cause and cited 2 Rolle's Rep. 59; March 45; 1 Mod. 167; Horton and Wilson; 1 Ventr. 165; 5 Mod. 238, Johnson and Lee; 4 Mod. 254; Johnson and Oxenden, 3 Keble 203, 441.

Bootle, contra, cited 4 Mod. 255; 2 Rolle's *Abr.*, 285, pl. 37; Easter 2 Ann., Hide and Partridge, and the last case he cited to enforce his argument for the prohibition, *viz.* that, if it was not granted, the Statute of Limitations would be in a great measure defeated. See 1 Rolle's Rep. 420; William Jones 230.

N.B. Mr. *Weldon*, in his original argument, besides the above-mentioned authorities, cited two cases to have been adjudged in this court between Skelton and Lee and Joslyn and Frogate, where it was held that no prohibition lay in such a case for fees.

But Lord Chief Baron [EYRE] said he could nowhere find any of these cases. And he said there was no case except that in Rolle's report where a prohibition had been absolutely denied. In all the other cases, prohibitions should have been granted. And so he determined it should in this. And let the plaintiff declare, and, then, the point might be solemnly settled. *Alii barones concordaverunt.*

488

Phillips v. Symes

(Ex. 1724-1726)

An omission in an answer can be cured by an allegation in a cross-bill.

A modus decimandi *in lieu of tithes in kind that is uncertain is void.*

Bunbury 171, 145 E.R. 636,
1 Rayner 207, 217, 2 Gwillim 654, 1 Eagle & Younge 800

15 June 1724.

A bill was brought by the rector of Stoke Abbots in the County of Dorset, among other things, for the tithe of furze, coppice and underwood, milk, calves, wool, and fruit, etc. of gardens.

The defendants insisted, first, that no tithe of furze ought to be, or ever was, paid, unless it was sold; secondly, nor any tithe of coppice or underwood, if cattle were depastured where the wood grew; thirdly, they insist upon a garden penny for the produce of the garden; fourthly, upon a *modus* of 8d. for every cow and 4d. for every heifer in lieu of the tithe of milk and calves of such cow and heifer; fifthly, that 3s. 4d. was payable for every score of sheep shorn out of the parish, and so proportionably for a less number than twenty, or for a less time than a year, for the wool and lamb of such sheep.

Note: The defendants omitted in their answer to specify the day whereupon the said respective *modus*es were payable. And, therefore, to supply that defect, they exhibited their cross-bill to establish these *modus*es and alleged the same to be payable at Easter and also to compel the rector to keep a bull, which, by custom, he ought to do for the use of the parishioners, and so it was admitted by the defendant to the cross-bill.

Upon hearing both these causes together, it was decreed *per* CURIAM, first, that the defendants ought to account for furze and coppice and underwood, for the defence, as to these, amounts, in effect, only to a *non decimando*; secondly, that, although the plaintiff in the original cause had a right to a decree for tithe in kind, because the defendants had omitted the day on which the *modus*es were payable, yet now that defect was supplied by their cross-bill, both causes being now but as one and it would introduce great inconsistency in the decree if the *modus*es should for that reason be adjudged void in the original cause and established in the cross-cause, provided they are good in other respects. Thirdly, the garden penny was allowed. Fourthly, the 8d. for a cow and 4d. for an heifer were adjudged good, though it was objected that it was not good for the milk and calf, for, then, it would be payable although there was no calf, to which it was answered that, then, the 4d. and 8d. would be payable, for it was payable for all the tithe a cow etc. produces, which is only milk and calf. Fifthly, to the 3s. 4d. for every score of sheep shorn out of the parish and so proportionably for a less number than twenty or for a less time than a year for the wool and lamb of such sheep.

It was objected, first, that this is too rank; secondly, it is payable for wool and lamb, though the lambs might be fallen before the sheep were removed, and the tithe of lamb would be payable before; thirdly, there is great uncertainty because of the fractions which might arise when a small number only was removed; fourthly, it is liable to fraud, for the parishioner might remove them out of the parish for a little way only just before shearing time and then bring them back again.

To these objections, it was answered *per* CURIAM, we cannot take notice of this, nor enter into the consideration thereof. (But query this reason.) Secondly, it is payable at Easter and is a satisfaction for all the wool and lamb before that time. Thirdly, the same objection might be made to arise from the fraction, where only a small quantity of wool was and tithe in kind paid. Fourthly, if fraud appeared, as it would be taken to be, under the circumstances put in the objection, then, the parishioner should pay tithe in kind, as well as if they had continued in the parish, to which the *modus* does not extend. So the defendants were decreed to account in the original cause for tithe of the furze and wood. But the bill was dismissed as to the rest, and the other *modus*es were established on the cross-cause. And the defendant was decreed to keep a bull pursuant to the custom.

But afterwards, 3 February 1725, this cause came on to be reheard and principally as to the *modus* of 3s. 4d. for every score of sheep shorn out of the parish etc. And, upon inspection of the cross-bill, the payment was alleged to be at Easter or otherwise when the sheep shall be sold, which being uncertain, *per* TOTAM

CURIAM, this *modus* was adjudged void. *Vide* 1 Rolle Rep. 38, 39; 2 Leonard 70; Moore 913; Hobart 107.[1]

Taussig MS. 311, vol. 2, p. 686

Monday, 15 June 1724. John Phillips, clerk, plaintiff v. John Symes, Thomas Studley, and John Hicks, defendants, *et e contra*.

The plaintiff, as rector of Stoke Abbots in the County of Dorset, exhibited a general tithe bill against the defendants, but the chief matters complained of were the subtraction of tithes of wood, furze, milk, calves, wool, lamb, and fruit.

The defendants, by answer, insist that no tithe is due for furze but when the same is sold nor for coppice or underwood where the beasts feed and depasture, otherwise where no feeding or depasturing. They insist on a *modus* of 8d. for every cow, 4d. for every heifer in lieu of tithes of milk and calves of every such cow and heifer, 1d. for every garden within the said parish, and 3s. 4d. *per annum* for tithes of wool and lamb for every score of sheep shorn out of the same parish and so proportionably for any less time than a year or number of sheep and lambs. But, in their answer, they alleged no day of payment for their *modus*es. But, in their cross-bill brought to establish their *modus*es, they set forth their *modus*es to be payable at Easter.

The court, upon hearing the causes, both coming on together, determined that the day of payment in the defendants' cross-bill would supply the want of alleging it in their answer and so they might allow the *modus*es as a good bar to the plaintiff's demand notwithstanding that defect. And they also decree an establishment of them upon the cross-bill too. And so they did, *viz.* they allowed all the *modus*es, but sent the defendants to account for the tithe of wood and furze, which by them are due though they are not sold and though beasts are fed or depastured in the wood or coppice grounds.

The *modus* of 3s. 4d. for a score of sheep shorn out of the parish was what was chiefly opposed, first, as being too rank, secondly, as being liable to perpetual fraud, thirdly, as making the payment of tithes of lambs dependent on the accident of the sheep's being shorn out of the parish. What answers were given by the court to these objections I know not, for I was not present at the hearing of the cause, but the court established all the *modus*es as is before-mentioned.

Harvard Law School MS. 1082, vol. 1, p. 208

Trinity term 1724.

---

[1] *Mascall v. Price* (1614), 1 Rolle Rep. 38, 62, 176, 81 E.R. 310, 328, 412, also 2 Bulstrode 238, 80 E.R. 1089, 1 Eagle & Younge 225; *Anonymous* (1587), 2 Leonard 70, 74 E.R. 366, 1 Eagle & Younge 91; *Stebs v. Goodlock* (1588), Moore K.B. 913, 72 E.R. 992, also 1 Leonard 99, 74 E.R. 92, 1 Gwillim 158, 1 Eagle & Younge 93; *Wilson v. Bishop of Carlisle* (1615), Hobart 107, 80 E.R. 256, 1 Gwillim 279, 1 Eagle & Younge 250.

The plaintiff Phillips, as rector of Stoke Abbots in the County of Dorset, brought his bill for tithes.

The defendants insist that no tithes are due for furze unless sold, 8d. for a cow yearly in lieu of milk and calf, 4d. for a heifer in lieu of the tithe thereof, 1d. for a garden in lieu of fruit, 2d. for Easter offerings, 3s. 4d. for and in lieu of the wool and lamb of every twenty sheep shorn out of the parish and so proportionable for a lesser number.

Note: In the answer, no time was fixed for payment of these [. . .]. But the defendants in their cross-bill supply that by fixing a particular time when such *modus*es were payable.

Pengelly, for the defendant, insisted that no tithes were due for furze unless sold. By common right, no tithe [is] due for sheep shorn out of the parish, so that 3s. 4d. is an additional recompense, which the occupier is not obliged to pay.

Serjeant *Hawkins*, for the plaintiff, insisted that tithe furze was due of common right. 1 Rolle, *Abridgment*, 653; March 26; Hicks v. Woodhouse.[1] The *modus* for every score of sheep is uncertain as to feeding out of the parish and is liable to a fraud. And so much paid for milk and calf is bad. Cro. Eliz. 446; Lutwyche 1051, 1052.[2]

Mr. *Ward*, for Syms: Tithe furze and wood is due of common right, and, to exempt wood spent in the house, a particular prescription ought to be laid. Tithe lambs are due when they fall and are independent of the tithe of wool when shorn. And this 3s. 4d. is so liable to a fraud, for, if fed out of the parish for half an hour, then, it is payable as well for wool as lambs and so [he might] shear them out of the parish at his election and so pay nothing for tithe of lambs. Here is no time fixed in the answer to the original bill as when these sums are payable, and the plaintiff ought to recover on his original bill and independently of the cross-bill.

Chief Baron [EYRE]: I take it that both causes must be considered together. Therefore, the time of payment being ascertained in the cross-bill, it is sufficient. And, in this case, the decrees would clash and be contradictory if they were separated. But I think that the defendants must account for the wood and furze. But I think the other *modus*es are good and must be established and even 3s. 4d. is

---

[1] *Barham v. Goose* (1619), 1 Rolle, Abr., *Dismes*, pl. H, 10, p. 653; *Anonymous* (1639), March 25, 26, 82 E.R. 395; *Hicks v. Woodhouse* (1697), Dodd 171, *sub nom. Hicks v. Woodeson*, 4 Modern 324, 336, 87 E.R. 422, 429, 1 Eagle & Younge 592, 2 Gwillim 550, 3 Lord Raymond 116, 92 E.R. 595, 1 Lord Raymond 137, 91 E.R. 987, 12 Modern 111, 88 E.R. 1200, Skinner 560, 90 E.R. 252, Comberbach 403, 90 E.R. 555, Carthew 392, 90 E.R. 827, Holt K.B. 671, 90 E.R. 1271, 2 Salkeld 655, 91 E.R. 558.

[2] *Grysman v. Lewes* (1595), Croke Eliz. 446, 78 E.R. 686, also Moore K.B. 911, 72 E.R. 991, 1 Gwillim 165, 1 Eagle & Younge 112; *Morton v. Briggs* (1696), 2 Lutwyche 1043, 125 E.R. 580, also 1 Lord Raymond 242, 91 E.R. 1058, 2 Gwillim 561, 1 Eagle & Younge 624.

good and not too high. And no fraud appears in this case. And when it does, a decree would be pronounced against the fraud. And this might have a good commencement. And, therefore, I shall establish the *modus*es. And the plaintiff is to have costs for wood and furze and to pay costs as to the others. And the plaintiffs in the cross-cause are to have costs.

And it was so ordered *per* CURIAM.

Harvard Law School MS. 1082, vol. 1, p. 261

Hilary term 1725/26.

The plaintiff, as rector of Stoke Abbots in the County of Dorset, by his bill, prays to have an account of tithes in kind. And the defendants insist on 3s. 4d. for every twenty sheep, and so proportionately, depastured within the parish and shorn out of the parish in lieu of tithe wool and lamb. And the defendants having omitted to fix the day for the payment of the *modus*, they exhibit a cross-bill to have this *modus* established and so fix Easter for the time of payment of otherwise as soon as they were sold, as it happened.

Pengelly, for the defendants, at first offered an issue.

Chesshyre, for the plaintiff: The *modus* of 3s. 4d. for every twenty sheep is not good.

Ward, for the plaintiff: The *modus* is not good. Lutwyche 222.[1]

Chief Baron [GILBERT] declared that a *modus* cannot be established without a trial and there being a cross-bill to establish it. Therefore, the *modus* must be admitted or sent to be tried.

Bootle, for the plaintiff: The practice has been that, if the *modus* is not good as insisted on for the plaintiff, to permit the plaintiff to make the objection, for we were told in Tyrrell v. Kennet[2] that, after a trial, we came too late.

Bunbury, for the defendants: The court has ruled it both ways, either to go to the matter of law or try the fact.

CHIEF BARON: I will not enter into the matter of law until the fact is admitted.

HALE [cited] Salkeld, tit. Tithes, Hicks v. Woodson. And I think it may be proper to see whether the *modus* is good at law or not, for it would be sending a vain thing to be tried if the *modus* is not good in point of law.

The court adjourned it to another day for the counsel for the plaintiff to answer whether they will admit the *modus* proved or not, and, if so, then the court would permit them to speak to the matter of law.

At another day, the counsel for the plaintiff, Phillips, admitted the *modus* proved. But then, he insisted that the *modus* was not good in point of law.

Chesshyre, for the plaintiff, Phillips: The question is, as to the tithe wool and lamb, which is insisted on for 3s. 4d. per score for all sheep depastured and shorn

---

[1] *Stinton v. Yates* (1685), 1 Lutwyche 222, 125 E.R. 116.

[2] *Tyrrell v. Kennett* (Ex. 1723-1725), see above, Case No. 378.

out of the parish and so proportionately for any greater or lesser number, no time was fixed in the original bill, but the cross-bill ascertains the time at Easter yearly or at selling as it happens. If anything is uncertain in this *modus*, the court cannot establish it. 3s. 4d. is uncertain. If there be forty lambs and forty sheep to be shorn, what is to be paid and how is it fixed? And it seems to be only for the wool as to shearing and not for the lambs.

The custom as insisted on extends to wool and lamb. And it is not good because the first confines it to sheep's wool and to the latter part for wool and lambs too. No *modus* can be good of one tithe in lieu of another; part of the thing itself cannot be good for the rest, as part of the wool cannot be good for wool and lamb. And the payment of a sum of money will not alter the case. 13 Reports 45; 2 Inst. 609; Moore 454, Munday v. Lewis; Sir Simon Degge 309, 312; 1 Rolle, *Abridgment*, 651, No. 17; 2 Lutwyche 1052, Moreton v. Briggs.[1]

And the time of payment is uncertain and not fixed and, therefore, not good. At Easter or at selling is not good because the sheep may be kept all the year within the parish and the day before shorn out of the parish and yet 3s. 4d. becomes due and the selling is made part of the custom. Whitehall v. Offley, Cro.,[2] as to time of payment.

It is entirely uncertain whether the money is to be paid at Easter after the shearing or before; if after, then it is carried on to another year. And therefore, it is not good, for a *modus* is to be annually paid, as well as the tithes.

In all events, the plaintiff is entitled to costs to the time of the answer because no time was laid.

Serjeant *Hawkins*, for the plaintiff: The custom is uncertain and unreasonable; at Easter or selling, when shall the parson have his recompense, for it seems to leave an election in the occupier. 1 Rolle, *Abridgment*, 647, 648; Hobart 107, Wilson v. Bishop of Carlisle; March 79; 1 Modern 229.[3]

Mr. *Edward Ward*, for the plaintiff Phillips: The law requires certainty in respect of the recompense and the person and the time of payment. And this fails in all. And a *modus* ought to be certain and durable. Hobart 40. This should be a certain recompense because it comes in lieu of a certain duty. The consideration of this *modus* is the shearing of the sheep out of the parish. And it is in the election of the occupier, and, therefore, it is unreasonable and as bad a *modus* as

---

[1] *Case of Modus Decimandi* (1609), 13 Coke Rep. 37, 45, 77 E.R. 1448, 1455; E. Coke, *Second Institute* (1642), p. 609; *Monday v. Lovice* (1596), Moore K.B. 454, 72 E.R. 690, 1 Eagle & Younge 118; S. Degge, *Parson's Counsellor*; *Sherrington v. Fleetwood* (1596), 1 Rolle, Abr., *Dismes*, pl. D, 17, p. 651; *Morton v. Briggs* (1696), *ut supra*.

[2] *Offley v. Whitehall* (Ex. 1717), see above, Case No. 28.

[3] *Wilson v. Bishop of Carlisle* (1615), 1 Rolle, Abr., *Dismes*, pl. B, 5, p. 647, and *ut supra*; *Weedon v. Harden* (1641), March 79, 82 E.R. 420, 1 Eagle & Younge 401; *Moor v. Field* (1677), 1 Modern 229, 86 E.R. 848, 1 Eagle & Younge 511.

absque visu et tactu et fraude. And, therefore, it should be disallowed because it is subject to fraud.

This *modus* could not have a reasonable beginning, and no such agreement could have been good. The parishioner is considered in the nature of an adversary, and so says Lord Holt in Lord Carlisle's Case.

No satisfaction was offered for dry sheep, for this is in lieu of tithe wool and lambs. But what becomes of wether sheep and by what rule is this shearing to be allowed? And this payment of 3s. 4d. is dependent upon the subsequent act of the parishioner, and, therefore, it is not good. March 79; Rolle, *Abridgment*, 650; Holt 107.[1]

And the law abhors the setting up of a *modus* if it lies only in the breast of the parishioner, which was the reason that the uncertainty of a pound rate was always disallowed. So was Startup v. Doderidge and Bean v. Lee.[2] And because this matter is laid only in the breast of the parishioner and the parson did not know what to demand, for the rule *id certum est quod certum reddi potest* is not good in the case of a *modus*. And so it was resolved in this court in Harrison v. Sharpe, in this court; Cro. Eliz. 446.[3]

So this *modus* is uncertain in point of recompense, liable to fraud, and uncertain in time of payment, for, as was before said, it was in the election of the occupier. And if the parishioner does not sell, would anything be due? No. But it must amount to a *non decimando*. And there is not one single instance as to such a *modus*.

To carry a load of peat is uncertain. Puller v. Kilner, in this court.[4] And it is uncertain in respect of the remedy for the parson, Bishop of Hereford v. Cooper,[5] for it would be a casual and contingent remedy, which is not good.

Easter offerings are due in all events. And, therefore, he prayed a decree for the plaintiff.

Bootle, for the plaintiff Phillips: According to this *modus*, if sheep are not shorn out of the parish, then the parson is entitled to tithes in kind. It must be admitted

---

[1] *Weedon v. Harden* (1641), *ut supra*; 1 Rolle, Abr., *Dismes*, p. 650; *Regina v. Weston* (1705), Holt K.B. 107, 90 E.R. 958, also 1 Salkeld 122, 91 E.R. 115, 2 Lord Raymond 1197, 92 E.R. 291.

[2] *Startup v. Dodderidge* (1705), 2 Lord Raymond 1158, 92 E.R. 266, 2 Salkeld 657, 91 E.R. 559, 11 Modern 60, 88 E.R. 885, 1 Eagle & Younge 666, note also *Doddridge v. Startop* (1690), Dodd 91, Public Record Office, E.126/15, f. 359v, 1 Wood 283, 1 Eagle & Younge 566; *Bean v. Lee* (1713), Dodd 231, 1 Rayner 120, 1 Eagle & Younge 703, 2 Gwillim 609, Public Record Office, E.126/20, f. 71, 1 Wood 537.

[3] *Harrison v. Sharp* (Ex. 1724), see below, Case No. 490; *Grysman v. Lewes* (1595), *ut supra*.

[4] *Tully v. Kilner* (Ex. 1723), see above, Case No. 386.

[5] Perhaps *Bishop of Hereford v. Cowper* (1730-1732), 3 Swanston 158, 36 E.R. 813, Bunbury 293, 145 E.R. 678, 3 Eagle & Younge 1236.

that one species of tithes cannot be given in satisfaction of another, so it shall not be in the power of the parishioner so to allot it. If one hundred lambs fall in the parish and are sheared out of the parish, then nothing is due, so that shearing the sheep out of the parish is to be a satisfaction for these tithe lambs, which is one species of tithes in lieu of another, *viz.* shearing for the lambs. Cro. Eliz. 446. In all *modus*es, nothing should be dependent on the will of the parishioner. And all tithes ought to be paid within the year, which, according to this *modus* as to the time of payment, *viz.* of selling, may be carried over to another year.

Chief Baron [GILBERT] seemed to think that the payment 'or otherwise at selling' was uncertain.

Pengelly, for the defendant Syms: This coming upon a rehearing and [there being] no complaint in the petition as to offerings, therefore, that is out of the case. As to costs to the time of the first answer, I must allow the answer was insufficient. But now, the whole case is to be considered as to both bills and answers. This *modus*, as laid, is good, which tends to supply and maintain the parson and to hinder a fraud by taking and carrying sheep out of the parish without making the parson a satisfaction.

I insist upon it that a sum of money may be a satisfaction for part of the tithe or for all of the tithe. And it is not to be compared to the case of one species of tithes in lieu of another. The *modus* of 3s. 4d. would be good for sheep sheared within the parish. And why not without the parish? A sum of money is good as to part or the whole. Bishop of Winchester's Case, in Coke's reports; Dr. Finch v. Sir Thomas Gerard; 1 Siderfin 443, Crouch v. Risden.[1] And this answers all the cases in Moore and Sir Simon Degge.

[To the] objection of Cro. Eliz., Jesmand v. Lewis,[2] [he] responded 1 Rolle Rep. 38, 39, 62.[3]

And a distinction has always been made between money and one tithe in lieu of another, and it was never determined against what I contend for, that a sum of money might be in lieu of the whole or any part of the tithes.

[To the] objection as to fraud, [he] responded this is to prevent fraud, *viz.* the sheep going out of the parish. The putting in of lambs will not vitiate the *modus*. The cross-bill confines it to sheep only.

[To the] objection as to time of payment, [he] responded there is no discharge unless the sheep were sold before Easter, and this payment vests in the parson at Easter unless the sheep are sold before.

---

[1] *Wright v. Wright* (1596), 2 Coke Rep. 38, 76 E.R. 501, also Moore K.B. 425, 72 E.R. 672, Croke Eliz. 474, 511, 78 E.R. 726, 760; *Finch v. Masters* (Ex. 1724), see above, Case No. 463; *Crouch v. Risden* (1670), 1 Siderfin 443, 82 E.R. 1207, also 1 Ventris 61, 86 E.R. 43, 2 Keble 612, 84 E.R. 385, 1 Eagle & Younge 481, Lincoln's Inn MS. Misc. 500, f. 114v (Edward Ward's reports).

[2] *Grysman v. Lewes* (1595), *ut supra.*

[3] *Mascall v. Price* (1614), *ut supra.*

Here is a sum of money in lieu of tithes. And the right of tithes in kind is generally the payment.

So he concluded for the defendants in the original cause, and the plaintiffs in the cross-cause.

The CHIEF BARON said that he thought otherwise. It opens the time of payment and leaves it indefinite. Is not a tithe due by the lamb's falling? And can anything the parishioner will afterwards do take away the right to those tithes?

PAGE: Is it not subject to fraud by feeding the poorest sheep in the parish and shearing the best sheep out of the parish?

Bunbury, for the defendants: it must be admitted that no tithes in kind were ever paid in respect of such sheep. Though much has been insisted on of one tithe for another, this is only in respect of the wool upon both bills and answers, which will be taken together. These tithes only happen once in a year; if at Easter, there is no uncertainty. 'Or otherwise sold' is only to be taken for such as are sold before Easter. 1 Rolle, *Abridgment*, [Dismes], 651.

[To the] objection it is liable to fraud, [he] responded that fraud is not to be presumed. 1 Rolle, *Abridgment*, 652; 1 Rolle, *Abridgment*, 648, a good *modus*.[1]

Probyn, for the defendant Syms: [See] Cro. Eliz. 475, Moore 603.[2]

CHIEF BARON: Though a custom is admitted, yet if it is unreasonable, it cannot stand in a court of equity, and so it is not to be established. And nothing can be good where it is in the power of the parishioner to supplant the minister's maintenance.

We must consider this case as it stands upon the cross-bill, and no critical interpretations are to be admitted. There is an interest vested by the falling of the lambs as to the tithe in the parson. And it cannot be divested by the act of the parishioner. The words 'or otherwise upon selling as it shall happen' are too uncertain, and the parson does not know when to come for a recompense. And these latter words leave it entirely uncertain. And if the words had been as above and joined 'within the year', it might have had another construction. I think that, in this case, it would put the maintenance of the minister in the power of the parishioner. And, therefore, I cannot establish it.

PRICE agreed it is a bad *modus*.

PAGE agreed that the cross-bill should be dismissed.

And they decreed [them] to account.

Note: There [were] long examinations by the plaintiff as to other matters, which were against the plaintiff, so that costs were waived on both sides, and the account was to be taken without costs.

---

[1] *Anonymous* (1619), 1 Rolle, Abr., *Dismes*, pl. G, 1, p. 652; *Delman v. Barton* (1609), 1 Rolle, Abr., *Dismes*, pl. C, 4, p. 648.

[2] *Sherington v. Fleetwood* (1596), Croke Eliz. 475, 78 E.R. 727, Moore K.B. 430, 599, 909, 72 E.R. 676, 784, 990, also Gouldsborough 147, 75 E.R. 1055.

Taussig MS. 311, vol. 2, p. 850

Hilary term 1725/26.

The court refused to hear the plaintiff's counsel on the validity of the *modus* unless they would first admit that the *modus* was well proved.

Taussig MS. 311, vol. 2, p. 853

Thursday, 3 February 1725/26.

The plaintiff now admitted that the *modus* was proved and went on to show that the *modus* was void in law.

Serjeant *Chesshyre, pro querente*: (But I did not hear him.)

Serjeant *Hawkins*: The *modus* is uncertain and unreasonable. First, it is uncertain as to the time of payment, which, in the cross-bill is laid at Easter or otherwise when sold. Second, *non constat* whether lambs shorn out of the parish are to pay and if not, then, it is a *non decimando* as to lambs. 1 Rolle's *Abr.*, 648, pl. 4; March's Rep. 79; 1 Mod. 229.[1]

Mr. *Ward*: In the cross-bill, the time supplied by the cross-bill is payable upon Easter yearly or otherwise so soon as they shall be sold as it shall happen.

(1) There is no consideration for this *modus*, for the shearing of the sheep out of the parish, which is alleged to be the consideration, depends upon the arbitrary and voluntary act of the parishioner himself and the parishioner is in the nature of an adversary to the parson.

(2) There is no satisfaction for dry sheep, for, if the lambs and sheep in the *modus* are to go together, then the sheep must be ewes.

(3) [As to] the tithe of lamb, which is a different species of tithe from wool [and] is to depend upon the shearing the wool, lamb is due when fallen [and] payable when yeaned. But, here, sheep shall not be paid at all if the sheep are not shorn in the parish. 1 Rolle's *Abr.*, 650, 652; Startup and Doddrige; Bean and Lee, adjudged void for uncertainty.

But *certum est quod certum reddi potest* in all other cases but in the case of *modus*es, Cro. Eliz. 446, because parishioners may put the less into the sheaves and leave the more for raking.

Secondly, they have failed in time of payment, for this is uncertain or otherwise when sold. Suppose he never [*blank*], then no tithe [were due] and yet there is no remedy to compel a sale, nor [is it] confined to any time.

Bootle: One species of tithe is no satisfaction for another species; so neither ought the management or ordering of one sort of tithes to influence the payment of another. Cro. Eliz. 446, Greisman and Lewis, is a case falling within the reason of this case.

---

[1] *Delman v. Barton* (1609), *ut supra*; *Weedon v. Harden* (1641), *ut supra*; *Moor v. Field* (1677), *ut supra*.

Mr. Serjeant *Pengelly*: If the 3s. 4d. had been laid as a *modus* for tithes of wool and lamb in the parish, it would certainly have been good. Mascall and Price, 1 Rolle's 37, 38, cites the Case of Greisman and Lewis, and it is denied by Lord Coke, so that the general doctrine is that, though tithes in kind of one sort cannot go in discharge of tithes of another, yet a sum of money may be in discharge of several sorts of tithes. And the case of Finch and Gerrard established a money *modus* for hay and all small tithes.

There is a difference between the bill and answer in point of laying it, for the bill leaves out the words 'and lambs' after the [word] 'proportionably', though the answer adds them.

As to uncertainty of time, 'on Easter or otherwise', the *modus* is expressly laid to be paid yearly or the yearly sum so that its not being payable if sheep are not sold within the year is out of the case.

Bunbury: The *modus* upon a whole record taking it upon the cross-bill and answer is no more than 3s. 4d. for tithe of wool and lamb of every score of [*blank*].

As to uncertainty, either of Easter or otherwise when sold, so if sold before Easter, they must pay at that time. If not, then they must be paid at Easter.

[There is] no case in law that I know of that prohibits or condemns a *modus* which puts it in the power to pay tithes in kind or a *modus*. 1 Rolle's *Abr.*, 652, letter G, no. 1.[1]

As to its being liable to fraud, [fraud] is not to be presumed and other cases are as liable to fraud as this and yet have been established, as the case in 1 Rolle's *Abr.*, 652, letter G, no. 1, and 648, letter C, no. 4; Moor 913; 2 Leonard 70; Stubbs and Goodlock.[2]

Robins: Cro. Eliz. 475, Moor 603.[3] Money is payable as a *modus* for several sorts of things. As to certainty of time, the bill supplies it and the same certainty is not a requisite in English as in law proceedings. The selling of the sheep is governed by the word 'yearly'.

Chief Baron [Gilbert]: If there be anything in a *modus* which would supplant any part of the maintenance of the minister, it is not to be established in a court of equity. And we are to take it upon the parishioner's bill and must establish it in the very words of that bill now in the *modus* laid, which is for wool and lamb. The parson's tithe for lambs is vested in him by law at the time of dropping. But, by this custom, it is to be divested by the shearing of the sheep out of the parish, which is purely at the parishioner's election. And as to time, we have no authority to supply the custom, but we must take it as laid. And it is not confined to selling within the year, as laid in the bill.

---

[1] *Anonymous* (1619), 1 Rolle, Abr., *Dismes*, pl. G, 1, p. 652.

[2] *Anonymous* (1619), *ut supra*; *Delman v. Barton* (1609), *ut supra*; *Stebs v. Goodlock* (1588), *ut supra*; *Anonymous* (1587), 2 Leonard 70, 74 E.R. 366, 1 Eagle & Younge 91.

[3] *Sherington v. Fleetwood* (1596), *ut supra*.

And all the court being of that opinion, they altered the former decree and dismissed the cross-bill and decreed an account upon the parson's original bill.

Costs were waived on both sides by consent.

[Order of 15 June 1724: 2 Wood 228.]

489

Laurence v. Jones

(Ex. 1724)

Easter offerings are due to the vicar only and never to an impropriator.

Bunbury 173, 145 E.R. 637,
1 Rayner 210, 217, 2 Gwillim 662, 1 Eagle & Younge 801

18 June 1724.

A bill was brought by the vicar of Brookworth in the County of Gloucester for tithes. It was decreed *per* TOTAM CURIAM that Easter offerings were due of common right to 2d. per head unless it had been customary to pay more, that the vicar ought to have a decree accordingly, though there was no proof of Easter offerings ever having been paid, there being a lay impropriator, who is not entitled to offerings, but only he who exercises the spiritual function.

And it was said by Baron GILBERT that offerings were a compensation for personal tithes.

Taussig MS. 311, vol. 2, p. 693, pl. 1

Trinity term 1724.

Per CURIAM: Easter offerings are due of common right, but the quantum is governed entirely by custom.

Per PAGE: 2d. is the common quantum unless there is a custom for more or less.

Per GILBERT: Easter offerings came in lieu of personal tithes. The canons for the paying of which sort of tithes were never received in England. That Easter offerings were due of common right was determined in the cause of Dodson and Oliver.[1]

And *per* CURIAM: Easter offerings are due to the vicar only and never to the impropriator.

Harvard Law School MS. 1082, vol. 1, p. 209, pl. 1

Trinity term 1724.

---

[1] *Dodson v. Oliver* (Ex. 1720-1724), see above, Case No. 128.

GILBERT said that offerings were in lieu of personal tithes and the canons in relation to tithes were never received.

490

Harrison v. Sharp

(Ex. 1724)

In this case, an alleged modus decimandi *in lieu of tithes in kind was held to be invalid.*

Taussig MS. 311, vol. 2, p. 688

Trinity term 1724. John Harrison, clerk v. John Sharp and Thomas Hurst.

The plaintiff, as vicar of North and South Grantham in the County of Lincoln, exhibited his bill for [tithes of] calves, lamb, sheep, [and] wool fed upon certain lands within the vicarage.

The defendants, by answer, insist that, time out of mind, it has been the usage and custom that, when any of the said enclosed pasture grounds in Harrowby within the vicarage of New Grantham and which were the lands in the defendants' possession are plowed or sown with corn or grain of any kind or when they are laid for meadow or mown and made into hay, the tithes in kind are paid and belong to the impropriator of the said rectory or his tenants, but, when the same are eaten and depastured with sheep or cattle, that, then, the occupier of such ground pays to the vicar 1s. in the pound of the yearly rent or value thereof and no more upon some day after Michaelmas yearly in lieu and discharge of all tithes whatever. And, in the same answer, the defendants insist that, in case the court should be of opinion that the plaintiff is not bound by this as a *modus*, he ought to give reasonable notice of his intention to break the said composition.

There was also a defense set up in relation to the tithes of a pingle in Sharp's possession, which was set forth in this manner, *viz.* that ever since he could remember and, as he has heard and believes, there has been paid yearly in lieu of the tithes of a small yard or pingle 1s. at Easter, that the same had been accepted in lieu of tithes.

Upon the hearing of the bill and answer opened in Hilary term last, the court ordered a case to be made with relation to the *modus*es. But there being some disagreement concerning settling a case, the court in Easter term ordered the cause should come on in the paper causes and stand to be heard as the other causes. But, at the first time the cause came on, the validity of the *modus* was shortly spoken to and the cases of Startup v. Doddridge and Bean v. Lee and Smith v. Rowcliffe, in this court Hilary 1717,[1] were cited as express authorities

[1] *Startup v. Dodderidge* (1705), 2 Lord Raymond 1158, 92 E.R. 266, 2 Salkeld 657, 91 E.R. 559, 11 Modern 60, 88 E.R. 885, 1 Eagle & Younge 666, note also *Doddridge v. Startop* (1690), Dodd 91, 1 Wood 283, 1 Eagle & Younge 566; *Bean v. Lee* (Ex. 1713),

in point against the validity of the *modus*. And on the other side, the case of Doctor Grant was insisted upon. And it was also argued that a custom to pay a year's value for a fine according to the improved rent at the time of admittance to a copyhold was a good custom and there is just the same uncertainty in that case as in this, and, therefore, unless there was a different rule in determining customs relating to tithes than to other things, this might be a good *modus*.

At the second time of mentioning the cause, Lord Chief Baron [Eyre] said that he had looked upon the case of Startup and Dodderidge and that he thought it was an express authority against the present *modus*, that, in that case, a [writ of] prohibition was upon argument denied in the King's Bench and afterwards in the Common Pleas and, according to the notes of the case, it came into this court by an English bill and it was held an ill *modus*. And, therefore, he thought the authority of that case was not now to be disputed and that it was not fitting to let the counsel debate it. And, therefore, unless this case could be distinguished from that, for his part, he should be against giving way to an argument.

And Mr. Baron Page said that the *modus* was ill upon another account, *viz.* that, as it was now stated, in case any part of the land was agisted, tithes were to be paid according to the *modus* though other parts of it was plowed.

Now, the cause coming to be heard in the paper on this day, the defendant's counsel gave up the argument as to the *modus*, the court having so strongly upon former occasions declared against the *modus*.

And the court now disallowed the *modus* and also determined that the defendants could not excuse themselves from costs upon the suggestion of its being a composition and that the parson had not given notice of determining it in case it was a composition because it was insisted on as a *modus*.

And as to the defense in relation to the 1s. for the pingle, it was not laid as a *modus*; so, as to that pretense, there was no color to dismiss the plaintiff's bill. And, though the defendant does say that the plaintiff had accepted the 1s., yet there was no allegation of payment during the time demanded in the bill nor any proof by witnesses of any such payment. And, therefore, upon the whole, the defendants were decreed to go to an account upon the whole of the plaintiff's demands and that with costs.

Bunbury 174, 145 E.R. 637,
1 Rayner 211, 217, 1 Eagle & Younge 801

Eodem die [18 June 1724].

A bill was brought by the plaintiff as vicar of Grantham in the County of Lincoln, who therein demands tithes of lands in the vill of Harrowby. The defendants insisted on this *modus, viz.* that, when any of the inclosed pastures in Harrowby were plowed and sown with corn or grain of any kind or laid for meadow

---

Dodd 231, 1 Rayner 120, 2 Gwillim 609, 1 Eagle & Younge 703, 1 Wood 537; *Smith v. Roocliff* (Ex. 1718), see above, Case No. 35.

and mown and made into hay, tithes in kind were paid to the rector, but, when eaten and depastured with sheep or cattle, then the occupier paid to the vicar 1s. in the pound of the yearly rent or value thereof, and no more, upon some day after Michaelmas, yearly, in lieu and satisfaction of all tithes whatsoever.

Per opinionem TOTIUS CURIAE, this *modus* was adjudged upon the authority of the case of Startupp v. Dodderidge; and, therefore, they gave no opinion upon the uncertainty of the day.

[Order of 18 July 1724: 2 Wood 224.]

491

Snowball v. Vicaris

(Ex. 1724)

In this case, a written contract was set aside in a court of equity in a suit to be relieved against it upon parol evidence that was contrary to the written memorandum.

Bunbury 175, 145 E.R. 638

22 June 1724.

A judgment was obtained at law in an action of *assumpsit* upon an absolute promissory note for £50 against the plaintiff Snowball, who brings his bill to be relieved, suggesting the note was really agreed to be conditional, *viz.* 'that unless Ram's Insurance rose to £100 percent. I [the now defendant] give you my word I will never trouble you for the money.'

It was objected by the defendant, first, that the plaintiff ought not to be permitted to enter into this evidence now because he might have done it at law, either upon the general issue or by pleading specially, secondly, that the plaintiff ought not to give parol evidence to prove the intent of a note in writing under hand.

But *per* CURIAM (*dubitante* EYRE, Chief Baron), the plaintiff was permitted to go into this evidence and was relieved.

And Baron PRICE said he could not distinguish this case from that of Lady Clarges v. Williams in this court, 20 February 1723.[1]

492

Murriet v. Lyon

(Ex. 1724)

Where a defendant's wife is hostile to him and friendly with the plaintiff, the defendant can answer without her.

---

[1] *Lady Clarges v. Williams* (Ex. 1724), see above, Case No. 465.

Bunbury 175, 145 E.R. 638

23 June 1724.

The defendant moved for liberty to answer without his wife, upon an affidavit made that she declared she should not answer with her husband, but that she loved the plaintiff better and would stand by him, which was ordered accordingly.

493

Blacket v. Finney

(Ex. 1724-1725)

An injunction can be granted to an ecclesiastical court to remove a tithes dispute into the Court of Exchequer where a modus decimandi *in lieu of tithes in kind is claimed.*

Where a modus decimandi *is pleaded to be paid at an uncertain date, the pleading can be amended to allege a certain date of payment.*

Bunbury 176, 145 E.R. 638,
1 Rayner 212, 217, 2 Gwillim 661, 1 Eagle & Younge 817

25 June 1724.

The bill suggested that there was a *modus* of 4d. per score of all sheep going on Gayerfield in the parish of Ryton in the County of Durham in lieu of tithe of lamb and wool, that the defendant libelled in the spiritual court for tithes in kind, that the plaintiff moved for a prohibition in the Court of Pleas in Durham, but it permitted a consultation to go, and he depended on relief in this court, and he prayed to have the *modus* established. The defendant, Doctor Finney, insisted there was no such *modus*, but that the 4d. was in lieu of the milk of the ewes, which was usual in that country.

Now, upon motion for an injunction to the spiritual court, the defendant's counsel insisted that this was proper matter of suggestion on a prohibition and also the defendant had in the answer denied the *modus*.

But *per* CURIAM, there being some dispute between the parties whether the *modus* is as alleged in the bill and as the spiritual court cannot try the *modus*, we will grant the injunction.

Harvard Law School MS. 1082, vol. 1, p. 240, pl. 3

Trinity term 1725. Finney v. Blackett.

The bill was to establish *modus*es, which were paid at or about the 25 April, being St. Mark's day, *viz.* 4d. per score and so proportionable.

[It was] objected that the *modus* was not good [because] 'at or about' [is] too uncertain. Harrison v. Sharp, in this court.[1]

[1] *Harrison v. Sharp* (Ex. 1724), see above, Case No. 490.

Chief Baron GILBERT and PRICE said that they would give leave to amend it since the *modus* is not denied as to the quantum or time of payment, but only for what such *modus* is.

PAGE thought that this ought not to be amended unless others were suffered to do the same.

But the court permitted it to be amended, *quod mirum est*. And at the sittings after this term, it being amended accordingly, an issue was directed whether there was such a *modus* or not.

Taussig MS. 311, vol. 2, p. 802, pl. 1

Trinity term 1725.

In a bill to establish a *modus* of 4d. for tithe wool and lamb, it was laid that that sum was immemorially paid or ought to be paid yearly at or about 25th April.

And the court were of opinion that, 'at or about' was uncertain, but they gave the plaintiff leave to amend his bill, paying costs, and the cause to stand over to the setting down of causes.

Taussig MS. 311, vol. 2, p. 808

Trinity term 1725.

The court directed an issue to try whether a *modus* of 4d. per score for sheep fed upon a parcel of ground called Gayer's Field in the parish of Ryton in the County of Durham was paid in lieu of wool and lamb of such sheep, for the rector insisted in his answer that the 4d. was only paid in lieu of the milk of such sheep.

Bunbury 198, 145 E.R. 646,
1 Rayner 221, 1 Eagle & Younge 817

10 June 1725.

A bill was brought to establish a *modus* for 4d. per score of sheep in lieu of the tithe of lamb and wool payable or which ought to be paid on or about the 25th day of April yearly. It was objected at the hearing to the uncertainty of the time of payment.

And the court allowed the objection, but gave the plaintiff liberty to amend upon paying the costs of the day.

8 Modern 375, 88 E.R. 267, 3 Rayner 1100

Upon a bill exhibited to establish a *modus*, the plaintiff set forth that this *modus* was payable on or about the twenty-fifth day of April etc., which is a void *modus* because it must be payable on a certain day, as was lately resolved in the case of Harrison and Clarke.[1] Besides, it is laid disjunctively in the bill, *viz*. that the parishioners of etc. 'constantly paid or ought to pay so much', whereas it should

[1] *Harrison v. Sharp* (Ex. 1724), see above, Case No. 490.

be 'constantly paid and ought to pay' etc. Then, as to the *modus* for sheep, it is laid that the parishioners usually paid 4d. for every score and so *pro rata*, but it does not show what they should have paid for a less number in case there were not so many as a score.

The defendant put in his answer and, amongst other things, admitted that the *modus*, as set forth in the bill was payable 'on or about' the twenty-fifth day of April etc.

But the plaintiff perceiving the faults in his bill, as before mentioned, moved for leave to amend. And he cited the case of Reynolds v. Rogers,[1] where the plaintiff suggested a *modus*, but did not lay it payable on any certain day, neither did the defendant in his answer confess any day of payment so that, no certain day of payment appearing, either in the bill or answer, the defendant, who was plaintiff in a cross-bill, having laid it to be payable on a certain day, it was held good.

THE COURT: This is a case where an amendment of these things will not alter the nature of the proofs. And the day being admitted by the defendant in his answer, it is reasonable that, on payment of costs, the plaintiff should amend, especially since his right appears upon the pleadings. Therefore, it would be too rigorous not to give him leave to amend, for, in such case, the decree must be founded on his bill, and, if his bill will not support it, though a day is confessed in the defendant's answer, he can have no good decree.

[Order of 24 June 1725: 2 Wood 250.]

494

Holden, *qui tam* v. Weeden

(Ex. 1724)

Where a criminal offense is created by a statute, every circumstance constituting the offense must be precisely alleged in the pleading and a general allegation of being contrary to the statute will not cure the defect.

An incomplete pleading can be cured by a verdict in a civil case, but not in a criminal case.

Bunbury 177, 145 E.R. 638

Eodem die [25 June 1724].

This was an information against the defendant upon the Statute 11 & 12 Will. III,[2] for having India silks in her custody knowing them to be such, whereby she became liable to the penalty of £200. There was a verdict for the plaintiff. And now, in arrest of judgment, several exceptions were taken to the information,

[1] *Reynolds v. Rogers* (Ex. 1717), see above, Case No. 26.

[2] Stat. 11 Will. III, c. 3 (*SR*, VII, 582-586).

but they were overruled. At last, an objection was made that this was no offence at common law, and, therefore, everything ought to be shown in the information to make it an offence within this Act of Parliament, and, though there was an averment that the commissioners had appointed warehouses etc., yet they have not averred that there were warehouses still continuing at the time of the seizure or that security was not given, as by the Act is directed, to which it was said that, the defendant being to have the benefit of them, it laid upon her part to show it.

But *per* CURIAM, the *contra formam statuti* is only a conclusion from the premises. And they thought the case in Sir W. Jones 156, Bedo v. [*blank*],[1] not to be law. So much ought to appear in the information, as to make this matter a complete offence within the Statute. Upon the Stat. 15 Eliz.,[2] it must be averred in an indictment that the defendant did not exercise the trade at the time of the Statute, although it is above one hundred years ago. And upon the objection that it did not appear that there were warehouses continuing or that the goods were not delivered out upon security, judgment was arrested.

And Lord Chief Baron EYRE seemed to think there was nothing in the distinction between an exception and proviso mentioned in 1 Levinz 26.[3]

Harvard Law School MS. 1082, vol. 1, p. 213

Trinity term 1724.

This was an information for prohibiting the using of East India goods and wearing apparel and furniture, being found in the defendant's house. She was found guilty upon the Stat. 12 Will. III and, thereby, incurred the forfeiture of £200, knowing the goods to be East India [goods].

Mr. *Hungerford* moved in arrest of judgment:

(1) [He] insisted on the Statute made the last sessions wherein the sense of the legislature was that goods made up into furniture before Christmas 1722 should not be liable to the forfeiture. And this is a new law; the informer ought to have taken notice of it;

(2) That wrought silks of China were the occasion of the Act of Parliament and, therefore, as laid in the information, *pecia serici* is not sufficient to convict the defendant. *Sericum* is silk generally, for *seres* is a silk worm.

So as to calicoes, it must be those painted or dyed in the East Indies, for all calicoes are not prohibited, and, therefore, it should be laid in the information painted and dyed there. And to incur the forfeiture, the silks must be manufactured there. And the words *operata et parata* only relate to the ginghams and not to the calicoes. In all penal laws, the information concludes *contra formam statuti*,

[1] *Bedoe v. Alpe* (1627), W. Jones 156, 82 E.R. 83.

[2] Stat. 5 Eliz. I, c. 4 (*SR*, IV, 414-422).

[3] *Whitwicke v. Osbaston* (1661), 1 Levinz 26, 83 E.R. 280, also 1 Keble 20, 83 E.R. 786.

but whether when [. . .] there are different acts of Parliament whether the conclusion ought not to be particular is submitted to the court. Cro. Jac. 141.[1]

Mr. *Bootle*, for the defendant: The verdict being general, if any part is not good, then the whole will be set aside. '*Pecia serici*' is not sufficient, and *operata et parata* only relate to the ginghams.

GILBERT thought those words took in the whole preceding words.

Chief Baron [EYRE] thought otherwise, for, if those words had been at the end of the sentence, it might have been so, but not where they come in the middle of the sentence, as here.

Bootle: There is a second clause in the Statute which gives a protection to such as are in the king's warehouse or in any other place where security is to be given and though attempted in the information as thought material, yet it was not sufficiently laid not to be in the warehouse or where security was given. And it is necessary to allege that there were warehouses *in esse*.

GILBERT: If one piece is within the Act of Parliament, then the forfeiture of £200 is incurred.

The court thought there was some weight in the objections and ordered it to be spoken to again.

Note: Upon the last objection of Bootle about the warehouses, judgment was arrested, *quod vide*.

Taussig MS. 311, vol. 2, p. 671

Trinity term 1724.

Mr. *Hungerford* moved in arrest of judgment upon this information, which was grounded upon 11 & 12 Will. III, ca. 10, that the information only charged that the goods were not made up into furniture before 29th September 1701, whereas the late Act of Parliament allows making up before Christmas last and so the prosecutor should have amended his information, the new Act of Parliament being made before the trial. Secondly, the Act of Parliament speaks of wrought silks, whereas the information is of a piece of silk called white damask and two pieces of silk called China tafaty without saying *operata* or any English word equivalent thereto.

EYRE, Chief Baron: Damask and tafaty are certainly wrought silks.

But the court doubted as to the sufficiency of the silks and whether they were sufficiently alleged to be wrought abroad and whether the allegation that warehouses were appointed was sufficient.

Et adjornatur for further argument.

Taussig MS. 311, vol. 2, p. 696

Trinity term 1724.

---

[1] *Broughton v. Moore* (1606), Croke Jac. 142, 79 E.R. 123.

First objection: That the goods described in the information are not prohibited by the Act, and it was laid down for a rule that, if part of the goods laid in the information are prohibited and another which are not, upon a general verdict, no judgment can be given for the prosecutor. Painting, printing, staining, and dying can only extend to calicoes.

Second objection: It is not alleged that there were warehouses continuing at the time these goods were found in the defendant's custody.

Thirdly, though there were such workhouses and these goods were found out for such warehouses, yet it will not follow necessarily that the goods are seizable, for they might be carrying to the waterside for transportation and, in such case, to be sure, they would not have been forfeited.

Hungerford on the same side: 11 & 12 King William is against wrought silks. And the information does not charge that the silks seized were wrought silks.

Secondly, the information only charges that the goods were not made up into furniture before 29th September 1701, whereas the late Act allows making up before Christmas last, and so the prosecutor should have amended his information upon the making of the new Act of Parliament since it was made before the trial.

Attorney General [*Yorke*]: The constant known distinction between crimes and contracts is that, in one case, judgment may be given for what was well charged, in contracts not.

Quod post 29em Septembris 1701 una pecia serici vocata Damask *duae peciae serici vocata* China taffeta *una toga et tunicula serici anglice* a taffeta gown and petticoat *sex peciae serici vocata* gingham *pictata vocata* painted *tincta vocata* dyed *impressa vocata* printed *vel depicta vocata* stained *in Persia, China, sive Indiis orientalibus in partibus transmarinis ante tunc parata et operata importata fuerunt in Magnae Britanniae viz.* Ratcliffe *non existentia ante importationem eorum factorum anglice* made up *vel usitata in aliquo genere apparati vel supellectilis quodque quaedam Elizabethae.*

Serjeant *Shepherd*:

[1.] If one crime be well charged, we may have judgment.

2. The *anglices* show that it was wrought silk.

3. The new Act extends only to furniture. Besides, this information was before the Act.

4. The warehouses, the most material exception, is not averred to be now continuing.

In answer to this, first, it is not material to make any averment at all. The Act is that such goods shall not be worn or used. And the appointing of warehouses is a matter of instruction by the officers in order to prevent the mischief. The offense is wearing or using or having the custody of them out of any warehouse, and this is a sufficient charge so that the allegation of warehouses being appointed is surplusage.

The allegation used by way of argument that these goods might be carrying to be exported again was matter of evidence and should have been taken advantage of at the trial.

If an averment was necessary, this is sufficient after the verdict.

Sed per Chief Baron [Eyre]: It might be so in civil cases, but not in criminal. There is no one instance of an averment in the latter case aided by a verdict. Sir William Jones 156; Butler reserved on a lease; Dyer 312; Cro. Eliz. 749.[1]

These cases were cited by Mr. *Ward* to show that the not being of warehouses should come by way of defense and that the prosecutor need not make such an averment. Raymond 487; Bradley, *qui tam* v. Long, in this court.[2]

Bootle: The case in Jones depends upon the words of the Act where the exception comes in by a proviso. 1 Lev. 26; the difference between an exception in the body of the act and a proviso; 1 Ventr. 134, Eaton v. Barker,[3] to the same effect.

Adjornatur.

Taussig MS. 311, vol. 2, p. 701

Trinity term 1724. Rex v. Weedon.

The court having taken time to consider of the exceptions taken to the information in this case, the Lord Chief Baron [Eyre] delivered the opinion of the court that judgment should be arrested for the insufficiency of the information and that in the two respects following, *viz.* because it was not charged in this information that there were any warehouses into which the goods censured in the defendant's custody might be properly lodged nor was it charged that she had not given security for the exporting of them and if there were in fact no warehouses appointed for receiving them or she had in fact given security for exporting them, then, the having them in her custody was not an offense within this Act.

The Statute on which this information was grounded is the 11 & 12 Will. III, ca. 10. The second clause prohibits the wearing or using the commodities therein mentioned, but under the limitations after-mentioned, the second clause for the better effecting the same provides the goods, after importation, shall be forthwith carried into warehouses etc. and shall not thence be taken but in order for exportation and not until security be given and that such of the aforesaid goods found in any other place other than the aforesaid warehouses shall be forfeited and the person in whose custody the same are found shall forfeit £200.

---

[1] *Bedoe v. Alpe* (1627), *ut supra*; *Dawson v. Alford* (1572), 3 Dyer 312, 73 E.R. 706; *Hill v. Langley* (1600), Croke Eliz. 749, 78 E.R. 980.

[2] *Hitchins v. Stevens* (1683), T. Raymond 487, 83 E.R. 254, also 2 Shower K.B. 233, 89 E.R. 909, T. Jones 232, 84 E.R. 1233; *Bradley, qui tam v. Long* (Ex. 1721-1723), see above, Case No. 203.

[3] *Whitwicke v. Osbaston* (1661), *ut supra*; *Eaton v. Barker* (1671), 1 Ventris 134, 86 E.R. 92.

It has been objected that the information alleging that these goods were found in the defendant's custody *extra aliquod repositorem contra formam statuti* was sufficient and that the defendant might have given in evidence upon it either that there was not any warehouse or else might have shown she had given security and then she could not have been found guilty, for that these are in the nature of excuses and ought to come of the defendant's side and the contrary need not be alleged in the information.

And to maintain this objection, the case in Dyer 312, [an action of] trespass under the Statute for distraining the *averia carucae*, the plaintiff need not show that he had other sufficient distress, but the defendant must, to excuse himself, say and show that the plaintiff had no other distress.

And the case in William Jones 157, an information upon the Statute of Edw. VI,[1] for engrossing butter, alleged that the defendant had obtained by emption divers parcels of butter to sell *contra formam statuti*, but did not allege that the defendant had not this butter by demise or *concess'* of the term, and yet it was held well.

And the case in Cro. Eliz. 749, which was an action of debt upon the Statute 1 Ric. III, ca. 3,[2] for taking a man's goods, who was imprisoned for felony before an attainder, and though the declaration did not set forth that the goods were taken *ea de causa*, yet it was held well and that the words *contra formam statuti* helped it.

As to the first of these cases, the Chief Baron said it was good law, but the reason of it was because the distraining the *averia carucae* was contrary to the rules of the common law. 2 Inst. 134; 1 Syd. 348.[3] But where an offense was created by a statute, there, every circumstance constituting the offense must be precisely alleged. And, therefore, he held that neither the case in Cro. Eliz. 749, which was determined by the authority of the case in Dyer, was law nor the case in Sir William Jones. And the case in William Jones was expressly held not to be [good] law in the case of the King and Alstone, Hilary 4 Will. & Mar., in the King's Bench.

And upon this ground, it was held that, upon the Statute for Exercising a Trade, 5 Eliz., ca. [*blank*], an averment that the defendant did not exercise the trade at the time of the making of that Statute, though it was then 100 years after it, was held necessary. 1 Syd. 203.[4]

Et nota: The book seems to warrant this notion *quoad* a prosecutor *sed nemi quoad* the king, for the book, *quoad* the king *contra formam statuti* is sufficient.

---

1 Stat. 3 & 4 Edw. VI, c. 21 (*SR*, IV, 120).

2 Stat. 1 Ric. III, c. 3 (*SR*, II, 478-479).

3 E. Coke, *Second Institute* (1642), p. 133; *Horthbury v. Levingham* (1667), 1 Siderfin 348, 82 E.R. 1149.

4 *Buxton v. Bateman* (1662-1664), 1 Siderfin 88, 201, 82 E.R. 987, 1056, also T. Raymond 52, 83 E.R. 29, 1 Keble 345, 370, 386, 420, 433, 457, 83 E.R. 985, 1000, 1009, 1029, 1037, 1051, 1 Levinz 71, 83 E.R. 302.

And the CHIEF BARON said that he could never understand what the books meant by distinguishing between exceptions coming in by way of a proviso and exceptions in the body of the clause, for, by him, judges must take the whole act together and, as the statutes are written upon the Parliament rolls, there are no breaks or paragraphs but one continued series of lines from the beginning to the end, and the breaks or paragraphs are made by printers. *In civile est nisi tota perspecta sententia de aliqua parte judicare.*

And so, by him, here, the offense being created entirely by statute and every circumstance requisite to constituting the offense not being shown, the *contra formam statuti*, which is only a conclusion from the premise well charged, will not supply the defect of any circumstance which is not charged if necessary to be charged. And, therefore, the information is faulty. And the judgment was accordingly arrested.

Perhaps, in a civil case, this omission would have been cured by the verdict, as want of attornment, but there are no instances of any material omission cured by the verdict in penal prosecutions. See the case of Northey, *qui tam* v. Levy, Trinity 1710, which seems to me to warrant this case and shows that defects in these informations are not aided or [. . .]d by verdict.

495

Thompson's Case

(Ex. 1724)

A person can be found in contempt of court for impugning the justice of the court in an insulting publication of a case.

Taussig MS. 311, vol. 2, p. 693, pl. 2

Trinity term 1724.

Mr. Attorney [General *Yorke*] moved the court for an attachment against Mr. Thompson for printing his case in a reflecting manner thereby impeaching the justice of the court. And he said that a partial state of the case was sufficient for the court's animadversions, but chiefly he insisted on the preface as ironical. And he cited the case of Doctor Browne[1] and the case of the author of *The True Briton*,[2] and that these sort of libels were of the most dangerous consequence as affecting the very foundation of a free government which depended on the faithful administration of justice in the several courts of Westminster Hall and the

[1] *Regina v. Brown* (K.B. 1706), Holt K.B. 425, 90 E.R. 1134, 11 Modern 86, 88 E.R. 911, British Library MS. Hargrave 66, f. 88, Harvard Law School MS. 4081, vol. 2, p. 88 (Herbert Jacob's reports).

[2] *Rex v. Payne*, cited in *Rex v. Charlesworth* (1730), 1 Barnardiston K.B. 342, 94 E.R. 230.

credit and reputation which they preserved by the justice of their proceedings. He said he might have exhibited an information in his own name for this offense, but he chose rather this method of attachment because it was past controversy that this court had the power to vindicate its own proceedings.

And to prove the fact upon Mr. Thompson, several affidavits were read from the persons concerned in presenting the case.

And upon the reading of these affidavits, the court granted an attachment against him.

And the Chief Baron [Eyre], who gave the rule, observed that, in such cases, it was not usual to give the offender a day to show cause, but he was to answer *in vinculis*.

496

Note

(Ex. 1724)

An information for a forfeiture can be amended but not so as to defeat a statute of limitations.

Taussig MS. 311, vol. 2, p. 695

Trinity term 1724.

Per Chief Baron [Eyre], it is certain that amendments may be made in informations as well as in actions and that after a plea is pleaded. But whether you can amend an information by taking a further compass of time backward, that is very doubtful to me.

And, at last, all the court agreed they could not amend so as to lay an importation so far back beyond the time mentioned in the information as would deprive the party of the benefit of the Statute which limits informations for forfeitures to be brought within two years of the importation, for this would be to set aside that Statute by a collateral act of the court.

497

Gould v. Pierce

(Ex. 1724)

A plaintiff cannot be dismissed from the action after a replication has been filed.

Taussig MS. 311, vol. 2, p. 700, pl. 1

Trinity term 1724.

The court would not give way to striking a plaintiff out of the bill after a replication.

498

Morey, *qui tam* v. Whaley

(Ex. 1724)

An information of seizure of forfeited goods should be grounded only on a single cause of forfeiture.

Taussig MS. 311, vol. 2, p. 700, pl. 2

Thursday, last day of the [Trinity] term 1724.

N.B. An information of seizure was brought for certain goods as forfeited. And, in the first part of the information, the cause of forfeiture was assigned on one Act of Parliament, then the information goes on and recites the seizure of the same goods by another, *bona et merchandiza*, and assigns another cause of forfeiture on another act of Parliament, and so a third.

And to this information, instead of demurring, the defendant pleads, that, as to the goods mentioned in the first part of the information, the general issue; and to the goods mentioned in the other parts of it, he disclaims any property in them, whereupon the officer seizing would have entered judgment for the two last parcels.

But the court was now moved that no judgment should be entered until the issue joined on the first part of the information was tried.

And so it was ordered by the court. And they entirely condemned this new invention.

Taussig MS. 311, vol. 2, p. 710

Trinity term 1724.

The Attorney General [*Yorke*] moved to amend his information and so to lay but one cause of forfeiture, which was granted, the party [being ordered] to plead anew and to give security to export or pay the duty.

N.B. This day there was another writ of delivery granted on the same terms, and the court thought it very reasonable because very often the appraised value did not amount to the value of the duties.

499

Fasting v. Pauncefort

(Ex. 1724)

A bond to indemnify for private debts and public debts is void as to the private debts but valid for the public ones.

It is not a fraud for a person to take a larger and better security for a person's behavior the more reason he has to doubt it.

Taussig MS. 311, vol. 2, p. 707

Sittings after Trinity term, Monday, 5 July 1724.

A bill [was brought] by Faiting *et al.*, the securities of one Ball, against Pauncefort. And it was brought to be relieved against a judgment which Pauncefort had recovered against them upon a bond to the king *solvendo eidem domino*, which they had entered into as securities for Ball's well-answering and accounting [for] the money he should receive as clerk to Mr. Pauncefort, who by the recital of the condition in the bond appeared to be Cashier of the Excise. And the condition of the bond was that Ball should answer to the crown and to Mr. Pauncefort [for] all moneys etc. This bond was entered into 10th December 1715, after which time, there were several new appointments of cashiers, *viz.* Lord Delaware and others were appointed with Pauncefort to be cashiers.

And there were two principal arguments insisted on the behalf of the plaintiff, *scil.* that this bond was to secure Pauncefort's private demands as well as the crown's money and so the bond was void.

Sed per CURIAM: This part of the condition, though it may avoid the bond as to the subject's money, yet cannot avoid the bond as to the crown, but it will still stand good for the crown money.

Secondly, they objected that the condition would only extend to such embezzlements as Ball should have been guilty of during the continuance of that appointment which was in being at the time of entering into the bond and not to any embezzlements during the appointments [of the others].

But *per* CURIAM: It appears that Mr. Pauncefort, during all this time, was cashier though other persons were added to him from time to time and Ball was not a deputy cashier, but only a clerk to Pauncefort in that office, so that this is not at all like the case of Lord Arlington and Merrick, in Saunders, nor to the case of Bartlett v. Attorney General, sittings after Michaelmas term 1709,[1] nor to the case of Seabrook v. Pauncefort, in late Lord Chief Baron Montagu's time, sittings after [*blank*].

Thirdly, they objected that Mr. Pauncefort had accumulated securities in this case and that, at the time of the bond entered into, Mr. Pauncefort knew him to be greatly in arrear so that the drawing the plaintiffs into this new security was a fraud.

Sed per CURIAM: It is no manner of fraud for a man to take larger and better security for a man's behavior the more reason he has to doubt it. And so the court decreed that the account should be taken of the state of the account between Pauncefort and Ball on the 10th December 1715 and then the plaintiffs to

[1] *Lord Arlington v. Merricke* (1672), 2 Williams Saunders 403, 85 E.R. 1215, also 3 Keble 45, 59, 84 E.R. 586, 593; *Bartlett v. Attorney General* (1707-1709), Eq. Cases Exch. 561, Dodd 218, Parker 277, 145 E.R. 779, Public Record Office, E.127/26, f. 70, E.127/27, f. 33.

account with Pauncefort for all the subsequent embezzlements of public money after that time until Pauncefort quit the Cashier's Office.

500

Vernon v. Minshull

(Ex. 1724)

A court of equity will grant an injunction to forbid execution of a final judgment at common law on the ground of newly discovered evidence.

Bunbury 178, 145 E.R. 639

At Serjeants' Inn, *post* Trinity 1724.

The plaintiff brought his bill against the defendant to be relieved against a judgment at law upon a suggestion and proof that two notes which would have been a proper defence at law were mislaid at the time of the trial and, since that time, have accidentally been found, whereupon the plaintiff was relieved, and an injunction was granted to stay execution on the judgment.

501

Anstruther v. Christie

(Ex. 1724)

In this case, a court of equity granted relief against a final judgment at common law that was founded upon a harsh bargain.

Where a contract for stock is registered, it need not be mentioned for whose benefit it is where the beneficiary is named in the contract.

Bunbury 178, 145 E.R. 639

At the same sittings [Serjeants' Inn, *post* Trinity 1724].

A bill was preferred by the plaintiff [Sir Alex Anstruther] against the defendant to be relieved against a judgment at law by default upon a South Sea contract for £9445 for £1000 stock to be transferred on the 21st of December 1720.

The plaintiff, by his bill, suggested that the defendant had not registered, was not possessed of the stock as the Statute requires, that he had not tendered, that it was an usurious contract, two notes being given for £1350 for continuing the contract for three months.

For the defendant, it was objected that these matters were all a proper defence at law, and, therefore, that the plaintiff ought not to be permitted to enter into this evidence, and that there was no difference that the judgment was by default, for that it was the plaintiff's own neglect that he did not plead and make his defence at law, of which he ought not to take advantage. And it was also insisted upon for the defendant that, since here was a contract in writing produced, the plaintiff ought not, by parol, to give evidence that it was a continuance of a former contract.

But notwithstanding these objections, the court permitted the plaintiff to go into proof of the before mentioned several matters. But afterwards, an issue was directed to try whether the defendant was possessed of stock as the Statute requires.

Note: It appeared in this cause there had been the most shameful subornation of perjury that ever appeared to a court, Sir Alexander [Anstruther] having, in his own handwriting, dictated what his witnesses were to swear, with a description of the defendant's person, time, place, sums, etc.

Taussig MS. 311, vol. 2, p. 713

Trinity term 1724.

In this case, it was said by Chief Baron [EYRE] and agreed to by the other barons that, where a contract for stock was made between A. and B. and a memorial thereof signed by B. was registered, the registry or memorial registered need not mention that the contract was made for his benefit, but it should be presumed. But if it be registered by any other person whose name was not in the contract, there ought to be an express assertion that the contract was made for his benefit, *quod mihi videtur consentaneum juri et rationi*, though Sir Peter King, Chief Justice of the Common Bench, seemed, as I was told, clear in his opinion that, where the contract was registered by one of the parties to the contract itself, yet it ought to be expressed that it was made for his benefit.

502

Miles v. Webber

(Ex. 1724)

Where a parson made a contract for a parishioner to retain his tithes and pay a sum of money at a certain date and the parson dies before the date for the payment, a court of equity will grant relief on account of the accident of the death and order the other party to pay the sum agreed to with a deduction for the tithes that accrued after the death of the parson.

Harvard Law School MS. 1082, vol. 1, p. 214, pl. 2

Sittings after Trinity term 1724.

This was a bill brought by the plaintiffs [Miles and Brandon], as executors of Henwood, who was rector of Satterley in the County of Devon, who died the 10th of September 1721. And this bill was brought for tithes or a composition due for tithes for the half year ending the 29th of September 1721. The defendant Webber insisted upon it that he was under a composition with the said Henwood at £1 8s. 0d. *per annum* payable half yearly at Lady Day [25 March] and Michaelmas [29 September] and that he constantly paid the same to the rector until the living was under a sequestrator and then he paid it to the sequestrator which was to Lady Day 1721, but that, Henwood dying the 10th of September 1721 and not living to Michaelmas, there was nothing due. But yet the plaintiffs insisted on that half year and that an equitable construction ought to be put upon it that, since the defendant had the whole tithes, most of which accrued in this half year, that, therefore, the defendant ought at least to pay his composition or to account for the tithes that so accrued in the meantime, *viz.* from Lady Day to Michaelmas.

There was some question in this case as to the deprivation or sequestration, but the Act of Pardon[1] intervening and having relation to the first day of the sessions, *viz.* 8 October 1720, therefore, the court was of opinion that this temporary deprivation was gone. So the single question remained as to this half year from Lady Day to Michaelmas where the rector died the 10th of September, as before set forth.

We that were for the defendant insisted upon it that Henwood, the former rector, could not have his tithes in kind because he was barred by the composition and that he could not have the composition money because he did not live to Michaelmas, but died the 10th September preceding, and that the occupier is obliged to pay the half year due at Lady Day, though no tithes arise during that time, and so we compared it to a rent that was not due.

PRICE inclined that the most equitable construction was to decree for the plaintiffs [Miles, Brandon, *et al.*], for that it would be too hard for the occupier to have the whole tithes and yet to pay nothing for them. And the successor cannot have them because they were severed during the lifetime of the former parson, and neither can he have the composition because that is determined. Therefore, if any other construction should be put upon it, then, the occupier is to run away with the whole tithes and to pay nothing for them.

Baron PAGE: I cannot agree with my brother though it may seem hard that the defendant should receive the whole tithes and pay nothing for them. But this is an accident that happens for the benefit of the tenant, as another may be for the benefit of the executors, as if the parson dies the 26th of March; though no tithes arise between Michaelmas and Lady Day, yet the executors shall have the composition due at Lady Day. And the tenant must have the benefit of this half year. And the Lord Somers would not relieve against it.

GILBERT: This is in the nature of a lease and the enjoyment of the land by the party under a tenant for life. And a court of equity will not relieve in that case. And why in this? And it will be difficult to rate and apportion it. And, therefore, he then inclined for the defendant.

---

[1] Stat. 7 Geo. I, c. 29.

Chief Baron EYRE: I admit that, if it is considered as a rent, then, I must agree that it is gone. But this is a contract for sale of the tithes, and it cannot be considered as a rent, but as a bargain and sale of the tithes and the payment of a sum in gross to be paid at a day *in futuro*. But he desired to consider of it at another day.

And within two days afterwards, the court gave their opinion, *absente* Page.

GILBERT: A retainer though by parol is good for life, and so it is not to be taken as a lease. And so he thought the most equitable construction would be for the defendant to pay the composition to the executors deducting what tithes arose between the 10th of September and Michaelmas.

PRICE: The payment to the sequestrator was good as to the first half year due at Lady Day, but, though the other half year was not due but since the lessee had the tithes, I think that he ought to pay the executors of the old parson. And I think that it is unreasonable for the lessee to take the tithes and pay nothing for it.

Chief Baron [EYRE]: A retainer for one year is good, and so is Hobbs v. Braisfield. But there, it was settled in the nature of a sale for tithes. Cro. Eliz. 188, 249; 2 Rolle, *Abridgment*, 63; Yelverton 94.[1]

GILBERT said that no law could set aside a parol contract.

CHIEF BARON: It cannot be discharged without a deed because tithes lay in grant.

GILBERT said that a composition or a personal contract does not sound in grant.

CHIEF BARON: As long as the parishioner enjoys, he ought to have paid the consideration. And this is a sum in gross payable *in futuro*. And he ought to pay to Michaelmas.

So, upon the whole, a decree was given for the plaintiffs [for the defendant] to account for the composition money deducting for the tithes that arose between 10 September and Michaelmas Day. *Quod vide*. And the best opinion seems to be Page's in this case.

Taussig MS. 311, vol. 2, p. 711

Wednesday, July 7th or 14th, 1724.

The plaintiff, as executor of Henwood, who was rector of Saterby in County of Devon, exhibits his bill against the defendant for composition money for tithes or else for the tithes in kind arising *infra* Lady Day 1721 and 10th September 1721, on which day the rector died. And the case was that the rector had made an agreement with the defendant for the defendant's own tithes from three years to three years at 28s. *per annum* payable half yearly, 14s. at Lady Day and 14s. at

---

[1] *Bugg v. Woodward* (1590), Croke Eliz. 188, 249, 78 E.R. 444, 504, also 2 Leonard 29, 74 E.R. 331, 3 Leonard 257, 74 E.R. 669, Owen 103, 74 E.R. 931, 1 Eagle & Younge 99; 2 Rolle, Abr., *Graunts*, p. 63; *Hawkes v. Brothwith* (1606), Yelverton 94, 80 E.R. 64, also Croke Jac. 137, 79 E.R. 119, Hobart 176, 80 E.R. 323, 1 Eagle & Younge 165.

Michaelmas Day. And it appeared that the rector had been suspended *ab officio et beneficio* for some time before his death and died, that the suspension not being taken off and the profits of the living were sequestered and the 14s. due at Lady Day were paid to the sequestrator. And the defendant took advantage thereof and insisted by his answer that the rector's executor had no right *causa qua supra* and also because, he dying before the day for the payment of the second one half yearly payment, the same never became due to the testator. And this was the main question, whether it was or no.

N.B. It was admitted that the harvest was [. . .]ed before the testator died.

And the court, doubting, adjourned the debate of the case to another day. And, afterwards, they determined that the executor of Henwood should have the 14s., but should deduct thereout for the value of the tithes arising between 10th September and Michaelmas Day.

503

Anonymous

(Ex. 1724)

The question in this case was whether a general search warrant was legal.

Harvard Law School MS. 1082, vol. 1, p. 217, pl. 1

Sittings after Trinity term 1724.

A general bench warrant was given to a constable and certain other persons to search generally all suspected houses as well out of their jurisdiction or elsewhere. And the question was whether such was a legal warrant and whether a constable had power to commit. Query Lord Chief Justice Holt's opinion on this.

504

Robinson, *qui tam* v. Butler

(Ex. 1724)

In a lawsuit involving a seizure of goods allegedly imported unlawfully, if a party wishes to have a commission to examine witnesses, he must produce an affidavit that the witnesses are material and are unavailable to testify being abroad.

Harvard Law School MS. 1082, vol. 1, p. 217, pl. 3

Michaelmas term 1724.

The Attorney General [*Yorke*] showed cause against an order for a commission grounded on the Statute of Frauds, sec. 24,[1] where a bill was exhibited in

[1] Stat. 14 Car. II, c. 11, s. 27 (*SR*, V, 399).

this court. The defendant, who is the plaintiff at law, has answered and says that he believes the copper in question was forfeited, and, likewise, he insists that the defendants are partners. I may admit that, though this court is not named in the Act of Parliament, yet that such a commission is grantable by this court.

This case is of greater consequence than just putting off a trial, for, if such a commission is grantable of course, then it will be a dilatory [step] in every case and so for a year together until the king's witnesses are gone or dead. But surely, there ought to have been affidavits made, and commissions are not to be granted for the asking, and a motion for a commission before issue joined is irregular. Lowther v. Whorewood, in this court.[1]

Mr. *Ward*, for the plaintiff in equity: That which I go upon is the letter of the law and such a commission is given as some recompense for the hardship that the *onus probandi* lies on the owner and claimer of the goods and likewise in recompense for the crown's liberty of trying all their causes at Westminster.

[To the] objection that it may be dilatory, [he] answered, where a matter arises upon these mercantile affairs, that makes it necessary in order to have justice done and to have the fact fairly set forth. And the practice has been to grant such a commission without an affidavit. And so is Jenkins v. Larwood, Trinity 1717, Exchequer.[2]

The court has sometimes granted such a commission without a bill being exhibited, and, then, affidavits are necessary. But here being a bill, there is no occasion for affidavits. And Lowther v. Whorewood is not like this case.

Mr. *Bootle*, for the plaintiff in equity: It is a matter of great consequence to the crown and to the party. The bill is proper if the ship had been named. And it is not in the power of the party to know the several transactions abroad. And I never knew affidavits to be required, and so I do not know upon what foundation as affidavit is required, for the Act does not direct it.

What can be done more by the merchant here to whom the goods are consigned? And what affidavit can such a correspondent here make?

This commission is only grounded on the Act of Navigation.[3] [There is] no delay, for it cannot be presumed that the party will be so long out of [possession of] his good. And the expense of a commission must be on the plaintiff's part. The crown cannot suffer, for the goods are in their custody. And this is a proceeding *in rem*. In the case of Sir Sebastian Wines, a commission was granted.

Chief Baron [Eyre]: I will consider [in] this case whether there ought to be affidavits or not. It is insisted that a commission is grantable of course, for, if without affidavits it is so, I cannot think it to be grantable of course. But it seems to be discretionary in the court. Double pleading on the Statute for Amendment

---

[1] *Lowther v. Whorwood* (1722-1723), see above, Case No. 358.

[2] *Jenkins, qui tam v. Larwood* (1717), see above, Case No. 23.

[3] Stat. 12 Car. II, c. 18 (*SR*, V, 246-250).

of the Law[1] is discretionary in the court. And so is the natural construction of the Act of Parliament. If a commission is to issue, there ought to be a proper foundation, which I take an affidavit to be, that there are material witnesses. And, therefore, I cannot construe that Act of Parliament unless there is such a foundation. And, therefore, I shall expect it. If the course of the court has been that putting the case into a bill will supply an affidavit, that I must submit to the practice of it.

PRICE: The practice of this court is as regular as any other court. And I think that the intention of the Act was to give the commission to the defendant in lieu of the *onus probandi*. But yet I think that it cannot be done without affidavits and so I shall expect in this case. The case about Sebastian Wines is against all commissions being granted, for nobody that heard the witnesses examined upon that commission would believe them.

PAGE: I am of the same opinion that such a commission ought not to be granted without affidavits to show that there are material witnesses and [they] cannot be had by the time of the trial.

And, therefore, for the want of them, the commission was denied *per* TOTAM CURIAM.

Note: Mr. Ward had the affidavits in his hand but would not produce them because he insisted that, by the practice of the court, there was no occasion for them.

Taussig MS. 311, vol. 2, p. 742

Michaelmas term 1724. Butler v. Robinson.

There was a seizure by Robinson of copper imported from Cadiz contrary to an Act of Navigation. And, thereupon, he exhibited his information of seizure upon that Act. Butler claimed the copper and exhibits an English bill in this court suggesting that the copper was brought from Barbary in an English vessel and driven by necessity into Cadiz and from thence came hither. And in the bill, he named two persons who were at Cadiz and capable of proving this fact. And so he prayed a commission under the seal of this court to examine these witnesses, but he annexed no affidavit to prove the facts suggested.

The Attorney [General, *Yorke*,] now came to show cause why such a commission should not go. And he objected that there was no affidavit and that encouraging these commissions would be for the future a constant dilatory and be used as a means of putting off all trials upon informations grounded on the Act of Navigation.

Ward: Before the Act of Navigation, the *onus probandi* lay upon the informer and, therefore, the Statute alters the law with respect to the crown and is for the benefit of the crown in two respects, *viz.*, it lays the *onus probandi* on the merchant and makes the cause triable at Westminster, in recompense whereof the

[1] Stat. 4 & 5 Ann., c. 3, s. 4 (*SR*, VIII, 458).

Statute gives the merchant this advantage by commission. And the case is within the express words of it.

This point does not depend entirely on the bill for the information shows it to be an information on the Statute. The bill in equity is only to found the jurisdiction of the court's granting such commission. In the case of Jenkins v. Larwood, in Trinity term 1717, which was upon a seizure of coffee, a commission was granted on a like bill without any affidavit.

Chief Baron [EYRE]: The Act of Parliament says the commission is to be granted upon a request. This request is to be made to the court, and, consequently, the court is to judge of the circumstances of the case laid before them for a commission. And this is like the Statute that allows the court to give leave for double pleas. By him, I think there is no better rule to determine the discretion of the court by in this case than the rule they go by in putting off trials where a man must make an affidavit that his witnesses are material and abroad.

PRICE has known this point debated in this court. An affidavit is always necessary upon a motion. And so he thinks the same ought to be where the proceeding is by bill. And he never knew the contrary.

PAGE was of the same opinion.

So the commission was denied.

505

Larnego v. Grice
Lynch v. Grice

(Ex. 1724)

In a lawsuit involving a seizure of goods allegedly imported unlawfully, if a party wishes to have a commission to examine witnesses, he must produce an affidavit that the witnesses are material and are unavailable to testify being abroad.

Taussig MS. 311, vol. 2, p. 745

Michaelmas term 1724. Two cases.

This was a motion now, originally made by Mr. *Ward*, for a like commission grounded on a bill as in the former case.[1] But here, an affidavit was produced naming the witness and that he was a material witness, was abroad, and could not be over soon enough. The ship came in on 4th August and the seizure was on the 12th. The question is whether the cocoa nuts were of French or Spanish growth.

Chief Baron [EYRE]: I think the court ought to settle some time after a seizure for applying for a commission. But in this case, the court granted a commission to Bilbao returnable the last day of the next term, as in Chancery. And the trial was put off to the next term.

[1] *Robinson, qui tam v. Butler* (Ex. 1724), see above, Case No. 504.

N.B. Grice was the seizer in both these cases.

Harvard Law School MS. 1082, vol. 1, p. 219, pl. 1

Michaelmas term 1724.

There being affidavits in this case, a commission was granted.

Lynch v. Grice [was] the same.

506

Woodnoth v. Lord Cobham

(Ex. 1724)

Account books kept by a party's steward in the usual course of business are admissible in evidence where the steward is dead.

Taussig MS. 311, vol. 2, p. 716

Monday, 26 October 1724, first equity day in term; EYRE, PRICE, PAGE, GILBERT *praesentibus*.

The plaintiff, as impropriator of Thornborough in County of Bucks, exhibits his bill for tithes of certain lands called Chantry Pastures and a certain meadow called Lott Meadows. The defendant insisted on a *modus* of 16s. 4d. paid constantly to the vicar of Thornborough in lieu of all tithes for those lands and no tithes were ever paid to the impropriator, and he insisted on a real composition of about five or six acres called Parsonage Meadow in lieu of all tithes of Lott Meadow.

To prove the constant payment of the 16s. 4d. to the vicar, the defendant produced the books of account kept by the steward of the Lord Cobham's family and allowed and cast up by Lord Cobham's auditor, in which books the steward entered the payment of this 16s. 4d. to the vicar. And the question was whether this was evidence.

EYRE, Chief Baron, thought it was evidence.

PRICE, *contra*. And [he though] that the allowance of vicars' and rectors' books of entries was a peculiar indulgence of this court.

PAGE and GILBERT thought it was, and particularly by GILBERT, because the question here is only whether actual payment has been made or no and these are entries by a steward who is disinterested and dead. If alive, it had not been evidence, or, if it had been the lord's writing, it had not been evidence, but now it is, and, by him, nothing is evidence in equity which is not so in law.

And by the CHIEF BARON, that is certainly evidence of an actual payment of a *modus* which is evidence of payment of anything else.

These were books of all sorts of the lord's steward's accounts, *viz.* payments to workmen, of annuities, of servants' wages, to ministers. And the books were accordingly read.

N.B. It was sworn in this case that the vouchers were lost or else I should have thought it hard to have admitted them as evidence, for it is certain that the vicar's receipts had been better evidence of this payment than an entry in the book, which ought to have been warranted by such a receipt as a voucher thereof.

Pengelly, pro querente, seems to give up the point as to Lott Meadows, there being evidence read by depositions of the enjoyment of Parsonage Meadow in lieu of the tithes of Lott Meadow. But as to the tithes of the Chantry Pastures, by him, the payment of a *modus* to the vicar is not evidence of a discharge of tithes against the rector; otherwise, had it been of tithes in kind, for it may be intended and it is most natural to intend that this money is only paid for the small tithes due to the vicar unless it had been paid for all tithes, both great and small, and though it is true that we are not able to prove many instances of the actual payment of great tithes to the impropriator, yet that defect is accounted for by the long unity of possession there has been of the rectory and lands, out of which etc., in the family of the Temples. Besides, non-payment is not to be admitted against common right. And to this purpose, the plaintiff showed an ancient deed or settlement whereby this unity was proved antecedent to any evidence given by the defendants of the payment of 16s. 4d. to the vicar, but, under the same settlement, there was afterwards a separation of them, the one, i.e. the rectory, came into the hands of the Lady Baltinglass and the other to Sir Richard Temple. And during this separation, it appeared by the evidence there had been disputes and controversies between the Lady and Sir Richard, the Lady claiming the great tithes and Sir Richard opposing her demands. But these disputes never came during all this time to any legal decision.

Wherefore the court was unanimously of opinion that the payment of 16s. 4d. in lieu of tithes of these lands to the vicar, which, by the generality of the depositions, was sworn to be a payment in lieu of tithes generally and by a few of them to be in lieu of all tithes together with the actual non-payment of great tithes to the impropriator was sufficient evidence to satisfy them that the *modus* of 16s. 4d. to the vicar was a discharge of all the tithes of those lands, both great and small. And so they dismissed the plaintiff's bill.

N.B. The plaintiff did not so much as desire a trial at law.

Harvard Law School MS. 1082, vol. 1, p. 219, pl. 2

Michaelmas term 1724.

Chief Baron [Eyre] said that he thought that the books between the steward and the defendant's ancestors should be read in evidence to prove the *modus* in question. And he compared it to the case of goldsmiths' books.

Price was of a different opinion, and he never knew them to go further than parsons' books.

PAGE was of opinion that it was evidence. And I cannot suppose a fraud between a lord and his steward. In 1706, in a case of tithes,[1] non-payment is evidence of a discharge.

GILBERT: When a court of equity directs evidence to be read *de bene esse*, it is only to see what it is, and that is the meaning of the court trusting themselves with evidence. The question in this case is payment or not. If these books had been in the custody of the lord himself, or his ancestors, perhaps it might not be evidence. But, in this case, they were in the hands of a person not interested and a person that made up the account so, when dead, it may be given in evidence. So the books of a vicar are evidence, and the reason is because the vicar is dead.

So they admitted it to be given in evidence, *per* CURIAM, *dissentiente* PRICE.

Note: In this case, the defendant insisted on a payment of 16s. 4d. payable to the vicar in full [discharge] of all great and small tithes. And though no proof was made but only the vicar's receiving 16s. 4d generally for tithes without saying for what, yet there having been a long non-payment and though that was answered by the unity of possession of the lands and tithes in Sir Peter Temple, who was the defendant's ancestor; yet, upon the whole, the court dismissed the plaintiff's bill, who was impropriator of the rectory of Thornburgh in the County of Buckingham, *quod mirum est*.

Bunbury 180, 145 E.R. 639,
1 Rayner 213, 217, 2 Gwillim 653, 1 Eagle & Younge 802

26 October 1724. Woodnoth v. Lord Cobham and Gibbs, his tenant.

A lay impropriator prefers his bill for great tithe of the parish of Thornborough in the County of Buckingham. The defendant insisted that there was a payment of 16s. 4d. to the vicar in lieu of the tithes of the Chantry Pastures, which were in demand. And to prove this, he produced accounts of one Edward Chaplin, who was steward to the defendant's father, wherein there were entries of this payment.

But it was objected for the plaintiff that, though a parson's or a vicar's book where it appeared that payments were made were evidence, yet it was never admitted in the case of him who has the fee.

But *per* CURIAM (*dissentiente* Baron PRICE), even old rent rolls, where it appears payments have been made etc., are good evidence. And they ordered these entries to be read.

But note: It was said by Baron GILBERT they ought to be read because no better evidence can be had, but, if Edward Chaplin had been alive, they ought not.

N.B. In this case, it seemed to be the opinion of the court that the payment of a *modus* to the vicar is good evidence of an exemption against the parson.

[1] Perhaps *Dean and Chapter of Worcester v. Seabright* (1707), 1 Wood 491.

507

Spendler v. Potter

(Ex. 1724)

The owners of the servient freehold must be parties to a suit to establish a custom.

Bunbury 181, 145 E.R. 640, 1 Eagle & Younge 802

12 November 1724.

A bill was brought to establish a custom, whereby the owners and occupiers of certain lands in the parish of Tort Baldwin in the County of Oxford were obliged to keep a bull and boar for the use of the parishioners. It was objected at the hearing that a custom which binds the inheritance of the lands can never be established in a court of equity without the owners of the inheritance are made parties, as Queen's College, who were owners etc., ought to have been here, upon which objection, the bill was dismissed, *per* TOTAM CURIAM.

Note: Also it was objected that, as to the occupier, an action on the case would be proper.

508

Williams v. Evans

(Ex. 1724)

An arrest warrant on the ground of a rescue is absolute and is not a mere show cause order.

Bunbury 181, 145 E.R. 640

Upon the return of a rescue, the court, upon motion for an attachment, will make it absolute at first as against those mentioned in the return.

509

Lord Bristol v. Hall
Lord Strafford v. Jones

(Ex. 1724)

A motion for permission to plead double must be supported by an affidavit.

Taussig MS. 311, vol. 2, p. 720

Saturday, 31 October 1724.

Mr. *Bootle* had a day to show cause upon a motion made by him in a cause between Lord Bristol and Hall that the Lord Bristol might plead double *non assumpsit* and *plene administravit*, to which the Chief Baron [EYRE] objected that he ought to have produced an affidavit of the truth of his plea of *plene administravit* and that this was always expected in other courts, to which he [*Bootle*] said that the motion had been granted here without an affidavit.

And to this Baron PRICE agreed.

But the CHIEF BARON insisted that, in the nature of the thing, it was reasonable to expect such an affidavit.

And it was ruled it should be so done, not only in this cause, but also in another moved by Mr. *Williams* between Lord Strafford and Jones, where he would have been admitted to plead *plene administravit* and *solvit ad diem*, the bond being twenty-nine years old. But the court made the same rule in this cause as in the former.

Bunbury 181, 145 E.R. 640

Jones, administrator *cum testamento annexo* of Bromhall v. Lord Strafford, administrator of Sir [*blank*] Johnson.

Mr. *Peere Williams* moved, on the behalf of the defendant, for leave to plead to this action, which was debt upon a bond (and it appeared by the declaration to be twenty-nine years standing) *solvit ad diem* and *plene administravit*.

But the court refused to grant the motion unless the defendant would make an affidavit that he had fully administered, and this, they said, had been the practice of both the King's Bench and Common Pleas.

The like rule was made the same day between [*blank*] and Lord Bristol, in an action of *indebitatus assumpsit*, who moved to plead *non assumpsit* and *plene administravit*.

[Related case: Jones v. Earl of Strafford (Ch. 1730), 3 Peere Williams 79, 24 E.R. 977.]

510

Simmons v. Mullins

(Ex. 1724-1726)

Even though there has been an interlocutory injunction against an arbitral award that was made a rule of the common law court, the equity court will not forbid the defendant at common law to be examined as to his alleged contempt of the common law court in not performing the award.

A defendant can be allowed to amend an answer before the parties are at issue.

The answer of one defendant can be used against another defendant for the purposes of an interlocutory injunction.

A court of equity cannot set aside an arbitral award that was made a rule of a common law court.

Taussig MS. 311, vol. 2, p. 729

Tuesday, 17th [November 1724]. Mullins v. Symonds.

The plaintiff's bill was to be relieved against an award, and it suggested several matters to show corruption in the arbitrators. And he annexed an affidavit to the bill to this purpose. This award being made by a rule of the court of King's Bench according to the Statute [*blank*] Will. III,[1] and an attachment was granted against the plaintiff for contempt in not performing the award. So his bill prayed an injunction.

The defendant put in an answer, which, upon exceptions, was adjudged an insufficient answer. And an injunction was obtained. But now, it was moved that the plaintiff might be examined on the attachment notwithstanding the injunction, which *per* EYRE, Chief Baron, PAGE, and GILBERT was thought reasonable, PRICE dissenting. And the reason was, unless they permitted such an examination, the parties did not stand equal in court, for, if the award was not to bind, then the injunction would be perpetual. If, upon hearing the cause, the court should think the award ought to stand, they could only dismiss the plaintiff's bill, but they must leave it to the King's Bench to enforce the performance of the award. And, therefore, they thought they could not do the same justice to the defendant unless they permitted the examination to go on with a stay of any punishment to be inflicted on him as they could to the plaintiff. And so the motion was granted.

Ward was for the defendant in equity; *Lee* was for the plaintiff.

Bunbury 182, 145 E.R. 640

17 November 1724.

Simmons preferred his bill to be relieved against an award, which was made a rule of the Court of King's Bench pursuant to the Stat. 9 & 10 Will. III and whereupon an attachment was granted against him for not performing it, suggesting corruption in the arbitrators. And the plaintiff obtained an injunction, the exceptions to the answer being allowed.

The defendants now moved for liberty to proceed to examine the plaintiff upon interrogatories in the King's Bench, notwithstanding the injunction, as is often done where the defendant applies for leave to affirm his judgment or to proceed to trial only.

And by three barons, it was granted because the plaintiff was the occasion of the delay. He comes here where he need not, for he might have had the same remedy in the court where the rule was made, as here, and, therefore, it would be against conscience to tie the defendants up; but the defendants were not to proceed to have a report on the examination (*dubitante* PRICE).

[1] Stat. 9 Will. III, c. 15 (*SR*, VII, 369-370).

Bunbury 186, 145 E.R. 642

26 January 1724[/25]. Mullins v. Simmonds.

Mr. *Ward* moved for leave to amend an answer in three particulars wherein the defendant found herself mistaken.

And *per* CURIAM, we often do it where issue is not joined. And it was ordered accordingly.

Harvard Law School MS. 1082, vol. 1, p. 230

Easter term 1725.

This was a bill to be relieved against an award, and the arbitrators were made defendants. And one of the defendants confessed some corruption in making the award. The question was whether the answer of one of the arbitrators can be read against the said other defendant Simons so as to grant an injunction upon it.

Chief Baron [EYRE] thought that the answer might be read.

PRICE agrees the same, for the answer of an attorney is evidence against the person that employed him. And I take it that the arbitrators and defendants are the same. But upon hearing the cause upon the merits, it may have another consideration, but, surely, it is sufficient to ground an injunction. If there are two obligees in a bond and one of the obligees confesses it to be a forged bond, that is sufficient to ground an injunction.

PAGE: [There are] no precedents that an answer of one defendant can be read against another. And it will be of dangerous consequence to admit because the plaintiff may make as many persons defendant as he pleases, and if one of those defendants proves to be a friend of the plaintiff and confesses anything in favor of the plaintiff, then, according to this rule of reasoning, there ought to be an injunction. The reference of the answer is immaterial, for, though a person may join at first, yet he may afterwards refuse. The defendant's answer cannot be read on the hearing; neither can an affidavit be read to support an injunction because it is evidence of one side. Harkness v. Wallis, before Lord Cowper, and though there appeared to be fraud on the part of the plaintiff, yet the arbitrators were examined in that cause. And, from the consequence, I am against reading this answer.

The CHIEF BARON replied and said that there was a difference between the final hearing of a cause and granting an injunction upon a motion. Affidavits of these persons might be read in the King's Bench upon this award. Why not in this case? Upon motions, the affidavits of the parties are admitted.

So by the CHIEF BARON and PRICE against PAGE, the answer was read and an injunction was granted.

Fenwick said that in Simpson v. Dixon, in Chancery, before this term, this was denied to be read.

Taussig MS. 311, vol. 2, p. 784

Friday, 15 April 1725.

The plaintiff exhibited his bill against the defendants, who were the arbitrators made by a rule of court at the assizes and the person in whose favor the award was made and who had taken an attachment against the plaintiff for nonperformance of it, suggesting corruption and malpractice in the arbitrators. And he prayed an injunction to which bill. All the defendants answered jointly, but the answer being insufficient and they were obliged to answer again. The party amended his bill, and then the party and the arbitrators answered severally. And the plaintiff, apprehending that the arbitrators, by their answer, had confessed sufficient [matter] to show the court that the arbitration was bad upon the aforesaid account, moved now to continue the injunction to the hearing of the cause. And, to support this, he would have read the answer of the arbitrators to make out the facts. But this was opposed upon the common rule that one defendant's answer is not to be read against the other no more to support or obtain an injunction than at the hearing of the cause and, therefore, not in this case.

E contra: There ought to be a distinction in the case before the court, for, here, the gist of the equity was the misbehavior of the arbitrators and the facts and proceedings of the arbitrators can only be discovered by their own answer and they having discovered so much as to make good the suggestion of the party, the plaintiff cannot read it. The award, though by their own account of it is voidable and, therefore, unjust and improper to be executed must, notwithstanding, be carried into execution.

Price was of opinion that the arbitrators' answers might be read.

Page, *contra*.

The Chief Baron [Eyre] went out of court before the motions were finished, and so he gave no opinion, but the matter was adjourned, the two barons differing.

Taussig MS. 311, vol. 2, p. 787

Easter term 1725.

9 & 10 Will., ca. 15, was again stirred. And Mr. *Williams* said that the rule of not reading one defendant's answer against another had many exceptions, as in case one defendant refers to the answer of the other. Secondly, an agent's or attorney's answer has been often permitted to be read against his principal. Thirdly, where a man is a purchaser as he says without notice, the person of whom he purchased his answer may be read against him even as to the point of notice.

Chief Baron [Eyre]: I think the arbitrator's answer may be read as to the question relating to the injunction.

Price: It may be read. Otherwise we may do injustice to the plaintiff in equity. And I think, as to this question, Symonds and the arbitrators are one. He agreed also to Peere Williams' case of the principal or his agent or attorney. So from the nature and circumstances of this case and the necessity of it, the answer may be read.

Page: I doubted it before and doubt it now. He admits, where there is a joint answer or where answers refer to one another, there they may be read. And

I think he admitted the case of the attorney or agent and the principal. But he insisted on the inconveniences of making one answer evidence against the other defendant for, then, you may make any man a defendant whom you believe will confess matters against the principal defendant.

[It was] agreed by Chief Baron [EYRE] and PRICE that it cannot be read at the hearing of the cause. What is the reason of it? Why, because it is not evidence in its nature? Are not we then saying that what is not evidence shall be admitted as evidence for an injunction?

Chief Baron [EYRE]: In the proceedings of a cause, several things are admitted as evidence which are not evidence at the trial, as the affidavits of the parties themselves.

And so the answers were read. And the answers did discover enough for continuing the injunction. And it was accordingly continued.

Bunbury 196, 145 E.R. 645

A bill was brought to set aside an award, as being unduly obtained. Now, upon motion for an injunction upon the merits, the answer of the arbitrators, the defendants, was admitted, by Lord Chief Baron EYRE and Baron PRICE, to be read against the other defendant, who was party to the award and for whose benefit it was.

Note: All the defendants joined in their first and second answers to their original bill. But the arbitrators [were] severed in their answers to the amended bill.

Baron PAGE, *totis viribus contra*, thought it a dangerous precedent, for a man might add a sham defendant and, by his answer, at any time, obtain an injunction, and it was never done before, and so admitted.

Taussig MS. 311, vol. 2, p. 944

Trinity term 1726.

The court dismissed a bill which was brought to set aside an award made upon a rule of court in the King's Bench purely on want of jurisdiction, for they said the Act of Parliament was intended to make an end of everything.

511

Whitehead v. Murat

(Ex. 1724)

Where a defendant has appeared and answered, he will not be required to give security to pay any decree before leaving the jurisdiction pendente lite.

Bunbury 183, 145 E.R. 641

17 November 1724.

Mr. *Kettleby*, on behalf of the plaintiff, moved that the defendant might be obliged to give security to abide the event of the suit before he went to Oporto, where he lived, and, as was suggested in the bill, that the defendant owed the plaintiff £400. But the answer of the defendant being come in, the court would make no order.

But upon the 8th of December following, in another cause where the defendant had not answered, but was in contempt, the court obliged the defendant to give security until answer and further order.

Harvard Law School MS. 1082, vol. 1, p. 217, pl. 2

Michaelmas term 1724.

Mr. *Kettleby*, for the plaintiff, moved that the defendant might give security before he leaves the kingdom.

But, in this case, the court said that there was no color for an injunction because the defendant had sworn a balance due to him, and, therefore, there was no color for the motion.

Query if a writ of *ne exeat regno* can be granted by this court because it seems to be a writ only grantable by the person or persons having the custody of the great seal. The court was divided in a former case. See Tutt v. Mercer.[1]

512

Attorney General, ex rel. Bailey v. Cornes

(Ex. 1724)

The Court of Exchequer has the jurisdiction to decide a dispute over an ecclesiastical pension.

Taussig MS. 311, vol. 2, p. 732

Michaelmas term 1724.

The Attorney General, at the relation of Francis Bailey, the curate of Saint Leonard's in Bridgnorth, exhibits an information against the defendant Cornes, who was the curate of St. Mary Magdalene in Bridgnorth to have a payment of a pension of £5 reserved by Queen Elizabeth upon a grant to Sir Christopher Hatton and by that grant is made payable *praecedicatoribus ibidem*. The fact was that both of these churches were within the royal peculiar of the deanery of Bridgnorth, which was now vested in Mr. Whitmore from the family of the Hattons and so both these churches did belong to him and both the plaintiff and the defendant were only curates. The relator pretends that he, being curate of St. Leonard's, which was a parish church, should be entitled to this pension for that the other, *viz*. St. Mary Magdalene's, was formerly only a chapelry belonging to

[1] *Mercer v. Tutt* (Ex. 1723), see above, Case No. 436.

the Castle of Bridgnorth, though now it is looked upon as a parish church [and] keeps its own poor and has sacraments etc.

Bunbury 183, 145 E.R. 641

A bill was preferred for a pension only, payable to the preacher of Bridgnorth. And upon the hearing of the cause, which was afterwards ended by compromise, it seemed to be admitted that a bill might be brought for a pension only.

513

Chapman v. Barlow

(Ex. 1724)

Cherries, whether wild or otherwise, if gathered, pay tithes.

A new mill erected after the Statute of 2 & 3 Edw. VI pays tithes.

Bunbury 183, 145 E.R. 641,
1 Rayner 216, 2 Gwillim 657, 1 Eagle & Younge 803

1 December 1724.

A bill was brought by the rector of Radnage in the County of Buckingham for the tithe of headlands, of a mill, and cherries.

The defendant insists the headlands were only large enough to turn the plow upon, and, as to this, the bill was dismissed.

As to the mill, no tithes thereof having ever been paid and being an ancient mill, it was adjourned to consider whether the tithe of a water corn mill was a praedial or a personal tithe.

As to the black cherries, the defendant insisted they grew wild in hedges and waste places and served for fencing his grounds. But the defendant was decreed to pay the tithe of these cherries.

Taussig MS. 311, vol. 2, p. 751

8th December 1724, sittings after Michaelmas term.

The plaintiff, as parson of Radnege in the County of Bucks, exhibited his bill for tithes of hay, milk, mills, [and] cherries. The defendants insist that grass made into hay grew upon headlands; second, on a *modus* of 3d. for milk of every cow; third, that the mill was an ancient windmill and only removed from out of one field into another in the same parish, 1 Rolle's *Abr.*, 652,[1] fourth, that the cherries are wild, and Rolle's *Abr.* holds that acorns fed on by hogs do not pay tithes.

As to the mill, it was proved that it was removed into another parish, *viz.* from Risborough into the plaintiff's parish.

[1] 1 Rolle, Abr., *Dismes*, F, 'A quel chose ceo extendera', p. 652.

And so the court thought it could bear no dispute, but that it was to be considered as a new mill; so they decree for that [*blank*].

As to cherries, *per* CURIAM, whether wild or otherwise, if gathered, they must pay tithe.

As to the headlands, the proofs in the cause being that they were no larger than necessary or usual, the bill was dismissed as to the hay growing upon them.

Bunbury: As to the mill, it is a particular tithe and then not having paid any tithes for forty years, it is discharged by the Statute Edw. VI. 1 Rolle's Rep. 405; Chamberlain and Newte, in this court.[1]

Per CURIAM: This mill was not in being at the time of the Statute of Edw. VI, and so it cannot be discharged by it.

2 Rolle's Rep. 83,[2] that cherry trees are timber in Buckinghamshire.

The court decreed an account as to the mill, reserving the consideration how the accounts should be taken, *scil.* whether *deductis expensis* as a personal tithe or as a praedial tithe.

PAGE [held] that it is a personal tithe.

PRICE [held] that it was praedial, that the case of Newte and Chamberlain was of a horse corn mill and, for that reason only, the Lords held it to be a personal tithe.

514

Baily v. Gregg

(Ex. 1724)

A sheriff's return of a writ of fieri facias *cannot be that the goods were stolen after the execution.*

The question in this case was whether a sheriff is liable in tort where a judgment debtor's goods are stolen after execution.

Harvard Law School MS. 1082, vol. 1, p. 222

Michaelmas term 1724.

This was an action brought against the defendant, the sheriff of Lancashire, for making a <false> return, *viz.* that of a rescue upon a *fieri facias* and for suffer-

---

[1] Stat. 2 & 3 Edw. VI, c. 13 (*SR*, IV, 55-58); *Jakes v. Anonymous* (1616), 1 Rolle Rep. 405, 81 E.R. 568, also 3 Bulstrode 212, 81 E.R. 178, 1 Eagle & Younge 257; *Newte v. Chamberlaine* (1705), Dodd 208, Eq. Cases Exch. 552, 1 Eagle & Younge 679, 7 Brown 3, 3 E.R. 2, 1 Eq. Cas. Abr. 366, 21 E.R. 1107, 2 Eq. Cas. Abr. 731, 22 E.R. 617, 1 Rayner 101, 106, 3 Rayner 1087, 1090, 2 Gwillim 596, Public Record Office, E.126/18, f. 580v, 1 Wood 482.

[2] *Wright v. Powle* (1619), 2 Rolle Rep. 83, 81 E.R. 674, 1 Gwillim 357, 1 Eagle & Younge 305.

ing the goods to be purloined. It was objected in arrest of judgment that an action did not lie because, upon application, the court would have quashed the return. Shower 180; Dalton 534; Cro. Eliz. 624, Barton v. Hedworth; 852.[1]

Mr. *Bootle*, for the plaintiffs, answered the objections. The action arises from the damage received. 1 Inst. 145.[2] The cases in Cro. Eliz. do not come up to this case because they were upon contempt to the court only. But here is a special damage to the plaintiff. An action will lie though the return is false. 2 Inst. 452.[3]

Where a sheriff makes an insufficient return, there, it is as if no return at all was made. So it is a nullity. So the cause of action arises for suffering the goods to be purloined. The plaintiff has his election either to bring his action or to apply to the court. Noy 22; 2 Saunders 59, Foster v. [*blank*]; Hobart 209, Parkhurst.[4]

By the common law, the sheriff is liable either for a false return or no return. 1 Siderfin 23; 1 Modern 245; 2 Saunders 343.[5] I admit that the return of a rescue is not good upon a *fieri facias*, but it is good so far as to charge the sheriff in this action. Cro. Car. 540.[6]

In some cases, the plaintiff may have his election of an action of debt or an escape. 4 Coke, Slade's Case; Fitzherbert, *Natura Brevium*, 95.[7]

Mr. *Starkie*, for the plaintiffs, said that the party has his election either to have his action or to quash the return. That [matter] mentioned in the declaration about the return is only by way of inducement. But there is sufficient [matter] without it to maintain this action.

---

[1] *Rex v. Bill* (1691), 1 Shower K.B. 180, 89 E.R. 524; M. Dalton, *Officium Vicecomitum*; *Barton v. Aldeworth* (1598), Croke Eliz. 624, 78 E.R. 865; *Boles v. Lassels* (1601), Croke Eliz. 852, 78 E.R. 1077, also Noy 39, 74 E.R. 1009.

[2] E. Coke, *First Institute* (1628), f. 145.

[3] E. Coke, *Second Institute* (1642), p. 452.

[4] *Spark v. Richards* (1617), Noy 22, 74 E.R. 992, also Hobart 206, 80 E.R. 353, Moore K.B. 886, 72 E.R. 974, 2 Shower K.B. 281, 89 E.R. 940, Hutton 11, 123 E.R. 1065, 1 Brownlow & Goldesborough 51, 123 E.R. 659; *Posterne v. Hanson* (1670), 2 Williams Saunders 59, 85 E.R. 658, also 2 Keble 607, 84 E.R. 282; *Parkhurst v. Powell* (1617), Hobart 209, 80 E.R. 356, also Croke Jac. 532, 79 E.R. 456, 1 Brownlow & Goldesborough 12, 123 E.R. 634.

[5] *Allen v. Robinson* (1661), 1 Siderfin 22, 82 E.R. 946; *Cockram v. Welby* (1677), 1 Modern 245, 86 E.R. 858, also 2 Modern 212, 86 E.R. 1031, 1 Freeman 236, 89 E.R. 169, 2 Shower K.B. 79, 89 E.R. 806; *Mildmay v. Smith* (1671), 2 Williams Saunders 338, 85 E.R. 1136, also 2 Keble 789, 821, 84 E.R. 499, 519, Lincoln's Inn MS. Misc. 500, f. 156 (Edward Ward's reports).

[6] *Perkinson v. Gilford* (1639), Croke Car. 539, 79 E.R. 1064, also W. Jones 430, 82 E.R. 226, March 13, 82 E.R. 389.

[7] *Slade v. Morley* (1602), 4 Coke Rep. 91, 76 E.R. 1072, also Moore K.B. 433, 667, 72 E.R. 677, 827, Yelverton 20, 80 E.R. 15; A. Fitzherbert, *Natura Brevium*.

Mr. *Philip Ward*, for the defendant, [argued] to justify the objections in arrest of judgment. And he cited 2 Saunders 154.[1] An action will not lie for the purloining of goods, and the plaintiff ought to have applied to quash the return. And there is no such election as is contended for.

Chief Baron [Eyre]: There is no weight in the objections. I allow [that] the return of a rescue to any execution is not good. But, if laid whereby the plaintiffs are damaged, an action will lie. If a sheriff has a *capias ad satisfaciendum* against a man and is in company with him and will not take him, an action will lie for the neglect, and it is not necessary to allege it to be a false return. And, therefore, the objection has no weight.

Price: This seems to me to be an action for a false return. And, if the sheriff has levied, he is liable. The party has an election in many cases, but, whether in this case, I am doubtful. Cro. Jac. 514, Ely v. Beach.[2] The proper remedy was by *distringas*. And it was agreed that the rescue was bad, but, there, it was agreed a *scire facias*, [writ of] debt, or *distringas* would lie. But I am at present doubtful.

Page: I own that the case in 2 Saunders 343 raised this doubt with me. And I am inclined to think that this action will not lie, for it will not be any damage to the plaintiff, for, if the sheriff has made himself liable, how can the plaintiff suffer by having his money? This action is grounded on the tort, and here is no tort.

Gilbert: Every action on the case is grounded on the tort or injury to the plaintiff. And here is no injury. And whether a false return will be an injury I think not because the sheriff has thereby taken it upon himself, and there are no instances of such an action.

Chief Baron: It seems to me not to rest on the false return, for without it an action will lie. And it is not doubted but, in cases of *capias ad satisfaciendum*, that an action on the case or debt will lie.

515

Reeves v. Butler

(Ex. 1724-1726)

In a action for property, if there are separate and distinct counts and entire damages are given, the plaintiff shall have his full court costs, even without a certificate. However, if a plaintiff in an action of trespass counts of a clausum fregit *and in another count* de bonis asportatis, *if the defendant is found not guilty as to the last count and guilty as to*

[1] *Benson v. Welby* (1670), 2 Williams Saunders 150, 85 E.R. 887, also 2 Keble 632, 670, 84 E.R. 398, 421, *sub nom. Parker v. Welby*, 1 Ventris 55, 85, 86 E.R. 39, 59, 1 Siderfin 439, 82 E.R. 1204, 2 Keble 591, 626, 630, 657, 84 E.R. 372, 394, 397, 413, 1 Modern 33, 57, 86 E.R. 710, 728, Lincoln's Inn MS. Misc. 500, f. 96 (Edward Ward's reports).

[2] *Sly v. Finch* (1618), Croke Jac. 514, 79 E.R. 439, also 2 Rolle Rep. 57, 81 E.R. 657.

the clausum fregit, *then the plaintiff shall have no more court costs than damages unless the trial judge certifies that full costs should be awarded.*

Taussig MS. 311, vol. 2, p. 721

Michaelmas term 1724.

Per Chief Baron [Eyre], the clause of the Statute 22 & 23 Car.[1] only extends to such cases where the judge can certify, which he cannot as in the case of an *asportavit* and, by him, an *asportavit* for which an action of trover will lie. And he thought that trover was maintainable for the taking and detaining the goods, as in the declaration, and so within the same reason as an *asportavit.*

Price [held] *contra* that an *asportavit* in the declaration was a stretch and this is still carrying it further.

Page: I do not think trover would lie in this case, for if it did, it might be brought in every case where a man enters into another's close or house and any goods are in the close or house.

Gilbert: This Stat. of 22 Car. has been construed by relation to the Stat. 43 Eliz.,[2] and both are taken together.

Harvard Law School MS. 1082, vol. 1, p. 252, pl. 1

Michaelmas term 1725.

Owen [moved] for the plaintiff for costs for that *cepit bona et catalla* is as much as *asportavit.* The words do amount to it on the Stat. 22 & 23 Car. II; 2 Ventris 215; Raymond 487, Sir Thomas Jones 232; 3 Modern 39, 40; 2 Levinz 234, Asser v. Finch.[3]

Philip Ward, for the defendants [said] that there should be no more costs than damages.

[To the] objection of 2 Ventris, [he] responded there is laid a *clausum fregit* and an *asportavit.*

[To the] objection of Raymond 487, [he] responded that was not a *clausum fregit.*

[To the] objection of 3 Modern, [he] responded it was determined in the case of Lane v. Browne, Hilary 1 Geo. [1715], King's Bench.

The ordering of an *asportavit* to carry costs is further than I should go. Mitchell v. Soper, Easter 10 Geo. [1724] in the Exchequer;[4] Bauclarke v. F[. . .]d.

---

1 Stat. 22 & 23 Car. II, c. 9, s. 9 (*SR*, V, 719).

2 Stat. 43 Eliz. I, c. 6 (*SR*, IV, 971).

3 Stat. 22 & 23 Car. II, c. 9, s. 9 (*SR*, V, 719); *Anonymous* (1690), 2 Ventris 215, 86 E.R. 401; *Smith v. Batterton* (1683), T. Raymond 487, 83 E.R. 255, T. Jones 232, 84 E.R. 1232, also Skinner 100, 90 E.R. 47, 2 Shower K.B. 258, 89 E.R. 927; *Barnes v. Edgard* (1684), 3 Modern 39, 87 E.R. 24; *Asser v. Finch* (1678), 2 Levinz 234, 83 E.R. 534.

4 *Mitchell v. Soaper* (Ex. 1724), see above, Case No. 474.

Chief Baron [Gilbert]: This case must be interpreted on the several statutes. The Statute of Gloucester[1] gave costs and damages. The Stat. 43 Eliz.[2] [gave] no costs under 40s. And [there were] no judges' certificates from [the time of] Queen Elizabeth until the Statute of 22 & 23 Car. II,[3] for this last Statute directs the judge's certificate.

If anything is fixed to the freehold or [there is] an *asportavit*, costs [will be granted]. 8 Will. III, cap. 10.[4] The interpretation of *asportavit* [was] right, and the legislature has confirmed that opinion. And I think there ought to be costs, fixed or not fixed to the freehold is a right distinction. But I will look into cases. 1 Salkeld 208, Venn v. Phillips.[5]

Page: There is a rule fixed. Statute of 21 Jac. I.[6] An action of trover will not lie in this case. The locking of the door is no conversion. I think that [an action of] trover will not lie. And, therefore, I cannot order costs [to be paid].

Hale: This was tried amongst the other trifling actions at Shrewsbury.

Chief Baron: I so far agree with my brother Page, that, if trover would not lie, I should not order costs. But I, at present, think that trover can be maintained.

Adjourned.

Harvard Law School MS. 1082, vol. 1, p. 258, pl. 1

Hilary term 1725/26.

Chief Baron Gilbert gave the opinion of the whole court whether any more costs than damages in an action of trespass without the certificate of the judge or where there is no particular *asportavit* laid. And he thought, without one or the other, there should be no more costs than damages.

Costs *de incremento* are taxed above and not by the jury. See the Statute of Gloucester. The Statute of Queen Elizabeth was very doubtful, and, then, [there were] very few certificates. But [see] the Statute of 21 Jac. I, about words, and that takes away costs *de incremento* where under 40s.

This question arises on the Statute of Car. II. And this Statute has made it necessary that there must be a certificate unless the title comes in question. And the construction is from the words of the Statute, *de bonis asportatis*; the plaintiff must have his costs without a certificate. And there, the Statute of Gloucester carries costs. And that part is not repealed by any subsequent statutes. 9 Geo., Keen v. [*blank*], Common Bench.[7] In breaking the close chasing his bull, the defendant had his costs because the freehold might have come in

[1] Stat. 6 Edw. I, c. 1 (*SR*, I, 47).

[2] Stat. 43 Eliz. I, c. 6 (*SR*, IV, 971).

[3] Stat. 22 & 23 Car. II, c. 9, s. 9 (*SR*, V, 719).

[4] Stat. 8 & 9 Will. III, c. 11 (*SR*, VII, 201-203).

[5] *Ven v. Phillips* (1703), 1 Salkeld 208, 91 E.R. 185.

[6] Stat. 21 Jac. I, c. 16, s. 6 (*SR*, IV, 1223).

[7] *Keen v. Whistler* (1722), 1 Strange 534, 93 E.R. 683.

question. Thompson v. Berry, Common Bench; Bland v. Miller, 12 Geo., Common Bench.[1] So by this, all the books are reconcilable. Wherever a *clausum fregit* is and, in the same count by way of aggravation, *bonis asportatis*, there are no more costs than damages. But if there is a separate count and it is substantiated by itself, there shall be more costs than damages and there is no occasion for the certificate of the judge. In [an action of] *detinue*, the freehold may come in question; therefore, costs are allowed.

In the principal case, [there was] only locking the barn and this is not touching the property of the goods, so he declared the opinion of the court was no more costs than damages.

Bunbury 207, 145 E.R. 649

29 January 1725[/26].

This was an action of trespass *quare domum et horreum fregit et bona et catalla etc. cepit et detinuit et deprivavit querentem de usu horrei et domus et bonorum etc.*[2] There was a verdict for the plaintiff and 2d. damages.

This case was argued in Michaelmas term 1724 by Mr. *Owen*, for the plaintiff, and Mr. *Philip Ward* for the defendant. And the single question was whether the plaintiff should have more costs than damages.

Lord Chief Baron EYRE thought that the plaintiff was entitled to full costs; PRICE, PAGE, and GILBERT, barons, doubted. So it was adjourned to be further considered.

And after time taken, GILBERT being now Lord Chief Baron, gave the opinion of the whole court this day and went over all the statutes relating to costs, as the statutes of Gloucester, Eliz., 21 Jac. I, 16 Car. II,[3] and, upon comparing and considering them, founded his opinion on this distinction, which the court agreed to, *viz.* where an action of trespass is brought *quare clausum fregit* and there is anything laid by way of aggravation of damages, there can be no more costs than damages, though the freehold might come in question, unless the judge certifies. But if there are separate and distinct counts and entire damages are given, there, the plaintiff shall have his full costs, even without a certificate. If a plaintiff in trespass counts of a *clausum fregit* and in another count *de bonis asportatis*, if the defendant is found not guilty as to the last count and guilty as to the *clausum fregit*, then the plaintiff shall have no more costs than damages.

---

[1] *Thompson v. Berry* (1723), 1 Strange 551, 93 E.R. 694; *Blunt v. Miller* (1725), 1 Strange 645, 93 E.R. 755, Gilbert Rep. 197, 25 E.R. 138.

[2] whereby he broke into the house and barn and he took and detained goods and chattels etc. and he deprived the plaintiff of the use of the barn and house and goods etc.

[3] Stat. 6 Edw. I, c. 1 (*SR*, I, 47); Stat. 43 Eliz. I, c. 6 (*SR*, IV, 971); Stat. 21 Jac. I, c. 16, s. 6 (*SR*, IV, 1223); Stat. 22 & 23 Car. II, c. 9, s. 9 (*SR*, V, 719).

Taussig MS. 311, vol. 2, p. 851, pl. 2

Saturday, 29 January 1725/26.

Chief Baron [GILBERT] gave the opinion of the court. The construction upon the statutes has been exceeding right and it is not political to restrain the laws made against the increase of actions and business of Westminster Hall. Statute of Gloucester. The last words of the Statute let in all personal actions, and costs *de incremento* come in upon this Statute in all cases where damages are recoverable.

The Statute of Eliz. is darkly penned, and [there is] little practice upon that Statute. 21 Jac. I, ca. 16, this Statute takes away all costs *de incremento*, and so it is a repeal of the Statute of Gloucester as to the actions therein mentioned. Car. II [*blank*], there must be a certificate of a judge in order to entitle one to full costs. In all actions where the freehold may come in question and upon Eliz., there must be a certificate to prevent costs.

Where there are distinct counts in trespass, one for a *clausum fregit* and another for *bonis asportatis* and entire damages [are awarded, there] must be full costs, for this case is not within the Stat. [*blank*] Car. [*blank*], but still remains within the Statute of Gloucester.

Keen and Christ or Crisp, 9 [*blank*]. Thompson and Bury, where the taking of a chattel is comprehended in the same count, there [can be] no more costs than damages; it is otherwise if in a distinct count. Blount and Miller, 12 *regis, per quod* is only in aggravation [of damages]. Then, he cites the case in the Common Bench of the *quendam taurum*[1] of no more costs than damages. All the former cases cited at the bar agree with these notions. See also for aggravation Lib. J, fo. 11.

In the principal case, the damage to goods is laid by aggravation and not in a substantial clause, the freehold may come in question.

Secondly, by way of detention, there are no more costs than damages, as the Case of Barnes and Edgar.[2]

Where a count *de bonis asportatis* is in a declaration of a *clausum fregit*, if there are no damages on the *bonis asportatis*, it is proper to have a verdict of not guilty.

So, the court concluded there should be no more costs than damages.

Gilbert Rep. 195, 25 E.R. 136

The Lord Chief Baron GILBERT's argument: This is an action of trespass, wherein the plaintiff declares, first, for breaking and entering his close. And then there is a count that the defendant, Richard Butler, *infra tempus praedictum, viz. 10 die Januarii anno regni dicti domini regis nunc 10, vi et armis, etc. unum domum et unum alium horreum ipsius Thomae Reeves apud Iscoy praedictum in comitatu praedicto fregit ac ostia domus et horrei predicti obserravit et bona et catalla, viz. centum*

1 *taurina MS.*

2 *Barnes v. Edgard* (1684), 3 Modern 39, 87 E.R. 24.

carecta tritici, centum carecta seisigir., centum carecta hordei, centum carecta tabap., centum carecta foeni ipsius Thomae Reeves ibidem inventa cepit ac eadem bona et catalla per quattuor septimanas tunc proximas sequentes de eodem Thoma Reeves in domo et horreo illo detinuit. And the jury find 2d. damages. And the question is whether there shall be full costs or not.

And I think there should not be full costs. The case depends upon the interpretation of several statutes compared one with the other. To understand it rightly, we must go back as far as the Statute of Gloucester,[1] which says that:

> whereas before time, damages were not taxed but to the value of the issues of the land, it is provided that the demandant may recover against the tenant the costs of his writ purchased together with the damages aforesaid. And this Act shall hold place in all cases where the party is to recover damages.

That Statute was that which gave costs *de incremento*, for, at common law, if the defendant prevailed, the plaintiff was only amerced *pro falso clamore*. But this Statute gave the costs of the writ, which, by a benign interpretation, they extended to all legal proceedings, as being founded upon that writ.

And the interpretation was that, though the jury were to settle the damages for the wrong done, yet the court were to settle the costs of the legal proceedings because these were matters of law to which the jury could not answer.

Thus it stood until the [Stat.] 43 Eliz., c. 6,[2] which enacts that, in all:

> personal actions to be brought in any of Her Majesty's courts at Westminster, not being for any title or interest of lands . . . nor for any battery, [if] it shall appear to the judges of the same courts, and is so signified or set down by the justices before whom the same shall be tried that the debt or damage . . . shall not amount to 40s. or above, then . . . .

there shall be no more costs than damages.

This Statute is pretty darkly penned, and, therefore, I believe had very little or no effect. The intention of it, no doubt, was to bring back these small actions into the country courts, but, by the words of the law, the judge that tried it was to signify the damages not to be above 40s., which is making the judge that tried the cause judge of the fact and to certify in approbation of the verdict.

And it was very hard that, when a man pursued his remedy for a debt or damage which happened within the compass of 40s. that he should be punished for bringing his action and, therefore, I suppose, unless the action appeared exceeding frivolous, the judge seldom certified to cut off the plaintiff's costs.

---

[1] Stat. 6 Edw. I, c. 1 (*SR*, I, 47).

[2] Stat. 43 Eliz. I, c. 6 (*SR*, IV, 971).

By 21 Jac. I, c. 16,[1] in all actions of slander to be sued in any courts of Westminster or in any other court whatsoever, if the jury upon trial of the issue find the damages under 40s., the plaintiff shall recover no more costs than damages, without any further increase of the same. This is a direct repeal of the Statute of Gloucester *quoad* these actions of slander, where there were no more costs than damages. And it takes away these costs *de incremento* by express and positive words.

We come now to 22 & 23 Car. II, c. 9, s. 149,[2] which says that, to make the Statute of Elizabeth more effectual, it was enacted that in all actions of trespass, assault and battery, and other personal actions, if the judge did not certify that the title of the land was in question or that the battery was sufficiently proved, if the damages were found under 40s., the plaintiff should recover no more costs than damages. Salkeld 208, Ven v. Philips.

The construction upon this Statute was that, in all actions of battery and in all actions of trespass where a freehold could come in question, if the damages were under 40s., the plaintiff must procure a certificate from the judge in order to obtain his costs, but, in all other personal actions, the law stood as it did before the Statute of Elizabeth, that the judge must certify the action as frivolous to strip the plaintiff of his costs, the plain consequence of which is that, if there be several counts in trespass and one relates to the freehold in which the title may come in question and another relates to chattels *de bonis asportatis* in which no title of land can come in question and entire damages be found under 40s., the plaintiff must have costs by the Statute of Gloucester because the costs are not remitted by the Statute of Elizabeth without a certificate from the judge.

And this is not within the Statute of King Charles II, wherein there is a necessity there should be a certificate of the judge to entitle to costs. And, therefore, when entire damages are found, there must be some damage proportioned to that count. And, if there be any damage proportioned to the count relating to the goods, the Statute of Gloucester carries costs of course.

This, I say to vindicate the resolutions of the law, for men have thought that some of the resolutions on the Statute of King Charles have impugned the Statute in order to enlarge the jurisdiction of Westminster Hall. God forbid that judges upon their oath should make resolutions to enlarge jurisdiction! These are just and genuine resolutions, according to the plain intention and meaning of these statutes, considered one with another. And all resolutions, both ancient and modern, have turned upon this reasoning. I will only mention some of the modern ones because they come close to the present case.

The first is Keen v. Whistler, 9 Geo. I, Michaelmas [1722], in the Common Bench, an action of trespass for chasing his cow and his domestic fowls, *viz.* hens, geese, etc. with dogs, which dogs were used to bite tame fowl, by whose biting they were killed. On a plea of not guilty, a verdict was found for the plaintiff;

---

1 Stat. 21 Jac. I, c. 16, s. 6 (*SR*, IV, 1223).

2 Stat. 22 & 23 Car. II, c. 9, s. 9 (*SR*, V, 719).

and he had his full costs because this is not a trespass wherein the right of freehold may come in question.

The next is Thompson v. Berry, 9 Geo. I, Easter [1723], in the Common Bench, an action of trespass for breaking his close and chasing his bull. There was a verdict for the plaintiff and 1d. damages. And the question was if he should have any more costs than damages. And it was held by the court that he should have his full costs because the 22 & 23 Car. II, c. 9, extends only to such actions of trespass where the freehold may come in question. Raymond 487; 3 Modern 39.[1] And how could the freehold come in question on chasing a bull?

Beck v. Nicholls, 10 Geo. I, Michaelmas [1723], in the Common Bench,[2] an action of trespass of assault, battery, wounding, and imprisonment, as also for entering and breaking his house and opening the doors of the said house and breaking three locks and three bars belonging to the said doors. The defendant pleaded not guilty to all, except the imprisonment, and, for that, he justifies. And, on the trial, the justification was found for the defendant and the plea of not guilty was found for the plaintiff and the damages were 2s. 6d., and it was held by the court that, the damages being under 40s., he could not have full costs for the battery because the judge had not certified the battery to be well proved; neither could he have full costs for breaking the house etc. because this is a trespass relating to the freehold, the construction of 22 & 23 Car. II, c. 9, s. 149, having been that it extends to a trespass relating to the freehold and inheritance and to such trespasses only, which is collected from the exception, where the judge certifies that the title came in question, which shows that the Act extends only to such trespasses where the freehold might come in question, and not to trespasses of chattels.

Blunt v. Miller, 12 Geo. I, Michaelmas [1725], in the Common Bench, an action of trespass for breaking and entering and breaking the plaintiff's house and keeping the plaintiff out of possession and use of the said house, with a *continuando* for a month, whereby the plaintiff was put to great expenses to gain the possession of his house and, in the meantime, lost the profit and use of his house, there was a verdict for the plaintiff and 2s. 6d. damages. And upon a motion for full costs, it was denied by the court, for this is a plain trespass *quare clausum fregit* and the *per quod* is only an aggravation. And in this case, the title of the freehold might have come in question, and, if so, there should have been a certificate of the judge, which not being in this case, the plaintiff can have no more costs than damages.

11 Geo. I, Trinity [1725], in the Common Bench, an action of trespass *quare clausum fregit et quendam taurum personae ignotae fugavit, per quod* the plaintiff's gooseberry bushes, *necnon quinque particas* (*Anglice* poles) *in eodem clauso erecto officiente et existente fregit laceravit et spoliavit*. There was a verdict for the plaintiff

[1] *Smith v. Batterton* (1683), *ut supra*; *Barnes v. Edgard* (1684), *ut supra*.

[2] *Beck v. Nichols* (1723), 1 Strange 577, 93 E.R. 710, Cooke C.P. 24, 125 E.R. 934.

and 1d. damages. And on a motion for full costs, the court held that these words in this declaration did not import an actual asportation, which must be an entire carrying away, and that the taking and pulling up the poles was not such an asportation, that this was a case in which a certificate might have been made because the freehold might have come in question and, though the trespass was begun by chasing the bull, yet damages is laid to be done to the freehold, and so the title of the freehold might there have come in question.

My Brother Denton, who gave me this report, says that the court doubted of the case in 2 Ventris 215, which was an action of trespass *quare clausum fregit* for digging up and carrying away his trees. And it was found upon evidence that they were roots of trees and carried from one part of the ground to the other. The court there doubted whether this was finding an asportation, for, if the jury only found that which was evidence of an asportation and not an actual asportation, it would not carry costs. But they agreed in the principal case that, if anything were carried off from the grounds, though of never so little value, it would be an *asportavit*, for the words *abcariavit* and *asportavit* in declarations mean such a carrying as amounts to a conversion to the defendant's use. So, where the declaration in a *clausum fregit* for breaking of hedges and an *asportavit* is laid by way of aggravation, that will not carry costs.

But in Smith v. Batterton, Raymond 487, an action of trespass for breaking stalls in a market, they gave full costs because it is a damage to a chattel, for the freehold of the market could never come in question in that action. 2 Shower 258. And it appears by 2 Jones 232 that the trespass was *quoad* the goods only.

And yet, in the case of Barns v. Edgar, 3 Modern 39, 40, where the trespass is only for impounding, the court would not allow full costs because the freehold would not be in question.

But in the case of Asser v. Finch, 2 Levinz, where the question was touching the right of a way and that appeared by the defendant's justification, though the plaintiff replies that it was done *extra viam*, yet the defendant had full costs. But this, though it was a case quoted at the bar, is not to our present purpose because, there, the matter of title appeared on the record itself.

We come, therefore, now, upon the foundations and principles before mentioned, to consider the case before us. Though I doubted somewhat of it at the first, yet I am now clearly of opinion with my brothers that there can be no more costs than damages.

In the present case, there is no count but where the freehold might possibly come in question, for this count is for breaking the barn and locking up the door of the house and barn and detaining several of the plaintiff's goods mentioned in the declaration in that house and barn. Now, here is no substantive and independent count *quoad* the goods and chattels because it is connected with the breaking and locking up of the barn. And in that case, the freehold of the barn might come in question, and, then, locking up the goods in the barn is but mere aggravation in that count.

If a man will put his goods into my barn without my leave, he cannot enter and break my barn in order to come at his own goods. And, therefore, upon this count, the property of the goods might not be in question, but merely the barn that was thus broken.

Another and still a stronger reason, in my opinion, is that it is laid by way of *detinuit*, and not by way of *asportavit*, for, where it is laid by way of *detinuit*, he may detain it as a distress and *contra vadios et plegios*, and not by way of asportation and conversion. And then, even on the face of the count, touching the goods and chattels, the freehold might come in question and whether such distress were lawful, so that taking this as an aggravation of the breaking of the barn, as indeed it ought to be, the freehold might come in question in this count. Or, if it had been put into an independent count in the *detinet* only, and not by way of asportation and conversion, such count would not be good in trespass, and, therefore, no damages could have been recovered for it. And, therefore, there could be no costs *de incremento*, and, consequently, there can be no costs in that case.

I think it very proper to be considered by all practitioners that, if there be a trespass upon the freehold and likewise a count laid *de bonis asportatis*, in order to put in for the costs merely, if there be no evidence of the carrying away of the goods and converting them, to take a verdict of not guilty upon that count, for then, where the jury bring in the damages under 40s., the plaintiff cannot have costs upon the other count of the *clausum fregit* without the certificate of the judge.

I am exceeding clear that, in this case, there ought to be only ordinary costs.

This was the opinion of the whole court, delivered by the Lord Chief Baron Gilbert.

516

Helbert v. Moreing

(Ex. 1724)

A judgment of a lower court is not superseded by a writ of error if the plaintiff in error does not transcribe and certify the record into the appellate court in a timely manner. If a lower court judgment is not superseded in a timely manner, a writ of execution can be issued upon it.

Taussig MS. 311, vol. 2, p. 725

Michaelmas term 1724.

Bootle moved for a rule that the plaintiff in error should transcribe and certify the record into the Parliament within eight days or else the defendant might take out execution.

Baron Price doubted upon the rule of the House of Lords, the error being returnable before them, and they should non-pros. The writ for the error is a *supersedeas* until non-prossed.

But the court thought it right and the motion proper, Eyre, Chief Baron, being now present though absent the day before when this was first moved.

N.B. This is done in the King's Bench by a rule in the office.

517

Ram v. Bradbury

(Ex. 1724-1726)

A defendant cannot refuse to answer interrogatories on the ground of misjoinder of defendants.

It is a sufficient answer to an interrogatory to say that one does not know the answer and has no means of knowing the answer.

Taussig MS. 311, vol. 2, p. 726

Michaelmas term 1724.

The plaintiff exhibits his bill against B. and thirteen others and thereby charges that one G. projected the Brunswick Lottery and that he, the plaintiff, by his appointment, was to receive the subscriptions of such who designed to engage in this lottery 40s. per ticket, 2s. 6d. to be paid down on subscription, that he did not accordingly receive to the amount of £13,000, that there were others also, *viz.* M., N., O., P., etc. who were appointed to receive subscriptions and did take in subscriptions to the amount of £20,000, that the lottery was never drawn. And the plaintiff alleges he repaid all the money he received, but that Bradbury and some of the rest of the defendants who were only subscribers to the other receivers and others of the defendants who were such receivers combining and confederating to charge him with all the money, or at least with their particular money, which had been paid into the said lottery, though not to his hands, had brought actions against him, and so by his bill interrogates Bradbury, to whom he paid in the money for his tickets and so the rest of them.

Bradbury demurs to the whole bill, not denying the combination, and he shows for the cause of the demurrer that the bill was for several independent, incoherent matters and intermixed with the concerns of other defendants, immaterial for him to answer and that he was thereby to be at the expense of taking out a copy of the whole bill etc.

Sed per curiam: The demurrer is improper and ought not to stand in the way of the discovery sought by the plaintiff's bill. And so they overruled it.

Taussig MS. 311, vol. 2, p. 927, pl. 2

Trinity term 1726. Ram v. Turton.

The question was whether he does not know, has heard, or believes what number of tickets were printed.

The defendant answers that he does not know nor has heard save by the bill nor can he set forth as to his belief, he knowing nothing thereof what number of tickets [there were].

And this exception was allowed.

Taussig MS. 311, vol. 2, p. 1010, pl. 1

Michaelmas term 1726.

N.B. Upon arguing the exceptions between Ram and Turton, I insisted on it that the injunction which was continued by setting down exceptions to the third answer would fall of course by overruling the exceptions. And I cited the case of Thompson and Paul.[1]

But Mr. *Aris* got up and contradicted this rule and said that the constant rule was that the injunction stood unless discharged by a motion.

518

Thompson v. Paul

(Ex. 1724)

Where exceptions to continue an injunction are argued and overruled, the injunction is discharged as a matter of course.

Taussig MS. 311, vol. 2, p. 728, pl. 1

Michaelmas term 1724.

If exceptions are put in to continue an injunction and are argued and overruled, the injunction falls of course. And, if the plaintiff would continue the injunction on the merits, he must do it immediately.

Decree Book, Saturday, 24th November 1724.

519

Rex v. Clay, *ex parte*

(Ex. 1724)

The king cannot charge lands seized and extended into his hands on a subsequent debt with a prior debt.

[1] *Thompson v. Paul* (Ex. 1724), see below, Case No. 518.

Taussig MS. 311, vol. 2, p. 746

Michaelmas term 1724.

Clay, being Postmaster of Derby and, as such, having given security to the crown by a bond of [*blank*] and being then seised of certain lands in Derby, *inter alia* of three acres of ground and two roods, which he sold to one Benjamin Blundell, Jr., who was made Receiver General of Leicestershire and, as such, gave security to the crown, and, failing, a [writ of] extent issued against him. And by an inquisition thereon, he was found seised of a considerable estate in Derby and *inter alia* of the close of three acres etc. The Lords of the Treasury order Blundell's estate to be sold. And, accordingly, it was sold to the best bidder before the Deputy [Remembrancer], and the terms of sale were agreed upon and certified to the Treasury, and the money was paid. But before the patent passed the Great Seal, an extent issued against Clay. And, by an inquisition thereon, he is found to have been seised of the aforesaid close of three acres in Derby at the time he entered into his bond and Locker, by this inquisition, is found to be a terre tenant of the same. Hereupon, Mr. Locker applies to the Treasury by a petition to be quieted in his possession. The Treasury refer the matter to the Attorney General.

And the point debated before him was whether the king could charge lands seized and extended into his hands on a subsequent debt with a prior debt. And, upon authorities cited before him, he was of opinion that the lands ought to be discharged from the former debt. And in his report to the Lords of the Treasury, he certified that Locker ought to be quieted in his possession under the extent against Blundell and that, if Locker pleaded this to the inquisition against Clay, they might authorize him to confess the plea, and, thereupon, the Court of Exchequer would award a [writ of] *amoveas manus*. The Lords of Treasury accordingly direct him to do this or take any other method for quieting Locker in his possession.

Whereupon, I moved this day for an order from the court that no further process might issue against Locker on the inquisition found upon the extent against Clay. And the Attorney General [*Yorke*] being in court and consenting to my motion, it was ordered accordingly.

N.B. This motion was made to prevent the charge of pleading, the defendant Locker having already expended the value of the close in his applications to the crown to defend his title. *Et nota*: The Attorney General and myself very much doubted whether the court would come into this method, for we thought they would oblige Locker to plead and not stay process without such title pleaded. But the court granted the motion without any difficulty whatever.

520

Rogers v. Willis

(Ex. 1724)

In this case, a clerk of a corporation entered the wrong name of a shareholder in the company books so that the true owner could not sell it as it declined in value, and the court ordered the corporation to buy the stock from the owner for the amount he paid for it even though there was no evidence that he would have sold it during the time of the erroneous entry in the company books.

Taussig MS. 311, vol. 2, p. 749

Michaelmas term 1724. Rogers v. Willis, Molineer, and the London Assurance Company.

Rogers contracts with Willis for £500 stock in the stock of this Company. Willis, the broker, was to have £1000 delivered to him on 7th September, which he had bought for one Poulter. And Poulter telling him that he was willing to part with £500, Willis agrees to transfer £500 to Rogers. On the 7th September, Willis procures Molineer to transfer £500 to Robert Poulter and £500 to Rogers, and receipts were given by Molineer to Rogers for £500 and to Poulter for £500. But both these receipts were actually given to Willis. And upon producing this receipt to Rogers's bankers, they paid the money to Willis and Molineer. After this, Willis and Molineer go to the office and desire that the stock transferred to Poulter might be altered and Adams' name inserted instead of Poulter's. This was done because Poulter's being one of the Exchange Insurance by the by-laws of the Corporation, he could not have stock in this Company. The clerk belonging to the company, by mistake, for aught appeared to the contrary, instead of striking out Poulter's name, strikes out the name of Rogers and inserts Adams. Rogers, on the 19th of September, goes to the Office and offers to pay in a call, but he was informed he had no stock in the books, but afterwards, *viz.* on 6th October following, the aforesaid mistake was rectified, and the £500 stock was replaced to Rogers's account. But he having been deprived, as he suggested by his bill, of the use of this stock, for which he paid £480 and the stock sinking considerably in value between the 7th September and the 6th October, he now refused to take the stock. And he brought his bill against Willis, Molineer, and the Company.

But as to the two first, the court dismissed the plaintiff's bill. And as to the Company, they decreed that the Company should pay Rogers the £480 and take the £500 stock themselves and this though there was evidence that Rogers declared he did not intend to part with the stock and never went in person to accept the stock until 19th September, *quod mirum mihi videtur*, for I think there is no color for making the Company pay to Rogers any more than the difference of the stock between the time of the mistake and when it was set right.

But EYRE, PRICE, and PAGE were unanimous in the former decree. Gilbert was absent.

521

Foot v. Hurst

(Ex. 1724)

It is a sufficient answer to a bill for tithes in kind to say that they were never paid by the defendant and therefore he, the defendant, kept no records but he believes the value to be such.

Taussig MS. 311, vol. 2, p. 753

Michaelmas term 1724.

[To a] vicar's tithe bill, the defendant insisted that, having paid a *modus* for milk and all other small tithes, he could not set forth an exact account of quantities of milk he had in the years under demand, but he set forth the number of cows he had in each of the said years. And an exception being taken that he has not set forth the quantity and value of the milk, by a second answer, he said he kept no account thereof nor could he set forth the quantity thereof for the reason in his former answer, but he verily believed that in the year [*blank*], the tithe or tenth of his milk was worth about 20s. and no more, in another year 30s. and no more.

And upon the former exception set down to this answer, the court overruled the exception and held the answer sufficient upon the circumstances of the case, though he did not set forth the quantities of milk in every year by gallons or quarts.

I [*Philip Ward*] was for the defendant.

522

Allen, *qui tam* v. Anonymous

(Ex. 1725)

Where unlawfully imported goods have been seized, where there is no bidder, the court can order a re-appraisal if it appears by an affidavit that the original appraisal is false.

Bunbury 185, 145 E.R. 641

23 January 1724[/25].

It was this day moved on the behalf of Allen and others, officers, who had seized a quantity of opium, that there might be a re-appraisement, the first appraisement being at 15s. per pound, which was too much by 5s. per pound, as appeared by an affidavit, and, if the first appraisement stood, it would be a great loss to the officers who seized, for they must pay the king's moiety according to the appraised value.

Per CURIAM: There being no bidder in this case, let there be a re-appraisement.

But query in what respect the case would differ in the reason of the thing if there had been a bidder.

523

Rolfe v. Budder

(Ex. 1725)

Personal property bequeathed to a married woman to her sole and separate use vests the interest in her, in a court of equity, as much as if the bequest has been to trustees for her separate use.

Where the intent of a testator is clear, but the will, being inops consilii, *is defective, a court of equity will correct the obvious defect.*

Bunbury 187, 145 E.R. 642

1 February 1724[/25].

A man and his wife, after many years cohabitation, parted and lived separate. About the year 1714, she being then above sixty years of age, the wife, being destitute of a place to live in, was at last received by the defendant at his house at Dulwich. After the separation, a son of them dies. And, by his will, he devises an £100 bond to his father and £100 East India bond, marked 'No', to his mother, whom he made executrix, and her assigns forever, to her sole and separate use. The bond devised to the father, after the son's death, was paid. The mother being indebted to the defendant for lodgings, necessaries, etc., agrees to let him have her East India bond and that it should be changed for another in the defendant's own name, which was accordingly done. The mother dies. And now the husband exhibited his bill to have an account and satisfaction for this £100 East India bond, suggesting she had eloped and that he was possessed of the bond.

To which the defendant answered as above, denying the elopement or any indirect practice to draw away the wife, but that she was forced to leave him upon the account of his cruelty to her. But no proofs were entered into, so it stood singly upon the point, whether, under these circumstances, she had not such a separate property in the bond, as that she could dispose of it.

And *per* CURIAM, clearly, she is not only executrix, but the bond is devised to her sole and separate use, which vests the interest in her in a court of equity, as much as if the son had vested it in trustees for her separate use. And there are many instances where a court of equity has decreed an husband to stand as a trustee for the separate use of his wife. Lady Suffolk's Case, who married Serjeant Maynard;[1] Sir Joseph Hern's Wife; Seymour v. Dilkes, 17 November 1718. And they said it would have made no alteration in this case if the plaintiff had taken out administration to his wife. And so, the bill was dismissed with costs.

Harvard Law School MS. 1082, vol. 1, p. 224

Hilary term 1724/25.

The question arose upon an East India [Company] bond which was given to the separate use of the wife by the will of her own son. And a bill was exhibited by the husband against the defendant, who had accepted of the bond from the wife, upon allowing so much to her during her life. And there being no trustee named in the will for to keep up the interest of the wife, therefore, it was insisted by the plaintiff that all chattels given to the wife vest in the husband by the marriage.

Chief Baron [EYRE]: I think that this is well vested for the separate use of the wife and that the husband ought not to intermeddle with it. And it is agreed by all that, if a trustee had been named for the use of the wife, it had been good. But I shall supply the want of a trustee in a will and direct it to go according to the will of the testator, *viz.* to the separate use of the wife. And the bill being brought by the husband ought to be dismissed.

PRICE: The wife has the interest in a court of equity, and, as executrix, she can pay debts for her own use. And the condition or a want of a trustee will be supplied and especially in the case of a will. And there is no difference whether [there is] a trustee or not. Lady Suffolk's Case; so much for housekeeping where the contest was between the executor and Lady Suffolk.

PAGE agreed.

And so the bill was dismissed.

Taussig MS. 311, vol. 2, p. 768

Hilary term 1724/25.

The plaintiff [Relffe] demands an East India bond of £100 against the defendant as assignee of his wife of the said bond. And the case was this, that the plaintiff and his wife parted and lived separately. And the husband provided no maintenance, but she went to service and, thereby, gained her livelihood. A son of the plaintiff makes his will, and, by his will, he devises one East India bond

[1] *Hobart v. Countess of Suffolk* (1709), 2 Vernon 644, 23 E.R. 1020, 1 Eq. Cas. Abr. 272, 21 E.R. 1040, *sub nom. Earl of Stamford v. Hobart* (1710), 3 Brown P.C. 31, 1 E.R. 1157, note also *In re Maynard's Will* (1691), Dodd 101.

to the plaintiff, his father, and the India bond in question to his mother and her assigns forever for her own separate use without any title, claim, or demand from her husband, any law or usage to the contrary notwithstanding. And he makes the wife executrix. And the husband gives her a receipt for the bond devised to him and a general release. And then, the wife, being old, goes to the East India House [and] delivers up the bond devised to her. And they give her a new bond for the same sum, which was by her direction made out in the name of the defendant, with whom she lived and who had supported her for some time and promised to bury her when she died and did so. And now, the plaintiff supposing that he, as husband, had a right to this bond, especially since his wife was deceased, exhibits his bill against the defendant for the same.

But the court, *viz.* Eyre, Price, and Page were unanimous that the bill should be dismissed. And they said that, had the will vested this bond in trustees, there had been no color to say the husband had any interest in it even at law and it was as plain as words could make it that it was the intent of the testator that his father should have nothing to do with it, but by his will being *inops consilii*, he had not hit upon the usual method of doing it, which defect it was the duty of a court of equity to supply.

And Price cited the case of Lady Suffolk, Serjeant Maynard's widow, and Page the case of the Lady Herne, in both which cases, it was determined in Chancery that a wife by her husband's consent might have a separate property in money and securities and their being so esteemed in the husband's lifetime was sufficient to secure them against the demands of all other persons except creditors.

And the bill was accordingly dismissed with costs.

524

Hodges v. Beverley

(Ex. 1725)

A gift to a married woman becomes the property of her husband and can be levied on by his creditors.

Bunbury 188, 145 E.R. 642

Hodges v. Mary Beverley and Burton, 11 February 1724[/25].

A man, as principal creditor, takes out administration to J.S. and prefers his bill against the widow and also against Burton for a discovery of the assets of the husband.

Burton, in his answer, insists he has no other assets than £500 and £100, which he submits to the court whether they are the husband's assets or not.

As to the £500, he says that he, being a relation of the wife and observing her to live in great straits and difficulties, out of mere kindness and compassion, proposed to give her £500 to her own separate use for her better support and maintenance. But this, as appeared by the defendant's proofs, was without the husband's privity. And in order to make such gift certain and sure to her, he gave her a promissory note dated 4 February 1707, 'I acknowledge to have received of Mary Beverley £500 to be laid out upon the public funds, and for which I promise to be accountable. /s/ *Bartholomew Burton*'.

As to the £100, he says that, in the year 1709, the wife delivered and deposited in his hands £100 to be kept and secured by the defendant for her separate use.

He insisted also that he frequently paid her sums of money in her husband's lifetime and gave her clothes, which he prayed an allowance for out of the £500 and £100. He submitted to account, but whether to the widow or to the administrator of the husband, he referred to the judgment of the court.

This cause came on to be heard on Thursday the 11th of February 1724, and *per* TOTAM CURIAM, Lord Chief Baron EYRE, PRICE, and PAGE only in court, it was decreed for the plaintiff that this note of £500 and the £100 should be taken as part of the assets of the husband, but they gave the defendant Burton allowance for what sums he had advanced to the wife in her husband's lifetime in discharge of so much of the principal sums of £500 and £100. And it not appearing that he had made any advantage of this money, they would not decree him to account for the interest.

525

Bryan, *qui tam* v. Chamberlain

(Ex. 1725)

In this case, the defendant was found guilty of violating the trading privileges of the East India Company.

Harvard Law School MS. 1082, vol. 1, p. 225, pl. 1

Hilary term 1724/25.

This was a motion in arrest of judgment upon an information on the East India Act. And the information sets forth that the defendant traded beyond the Cape of Good Hope and the Straits of Magellan and, in his homeward bound voyage from the East Indies, the defendant broke bulk.

[To the] first exception [that] it does not appear that the Cape of Good Hope and the Straits of Magellan are part of the East Indies, [it was] answered the Statute of 9 & 10 Will. III, 6 Queen Anne, 5 Geo., 7 Geo.[1] have given those parts to the East India Company.

---

1 Stat. 9 Will. III, c. 44 (*SR*, VII, 429-446); Stat. 6 Ann., c. 71 (*SR*, VIII, 824-829); Stat. 5 Geo. I, c. 21; Stat. 7 Geo. I, stat. 1, c. 21.

The second exception [was that] it is not said that the defendant was not a member of the Company trading to the Levant Seas and such a person was capable of trading there.

But the court overruled that and the other exception and gave judgment for the plaintiff.

526

Downes v. Mooreman

(Ex. 1725)

In this case, a right to tithes was established by the court.

In this case, a sworn copy of an old contract was allowed to be read as evidence because the original could not be produced in court.

Bunbury 189, 145 E.R. 643,
1 Rayner 202, 2 Gwillim 658, 1 Eagle & Younge 803

11 February 1724[/25].

A bill was brought by the rector of Bonchurch in the Isle of Wight in the County of Southampton for the great and small tithes of a farm called Luccomb Farm in the defendant's possession.

The defendant insists that Lovecomb, *alias* Luccomb, Farm formerly belonged to the Abbey of Quarr, that the abbot of Quarr was seised in fee of the manor and farm of etc. and all the tithes renewing thereon as of a portion of tithes in gross, that this abbey, by surrender and by the Stat. 27 Hen. VIII,[1] came to the crown, that, after King Henry's demise, the same descended to King Edward VI, who in the seventh year of his reign, by his letters patent, granted *manerium de Lovecomb ac grangiam etc. ac omnes et omnimodas decimas etc. in dicto manerio de Lovecomb etc., parcella reventionum dictae abbatiae de Quarr dudum existentis* to Cotton and others, and so he derives the title down to Knight, to whom the defendant was lessee for twenty-one years. And in his answer, he set forth the clause in the Stat. 27 Hen. VIII, that all persons etc. who should have by any letters patents lands, etc., tithes, etc. belonging to any monastery etc. dissolved by that Statute, should hold the same in like form, manner, and condition, as the abbots etc. held the same and might have held the same if the said abbeys had not been suppressed.

This cause was heard 11 February 1724. And the defendant carried his proof down from the year 1289 in a regular method to the hands of the defendant's lessor, the Knights.

[1] Stat. 27 Hen. VIII, c. 28 (*SR*, III, 575-578).

But note: All the written evidence produced mentioned the tithe only '*omnes vel omnimodas decimas*' etc. but, in none of the instruments, was mention made of a portion of tithes, upon which the plaintiff founded his objection, that no title appeared in the defendant, *portio decimarum* being a thing distinct from tithes in the general acceptation.

But the proof being so clear, *per* TOTAM CURIAM, the plaintiff's bill was dismissed, and the party had a decree on his cross-bill to enjoy his tithes pursuant to his grants etc.

Note: A copy of an agreement between the abbot of Quarr and the monks of Lyra was produced in evidence, to which it was objected for the plaintiff that, by the rules of evidence, it could not be read, being neither a record nor a public thing. But the defendant produced a copy of the statutes of Oxford,[1] that no book etc. should go out of the Bodleian Library. And the court gave leave to read this copy of agreement in evidence, though they admitted it not to be within the general rules of evidence, but upon the very particular circumstances of this case.

Harvard Law School MS. 1082, vol. 1, p. 225, pl. 2

Hilary term 1724/25.

The original bill was brought by the plaintiff against the defendant, setting forth that he was rector of Bonchurch in the Isle of Wight, against the defendant occupier of a farm called Luccombe, *alias* Lovecombe, Farm within that rectory. The defendant insisted that he was tenant of that farm under Mrs. Price and Sarah Knight, daughters and co-heirs of Richard Knight. And he insisted that the Abbey of Quarr was before the Dissolution of the Monasteries seised in fee of this manor of Lovecombe *alias* Luccombe and likewise of all the great and small tithes arising therefrom as a portion of the tithes in gross and that this abbey was dissolved by Stat. 27 Hen. VIII. And then he recites the clause in the Statute that such lands and other things came to the crown and the patentee in the same manner as the abbot held them, that Henry VIII died, and the same descended to Edward VI, who, by letters patent dated 18 May 7 *regni* granted the same to Reve and Lofton, under whom the Knights, the landladies of the defendant Moreman, claimed the same so insisted upon, that they were seised of these tithes as a portion of the tithes in gross and that no tithes had ever been paid for these lands but by a collusive decree once obtained by the plaintiff against Rolfe.

The defendants'[2] cross-bill was to be quieted in the perception of the tithes against the plaintiff as rector or any of his successors. And upon the proof, several old leases before the dissolution were produced where the tithes were let separately from the lands, and likewise, in the minister's accounts, there was a separate account of the tithes and another for the lands. And as full a proof as

[1] *Parecbolae sive Excerpta e Corpore Statutorum Universitatis Oxoniensis.*

[2] Plaintiff's *MS.*

the case could admit was made in the original cause by the defendant and the plaintiffs in the cross-cause.

But the counsel said for the plaintiff Downes that this was a new-fangled invention to excuse the lesser monastery under Stat. 27 Hen. VIII from being exempt. And so he seemed to ridicule the notion of it.

But the court was of a different opinion.

Chief Baron [Eyre]: The question was who had a right to the perception of these tithes, which he thought was well vested in the defendants, who, by their own cross-bill, were entitled to be established in that right. In 1289, the tithes were in the hands of the Abbey of Quarr, and it is a portion of the tithes and they were granted as a separate interest. And tithes will subsist as collateral to the land, and the accounts proved in this cause are very material. And the king is not deceived in his grant, and it is a portion of the tithes in gross and nothing else. The right is well established ever since 1289. And the evidence is very strong. And the Knights might grant away the tithes separate from the land. And I think that the cross-bill is well founded as to the pernancy of the tithes. And, therefore, the rector's bill must be dismissed and the cross-bill retained.

Price: I admit that the non-payment alone will not be sufficient against a rector. And there have been but few if any cases of this kind. But I never saw a defense more fully made out than this before us. Before the Council of Lateran, every person might pay to whom they would, and, before that, the former owner of the lands might grant these tithes to the Abbey of Quarr or Lyra. And I must call this a portion of the tithes. And it is separated from the rectory. And I will intend it before the grant of Richard I. And here has been indisputable possession against the plaintiff. This is not by way of discharge. And I think that the cross-bill is proper, founded on the notion of a bill of peace.

Page: The reasons and rules given by my brethren are agreeable with my opinion. And a religious house was capable of a discharge. If the abbey had only the perception of the tithes and not the lands, they were well vested in the crown.

So upon the whole, the court decreed the plaintiff's bill as rector to be dismissed, and they established the pernancy of the tithes upon the defendant's cross-bill, which was ordered to be retained.

Taussig MS. 311, vol. 2, p. 778

Hilary term 1724/25.

N.B. The Abbey of Lyra in Normandy had the Church of Carisbrooke in the Isle of Wight, and this was a cell to the said Abbey.

The plaintiff, as rector of Bonechurch in the Isle of Wight, exhibits his bill for tithes.

The defendant insists by an answer that the farm of Luckhome and the tithes thereof were in the possession of the Abbey of Quarr, one of the lesser abbeys, as a portion of tithes in gross, which Abbey was dissolved by 27 Hen. VIII, and thereby the lands and tithes came to Henry VIII, then to Edward VI, and he conveys title under letters patents to two sisters, the Knights, and to himself as lessee under them. The defendant and the two Knights bring a cross-bill to be quieted in possession of the lands and tithes.

There was an agreement 4 Ides of March 1289 under seal between the monks of Quarr and the monks of Lyra in Normandy concerning these tithes. The instrument was in Latin, *Religiosi de Lyra et Religiosi de Quarra*, 29 September 4 Hen. VII [1488], a lease of the manor of Luchouse and tithes. 20 Hen. VIII [1528 x 1529] was another lease.

A question arose whether a copy of this agreement might be read as evidence upon these circumstances, *viz.* because the agreement itself was in the Bodleian Library and there bound up in a book together with several other original deeds and writings for the better preserving of them and, by the Statutes of the University of Oxford made for the preservation of the books and manuscripts of the said library, it was expressly provided that none of them should be removed or carried out of the Library on any occasion whatsoever unless for the binding of them, and upon an oath that due application had been made to the library keeper etc.

And upon a return of the aforesaid answer and producing a copy of the said statute, which was agreed to be evidence of the statute and swearing that the copy produced was a true copy, the court permitted it to be read, there being no method which the court could previously take to compel the producing of the original. The agreement being read and purporting that the tithes arising out of the particular lands in question did belong to the monks of Quarr and there being old leases of the land and of the tithes with distinct rents reserved for the same and in some of them a reservation of part of the tithes themselves and there being distinct accounts for the lands and tithes and distinct rents answered for them in the minister's accounts in the Augmentations [Office] and grants from the crown particularizing the tithes as tithes arising out of and for those particular lands, the court thought the evidence full to prove the tithes in the convent and in the crown as a portion of the tithes. And, therefore, they dismissed the rector's bill and decreed that the plaintiff's in the cross-cause should be quieted in the enjoying of these lands and of the tithes.

N.B. The Abbey of Lyra in Normandy had the church of Carisbrooke in the Isle of Wight, and this was a cell to the said Abbey.

[Order of 11 February 1725: 2 Wood 238.]

527

Rickson, *qui tam* v. Sandford

(Ex. 1725)

Upon a prosecution for a forfeiture for not paying customs, the possessor of the goods need not plead that the goods had been already condemned before he bought them.

Bunbury 191, 145 E.R. 644

17 February 1724[/25].

Upon an information of seizure of a parcel of wines, the defendant gave in evidence that he bought them of Boys, and Boys bought them at the Custom House in Portsmouth, being condemned wines.

The Attorney General [*Yorke*] objected at the trial that the condemnation should have been pleaded, or at least they should have produced the condemnation.

But *per* Lord Chief Baron EYRE, the defendant now is a third person, and he bought the wines of Boys, and it would be hard to put him to show, much more so to plead, the condemnation, whatever might have been done in case Boys had been the defendant, who was the first purchaser after the condemnation. And, therefore, he thought it ought to be left to the jury. And so it accordingly was, and they gave a verdict for the defendant.

(But the point of pleading was reserved for the judgment of the court. See the Exchequer rules.)

528

Anonymous

(Ex. 1725)

The question in this case was whether the defendant should be required to accuse himself of forgery in his answer to the bill of complaint.

Taussig MS. 311, vol. 2, p. 758

Saturday, first day of Hilary term 1724/25.

A bill suggesting that, in order to induce the plaintiff to lend money, the defendant mortgagor, by the advice of his solicitor, had made an affidavit that the estate was free from mortgage and mortgages and then followed a blank, which after swearing was filled up with these words 'and incumbrance and incumbrances'. And, by the bill, this was charged to be done by the advice of the defendant's solicitor, who was also made a party to the suit. And the bill inquired particularly into this circumstance.

And hereupon last term, the bill was referred for scandal, and the Master reported the fact specially as above. And now it was alleged that this charge was proper as being the gist of the plaintiff's equity and, though it was a charge of forgery, yet it was proper to be inserted in order to give the plaintiff an opportunity to prove it. But whether the defendant should be obliged to answer it was another question, which the court would not now determine. But they discharged the former order for the reference.

EYRE, Chief Baron, seemed to think it would be too hard to make the defendant to answer.

PAGE seemed to think otherwise and cited a case between [*blank*].

529

Jones v. Barrett

(Ex. 1725)

When a sequestrator of a church is sued, the bishop who appointed him must be joined as a co-defendant.

Harvard Law School MS. 1082, vol. 1, p. 227, pl. 2

Sittings after Hilary term 1724/25.

The plaintiff, as vicar of West Dean in the County of Sussex, brought his bill for tithes against the sequestrator, which incurred during the vacancy of the living in the former predecessor's time, which vacancy was from January 1714 and the [date the] plaintiff was inducted, 25 November 1719.

[It was] insisted for the plaintiff that, by the Stat. 28 Hen. VIII, cap. 11,[1] the successor is entitled to all tithes and dues incurred during the vacancy and there is a penalty in that Statute for not accounting. If the surplusage profits had been applied for the repairing of the vicarage house, the plaintiff would not have brought this bill.

Mr. *Ward*, for the defendant: This is an unprecedented bill and very improper and especially against the defendant alone. And it has been often held in this court that a sequestrator's title is too feeble to bring a bill alone without the bishop as ordinary because the sequestrator is only a servant to the bishop and the bishop is only to take care of the profits. See the Statute of Hen. VIII.

The penalty of the Statute is only against the bishop after deduction of expenses. The bishop of the diocese is the person to judge what is proper to be allowed, and the ordinary is the only person. It is a very hard case, for the plaintiff himself officiated as curate for the defendant and, by way of return got the scales for this living. And this living has been so poor that it has been held under sequestration for forty years. I allow that the plaintiff seems to allow and to secure the rents and profits to the next incumbent, yet, when the bishop grants a sequestration, then there is a relaxation as to those profits and the account only [is] proper and what ought to be allowed in ecclesiastical courts.

Bootle, for the defendant: The bill is improper because what was prayed cannot be decreed as to allowances, for the Act of 28 Hen. VIII, cap. 11, sec. 5, has prescribed the method and the bishop is judge of the allowances. But if a decree is to be obtained, then the Deputy [Remembrancer] is to be the judge of these

[1] Stat. 28 Hen. VIII, c. 11 (*SR*, III, 666-667).

allowances where the Statute has appointed the ordinary. The original cause of giving jurisdiction to this court of all tithes was as *debitor domini regis*. See Bartlett v. Bishop of Norwich and Nichols.

Chief Baron [EYRE] thought the application was proper in this court and he agreed that it was made a legal right by the Statute of Hen. VIII. And so he agreed. And in the case of Champernon v. Jeffreys, the King's Bench granted a [writ of] prohibition. The bishop is only ministerial and not judge, for, if so, he would be judge and officer too, which is inconsistent. And an action will lie against the bishop.

PRICE: Surely, the bishop ought to be a party.

Upon the whole, the court recommended the parties to refer the matters in difference to their diocesan, and so it was agreed by the parties to do. Query this case, it being *primae impressionis*.

Taussig MS. 311, vol. 2, p. 781

Hilary term 1724/25.

The bill by the plaintiff, as vicar of West Dean in the County of Sussex, as presented, instituted, and inducted thereto 5 November 1709, demands an account of the tithes from November 1714. The defendant, in November 1714, entered into the living and held the same by a sequestration under the bishop of Chichester to the time of the plaintiff's institution and induction and served the cure by himself and one paid by him all that time and this living had been under a sequestration for forty years before the defendant's time by one Mr. Richardson.

N.B. The plaintiff offered to make all reasonable allowances for serving the cure and repairs.

Ex parte the defendant, it was objected that the bishop of Chichester should have been made a defendant.

The court gave no opinion about the matter, but recommended it to the parties to refer it by consent to the bishop of Chichester to settle the controversy between them and the cause to stand over to the next term. And, if the bishop did not determine it in that time, then the court would.

Bunbury 192, 145 E.R. 644,
1 Rayner 204, 2 Gwillim 657, 1 Eagle & Younge 804

22 February 1724[/25].

A bill was brought by the vicar of West Dean in the County of Sussex against the defendant, who was sequestrator, for an account of the profits received during the vacation. It was objected for the defendant that the bishop ought to have been made a party, since the sequestrator is accountable to him for what he receives by the Stat. 28 Hen. VIII. The court seemed to think the bishop should have been a party.

But, by consent, this cause was preferred to the bishop of the diocese.

Note: It was said a sequestrator could not bring a bill alone for tithes.

[Order of 22 February 1725: 2 Wood 235, 1 Eagle & Younge 804.]

530

Reynell v. Wills

(Ex. 1725)

The question in this case was the validity of a modus decimandi *in lieu of tithes in kind alleged by the defendants.*

Taussig MS. 311, vol. 2, p. 762

Thursday, 28 January 1724/25. Reynell v. Dennis, Moore, Wills, and Wyche.

The plaintiff, as impropriator of Broadclist in the County of Devon, exhibits his bill for tithes of all sorts of [*blank*]. The *modus*es set out and insisted upon by the answer were:

2d. per hogshead for cider and so proportionally;

2d. for every hoard of apples;

2d. for every milk cow or heifer;

2 for every winter cow;

1d. for garden stuff consumed in the house, but not for stuff sold;

1d. per hearth for wood burnt in the house.

As to Easter offerings: 2d. for a man, 2d. for a wife, 2d. for every child unmarried above sixteen.

Custom to mow and cut, ted and spread, the grass and then gather and set it up into cocks in lieu of tithes of the first and second moath.

A cross-bill [was filed] by Sir Hugh Ackland etc. v. Sir William Reynell and Long[1] to establish the *modus*es both against Reynell and against Long, the vicar of Broadclift.

The parish is divided into thirds, two-thirds are enjoyed by the impropriator and one-third by the vicar alternately.

The defendants insisted on the 2d. for a hogshead of cider and 2d. for a hoard of apples as extending to all apples, as well in new-planted orchards as old and to apples sold, as well as such as are made into cider or spent in the family. Hutton 58.[2]

Pengelly: The vicar is not a party to the original bill, but he demands all the tithes for ten years last past whereas the right to the tithes in the three several parts of the parish is alternate between the vicar and him.

The first *modus*, 2d. per hogshead for cider and so proportionably, this extended to new orchards or new enlargements of old orchards.

---

[1] Perhaps *Reynell v. Ackland* (Ex. 1726), see below, Case No. 613.

[2] *Poole v. Reynold* (1621), Hutton 57, 123 E.R. 1098, also Winch 1, 44, 124 E.R. 1, 38, 1 Eagle & Younge 322.

The *modus* for a hogshead is not annexed to the land, but to the produce. And so the case in Hutton is not like this, for, there, the *modus* is annexed not to the hay, but to the hay ground.

2d. for every hoard of apples;

8d. for every calf;

2d. for every ill heifer;

1d. for every colt;

1d. for eggs of all poultry except geese;

The two mills are ancient mills, and [they] never paid tithes.

[They] put off to make the vicar, Mr. Long, party to the original bill.

Taussig MS. 311, vol. 2, p. 776

Monday, 8 February 1724[/25]. Reynell v. Wills.

Serjeant *Pengelly*: In Michaelmas 8 George [1721], a bill was filed. [There was] satisfaction for tithes by receipts under the hands of Reynell or his agents.

As to wood spent in the house, 1d. called a hearth penny. As to other wood sold, the defendants say it was cut from old timber stools;

2d. per hogshead for cider, and the defendants say it extends to what is sold as well as spent in the family;

2d. for every hoard of apples, ditto;

2 for every [*blank*];

8 for every calf fallen;

2d. for every [*blank*];

1d. for garden stuff; this does not extend to turnips or cabbages sold;

2d. for offerings, as before;

1 for every [*blank*];

2 for cheese, honey, and wax;

Hay; there is a *modus* that the parishioners mow and cut, ted and throw it abroad in windrows, and then gather it into cocks, and this is in lieu and satisfaction of said tithes of the second crop.

As to mills, two of them, they are ancient mills. And no tithes were ever paid for them. They are immemorially discharged.

The chief controversy will be as to the *modus* for cider, hoard of apples, and hay, whether the two first extends to new orchards or an enlargement of old orchards, to apples sold as well as spent in the family, and whether the *modus* for hay is good.

8d. for every calf fallen is too rank.

The court directed issues to try whether there was a *modus* for 2d. per hogshead for all cider made of apples throughout the parish; secondly, whether 2d. per hoard of all apples not made into cider [was due].

Chief Baron [EYRE]: I take it that the word 'hoard' signifies every collection of apples not made into cider.

The first issue is one issue as to apples, *viz.* whether 2d. per hoard for every hogshead of cider made of apples grown in the parish and 2d. for every hoard of apples not converted into cider. The second issue is whether the tedding etc. of the first crop of grass is a *modus* in satisfaction of the tithe of after-moath whether made into hay or threshed and made into seed.

[Order of 8 February 1725[/26]: 2 Wood 244, 1 Eagle & Younge 808.]

531

Hanson v. Green

(Ex. 1725)

An amendment to a bill of complaint can extend the time upon which damages can be awarded.

Taussig MS. 311, vol. 2, p. 764

Hilary term 1724/25. Hanson and Parrot v. Green *et al.*

A bill was filed by the plaintiff setting forth that his brother, to whom he was heir, made a lease to the defendant's father of the impropriate tithes of the parish of Sow in the County of [*blank*] to commence from 26 March 1701 for twenty-one years and, therefore, ended 26 March 1722, and that he the plaintiff made a new lease to the other defendant Parrot to commence from 26th March 1722 and that the defendant to avoid the plaintiff's taking possession by virtue of this second lease held on and pretended that his lease did not end until 26th March 1723. Therefore, he demanded a discovery of the lease and prayed an account of the tithes for that year, *viz.* from Lady Day 1722 to Lady Day 1723. And the bill suggested that, if the original lease in the defendant's hands was made to commence from 1702, that it had been altered, since it was signed by the plaintiff's brother. The defendant put in his answer whereby he insisted that his lease was to commence from 1702 and not from 1701 and, consequently, did not expire until 1723. He denied any alteration of the lease. Then, the plaintiff amends his bill and, by that amended bill, he takes in another year, *viz.* all the year 1723 and prays an account of the tithes in that year as well as in the former year. To this, the defendant put in his second answer and very imprudently insisted that the plaintiff might have no right at all to the tithes because he had purchased the manor of Sow with all its appurtenances and so would have thought that he was also entitled to the tithes.

Upon the hearing of the cause this day before the Chief Baron Eyre, Price, and Page, the original lease and counterpart were produced. And the plaintiff gave up the point, that is to say would not go to a trial at law whether the lease was to determine at Lady Day 1722 or 1723, but prayed they might have their rent for the year 1722 and that the defendants might account for the tithes of the year 1723.

To this, it was answered that the court could not decree them the rent because there was no such demand by their bill. Secondly, if there had been such a demand, it would have been a very improper one because that was at law, second, that the court could not decree them an account for the tithes, even of the year 1723 for that the first bill being exhibited Michaelmas 1722, though the year 1723 was inserted in the amended bill, it was perfectly irregular and, by the rules of the court, an amended bill can never carry a demand to a further time than the original bill. And this always was esteemed the common practice.

But notwithstanding, the court made a decree that the defendant should pay to the plaintiff his rent of £60 for the year 1722 and should account for the tithes of the year 1723. And they said that the counterpart signed by the defendant's father being wrong gave the plaintiff occasion for this suit and, therefore, in equity, he ought to make him amends for it and the bill was for tithes or some satisfaction for them and prayed a general relief.

Second, the Chief Baron said it was now too late to object to the amended bill since the defendant had answered to it and had submitted to account in the case. The court was of opinion the plaintiff had a title, which it was certain he had after the defendant's lease was expired and, by our own acknowledgement, it did expire at Lady Day 1723. And, consequently, the plaintiff was well entitled for the year 1723. And by the Chief Baron, if it is irregular to carry the demand further by an amended bill than was originally intended by the bill, he should have objected to the amendment and not have answered to it, but now the court may well decree upon the amended bill.

And Page said that such amendments to carry the demand further had been often allowed in this court because they prevented the vexation of a perfect new bill.

And the court decreed the defendant to pay costs even though the chief matter in controversy was the determination of the lease, which point was now entirely given up, *quod mihi et aliis domorum [?] videbantur.*

532

Warren v. Hooper

(Ex. 1725)

The filing of a bill in equity for tithes is ipso facto *a waiver of the statutory penalties.*

Taussig MS. 311, vol. 2, p. 774

Hilary term 1724/25.

The defendant demurred to the plaintiff's bill for tithes, for that he had not waived the penalties of the Statute[1] for the treble value. And 3 Leon. 204[2] was cited.

But the court overruled the demurrer because the bringing of the bill was a waiver of those penalties and this court would enjoin against an action brought for the penalties and decree for the single [damages]. It is otherwise upon a bill to stay waste. There, the penalties must be waived. So in the ecclesiastical court, penalties must be waived or [a writ of] prohibition must go because the ecclesiastical court can enjoin in the case of an action brought at law. It was overruled with costs though the plaintiff had no counsel to oppose the demurrer.

533

Page v. Chester

(Ex. 1725)

The question in this case was whether a defendant can object to discovery without alleging specifically a title in himself to the property in issue.

Taussig MS. 311, vol. 2, p. 775, pl. 2

Hilary term 1724/25.

Eyre and Page: In a bill to discover a title, the plaintiff claims as heir or administratrix to A. [and] makes a title. The defendant pleads a title from the original owner to C., but did not show that C. was a purchaser for a valuable consideration, and shows no title from C., only insists that he has a title under him and so pleads in bar of discovery. The plea is good.

Price, *contra*, [held] that he ought to show a title to defend himself against a discovery.

But the court took further time to determine the question.

534

Bibye v. Huxley

(Ex. 1725)

The question in this case was whether beech trees were considered timber in the county for the purpose of tithes.

Harvard Law School MS. 1082, vol. 1, p. 229

Sittings after Hilary term 1724/25.

---

[1] Stat. 2 & 3 Edw. VI, c. 13, s. 1 (*SR*, IV, 55-56).

[2] *Anonymous* (1588), 3 Leonard 204, 74 E.R. 634.

This was a bill for tithe of wood. The defendant insisted upon that the woods in question were timber woods and so preserved for that purpose. And though they did cut some wood as the loppings and prunings of trees of oak, ash, and elm and likewise cut down great quantities of beech, which was used for timber in this county, *viz.* of Bedford, therefore, no tithes were due.

The court offered the plaintiff to try whether beech was timber or not in this county, which he declined. So they ordered the defendant to account of such woods cut as was not toppings, loppings, or prunings of trees above twenty years growth and that was not beech wood.

Bunbury 192, 145 E.R. 644,
1 Rayner 201, 2 Gwillim 657, 1 Eagle & Younge 805

Eodem die [22 February 1725].

In a bill for tithes of wood by the rector of Whipmeed in the County of Bedford, the question was whether beech was esteemed timber in this county, which went to an issue to try. See the cases cited: Plowden, *Commentaries*, 470; 2 Inst., commentary upon the Stat. 45 Edw. III; Stat. 35 Hen. VIII; Cro. Jac. 100, Moore 908; 2 Croke 199; 1 Rolle, *Abridgment*, 640, P.5; 1 Inst. 53.[1]

[Order of 22 February 1725: 2 Wood 237.]

535

Attorney General, ex rel. Waters v. Vincent

(Ex. 1725)

A discovery that may lead to penalties and forfeitures at common law will not be compelled in equity.

Harvard Law School MS. 1082, vol. 1, p. 228

Sittings after Hilary term 1724/25.

This was a bill at the relation of Walters, lord of the manor of Woking in the County of Surrey, against the defendant for a discovery of what waste was committed by the defendants, who were copyholders of that manor. And the bill included several other matters besides that of committing waste.

The defendants demur and, for cause of demurrer, show that committing waste by a copyholder is a forfeiture, and, therefore, it is to be demurred to be-

[1] *Soby v. Molins* (1574), 2 Plowden 468, 75 E.R. 700, 1 Eagle & Younge 60, 1 Gwillim 133; E. Coke, *Second Institute* (1642); Stat. 45 Edw. III, c. 3 (*SR*, I, 393); Stat. 35 Hen. VIII, c. 17 (*SR*, III, 977-980); *Brook v. Rogers* (1605), Croke Jac. 100, 79 E.R. 86, Moore K.B. 908, 72 E.R. 989, 1 Eagle & Younge 158; *Anonymous* (1607), Croke Jac. 199, 79 E.R. 174, 1 Gwillim 228, 1 Eagle & Younge 167; *Leonard's Case* (1596), 1 Rolle, Abr., *Dismes*, pl. Q, 5, p. 640; E. Coke, *First Institute* (1628), f. 53.

cause there is no waiver of penalties and it is to aid a party to recover a forfeiture, for when that is discovered, the plaintiff may bring his [action of] ejectment and recover the copyhold. And there can be no case in equity for the copyhold defendant to accuse himself and to subject himself to a forfeiture.

Attorney General [*Yorke*], for the plaintiff: This bill is to establish certain customs as well as for discovery of what timber was cut down. And there is a difference between this case and a penalty directed by an act of Parliament, for this is not an offense so created. Bills are proper for discovery of a bond, though the penalty is annexed, and so where a condition is annexed for the holding of an estate, a bill is proper for a discovery of such a condition. This is a common case of a tenant for life and suggesting of committing waste. And this demurrer is improper because it covers too much, for there are other customs that this demurrer covers. And, therefore, it ought to be overruled.

Bootle, for the plaintiff: The form of the demurrer is not good, and it covers too much because several infringements of the customs are covered by this demurrer. But I think I need not insist upon that because the court last term overruled the demurrer which was for want of waiving of penalties to a tithe bill and the bringing a bill is a waiver. And it was so adjudged in Warren v. Hopper heard last term.[1] And so [it was] adjudged in the cases in this court about the duties of malt and other excise duties. Attorney General v. Phipps.

Cox replies for the defendant: The tithe bill prays the single value only and that is in consequence a waiver of penalties, which is an answer to that case about tithes. But, if the lord brings an ejectment in the present case, the answer of the defendants will be evidence against the defendants to enable the lord to recover a forfeiture.

Chief Baron [Eyre]: I think that the penalties must be waived, and it is not like the case of a tithe bill. And no satisfaction can be given for the waste in this court. And, therefore, we cannot stop the lord by an injunction if he should bring his [action of] ejectment for the forfeiture. The common forms of bills are with a waiver of penalties. So I think the demurrer is good.

Price agreed [and] so allowed the demurrer.

Bunbury 192, 145 E.R. 644

25 February 1724[/25].

An English information was brought to discover copyhold lands and also what timber had been cut down and what waste [was] committed etc.

The defendant demurs because there is a forfeiture of the place wasted and treble damages and yet the Attorney General has not waived forfeitures.

---

[1] *Warren v. Hooper* (Ex. 1725), see above, Case No. 532.

Per CURIAM, the demurrer was allowed, and this differs from the case of a tithe bill, which used indeed formerly to be with a waiver of penalties, but has of late been discontinued because the bill prays only the single value of the tithes.

536

Soper v. Morris

(Ex. 1725)

A general release must be made within a set short period of time after a judgment.

A person can release the costs in an ecclesiastical court, but not the judgment itself.

Taussig MS. 311, vol. 2, p. 789

Easter term 1725. In prohibition.

1 Mod. 21, 22, Worthy v. Liddall;[1] Cro. Car. 10.

Whether the general release is good: first, it came too late after the conclusion of the cause according to our forms and, therefore, the remedy is by way of an appeal; secondly, the husband cannot discharge this suit. Indeed, he may discharge the costs, but not the sentence of penance. Cro. Car. 222, to this very point; Rolle, *Abr.*, 343, [*blank*] 9.[2]

E contra: 1 Salkeld, Chamberlain and Howson's Case, 7 & 8 Will. III, fol. 115,[3] is express authority that prohibition will lie *quoad* the costs after a release. Cro. Eliz. 908, Moor 665.[4]

537

Farr v. Butcher

(Ex. 1725)

In this case, the executor of a decedent's will was ordered to make his accounts with the court and to pay the plaintiffs that which they were due.

---

[1] *Worthy v. Liddall* (1669), 1 Modern 21, 86 E.R. 700, also *sub nom. Worsley v. Lyddal*, 1 Siderfin 433, 82 E.R. 1201, 2 Keble 577, 581, 84 E.R. 363, 366, 1 Ventris 61, 86 E.R. 43, Lincoln's Inn MS. Misc. 500, f. 62v (Edward Ward's reports).

[2] *Anonymous* (1631), Croke Car. 222, 79 E.R. 794; *Motam v. Motam* (1616 x 1617), 1 Rolle, Abr., *Baron & Feme*, pl. F, 9, p. 343.

[3] *Chamberlain v. Hewson* (1696), 1 Salkeld 115, 91 E.R. 107, also 1 Lord Raymond 73, 91 E.R. 945, 5 Modern 69, 87 E.R. 524, 12 Modern 89, 88 E.R. 1184, Holt K.B. 99, 90 E.R. 953.

[4] *Stephens v. Totty* (1602), Croke Eliz. 908, 78 E.R. 1130, Moore K.B. 665, 72 E.R. 826, also Noy 45, 74 E.R. 1014.

Public Record Office E.126/23, f. 277, pl. 1

29 April 1725, Surrey.

Whereas by an order of this court made on the hearing of this cause the 11th day of July 1723, it was then ordered that the said defendants [Robert Butcher, Richard Amery, and Richard Starkey, executors of John Marshall] should come to an account with the plaintiffs [Thomas Farr and Eliza, his wife] before the Deputy Remembrancer of this court for all such money, household and other goods, plate, jewels, rings, and other effects late of the said John Marshall which at any time since the death of the said John Marshall anywise came to the defendants' hands, custody, power, or possession or of any or either of them or of any other person or persons for their use by their order or in trust for them or any or either of them and for the better discovery and taking of the said account of the estate of the said John Marshall or come to their hands, the said defendants were to be examined on interrogatories and the said Deputy was to be armed with a commission and commission or commissions might issue into the country if need was for the better taking of the said account and the said Deputy Remembrancer was to make his report with all convenient speed, which said cause standing in the paper of causes came on this day to be heard upon the Deputy's report before the Rt. Hon. Sir Robert Eyre, Kt., Lord Chief Baron, Mr. Baron Price, Sir Francis Page, Kt., and Sir Jeffrey Gilbert, Kt., three other of the barons of this court, and upon hearing of Mr. Fane and Mr. Short, for the plaintiffs, nobody attending for the defendants and upon reading of the said order on hearing of the 11th day of July 1723 and of the report of John Harding, Esq., Deputy Remembrancer of this court, dated the 23d day of February last, who thereby certified that he found the sum of £54 18s. 4d. of the estate of John Marshall in the said order mentioned came to the hands of the defendant Robert Butcher and has thought fit to allow the said defendant Butcher for his disbursements in the whole amounting to the sum of £28 15s. 8d. which being deducted out of the sum of £54 18s. 4d. reduces the same to the sum of £26, 3s. 4d., it is thereupon this day finally ordered by this court that the said defendant Robert Butcher do upon notice of this order or a true copy thereof forthwith pay or cause to be paid to the plaintiffs or their assignees the sum of £26 3s. 4d. so reported to be in the said defendant Robert Butcher's hands, which is due to the plaintiffs together with their costs to be taxed by the Deputy Remembrancer of this court.

538

Raine v. Hughes

(Ex. 1725)

At common law, a contempt of court can be denied by the contemnor's own interrogatory answers alone, but, in equity, a person can use the interrogatory answers of third persons to prove a contempt.

Harvard Law School MS. 1082, vol. 1, p. 232

Easter term 1725.

There being an attachment against Cradock for a contempt and, thereupon, Cradock had been examined on interrogatories on the law side of this court, Mr. *Aris* moved for a commission on the law side for liberty to examine witnesses to prove the contempt upon Cradock and to falsify his examination.

Mr. *Bootle*, for Cradock: All this proceeding is on the plea side. And the method should be according to all the other courts at law. And the defendant in this case having denied this contempt upon his oath, such party is cleared without any further examination; so in this case. And though precedents were produced that such a commission had issued, yet they appeared to be granted by consent.

The court, in this case, declared that, upon contempts in causes in equity, it was usual to grant a commission to falsify his examination because contempts in equity affect the very merits of the cause itself, but not so at law. So the motion was denied.

539

Johnson v. Firebrace

(Ex. 1725)

Where the amount of the tithes due for past years for agistment of cattle cannot be determined, the amount due will be based on the rental value of the land.

3 Eagle & Younge 1234

By the decree in this cause dated the 11th of July 1723, it was referred to John Hardy, Esq., the Deputy Remembrancer, to take an account of the several tithes demanded by the plaintiff's bill. The Deputy Remembrancer made his report dated 22nd April 1725 and thereby certified he had taken an account of the several tithable matters therein mentioned and found the several sums of money therein mentioned to be due to the plaintiff for such tithes. And he further certified that there was due to the plaintiff from the defendant Ambrose Death for the tithe of agistment on Melford Hall Park from Michaelmas 1713 to Michaelmas 1716, being three years, which Park had been constantly fed and depastured in each of the said three years with divers sorts, numbers, and kinds of barren and unprofitable cattle. But the quantities of the said cattle or the value of the said tithes, as it appeared, could not be ascertained, but it appeared to the said Deputy Remembrancer that the said defendant, during the time aforesaid, rented the said Park at the yearly rent of £110. Therefore, he had reported the same specially to the court and had allowed the said complainant, in lieu of the said tithes, 1s. 6d. in the pound, according to the aforesaid rent for the said three years, which, if the court should think it fit to approve of, the tithes for the time aforesaid amounted to £24 15s. The Deputy Remembrancer then made a similar report as to another defendant, Mitchell, who occupied the Park as tenant thereof for five years subsequently to the defendant Ambrose Death. The court confirmed the report and decreed payment according to it.

2 Gwillim 660

The Deputy Remembrancer reported that the number or kinds of cattle agisted could not be ascertained. But, it appearing to him that the lands were rented at £110 *per annum*, he had allowed to the plaintiff 1s. 6d. in the pound of the said rent.

The court confirmed the report, which was special, and ordered payment.

540

Greaves v. D'Acastro

(Ex. 1725)

Where a seizure upon a writ of outlawry is for the benefit of a private party, the landlord is entitled to his one year's rent out of the goods seized.

Bunbury 194, 145 E.R. 644, Conroy 117

17 April 1725.

D'Acastro, who was tenant to Webster, was outlawed at the suit of the plaintiff Greaves, and his goods and money were seized by the process on the outlawry, but still remained in the sheriff's hands.

It was now moved upon the Stat. 8 Ann., c. 14,[1] on behalf of the landlord Webster that he might be satisfied one year's rent in arrear out of the money in the sheriff's hands.

And the court thought it ought to be granted because a *capias utlagatum* at the suit of the party is to be considered only as a private execution and is only auxiliary to the party. And they ordered the sheriff to show cause.

---

[1] Stat. 8 Ann., c. 18 (*SR*, IX, 247-248).

On the first of June 1725, this order was made absolute, Baron PRICE only then in court. But, on the 9th of June 1725, it was stirred again before Lord Chief Baron GILBERT, PRICE, and PAGE, when the order was made absolute *per* TOTAM CURIAM. But *vide antea*, pl. 3.[1]

Harvard Law School MS. 1082, vol. 1, p. 233, pl. 1

Easter term 1725.

Mr. *Foley* moved for Webster, the landlord, to have a year's rent paid him upon a seizure of goods on an outlawry upon the Stat. 8 Queen Anne.

PRICE said that it was formerly controverted whether, in the case of an outlawry, a year's rent should be allowed because there is a proviso in the Stat. 8 Queen Anne that, in the case of the crown, no allowance should be made to the landlord, but we have settled it to be a just demand for a landlord in the case of a sequestration. And an outlawry is in the nature of a private suit.

PAGE: I think it clear that no allowance ought to be made where it is at the crown's suit. But this is not to be so considered. And the *capias utlagatum* is only by way of remedy to the party.

So notice was ordered to be given to all parties, and the secondary is to show cause, for the goods being in his hands, why Mr. Webster should not have the year's rent.

Note: It has been adjudged in this court the very reverse of this and that an outlawry is the crown's suit, and, therefore, no allowance ought to be made to the landlord. *Vide ante.*

541

Rodd v. City of Exeter

(Ex. 1725)

In this case, a suit in equity was allowed to determine the amount of damages suffered by the plaintiff by a taking of his land for public purposes and the issue was sent to a jury for the determination of the amount.

Harvard Law School MS. 1082, vol. 1, p. 233, pl. 2

Easter term 1725.

The plaintiff's bill was for damage done by the defendant and to have an account after the rate of twenty year's value for such land taken away by the defendants as directors of the Navigation for the River Exe, according to the Stat. 31 Hen. VIII,[2] which directs twenty year's value or upon application to the justices of assize to settle the value, we that were for the defendants insisted upon it that

[1] *Franklyn v. Jenkins* (Ex. 1721), see above, Case No. 204.

[2] Stat. 31 Hen. VIII, c. 4 (*SR*, III, 720).

this bill in equity was a mere action for damages and that a bill in equity was not proper for relief.

But the court overruled the objection. And an issue was directed [to find] how much land and of what yearly value was taken from the defendants. And a *quantum damnificatus* [was] directed to be tried.

542

Robinson, *qui tam* v. African Company

(Ex. 1725)

Horns cannot be exported without giving the Company of Horners a right of first refusal to purchase them.

A motion cannot be heard where all of the parties have not been given notice of the hearing.

Harvard Law School MS. 1082, vol. 1, p. 233, pl. 3

Easter term 1725.

This was an information grounded on the Stat. 7 Jac., concerning the prohibiting of unwrought horns,[1] which is relatory to the Stat. 4 Edw. IV[2] and part repealed by that Stat. 1 Jac. I.[3]

And it was now moved in arrest of judgment for the defendant by *Philip Ward* that the Stat. of 7 or 1 Jac. I only orders the Statute of 4 Edw. IV to be revived whereby the Company of Horners are to have the refusal of horns, and, if so, then such unwrought horns might be sold to strangers or exported beyond the sea. See the proviso of the Statute.

Now, upon this information, no offense is charged. And this is only a prohibition *sub modo*, but not a total prohibition. And, therefore, it not being averred that these horns were not offered to the Company of Horners, for *contra formam statuti* is only a conclusion of the premises, and if it is not well alleged before, then this will not help it. He cited Attorney General v. Weedon.[4]

Bootle, for the defendant: It is not laid as the Statute prescribes, for unwrought horns may still be exported and the general clause is only relatory to the former Act and is in the same manner as if the former Statute was incorporated in this. And it depends on the Stat. 4 Edw. IV. And this Stat. 4 Edw. IV is totally revived by Stat. 7 Jac. And it ought to have been alleged in this information that these horns were not offered to the Company of Horners.

---

1 Stat. 7 Jac. I, c. 14 (*SR*, IV, 1170-1171).

2 Stat. 4 Edw. IV, c. 8 (*SR*, II, 415).

3 Stat. 1 Jac. I, c. 25, s. 7 (*SR*, IV, 1051-1052).

4 *Holden, qui tam v. Weeden* (Ex. 1724), see above, Case No. 494.

Chief Baron EYRE: I am of opinion that the intention of this Act was a general prohibition of all unwrought horns and that, therefore, the information is well laid. And it ought to have come on the part of the defendants that these were such horns as were offered to the Company.

But there is no notice in this case, and, therefore, the *postea* cannot be stayed.

PRICE: This seems to be a general prohibition by the Stat. 7 Jac. I. And this ought to have been on the defendant's part. And it is not necessary to be alleged on the part of the crown, and this is to be so construed in all prohibitory acts.

PAGE: I doubt this case very much. And wherever it is joined in the same clause, there, the whole must be set forth to bring it within the prohibition. If all horns were prohibited, then, I would agree that the information was right, but it is only a prohibition *sub modo*. And I must compare this case to that cited of Attorney General v. Weedon, for, there, for want of averring that there were warehouses for East India goods, the judgment was arrested.

CHIEF BARON: This case does not rest on the Statute of Edw. IV. But I think it is a general prohibition intended for keeping the manufacture within the kingdom.

PRICE said that there was a difference between two acts of Parliament and two clauses in the same act of Parliament.

CHIEF BARON: If worked up in the same act, something might be said, but this is upon different acts.

PAGE: There is no occasion for the former Act of Edw. IV, and this [Act of] 7 Jac. is incorporated as one act. And the Company of Horners seem only to have the preemption.

Note: Page seemed right in his opinion.

But, upon the whole, there being no notice, the judgment was not ordered to be stayed.

Taussig MS. 311, vol. 2, p. 791

Easter term 1725. In Middlesex. Friday, the last sittings in the term.

An information [was exhibited] against the Company for that the Company *inter et exhibitum informationis misit et mitti causavit parcellam cornum Anglicanum non operatam, anglice* English horns unwrought *ultra mare in partes forinsecas extra Magna Britannia contra formam statuti*. And upon the trial, it appeared that the horns thus exported were shaved and cut at the ends by a horn turner so as to make them worth 1d. a horn more than they were when taken from the hide, that is 8s. 4d. per hundred and there was a profit of £36 *per centum* even gained by this sort of working.

But EYRE, Chief Baron, was very clear that this was not a working of them within the meaning of the Statute. And, therefore, he directed the jury accordingly and expressed some uneasiness at the trial that the defendant's counsel should insist upon it that this sort of working of the horns should exempt them out of the Statute, notwithstanding the words of the Statute are so very general.

And on Monday, being the last day of the term, it was moved in arrest of judgment that there was no offense laid in the information for that the Statute was not an absolute prohibition to the exporting of horns, but a qualified one, *scil.* if the Company of Horners would buy them and if they would not or they were such as were not fit to be wrought here in their business, then, by the express words of the Statute, they are exportable.

But notwithstanding the case of the King and Weedon, here before, f. [*blank*], which, in my apprehension, is an authority in point against the validity of the information, the Chief Baron and Price seemed to make slight of the objection.

But Page differing, the court laid hold of the omission in the defendant's attorney for not giving notice to the plaintiffs to bring in the *postea*. And so the defendant lost the opportunity of any further debating of this point.

N.B. *Bootle* and myself were of counsel with the defendant, both at the trial and upon the motion in arrest of judgment. See the Stat. 7 Jac., ca. 14. N.B. The information does not so much as allege that they were bulls' or oxen's horns.

543

Griffith v. Jones

(Ex. 1725)

The question in this case was whether a clerk to a prothonotary of the Court of Common Pleas has a privilege to be sued in that court only.

A demurrer admits the truth of the facts pleaded in the preceding pleading.

Harvard Law School MS. 1082, vol. 1, p. 235

Easter term 1725.

The defendant pleaded that he was clerk to Mr. Foley, the prothonotary of the [Court of] Common Pleas [and] so claimed privilege. And the plaintiff demurs.

Bootle, for the plaintiff: The plaintiff is the king's debtor. That gives privilege. 1 Inst. 131; 25 Edw. III.[1] It is a privilege, though not a special privilege. And I would confine it to such persons that are entitled to a writ of privilege, but [it is] not so in this case. Hardres 365, 188.[2] *Licet tangit nos* are the words.

Mr. *Weedon*, for the defendant: The jurisdiction of the Common Pleas is pleadable to a *quo minus*. It is admitted that, as debtor [to the crown], that is only a general privilege, and those words are not always in writs of privilege. The case in Hardres is [. . .]. The clerk to a prothonotary is a good minister of the court.

---

1 E. Coke, *First Institute* (1628), f. 131b; Stat. 5 Edw. II, c. 25 (*SR*, I, 163).

2 *Clapham v. Lenthall* (1664), Hardres 365, 145 E.R. 499, also British Library MS. Hargrave 62, f. 4v, pl. 2; *Wilkins v. Shalcroft* (1661), Hardres 188, 145 E.R. 445.

2 Rolle, *Abridgment*, 274, 272; Bro., Priv., 40.[1] A filazer's servant is entitled to the privilege.

The defendant has pleaded his privilege and his attendance in the court. And by it, such persons are not liable to be a churchwarden. And the office of a clerk must be [performed] in person. 3 Levinz 398 (or 98); 2 Salkeld 543, 544.[2] And by the demurrer, the attendance on the Court of Common Pleas is admitted.

Bootle replies. By the writ of privilege *quae nos non tangit* saves the jurisdiction of this court. There is a great difference between attorneys of the Common Pleas and clerks to a prothonotary. In the first [case], there is a privilege, but not in the latter.

Price: The plea of prothonotary's clerk's privilege I am a stranger to. But you have admitted attendance on the court by the demurrer. Lightbound v. Russel.[3] A general privilege will not do in this case.

Page: The clerks to a prothonotary are not entered upon record. The attorneys are sworn, but the clerks are only menial servants to the prothonotary and not officers upon the records of the court. A person may be as easily clerk to a prothonotary as the king's debtor. And this seems to be only a general privilege.

[It was] adjourned to be considered next term.

Taussig MS. 311, vol. 2, p. 790

Easter term 1725.

The defendant pleaded to a *quo minus* that he was *unum clericorum* of Mr. Foley, one of the prothonotaries in the Common Bench. And the plaintiff[4] demurred thereto.

It was said for the plaintiff that this is no privilege at all. 1 Inst. 131; Hardr. 188, 365.

Weldon, contra, cited 2 Rolle's *Abr.*, 272, 274; Brook, Privilege, 40; 3 Lev. 398; 2 Salkeld 544, is express for a clerk of a prothonotary.

Price, baron: I am a stranger to the privilege claimed on behalf of a clerk of a prothonotary, but, if there is any such privilege, it must be special, whereas that of a debtor of the king is general and does not exclude a special privilege. I have

---

[1] *Butt's Case* (1606), 2 Rolle, Abr., *Priviledge*, pl. F, 3, p. 274; *Wilson's Case* (1636), 2 Rolle, Abr., *Priviledge*, pl. A, 1, p. 272; YB Pas. 10 Edw. IV, f. 4, pl. 9 (1470), Brooke, Abr., *Privilege*, pl. 40.

[2] *Baker, qui tam v. Duncalfe* (1694), 3 Levinz 398, 83 E.R. 749, also 1 Lutwyche 193, 125 E.R. 101; *Kirkham v. Wheely* (1695), 1 Salkeld 30, 91 E.R. 31, 2 Salkeld 543, 91 E.R. 459, also 1 Lord Raymond 27, 91 E.R. 914, Comberbach 319, 90 E.R. 502, 12 Modern 74, 88 E.R. 1173, 3 Salkeld 282, 91 E.R. 825, Fortescue 342, 92 E.R. 882; perhaps *Anonymous* (1704), 2 Salkeld 544, 91 E.R. 461.

[3] *Lightbound v. Russell* (Ex. 1721), see above, Case No. 170.

[4] defendant *MS.*

heard that, where the king's debtor recovers, the king might arrest the money recovered.

PAGE, baron, doubted whether there is any privilege for a prothonotary's clerk.

Adjourned.

Harvard Law School MS. 1082, vol. 1, p. 240, pl. 1

Trinity term 1725.

The defendant in this case pleaded that he was clerk to the prothonotary of the Common Pleas. And the plaintiff demurs.

It was urged on the part of the plaintiff that clerks to prothonotaries are without number and that such a privilege ought not to be honored. But in regard that it was alleged in the plea that his attendance was necessary in court and admitted by the plaintiff's demurrer, judgment was given for the defendant.

Taussig MS. 311, vol. 2, p. 800, pl. 1

Trinity term 1725.

N.B. In the pleading of this privilege, the plaintiff instead of insisting on the defendant's producing an affidavit that he was a clerk attending in the office, which is always required in the King's Bench upon a plea of this sort, the plaintiff demurred. And so the plea was confessed as true, and the court allowed it. Rolle's *Abr.*, 275, 6; Hard. 316; Salkeld 543.[1]

544

Samber v. Noke

(Ex. 1725)

Even though a testator devises land to be sold to pay debts, legacies, and funeral expenses, the testator's personal estate will be charged with these payments first.

Harvard Law School MS. 1082, vol. 1, p. 236

Easter term 1725. Penn Samber and Selwyn Samber *alias* Darby v. Noke *et al.*

Judith Medlycot, being seised of several messuages and likewise possessed of a personal estate, made her will bearing date and after having given some legacies to the plaintiff Selwyn [Samber] and, to the intent that all her debts, legacies, and funeral expenses might be justly and honestly satisfied and paid, she did give and desire all that her moiety, part, or share of all that her mansion house called Bechington in the parish of Friston and also all that the manor of Peak Dean and all her estate within several parishes therein mentioned unto the defendants Willard

[1] *Reeve v. Jacey* (1635), 2 Rolle, Abr., *Priviledge*, pl. G, 6, 7, pl. I, 6, p. 275; *Carterett v. Massam* (1663), Hardres 316, 145 E.R. 475; *Kirkham v. Wheely* (1695), *ut supra*.

and Gilbert in trust that they should within two years next after the testatrix's death sell and pay all her debts, legacies, and other expenses which they should be at, in, and about her funeral and selling the said estate. And then she gave the overplus of such money after such her debts, legacies, and other expenses whatsoever paid and discharged to the defendant Juke upon condition that he should purchase her moiety of Peak Dean and the Monts and come and inhabit at Friston and, if he had a son, to baptize him by the name of Selwyn and that the defendant should not have the overplus of the money until after the sale of the estate and payment of her debts and legacies. And all the rest and residue of her goods and chattels, money, plate, and personal estate whatsoever not herein before given away nor disposed of, her debts, legacies, funeral and other expenses being paid and discharged, she gave to the defendant Noke. And she made him executor.

So the question was whether this estate so devised to Willard and Gilbert was not a particular fund intended by the testatrix for the payment of the debts and legacies so as to exclude the personal estate from being subject thereto.

Fazakerly, for the plaintiff, insisted upon it that there were no words to exclude the personal estate. And in all cases where the personal estate is not particularly excluded, it shall go in aid so far as to unload the real estate and that the testatrix's intention was that her debts and legacies should be paid in all events so that, if the personal estate should not be sufficient, that then, if the estate so devised should likewise be liable but that the personal estate was the primary fund. 1 Can. Cases, Ford, Lord Grey v. Lady Grey; Popley v. Popley.[1] And this estate so devised is only to be esteemed a supplemental fund.

We, that were for the defendant, insisted that the defendant was heir at law and, therefore, a favorable construction ought to be made. And there being no occasion to resort to the personal estate, it ought not to come in aid. And here is a provision made for the plaintiff by other parts of the will, and, by the devise, the rest and residue is devised over, and that this was the fund intended for the payment of her debts and legacies and not the personal estate, which was intended by the will for the defendant Noke and that the personal estate was specifically devised to the defendant. And though sometime the personal estate has been ordered to come in aid, that construction has been in favor of an heir at law or for the benefit of creditors, but not so in this case. And as it was in the power of the testatrix to charge the real estate, so she has done it in the present case. And the estate thus devised to Willard and Gilbert is made assets for this particular purpose. If the trust estate had fallen short, then, perhaps, the personal estate might have come in to have been auxiliary to it. But, in this case, the personal es-

[1] *Lord Grey v. Lady Grey* (1677), 1 Chancery Cases 296, 22 E.R. 809, also Reports *tempore* Finch 338, 23 E.R. 185, 2 Swanston 594, 36 E.R. 742, 2 Freeman 6, 22 E.R. 1020, 1 Eq. Cas. Abr. 270, 381, 21 E.R. 1117, 73 Selden Soc. 393, 79 Selden Soc. 481, 657, British Library MS. Stowe 406, f. 93; *Popley v. Popley* (1681), 2 Chancery Cases 84, 22 E.R. 858, also 1 Vernon 36, 23 E.R. 290, 1 Eq. Cas. Abr. 270, 21 E.R. 1038.

tate amounted to but £514 10s. 8d. and the debts and legacies to £2979 11s. 10d. And, therefore, the devise of the residuum could not be meant the £514 10s. 8d. We cited Sir John Tyrwhit v. Trotman and Dame Drake, heard in Chancery, 17 December 1712, and in the House of Lords, May 1714; Adams v. Merrick, 19 February 1724; Wainwright v. Bendlow, 3 Geo.; 2 Levinz 203.[1] And we insisted not one case was otherwise since My Lord Chief Baron's will.

This case came to be heard above a year ago, and, then, MONTAGU, PRICE, PAGE, and GILBERT were in court, and PRICE decided against the other three, so we petitioned for a rehearing, and it came this day before.

EYRE, Chief Baron: And he thought that the original estate ought first to come in aid and that there were no words to exclude it.

PRICE: I desire to look into the cases, for the whole scheme seems to me that the testatrix intended to make only the real estate the fund for the payment of debts and legacies. Chief Baron Montagu's will and Wainwright's Case are very strong in favor of the defendant.

PAGE: I cannot alter my former opinion. And I think it was right that there are no words to exclude the personal estate, and, therefore, it must come first in aid. And it seems that both were intended to be liable to debts and legacies, and the settling of the family of Selwyn seems to be her first intention.

GILBERT: The rules of equity are right. The testatrix has a disposition over the real and personal estate. And she has subjected both for debts and legacies by this will, and there are no words to exclude the personal estate. And their being no such exemption, the personal estate must first go in aid.

Note that in Trinity term following, judgment was given by Chief Baron GILBERT and PAGE against PRICE's opinion that the personal estate must first go in aid.

It was observed by Lord Chief Baron GILBERT that, by devise of land to be sold, the money was to be raised in two years, whereas the debts and legacies were to be paid immediately, so that could not be esteemed the first fund for the payment of debts.

[Affirmed on appeal: 1 Brown P.C. 506, 1 E.R. 720.]

---

[1] *Tyrwhitt v. Trotman* (1714), 3 Brown P.C. 52, 1 E.R. 1171; *Adams v. Meyrick* (1724), 1 Eq. Cas. Abr. 271, 21 E.R. 1039; *Wainwright v. Bendloe* (1716), Precedents in Chancery 451, 24 E.R. 201, Gilbert Rep. 125, 25 E.R. 87, 2 Vernon 718, 23 E.R. 1071, 1 Eq. Cas. Abr. 271, 21 E.R. 1039; *Feltham v. Harlston's Exors.* (1667), 1 Levinz 203, 83 E.R. 369, also 1 Eq. Cas. Abr. 271, 21 E.R. 1039.

545

Lord Digby v. Meech

(Ex. 1725)

In an action to establish a property right, the plaintiff must plead specifically how his claim is vested in him.

In this case, a defective pleading was allowed to be amended.

Bunbury 195, 145 E.R. 645

26 April 1725.

A bill was brought to establish the plaintiff's right to the manor etc. of Sherborn Castleton in the County of Dorset and the liberties and hundred of Sherborn, to green wax fees, fines, amercements, post fines, and fines set at the assizes upon the inhabitants within the liberty, and also poundage fees on executions, and *retorna brevium* etc. by virtue of a grant 14 Jac. I. The bill was brought against three succeeding sheriffs of the county and Templeman, who had been the under sheriff for three or four years, and, as to him, to have an account of what poundage fees etc. he had received within the liberty. The title set forth by the plaintiff was that of King James I to Sir John Digby, afterward earl of Bristol; from him, they descended to George, from him to John, earl of Bristol, and, on his death, vested in the now plaintiff.

It was objected at the hearing that here was not a sufficient title set forth, it not appearing how the premises vested in the plaintiff, whether by descent, settlement, or how.

And *per* TOTAM CURIAM, Lord Chief Baron EYRE, PRICE, and PAGE, the bill ought to be dismissed for that reason, the bill being to establish a right, as well as for an account. And upon this, the cause went off. But the plaintiff had liberty to amend his bill.

546

Anonymous

(Ex. 1725)

An injunction against a judgment in another court will be dissolved where the matter is in issue in the court of equity.

Taussig MS. 311, vol. 2, p. 794, pl. 1

Trinity term 11 Geo., 1725. EYRE, PAGE *praesentibus*.

A motion was made to dissolve an injunction upon coming in answer *in causa* and that the defendant might be at liberty to affirm the judgment in the meantime, *quod fuit concessum*.

547

Frankland v. Frankland

(Ex. 1725)

Upon a motion for an injunction, the defendant can argue all of his exceptions.

Taussig MS. 311, vol. 2, p. 794, pl. 2

1 June 1725.

The question upon a motion for an injunction upon opening a material exception was whether, after the counsel had opened the first, which the court, upon debate, adjudged not to be material, they might go to another, which *Browne* said they could not.

Per CURIAM: For that this would oblige the court to go through twenty exceptions upon a motion.

Sed per Chief Baron [EYRE] and PAGE, they were admitted to go to another.

548

Cosby v. Pakenham

(Ex. 1725)

The question in this case was whether the Court of Exchequer can grant a writ of ne exeat regno.

Taussig MS. 311, vol. 2, p. 795

Trinity term 1725. Mr. Baron PAGE only was present.

Mr. *Bootle* moved him for a [writ of] *ne exeat regno.*

The BARON gave a rule to show cause, but did not take any notice of the court's jurisdiction in this matter.

549

Egerton v. Still

(Ex. 1725)

Easter offerings are due to the rector of the parish by common right.

Where less than ten offspring are born in a year, the tithe payable is the value of the tenth part.

Harvard Law School MS. 1082, vol. 1, p. 239, pl. 1

Trinity term 1725.

The plaintiff, as rector of Cowden in the County of Kent, brought his bill for tithes and Easter offerings as due by custom. The defendant insisted that no Easter offerings were due as laid by the bill and that, as to calves, lambs, etc., he had not the number of ten during the time by the bill demanded and, as the plaintiff insisted to have tithes in kind, the defendant could not pay them until the number came to ten and, when so, the defendant intended to pay the tenth. And, as to the other part, an exemption was insisted upon for such as were bred for the plow and pail.

But notwithstanding this defense, the defendant was decreed to account for the tithes in kind for that offerings were due of common right and that tithes were annually renewing unless [there was] a custom to the contrary which might be good. And, therefore, the defendant must account for the tenth part of the value of his calves, lambs, etc. without staying for making up the number ten, for, to the contrary, it would be attended with very great inconvenience, for then, if a new incumbent happens in the second year, then, such new incumbent would reap the advantage of his predecessor's first year's tithes. And the custom of tithing by the second year would not be good unless the same parson and occupier continued. The parson has his election, and that the law has settled the tithe at the tenth part of the value. And the court seemed to think that, as to such cattle brought up for the plow and pail, it was only an excuse as to the pasturage, for that tithes were due for such things when fallen.

Taussig MS. 311, vol. 2, p. 796

Monday, 7th June 1725. GILBERT and PAGE only present.

The question was whether, when there was under ten calves, lambs, pigs, or geese, the rector was to expect to the next year.

And *Bunbury* said he should because, by the Statute 27 Hen. VIII, ca. 6,[1] tithes are provided to be paid by the ecclesiastical law. And the Canon of Robert Winchelsea, *anno* 1305, appoints *quod expectat rector.*

GILBERT, Chief Baron: Offerings are due of common right, but perhaps a householder may not be obliged to pay for all his household without a custom. As to accounting over, if there be a custom for it, then they may go over; otherwise, he must pay it according to the value of the tenth part of the odd tithable matters.

PAGE was of the same opinion and, though they had laid it by a custom, yet it appearing to be due at common law, we may decree for it.

The defendant was decreed to account.

Bunbury 198, 145 E.R. 646,
1 Rayner 220, 2 Gwillim 661, 1 Eagle & Younge 818

7 June 1725.

[1] Stat. 27 Hen. VIII, c. 20 (*SR*, III, 551–552).

It was decreed *per* CURIAM in this cause, first, that the plaintiff should have Easter offerings, as due of common right, although he demanded them as due by custom; secondly, that where there are above ten calves, lambs, pigs, etc., the tithe of the odd number above ten shall be paid according to the value, and not be carried over to the next year.

[Order of 7 June 1725: 2 Wood 251.]

550

Wright v. Cook

(Ex. 1725)

There must be a transcript of the record in order to perfect a writ of error.

In this case, the writ of error was not perfected and the performance bond to so do was thus forfeited.

Taussig MS. 311, vol. 2, p. 798

Trinity term 1725.

[Upon a] *scire facias* upon a recognizance *quare executionem non*, the recognizance was entered into by the defendants that A. should prosecute his writ of error, which he had brought upon a judgment recovered against him by the plaintiff and the *scire facias* set forth that A. did bring his writ of error which was non-prossed in the Court of Exchequer Chamber. So he prays execution. The defendants plead a writ of error in Parliament brought by A. *per quod* the record in Exchequer *transmissus fuit in Parliamento*. The plaintiff replies *nul tiel record* by which the judgment and proceedings were transmitted into Parliament. The defendant rejoins *quod habetur tale recordum* and had a day to bring it in by a rule and bring in a record of the judgment of the Exchequer Chamber, on which there was an entry of a writ of error into Parliament, but no transcript of the record. And the question was whether this record warranted the plea pleaded by the defendants.

Et per TOTAM CURIAM: It did not. And so judgment [was given] for the plaintiff.

Comyns, pro querente, Kettleby, pro defendente, Owen, attorney, *pro querente.*

Harvard Law School MS. 1082, vol. 1, p. 239, pl. 2

Trinity term 1725.

Upon a *scire facias* upon a recognizance and upon a writ of error, the record was transmitted [by] the defendant. And it was alleged that there was *nul tiel record.*

Kettleby: It is not proper to pray upon a *nul tiel record* pleaded, and this ought to be brought into court by the Master.

Chief Baron [GILBERT]: If there be a record of another court, then a [writ of] *certiorari* [ought] to be allowed to remove it, and the Master cannot go further than to see the record itself. It is incumbent on the pleader to show the record, and the Master must certify.

PRICE: [Give] judgment for the plaintiff.

551

Patterson v. Lord Forrester

(Ex. 1725)

The question in this case was the sufficiency of the pleadings of this contract action.

Taussig MS. 311, vol. 2, p. 797

Wednesday, 9 [June] 1725.

A declaration in [an action of] covenant upon a deed of 26 March 1702, reciting that Paterson became bound in £12,000 with a condition for £6000 [*blank*] 1721 and that Paterson became bound for Lord Forrester to Sir John Anstruther as aforesaid, Lord Forrester agrees to pay the money that Patterson should compound this bond for £2000, sets forth that [*blank*].

The demurrer shows several special causes.

The first cause is want of an *alias dictus*. This is the constant form.

Second, the deed is only set forth by way of a recital under a *testatum sit quod idem* Forrester etc. Now, though the form of the deed is it is witnessed, yet in pleading, it must be alleged that he was bound, not that it witnessed that he was bound. 1 Saunders 273; 2 Saunders 319, Bennet and Holbetch.[1]

Thirdly, one cannot compound a bond, but, if it may be compounded, yet he does not show how he compounded it, which he ought to have done.

Serjeant *Pengelly*: It is said that George, lord Forrester, *per* [. . .] became bound. *Testatum existit* is good in [an action of] covenant though perhaps not in avowry or debt upon a demise. But here, the declaration goes further and says *ac etiam per idem scriptum obligavit se*[2] so that this question is out of doors.

By Chief Baron [GILBERT] and PRICE: If the composition of the bond be such as will oblige Sir John Anstruther either in law or equity and Paterson has actually paid it, Lord Forrester will by this deed of covenant be obliged to pay the money.

Adjornatur upon a seeming doubt of Page.

---

[1] *Rex v. Sutton* (1670), 1 Williams Saunders 269, 85 E.R. 327, also 1 Ventris 32, 86 E.R. 23, 1 Siderfin 420, 82 E.R. 1193, 2 Keble 526, 533, 84 E.R. 329, 343; *Bennet v. Holbech* (1671), 2 Williams Saunders 309, 85 E.R. 1108, also 2 Levinz 11, 83 E.R. 429, 2 Keble 750, 769, 789, 825, 84 E.R. 474, 486, 499, 522.

[2] and also, by the same writing, he bound himself.

Harvard Law School MS. 1082, vol. 1, p. 240, pl. 2

Trinity term 1725.

The declaration sets forth that the defendant being obliged to pay a considerable sum to Anstruther and that, if the (*vide*[1] next term).

Cited for the demurrer [were] 1 Saunders 273; 2 Saunders 319.[2]

It was answered for the plaintiff those cases by saying that a *testatum existit* is good in a declaration in covenant, but not in an avowry, which were the cases cited in Saunders.

552

Attorney General v. Elwell

(Ex. 1725)

Debts are not bound by a writ of execution before the date of the inquisition.

Notes of hand are not merged by an interlocutory judgment, the debt not being ascertained upon a writ of execution before the writ of inquiry be returned and final judgment be entered thereon.

Bunbury 199, 145 E.R. 646

At the sittings at Westminster. 14 June 1725.

A *scire facias* was brought in the name of the Attorney General against Sir John Elwell, setting forth that there he had a [writ of] extent issued against Sir Matthew Kirwood and an inquisition was taken thereon, which found Sir John Elwell indebted to Sir Matthew Kirwood by two promissory notes, one for £150 and the other for £100, and he prays that the defendant should show cause why the crown should not have execution for this debt.

The defendant pleads that he was not indebted by those notes or either of them *die inquisitionis*. The Attorney General proved only Sir John's hand to the notes. The defendant gave in evidence that Kirwood, before he failed, brought an action on these notes and obtained judgment by *nil dicit* and that a writ of inquiry of damages issued and was executed, and, thereupon, a final judgment was had and, therefore, that he could not be indebted on those notes because they were merged in the judgment, according to Higgins's Case.

But it appeared that, although the interlocutory judgment was entered before the inquisition was taken upon the extent, yet the writ of inquiry and final judgment were not executed and obtained until a long while afterwards, for the inquisition on the extent was upon the 28th of November, 5 Geo. [1718], the

[1] *Sic* in MS.

[2] *Rex v. Sutton* (1670), *ut supra*; *Bennet v. Holbech* (1671), *ut supra*.

interlocutory judgment was before, but the writ was not executed until the 7th of February, 5 Geo. [1719].

And, thereupon, the Lord Chief Baron GILBERT, who tried the cause, immediately directed the jury to find, as they did, for the crown.

Note: First, by this plea, it appears that debts are not bound until the *teste* of the inquisition; secondly, that notes of hand are not merged by an interlocutory judgment, the debt not being ascertained before the writ of inquiry returned and final judgment entered thereon.

553

Rogers v. Linton

(Ex. 1725)

In this case for an accounting and settlement of a decedent's estate, where one of the principal defendants could not be served with process, the court allowed the case to proceed without him.

Bunbury 200, 145 E.R. 647

16 June 1725.

A bill was brought for an account of Charles Rogers's personal estate, who was a freeman of London, and, having had three wives and issue by the first wife two children, by the second, one, and by the third, four, devised one third to his wife and one third to all his children and the other third to the children by the last wife. These last were plaintiffs, and they demand the share devised to all the children, alleging that the children by the two former wives were provided for in the testator's lifetime. Charles, the son by the second wife, was named a party, but he never answered, nor was he served with process.

The plaintiffs moved the court that they might hear the cause without Charles, he being beyond the sea, and, if it appeared he had any right, he might come before the Deputy [Remembrancer] on the account.

And, though no precedent was produced to such an allowance before, the court, *viz.* Lord Chief Baron GILBERT and PRICE, *contra* PAGE, gave liberty to hear the cause without Charles.

554

Walton v. Terry

(Ex. 1725)

A modus decimandi *in lieu of tithes in kind that is too large is invalid.*

A modus decimandi *must be proved to be payable at a certain date.*

Harvard Law School MS. 1082, vol. 1, p. 242, pl. 1

Sittings after Trinity term 1725.

The plaintiff, as rector of Botley in the County of Southampton, brought a suit against the defendants for tithes. And the defendants insist upon the following *modus*es, *viz.* 1s. for a calf, 11d. for a heifer, 1d. for a dry sheep, 2d. for lamb, and 1d. for every ewe or 3d. for an ewe and lamb.

And though I cited the case of Rowe v. Bishop of Exeter, Hilary 7 Geo., which *vide ante*,[1] in relation to the heifer, yet the court overruled all the *modus*es as too high and likewise for not proving when the times of payment were, which being laid right in the answer, yet not so proved.

Taussig MS. 311, vol. 2, p. 807, pl. 2

Trinity term 1725.

The plaintiff, as rector of Botley in Hampshire, exhibits his bill for tithes.

The defendants insist on a *modus* of 6d. for every calf fallen, 1s. for every milk cow and in lieu of milk, 1d. for the agistment of every day sheep, 2d. for every lamb fallen, and 1d. for every ewe, or 3d. for every ewe and lamb.

The case of Frankland and Jenkin *et al.*, vicar of Farnham,[2] was cited as a case in point for the invalidity of the *modus*es.

E contra, it was said that, in the case of Roe *et al.* v. Bishop of Exeter, Hilary 1719/1720, 1s. 5d. was established for a cow and calf, so [there was] only 1d. difference.

The court did not think fit to determine the point whether 12d. was a good *modus* for a milk cow or 6d. for a calf, but made the defendants go into their evidence. And not being satisfied with the proof of the *modus*, they decreed an account as for the tithes in kind.

555

Fisher v. Crooke

(Ex. 1725)

Where leave of court is given to prove exhibits ore tenus, *notice of the exhibits, including leases by deans and chapters, must be given to the opposing parties prior to the hearing.*

Taussig MS. 311, vol. 2, p. 800, pl. 2

Thursday, June 10th, 1725. Gilbert, Chief Baron, Price, and Page.

A bill was brought by the plaintiff as lessee of the Dean and Chapter of Christchurch, Oxford. And, in his bill, he sets forth that the Dean and Chapter,

[1] *Roe v. Bishop of Exeter* (Ex. 1720), see above, Case No. 119.

[2] *Franklyn v. Jenkins* (Ex. 1721), see above, Case No. 204.

by indenture of 1st August 172,[1] leased the premises. And after opening the bill and answers, the plaintiff would have read his lease, which was under seal, but the defendants objected that, though we had a rule to prove exhibits *viva voce* at the hearing of the cause, yet we had not given notice to them of this lease among our other exhibits, which ought to have been done two days before the hearing of the cause according to the course of the court, to which it was answered that the lease, being under the seal of the corporation, needed no proof, no more than a bishop's lease etc., which were never signed or delivered otherwise than by putting the seal to it and no witnesses ever endorsed.

For that reason, the Chief Baron [GILBERT] admitted it in the case of a sole corporation, as a bishop etc., but doubted it as to a corporation aggregate.

But PRICE and PAGE thought there ought to be a witness to prove it was the dean and chapter's seal and, if so, then, not having given notice of it, we could not now be at liberty to do it and, though it was insisted that, if notice were necessary, it was given in this case by the bill itself wherein the date and the parties' names were set forth as our title.

The court thought this was not sufficient. And so they adjourned the cause over to Michaelmas term.

Taussig MS. 311, vol. 2, p. 816, pl. 1

Michaelmas term 1725.

This cause was heard in part on Thursday and then adjourned over to Thursday, November 18, and heard again in part on that day and on Friday morning following in the Exchequer Court. And the court took time to consider of it and give their opinions of it the next term.[2]

556

Wood v. Spencer

(Ex. 1725)

A suit in equity to discover manorial fines and quit rents must be limited to a single manor.

Taussig MS. 311, vol. 2, p. 805, pl. 1

Trinity term 1725.

The plaintiffs, being joint-tenants of several distinct manors in the County of Suffolk, exhibit their bill against all the tenants of the said manors to discover what of their lands within the said manor were copyhold and what freehold and what fines and quit rents were due and owing to the lords. To this, it was

[1] Sic in MS.

[2] Perhaps *Fisher v. Lord Somerville* (Ex. 1725–1726), see below, Case No. 580.

demurred because the bill contained demands of different natures and complicated the defendants' several offenses.

And the court allowed the demurrer and said, if they might inquire into the fines and quit rents of more than one manor by one bill, they might for twenty, which would be endless.

557

Williams v. Williams

(Ex. 1725)

A modus decimandi *is payable by the occupiers of land not by the land in issue.*

Taussig MS. 311, vol. 2, p. 807, pl. 1

Wednesday, 23 June 1725. First day of setting down of causes.

A bill was exhibited for tithes of hay. A *modus* [was alleged], *viz.* immemorial custom that several pieces of ancient meadows, naming them in particular, ought to pay two horse sledge-fulls or carloads or a composition for the same in lieu of tithe hay.

Chief Baron [GILBERT]: The custom laid is that the meadows ought to pay, not that the occupiers of the meadows ought to pay. So the *modus* was overruled.

558

Note

(Ex. 1725)

A ship will not be forfeited where a small item was smuggled in it without the knowledge of the master of the vessel.

Taussig MS. 311, vol. 2, p. 809

Trinity term 1725.

38 Edw. III, ca. 8.[1] 'Whereas the ships of divers people of this realm be arrested and held forfeit because of a little thing put in their ship, not customed, whereof the lords of the same ship be ignorant, it is accorded that no lord shall lose his ship from 15 February next coming for such a small thing put within the ship not customed without his knowledge.'

[1] Stat. 38 Edw. III, stat. 1, c. 8 (*SR*, I, 384).

559

Jones v. Tuffnell

(Ex. 1725)

A court of equity will not specifically enforce a contract for the sale of land that is harsh.

Harvard Law School MS. 1082, vol. 1, p. 242, pl. 2

Sittings after Trinity term 1725.

This was a bill brought by the plaintiff to oblige the defendant to perform an agreement for land after the rate of forty years purchase or thereabouts, And it was urged for the defendant that a court of equity will not help a hard bargain, but leave the plaintiffs to go to law so that, if there is the least deficiency in want of producing the writings on time or the want of title in never so minute a matter, the court of equity will not assist, as in the case of Hicks v. Phillips, in Chancery,[1] where, in a contract to sell a considerable parcel of lands in fee, yet there being 16s. copyhold, though the plaintiff offered to enfranchise it, yet the court would not compel an execution of the agreement, so for not producing writings in time, as in the case of Lewis v. Lord Lechmere, in Chancery. Eyles v. Hanger, in Chancery.[2]

And in this principal case, there not being shown a title to a piece of a yard leading to one of the houses in question, only under a lease for years, whereas it ought to have been a freehold, and, therefore, the court would not oblige the defendant to perform this agreement, but dismissed the bill without costs.

But this seemed against the opinion of the court in Tendring v. London, last term,[3] where the court ordered a specific performance of the agreement, where I was counsel for the plaintiff (but I cannot find my notes or the brief).

560

Rex v. Pixley

(Ex. 1725)

A debt to the crown cannot be discharged by bankruptcy proceedings.

Bunbury 202, 145 E.R. 647

16 November 1725.

---

[1] *Hicks v. Phillips* (1721), Precedents in Chancery 575, 24 E.R. 258, 2 Eq. Cas. Abr. 18, 688, 22 E.R. 15, 579.

[2] *Lewis v. Lord Lechmere* (1722), 10 Modern 503, 88 E.R. 828, 2 Eq. Cas. Abr. 20, 688, 689, 22 E.R. 17, 579; *Hanger v. Eyles* (1721), 2 Eq. Cas. Abr. 20, 689, 22 E.R. 17, 579.

[3] See *Tendring v. London* (1718), above, Case No. 63.

In 1715, Ball was made one of the clerks to Mr. Pauncefort, the Treasurer of the Excise. And he and Pixley entered into a bond of £2000 penalty to the crown with condition that Ball should duly account with Pauncefort for what moneys etc.

Pixley, in May 1721, became a bankrupt and surrendered himself and complied in every respect with the Stat. 5 Geo.[1] and had a certificate, which was confirmed. And he was actually discharged.

In the last vacation, a *capias* was taken out upon this bond against him, and he was arrested thereon, and he was in the custody of the sheriffs of London.

And this day, I [*Bunbury*] moved that Pixley might be discharged out of custody by virtue of the Stat. 5 Geo. and another Stat. 6 Geo.[2] and also upon producing a copy of the certificate confirmed as the Statute directs.

But *per* CURIAM, the statutes of bankrupt do not bind the crown, and, therefore, we cannot discharge him. And it was ruled so, not only in the case of an extent, but even of an extent in aid, in which last case, the court refused to relieve.

Note: It was objected that a *scire facias* should have issued first upon this bond, being for the performance of covenants. But it was said to be everyday's practice that a *capias* issues immediately where an oath is first made of the debt, as was done in this case.

Harvard Law School MS. 1082, vol. 1, p. 254, pl. 1

Michaelmas term 1725.

Mr. BROWNE, for the defendant, moved to discharge the defendant out of the custody of the sheriffs of Middlesex because the defendant had submitted to the Acts of Bankruptcy and obtained a certificate according to the Stat. 5 Geo.

The court refused the motion because the crown cannot come in under the commission of bankruptcy. See Salkeld 108.[3]

Taussig MS. 311, vol. 2, p. 815

Michaelmas term 1725.

Mr. *Bunbury* moved the court to discharge the defendant Pixley, who was taken upon a *capias* on a bond to the crown for Pauncefort's good performance of his office, the said Pixley having been a bankrupt and discharged from the commission and, therefore, says *Bunbury*, he is discharged from all debts owing before. *Vide* 5 Geo., fol. [*blank*].

The Act does not extend to a case of the crown nor can the king come in as a creditor upon a commission of bankruptcy, so the motion was denied.

---

[1] Stat. 5 Geo. I, c. 24.

[2] Stat. 6 Geo. I, c. 22.

[3] *Paine v. Teap* (1691), 1 Salkeld 108, 91 E.R. 99, also Dodd 92, 104, Public Record Office, E.126/15, ff. 338v, 367v.

561

Harman v. Immins

(Ex. 1725)

Where a defendant files two insufficient answers to a bill of complaint and an insufficient answer to an amended bill of complaint, the defendant will be liable to pay court costs at the amount of a third insufficient answer.

Taussig MS. 311, vol. 2, p. 815 [bis]

Michaelmas term 1725. Immins and Harman.

The plaintiff took exceptions to the defendant's answer, which were allowed and set down to the second answer and also allowed. And then, the plaintiff moved to amend his bill, and he amended it accordingly. And the defendant put in a third answer, and the plaintiff filed exceptions to it, *viz.* exceptions taken to the answer of the defendants to the plaintiff's amended bill, which exceptions were the same, word for word, as the exceptions to the original bill save in one particular sentence.

And upon arguing these exceptions, they were allowed to this third answer and not upon the point wherein the amendment was made, but upon the old point of the former exceptions. And, therefore, the court looked upon this as a third answer, though, in truth, it was the first answer to the amended bill. And they ordered the defendant to pay £9 costs, as for a third insufficient answer, though this was thought hard and that the regular way for the plaintiff would have been to have kept the first exceptions on foot and not have confounded the exceptions of the amended bill with the exceptions to the original one and then, no doubt, the allowance of the original exceptions to this answer would [not] have carried costs as to a third insufficient answer.

Bunbury 203, 145 E.R. 647

20 November 1725.

Exceptions were allowed to two answers to the original bill. And then, the plaintiff amended his bill, as he might do without costs. The defendant put in an answer to the amended bill. And the plaintiff set down the exceptions, with some little additions, to that answer. And they were allowed. And the question was whether the defendant should pay £9 costs, as upon a third insufficient answer, or only £3, as upon a first insufficient answer, to the amended bill.

And *per* CURIAM, the defendant was ordered to pay £9.

562

Lister v. Baxter

(Ex. 1725)

In this maritime case, a writ of prohibition to the Court of Admiralty was denied.

Harvard Law School MS. 1082, vol. 1, p. 244, pl. 1

Michaelmas term 1725.

Mr. *Ward* shows cause against the order for a [writ of] prohibition, for though I agree that, on warrants generally, where the property of the ship comes in question, that a prohibition has been granted out, on this warrant, it is *in causa maritima*, which differs from the other warrants. Tranter v. Watson, Salkeld 35; Johnson v. Shippen, *idem*.[1]

Bootle, for a prohibition: There ought not to be a greater power in the Admiralty than in any other court. As for the objection the warrant was to defend the possession, [he] responds *in quadam causa maritima* does not alter the case. And if this is allowed, it is an execution in the first instance, and it appears by the cases cited by Mr. Ward that *causa salvagii* or *hypothecatum* appeared by an affidavit.

Chief Baron [Gilbert]: The court formerly differed upon granting these prohibitions. And I am doubtful.

Price: This is carrying it further than was ever asked for a prohibition, since it is *in causa maritima*.

Page: I am against a prohibition, for this warrant is only until security be given and the ship may not be stayed three hours.

Hale [was] against a prohibition.

So the former rule for a prohibition was set aside.

Taussig MS. 311, vol. 2, p. 819

Michaelmas term 1725.

Ward shows cause why a prohibition should not go to the Admiralty Court. We are here before a libel and, though the court has formerly granted prohibitions before the libel, yet, then, the form of the warrants were very different from the form in this case. The form of the former warrants was *causam ostensuras quare in possessionem dictae navis mitti seu saltem l[. . .]eri sive defendi non debeat*. So that it appeared upon the face of those warrants that the property of the ship was in *quidam*.

But, in this case, the warrant is *Roberto Rotterdamiae, mercatori, in quadam causa civila et maritima de justitia responsuro*. So that here it may be a matter proper for the jurisdiction of the court, as an hypothecation. Rolle's *Abridgment*, 670.

---

[1] *Transer v. Watson* (1703), 1 Salkeld 35, 91 E.R. 36, also 2 Lord Raymond 931, 92 E.R. 122, 6 Modern 11, 87 E.R. 776; *Johnson v. Shippen* (1703), 1 Salkeld 35, 91 E.R. 37, also 2 Lord Raymond 982, 92 E.R. 154, 11 Modern 30, 88 E.R. 863.

In all other courts, even on the former warrants, the prohibition used to be granted before the libel.

Bootle, contra: It is admitted that prohibitions formerly went before the libel and for the same reason now as formerly. He takes notice of the words in the warrant, which cites all persons claiming *jus, titulum, seu interesse in dicta nave*. And, therefore, this is in the nature of an execution in the first instance.

Secondly, though this warrant does express it *in quadam causa civili*, yet this is not more certain than before, for, whether this be *in causa salvagii* or for hypothecation or for mariners' wages, *non constat*.

Third, this will prevent a voyage.

Chief Baron [GILBERT]: In our law, we do proceed *in rem* even in our first process at common law, as, upon an attachment of goods, they are forfeited by non-appearance. It is difficult to overturn and make them alter this form.

PRICE: They have now altered their warrant and have now alleged a cause civil and maritime, which was omitted in the former warrants.

PAGE: Putting in a caution discharges the ship against a prohibition.

So the court allowed the cause to be shown and discharged the rule.

563

Rex, *ex rel.* Derby v. Railand

(Ex. 1725)

The question in this case was whether the court should discharge a writ of extent against a discharged bankrupt who owed money to the crown.

Harvard Law School MS. 1082, vol. 1, p. 244, pl. 2

Michaelmas term 1725.

Serjeant *Comyns*, for the defendant, moved to discharge the defendant, who is a bankrupt and owes the crown money, according to the Stat. 6 Geo,[1] that this was only a debt in aid to the crown. The certificate discharges the bankrupt generally. Hardres 403;[2] Rules 15 Car. I. The defendant, by the Statute, is obliged to discover and deliver up all, and it would be hard to keep the defendant in custody when there cannot be anything to pay [over].

Ward, pro eodem: This is a case of compassion. And this Derby [receiver of Dorset], at whose suit this is, is a trader, which he ought not to be according to the Rules of 15 Car. I. [There was] no commission of bankruptcy until 13th of November, and the *teste* of the extent [was] 14 November. This was a debt arising upon a simple contract. And no [writ of] extent is to issue in term time but

[1] Stat. 6 Geo. I, c. 22.

[2] *Attorney General v. Poultney* (1665), Hardres 403, 145 E.R. 519.

by motion in court, and there was no such motion. And it is not known that this was a debt originally due to the king's debtor.

Fazakerly, pro eodem: The Rules of 15 Car. I were not pursued. No extent will lie on a bill of exchange.

Bootle, for the extent: This is a new attempt to trip up the practice of the court. The Act of Parliament is out of the case, for the certificate is not obtained until after the defendant was in custody.

[To the] objection that this extent issued irregularly because the receiver was a trader, [he] responded the affidavit does not say that this debt was contracted in the way of trade.

[To the] objection of [being] contrary to the Rules of 15 Car. I, [they are] not applicable to this case. In this case [of a] sum of money received by the king's receiver, an extent was taken out against himself, and an inquisition binds this debt. An affidavit was made and a proper warrant for the extent.

Chief Baron [GILBERT]: It did not appear to him to be irregular.

But yet the court referred it to the Deputy [Remembrancer] to state.

564

Cheval v. Nichols

(Ex. 1725)

The recording statute does not protect a purchaser for value who has notice of prior unrecorded liens and encumbrances.

Taussig MS. 311, vol. 2, p. 839

Friday, 10th December 1725.

Cheval, being about seventy, applies to Hall to grant him an annuity for the residue of his life. Hall was his brother-in-law, and he had a garden ground of about nine acres walled in and planted with fruit and a house in it. One half of the ground was freehold, one half copyhold, and it had been improved by Hall. Hall, accordingly, on 13 May 1720 in consideration of £30, grants him £40 *per annum* to be issuing out of the freehold part of this garden ground, particularly mentioning it with a clause of distress and covenants that he was seised in fee. At this time, Hall was possessed of the residue of a term of 31 years assigned to him from one Bedford, which was to expire at Christmas 1725. But, in the year 1717, one Walcott, who made the former lease to Bedford, was seised of the reversion of the premises, [and he] offered Hall to sell him the reversion. Hall, having not money enough of his own to purchase the said reversion, applies to the defendant Nicholls to borrow the money of him and, accordingly, Nicholls lends him £400 and takes a conveyance to himself and Storer, his trustee, in fee from Walcott, which, though it was an absolute purchase on the face of the deed and though Hall was no party to the conveyance, yet it was acknowledged to be taken as a security only for the repayment of the said £400 and interest. And this conveyance was duly registered according to the Act of [*blank*] Anne, ca. [*blank*], for registering deeds in Middlesex.[1] On 24 June 1718, Nicholls lends Hall £200 more and makes a bond for the £200 and also enters into a defeasance that, if Hall paid him the £600 and interest on 24 June 1720, then he and his trustee would reconvey to Hall. In December 1720, Nicholls lends Hall £200 more, and then, in May 1721, Nicholls had notice of the grant of the rent charge and, after that, lends Hall about £300 more or so much as with the interest made up the whole £1000 and, in December 1723, takes an absolute conveyance and release of the equity of redemption from Hall in consideration of £1000.

Chevall brings a bill to have the arrears of the annuity paid him which accrued after Hall's death, who died in 1723, and to have the annuity charged upon the land for the future or to have other relief *prout* equitable. Nicholls, by an answer, insists that he was a purchaser for a valuable consideration and sets forth the case as above with this further that, on the 24 June 1720, when the defeasance was executed, the original lease from Walcott to Bedford and the assignment thereof from Bedford to Hall were delivered up to him by Hall. And, in that defeasance, Hall covenanted for further assurance and that, as he remembered and believed, they were intended to be made a security together with the reversion for the repayment of the money mentioned in the defeasance. But he admits there was no direct assignment of them to him for that purpose. And by his answer, the defendant admitted that, between the advancement of the £200 on the 24th June 1718 and the other £200 in December 1720, Hall paid him off £100 of the principal money so that, in May 1720, when the annuity was granted, there was but £500 lent by Nicholls which was strictly speaking chargeable on the premises. And the defendant insisted by his answer that the deed of grant of the rent charge was void against him, never having been registered, and he also said that, though he had notice of it in May 1720, yet he never promised the plaintiff that, in case Hall did not pay the annuity, he would and that, in case he was prevailed upon to lend Hall any more money, the same should not be to the prejudice of his annuity.

But his answer was disproved in this last particular by three positive witnesses examined on the part of the plaintiff. And upon hearing the cause, it was insisted for the plaintiff that, as to the term of years subsisting and which would not expire until Christmas 1725, the rent charge was a lien on the land even in point of law for that this term was never vested in the defendant Nicholls according to his own account of the matter.

And this was agreed to by the court.

Secondly, it was said that, if Hall had purchased the reversion in his own name, the reversion would certainly have been subject to the rent charge as well

[1] Stat. 7 Ann., c. 20 (*SR*, IX, 89–93).

as the term, even though the reversion had been purchased after the grant of the rent charge. *Quod etiam concessum fuit*. And that, in equity, Nicholls stood in the same place with Hall, it being admitted that the purchase was made in Hall's right, and, therefore, Nickolls could only claim the reversion as a security for the £600 which he lent to Hall prior to the rent charge and which, by the defeasance 24th June 1718, was made chargeable on the same and, £100 being paid off of this £600, he could only claim the same as security for the remaining £500.

And of this opinion was the court. And Lord Chief Baron [GILBERT] said that it was a known rule in equity that though a mortgagor or his heir should not redeem without paying the mortgagee the money lent on the mortgage and the subsequent sums lent him on a bond also because the bond would affect the land and might be made a lien of the lands in the hands of the mortgagor or his heir, yet, as against a subsequent mortgagee, no bonds or money which was not originally lent on the security of the land itself could be charged upon it so as to prevent or delay the satisfaction which the second mortgagee was entitled to. And as I understood him, no money lent by a first mortgagee, though agreed to be charged on the land at the time of lending it, would be admitted so to do as against a subsequent mortgagee where the first mortgagee had notice at the time of lending such additional sums of the second mortgagee.

And the Chief Baron [GILBERT] and PAGE and HALE also said that, though, by the words of the Statute [*blank*] Anne, a prior conveyance or mortgage not registered was made void against a subsequent conveyance which was registered, yet it was not nor could be the intent of the Statute to make such prior conveyance void when the purchaser under a subsequent conveyance knew and was apprised of the former conveyance or mortgage, for that would be to encourage and establish frauds instead of preventing them.

And upon the whole, the court decreed the payment of the annuity to Christmas 1725 and that, then, it should be at the defendant's election to confirm the annuity or it to be redeemed by the plaintiff on the plaintiff's paying him the £500 and interest thereof to the time of the bill etc.

Note: I [Philip Ward] was of counsel for the plaintiff.

Lincoln's Inn MS. Misc. 177, p. 20 (Jodrell's reports)

In 1717, the defendant took a mortgage from one Hall for £400. In 1718, he lent £200 on the same estate, both of which were registered. In 1720, he lent him £200 more upon a bond. In May following, Hall granted an annuity for £40 *per annum* to the plaintiff, which was not registered, but the plaintiff gave the defendant notice of it and desired him to lend no more to Hall. The defendant promised he would not and, if he did, he would take care of him, yet, after that, he lent Hall many more sums and, at last, purchased the equity of redemption, which he registered, yet the court held that the plaintiff's title to the annuity [was] good against the equity of redemption.

1 Strange 664, 93 E.R. 768

One John Hall was possessed of a term for years in certain lands lying in the County of Middlesex, and he granted an annuity of £40 to the plaintiff to be issuing out of the lands. The defendant, being concerned for this Hall in the management of some of his affairs, knew that Hall had granted this annuity to the plaintiff and had seen the deed and paid him part of the annuity upon Hall's account. Afterwards, Hall purchases the reversion of these lands, and then the defendant purchases the term and the reversion of Hall. Hall dies. And the defendant refused to pay the plaintiff his annuity because the deed by which Hall had granted it was not registered according to the Statute 7 Ann., c. 20,[1] which requires that all deeds or conveyances of, and all encumbrances upon, lands lying in the County of Middlesex shall be registered within such a time at the office; otherwise, every such conveyance shall be void against any subsequent purchaser for a valuable consideration. The defendant, therefore, insisted that he was a subsequent purchaser for a valuable consideration and that the plaintiff's claim of an annuity could not affect him because it was not registered.

The whole court were clearly of opinion that the plaintiff was entitled to have his annuity out of these lands against the defendant, notwithstanding this Statute, for the Statute only intended to give such notice of former encumbrances to purchasers that they might not thereby be defrauded. But, if a man knows of his own knowledge that there is a prior incumbrance and, notwithstanding that knowledge, will be a purchaser, the Statute was never intended to relieve such, though the first incumbrance was not registered, for, where a man purchases with notice of a prior incumbrance, he purchases with an ill conscience, and, in a court of equity, his purchase shall never be established.

Therefore, they decreed [to] the plaintiff his annuity and the arrears.

565

Spong, *qui tam* v. Fasting

(Ex. 1725–1726)

A person who has even a remote interest in the outcome of a case is incompetent to testify as a witness therein.

Taussig MS. 311, vol. 2, p. 805, pl. 2

Thursday, 17 June 1725. Spong, Sands, and Speed, *qui tam* v. Fasting.

[There was an] information against the defendant, the claimer of a parcel of brandy, upon the Statute for importing brandy in casks under sixty gallons. The defendant would have called the master [of the vessel] as an evidence. But the

1 Stat. 7 Ann., c. 20 (*SR*, IX, 89–93).

Attorney [General *Yorke*] objected that he was liable to the duty if the brandy was put on shore and so was biased in point of interest.

And of this opinion the Chief Baron [Gilbert] was. And so he was not permitted to be examined, for he said, whether the interest was immediate or mediate, it might bias the witness and so make him incompetent. But he permitted us to make a case of this point.

N.B. The aforesaid information was grounded upon 4 & 5 Will. & Mar., ca. 5, § 8,[1] but this clause gives no penalty against the master, but only forfeits the brandy. The penalty upon the master, I suppose, is grounded upon 6 Geo., which imposes, [at] fol. 412,[2] a penalty of imprisonment for six months on the master of the ship for suffering the brandy to be put out of the ship. See the clause and query whether it extends to any suffering, *viz.* by negligence, or only to a voluntary one. And it seems by the prior clause it only extends to masters of vessels of fifty tons or under, but not to greater vessels.

Taussig MS. 311, vol. 2, p. 814

Saturday, 6 November 1725.

The point of evidence was whether the master might be a witness.

Price: It seems to me that the master is no witness because the master has brought the brandy in an unsizable cask. But I would think of it because the precedents are otherwise, as it is said at the bar.

Page was of the same opinion because whether the master has done ill or well is the question and, therefore, he is no witness. It is not to be supposed that the ship sailed by the master alone; so there is no necessity of making use of his evidence. It is an objection even without an act of Parliament. Importation is not the only question, but the breaking of bulk.

Hale thinks the court should not make any general rule.

Chief Baron [Gilbert]: The master is the principal importer. And I do not think there is any distinction between an information filed against the master and where it is not. This is no case of necessity because others may be witnesses of the stress of weather.

The court will consider of it.

Harvard Law School MS. 1082, vol. 1, p. 252, pl. 2

Michaelmas term 1725.

Mr. *Bunbury*, for the defendant, moved for a new trial, the benefit being reserved on the trial, because Thomas Falkner, the master [of the vessel], was refused to be a witness. This objection was only started since 1723. And, out of necessity, the master ought to be evidence for the sale of the trade and, perhaps,

---

[1] Stat. 4 Will. & Mar., c. 5, s. 6 (*SR*, VI, 384).

[2] Stat. 6 Geo. I, c. 21, s. 32.

there was no person in the vessel but one or two sailors and the master. The master is but in the nature of a servant. He receives wages from the owners. If an information had been depending against the master, it might have varied the case. The former verdict against the defendants could not be given in evidence against the master.

Philip Ward, pro eodem: In several cases, the master has been admitted, *viz.* Williams, *qui tam* v. Worth, Exchequer 1702; Clap, *qui tam* v. Patrick Walsh, July 1704. In the last case, the master was refused because he was a part owner. But in Leslie, *qui tam* v. Gray and Corbet,[1] Chief Baron Eyre did admit the master as a witness. The Stat. 6 Geo.[2] imposes a penalty of imprisonment where the master suffers goods to be run, and the master lies on no other penalty.

Mr. *Bootle*, for the defendant: This case is of very great consequence to trade and merchants in general. The master is under no influence. And whether a consequential objection will be sufficient to take away in consideration of the consequence of trade must be submitted. This is an information *in rem* where the master is not affected. This is a remote objection, and he ought to be admitted, as in the case of a remote remainderman in tail, where such a person has been admitted. Lord Rochford's Case; Layton v. Layton; 1 Ventris 49, 1 Siderfin 431, 2 Keble 572.[3]

For the necessity that a master should be admitted, [see] Michaelmas 12 Will. III, Rex v. Weedon Ford,[4] where Emerson, the party escaping, was admitted to prove the voluntary escape. Jenkins, *qui tam* v. Larwood, 1717.[5]

Attorney General [*Yorke*], for the king: I am surprised to hear it said that the master is not subject to any penalty but that of imprisonment by [Stat.] 6 Geo. I insist that he is liable to the penalty of £100 by Stat. 14 Car. II.[6]

[To the] objection that the former verdict cannot be given in evidence against the master, [he] responded that is not the rule of evidence, as in a case of a right of common. There, a commoner cannot be an evidence, yet the former verdict cannot be read against him. What the master said can be given in evidence in relation to the penalty. And, therefore, he cannot be indifferent in delivering his evidence.

[To the] objection of no information filed, but, if there was one against the master, it is admitted a good objection, [he] answered no reason is given for that difference, and the master is affected by the question.

---

[1] *Lesley, qui tam v. Gray* (Ex. 1724), see above, Case No. 479.

[2] Stat. 6 Geo. I, c. 21, s. 32.

[3] *Rex v. Parris* (1669), 1 Ventris 49, 86 E.R. 35, 1 Siderfin 431, 82 E.R. 1200, 2 Keble 572, 84 E.R. 360.

[4] Perhaps *Regina v. Ford* (1703), Colles 332, 1 E.R. 312, or *Attorney General v. Mason* (1708), Eq. Cases Exch. 577, 4 Brown P.C. 133, 2 E.R. 90.

[5] *Jenkins, qui tam v. Larwood* (1717), see above, Case No. 23.

[6] Stat. 14 Car. II, c. 11 (*SR*, V, 393–400).

[To the] objection of the necessity of the master's evidence, [he] responded it is a necessity only lying in the cognizance of the party, for any sailor may be a witness.

[To the] objection of matters of privity between the master and sailors and known by no other party, [he] answered, as to sailing, the master knows no more than the mariners.

[To the] objection of Williams, *qui tam* v. Worth, [he] responded [and] admitted that the objection was not taken.

Bunbury replies that this was too distant a consideration to take away the master's evidence and the master was under no influence at the time of the examination. And, therefore, there is a great difference between an information filed or not against the master. The Attorney General admits it is a distant consideration in a case of the owners' bringing an action against the masters. And this is the same case, there being no information filed.

Bootle replies: By the Statute of 14 Car. II, if the master did not consent, the master might be a good witness whether this was an importation or not.

PRICE: I would consider of it, but my present thoughts are that the master cannot be an evidence, for the master seems to be more interested than the defendant, who is only to prove his property. I admit that the verdict in this case cannot be read in evidence against the master. And that is not the rule of evidence. The argument of necessity cannot be used, for the sailors may be witnesses and who may know as well concerning the voyage as the mariners.

PAGE: I agree that the master cannot be an evidence, but, wherever the party is concerned in interest, though remote, he cannot be a witness, as in the case of a parishioner or a commoner.

HALE: I am far from laying down a general rule that the master cannot at any time be an evidence. See Browne's Case, in Ventris.[1] In this case, the sailors are as good evidence of the stress of weather as the master.

Chief Baron [GILBERT]: The question is whether there was an importation or not, and the master is concerned as an importer. And there is no difference whether an information is actually filed or not, for the master is liable to an information. And after the argument of necessity, it has no weight, for the common law is broken into by the Statute of Winchester,[2] where the party robbed is admitted.

So it seemed to be agreed *per* TOTAM CURIAM that the master could not be a witness.

---

[1] *Rex v. Brown* (1673), 1 Ventris 243, 86 E.R. 163, also 3 Keble 193, 84 E.R. 671.

[2] Stat. 13 Edw. I, Winchester (*SR*, I, 96–98).

Taussig MS. 311, vol. 2, p. 868, pl. 1

N.B. The Chief Baron [Gilbert] at the sittings on Thursday evening, the 10th February, said that the court had determined it in the Case of Spong etc. v. Fasting, that the master could not be admitted as a witness, though my notes are that the court would consider of it. And I am pretty sure the fact was so, though I agree that every one of the barons inclined to think that the master was not an evidence. [See] above.

Bunbury 203, 145 E.R. 647

[In an] information for importing brandy in casks under sixty gallons, upon the trial, the defendant produced the master of the vessel as a witness. But it was objected by the Attorney General [*Yorke*], that the master was liable to a penalty of £100 for breaking bulk, by the Stat. 14 Car. II and, therefore, [was] concerned in the question, of which opinion was the Chief Baron. But he reserved this point for the opinion of the court. And now *per* totam curiam, [it was held that] the master ought not to be admitted as a witness, though no information was filed against him. And it seemed to make no difference where it was or was not filed, though many instances were mentioned on this distinction before. There were cited for the defendant: Williams, *qui tam* v. Ward, 1702, for importing in unsizable casks; Knapp v. Walsh, 1740, on the Act of Navigation; Lesley, *qui tam* v. Grey, 9 Geo. [1722 x 1723], tobacco; Jenkins, *qui tam* v. Larwood, on the Act of Navigation.

566

Talbot v. Whitfield

(Ex. 1725)

The question in this case was whether a court of equity will allow a testamentary trust of funds that are directed to be invested in land in tail to be distributed directly to the first beneficiary without joining the remainderman beneficiary as a party to the suit.

Harvard Law School MS. 1082, vol. 1, p. 251

Michaelmas term 1725.

The bill was to desire that money directed to be laid out in lands, which were to be settled for the plaintiffs' benefit and thereby made tenants in tail. And the plaintiffs by their bill insisted that, since, by the will, if the lands were to be so settled, that they could suffer a recovery, so they desired to have the money without such a settlement.

Price and Hale [were] against decreeing the money because there may be a chance that the plaintiffs will not suffer a recovery. And, this bill being to execute a trust, we cannot alter the will of the testator and act contrary to it.

Chief Baron [Gilbert]: A court of equity esteems a person that is tenant in tail to have an entire dominion over his estate, and this suffering of a recovery is only a ceremony and may be supplied in a court of equity.

Price: If any precedents can be showed that a court of equity did ever do it, I should agree.

Page agreed with the Chief Baron.

But Hale said it cannot be done without that the remainderman shall desire the court [to do it]. This matter has been always denied in a court of equity.

It was referred to the Deputy [Remembrancer] to find out a purchaser.

Then, this being a matter by consent, the plaintiffs agreed to dismiss the bill without costs.

Taussig MS. 311, vol. 2, p. 821, pl. 2

Thursday, 25 November 1725.

A man devises that, when A. comes of age, the £400 should be invested in land and settled to the use of A. and the heirs of his body and the remainder over to B. A. comes of age and brings his bill against Whitfield, who was the trustee, to have the money, and he does not make the remainderman a party. The trustee submits to do as the court directs. And for the plaintiff, it was said that, he being to be tenant in tail and so capable of docking the entail and the sum of money being so small, a great part of it would be exhausted in the purchase and suffering the recovery and it being more convenient for the first devisee to have the money and the trustee consenting, the court might decree the executor or trustee to do it.

And Chief Baron [Gilbert] and Page inclined to think they might.

But Price and Hale thought not because the remainderman was no party and he had a chance for it in case A. should die before he had an opportunity of suffering a recovery.

So the bill was dismissed without costs by consent.

Et nota: Paul Foley told me on this occasion that it was his own case, his father leaving his fortune in money with a direction that, when he came of age, his eldest brother, who was his father's executor, should lay out the money in land to the same uses as in this case and Paul choosing to have his fortune in money and his brother consenting to pay it in case the court of equity would indemnify him, they, thereupon, consulted and advised with Sir Simon Harcourt and Master How, and they told them it could not be done. However, a bill was exhibited in Chancery, and the eldest brother, who was both executor and remainderman, submitted to do as the court should approve, but Lord Cooper dismissed the bill, refusing to give any such directions.

Bunbury 204, 145 E.R. 648

25 November 1725.

A man by his will devises a sum of money in trust, that the same should be laid out in a purchase of lands by his trustee, which lands should be to the use of the mother for life, remainder to her first and other sons in tail, remainder to A. in fee. The mother died. The son, who, by the will, was to be tenant in tail, preferred his bill, setting forth this case and that the trustee had not laid out the money, and he prayed that it might be paid to him, being more advantageous to him in his way of business than lands, and likewise to save expense, for, if it was laid out in land, the plaintiff now being of age, could suffer a recovery and, thereby, bar the remainderman and sell the land. The defendant trustee, in his answer, agreed to this prayer.

But note: The remainderman was not made a party, and, therefore, it was objected that the plaintiff might die before he suffered a recovery and it would be wrong in a court of equity to deprive the remainderman of this chance without being heard.

Lord Chief Baron GILBERT and PAGE thought they might decree in this case, as there was no infant concerned. But PRICE and HALE [were] *totis viribus* of another opinion. So, the court being divided, the bill was dismissed by consent.

567

In re Will of Shelmer

(Ex. 1725)

The word 'money' as used in a will means ready money, cash, and money due and payable, but not shares of stock, annuities, or the proceeds of a sale of property.

Gilbert Rep. 200, 25 E.R. 139

18 December 1725. The case of Mary Shelmer's will and the award of Baron GILBERT made thereupon.

Mary Shelmer, widow, by her will, dated the 27th of August 1722, gives to her own nieces, Gwyn, etc., £50 apiece, and, after several other legacies to her husband's relations, and also to her own more distant relations, and particularly £100 to her husband's nephew, Philip Gibbons, Esq., whom she made sole executor, she gives a direction in the following words, concerning a house she held by a long lease from the Town of Bedford at a small ground rent, *viz.*:

> also I will that my house in Bedford Buildings with the marbles and cisterns thereto belonging be sold by my executor hereafter named with all convenient speed, and, out of the purchase money thereby arising, I give to my cousin John Lloyd of Westminster £100, and, if he should die in my lifetime, I give the said £100 to his child or children equally to be divided between them.

But she says nothing farther touching the money to arise by the sale of this house. Then, she proceeds and gives her own niece, Elizabeth Bernard, her executors, and assigns, her tenement in Fleet Street for the remainder of the term therein to come chargeable with £20 apiece to her three sons. To her own nephew, Owen Brigstock, Esq., she devises an estate of inheritance in Wales, subject to pay his brother William £100, and, after some other legacies, she bequeaths to her man and maid servant, in the following words:

> Item, I give to my servant Philip How £200;
> Item, I give to my servant Elizabeth Pilgrim £100 and all my wearing apparel;
> Item, I farther give to the said Philip How and Elizabeth Pilgrim all my household goods, money, and plate, that I shall leave behind me at the time of my death undisposed of, and not bequeathed to others, my funeral expenses, debts, and legacies being first paid;
> Item, to Mary, [my] servant, £20, and to James, [my] servant, £10, provided they respectively dwell with [me] at the time of [my] decease.

And after these bequests to her servants, she gives several legacies in money, several specific legacies out of her household goods and plate to other legatees and, particularly, to her niece Bernard, and to the wives of her nephews Brigstock, several pieces of plate, and to Mr. Gibbons, her executor, and his lady, each a diamond ring, and to him a pearl necklace and some movables, and to his daughters, each a specific legacy.

The testatrix gives about seventy specific legacies by her will, twenty-eight whereof preceded the said bequest to her servants, Philip How and Elizabeth Pilgrim, and about thirty followed. And, in the last clause of her will, she directed that whatever money she owed any of her servants at her death, either for wages or notes under her hand, should be paid them over and above their respective legacies therein left them and that her servants living with her at her decease should be permitted to continue in her house one month next after her decease, being the house in Bedford Buildings directed to be sold. And of her will, she appointed the said Mr. Gibbons sole executor, without devising or taking any other or further notice of the residuum of her estate, except what is mentioned in the above recited bequest to her man and maid, Philip How and Elizabeth Pilgrim, in the middle of her will.

The testatrix owed none of her servants any money, besides a trifle for wages, except to Philip How, to whom she owed £100 by a note given to him for the debt of another person, and also the balance of an account for money laid out, besides what she owed him for wages.

Her said man Philip How had lived with her husband and herself twenty-six years, and her maid had lived with her about ten years.

The testatrix had three sisters, who died before her, but left children living at the testatrix's death, *viz.* Mr. Gwyn's mother, Mr. Bernard's mother, and the mother of the two Brigstocks. And these nephews and nieces are the next of kin to the testatrix, according to the due course of law, and were most of them in good esteem with the testatrix.

The testatrix during her life was seised of an estate of about £800 a year, part by jointure and part by her husband's will, which she enjoyed from the time of his death, which happened about twenty-six years before her own.

She died the 7th of September 1724, about two years after making her will, aged 77 years or thereabouts. And it is thought she had at the time of making her will computed specifically, giving away as much as she was worth and, therefore, did not close her will with any devise or direction concerning the residue of her estate.

The house in Bedford Buildings has been sold for £400, whereas she has but specifically given away £100 of that money.

And she died possessed of £500 or £600 South Sea stock and annuities, of a considerable sum due in arrear for the rent of her freehold estate, which she held for life, and also for considerable sums due to her upon bonds and mortgages.

She likewise left a considerable quantity of plate undisposed of by her will and also 100 guineas in ready money in her house at the time of her death, so that the specific devise to her servants Philip How and Elizabeth Pilgrim, without taking in the residuum of her estate, will amount to near £400 apiece, which is much more than she has given to any other legatee or person of her family or her nearest relations.

And it is thought the testatrix intended her said servants nothing beyond their specific money legacies, than household goods, plate, and such ready money, as should be in her dwelling house at the time of her death, she usually having £100 or £200 in ready money by her. And not even those until her debts and all her other legacies were paid because, as by her will she has given several particular legacies out of her household goods and plate to other persons, it was for that reason she added in the devise to her servants Philip How and Elizabeth Pilgrim the words 'undisposed, and not bequeathed to others' and not with an intent to give them the whole residue of her estate in general.

And this is the rather to be supposed from the last clause in her will, which declares that her servants should be paid their legacies over and above what she owed them for wages or by note and that they should live in her house a month after her death, which clause was in a manner useless if she had intended the residuum of her estate to Philip How and Elizabeth Pilgrim, the testatrix having but four servants at the time of her death, of whom they were two, and being little or nothing indebted to any of them, except to Philip How, in which case, Philip How would have had the control over her dwelling house in Bedford Buildings, as well as an absolute power to himself to secure his specific legacies.

The residuum of the testatrix's estate, after payment of her debts and legacies, will amount to £400 or £500.

Whether the testatrix's servants Philip How and Elizabeth Pilgrim or the testatrix's next of kin are entitled to the residue of the money arising by the sale of the house in Bedford Buildings and the remaining part of the residuum of her personal estate or either and which of them is the question.

I have considered of the matter referred to me between Mrs. Shelmer's relations and servants touching her will. And I am of opinion that the word 'money' mentioned in the bequest to the servants in her will is a general word, but yet not so large and comprehensive as the word *pecunia* in the Roman tongue, for such word in that language [means] all the testatrix's substance, both real and personal, that can be converted into money. But the word money in our language answers to the barbarians' Latin word *moneta*, and it is a genus that comprehends two species, *viz.* ready money and money due, that is to say, the money in her own hands or her money in the hands of anybody else. And, therefore, in this case, the bequests to her servants will comprehend Mr. Wood's mortgage and the arrears of rent, since these must be looked upon by all the rules of construction to be Mrs. Shelmer's money at the time of her death. But the word money will not comprehend South Sea stock or annuity stock because that is an interest arising out of funds, settled by public laws, and, though it be redeemable by money, or saleable for money, yet it can be no more looked upon as money at the time of Mrs. Shelmer's decease than a term of years, a coach and horses, or any other real or personal chattel whatsoever can. And, therefore, I am clearly of opinion it cannot be comprehended in the word 'money'. I am likewise of opinion that the money arising by the sale of the house in Bedford Buildings will not be comprised by this bequest because that was not money left behind her at the time of her decease, for, then, it was a chattel real, and it could not by the frame of the will be sold until a month after her decease, since the servants are by an express clause in the will to remain there during that time.

I am, therefore, of opinion that the blended and liquidated residuum that is composed of all these species that remain in the hands of Mr. Gibbons, the executor, is to be divided in the proportion that the relations' residuary part bears to the residuary part of the servants. The residuary part of the relations consists of the annuity stock and this money arising by the sale of the house in Bedford Buildings, which is the first proportion, by which the ultimate residuum in Mr. Gibbons's hands is to be divided. The residuary part of the servants consists of Mr. Wood's mortgage and the arrears of rent and likewise the ready money, which is not to be considered specifically as a part and share due to the servants at all events, but as one of the 'items' that is to make a part of the computation of their proportion, so that the second proportional to divide this blended residuum is the residuary part or share of the servants. And the apportionment stands thus: as the relations' part is to the part of the servants, so the residuary part in Mr. Gibbons's hands is a fourth proportional.

Note: This is to be computed by the rule of three, either direct or inverse; and, accordingly, the shares of the relations and servants will come out by the aforementioned additions.

Therefore, I do award, order, and determine that the respective shares be paid to the servants according to their proportion and that, likewise, the residuary part or share of the relations be paid to them according to this proportion, but to be subdivided among them, according to the Statute of Distributions of Intestates' Estates.[1] And I do likewise order and determine that the said relations and servants, upon receiving such their shares and proportions, shall give to the said Philip Gibbons, Esq., the executor, proper releases. And I likewise do order that these proportions be forthwith calculated, settled, and adjusted, and the award drawn up in form with all convenient speed.

Witness my hand this present 18th Day of December in the 12th year of the reign of our sovereign lord King George I, in the year of our Lord God 1725. /s/ *Jeffrey Gilbert.*

568

Allport v. Thomas

(Ex. 1725)

Where discovery is prayed and a liquidated debt is admitted by the answer, a court of equity may give relief, but, where the debt is uncertain and sounds in damages, it is proper for a jury to ascertain it.

The owners of a ship are liable to pay for the necessary tackling of their ship, and the Court of Exchequer has concurrent jurisdiction with the Court of Admiralty to enforce such a debt.

Gilbert Rep. 227, 25 E.R. 158

A person that had furnished necessary tackling for a ship that was afterwards sold, by his bill, prays a discovery of the personal estate of one of the part owners, who was dead, and to have relief against his executor and the surviving part owners.

Mr. *Ward*, senior, for the plaintiff, said that, by the civil law, the bottom of the ship was liable to answer for the tackle and furniture which the defendants had contracted for. And here, they having sold the ship, they were very proper to demand satisfaction out of the profits arising by such sale. And as their bill was proper to have a discovery of the personal estate of the part owner that was dead, so, from thence, they would be entitled to relief against the others, for, in the case of Dupins v. Duke of Kingston, which was a bill brought by a milliner against the duke, as administrator of his son, for a discovery of assets and to have a debt which was due to her from his son discharged, it was laid down as a rule that discovery should draw with it relief.

---

[1] Stat. 22 & 23 Car. II, c. 10 (*SR*, V, 719–720).

Mr. *Bunbury*, for the defendant, said that, if that was to be taken as a general rule, the common law would be of little use, for, then, always after the death of one of the parties, they might bring their bill here upon any contract; besides, here they should have proceeded in the Court of Admiralty to have subjected the bottom of this ship, and that this court could not do it.

Chief Baron Gilbert said that the chief distinction upon the rule that discovery should draw with it relief seemed to be that, where a discovery is prayed and a liquidated debt is admitted by the answer, the court might then proceed to give relief, but, where the debt was unliquidated, being uncertain, and sounding in damages, it was proper for a jury to ascertain it, there being nothing for a court of equity to found a determination on; that though this case was within the mercantile law, yet it being admitted by the answer that the charge was for tackling etc., a court of equity must grant them the redress as a Court of Admiralty would, *viz.* upon the bottom of the ship, and that it would be very hard to send them back again there to obtain relief; and that all the part owners ought to make satisfaction, having received the profits of the voyage, which the ship was enabled to perform by the plaintiff's furnishing the tackle etc.

Baron Hale thought the Case of the Duke of Kingston should have gone no further than a discovery and, after that, should have proceeded at law, that, in this case, the proceeding in this court was very proper, and they might go on, for, in the Court of Admiralty, seamen's wages are recoverable, and they are likewise chargeable properly upon the bottom of the ship, and yet the Court of Chancery retains bills for them. And Sir John Trevor, late Master of the Rolls, used to say that a court of equity had a concurrent jurisdiction with them.

569

Marriot v. Marriot

(Ex. 1725–1726)

A court of equity has the power to supervise the administration of wills.

The question in this case was whether a will can be set aside only partially on the grounds of lack of capacity of the testator or undue influence.

Harvard Law School MS. 1105, p. 1

Michaelmas 11 Geo. I.

A bill was brought by two of the sons of one Mr. Marriot, deceased, for setting aside his will, suggesting the same to be unfairly and fraudulently obtained by the defendants, Kimbra, his executrix and widow, Ann Deacon, her mother, and Yates, the drawer of it, and that the testator was insane at the time of making it etc. The defendants answered, and many witnesses were examined on both sides. And the case, upon the whole, appeared to be in substance thus.

Mr. Marriot, a very eminent clerk in the Exchequer office and a very prudent person, being in his declining years and infirm, married Kimbra, one of the defendants, and declared to his friends that he married her only for a nurse. He settled her whole fortune upon her, which was £2000, and agreed also to leave her by will £2000 and also a copyhold estate of about £50 *per annum*, which settlement, he afterwards said, he had made that she might expect no more from him, intending to leave the rest of his estate to his children by a former wife, to whom he had actually given it by a will made before this last marriage. All these children, except Samuel, had always behaved very dutifully to their father and been very serviceable to him and were much beloved by him. But their mother-in-law kept them off from their father as much as possible, and she and her friends would frequently tell him that they did not behave affectionately towards him, that he had already provided sufficiently for the sons, who were all set up in business, that they were prodigals, and that they had deserted the true church, meaning the Dissenters, Mr. Marriot being one. The testator would also sometimes complain of being very much plagued and disquieted by his wife and her mother, Mrs. Deacon, another of the defendants.

Soon after this marriage, Mr. Marriot made a new will, but, concerning this there was a great contrariety of evidence between the defendants' own witnesses, one swearing that herein nothing was left to the children and the residue of the estate to his wife and another swearing that £1000 was left to such of his children and nothing to the wife. However, after this, Mr. Marriot made another will which was prepared by Yates, an intimate of Kimbra, and executed with all possible secrecy, whereby he gives to his wife the said copyhold estate, which he had surrendered to the use of his will, and her heirs, to his disobedient son, Samuel, £20 *per annum* for life, to his three other sons £400 apiece, to Elizabeth, his daughter, £1500, all these legacies to be paid in three years time after his decease. And there is a proviso that, if the said children do not execute a general release to his executrix within three months after his death, their legacies should be forfeited and go to her. The testator gives to his wife's mother £100 and to others some such legacies, all of which, including the children's, he charges upon the money secured to him by Sir John Hobart's mortgage. And lastly, he gives the residue of his real and personal estate to his wife, her heirs, executors, and administrators, whom he makes executrix. This will was drawn and prepared by Yates. And the testator [was] very much disordered in body and very peevish and passionate, and some parts of the will were written by the testator himself, but these were exceedingly misspelled.

About half a year after the making of this will and one year and a half after the marriage, the testator died leaving a very considerable real and personal estate. The defendant Kimbra [. . .] in her answer she had already received £15,000. The widow proves the will.

In this case, besides the question on the merits, whether the plaintiffs are entitled to relief, it was very largely and elaborately argued whether this court has any jurisdiction or power to give any.

And it was argued by Serjeant *Pengelly*, Serjeant *Carter*, Mr. *Williams*, Mr. *Hungerford*, and many others for the plaintiffs that, though the spiritual court has the sole power of setting aside wills of personal estates where they are void *in toto*, as for infancy etc., which seemed clearly admitted, yet, when part of a will is obtained by fraud, a court of equity has, in such case, a power of giving relief not by way of sa[. . .]ing the will but only by making the legatee stand as a trustee for those who are entitled by law to what is by fraud thus nominally given away from them. In such case, an implied trust arises *ex delicto*. And all trusts upon wills, whether *expresse* or *constructive*, are the proper objects of the jurisdiction of a court of equity, as is plain by the common case where an executor is a legatee and there is no disposition of the residuum; there, in equity, the executor is a trustee of the residue for the next of kin, though, by the spiritual law, it belongs wholly to the executor.

In the present cases, if courts of equity could no way interpose, the plaintiffs would have a right without a remedy, for the spiritual court has not, nor ever exercised, a power of setting aside part of a will. And this would be very injurious to the children who, by the civil law, are very much favored, Swinburne, 1st part, 15; Godolphin, *Orphan's Legacy*, 17, and are according to that law, entitled to *legitima portio*. Justinian's *Institute, Corpus Juris Civilis*, 2 lib., 18, *De testamentis inofficiosis*.[1]

As to the jurisdiction of the spiritual court in the case of wills, it was urged that this is *non de jure sed de consuetudine Angliae et consensu regis et procorum communitatae*[2] and personal estates being temporal things. Linwood 114; Bacon's *Ecclesiastical Causes*, published 1632;[3] Selden, *Of Testaments*, 9, 10; 5 Coke 16a; 9 Coke 37, 38; Godolphin, *Orphan's Legacy*, 1st part, 58, 59; Shower 173, Salkeld [*blank*].[4]

And as to the extent of it, it is not unlimited and exclusive, but in many cases, subject to the control of the temporal courts, who have a concurrent jurisdiction therewith, as in the case of legacies, revocations, and the exposition of wills. And sometimes those courts determine in a different manner from what the ec-

[1] H. Swinburne, *Brief Treatise of Testaments and Last Wills*; J. Godolphin, *Orphan's Legacy*; Justinian, *Institutes*, 2, 18.

[2] not of right but by the custom of England and the consent of the king and of the representatives of the community.

[3] W. Lyndwood, *Provinciale* (1929); F. Bacon, *A Letter to a French Gentleman Touching the Proceedings in England in Ecclesiastical Causes* [this was published in *Cabala sive Scrinia Sacra* and in G. Burnet, *History of the Reformation*].

[4] *Spencer v. Clark* (1583), 5 Coke Rep. 16, 77 E.R. 72; *Hensloe v. Gage* (1600), 9 Coke Rep. 36, 77 E.R. 784; *Shatter v. Friend* (1691), 1 Shower K.B. 158, 172, 89 E.R. 510, 518, 2 Salkeld 547, 91 E.R. 462, also 3 Modern 283, 87 E.R. 188, Carthew 142, 90 E.R. 687, Holt K.B. 752, 90 E.R. 1313, Comberbach 160, 90 E.R. 404.

clesiastical judges would do. Cro. Ch. 115; Cro. Jac. 346;[1] Bagnall v. Dry, Trinity 1719, by Macclesfield, Chancellor. There a man, by his last will, made three executors, one of whom died in the testator's lifetime, and after the testator's death, his children brought a bill insisting that the legacy given to the executor who was dead was lapsed and ought to be distributed according to the Statute,[2] and so it was decreed, though, by the spiritual law, this belongs to the surviving executors who, according to that are entitled to the residuum.

Edwards v. Grover [was a] suit in a court Christian for a legacy payable by the executor out of lands devised to be sold by him, and a [writ of] prohibition was granted.

Clark v. Clark, in the time of Lord Holt.[3]

Brown v. Wentworth[4] [was a] suit in the spiritual court for a legacy given by a will against an administrator, who insisted that the will was revoked and attempted to prove the revocation by one witness. But the spiritual court refusing this proof, a [writ of] prohibition was granted, a single witness being in such cases sufficient by the law of the land.

[In] Richardson v. Desborrow,[5] [a writ of] prohibition [was] granted for the same reason to a suit in a court Christian for a legacy because they refused a single witness to prove the payment of it.

Even in the case of marriage, which is originally of canonical jurisdiction, this is frequently tried in the temporal courts without sending to the bishop for his certificate. And issues have been directed by the Court of Chancery to be tried there, particularly in the cases of Monday v. Sacheverell and Hillyard v. Grantham, which were before Lord Macclesfield. And there, at the trial, a sentence of the spiritual court was produced for annulling the marriage because the ceremony was performed by a Romish priest and according to the Romish manner, but this evidence was rejected. [See] Lady Ogle v. Thynne, and many others.

So in the case of an excommunication, it is frequent for the temporal court to quash the writ *de excommunicato capiendo*. And there are many cases where courts of equity exercise concurrent jurisdiction with other courts, as in the case of wills of real estate, bonds, and deeds, and even judgments where, if there be any fraud, equity always interposes. And yet, in all these instances, the courts of common law have as proper a jurisdiction as the spiritual court can claim in the case of wills of personal estates. And, therefore, *pari ratione*, where these are

---

[1] *Denne v. Burrough* (1628), Croke Car. 115, 79 E.R. 701, also Hetley 105, 113, 148, 124 E.R. 378, 384, 413; *Egerton v. Egerton* (1614), Croke Jac. 346, 79 E.R. 296, also 2 Bulstrode 218, 80 E.R. 1074.

[2] Stat. 22 & 23 Car. II, c. 10 (*SR*, V, 719–720).

[3] *Clerke v. Clerke* (1700), 1 Lord Raymond 585, 91 E.R. 1291.

[4] *Brown v. Wentworth* (1606), Yelverton 92, 80 E.R. 63.

[5] *Richardson v. Desborough* (1675), 1 Ventris 291, 86 E.R. 188, 3 Keble 570, 576, 579, 84 E.R. 884, 888, 889.

fraudulently obtained, they may be relieved against in equity, all one as other fraudulent conveyances, a will being in the nature of a conveyance.

Upon the whole, therefore, it was urged that this court may and ought to interpose in this case by making the executrix accountable to the next of kin for the residuum of the testator's estate, the same being not properly disposed of, which is all one as if it was not disposed of at all. And to this point, the following cases were also cited, *viz.* Ainsworth v. Pollard, 1 Chancery Reports 101; Smallpeace v. Anguish, 1 Chancery Cases 75.[1] In this last case, as it appears by the decretal order, a bill was brought to discover the estate of Mary Smallpeace, the plaintiff's sister, and to set aside a will unfairly obtained in the time of her last illness by the procurement of one of the defendants, who had, by many solicitations, gotten her to his own house and cohabited with her and had, in her last illness, placed his own friends about her against her liking and excluded her own and afterwards concealed her death until he had proven her will in common form. And the bill was also brought to stay proceedings upon a bond given by another of the defendants to the testator. The defendants demurred for that, by the plaintiff's own showing, it appears they have already proved the will, which, being of personal estate, is properly examinable in the spiritual court and that the plaintiff is neither an executor nor a legatee. But the court overruled the demurrer and ordered that the said bond debt should not be paid until further order, and, in the meantime, an injunction was granted to stay proceedings thereon.

Hatter v. Newburgh, Style 497; Thynne v. Thynne, 1 Vernon 296; Maundy v. Maundy, 1 Chancery Reports 123; Herbert v. Lowndes, 1 Chancery Reports 22; Oldham v. Litchford, 3 Vernon 506; Hayward v. Bacon, 1692; Bransby v. Kerrish *et al.*, 5 Geo. I, *coram* Macclesfield, Chancellor.[2] There, as it appears by the decretal order, an extravagant son, after he had by two former wills given all his real and personal estate to his father, who had always used him very kindly and very handsomely supported him, was prevailed on by the defendant Kerrish, whom the father had placed with his son in his last illness to take care of him, the son being from home and the father absent, to make a will a few days before

[1] *Aynsworth v. Pollard* (1635–1636), 1 Chancery Reports 101, 21 E.R. 519; *Smallpiece v. Anguish* (1666), 1 Chancery Cases 75, 22 E.R. 702, also 1 Eq. Cas. Abr. 238, 21 E.R. 1016.

[2] *Hacker v. Newborn* (1653–1654), Style 413, 427, 82 E.R. 822, 834; *Thynn v. Thynn* (1684), 1 Vernon 296, 23 E.R. 479, also 1 Eq. Cas. Abr. 380, 21 E.R. 1116; *Maundy v. Maundy* (1638–1639), 1 Chancery Reports 123, 21 E.R. 526; *Herbert v. Lownes* (1628), 1 Chancery Reports 22, 21 E.R. 495, also 118 Selden Soc. 578, Cambridge Univ. Lib. MS. Mm.6.69, f. 17; *Oldham v. Litchfield* (1705), 2 Vernon 506, 23 E.R. 923, also 2 Freeman 284, 22 E.R. 1214, 1 Eq. Cas. Abr. 231, 21 E.R. 1011, 2 Eq. Cas. Abr. 44, 22 E.R. 39; *Bransby v. Kerrick* (1718), Misc. Chancery Repts. (1714–1730), 15, 1 Eq. Cas. Abr. 133, 406, 21 E.R. 937, 1136, 2 Eq. Cas. Abr. 421, 508, 767, 22 E.R. 358, 430, 652, 7 Brown P.C. 437, 3 E.R. 284.

his death, being very weak in body and mind, whereby he gives all his personal estate, except a small legacy, to Kerrish and also all his real estate on trust to pay his debts and makes him executor, the defendant Kerrish having taken occasion from the plaintiff's not remitting £30 to his son, as was expected, and which he was by accident prevented from doing, to say to the son that this was done with a design to defer the payment of his debts until his death and that then he, his father, would not pay any, and he told the son he desired or intended no benefit to himself by the will, but only that he might die like an honest man by his, the said Kerrish's, paying all his debts. And after the will, the son declared he intended no other alteration by it than that his debts should be paid. A bill was brought by the father to be relieved against this will, after the probate thereof by Kerrish, to which the defendants put in an answer. And on hearing the cause, the Lord Chancellor declared that the will was fraudulently obtained and, therefore, the defendant Kerrish ought not to take any benefit thereby, and he decreed that Kerrish and the other defendants, who were the testator's heirs at law, should join in a surrender of the copyhold and in a conveyance of all the freehold and other estates of the son in possession, reversion, or expectancy to the plaintiff and his heirs and that Kerrish should come to an account for the personal estate, for the better discovery whereof, he was to be examined on interrogatories as a Master should direct and to produce all books and papers relating thereto upon oath before the said Master and that, upon the said account, after allowances of debts, legacies, and funeral expenses paid by the defendant Kerrish, he should pay the surplus to the plaintiff. And he was also ordered to pay the plaintiff his costs. But in this case, as it was said by the defendants' counsel, it appears by the depositions, which are in court, that the will was read over to the son while he lay *in extremis* as if the estate was given to the father and his heirs, when, in fact, it was given to Kerrish.

Pope v. Tracey, in Chancery, 3 November 1716.[1] After a son had by his will devised lands to his mother forever, the defendant Tracey, the drawer of it, came and told her that, as the will was worded, the estate would not descend to her heir and therefore, he pretended a necessity for making a new will to remedy this defect and offered to prepare such will, which was agreed to. Accordingly, a new will was made and executed by the son when he was almost in extremity, wherein the lands were devised to the mother for life only and then to the defendant Tracey and his heirs. After the son's death, the mother brought a bill to set aside this will for fraud and to establish the former [will]. And Lord Chancellor Cowper said that a will may be set aside in equity for fraud, though it be good in law, as for instance, if a man agrees, in consideration of £1000 paid him by J.S., to devise his estate to him and his heirs, which he does accordingly, receiving from him a

[1] *Gosse v. Tracy* (1715), 2 Vernon 699, 23 E.R. 1052, 1 Peere Williams 287, 24 E.R. 392, 1 Eq. Cas. Abr. 406, 21 E.R. 1136, 2 Eq. Cas. Abr. 396, 491, 767, 22 E.R. 338, 416, 651.

Bank bill for £1000, and after the testator's death, the bill appears to be a forged one, the Court of Chancery will set aside this will, though it be duly executed and the testator was *compos* [*mentis*]. And in the principal case, he was of opinion that there was fraud in obtaining the second will and there being some proof that the son was not *compos* [*mentis*] at the time of making it, he directed an issue at law to try whether a will or no will,[1] and there was a verdict against it.

Savile v. Blacket, in Chancery, 18 July 6 Geo. I [1720],[2] Sir Edward Blacket, having by his will given to his two daughters £2000 apiece, one Beaumont, a little before the testator's death representing what a large estate he had, desired him to augment their fortunes, which the testator declared he thought reasonable and that he would give each of them a bond of £500 besides their said legacies. Thereupon, he ordered a lawyer to be sent for to bring such bonds, who coming without them, the testator declared to the lawyer and to his son, the defendant John Blacket, who was present and was to take a very great estate by his will and was made residuary legatee and executor thereof, that he was determined his daughters should have £500 apiece above what he had given them by his will, upon which the defendant desired his father to give himself no further trouble about that matter and promised him to pay the plaintiffs, his daughters, £500 apiece accordingly. And the testator afterwards spoke of this additional provision as a thing actually settled. And it was decreed by Lord Macclesfield that the defendant Blacket should pay his two sisters, the plaintiffs, £500 apiece over and above the money given to them by the will. To this point were also cited Nock v. Waters and Chichester v. Phillips and Hayward v. Colley, Trinity 11 Geo. I,[3] where several conveyances were decreed to be set aside upon this foundation, that a sentence of divorce obtained by fraud in the spiritual court is null and void, and so Lord Chancellor Macclesfield expressly said it is.

It was further objected in this case that, as the defendants have put in an answer, examined witnesses, filed a cross-bill for establishing this will, and the same is now come to a hearing, they have submitted to the jurisdiction of the court, all one as in the courts of common law, after the defendant has pleaded *defendit vim et injuriam*, he cannot object to the jurisdiction. If the defendants had a mind to contest this, they should have demurred, as was done in Smallpeace v. Anguish, 1 Chancery Cases 75.

On the other side, it was argued by Mr. Attorney General [*Yorke*], Mr. *Cowper*, Mr. *Keeve*, Serjeant *Comyns*, and several others that, though, in the case of wills of real estate, the temporal courts have a jurisdiction, because these were originally

1 I.e. *devisavit vel non*.

2 *Savile v. Blacket* (1721), 1 Peere Williams 777, 24 E.R. 610, 2 Eq. Cas. Abr. 568, 672, 22 E.R. 479, 564.

3 *Chichester v. Philips* (1680), T. Raymond 404, 83 E.R. 211; *Hayward v. Colley* (1724), Dickens 43, 21 E.R. 183, Select Cases *tempore* King 24, 25 E.R. 201, 2 Eq. Cas. Abr. 81, 491, 22 E.R. 71, 417 (deciding other points).

devisable by Act of Parliament,[1] yet in the case of personal estate, the spiritual courts have a final and exclusive jurisdiction, especially where such wills are absolutely void, as they certainly are when they are obtained by fraud and circumvention. Swinburne, part 1, sect. 3, pl. 15, pt. 7; Godolphin, *Orphan's Legacy*, 3, 4, 49.

If this were otherwise and after the probate of a will in the ecclesiastical court and a confirmation thereof upon an appeal, it might be litigated in courts of law or equity, who have in such a case an equal jurisdiction, it would be attended with very great confusion and uncertainty in relation to the property of the subject. The question, therefore, in the temporal courts over such wills can only be whether it has the ordinary's seal to it or not. If it has, they are concluded thereby. And by the same reason that they cannot set aside wills *in toto*, they cannot in part because this would be in effect making a new will different from that which was proved below. Besides, if part of a will be obtained by fraud, this must extend to the whole and make it void *in toto*.

In the present case, the whole will ought not to be set aside (1) because all the legatees are not made parties to the bill as, in such a case, they ought to be; (2) if this will be set aside, the former will made by the testator ought to be set up, according to Onions v. Fiers;[2] neither ought the bequest of the residuum only to be set aside and the next of kin let in for this part (1) because the bill is brought to set aside the whole will and suggests things proper for that purpose, as insanity, fraud, etc. and, on the bill, the decree must be founded, (2) if this should be set aside, the defendant Kimbra will be entitled to the residue as executrix, she having no specific legacy. And this court will scarcely strike out the nomination of her as executrix after she has actually proved the will. (3) It is not agreeable to the intention of the testator that the same person to whom he has given particular legacies should also have their distributive shares of the residuum and that Samuel, the undutiful son, should fare equally well with the others. In this respect, therefore, it differs materially from most of the cases cited *contra*, in those there being evidence of a trust but, here, none at all but a violent presumption of the contrary. (4) It is against the Statute of Frauds[3] that a bequest may be averred to be upon trust and parol evidence given thereof. Salkeld 162.[4] And it is plain by the acts[5] directing all nuncupative wills to be reduced to writing that it extends to wills of personal estates as well as real.

---

[1] Stat. 32 Hen. VIII, c. 1 (*SR*, III, 744–746).

[2] *Onions v. Tyrer* (1716), 2 Vernon 741, 23 E.R. 1085, 1 Peere Williams 343, 24 E.R. 418, Precedents in Chancery 459, 24 E.R. 205, Gilbert Rep. 130, 25 E.R. 91, 1 Eq. Cas. Abr. 407, 21 E.R. 1138.

[3] Stat. 29 Car. II, c. 3 (*SR*, V, 839–842).

[4] *Rex v. Lady Portington* (1694), 1 Salkeld 162, 91 E.R. 151, also 3 Salkeld 334, 91 E.R. 856, 1 Eq. Cas. Abr. 96, 21 E.R. 906, 12 Modern 31, 88 E.R. 1144, Eq. Cases Exch. 338, Dodd 137, 337.

[5] Stat. 29 Car. II, c. 3, ss. 18–20 (*SR*, V, 841–842); Stat. 4 & 5 Ann., c. 3, s. 14 (*SR*,

On this side were cited to the point of jurisdiction the following books and cases, *scil.*, Glanvill, l. 2, pl. *Testamenta coram judicae ecclesiasticae*; *Fleta*, l. 2, 37; *Bracton*, l. 3, c. 16; Gibson's *Codex* 560; 2 Croke 346; 3 Croke 391, 395; 3 Chancery Cases 107; Roberts v. Wynne, 1 Chancery Reports 236, same case 3 Chancery Cases 61; Lord Montagu v. Maxwell, in Chancery, 1718; Shrimpton v. Wycherley, 7 March 8 Geo. I [1722], in Chancery.[1] Mr. Wycherley, being very old and bedridden, married a young woman a few days before his death, not being then able to repeat the marriage service, and in three days after his marriage made a will wholly in her favor. And on a bill brought by his heir at law for setting aside the will and also a settlement made by Mr. Wycherley, though there was great fraud proved to have been used in obtaining them, yet the bill was dismissed.

But the Lord Chief Baron [GILBERT] said that the reason of denying relief in that case was because the plaintiff had refused to lend Wycherley any money or to join with him in settling part of the estate in order to pay his debts, which Wycherley very much resented, and, therefore, he married in order to give his estate away from him to his wife, which he had a power of doing, and with her portion to pay his debts.

[They cited] Noell v. Wells.[2] It was there laid down that a probate is conclusive, even though the will was forged.

Kinsman v. Woodcock; a man gave away all his estate, *scil.* £3000, except £20 from his son to a common sailor, though it did not appear that the son had ever disobliged him and, the father being asked the reason of his doing thus, he answered that he would do so and so. And a bill was brought to discover the testator's intention in saying these words, suggesting that they amounted to a trust, and, upon a trial at law, it was found for the will, and it was decreed accordingly. But afterwards, by the recommendation of the court, the devisee gave the heir somewhat more.

Eldred v. Chapp, June 11 Geo. [1725], before the Master of the Rolls. A bill was brought against an administrator suggesting that there was a will and that the defendant suppressed it, but it appearing that he had obtained letters of administration, the bill was dismissed, for that the party ought to apply to the

---

VIII, 459).

[1] E. Gibson, *Codex Juris Ecclesiastici Anglicani*; *Egerton v. Egerton* (1614), Croke Jac. 346, 79 E.R. 296, also 2 Bulstrode 218, 80 E.R. 1074; *Roberts v. Wynn* (1663–1664), 1 Chancery Reports 236, 21 E.R. 560, and cited in *Earl of Mountague v. Earl of Bath* (1693), 3 Chancery Cases 55, 61, 22 E.R. 963, 967; *Shrimpton v. Wycherly* (1720), Misc. Chancery Repts. (1714–1730), 40, *sub nom. Wycherly v. Wycherly*, 2 Eq. Cas. Abr. 391, 22 E.R. 334.

[2] *Noell v. Wells* (1668), 1 Levinz 235, 83 E.R. 385, 1 Siderfin 359, 82 E.R. 1156, 2 Keble 337, 343, 641, 84 E.R. 210, 214, 403.

spiritual court, and on appeal to the Lord Chancellor, the decree was confirmed in August last for the same reason.[1]

Sands and Loyd v. Price, in Chancery, before Lord Harcourt. A bill [was brought] to set aside a will and also some deeds unduly obtained, and though there was plain proof of fraud used in obtaining both, the deeds only were set aside, but the will was sent by him into the Prerogative Court to remain there during the testator's life, and, after his death, it was set aside by the [Court of] Delegates, which case is contrary to that of Herbert v. Lowndes.

Hatfield v. Hatfield.[2] Upon an appeal from Ireland to the House of Lords, 10 Geo. [1723–1724], the question there was whether a sentence of divorce was void as being obtained by collusion, but the House of Lords, upon debate, held that they were bound by the sentence and, if it was erroneous, it must be certified in the spiritual court.

As to the case of Herbert v. Lowndes, 1 Chancery Reports 22, cited *contra*, it was objected that this is a very extraordinary one, a will being there set aside in the testator's lifetime. And it differs materially from the present, for, in that case, it appeared in the proof, which is not stated in the printed book, that the testator was so weak as not to know his most intimate friends and, after being told, he would ask again who and what they were and whatever a servant who attended him said he would repeat after him like an echo and, in speaking a sentence of twelve words only, he often forgot himself, asking what he said last. Neither did it appear that Bland ever found fault with the former will or that he ever declared any intention of advancing Lowndes with any part of his estate or that there was ever any discontent between the testator and his children after the said will [was] made, but, after the last will, he had expressed much sorrow when he heard what was done, saying that Lowndes had cozened him. The consideration also appeared to be inadequate to the value of the estate. And it did not appear that the testator had ever given any instruction for the alteration.

[It was] objected in the present case that, if this court has no jurisdiction, it ought to have been taken advantage of by way of a demurrer. [It was] answered, if the court cannot interpose, to be sure, they will not, notwithstanding the defendant's answer. Besides, if the bill had been demurred to, the allegation therein, that the defendant Kimbra promised the testator to be a trustee for the children, would be confessed, in which case the plaintiffs would be clearly entitled to relief.

But, as to this point, it was said by way of reply that the defendant might and ought to have denied this allegation and have demurred to the rest of the bill.

And as to the objection taken from the particular circumstance of this case against setting aside the residuary bequest, which is the thing contended for, and

[1] *Eldred v. Child* (1725), Select Cases *tempore* King 49, 25 E.R. 216.

[2] *Hatfield v. Hatfield* (1725), Brown P.C. 100, 2 E.R. 559, 2 Eq. Cas. Abr. 585, 22 E.R. 492.

not the setting aside of the whole will, it was answered (1) that, though the bill prays that the will may be set aside, yet the general prayer, which the bill concludes with of 'such other relief as the court think fit', entitles the plaintiffs to such relief as is proper, though different from that particularly mentioned. And there are cases where the decrees are made according as the case is and directly contrary to the prayer of the bill. (2) If this bequest is set aside, the defendant Kimbra cannot take the residuum as executrix because she takes a copyhold estate by the will and is also entitled to £2000, which the testator was obliged by the settlement to leave her by his will. Besides, she waives this implied right by her claim under the express devise. And the fraud used by her ought to affect her so far as to exclude her from taking the residuum as executrix. (3) There is no inconsistency in setting aside the residuary bequest as an unjust and inofficious one and letting the others to the innocent legatees stand. Raymond 334. And it is no objection that Samuel, the undutiful son, will be let in, this being by operation of law. (4) Though, in the case of lands, a devise cannot be averred to be to an use because this is implied in the devise itself, yet, in the case of a personal estate, such an averment is not taken away by the Statute of Frauds.[1] And there are many decrees in Chancery founded upon this very thing. Raymond [*blank*].

The court were very clearly of opinion that they have a power of giving relief in the present case.

And GILBERT, Chief Baron, said it did not deserve so much litigation.

They declared also that this was a very strange and extraordinary case and of a very black aspect and highly deserved the interposition of the court. As the evidence was not in all points full and satisfactory and, in some, contradictory, the court, therefore, ordered that the defendant Kimbra shall be examined upon interrogatories whether the two first wills are in her possession or not (and, if they are, to bring them into court), when the last will was delivered to her and by whom, and whether it continued in her possession to the time of the testator's death, who first acquainted her she was executrix [and] residuary legatee, whether she said anything to her hus[band] or used any means by herself or others and what and when and on what occasion and by whom to prejudice him against the children, and, particularly whether she used the expressions mentioned in the depositions, and with what intent, whether she made any and what application to the testator and by whom and in what manner to obtain the bequest of the residuum, also what is the quantum of the testator's personal estate, and whether anything and what is come to her hands since her answer, and whether any inventory is taken of the personal estate, and, if so, that she may bring a copy thereof into court.

And after her examination, the court directed a trial at law whether the testator gave any instructions to Yates about the residuum and whether the will was

---

[1] Stat. 29 Car. II, c. 3 (*SR*, V, 839–842).

wholly read over by or to him and whether, at the time of giving the instructions, if any, and of executing the will, he fully understood them and also whether the residuary bequest was obtained by any artifice and practice.

The court also declared that the testator's daughter, who attended him at the time of his death, would be a very proper witness and, after executing a release to the plaintiffs, might be examined. But this having not been yet done, her deposition, which related to the expressions of affection used by the testator towards his children and of resentment towards his wife, were, by order, suppressed, she being a party interested.

Note: It was moved afterwards, *scil.* 29 November 1725, by Serjeant *Pengelly* that the defendant Kimbra may bring into court all the mortgage deeds upon Sir John Hobart's estate, whereby £14,000 is secured to the testator upon an affidavit that she had declared she would spend all she had rather than that the plaintiffs should gain their ends. And it was urged that this was very reasonable because the defendant Kimbra is plainly a trustee for the specific legacies, which are all charged on these securities, and perhaps for the residuum and she has been guilty of a great fraud. Besides, she can suffer no inconvenience by this, she having a sufficient provision by the marriage settlement and having also received a considerable part of the personal estate already.

It also appeared that the testator died indebted to the court in £120 in causes wherein he had been concerned, besides which there did not appear to be any debts payable out of his estate unless it was the £2,000 he agreed by his settlement to leave the defendant Kimbra to be paid in two years after his death.

On this side was cited Powell v. Andrews, before Lord Macclesfield;[1] a suit was instituted in the spiritual court for setting aside a will for insanity and the probate was called in and an order [was] made for bringing the assets into court, and, upon an appeal to the [Court of] Delegates, they were of opinion that the court below had no power to make such an order, whereupon a bill was brought in Chancery for bringing in the assets suggesting very great poverty in the executor and that he would be in all events a trustee for the children, the estate being given to them by the will; to this bill, the defendants demurred, but the Lord Chancellor overruled it as frivolous and ordered the effects to be brought before a master because there had been a fraud committed and the executor could be no other than a trustee. And, upon an appeal to the House of Lords, they confirmed this decree.

It was argued by Mr. Attorney General [*Yorke*] and others that the defendant Kimbra ought not to be compelled to bring in these deeds, she being an executrix and residuary legatee and also a creditor for £2000 and she is not in a state of indigence.

---

[1] *Andrews v. Powys* (1723), 2 Brown P.C. 504, 1 E.R. 1094, 2 Eq. Cas. Abr. 377, 421, 22 E.R. 321, 358.

But the court said that dishonesty in an executor is a stronger reason for ordering securities to be brought into court than poverty, for poor people may be honest, and it appears by the declaration now sworn to that the defendant Kimbra is not fit to be trusted. No harm can be done by it. It was, therefore, ordered that the deeds be brought into court in a week's time.

Harvard Law School MS. 1082, vol. 1, p. 245

Michaelmas term 1725.

Serjeant *Pengelly*, for the plaintiff: This is a bill to be relieved against a very unnatural will obtained by fraud and circumvention and so much only as was so obtained by the defendant Kimbra Marriot, the step-mother of the plaintiffs. In a court of equity, whatever is given by the misrepresentation and fraud of Kimbra, the party using such fraud or misrepresentation shall have no advantage thereby. But in such case, it shall be esteemed a resulting trust for the benefit of the plaintiffs, the children of the testator. Kimbra has a very considerable provision without this fraudulent proceeding, and, by the articles, though she died before her unhappy husband, she could dispose of £1000.

Kimbra married 5 May 1722; 2 January 1723, the will was obtained; June 1723, the testator died. Yates is Kimbra's agent, and he alone is to support this unnatural will, for, though the will was executed at Mr. Marten's chambers, yet no person heard it read over or pretends to testify to the same but Yates. And though perhaps this man was not strictly *non compos*, yet the poor man was so weak and feeble that any misrepresentation had the greater weight.

Secondly, the very recital in this will is *felo de [se], viz.* to settle his affairs and to prevent uneasiness in his family and so he gives away £20,000 from his own children and the taking care to bring them up handsomely, and, therefore, he gave away the whole estate.

Thirdly, [there is a] mistake in the value of the offices of the two sons, and then he gives them £400 each to be paid within three years without interest.

Fourthly, the legacies are encumbered with a general release.

Fifthly, the legacies to the famous Kimbra's mother and daughter are to be paid within a year.

I cannot but think that the law of nature is very much to be regarded in this case. And, therefore, the whole frame of the will does show a management and misrepresentation in this affair. There is no instance of undutifulness in these children. The constant declarations are to the contrary; the plaintiffs have a natural right and likewise to be paid for their labor and pains, which was constantly spent by them in their father's service, the frequent declaration of leaving the grandson all and making a Tom Marriot of him, the proof of vile practices used by Kimbra, A. Deacon, A. Sampson, and Yates, one of the plaintiffs, Benjamin Marriot, was turned out of the house, and the children and grandchildren were not permitted to come to him, the misrepresenting of the plaintiff Richard's wife as extravagant and the children as popishly inclined and that asking a blessing was popery, continually disturbing him and his declaration of marrying three plagues. The poor man had his death bed resentment by declaring, *viz.* 'You have been the ruin of me and my family.' The extraordinary preparation of Kimbra, Deacon, and Sampson was to get the whole family out of the way when directions were to be given for making a will. These were all actors in the fraud. No actual distress or absolute insanity is necessary, for, if so, at common law, the whole will might be set aside. Style 427, Hacker v. Newborne.

A court of equity should give a mutual defense, and it is the same reason for protecting a man when weak, as a wife in respect of her weakness that is *sub potestate viri.* So upon the same reason was the decree pronounced in Chancery in Bransby v. Kerridge, 5 Geo. 14 November; it was decreed there for the executor to be a trustee for the father. Herbert v. Lowndes, 3 Car. I, 1 Can. Rept. 665; Aynesworth v. Pollard, 11 Car. I, fo. 101, Can. Rept. *octavo.* Courts of equity have frequently interposed in these cases. And if ever there was a proper case for such relief, that now before you is proper.

And so he prayed that Kimbra might stand as trustee for and on the behalf of the plaintiffs, the infants.

Serjeant *Carter* cited Thynn v. Thynn, Lord Keeper North, 1684; Oldham v. Litchford, and Goss v. Tracey, Lord Chancellor Cooper, 17 November 1710; Sir Robert Janson's Case concerning Mr. Rose's will before the late Master of the Rolls, Trinity 1720; Savile v. Blacket, in Chancery; Bransby v. Kerridge, already cited; and, in the latter case, though it was done in favor of the heir at law, yet being circumstanced with fraud, it was set aside.

Wills, pro eisdem: Courts of equity have interposed in relation to wills concerning personal estates only. Herbert v. Lowndes, Can. Rept. *octavo* 2d 22. The ecclesiastical court cannot try a fraud and can only go to [the issue of] *non compos.* And the ecclesiastical court cannot reject part of a will and let the other part stand. Smallpiece v. Anguish, Can. Cases.

Hungerford cited Haywood v. Colley, Trinity, Chancery; Hayward v. Baines; Maundy v. Maundy, *octavo* ed., 123.

Peere Williams, Bunbury, and *Bootle* [were] *pro eisdem.*

Attorney General *Yorke*, for the defendant: The first question in this case is whether this matter only being concerning a will relating to personal estate and the ecclesiastical court having granted a probate, whether this court has jurisdiction, (second question) and, if the court has jurisdiction, whether this is a proper case for relief.

As to the first, this bill would have been demurred to if it was not therein suggested that the testatrix[1] had promised to be a trustee for her children. *Non compos* is indeed alleged in the bill, which prays to set aside the whole will. All these points suggested in the bill are properly cognizable in the ecclesiastical

[1] Sic in MS.

court. No temporal courts can intermeddle in the probate of wills concerning personal estates. Probate in common form is final, and, if not appealed from, is conclusive. And the court of equity is as much bound by such probate as the common law. And there might be a clash of jurisdictions in the different courts if they had a concurrent jurisdiction.

As to insanity, relief is in the ecclesiastical court and so likewise [they are] judges of the threats, frauds, and misrepresentations, and, then, it is not the will of the testator. Swinburn, cap. 3, p. 16, 106, 160, cap. 7, 49.

[As to the] objection that executors may be construed to be trustees in a court of equity, [he] responded that may be so in some cases, and it is artfully turned by Serjeant Pengelly, yet the bill, and so is the prayer of it, is to set aside the whole bill.

I believe I may defy the gentlemen on the other side to show the setting aside of a will for a personal estate only.

[To the] objection of Style 427, [he] responded that related to real estate.

[To the] objection of Herbert v. Lowndes, 1 Can. Rept. 122 or 22, [he] responded that it concerned real estate.

[To the] objection of Aynesworth v. Pollard, [he] responded the defendants admitted that they apprehended themselves to be trustees for the wife and children.

[To the] objection of Thynn v. Thynn, [he] responded [it is a] plain trust by the express promise of the son.

The court of equity may decree a gift or trust of personal estate where a party is so appointed by his own declaration, apprehension, or proof in the cause, but it is never done on a suggested misrepresentation or fraud, and this distinction will go through all the cases.

[To the] objection of Oldham's Case, [he] responded a plain trust was intended.

[To the] objection of Gosse v. Tracey in November 1710, there was the declaration of the executor to that purpose.

[To the] objection of Bransby v. Kerridge, [he] responded it was proved that the executor declared that he was to have no interest in the estate but to pay debts.

None of the cases come up to give jurisdiction to a court of equity in this matter where the case stands naked without any declaration of a trust either in the executor or the testator.

[To the] objection of Harward v. Colley, [he] responded, in that case, the sentence was not produced, only an inhibition; if the will had been proved, it had been otherwise.

The law has always the greatest regard for the sentence of ecclesiastical courts in cases where they have jurisdiction, for, in the case of that Hatfield and *idem*, last sessions before the House of Lords after a sentence of the ecclesiastical court in the case of a marriage, the parties were bound by it. In *causis matrimonii vel testamenti*, the ecclesiastical court has jurisdiction. We have precedents full in our favor. Roberts v. Wynn, 1 Chan. Cases, taken notice of in Bath v. Montagu. This was of a will of a real and personal estate, and the court of equity would not interfere, but returned it back to the Chancellor with a sort of recommendation to set aside the will, but the Chancellor refused, and the bill was dismissed in Chancery, and a private act of Parliament was afterward obtained. Montagu v. Sir George Maxwell, 1718; where the issue was *devisavit vel non* and it was found by the verdict *quod non devisavit*, yet the will stood as to the personal estate because it was there proved.

Shrimpton v. Mitcham, 5 Geo., upon Wycherley's will, where it was made *in extremis* by the contrivance of a man in favor of a wife, whom he afterwards married, and the Chancellor refused to set aside the will.

It leaves too great a latitude, and this proceeding would be carrying the thing further than ever was before attempted. I humbly insist upon it that, if they were to go into proofs, [there would be] no ground to set aside a will, no proof of insanity, and no reason to set aside a will because the party was dull and peevish and did not attend Westminster.

[To the] objection of fraud and misrepresentation, [he] responded but this had no effect upon the testator and no time was mentioned by witnesses when sued.

The testator had a disgust to these children; whether reasonable or not, the court is not the judge of. There cannot be a distribution in this case.

Chief Baron [GILBERT] desired the Attorney General to answer whether a wife that has been party to a fraud shall have the residue.

Mr. *Cowper*, for the defendant: There is no instance of a will being void in part and good in part.

Reeves, for the defendant: This matter as to *non compos*, fraud, and concerning personal estate is proper in the ecclesiastical court. It is prayed at the bar to set aside the will in part, but the bill strikes at the whole, and, if one clause is set aside, why not the whole, for setting aside a part is altering the whole will, so that one will is to be established in one court and a different will of the same testator established in another court. It must be agreed that a court of equity has the power to see trusts performed if the trust is proved or admitted by the executor's answer or declaration, for trusts may be declared by parol since the Statute of Frauds. But, in this case, no trust was implied or expressed or admitted by the executrix, but flatly denied. The ecclesiastical court may examine into all these matters on oath. There is no proof to set aside the will. And the cases cited by the plaintiff are where the trust has been proved or confessed. And without either, it was never done. The evidence endeavoring to prove a misrepresentation is very loose. No particular time was fixed. And if such evidence should be admitted to set aside a will, no will can stand. In the proof, the daughter was as much spoken against as the sons, yet there was no complaint on her behalf.

[To the] objection [of the case in] Style, [he] responded that goes to the whole will, and it appeared that the wife obtained it by leaving the husband in his sickness.

It was never the testator's intention to give the whole estate to the sons by the former will. Each was to have only £1000. But there is no notice where the residue should go. There was a will made in the defendant's favor, so there was no occasion to te[. . .] the testator to make a new one [. . .] in her favor. No will can be made with greater deliberation than this was. And the blanks were filled up by himself. And the will was made five months before his death, so he had an opportunity of altering it if he had disliked the will. Every Englishman has a power to make his will by law and to dispose of his estate as he thinks proper. And whether it is a reasonable or hard will, the court has no power to alter it.

Serjeant *Comyns*, for the defendant: There is no difference between a court of equity or law as to wills, and that which relates to a personal estate belongs to the ecclesiastical court. Levinz, Nowel v. Webb.

The probate is conclusive. And though the will should be forged, yet the probate concludes it. And it was in the power of the plaintiffs to controvert this will in the ecclesiastical court. I admit a will as a voluntary conveyance, so, if it be obtained by fraud or misrepresentation, it is not his will. But whenever it goes to the avoidance of a deed, it goes to the whole. Hardship of the will is no argument in this case, and the testator has a power to dispose at his will and pleasure. And though it be foolishly disposed of, it is no argument to set aside a will. King v. Lady Falkland, Salkeld 162; Bodwill v. Roberts, the Statute of Frauds sets aside the whole; Kinsman v. Woodcock, where the eldest son was disinherited.

Browne and *Kettleby, pro eodem; Fazakerly, pro eodem*: This court cannot have a jurisdiction unless there is a defect in jurisdiction in the other court, which is not pretended. If the residue is to be divided, then his unworthy son, Samuel, is to have a share, which could never be his intention. If it be a resulting trust, it results to the executrix.

Hamilton, for the defendant: The ecclesiastical court can examine into these very points of fraud and misrepresentation. Jones v. Owen, 1723, will of Michael Rhodes. The civil law calls fraud and misrepresentation surreptitiously obtained.

Page asked whether the ecclesiastical court can set aside a will in part or not.

Serjeant *Pengelly* replies for the plaintiffs: A bill is proper which prays such relief as the court will please to give. The jurisdiction of this court arises from the *delicto* of Kimbra.

[To the] objection the ecclesiastical court has jurisdiction, [he] responded this court has a concurrent jurisdiction, as in cases of legacies. And this whole case is proper for the examination of a court of equity.

The ecclesiastical court has only a derivative jurisdiction from the temporal courts. The probate does not belong *de jure* to the ecclesiastical court, but *de consuetudine*. Linwood, *De Testamentis*, 170, 174, 176, but cases *de matrimoniis* are *de jure* in ecclesiastical courts, but not so in probates. Temporal courts did proceed upon probates until within these one hundred years. Hensloe's [Case], 9

Rept. 38; Selden, *De Testamentis*; Godolphin, *Orphan's Legacy*, 59; Vaughan 207; Shower 173.[1]

[To the] objection of Nowel v. Webb, 1 Levinz 135, [he] responded 1 Siderfin, Chichester v. Philips, Raymond 405, 71.

If a probate was obtained by surprise, the temporal courts have jurisdiction and sometimes interpose in cases of a personal estate; so in a case of a legacy. Yelverton 92, 93, Browne v. [*blank*]; 1 Ventris 291, 292, Shower 158, 72, Shotter v. Frend, 3 Modern 283.

The question in this case is whether the ecclesiastical court has an exclusive power and whether this court has not a concurrent jurisdiction. The ecclesiastical court could never judge of part of a will. The will in this case is proved *in toto* and so far being proved, the executrix Kimbra must receive the estate. But she having procured the residue by unjust means, the court will decree her to be a trustee for the children.

This will arise as well from *delicto* as *de contractu*. If she has been guilty of imposition, she cannot be entitled to the residue. And in a court of equity, she is accountable. What is specifically devised to Kimbra, except the residue, she must take. The cases cited for the defendant in the ecclesiastical court go to the whole will, which ought to stand for the benefit of the honest legatees. 2 Rolle, *Abridgment*, 299.[2]

The ecclesiastical court cannot proceed for matters *dehors*. Holt 265; 2 Rolle, *Abridgment*, [Prohibition], 285, pl. 55; Clarke v. Clarke, Rolle Rept.; Trinity 12 Will. [*blank*]. It has been the constant practice of a court of equity to divide the residue upon an implied trust where the executor has a specific legacy. Though a person as executor stands in the will, yet he is a trustee for another. And a court of equity does not alter the probate of the will, but only declares him a trustee. If a testator directs a bequest to J.S. and the writer gives it to himself, he shall be deemed a trustee for J.S.

None of the cases in Swinburne do come up to show that the ecclesiastical court will intermeddle in cases of misrepresentation and trusts, for the ecclesiastical court cannot substitute another person *dehors* of the will to have the benefit, though a court of equity may. And the objections as to danger and inconvenience will be of no weight. And, in this case, it is only exercised for the next of kin. Though the testator has an absolute power over his estate, yet a misrepresentation governed in this particular, which ought not to take place. And, therefore, as to this point, it was not the testator's will.

[To the] objection that Herbert v. Lowndes went too far, [he] responded it proves the exercise and jurisdiction of a court of equity.

---

[1] *Hensloe v. Gage* (1600), 9 Coke Rep. 36, 77 E.R. 784; *Harrison v. Burwell* (1668), Vaughan 206, 124 E.R. 139, also 2 Ventris 9, 86 E.R. 278, Lincoln's Inn MS. Misc. 500, f. 96v (Edward Ward's reports); *Shatter v. Friend* (1691), *ut supra*.

[2] *Wilson v. Wilson* (1617), 2 Rolle, Abr., *Prohibition*, pl. Q, 1, 2, p. 299.

Bransby v. Kerridge is a full case for us.

[To the] objection of Hatfield v. Hatfield, [he] responded that was a matter merely ecclesiastical concerning matrimony.

[To the] objection of Montagu v. Sir George Maxwell, the objection went to the whole will for insanity. And though the personal estate went one way, yet the real estate went another.

[To the] objection of Roberts v. Wynn, [he] responded that was triable at law whether a will or not and that was a disposition of lands, and this case was just after the Restoration [1660], and cases in Chancery have gone further since. In cases mixed, as concerning real and personal estate, the courts of law and equity will retain such suit. The declaration in Roberts v. Wynn in the Act of Parliament is strong for us.

He observed on the evidence [that] ours is full and strong and founded on facts. The will made after one of the former wife's death gave all to the children. And these practices had the greater effect over a feeble and infirm body. This wicked scene is fully disclosed that, from the time of her marriage, of her alienating his affections from his family and the consultations for that purpose. Yates was the only reader of this will. And Yates is so concerned in this fraud that his testimony cannot be of weight. The defendants witnesses are either parties interested or are of no credit, all being related to the defendant except Yates, but confirm the testator's weakness and inability.

He observes on the draft where no notice is taken of the residue.

A trust of a personal estate may be decreed by parol.

So, upon the whole, he prayed that the executrix, as to the residue, may be deemed a trustee for the children and that she may be decreed to account accordingly.

Serjeant *Carter* replies: The jurisdiction is admitted by the cross-bill exhibited by her. Smallpiece v. Anguish, in Chancery Cases; Bagnall v. Dryden, Trinity 1719; Cro. Car. 115; 2 Croke 246.

Hungerford replies: the writ *de rationabili parte bonorum* shows a distribution before by the common law without going to the ecclesiastical court. *Vide* Stat. 31 Edw. III.[1] This jurisdiction arises by a grant from the crown and from acts of Parliament to the ecclesiastical court. And what was not granted remains with the temporal courts. And trust and fraud are properly examinable in the ecclesiastical court. In the case of marriages, the courts of law do not depend on the certificate of the ecclesiastical court, but direct an issue. Linwood 124.

Williams replies: In the case of a deed, it would be construed a trust, and it is much stronger in a will.

So they prayed that the defendant, the executrix might be deemed a trustee for the children and that she might [give] security to account with them.

[1] Stat. 31 Edw. III, stat. 1, cc. 4, 11 (*SR*, I, 350, 351).

Note that the court afterwards directed the estate to be brought into court and for her to be examined touching any former will or wills and what discourse passed between her and the testator.

Note: This last order procured an accommodation. And at last, as I am informed, the residue was agreed to be distributed as if the testator had died intestate.

Lincoln's Inn MS. Misc. 506, p. 81

Michaelmas and Hilary 12 Geo. [1725–1726].

This was a bill brought by the children of the testator, being officers of the Court of Exchequer, against the widow, their mother-in-law, who was the residuary legatee of a very considerable personal estate, to have a distribution of the residue, insisting that the widow was to be considered as a trustee for them, suggesting that she had misrepresented them to their father at the time of making his will, which was but about six weeks before his death, and at several other times before and after, which was the reason he had cut them off with such small legacies. There was no proof of any declaration of trust from the widow or that she had made the testator believe that what he left to her should be for the benefit of his children, but only that she had represented them as haunters of taverns and as leaving the true religion because they went to the Church of England, the father being a rigid Presbyterian, and such like.

It appeared in proof that he had often declared he would leave but little to his sons before he was married to the defendant, that he had been offended with them for not coming near him when he lay ill at his house in the country, that he had made another will before this wherein he had left them less, that he was so far from being angry at their going to church that he made answer he thought there might be as good preaching at church as at meeting. It was also proved that the will was a very deliberate act. It was read over to him, and he declared that he intended his children should have no more than was there given them.

The court desired to see precedents. Some cases were produced, which were again repeated and answered by the counsel for the defendant and some other cases cited by them as follows.

Roberts and Wing was the case of a real estate and yet relief was denied by Clarendon, Chancellor, because a will or no will of lands was triable by law so that at last an Act of Parliament was thought necessary. The same reason would hold with respect to personal estate, that the spiritual courts are the proper judges whether a will or no will.

Hatfield and Hatfield; the House of Lords declared they could not alter a sentence in a matrimonial cause.

Mountague and Maxwell was where the party had a remedy at law and, upon an [action of] ejectment, was relieved.

Thynn and Thynn; the father having made his wife executrix and residuary legatee, the son prevailed with his mother to desire the father to put him in her room, telling him that there would be a great many debts which would occasion a great deal of trouble, that it was not fit for her to manage it, that he was a Member of Parliament and could manage it much better. Accordingly, another will ready drawn in which his mother was left out and he put in was brought to the father, who executed it. The father died, and the son kept all to his own use. Upon a bill brought by the mother, this was declared a trust in the son for her.

Goss and Tracey [and] Bransby and Kerridge, Chancery, 5 Geo.; the testator had been in Ireland and was returning to his father, who lived at Norwich. The father met him at Leicester, where he fell ill, and he made his will and his father executor. The father's business would not permit him to stay long with him; so he left Kerridge to take care of him. The father was to have sent his son a bill for £30, which he did not send at the time, but he sent to Kerridge to excuse it to his son and tell him he would send it soon. Instead of that, he tells him that his father would send none and would take no care of him, that he had made no provision in his will for the payment of his debts, that he could not die like an honest man without it, and so persuaded him to make a new will to provide for the payment of his debts and to make him executor. The testator declared that it was his intention his father should have all; Kerridge [said] that he desired no benefit to himself, but only to pay his debts. There was a proof of the will in the spiritual court *per testes* and an appeal, but there was an injunction to the appeal on a bill in equity. This was decreed a trust in Kerridge for the father.

Salmon and Blacket was mentioned as declared by the court that, though the son had not promised, yet he had put a trick upon his father and no one shall have advantage of his own fraud.

Bagnal and Dry, Chancery, Trinity 1719; there were three executors, one dies in the life of the testator. The surviving two prove the will. The residuum was devised to the executors; as to a third part, it was decreed a lapsed legacy in favor of the children. Cr. Car. 115; 2 Cr. 346.

Trevor and Trevor; the late Master of the Rolls, according to the words of the articles of his marriage settlement, might by fine and recovery bar his eldest son from inheriting, which he was afterwards solicited by some people to do and, at last, against his own inclinations, by frequent importunities, he was prevailed on to do so, but he did not destroy the articles as he might and would in all probability have done had he intended his eldest son should be barred, but, on the contrary, he put them up safely in a strong box and told a friend of what he had done and desired that the box should be looked into on his death. And it appeared that this was done with a design that the fine and recovery might be set aside in a court of equity. Accordingly, there was a decree in Chancery that they should be set aside, and that decree was confirmed in the House of Lords.

Haywood and Collins, Trinity 11 Geo. [1725], Chancery; upon an intermarriage, both the man's and the woman's lands were so settled that neither of them could sell. Being thus entangled by the settlement and not knowing how to get rid of it, a cunning attorney found them out this method, that they should be divorced as for precontract and then, the marriage being null, the settlement which was made in consideration of marriage must, of course, be void too, which was accordingly done and conveyances in fee simple were executed. There was a bill brought to set aside those last conveyances. In that case, the conveyances were set aside, but then the sentence of divorce was not produced to the court. It appeared only by way of recital in an appeal. Besides, the divorce was void, the man being cited into Middlesex when he lived in a remote country.

It was insisted on for the defendants that, to declare her a trustee in this case for the children, would be really setting aside the will and declaring it void, that the spiritual court is the only proper court for examining wills, which relate only to the personal estate, that as to insanity, misrepresentations, cajoling, or such like, it is as far as they can prevail. If the facts are made out, relief may be had in the spiritual court, that all the cases quoted turn upon this distinction, whether the legatee had declared a trust himself or no, as he did in the cited cases.

In Smallpeace and Anguish, there was no dispute whether the executor was a trustee or no, but he admitted himself a trustee, and the question was for whose benefit the trust was, whether for the widow or the children, that there could be no instance produced where a legatee was declared a trustee only for using arts to prevail on the testator to bequeath the legacy to him without making himself any declaration of a trust. In the cited cases, there was no fraud practiced on the testator as to the will or any clause of it, for the testator's intent to dispose of his estate in that manner remained still the same. He knowingly bequeathed it to another person, but still to answer the same end and relied on the faith and integrity of the legatee to perform his engagement.

The court were strongly inclined to favor the plaintiffs and, at first, recommended a reference. But, when that did not do, they asserted a concurrent action with the spiritual court as to the trial of wills of personal estate and ordered the defendant to be examined further on interrogatories touching the suggestions of the bill.

This was afterwards compounded between the parties, which seemed to be the design of the court to force the defendant to comply with.

Taussig MS. 311, vol. 2, p. 811

Michaelmas term 1725.

Precedents were cited for the plaintiff in this case to justify setting aside the devise in the will to Kimbra Marriot of the residuum and making her a trustee for the same. Styles 427, by Lord Rolle in the case of Hacker v. Newborn; Hayward and Barne, in 1691, 1692; Hayworth and Colley in Chancery, last Trinity term; in Bath and Montagu's Case, by Treby, Chief Justice, page 124 [*blank*]; Goss and Tracy, 2 Vernon 699, 17 November 1715, *coram* Lord Cowper; a will may be set aside for fraud in equity, though good in law; Maundy v. Maundy, 1 Chan. Rep. 1 vol. 123, edit. octavo; Bransby and Kerrick 14 November 5 Geo., *coram* Lord Macclesfield, in Chancery; and Thyme, 9 February 1684, before Lord Keeper North, 1 Vernon 296; Smallpiece and Anguish, 1 Chan. Cases page 75;

Godolphin's *Orphan's Legacy*, 4, definition and account of a will; Godolphin, *Orphan's Legacy*, 17, a will in favor of children; whether a court of equity may set aside part of a will, *Corpus Juris*, 3 book, title de *inofficioso testamento*. The civil law is a pattern to our law in many cases, as, for example, in distribution and attestation of wills.

Attorney General [*Yorke*]; Swinburn, ca. 3, page 16, ca. 7, pa. 106 or 160; Godolphin's *Orphan's Legacy*, ca. 17, pag. 49, edit. octavo; Herbert v. Lownes, a decree that a scrivener making himself a trustee should not have a benefit by the conveyances of the land nor meddle as executor without his co-executors; 1 Chancery Reports 105, Ainsworth v. Pollard, the executors agree themselves to be trustees; the question was to and for whom; Thynne and Thynne, an express promise by the son that he would be an executor in trust for his mother; Oldham v. Litchford, 2 Vernon 506, in this case, there was also an express promise from the executor; Gosse and Tracey, 17 November 1715, to the same purpose; so is Saville and Blacket [*blank*]; Bransby v. Kerrick, 5 Geo., in Chancery, an executor declared that he pretended only to pay debts and, therefore, declared he would not leave his estate from his father; Hatfield v. Hatfield, in the House of Lords, the Lords thought themselves bound by the sentence in the ecclesiastical court, though the will should be obtained by collusion; Roberts and Wynn; 1 Chancery Cases; and it was also cited in the argument upon the case of Bath and Mountagu, lord Mountagu and Sir George Maxwell, 1718, upon a *devisavit vel non* and found *non compos* and yet the will stood as to the personal estate; Shrumpton and Mitcham, 3 March 6 Geo.; Wicherley's Case.

Taussig MS. 311, vol. 2, p. 817

Michaelmas term 1725.

Pengelly replies that the spiritual court had no original, but only a derivative jurisdiction. Godolphin's *Orphan's Legacy* 57; Vaug. 207; Lindwood *de [blank] testamenti insinatione* 170, *verbo 'approbatis'* 174; Raymond 405, 407; Linwood 176, *verbo 'Eccleiasticarum Libertatum'*. The will is of a temporal nature. Yelverton 92, 93, confirmed by Hale, 1 Ventr. 291, 292; Michaelmas 2 Will.; Shores 158, 172; 3 Modern 283, Shotter and Friend.

False representations, untrue suggestions, [there are] no instances of that nature in Swinburn. There is no instance of setting aside part of a will in an ecclesiastical court. Implied trusts are as proper for a court of equity as express trusts. Even law raises a remedy by an action *ex delicto*, as actions against carriers and promises to pay for goods.

Secondly, if she does not take the residue as by the express devise, she shall not take as executrix.

Ecclesiastical courts have no jurisdiction as to trusts and conditions. 15 Jac. I; 2 Rolle's *Abr.*, 299, pl. 1, 2; Edwards [*blank*]; Hob. 165; 2 Rolle's 285, pl. 35; Clarke and Clarke, Trinity 12 Will., in the King's Bench, an ecclesiastical court has no jurisdiction as to secret or implied trusts. The disposition of the surplus to the next of kin is upon the supposition that there is an implied trust for the relations. Chancery, every day, compels such a distribution.

Taussig MS. 311, vol. 2, p. 823

Friday 26th [*blank*], Michaelmas term 1725.

Mr. *Wills* admitted that the will is good in part and only to be set aside as to this devise as to the residuum of Kimbra. This cannot be done in an ecclesiastical court. Therefore, if done at all, it must be done in a court of equity. Suppose a woman should agree upon her marriage not to take anything by her husband's will, but should after[wards] prevail upon him to give her a good part of his personal estate, the will is good, but equity would prevent the effect of it.

Courts of equity relieve against a judgment at common law though they do not set aside or reverse the judgment. So here, a court of equity does not set aside the will, but, upon the injustice and unconscionableness of the thing itself, it interposes and prevents the effect of it. The case of Bransby and Kerrick was a trust arising from a fraud and no express promise.

He insists on the case of Roberts and Wynne as a strong case for the plaintiffs, though cited on the other side. The Act of Parliament made in the case of Roberts and Wynne is declaratory of the common law. See the words *inde* to prevent such like frauds for the future.

Hungerford cited Bacon's book[1] published about thirty [years ago], concerning the beginning of the ecclesiastical court's jurisdiction.

Baron Price: That book was burnt.

He cites then Henloe's Case. And the writ of *rationabili bonorum* to prove that the jurisdiction of the courts of Westminster Hall as to these sort of causes was prior to the ecclesiastical courts. He cited Linwood 124. And he said that the Church had stolen all the petitions on which the acts of Parliament against them had been made.

British Library MS. Add. 35997, f. 24

Michaelmas 12 Geo. I.

The plaintiffs, Richard Marriot, son and heir of Thomas Marriot, Esq., and Benjamin Marriot, another son of the said Thomas Marriot, bring their bill against Kimbra Marriot, widow of the said Thomas, Ann Deacon, widow, mother of the said Kimbra, Ann Sampson, spinster, daughter of the said Kimbra, Thomas Yates, Thomas Judd, Elizabeth Marriot, sister, and Samuel and John Marriot, brothers of the plaintiffs, to be relieved against a certain pretended will of the said Thomas Marriot, whereby he confirms the settlement made before

[1] F. Bacon, *A Letter to a French Gentleman Touching the Proceedings in England in Ecclesiastical Causes* [this was published in *Cabala sive Scrinia Sacra* and in G. Burnet, *History of the Reformation*].

his marriage with the defendant Kimbra 4 May 1722 and makes her executor of his will and then gives to his sons, being desirous to give them such parts of his estate as to the best of his judgment will be for their real good and incite them to diligence in their several stations, to his son Richard, to whom he says he had given an employment £500 and £100 in money, £400; to his son Samuel, who had disobliged him by his dissolute course of life, an annuity of £20 for his life; to Benjamin, whom he says he has bred up in the Exchequer Office and to whom he had given £1000, £400; to John, whom he had bred a merchant and put forth to trade at the expense of £1000, a like sum of £400, the said several sums of £400 to be paid within three years after his decease. And then he gives to his daughter Elizabeth £1500 payable likewise within three years, the interest to be paid her in the meantime. And [he] orders that the said legatees shall release to his executrix all their right to his real and personal estate upon a condition of forfeiting their legacies. Then [he] gives to the defendants Deacon, Sampson, and Judd £100 apiece payable within twelve months and to Judd his chambers in Clifford's Inn. Then [he] gives £100 to be distributed by his executrix in charity and £20 *per annum* to the poor widow Gursman for life. And then [he] appoints Kimbra residuary legatee. And [he] wills that all his legacies be paid out of Sir John Hobart's mortgaged lands in Cornwall and Devon. And [he] revokes all former wills.

The charge of the bill was that the plaintiffs had always behaved themselves dutifully to their father and that he himself had declared his satisfaction in their conduct, that notwithstanding, the defendants, by fraud, circumvention, and indirect practices, had managed and inclined their father to make the said pretended will, that, at the time the said will bears date, their father was not of sound and perfect disposing mind and memory, that, by the contrivance of the defendants, he was drawn in to execute the same when he was *non compos mentis* or did it by compulsion for peace and quiet sake and to avoid his being perpetually tarried by the defendant Kimbra etc. The prayer of the bill was that Kimbra might account for the residuum, amounting to near £20,000.

Serjeant *Pengelly*, counsel with the plaintiffs, said they could not pretend to give evidence that the testator was under actual force or absolute insanity, but that he was very ancient and infirm in his understanding and worked upon by the arts and unfair practices of his wife and her accomplices and was induced by their false representations to bequeath the bulk of his fortune to Kimbra, who was his third wife, for whom he had already made a sufficient provision by a marriage settlement and to leave little or nothing to his sons, who were almost unprovided for and had always behaved themselves dutifully to him and with reputation in their businesses and for whom he himself had expressed great affection and, therefore, he desired not that the will should be entirely made void, but that the will as to all the parts of it except the devise of the residuum should stand, that the widow might not take advantage of her own iniquity, but account for the residuum as a trust subject to distribution.

And he cited the opinion in the case of Hacker v. Newburn, Style 427, to show that a will made by the importunity of a wife in a man's last sickness ought to be set aside. And the following cases were quoted to prove that courts of equity have obliged executors and residuary legatees to account to the next of kin where the residuum was disposed in favor of strangers to the prejudice of the kindred by fraud and circumvention: Bransby v. Kerrick, *coram* Macclesfield, 5 Geo., 14 November; Herbert v. Lownes, Chancery reports, 1st volume, octavo, second edition, f. 22.

Gilbert Rep. 203, 25 E.R. 142,
1 Strange 666, 93 E.R. 770

Lord Chief Baron GILBERT: In this case is observable, Mr. Marriot, Master of the Exchequer of Pleas, made his will, and left his wife executrix and residuary legatee. His sons were plaintiffs in this cause, and they contended that this devise was gotten by fraudulent means and by surprise. The wife produced the probate of the will. And counsel, in behalf of the wife, the defendant, contended that the probate of the will was conclusive evidence touching this disposition of the residuum and that a court of equity could not look into the same, but that it was merely of ecclesiastical jurisdiction and to be determined there.

And in this question, four things are considered: first, how the jurisdiction of the testamentary matters stood by the civil law; secondly, how it stood by the canon law; thirdly, upon what foot it stood by the law of England; fourthly, what have been the several distinctions in our law touching this jurisdiction.

First, how the jurisdiction of the testamentary matters stood by the civil law. The way of authenticating wills in the civil law was first before the Praetor and, afterwards, before the Magister Census, for they reckoned wills to be in the nature of judgments in the divisions or distributions that a man himself made touching his estate, and, therefore, they were shut up with the Magistrate during the life of the person for the quiet and repose of the family, but they were opened after his decease. They were signed by the testator and sealed by him and by the witnesses upon a thread and carried in to the Praetor. After the death of the party, the witnesses were called, if living, to acknowledge their seals; if they were not living, then the seals were broken and the will [was] opened in the presence of other sufficient witnesses, and the will was read and registered, and a copy of it delivered over to any person that would ask for the same, for it was reckoned as a matter of record, and, therefore, any person might have access to it. Of this, *vide Digesta*, lib. 28, tit. 1, *Qui testamenta facere possunt et quemadmodum testamenta fiant*, and *Codex*, lib. 6, tit. 32, *Quemadmodum testamenta aperiantur*, etc.[1] And when any legacy was disposed of to pious uses for the use of the church or for monasteries or for the poor, the bishops were to sue for the same and see to the

[1] *Digesta*, 28. 1; *Codex*, 6. 32.

administration thereof. This appears by the *Codex*, lib. 1, tit. 3, law 42, § 6, *Vid. Necessarium*, § 7, *Amplius*, § 8, *Si autem contigerit*, § 9, *Praeterea sancimus.*

Upon this, the bishops began to intermeddle with the probate of wills, which was a mere temporal authority. But this invasion of the prelates Justinian would not endure. And, therefore, in his Code, he puts the law against the bishops' probate of wills before the laws herein before mentioned and in this *Codex*, lib. 1, tit. 3, *Repetita promulgatione, non solum judices quorumlibet tribunalium, verum etiam defensores ecclesiarum huius almae urbis, quos turpissimum insinuandi ultimas deficientium voluntates genus irrepserat, praemonendos esse censemus ne rem attingant, quae nemini prorsus omnium, secundum constitutionum praecepta, praeterquam Magistro Census, competit; absurdum etenim clericis est, immo etiam opprobrium, si peritos se velint (ostendere) disceptationum esse forensium; temeratoribus huius sanctionis poena quinquaginta librarum auri feriendis. Datum XIII Kalendis Decembris C. P. Justino A. 11, et Opiliano Conss.* 524. Thus things stood by the civil law.

Secondly, we come now in the second place to see how things stood by the canon law. The popes, as their power increased, endeavoured to get the jurisdiction over testaments, etc. This appears by the *Decretum*, lib. 3, tit. 26, c. 26, *Si haeredes jussa testamentoris non adimpleverant, ab episcopo loci illius omnis res quae eis relicta est canonice interdicatur, cum fructibus et caeteris emolumentis, ut vota defuncti adimpleantur*; and likewise *Decretum*, lib. 3, tit. 36, *De Testamentis*, c. 17, *Tua nobis fraternitas intimavit quod nonnulli tam religiosi quam clerici seculares, et laici, pecuniam et alia bona, quae per manus eorum ex testamentis decedentium debent in usus pios expendi, non dubitant aliis usibus applicare; cum igitur in omnibus piis voluntatibus sit per locorum episcopos providendum, ut secundum defuncti voluntatem universa procedant, licet etiam a testatoribus id contigerit interdici, mandamus quatenus executores testamenti huiusmodi ut bona ipsa fideliter et plenarie in usus praecedictos expendant monitione praemissa compellas.* Pope Innocent IV, upon this law, fo. 152, says that the bishop may dispense this charity if there be no executor appointed by the will, and, if there be an executor and he does not fulfill the will, that, then, he may take it to himself. *Decretum*, lib. 3, *De testamentis*, tit. 26, c. 19, *Johannes Clericus et P. Laicus executores ultimae voluntatis. O Clerici Sanctae Crucis, qui venerabilibus episcopis locis de bonis suis in ultima voluntate legavit, mandans inde supersatisfieri creditoribus per eosdam, post mandatum susceptum per diocesanum cogi debent testatoris explere ultimam voluntatem.* See Innocentius, *In Legem*, 153. Panormitanus[1] (Panormitanus, tit. 4, fo. 157), upon the law of *Si haeredes*, says that this matter of wills, even where the devise is to pious uses, is *mixti fori* and that the heir or executor is to have a year's time to fulfil the will before he can be compelled to do it by ecclesiastical censure.

Upon the same law, *Tua nobis*, Panormitanus says that the bishop is to compel by ecclesiastical censure the executor to the performance of a will to pious

[1] Nicholas de Tudeschis (d. 1445).

uses, although the will itself says that the bishop was not to intermeddle, for they look upon that as an irrational part of the devise, which is in itself void.

The last chapter [of] *verbo Johannes*, the case, as Panormitanus states it, was, where after debts [are] paid, the residue was left to pious uses and, then, the bishop was to compel the payment of debts and, afterwards, to see the disposition of the residuum. I do not find that any of the canonists pretend that wills are of ecclesiastical conusance *sua natura*, but only such wills as were made for pious uses. And Lynwood, fo. 174, *verbo Approbatis*, says that the jurisdiction of the ecclesiastical courts touching testamentary matters is by the custom of England, and not by the ecclesiastical law.

We are, thirdly, to consider upon what foot the ecclesiastical jurisdiction stood by the law of England. In England, the bishop and sheriff sat together in the county court, as it appears by the Laws of King Edgar, c. 5, *De comitiis* (Wilkins, 78; Lambard, *Saxon Laws*, 64). *Centuriae comitiis quisque (ut ante praescribitur), interesto; oppidana ter quotannis habentur comitia; celeberrimus autem ex omni satrapia bis quotannis conventus agitur, cui quidem illius diocesis episcopus et senator intersunto, quorum alter jura divina alter humana populo edoceat. Leges Canuti*, c. 17, *de comitiis municipalibus; ter in anno habeantur comitia municipalia, et duo conventus (aut plures etiam) ex omni provincia, et illis intersint episcopus et senator, et ibi ubique doceatur tam jus divinum quam humanum.* (*Ibid.* 136; Lambard, *Saxon Laws*, 111.) From these laws, it plainly appears that the probate of testaments was in the county courts.

William the Conqueror was the first that separated the ecclesiastical court from the civil. Selden, in his *Notes upon Eadmerus*, 167, gives us the very charter of such separation; *Propterea mando et regia authoritate praecipio, ut nullus episcopus aut archidiaconus de legibus episcopalibus amplius in hundredo placita teneat, nec causam, quae ad regimen animarum pertinet, ad judicium secularum hominum adducant.* This Charter, as Mr. Selden has told us, was recited in a close roll of Richard II and then confirmed; but the Charter of William I does not mention matters testamentary or the probate of wills to be of ecclesiastical conusance, but only says that the crimes that were to be prosecuted *pro salute animae* were to be of that conusance.

That which seems first to have given birth to the ecclesiastical jurisdiction was the Charter of Henry I, which says *Si quis baronium vel hominum meorum infirmabitur, sicut ipse daret vel dare disposuerit pecuniam suam, ita datum esse concedo quod si ipse confectus vel armis vel infirmitate pecuniam suam nec dederit nec dari disposuerit uxor sua sive liberi aut parentes et legitimi haeredes sui pro anima ejus eam decidant.* This let in the several canons herein before mentioned into England, for, since the personal estate was to be disposed of for the good of the soul, they looked upon every will to be a disposition of the testator in a gratuitous or charitable manner, that whatever was left was to be disposed of by the executor for the good of his soul, so that all the canons touching charitable dispositions were to take place in England.

In the time of Richard I, when he was in confinement, the clergy got a confirmation from him of the ecclesiastical immunities. This is mentioned by Matthew Paris, 161, *item, distributio rerum quae in testamento relinquitur authoritate ecclesiae fiet, nec decima pars ut olim subtrahetur si quis enim subitanea morte vel quolibet casu praeoccupatus fuit, ut de rebus suis disponere non possit, distributio bonorum ejus ecclesiastica authoritate fiet.* This charter is likewise mentioned in the same terms in Radulphus de Diceto, one of the *Decem Scriptores*, fo. 658. These ecclesiastical immunities were confirmed by the pope, and the confirmation appears in [T. Rymer], vol. 1, *Foedera*, 104, though there is no express mention of a testamentary jurisdiction.

Note: Also it appears by the charter that the king releases the tenth that used to be taken on the death of the tenant, and, thenceforward, the king and his lords only took heriots, as an acknowledgment in lieu of such decimation.

From henceforth, the ecclesiastical court began to consider a proper method for the publication of wills. Therefore, when any person died, they summoned in the executor or next relation to take care of his soul. And the executor was obliged to bring in the will, and both executors and administrators were obliged to bring in an inventory of his goods. And the charges were lightened by the canons in order to bring everything into the ecclesiastical court. Lynwood, 176, Canons of Simon Mepham. And it appears by the Canons of Stratford that the residue in the hands of the executor was to be distributed for the good of the soul. Lynwood, 178. And by the Canons of Ottobon, an inventory was to be, exhibited. Lynwood, 167.

Notwithstanding all this, the jurisdiction of the county court still continued, for this was acknowledged to be a matter *mixti fori*. And, therefore, they could not hinder the county court from proceeding, even according to their own canon law.

But in order to get the whole jurisdiction, in the time of Richard II, as is mentioned by Selden in his *Notes on Eadmerus*, they got the king to publish the Law of William the Conqueror and confirm the same, that no matters of ecclesiastical conusance should be transacted in the county courts. This is the Charter of 2 Richard II, membrano 12, N. 5, and is mentioned in Selden's *Eadmerus*, 168.

From henceforward, the clergy had the whole jurisdiction of wills because the county court could not receive the probate, etc. and the king's courts had never intermeddled with it because, by the Charter of Henry I, herein before mentioned, and likewise by Magna Charta, c. 18, the king had granted the liberty to his own tenants to dispose of their goods. And, therefore, the will touching the personal estate never received any sanction in the immediate court of the king.

This reconciles that case of Fitzherbert, *Abr.*, tit. Testament, fo. 148,[1] where it is said by Fairfax that it was but of late that the Church had the probate of

[1] Mich. 2 Ric. III, Fitzherbert, Abr., *Testament*, pl. 4; cf. YB Mich. 2 Ric. III, f. 22, pl. 51 (1484).

wills, which was by an Act. (I suppose he must mean the Confirmation of Richard II, herein before mentioned, for there is no act of Parliament that gives them that probate.) And he says that, in other countries, the probate was of temporal conusance, which Selden notes to be true in all countries except France. And Tremaile, in that case, asserts the usage of proving wills in courts baron, which certainly may be where the custom prevails.

In the 11th of Henry VII, 12,[1] Fyneux asserts that the probate of wills did not belong to the spiritual court by the ecclesiastical law, but came to them by custom and usage. And these are the foundations on which my Lord Coke, in Henslow's Case, 9 Rep. 38,[2] concludes that, when the will is proved in the ecclesiastical court, the court has executed its authority, but the executors are to sue in the temporal courts, to get in the estate of the deceased.

Fourthly, we are to see what have been the several distinctions in our law touching this jurisdiction, which will fall under five heads:

First, that the spiritual court is the only court now that has authority to receive the probate of wills and to give a sanction to them because the jurisdiction of the county court is lost by non usage and, since Magna Charta, c. 18, the king's courts did not intermeddle with the goods of a deceased tenant. But here must be excepted all courts baron that have had probate of wills time out of mind and have always continued that usage.

Secondly, the seal of the ecclesiastical court does authenticate the will, for, there, the will is to be brought in and proved. (3 Rolle 299.[3]) And, therefore, the case in Raymond 406, 407,[4] is certainly good law that the seal of the ordinary cannot be contradicted because, if there be no way in the temporal courts to prove the will relating to chattels, it must go on in the spiritual court and the determination there must be final, for the temporal courts cannot make a judgment concerning the will contrary to what was made in the ecclesiastical court. And, therefore, it is certainly good law that, if they show a probate under the hand of the ordinary, they cannot prove in evidence that the will was forged or that the testator was not *compos* [*mentis*] or that another person was executor; but they may give in evidence that the seal was forged or the will was repealed or that there were *bona notabilia* because that is not in contradiction to the real seal of the courts, but it admits the seal and avoids it. Levinz 235; Vaughan 207; 1 Shower 293.[5] And since the ecclesiastical court has the probate of wills now settled by custom, the temporal court cannot prohibit them in their inquiries whether the

[1] YB Hil. 11 Hen. VII, f. 12, pl. 1 (1496).

[2] *Hensloe v. Gage* (1600), 9 Coke Rep. 36, 77 E.R. 784.

[3] *Wilson v. Wilson* (1617), 2 Rolle, Abr., *Prohibition*, pl. Q, 1, 2, p. 299.

[4] *Chichester v. Philips* (1680), T. Raymond 404, 83 E.R. 211.

[5] *Noell v. Wells* (1668), *ut supra*; *Harrison v. Burwell* (1668), *ut supra*; *Hill v. Mills* (1691), *ut supra*.

testator was *non compos* or not or whether the will be revoked or not because that is necessary for the authenticating the will. Hardres 131, 313.[1]

Thirdly, if a temporal matter be pleaded in bar of an ecclesiastical demand, they must proceed in the ecclesiastical court according to the temporal law or else the temporal courts will hinder them, as if payment be pleaded in bar of a legacy and there is but one witness, which the ecclesiastical court will not admit, there, the temporal courts will prohibit them because it is a matter temporal that bars the ecclesiastical demand. Shutter *et ux.* v. Friend, Shower 158, 173; 1 Ventris 291; 3 Modern 283.[2] But if, upon a probate of a will, they allege on the other side that the will was revoked and they would prove the revocation by one witness, according to the resolution in Yelverton in the case of Brown v. Wentworth, fo. 92 or 96,[3] which is but that of three judges against two and seems against the opinion, 2 Rolle's *Abr.*, 299, they might be prohibited. This seems to intrench upon their jurisdiction, for, if they cannot judge by their law whether the will is revoked or not, they cannot judge whether there is a will or no will. Indeed, the judges there say that the revocation is a temporal matter, and, therefore, it is to be proved according to their law by one witness. But then, we do not suffer them to determine touching the validity of a will of a personal estate, which everybody allows to be of ecclesiastical conusance. But if the spiritual court do admit a will, but yet will not give the probate to the executor because he cannot give security for a just administration, it seems that a *mandamus* will lie. And this was resolved in the case of the King v. Sir Richard Raines, Mich. 10 Will. [1688], in the King's Bench, MS. Rep., fo. 1,[4] for, though they are to determine whether there be a will or not, yet, if there be a will, the executor has a temporal right, and they cannot put any terms upon him but what are mentioned in the will. And, therefore, if they will not grant the probate, where they admit there is an executor, the court will grant a *mandamus*.

Fourthly, if a man gives lands to be sold for the payment of debts and disposes of the money to several persons, that cannot be sued for in the ecclesiastical court, but only in a court of equity because that is not a legacy merely of goods and chattels, but it arises originally out of lands and tenements and they have a

---

[1] *Minshal v. Spicer* (1658), Hardres 131, 145 E.R. 416; *Hobart v. Barrow* (1662), Hardres 313, 145 E.R. 474.

[2] *Shatter v. Friend* (1691), 1 Shower K.B. 158, 172, 89 E.R. 510, 518, 3 Modern 283, 87 E.R. 188, also Carthew 142, 90 E.R. 687, Holt K.B. 752, 90 E.R. 1313, 2 Salkeld 547, 91 E.R. 462, Comberbach 160, 90 E.R. 404; *Richardson v. Desborough* (1675), 1 Ventris 291, 86 E.R. 188, also 3 Keble 570, 576, 579, 84 E.R. 884, 888, 889.

[3] *Brown v. Wentworth* (1606), *ut supra*.

[4] *Rex v. Raines* (1688), 12 Modern 136, 205, 88 E.R. 1218, 1265, Carthew 457, 90 E.R. 864, Holt K.B. 310, 90 E.R. 1071, 1 Salkeld 299, 91 E.R. 265, 3 Salkeld 162, 233, 91 E.R. 752, 796, 1 Lord Raymond 361, 91 E.R. 1138.

testamentary jurisdiction touching chattels only. Hobart 365, Case 345; 2 Rolle, *Abr.*, 285.[1]

Fifthly, the courts of equity can hold a plea concerning a legacy and, likewise, concerning the devise of a residuum, which is but a legacy. They may in notorious cases declare a legatee that has obtained a legacy by fraud to be trustee for another, as, if the drawer of a will should insert his own name instead of the name of a legatee, no doubt he would be a trustee for the real legatee. As to the devise of the residuum, nothing can be more clear, for, since the case of Foster v. Munt, 1 Vernon 473,[2] wherever an executor has had a specific legacy, he was looked upon as a trustee of the residuum for the relations in a course of distribution. And nobody ever attacked these decrees in favor of the relations upon this head of argument, that they were contrary to the ecclesiastical jurisdiction. (See 2 Vernon 648.[3])

But in all cases, a court of equity must consider what was the real intent of the testator. And they cannot declare a trust according to their own fancy nor according to what the testator should have willed, for, then, they make the will, and not the testator. But they may, according to the real intention of the testator, declare a trust upon such wills, although it be not contained in the will itself, which is in these three cases:

First, in the case of a fraud upon a legatee, as before is mentioned;

Secondly, where the words imply a trust for the relations, as in the case of a specific devise to the executors and no disposition of the residuum;

Thirdly, in the case of the legatee's promising the testator to stand as a trustee for another.

And nobody has thought that declaring a trust in these cases is an infringement upon the ecclesiastical jurisdiction.

The court being thus of opinion that they had a power to relieve against the devise of the residuum, they directed proper issues to try the matters of fraud and surprise insisted on by the plaintiffs, against which decree the defendant brought an appeal, but, before anything further was done upon it, the plaintiff and defendant agreed to divide the residuum between them.[4]

N.B. This cause was agreed. But, if the point of jurisdiction had been insisted on by the executrix, my Lord Chief Baron GILBERT had prepared this argument.[5]

---

[1] *Edwards v. Graves* (1619), Hobart 265, 80 E.R. 410, 2 Rolle, Abr., *Prohibition*, pl. F, 32, p. 285.

[2] *Foster v. Munt* (1689), 1 Vernon 473, 23 E.R. 598, also 1 Eq. Cas. Abr. 243, 21 E.R. 1020, 2 Eq. Cas. Abr. 433, 443, 22 E.R. 368, 378, Dodd 78.

[3] *Lady Granville v. Duchess of Beaufort* (1709), 2 Vernon 648, 23 E.R. 1023, also 1 Peere Williams 114, 24 E.R. 317, 1 Eq. Cas. Abr. 245, 21 E.R. 1021, 2 Eq. Cas. Abr. 415, 22 E.R. 352, 3 Brown P.C. 37, 1 E.R. 1161.

[4] This paragraph comes from Strange's report of the case.

[5] This paragraph comes from Gilbert's report of the case.

570

Earl of Cardigan v. Bishop of Peterborough

(Ex. 1725)

The question in this case was whether the parson and patron of a parish can, with the consent of the bishop, agree to a composition in lieu of tithes that is binding on successor parsons.

Taussig MS. 311, vol. 2, p. 845

10 December 1725. Lord Cardigan v. Bishop of Peterborough, and Henry Goode, clerk, rector of Dean in the County of Northampton.

The plaintiff being patron of the parish church of Dean and lord of the manor *inde*, made an agreement with Goode, who was presented by his ancestors to the said living thirty-five years since to give him £110 *per annum* clear of all taxes, parochial and others, except the land tax and to let Goode enjoy tithe eggs, churchings, christenings, burial mortuaries, etc. in lieu and discharge of all the tithes arising on the lands of the plaintiff in the hands of the plaintiff and his tenants. And to secure the payment of the composition, the plaintiff agreed to settle the whole manor *prout* counsel should advise. Goode agreed thereto. And an application was made to the bishop, and he awarded a commission to inquire whether the composition was reasonable. And upon an inquiry, the commissioners certified it would be a beneficial composition for the parson and his successors. And, upon this return, the bishop, by an instrument under his episcopal seal, grants his license and consent to the said composition. And now, this bill was exhibited to have the same established by a decree of the court. Goode and the bishop put in several answers testifying to their several consents to the prayer of the bill. And Goode acknowledges his said agreement to have been entered into with an express intention to make a perpetual composition binding on the present parson and his successors also.

And yet notwithstanding this, the court, *viz.* GILBERT, PAGE, and HALE, told the Lord Cardigan's counsel on opening the cause they could not do it. And, therefore, they only decreed the execution of the agreement for the life of the present incumbent, Goode.

But note this seems strange to me for I cannot find anything in the Statute of 13 Eliz., ca. 10,[1] which disables the parson, patron, and ordinary to make such a composition. And several such compositions have been made and established by a decree of the Court of Chancery long since the making of that Statute. [*blank*] Stoke; Gibson's *Codex*, 687, 688.[2] Query of this matter.

---

[1] Stat. 13 Eliz. I, c. 10 (*SR*, IV, 544–545); note also Stat. 13 Eliz. I, c. 20 (*SR*, IV, 556).

[2] *Llen v. Seymour* (1628?), Palmer 525, 81 E.R. 1202; E. Gibson, *Codex Juris Ecclesiastici Anglicani* (1713).

Harvard Law School MS. 1082, vol. 1, p. 257

Sittings after Michaelmas 1725.

This was a bill to have the performance of an agreement made by the consent of the parson, patron, and ordinary in relation to a payment in lieu of tithes, which the defendant by his answer admitted and consented to.

But yet the court would only decree such payment during the present incumbent's life.

571

Guavas v. Kelynack

(Ex. 1725)

Witnesses can be examined de bene esse *before the parties are at issue.*

Taussig MS. 311, vol. 2, p. 816, pl. 2

Michaelmas term 1725.

The plaintiff exhibited his bill in Hilary term last. The defendants answered in Trinity, and exceptions were immediately filed and set down to be argued the same term. But before argument, they submitted an answer and put in a second answer at the beginning of this term and, at the same time, filed a cross-bill against the plaintiff and served him with process returnable 6th November, to which he appeared. Then, the plaintiff, by a motion, set down further exceptions to the second answer. And this day, the defendants moved for liberty to examine witnesses *de bene esse* on their cross-bill though the time for Guavas answering the cross-bill was not expired and the exceptions to the defendants' two answers to the original bill were set down to be argued this very term.

And the court gave leave to his examining his witnesses *de bene esse* notwithstanding the circumstances aforesaid.

[Later proceedings in this case are reported at Taussig MS. 311, vol. 2, pp. 1110, 1148, 1152, Harvard Law School MS. 1082, vol. 2, p. 42, Bunbury 239, 256, 145 E.R. 660, 665, 2 Wood 284, 1 Rayner 240, 247, 251, 278, 2 Gwillim 691, 2 Eagle & Younge 1, 2 Brown P.C. 446, 1 E.R. 1054.]

572

Rogers v. Quin

(Ex. 1725)

An answer must respond to the entire bill of complaint.

Taussig MS. 311, vol. 2, p. 816 [bis]

Michaelmas term 1725.

A bill was exhibited by a bail against the creditor, her attorney, the under-sheriff, and the principal, suggesting that the principal had paid the money and yet that the creditor and other confederates threatened to take out execution against them for the whole penalty of the bail bond and they had recovered judgment against them on the bail bond for that purpose. The creditor by an answer denies the payment of any money and confesses that she had given an order to her attorney to sue the bail on their bail bond etc. and hopes she might lawfully take out execution against them for the debt and costs. And an exception was taken that she had not expressly answered whether she threatened to take out execution for the whole penalty.

And the court allowed the exception without any hesitation.

573

Morgan v. French

(Ex. 1725)

An ecclesiastical court has jurisdiction where a person is accused of being a prostitute.

Taussig MS. 311, vol. 2, p. 821, pl. 1

Michaelmas term 1725.

[The words spoken were] 'Thou art a whore and a whore upon record.'

Mr. Serjeant *Webb* moved for a [writ of] prohibition and [cited] 2 Inst. 492; 1 Syd. 404.[1]

The court denied a prohibition for it was inconceivable how a woman should be a whore upon record and, without controversy, if the words 'upon record' are omitted, the spiritual court has jurisdiction.

574

Rex v. Anonymous

(Ex. 1725)

The Statute 33 Hen. VIII, c. 39, s. 55, does not extend to suits concerning the king's lands.

A warrant from the Lords of the Treasury for a lease is, without more, neither a lease nor a license.

[1] E. Coke, *Second Institute* (1642), p. 492; *Mellet v. Herbert* (1669), 1 Siderfin 404, 82 E.R. 1183, also Lincoln's Inn MS, Misc. 500, f. 8 (Edward Ward's reports).

Taussig MS. 311, vol. 2, p. 825

Saturday, 27 November 1725.

Upon an information of intrusion for intruding into a house and a rood of ground in [*blank*], the defendant pleaded a warrant from the Lords of the Treasury to authorize the making of a lease to him of the premises and so he entered.

Ward, pro defendente: The defendant is not a stranger, but affirms the king's title and claims under the king's title. And, therefore, his plea here amounts to a license and there is no *continuando* in the information; so it is only a single act of trespass.

Bracton's definition of intrusion: [*blank*]. An information of intrusion is the king's action of trespass. And, to be sure, a license may be pleaded in [an action of] trespass.

Secondly, matter of equity may be pleaded by 33 Hen. VIII,[1] and this is certainly a matter of equity.

But the court was clear that there was nothing in the plea, and they so gave judgment for the king.

And by the Attorney [General, *Yorke*]: The Statute 33 Hen. VIII does not extend to suits concerning the king's lands *quod fuit concessum per* CURIAM and likewise, by him, a warrant from the Lords of the Treasury for a lease is neither a lease nor a license, but only preparation and, upon such warrants, the Attorney General hears counsel, and very often reports that the lease ought not to be made.

575

Anonymous

(Ex. 1725)

The question in this case was whether an action upon the case lies for suing a false action, i.e. a non-meritorious claim.

Taussig MS. 311, vol. 2, p. 827

Monday, 29th day of November, last day of term.

Cases were cited to show that an action of case will not lie only for a false action: Hob. 266; Rolle, *Abr.* [*blank*]; 1 Salkeld 15; 1 Sand. 228, 2 Keble 476.[2]

---

[1] Stat. 33 Hen. VIII, c. 39, s. 55 (*SR*, III, 891).

[2] *Waterer v. Freeman*, Hobart 205, 266, 80 E.R. 352, 412, also Noy 22, 74 E.R. 994; 1 Rolle, Abr., *Action sur Case*, pl. C, 6, 8, 9, p. 34; *Robins v. Robins* (1699), 1 Salkeld 15, 91 E.R. 15, also 1 Lord Raymond 503, 91 E.R. 1236, 12 Modern 273, 88 E.R. 1316, 2 Salkeld 728, 91 E.R. 609, 3 Lord Raymond 298, 92 E.R. 698; *Skinner v. Gunton* (1669), 1 Williams Saunders 228, 85 E.R. 249, also 1 Ventris 12, 18, 86 E.R. 9, 13, T. Raymond 176, 83 E.R. 93, 2 Keble 473, 476, 497, 84 E.R. 297, 298, 312, Lincoln's Inn MS. Misc. 500, f. 30v (Edward Ward's reports).

Secondly, the allegation of the defendant's being nonsuited in the action brought, *viz. 'quod praedict. devenit non pros.'* is nonsense. *Vide* Rastall's *Entries*, 178, 355, 663; Aston's *Entries*, 245. *E contra*, 3 Lev. 210; Thomas Jones 132; 5 Mod. 405.[1]

576

Charles Doe, *qui tam* v. Thomas Rhodes
Charles Doe, *qui tam* v. Samuel Roe

(Ex. 1725)

A person can be convicted of aiding and abetting the receiving of smuggled goods.

Counsel in their arguments should not appeal to the sympathy of the jury.

A motion in arrest of judgment need not allege the reason therefor.

Taussig MS. 311, vol. 2, p. 828

Tuesday, 30th November 1725, sittings after term.

Two separate informations were exhibited against the defendants charging each of them with a parcel of brandy and wine that came to the hands of each of them, knowing the duties were not paid, upon 8 Anne.[2] And the question was whether, after Roe had been convicted upon the first information, there being a verdict given against him on his information, which was first tried, that the goods came to his hands, the crown may convict the other defendant Rhodes upon the other information for the self-same goods.

And the Chief Baron [Gilbert] ruled that it might. *Sed multum dubito.*[3]

It seemed that the Chief Baron's reason was this, that for aiding and assisting upon that Act, every person was liable by the express words of the Act to the whole penalty. And so, says he, is every person to whom the goods knowingly had come *toties quoties*. And, therefore, he overruled the objection and directed the jury to find the second defendant guilty of the information against him.

N.B. The evidence upon both informations was exactly the same, the fact one and single, and both the defendants were present and acting together in carrying off the same parcel of wine and brandy so that the wines etc. *devenerunt* to them at the same instant of time.

---

[1] *Gray v. Degge* (1680), T. Jones 132, 84 E.R. 1183, also T. Raymond 418, 83 E.R. 219; *Saville v. Roberts* (1698), 5 Modern 394, 405, 87 E.R. 725, 733, also 1 Salkeld 13, 91 E.R. 14, 3 Salkeld 16, 91 E.R. 664, 1 Lord Raymond 374, 91 E.R. 1147, 3 Lord Raymond 264, 92 E.R. 679, 12 Modern 208, 88 E.R. 1267, Carthew 416, 90 E.R. 841, Holt K.B. 8, 150, 193, 90 E.R. 902, 981, 1005.

[2] Stat. 8 Ann., c. 14, s. 1 (*SR*, IX, 233–234).

[3] Sic in MS.

N.B. On the aforesaid 30th November 1725, the Lord Chief Baron GILBERT, before he entered upon the trial of the causes, declared that he had considered with himself and was come to a resolution which he thought fit to mention to the counsel before he entered upon the trial of any cause lest his taking notice of it in any particular cause, it was this, *viz.* that it was not proper for the defendants' counsel to endeavor to influence the juries' affections and passions by telling them that the laws on which etc. were hard and severe laws, that their client was a poor trader, etc., and must be absolutely ruined in case they found him guilty, the penalty being so very great that neither he nor his family and his friends could be able to raise it or such like topics, for this was only an application to the passions of a jury. And if anyone should use such arguments to a jury out of court, he would lay him by the heels and what was not fit to be urged to them out of court, he would not permit counsel to urge and insist upon before him in court.

Taussig MS. 311, vol. 2, p. 846 [bis], pl. 2

Hilary term 1725/26.

Mr. *Bootle* moved that the plaintiff might bring in the *postea* that the defendant might move thereon in arrest of judgment.

Mr. Attorney General [*Yorke*] said that the court, upon granting such a motion, expected that the defendant's counsel should mention some exception or other.

But *Bootle* insisted on the contrary.

And the court agreed with him, and so they would not oblige him to mention the exception.

Per Chief Baron [GILBERT]: The exception may arise upon the verdict as entered on the *postea*.

Taussig MS. 311, vol. 2, p. 859

Hilary term 1725/26. Doe, *qui tam* v. Rhoades.

A motion in arrest of judgment [was made] that, among the other goods [alleged] by the information to come to the defendant's hands and for which the information was brought, there were these, *viz. octo dolia vini*. And it was insisted that this was totally uncertain, neither expressing quantity nor quality, so much as whether red or white. That it was uncertain as to quantity, it was insisted that *dolium* signified either a tun, a pipe, or a hogshead and, therefore, it ought to have been ascertained either by an *Anglice* or by the number of gallons. And, for the maintenance of the exception, Playster's Case was urged and the Case of Natt, *qui tam* v. [*blank*], in this court.[1]

[1] *Playter v. Warne* (1583), 5 Coke Rep. 34, 77 E.R. 105; *Nat, qui tam v. Bartlett* (1710), Dodd 221, 223, Parker 278, 145 E.R. 779.

But Lord Chief Baron GILBERT and PAGE, the other two barons being gone away to the [House of] Lords, disallowed the exception. And they were so very clear in it that they said they would not give so much countenance to it as to take any further time to consider of it.

See the brief of this. Myself and *Bootle* were counsel with the defendants.

577

Davies v. Duke

(Ex. 1725)

In this case, a court of equity heard evidence of a payment by the plaintiff to the defendant's decedent and enjoined the defendant from trying the case in a court of common law.

Taussig MS. 311, vol. 2, p. 830

Michaelmas term 1725.

The case was, one Bowles being indebted to Ann Duke, to whom the defendant was son and administrator, by a bond of £150, she applies to him for payment thereof, and, accordingly, he pays her on 29th November 1723 £50 thereof in money and gives her a promissory note for the remaining £100, payable three months afterwards, before which time of payment, she, being ill, sends for Davies and desires him to take the note and apply to Bowles for payment thereof, who, at first and a second time, did not pay it because Duke had not endorsed her name on the said note. But she endorsing her name on it and he carrying it a third time to Bowles, he paid it. And Davies gave a receipt on the back of the note: '28 January 1723, received the contents for the use of Duke, *per me* /s/ *Davies*.' After this, Duke, the intestate, continued ill and died of that illness in March following. And her son and administrator, who appeared not to have lived with her nor to have visited her, she being disobliged by him, enquiring into her effects and finding out that Davies had received £100 for her in January preceding, supposing he had not paid the money to her, brought his action of *indebitatus assumpsit* against Davies for so much money had and received to the intestate's use. After this action was so brought, Davies brings a bill against him in this court suggesting that, when he had paid the money and that when she gave him the note to apply to Bowles for the payment thereof, she required a note from him of the receipt of that note and of his promising to return it or the money, that, accordingly, he gave such note dated 13th December 1723, that, afterwards, when he had received the money from Bowles, he paid it to her and she returned him the aforesaid note 13th December 1723. And he suggested further by his bill that Duke, the son, who had sued him in the aforesaid action, had papers and accounts of his mother in his hands whereby it would appear that he had actually paid this £100 to her. So he prays an injunction and relief.

Duke answers that he was a stranger to his mother's affairs during her life, and he denies that, by any papers or books of account which he could find, any such thing appeared pending these proceedings. The plaintiff in equity not moving for or not being able on motion to obtain an injunction, a trial is had. And a verdict is against Davies for the £100, but no defense was made at the trial by Davies; so it was a verdict by default and judgment thereon. And a writ of error was brought by Davies, on which said writ of error, one Mr. [*blank*] was bail for Davies. And after the writ of error was so brought, witnesses were examined in the cause in equity, and it came on to be heard this first day of the setting down of causes. And the plaintiff Davies insisted on the note of 18 December, which he produced as an exhibit in the cause, as strong evidence of his having paid the money. And also having examined the aforesaid Mr. [*blank*], and he swearing that he had heard the said Ann Duke, sometime before her death, acknowledge that Davies had paid her this very money, the court thought it was strong proof of his having so done.

And it was insisted on the other side that, if this were true, it was proper evidence to be used on his behalf at the trial at law and, consequently, he should not have declined such trial, which was the only proper method for determining the question, and instead thereof rely on his suit in equity wherein the whole merits of the case being a single matter of fact could not in the nature of it be so well and fully examined and tried as by a jury, that the permitting this method would set aside all actions of law and trials by juries. And though it was also urged that, as to Mr. [*blank*]'s evidence, little credit could be given to it, he appearing to be a party interested in the event of the suit, being bail on the writ of error, as he himself acknowledged in his deposition upon cross-examination and so he could not have been read as a witness at all had not the defendant unwarily examined him to the point of the payment of the money as well as to his being bail. And though, by the defendant's proofs, it was sworn that Davies had acknowledged he never gave a receipt for the £100 note, which disproved his main evidence from the note he now exhibited and also proved by the maid servant, who lived with the mother and who was the plaintiff's witness and was examined on his side as well as on the defendant's, that though she was a witness to a writing between Davies and her mistress, which she did not know the contents of, yet she never saw Davies pay any money to her, though she constantly attended her during all the time of her sickness and, if she went from her for a short time, she either took the key with her or else left her in the nurse's company. And though, if Davies had paid the money, the old woman must have received £150 within the three months or very little more of her death and yet no more than £20 or £30 [could] be found. And it was sworn by the same maid servant that she did not expend above £30 in the whole during the sickness.

Yet notwithstanding all this, Chief Baron Gilbert, Page, and Hale decreed a perpetual injunction against the defendant and would not so much as suffer him to have any trial at law upon the point whether Davies had paid the money or not, and this though the Chief Baron at first proposed that the verdict should stand as a security and a trial should be had at the peril of costs, but the defendant's going into his proofs, the court retracted their first proposal and decreed *ut supra. Quod mihi et aliis domorum [?] videbantur.*

578

Floyer v. Johnson

(Ex. 1725)

Where the parties to a contract for the sale of land have not agreed on the purchase price, a court of equity can send the case to an advisory jury to determine the reasonable price.

Taussig MS. 311, vol. 2, p. 835

Michaelmas term 1725.

In this case, Floyer's bill was to compel a specific performance of a contract made between him and Johnson whereby Floyer was to purchase a leasehold estate near Croydon at sixteen year's purchase of the annual value of the farm. Floyer, by a bill suggesting that Johnson would not assign to him unless he admitted the annual value to be £180 *per annum*, whereas it was not worth above £150, prayed a specific performance according to the real annual value. Johnson exhibited his cross-bill wherein he insisted that the real value was £180 *per annum* and that Floyer had agreed to take it at that rate, and, therefore, he prayed performance at that value. Floyer in his answer denied his having come to any certain agreement concerning an annual value and, by the same answer, said he had been far from agreeing to take the value at £180, that the premises were really worth about £150 or £160 as he had been informed and, though leased at £168 to an under-tenant, yet the said under-tenant was not restrained as usual from plowing etc. Upon hearing the cause, the single question was whether any value had been agreed upon and fixed between Floyer and Johnson.

And the court, being of opinion there had not, decreed that the agreement should be performed and that their having been no agreement between the parties whereby the value of the land was ascertained and fixed, the Master should state and adjust the account according to the true value of the land.

Hereupon, the parties went before the Master, but there was so very great variety of evidence about the value of the land that the Master made a special report and concluded that he could not gain any satisfaction as to this point. Hereupon, the court direct an issue to try what was the real annual value of the land in question and direct a view and a good jury. The issue was tried at the last assizes for Surrey *coram* Dormer, and there was a verdict for Floyer that the land was worth £130 *per annum* and the cause being set down to be finally heard on the *postea*, Johnson obtained an order for liberty to move for a new trial when the cause came on in the paper, which was granted.

And now, it was insisted by him that this verdict was a very extraordinary one and, to induce the court to believe it so, he made an offer to give Floyer 150 guineas and to pay him all his costs of suit if Floyer would release him from the bargain. And they also offered an affidavit concerning the trial, which contained a sort of imputation of his own counsel, *viz.* for not examining all his witnesses and for not having Floyer's bill and Floyer's answer to his cross-bill read in evidence as likewise for not having a letter or two of Floyer read and some other particulars.

But there being no certificate from the judge who tried the cause, the court would not suffer the affidavit to be read, but they were so strongly induced to believe the verdict had undervalued the lands because Johnson had made the aforesaid offer that, upon reading the bill and Floyer's answer to the cross-bill, they declared they would grant a new trial. And they pressed Mr. Floyer to accommodate the matter or to consent to a new trial in Middlesex or at the bar upon Johnson's consent to be bound down by such new trial, which proceeding of the court seemed new, *viz.* in impeaching the verdict barely from an admission in the bill etc. without any certificate from the judge of his dislike thereto when even these admissions etc. were before the court before the issue directed. And had they been to govern in the case, the court need not have directed an issue at all, at least they should not have directed the aforesaid issue and, of course, the present motion sent in impeachment of what the court had done previous to the trial as well as to the verdict.

See Parliament Cases of 16 February 1726[/27], where the trial was continued.[1]

579

Hall v. Tasker

(Ex. 1725)

In this case, the defendant was ordered to make an account to the plaintiff.

Public Record Office E.126/23, f. 349v, pl. 1

25 November 1725. London.

Whereas by an order of this court made the 10th day of June last on the hearing of this cause for the reasons therein mentioned, it was ordered, adjudged, and decreed by the court that the said defendant, William Tasker, should account with the said complainant [Thomas Hall] before John Harding, Esq., the Deputy of His Majesty's Remembrancer of this court touching the sum of £235 15s. due on the bond in question in this cause and all interest due for the same from the said defendant to the said complainant and the cause was to be continued in the paper of causes to be further heard upon the said Deputy Remembrancer's report unless the said defendant should show cause to the contrary on the first day

[1] *Floyer v. Johnson* (1727), 7 Brown P.C. 156, 3 E.R. 101.

of causes in this present Michaelmas term, he first paying unto the plaintiff or his clerk in court £5 costs for that day's attendance and this cause standing in the paper of causes came on this day to be further heard in the Exchequer Chamber at Westminster before the Rt. Hon. Sir Jeffery Gilbert, Kt., Lord Chief Baron, Robert Price, Esq., Sir Francis Page, Kt., and Barnard Hale, Esq., three other barons of this court, whereupon hearing of Mr. Davenport, of counsel with the plaintiff, informing the court that the said defendant had not paid to the plaintiff or his clerk in court £5 costs or any part thereof, the said plaintiff's counsel therefore prayed that the said decree of the 10th of June aforesaid may be made absolute, whereupon and upon reading of the said decree, no counsel attending for the said defendant, it is thereupon this day ordered, adjudged, and decreed by the court that the said decree of the 10th of June last shall be and is hereby made absolute and that the said defendant shall come to an account with the plaintiff for the sum of £235 15s. and all interest due for the same before the said John Harding, the said Deputy Remembrancer of this court, who is to make all parties all just allowances and to make his report herein to the court with all convenient speed, and this cause is to be continued in the paper of causes to be further heard upon the said report when this court will make such further order herein as shall be just.

580

Fisher v. Lord Somerville

(Ex. 1725–1726)

The question in this case was whether a constant non-payment of tithes is evidence of an exemption from tithes against a lay impropriator.

Harvard Law School MS. 1082, vol. 1, p. 254, pl. 2

Michaelmas term 1725.

The plaintiffs, as lessees under the Dean and Chapter of Christchurch of the rectory of Chipenham in the County of Wilts, bring a bill for tithes. Some of the defendants [Lord and Lady Somerville and their several tenants] insist that the lands in their occupation never paid tithes and that they did belong to and were part of the demesnes of the Abbey of Stanley and vested in the crown and so in King Henry VIII, who granted the same together with the tithes to Sir Edward Bainturn and his heirs, under whose grant the Lady Somerville claims the lands and tithes aforesaid.

My Lady Somerville in her answer insists on letters patent dated 28 Hen. VIII [1536 x 1537] to Sir Edward Bainturn and his heirs, under which she claims, and that no tithes had been ever paid for these lands.

Other defendants insist that they were part of the demesnes of Monkton, part of the Abbey of Farley, and that they never paid tithes.

Serjeant *Pengelly, Browne, Edlin, Thoresby,* and *Bootle* insisted for the defendants that there was no title in the plaintiffs to these tithes and no possession of these tithes, so we called on the plaintiffs' counsel to begin, for though the discharge was laid on the defendants' part, yet denying the title put the plaintiffs upon the proof.

Chesshyre, Bunbury, Philip Ward, for the plaintiffs, [said] that the plaintiffs were lessees under the Dean and Chapter of Christchurch, who claimed by virtue of a grant made 38 Hen. VIII and this grant takes in Stanley as well as Farleigh.

I must beg leave to say that a dean and chapter is no lay impropriator, and non-payment, if anything, in the argument, would hold as strong against a parson and vicar, for a spiritual person might alienate before the disabling statutes.[1] And a single person might have granted away the tithes, and now a dean and chapter are disabled from alienation by the disabling statutes. The Statute of Limitations[2] is not pleadable to a dean and chapter. See Dean and Chapter of Westminster v. Herbert, Exchequer.[3] Bateman v. Nunn[4] was the first case where this point was started.

These abbeys were of the Cistercian Order. And so there is no exemption but *quamdiu propriis manibus*. Perhaps our grant being in 38 Hen. VIII [1546 x 1547] and they, claiming Stanley under 28 Hen. VIII, may insist on a precedent grant, but there is no pretense of a preceding grant as to Monkton, for the grant of Henry VIII does not mention tithes and only 24 Eliz. [1581 x 1582], which is subsequent to our grant. Non-payment of tithes is only a neglect. The four defenses are inconsistent with each other, *viz.*, part of an abbey, non-payment, a portion of tithes in gross, and antecedent grants. The pleading is inconsistent. 4 Rept., Bozoun's Case.[5] And the defendants should be obliged to some certain rules of pleading [so] that the plaintiffs may be able to answer such defense by evidence.

Before the Stat. 32 Hen. VIII,[6] laymen could not sue for tithes. A mere layman cannot prescribe in *non decimando*. A lay person was not capable of a discharge of tithes. Bishop of Winchester's Case.[7] And there is no presumption that this was granted away between this and the disabling statutes.

A grant of tithes was set up in bar by Mrs. Rolt's answer.

---

[1] Stat. 13 Eliz. I, c. 10 (*SR*, IV, 544–545); Stat. 14 Eliz. I, c. 11, ss. 3, 4 (*SR*, IV, 602–603).

[2] Stat. 21 Jac. I, c. 16 (*SR*, IV, 1222–1223).

[3] *Dean and Chapter of Westminster v. Cross* (Ex. 1720), see above, Case No. 126.

[4] *Bateman v. Nunn* (Ex. 1722), see above, Case No. 312.

[5] *Bozoun's Case* (1584), 4 Coke Rep. 34, 76 E.R. 970, also *sub nom. Futter v. Boorome*, Godbolt 35, 78 E.R. 22, 1 Eagle & Younge 86.

[6] Stat. 32 Hen. VIII, c. 7 (*SR*, III, 751–752).

[7] *Wright v. Wright* (1596), 2 Coke Rep. 38, 76 E.R. 501, also Moore K.B. 425, 72 E.R. 672, Croke Eliz. 475, 511, 78 E.R. 726, 760, 1 Gwillim 167, 1 Eagle & Younge 119.

Serjeant *Pengelly*: We may have three or four defenses. These might be parcel of an abbey, and a dean and chapter has no other privilege than as a lay fee, and the Abbot of Stanley might grant away these tithes, and they might be held as a portion of tithes or by retainer. But we have an antecedent grant of 28 Hen. VIII as to these lands and tithes.

We for the defendants argued that it was properly insisted on by the defendants in their answer that this method of a general non-payment was good and [it was] so settled in the Town of Warwick v. Lucas, Easter 1710,[1] admitted because the difficulty of setting forth discharges and, therefore, by other lawful ways and means admitted. No possession of these tithes was showed in the plaintiffs, and, therefore [it is] barred. And in the Town of Warwick v. Lucas, it did not appear that the preaching friars of Warwick was one of the greater monasteries. Non-payment coupled with another defense has always been admitted. And though the part [about] the abbey may fail, yet the non-payment is a good defense. Downes v. Moreman, Hilary, Exchequer,[2] is a strong case as to tithes in gross. Hankin v. Gay, Hilary 1718[/19].[3]

There is no occasion to say how he was discharged. Collard v. Newton, Hilary 1681; Mompesson v. Ellis, February 1684; Medley v. Talmley;[4] Carrington, lessee of King's College v. Mascall, Trinity 4 Jac.

These tithes might be granted away before they vested in the Dean and Chapter of Christchurch. And the defendants' claim of the tithes is paramount to the plaintiffs' claim. Cro. Jac. 559; Cro. Eliz. 206; Dyer 349; Branche's Case, Moore 219.[5]

By the grant of 28 Hen. VIII, these tithes were vested in the grantee before the grant to Christchurch. As to Monkton, the grant of 24 Eliz. recites the grant of Hen. VIII, so of the tithes. The words in Hen. VIII are '*hereditamenta*'; that will carry tithes. The Dean and Chapter of Christchurch is become a lay fee, and is so to be considered. Tithes amounting to £150 *per annum* cannot be construed a neglect of the impropriator. That both these abbeys of Stanley and Farleigh

---

1 *See Corporation of Warwick v. Lucas* (1711), Eq. Cases Exch. 671, Public Record Office, E.126/19, ff. 191, 221.

2 *Downes v. Mooreman* (Ex. 1725), see above, Case No. 526.

3 *Hankin v. Gay* (Ex. 1719), see above, Case No. 76.

4 *Collard v. Newton* (1682), Eq. Cases Exch. 143, 1 Rayner 58, 2 Gwillim 530, 1 Eagle & Younge 526; *Medly v. Talmy* (1696), Dodd 164, 347, 1 Rayner 81, 2 Gwillim 559, 1 Eagle & Younge 620, Public Record Office, E.126/16, f. 360.

5 *Porter v. Bathurst* (1620), Croke Jac. 559, 79 E.R. 479, also 2 Rolle Rep. 142, 81 E.R. 712, Palmer 118, 81 E.R. 1006, 1 Gwillim 373, 1 Eagle & Younge 312; *Nash v. Molins* (1590), Croke Eliz. 206, 78 E.R. 462, also 1 Leonard 240, 74 E.R. 220, 1 Gwillim 162, 1 Eagle & Younge 100; *Parson of Peykirke's Case* (1576), 3 Dyer 349b, 73 E.R. 784, 1 Gwillim 136, 1 Eagle & Younge 66; *Branche's Case* (1585), Moore K.B. 219, 72 E.R. 541, 1 Gwillim 156, 1 Eagle & Younge 89.

were founded before time of memory, see Dugdale [*Monasticon Anglicanum*] 620, 1 vol., 867. And, therefore, they have a prescriptive right. Cro. Eliz. 763; Moore 219; Selden 294.[1]

Chief Baron [Gilbert]: The Council of Lateran in 1215 did no more than order that there should be no appropriation to a monastery without the bishop's consent. This must be esteemed a lay fee. But I think that a trial at law ought to be offered.

Price: This is a case of great consequence. And usage will govern much.

Page: The difficulty that sticks with me is whether a man can prescribe in *non decimando*. But I think that the answer is very proper. This now belongs to Christchurch. And colleges have been esteemed lay fees. This is a privilege running and belonging to the land. And, therefore, it is not personal. These lands were severed from the rectory and so granted away by 28 Hen. VIII prior to the plaintiff's title.

Chief Baron: There is a difficulty for a person to prescribe against a lay impropriator, which lay impropriation came and arose within time of memory. Non-payment is an evidence of a discharge. And the former cases have sent this [issue] to be tried.

Price: I think it so clear in favor of the defendants, I mean the non-payment, that I think there is no occasion for a trial.

Hale: It is a case of consequence. *Non decimando* has not been allowed in a layman. And whether the plaintiffs have ever had possession may be material, for they cannot show any.

The Chief Baron [said] that a lay impropriator must allege seisin of the tithes.

Note that, afterwards, the court gave an opinion that the lands of Stanley were discharged because there was an antecedent grant to the plaintiffs in 28 Hen. VIII. But as to Monkton, they decreed tithes to be paid because the grant of Elizabeth was subsequent. See below.

Harvard Law School MS. 1082, vol. 1, p. 266, pl. 1

Hilary term 1725/26.

The defendants, Croke *et al.*, insisted on the letters patent under Edward Baynturn and, by that grant, the tithes are granted prior to the plaintiff's title. As to the defendants Esmead and Whaley, in 24 Eliz. [1581 x 1582], [there were] general words as tithes, but here, in the first grant of Henry VIII, therefore, that is subsequent to the plaintiff's title. And no tithes are admitted to be paid in respect of these lands.

There might be a question whether non-enjoyment alone will not do against a lay impropriator. But this case does not turn upon it. The question will arise

[1] *Pigot v. Sympson* (1600), Croke Eliz. 763, 78 E.R. 994, 1 Eagle & Younge 148; *Branche's Case* (1585), *ut supra*; J. Selden, *History of Tithes*.

on the Stat. 32 Hen. VIII, which Statute gives two remedies. And it is plain the king had a remedy in his own court for the subtracting of tithes. But I think that this college, *viz*. the Dean and Chapter of Christchurch, is an ecclesiastical body and the king is *persona mixta*. And when it is granted to an ecclesiastical body, it becomes an ecclesiastical fee. But if it is granted to a lay person, it becomes a lay fee. Christchurch was erected in 1546 as a chapter for a bishop. Anthony Wood, [*Athenae Oxonienses*], 452. It came out of the crown to the chapter. But as to the manor of Stanley, the defendants have a discharge because of a prior grant. Personal privileges are only inherent to the bodies and, as such, discharged by the Statute 27 Hen. VIII.[1]

But as to Monkton, *viz*. the defendants Esmead and Whaley, they were ordered to account because those tithes were not granted to those under whom the defendants claimed until long after the grant to the plaintiff's lessors, the Dean and Chapter of Christchurch.

Bunbury 209, 145 E.R. 649,
1 Rayner 231, 1 Eagle & Younge 805

The case of Fisher *et al*., lessees of the Dean and Chapter of Christchurch in Oxford. 3 February 1725[/26].

This case stood for the judgment of the court this day, when it was expected that the long-controverted question, whether a constant non-payment of tithes is evidence of an exemption against a lay impropriator, would have been decided.

But the court gave judgment on the words of the patents mentioned in the cause, though they determined that the Dean and Chapter was a spiritual and not a lay body.

581

Attorney General v. Barry

(Ex. 1726)

Even though the crown does not receive court costs, the sheriff is still entitled to receive his official fees.

Taussig MS. 311, vol. 2, p. 865, pl. 2

Hilary term 1725/26. Rex v. Barry, *ad instantia* Kenneday.

The case was this. Kenneday was the collector of the customs at Exeter. And he sends up £1600 in a box which was put up in another box, and he so delivered to Barry, who was the Exeter carrier to carry the same to London. And Kenneday's correspondent in London and to whom the box was sent sending word to him that, when he opened the box here in London, there was nothing but stones

[1] Stat. 27 Hen. VIII, c. 28 (*SR*, III, 757–758).

in the same, thereupon, Kenneday applies to Baron Price in vacation time for a [writ of] immediate extent against Barry for this money. And to obtain it, he makes an affidavit that the money was the king's money collected for customs, that he put it up in the box, and sent it to Barry at Exeter by one Mr. Beaver, his clerk, who delivered it to Barry to carry thence to London as directed to Francis Stephens. And upon the box's coming to London, he has reason to believe that Barry had opened the box and taken out the money. Thereupon, an extent was granted and sent down to the sheriff and endorsed for £1600 bail. But the sheriff would not take the bail, but carried Barry to prison.

N.B. There were several affidavits *ex parte* Barry that, when the boxes were delivered to the carrier, they were said to be full of papers and writings. And the other box, for there were two separate boxes, was only a present to Stevens of woodcock pies and gammons of bacon. And there were some other affidavits to show the court that the carrier is always paid for the carriage of money a very different price than for other goods.

And it was now moved to set aside this extent following several objections made to the proceedings:

First, that the affidavit on which it was granted was taken before the solicitor in the cause;

Secondly, the affidavits of Kenneday, Beaver, and Biggs, 404 in Hardres's Reports,[1] the king's process should not be made upon a stale [*blank*] not sufficient, for nothing is sworn that the debt is not put in suit other ways nor that the defendant absconds;

Thirdly, that the debt from Barry to Kenneday was a simple contract debt and found by an inquisition on the extent against Kenneday in aid of him without a particular warrant for that purpose.

After reading all the affidavits on both sides, the court said that, since the question was whether the money was the plaintiff Kenneday's or not, they would not enter into the regularity of the issuing of the extent, but they would make the party traverse it and try that point and then the party might move what he pleased.

Harvard Law School MS. 1082, vol. 1, p. 258, pl. 2

Hilary term 1725/26.

Serjeant *Shepherd* moved to set aside a [writ of] extent, which was granted at the instance of Kennedy, the collector at Exeter, for £1600 in foreign gold sent up by the defendant, the Exeter carrier. And this money was directed to Francis Stephens in London. And the oath only is that he had received a letter that Stephens had not received it was insufficient. No extent should go but by motion in open court.

[1] *Attorney General v. Poultney* (1665), Hardres 403, 145 E.R. 519.

Bunbury, pro eodem, [said] that the oath is defective and there was no proper affidavit and it was not taken before a proper commissioner, being only before Kennedy's solicitor in this cause, contrary to the Rules of 15 Car. I; 35 Car. II. He cited Hardres 404.

An action was brought for this very money, and he is not to be twice vexed for the same thing. And the affidavit ought to have been that the defendant Barry absconded. Kennedy swears it to be the king's money, and Woodward swears it to be his and that Kennedy is paid, and so they are inconsistent.

PAGE: Though the first affidavit may be a little defective, yet the defendant Barry has not sworn that he knew nothing of the taking out of the money.

PRICE: I ordered the extent. And though the affidavit might be a little defective, yet I directed bail to be taken.

Chief Baron [GILBERT]: I will have this extent traversed.

Note: It afterwards was. And upon a trial and full evidence, a verdict was given for the king.

Harvard Law School MS. 1082, vol. 2, p. 3, pl. 2

Trinity term 1726.

The defendant was a carrier at Exeter. And Kennedy, the collector, entrusted him with £1600 of the king's money to bring to London. And the defendant pretended that he had never received it. And upon an extent issued, the defendant was found indebted to the crown in £1600. And upon a motion and recognizance entered into by the defendant's surety to pay the debt, restitution was ordered of his goods. And the question was now concerning costs.

And we that were for the defendant, though we admitted the verdict against us, yet that the king neither receives nor pays costs, so there should be no costs in this case. Rex v. Pocock; Attorney General v. Knight and Albert, Easter 1716;[1] Jones v. Oliver.

Ward, for the king: For an information *in rem*, there are no costs. 8 Geo.[2] [gives] costs in lieu of damages. In this case, Barry comes in after execution. And he is indulged with a favor, and he ought to pay costs.

Chief Baron [GILBERT]: Costs are in the breast of the court. And the sheriff is entitled to his poundage. And it would be hard to put it on the crown. The defendant ought to pay the costs of the poundage, but no costs at common law.

PRICE: It being for money due to the crown, I will carry it as far as I can. The person of the defendant is redeemed. And he ought to pay costs.

PAGE: There is no precedent of this case. If the king had brought an action of trover, costs would have been given by the jury in lieu of interest. And in this case, the court redeems the defendant upon condition.

---

[1] *Attorney General v. Pocock* (Ex. 1720), see above, Case No. 134; *Rex v. Albert* (Ex. 1716), see above, Case No. 9.

[2] Stat. 8 Geo. I, c. 25.

HALE: The defendant moves to vacate his recognizance and debt [?]; it is to ask a favor. And why not upon conditions?

Taussig MS. 311, vol. 2, p. 912

10 June 1726. GILBERT, PRICE, PAGE, and HALE *praesentibus*.

Mr. *Ward* [moved for] the king and Kenneday against Barry, the Exeter carrier, for costs on the trial of the plea to the extent against him [Barry].

On the other side, they cited the case of Attorney General v. Knight and Fletcher Albert, Easter 1716, wherein it was determined that no costs [lay] on either side in the case of a recognizance for pleading to an extent on a recognizance, and the case of the King v. Pocock and Bower, May 30, 1720, express to the same point.

But, *per Bunbury, Browne*, and *Bootle*, on a *scire facias* or extent on a bond entered into to the crown, the [Stat.] 38 Hen. VIII[1] expressly gives costs, but on a recognizance to try the plea, they never gave any costs *prout* the two cases *in rem*. But in personal informations, there are costs as in a *devenerunt*.

And the Chief Baron [GILBERT] seemed to agree with Mr. Ward that there is a difference between an extent actually executed and where he comes in originally and pleads to a *scire facias*. And, surely, says he, it is not reasonable to let him go quit without the payment of poundage. It is otherwise as to costs, for, as to that, he said he was not satisfied how the practice was.

PRICE: In an action of debt, the king has costs. (Query this.)

PAGE: I shall be glad to look into precedents, but, surely, none of the precedents will come up to this case, for, here, the king might have had [an action of] trover and, in such case, the king should have judgment for damages and costs. And in this case, the defendant Barry is in a less favorable case than if it had been tried upon a trover. He laid it down for a rule that though a subject cannot soften a felony into an action for a duty, yet the crown may bring [an action of] debt or trover for a felony. And he also insisted upon it that the court had favored the defendant Barry by letting him in to traverse the inquisition; so it is by way of redemption that he entered into the recognizance.

HALE: If the motion had been made that the recognizance should be discharged on bringing the money into court and the court would not have granted this without payment of the principal and interest, then I think we may give the crown liberty to put the recognizance in suit unless they will pay the principal and costs and the poundage.

And the court exhorted the defendant to submit to this and made a rule upon him so to do it, being, as they all said, a case of a very extraordinary nature. And they would not in such a case as this be obliged to consider and search for precedents to determine whether, by the course of the court, the defendant was

[1] Stat. 33 Hen. VIII, c. 39, s. 36 (*SR*, III, 886).

obliged to pay costs or no. And so, for fear of making a precedent upon consideration, they made one without consideration.

N.B. I think this was a most extraordinary case and determination as it now came before the court, for Mr. Ward's motion was that the crown might be at liberty to put the defendant Barry's recognizance in suit for the principal, interest, and costs. This recognizance was entered into by Barry by an order of this court made 26th January last, which recited that an extent had been awarded against him at the instance of F. Kenneday, His Majesty's collector of customs at Exeter, for £1600 as money received by him to His Majesty's use, that Barry's body and goods had been seized on this extent though Barry offered security to the sheriff to plead to the extent and inquisition, whereby he was found a debtor to the said Kenneday for this sum of £1600. Thereupon, it was ordered that Barry's person and effects should be discharged and all further proceedings should stay on the said extent and inquisition on Barry's giving security to be approved of by Kenneday to answer the debt which should appear to be due to His Majesty. In pursuance of this order, Barry entered into a recognizance before the commissioners in the country of £3200 dated 31st January with a condition in which was recited the order, above. Therefore, the condition of the recognizance was this, that, if John Barry, his heirs, executors, or administrators, in the case of his decease, should well and truly observe, perform, and obey such order and directions as the court should make upon the trial of the cause and pay and satisfy unto His Majesty or his successors all such sum or sums of money as shall be adjudged to be due from him to His Majesty, then the recognizance to be void etc.

Subsequent to the aforesaid order and recognizance, *viz.* on 8 February 1725, Barry moved to set aside the extent against him as being grounded on the first extent and inquisition against Kenneday because it was irregular, see before [*blank*]. And, thereupon, the court made an order (in my apprehension a very extraordinary one) that the irregularity of issuing the said extent and the execution of the same should be reserved to the giving of judgment in this cause.

Barry, according to the recognizance, pleaded to the first extent and inquisition *non indebitatus*. And the cause was tried before the Chief Baron at the sittings after Easter term last, and there was a verdict against Barry for the £1600.

And now it was moved by *Ward*, on behalf of Kenneday, that the court would give them leave to put Barry's recognizance in suit for the principal sum and for the interest of it together with the poundage paid to the sheriff and the costs of the proceedings. The intent of this motion was that, if they could put the recognizance in suit, thereupon, they should be able to get costs etc.

This motion was opposed by Barry's counsel and, in my apprehension, very unskillfully, though what they urged with relation to the costs of the proceedings was, in my notion of it, very right, for I apprehend it to be a very plain case that, according to the course of the court, if a debtor to the crown's debtor comes in and traverses the inquisition by which he is found to be a debtor in such a suit, the king neither pays nor receives costs, and the cases cited by the defendant's counsel, as before, were rightly urged to this point. And I apprehend the distinction is this, that, in an extent immediate against the debtor of the crown on a bond grounded upon 33 Hen. VIII[1] or in a *scire facias* on such a bond or on a recognizance, the crown has costs by the express words of the Statute, but the suit against a debtor of the crown's debtor is at common law where the crown not being subject to costs, receives none, no more than upon a *scire facias* to repeal patents etc.

Nor do I see how the putting of Barry's recognizance in suit was feasible, for it seems to me that it was not forfeited. The crown could not have assigned a breach upon it at the time of this motion, for the £1600 for which the verdict was given on the suit grounded upon the extent and inquisition for the payment whereof the recognizance was entered into was not at that time payable, no judgment being given on the verdict as yet, this being the first day of the term after which the verdict was had.

Secondly, the recognizance could not be forfeited with respect to any disobedience to any order made by the court on Barry, for the court had as yet made no order, but, on this opportunity, they took the hint and made an order upon him to pay the debt and interest, the costs of the suit, and poundage.

Third, if the court had granted the motion as made and the king could have assigned a breach, yet if, by the rules of the court and the former practice, the costs of the former suit were not payable, how could the court with any justice annex them to the suit upon this recognizance?

Query, therefore, of these matters.

The barons were far from being clear whether costs were payable in such a suit as before, and, therefore, if they were obliged to determine this point, they would search for precedents, but they seemed to think there might be a difference between coming in to plead to an inquisition, as they called it, voluntarily and out of custody and being taken up and then pleading upon giving security. And they thought that, by means of a recognizance, they had a greater power over the pleader than in other cases and that it was discretionary in them to discharge the recognizance and, consequently, upon what terms they would do it, *viz.* upon payment of costs only.

Now query by me, whether, in all cases, a pleader to an inquisition does not enter into a recognizance, secondly, if the court, for the reasons before, could tack the costs of the pleadings in the former suit to a suit on this recognizance, which was the true intent of the present motion.

N.B. The court was much scandalized at the nature of the cause itself, which, in truth, was a very scurvy one on Barry's side and such, perhaps, he might have answered for in a criminal way. And, therefore, the barons were not so scrupulous as perhaps they would otherwise have been. And, therefore, in order to

[1] Stat. 33 Hen. VIII, c. 39, s. 36 (*SR*, III, 886).

decide the present controversy, they now made a sort of an arbitrary order on Barry that he should pay the principal, interest, costs, and poundage. And they told his counsel it were better for him to do so than to give them a second opportunity of hearing anything further about him in this matter.

582

Cary v. Stafford

(Ex. 1726)

Where a person makes a grant of fictitious land, a court of equity will order him to convey land of equivalent value.

Taussig MS. 311, vol. 2, p. 861

Monday, 7th February 1725[/26].

The plaintiff brought her bill against the defendant to make good to her a settlement of lands of £22 *per annum* in Gloucestershire, which he made to her by way of a lease for life at a peppercorn rent with the usual covenants for the lessee's enjoyment. And on the back of the deed was endorsed a receipt for 5s. consideration of the deed. But there was no livery nor indeed any such lands *in rerum natura* as was confessed by the answer of the defendant. And the case was that the plaintiff was a maid servant who lived in the same town as the defendant in Christchurch, Southampton, with her uncle and aunt and was recommended to the defendant's service. She lived with him one month and then went away, but she came again and was received into his service about one half year after[wards]. And she lived with him about two years, in the middle of which time, he directed an attorney to draw the lease blank for the lessee's name, which he after[wards] filled up with the plaintiff's name and then sealed and delivered it in the presence of the said attorney who drew it. And the said attorney swore that he sealed and delivered it in earnest though he did not then see or know who was the lessee. And another witness swore that the defendant declared he executed the lease in favor of and also swore that he had also declared that he delivered the deed to the plaintiff with his own hand, though he, by his answer, swore that she took it out of his custody privately. And the defendant insisted he had no consideration for the deed, and so he insisted that, as no advantage could be taken of the deed, there being no livery of seisin, therefore, a court of equity would not decree an equivalent for it, there being no valuable consideration for it. And it was insisted at the bar that, if the plaintiff was a volunteer, a court of equity would not help her, much less if the consideration arose *ex turpi causa*.

Nota bene there was proof of an agreement for 50s. *per annum* wages for her service.

But the court were all of them very clear that the defendant should be obliged to make good the settlement and accordingly decreed it.

Note: I [*Philip Ward*] was for the defendant.

Ambler 831, 27 E.R. 522,
3 Swanston 482, 36 E.R. 935

Hilary, 12 Geo. I, 1725[/26].

The plaintiff was the defendant's servant at 50s. *per annum*, which was proved in the cause to be paid. And, during her service, the defendant procured a deed to be drawn by an attorney whereby lands of £22 a year were settled for life with the usual covenants to repair and for quiet enjoyment with a reservation of a peppercorn rent. And there was a receipt indorsed for 5s. as the consideration money, but blanks were left for the names of the parties. The defendant, afterwards, filled up the blanks with his own name as the grantor and the plaintiff's name as the grantee. But it appeared after to be all a fiction and that there were no such lands as were described in the deed. It was proved in the cause that, when the plaintiff came to demand where the lands were, the defendant laughed at her and said they were *in nubibus*, whereupon, the plaintiff brought her bill to be relieved and to compel the defendant to convey lands for the same estate and to the same value.

For the defendant, it was urged that, it appearing that the plaintiff was a mere volunteer, that she ought not to have the aid of a court of equity, that she did not come to be relieved against a fraud by which she was deprived of anything, but to force the defendant to give her what he never intended, that it was *turpis causa* and not to be favored in equity.

Some proofs were then read to show criminal conversation between the plaintiff and defendant, but not fully.

The court [was] of opinion that the plaintiff ought to have relief and that it should go to the Deputy [Remembrancer] to see a good conveyance made to the plaintiff of defendant's lands to the same value and to take an account of the rents and profits from the date of this fraudulent deed as if such lands had been really conveyed by it.

And *per* Gilbert, Chief Baron: This is not within the case of volunteers, for here is nothing at all given, and, therefore, no remedy can be at law. But, in the case of a volunteer where something is conveyed, damages may be recovered at law on the covenants, and, therefore, equity will interpose.

Hale, Baron: If the consideration did arise *ex turpi causa*, yet it is good in equity where there is no creditor etc. And courts of equity, in such cases, will decree performance, and that as a punishment to the party; and the man in this case is more criminal, for it must be supposed the solicitation first came from him.

From Mr. Coxe's MSS.

583

More v. Freeman

(Ex. 1726)

A married woman can exercise a power of appointment.

In this case, a contract by a married woman to exercise a power of appointment was found to be made without the duress of her husband and was thus valid.

Harvard Law School MS. 1082, vol. 1, p. 266, pl. 2

Hilary term 1725/26. More v. Ellis.

This was a bill brought against the defendant as executor of My Lady More, who was the plaintiff's wife, in order to establish an agreement between the plaintiff and his wife and to have £1000 according to the articles.

Pengelly, for the defendant Ellis: These were articles obtained by duress, on which this agreement was founded. And the wife being under the coverture of her husband, her agreement is, therefore, not good. And no encouragement ought to be given to carry into execution such an agreement, for no persons were parties to this agreement but the husband and wife. And it is of the worst consequence.

By the first agreement, where the trustees were parties, there, care was taken that her estate should not be liable to debts. But if this clandestine agreement should prevail, then her whole estate will be liable. And if this last agreement is good, the trustees must be decreed to be guilty of a breach of trust.

The law has taken care that the wife shall not dispose of anything without a fine and an examination in the most solemn manner.

Stevens, for the defendant, insisted that Ellis was not interested in this cause. And before he was examined and cross-examined by the plaintiff, he hoped he might be read though now he happened to be a defendant.

But that was overruled by the whole court.

Ward, for the defendant: This is a hard demand. And Mr. Edmonds, Lady More's father, left this estate to the separate use of his daughter. And if this agreement prevails, it will set aside the will of her father.

Hungerford, for the plaintiff: [To the] objection that these articles ought not to be carried into execution, [he] answered that would take away separate maintenance and articles between a man and wife. Where there is a separate estate, the man and wife are to be considered as different persons.

[To the] objection that the plaintiff never gave security according to the articles, [he] answered the lady had the benefit of it, for she was never molested.

Bunbury, for the plaintiff: My Lady More, by her own bill, offers £200 *per annum*. There is no merit in the defendant. He was no relation or acquaintance until August before. It does not set aside Edmonds's will, but [acts] rather to carry it into execution.

[To the] objection that it was against the decree, [he] answered that the decree was in 1717, and nothing could be in issue in relation to this matter.

The court inclined to think that articles fairly obtained between a man and his wife might be carried into execution.

Chief Baron [GILBERT]: This matter turns on the duress only, for there may be an agreement between a man and his wife in relation to separate maintenance and there may be a reason for a man to live separate from his wife.

Bunbury insisted that there was a difference between courts of equity and common law in relation to husband and wife. He cited Co. Litt. 52, 187.[1]

Note: The court afterwards directed an issue whether these articles were obtained by duress or constraint or not. And there was a verdict that they were fairly obtained. And Sir Cleave More obtained a decree.

Bunbury 205, 145 E.R. 648

26 January 1725/26.

Sir Cleave More having married the daughter of Mr. Edmonds of Hertfordshire, after some years cohabitation, Lady More eloped and lived in a scandalous manner with several persons, as appeared by proof. This marriage proving so unfortunate, Mr. Edmonds, by his will in 1696, devised, among other things, £6000 to three trustees in trust that the said trustees etc. should pay both the principal and interest to such person or persons as Lady More should by deed in writing subscribed by two or more witnesses appoint; and Sir Cleave or any after-taken husband [was] not to intermeddle therewith, nor the same to be subject to the debts of Sir Cleave or such after-taken husband.

After this, Lady More continued to live in the scandalous manner she had done. And Sir Cleave, on the 10th day of August 1716, met with her in a coach and took possession of her. And, on the next day, there was an agreement executed by Sir Cleave and his lady, the substance of which articles was that, in consideration Sir Cleave would permit her to live separate from him, she would settle upon him for his life £200 *per annum* and also pay him the sum of £1000 out of her separate estate, the first quarterly payment to commence three months after. And the articles being reduced into writing were subscribed by Lady More and Sir Cleave and witnessed by four persons. They met afterwards at the Middle Temple Hall on the 10th of November following, the day of the first payment, and, on the 24th of November, the said agreement was ratified by indorsement on the articles and subscribed and witnessed as before.

The morning of the day of the meeting at the Temple Hall, Lady More made her will and devised several specific legacies to Mr. Ellis, whom she also made executor and residuary legatee.

[1] E. Coke, *First Institute* (1628), ff. 52, 187.

There [was] a bill before by Lady More against Sir Cleave to set aside the articles or that he should make his election to take £300 *per annum* or according to the articles and a cross-bill by Sir Cleave against Lady More and her trustees to carry those articles into execution, which causes were heard. And the court [was] then equally divided, and so it went to the Chancellor of the Exchequer [SIR ROBERT WALPOLE], who referred them to the judges again. But before they were heard again, Lady More died.

And now, upon a revival of all the proceedings in both causes against Mr. Ellis, as executor of Lady More, *per opinionem* TOTIUS CURIAE, these articles were deemed a good execution of the power under the will of Mr. Edmonds and that Sir Cleave could not be excluded by the negative words, and, secondly, that, though the trustees were not parties to the articles, yet, in equity, it was good to bind her, it not being a direct transferring of an interest, but an appointment pursuant to a power. But a point arising whether these articles were obtained by duress, that was sent to an issue to try.

Note: Mr. Ellis was a witness to the force in the former causes. But it was now objected that he, being become the party interested by the act of Lady More herself, swore now to support a present interest, and, besides, his examination in the former cause was after the 10th of November 1716, the day he made the will, whereby he was made executor and residuary legatee. And for these reasons, though he might have been a good witness in the former causes, his deposition was now rejected.

Note: After a trial of the issue, which lasted nine hours, there was a verdict that the articles were fairly obtained without duress.

Upon the equity reserved, there was a decree for Sir Cleave, from which Mr. Ellis appealed to the House of Lords. But the decree was affirmed with £40 costs.[1]

Taussig MS. 311, vol. 2, p. 851, pl. 1

Hilary term 1725/26.

This cause was heard this day in the Exchequer chamber for the defendant and the next day heard out in the Exchequer court. And an issue was directed to try whether the agreement signed by Lady Moor for allowing Sir Cleeve [Moor] an annual rent out of her separate estate were freely and voluntarily executed by her.

N.B. Upon the trial, it was found by the jury to be freely executed.

[1] *Freeman v. More* (1728), 1 Brown P.C. 237, 1 E.R. 538.

584

Attorney General v. Randall

(Ex. 1726)

A judge will not order a writ of arrest for smuggling without an affidavit of the commission of the offense.

Bunbury 209, 145 E.R. 650

4 February 1725[/26].

Upon an information for the running of goods, a [writ of] *capias* issued as the first process, pursuant to the Stat. 8 Geo., c. 18,[1] by virtue of which the defendant was taken and put in prison. It was now moved to supersede this process because, although the information was filed, yet it was not entered in the book (so that the party might have notice) pursuant to the Rules in 1687 and 1700. And it was also said that the information was only the commencement etc. Cro. Eliz. 261, Regina v. Harris.[2] And it would be inconvenient to the subject not to have notice by the book. To which it was answered and resolved *per* TOTAM CURIAM that, to prevent the inconvenience etc., the baron never signs a warrant for a *capias* without an affidavit. And as to the Stat. 18 Eliz.,[3] there is a proviso in that Act, so that this case is not within that Statute.

And by Lord Chief Baron GILBERT and Baron PAGE, [who were] only in court, the motion was denied.

Taussig MS. 311, vol. 2, p. 858

Hilary term 1725/26.

A *capias* issued against the defendant upon the new Act, which gives it as the first process on an information, before the information was entered in the office, which is contrary to the Rule of 12 Will., Trinity, 26th June, that no process shall issue before entry in the book though the information was really on the file. Cro. Eliz. 261; 18 Eliz., ca. 5, directs that the information shall be deemed on the record from the time of its entry in the book.

N.B. The proviso is not to extend to informations exhibited by officers.

Chief Baron [GILBERT]: The Statute of Eliz. extends only to crown informers. And, if entry in the book should be necessary, it will entirely set aside the Act of Parliament. So there is no color or shadow for setting aside the process.

---

[1] Stat. 8 Geo. I, c. 18.

[2] *Regina v. Harris* (1591), Croke Eliz. 261, 78 E.R. 517.

[3] Stat. 18 Eliz. I, c. 5, s. 8 (*SR*, IV, 616).

585

Mills v. Etheridge

(Ex. 1726)

A lessee of tithes where the parson-lessor was in violation of the statute of non-residence does not have any title to the tithes.

A plaintiff who does not have a good title to receive tithes cannot have any discovery of them.

Harvard Law School MS. 1082, vol. 1, p. 259

Hilary term 1725/26.

This was a bill for tithes as lessee of [*blank*]. And the defendant pleads in bar to the discovery and account [by the] Stat. 13 Eliz., cap. 20,[1] for that the plaintiff's lessor was absent above eighty days in one year and so, by the said Statute of non-residence, the lease was void, so the plaintiff cannot recover.

Hungerford, for the plaintiff: The plea is bad in point of form as to the discovery and, likewise, it is not sufficiently averred that the plaintiff's lessor was voluntarily absent, which ought to have been, for there are some excuses which might be legal. And there are several exceptions in the Statute. And it is not averred that the plaintiff's lessor was comprehended within those exceptions.

Foley: The plea is bad because it goes to the discovery, so in a case of a *modus*, the defendant is obliged to answer to quantity, quality, and values. And so was the case of Gumley v. Fontleroy, Easter 1720.[2] So the plea covers too much.

Bunbury, for the [defendant], [said] that the plea is good and this law is made perpetual by 3 Car. I.[3] And there is no such word as 'voluntary' in the Statute. And as to the provisoes, it lies on the plaintiff to show that he comes within the exceptions. The absence need not be imputed as eighty days together. Noy 116, Adney v. Carver.[4] In the case of Gumley v. Fontleroy, there, the *modus* or agreement admits the right. But, in this case, by the Statute, it destroys the right itself.

Bootle, for the defendant: There is no occasion to aver a willful absence, for the Act has not directed it. The Statute of Hen. VIII[5] calls it a voluntary absence, but not this Statute of Elizabeth. Cro. Eliz. 100.[6] There is no occasion to show that the parson is within the provisoes, but it behooves the parson to show that he is. And there is a difference between an exception in the body of the same clause; there, the party must aver that brings his action. But where the proviso is

---

[1] Stat. 13 Eliz. I, c. 20 (*SR*, IV, 556).

[2] *Gumley v. Fontleroy* (Ex. 1720–1721), see above, Case No. 127.

[3] Stat. 3 Car. I, c. 5 (*SR*, V, 27).

[4] *Sidner v. Calver*, Noy 116, 74 E.R. 1081.

[5] Stat. 21 Hen. VIII, c. 13, s. 15 (*SR*, III, 294–295).

[6] *Collins v. Vaughan* (1588), Croke Eliz. 100, 78 E.R. 358.

a distant clause, then the defendant must show that he is within it. And by the Statute, the lease is *ipso facto* void.

Chief Baron [GILBERT]: The plea must be allowed and [the word] 'voluntary' is not within the Statute of Eliz., though it is within the Statute of Hen. VIII. In the case of provisoes, they being separate clauses, the defendant must show that he is within them. The question in this case is whether the plaintiff has a title or not. If he has not, there is no occasion for a discovery of quantities and values.

PRICE: I think that it is a good law to oblige parsons to residence. And it is laid as a penalty. No plea shall deprive the plaintiff of the benefit of a discovery. And because the defendant says that the plaintiff has no title, that ought not to debar the plaintiff of his discovery. And how can the plaintiff reply as to the exceptions. And I am not satisfied in another point, whether the defendant ought not to ascertain the particular days of absence, for this is in a case of a penalty. Statute of Recusancy.[1] So he seemed against the plea because it covered too much.

PAGE: This plea is well enough. And there is no occasion for a discovery where the plaintiff has no title, for in a case of a *modus* or agreement, the plaintiff's right is admitted *sub modo*. And I do not see any occasion to particularize the days of absence. In the case mentioned by Brother Price, that is only to particularize the months. There are no exceptions in the Statute that reach this case, which is only for letting to a curate. And here, it appears to be let to a layman.

HALE: The question does arise on the Act of Parliament. And the plea is good if true. And so he compared this case to the plea of a purchaser for a valuable consideration, and that goes to the discovery.

So the plea was allowed good, *dubitante* PRICE as to the discovery.

Taussig MS. 311, vol. 2, p. 863

Hilary term 1725/26.

The plaintiff, [lessee of Hawes, rector], brings a tithe bill as lessee of a rector and sets forth the lease so dated and prays a discovery and an account. The defendant pleads 13 Eliz., ca. 20, avoiding the lease of a non-resident and pleads that the lessor was absent eighty days.

[It was] objected to the plea first, it goes to discovery as well as relief; secondly, the plea should have been that the parson was willfully absent. The solution is the Act destroys the lease *ab initio* and, therefore, the lessee has no title at all and, therefore, it is not like the cases of a *modus* and a composition.

Secondly, there is no such word as voluntary or willful in the whole Act. And, therefore, there is no need to set it out in the plea, but it must come on the other side that the absence was involuntary, *quod fuit concessum per curiam; aliter* upon the Stat. Hen. VIII, for, there, the word 'voluntary' is inserted. If the exception is in the body of the clause, there, the party must aver the parson is not

[1] Stat. 35 Eliz. I, c. 2 (*SR*, IV, 843–846).

within the exception, otherwise as to a proviso, for that must be taken advantage of by the parson for whose benefit it was.

And the Chief Baron [Gilbert] agreed also to the distinction between this case and the case of a *modus* or a composition.

Price doubts whether the plea is good on account that it goes to the discovery as well as to the relief. And he also thinks the pleader ought to show what days the plaintiff was absent and that the allegation of eighty days' absence in the year is not sufficient.

Page agrees with the Chief Baron as to both points.

Hale also agrees.

And so the plea was allowed by three barons.

See Noy 160; Cro. Eliz. 100.

Bunbury 210, 145 E.R. 650,
1 Rayner 218, 2 Gwillim 660, 1 Eagle & Younge 806

3 February 1725[/26].

A bill was brought by the lessee of Matthew Hawes, clerk, setting forth his lease dated 4 February 1723, for the tithes etc. for 1724 and 1725 in the parish of Simpson in the County of Buckingham.

The defendant, as to the discovery of the quantity of lands he held and what tithes he had in those years and also as to the account, pleads that it appears by the plaintiff's bill that his lease was dated 4 February 1723. Then, he pleads the Stat. 13 Eliz., c. 20, touching leases of benefices and other ecclesiastical livings with cure, and he avers that Matthew Hawes, clerk, the lessor, was absent from his benefice eighty days and more in one year since the lease and before the filing of the bill, *viz.*, in 1724, that the church of Simpson is not impropriate and that it is a benefice or ecclesiastical promotion with cure, and, therefore, by such non-residence and by virtue of the said Act, the lease was absolutely void.

Now, upon arguing this plea, which was drawn by myself, Baron Price was for overruling the plea because it covered the discovery, which, according to the usage of the court, a plaintiff was entitled to, whatever exemption or discharge a defendant might have.

(And at the time of drawing the plea, I [Bunbury] was of that opinion and so informed my client.)

But the Lord Chief Baron [Gilbert], Page, and Hale were of opinion that the plea was good, extending even to discovery, because it amounted to an absolute incapacity in the plaintiff, which differed from the cases where the plaintiff was entitled of common right. And there is no necessity to aver that the absence was voluntary, for, if it was otherwise, it lay upon the plaintiff to show it, or to aver that the absence was eighty days together. So the plea was allowed.

586

Attorney General, *ex rel.* Bowling v. Bradley

(Ex. 1726)

A writ of extent can be had where the crown's debt is in danger of being lost.

Harvard Law School MS. 1082, vol. 1, p. 260

Hilary term 1725/26.

Mr. *Bunbury* [moved] to set aside a [writ of] extent, for, in this case, Bowling gave security by a recognizance for £4437 with two others and Bowling pays the money. This security was upon account of a writ of delivery 21 April upon an inquisition he obtains an immediate extent against Bradley and the inquisition then found goods to the value of £77 8s. 6d. and this proceeding is against the Rules of 15 Car. I and 35 Car. II, for that Bowling was no receiver, accountant, or farmer and this was only for the performance of covenants, and process of *scire facias* ought first to issue before the extent. And this was without a motion in open court. To find debts without a specialty, only a *scire facias* ought to issue. Rules of 35 Car. II. The extent was obtained on a false suggestion. And Bowling was no debtor because he had received the money of [. . .]. Hardres 404; Rex v. Taylour and Newman, Michaelmas 1723.[1]

Mr. *Philip Ward*, for Bowling: It must be admitted that this recognizance was forfeited and, after such forfeiture, it becomes a debt due to the crown. Sir Thomas Cecil's Case, Coke Rept.[2]

[To the] objection that no debts in aid can be found upon a simple contract without a motion in open court, [he] answered the second extent is by a motion in court and the Rules of 15 Car. I are not always strictly pursued.

[To the] objection that it appears the recognizance was satisfied, [he] answered but that was afterwards.

Bootle: They come too late to set aside an extent when the money has been paid in. And the recognizance to the crown is in the nature of a statute staple.

Chief Baron [GILBERT]: The first extent was regular, and the Rules cannot control an act of Parliament. And wherever there is a debtor to the crown, the usual practice of late has been to take out a commission to find debts and to avoid clandestine commissions of bankruptcy. And such Rules of 15 Car. I have been often dispensed with. And why is not a commission upon the first extent as good as a commission to find debts? As to the objection that the money was repaid, but that was not until afterwards.

---

[1] *Attorney General v. Poultney* (1665), Hardres 403, 404, 145 E.R. 519; *Rex v. Taylor* (Ex. 1723), see above, Case No. 394.

[2] *Cecil's Case* (1597), 7 Coke Rep. 18, 77 E.R. 440.

Bunbury replies: The inquisition is not well founded because there was no motion in court. And he insists on the Rules. The proceedings upon a commission are not applicable in this case because they have not proceeded in this manner.

Chief Baron: In the case of Rex v. Newman, there was a fraud by voluntarily entering into the bond, and there is no occasion for a motion. The old rule is right that extents should not issue but in the case of necessity, and that is supplied by an affidavit. But in all cases where the debt is in danger of being lost, an immediate extent should issue.

Price: They come too late to set aside an extent after an execution is executed though there might have been pleas to the inquisitions and *venditioni exponas.*

Page: the Rules of 15 Car. I were not intended to hazard the king's debts.

And, since it appears the debt was in danger and the king cannot come into the commission of bankruptcy, so the court decreed the motion and ordered Bowling his costs.

Taussig MS. 311, vol. 2, p. 847, pl. 1

Hilary term 1725/26. Bradley v. Bowling.

A motion [was made] to set aside a [writ of] immediate extent against Bradley, on which Bowling had got in a debt due from Bradley to him on a simple contract. See the Master's report among the papers of this term.

587

Geale v. Winter

(Ex. 1726)

A modus decimandi *in lieu of tithes in kind when established by a court is* res adjudicata.

Bunbury 211, 145 E.R. 650,
1 Rayner 219, 4 Gwillim 1584, 1 Eagle & Younge 806

11 February 1725[/26].

A bill for tithes as vicar of Bishop's Lyddiat in the County of Somerset sets forth a former bill in this court in 1717 and a decree in 1718 for these tithes after an issue to try *modus*es and a verdict for the plaintiff.[1]

The defendant pleads that, in Trinity term 1721, he preferred his bill in the Court of Chancery to establish the *modus*es etc., that issues were directed and found for the *modus*es, and it was decreed thereupon to be established, and he pleads the same verdict and decree in bar of the plaintiff's now demand.

And the plea was allowed *per* totam curiam.

[1] *Geale v. Winter* (Ex. 1719), see above, Case No. 79.

588

Anonymous

(Ex. 1726)

In this case for an unlawful importation, the defense of manufacturing and thus changing the nature of the goods imported was not allowed.

Bunbury 212, 145 E.R. 651

At the sittings after Hilary Term 1725[/26].

Upon the trial of an information for importing coconuts from Holland, not being the place of their growth etc. contrary to the Act of Navigation,[1] it appeared that the goods were only husks and shells and some little of the nut mixed with them, which they did in Holland, separating the husks from the nut by putting them over the fire. And this the defendant pretended was a manufacturing of the coconuts and so excepted out of the Act and that this was used only in water, which the French refugees drank.

But it was held by Lord Chief Baron GILBERT this is a plain fraud and no manufacturing.

589

Woodhouse v. Price

(Ex. 1726–1727)

An action lies for neglecting a duty to keep a watercourse clean.

'Neglecting rules of pleading is a worse inconvenience than a particular injury in a particular case.'

Taussig MS. 311, vol. 2, p. 880

Easter term 1726.

This case was argued by Mr. *Chauncy* and Mr. *Bootle.* The cases cited by Mr. *Chauncy* were Cro. Eliz. 445; 2 Lev. 163; Tenant v. Goldwin, Modern Cases 311; 1 Ventr. 274, St. John v. Moody; Salkeld 21.[2]

---

[1] Stat. 12 Car. II, c. 18 (*SR*, V, 246–250).

[2] *Upton v. Basset* (1595), Croke Eliz. 445, 78 E.R. 685; *Welby v. Herbert* (1676), 2 Levinz 163, 83 E.R. 500, also 3 Keble 606, 609, 84 E.R. 905, 907; *Tenant v. Golding* (1704), 6 Modern 311, 87 E.R. 1051, 1 Salkeld 21, 360, 91 E.R. 20, 314, also 2 Salkeld 770, 91 E.R. 634, 2 Lord Raymond 1089, 92 E.R. 222, 3 Lord Raymond 324, 92 E.R. 712, Holt K.B. 500, 90 E.R. 1175; *St. John v. Moody* (1675), 1 Ventris 274, 86 E.R. 184, also 2 Levinz 148, 83 E.R. 492, 3 Keble 528, 531, 84 E.R. 860, 862.

Bootle, contra, took notice that, in the case of 1 Ventr. 274, it was said that, before 7 King James I, the usage had been to prescribe, but not since, that this action was for a negligence in not repairing the channel, that a reversioner may have an action for the damage to his reversion and the possessor for the damage [to] his possession. Biddlesford v. Onslow, 3 Lev. 309, tenants and occupiers and not tenants or occupiers.[1]

Page, Baron: Between landlord and tenant, the tenant at will is not obliged to repair, but, as to others, he is, for the person who is prejudiced by not repairing cannot tell whether he is a tenant or an occupier.

Chief Baron [Gilbert]: Where owners are on the land, the charge is rightly laid on tenants and occupiers.

Adjornatur.

Harvard Law School MS. 1082, vol. 1, p. 268, pl. 2

Easter term 1726.

Chancey took exception upon a demurrer to a declaration for that the declaration is that the tenants and occupiers ought to repair the watercourse under the stable and that an occupier was too slight an interest. Cro. Eliz. 445; 2 Levinz 163; 6 Rept.;[2] 1 Ventris 274, St. John v. Moody.

Bootle, for the plaintiff: To maintain the declaration, ever since King James's time, *tenentes vel occupatores* is good. A base possession is sufficient to maintain the action, and an action will lie against a tenant whose duty it was to cleanse. And there is a difference between a prescriptive right to fix a demand and a discharge.

Chancy replies: This does not come by way of discharge or easement, but to ground a demand on the land by charging the freehold.

Price: It seems a repugnant prescription.

Chief Baron [Gilbert]: The reason in St. John v. Moody was because it was betwixt a landlord and a tenant. A tenant supposes a seisin. See Golding's Case in Salkeld.[3] Where there is an onus upon the land, it is good against tenant and occupier. Non-feasance is a misfeasance.

Taussig MS. 311, vol. 2, p. 1029

31 January 1726[/27].

Serjeant *Branthwaite*, for the defendant: Of late times, a general declaration on the possession is good against a wrongdoer as possessed of a common or watercourse etc. But then, such action must be brought against a wrongdoer, but not against the owner. Starr and Rokesby, Salk. 335, 360.[4]

---

1 *Bedingfield v. Onslow* (1685), 3 Levinz 209, 83 E.R. 654.

2 *Smith v. Gateward* (1607), 6 Coke Rep. 59, 77 E.R. 344, also Croke Jac. 152, 79 E.R. 133.

3 *Tenant v. Golding* (1704), *ut supra*.

4 *Star v. Rooksby* (1710), 1 Salkeld 335, 91 E.R. 295, 11 Modern 168, 88 E.R. 967.

Bootle: St. John and Moody, 1 Ventr. 274, and 3 Salk. 21, Tenant v. Goldney; Mod. Cases 211; 2 Ventr. 186. There is no distinction between the action being brought against a wrongdoer and against a lawful owner. This is the same case as the case of fences. 1 Lutw. 119[1] states the case of Tennant and Goldeney from his own report of the case, which he said was ill stated in Salkeld, *ubi supra*.

Branthwaite replies: A trespass is to the possession, and, upon this very principle, the case was determined. There was no annoyance from the defendant's ground or possession, as appears from the declaration, which did appear in the case of Tennant and Goldney.

Chief Baron [Pengelly]: Possession against a wrongdoer will certainly do. Two may declare against the owner of the soil, out of the privilege, where the profits arise. So are the cases of Sands and Trefusis, in Cro. Car.; Strode and Burk, 4 or 3 Mod.[2] In the case, this is an easement in the plaintiff and a duty in the defendant to repair. F.N.B., *curia claudenda*; Rastall's *Entries* 172; F.N.B. 127, *debet et solet reparare tenentes et occupatores debent et solent* is a formal and direct charge.[3] And so it was held in the case of Starr and Rokeby. And in this case, here is a right laid; an injury and damage are also charged. In the case of Starr and Rokeby, the court held that the plaintiff might have [an action of] trespass or case. In the case of a common, though it is against the owner of the soil, the practice is to declare that *communiam habere debet*.

Carter: There was a general demurrer, and so the fact in the declaration is admitted.

Baron Comyns: The plaintiff has sufficiently entitled himself by *debet* etc. If the defendant makes a title in the pleading, the plaintiff must reply and make a title whether there is enough in the declaration to charge the defendant to repair where, of common right, the defendant is to repair. The charge is sufficient where it does not appear that the defendant has any advantage for the current. There is no consideration for this repair, though so far as the watercourse goes under his stable, he is obliged to cleanse the watercourse *ad et subter*, which lays an obligation to go into the plaintiff's ground. But perhaps, this is cured by the assignment of the breach, which is tied up to the what repair *subter*. It is an entire prescription. [Query] whether there can be judgment for the plaintiff, for it might be perhaps an estoppel afterwards to the defendant to say that he is not to repair *ad* as well as *subter* the channel of the sink.

By the Chief Baron: It is not said the channel or the sink goes from the well, but this I apprehend is a mistake. Query of the showing of consideration.

Hale, baron: *Ad stabulum* may signify at the stable and not to the stable.

---

[1] *Blockley v. Slater* (1693), 1 Lutwyche 119, 125 E.R. 63.

[2] *Sands v. Trefuses* (1640), Croke Car. 575, 79 E.R. 1094; *Strode v. Birt* (1695), 4 Modern 411, 418, 87 E.R. 473, 476, also 12 Modern 97, 88 E.R. 1190, Skinner 621, 90 E.R. 279, Comberbach 370, 90 E.R. 534, 3 Salkeld 12, 91 E.R. 661, 1 Comyns 7, 92 E.R. 930.

[3] W. Rastell, *Collection of Entries*; A. Fitzherbert, *Natura Brevium*.

This is to be spoken to again next term.

Harvard Law School MS. 1082, vol. 2, p. 14, pl. 2

Hilary term 1726/27.

The plaintiff brings an action setting forth that all the occupiers of the stable in the possession of the defendant had time out of mind cleansed and repaired the drain running under the same and that the defendant had neglected so to do and, thereby, the watercourse of the plaintiff ran over and did damage to the plaintiff's cellar. The defendant demurs generally, and the plaintiff joins in demurrer.

Serjeant *Branthwaite*, for the defendant: I may admit that such a declaration generally is good against a wrongdoer. And the later resolutions have been in favor of such general pleading against the wrongdoer. But that is not this case, for there is a difference between the possession against a wrongdoer and one that claims a right in another's soil and the owner of it. But this is not against the wrongdoer, but a person that has the right. And in such a case as this, there must be something particularly set forth. And the declaration is too general. And the question is who has the right to compel this watercourse to be cleansed, whether the defendant is who has no interest in this watercourse. Salkeld 335, 360.

Bootle, for the plaintiff: Here is a sufficient admission by the demurrer as to the possession. Then it is against a wrongdoer. He objected 1 Rept. 27 [. . .]; Tenant v. Golding, Salkeld 21; 2 Ventris 186; 5 Modern, last case.[1] And there is no difference between a wrongdoer and a person that has a right. About fences or a way, [see] 1 Ventris 275. In that case, it was against the owner of the soil; 1 Lutwyche 119, Lockley v. Slater.[2] It being laid by presumption, it is good. And the question as to the Serjeants' Case is only whether an action of trespass would lie.

Serjeant *Branthwaite* replies: The difference in the case in Salkeld is with me. It does not appear that the plaintiff has any title to the watercourse or that this was contiguous to the plaintiff's estate.

Chief Baron [Pengelly]: I think that this case does come within the later resolutions, for, though, formerly, there was a difference between a wrongdoer and a person claiming right how far the defendant should be charged without setting forth a particular right. Sands v. Trefuses, in Cro. Car.; Strode v. Bush, 4 Modern.[3]

This is a charge, which is stronger than having an easement, for which the plaintiff may declare generally.

---

1 *Tenant v. Golding* (1704), *ut supra*; *Warren v. Sainthill* (1690), 2 Ventris 185, 186, 86 E.R. 383, 384; *Attorney General v. Prynne* (1690), 5 Modern 459, 87 E.R. 764, also Holt K.B. 362, 90 E.R. 1100, *sub nom. Rex v. Abraham*, Comberbach 141, 90 E.R. 392, 1 Shower K.B. 49, 89 E.R. 440, *sub nom. Rex v. Berchet*, 1 Shower K.B. 106, 89 E.R. 480.

2 *Blockley v. Slater* (1693), 1 Lutwyche 119, 125 E.R. 63.

3 *Sands v. Trefuses* (1640), *ut supra*; *Strode v. Birt* (1695), *ut supra*.

[To the] objection of no showing a title to the watercourse, [he] answered there is no occasion only to set forth *cursus currere [. . .]*. Possession is sufficient. And the charge is prescriptive.

There is a duty sufficiently charged on the defendant. And so it is like the case of Tenant v. Golding. Rastal 172; Fitzherbert 127. *Tenentes et occupatores* is a sufficient charge. And any man that receives the injury may bring the action.

The court did not go upon the distinction taken by Branthwaite, that it might be either by trespass or a special action.

Baron Carter: The demurrer admits the declaration. And there is a sufficient tort laid.

Baron Comyns: Part has not been spoken to, whether there is a sufficient title laid against a wrongdoer. If a person brings a general action [and] the defendant insists upon a title, then it is too late. Stroud v. Burle.[1] I do not know whether there is a sufficient charge in the declaration against the defendant, for, of common right, if it is not to be done and if there is no common right, then a particular title should be showed, for it does not appear that the defendant had any benefit by this watercourse, which should be particularly set forth that *ratione inde* the plaintiff ought to cleanse. If it was to keep the watercourse clean under the stable, there, it might have obliged the defendant of common right to cleanse the whole watercourse.

So he doubted whether this being an entire prescription and it was only assigned part by way of breach whether the defendant is not estopped to say that he is not obliged to cleanse the watercourse to the stable. I take a difference between where it is of common right and where there is a particular onus.

Chief Baron: There is a prescription to a way; no consideration is mentioned but to amend the way.

Hale: The declaration seems well framed. I cannot distinguish the case from Tenant v. Goulding.

[The case is] to be spoken to again.

Taussig MS. 311, vol. 2, p. 1034 [bis]

5th May 1727.

First, he ought to have laid a title because it was a demand against common right. This objection arose from the case of Strode and Birt, in [an action of] trespass. If he lay a charge on a terre tenant against a wrongdoer, Tennant and Golding, the difference is between a tenant and a wrongdoer. Starr and Rokeby. In this case, the defendant is not a wrongdoer. By common law, he is no wrongdoer. This is a prescription not in itself a prescription without a consideration. 6 Mod., Cudden and Eastwick;[2] a prescription must have a lawful commencement. This

[1] *Strode v. Birt* (1695), *ut supra*.

[2] *Cudden v. Estwick* (1704), 6 Modern 123, 87 E.R. 881, also 1 Salkeld 143, 192, 91 E.R. 132, 174, Holt K.B. 433, 90 E.R. 1138.

prescription carries no benefit to the defendant. Bro., *Abr.*, Presc., 49, A. and B. ought to repair; 78, *ratione tenurae*, he ought to repair.[1] A prescription for a toll; 1 Mod. 104; 1 Ventr. 71, 1 Mod. 47, no benefit to the defendant.[2] Secondly, the plaintiff is at no charge in the case of a toll traverse. Thirdly, it could not have a reasonable commencement. No [action of] trespass [lies] for entering a trench in another's soil. Secondly, Rolle's *Abr.*; Moor 644, 682; 2 Cro. 121; 1 Ventr. 45, unity of possession.[3] A prescription in itself is not good as laid in tenants and occupiers. Cro. Eliz. 435, 665; Holbet and Warner; 2 Lev. 163,[4] farmers to find ale and cake not only *ad et subter stabula*; so they insist *ad* is *terminus ad stabula* and the *terminus a quo*.

Reply: The word '*ad*' must signify 'to'.

Lord Chief Baron [Pengelly]: The point of showing the title settled is now past controversy. And there is no difference between a tenant of the land and a stranger. Both are equally wrongdoers; so possession only is necessary. If you would force the plaintiff to show a title, you must show your own title and pray judgment whether you should answer further without the plaintiff's showing his title. *Tenentes* is good in general because the plaintiff does not know the particular title, but not in the case of occupiers because occupiers' acts cannot bind the land. There is no necessity to allege a consideration in a prescription because it is supposed that there is a consideration unless the contrary plainly appears upon the face of the prescription. He agrees there may be a reasonable commencement. Secondly, it gives a title to the defendant to this watercourse and the plaintiff cannot stop it nor put down any filth in it. And a claim of a watercourse implies that the claimer shall repair and cleanse it. So is the very resolution in the case of 1 Ventr. The breach assigned is only in not cleaning it under the stable. And, if so, then, the case of Tenant and Golden [applies] for anything that appears in this declaration. The spring may be close to the stable into and through the channel and *subter* may be as right as 'to'. And generally speaking, where '*ad*' signifies

---

[1] YB 27 Edw. III, Lib. Ass., f. 134, pl. 8, Brooke, Abr., *Prescription*, pl. 49 (1353); YB Mich. 21 Edw. IV, f. 38, pl. 3, Brooke, Abr., *Prescription*, pl. 78 (1481).

[2] *Warren v. Prideaux* (1674), 1 Modern 104, 86 E.R. 766, also *sub nom. Prideaux v. Warne*, T. Raymond 232, 83 E.R. 121, 2 Levinz 96, 83 E.R. 466, 1 Freeman 355, 89 E.R. 264, 3 Keble 249, 275, 84 E.R. 704, 718; *Haspurt v. Wills* (1670), 1 Ventris 71, 86 E.R. 50, 1 Modern 47, 86 E.R. 722, also Lincoln's Inn MS. Misc. 500, f. 96, pl. 2 (Edward Ward's reports), 1 Siderfin 454, 82 E.R. 1214, 2 Keble 624, 665, 84 E.R. 392, 418.

[3] *Guy v. Brown* (1601), Moore K.B. 644, 72 E.R. 813; *Brown v. Nichols*, Moore K.B. 682, 72 E.R. 837; *Nicholas v. Chamberlain* (1606), Croke Jac. 121, 79 E.R. 105; *Pomfret v. Ricroft* (1669), 1 Ventris 26, 44, 86 E.R. 18, 32, also 1 Siderfin 429, 82 E.R. 1198, 2 Keble 505, 543, 569, 84 E.R. 317, 340, 357, 1 Williams Saunders 321, 85 E.R. 454.

[4] *Stile v. Butts* (1595), Croke Eliz. 434, 78 E.R. 675; *Holbetts v. Warner* (1623), 2 Rolle Rep. 288, 81 E.R. 806; *Welby v. Herbert* (1676), *ut supra*.

'to' or 'unto', it is '*usque ad*' upon a prescription for ways. The intermediate ground which is his own is not part of his prescription. 2 Rolle's Rep. 397, Palmer 387.[1]

HALE: The prescription is good though the charge was laid on the defendant to repair a *fontem usque ad*, for there is a benefit if he will make use of it by keeping the channel clean. [It is a] spring or fountain rather than a well, for a well is to be dug. But it is more true and natural to understand the word '*ad*' in the sense of 'at', though, in the other place of *fluere* and *currere*, it signifies 'to' because these words '*fluere*' and '*currere*' are words of motion. But the words '*refluere*' and '*ennudare*' are not so. Therefore, the word '*ad*' here may signify 'at'. *Ad Portam Hoctos ad Tiberim*. And the sense seems to be confirmed in that part that assigns the breach.

CARTER was of the same opinion. It is barely a possessory action. On a demurrer, if it is well laid, it is confessed if not contrary to common sense. It implies a consideration, for it is impossible to show the particular consideration at this time of day. A good consideration is by the water running there, but here it may carry away the filth of the stables. It is only to be understood in the sense of 'at', though in the first place it is meant 'to'.

COMYNS: Neglecting rules of pleading is a worse inconvenience than a particular injury in a particular case. Nothing is plainer than that the first objection is quite out of the case. And it has been overruled by a multitude of authorities. Second, because the charge ought to be extended as far as can be because the defendant has demurred and it is really a general demurrer because it gives no light to the plaintiff. To and under the stable and from the stable to a street in a presteigne does not lay the charge on the defendant to repair the channel of the whole watercourse, but only *ad et subter stabulum praedictum*. Nonfeasance does not import a wrong. Therefore, there must be a consideration laid, and the bare alleging of a prescription is not sufficient. Whether a consideration must be shown, Smith v. Shepheard,[2] a toll traverse implies a consideration, but the consideration must be shown for a toll through. Rolle's *Abr.*, 562; Jones 162; Syd. 654 or 254; 1 Mod. 47, 104; 4 Mod. 320.[3] Though it does run under the stable, it does not necessarily imply that it is for his benefit. But he thinks *ad et subter* signifies 'at'. So then, the repairing is confined at and under the stable. So he concludes for the plaintiff, for there is a reasonable ground for repairing under and at the stable, for he could not have built the stable without the consent of the owner of the watercourse.

[1] *Slowman v. West* (1623), 2 Rolle Rep. 397, 81 E.R. 876, Palmer 387, 81 E.R. 1136.

[2] *Smith v. Shepherd* (1599), Moore K.B. 574, 72 E.R. 768, Croke Eliz. 710, 78 E.R. 945.

[3] *Anonymous* (1615), 2 Rolle, Abr., *Trespas*, pl. G, 12, p. 562; *Haspurt v. Wills* (1670), *ut supra*; *Warren v. Prideaux* (1674), *ut supra*; *Warrington v. Mosely* (1694), 4 Modern 319, 87 E.R. 419, also Comberbach 295, 90 E.R. 487, Holt K.B. 673, 90 E.R. 1272.

Harvard Law School MS. 1082, vol. 2, p. 23, pl. 2

Easter term 1727.

This is a declaration wherein the plaintiff declares that the tenants of the stable in the possession of the defendant used to cleanse the si[. . .] watercourse. And, to this declaration, the defendant demurs.

Wilbraham, for the defendant: It is a demand against common right. Strode v. Burt, 7 Will. III, 4 Modern 418. There is not a proper title set forth in the plaintiff. And, therefore, the defendant cannot be a wrongdoer. St. John v. Moody, in 1 Ventris and Levinz and 6 Modern 313; 1 Salkeld 336, Stam v. Rookby.[1]

The prescription is not good as laid in the tenants and occupiers. 6 Modern 124. Prescriptions ought to have a good commencement. 6 Coke 61; Brooke, *Abridgment*, tit. 'prescription', 49, pl. 6. The defendant has no benefit from this. 1 Levinz 98; 1 Modern 104; Raymond 232; 1 Ventris 71; 1 Modern 47. This is a charge without any consideration or benefit laid for the defendant. And the same reason holds in the demands of tolls through. Moore 574; Cro. Eliz. 710. Suppose one person had been possessed of both houses. 2 Rolle, *Abridgment*, 567; Moore 664, 682; 2 Cro. 121; 1 San. 323; 1 Ventris 45.

It is not good, as this prescription is laid in tenants and occupiers *ad et subter stabulum*. Cro. Eliz. 435 or 445; 2 Croke 665; 2 Levinz 163; 6 Coke 60. *Ad* supposes a fountainhead. So he prayed judgment for the defendant.

Philip Ward, for the plaintiff: This, it must be remembered, is a general demurrer. As to the last objection of *ad vel subter stabulum*, [he] responded the word '*ad*' signifies 'at' and 'under', and not the course leading from the fountainhead. Moore 644; 1 Ventris 45.

A man is no trespasser for going into another man's ground to do a lawful act. From the [year] 8 Eliz. [1565 x 1566] to this time, the plaintiff, in an action upon the case, is not obliged to lay a special title. And in an action upon the case, [it] is a possessory action. Dyer 250, pl. 88; 1 Cro. 198;[2] More v. Elne, 1 Levinz 247, 466. In this action, it is only to recover damages. Yelverton 75; Cro. Jac. 43, 122, Dent v. Oliver.[3] Possession is sufficient. Babington's Case, Rolle Rept. 13; 2 Rolle Rept. 288; Cro. Jac. 499, 500, 575; 1 Ventris 174, St. John v. Moody, 2 Levinz 148; 1 Ventris 319; 2 Ventris 186; 1 Lutwyche 119; 4 Modern 418; Salkeld 360, 336, Tenant v. Goldney.[4]

---

[1] *St. John v. Moody* (1675), *ut supra*; *Star v. Rooksby* (1710), *ut supra*.

[2] *Yevance v. Holcomb* (1566), 2 Dyer 250, 73 E.R. 553, also 3 Leonard 13, 74 E.R. 509, 4 Leonard 167, 224, 74 E.R. 799, 835; *Leverett v. Townsend* (1590), Croke Eliz. 198, 78 E.R. 454, also 2 Leonard 184, 74 E.R. 463, 3 Leonard 263, 74 E.R. 674.

[3] *Faldo v. Ridge* (1605), Yelverton 74, 80 E.R. 51; *Dent v. Oliver* (1604–1606), Croke Jac. 43, 122, 79 E.R. 35, 106.

[4] *Babington's Case* (1614), 1 Rolle Rep. 13, 81 E.R. 292; *Holbetts v. Warner* (1623), 2 Rolle Rep. 288, 81 E.R. 806; *Thomson v. Field* (1618), Croke Jac. 499, 500, 79 E.R. 426; *Monk v. Butler* (1620), Croke Jac. 574, 79 E.R. 491; *St. John v. Moody* (1675), *ut supra*;

It is good to say 'tenants and occupiers time out of mind have and ought to repair'.

[To the] objection of 'occupiers', [he] responded, in the case of an easement or by way of discharge, it is good. 1 Salkeld 336, Stam v. Rokby; 'tenants or occupiers' is bad; Carter Rept. 32.[1] But it is good in this case.

[To the] objection of no consideration laid, [he] responded prescriptions carry a consideration with them, so there is no occasion to lay one. Where there is no apparent contradiction that appears on the face of it, no consideration is laid for repairing hedges. But the defendant has a benefit by the water if a consideration is necessary. And this may have a reasonable commencement.

And so he prayed judgment for the plaintiff.

Wilbraham: *Ad* must signify something or else *subter* would do it *a forte*. And the question is whether the defendant is obliged to do this of common right. But I admit the cases cited by Mr. Ward. But these cases are in actions grounded on the possession against wrongdoers. And these subsequent cases will have an influence. Burt v. Strode; Tenant v. Goldney; Starr v. Rookby. It does not appear to be the defendant's duty to cleanse this sink and no advantage can arise hereby to the defendant. And, therefore, this is a void prescription.

Chief Baron [PENGELLY]: This being a possessory action, I think that there is no occasion to set forth the title to recover damages. And so are all the cases. And if the defendant does omit to do what he ought to do, he is to be taken as a wrongdoer. Oswell v. Fryar. Possession is sufficient at first. If the defendant shows a title, then it will put the plaintiff to show his *tenentes et occupatores* is good. Starr v. Rook. [. . .] It is unnecessary to allege a consideration in a prescription unless there is an apparent contradiction on the face of it. No consideration is laid in a *curia claudenda* or repairing of hedges. This gives a title to the defendant to have a watercourse to and under the stable. The breach is only laid *subter* the stable, for, what appears by this declaration, the plaintiff's yard and stable may be all adjoining and no distance of place. *Ad* is expressed that no different intermediate ground appears. Upon a prescription to have a way, if there is an intermediate ground, it is only to be implied to have a way over that part that he has a power over. 2 Rolle Rept. 397; Palmer 387.

HALE: The prescription seems well laid. And there may be a benefit arising to the defendant by the flowing of the water. And there is no necessity to make *ad* relate to the fountainhead. *Ad* may only be a description to the place.

CARTER agrees. The defendant is a wrongdoer.

Saunders v. Williams (1677), 1 Ventris 319, 86 E.R. 206, also 3 Keble 820, 84 E.R. 1031; *Warren v. Sainthill* (1690), 2 Ventris 185, 186, 86 E.R. 383, 384; *Blockley v. Slater* (1693), 1 Lutwyche 119, 125 E.R. 63; *Strode v. Birt* (1695), 4 Modern 411, 418, 87 E.R. 473, 476; *Tenant v. Golding* (1704), *ut supra*; *Star v. Rooksby* (1710), 1 Salkeld 335, 91 E.R. 295.

[1] *Star v. Rooksby* (1710), *ut supra*; *Gold v. Barnsly* (1665), Carter 30, 124 E.R. 805.

Comyns: I would not be too curious in carrying the nicety of pleading too far. But yet rules of pleading are necessary. And if such rules are totally set aside, it may be of dangerous consequence. I do not think there is any weight in the first objection as to the prescription, for this is an action founded on the possession. The charge upon the defendant ought to be extended as far as possible, for, by the demurrer, the defendant has admitted everything. The charge is only for the defendant's cleansing *ad et subter stabulum*. And the damages prayed are only for the want of cleansing *subter stabulum*. And there should be some reason assigned that the defendant is obliged to do this. 4 Modern 320; Smith v. Shepherd; Rolle, *Abridgment*, 562; Jones 162; Siderfin 154; 1 Modern 71; 1 Ventris 71.[1] But at last, he said that judgment ought to be given for the plaintiff for it does imply some benefit to the defendant by cleansing the watercourse.

590

Anonymous

(Ex. 1726)

A pleading can give dates and sums in numerals as well as in letters.

Taussig MS. 311, vol. 2, p. 846, pl. 1

Monday, 24th January 1725[/26], being the first day of term. Gilbert, Chief Baron, Price, Page, and Hale *praesentibus*.

Foley moved to suppress an answer for that the dates and sums therein mentioned were written in figures.

Sed per curiam: In Latin proceedings, Roman figures are allowed. Therefore, by parity of reason, English figures are good in English proceedings.

591

Priestly v. Clarke

(Ex. 1726)

A new trial can be granted where evidence was improperly admitted at the first trial.

[1] *Warrington v. Mosely* (1694), 4 Modern 319, 87 E.R. 419, also Comberbach 295, 90 E.R. 487, Holt K.B. 673, 90 E.R. 1272; *Smith v. Shepherd* (1599), *ut supra*; *Rex v. Corporation of Boston* (1627), W. Jones 162, 82 E.R. 87; *Rex v. Leginham* (1670), 1 Modern 71, 288, 86 E.R. 740, 890, also 1 Ventris 97, 104, 86 E.R. 67, 72, T. Raymond 193, 205, 83 E.R. 101, 108, 1 Levinz 299, 83 E.R. 416, 2 Keble 687, 697, 84 E.R. 432, 439; *Haspurt v. Wills* (1670), *ut supra*.

Taussig MS. 311, vol. 2, p. 847, pl. 2

Hilary term 1725/26.

Mr. Drax, in his lifetime after his return from Jamaica upon visiting at Mr. Clarke's, whose wife was a cousin, observed she had no plate. And so he sent in some plate he then had by him to their house and had bespoken some new plate from the goldsmith, which was marked with his own arms and also sent in to Mrs. Clarke. There were three several deliveries of the plate from May to the end of August. Sometime after this and before his death, he made his will and gave his cousin Smith all his plate undisposed of. And the question was between Clarke and Smith. And by an English bill in this court, [the question] is whether the plate sent in to Mr. Clarke was a gift or a loan only.

And several witnesses were examined on both sides who spoke to declarations of Mr. Drax both precedent to the delivery of the plate and subsequent to the delivery of the last part thereof, *viz.* after August to the time of his death as well as to what fell from him at Mrs. Clarke's during the time the plate was delivering. And a young Negro woman was examined in the cause about twelve or thirteen years old. She was sent over after her examination into Jamaica not being examined on the part of the plaintiff, Mr. Smith.

The court, upon hearing the cause in equity, being doubtful whether the plate delivered to Clarke was a gift or a loan, directed an action of trover wherein the executors of Drax, *viz.* Priestly and Tobtoft, should be the plaintiffs and Clarke the defendant and the defendant was to admit the property to have been in Drax. At the trial, the plaintiffs would have given evidence of a declaration made by Drax after all the plate was delivered to Clarke.

But the Chief Baron [GILBERT] ruled it against them, that they should not and so, being prevented in this part of their intended evidence and the defendant producing a servant maid who lived at Mr. Clarke's at the time of the plate's being sent in and delivered, who had not been examined on either side in the cause in equity and swore very strong for the defendant, the jury found a verdict for the defendant.

And this day, the plaintiff moved for a new trial on the point of evidence and also produced affidavits of the character of the woman servant who was examined at the trial. As to the point of overturning the evidence, the plaintiffs' counsel admitted it was right as the action was in trover and so the executors were plaintiffs, and, therefore, they could not give in evidence what their testator said after the delivery of the plate, but this difficulty upon them proceeding from trying the point in doubt with the court in a formed action of trover and not upon a feigned action and the trial being for *ad informandum conscientiam* and the surprise upon them in producing a new witness not examined whose character was impeached on reading the affidavits, the court saw fit to give way to another trial of the question.

N.B. All the court thought the Chief Baron's opinion in point of evidence was right.

And Page thought what Drax had said after the delivery could not be given in evidence in any writing whatsoever. He said he had ruled it that, where there were two bills of sale, the vendor is not to be a witness to set up or establish either of the bills of sale.

N.B. The reason why what Drax said of the plate during the time the same was in delivery, *viz.* between May and September, was, as My Lord said, because [*blank*] *tua nomen imponit operi tuo.*

592

Mayor of Yarmouth v. Andrews

(Ex. 1726)

The issue of whether a local custom as to a trade is inconsistent with a statute should be raised by an answer rather than a plea in a suit in equity.

Taussig MS. 311, vol. 2, p. 860

Hilary term 1725/26.

The Town of Yarmouth brings a bill to establish their custom concerning their herring trade. And the defendant pleaded several statutes, *viz.* 35 Edw. III, an ordinance for herrings; 5 Eliz., ca. 5, politic constitutions for the maintenance of the Navy; 39 Eliz., ca. 10; 10 & 11 Will. III, ca. 24.[1]

The court did not think fit at this time to determine the point whether the acts of Parliament were inconsistent with and consequently destructive of the customs alleged in the bill. And, therefore, they proposed [that] the plea should stand as an answer with liberty to except to it, and so it did.

593

Anonymous

(Ex. 1726)

The absence of a material witness is a good cause for a continuance.

The question in this case was whether the absent witness was actually a material one.

[1] Stat. 35 Edw. III (*SR*, I, 369–370); Stat. 5 Eliz. I, c. 5 (*SR*, IV, 422–428); Stat. 39 Eliz. I, c. 10 (*SR*, IV, 910–911); Stat. 11 Will. III, c. 14 (*SR*, VII, 603).

Taussig MS. 311, vol. 2, p. 865, pl. 1

Hilary term 1725/26.

Saying of a witness that he is the most material witness is not saying he is a material witness, and so it is not a cause of putting off a trial. But the Attorney [General *Yorke*] consented upon undertaking to try it next term at all events.

594

Attorney General v. Reeves

(Ex. 1726)

The term 'unload' includes taking away the goods from the shore after they have been put off the ship.

Taussig MS. 311, vol. 2, p. 868

Hilary term 1725/26.

An information was exhibited against the defendant upon [Stat.] 8 Ann.[1] for being concerned, aiding, and assisting in unshipping six hogsheads of wine, customs not paid. And the evidence was that the wine was unshipped and brought up in boats to the shore about two miles from the ship and the defendant was only concerned in rolling up the hogsheads from the shore and carrying them off in his wagon. And it was insisted that this did not prove him guilty of the information, but he might have been convicted on an information of *devenerunt* or else, bringing his cart for the hogsheads, he was liable to a forfeiture of the cart and horses.

But Chief Baron [Gilbert] ruled it that his rolling the hogsheads from the shore when they were put out of the boat maintained the information against the defendant for unshipping.

595

Stanfield v. Miller

(Ex. 1726)

The question in this was whether a gift causa mortis *of a chose in action is invalid.*

Taussig MS. 311, vol. 2, p. 873

Thursday, 28 April 1726, second day of term, by an English bill. Stanford v. Miller.

[1] Stat. 8 Ann., c. 14, s. 1 (*SR*, IX, 233–234).

Chief Baron [GILBERT]: A court of equity will never establish a *donatio mortis causa* of a chose in action because the property of such a thing does not pass even at law by the bare delivery; [it is] otherwise of things the property whereof does pass by delivery.

PAGE and HALE were of the same opinion.

N.B. The above was said by the Chief Baron, though, in fact, the case was not of a *donatio mortis causa* but a gift of the bonds absolute to the defendant by the testator in his lifetime. But the Chief Baron laying down the aforesaid rule, I inquired of the Chancery practicers concerning the point. And Mr. *Ryder* told me he had been actually concerned in two causes, one before the present Master of the Rolls [Jekyll] and another before the Lord Macclesfield, which upon rehearing was confirmed by the present Chancellor King, where a *donatio causa mortis* of choses in action had been decreed in Chancery and not so much as any objection or difference was taken between choses in action and other chattels. *Ideo quaere* of the Chief Baron's opinion which was certainly extra judicial.

Harvard Law School MS. 1082, vol. 1, p. 272, pl. 1

Easter term 1726.

A bill was brought as administrator of William Stanfield against the defendant to have an account of some bonds and notes, which the defendant swore to be given him by the intestate. But there was no proof of any consideration for the gifts.

Chief Baron [GILBERT] [said] that a gift of choses in action is not good without a consideration, even against an administrator. Perhaps, if it had been money, which passes by the delivery, it might be a good *donatio causa mortis*, but not so in choses of action.

PAGE and HALE agreed, so it was decreed for the plaintiff.

596

Marston v. Cleypole

(Ex. 1726)

The Statute of Limitations is not a defense to discovery.

The Statute of Limitations applies to suits in equity but not to suits in an ecclesiastical court.

The Statute of Limitations does not apply to a suit in equity for tithes nor to a receiver or bailiff of a plaintiff.

Harvard Law School MS. 1082, vol. 1, p. 269, pl. 2

Easter term 1726.

The plaintiff, as impropriator of Belton in the County of Rutland, brings his bill for twenty-four years tithes. And the defendant pleads the Statute of Limitations[1] in bar to the demand.

Ward, for the defendant: The Statute of Limitations is a general law and a very good one. Cro. Car. 115, Browne v. Hancock.[2] He pleaded no promise within six years or cause of suit to arise within that time. And a bill in equity is only a waiver of the Statute of Edw. VI.[3]

Chief Baron [Gilbert]: Tithes are an inheritance.

Ward: There are but these ways to recover tithes: either upon the Statute or by a suit in the ecclesiastical court or a bill in equity. And the plaintiff, by his bill, waives the penalty given by the Statute. If an action of *detinue* was brought, the Statute would operate upon it; so of an action of trover.

The Statute of Limitations will operate on a suit at equity as well as at common law. And the plaintiff cannot have an execution where it appears the cause of action was above six years before. Hetley 111.[4]

The case would differ between an ecclesiastical rector and a lay impropriation now turned into a lay fee. The reason of the Statute is because the plaintiff neglected to make his demand. And the Statute of Frauds and Perjuries[5] is similar to it. In an action of debt without a special[ty], this Statute is pleadable, but not where it is by an indenture. And a rent savors as much of the inheritance as tithes.

Bootle, for the defendant: An action is synonymous with this suit, which is a matter of account. And the Statute relates to all matters of account. 1 Saunders, Jones v. Pope.[6] This bill is not founded on the inheritance, but on the possession being only against the occupier. An assize will only lie against a terre tenant and not against the occupier as for tithes. If the suit was founded on the Statute of Hen. VIII[7] and so construed as a specialty and, therefore, not within the Statute of Limitations, if this was not allowed to be good, then, as the lay impropriator brings a bill for twenty-five years, so it may be for fifty or one hundred years. And how can the defendant answer to such a number of years?

---

[1] Stat. 21 Jac. I, c. 16 (*SR*, IV, 1222–1223).

[2] *Brown v. Hancock* (1628), Croke Car. 115, 79 E.R. 701, also Hetley 111, 124 E.R. 383.

[3] Stat. 2 & 3 Edw. VI, c. 13 (*SR*, IV, 55–58).

[4] *Brown v. Hancock* (1628), *ut supra*.

[5] Stat. 29 Car. II, c. 3 (*SR*, V, 839–842).

[6] *Jones v. Pope* (1666), 1 Williams Saunders 34, 85 E.R. 45, also 1 Siderfin 305, 82 E.R. 1122, 2 Keble 93, 84 E.R. 59, 1 Levinz 191, 83 E.R. 363.

[7] Stat. 32 Hen. VIII, c. 8 (*SR*, III, 537–538).

Bunbury, for the plaintiff: This plea was never allowed. This plea goes too far because it goes to the discovery and the Statute of Limitations is not pleadable to a discovery. Dean and Chapter of Westminster v. Railton and Mr. Herbert.[1]

[To the] objection it is in the nature of an action of *detinue*, [he] answered this demand subsists upon single damages and so upon the Statute and the Statute of Limitations is not pleadable to a matter arising on the Act of Parliament, which is a specialty. Cro. Car. 513.[2]

And it cannot be a good plea because it goes to the discovery.

Ward replies: I cannot remember any case of the Statute pleaded. Here is a distinction between a discovery of deeds, which was the Case of the Dean and Chapter of Westminster, and a bill for tithes.

[To the] objection this suit is in the nature of the Statute, [he] answered it is a contradiction, for it is grounded on the Statute. 2 Saunders 174.[3]

Bootle replies: [To the] objection of a plea to the discovery and so compared to a *modus*, [he] answered, as to a *modus*, it is not like this case because that might be fictitious and can thus be the case here when it appears upon the complainant's bill that his demand is for twenty-five years and nothing consequential can be drawn from it. And the case may vary where the discovery may alter the case, which it cannot be in the present case.

Chief Baron [GILBERT] [and] PRICE: If it should come out that the defendant promised within six years, the Statute of Limitations is not pleadable to this bill. And it is never pleaded to a discovery. And if the defendant discovers, the plaintiff may proceed on the Statute of Edw. VI. The Dean and Chapter of Westminster is a proper case before us as to the discovery. I may admit that the Statute of Limitations does extend to equity as well as law. Tithes are always favored here. And it is annually renewing. And though the Statute of Non-Residence[4] is a good plea, yet I cannot allow this to be good.

PAGE: The Statute of Edw. VI does not give the duty, but the penalty. But this plea might good if well pleaded. And this is a good discharge of the demand, which is a debt. This demand is not founded on the Statute, but the plea is bad in point of form.

Baron HALE: Query if the Statute of Limitations has been allowed. If the plea was good in point of law, I think the discovery of little use, for it appears on the face of the bill whether the Statute of Limitations may be pleaded in this case. And [he] considered the case as a matter of an account or a receiver.

---

[1] *Dean and Chapter of Westminster v. Cross* (Ex. 1720), see above, Case No. 126.

[2] *Talory v. Jackson* (1638), Croke Car. 513, 79 E.R. 1043.

[3] *Webber v. Tivill* (1670), 2 Williams Saunders 121, 85 E.R. 840, also 1 Levinz 287, 83 E.R. 410, 2 Keble 622, 634, 84 E.R. 391, 399, Lincoln's Inn MS. Misc. 500, f. 82 (Edward Ward's reports).

[4] Stat. 13 Eliz. I, c. 20 (*SR*, IV, 556).

CHIEF BARON: This case seems to differ from the common case of discovery because it must come out of the defendant's answer. But it is not so here.

[To the] objection that the Statute of Limitations has discharged this demand, [he] answered, I cannot think but the demand for tithes is a subsisting demand, and I must consider the original right of tithes and the Stat. 32 Hen. VIII, cap. 7.[1]

The process of the Exchequer went out before the king granted the tithes away; so the Statute was made to give a remedy for the lay impropriator, for that he had no remedy after the crown had granted them away. And by that Statute, the lay impropriator and the ecclesiastical person have an equal remedy to recover their tithes. And the Statute of Edw. VI gave the penalty because suits in an ecclesiastical court by a lay impropriator had little or no encouragement, and the Statute of Limitations cannot operate on a suit in an ecclesiastical court.

I think that tithes are profits of the inheritance, and so in the case of a bailiff and landholder, who brings a bill for twenty years' profits, and it is construed as a trust. And so in this case and in such a case, if the defendant owned the debt, it will take it out of the Statute. If the defendants owns himself a bailiff for twenty years, the Statute of Limitations will not operate upon it. And so I think if the defendant receives the tithes.

The plea was overruled, for different reasons, as to form and substance.

Taussig MS. 311, vol. 2, p. 886

Easter term 1726.

There was a plea of the Statute of Limitations to a tithe bill for not setting out tithes, *viz.* to so much of the demand as is beyond six years last past before exhibiting the bill.

Ward: The Statute of Limitations is not pleadable to an action upon the Statute because the Statute is a specialty. But in equity, the party waives the penalty on proceeding upon the Statute. This bill is for twenty-four years backwards, and it is different from the case of a rector because this is a lay impropriator. It is beyond the time of limitation by the plaintiff's own showing. Cro. Car. 115, Hetley 111. The Statute of Limitations is to be construed by equity, and so it will extend to courts of equity. It is pleadable to an action of debt for rent upon a parol demise.

Bootle, on the same side: 'Action' and 'suit' are synonymous. Therefore, the Statute of Limitations is pleadable to a bill in equity as well as to an action at law. Now, this is a suit for an account, and it does not concern merchandise. And it is very reasonable to allow the Statute on the account of the strictness the court holds the defendant to in quantities, qualities, and values. It is the plaintiff's own

[1] Stat. 32 Hen. VIII, c. 8 (*SR*, III, 537–538).

fault or laches not to bring his bill sooner. At common law, the proof lies on the plaintiff, but here in equity on the defendant.

Chief Baron [Gilbert]: How do you distinguish between the lay and the spiritual impropriator?

Bunbury: The plea is that they made no promise within six years next before the exhibiting of the bill or suing out process, and it extends to cover or prevent discovery. The Statute of Limitations is never pleaded to a discovery. Dean and Chapter of Westminster v. Doctor Cross is a case in point. This suit here by a bill is in the nature of an action of debt. Cro. Car. 513; 'account' in the bill signifies nothing but to discover and pay, but the word 'account' in the Statute signifies an account where there is a mutual dealing, which is certainly not this case. 2 Sanders 124.

Price: The Statute of Limitations is never pleaded to a discovery. If the party had brought his bill for a discovery, he might upon discovery have brought his action upon the Statute. Secondly, it is no bar to relief, for though the Statute of Limitations is pleadable to suits in equity, yet the nature of the demand must be the same as at law, which is here in the nature of a debt.

Page: Though I do not like this going back so far, yet this plea is ill as pleaded. This suit is not for a duty arising by an act of Parliament, but for a common law duty. And the Statute of Limitations was intended to prevent going back above six years. And, therefore, I do not see why, if a plea is well pleaded, it is not as well pleadable in a case of tithes as in any other case, for, if the plaintiff may go back for seven years, he may for seventy years. And why is not the Statute pleadable in this case as well as for rent upon a parol demise? But as I said before, the plea was not well pleaded.

First, it ought not to be pleaded to the discovery.

Secondly, it is not well pleaded because the protestation goes to the whole bill, whereas it ought to have been bounded with the exception of 'except what is hereafter pleaded to'.

Third, you should not have pleaded that you made no such promise, though, perhaps, that is well enough.

Hale: Substance is to be considered. And I should think it a reasonable plea to be allowed. If the plea is good in substance, there is no need of discovery, for there is a great difference between this case and a *modus*, for the *modus* may be good or bad, but it is certain if the plea is good in substance that the plaintiff can have no remedy. I query how would it stand with a receiver of rents or a bailiff? I think this is like that case.

Chief Baron: This case differs from the case of a common discovery, for here, if the argument is right, the defendant says you have no title to the thing concerning which you seek a discovery. But I cannot think the Statute has discharged the duty or debt, but it is yet a subsisting duty. We must, therefore, consider the Stat. 32 Hen. VIII and the remedy given for tithes to the lay impropriator under that Statute. And in a case of subtraction, a layman may sue in a spiritual court as well as an ecclesiastical person. The Stat. of Edw. VI gives the election to sue at law or in an ecclesiastical court. The Statute of Limitations cannot run against a parson if he sues in the ecclesiastical court, nor was it ever intended to run to the profits of an estate because the receiver is a trustee. Now here, the defendant admits the receipt of the profits and, if so, a court of equity will not bear that, but will make him refund them.

The plea was overruled, but without costs.

Bunbury 213, 145 E.R. 651,
1 Rayner 235, 2 Gwillim 674, 1 Eagle & Younge 812

11 May 1726.

To a bill by a lay impropriator for tithes for about twenty-four years, the defendant, as to such part of the bill as prays discovery and relief for any time before within six years next before the filing of the bill or serving the subpoena, pleads the Statute of Limitations and that he did not promise to make any satisfaction for any tithes before the said six years.

This plea was now argued and overruled *per* TOTAM CURIAM, for the defendant, as to the tithes is in the nature of a receiver or bailiff for the plaintiff, in which case the Statute of Limitations does not operate.

Cases cited for the plaintiff [were] Cro. Car. 513; 1 Saunders 38; 2 Saunders, Webber v. Tyrrell.

Cases cited for the defendant [were] Cro. Car. 115; Hetley 111.

597

Davies v. Strange

(Ex. 1726)

A vicar can be compelled to produce his predecessor vicar's account books for the inspection of an opposing party.

The question in this case, the validity of a modus decimandi *in lieu of tithes in kind, was tried upon an issue to a jury.*

Taussig MS. 311, vol. 2, p. 879

Easter term 1726.

The court obliged the vicar of the parish of Tunbridge to produce the books of his predecessor which the executor had delivered to the present vicar and in which the vicar had written several things relating to his own private affairs. But the plaintiff Strange having by his bill alleged that there was evidence in these books which would make out the *modus* or which did relate to the *modus* in question and desiring the vicar to answer to this point, though the vicar did in his answer to the bill set forth in a schedule the whole contained in such book relating to *modus*es and though it did not appear to the court of what standing the book was or that the vicar intended to make use of it as evidence for himself, yet having submitted to produce it at trial, the court now, upon Mr. *Foley*'s motion, ordered the book to be produced and that the plaintiff Strange should have liberty to inspect the same before the executing of the commission *ad examinandum testes* as to what the vicar had sworn in his answer that the schedule contained the whole in the book relating to the *modus*es.

It was said from the bar and bench that this was only the vicar's judgment of it, but it ought not to preclude the plaintiff from seeing with his own eyes.

N.B. This was thought a very extraordinary rule by the practicers at the bar.

Harvard Law School MS. 1082, vol. 1, p. 272, pl. 2

Easter term 1726.

Mr. *Foley* and *Bootle* moved for the defendant in the original cause and the plaintiff in the cross-cause to oblige the parson to produce his books in order to be examined to fish for a *modus* insisted upon by Strange.

The court said that, in all public books and rolls of manors, they were produced on either side. And though this motion was decreed in Chief Baron Ward's time in the Case of the Bishop of Exeter v. Rowe[1] and Hughes v. Walker, yet in this case, they granted the motion that the parson should produce his predecessor's books.

Taussig MS. 311, vol. 2, p. 928

Trinity term 1726.

The plaintiff, as vicar of Tunbridge in the County of Kent, exhibits his bill against the defendant as occupier of a cherry garden or orchard of three acres. The defendant by an answer insisted that the cherry garden had been formerly always held with a messuage in the possession of J.S. etc., that there was and had been an immemorial payment of 3s. *per annum* payable at Michaelmas to the vicar in lieu and satisfaction of all small tithes arising in and upon the said messuage and three acres.

The plaintiff's counsel, Mr. *Ward* and *Edlin*, insisted that this *modus* was too rank upon the very face of it, for, supposing the land worth 20s. an acre, it was the full tithe, much more so when it was laid to be in satisfaction only of vicarial or small tithes. But they also insisted that the proof in the cause manifestly showed it to be a composition.

But failing herein, the proof being pretty strong on the other side that it was paid as a *modus*, the counsel for the defendant proposed a trial whether *modus* or no *modus*.

---

[1] See *Roe v. Bishop of Exeter* (Ex. 1720), above, Case No. 119.

And to this, the court, *viz.* GILBERT, PAGE, and HALE agreed, Price absent, though the plaintiff's counsel made a strong opposition thereto on account of the value. And the court seemed to think the 3s. too much for the land only. But inasmuch as the owner of the house might have many tithable matters independent of the land, they thought it was not fit to reject the *modus* entirely.

N.B. Chief Baron [GILBERT] said that, though these exceptions to *modus*es on account of being too near the value of the tithes in kind had obtained in this court, yet he did not apprehend that the objection was above sixty years old, and Lord Chief Justice Treby had overruled it upon a trial before him; so he seemed to doubt the reasonableness of the objection.

And a trial was ordered.

N.B. In this case, I insisted that, before the plaintiff should be heard to the validity of the *modus*, he should admit the fact of it, as was done on debate in Phillips and Symens' Case.[1]

But now, PAGE thought that rule was not reasonable and that it was more properly and orderly to debate the validity of the *modus* in point of law in the first place. And it was so done.

Harvard Law School MS. 1082, vol. 2, p. 1, pl. 3

Trinity term 1726.

The plaintiff, as rector of Hallingbury in Essex, brings a bill for tithes. The defendant insists on 3s. *per annum* for three acres of land as a *modus* and 2s. 4d. for a quarter [?] of an acre.

And though these seemed so rank on the face of them, yet the court permitted the defendants to read their evidence. And as to one part, they directed an issue.

598

Hastings v. Bowles

(Ex. 1726)

In this case, a customary method of paying tithes of milk was held to be invalid.

Taussig MS. 311, vol. 2, p. 869

Friday, 18 February 1725[/26], setting down of causes after Hilary term. Hastings, rector of Dailsford in the County of Worcester v. Bowles.

The defendant in this cause set forth in his answer that, within the Parish of Dailsford, there is and has been time out of mind immemorial an ancient and well established customary payment of tithe milk, which customary payment is for the rector to receive from every inhabitant of the said parish who has milk

[1] *Phillips v. Symes* (Ex. 1724–1726), see above, Case No. 488.

cows tithe milk in kind every tenth day beginning every second of May and continuing to the first of August following in every year and to receive the whole milk of all the cows every such tenth day in lieu and full satisfaction of his tithe of milk.

The *modus* was adjudged to be naught upon the hearing. It was read and so ordered to account for milk. But the plaintiff having heretofore accepted it, the Chief Baron [Gilbert] etc. seemed to think he ought to be bound for the years he accepted.

Sed quaere per me how this can be, for this *modus* is only a part of the very tithes *in specie*. It seems, therefore, no manner of conclusion against him as to the residue of the year.

599

Wilkins v. Wilkins

(Ex. 1726)

The question in this case was whether a father must support his minor child who has assets of his own.

Taussig MS. 311, vol. 2, p. 881

9 May 1726.

If a child has a legacy, [query] whether the father is obliged to maintain the child *ex proprio*.

600

Grosvenor, *qui tam* v. Bean

(Ex. 1725–1726)

The question in this case was whether the Attorney General, upon an information qui tam, *can withdraw a juror.*

Taussig MS. 311, vol. 2, p. 826

Sittings in Middlesex on Thursday, 25 November 1725. Before Gilbert, Chief Baron.

The informer had laid his seizure wrong, *viz*. two days after the information was exhibited, and, therefore, the Solicitor General [*Wearg*] insisted upon withdrawing a juror.

And I objected for the defendant that an informer *qui tam* has no such privilege.

Solicitor [General, *Wearg*]: The issue is joined by the Attorney General though the information is in the name of the informer so the issue to be tried is the king's issue.

The Chief Baron [GILBERT] said that the reason why the king may withdraw a juror is because the king cannot be nonsuited.

Query whether the king, even in his own causes, has any such a prerogative. Query, if he has, whether it extends to an information *qui tam* in such circumstances as before.

The CHIEF BARON, being doubtful, saved the point to us.

Harvard Law School MS. 1082, vol. 1, p. 273, pl. 2

Easter term 1726.

The question was whether, when there was an informer, a juror might be withdrawn.

Mr. *Ward*, for the defendant: Though the crown may enter a *non vult ulterius prosequi* and though the king cannot be nonsuited, yet an informer may [withdraw a juror]. 1 Inst. 139;[1] Mead, *qui tam* v. Drury, Easter 14 Jac. I, ro. 42, Trinity 11 Jac. I. If a juror can be withdrawn, then the defendant cannot have costs. Baspole's Case, 2 Shower 487.[2]

Bootle cited 18 Eliz., cap. 3, sec. [*blank*].[3]

Solicitor General [*Talbot*], for the king: The issue is joined by the crown, and the crown has the sole power of trial. And in Farewell, *qui tam* v. Norris, a juror was withdrawn.

Ward and *Bootle* reply: No answer is given to the Act of Parliament[4] that says an informer may be nonsuited.

Chief Baron [GILBERT]: The king's prerogative will extend to his part, though the informer may proceed for his. It is no consequence that, because the informer may be nonsuited, therefore, the crown cannot withdraw a juror.

PRICE: I always thought that it was only in the case of the crown to withdraw a juror. The practice of the court supplies the joining of issue. I shall not hinder the defendant from proceeding.

CHIEF BARON: I have some doubts. And I do not know but that an informer, as to his part, may be nonsuited and [as] such an informer *non pros* himself. When an information is begun, an interest is vested in the crown. And whether the crown, having an interest in the penalty, has not a prerogative to withdraw a juror, it is a reasonable prerogative, and there seems to be the same reason for the one as the other.

Taussig MS. 311, vol. 2, p. 901

Easter term 1726.

---

[1] E. Coke, *First Institute* (1628), f. 139.

[2] *Rex v. Baspoole* (1686), 2 Shower K.B. 486, 89 E.R. 1057, also Comberbach 38, 90 E.R. 329.

[3] Stat. 18 Eliz. I, c. 5, s. 4 (*SR*, IV, 616).

[4] Stat. 18 Eliz. I, c. 5, s. 4 (*SR*, IV, 616).

Chief Baron [Gilbert]: The Attorney General joins issue. The Attorney General is an informer *qui tam*. In Co. Lit., he is an informer in an action of debt *qui tam*.

Chief Baron: Suppose the informer may be nonsuited, will it thence follow that the crown may not withdraw a juror? There are two cases to be considered, first, if the penalty is wholly in the informer, then he may be nonsuited. If the penalty moiety is in the informer, query whether he may be nonsuited without leave of the crown, for then there is an interest which he has vested in the crown.

It is certain an informer may be nonsuited; else, the statutes speaking of his being nonsuited would be absurd. But the query is whether this is not to be understood of the first case only.

The question is whether the crown may not withdraw, for the Attorney [General] may see faults in the information, and, therefore, he may nonsuit it.

Secondly, why may the crown discharge a juror if [it has the] whole [forfeiture] and yet may not where it has but half?

Bunbury 220, 145 E.R. 653

Note: A question arose, whether the Attorney General, upon an information *qui tam* etc., could withdraw a juror.

Upon an information in the Attorney General's name only, it was admitted he could enter a *non prosequitur* upon that information, which in effect amounted to withdrawing a juror.

1 Inst. 139,[1] was mentioned for the defendant, but, to that, the Attorney General [*Yorke*] said it related only to actions *qui tam*, not to informations, and, in these informations, the Attorney General only joined issue.

Baron Price: Nothing but the practice of the court can justify that, which is only to save the king's right.

601

Attorney General, *ex rel.* St. John's College v. Town of Shrewsbury

(Ex. 1726)

A court of equity can regulate a charity according to its bylaws without interfering with the powers of a visitor of the institution.

[1] E. Coke, *First Institute* (1628), f. 139.

Bunbury 215, 145 E.R. 652

King Edward VI, by letters patent, erects a free school in Shrewsbury and gives the bailiffs and burgesses power *nominandi et appunctuandi* a schoolmaster and of making laws *concernentem et tangentem ordinem, gubernationem, et directionem paedagogi* with the advice of the bishop of Lichfield and Coventry and also for the preservation of the revenue etc.

Queen Elizabeth, *anno 13 regni* [1570–1571], increases the revenue of the school, in consideration whereof the bailiffs and burgesses agree to such ordinance as Mr. Ashton, then the head master, should, with the advice of the bishop, make, who did accordingly make several relating to the disposition of the revenues and qualification of the master.

Anno 20 Eliz. [1577–1578], the bailiffs and burgesses made by-laws, the seventh and eighth of which were 'that upon every vacancy of a master, the college should elect and nominate a proper person (qualified as by Ashton's ordinance) to the bailiffs, who should nominate such person'. But by the eighth by-law, they had power to approve or disapprove. And by an indenture 20 Eliz. between the bailiffs and burgesses and the bishop of Lichfield and the college, they covenant to perform the said bylaws and enter into bond of £1000 for that purpose. And this method of election had been observed for one hundred and fifty-two years without any interruption until lately.

And now upon an information by the Attorney General at the relation of the College of Saint John [Cambridge] to compel the town to nominate according to the by-laws and usage, it was first objected by the court that, by the letters patent of Edward VI, he, being the founder, is consequently visitor and the decree now prayed is interfering with the visitatorial power and the crown can visit only under the great seal.

But upon the second hearing, the court thought there was no weight in this, but that the court might proceed to establish this as a charity.

Secondly, it was objected that the power of nominating by the letters patent of Edward VI was vested in the body as a trust or naked authority and, therefore, could not be delegated, to which it was answered that this was not a total delegation of the authority, but only a regulation to prevent confusion, as in the Case of Corporations, Lib. 4,[1] to which it was said that the same objections might be made as to this. And the usage of two hundred and fifty-two years did much corroborate this case.

And of that opinion was the whole court, and they decreed for the plaintiff.

[1] *The Case of Corporations* (1598), 4 Coke Rep. 77, 76 E.R. 1052, also Jenkins 273, 145 E.R. 197.

Harvard Law School MS. 1082, vol. 1, p. 274

Easter term 1726. [From] loose notes. Bylaws about turning out a schoolmaster at Shrewsbury. And I was counsel in the case, but have lost the first notes.

Serjeant *Comyns*, for the plaintiff, [moved] to have an establishment of an agreement according to certain bylaws acquiesced in for several years that they should send to the college to nominate a proper person to be head schoolmaster at Shrewsbury. This does not interfere with the visitorial power. It neither tolls nor prejudices it. And the crown as visitor may disannul these ordinances. I admit that a visitor has an absolute authority and the visitor may make new rules.

Ward, for the plaintiff: The Attorney General's bill is proper. And this court has a proper jurisdiction.

[To the] objection that it is interfering with the visitatorial power, [he] answered, to settle charities, it is always allowed, and it is proper to be demanded in any court. Trinity 1687, Attorney General, *ex rel.* Lloyd v. Executors of Dr. Barrow,[1] for settling a free school of St. Asaph. And the settlement of a charity is proper in this court.

[To the] objection that the bylaws are void and of no proper authority because it cannot be delegated, [he] answered the right of nomination is left, and this is only a regulation and a proper method of completing the intended charity.

Bunbury: The Stat. 43 Eliz.[2] does not extend to this case. If it was a trust and a naked authority, then I admit that it could not be delegated.

Wills: If they proceeded in this court, it might occasion a clashing of jurisdictions. Phillips v. Bury,[3] *ratione fundatoris*. The method of proceeding is chalked out, and the crown visits by the Chancellor. Coke Litt. 96.[4] The Chancellor, in a summary way, may alter whatever decree is made.

Probyn: This is not a proper case before this court. Bylaws may restrain to a select number, but cannot interfere with the original authority. And this is a naked authority without an interest. And, therefore, it cannot be delegated and usage cannot create a power, though it may model it.

In the beginning, when this ordinance was made, it was null and void. And though it may be thought convenient, yet such convenience will not create a right. This authority is personally vested in the Chancellor. And it is not examinable by a bill of review, as the representative of the crown. *Ordinem* will not include a nomination and app[ointment].

---

[1] *Attorney General, ex rel. Lloyd v. Clopton* (1687), Eq. Cases Exch. 281.

[2] Stat. 43 Eliz. I, c. 4 (*SR*, IV, 968–970).

[3] *Phillips v. Bury* (1694), Skinner 447, 90 E.R. 198, Shower P.C. 35, 1 E.R. 24, 1 Shower K.B. 360, 89 E.R. 624, Comberbach 265, 314, 90 E.R. 469, 499, Carthew 180, 319, 90 E.R. 709, 788, 1 Lord Raymond 5, 91 E.R. 900, 2 Term Reports 346, 100 E.R. 186, 1 Salkeld 403, 91 E.R. 349, Holt K.B. 402, 715, 90 E.R. 1122, 1294, 4 Modern 106, 87 E.R. 289.

[4] E. Coke, *First Institute* (1628), f. 96.

Serjeant *Comyns* replies: This is a proper bill. And the ordinances are proper regulations not interfering with the original right, but pursuant to and to prevent tumultuous elections.

Chief Baron [GILBERT]: The decree must be for the plaintiffs. And, though lodged in the corporation, yet all the words must be taken together. I cannot consider this as a naked authority. The court will consider what was the true intent and meaning of this charity and what the best method for the supporting of it is. And these ordinances seem to answer the original intent. And I think that this usage will be of benefit and that these bylaws are of benefit to the charity. And it would be too hard to overturn them. And he thought that *ordinem pro tempore existente* will do under their seal, and the bailiffs and burgesses have covenanted to perform it.

I allow that no new person can be appointed contrary to the charter. But it may be narrowed and regulated. And, therefore, he thought the seventh and eighth bylaws were reasonable and proper. And, therefore, Owen, the present schoolmaster, ought to be displaced.

PRICE agreed.

PAGE: It is a prudent regulation.

HALE agreed.

So they directed the bailiffs and burgesses to give notice to the College when a schoolmaster was wanted.

Taussig MS. 311, vol. 2, p. 899

Monday, 16 May 1726.

Two questions were proposed by the court to be spoken to and considered, first, whether the application to a court of equity [is proper] or it does not fall under the king's visitatorial power.

Serjeant *Comyns*: The decree of this court will no ways influence the king's visitatorial power, for the decree of the court will only bind down the agreement as between the parties and not with respect to the king. The decree of 11 King James, though not evidence, yet it is an authority for the jurisdiction of a court of equity, for, there, the Court of Chancery established the ordinances now in question.

Secondly, what we pray here cannot be done by a visitor, for he has no power to confirm or annul the agreement as an agreement, but he may make an ordinance or rule contradictory to the agreement, which is indeed avoiding the decree *per obliquum*, but *non ex directo*.

Mr. *Ward*: It was never doubted, but bills to establish charities [lie] in courts of equity, and this notwithstanding the Stat. of Queen Eliz. concerning charities. [See] Trinity term 1687, Attorney General, *ad relatione* Doctor Lloyd, bishop of St. Asaph v. Executors of Dr. Barrow, to show that the king may proceed in equity or by commission. The like he infers as to the visitatorial power and a court of equity, for the king may choose his jurisdiction whether by visiting or by proceeding in a court of equity.

The second question is whether the Town of Shrewsbury can delegate their authorities. See 4 Rep. [*blank*] and 1 Salkeld 190.[1] Nor is there any delegation of power here, for the Corporation made this bylaw and, now, they qualify it, which is the same case as that determined in the 4th Report. These bylaws have obtained a long time, and overturning them would be of very ill consequence.

Mr. *Bunbury*: By [Stat.] 43 Eliz. [*blank*], there is an express proviso that the Statute does not extend to corporations.

As to the second point, whether a power can be delegated, the objection is that it is a trust or naked authority so it is not capable of being transferred, but the power of nominating is in the bailiffs and burgesses and the bylaw restrains it to the bailiffs. And the bailiffs have still the power. So it is only a regulation or qualification of that power. And it is exactly the case of 4th Report.

Adjornatur.

602

West v. Erisey

(Ex. 1726)

A marriage settlement can be modified to express the intention of the original parties thereto.

A court of equity can appoint trustees to preserve contingent remainders.

Taussig MS. 311, vol. 2, p. 905

Saturday, 21st [May] 1726.

Articles of agreement were made before marriage that a settlement should be made to the husband for life without impeachment of waste, then to the heirs male of that marriage, then to the heirs male by a second wife, then to the heirs female etc. A settlement is made before the marriage and it recited that it was made in pursuance and performance of those articles. And, by that settlement, the uses are limited so as to make the husband tenant in tail. And after[wards], he levies a fine and suffers a recovery, and, by a will, he devises to A., B., C. The granddaughters, he dying in 1722, bring a bill to set aside this settlement as not agreeable to the intention of the first articles, for, by them, the husband should have been only a tenant for life. And the settlement was pleaded in bar to the bill.

And there were two questions. Whether, if a settlement had now been to have been made, a court of equity would not have made a settlement to the husband for life with remainders to trustees to preserve contingent remainders; secondly, though if that would have been the case, suppose the settlement had been

---

[1] *The Case of Corporations* (1598), *ut supra*; *Butler v. Palmer* (1699), 1 Salkeld 190, 91 E.R. 172.

in fieri, yet now the settlement is made above forty years ago, whether the court can go back to the articles.

That a court of equity would go back were cited the cases following: Trevor and Trevor; Lady Dacres and Chaloner Shute; Vernon 217; Honor and Honor, Trinity 1710 *coram* Cooper, Vernon's Reports; Seymour and Fotherby, 320;[1] 10 November 1698, Jones and Wharton, that the case of daughters is not considered by a court of equity as that of sons, for the last preserve the name of the family.

Chief Baron [Gilbert]: The plea is overruled as such, and [it is] to stand as an answer with liberty to except.

Lincoln's Inn MS. Misc. 12, p. 258

9 December 1726.

The plaintiff's grandfather, before his marriage, entered into articles whereby he agreed to settle lands to the use of himself for life, then to his intended wife for life, remainder to the heirs male of his body begotten on the wife, remainder to the heirs male of his body begotten on any other wife, remainder to his heirs female begotten on the intended wife, remainder to himself in fee. Before the marriage, he makes a settlement, which is said to be in pursuance and performance of the articles whereby he settles the lands to the use of himself for life, then to the wife for life, remainder to his first and other sons begotten on the wife in tail male, remainder to his first and other sons on any other wife begotten in tail male, remainder to the heirs of his body begotten on his intended wife, remainder to himself in fee.

The marriage took effect. And the wife died leaving one daughter only and no son. And afterwards, the husband suffered a recovery and sold part of the lands and died having by his will given the rest of the settled lands from his daughter to his sister. The daughter died about ten years after her father having never controverted the settlement.

And the plaintiffs who are her daughters and co-heirs bring their bill against the devisee complaining that the settlement was not made agreeable to the articles for that, instead of the limitation to the heirs of the body of the husband begotten on the wife, it ought to have been to the daughters of the marriage in tail

[1] *Trevor v. Trevor* (1719), 1 Peere Williams 622, 24 E.R. 543, 9 Modern 161, 88 E.R. 377, 10 Modern 436, 88 E.R. 798, 1 Eq. Cas. Abr. 185, 387, 21 E.R. 977, 1122, 2 Eq. Cas. Abr. 475, 505, 22 E.R. 404, 427, 5 Brown P.C. 122, 2 E.R. 574; *Lady Dacres v. Chute* (1683), 1 Vernon 160, 23 E.R. 387, also 2 Chancery Cases 104, 22 E.R. 867, 1 Eq. Cas. Abr. 352, 21 E.R. 1097, 3 Chancery Reports 6, 21 E.R. 711, 2 Freeman 148, 22 E.R. 1120, *sub nom. Lady Darcy v. Chute*, 1 Chancery Cases 21, 22 E.R. 673, 1 Eq. Cas. Abr. 63, 21 E.R. 877; *Lady Speake v. Lady Speake* (1684), 1 Vernon 217, 23 E.R. 425, also Skinner 158, 90 E.R. 73, 1 Eq. Cas. Abr. 221, 21 E.R. 1004; *Honour v. Honour* (1710), 2 Vernon 658, 23 E.R. 1028, also 1 Peere Williams 123, 24 E.R. 321, 2 Eq. Cas. Abr. 38, 22 E.R. 33; *Seymour v. Fotherly* (1685), 1 Vernon 320, 23 E.R. 496.

for so the words in the articles do import and, if the settlement had been made in that manner, the father could not by a recovery have barred his issue female. And, therefore, it was prayed that the lands which the grandfather had devised by his will (for, as for the lands which were sold, the plaintiffs did not go about to disturb the purchaser) might be settled according to the articles.

Lord Chief Baron PENGELLY recommended it to the defendant to do something for the plaintiffs, but he not coming readily into it, the bill was dismissed.

Note the settlement was made forty years ago and the plaintiffs' mother, though she lived ten years after the father, never questioned it. In this case were cited Honor and Honor, *quod vide* in Vernon's reports, and Trevor and Trevor, *quod vide* Liber C, 129; *vide* the case of White and Thornburgh, Liber C, 63, and the case of Pin and Pin, there cited, and Baker and Norton, 194.[1]

Harvard Law School MS. 1082, vol. 2, p. 10, pl. 2

Sittings after Michaelmas term 1726.

HALE: There is no ground for to grant the plaintiff any relief. The agreement has no relation to Richard Erisey, but only to the party to the marriage, but the estate does not proceed from him. The settlement is declared pursuant to the articles and that must be taken according to the intention of the parties. A settlement was made before marriage at three months distance between the date of the articles and the settlement, and this settlement ought to be construed [by] the agreement of the parties. If there was a mistake, then a court of equity might alter it, as in the case of Honum and Honum.[2] The construction seems to be pursuant to the agreement of the parties and, therefore, the bill that prays a settlement according to the articles must be dismissed.

CARTER: I take these articles only to be short heads of an agreement. And I shall suppose this as being a settlement made before marriage that the parties themselves waived some particular parts in the articles. And in all the cases cited for the plaintiff, the settlement is made subsequent to the marriage.

This settlement is the new agreement of the parties. And the articles seem to be under consideration at the time of the settlement. And the omission of trustees has been often supplied in a court of equity. Sir John Hobart v. Lord Stanford.[3] The liberty to make a settlement on a second wife is only in the case of a

---

[1] *Honour v. Honour* (1710), *ut supra*; *Trevor v. Trevor* (1719), Lincoln's Inn MS. Misc. 11, p. 129, and *ut supra*; *White v. Thornburgh* (1714), Lincoln's Inn MS. Misc. 11, p. 63, also Gilbert Rep. 107, 25 E.R. 75, Precedents in Chancery 425, 24 E.R. 190, 2 Vernon 702, 23 E.R. 1056, 2 Eq. Cas. Abr. 231, 714, 22 E.R. 196, 601; *Baker v. Norton* (1721), Lincoln's Inn MS. Misc. 11, p. 194.

[2] *Honour v. Honour* (1710), *ut supra*.

[3] *Earl of Stamford v. Hobart* (1710), 3 Brown P.C. 31, 1 E.R. 1157, *sub nom. Hobart v. Countess of Suffolk* (1709), 2 Vernon 644, 23 E.R. 1020, 1 Eq. Cas. Abr. 272, 21 E.R. 1040, note also *In re Maynard's Will* (1691), Dodd 101.

defect of issue male. Pym v. Pym, settlement after marriage; Trevor v. Trevor, there was a fraud; Sir Edward Turner's Case, Lord Cowper's time.[1]

Comyns: I agree that the bill must be dismissed. And it is not fit for a court of equity to break into the settlement.

Chief Baron [Pengelly]: It is necessary to stop somewhere and upon the same reason that, if the plaintiff might have relief, so he might against purchasers for a valuable consideration. Richard is a purchaser in consideration of marriage, and that is preferable to the consideration of money. Bate v. Coleman, reversed by Lord Harcourt.[2] An estate in this case moved from another person. This settlement is made in pursuance of John Erisey's part of the articles and so ought to be construed. Here is an alteration by virtue of an endorsement, to which Killigrew, the wife's father, is a witness. See the settlement. The plaintiff comes to have a settlement broken into after forty-one years' acquiescence, which I cannot do. Therefore, the bill must be dismissed.

Note this decree was reversed in the House of Lords.[3] See Cases.

1 Comyns 412, 92 E.R. 1135

Frances West and Mary West, by their father, John West, Esq., plaintiffs, and Frances Erisey, Mary West, and Thomas Barrable, an infant, by his guardian, defendants.

A bill was exhibited in September 1725, by which it was alleged that, on a treaty of marriage between Richard Erisey and Frances, the daughter of Sir Peter Killigrew, it was agreed by articles dated the 23rd of December 1685 between James Erisey, uncle of the said Richard, and the said Richard Erisey, of the one part, and Sir Peter Killigrew, of the other part, that, in consideration of the said marriage and £1700 marriage portion, James Erisey would settle lands in the counties of Cornwall and Devon to the use of Richard Erisey for life without impeachment of waste and to the heirs male of his body on the said Frances to be begotten and, for want of such issue, to the heirs male of his body by any other woman and, for want of such issue, to the heirs female of his body by Frances and, after, to his heirs female by any other wife and, for want of such issue, to Charles Vivian etc. with divers remainders over. And, by the same articles, the lands in Devon were to be settled to James Erisey for life without impeachment of waste, remainder in part to Mary, his wife, for life, remainder of the whole to Richard Erisey as aforementioned. And, by the same articles, it was agreed that

[1] *Trevor v. Trevor* (1719), *ut supra*; *Turner's Case* (1678–1681), 1 Vernon 7, 23 E.R. 265, also 1 Eq. Cas. Abr. 58, 21 E.R. 871, *sub nom. Turner v. Turner*, Dodd 38, 79 Selden Soc. 711, *sub nom. Turner v. Bromfield*, 1 Chancery Cases 307, 22 E.R. 814, Lord's Journal, vol. 13, p. 681.

[2] *Baile v. Coleman* (1711), 2 Vernon 670, 23 E.R. 1036, 2 Peere Williams 142, 24 E.R. 330, 2 Eq. Cas. Abr. 309, 472, 717, 22 E.R. 261, 402, 603, Lincoln's Inn MS. Misc. 383, p. 51, British Library MS. Hargrave 80, p. 47.

[3] *West v. Erisey* (1727), 1 Brown P.C. 225, 1 E.R. 530.

James Erisey might nominate counsel for settling the said estates and jointure and that Sir Peter Killigrew might advise likewise with his counsel, so that the same may be effectual in law. By an indenture dated the 23rd and 24th of March 1685, 2 Jac. II, between James Erisey, of the first part, Hugh Boscowen and another trustee, of the second, and Richard Erisey, of the third part, James Erisey, in consideration of love to Mary, his wife, and for confirming and setting her jointure and for love to Richard Erisey and conveying and settling the lands and tenements afternamed in his name and blood and in pursuance and performance of the said articles, conveys the lands and tenements in the county of Devon to the use of himself for life without impeachment of waste, then, as to the barton of Erisey etc., to the use of Mary, his wife, for her life for her jointure and in satisfaction of dower and, as to the said barton etc., after her decease, and as to the residue of the premisses from and after his own decease, to the use of the said Richard Erisey for life without impeachment of waste and, from and after his decease, to the use of his first and other sons to be begotten on the body of Frances, his wife, in tail male and, for want of such issue, to the use of his first and other sons by any other wife in tail male and, for want of such issue, to the use of himself and the heirs of his body on the body of the said Frances to be begotten and, in default of such issue, to the use of the heirs of his body and, for want of such issue, to the use of Charles Vivian etc. And he gave a power to himself and Richard Erisey to make leases etc. And, by an indenture of lease and release dated the 25th and 26th of March 1686, 2 Jac. II, which were the ensuing days, James Erisey settled the lands in Cornwall to the use of Richard Erisey in possession for life without impeachment of waste with such remainders as before and gave him power to make a jointure for another wife and to make leases etc., and James Erisey covenants for him and his heirs that the trustees shall be seised to the same uses according to the intent of such leases and estates and, after the determination of such leases and estates, to the use of such persons and for such estates and in such manner as the same lands were settled before.

In the deed of this settlement produced, several lines were erased and memorandums [were] made of it.

In April 1686, the marriage took effect between Richard Erisey and Frances Killigrew, by whom he had issue Mary only, afterwards married to John West, father of the plaintiffs, for the plaintiffs were daughters and heirs of John West and Mary, his wife, the daughter and heir of Richard Erisey and Frances, his wife. And, in two years after the marriage, Frances, the wife of Richard Erisey, absented herself from her husband.

After the death of Sir Peter Killigrew and James Erisey, by indenture of the 18th and 19th of January 1697, 9 Will. III, Mary, late wife of James Erisey, conveyed to Richard Erisey and his heirs, during his life, the premises settled to her for her jointure in consideration of an annuity for her life pursuant to articles between them dated the 17th of January 1697. And, afterwards, Richard Erisey, having the freehold of all the estate in him, did, by indenture of lease and release, bearing date the 25th and 26th of April 1698, 10 Will. III, grant and convey the whole estate to two persons to make them tenants to the *praecipe* in order for a fine and common recovery. And, in Easter term, 10 Will. III, a fine was levied and a common recovery suffered accordingly, and, by that deed, the uses are declared to Richard Erisey in fee.

After this recovery, Richard Erisey alienated in fee several parcels of the estate. And, by his will dated the 20th of December 1722, he devised the residue of the estate to the defendant Mary Erisey in fee.

James Erisey, who made this settlement, had two brothers Richard and William. James died without issue. Richard had no issue male, but left a daughter Mary, then alive. And William had issue, Richard Erisey, upon whom the settlement was made. And now, the plaintiffs Frances and Mary, infants, exhibit their bill and, by it, pray that such part of the estate as was not sold by Richard Erisey, their grandfather, may be settled upon them, according to the intent of the articles, and that the defendant, as executrix and devisee of Richard Erisey, shall make them satisfaction out of her personal estate for the value of the estate sold by him in his lifetime.

The defendant pleaded the marriage settlement, the fine and common recovery, the deeds which lead the uses of them, and the will of Richard Erisey in bar of the relief prayed by the bills. But the plea was ordered to remain for an answer, with liberty to except to it. And then, the cause was heard upon the merits. And it was insisted for the plaintiffs that the intent of the articles was that provision should be made for the issue male and female of this marriage, that no provision was made for issues female, only by the limitation in the articles to heirs female of the body of Richard Erisey, and, therefore, when those articles were put in execution, the settlement ought to have been made in such a manner that the issues female might have the benefit of the provision intended for them, and, then, the estate ought not to have been limited to the heirs female of Richard Erisey, by which it was in his power to bar his daughters by fine and recovery, but should have been to all and every the daughters of the body of the said Richard Erisey on the body of Frances, his wife, to be begotten, and, then, it would not have been in the power of Richard Erisey to bar Mary, his daughter, to whom the plaintiffs are heirs, that the settlement was intended in pursuance and performance of the articles, and, then, when the intent is not well pursued, it ought to be rectified in equity, and the plaintiffs, who are entitled by the proper limitation, may enforce the execution of the articles. And it is the constant experience in courts of equity that, if the settlement in pursuance of marriage articles is contrary or defective, it shall be reformed by the court.

Trevor v. Trevor, in Chancery, 5 June 1719, and afterwards affirmed in the House of Peers, February 1719,[1] is a case expressly to this purpose, for, there, by

[1] *Trevor v. Trevor* (1719), *ut supra*.

articles in 1669, made by Sir John Trevor, late Master of the Rolls, upon his marriage, it was covenanted to make a settlement of lands to the value of £250 *per annum* within two years to the use of himself for his life without impeachment of waste and, afterwards, to the use of his wife for her life and, then, to the use of his first, second, and other sons by such wife in tail etc. and, in case no settlement was made in two years after the marriage, the persons seised should stand seised to the same uses. After the two years, he suffered a recovery and disposed of the estate by will. But all was set aside, and the construction made was that the articles should have been executed so as not to have enabled the Master of the Rolls to defeat the children of the marriage, and, although it was insisted that, by the covenant to stand seised, the estate was now executed to the limitations as expressed in the articles, it was held that ought to make no alteration.

But Pengelly, Chief Baron, Hale, Carter, and Comyns, barons, held that it was dangerous to set aside settlements made upon great deliberation, for, though, according to the case of Trevor v. Trevor, if articles are made to settle an estate to a man and the heirs male of his body, a settlement in pursuance of such articles will be decreed in equity to be made in common form, to him for life and to trustees to preserve the contingent uses, and, then, to the first and other sons successively in tail, yet the rule does not hold with respect to females, who are less regarded because the name of the family will not probably be preserved by them. And, by these articles, the daughters of this marriage are postponed to the sons of a subsequent marriage. So the bill was dismissed without costs.

But upon an appeal to the House of Lords, the decree of dismission was reversed in February 1727,[1] principally because the settlement, being expressly mentioned to be made in pursuance and performance of the articles, showed that the parties did not intend to vary the agreement. And the Lords held that the expression of heirs female in marriage articles should have the same construction in favor of daughters as heirs male should in favor of sons, especially as no other provision was made by the settlement for daughters. And the Lords decreed a conveyance to trustees to the use of the appellants and the heirs female of their bodies as tenants in common with cross-remainders to them in tail female; and the appellants were to have an account of the profits and of the purchase money for the premisses sold and interest, the principal money to be laid out in land to the same uses, but the interest to be paid to the use of the appellants, all writings to be brought into the Court of Exchequer and possession delivered to the appellants.

2 Peere Williams 349, 24 E.R. 760

The bill was to have the benefit of marriage articles dated 23 December 1685 and made on the marriage of Richard Errissey with Frances, the daughter of Sir Peter Killigrew, and that the settlement which, either through mistake or fraud,

[1] *West v. Erisey* (1727), 1 Brown P.C. 225, 1 E.R. 530.

was made in a different manner from what was contained in the articles might be set right.

The two plaintiffs, Mary and Frances West, were the granddaughters and coheirs of this Richard Errissey and Frances, his wife. And, by the said marriage articles, James Errissey, the plaintiff's grandfather's uncle, being seised in fee of divers manors and lands in Cornwall and Devonshire, did, in consideration of the marriage and marriage portion, covenant to settle a great part of the premises, mentioning the parcels, to the use of Richard Errissey, the plaintiff's grandfather, the then intended husband of Frances, for life without waste, remainder as to part to the use of Frances, the intended wife, for life, remainder of the whole to the heirs male of the body of the said Richard Errissey by Frances, remainder to the heirs male of the body of the said Richard Errissey by any other wife, remainder to the heirs female of the body of the said Richard Errissey by Frances, remainder over, with a power for the said Richard Errissey to make leases for three lives and to make a jointure.

Afterwards and before the marriage, by indenture dated the 24th of March in the same year 1685, a settlement was made of the premises and mentioned to be in pursuance and performance of the articles, by which James Errissey, the uncle, conveyed the premises to the use of Richard Errissey, the husband, for life without waste, remainder to Frances, his wife, for her life for her jointure, remainder to the first etc. son of the marriage in tail male successively, remainder to the first and every other son of the said Richard Errissey by any other wife in tail male successively, remainder to the heirs of the body of the said Richard Errissey by the said Frances, remainder over, by which settlement, there was an omission of trustees for supporting contingent remainders and, instead of limiting a remainder to the daughters of the marriage, the limitation was to the heirs of the body of Richard Errissey by the said Frances, which plainly gave an estate tail to Richard Errissey and, consequently, a power to bar the daughters of that marriage and also the remainders over by a recovery.

Richard Errissey had issue by the said marriage one only daughter Mary. And, in Trinity Term 1698, taking advantage of this mistake, he sold part of the premises to the amount of £6000 and upwards, and, having suffered a common recovery of such part of the premises as remained unsold, by indenture of the 16th of February 1709, he conveyed the premises unsold to trustees, Worth and Herle, and their heirs in trust to himself for life, remainder to such trusts as he should declare by will.

Afterwards, the said Richard Errissey, by will dated the 27th of December 1722, devised the premises to his sister, the defendant Mary Errissey, and her heirs, except a small tenement which he devised to one Barrable and his heirs. And having made the defendant Mary Errissey executrix, he died in January following.

Mary, the daughter of Richard Errissey by Frances, married Colonel West, and they had issue, the now plaintiffs Mary and Frances West, both infants. Mary West, the mother, died, and the two plaintiffs, Mary and Frances West, brought their bill against Mary Errissey in order to rectify the mistake in the settlement, whereby the premises, instead of being limited in strict settlement as they ought to have been in compliance with the articles and the intent thereof, were settled in tail upon the said Richard Errissey. But, as to the premises sold, the bill did not seek to disturb the purchase, only to recover the purchase money out of the assets of Richard Errissey.

The defendant, Mary Errissey, pleaded the settlement of 1685, the common recovery, the will of Richard Errissey, and the long enjoyment of the premises. And the plea being argued before the Lord Chief Baron Gilbert and the other barons, the same was overruled unanimously.

Afterwards, the cause coming on to be heard before Lord Chief Baron PENGELLY, who had succeeded to that place on the death of Lord Chief Baron Gilbert, and the Barons HALE, CARTER, and COMYNS, the bill was dismissed without costs in December 1726, it being dangerous, as it was said, to set aside a settlement which seemed to have been deliberately and solemnly made, that it appeared the daughters of this marriage were postponed to the sons of a subsequent marriage and so their advancement by this reversion was not so much regarded, that though the case of Trevor v. Trevor was an instance in point, where marriage articles for settling lands on the husband for life, remainder to the heirs male of his body by his then intended wife had been construed to mean his first and every other son in tail male, yet where there had been another remainder, whereby the premises were agreed to be limited to the heirs female of the body of the husband by the wife, this had never been construed to mean daughters, the sons being more to be regarded than daughters, as they preserve the name of the family, besides that the settlement of 1685 had been attested by Sir Peter Killigrew, father of the said Frances.

From this decree, an appeal was brought in the House of Lords,[1] where it was insisted:

First, that, by the marriage articles, it was agreed that the estate should be limited to Richard Errissey for his life without waste and that he should have power to make leases, which was a plain evidence that the estate was intended to be limited in strict settlement and that Richard Errissey should be but tenant for life and have no power to bar either his sons or daughters by fine or recovery;

Secondly, that the settlement took notice of the articles and was expressly mentioned to be made in pursuance and performance thereof, which words were a demonstration that the parties did not design to depart from or vary the terms of the articles, nor had come to any new agreement for that purpose, and that it was apprehended the limitations in the settlement under which Richard Errissey, by construction of law, became tenant in tail had proceeded from the mistake or negligence of the counsel who drew the same and not from any agreement or

[1] *West v. Erisey* (1727), 1 Brown P.C. 225, 1 E.R. 530.

design of the parties to vary the terms of the articles, of which mistake or neglect, the omission of the common limitation to trustees to preserve contingent remainders was a plain proof;

Thirdly, that the respondent was a volunteer under the will of Richard Errissey, who took advantage of the mistakes in the settlement and suffered a common recovery to bar his issue, although Mary, his daughter, was then living, which was apprehended to have been a manifest breach of trust in him.

Indeed, it had been objected that, although courts of equity had in like cases decreed an execution of marriage articles in strict settlement in favor of sons, yet had they not extended it in favor of daughters, who were most commonly provided for by a term for years to raise portions for them in case of issue male. But surely, the reason seemed to be as strong that the expression of heirs female of the body, contra-distinguished from sons, should in marriage articles have the same construction in favor of daughters as the expression of heirs male in favor of sons, since both were equally under the contemplation of the parties and, especially, since, in the present case, there was no other provision for daughters besides the limitation intended them by the marriage articles. And according to the common course where a provision is made for daughters by a term for years, it is always so limited as to be out of the power of the father to bar it.

It had been objected, secondly, that the settlement being made before the marriage, it was to be presumed that the parties came to some new agreement to vary the terms of the articles and that the settlement was made to the satisfaction of Sir Peter Killigrew, who was a witness to the settlement, as he had been a party to the articles.

Response: But, it seems, the settlement was not only expressed to be in pursuance and performance of the articles, but the appellants by their bill charging that the parties came to no new agreement after the date of the articles to vary the terms thereof, the respondent Errissey, by her answer, had admitted she never pretended that the parties after the articles came to any new agreement to vary them. And as to Sir Peter Killigrew's being a witness to the said settlement, he, as most gentlemen in like cases, relied upon his counsel's framing the settlement so as to answer the intent of the articles, being himself a stranger to the forms and method thereof.

Objection: Thirdly, but after such a length of time and an acquiescence under the settlement, the appellants ought not at this time of day to have resort to the articles of marriage.

Response: The appellants were infants, whose title did not accrue until after the death of Richard Errissey, the grandfather, in January 1722, and they filed their bill for relief within a short time after.

Fourthly, it had been objected, if the articles of marriage should be allowed to control and vary the settlement, the purchasers under Richard Errissey would in consequence be affected.

To which, it was answered that the appellant's bill was not brought against any purchaser, since, as to those parts of the estate which were sold by Richard Errissey, the appellants only prayed that they might have satisfaction for the same out of the personal estate of the said Richard Errissey, which had been principally acquired by those sales in breach and violation of the trusts, and that, by the conditions in his will annexed to the trifling and fruitless bequests to the appellants, his granddaughters and heirs at law, he seemed to be aware of the injury he had done them and that his personal assets would be liable to their demands in respect thereof.

Whereupon, the House of Lords reversed, in February 1727, this decree of dismission and decreed that the trustees, Worth and Herle, and the respondent, Mary Errissey, should convey such of the premises as were comprised in the articles to trustees to the use of the appellants, Mary and Frances West, and to the heirs female of their bodies as tenants in common with cross-remainders to them in tail female, and the respondents, Mary Errissey and Barrable, to account for the profits and to pay the same to the appellants, the infants, also Mary Errissey, the executrix, to account for the purchase money that had been received by the said Richard Errissey for such part of the premises as he had sold and pay the interest thereof to the appellants, Mary and Frances West, and the respondents to bring their writings into the Court of Exchequer and deliver up the possession to the appellants, the infants. But, as to the principal monies arising by the said sales, these were to be laid out in the purchase of lands in fee to be settled to the same uses as the lands unsold were decreed to be conveyed.

2 Eq. Cas. Abr. 39, 22 E.R. 33

Articles [were made] on marriage to settle lands on the husband and wife for their lives, remainder to the heirs male of the body of the husband by the wife, remainder to the heirs male of the body of the husband by any other wife, remainder to the heirs female of the body of the husband by this wife. A settlement is made before the marriage, *viz.* in 1685, and said to be in pursuance and performance of the said articles, whereby the lands are limited to the husband for life without waste and with a power to make leases, remainder to the wife for her life for her jointure, remainder to the first etc. son of the marriage in tail male successively, remainder to the first etc. son of any other marriage in tail male, remainder to the heirs of the body of the husband by this wife, remainder over. By this settlement, there was an omission of trustees for supporting contingent remainders, and, instead of limiting a remainder to the daughters of the marriage, the limitation was to the heirs of the husband of the marriage, which gave the husband an estate tail and, consequently, a power to bar the daughters of that marriage and also the remainders over by a recovery. The husband had issue of this marriage one only daughter, Mary. And, taking advantage of this mistake, he sold part of the premisses to the amount of £6000 and upwards, and having suffered a recovery of such part as remained unsold, by indenture 16 February 1709, he conveyed the same to trustees, Worth and Herle, in trust for himself for life, remainder to such trusts as he should declare by will. And accordingly, 27 December 1722, he devised the premises to the defendant in fee, except a small tenement which he devised to one Barrable in fee, and made her executrix. Mary, the daughter, married B., and they had issue, the plaintiffs, Mary and Frances, both infants. Mary, their mother, being dead, the plaintiffs brought their bill against the devisee in order to rectify the mistake in the settlement. But as to the premises sold, the bill did not seek to disturb the purchase, only to recover the purchase money out of the assets of their father. The devisee pleaded the settlement of 1685, the recovery, the will, and the long enjoyment of the premises. And the plea being argued before GILBERT, Chief Baron, and the other barons, the same was overruled unanimously. But upon hearing the cause before all the barons, the bill was, in December 1726, dismissed without costs, it being dangerous, as it was said, to set aside a settlement which seemed to have been deliberately and solemnly made.

But upon an appeal to the House of Lords, this decree of dismission was in February 1727 reversed.[1] And it was decreed that the trustees and the devisee, Mary Erressey, the respondent, should convey such of the premises as were comprised in the articles to trustees to the use of the appellants, Mary and Frances, and to the heirs female of their bodies as tenants in common with cross-remainders to them in tail female, and the respondents, the devisees, Mary Errissey and Barrable, to account for the profits and to pay the same to the appellants, the infants, and the respondent, the executrix, to account for the purchase money that had been received by her testator for such part of the premisses as he had sold and pay the interest thereof to the appellants, and the respondents to bring their writings into the Court of Exchequer and deliver up the possession to the appellants. But as to the principal monies arising by the said sales, these were to be laid out in the purchase of lands in fee to be settled to the same uses as the lands unsold were decreed to be conveyed.

603

East India Company v. Mathews

(Ex. 1726)

The East India Company had an exclusive trade coastwise as well as an exclusive trade to and from the East Indies.

Harvard Law School MS. 1082, vol. 1, p. 269, pl. 1

Easter term 1726.

[1] *West v. Erisey* (1727), 1 Brown P.C. 225, 1 E.R. 530.

An information was grounded on 9 & 10 Will. III[1] for the defendant's trading in the years 1722 and 1723 between the Straits of Magellan and the Cape of Good Hope and he gained by this clandestine trade £15,000. And a special verdict finds that the defendant was the commodore over several ships to suppress pirates. But instructions were given to the defendant not to trade or bring home anything but gold and silver. And the defendant traded coastwise from place to place in goods and disposed of such goods there in the East Indies within the limits of the East India Company. And whether this trading is contrary to the Statute the jury doubt.

'In, to, or from the East Indies'; see Stat. 9 & 10 Will. III, par. 81. Trading in the East Indies is the same as into and from; see sec. 61. The trade within those limits is granted; see Stat., sec. 61. This trade is granted exclusive of any other and upon a consideration of £2,000,000. The words of an act are taken so as to include the whole. 10 Rept. 101; Sir Thos. Jones 108, 2 Levinz 127; 1 Ventris 62, Hill v. Phillips; 5 Rept., Mallory's Case.[2]

Serjeant *Belfield*, for the defendant: The information is only '*ad vel in orientalis*', and *ad*, the preposition, signifies into. This is a penal law, and it ought to be taken in favor of the defendant. And it rests upon the penal clause 81; the parts before mentioned are only relatory. If construed as contended for, it would hinder the parties dwelling in these parts to trade there. 12 Car. II, cap. 18; 7 & 8 Will. III, cap. 22,[3] explains this and alters it, which shows that the first Act was defective upon the point now in question. And the same Parliament made the Stat. 9 & 10 Will. III.

Bootle replies: Hall v. Phillips, in 1 Ventris, answers the objection as to a penal statute.

[To the] objection of Stat. 7 & 8 Will. III to alter 12 Car. II upon that point, [he] answered from port to port, which is in the East India Act, and these words are wanting [in] 12 Car. II, which was the occasion of making the Statute 7 & 8 Will. III.

Chief Baron [Gilbert]: *Ad et in*, first [as a] preposition governs the accusative case. The question is whether the defendant is within the letter of the Act. And it was truly observed by Brother Belfield that 'parts' before mentioned is

---

[1] Stat. 9 Will. III, c. 44 (*SR*, VII, 429–446).

[2] *Beawfage's Case* (1612), 10 Coke Rep. 99, 101, 77 E.R. 1076, 1079–1081; *Gilmore v. Shutter* (1678), T. Jones 108, 84 E.R. 1170, 2 Levinz 227, 83 E.R. 531, also 1 Ventris 330, 86 E.R. 214, 1 Freeman 466, 89 E.R. 348, 2 Shower K.B. 16, 89 E.R. 764, 2 Modern 310, 86 E.R. 1091; *Hall, qui tam v. Philips* (1670), 1 Ventris 62, 86 E.R. 43, also 2 Keble 613, 84 E.R. 386; *Mallory v. Payn* (1601), 5 Coke Rep. 111, 77 E.R. 228, also Croke Eliz. 805, 832, 78 E.R. 1033, 1058.

[3] Stat. 12 Car. II, c. 18 (*SR*, V, 246–250); Stat. 7 & 8 Will. III, c. 22, s. 1 (*SR*, VII, 103).

only relative to the first limits described. It goes to the whole, and 'coastwise' takes in the whole.

So the Chief Baron [GILBERT] and PAGE thought there is very little in the objection.

Taussig MS. 311, vol. 2, p. 894

Easter term 1726.

Attorney General [*Yorke*] opens the record. There are two questions: first, whether the facts found by the verdict are within the information '*ad et in Indias Orientales*'. In cases of law proceedings, where there are two prepositions, the noun following may be in either case. But the other part of the information helps this, for the information specifies several particular places in which he traded. Second, the next and main point is whether the fact found is within the Act.[1]

The first consideration is what is granted to the Company.

§ 61 explains this; so reads the clause, and he insists upon the word 'in' in that clause and takes notice that the Company is a purchaser of this trade. So if the Act had gone no further, here is an exclusive trade to and from and in the East Indies.

§ 81 [is] 'to and from the East Indies and to and from all the ports, havens', etc. and these places shall not 'be visited . . . haunted, etc. by any others'.

Secondly, the next consideration is how this trade granted is secured. And it is naturally to suppose that the security was intended to be co-extensive with the grant of the trade or else it is not an adequate security; so reads § 81 which gives the penalty [and] takes notice of the words 'and other the parts before mentioned'.

Now, for the *terminus a quo*, it must not be understood of England, Europe, or Africa. Therefore, since no *terminus a quo* is particularly mentioned, it excludes all.

As to the parallel case from the Act of Navigation,[2] the Act of Navigation does not directly extend to trade, but only to carriage or navigation of goods and merchandises.

'Imported into or exported out of', and these words are technical words relative to England only. And, therefore, a coast-wise trade from one place of England to another place in England is not either importation or exportation into or out of England. This way of reasoning if applied to the plantations is the same.

Chief Baron [GILBERT]: Is not carrying out of a port an exportation?

Attorney General [*Yorke*]: In strictness it is so but in legal understanding, for, if an information was brought against a man for importing goods and the evidence was only of bringing from Newcastle, this would not be within the penalty of the Statute of Tonnage and Poundage, 9 Will. ca.,[3] that if any of the king's subjects

[1] Stat. 9 Will. III, c. 44 (*SR*, VII, 429–446).

[2] Stat. 12 Car. II, c. 18 (*SR*, V, 246–250).

[3] Stat. 9 Will. III, c. 23 (*SR*, VII, 382–385).

who had gone into France etc. Lindsey's Case, tried in 3 Queen Anne.[1] And there are many cases wherein the facts are not within the strict words, as Alexander Poulter's Case and Magdalen College Case.[2] If within the plain intention, though penal, they have been construed to be within the prohibition of the Act that this fact is within the meaning of the Act or else it is manifestly absurd.

Fazakerly: Everyone is not prohibited. Therefore, it ought to set forth that Mathews is one of those who come within the prohibition. It is not said *non habens authoritatem negotiandi*, but only *negotiatus fuit non habens authoritatem* without saying for what.

As to the main point, the Act settles an English company, and all the places particularly mentioned are a description only of the *terminus ad quem*.

The first name of the Company was *Societas Mercatorum Negotiandum ad Indias Orientales*.

The preamble settling a trade to the East Indies [*blank*] then reads § 61 and construes all the places to be only a description of the East Indies.

The *terminus a quo* is from England or any other place; that must be understood any other place exclusive of limits or else it cannot be a *terminus a quo*, for all places within the limits are a *terminus ad quem*.

§ 64 takes notice of the oath directed and before whom must he take the oath and secures the trade to the *terminus ad quem*;

§ 67 are by-laws for regulating the trade to the East Indies not within the East Indies;

§ 68 the Company cannot trade there themselves;

§ 69 [goods] shall be landed in England;

§ 81 is the immediate clause on which the question arises. An Englishman's trading within the limits is no more damage than the natives and no damage at all from neither, for all the goods carried from one place to another within are still within the limits and liable to be bought up by the Company to be imported hither.

He takes notice of the Attorney [General]'s answer to the Act of Navigation and his sense of the word 'exportation'. And he answers it thus, *viz.* that if this were the sense of the word, then the re-landing in England would be unnecessary, for re-landing in England makes it not to be an exportation.

And the Case of Lindsey is nothing to this purpose, for the being in any county is a continuance of the same offense.

The *Attorney General* replies: Not being *ad inde licentiatus nec habens et negotiatus fuit* is the same as not being *licentiatus ad negotiandum*. Fazakerly's argument from the name of the Company, *viz.* England, and from the oath and books would imply that an Englishman may trade thither from any place out of

---

[1] *Lindsay's Case* (1704), Holt K.B. 693, 90 E.R. 1283.

[2] *Rex v. Powlter* (1610), 11 Coke Rep. 29, 77 E.R. 1181; *Warren v. Smith* (1615), 11 Coke Rep. 66, 77 E.R. 1235, also 1 Rolle Rep. 151, 81 E.R. 394, 2 Bulstrode 146, 80 E.R. 1021, Croke Jac. 364, 79 E.R. 312.

England. The regulations of the trade are of a very different consideration from the grant of the trade, and the clauses mentioned by Fazakerly only extend to regulating the trade.

CHIEF BARON: The latter end of § 61 fortifies the construction contended for by the defendant.

Adjornatur for judgment until next term.

Taussig MS. 311, vol. 2, p. 921

17 June 1726.

Chief Baron [GILBERT] gives the judgment of the court. He opens the information and the special verdict. First, he considers the general view of the Act and the state of the Company at that time, *viz.* that they were a company by a charter only and could not exclude others. The nation being in an expensive war, there was a necessity of raising money. And this Act was a plan for that purpose. And the money was subscribed for and is a purchase of an exclusive trade.

And the question is whether it was an exclusive trade coastwise as well as an exclusive trade to and from. If this case was not within the letter of the Act, judges ought not to extend it, it being a perpetual act. But we are all of opinion that this case is within the letter of the law.

§ 61, this extends to coastwise trade as well as to and from.

§ 81 is the effectual clause and consists: (1) of a positive clause that they shall have the sole trade; (2) of a negative clause that others shall not trade; (3) of a penalty to secure their sole and exclusive trade.

Words could not be found out to make it plainer, for they go expressly to the places within the surround, *viz.* islands, creeks, havens, and places within. And the proviso in behalf of the old East India Company which gives the old East Company liberty to trade within the limits proves this further.

Objections have been made from the difficulty of apportioning the coastwise trade to the capital of £100. He admits the subscribers might have had a coastwise trade and so might have an opportunity of increasing his £100 by a coastwise trade.

The *terminus a quo* is any country whatsoever, not any country without the limits, but any country at all. He takes notice of the case parallel put upon the Statute of Navigation. The Act of Navigation says exported or imported to and from the plantations and the word plantations there is to be taken as a generical name, and, therefore, that Act does not exclude coastwise trade. But here are the words 'shall not visit, haunt, or frequent'. The words of the Navigation Act go to the thing. The words of this Act go to the person. And this Statute is penned not only in a generical way, but particular places are mentioned so as to be sure to comprehend the coastwise trade. So there must be judgment for the king and the Company.

Chief Baron [GILBERT] delivered the opinion of the court.

Harvard Law School MS. 1082, vol. 2, p. 3, pl. 1

Trinity term 1726.

Chief Baron [Gilbert]: This came for the judgment of the court. And the question arises on the Stat. 9 & 10 Will. III so [. . .]ated the case on the special verdict. And the true question is whether the coastwise trade is within the Act of Parliament. The general view of the Act and, likewise to be considered, before the Statute, for then there was an old company called the East India Company, but then such old Company had not an exclusive trade. But this Statute of Will. III was a plan to raise £200,000 and subscribers were admitted at 8 percent. And by that subscription and complying with the Act of Parliament, it had an exclusive trade.

[To the] objection it only purchased a trade within such limits and that coastwise trade is a *casus omissus*, [he] answered it is not within the words. I own that, by construction, it ought to affect the defendant, it being a penal law, but we are of opinion that this case is within the words of the Act of Parliament. And we think, [by] Clause 31 of the Statute of Will. III, the coastwise trade is included, for that clause gives an exclusive right. And the proviso for the old East India Company corroborates this opinion.

[To the] objection of the Stat. 12 Car. II and so the occasion for the Stat. 7 & 8 Will III, [he] answered the Act of Car. II is worded as this Act, but not as to exported out of the East Indies. The coastwise trade here is no exportation from England; so of the West Indies; unless the words are the same in the Act, there is no consequence from it. The penners of the East India Act took the words of 7 & 8 Will. III under their consideration.

We are of opinion that this offense is within the words of the Act. Although the East India Company does not use the coastwise trade, yet judgment ought to be given for the Company.

Gilbert Rep. 213, 25 E.R. 149

This is an information exhibited by the East India Company against Thomas Mathews on the Statute of 9 & 10 Will. III, c. 44.[1] And it sets forth that the defendant, between the first of April 1722 and the first of June 1724, being a subject of this kingdom and being neither factor nor agent or servant of the said Company or thereunto licensed by the said Company nor having any lawful authority, did trade and traffic *ad et in India Orientali* and divers other places within the limits where none except the said Company, their factors, agents, or servants, or persons by them authorized, ought to exercise any trade or merchandize and did acquire goods to the value of £3000 in the East Indies and other places within the limits and time aforesaid, and the said goods did put on board the *Lyon* and *Fancy*, which said ships, with their furniture, valued at £5000, and, with these

[1] Stat. 9 Will. III, c. 44 (*SR*, VII, 429–446).

goods so put on board, did trade, traffic, and adventure, the proceeds and effect of which was to the amount of £15,000, for which offence they claim the forfeiture of the said ships and all the proceed and effects of the same and also the sum of £6000, being double the value of the goods.

To this information, the defendant pleaded not guilty. It was tried, and a special verdict was found that, on the 23rd of January 1720, the defendant Thomas was appointed commander of a ship called the *Lyon*, a man of war, and three other ships, which were sent out for the security of the trade of the East India Company from pirates. And, for that purpose, the defendant received several instructions from the Lords of the Admiralty, and, among other things, that he should take care that neither himself nor any of the officers in company belonging to any of His Majesty's ships under his command should take on board any goods or merchandises upon any pretence whatsoever, gold and silver only excepted, as he and they should answer the same at their peril, and that, on the receipt of these instructions, the said defendant sailed from England for the East Indies in the said man of war called the *Lyon* and, on the 30th of March 1721, arrived there, and that, after his arrival, being neither factor, agent, nor servant unto the said Company, nor being thereto licensed by the said Company, he did trade with the said ship at the East Indies and other places within the limits in the information mentioned from port to port and from place to place, and acquired goods to the value of £13,676 17s. 6d. and that the said goods were shipped on board the *Lyon*, a man of war (value 20), within the limits aforesaid. And whether this is within the Act is the question.

In order to consider this case, it will be proper to look into the state of things at the time of making this Act. There was then an old East India Company incorporated by charter, but the charter of the crown could not exclude any person to and from the East Indies, for nothing can exclude the subject from trade but an Act of Parliament.

The crown, at the time of making the Act, had occasion for two millions of money for carrying on the war, and the Act is a plan for raising that sum in this manner. Books are to be laid open to subscribers for raising these two millions, and every subscribing person, both subject and foreigner, is to have an annuity of £6 percent and a fund is settled. Besides, such subscribing persons have a right to trade, within certain limits, exclusive of all others, from the Cape of Good Hope to the Straits of Magellan, so that the new right, purchased by subscription in pursuance of the Act, is a right to exclude every unsubscribing person.

Those that have argued for the defendant do admit that the power of trading to and from the limits is taken away from all unsubscribing persons, but they say that the right of trading coast-ways within the limits is not taken away by this Act. That is a *casus omissus* and not within the law, so that, if a man does not pass the limits or transport any wares, commodities, coin, or bullion from a place out of the limits to a place within the limits, he is not within the letter of the law.

If it were so, that the coast trade were a *casus omissus* and out of the letter of the law, I could not construe it to be within the intent, for that were to torture a penal law by excluding it in point of construction. And, if there be a *casus omissus*, the parties concerned in interest had better apply to Parliament, which are sitting every year, than for the judges to stretch the law in point of construction. So that the question is reduced to this, whether the coast-ways trade is within the letter of the law.

Now, plainly, the 61st Section does grant a coastman's trade to the subscribers, as well as a trade to and from the limits, for it is that they shall freely traffic and use the trade of merchandize in such places and by such ways and passages as are already frequented, found out, or discovered, or which hereafter shall be found out or discovered and as they severally shall esteem and take to be fittest or best for them into and from the East Indies in the countries and ports of Asia and Africa and into and from the islands, ports, havens, cities, creeks, towns, and places of Asia, Africa, and America or any of them beyond the Cape of Bona Esperanza to the Strait of Magellan, where any trade or traffic of merchandize is or may be used or had and to and from every of them.

Indeed, if there were no more in the Act than this grant, it would have given them no more than what they had as subjects originally and before the making of the Act, for they had a power of trading to and from the limits and likewise a power of trading coast-ways. So this case is only preparatory to the 71st clause, which runs thus:

> That such persons or corporations as in pursuance of this Act shall have a right and power to trade to the East Indies and other the parts aforesaid according to such provisions, proportions, and restrictions as are in this Act contained and subject to the condition or power of redemption before mentioned from and after the [date of the] said 29th of October 1698 shall have, [sell], use, and enjoy the whole and sole trade and traffic and the only liberty, use, and privilege of trading, trafficking, or exercising the trade or business of merchandize to and from the East Indies, and [other the parts aforesaid, according to such provisions, *viz.*] to and from all the islands, ports, havens, cities, towns, and places within the limits aforesaid, or any of them, as shall after the said 29th of October 1698 be visited, frequented, or haunted by any other of the subjects of His Majesty, his heirs, or successors, during such time as the benefit of trade hereby given or intended to be given to the subscribers or others, as aforesaid, ought to continue by virtue of this Act. And if any of the subjects of His Majesty, his heirs, or successors of what degree or quality soever they be, other than such as may lawfully go and trade to the East Indies or other the parts aforesaid, by virtue of this Act, and their factors, agents, or servants respectively who shall be employed according to the true meaning hereof, shall directly or indirectly visit, haunt, frequent, trade, traffic, or adventure into or from the said East Indies or other the parts before mentioned, contrary to the true meaning thereof, all and every such offender and offenders shall incur the forfeiture

> and loss of all the ships and vessels which shall be employed in such trade with the guns, tackle, apparel, and furniture thereunto belonging and also all the goods and merchandize laden thereupon and all the proceeds and effects of the same and also double the value thereof, *viz.* one fourth part thereof to such person or persons as will seize, inform, or sue for the same, to be recovered in any court of record as aforesaid and the other three fourth parts to the said general society, until etc. as aforesaid and after the erecting [uniting] thereof, if any such be, then to the use of the said Company without account, the charges of prosecution being borne by the said Society or Company.

If the 61st Clause had stood alone without the 71st, it would have been no grant at all, for the 61st would have granted no more than that which all subjects had before the making the Act. But the 71st is the effectual clause, which excludes all other subjects in as large terms as the 61st clause grants the whole and sole trade to and from the East Indies, and to and from all the islands, ports, havens, cities, towns, and places within the limits and then came the words which inflict the penalty, which say that 'if any person of what degree or quality soever shall directly or indirectly visit, haunt, frequent, trade, traffic, or adventure to and from the East Indies or other parts aforementioned, contrary to the true intent and meaning thereof', they shall incur the forfeiture etc., so that the words of the law do as well extend to the trading within the limits as to and from the limits, for trade, traffic, and adventure to and from the East Indies and other parts aforementioned are relative words and relate to any island, port, haven, city, town, or place within the limits.

I cannot see how plainer words could have been made use of, both to grant a coast-ways trade to the subscribers and to exclude all other subjects from it. And indeed, the grant would have been nothing if the exclusion had not been equal and parallel to the grant, for the subscribers would have no more than they had before if all other subjects had not been excluded. And so it was necessary to pen the exclusive clause in these strong terms, in order to make the grant itself any way effectual.

There is another clause that manifests the same intent. I cannot say it makes it plainer, for no words could, I think, be plainer. And that is Clause 73.

> Provided also and be it enacted by the authority aforesaid that nothing in this Act shall extend or be construed to extend to hinder and restrain the Governor and Company of Merchants in London trading into the East Indies to continue to trade within the limits aforesaid until the 29th of December 1701, anything in this Act contained to the contrary notwithstanding.

By this Clause, it is plain that the old East India Company were excluded from a coast-ways trade after the time appointed, for, though they had a settlement under the king's charter and had effects in the East Indies, yet they could not make any advantage of the effects after the time limited. And if the Act excluded them from a coast-ways trade, to be sure it must be designed to exclude all other persons whatsoever.

Those that argue for the defendant argue from the intermediate clauses between the 61st and 71st. And they say that every person that subscribes £100 shall have power to sell £100 in goods, wares and commodities or coin within the limits.

This is the 61st Clause. And indeed, all the rest of the clauses go upon the supposition that any person that would trade to the East Indies would freight his ship with commodities and not go out empty to carry on a coast-ways trade, for no man in his wits that ever traded to the East Indies would carry on a trade in such manner, for that would be to lose the profits of his outward voyage.

But certainly, any subscribing person that had carried out £100 might make the best of it by a coast-ways trade, for, otherwise, if he had not found a market for the commodities at one haven or port, he could not carry them to another, for, if the Act were interpreted that the subscriber was to carry the commodities from a *terminus a quo* without the limits to a *terminus ad quem* within the limits and that was the whole power given to the subscribers, then, if a subscriber could not find a market in one port, he could not carry them to another. It would be the most absurd construction of the Act that could be.

So if a subscriber of £100 had carried out a cargo of that value from a place out of the limit and, within the limit, the ship should meet with a storm and it were necessary to lighten the ship by throwing the cargo overboard, no man will say but that he may take in goods to freight or take up goods on credit to the value of £100 that any person might do before the Act and the subscribers too had the same power and liberty of the Act made.

And whatever power the subscribers had after the Act, they were by the Act to have and enjoy the same, exclusive of all other, for, if a subscriber might carry on a coast-ways trade, as they that argue for the defendant must admit, he must by the 71st clause enjoy it sole and separate and exclusive of any unsubscribing subject.

Indeed the 61st Section, that begins to settle the proportions, says that persons subscribing shall not ship, lade, or put on board to or for the East Indies or other parts within the limits aforesaid from England or any other country or place whatsoever any goods of greater value than as in the Act is expressed, *viz.* that he that has subscribed £100 shall and may ship, lade, and put on board yearly for the said East Indies or parts within the limits aforesaid goods, wares, and merchandises that shall amount to the value of £100, so that, though, in this clause, the *terminus ad quem* is the East Indies or a place within the limits, yet the *terminus a quo* is England or any country whatsoever, which comprehends all places, either within the limits or without.

So, when the oath is limited in the 64th clause, they are to swear not to ship or cause to be sent from England or any other country to the East Indies or other places within the limits any goods of a greater value than such as they may lawfully send. Here, the *terminus a quo* is left at large, for the goods may be shipped from any country, either within the limits or without, so that the penning of these clauses does comprehend a coast-ways trade, as well the trade from places without the limits, as to places within; and the *terminus a quo* is left at large, that it may comprehend all sorts of trade whatsoever.

Indeed, the 66th Clause says that every person that shall send any goods to the East Indies or other parts within the limits shall enter the quantity and value of such goods in a book and likewise the name of the ship and commander.

Now, it is argued that no subscriber could carry on a coast-ways trade because he could not be able to make these entries. Indeed, the law is here adapted to the common manner of the trade, for no subscriber that was fitting out a ship would carry her out empty to the East Indies in order to freight her there. The law does not suppose anything so absurd as that he would lose the profit of his outward-bound voyage.

But there is no doubt that, if any person had by storms lost the cargo of his ship, he might take goods to freight to the value of his subscription within the limits; and, if he enter such goods *ex post facto*, he would be within the equity of the law, for the Statute does not put any cases upon particular accidents. But the regulation of the proportion is adapted to the general course of trade, that is, to carry out goods to the East Indies and not merely to take in goods to freight there.

But the regulation of subscribers in this manner, by these entries, cannot induce a consequence that the coast-ways trade is not within the Act, since it is within the express letter of the law as aforesaid. And, if a man were to trade with goods to the value of £100 from a place without the limits to a place within the limits, he must be obliged to unload at some one place to make his market there in case the subscriber was excluded from making the best of his £100 by a coast-ways trade within the limits.

From all which it is plain that the sole coast-ways trade is by this Act sold to the subscribers as well as the trade to and from the East Indies.

It has been likewise argued for the defendant that 12 Car., cap. 18, concerning navigation,[1] is of as large extent as the Act, and yet it did not comprehend a coast-ways trade, that no goods or commodities whatsoever shall be imported into or exported out of any lands, islands, plantations, or territories but in English built ships and whereof the master and three fourth parts are English. This Act did not comprehend the coast-ways trade, for 7 & 8 Will. III, c. 23, was forced to be enacted to prevent this abuse in a coast-ways trade, which enacts 'That no goods shall be exported or imported into any part or place in the said colonies or plantations, but in English built ships'.[2]

But the answer is very plain, for, indeed, 12 Car. did not comprehend a coast-ways trade of the plantations, for the goods were carried from one port to

[1] Stat. 12 Car. II, c. 18 (*SR*, V, 246–250).

[2] Stat. 7 & 8 Will. III, c. 22, s. 1 (*SR*, VII, 103).

another within the same plantation, and, though the goods are imported and exported, yet they are not exported from the plantations. As if goods are carried from Portsmouth to London coast-ways, though the goods are exported and imported, yet they are not exported from England. So, the word 'plantations' in the Statute is a general name. And though goods are carried there from one port to another, yet they are not exported from the plantations.

But there is no arguing from the words of one statute to another, unless the words were exactly the same because the difference of the words will alter the sense and intent of the law. And it is not right reasoning to say that, because as the Statute 12 Car. is so penned as not to prohibit a coast-ways trade in foreign built ships within the plantations, that so the 9 & 10 Will. III does not give a sole coast-ways trade to the subscribers within the limits, where the language, the penning, the sense, and signification of the words and intent of the Statute is perfectly different, for no subject by the Act is directly or indirectly to visit, haunt, frequent, trade, traffic, or adventure into or from the said East Indies or other the parts aforementioned.

As the words are not the same in any particular, so there is no similitude between them. The Statute of Car. respects the thing; this Statute respects the person.

It is penned in as strong a language as I think is possible to be used to forbid all subjects all manner of trading within the limits. There is no ambiguity in the words. I do not see how they can be tortured or represented in any manner to let a subject into a coast-ways trade. The sole trade is granted to the subscribers. They are to execute it in the manner they think proper.

The subscribers, before the making of this Statute, had a right to trade coast-ways. By their subscription, in pursuance of this Statute, they have the sole right of trading coast-ways and excluding all others, so that which was before the general right of all subjects became the property of the subscribers by this Act. Whatever the law granted to them, it excluded all other persons from it. And the exclusive words are penned in the most forcible manner and in the most significant language to exclude all other subjects from trading within the limits.

And it is highly probable that this Act of the East India Company being made after the 7 & 8 Will. III, which makes use of these words that they shall not carry goods from one port or place to another port or place in the said colony; so, in this subsequent law, they thought it enough to say in general that no subject should carry goods within the limits, but into or from any creek, haven, port, or city within the same.

604

Hanson v. Fielding

(Ex. 1726)

The question in this case was whether lands that were formerly owned by the Hospitalers of St. John of Jerusalem were discharged from the payment of tithes.

However, in this case, the plaintiff could not prove his alleged claim to the tithes.

Harvard Law School MS. 1082, vol. 1, p. 273, pl. 1

Easter term 1726.

The plaintiff, as impropriator or lessee of the rectory of Shelton in the County of Warwick, brings his bill for tithes against the defendant, who insists that he is the lord of the manor of Barnewell containing 223 acres at £96 *per annum* and that the manor and lands were part and parcel of the possessions of St. John of Jerusalem and they were so granted by Edward VI to Sir Ralph Sadler and so, by several mesne conveyances, the same vested in the defendant. And he insists on the Statute of 32 Hen. VIII[1] by way of discharge.

We that were counsel for the defendant showed the grant of Edward VI to Sir Ralph Sadler, which called the place in question Tene Place in Barnangle, *alias* Barnacle, together with all privileges, but no tithes were granted. And then we produced the grant of 5 Edw. VI, whereby tithes were granted with the manor of Barnacle to Nichols and Bullock, who granted to Michael Fielding, grandfather of the defendant. And then we showed the descriptions of the parcels of lands only by a settlement in 1653. Then we produced some old court rolls belonging to the manor of Barnacle, whereby some of the fields in question were mentioned. We insisted on the matter of law and that this was a good exemption and relied on the case in Raymond 225, Fosset v. Franklin, and Dyer 277.[2]

But then [were] objected by the plaintiff the cases following: Sir Wm. Jones 181; Cro. Jac. 57; Latch 89, Bridgman 32,[3] and that it was agreed by these cases that, though in the first clause of 31 Hen. VIII,[4] the word 'privileges' was

---

[1] Stat. 32 Hen. VIII, c. 24 (*SR*, III, 778–781).

[2] *Fosset v. Francklin* (1673), T. Raymond 225, 83 E.R. 117, also 3 Keble 208, 217, 84 E.R. 679, 684, 1 Eagle & Younge 501; *Stathome's Case* (1568), 3 Dyer 277, 73 E.R. 621, 1 Gwillim 132, 1 Eagle & Younge 59.

[3] *Whitton v. Weston* (1627), W. Jones 182, 82 E.R. 96, Latch 89, 82 E.R. 289, J. Bridgman 32, 123 E.R. 1179, also Godbolt 392, 78 E.R. 231, Benloe 168, 185, 73 E.R. 1031, 1043, 1 Gwillim 410, 1 Eagle & Younge 340, H. Winch, *Le Beau Pledeur: A Book of Entries* (1680), p. 342, Paynell K.B. 35, 44, 258, 342; *Cornwallis v. Spurling* (1602), Croke Jac. 57, 79 E.R. 48, 1 Gwillim 224, 1 Eagle & Younge 157, *sub nom. Quarles v. Spurling*, Moore K.B. 913, 72 E.R. 993.

[4] Stat. 31 Hen. VIII, c. 13, s. 1 (*SR*, III, 733).

mentioned, yet that would not be an exemption within the second clause, and, therefore, the word 'privileges' did not discharge it by the Stat. 32 Hen. VIII.

However, the whole court thought the last resolution was right, in Raymond 225, and another case cited by Mr. Ward, in Trinity 1687, Vicar of Bengoe v. Sir John Gore,[1] where this exemption was allowed. But as for the plaintiff, when they came to show their grant, it was subsequent to both our grants, and, therefore, the court dismissed the bill.

Taussig MS. 311, vol. 2, p. 890

Thursday, 12 May 1726, by English bill.

The plaintiff and his lessee of the impropriation of Shilton and Barnacle in County of Warwick demand tithes of corn and grain arising out of particular lands lying within that rectory. The defense is that the lands lie in the manor of Barnacle, being about 223 acres, that they were part of the possessions of the Hospital of St. John of Jerusalem. Their exemption was *quamdiu propriis manibus*.

Serjeant *Pengelly*: All the lands of the Hospital of St. John of Jerusalem did not come to the crown by [Stat.] 32 Hen. VIII, but some by [Stat.] 31. But he waived this point. And he said he would rely entirely on the Statute of 32 Hen. VIII and an exemption under that. And he insisted on the authorities following, *viz*. Dyer 77; Plowden 60.[2] Afterwards, in King James' time, as it appears by Cro. Jac. 57, it came to be doubted, but, there, the point was only debated on the foot of 31 Hen. VIII.

Sir William Jones 182 is a debate of 32 Hen. VIII, and the judges were divided, but three of them resolved the point against Whitlock. Raymond 225, Fosset and Franklyn, absolutely determined that the word 'privileges' in 32 Hen. VIII carries the discharge. And so the point was fluctuating between the time of Elizabeth and Charles II. It was then settled, and, by him, there was no dispute of it since unless, perchance, in this court, which cases, if any there are, being not printed, will be cited on the other side.

So we will go on to our proof to make out the fact. 15 December 4 Edw. VI [1550], there were letters patent to Sir Ralph Sadler *et al.*, but no tithes were therein mentioned.

N.B. *Quaere per me*, if the abbot etc. has the rectory and also the manor etc. within the parish and the demesnes of the manor are in hand *tempore dissolutionis* and so come to the crown by the dissolution, then the crown grants parcel of the manor to A. *cum omnibus juribus, emolumentis, privilegiis in tam amplis modo et forma quam abbas*[3] etc. and also grants the rectory to B., whether the grant to A., supposing it to be prior, will carry a grant of the tithes, for the discharge in

[1] *Daniel v. Gore* (1687), Eq. Cases Exch. 278, Public Record Office, E.126/15, f. 106v.

[2] *Abbot of Kingswood's Case* (1552), 1 Dyer 77, 73 E.R. 166; *Dive v. Maningham* (1550), 1 Plowden 60, 75 E.R. 96.

[3] with all rights, emoluments, privileges in as ample manner and form as the abbots.

this case at the time of the dissolution may be as well owing to the unity as to the order. And I should think in a such case, if it can be proved that the rectory came first and then the lands, it would be a plain case that the lands can have no discharge. But if the lands *ex quibus* come first and then the rectory is appropriated, there the first right of discharge being *ratione ordinis* perhaps may not be destroyed by the right of discharge arising from the unity.

The manor of Barnacle *visus francplegii Prioris Sc. J.J.* 15 May 1 Hen. V [1413], so that it did not appear that this manor came into the possession of the prior before this time.

Mr. *Ward*: As to the point of the discharge of the lands of St. John of Jerusalem, it was determined in Trinity 1687, Daniel, vicar of Benjeo in the County of Hertford v. Sir John Gore upon a case made and debated 10 May 1688.

Bunbury: The defense is of an exemption. And now, they insist on a title to the tithes themselves, and these are distinct and separate things.

Chief Baron [GILBERT]: If they have a right to them *in prendre*, we cannot decree for you as impropriator.

As to the point of law, *Bunbury* said that the case in Dyer is an authority that the land is discharged by 31 Hen. VIII. Cro. Jac. 57; Moor 913. As to Raymond 25, a short note of a case and as to the word 'privileges', the same word is in the first part of the Statute 31 Hen. VIII, and yet it has been determined that, without the other express clauses of discharge, the lands would not have been discharged. And if this be true, then the 32 Hen. VIII having not any express clause of discharge, the word 'privileges' alone will not do.

Sed per CURIAM: We look upon it now that this is not to be disputed.

And when the plaintiff came to reply, he could prove no title at all to his tithes. And so his bill was dismissed.

Bunbury 214, 145 E.R. 651

A bill [was brought] by a lay impropriator for tithes within the parish and boundaries of Shilton and Barnacle in the County of Warwick.

The defendant, as to the manor of Barnacle, by his answer, insists that the manor was part of the possessions of the priors of Saint John of Jerusalem, whose possessions were exempt from payment of tithes *quamdiu propriis manibus etc.* Then he sets forth the Stat. 31 Hen. VIII with the clause of discharge and also the Stat. 32 Hen. VIII, whereby these priories with all privileges etc. were vested in the crown, and that no tithes in kind had been paid for this manor.

Upon the debate of this exemption were cited for the plaintiff: lib. 2, 47a; Cro. Jac. 57, Moore 913; Degge 346.[1] For the defendant: Dyer 277b; Bridgman

[1] *Green v. Balser* (1596), 2 Coke Rep. 46, 76 E.R. 519, 1 Gwillim 189, 1 Eagle & Younge 113; *Cornwallis v. Spurling* (1602), *ut supra*; S. Degge, *Parson's Counsellor.*

32, Latch 89, Sir W. Jones 182; Raymond 225; Daniel, Vicar of Bengo *in Comitatu* Hertford v. Sir J. Gower, Trinity 1687.[1]

The court seemed all of opinion that it was a good discharge.

But the plaintiff, afterwards, failed in making out his title. And the bill, upon that, was dismissed.

Gilbert Rep. 225, 25 E.R. 156,
1 Rayner 231, 2 Gwillim 663, 1 Eagle & Younge 812

A bill was brought by an impropriator claiming under a grant from the crown after the dissolution of the religious houses for the tithes of corn, grain, wool, and lamb for the year 1723. The defendants, as to the tithe for wool and lamb, say they are lessees of the vicar of Austis and that the small tithes did not belong to the mother church, but were received by the chaplain of Austis long before the dissolution of religious houses and that, after they came into the hands of the crown, they were also enjoyed distinctly. As to the tithes of corn and grain, they say that the lands were formerly part of the possessions of the Hospitalers of St. John of Jerusalem and that their lands were discharged from the payment of tithes, while they continued in their own manurance and occupation, that their lands, by virtue of some acts of Parliament, 27,[2] 31, and 32 Hen. VIII, were vested in the crown and were to be held and enjoyed by the king and his grantees in as large and ample manner as the late religious houses held them, that they were grantees under the crown and, consequently, entitled to hold them discharged from tithes.

Mr. *Bunbury*, for the defendant, objected that the lands of the Hospitalers of St. John of Jerusalem coming to the crown by the Statute 32 Hen. VIII, c. 24, they could not claim the privilege of the clause of exemption in Statute 31 Hen. VIII, c. 13, by which it is appointed that all monasteries, abbeys, etc., which before had come or hereafter should come to the king by suppression, surrender, etc. should be held and enjoyed by him in as large and ample manner as the religious houses held them and, whereas many of them were discharged from tithes, they should be held by the king and his grantees discharged etc. And he cited 2 Coke 47, Bishop of Canterbury's Case,[3] where it was resolved that the clause of discharge should extend only to those possessions, which come to the king by the said Act and that it would be absurd that the branch of the Act of 31 Hen. VIII should extend to a future act of Parliament, which the makers of the said Statute 31 Hen. VIII, without the spirit of prophecy, could not have foreknowledge of.

---

[1] *Stathome's Case* (1568), *ut supra*; *Whitton v. Weston* (1627), *ut supra*; *Fosset v. Francklin* (1673), *ut supra*; *Daniel v. Gore* (1687), *ut supra*.

[2] Stat. 27 Hen. VIII, c. 28 (*SR*, III, 575–578).

[3] *Green v. Balser* (1596), 2 Coke Rep. 46, 76 E.R. 519, 1 Gwillim 189, 1 Eagle & Younge 113.

And he insisted strongly upon the case of Cornwallis v. Spurling, Croke Jac. 57; Moore 913, as an express authority in point.

Serjeant *Pengelly*, for the defendant, made use of two ways to take off the objection: first, that part of the land of the Hospitalers of St. John of Jerusalem were vested in the crown by the Stat. 31 Hen. VIII and that the Stat. 32 Hen. VIII was only made because of the great compass of their estates, some of which were in Ireland, and to be so general as to comprehend all that might be omitted in Stat. 31 Hen. VIII, and then, without doubt, the branch of the Act concerning discharge from tithes extends to them. But, if the court should think these lands passed only by the 32rd, he thought, secondly, that, even upon that Statute, the grantee should hold them discharged from tithes, and seeing it had been resolved by some judges that the clause of exemption in the Stat. 31 Hen. VIII should not extend to latter Statutes, though at first that was a doubt upon the words 'or hereafter' shall come, he would, therefore, waive that and rely upon the Stat. 32 Hen. VIII, by which they are vested in the crown with all privileges etc. Now, one of their privileges was that they should hold the lands discharged from tithes whilst they continued in their occupation, which being continued to the crown by the said Statute 32 Hen. VIII, we say is a real discharge annexed to the land and going along with it. And it has been accordingly expressly granted to us, for we have a grant dated the 15th of December 4 Edw. VI [1550], of this manor of Barnacle etc. with the very same words as are in the Statute, *viz.* with 'all privileges' etc., and we have enjoyed it ever since with the benefit of this exemption. And he cited Raymond 225, Fosset v. Franklin, where it is said by Hale, Chief Justice, that, by reason of the word privileges, they shall not pay tithes, and it was resolved accordingly by the court.

Serjeant *Comyns*, senior, and Mr. *Ward*, senior, on the same side, cited Dyer 277, pl. 60; W. Jones 182; Bridgman 32; Latch 89, and by *Ward*, in Trinity term, 1687, the Case of Daniel, Vicar of Bengeo in Hertfordshire, and Sir John Gower, where, upon considering all the cases, this court held all the lands discharged and dismissed the bill.

Mr. *Bunbury* said in reply that, in the case in Dyer, the lands came to the crown by Stat. 31 Hen. VIII, and then they were immediately exempt, as Bridgman 32; Latch 89; W. Jones 182. As the case appears, the court was equally divided upon the point of discharge. As to Raymond 225, it was a very short report, and it does not appear upon what reasons the court went. The great stress is laid upon the word privileges in the Statute 32 Hen. VIII, and yet that very word is used in Statute 31 Hen. VIII. And if that of itself had been sufficient, for what reason did they insert a particular clause of exemption from tithes? He insisted upon the case of Cornwallis v. Spurling, which, being determined upon a special verdict, the book also taking notice that the like judgment was given upon a demurrer, is of great authority.

Gilbert, Chief Baron: Those privileges were granted to these ecclesiastical corporations by bulls from the pope. But these discharges, for want of a special clause to continue them, were extinguished in as many of them, as were dissolved by the Stat. 27 Hen. VIII, but that cramping the king in his alienations, in Stat. 31 Hen. VIII, they put a clause to continue to the crown the privileges that were in them as special corporations. Now, the question is whether the word privileges in Stat. 32 Hen. VIII has not the same intent to carry all the other privileges to the crown. If the point had been resolved, we should not have disputed it.

Note: It was no further settled, for, when the plaintiff went into his proof of the grants of the tithes of these lands, they appeared to be grants of different possessions. Therefore, his bill was dismissed.

[Order of 21 February 1726: 2 Wood 255.]

605

Quilter v. Mussendine

(Ex. 1726)

The statutory requirement that parsons not be absent from their parishes more than eighty days in a year means any eighty days, not eighty consecutive days.

The word year means a calendar year, not an aera.

Harvard Law School MS. 1082, vol. 1, p. 271

Easter term 1726.

A bill was brought, as lessee of White, rector of Little Oakley, for tithes. The defendant pleads the Statute of 13 Eliz.,[1] that the lease being made by Thomas White, the rector, and that this was a benefice with cure and that Thomas White was absent above eighty days in the year.

Bunbury, for the defendant, [said] that he thought Mills v. Etheridge, 3 February 1725,[2] [is] in point.

Ward, for the plaintiff: This is no good plea, for the Statute of Limitations[3] ought not to be pleaded to the discovery. And to make this plea a complete bar, it ought to be averred that the absence continued for eighty days together. Moore 448; 1 Bulstrode 111.[4] Absence may be justifiable, as in sickness or where there is an inhibition from the ordinary [or] lawful imprisonment. 6 Rept., Butler and Goodal.[5] And, in these cases, absence is excusable. And the lease is not void until

[1] Stat. 13 Eliz. I, c. 20 (*SR*, IV, 556).

[2] *Mills v. Etheridge* (Ex. 1726), see above, Case No. 585.

[3] Stat. 21 Jac. I, c. 16 (*SR*, IV, 1222–1223).

[4] *Robins v. Gerrard* (1596), Moore K.B. 434, 448, 71 E.R. 678, 686; *Shepherd v. Twoulsie* (1611), 1 Bulstrode 111, 80 E.R. 808.

[5] *Goodale, qui tam v. Butler* (1598), 6 Coke Rep. 21, 77 E.R. 258, also Moore K.B. 540, 72 E.R. 744, Croke Eliz. 590, 78 E.R. 83, Gouldsborough 169, 75 E.R. 1071.

eighty days are elapsed. And it would be hard to permit this plea to be good to the discovery because, upon the traversing of this plea, if it is found that it was a lawful absence, then the plaintiff is turned around to begin again. And if the party is to be examined upon interrogatories, that cannot be obtained if the party dies, and, [by] this method, the plaintiff may be kept out three years before he can obtain an answer.

Edlin, for the plaintiff: This is no good plea to the discovery. Gumley v. Fontleroy, Easter 1720.[1] And the practice of the court is grounded on good reason, for tithes are multifarious and only within the cognizance of the party. In all cases of *modus*es, there must be a discovery; so in this case, for, in that of a *modus*, the right is decreed. Stat. 18 Eliz., cap. 11,[2] to enforce the penalty says that this last Statute only relates to one year's tithes.

Bunbury, for the defendant: The words are to be taken [as] within the year before making the lease.

[To the] objection of the Stat. 18 Eliz., [he] answered, though a jurisdiction is given to the ordinary, yet there are no exclusive words.

[To the] objection that the absence ought to be continuing, [he] answered the plea is according to the [words of the] Statute. Noy 116;[3] the absence need not be eighty days together.

The Stat. 21 Hen. VIII[4] is worded in a different manner. Cro. Eliz. 100.[5] The excuse lies on the plaintiff. And they have not answered the objection and the distinction between a *modus* and this case, for a *modus* admits the plaintiff's title, but it is otherwise in the present case.

Bootle, for the defendant: [As to the] objection [of the case in] Moore,[6] [he] answered Yelverton 106, Jennings v. Hathway.[7]

Chief Baron [GILBERT]: I deny the case in Bulstrode to be [good] law. And that Statute would be totally evaded if it was. The distinction is right. The *modus* admits the right; this plea denies it. Mills v. Etheridge, in this case, [is] in point. The Statute of Limitations is not good in bar of a discovery. I allow the plea.

PRICE: The case does not differ from Mills v. Etheridge; only the plea is better in this case. I allow the plea because it takes away the plaintiff's foundation for his demand. I have some scruple upon the [issue] in relation to the continuance of the absence of eighty days.

---

1 *Gumley v. Fontleroy* (Ex. 1720–1721), see above, Case No. 127.

2 Stat. 18 Eliz. I, c. 11, s. 5 (*SR*, IV, 623).

3 *Sidner v. Calver*, Noy 116, 74 E.R. 1081.

4 Stat. 21 Hen. VIII, c. 13, s. 15 (*SR*, III, 294–295).

5 *Collins v. Vaughan* (1588), Croke Eliz. 100, 78 E.R. 358.

6 *Robins v. Gerrard* (1596), *ut supra*.

7 *Jennings v. Haithwaite* (1607), Yelverton 106, 80 E.R. 72, also 1 Brownlow & Goldesborough 208, 123 E.R. 758.

PAGE: The plaintiff has no right to his demand if his lessor was absent. The plaintiff brings a bill for rents and profits. The defendant pleads a purchase for a valuable consideration. That is a good plea in bar of a discovery because it denies the plaintiff's right.

HALE: I agree that the plea is good.

And so it was allowed by the whole court.

Taussig MS. 311, vol. 2, p. 907

Easter term 1926.

The objections to the plea were, first, absence or non-absence is issuable. And by the authorities following, the absence must be continual. Moor 448; 1 Bulstr. 111. But supposing it is well pleaded in this respect, yet it is not well pleaded in another because it is pleaded to the discovery.

Edlin, of same side: This case is different from that in last term. The absence laid is an absence of above eighty days, *viz.* between 1st September 1723 to the last day of August then next following. In the case of Gumley and Fauntleroy, Hilary 1720, it was resolved that a *modus* could not be pleaded without discovering quantities and values, and there is no difference between the case of a *modus* and a plea of absence. As to the point of discovery, there ought at least to be a conviction before the ordinary.

Bunbury: There are no negative words in the Stat. 18 Eliz., ca. 11. And Yelverton 106 proves that there need not be a continued absence for eighty days together.

Chief Baron [GILBERT]: The case in Bulstrode is certainly not law. And, if there were not any authorities to the contrary, I should make no scruple of overruling it; much more when authorities are expressly contrary, as in Noy and Yelverton, for the construction in Bulstrode would wholly overturn the very intent and whole design of the Statute.

PRICE agrees and comes off from his former objection as to discovery.

PAGE, ditto: There may be an occasion for a discovery though there is a *modus*, for if the *modus* is 1d. for a load of hay etc., [in] such case, a discovery is necessary even to direct a recovery upon the foot of the *modus* supposing it to be true.

So *per totam* CURIAM, the plea was allowed.

HALE: *In casu supradicto*, the point is that the plaintiff has no title at all and in a case of limitation, I should have thought that the statute is pleadable, but only for this reason, that tithes are of a superior nature to simple contracts and the statutes extend not to any specialties.

N.B. On the same day, another plea of the same nature was allowed.

Gilbert Rep. 228, 25 E.R. 158,
1 Rayner 225, 2 Gwillim 668, 1 Eagle & Younge 816

A bill was brought for a discovery of tithes by the lessee of a parson. The defendant pleads the Stat. 13 Eliz., c. 20, against non-residence, in bar.

Ward, for the plaintiff, objected to the plea:

First, that it was bad in substance, for that it did not show that he was not of necessity or justifiably absent, barely saying he was voluntarily absent not being sufficient, as he might have done, according to Butler and Godall's Case, 6 Coke 21b;

Secondly, the time of absence the Statute requires to avoid the lease is eighty days and more, which ought to appear to be a continual absence for eighty days altogether and at one time. 1 Bulstrode 111, Shepherd v. Townslie; Modern 436.

Thirdly, though the plea should be thought good in substance, yet it could be no bar to the discovery, though it might as to the relief, to prove which he mentioned the case of a *modus* pleaded in bar to a bill for tithes, in which case, it was held that, although the plea was good as to the relief, yet it was no bar as to the discovery; but that the defendant must answer and show the quantity, quality, and value of the tithes; and the reason upon which that has been so resolved is because, if the defendant's plea in bar should prove to be false, the plaintiff then is to have a discovery from the defendant upon oath, and they will not let him run the hazard of losing such discovery, which he might do if the defendant should die in the meantime; and that, in Hilary term last, the court would not allow a plea of the Statute of Limitations to be a good bar to a bill for tithes.

Fourthly, *Edlin* objected that they had set out the year wrong in the plea and that it did not appear that he was absent for above eighty days in any one year, taking the year to commence according to the computation of the *aera* upon the 25th of March, as he insisted it ought.

Bunbury and *Bootle*, for the defendant, to what had been said, gave the following answers.

As to the first objection, that, if he had any good excuse for his absence, it being a thing lying entirely within his own cognizance, they need not take notice of it, but he must show it in his replication.

And the whole court held the same.

Secondly, the construction they contend for would entirely defeat the Statute, for, at that rate, he need only be there five days in the whole year. As to the opinion in Bulstrode, it is only that of two judges' *obiter*; and as to Moore 436, the *insimul ac pariter* are in the special verdict, but no notice was taken of it, that it was necessary they should be in.

Thirdly, they distinguished this from a plea of a *modus*, for that admits the plaintiff's title to the tithes, but only avoids the payment of them in kind, for that, by custom, he was to have something else in lieu of them. In that case, the demand is allowed to be just, and the only question is in what manner that demand is to be satisfied. But the plea in the present case denies and defeats all the plaintiff's right and title to the tithes and to any manner of satisfaction for them. The plea of the Statute of Limitations was also very different from this, for that Statute could not be extended to a demand for tithes.

Fourthly, that the year was to be 365 days without reckoning it from the 25th of March; and they insisted upon the case of Etheridge v. Mills,[1] in this court, being in point.

GILBERT, Chief Baron: The case of Etheridge v. Mills cannot be distinguished from this.

Secondly, The case in Bulstrode is not law, for that would defeat the Statute *causa qua supra*.

Thirdly, that this was a good plea in bar, both as to the discovery and relief; as to the case of pleading a *modus*, that allows the plaintiff's title, and so that is pleading against what you allowed before.

The reason why the Statute of Limitations was not allowed to be pleaded in bar to a bill for tithes was that tithes were not of the nature of those demands that are intended to be barred by the Statute; besides, that plea allows the title. Years shall not refer to the *aera*, but must be intended a solar year, 365 days.

PRICE, Baron, agreed the year shall be 365 days and the absence any eighty days within that compass.

As to the second objection, how inconvenient it might be to allow such plea a good bar as to the discovery, for that supposing the plea to be false, if the defendant should die, the plaintiff might lose the benefit of a discovery. The answer was very plain, for the defendant having here shown that the plaintiff has no title to the tithes themselves, he, in consequence, can have no title to a discovery concerning them.

PAGE, Baron. The plea of a *modus* is an acknowledgment of the title of the plaintiff and is in part a discovery itself, for it sets out he is to pay so much for corn, so much for pigs, etc., and, then, it is nothing strange he should be compelled to go on a little farther and show the quantity and number of his corn, pigs, etc.

He took the distinction to be between a plea acknowledging the title and one which absolutely denies it. If a bill be brought by an heir claiming by descent against another, suggesting some fraud and praying a discovery, there, if the defendant pleads he is a purchaser for valuable consideration, such plea which goes to the plaintiff's title is always good, both as to the relief and discovery. So in the case of a bill for an account against one as bailiff, suggesting fraud, if the defendant pleads that, at such a time, he did account, he need not go on and set out an account. And he also agreed as to the computation of the year.

HALE, Baron, [held] that the plea is a good bar to the discovery and that the case of a *modus* had been rightly distinguished from this.

As to the Statute of Limitations, he thought it might have been pleaded in bar to the discovery if it could have been pleaded at all, which it could not, for that specialties are not barred by the Statute and tithes are of a higher nature.

---

1 *Mills v. Etheridge* (Ex. 1726), see above, Case No. 585.

And he farther said that no construction could be too liberal to make parsons reside and take care of their parishes.

606

Cuthbert v. Westwood

(Ex. 1726)

A suit in equity for a modus decimandi *in lieu of tithes can be brought against only the owners of the lands in question and the occupiers will be bound by the decree as well as the owners.*

Gilbert Rep. 230, 25 E.R. 160,
1 Rayner 224, 2 Gwillim 666, 1 Eagle & Younge 815

A bill was brought against land owners to establish a right of £40 *per annum* and in lieu of tithes, which, by a decree in the time of Charles I, was to be paid out of particular lands, which were formerly part of the Forest of Braden, to the vicar of Churchlade in Wiltshire.

Two objections were taken for want of parties, first, that these land owners were tenants to the crown of lands lying within the bounds of the forest, which formerly paid no tithes, and that so the Attorney General ought to have been made a party.

Response: It does not appear by the bill that they are lessees under the crown and the defendants have not insisted upon it in their answers, and so that is out of the case.

Second objection: It is not sufficient to make the land owners only, but they should have made the occupiers, parties to the bill, for a decree against the land owners could not affect them.

Response by *Bunbury*. That it would be endless to make all the occupiers parties and, if that was necessary to be done, the plaintiff could never come at his right, for there were great numbers of them and any single one dying would put the plaintiff to his bill of revivor. And he cited the Case of Biscoe against the Undertakers of the Land Bank,[1] before Lord Keeper Wright, who said he would not oblige them to bring all before the court, since the right might be determined by having a view, which the court thought reasonable.

Per CURIAM: Though we can decree only against the land owners, who are before the court, yet that will affect the lands. The £40 *per annum* ought to be apportioned among the owners, and the original decree may be carried against the occupiers. And they decreed a commission should go to inquire into and ascertain the value of the lands, the owners' and occupiers' names, and what proportion of the £40 *per annum* each tenement ought to pay.

[1] *Anonymous v. Briscoe* (Ch. 1706), Lincoln's Inn MS. Misc. 383, f. 8.

[Order *sub nom.* Cuthbert v. Pleydell (5 May 1726), 2 Wood 280.]

607

Gerrard v. Williams

(Ex. 1726)

An action for defamation lies for saying that a woman committed fornication.

Taussig MS. 311, vol. 2, p. 902

Easter term 1726.

The words were 'I fucked Nanny Gerrard as often as she has fingers and toes. As I was fucking Nanny Gerrard, her father had like to have caught us.'

Probyn, Serjeant, in arrest of judgment, said the words were to no more [intent] than calling her a whore or charging her with fornication; so they are not actionable because they are words only of spiritual cognizance.

2 Lutw. 1295;[1] one must lay special damages, that is one must specify who courted and afterwards refused to marry, for a general allegation that several persons refused is not sufficient. Cro. Eliz. 786;[2] it must affect the particular person refusing with notice.

Second, the damage is that her father turned her out of doors. 1 Ventr. 4, 1 Syd. 390.[3]

Probyn: This [allegation] of the father's anger may be only a windlass to wind up the action.

But the court gave judgment immediately for the plaintiff because the law is much altered in these cases of scandal. And so they would not so much as put the plaintiff's counsel to reply to the objections.

608

Gwinn v. Hutton

(Ex. 1726)

An action for defamation lies for saying that a man is a cuckold.

Taussig MS. 311, vol. 2, p. 904, pl. 1

Easter term 1726.

---

[1] *Wetharald v. Clarkson* (1700), 2 Lutwyche 1295, 125 E.R. 717, also 12 Modern 597, 88 E.R. 1544.

[2] *Royal v. Peckham* (1600), Croke Eliz. 786, 78 E.R. 1015.

[3] *Barnes v. Bruddel* (1669), 1 Ventris 4, 86 E.R. 4, 1 Siderfin 396, 82 E.R. 1178, also 1 Levinz 261, 83 E.R. 397.

The court granted a rule to show cause why a [writ of] prohibition should not go to the spiritual court of Llandaff to prohibit a suit there for these words, 'If the horned fellow or hornified man' etc., *ex mea motione*.

609

Gravenor, *qui tam* v. Dent

(Ex. 1726)

The question in this case was whether brandy can be carried by sea from one port to another within England without the permission of the officers of the customs.

Taussig MS. 311, vol. 2, p. 909

Easter term 1926.

An information was exhibited for carrying a parcel of brandy from the Port of London to another part of England by sea without a Custom House sufferance.

The defense was that there was an excise permit so that the defendant's counsel insisted that this was sufficient within 6 Geo., ca. 21, § 18,[1] and that it was the single question.

N.B. and query of the case of Morey, *qui tam* v. Coates, which, in my brief, was said to have been ruled in point in Trinity term last by the present Chief Baron.

And the Chief Baron [GILBERT] now seemed strongly of opinion that the point was with the informer *pro rege*; otherwise, says he, this new Act would weaken the security which the king had under the former Act of 14 Car.

The CHIEF BARON, however, gave way for a case [to be made] upon the point.

610

Coleman v. Barker

(Ex. 1726)

Tithes are due for agistment of sheep.

Harvard Law School MS. 1082, vol. 1, p. 268, pl. 1

Easter term 1726.

The plaintiff, who was seised of the rectory of Thompson in the County of Norfolk, brought his bill for the feeding of wetter sheep on turnips, which sheep had paid tithe wool.

Pengelly and I, for the plaintiff, insisted that there were twenty-five acres so consumed so that, from the time they were sheared to the time they were sold, they were unprofitable cattle to the rector, and, therefore, they ought to pay an

[1] Stat. 6 Geo. I, c. 21, s. 17.

agistment tithe. And we cited Dummer v. Wingfield, 1 Will & Mary, Hilary, in the court.[1]

Ward and *Bunbury*, for the defendant: This is only a manner of husbandry. And there are always kept the same number of sheep. Tithes only arise *annuatim*. And if this was to be allowed, it would be a double tithe. Rolle, *Abridgment*, 642.[2] No tithes are due for herbage of sheep where they are shorn, 2 Inst. 651,[3] nor of cattle that manure the ground. Shower 193.[4] If this demand was to be encouraged, it would be a double tithe. The case of Dummer v. Wingfield differs because that was founded on a custom and a fraud.

Price: Dummer v. Wingfield is a case in point, and these sheep are unprofitable from June to April. And so the tithe ought to be paid.

Page: This comes within the rule of unprofitable cattle. And [tithe] wool is for the year preceding. And it might happen that they might be fattened and sold.

Hale: Here is an adventitious [gain] to the owner by feeding these sheep. And, therefore, he ought to pay his tithes.

So, by the whole court, he was decreed to account for the tithe, *quod vide*.

Taussig MS. 311, vol. 2, p. 960

Trinity term 1726.

The rector of Thompson in the County of Norfolk exhibits his bill for tithes of feeding sheep on turnips. The defendant insists he fed his sheep on them as unsevered from the ground. There were twenty-five acres of turnip ground, and the sheep fed from June to April. 1 Will. & Mar., Dummer and Wingfield, Hilary term, 11 February; Shower 163 or 193; Rolle, *Abr.*, 642. So he insists upon a pasturage tithe for 300 sheep. These were bought in May [and] shorn there, and the rector had the tithe of wool of all these sheep. In April following, he sells out 100 of these sheep fold and then replaces 100 fresh sheep and so on. Rolle, *Abr.*, 642; 2 Inst. 651. [There is] no agistment of such cattle as the parson has the tithe of, 2 Inst. 651, as to fruit, *sed quaere*, Rolle, *Abr.*, 648; Popham 197.[5]

Price was formerly of opinion that no pasturage tithe was due for sheep. But I am convinced of the contrary by the case of Dummer and Wingfield.

Page: The rule is [they are] not profitable and unprofitable cattle in their nature, but profitable to the parson. And these sheep are not profitable for part of the year unless you will give him an agistment tithe.

Hale was of the same opinion.

---

[1] *Dummer v. Wingfield* (Ex. 1690), Dodd 94, Eq. Cases Exch. 328, 1 Eagle & Younge 566, Public Record Office, E.126/15, f. 302v, 1 Wood 273.

[2] *Marskall v. Price* (1614), 1 Rolle, Abr., *Dismes*, pl. R, 8, p. 642.

[3] E. Coke, *Second Institute* (1642), p. 651.

[4] *Eastmond v. Sandys* (1696), Shower P.C. 192, 1 E.R. 129, 2 Gwillim 558, 1 Rayner 78, 1 Eagle & Younge 616, 1 Wood 364.

[5] *Anonymous* (1626), Popham 197, 79 E.R. 1289, 1 Eagle & Younge 356.

So the court decreed that sheep kept in the parish from shearing time, i.e. June in 1720, and sold out in April 1721 shall pay a pasturage tithe, though at the time when those sheep were sold out, there were an equal number of new sheep brought in, of which he had the whole wool [tithe] in June 1721.

Quod multum dubito.

Gilbert Rep. 231, 25 E.R. 160,

1 Rayner 222, 2 Gwillim 665, 1 Eagle & Younge 814

The plaintiff [Coleman, impropriator of Thompson in Norfolk], by his bill, demanded tithe for the depasturing of sheep on turnips remaining on the ground unsevered.

The defendant said the sheep paid tithe of wool and that tithes ought not to be paid twice.

It appeared that, after shearing time, the defendant fed his sheep with turnips, whereby they were bettered 5s. per sheep, that they went about five months on the turnips, and then were sold for the butcher. And the defendant brought in a like quantity of new sheep before shearing time came again so that the plaintiff always had tithe wool of the full number.

Pengelly, for the plaintiff, said this improvement of the sheep by the turnips was a new increase and that consequently tithe ought to be paid for the improvement and increase. And, if the turnips had been severed, there had been no doubt but tithes had been due. He cited three cases which he relied on:

First, the case of Nicholas v. Hooper, 1 Rolle, *Abridgment*, tit. Dismes, 642, pl. 7,[1] where it is adjudged that, if a man pays tithes of lambs and, two months after, shears the other nine parts, he shall pay tithe wool, although he had before paid tithe of the lambs; for, says the book, it is a new increase.

Secondly, the second case which he quoted was Shower's Parl. Cases 192, Eastmond v. Sandys,[2] a demand for tithe herbage of oxen, which were depastured to be fatted. The defendant insisted that these oxen had been used for the plow, and so were exempted, that their labor improved the parson's tithe, and so to pay tithe for their agistment would be double tithing. But the Court of Exchequer decreed, and it was affirmed in the House of Lords, that tithe herbage was due from the time they were taken from the plow, they being then no otherwise beneficial to the parson in tithes.

Thirdly, the case most relied on was a decree in this court, Hilary 1 Will. & Mar. [1689], Dummer v. Wingfield,[3] which was a demand of tithe for pasturage of sheep from the time of shearing until they were sold. The defendants insisted that, by the sheep's depasturing on the land, it was improved and the plaintiff's tithes bettered thereby. But the court decreed an account and said that was no bar to the plaintiff's demand. And this decree, upon a rehearing, was affirmed.

---

1 *Nicholls v. Hooper* (1618), 1 Rolle, Abr., *Dismes*, pl. R, 7, p. 642.

2 *Eastmond v. Sandys* (1696), *ut supra*.

3 *Dummer v. Wingfield* (Ex. 1690), *ut supra*.

Ward and *Bunbury*, for the defendant, argued that, if this demand prevailed, it would be double tithing, which was contrary to the whole tenor of the law. And they cited many cases for that purpose.

But the court agreed that it was a new increase, that they could not distinguish it from the case of Dummer v. Wingfield, that the distinctions laid down in the case of Eastmond v. Sandys, Shower's Parliament Cases 192, were good. And they decreed that the defendant should go to an account.

2 Eq. Cas. Abr. 733, 22 E.R. 620

The bill demanded tithe for the depasturing of sheep on turnips remaining on the ground unsevered. The defendant said the sheep did pay the tithe wool and that tithes ought not to be paid twice. It appeared that, after shearing time, the defendant fed his sheep with turnips, whereby they were better 5s. per sheep, that they went about five months on the turnips and then were sold to the butcher, and the defendant brought in a large quantity of new sheep before shearing time came again, so that plaintiff always had tithe wool of the full number. It was strongly insisted that this was a double tithing, but the court agreed that it was a new increase and decreed that the defendant should go to an account.

611

Torrent v. Burley

(Ex. 1726)

A bill in equity lies for discovery as to payments of mortuaries, but a bill in equity against a single parishioner only cannot establish a general right to receive mortuaries.

Where a bill in equity is dismissed generally, the plaintiff is liable to pay court costs even if the defendant did not demur.

Harvard Law School MS. 1082, vol. 2, p. 1, pl. 2

Trinity term 1726.

This was a bill for a mortuary and to be relieved against an action at law for £3 4s. 0d.

The court inclined to dismiss the bill upon the opening, though there was no defense. But, at last, they made a decree *nisi*.

Harvard Law School MS. 1082, vol. 2, p. 7, pl. 1

Michaelmas term 1726.

Torrent, as vicar of St. Giles in Reading, brought a bill against the defendant for a mortuary, setting forth that the plaintiff was entitled to mortuaries by custom according to Stat. 21 Hen. VIII[1] and that the defendant's testator died possessed of an estate to the value of £40, so he demanded 10s., setting forth that 10s. was paid by the direction of the defendant to the plaintiff, but that she brought an action for money had and received and she recovered by a verdict for £3 4s. 0d. and that the plaintiff moved for a new trial and had an order for that purpose upon payment of costs. And this bill prays an injunction to stay the proceedings for the costs and to have a decree for the mortuary. The defendant answered and denied the custom and examined several witnesses.

But *Wills*, myself, and *Bootle* insisted that this was a matter properly triable at law. And, since the plaintiff had gotten the discovery, he ought to go to law.

For the plaintiff, [it was] insisted that a bill for mortuaries was proper. And as they prayed for an establishment of that demand, it was proper for the court to direct an issue and to settle it *in futuro*.

But the court said that, though the bill was proper for a discovery, yet it was not for relief in regard that the matter was properly triable at law and the bill was not proper for the establishment of a right against one defendant only. So they dismissed the bill.

But HALE said that, in regard that the defendant did not demur at first, he had forfeited his costs, and so was the rule in the Court of Chancery, to which I answered that the rule was otherwise here and it was here thought too hard that, because the defendant might happen to be in contempt, that he should forfeit his costs when he had lost his time for demurring.

So the answer was allowed to be right, and the bill was dismissed.

Taussig MS. 311, vol. 2, p. 969, pl. 2

Michaelmas term 1726.

The plaintiff's bill set forth that, by custom in the parish of St. Giles in Reading, of which he was the vicar, a mortuary was due to him upon the death of a parishioner, that the defendant's testator died worth £40 over and above debts paid, so, by custom and statute, he was entitled to 10s., that he demanded it of the widow. She paid it and, afterwards, brought [an action of] *indebitatus assumpsit* for money had and received to her use.

And, upon this, a trial was had before Mr. Justice PRICE in the Oxford Circuit, on which trial, there was full proof of the custom. But the jury not being satisfied with the quantum of the testator's estate, found that the vicar was only entitled to 3s. 4d. and so they found a verdict for the plaintiff for 6s. 8d. But Mr. Justice PRICE being dissatisfied with the verdict, Torrent applied for a new trial and had a rule for a new trial. But instead of proceeding thereon, the vicar brings his bill both for discovery of what the widow's testator died worth and also for relief and prays an injunction. And upon the answer of the widow admitting

[1] Stat. 21 Hen. VIII, c. 6 (*SR*, III, 288–289).

he died worth £40 over and above debts, both parties went to proof and examined witnesses as to the custom, which was the chief matter of the depositions. And upon opening the bill and answer, the defendant's counsel objected that the plaintiff's bill was not proper for relief, though it was for discovery, for, first, as to the custom in general, it could not be established by a decree of this court the vicar having only made one of the parishioners party to it. And as to this defendant, it was not proper because they were already at law where the right was properly determinable, as properly as it could be on an issue directed by the court if the court should think fit to direct one. And, therefore, though a bill in equity lies for a mortuary, yet never after an action at law. And the plaintiff here had a rule for a new trial in his favor, on which he should have proceeded.

E contra by the plaintiff's counsel: Many bills [have been filed] for a mortuary, and, in the case before the court, the plaintiff was under a necessity to come here for discovery of the personal estate [and] the quantum whereof the quantum of the mortuary must depend. And it is a rule that, if discovery is necessary and the demand is a liquidated demand and is certain, the court will proceed and decree; otherwise, where the demand is uncertain and consists in damages. Besides, the defendant should have demurred and not have submitted to the relief prayed and gone on to proof and examination of witnesses as to the custom. And it was further said it was doubtful whether an action at law would lie for a mortuary. *Vide* Watson 1053 (octavo edition).[1]

But as to this last point, Pengelly, Chief Baron, and Page thought an action is well maintainable.

For as to the defendant's not demurring to the relief, Hale, Baron, thought on this account that the plaintiff ought to be excused his costs and that was the rule in [the Court of] Chancery.

But by the Chief Baron and Page, the bill was dismissed generally, which carries costs of course.

And Mr. *Browne*, with whom Page agreed, said that, though the practice was so in Chancery, yet it never obtained here. And the reason was because the defendant could not demur, for, if an attachment is once taken out against a defendant for not answering, he can never be permitted to demur. And, therefore, it would be very hard that the plaintiff should be excused costs for an improper demand because not demurred to when perhaps, by the rules of practice, the defendant had not the power of demurring.

Semble in this case the court implicitly determined that the right of a mortuary might be determined on the action of *indebitatus assumpsit* brought by the person who had paid it.

Quod multum dubito.

---

[1] W. Watson, *Clergy-man's Law.*

2 Strange 715, 93 E.R. 803

A bill was brought to discover whether the defendant's husband died worth £40 so as to be liable to pay the plaintiff a mortuary and praying relief. Upon an answer admitting assets, but denying the custom, the plaintiff went into a proof of his right. And several witnesses were examined on both sides. And at the hearing, the bill was dismissed with costs as to the relief because that was properly at law or in the spiritual court and, in a bill against one person only, the right could not be established. The dismission was generally with costs, though the defendant had not demurred to the relief, but run into a proof of the right.

Strange, pro querente.

612

Reynell v. Moore

(Ex. 1726)

In this case, a modus decimandi *in lieu of tithes in kind of hoard apples was established.*

Taussig MS. 311, vol. 2, p. 961

Trinity term 1726.

The issues in this case were three, *viz.* 2d. per hogshead, 2d. per hoard, [and] whether tithe of the first moath was in lieu of after-moath. The two first issues were found against the parson; the last was with him.

And now, for the plaintiff, it was insisted that the *modus* for the hoard is void because the word 'hoard' is uncertain. And ten bushels is a hoard and twenty bushels or one hundred bushels is a hoard, and also that the 2d. per hogshead is confined to ancient orchards. July [*blank*] 1716 [*blank*].

Sed per PENGELLY: Hogshead has been determined to be good in the case of the Bishop of Exeter v. Roe, *quod fuit concessum per curiam*; Hetley 93, 85; *Compleat Incumbent* 447,[1] as to the fruit of an orchard; 2d. as to a hoard. Hoard is a term of art and must be understood in the sense of the country, as wintering sheep. And though one hoard is larger than another, yet that makes no difference no more than 1d. for a hearth, though one house burns twenty times as much as another or one yard, orchard, or garden is twice as large as another.

Browne: The second *modus* of 2d. per hoard was also established in the case of the Bishop of Exeter and Roe.

PRICE: I remember at the trial it was very difficult to describe what a hoard was. And I own that, unless that point was absolutely determined in the Case

[1] *Roe v. Bishop of Exeter* (Ex. 1720), see above, Case No. 119; *Thornhill's Case* (1628), Hetley 93, 124 E.R. 369, 1 Eagle & Younge 362; *Woolmerston's Case* (1628), Hetley 85, 124 E.R. 362, 1 Eagle & Younge 362; W. Watson, *Clergy-man's Law.*

of the Bishop of Exeter, I should not think it a good *modus*. So they directed the Decree Book to be brought into court.

N.B. In the Case of the Bishop of Exeter and Rowe, the *modus* for a hogshead of cider was 8d. and, for the tithe of all hoard apples of every tenement gathered within the said parish in every year and not made into cider, 1d. payable at Easter. The Case of the Bishop of Exeter and Roe is entered of the 22 February 1719, fol. 376, of the Decree Book.

Friday, 8th July 1726.

The Decree Book was now produced to the court. And the parishioner's bill and answer and the *modus* as to the hoard of apples in that case ran thus, *viz.* as before.

Serjeant *Belfield*: This Case of the Bishop of Exeter is very different from the case before the court in two respects, for, in this case of Reynell, the *modus* is thus laid, 2d. for every hoard of apples had or kept by every landholder, owner, or occupier of orchards or lands within the said parish in lieu of tithes of all apples grown and received yearly in such orchards or lands and which are not converted into cider but gathered in and kept for their hoard. But in that case, it was a *modus* for hoard apples and the sort of apples called hoard apples is well known. Second, the hoard apples in that case are confined to every distinct tenement, but this is for all apples whatsoever if hoarded.

But PRICE and PAGE thought that this custom and that in the Case of the Bishop of Exeter was the same in substance. And so they established this *modus*.

But HALE seemed strongly of another opinion.

It seems to me there is a plain difference between the cases and that a hoard of apples are winter apples and kept for the winter.

N.B. In this case, Baron HALE expressed himself as very much dissatisfied with the way of sending *modus*es to a trial without being perfectly well-satisfied of the validity of them, for he was very much afraid that the country juries would find any *modus* that could be invented by the parishioners.

613

Reynell v. Ackland

(Ex. 1726)

A modus decimandi *in lieu of tithes in kind must be certain.*

3 Eagle & Younge 1235

To a bill for tithes, the defendant insisted on a *modus* of 2d. per hogshead of cider in lieu of the tithe apples that make that cider, and also on 2d. per hoard for all apples had and kept by every occupier, tenant, of an orchard within the parish, which *modus*es were found on an issue and now established *per* CURIAM, though it was objected that 2d. per hoard was uncertain, the quantity being uncertain.

But [it was said] by PRICE and PAGE, barons [that] the word is known in the country and was well understood by the jury. It may be compared to a smoke penny, which is in lieu of all wood burnt in the house. So, a hoard of apples is all the apples the occupier keeps in his house for his own use that year. And they mentioned a case of Rowe v. Bishop of Exeter, Hilary 1719,[1] where such a *modus* was established.

But HALE, Baron, seemed to think it unreasonable, for one man might have all the tenements, orchards, in the parish and pay but one *modus*.

614

Bridges v. Mitchell

(Ex. 1726)

A suit for a settled account will be barred in equity by a great length of time in enforcing it.

Taussig MS. 311, vol. 2, p. 927, pl. 1

Trinity term 1726.

There was a plea to an English bill seeking an account of dealings and transactions between merchants that it was twenty-five years since they had any dealings together. So he pleaded the length of time.

And this plea was allowed because, the accounts lying unclosed for such a length of time without any promises since, it was unreasonable to allow a bill. So the plea was allowed.

Bunbury 217, 145 E.R. 652

18 June 1726.

The bill sets forth that the plaintiff and defendant, many years ago, were partners as merchants and that, upon settling accounts between them in 1701, there was due upon the balance of that account from the defendant to the plaintiff £190, and it prays a discovery, an account, and satisfaction.

The defendant pleads to so much of the bill as seeks an account and satisfaction, that it appeared upon the plaintiff's own showing that the pretended balance was due above twenty-four years before the filing of the bill and that, in all that time, he never commenced any suit for it. And he also pleaded the Statute of Limitations.[2]

And *per* TOTAM CURIAM, the plea was allowed on the long acquiescence of the party. And after such a length of time without suit, it shall be presumed the balance was satisfied. And the court seemed to think this was not a merchant's account within the Statute of Limitations, these persons not dealing as

[1] *Roe v. Bishop of Exeter* (Ex. 1720), see above, Case No. 119.

[2] Stat. 21 Jac. I, c. 16 (*SR*, IV, 1222–1223).

merchants with one another, but as one merchant with others. But they gave no positive opinion on this head, but allowed the plea on the other.

Gilbert Rep. 224, 25 E.R. 156

A bill was brought for an account by the plaintiff, a merchant, against the defendant, another merchant, who was his partner. The defendant pleads that the dealings, concerning which the plaintiff prays an account, were transacted above twenty years before the bill was brought, and he pleads such acquiescence without suit and also the Statute of Limitations, 21 Jac. I, c. 16, in bar of the account.

Per CURIAM: Forbearance of suit for twenty years will in equity be a good bar, though in a demand by one merchant upon another. Secondly, It is not necessary in the answer for the defendant to aver his having not promised within six years to account etc. unless such promise is particularly charged in the bill, as was resolved *inter* Bodvil and the Bishop of Meath[1] in this court, and further, that though the Statute has been always construed to except accounts open between merchant and merchant, yet that is to be understood with this distinction, that, if open accounts be by subsequent acts continued, they are not barred by the intervention of such length of time from the original transaction; but, if such an account is by the complainant deserted, then, in such case, it is barred.

And they held the defendant's plea good.

615

Case of the County of Nottingham

(Ex. 1726)

The question in this case was whether the inhabitants of a county have a duty to keep in good repair a town hall where the courts sit.

Taussig MS. 311, vol. 2, p. 933

Wednesday, 22 June 1726.

Mr. *Bootle* moved on behalf of the inhabitants of the County of Nottingham to discharge a fine of £2000 set upon them by Mr. Justice POWYS for the not repairing the Town Hall where the assizes are had. And Mr. *Bootle* seemed inclinable to go into the question whether, by 6 Ric. II, ca. 5,[2] the judge of assize had any power to set such a fine and, secondly, whether it was well imposed on the inhabitants of the county.

The court said they would not determine the question whether the fine was well imposed by the judge on a motion, for, if they would go into that matter, they should plead to the process, as the court obliged the South Sea directors to

---

[1] *Bodwell v. Bishop of Meath* (Ex. 1721), see above, Case No. 174.

[2] Stat. 6 Ric. II, stat. 1, c. 5 (*SR*, II, 27).

do.[1] But so far, they would stay process for a time upon a motion. But at the same time, they gave a hint the county would do well to repair, for it seemed as if such a fine and the power of imposing it might be maintained.

As to the power of a justice of assize by the Stat. Ric. II, if the Act obliges the justice of assize to hold the assizes at the shire court, it implies it should be kept in such order as to be convenient for that purpose.

But whether the county at large is chargeable herewith, as in a case of bridges, query.

Process was respited for a year.

616

Thompson v. Holt

(Ex. 1726)

In this case, the defendants were ordered to account for various tithes and moduses *payable to the rector of the parish.*

Taussig MS. 311, vol. 2, p. 935

Thursday, 23 June 1726.

The plaintiff, rector of Lowton in the County of Buckingham, exhibits his bill for [tithes of] milk, wool and lamb, garden fruit, pigeons, wood, calves.

The defendants set up *modus*es. A *modus* for milk while the cows go in the commons or common fields, *viz.* 2d. for a new milk cow and 1½d. for an old one payable at Christmas, but they agree milk is tithable in kind while they feed in enclosures payable every tenth day. As to wood, they set up a *non decimando* for wood in hedgerows in the hundred and a *modus* for the garden, 1d. for fruit except pears and apples, 8d. per score for wool of sheep wintered in another parish. Rolle, *Abr.*, 645, was cited that this *modus* is good. As to wood spent in the house, a smoke penny, Rolle, *Abr.*, [Dismes], 644, is good. Wood spent in the fencing grounds of the parishioners, Rolle, *Abr.*, 644, is good.[2] Loppings and toppings of oak, ash, and elm, these are privileged by law being timber. Pigeons sold pay tithes; otherwise, when spent in the house. Rolle, *Abr.*, 644,[3] and Jones and Calvert in this court. [There is a] *non decimando* as to the wood of hedges, bushes, [and] furze in the parish of Lowton lying within the hundred of Newport Paganel; ½ for a calf weaned. Case of Reeves and Fitzherbert, the hundred of Pipehill in the County of Stafford.[4]

---

[1] *Rex v. Astell* (Ex. 1723–1724), see above, Case No. 430.

[2] 1 Rolle, Abr., *Dismes*, pl. Z, 2, p. 644.

[3] *Watley v. Hanberrie* (1616), 1 Rolle, Abr., *Dismes*, pl. Z, 4, 5, p. 644.

[4] *Rives v. Fitzherbert* (1725), 1 Eagle & Younge 811, 2 Wood 249.

Mr. *Bunbury*, for the plaintiff: [There are] three commons in this parish on which cattle go all the year round, and there are common fields on which cattle go after the corn is taken away. This is not proved in the cause. And the *modus* laid is in lieu of the tithe arising while they are fed on the commons or common fields, and the proof goes to the common fields.

But *per* CURIAM: Since you have not shown that there are not commons in this parish, we must take it that the expression of commons or common fields is only in contradistinction to enclosures.

As to the *modus* of 8d. for wool of sheep wintered, by him, 'winter' is uncertain, so the *modus* is void.

Sed per PAGE: The Canons of 1601 and the tithe table takes notice of winter and summer.

The defendant gave up the *non decimando* as to the wood of hedges etc.

Per Edlin: In the case of Dummer and Winkfield,[1] it was determined that the year for wool begins from mid-summer to mid-summer and, if the sheep continue in after mid-summer, the parson must have agistment tithes.

So they decree an account for apples and pears, milk, enclosures, lambs, wood (except wood in fencing or burnt in their houses or faggots made of loppings and toppings of timber trees), for furze, and they must account for Easter offerings and for calf according to the *modus* of ½ a calf.

2 Gwillim 671, 1 Eagle & Younge 826, 2 Wood 269

23 June 1726.

The rector of Loughton in the County of Buckingham claimed the tithes of garden stuff, apples, pears, pigeons, cows, milk, lambs, sheep, wool, faggots, furze, calves, and the loppings of oaks, ash, and elm.

The defendant Holt said that he held an ancient garden in the said parish, but that no tithe in kind was due to the rector for the fruit thereof, for that, time out of mind, gardens in the said parish had paid and ought to pay to the rectors of the said parish at Easter yearly 1d., called a garden penny, in lieu of all garden stuff or fruit, except apples and pears, yearly arising in such gardens. And he tendered the same with his proportionable costs. He also admitted that he had several dozen of pigeons, but he denied that he had sold any, and he insisted that no tithes were due for them. He also admitted that he had several cows, which he had kept sometimes upon his enclosures and sometimes in the common fields belonging to the said parish. And he insisted that he was not accountable to the plaintiff for the tithe of such milk as was milked from the cows while they were depastured upon the common fields, for that, time out of mind, there had been due and payable to the rector of the said parish for the time being at Christmas

[1] *Dummer v. Wingfield* (Ex. 1690), Dodd 94, Eq. Cases Exch. 328, 1 Eagle & Younge 566, Public Record Office, E.126/15, f. 302v, 1 Wood 273.

yearly for every new milk cow, 2d., and for every old milk cow, 1½d., depastured on the common fields, which he, by his answer, tendered accordingly, as also a tenth part of the value of the milk milked from his cows while depastured on his enclosures, with his proportionable costs. He also set forth that he had two lambs, and he tendered the plaintiff a halfpenny apiece for them. He also stated that, in April 1723, he had brought into the parish several sheep that had been wintered in other counties and were by him shorn in the parish in that year. But he insisted that he was not accountable for the tithe wool of them, for that, time out of mind, there had been due and payable at Christmas yearly 8d. a score and so proportionably for a greater or less number which were so brought into the parish, and not wintered there, in full satisfaction of the tithe wool of such sheep so brought in. He also said that, in the said year, he had caused several hundreds of furze faggots to be cut upon Loughton Common, that some thereof were sold and the rest burnt in his family, and that there had been due and payable at Easter yearly to the rector of the said parish 1d., called a smoke penny, in lieu of all wood, furze, and fuel burnt and spent in the house of every inhabitant within the said parish. And he tendered the same by his answer with his proportionable costs. He also said that the said parish of Loughton lay within the hundred of Newport Pagnell and that no tithe for wood of hedges, hedgerows, bushes, willows, and furze, which were either sold or used for firing, were ever paid within the said hundred, that he had lopped from oak, ash, and elm trees of above twenty years growth several hundred faggots, had sold some, and spent the rest in his family. And he insisted that no tithe was due for the same or anything in lieu thereof. He also set forth an account of his calves and the price for which he had sold them, and he stated that two thereof were weaned for the pail, and he insisted that a *modus* of 1½d. a calf for each calf weaned for the purpose aforesaid was due to the rector in lieu of the tithes of such calves, which he also tendered to the plaintiff.

The other defendants, by their answers, also insisted upon the said *modus*es.

The court ordered the defendants to account for tithe milk in kind during the time the defendants' cows were kept on their enclosed grounds and pasture lands, for the tithes of their wood and furze, except for the loppings and toppings of timber trees above twenty years growth or burnt in their houses or used in fencing, for the tithes of apples and pears, lambs, Easter offerings, pigeons sold, and such dry cows as were altogether unprofitable and through which no tithe did otherwise accrue to the rector of the parish. But, as to the other matters, they were ordered to account, according to the *modus*es set forth in the answers.

617

Somerville v. Wise

(Ex. 1726)

In this case, the court found an alleged modus decimandi *in lieu of tithe hay to be uncertain and invalid, and the court found a custom as to the method of paying tithe milk to be invalid.*

Taussig MS. 311, vol. 2, p. 956

Trinity term 1726.

The plaintiff [being] rector of Abberbury in the County of Gloucester, the court determined three points, *viz.* that a *modus* or custom to have tithe milk for part of the year only is not good; secondly, that a *modus* of 2d. a mower or so much as a man can mow in a day is naught because it is uncertain, like the case in Keble 612;[1] otherwise, perhaps, of a man's moath, for that may signify a particular quantity of land; thirdly, that, if the defendant insists upon 6d. per yard land in his bill, he cannot prove it by an evidence that two particular yard lands pay 1s. nor, *e contra*, for 6d. per yard land is a distinct *modus* from a *modus* of 1s. for two yard lands [*blank*].

2 Gwillim 671

5 July 1726.

A bill was brought by the vicar of Adderbury in Oxfordshire for the tithes, *inter alia*, of hay and of milk. The defendants, as to the tithes of hay in certain meadows, called Lott Meadows, insisted on a *modus* of 2d. a mower or man's moath and so in proportion for any other quantity of meadow in lieu of all tithes thereof, payable at Michaelmas. And with respect to the milk, they said that the vicars had immemorially taken every tenth meal, or morning and night's milk, from all milk cows in the parish from their first going upon the common, which happened usually on the 3rd of May, for ten tithe meals or turns of morning's and night's milk in lieu of all tithe milk.

The court declared both customs to be void and decreed the defendants to account.

[Order of 5 July 1726: 2 Wood 263, 1 Eagle & Younge 822.]

---

[1] *Took v. Ledgierd* (1663), 1 Keble 612, 83 E.R. 1142, 1 Eagle & Younge 440.

618

Tandy v. Tandy

(Ex. 1726)

Where a testator directs his debts and legacies to be paid out of his real estate, his personal estate is not liable therefor (if the real estate is sufficient).

Harvard Law School MS. 1082, vol. 2, p. 1, pl. 1

Trinity term 1726.

Chief Baron [GILBERT] said that, if the real estate was made subject, then the personal estate should be excused.

PAGE: He said that it was a mere charge on the real estate.

HALE: It was a settled point in a court of equity, if another person is made an executor in favor of an heir, to order the personal estate to come in aid. And in the case of the Mayor of London v. Garraway, in Chancery,[1] the whole personal estate was ordered to be applied. And without negative words to exclude the personal estate, the personal estate must come in aid in favor of an heir at law.

But in this case, the court decreed this an onus on the land, *quod vide*.

619

Attorney General v. Champion

(Ex. 1726–1627)

There may be a judgment for the crown upon a general demurrer whatever the question might be if causes had been assigned.

Where a defendant pleads performance of a contract or bond and the plaintiff replies with an allegation of a breach, the defendant cannot rejoin.

Where there is an express condition to pay, then there is no need of a demand for payment.

Harvard Law School MS. 1082, vol. 2, p. 1, pl. 4

Trinity term 1726.

A *scire facias* was brought on a bond the condition whereof was that Halliwell should faithfully account. And the defendant pleads conditions performed. And the Attorney General replied that Halliwell received £300 on account of licenses and had not accounted. And the defendant demurs.

[1] *City of London v. Garway* (1706), 2 Vernon 571, 23 E.R. 972, 1 Eq. Cas. Abr. 196, 272, 21 E.R. 985, 1040.

Fazakerly, for the defendant: There was nothing in the condition of the bond to account for licenses, and, if he was accountable, the minute he receives them, he forfeits his recognizance, but if he is accountable, it should be on a demand. But in the case of a penalty, there should be a demand previous. 1 Rolle, *Abridgment*, 459, pl. 1; Hobart 82.[1] And it does not appear but that an account had been made, for though Halliwell did not account, yet others might.

Serjeant *Comyns*, for the king: The condition of the bond is fully explained, and, in the second clause, Halliwell is accountable.

Chief Baron [Gilbert]: Judgment must be given for the king.

Price cited Lord Arlington's Case, in 2 Saunders,[2] about the Post Office; there was no necessity for a demand, and the account is incident to the office.

Page doubts, for it ought to appear that this was part of the office and there should be a demand and the general demand is not good.

Hale inclined for the king.

The Chief Baron doubted whether this was a power so delegated by the commissioners that they are authorized to give such licenses.

Price: If they were blank licenses, yet I have no difficulty.

Taussig MS. 311, vol. 2, p. 930

Trinity term 1726. Attorney General v. Campion.

Fazakerly: Nothing is expressed in the condition that the licenses themselves are part of the duty of his office, nor does it in any way appear that it is so. And, therefore, though he ought to account for the licenses, yet he is not under the penalty of forfeiting his bond.

Secondly, there ought to have been a previous demand of the licenses. 1 Rolle, *Abr.*, 459, pl. 1; Hob. 82 are authorities that you must demand before you enter for non-payment of rent or a *nomine poenae*. And the consequence would be very extraordinary if it were not so, for then, receiving any license, if he keeps it an hour, it would be a forfeiture.

Third, it is not averred that the others named in the bond have not returned the licenses, but only that Halliwell has not returned them.

Serjeant *Comyns* answers the first objection by reading the record, by which it appears that he was accountable for the licenses. Secondly, the breach assigned is not only that he has not accounted, but also that he neglected and refused to account for them.

The reply was that it ought to have been averred that this was part of the office and, then, we might have an issue taken upon it. *Neglexit et recusavit* is not sufficient without alleging a demand, for, if a demand is not legal, then a refusal

1 1 Rolle, Abr., *Condition*, pl. Z, 1, p. 459; *Grobham v. Thornborough* (1613), Hobart 82, 80 E.R. 232.

2 *Lord Arlington v. Merricke* (1672), 2 Williams Saunders 403, 85 E.R. 1215, also 3 Keble 45, 59, 84 E.R. 586, 593.

is no fault and a general demand is not sufficient. But it must be particular, and the party may either traverse the demand or the refusal.

Chief Baron [GILBERT]: You plead that you have rendered an account of all your proceedings. They reply you have neglected etc. So then, they have taken away or avoided your bar. If delivering out these licenses and giving an account of them is part of your office, the bar is avoided. And this appears by the nature of the thing itself.

PRICE: Performance of a condition is incumbent on a defendant. He cites Lord Arlington's Case, in 2nd Sanders. *Neglexit et recusavit* implies a demand.

PAGE doubts, for it must appear that it is part of the office. The Act of Parliament does not mention the duty of the office. Therefore, it must appear by the condition, for we cannot understand otherwise what the duty of his office is. Query whether the commissioners have authority to deliver out blank licenses. '*Negavit*', in his opinion, is not traversable.

HALE: If the accounting for the licenses is not part of his office, I do not know what is. If he is to account for the money he receives for licenses delivered out, he must account for the licenses themselves which he does not deliver out.

Harvard Law School MS. 1082, vol. 2, p. 21, pl. 1

Easter term 1727.

[There may be a] judgment for the king upon the general demurrer whatever the question might be if causes had been assigned.

Harvard Law School MS. 1082, vol. 2, p. 23, pl. 1

Easter term 1727. Rex v. Champion.

The defendant pleads performance. And the Attorney General [*Yorke*] replies, and he assigns two breaches, that Halliwell had received £359 and not returned it to the Commissioners and likewise received several horse and foot liveries and not rendered any account in that respect. As to the first, £359, the defendant pleads that he had returned the money, and issue was joined upon it. But as to the latter breach, the defendant demurs, and the Attorney General joins in demurrer.

Bootle, for the demurrer, [said] that it does not appear that Halliwell was authorized to receive money due on these licenses and the court cannot take notice of it. Halliwell only appears as a riding surveyor, and it is not explained by the bond or the record.

Attorney General [*Yorke*]; It is a breach within the condition of the bond and is well assigned. There are no negative words to restrain this. The office is not to be confined to the recital in the bond only, but it is alleged that Halliwell should do the business of the office. And by the condition of the bond, Halliwell was obliged to return all such money as he should receive by virtue of any licenses. And that shows it to be part of his duty.

[To the] objection that there ought to be a request, [he] responded there was no occasion, for it was a duty incumbent in Halliwell to do it without a request.

The defendant has pleaded performance. Cro. Car., Chapman v. Chapman.[1]

Bootle replies: A request is necessary. In Chapman v. Chapman, payment was insisted on. And, therefore, to say it was not requested was a departure.

Chief Baron [Pengelly]: This seems to be sufficient to show that this was the business of Halliwell's office. And there are several things required by Halliwell to do and not contained in the recital of the bond. It is admitted by the demurrer that Halliwell was concerned in these licenses and the distributing of them. There is no occasion for a request where performance is pleaded. In the performance of an award, it is a single case where the whole must be set forth and notice and request.

I am doubtful as to the latter part of the breach, *sive administrationem eorundem*. It is too general and seems to be a disjunctive issue by the word *sive* and so uncertain. And the defendant is obliged to follow the words of the breach assigned. Stat. 8 & 9 Will. III. The question is whether it is not an entire breach.

Hale seemed to think it right.

Baron Comyns: It appears to be within his office and well assigned.

Taussig MS. 311, vol. 2, p. 1030 [bis]

2 May 1727.

Bootle, for the defendant: The question is upon the latter breach. The breach assigned is not within the compass of the bond nor within the compass of the office so far as the office appears to the court. A riding surveyor, *viz.*, is to travel into such places as the commissioners shall appoint to take and apprehend persons trading without licenses. The breach assigned is that he has not given an account *de et concernente easdem seperales licentias*. So it does not say that he received the money on the licenses nor has any ways supplied the generality of the condition. By the breach assigned, he must either return the licenses he has received or else the money which he received for them. Therefore, it ought to be shown in certain which of these two things he has not done. And perhaps he has done one and the not doing the other is the cause for which the action was brought. 2 Rolle's *Abr.*, 460, § 10.[2] This case was cited to show that there ought to have been a request of one of them whether a reply that he had rendered an account; *de et concernente easdem licentias sive administrationes earundum* would this make an issue.

Attorney General [*Yorke*]: Though the whole of the office is not recited in the condition, yet there are no restrictive and limiting words. The condition is not in the disjunctive as Bootle states it, but it is expressly in the conjunctive. And

[1] *Chapman v. Chapman* (1626), Croke Car. 76, 79 E.R. 667, also Hutton 90, 123 E.R. 1122.

[2] YB Hil. 9 Hen. VI, f. 57b, pl. 2 (1431), 2 Rolle, Abr., *Return*, pl. L, 1, p. 460.

this also answers the objection of no request. Cro. Car. 76; where one pleads performance and the plaintiff replies with a breach, he cannot rejoin. The thing not done was not requested to be done, for that would be a departure.

Chief Baron [PENGELLY]: What follows after the words to do the duty of the office of riding surveyor may be explanatory of, but must not be understood to be restrictive or comprehensive of, the whole duty. You have admitted by your demurrer that you did receive the licenses; so that is admitted to be within your office and you shall not now controvert it. As to the request, there is no need after a general performance has been pleaded. And the case in Cro. Car. 76 is express in point. But I think a request is not necessary, for it is agreed in the case of Rolle and twenty others that, if the condition be to perform covenants, there, indeed, the condition leaves the payment of the rent on the same foot exactly as it stood upon the deed. But if the condition is express to pay the rent, then there is no need of a demand. But I do somewhat doubt of the generality or disjunctiveness of the breach assigned, that he did not render an account of those licenses *sive administrationis* of them. But this seems to me not to be an assignment of two breaches, but a disjunctive breach.

HALE: You have not given an account of the receipts and how you disposed of them. This is not such a duplicity, in my apprehension, as will avoid the replication.

COMYNS: It is plainly within the duty of the office, for, by his office, he is to deliver out licenses. Why then delivering out licenses is part of the duty of his office. Therefore, the condition expressing that he should account for them is certainly shown to be part of his office. And, as to the disjunctive, *sive administrationis*, suppose a condition to pay *summa sive redditum*. Would it not be a good breach that he had not paid *summa sive redditum* 20s.? And the defendant might have replied that he had given an account of the licenses and management.

CHIEF BARON: This seems to be an entire breach of two parts. It might have been made good by a rejoinder, but here is a demurrer.

N.B. On 10th May 1727, the court gave judgment for the king, the defendant's demurrer being general. So they did not give any express opinion whether the Attorney [General]'s replication was good in the disjunctive had the demurrer assigned this for a special cause.

620

Reynell v. Cooper

(Ex. 1726)

The Statute of Frauds covers promises for the default of another.

The Statute of Frauds covers contracts for grants of hereditaments, such as offices.

A oral promise to be performed upon a contingency which may or may not happen within one year after the making is made unenforceable by the Statute of Frauds.

Harvard Law School MS. 1082, vol. 2, p. 2

Trinity term 1726.

A bill was brought as in the margin, [i.e.] for being concerned in getting the office for William Cooper for which the defendant promised to make satisfaction. The defendant pleads the Statute of Frauds,[1] that there was no agreement in writing, and the Statute of Limitations,[2] no promise within six years.

The court said this seemed to be upon the default of another. 1 Salkeld 280.[3]

Shepherd, for the plaintiff: This was a contingency, and it was not known when it was to be performed, which might be within the year. The Statute of Limitations only commences from the time that the cause of action accrued. Cro. Car. 139, Godbolt 437, Sir William Jones 194; 1 Levinz 48.[4] The agreement was to be perfected only on the death of Johnson, which did not happen until 1723. 2 Salkeld 422.[5]

Ward, for the plaintiff: This is a plea of two statutes to the same thing. This agreement is dependent on the death of Johnson. And in an action, the plaintiff must have averred the death of Johnson or he would have failed. This was an original undertaking in Spencer Cowper, the defendant. 3 Levinz 303 or 103; Comberbach 304;[6] the contingency is a *casus omissus*. The cause of action arose above six years before the bill was filed. The cause in this case did not arise until the death of Johnson, which was in 1723. This plea is overruled by the answer. The plea is in bar of the action,[7] yet the defendant, by way of an answer, submits whether the court will give relief.

Pengelly, for the defendant: This is plainly for the miscarriage of another, *viz.* William Cooper. And in such a case, it must be in writing. And it was so ruled in the case in Levinz cited by the plaintiff. In this case, a certain time was fixed. The Statute of Limitations was well pleaded as no cause of action was brought within six years.

---

[1] Stat. 29 Car. II, c. 3 (*SR*, V, 839–842).

[2] Stat. 21 Jac. I, c. 16, s. 3 (*SR*, IV, 1222).

[3] *Anonymous* (1693), 1 Salkeld 280, 91 E.R. 244.

[4] *Shutford v. Penow* (1628), Croke Car. 139, 79 E.R. 722, Godbolt 437, 78 E.R. 257, W. Jones 194, 82 E.R. 103; *Webb v. Martin* (1661), 1 Levinz 48, 83 E.R. 291, also 1 Keble 177, 197, 83 E.R. 885, 897.

[5] *Gould v. Johnson* (1703), 2 Salkeld 422, 91 E.R. 367, also 2 Lord Raymond 838, 92 E.R. 60, 1 Salkeld 25, 91 E.R. 24, Holt K.B. 34, 90 E.R. 916, *sub nom. Booth v. Johnson*, 7 Modern 143, 87 E.R. 1152, 3 Lord Raymond 7, 92 E.R. 533.

[6] *Haight v. Langham* (1691), 3 Levinz 300, 303, 83 E.R. 699, 701; *Hellier v. Condy* (1694), Comberbach 304, 90 E.R. 493.

[7] agreement *MS*.

Wills, for the defendant: [To the] objection it was not for the miscarriage of another, [he] answered in the nature of the thing, the promise is on the default of another, for in case William Cooper does not perform it, the defendant is to do it. The case of marriage differs because the party shall not take advantage of his own laches, and so it may be the case of a person that navigates a ship.

[To the] objection that there were six years before serving process, [he] answered that the cause of the suit did not arise within six years before or process served. The plea is good in point of fact.

Bunbury, for the defendant: The contract or sale for an office is an hereditament and so included within the Statute. Within six years or serving the process is a good plea. Marston v. Cleapoole, last term.[1]

Bootle enlarged on the Statute of Frauds.

Chief Baron [GILBERT]: The Statute of Frauds was to prevent such things, and, where the promise is for the default of another, it should be in writing. An office is an hereditament, and there should be something in writing to authenticate the agreement. Uncertain interests have been construed out of the Statute. I would consider the case.

PRICE, PAGE, and HALE agreed that the plea should be allowed. And it was allowed accordingly.

Taussig MS. 311, vol. 2, p. 937

Trinity term 1726.

Serjeant *Shepherd*, for the plaintiff, [argued] that promises which may or may not by accident be performed within a year are not within the Statute of Frauds. Comberbatch 463; 1 Salk. 280.[2]

Chief Baron [GILBERT]: There is another point, *viz.* this promise was made in default of another.

To this, the plaintiff's counsel answered that the Statute extended to both cases. The agreement must be in the nature of it within the Statute.

Secondly, it is not within the Statute of Limitations because the six years must incur from the cause of action. Cro. Car. 139; Jones 194; Godb. 437; that is, a complete cause of action; 1 Lev. 48 is to the same purpose; Webb and Martin. Here, the complete cause of suit did not arise until the death of Johnson, which was in 1723. 2 Salkeld 242;[3] in consideration that he would entertain the defendants *ut hospites* with diet etc., the consideration is executory and so was not within the Statute of Frauds and Perjuries, and it was so adjudged upon a demurrer.

Ward, for the plaintiff, objects that here are two pleas.

---

[1] *Marston v. Cleypole* (Ex. 1726), see above, Case No. 596.

[2] *Anonymous* (1697), Comberbach 463, 90 E.R. 593; *Anonymous* (1693), 1 Salkeld 280, 91 E.R. 244.

[3] *Gould v. Johnson* (1703), *ut supra*.

This was immediately overruled as soon as stated.

So he goes on the other two points. Here is no undertaking for the debt or default of William Cowper, but it is an original and independent promise of Spencer Cowper. 3 Lev. 303; Masters v. Marriot.[1] And the case stated in Salkeld that, if a man goes into a shop and tells the shopkeeper that, if he delivers such goods to A., he will see him paid, this is an original promise.

Secondly, the agreement is not certainly to be performed within a year and yet it might be performed in one half a year. And so he insists on the cases cited.

The third objection to the plea is that it is pleaded in bar of the relief and yet the bill desires to know whether there is any other agreement.

Four, the surrender of Johnson shall not defeat the agreement.

Five, if a court of equity cannot decree a specific performance, it may direct a [writ of] *quantum damnificatus* within six years before the filing of the bill or before the serving of process that is informal.

Six, they have overruled the plea by the answer, for he answered and submitted it to the judgment of the court whether the plaintiff ought to have any relief on account that this was an office of trust and dependent on the rules of the House of Lords.

Seven, they insist on the order of the Lords in January 1723[/24], yet the defendant might have performed the promise between the death of Johnson, which was in July 1723, and this order of January 1723[/24].

Wynne, of the same side, cited 4 Co. 10, a case of avowry for services.[2]

Serjeant *Pengelly*: It appears from the circumstances of the case itself that this was an undertaking for the default of William Cowper, for William Cowper was to have the office and to do the specific thing to the use of Spencer Cowper. The promise is only to answer for the non-performance of the thing *in specie*. The intendment is that the promise will not be performed within a year because the life of a man is intended to exceed any term of years, much more one year.

The plea avers that the cause of action did not accrue within six years, so he ought to reply to this and take issue thereupon.

Wills admits it is not to answer for a debt, but it is as plain that it is to answer for his default. In the cases cited, the thing promised was in the power of the promisor[3] to do *in specie*, but here, it is otherwise. Marriage is entirely uncertain, and a man's not marrying shall not defeat his own promise.

Wills: The plea must be taken to be true if not replied to, so that what they say with relation to the fact is not material for they may reply.

---

[1] *Haight v. Langham* (1691), *ut supra*; *Masters v. Marriot* (1693), 3 Levinz 363, 83 E.R. 732, Skinner 347, 90 E.R. 154, Holt K.B. 26, 90 E.R. 912, 12 Modern 44, 88 E.R. 1154.

[2] *Parker v. Francis* (1575–1583), 4 Coke Rep. 8, 76 E.R. 862, also 1 Anderson 57, 123 E.R. 352.

[3] promisee *MS*.

Bunbury insists they ought to reply and the fact is confessed to be otherwise by setting down the plea to be argued. Also he insists upon it that it is in defense of another person. He insists that this is a contract concerning an hereditament, nay, it is within the word 'tenement'; an office is a tenement.

Before filing the bill or serving process, the court ruled it was well in the case of Marston and Claypole.

Fazakerly: As to discovery, the plaintiff is at liberty to except to the answer and so may have any further discovery.

Foley, ditto.

Bootle cites a case out of Hutton that, if an *assumpsit* be laid fifty years since and the Statute of Limitations is pleaded, he may reply with a promise on another day different from the declaration and which is within six years because the day is material. Then, he goes on to enforce Bunbury's objection of tenement and hereditament.

Chief Baron [Gilbert]: [It is] very clear that this promise of Spencer Cowper is a promise for the default of another.

[To the] objection but Spencer Cowper promises to procure, the solution is this is blowing up the Statute at once, for all undertakings for another may be laid in this way, *viz.* that the party promised to procure.

Secondly, the plea ought to be allowed upon the part of the Statute mentioned by Bunbury because the office or deputation to it must not be intended of a deputation for a day or two but must be understood of a deputation to the office during the deputer's enjoyment of it.

But as to the third point, *viz.* whether the agreement is an agreement not to be performed within a year and so within the Statute, I would look into the former cases adjudged, though he seemed to think it a strange construction and perhaps did depend upon the party's being to perform the contract himself.

And they all agreed that the plea should be allowed.

N.B. None of the judges took any notice of the objections to the form of the plea.

Chief Baron [Gilbert] said the plea of limitations was well pleaded by saying that the cause of action did not arise *infra sex annos*.

C. Viner, Abridgment, vol. 5, p. 524, pl. 47

Trinity term 1726, Reynolds v. Spencer Cowper, Esq.

A bill [was brought] for a specific performance of a promise by the defendant to procure the plaintiff to be made deputy to the defendant's son as clerk of the House of Peers or otherwise to provide for the plaintiff a consideration of plaintiff's insisting upon and soliciting in procuring a reversionary grant of that place for defendant's son, which the defendant now enjoyed etc.

The defendant pleaded the Statute of Frauds and Perjuries and that the promise was not in writing nor to be performed within one year and also the

Statute of Limitations, that the promise was made above six years before the bill was filed.

Per CURIAM: The plea was allowed in both respects. And they held, first, that a parol promise to be performed upon a contingency which may or may not happen within a year after the making is void within the Statute of Frauds; secondly, and so, if made above six years before the bill or action be brought, it is barred by the Statute of Limitations, though the contingency or time of performance happens within the six years.

621

Christie v. Crookshanks

(Ex. 1726)

The question in this case was whether a creditor who sells the security given for a loan for a greater sum than the amount of the loan should pay the difference to the debtor.

Taussig MS. 311, vol. 2, p. 943

Monday, 27th [June] 1726. By English bill.

Christie borrows £1000 of Dawson, who was a trustee for Crookshanks, and conveys £200 South Sea stock for a security. This was on 29 August 1720. Within three days after, Dawson sells this stock at £1670, and, then, at the day of payment of £1000, he comes to Christy and insists upon further security, and Christy gives him a South Sea subscription receipt. And this the defendant also sold. And the bill was to have an account for the surplus for which the South Sea stock and the subscription receipt were sold for over and above the £1000 borrowed by Christie. The £1000 was to be repaid on 29 September 1720.

Ward cites the case of Tutt and Mercer, in this court and afterwards in the House of Lords; Helbut and Philpott, in Chancery and afterwards in the House of Lords, as parallel cases to the present case.[1]

622

Berney v. Chambers

(Ex. 1726)

Damages are payable for interfering with the collecting of tithes.

[1] See *Mercer v. Tutt* (Ex. 1723), above, Case No. 436, and 2 Brown P.C. 563, 1 E.R. 1134; *Philpot v. Helbert* (1722), 2 Eq. Cas. Abr. 746, 22 E.R. 633.

2 Gwillim 673

The bill stated that the plaintiff sent a cart and horses to fetch away the tithe of wheat, that, the cart being loaded and going out of the field, the defendant locked up the gate and would not suffer it to be drawn out, but, at length, permitted the horses to go out, but stopped the cart, and that on the third day after, the plaintiff was obliged to take away the same by an action of replevin, whereby he suffered great damages. And he brought his bill for the value of the tithes.

The defendant, by his answer, confessed that he, on the Saturday, stopped the cart and horses as they were carrying away the tithes and locked up the gate, they being trespassers and *damage feasant* because the cart wheels were shod with iron, which, as he was advised, ought not to be because such wheels cut the soil and much spoiled the clover sown among the corn, but he permitted the horses to be taken away immediately, that being told he could not justify the detaining of the cart, he, on Monday morning early, sent notice to the tithe gatherers that they might take away the cart, and he tendered 5s. for damages for stopping it, but the plaintiff would not take it away until Tuesday, when he brought a replevin, that he had since offered to pay the charges of the replevin.

The court ordered the Deputy Remembrancer to inquire into the damages sustained by the plaintiff by the defendant's stopping his cart and horses.

[Order of 1 July 1726: 3 Eagle & Younge 1235.]

[Later proceedings in this case are reported at Bunbury 248, 145 E.R. 663, 2 Gwillim 674, 3 Eagle & Younge 1236.]

623

Bate v. Howland

(Ex. 1726)

The question in this case was the validity of various alleged moduses *in lieu of tithes in kind.*

Harvard Law School MS. 1082, vol. 2, p. 4

Trinity term 1726.

The plaintiff brings his bill for tithes. The defendant insists on the *modus*es in the margin [i.e.] 12d. per acre for marshland and 8d. per acre for upland for all tithes except corn, grain, and crops.

It was objected by *Ward* and *Edlin*, for the plaintiff, that these *modus*es were too rank and bad by the rules of law. The tithes of this whole parish by the survey of 26 Hen. VIII was £3 13s. 4d. And if this was a *modus*, the tithes would be worth £100 per acre, and, if this survey is of any weight, then all the *modus*es must fall.

First, it covers too much. Every satisfaction must go to the thing for the thing, and not one tithe for another. Cro. Eliz. 446; Rolle, *Abridgment*, 134; 2 Lutwyche 1052; Hicks v. Woodson; the court will not establish a bad custom.[1]

These *modus*es are only for uplands and marshland. And that cannot include gardens, which is of neither sort. And there was no tender for the gardens. Exception [?] is incorporated with the *modus*.

The third objection was it is not laid proportionably. 1 Rolle, *Abridgment*, 648; Harrison v. Sharpe, in this court.[2] 1s. for all pasture or swath ground is not good because it was not laid proportionably.

The fourth objection was it is too rank, as in Grascomb v. Jeffreys, 17 November 1684;[3] 12d. per acre for all marshland was in lieu of all tithes; a trial was denied because the *modus* was too high.

That [it was] due and payable was uncertain; it ought to be laid [to be] paid at such a time. The modus is unequal. [It is] one tithe for another. Barker v. Cockram, Hobart 329.[4]

1 or 2d. for a hogshead, it is not good; if it be tied down for apples made into cider, it may be good. Sherrington v. Fleetwood; Cro. Eliz. 139; Moore 454, Monday v. Lewis.[5] This is not cont[. . .]ed to the acre.

It was objected that small tithes is too uncertain a term.

It is in the power to make it a *non decimando*. If converted into orchards, nothing is [due], so it is liable to a fraud.

Serjeant *Pengelly*, for the defendant: This is not the payment of one tithe for another, but a sum of money may be paid for all tithes. Dr. Finch v. Sir William

---

[1] *Grysman v. Lewes* (1595), Croke Eliz. 446, 78 E.R. 686, also Moore K.B. 911, 72 E.R. 991, 1 Gwillim 165, 1 Eagle & Younge 112; *Hicks v. Woodson* (1697), 4 Modern 324, 336, 87 E.R. 422, 429, 1 Eagle & Younge 592, 2 Gwillim 550, 3 Lord Raymond 116, 92 E.R. 595, 1 Lord Raymond 137, 91 E.R. 987, 12 Modern 111, 88 E.R. 1200, Skinner 560, 90 E.R. 252, Comberbach 403, 90 E.R. 555, Carthew 392, 90 E.R. 827, Holt K.B. 671, 90 E.R. 1271, 2 Salkeld 655, 91 E.R. 558, Dodd 171.

[2] 1 Rolle, Abr., *Dismes*, p. 648; *Harrison v. Sharp* (Ex. 1724), see above, Case No. 490.

[3] *Grascomb v. Jeffreys* (1687–1688), Eq. Cases Exch. 285.

[4] *Barker v. Cocker* (1620), Hobart 329, 80 E.R. 471, 1 Gwillim 385, 1 Eagle & Younge 321.

[5] *Sherington v. Fleetwood* (1596), Moore K.B. 430, 599, 909, 72 E.R. 676, 784, 990, Gouldsborough 147, 75 E.R. 1055, Croke Eliz. 475, 78 E.R. 727; *Perry v. Soam* (1589), Croke Eliz. 138, 78 E.R. 395, also 2 Leonard 27, 74 E.R. 330, 1 Eagle & Younge 96; *Monday v. Lovice* (1596), Moore K.B. 454, 72 E.R. 690, 1 Eagle & Younge 118; 1 Rolle, Abr., *Dismes*, pl. D, 16, p. 651.

Gerrard.[1] [The meaning of] small tithes is well known. [See] the case of Siderfin, Crouch v. [. . .]son, for all minute tithes.[2]

Taussig MS. 311, vol. 2, p. 1005

Setting down of causes in Serjeants' Inn in Chancery Lane, 8 December 1726.

It was admitted by Mr. *Edlin*, of counsel with Bate, that the parishioners had proved the payment of the *modus* for as long as any man living remembers.

But they said they could overreach this sort of proof by books of former rectors and hearsay evidence as well as from the nature of the *modus* itself, it appearing on the face of it that it was too rank.

After long debate, it was sent to an issue.

[Order of 6 July 1726: 2 Wood 257, 1 Eagle & Younge 819.]

624

Attorney General v. Houghton

(Ex. 1726)

The question in this case was whether, in an information to recover import duties, the date of the importation as alleged is material to the case.

Taussig MS. 311, vol. 2, p. 950

Trinity term 1726.

An information of debt set forth that the defendant, in 1722, imported and brought into England such and such goods for which duties were payable and, not having paid such goods, *actio accrevit*. The evidence was that the goods were imported in March 1719.

And Mr. *Ward* objected that this evidence did not maintain the information because the duties arise upon importation. The duties demanded arise upon goods imported in 1722 and, consequently, cannot be the duties arising upon goods imported in 1719.

But the Chief Baron [GILBERT] overruled the objection because the time of importation is not material in this case any more than in the case of an *indebitatus assumpsit* for goods sold and delivered or money lent.

Sed tamen quaere, for the cases are not alike, for, in an [action of] *indebitatus assumpsit*, there never is any time laid for the delivery of the goods or the lending of the money, but only a time for the being indebted or for the promise, *viz. quod*

1 *Finch v. Masters* (Ex. 1724), see above, Case No. 463.

2 *Crouch v. Risden* (1670), 1 Siderfin 443, 82 E.R. 1207, also 1 Ventris 61, 86 E.R. 43, 2 Keble 612, 84 E.R. 385, 1 Eagle & Younge 481, Lincoln's Inn MS. Misc. 500, f. 114v (Edward Ward's reports).

cum such a day *indebitatus fuit* to the plaintiff *pro bonis ante tunc debitatus* or else *quod cum vendidisset bona* the defendant *in consideratione inde* such a day promised. Therefore, in an *indebitatus assumpsit*, no time being expressly laid for the consideration, it cannot be material whether it was in one year or another if sobeit it be previous to the promise made. But, in the case before us, there is a fine laid and the question is whether they can go backward beyond that time. If they can, this is most certain that they may prove another debt than the debt described in the information. Therefore, I much doubt the point.

625

Vaughan v. Goodwin

(Ex. 1726)

Evidence of usage as to exemptions and discharges of tithes will prevail against an endowment of tithes.

Taussig MS. 311, vol. 2, p. 952

5 July 1726, first day of sittings at Serjeants' Inn in Chancery Lane after Trinity term.

The plaintiff, as vicar of Powlet, brings his bill for small tithes arising upon certain lands called Southam within his parish in the County of Somerset. The defendants set up an exemption and discharge from tithes arising on these lands because the lands called Southam are parcel of a tract of land called Gauntesham, that, by the dissolution of the monastery of St. Augustine in Bristol, these lands came to the crown, that King James by his grant 7 *regni* grants them *M. et P. omnes illas decimas nostras quascunque tam majores quam minores provenientes, renovantes, sive emergentes in Gauntesham in Comitatu nostro Somerset ac etiam omnes illae decimarum nostrum garbarum totius parochiae de Pawlet cum suis pertinentibus universis ac omnia particularia et commoda de praedictis decimariis provenienibus sive emegentibus per particularia inde annuatim reddit, sive valore 14 libri nuper monasterio Sancti Augustini juxta Bristol quondam spectante.*

The plaintiff insisted on an endowment, a transcript whereof was registered in a register book belonging to the Dean and Chapter of Wells in these words following, *viz. Reverendo Domino et Patri J., Dei gratia Bathoniensis episcopo W. permissione divina Abbas Sancti Augustini de Bristol et ejusdem loci conventus cum omni reverentia et devotione, salutem, praesentamus vobis ad perpetuam vicariam ecclesiae de Poulet Dominum Antonium presbiterum quae quiddam vicaria in subscriptis portionibus consistit, viz. in omnibus oblationibus et minutis decimis et decima molendini et decima de dominico nostro, viz. bladi et foeni dominici nostri quod habuimus anno incarnationis Dominicae 1239 et in decimis foeni acquisitis et acquirendis et in decima sex acrarum quas Hugo Trevet nobis dedit ac in quattuor acris prati dimidium in viteri mora et in una acra prati juxta Horseacram in una acra terrae arabilis in quam mansum vicarii est constructam et debet vicarius de praedictis annuatim pro nobis solvere unam mariam argenti socoribus de Bockland, scil. ad festum Sancti Michaelis dimidium marcae et ad Pascha dimidium marcae et respondebit Domino Archidiacino Wellensi de procuratione sua et de 12 de dono et debet solvere 15 denarios ecclesiae de Pereton de consuetudine Paschali sustinebit etiam idem Antonius cetera onera ordinaria dictae ecclesiae extraordinaria vero pro sua portione supplica. Igitur sanctitati vestrae quatenus in hac parte quod vestrum est exequamini, in cujus rei testimonium praesento scripto sigillum nostrum duximus apponendum valeat sancta paternitas vestra semper in Domino* of the register book, fol. 157.

The plaintiff proved in affirmance of this endowment his having great tithes in some parts of the parish and his having all small tithes throughout the rest of the parish except Gauntesham and also proved perpetual payment of the 13 and 4 *per annum* reserved upon making this endowment and one or two particulars more. But he did not prove any tithes in fact out of lands in Gauntesham except in the years 1714 to 1715 of one or two of the tenants.

The defendants, on the other side, proved constant payment of their proportion of the £14 *per annum* towards the rent charge and the constant non-payment of tithes to the vicar.

It was insisted for the plaintiff that, though the usage had been against the plaintiff, yet usage could not contradict an express endowment, secondly, that here was no express contradiction, for that there was no evidence that the small tithes of Gauntesham were in the monastery *tempore dissolutionis* nor do the leases then in being speak of any small tithes, but only tithes in general in Gauntesham, but indeed King James's grant does mention the *decimas tam majores quam minores*, which shows that the title under the monastery as to the tithes of these lands was enlarged afterwards.

But the court, *viz.* PRICE, PAGE, and HALE were all of opinion that usage must explain the endowment; nay, they thought it would control it. And so, they dismissed the plaintiff's bill. See 2 Rolle's *Abr.*, 269, M, 17.[1] Chief Baron Gilbert was absent *propter aegrotudinem*.

[Order of 5 July 1726: 2 Wood 267.]

626

Taylor v. Oates

(Ex. 1726)

In this case, the plaintiff failed to prove his title.

[1] *Pringle v. Child* (1605), 2 Rolle, Abr., *Prescription*, pl. M, 17, p. 269.

Taussig MS. 311, vol. 2, p. 957

Wednesday, 6th July 1726.

The plaintiff sets forth by his bill that he was by and under a grant of the [. . .] seised in fee of the rectory of Foulforth etc. or otherwise entitled to them. And, upon the hearing of the cause, he begins to show his title by a deed of May 1713.

And it was held this was not sufficient proof of his bill, PAGE doubting and seeming to be of a contrary opinion.

627

Gouge v. Clarke

(Ex. 1726)

A rector cannot object to the validity of a modus decimandi *in lieu of tithes in kind before it has been proved by the parishioner.*

Taussig MS. 311, vol. 2, p. 958

Thursday, 7th July 1726. Gouge, rector of Gilling in the County of York v. Clarke.

The court now determined again that the plaintiff should not go into the validity of the *modus* before the fact of it was proved and, therefore, they should admit the fact or else go to issue or else the court would not hear their objections.

N.B. The *modus* laid in the answer was this, all the hay growing yearly on three acres of meadow lying in a close or meadow called Low Ings, which three acres have been always enjoyed in lieu [of tithes].

The proofs went to the hay, *scil.* grass or the sweep of the meadow growing in the three acres. And after the proofs were read, *Bunbury* objected, first, that the *modus* laid is uncertain, *scil.* whether it was the soil or the vesture of the land, and there is a considerable difference between these, for, by this proof, the rector is not to have the after-moath or the trees or the employing of it in any different manner than in meadow. 1st Inst. 4b.[1] Secondly, the *modus* is too small, which is a good objection in all *modus*es except money *modus*es.

Per CURIAM: We understand that the *modus* is of hay and not of the land and the words 'which acres are received' are improper, for one cannot receive acres.

Thirdly, as to value, it is laid in lieu of tithes arising on demesne lands. Demesne lands formerly yielded little or nothing, being generally only downs or commons etc.

That the rector of the said parish *pro tempore existente* [was] entitled unto and time out of [mind] etc. has received yearly in lieu of the tithes arising on the demesne lands of the manor all the hay yearly growing on three acres of meadow in

[1] E. Coke, *First Institute* (1628), f. 1b.

a close in Gilling called Low Ings, which three acres of meadow he believes has been enjoyed time etc. in lieu of the tithes in kind arising on the demesne lands.

[Order of 7 July 1726: 2 Wood 268, 1 Eagle & Younge 825.]

628

Howell v. Lord Coningsby

(Ex. 1726)

If a defendant, after an appearance, stands out to a sequestration in contempt, the court will take the bill pro confesso *and make a decree* nisi.

Bunbury 219, 145 E.R. 653

28 October 1726.

A defendant, after an appearance, stands out to a [writ of] sequestration for want of an answer. Upon motion, the bill was taken *pro confesso* and then set down in the paper of causes to be heard. And yesterday, upon the hearing, the question was whether the decree should be absolute or only *nisi*.

Barons PAGE and HALE, then only in court, doubted and deferred giving judgment on this point until the Lord Chief Baron came up. And this day, it was stirred again, when the new Lord Chief Baron [PENGELLY] and PAGE were of opinion it should be *nisi* only, *hesitanter*. But Baron HALE, upon the precedents produced, was clear that it ought to be absolute.

Which, I [Bunbury] think, seems to be the better opinion, for, when a bill is taken *pro confesso* after an appearance, it is giving time to a defendant for no purpose, for, when be comes, he can be admitted to say nothing.

Baron PAGE made a difference arising from the quick process against a peer, which is not in the case of a common subject. But the reason has but little weight (*ut videtur*).

Harvard Law School MS. 1082, vol. 2, p. 6, pl. 2

Michaelmas term 1726.

A bill was brought by the plaintiff against the defendant for fees. And the defendant stood so long in contempt that the bill was taken *pro confesso*. And it was set down in the paper.

Owen, for the plaintiff, moved for an absolute decree against the defendant.

But PAGE, [being] alone in court, doubted, so it was moved again.

Owen, afterwards, cited several precedents in Chancery where it was done, Lee v. Lord Coningsby, and one in this court, *viz*. Crossman v. Goodrich, 3 & 4 Jac. II,[1] where the decree was made absolute.

[1] *Crossman v. Goodrich* (1688), 1 Rayner 66, 1 Eagle & Younge 554, 1 Wood 254.

PENGELLY and PAGE agreed to have it only *nisi*.

HALE was for having it absolute, for it would be strange to give a day to the defendant when, if he comes in, being in contempt, he cannot be heard.

Though the decree was only *nisi*, as above, yet that is contrary to the rules in this court, for in the cause of Bilson v. [*blank*], where Thompson and Combs were concerned, I had an absolute decree for a foreclosure upon a bill taken *pro confesso*.

Taussig MS. 311, vol. 2, p. 967

Michaelmas term 1726.

Crossman v. Goodritch, Hilary, 3 & 4 Jac. II; Nicholas v. Plunket, in Chancery, Michaelmas 1725, 1 December; Leigh v. Lord Coningsby, Trinity 1726, before the Master of the Rolls, 12 George. These authorities and precedents were cited by Mr. *Owen* to show that, if the defendant, after an appearance, stands out to a sequestration in contempt, the court will take the bill *pro confesso* and make an absolute decree against him and not a decree *nisi* only. 1 Chancery Reports 204, 205; 2 Canc. Rep. 133; Vernon 247, 248.[1]

Sed per Chief Baron [PENGELLY]: In the case where there is a decree against a man that stands out to a sequestration so that the defendant has no day in court to move against it, the court ought to pronounce the decree and not leave the party to draw it up himself.

And after some debate, the court pronounced the decree *nisi*.

And it was said by PAGE, and all the clerks in court agreed, that the time to show cause was not necessarily to be adjourned to another term, but cause might be shown in the same term if the court thought fit.

629

Blunt v. Vaughan

(Ex. 1726)

Where land in a decedent's estate is charged with the payment of a legacy and the court orders a sale and payment, the court fees involved are part of the court costs and are to be paid out of the decedent's estate and not by the legatee.

British Library MS. Hargrave 70, f. 42, pl. 229,
Harvard Law School MS. 1162, p. 69, pl. 375

28 October 1726.

---

[1] *Salmon v. Hamborough Company* (1671), 1 Chancery Cases 204, 22 E.R. 763; *Denny v. Filmer* (1663, 1682), 2 Chancery Cases 133, 22 E.R. 881, also 2 Freeman 172, 22 E.R. 1138, Nelson 64, 21 E.R. 790, 1 Eq. Cas. Abr. 81, 21 E.R. 894, *sub nom. Dunny v. Filmore*, 1 Vernon 135, 23 E.R. 369; *Gibson v. Scevengton* (1684), 1 Vernon 247, 23 E.R. 445.

A legacy of £3000 was left to the defendant [Charlotte Vaughan], daughter of the testator. The widow and executrix preferred a bill against the heir upon an agreement between them, to which the defendant was no party, and made her a party to the bill. She prefers a cross-bill for her legacy, which was decreed with interest and costs in both causes. The estate, on which the legacy was charged, was ordered by the court to be sold and the money brought into court, by which the Deputy [Remembrancer] became entitled to poundage, 2d. per pound, which came to £25. Now, upon motion, the court ordered that the poundage should be allowed to the defendant as costs and that it should be charged on the testator's estate and that, though it bore the name of poundage, yet it was as much costs as if she had paid it out of pocket.

630

Watts v. Robinson

(Ex. 1726)

A widow can recover lands that belong to her but which were sold upon an outlawry of her deceased husband.

Harvard Law School MS. 1082, vol. 2, p. 6, pl. 1

Michaelmas term 1726.

Serjeant *Chesshyre*, for the defendant, [moved] for leave to plead to an inquisition taken upon an outlawry against the defendant's husband after a [writ of] *venditioni exponas* granted near two years since.

Kettleby and *Bootle* insisted upon it that this, being a term, was regularly sold and *bona fide* according to a *venditioni exponas* awarded and that it would be hard to trip up the heels of such a purchaser who depended on the title granted by the court and the rather since there has been an [action of] ejectment brought by the defendant and a verdict given for the plaintiff and then a writ of error and that spent and, then, a bill was exhibited by the defendant in the Court of Chancery against the now plaintiff, who pleaded these several proceedings, and the plea was allowed and the bill was dismissed.

But the court resolved that the defendant should be permitted to plead or else it would be the greatest hardship on the defendant, who was a wife, and nothing against her husband could bind her, not even a recovery. And the Statute of Hen. VIII[1] has given all manner of advantage to the wife's right. If this method could prevail, even though a settlement was made upon a marriage, yet the husband by this contrivance might defeat such a settlement for it was only taking and contriving an outlawry and so procuring the term to be sold and so defeat

[1] Stat. 27 Hen. VIII, c. 10 (*SR*, III, 539–542), note also Stat. 32 Hen. VIII, c. 1, s. 10 (*SR*, III, 746).

the wife. As for the proceedings at law and in equity, the woman was ill advised to go on in that way, for which she has paid costs. And the judgment given in those cases was right because, as long as the inquisition and *venditioni exponas* remained, there must be a verdict for the plaintiff, who was the purchaser. But now, the woman comes in a regular way to plead her title. She ought to be permitted to do it, which was ordered accordingly.

Taussig MS. 311, vol. 2, p. 969, pl. 1

Michaelmas term 1726.

A married man seised of the estate of freehold in the right of his wife is outlawed, and, upon the judgment upon the outlawry, this estate is found to be a term for years and is seized and afterwards is sold by [a writ of] *venditioni exponas* and, thereupon, an [action of] ejectment was brought by the vendee and recovery was had and, now, the husband being dead, the wife came and prayed that she might be admitted to plead her title.

And the court gave her leave so to do.

Bunbury 220, 145 E.R. 653, Conroy 118

29 October 1726.

A. was outlawed, and, by an inquisition taken thereon, it was found that he was possessed of a term for years *in jure uxoris*. After his decease, a *venditioni exponas* issued, and the term was sold.

Now, the widow moved that she might be at liberty to plead to the inquisition, which was granted, although it was objected in behalf of H., the purchaser, that he had purchased under the sanction of the court, had since brought an ejectment which was defended by her, that she had brought a writ of error and also a bill in Chancery relating to this matter.

But it was said *per* CURIAM, though she has been wrong advised, we will not deprive her of the liberty of pleading now.

631

Rex v. Clarke

(Ex. 1726)

In this case, a writ of immediate extent to enforce a private debt was quashed as improperly sworn out.

The crown cannot be a trustee for a private person.

Harvard Law School MS. 1082, vol. 2, p. 7, pl. 2

Michaelmas term 1726.

This was a motion for a [writ of] extent grounded on an affidavit made by Robert George, one of the executors of Mr. Pauncefort, deceased, who was Cashier of the Excise. And the affidavit set forth that Clarke was the billman to Pauncefort and was so authorized to receive the money due to the Excise and that the defendant for eighteen years received the same but had not accounted. And Baron Page granted the extent but not to execute it but upon four days' notice to the assignee of the commissioner of bankruptcy against Clark.

Bunbury, Kettleby, and myself moved to set aside the extent. And we showed that, by the affidavit of George, no money was sworn to be due to the king, and, though Pauncefort might be an officer, yet nothing might be due. And we produced Clark's affidavit, which showed that Pauncefort had paid the whole money to the crown and that Pauncefort was discharged and his bond delivered up. And even Pauncefort, by George, his agent, took a new bond from Clarke for this money and had received part thereof, which was endorsed on the bond. We likewise produced proper certificates of Pauncefort's discharge. And we insisted on no money being sworn due, according to the Rule of 3 Jac. II.

Chief Baron PENGELLY: It appears by George's own experience as servant to Mr. Pauncefort what was proper to be sworn. But this affidavit is cloaked under general terms to deceive the court. There is a fallacy in the affidavit. And I think the extent must be set aside. But if Pauncefort had been unable and the crown had directly applied for an extent, it might have had a different construction. But here is no debt due to the crown. And here is new credit taken and security accepted by Pauncefort by a new bond so that Pauncefort has waived the benefit. If an extent should issue, the crown would only be a trustee for Pauncefort's executor. And if this method was to prevail, it is setting up a private person to have the privilege of the crown.

HALE: Immediate extents are only for immediate debts. Lane 112; Attorney General v. Pultney, in Hardres.[1]

CARTER: I agree that the order for an extent shall be discharged.

Baron COMYNS: The case of the crown ought to be considered and likewise the case of a subject. The first bond from Clarke to the crown is good. And the prerogative process might have gone on that bond. But it plainly appears by an affidavit that Pauncefort has taken a new bond; so new credit was given. And private money might be paid and yet apply that to the private account and so let the crown debt remain. In the case of receivers, where the surety pays the money, it is but natural equity that they should stand in the place of the crown. The affidavit is defective.

And by the whole court, the extent was set aside.

[1] *Sawyer v. East* (1611), Lane 74, 108, 145 E.R. 311, 339; *Attorney General v. Poultney* (1665), Hardres 403, 145 E.R. 519.

Taussig MS. 311, vol. 2, p. 977

Michaelmas term 1726.

Mr. *Bunbury* moved to set aside a [writ of] immediate extent against Clarke in aid of Pauncefort, Cashier to the Commissioners of the Excise.

On 14 March 1715, there was a bond to the king with a condition that, whereas Pauncefort had agreed to employ Clarke as his billman in receiving money due upon the account of the excise and also due upon his own private account, therefore, the condition of the obligation was that Clarke should duly and from day to day account for and pay all such monies, then the bond to be void. The affidavit, upon which the application was made for an immediate extent, was made by one Robert Georges, one of the executors of Mr. Pauncefort and was that Pauncefort was cashier of the Commissioners of the Excise, that Clarke was employed by him as his billman and receiver of the revenues of the excise, that Clarke and Atkinson were bound by a bond to the king 14 March 1715 [in a] £1000 penalty conditioned for Clarke's performing the office of a billman to Pauncefort and for Clarke's paying all sums of money, bills of exchange, etc. that Clarke or any by his order should receive relating to the said revenue, that Clarke did receive £1876 arising from monies of the excise, which he embezzled, and, afterwards, he paid £398, but the residue, amounting to £1478, he had converted to his own use and had not yet paid the same to His Majesty's use, but the same still remains due and unpaid by him and is in danger of being lost.

Bunbury: The affidavit for obtaining the extent is imperfect, Hardres 404, for the affidavit is not that the money was not paid to the crown, but is only that Clarke has not paid the money to the crown. But upon the defendant's affidavit, it appears that the money is paid to the crown; it was paid by Pauncefort, and he took a private bond from Clarke for the whole money paid in. And there is a certificate from the Commissioners of the Excise that all Pauncefort's bonds are delivered up to his executors. 3 Jac. II Rules of court then made. The third rule is that the party applying for an extent must swear that the crown's debt is not satisfied.

Attorney General [*Yorke*]: This bond is given to the king and there is no pretense that the money is paid to the crown by the obligor.

First, that, as to taking this bond, it was justified, as by the Case of the King and Elihu Yale.[1]

Secondly, upon the affidavit made for obtaining this extent, it does appear that it is the crown's debt, for it is the money received by the obligor himself.

Thirdly, as to what is said by Hale, it is said with relation to bonds assigned to the king not upon bonds immediately entered into to the king himself.

Fourth, as to Clarke's affidavit, he has not sworn such a payment to the crown as could be pleaded in discharge of this bond.

---

[1] *Rex v. Yale* (1720–1721), see above, Case No. 121.

Fifth, the Rules of 3 Jac. relate to debts in aid, but this is an immediate debt to the crown.

And, therefore, he submits whether the court will set aside the extent and not rather put them to plead.

Chief Baron [Pengelly]: Upon the face of the affidavit, it might appear to be a debt due immediately to the crown; so he has not fully represented the condition of the bond, for the condition is not to pay to the crown or to account with the crown but to account to Mr. Pauncefort. So there is a fallacy in the affidavit. And the crown has two persons liable, *viz.* Pauncefort immediately and Clarke mediately. And, therefore, this affidavit is not a fair affidavit and it shows to me that the party making it was suspicious. If he had truly stated the case, he would not have been able to maintain his motion for an extent. But now, it appears on the other side that the crown is satisfied. Then, this is making the king a trustee for the executors of Pauncefort. And if this debt was really levied by the process of the crown, how must this money be paid to the executors of Pauncefort? And is not this prostituting the process of the crown?

This, in my apprehension, is giving up the prerogative of the crown and laying it open to the benefit of others in common with him. Hale's saying in Hardres is grounded on what Lord Coke says in his 4 Inst., treatise of the Exchequer.[1] Whoever assigns a breach of the condition must assign it in not paying or accounting with Pauncefort.

N.B. by the Chief Baron, in the Case of the King and Yale, it is a *scire facias* against Sir Matthew Kirwood.

Hale: Lane 112 [and] Hardres are of the same opinion.

Carter agrees and says that the bond to the crown [that was] entered into ought to have been discharged, the debt being paid.

Comyns: I do not in the least doubt but that it is reasonable that, where the immediate officer employs another to receive the crown monies and takes a bond *in nomine regis* to pay this money, the immediate officer may have the benefit of the crown process. But, in this case, there is now no debt due to the king, for the immediate officer has paid the money and taken a new security from Clarke [to] himself. This is plainly a waiver of his advantage under the first bond. And he takes notice of the great inconvenience of mixing an account of the crown money with private money, for then there may be eternal disputes about what monies they are and from what occasion they sprung, especially after any length of time.

So the rule for an immediate extent was discharged.

Vide Savile 15, that the privilege of the Exchequer ceases when the debt to the crown is satisfied. Savile 11, same position.[2]

---

[1] E. Coke, *Fourth Institute* (1644), p. 115.

[2] *Ragland v. Wildgoose* (1580), Savile 11, 15, 123 E.R. 984, 986.

Bunbury 221, 145 E.R. 654

11 November 1726.

Pauncefort, Cashier of the Excise, employed Nicholas Clarke as his billman to receive money arising by the revenue of the excise. And he took a bond from him to account and pay what money he should receive of the revenue money and also on his own private account.

In 1724, Clarke was called upon to account to the Commissioners of the Excise. And, being in arrear £1800, he applied to Pauncefort to help him to the money to answer the demand. And Pauncefort did, by Mr. Georges, pay the whole money to the commissioners, and he took a bond from Clarke to him for that money. Mr. Pauncefort, afterwards, dies. And Mr. Georges, one of the executors of Mr. Pauncefort, makes an affidavit that he, Clarke, had not paid the money due to His Majesty, that the same was unpaid and in danger of being lost. And, thereupon, he obtains an order for an immediate extent against Clarke.

Now, this day, we moved to discharge the order, first, because the affidavit upon which it was granted was fallacious, for that it only said he had not paid etc.; secondly, that the same was unpaid, but it was not said to the crown; thirdly, in danger of being lost, but it was not said to the crown. And by our affidavit, it appeared as above that Georges himself had paid the money to the crown, that nothing was in arrear to the crown, for, as appeared by certificate from the excise officer, Pauncefort had his discharge and all his bonds and securities delivered up, and, therefore, there was nothing to found this extent upon. And lastly, that any benefit Pauncefort or his executors might have by the prerogative process was waived by taking a private bond for Clarke for the payment of the money.

And of this opinion was the whole court, and they discharged the order for an extent.

But *nota bene*, upon Mr. Attorney General's [*Yorke*] request, they declared it should not be a rule that a debtor of the crown, though the crown debt was satisfied, should not have the benefit of the crown process to reimburse himself, though it could not be granted under the circumstances of this case.

1 Comyns 388, 92 E.R. 1124

Edward Paunceford, being appointed Cashier to the Commissioners of Excise, employed Nicholas Clark to be his billman or receiver, who, by his obligation of the 14th of March 1715, was bound to the king in £1000 with a condition to satisfy, pay, and deliver each day unto the said Edward Paunceford, his agent, executors, or assigns all such sums, bills, bonds, notes, and other papers as the said Nicholas Clark should receive by virtue of any bills of exchange, notes, etc. relating to the excise or on any account belonging to His Majesty or to the said Edward Paunceford on his own account and should due accounts make with the said Edward Paunceford of or concerning any bills of exchange etc. belonging to His Majesty or relating to the said Edward Paunceford and should follow all such orders etc. as he should receive from the said Edward Paunceford etc.

And by another obligation of the same date, Nicholas Clark and others where bound to the king in £500 upon condition to the same intent and purpose.

Upon the motion of the Attorney General [*Yorke*] and an affidavit that Nicholas Clark had received £1876 arising from the revenue of the excise and had paid only £398 and the residue £1478 was by him embezzled and converted to his own proper use and that a commission of bankruptcy then was awarded against him, it was ordered by the court that a writ of extent should immediately be awarded to extend the estate and effects of the said Nicholas Clark, bearing date the 26th of October, which was the day of the motion, but that it should not be executed until four days after notice given to him and the commissioners of bankruptcy.

And then, it was moved to discharge this order because it did not appear that the debt to the king remained due. And it was shown by affidavit that the king was paid all his dues by Edward Paunceford, who settled accounts with Clark and took his obligation for the balance and paid all the debt due to the king, and, on the 3d of July 1724, had the bond restored to him, which the said Edward Paunceford had given to the king. And it was insisted that this obligation was made for the benefit of Paunceford himself and the king's prerogative ought to be used only for the king's debts. In Hardres 404,[1] it is said by Chief Baron Hale that it 'would be unreasonable, inconvenient, and mischievous to the subject' to make the king's prerogative instrumental for obtaining the debts of the subject. And by a rule 3 Jac. II, 1687, no extent shall issue where a bond is not due and brought into court and an affidavit made that the debt to the king is still due. And it was also said that an extent shall not be upon an obligation with condition without a *scire facias*. Savile, pl. 95; 2 Leonard 55, Owen 46.[2]

And on the other part, it was insisted by the Attorney General [*Yorke*] and others that an extent shall issue upon a bond, as here, and so it was adjudged in 1721, between the King and Yale,[3] referred to the Chief Justices Pratt and King and afterwards affirmed in Parliament, where the condition was to the same effect as this is; if a man be bound to the king with sureties and the principal prove insolvent, upon which, the sureties pay the debt to the king, it would be very mischievous if they could not have the prerogative process against their principal. If monies due to the king are delivered to a common carrier who loses or embezzles them, extents shall issue against him for the recovery of these monies. And, if the receiver die indebted to the king and his executors pay the debt, they shall have the prerogative process for the recovery of the debts due to their testator. As to the case of Hardres 404, it was mentioned by Chief Baron Hale in regard of debts in aid, and the rules

[1] *Attorney General v. Poultney* (1665), Hardres 403, 404, 145 E.R. 519.

[2] Note (1583), Savile 45, 123 E.R. 1003; *Beaumont's Case* (1587), 2 Leonard 55, 74 E.R. 353, Owen 46, 74 E.R. 899.

[3] *Rex v. Yale* (1720–1721), see above, Case No. 121.

made 3 Jac. II were never enrolled and regard only extents in aid. But it was never doubted before that, if a man be indebted by bond to the king, an extent might issue before it be proved that the debt remains unsatisfied.

And it was agreed by the court, if a man be a receiver for the king and employ others as his agents or deputies, that he can take their obligation in the king's name for the king's monies which shall come to their hand, and, to me [Comyns], it seems that it was never denied that, if it be added to the condition that they shall account also to the receiver for the proper monies that they have received, that this should not vitiate, but, if the obligor embezzles or converts the king's monies, an extent shall be issued upon such obligation.

It was also agreed that, if a common carrier embezzle the king's monies, an extent may issue against him; so, if the principal debtor to the king fail and his sureties pay, it was agreed by Baron Carter and myself [Comyns], and not denied by the others, that the sureties shall have the prerogative process against the principal.

But, in the principal case, this rule was discharged upon consideration chiefly of the circumstances of this case, for, when this obligation was made in 1715, by which Nathaniel Clark was bound to pay each day such sums etc. as he should receive, the monies then due were converted by him many years past, and, after an account was settled between Paunceford and Clark and the monies due to the king by Clark were paid by Paunceford and he had his security given to the king cancelled and restored to him and, then, took an obligation of Clark for the balance upon that account, so that he did not rely upon the bond given by Clark to the king.

And the Chief Baron [Pengelly] added that, by the condition of the obligation, Nathaniel Clark was not bound to pay to the king or account to the king for the monies by him received, but to pay to Paunceford and account to him, not only for the king's monies, but also his own proper monies, and, therefore, the king's name seems to be used solely on trust for Paunceford, but the king cannot be trustee for another person.

632

Burkett v. Stratton

(Ex. 1726)

A defendant can pay into court money claimed before a plea is actually pleaded and then be not liable for further court costs.

Taussig MS. 311, vol. 2, p. 975

Friday, 11 November 1726.

The defendant obtained the common rule to bring money into court and that the plaintiff might proceed further at his peril.

Mr. *Bootle* now moved the court to set aside the rule, suggesting that the defendant had, after the declaration was delivered, put in a plea in abatement that he was one of Foley's clerks. But upon the application of the plaintiff, the court made a rule for discharging this plea and that the defendant *respondeat ouster indilate*; therefore, the defendant should have pleaded immediately and not have come to the court to bring in money.

Sed per Chief Baron [PENGELLY]: The rule in this court and the King's Bench is that, until the plea is actually pleaded, the defendant may bring money into court, but, in the Common Bench, he cannot do it after the rules for pleading are out. And, therefore, the defendant is proper in this case, not having pleaded, and the court having discharged the plea, it was no plea at all. And the words of the rule in *respondeat ouster* are not proper, but they should have been that he should plead immediately.

633

Evans v. Viscountess Dowager Fauconberg

(Ex. 1726)

In an action of debt for rent, upon a defendant's plea of general nil habuit in tenementis, *a plaintiff can demur where an estoppel of the defendant appears in the plaintiff's declaration and is thus in the record and where the defendant has not alleged any dispossession.*

Harvard Law School MS. 1082, vol. 2, p. 10, pl. 1

Michaelmas term 1726.

An action of debt was brought for rent for a house in New Bond Street [Westminster], to which the defendant pleads that, before the making of the lease, the plaintiff assigned to Alice Coville and that Alice entered and was possessed, to which plea the plaintiff demurs.

Serjeant *Chapple*, for the plaintiff, who demurred: This is, if anything, a plea of *nil habuit in tenementis*, which the defendant is estopped to do where it is a lease by indenture. If this is anything, it is a suspension of the rent, and the defendant should have showed an actual expulsion and an amotion. 3 Levinz 193; Coke, *Entries*, 561;[1] Rastal 183.

Whitaker, for the defendant: I agree that it would not have been good upon a general plea of *nil habuit in tenementis*, but the plaintiff should not have demurred. 1 Inst. 47; a lessee may confess and avoid. Cro. Eliz. 700, 701, Brereton v. Edwards. Non tenure in a *scire facias*, it may be pleaded specially. 3 Levinz 205.[2]

---

[1] *Aylet v. Williams* (1684), 3 Levinz 193, 83 E.R. 646; *Attorney General v. Fanshawe* (1585), E. Coke, *A Booke of Entries* (1614), 'Quo Warranto', pl. 12, f. 561.

[2] E. Coke, *First Institute* (1628), f. 47b; *Brereton v. Evans* (1599), Croke Eliz. 700,

And though *nil habuit in tenementis* cannot be pleaded, yet the defendant is at liberty to show a prior title, and the plaintiff should have replied to this plea. Coke, *Entries*, 603; Perry v. Stevens, Michaelmas 11 Ann.; Hobart 206, Steed v. Richards; 4 Coke 53.[1]

Serjeant *Chapple* replies: There is no difference between a general *nil habuit in tenementis* and a particular one. The lease appears on the record itself and the estoppel. And therefore, a demurrer is proper. The case of Perry v. Stevens was an acquittance, which was a matter *dehors* of the record.

Chief Baron [PENGELLY]: I think that this special plea is worse than a general plea of *nil habuit in tenementis* because, upon a general plea, the plaintiff is at liberty to reply [with] any prior title. But this is confined to the particular plea. The difference is right between a matter on record and a matter that arises *dehors*. But where it appears upon the record itself, there, a demurrer is proper, and not by way of plea. Salkeld 277, Kemp v. Goodal.[2] The demurrer ought to be allowed and judgment [given] for the plaintiff.

COMYNS agreed and cited 3 Levinz 147; 2 Ventris 67.[3]

Taussig MS. 311, vol. 2, p. 988

Wednesday, 16th November 1726.

An action of debt [was brought for that, on] 27 September 1723, the plaintiff demised to the defendant a house in Bond Street for seven years, that she entered and held to Lady Day 1725 and for [*blank*] rent. The defendant pleads that the plaintiff, before the making of the said lease, was possessed of the premises *pro residuo termini 90 annorum* and, being so possessed before the lease, assigned to Alice Calwell, *virtute cujus* she entered etc.

Serjeant *Chappell*, for the plaintiff: The defendant cannot plead *nil habuit in tenementis*; the lease is an estoppel. If this is intended as a plea of suspension, he ought to have pleaded an entry and expulsion, as all the precedents are. *Vide Subsequentia* Co. *Entr.* 561; Rast. 183, 184; 3 Lev. 193.

---

78 E.R. 936; *Barret v. Trotman* (1684), 3 Levinz 205, 83 E.R. 652.

[1] *Colgate v. Blythe* (1585), E. Coke, *A Booke of Entries* (1614), 'Replevin et Avowrie', pl. 18, f. 603; *Speake v. Richards* (1617), Hobart 206, 80 E.R. 353, also Moore K.B. 886, 72 E.R. 974, 2 Shower K.B. 281, 89 E.R. 940, Hutton 11, 123 E.R. 1065, 1 Brownlow & Goldesborough 51, 123 E.R. 659, Noy 22, 74 E.R. 992; *Rawlyns v. Somerford* (1587), 4 Coke Rep. 52, 76 E.R. 1007, also 4 Leonard 116, 74 E.R. 767, Gouldsborough 89, 93, 75 E.R. 1015, 1018, Jenkins 254, 145 E.R. 180.

[2] *Kemp v. Goodal* (1705), 1 Salkeld 277, 91 E.R. 242, also 2 Lord Raymond 1154, 92 E.R. 263.

[3] *Heath v. Vermeden* (1683), 3 Levinz 146, 83 E.R. 622; *Baynton v. Bobbet* (1689), 2 Ventris 67, 86 E.R. 312.

Whitaker: I agree that *nil habuit in tenementis* generally is not a good plea. 1 Inst. 47.[1] But a case may be where a lessee may confess and avoid. Cro. Eliz. 700, 701, is as strong a case as the present; so there may be a special *nil habuit*. Non tenure in a *scire facias* is not a good plea, but non tenure specially may be good. 3 Lev. 205 is in point on the reservation in the lease to the lessor and his executors.

Secondly, the plaintiff ought to have relied on the estoppel, as Co. *Entr.* 603, and not have demurred. Perry and Stevens, Michaelmas 11 Anne; Hob. 206, Speak v. Richards; 4 Co. 53a, Rawlins's Case, estoppels must be relied on; so, *quacunque via*, either we may show a special *nil habuit* or else the plaintiff ought to have replied and relied on the estoppel.

Serjeant *Chappell*: There is no difference between a special and a general *nil habuit*. And the case in Croke is nothing to the purpose, for the deed was made by a husband and wife and, if it was not an estoppel to the wife, then [there is] no estoppel. As to relying on an estoppel, the indenture appears on the record, so he may take advantage of it; it is otherwise of an estoppel *dehors* the record.

Chief Baron [Pengelly]: Salkeld 277, but it is not very accurately reported. If the plaintiff will declare generally on a demise without showing it by an indenture and the defendant pleads *nil habuit in tenementis*, the plaintiff must reply that the demise was by an indenture and demand *si contra indenturam suam etc.* But if he declares on the indenture at first, the plaintiff may take advantage of the estoppel by a demurrer; so, by him, the plaintiff must have judgment.

Comyns was of the same opinion and cited 3 Lev. 147 in point. And he said further that the defendant should have traversed the enjoyment. 2 Ventr. 67, is in point as to this purpose.

Judgment was *pro querente per* TOTAM CURIAM.

1 Comyns 391, 92 E.R. 1125

This was an action of debt for rent. And the plaintiff declared that, by an indenture of the 27th of September 1723, he demised to the defendant a messuage in Bond Street for seven years at £160 *per annum*, by virtue of which demise, the defendant entered and was from thence in possession to the day of the Feast of the Annunciation of the Blessed Virgin in 1726, and, for a year's rent due at the said feast, this action was brought etc.

The defendant pleaded that, before the demise, *viz.* on the 24th of January 1722, the plaintiff was possessed of the same messuage for the term of 99 years to come and, the same day, assigned his term to Anne Colwell, who afterwards, *viz.* on the 25th of July 1723, entered and was, and is still, in possession, and this she is ready to prove, to which the plaintiff demurred and showed for cause that the plea does not confess and avoid, nor deny, the matter in the declaration, that

[1] E. Coke, *First Institute* (1628), f. 47b.

it does not show expulsion of the defendant, and that it is argumentative, etc. The defendant joined in demurrer.

And it was argued by Serjeant *Whitaker* that the plea is a special *nil habuit in tenementis* and, therefore, the plaintiff ought to have replied and relied upon the estoppel and not demurred. Coke, *Entries*, 103; Hobart 206. And perhaps, the plaintiff had an interest and, therefore, the defendant might confess and avoid. Co. Lit. 47b; Cro. Eliz. 700.

Sed non allocatur, for, upon a plea of general *nil habuit in tenementis*, the plaintiff might demur, where the estoppel appears in his declaration. 3 Levinz 146; 1 Salkeld 277.[1] *A fortiori*, in a special *nil habuit* etc. And the defendant here does not show that the plaintiff had an interest which could be avoided. And also, the defendant did not answer to the possession as she ought. 2 Ventris 67.[2] And, therefore, judgment was given for the plaintiff.

634

Attorney General v. Burges

(Ex. 1726)

A person is liable for the full penalties for smuggling where the actual importation was done by his agent at his direction.

Taussig MS. 311, vol. 2, p. 997

Sittings at Westminster, 29 November 1726, *coram* Pengelly, Chief Baron.

Upon an information of *devenerunt* for the treble value of 3000 pounds weight of tea and 200 pounds weight of coffee which came to the defendant's hands knowing the duties were not paid, the evidence for the king proved that, in April 1724, the defendant, one Hunter, who was the witness, and two others entered into an agreement that the defendant should buy a parcel of tea and ship it to Dunkirk, that Hunter should go over to Dunkirk and reship it from thence to a seller in Hampshire and there run it, that, accordingly, in May 1724, the defendant Burgess entered 680 pounds weight of tea shipped on board the Dunkirk pacquet and 2724 pounds weight of tea shipped on board the *Neptune* for Dunkirk making *in toto* of 3404 pounds weight of tea, which was accordingly carried to Dunkirk and was received there by Hunter. And certificates were sent over of the landing of both of the said parcels. And, upon those certificates, the proper officer of the customs delivered up the defendant Burgess's bonds and they were cancelled, that the very same tea was put into other packages at Dunkirk and was shipped by Hunter on board two vessels consigned to a seller, who was

---

[1] *Heath v. Vermeden* (1683), 3 Levinz 146, 83 E.R. 622; *Kemp v. Goodal* (1705), 1 Salkeld 277, 91 E.R. 242, also 2 Lord Raymond 1154, 92 E.R. 263.

[2] *Baynton v. Bobbet* (1689), 2 Ventris 67, 86 E.R. 312.

one of the persons engaged in this project, that the same was accordingly carried over in these vessels, and the greatest part of it, together with 700 pounds weight of coffee bought by Hunter at Dunkirk, by the direction and agreement between the parties, was landed at different times upon the coast under the direction of the seller, who lived there, though one or two of the boats which were bringing it off from the vessels were chased by the Custom House boat and forced thereupon to throw part of their cargo overboard. However, the tea proved to be landed, some in one and some in other places of the coast, was more in the whole than the quantity contained in the information. But there was no direct and positive proof that the same came into the actual possession of the defendant in London, who kept a druggist's shop at the Sign of [*blank*] in Fleet Street, though there were many instances of his acknowledgment of his having part of the said tea and of his directions from time to time for the conducting and managing the affair in the country and being often there in person during this transaction. And there was an account under his own hand produced by Hunter wherein there was an article or two including the whole quantity of tea. There was no evidence for the defendant, but it was objected that this was a personal offense and, therefore, the coming to the hands is the gist of the information.

But it was answered by the Attorney General [*Yorke*] and agreed to by Chief Baron [Pengelly], and he so directed the jury, that, if they believed the goods have come to the seller's hands with the privity, direction, and consent of the defendant, that then such coming to the seller's hands must be looked upon as a coming to the defendant's hands, for an agent, in such a case, it is the same as one's self where he acts by the direction and authority of the principal.

And the jury found a verdict for the king, the treble value whereof amounted to £3270.

Bunbury 223, 145 E.R. 654

29 November 1726.

Upon an information by way of *devenerunt* for the treble value on the Stat. 8 Ann.,[1] for goods that came to the hands of the defendant, knowing they had not paid the duties, it was determined at the trial at the sittings by Lord Chief Baron Pengelly that, if several persons were concerned, either in partnership or otherwise, yet the crown might come against any one of them for the whole penalty, it being in the nature of a tort, and not a contract, as, in cases of tort, a subject might come upon anyone concerned in the tort. And it was also resolved that, on such an information, there was no necessity that the goods should be proved to come actually into his hands if they came into his power or into the custody of any agent of his or to any person by his direction.

[1] Stat. 8 Ann., c. 12, s. 17 (*SR*, IX, 221).

635

Attorney General v. Weeks

(Ex. 1726)

A factor, as opposed to an agent or servant, is an importer and is liable to pay customs duties as well as the owner of the goods imported.

No evidence of an importation of goods can admitted for an importation that was outside the dates pleaded in the information.

Taussig MS. 311, vol. 2, p. 1000

Michaelmas term 1726.

An information of debt [was brought] for the importation on 12 April 1726 of 1000 pounds weight of licorice [and] 100 of nutmegs and cloves. And, for the duties of these goods, the information was brought.

The evidence was of an importation in 1719, but this objection was not taken. But it appear[ed] that the goods were imported jointly for the mutual risk of the defendant [Charles Weekes] and of Randall, who was the witness, and so the information ought to be against both. And this is also a strong objection to the credit of the witness.

Attorney General [*Yorke*]: This is an information of debt which arises *ex delicto* and the duties must be paid or agreed for before the landing. And these sorts of informations have been held good even against a factor. And the crown may maintain an information against each of the importers, but can make but one levy.

And the Chief Baron [PENGELLY] said that, where there are several part-owners in the same goods at the time of landing, he thought the crown may have the duties from either but *fiat nisi unica executione* as matters of two obligors in a joint bond. As to the case of a factor, if it be that a factor for one who is abroad, no doubt the law is so, for he is the consignee of the goods. And as to a factor to one at home, he is more than a servant or laborer and has a sort of interest in the goods, and, if the factor comes and enters, he must pay the duties, and, if he secretly and clandestinely takes upon himself to take up the goods without an entry, there can be no reason to discharge him from the duties nor any description or evidence of his ownership otherwise than by ordering, managing, and directing, for a mere servant perhaps may be only prosecutable as aiding and assisting and not as an importer, but one who takes upon himself to order or manage as a factor or person interested may be looked upon as an importer. If a merchant sends for goods which are consigned to himself and sells them before arrival to another merchant and he is to take them up and does so, he must pay and be answerable for the duty. And, by him, the debt here arising *ex delicto*, the crown may charge either.

There was a verdict for the king.

Bunbury 223, 145 E.R. 654

1 December 1726.

Upon an information in debt for non-payment of duties, it was laid in the information that the defendant imported the goods in 12 Geo. [1725–1726]. The plaintiff gave in evidence an importation in April 1719.

In this case, two objections arose, first, whether they could be permitted to give evidence of importation at any time before the day laid in the information; secondly, whether any person can be charged on such an information in debt for the duties but the actual importer.

To the first objection it was answered, and resolved by the Lord Chief Baron [PENGELLY] that this might have been made easy to the defendant by application to the court, who would have made an order for confining the evidence to a certain time. And the CHIEF BARON thought the case in Cro. Eliz. 660[1] not to be [good] law, that the day is not material, and constant experience had justified this practice.

To the second objection, though upon a *devenerunt*, which is a criminal prosecution, every person to whose hands the goods come may be charged, yet, in debt, the person to be charged as importer must have such an interest in the goods, as to be liable to pay the duties, and it will not extend to a mere agent or servant. But, if he is jointly interested with another, the crown may recover the whole against one, as, in the case of several obligors in a bond, the obligee may sue one or all, though he can have but one satisfaction. A factor for a person abroad is in this case undoubtedly liable because the crown cannot get at the principal; and a factor for a merchant here has some sort of interest in the goods and has some share and allowance for his factorage and has a special property in the goods; he is to take the goods and pay the duties and, therefore, must be taken to be the importer; *aliter*, in the case of a mere agent or servant.

636

Attorney General v. Jewers

(Ex. 1726)

After goods that were imported without paying customs duties have been seized for that reason, the crown cannot sue to collect the duties, but, if there was no seizure and forfeiture, the crown can sue for the duties.

Bunbury 225, 145 E.R. 655

2 December 1726. *Coram* Lord Chief Baron Pengelly.

[1] *Munday v. Martin* (1599), Croke Eliz. 660, 78 E.R. 899, also Hetley 120, 124 E.R. 391.

Upon an information of debt for the duties, it was objected as to part, *scil.* the French wines coming from Holland, that they are prohibited and forfeited and so no duties are payable. Simms v. Kennison.

But it was said by the Lord Chief Baron [PENGELLY], after a seizure is made, the crown cannot make an election because the right is attached in the informer as to his share. And this is not an absolute prohibition, but a prohibition *sub modo*, as, in the case of brandies, had been resolved since the case of Doe, *qui tam* v. Cooper, Michaelmas 2 Geo.[1]

Taussig MS. 311, vol. 2, p. 1003

Michaelmas term 1726. Attorney General v. Jewers and Batty.

An information in debt [was brought] for duties laid in the information to be imported in October 1725, and the evidence of the importation [was it was] in 1719. And I made the objection [. . .] was or seemed to be of opinion against me.

In the same case, it was debated whether duties can be demanded for wines from Holland. And I cited Symms and Reynardson [Exchequer, Michaelmas term 1709], and Mr. Attorney General [*Yorke*] cited the case of Doe, *qui tam* v. Cowper.

The Chief Baron [PENGELLY] thought that, in this case, which is only a prohibition *sub modo*, the king had an election, but it is otherwise where there is a total prohibition. And this case differs not from every other case where the goods are forfeited by the express words of the Statute for being landed without the payment of duties and yet the crown prosecutes for the duty, for, in those cases, the goods themselves are forfeited *in toto* and therefore ought not to yield a duty if the aforesaid argument is good. If there is a forfeiture of the goods themselves and an information *qui tam* is exhibited for the goods themselves as forfeited, then, by the CHIEF BARON, I do not think that the king can sue for the duties, for that would perhaps destroy the informer's prosecution. But when that time is over, the king may sue for the duties.

There was a £220 verdict for the king; 2s. 7d. for the defendant.

637

Rex v. Bowling

(Ex. 1726)

A writ of execution does not lie to recover a debt assigned to the defendant's surety.

Bunbury 225, 145 E.R. 655

At the sittings at Serjeants' Inn.

[1] *Doe, qui tam v. Cooper* (Ex. 1719), see above, Case No. 88.

Bowling became surety with Acock on his obtaining a writ of delivery for a ship, and he entered into a recognizance for that purpose, according to the course of the court.

Bowling, after a *scire facias* on the recognizance against him, takes out a [writ of] extent against himself to find debts. And upon an inquisition, it was found that Harrison was indebted to Sandys in £220 for goods sold and delivered and that Sandys had, three days before the extent, by deed poll assigned this debt to Bowling for a valuable consideration. And the inquisition concluded that *die captionis inquisitionis Harrison indebitatus existit* to Bowling in £220; upon that, Bowling, upon making an affidavit that this debt was really and *bona fide* due to him, obtains an extent against Harrison.

And this matter coming before the court on the Master's report, wherein it appeared that no evidence was given upon the inquisition that any debt was due from Harrison to Sandys, and that the solicitor for Bowling had only sworn that the consideration of the assignment from Sandys to Bowling was a promissory note to the best of his remembrance, I [*Bunbury*] now moved that the extent against Harrison might be set aside because it appeared that there was no original debt due from Harrison to Bowling, as the Rules of the 15 Car. I direct, upon which reason, the extent was discharged. I also objected that the interest of Bowling by the assignment from Sandys was only an equitable interest and that debts in equity cannot be seized upon an extent. But, in this, the court would give no opinion.

638

Bryerley v. Pendlebury

(Ex. 1726)

Where the plaintiff alleges that the defendant is to do a particular act, the defendant must show in his responsive pleading an exact and punctual performance.

Harvard Law School MS. 1082, vol. 2, p. 8

Michaelmas term 1726.

An action of debt was brought upon a bond whereby the defendant was obliged to provide proper habitation, bed and bedding, and household goods, tools and materials for his trade. The defendant pleads that he did perform the condition of the bond and offered to provide. And the plaintiff replies that the defendant did not offer to provide. And the defendant demurs, and the plaintiff joins in demurer.

Bootle, for the defendant. The replication puts a matter in issue that is immaterial. And this bond is on a condition only to find and provide a sufficient place for habitation, bed, bedding, and some household goods and tools and material for this trade. And the defendant is not obliged to offer such habitation. And the defendant has pleaded that he did provide. It is material in pleading that there should be an affirmative and a negative. And the defendant having pleaded that he did do it, the plaintiff has departed from the material part by saying that the defendant did not offer. Dyer 31; Lutwyche 1480.[1]

Ward, for the plaintiff: I agree that, if it is entirely immaterial, then the replication is wrong. But, if the defendant pleads immaterially, the plaintiff is entitled to his judgment. And the defendant says he has performed generally, and that is not good. And if *obtulit* makes it good, then the replication is good. And when the defendant pleads performance of an agreement consisting of several parts, it must be according to the sense and meaning. Plowden 23.[2]

It was incumbent on the defendant to put the plaintiff in possession and security to enjoy. Style 263, 273, Peck v. Ingram; Yelverton 49, Allen v. Randal; Hobart 69; 2 Leonard 125; Cro. Eliz. 477; Bendlow 65, 66; Nichol's Case, 5 Rept.[3]

Bootle replies: The defendant pleads *secundum formam et effectu conditionis*.

[To the] objection that the plea is not good without *obtulit*, [he] answered the instances cited are only personal and there is no fixed time for doing it. When the covenants are in the affirmative, performance generally will be good. 2 Cro. 104, 107, 138.[4]

Chief Baron [Pengelly]: By the form of the pleading, it is admitted that you must answer specially where several matters are alleged. And a special performance ought to be shown. And the knowledge of this matter is within the privity of the defendant. And the plea seems defective *quacunque via data*. Judgment must be given for the plaintiff, for, if the plea is not good, then judgment is for the plaintiff; if it is made good by *obtulit*, then the replication is proper.

Hale and Carter agree.

---

[1] *Anonymous* (1537), 1 Dyer 31, 73 E.R. 69; *Talbot v. Woodhouse* (1699), 2 Lutwyche 1471, 1480, 125 E.R. 811, 816.

[2] *Colthirst v. Bejushin* (1550), 1 Plowden 21, 75 E.R. 33.

[3] *Peck v. Ingram* (1651), Style 263, 273, 82 E.R. 696, 705; *Allen v. Randall* (1604), Yelverton 49, 80 E.R. 35; *Boothly v. Baily*, Hobart 69, 80 E.R. 218; *Venable's Case* (1586), 2 Leonard 122, 185, 74 E.R. 410, 621; *Ewer v. Hayden* (1596), Croke Eliz. 476, 658, 78 E.R. 727, 897, also Moore K.B. 359, 72 E.R. 629, Owen 74, 74 E.R. 912; *Lord Evers v. Buckton* (1558), Benloe 65, 123 E.R. 51; *Chamberlain v. Nichols* (1595), 5 Coke Rep. 43, 77 E.R. 121, also Croke Eliz. 455, 78 E.R. 694, Moore K.B. 692, 72 E.R. 844, Jenkins 257, 145 E.R. 183.

[4] Perhaps *Peterson's Case* (1588), Croke Eliz. 104, 78 E.R. 362; *Bellicote v. Taylboys* (1588), Croke Eliz. 107, 78 E.R. 365; *Warcop v. Morse* (1589), Croke Eliz. 138, 78 E.R. 394.

COMYNS: Where the defendant is to do a particular act, the defendant must show an exact and punctual performance. And the words of the condition are not sufficient without answering the intent of the condition.

Judgment was given for the plaintiff.

Taussig MS. 311, vol. 2, p. 993, pl. 2

Michaelmas term 1726.

This case was argued between Mr. *Bootle*, for the defendant, and myself, for the plaintiff.

And the point of the case was no more than this. Pendlebury was bound by a bond of £50 with a condition that, if he, immediately upon Brierly's return from Lancaster Castle to Bolton, should find a sufficient place of habitation for Brierly at Bolton so and so furnished, then the obligation to be void. The defendant, taking notice that the plaintiff returned on such a day in certain, says that he *invenibat et providebat* a sufficient place of habitation for him etc. in the very words of the condition, concluding it with a *secundum formam et effectum conditionis praedictis et adtunc et ibidem obtulit eundem sufficientem locu habitationis etc.* And the plaintiff replied and traversed the *obtulit*. The defendant demurred, and the plaintiff joined in demurrer.

Et per TOTAM CURIAM, it was adjudged that the plea was not good without the *obtulit*, for it was absolutely necessary to the true performance of the condition that Pendlebury should give notice of the house found or else the finding and providing was to no purpose.

And PENGELLY, Chief Baron, said he apprehended the replication was good because the *obtulit* implied notice, according to the authorities cited by me. But he was clear that the plea was not good without notice.

COMYNS, ditto, and HALE and CARTER agreed in the main. And judgment [was given] for the plaintiff *nisi causa* on Monday next, the last day of term.

639

Thomas v. Duke of Beaufort

(Ex. 1726)

Tithes of wood are due by common right.

Whether tithes are payable out of certain land must be established by a jury.

Taussig MS. 311, vol. 2, p. 974

Thursday, 10 December 1726; PENGELLY, Chief Baron, HALE, CARTER, COMYNS, *praesentibus*.

The plaintiff, as rector of Llandvaches in the County of Monmouth, exhibited his bill against the duke of Beaufort and the other [defendant] for the tithe of wood cut down within the parish. The duke defends in this manner, *scil.* that the place where the wood grew was part of Wenwood Forest and not within the parish of Llandvaches, but extra-parochial, and that he hoped, by divers grants and records, that he was entitled to the tithes of the lands lying in the Forest. The other defendant was a tenant of certain iron mills belonging to the duke and the purchaser of the wood after the same was felled and corded for the use of the mills.

Wills, for the defendant, took an exception that the plaintiff ought to have alleged a custom for the payment of tithe wood, for that it was not tithable of common right. And he cited the Case of Hicks and Woodson, Salkeld 655, 3rd fol., for that purpose.[1]

Sed per PENGELLY: It is true that there is such an assertion in that case and that was the Lord Chief Justice Holt's opinion, but the contrary has been frequently adjudged in this court, and that the Statute *Silva Caedua*[2] was in affirmance of the common law, declaring what sort of wood was tithable at common law. So this exception was overruled.

Browne took another exception, *viz.* that it appearing by the answer that the lands on which were extra-parochial, the Attorney General ought to have been made a party.

Sed per Chief Baron [PENGELLY]: You only defend as the lands are out of the plaintiff's parish and that is the matter in issue.

Et per TOTAM CURIAM: We must direct an issue to be tried at law, for we can never bind the inheritance by depositions, but it must be tried at law.

640

Lannego v. Goodeere

(Ex. 1726)

A court of equity will not enforce a harsh bargain or a usurious loan.

Taussig MS. 311, vol. 2, p. 982

Monday, 14 [December] 1726; all the barons present.

In August 1720, the defendant, having occasion to borrow £8000, applies to Cardosso, a broker, for that purpose, who recommends the plaintiff. On 25 August 1720, an indenture is drawn up between them to this effect, *viz.* that the defendant, having, upon receipt of £8325 6s. 3d., transferred £1000 South Sea

[1] *Hicks v. Woodeson* (1694), 2 Salkeld 655, 91 E.R. 558, also 4 Modern 324, 336, 87 E.R. 422, 429, 1 Eagle & Younge 592, 2 Gwillim 550, 3 Lord Raymond 116, 92 E.R. 595, 1 Lord Raymond 137, 91 E.R. 987, 12 Modern 111, 88 E.R. 1200, Skinner 560, 90 E.R. 252, Comberbach 403, 90 E.R. 555, Carthew 392, 90 E.R. 827, Holt K.B. 671, 90 E.R. 1271, Dodd 171.

[2] Stat. 45 Edw. III, c. 3 (*SR*, I, 393).

stock with the midsummer dividend to Lannego as also £500 of the third subscription, that Lannego should re-transfer the said stock within a month's time to the defendant, and the defendant should repay him the sum of £8360. Goodeere covenants in the said deed to accept of a re-transfer of this stock and subscription receipt within a month and he would repay the money.

And the plaintiff's bill was to compel the defendant to take a re-transfer of his stock and pay the money or that the stock and produce thereof may be sold and the plaintiff may have what it sells for and [the defendant] may be obliged to pay the residue of the money.

On 26th August 1720, by an indenture, Lannego covenants with Goodeere to transfer to Goodeere within a month's time £1000 South Sea stock with the midsummer dividend. Goodeere covenants to accept thereof at any time within a month and to pay the said Lannego the said £8360. And it was agreed that the plaintiff Lannego should, upon the payment of the £8360, return the £500 subscription receipt. Upon the back of the indenture was endorsed a receipt from Mr. Goodeere to Mr. Lannego for the £8325 6s. 3d. in full for the purchase of £1000 South Sea stock with the midsummer dividend this day transferred to the said Lannego by the said Goodeere.

It was proved by Martin and Cardosso that the stock and £500 subscription was transferred as a security for the £8000 lent and by Cardosso that the plaintiff was ready before the day to re-transfer the stock, but the defendant said he could not pay the money and so desired the plaintiff would keep the stock longer and, several times after the day, the defendant promised to give further security. [On] April 6, 1721, [there was] a letter from Goodeere to Lannego, the substance whereof was a direction that the plaintiff should take the stock which the company gave for the subscription receipt.

Wills, for the defendant: This bill is not proper, for it is a plain action at common law and a court of equity will not intermeddle in the compelling of so hard a bargain. And by him, if the plaintiff has done all in his power to make a transfer before the day, this is good at law. But if it is not good at law, then equity will not help it. It must be taken upon the face of the contract either to be a sale for £8325 6s. 3d. or else as a loan upon the security of the stock transferred; if it is a loan, as is now contended for, then it appears £8000 only was paid. And here is a covenant to repay £8360 which is above £50 *per centum*. In the case of a mortgage, all that the court of equity can do is to direct the mortgaged premises to be sold, but it cannot make the security better and more valuable than it really is.

Reeves replies: We could have had no remedy at common law, for we must have proved a precedent transfer at the day and the agreement of the defendant to waive the precise terms of the contract would not do at law. So he takes it not to be a contract for a sale, but for the loan of the money. I do not insist by the answer upon the contract's being usurious, and we do not insist by our bill to have the whole £8360, but only what is justly due for principal and legal interest.

Chief Baron [Pengelly]: I do not think a court of equity is to interpose. If the law will not help these sort of contracts, a court of equity will not. The plaintiff says that his not having transferred on the defendant's desire [*blank*]. Now, this does not appear by the evidence, for there was no agreement to adjourn the performance of the contract to another day, but it does appear by Cardosso's evidence that the defendant said he could not take it and he desired the plaintiff would keep it longer. That should by no means have hindered the plaintiff from doing what was necessary on his part to take his advantage of the contract, and, if he did not, it was not his laches. It was in the lender's power to have stipulated that he might have sold it at the day. But, in this case, the plaintiff seems to have taken the £500 receipt subscription of £500 instead thereof. And the plaintiff has laid by all this while, from 1720, and would now lay the whole upon the defendant. So I cannot agree to make a decree for more than the produce of the stock and the subscription.

Hale: I think a court of equity is not to decree a very hard contract and that we are not to consider the general rules of mortgages in the determining of these sort of cases, for they are peculiar to the time.[1] And I believe such things will never happen again. So the plaintiff must have a decree either for the sale of the stock and take it for his satisfaction or else his bill must be dismissed.

Carter: We must now look upon it as a loan, and, if so, it is usurious, £8360 for £8000. But in a court of equity, he can have nothing but a sale or a foreclosure. The defendant, indeed, has dealt somewhat hard with the plaintiff, but it was the plaintiff's own folly to have so much reliance on the defendant when Cardosso informed him that the defendant would not accept.

Comyns: It appears to us to be an usurious contract. And we must then decree a usurious contract.

And the court proposed that the plaintiff should take a decree for the stock and the produce of the subscription or else the court must dismiss the bill, though they were inclined to dismiss without costs.

But the plaintiff's counsel desired time to speak with their client, which was granted.

Taussig MS. 311, vol. 2, p. 990

Michaelmas term 1726.

The plaintiff in the cause chose to have his bill dismissed.

But the court declared it should be without costs. The Chief Baron [Pengelly] said that he saw no reason to alter his former opinion and said that, upon the face of the pleadings, it was a manifest trick to elude the Statute of Usury.[2]

---

[1] I.e. the burst of the South Sea bubble in 1720.

[2] Stat. 13 Ann., c. 15 (*SR*, IX, 928).

641

Patten v. Humphreys

(Ex. 1726)

The Statute of Frauds does not apply to a suit in equity for an account.

Taussig MS. 311, vol. 2, p. 991

Michaelmas term 1726.

The plea of the Statute of Frauds and Perjuries[1] in this case was overruled. The bill was for a specific performance of an agreement between the plaintiff's testator and Humphreys concerning the working of a lead mine and for an account of the profits thereof since the last account was made up in the testator's lifetime. And the case was this. Humphreys was the owner of the land for life in which [*blank*] and made up an agreement with the plaintiff's testator and another that, if they two would undertake the working of this mine and pay proportionally towards the charges thereof, they should, each of them, have two-fourths of the profits and he would pay the two other fourths of the charges and have two-fourths of the profits. The mine was worked. And for twenty-two years, together, accounts were made up in writing, as alleged by the bill, and stated and adjusted between them all. But now the plaintiff's testator being dead, the defendant Humphreys would not permit the plaintiff to have any benefit of the mine. And to this bill, the Statute of Frauds and Perjuries was pleaded.

Sed per CURIAM, the accounts made up in writing between the parties will, if true, bring the case out of the Statute; therefore, to be sure, that part of the bill must be answered.

642

Wragg v. Clements

(Ex. 1726)

A plaintiff in an action of trover does not have the right to inspect the goods claimed before the trial.

Taussig MS. 311, vol. 2, p. 992

Michaelmas term 1726.

I showed cause against the rule the plaintiff had got for inspecting a bag of foreign money in the Custom House, *viz.* that this was an action of trover by the plaintiff for so many pieces of silver, foreign coins, etc. and that, though, in the case of an information of seizure where the proceedings were *in rem*, the court

[1] Stat. 29 Car. II, c. 3 (*SR*, V, 839–842).

had often permitted the defendant to have samples and a view, yet it was never done in the case of a private action of trover.

And of this opinion was the court. And so the plaintiff was defeated of his intention, and the rule was set aside.

N.B. The motion was made on the defendant's behalf. Clements, the officer, having seized a parcel of foreign silver which was carried into the king's warehouse, Wragg, the owner, brought [an action of] trover against him for the same and moved that his witnesses might have access to it to view it or that it might be produced at the trial. *Sed negatur* upon the reasons before.

643

Gough v. Harrison

(Ex. 1726)

Although a litigant is privileged from arrest while going to and from court, the defendant in this case, when arrested, was no longer going home from court.

Taussig MS. 311, vol. 2, p. 995

Michaelmas term 1726.

Colonel Harrison, who was plaintiff in the cause against Hart,[1] when he went away from the court on Wednesday between 2 and 3 o'clock at noon went to the Baptist Head Tavern in Chancery Lane and was there from 5 in the evening and stayed there until between 10 and 11 at night. And, as he went out of the tavern, he was arrested by one Cole, a bailiff, upon a [writ of] *capias ad satisfaciendum* on a judgment obtained against the said Harrison at Sir Richard Gough's suit. And, thereupon, on Thursday morning, Mr. Collier, Harrison's solicitor, and Traverse and Periam, two accountants, made affidavits that Harrison and the others were together at the tavern in order to make up some accounts there which were to be delivered to the barons on Thursday morning and that they were employed at the tavern on this business. And, therefore, it was moved that Harrison might be discharged and the officer committed for a contempt in arresting the said Harrison, being, as they suggested, under the protection of the court *eundo et redeundo*. And the court made a rule to show cause why Cole should not discharge him.

And this day, Serjeant *Darnall* and *Fazakerly* came to show cause against the rule made by the court. And they insisted that the privilege did not extend further than to the party's going home to his own house or, if he might go to his solicitor's or attorney's house, that could not protect him further. And Serjeant *Darnall* also said that Holt, Chief Justice, had held that, unless the party's attendance on the court was necessary and by way of compulsion, it would not privi-

[1] *Harrison v. Hart* (Ex. 1722–1727), see below, Case No. 649.

lege him, and he cited the case in Salkeld [*blank*].[1] And they produced affidavits that it was about 11 o'clock at night that Harrison was arrested.

And upon the whole, the court refused to do anything in the matter, *viz.* either to discharge Harrison or to censure the bailiff.

1 Comyns 411, 92 E.R. 1135

Harrison, after his attendance in court upon the cause aforementioned, went about 3 o'clock in a coach from Westminster to Chancery Lane with his solicitor and others to give instructions for procedure in the cause and there continued until 10 or 11 o'clock, and then was arrested by a bailiff upon a [writ of] *capias ad satisfaciendum*, upon a judgment in *scire facias* upon a judgment against him in the Court of Common Pleas. And now, it was moved that he should be discharged, for each party has privilege to attend his cause and, if he be arrested in going or returning, it shall be a contempt of the court, upon which the officer shall be punished and the party discharged. But it was not allowed, for, here, it does not appear that there was any contrivance by the defendants or any concerned in the cause to procure this arrest, in which case, the court perhaps will extend its power against the procurers. Nor does it appear that the officer knew that he had attended his cause at Westminster, for his warrant was dated before the arrest and there was another *capias ad satisfaciendum* taken in Trinity term preceding, returnable in London where the action was brought, and a *testatum capias* afterwards in London the first return of this term before the *capias ad satisfaciendum* upon which he was then taken, and the arrest here was not in his attendance upon that cause, but he had continued many hours in another place. And, if the court should discharge him, how shall the sheriffs be defended against an action for the escape? In 1 Brownlow, p. 15, in the case of Wilson v. The Sheriffs of London,[2] in an action for an escape, it was said that the court can discharge if the arrest was in view of the court, otherwise not; and in 2 Salkeld 544,[3] where a man went to confess an indictment in the King's Bench and was arrested in his journey, the court would not discharge him, for he went of his own head. And there is a difference where a man attends upon the court by process and when not.

[1] *Anonymous* (1704), 2 Salkeld 544, 91 E.R. 461.

[2] *Wilson v. Sheriffs of London* (1620), 1 Brownlow & Goldesborough 15, 123 E.R. 635.

[3] *Anonymous* (1704), 2 Salkeld 544, 91 E.R. 461.

644

Snow, *qui tam* v. Hatton

(Ex. 1726)

Where an information is brought for the seizure of goods imported unlawfully between such a time and such a time, then the plaintiff cannot prove a seizure at any other time.

Taussig MS. 311, vol. 2, p. 1002

Michaelmas term 1726.

'*Parcella serici holoserici vocata* velvet.' In Littleton's *Dictionary*, '*holosericus*' is only used as an adjective, but in Cote's *English Dictionary*, it is used as a substantive, though, in the Latin part of the *Dictionary*, it is used as an adjective. However, the defendant went into his evidence as to the whole of the silks seized as well as the velvet.

And in this case, Mr. Attorney [General *Yorke*] admitted that, where he lays an information for goods as *adducta et importata* between such a time and such a time, that then he is confined to that time and cannot go out of it. And, therefore, if the defendant shows that the goods were in his possession before the first time in the information, he must be acquitted as to them or more properly the goods cannot be condemned on such an information.

There was a verdict for the defendant.

645

Bannastre v. Webb

(Ex. 1726–1727)

Where a vicar sues the lessee of an impropriator in a dispute over tithes, the impropriator is a necessary party.

The Court of Exchequer has jurisdiction over tithes cases where the tithes are not set out or paid but not where they are detained except where the king or his lessee is concerned.

Taussig MS. 311, vol. 2, p. 1006, pl. 2

Michaelmas term 1726. Banister, vicar of Wonersh in the County of Surrey v. Webb, lessee of the impropriator of the rectory of the same parish.

The plaintiff brings his bill against the defendant to account for great quantities of tithes of pease and beans which the lessee of the impropriator had taken and carried away after the said tithes were set out by the occupiers of the land whereon they grew. And the great question made upon the pleadings was whether the vicar had the right to these sort of tithes, the pease and beans being set in the open fields in a garden-like manner. And the depositions *ex utraque parte* went to this right.

But after opening the bill and answer, *Bunbury*, *Browne*, and *Edlin*, for the defendant, objected, first, that the impropriator ought to be made a party. And this seemed to be agreed to by the court. But they said that they would let the cause stand over upon payment of costs of the day until next term in order to let the plaintiff make the impropriator a party.

But then they objected that the plaintiff could never maintain this bill though the impropriator was made a party, for the jurisdiction of this court was for subtraction of tithes by the occupiers and there was no instance of a bill but where the occupier was made a party. But in the case before the court, the tithes being actually set out and taken away afterwards, it was only an action of trespass or trover. And they cited Noy 44; Cro. Eliz. 607.[1]

And Mr. *Browne* cited the case of Cross and Pointz, sittings after Hilary term 1719, where a vicar's bill was dismissed upon this very point, *viz.* because it was brought against the impropriator only, and the case of Nicholas v. Sweethurst, same sittings, where the court would have allowed the same objection, but that the defendant had in his answer submitted to account. And of this point, the court took time to consider. See 2 Chancery Cases 31, 32.[2]

Next morning, the Chief Baron [PENGELLY], who had looked into this point, said that originally the right of tithes was determinable by the common law. Cawdry's Case, 5 Rep. 16a. Westminster II, ca. 5,[3] recites that they could not proceed in the ecclesiastical court, for the writ of *indicavit* lay in such a case, 2 Inst. 364,[4] to prohibit the ecclesiastical court. The Statute of *Circumspecte Agatis*, 13 Edw. I,[5] gives the jurisdiction to the spiritual court, even of the mere right in case it does not amount to the fourth part of the advowson. 2 Inst. 491. And 18 Edw. III, ca. 7, takes away the *scire facias* against clerks, 2 Inst. 640, to answer in Chancery for tithes.[6]

But neither the Statute of *Circumspecte Agatis* nor 18 Edw. III break in upon the prerogative. And the king might controvert the mere right, and so might the

[1] *Webb v. Petts* (1601), Noy 44, 74 E.R. 1013, 1 Eagle & Younge 153; *Leigh v. Wood* (1598), Croke Eliz. 607, 78 E.R. 850, also Moore K.B. 912, 72 E.R. 992, 1 Eagle & Younge 139.

[2] *Perne v. Oldfield* (1680), 2 Chancery Cases 19, 31, 22 E.R. 826, 832, also 2 Ventris 349, 86 E.R. 349, 1 Eagle & Younge 526.

[3] *Caudrey v. Atton* (1591), 5 Coke Rep. 1, 77 E.R. 1, also Popham 59, 79 E.R. 1175; Stat. 13 Edw. I, Westminster II, c. 5 (*SR*, I, 75–77).

[4] E. Coke, *Second Institute* (1642), p. 364.

[5] Stat. 13 Edw. I, *Circumspecte Agatis* (*SR*, I, 101–102).

[6] E. Coke, *Second Institute* (1642), p. 491; Stat. 18 Edw. III, stat. 3, c. 7 (*SR*, I, 303); E. Coke, *Second Institute* (1642), p. 640.

farmer in this court. 38 Ass. 20, cited in 2 Rolle's Rep. 301; 1 Rolle's *Abr.*, 538, D, 1, *et ibidem*, D, 2, 'If J.S. be the parson impropriate of A. and B. be the vicar there and the king be the patron of the vicarage and [there is a] dispute between the parson and the vicar touching the tithes there, the suit must be for these tithes in the Exchequer', Hilary 8 Jac. [1611].[1] And by Lane 100,[2] it may be by an English bill or by an action in the Office of Pleas, for the king is the supreme ordinary. And it appears by Rolle, *Abr.*, Prohibition, 311 and 312,[3] that, in 12 Jac., it was doubted whether an impropriator and vicar could controvert the mere right of tithes in the ecclesiastical court without the parishioner, and the doubt was because the Stat. 31 Hen. VIII[4] had made impropriations lay fees and, therefore, the impropriator did not, as they apprehend, stand perfectly in the same case as a rector, but the Statute, as it was afterwards observed, having saved the jurisdiction of the spiritual court, a [writ of] prohibition was denied in the case of an impropriator and a vicar. The case in Noy 44 and Cro. Eliz. 607 is only to this effect, that, when the tithes are once set forth, the remedy for him that right has to such tithes is at common law only, for, by the setting forth, they become lay chattels and [there is] no remedy in such a case in the spiritual court.

And upon this, the Chief Baron [Pengelly] concluded that the remedy in this court by an English bill was not proper, but in cases where the tithe was not set out.

So the bill was dismissed unless the plaintiff would amend it by joining a parishioner.

Harvard Law School MS. 1082, vol. 2, p. 11

Sittings after Michaelmas term 1726.

A bill was brought as in the margin [i.e.] for tithes after [they are] duly set out.

Chief Baron [Pengelly] declared that the bill could not be maintained. The whole right of tithes so as to give jurisdiction to this court is only where they are detained, not where they are set out. Stat. Edw. I, Westminster, cap. 6.[5] Temporal court had jurisdiction. The Statute of *Circumspecte Agatis*[6] takes away the jurisdiction of temporal courts. 9 Edw. II, cap. 2, confirms the Statute of

[1] YB 38 Edw. III, Lib. Ass., f. 227, pl. 20 (1364); *Coke's Case* (1623), 2 Rolle Rep. 294, 301, 81 E.R. 809, 814, also Benloe 108, 117, 73 E.R. 976, 983, Godbolt 289, 78 E.R. 169; 1 Rolle, Abr., *Court*, pl. Q, 1, p. 538; *Anonymous* (1611), 1 Rolle, Abr., *Court*, pl. Q, 2, p. 538;

[2] *Anonymous* (1611), Lane 100, 145 E.R. 332, 1 Eagle & Younge 199.

[3] *Winter v. Pierce* (1635), 2 Rolle, Abr., *Prohibition*, pl. A, 3, p. 311.

[4] Stat. 31 Hen. VIII, c. 13 (*SR*, III, 733–739).

[5] Stat. 13 Edw. I, Westminster II, c. 5 (*SR*, I, 75–77).

[6] Stat. 13 Edw. I, *Circumspecte Agatis* (*SR*, I, 101–102).

Westminster II.[1] Spiritual courts had jurisdiction. 18 Edw. III, cap. 7; 1 Rolle, *Abridgment*, 538; 2 Rolle Rept. 301; Littleton's Rept., Bruges' Case.[2]

The court had a jurisdiction for subtraction of tithes before the Statute of Hen. VIII where the patronage is in the crown. 2 Rolle 310, 311, 312, 467. The Stat. 31 Hen. VIII saves a right to the spiritual court. 32 Hen. VIII[3] gives the lay person leave to sue as ecclesiastical persons. The statutes seem to exclude the temporal unless it is a privileged case where the crown is concerned.

This bill takes away the right of the temporal and ecclesiastical court. And it seems a conversion of the tithes, which is proper for an action [at law]. 2 Chancery Repts. 31, 32, Fern v. Coldfield.[4]

Baron Comyns: If ever there was any instance since 18 Edw. III unless there is something of the crown concerned, 2 Inst. 650; Rolle, *Abridgment*, 538; Hardres 116,[5] because the king was patron, there is no instance unless where the king or his farmer is concerned.

Carter: The exception only is for want of parties. The occupier has set out his tithes. And I do not see any objection. If it is only in the spiritual court, there, he cannot proceed because the tithes were set out.

Baron Hale: Where the objection is made to the jurisdiction, there the court ought to consider of it.

Baron Comyns agreed it was proper for a discovery.

Taussig MS. 311, vol. 2, p. 1013, pl. 2

6 February 1726[/27].

The case of Dewy and Price, Easter 5 Will. & Mar. [1693], was cited in this cause and so was the case of Norton Hanson v. Green.[6]

And the cause came now to be mentioned again whereon the Chief Baron [Pengelly] observed that the case of Norton Hanson and Green was not to this point because there was no controversy in that case between the parties as to the mere right of the tithes. And the Chief Baron adhered to his former opinion, *viz.* that the court could not retain the bill upon the present foot it now stood on this account, that the case was at law and not in equity.

---

[1] Stat. 9 Edw. II, *Articuli Cleri*, c. 2 (*SR*, I, 171); Stat. 13 Edw. I, Westminster II, c. 5 (*SR*, I, 75–77).

[2] Stat. 18 Edw. III, stat. 3, c. 7 (*SR*, I, 303); *Coke's Case* (1623), *ut supra*; *Burgess v. Symons* (1628), Littleton 102, 141, 124 E.R. 158, 177, 1 Rayner 13, 2 Gwillim 433, 1 Eagle & Younge 365, 118 Selden Soc. 565, Paynell Exch. 198, 246.

[3] Stat. 32 Hen. VIII, c. 7, s. 5 (*SR*, III, 752).

[4] *Perne v. Oldfield* (1680), *ut supra*.

[5] E. Coke, *Second Institute* (1642), p. 650; *Langham v. Baker* (1658), Hardres 116, 145 E.R. 408, 2 Gwillim 511, 1 Eagle & Younge 428.

[6] *Dewey v. Price* (1693), 1 Eagle & Younge 577, 1 Wood 308; *Hanson v. Green* (Ex. 1725), see above, Case No. 531.

So the court pronounced this rule that, upon payment of costs, the plaintiff should have liberty to amend his bill by adding proper parties, *viz.* that they might add an occupier. *Omnibus barones presentibus.*

646

Atkinson v. Niesley

(Ex. 1726)

The question in this case was whether a lease of tithes is void ab initio *where the rector is absent more than eighty days from his parish.*

Harvard Law School MS. 1082, vol. 2, p. 12

Sittings after Michaelmas term 1726.

The plaintiff, as rector of Hampton Powel in the County of Oxford, brings a bill for tithes, which were demised to Rogers. The defendant pleads the Stat. 13 Eliz.,[1] of non-residence.

Bootle, for the defendant, cited Mills v. Etheridge [and] Quilter v. Mussendine, last term.[2]

Chief Baron [PENGELLY]: The making of the lease was void, yet it will not extinguish the right of tithes.

Edlin: Though the plea may be good if well pleaded, yet it is not so in this case, for this plea does not answer the time alleged by the bill. The lease ceases only on the eighty days' absence. The bill was from Michaelmas 1723 to Michaelmas 1724. The bill was filed in Trinity 1725, and this plea confines it only to 1724.

CHIEF BARON: It may be a question whether the absence does not make the lease void *ab initio.*

Edlin: The lease is to be void upon the absence, though the lessor was eighty days absent in 1724, yet the lease might be good for part of the year demanded by the bill.

Baron COMYNS: the question is whether the lease is absolutely void *ab initio.*

Edlin: The lease continued good until Michaelmas 1724. The right of tithes reverts to the rector. See the Stat. 18 Eliz.[3] This lease is no bar to destroy the plaintiff's right. The cases cited by the defendant were of no minister before the court. The Stat. 18 Eliz. is an appendix to the Stat. 13 Eliz.

CHIEF BARON: the question is whether the lease was not expired before the non-residence operated upon it.

---

[1] Stat. 13 Eliz. I, c. 20 (*SR*, IV, 556).

[2] *Mills v. Etheridge* (Ex. 1726), see above, Case No. 585; *Quilter v. Mussendine* (Ex. 1726), see above, Case No. 605.

[3] Stat. 18 Eliz. I, c. 11, s. 5 (*SR*, IV, 623).

The plea was overruled because it was uncertain to what time the non-residence was continued to.

Taussig MS. 311, vol. 2, p. 1010

Michaelmas term 1726. Atkinson and Rogers v. Peisley *et al.*

A bill for tithes [was brought] by the plaintiffs, Rogers, as lessee of the tithes by a lease from the other plaintiff, Atkinson. There was a plea of non-residence. The lease was in 1723 from Michaelmas 1723 to Michaelmas 1724. The demand of tithes was from Lady Day 1723 to Lady Day 1724. And the defendant assigns the absence of Atkinson eighty days in the year 1724.

Edlin: No lease shall endure longer etc. so it only ceases from the time of the absence and, if so, then the lease may be good for all the time demanded by the bill.

Secondly, supposing the lease to be void, yet the rector is the plaintiff and the only penalty imposed is the destruction of the lease. The bill was filed Trinity term 1725.

The practice of joining the lessor and the lessee is admitted in this court to prevent multiplicity.

The forfeiture of profits must attach upon the subsequent profits.

Chief Baron [PENGELLY]: You do not bring the absence within the continuance of the lease, for he may be absent eighty days in the year 1724 though he was not absent one day in Michaelmas 1725.

647

Ley v. Nicholson

(Ex. 1726–1727)

A dispute over an election of a minister of a church pursuant to a deed of trust must be litigated in a court of equity and not in an ecclesiastical court.

Though a notice of a meeting for a particular purpose is only notice for that purpose, yet, if all who are of interest are present on that occasion and another matter is proposed and consented to by all, that act may be established though particular notice was not given thereof in the original summons.

Notice of a meeting given to one will not serve for any other person, nor will notice to the majority be notice to all though the consent of all is included in that of the majority.

Harvard Law School MS. 1082, vol. 2, p. 13

Sittings after Michaelmas term 1726.

This was in relation to the election of a minister of Clerkenwell, which election is made by the parishioners in general by virtue of a deed of trust from Drake in 1656. The churchwardens refused to call an election. And, thereupon, the other parishioners at a parish meeting ordered an election to be on 2nd May, where the plaintiff had 457 votes and the defendant only three. The churchwardens gave notice for another election 12 May. And there, the defendant had 237 and the plaintiff three. And there being a proceeding in the ecclesiastical court and this matter arising on the deed of trust, the court granted an injunction to stay proceedings in the ecclesiastical court.

Taussig MS. 311, vol. 2, p. 1045

8 June 1727. The court was full.

Rex v. Nevison, Easter 10 George [1724].

Chief Baron [Pengelly]: See the Case of Birmingham School.[1] He thought though perhaps the parish meeting summoned on one legal purpose may, if there be no surprise or fraud, take into their consideration other parish affairs, yet a court would scarcely establish an act done at an assembly by particular persons for a particular purpose. The plaintiff must prove notice and good notice, and the notice must be antecedent to the election. If a churchwarden refuse to give notice, another parishioner may give notice in the church, as in the case of the dispute between the select vestry and the parishioners at large of the parish of Saint Olave's Southwark. So he was for dismissing the bill.

Hale thought in this case the churchwardens would have had no election at all. And though notice in church is the best notice, yet the particular place of giving notice is not so material since there is real notice and the behavior of the defendants is so refractory that I am for establishing the plaintiff's election.

Carter: The churchwardens are to blame, but yet I cannot think the plaintiff has been regularly elected. General notice ought to have been given in the church precedent to the election. If notice of the assembly is not good, the assembly could not be a legal assembly for that purpose. I am of opinion that both elections are naught. So the plaintiff's bill ought to be dismissed.

Comyns: The court must go upon the right of the thing. The election that has been made is irregular; so it is not proper to establish it for fear of precedent. He was of the same opinion with the Chief Baron. The rule is that, though a notice for a particular purpose is only notice for that purpose, yet, if all who are of interest are present on that occasion and another matter is proposed and con-

[1] *Eden v. Foster* (1725–1726), 2 Peere Williams 325, 24 E.R. 750, Gilbert Rep. 178, 25 E.R. 125, Select Cases *tempore* King 36, 25 E.R. 208, 2 Eq. Cas. Abr. 199, 202, 751, 22 E.R. 171, 173, 636.

sented to by all, that act may be well established though particular notice was not given thereof in the summons. Notice in the church is general notice to all the parishioners, as notice at the manor is notice to the tenants thereof. Notice to one will not serve for others, nor will notice to the majority be notice to all though the consent of all the parishioners is included in that of the majority. Therefore, he was for dismissing the bill. There were a great many niceties before the Revolution which are since got over, and the Birmingham School Case is a set of good rules.

The plaintiff is an indifferent person, but the churchwardens have been in fault. And so no costs were awarded to the churchwardens, but there must be costs as to Nicholson and as to Barners, the trustee.

[Related cases: Attorney General and Turner v. Rose and Hill (Ex. 1728), British Library MS. Hargrave 83, pt. 2, f. 122.]

648

Bokenham v. Bentfield

(Ex. 1726)

To a bill for tithes, a parishioner need not answer as to the value and quantities of the tithes where he denies the plaintiff's right to receive tithes, as where the lessor of the tithes was non-resident in the parish.

1 Comyns 392, 92 E.R. 1126,
1 Rayner 238, 1 Eagle & Younge 828

This was a bill by the lessee of the parson of [*blank*] for tithes against the defendant, a parishioner, to which the defendant pleaded the Statute 13 Eliz., c. 20,[1] by which it was enacted that no lease of any benefice or ecclesiastical promotion with cure, or any part thereof, shall endure any longer than while the lessor shall be ordinarily resident and serving the cure of such benefice without absence above eighty days in any one year, but that such lease immediately upon such absence shall cease and be void etc. and that the lessor was absent above eighty days in such year, whereby his lease to the plaintiff did become void. And the plea being admitted to be heard according to the rules of court, no one then appeared to defend or maintain the title of the plaintiff, for it was said by the counsel for the defendant that such plea was formerly allowed, that it was allowed on the 5th of February Hilary 12 Geo., in the case between Mills and Etheridge,[2] that it was allowed also Easter 12 Geo. in the case between Quilter and Missendine,[3] and between Quilter and Lowndes, that the sole question in those cases was, if the

[1] Stat. 13 Eliz. I, c. 20 (*SR*, IV, 556).
[2] *Mills v. Etheridge* (Ex. 1726), see above, Case No. 585.
[3] *Quilter v. Mussendine* (Ex. 1726), see above, Case No. 605.

defendant should not answer to the quantities and values alleged by the bill at the same time that he tenders his plea, so as where the defendant insists on a *modus* as a discharge of his payment of tithes *in specie*, yet the defendant ought to answer to the quantity and value of the tithes charged in the bill; otherwise, if it were afterwards found that there was no such *modus*, the plaintiff cannot have a decree against the defendant because it does not appear how much is due by him for his tithes to the plaintiff. But it was then resolved by the court that, upon such plea of non-residence of the lessor, the defendant need not answer to the quantities and values, for such plea goes to the right and title of the plaintiff, but, where a *modus* is alleged, that admits the title of the plaintiff to take tithes of the defendant, but only goes to the manner of payment, if tithes should be paid in specie or not.

And upon all those authorities alleged, the plea in the present case was allowed.

649

Harrison v. Hart

(Ex. 1722–1727)

The question in this case was whether a pawnee of shares of stock who sells them should account to the pawner for any profits received thereby.

Taussig MS. 311, vol. 1, p. 283

Easter term 1722.

A motion [was made] that Mr. Hart might be taken upon an attachment if he did not answer by the time given him. He had had time granted him by the court, first for two months and afterwards in this term for a fortnight which would end in the vacation time between this and the next term. And now the motion was made *ut supra* and defended.

But the court, being today all for expedition, granted the motion, *viz.* that Hart should appear before the Master if he did not answer by the day given. And, as I think, did all of them agree that, for the future, whenever they granted a second further time, the defendant should upon such indulgence appear before the Master and, in case he did not answer by the time given him, a messenger should go.

1 Comyns 393, 92 E.R. 1126

This was a bill for an account of the produce of £20,000 South Sea stock transferred by the plaintiff to the defendant Hart for the security of £70,000 and interest and, after deduction of principal and interest, that Hart pay the balance to the plaintiff and also that the defendant Franks shall account to the plaintiff for the said £70,000 which was paid to him to be disposed of for the use of the plaintiff.

And the bill suggested that the plaintiff applied to the defendant Hart on the 25th of May 1720 for a loan of £30,000, who advanced that sum to the plaintiff. And, for security, the plaintiff agreed to give his bond and also to transfer to him £10,000 South Sea stock. And, accordingly, the plaintiff was bound the 25th of May 1720 in a penalty of £60,000 under the condition that the plaintiff should pay to Hart £30,000 on the 25th of September next with interest after the rate of £5 percent, being the same sum mentioned in a defeasance of the same date made between the plaintiff and the defendant Hart.

That on the same day, the plaintiff transferred to the defendant Hart or his order £10,000 South Sea stock, and, by a defeasance dated the 25th of May 1720 between the defendant Moses Hart on the one part and the plaintiff Thomas Harrison on the other part, reciting the said obligation and transfer, it was agreed that the £10,000 stock so transferred was transferred to the intent that the same should and might remain and be as and for a collateral or further security for the more sure payment of the said sum of £30,000 according to the condition of the said bond.

And by the same deed, the defendant Hart covenants that, if the plaintiff should pay the said £30,000 etc., he would on the payment of the said sum transfer the said £10,000 stock to the plaintiff and deliver up the bond. And the plaintiff covenants that he will pay all calls etc. upon the said stock, until payment of the money becomes due, and he authorizes the defendant, if the money be not paid, to sell and dispose absolutely of the said stock and keep the monies arising by the sale towards the payment of the said sum of £30,000, interest, and charges, returning the overplus, which the defendant agrees to do.

And it is agreed that all gains, dividends, interest, and advantage, which shall arise by reason of the said stock in the said Company from the date hereof, shall be for the only use and benefit of the plaintiff, unless default shall be made in the payment of the said £30,000 etc. And if the stock of the Company, before the £30,000 shall grow due as aforesaid, shall fall in value, so as to be sold at or under the rate of £350 percent in Exchange Alley, the plaintiff on three days notice shall give further security etc. or, in default thereof, it shall be lawful for the defendant Hart to sell the said stock and keep the money arising by the sale towards the payment of the said £30,000 though not then due, according to the bond, returning the overplus, if any, to the plaintiff.

That the defendant on the 10th of June 1720 advanced £40,000 more to the plaintiff, who gave his bond in £80,000 with condition to pay etc. on the said 25th of September, and another defeasance was executed in the same terms as the former, save that a power of sale was given if the stock lessened to £500 percent etc.

That the defendant Hart afterwards disposed of this stock for great prices, for which he ought to account.

That the whole £70,000 was paid into the hands of the defendant Franks, for which he ought to account to the plaintiff.

The defendant Hart, by his answer, confesses the loan of £30,000 on the 25th of May 1720 and the bond and defeasance accordingly and another loan on the 10th of June 1720 and the bond and defeasance accordingly. And he says that he has, and always had, in his own hands or in the hands of others in trust for him sufficient stock to answer the plaintiff's demands, which the defendant kept on purpose without making any sale or disposition thereof ready to be transferred to the plaintiff or his order when he should require on his payment of the £30,000 and £40,000 and interest etc.

And by his second answer to the original bill and three other answers to the amended bill, it appears that, on the 25th of May 1720, when the first loan was made, the transfer of the first £10,000 by the plaintiff was in this manner:

£2000 was transferred to Benjamin Collier for £9600	
£2000 to Robert Sawbridge, at £482 percent, £9640	£24,040
£1000 to Wolfe, at £480 percent, £4800	
£5000 to the defendant Hart himself, who paid to the plaintiff only	£5,960
Total	£30,000

That on the second loan on the 10th of June 1720, the transfer of the second £10,000 South Sea stock was made by the plaintiff in this manner, *viz.*:

£1000 to Robert Mann, at £745 percent, for £7450	
£1000 to Count Nassau, at £735 percent, for £7350	£22,200
£1000 to John Mark, at £740 percent, for £7400	
That the remaining £7000 was transferred by the plaintiff or order to Moses Hart, who paid	£17,800
Total	£40,000

And it appears by the depositions of James Travers and Benjamin Periam, two witnesses examined in the cause, that Moses Hart had raised by the sale of the £20,000 South Sea stock transferred to him by the plaintiff on the 25th of May and on the 10th of June 1720, the full sum of £86,291 17s. 8 3/4d., *viz.*:

By sale of £5000 to Collier, Sawbridge, and Wolfe	£24,040
By sale on the 30th of May 1720 of £4000 to James Sawbridge at £520 percent, of which £3659 4d. was the plaintiff's stock (for he had only £340 19s. 8d. of his own proper stock) the sum of	£19,026 17s. 8d.
By sale on the 3d of June 1720 of £500 stock of the plaintiff at £520 percent (for the defendant had then no other stock in his own name)	£2,700

By sale on the 10th of June, as above, to Mann, Count Nassau, and Mark	£22,200
By sale on the 15th of June 1720, to William Dale £500 at £750 percent, for M. Hart had not stock in his own name, only £1000 purchased of Lord Grimston for £8000, of which he had sold £100 to Charles Goodwin, and £400 to Bartholomew Zolocastre on the 10th of June 1720, and then sold £1000 to William Dale, of which £500 must be of the plaintiff's stock	£3,750
By sale on the 15th of June to Henry Hankey £1000 at £700 percent	£7,000
By sale on the 20th of June to William Bateman £500 at £765 percent	£3,825
And to John Baker £500 as £750 percent	£3,825
Total	£86,291 17s. 8 3/4d.

So, by the depositions of the same witnesses, it appears that the defendant Moses Hart had in his own name upon the 25th of May 1720, no stock, except £340 19s. 8d. and the annuity stock.

That upon the 25th of September 1720, he had no stock in his own name, except £20,885 1s. 7d. and the annuity stock.

That £4400, part of the £20,885 1s. 7d. was pledged to Hart by lord Hillsborough.

That £9100, another part of the same, appears to be in trust for the South Sea Company, for, on the 16th of September 1720, the sum of £48,140 was delivered to Hart by Robert Knight, cashier to the South Sea Company, with an intent to purchase stock for the use of the Company, and that Hart, with this sum, made a purchase of £9100 South Sea stock, and on the 27th of September 1720, £9100 of this stock was transferred by Hart to the South Sea Company.

So by the depositions of William Walmsley, another witness, it appears that lord Newburgh said to him on the 24th of August 1720 in Exchange Alley that Hart had purchased £2000 South Sea stock for him of Isaac Fernandez Nunes at £850 percent to be transferred the next transfer day after Michaelmas, and, for his security upon the 26th of August 1720, the aforesaid lord transferred to Hart £1000 South Sea stock in trust for himself, and, in a short time after the expiration of the time to perform the bargain, the said lord Newburgh gave satisfaction to Hart, who detained the £1000 stock in part thereof.

By the deposition of Sir William Stapleton, it appears that, on the 23rd of June 1720, he purchased of Hart £1000 South Sea stock and of Walter £600

South Sea stock at £1000 percent, which Hart took to himself upon the 27th of September at £400 percent.

By the deposition of Thomas Edwards, it appears that Hart, upon the 20th of August 1720, purchased for him £500 South Sea stock at £800 percent and kept it in trust for him for two years following, when Hart took the same stock for part of the monies due to him by Edwards, which several parcels of stock, *viz.* £4400, £9100, £1000, £1600, and £500, with the Midsummer dividend for the two last parcels, amount to £16,810 and reduce the stock which the defendant Hart had in his own right upon the 25th of September 1720 to £4075 1s. 7d.

By the deposition of George Harrison, brother to the plaintiff, it appears that, upon the 19th of August 1720, Hart contracted to sell him £1000 South Sea stock at £910 percent to be transferred to him within a month after the next opening of the books and deposited for security of his performance of the contract one subscription receipt of the value of £3000, and Hart had also contracted to deliver to the lord Newburgh the £2000 stock mentioned in the deposition of William Walmsley for £850 percent upon the 22nd of September 1720 and to Col. Lumley another £2000 at the same time and for the same price.

That by the Statute 6 Geo.,[1] enabling the South Sea Company to increase the capital stock, power was given to the Company to take in the annuities etc. and, by a resolution of the 19th of May 1720, the Company agreed to make allowance for each £100 of long annuities, subscribed before the 27th of May £700 percent and £575 in monies and South Sea bonds and for each £98 *per annum* of the £14 percent annuities and £511 in monies and bonds.

That Hart, upon the 28th of April 1720, subscribed £1460 *per ann*um of the long annuities and £1040 *per annum* of the £14 percent and, by the hands of Edward Harris, £200 *per annum* long annuities and, by the hands of Wymondsell, the same sum, for which he was allowed £700 percent, *viz.*:

For £1860 long annuities	£13,020
£1040 of £14 percent	£7,428 11s. 5d.
Midsummer dividend	£2,044 17s. 1d.
In all	£22,493 8s. 6d.

That, by an order of the South Sea Company, the books were not opened for the transfer of the South Sea stock until the 5th of October 1720.

And on the part of defendant Hart, it was proved by the deposition of Lazarus Simon, Moyer Wagg, and Isaac Franks, the other defendant, that, on or about the 10th of June 1720, the plaintiff discoursing with the defendant Hart, who said that perhaps he could not re-transfer to him at the time agreed the £20,000 stock in other than annuity stock, having sold to others the said £20,000,

[1] Stat. 6 Geo. I, c. 4.

declared that he well knew that he could not have the same stock and would be content with annuity stock, for he did not regard which stock he had and knew well the sufficiency of the defendant.

That annuity stock was equal in value to the other and was apprehended to be transferrable before the 25th of September, and some parcels were actually transferred before the said day.

And Franks added that, since the loan of the said sums, when stock was considerably advanced in price, the defendant Hart advised the plaintiff to sell all his stock, by which he would acquire a great estate and, therefore, offered to him to deliver the whole £20,000 stock with the dividends, but the plaintiff refused, saying that stock would rise to the price of £1500 or £2000 percent.

And Simon Lazarus added that he, being directed by Sir John Lambert, a director of the South Sea Company, to purchase stock, offered to the plaintiff to give £900 percent for all the £20,000 that Hart had of him and to take the security which was given to Hart for it.

And Isaac Helbert added that he offered to Hart by the order of Knight and Grigsby for all his stock, annuity stock and other stock, £950 percent who refused to depart with all his stock by reason of his engagement with the plaintiff.

As to the defendant Franks, he admitted by his answer that he received for the use of the plaintiff the £30,000 and £40,000 of Hart and such others, to whom the plaintiff transferred the £20,000 stock, but he says that he disposed of it pursuant to the orders of the plaintiff in South Sea stock or subscriptions and, from time to time, gave to the plaintiff an account in writing how he had disposed of it, which writing the plaintiff perused, and it was left with him, and, afterwards, he declared his approbation of the account. And after all the monies were disposed of for the plaintiff, a balance of £56 remained due to the defendant Franks, which was demanded of the plaintiff, who admitted such sum due and promised payment; that, by a fire the 17th of January 1723, all his papers and accounts were destroyed or lost, wherefore he could not now account.

And it appeared that Franks was not made a defendant to the original bill of the plaintiff filed in Michaelmas 1721, but, afterwards, in Michaelmas term 1722, Franks was made one of the defendants.

And by the deposition of Abraham Solomon, who was employed to purchase the stock and subscriptions for the plaintiff, it appeared that he delivered an account to the plaintiff in writing of all the sums for him expended and of all the stock or subscriptions for him purchased in the South Sea Company or other companies, and he apprehended that the account was just, that the plaintiff perused them, and, about two days after the delivery of each account, the plaintiff declared that he had inspected and was satisfied. And Abraham and Benedict Solomon testify that the plaintiff promised payment of the monies demanded as the balance due upon those accounts to the defendant Franks and the sum demanded exceeded £50.

Upon this case, it was insisted by the Attorney General [*Yorke*] and other counsel with the plaintiff that the defendant Hart ought to render an account to the plaintiff for all the monies which he had raised by the sale of any part of the £20,000 alleged to be transferred to him by the plaintiff and, after a deduction of the principal sums and interest, to answer for the residue of the profits to the plaintiff.

First, this seems agreeable to the nature of the transaction, for, when a pledge of stock is made by the plaintiff to the defendant, it is consonant to law and reason that the defendant shall render to the plaintiff upon mutual payment of monies the stock and all the profits arising from it. If a man distrain his tenant and labor the distress, he shall give damages to the party to the value of the labor.

So, by the civil law, the fruit and profit arising from a thing in pledge ought to be accounted for to the debtor, and, after deduction of its principal and interest, the surplus arising from the sale of the pledge ought to be restored to him. Domat, 1 vol., 345, *De deposito*, 1, 3.[1] All that shall arise or accrue from the thing which is mortgaged, or that shall augment it, accrues to the mortgagor. So tit. 3, § 15. *Cum sortis nomine et usurarum aliquid debetur ab eo, qui sub pignoris nomine pecuniam debet, quicquid ex venditione pignoris recipiatur primum usuris quas jam tunc deberi constat, deinde si quid superest, sorti accepto ferendum est.*

So, in the case of a mortgage, the mortgagee shall answer for all casual profits. If a man pledge a diamond for £100 and it is sold for £500, shall not he have an account given him of the surplus? By the common law, he who receives a pledge has no other property in it than to detain it until his debt is paid, nor can he use or sell it. 2 Croke 244.[2] So by the canon law, Lindwood 60, the Canon of Pledges says *Inhibemus ne pignus retinere quisquam contendat postquam de fructibus sortem perceperit, deductis expensis, quoniam usura est.*[3]

And it seems to be confirmed by a resolution in this court, in the case between Mercer v. Tutt, which was afterwards affirmed by Parliament upon an appeal on the 2nd of March 1725.[4] Mercer had borrowed £1100 of Tutt and, for his security, gave his bond for payment, and also he pledged a second subscription No. 195, and it was agreed that, if Mercer paid the money, Tutt should restore the subscription, and, if he did not pay it, that Tutt might sell; afterwards,

---

1 J. Domat, *Civil Law* (1722).

2 *Ratcliff v. Davies* (1610), Croke Jac. 244, 79 E.R. 210, also Noy 137, 74 E.R. 1100, Yelverton 178, 80 E.R. 118, 1 Bulstrode 29, 80 E.R. 733.

3 We forbid any man to strive or contend to keep the gage after he have received the principal debt of the fruits of the said gage above all expenses for its usury. J. V. Bullard and H. C. Bell, trans., *Lyndwood's Provinciale* (1929), p. 62.

4 *Mercer v. Tutt* (1723–1725), see above, Case No. 436, 2 Eq. Cas. Abr. 6, 22 E.R. 6, 2 Brown P.C. 563, 1 E.R. 1134.

Tutt sold the subscription, whereupon Mercer exhibited his bill in this court for an account of the money raised by the sale. The defendant insisted that he had preserved another second subscription No. 194, in lieu of that; and, upon debate concerning the subscription pledged, a trial was directed, and a verdict found for the plaintiff, whereupon an account was decreed.

So in the case of Merrick v. Spark, Michaelmas 1723,[1] stock was mortgaged by Merrick for £1000; the mortgagee, after this, mortgaged it for £1200, whereupon Merrick exhibited his bill for an account of the overplus, and an account was decreed.

Secondly, this was the express agreement of the parties, for, by the defeasance, it is said that the stock shall be and remain a further security for payment, which shows that the intent was not that it should be sold, for, then, it would not continue a security, and it was pledged only as a collateral security for the obligation, which was principally intended for the security of the defendant.

Therefore, by the same defeasance, the defendant Hart covenanted upon repayment etc. to transfer the said stock to the plaintiff, and the plaintiff covenanted to pay all calls upon the said stock; but, if the stock was intended to be sold, it could not be transferred to the plaintiff, nor could there be any calls upon it; and it appears more fully by the covenant and agreement, which says that all gains, dividends, etc. arising by the said stock shall accrue to the plaintiff, and, by the subsequent covenant, which shows in what cases it should be sold, *viz.* if it fall to £350, but, in that case, the defendant is to account for the overplus, and when the parties expressly agreed that, upon such diminution in value, it shall be sold and that, in such case, the defendant ought to account for the sale, it can never be intended that, in any other case, it may be sold without account. If the plaintiff ought to have an account of the profits which arise from the sale, when the sale was allowed by the consent and agreement of the parties, shall it be said that he is not accountable for the sale when sold by himself and in breach of the trust reposed in him?

Thirdly, this construction of the articles is very reasonable, for, if the plaintiff would sell the stock, he might have sold it himself. It would be very dangerous that he to whom the stock is pledged might traffic with it. Where should the stock have been found if the defendant had become a bankrupt? Whilst the specified stock remained in his hand, the plaintiff, in case of bankruptcy, could resort to it and take the stock out of the hands of the commissioners or assignees. But if it be sold, what remedy shall he have? And it is, therefore, necessary that the party be strictly bound to his agreement. The agreement in writing should always be the rule of the action, but it is more necessary in things which fluctuate in the manner that stock fluctuates, and it is more requisite in the case of a broker, who, by an Act of Parliament,[2] is to be sworn and ought not to intermeddle

[1] *Merrick v. Spark* (1723), 2 Eq. Cas. Abr. 6, 22 E.R. 6.

[2] Stat. 8 & 9 Will. III, c. 32 (*SR*, VII, 285–287).

with stock. And, therefore, when he acts contrary, he ought to be strictly obliged to the letter of his agreement.

Fourthly, if it be said that the agreement in writing is varied by the subsequent transactions, because the plaintiff himself transferred part of his stock to others, therefore, the defendant Hart reserved other stock for the performance of his contract. It does not appear that he apprehended the persons to whom the plaintiff transferred his stock were other than trustees for Hart. And the plaintiff, by his answer, swore that he took them to be his trustees. But if it made any variation, can an agreement in writing be varied by word?

Fifthly, as to the allegation that Hart reserved equal quantity of stock at all times out of which he could answer to the plaintiff, it was agreed by Mr. Cowper that, if the allegation was true, it was a good answer, for, if a man having £10,000 takes other £10,000 on pledge and then disposes of £10,000 only, it is not any inconveniency to the party and it cannot be known if the plaintiff's stock be transferred or his own stock.

But it was insisted that, upon the 25th of May 1720, the defendant Hart had only £340 in his own name and, upon the 25th of September 1720, although he had £20,885 in his own name, yet he was only a trustee for others as to the greatest part of it, and the annuity stock ought not to be regarded because it was not transferrable until the fifth of October 1720 and, therefore, could be of no use to answer the demand of the plaintiff upon the 25th of September preceding.

Sixthly, the defendant Hart himself was conscious that he had sold the plaintiff's stock contrary to his agreement and that he had not sufficient stock of the same nature whereby he could answer the plaintiff, as it appears by his varying defenses and by his varying answers, for, by his first answer, he says that he has always had in his own hands or others in trust for him sufficient to answer the plaintiff's demands, which he kept on purpose, without making any sale or disposition thereof, ready to be transferred to the plaintiff or his order, by which everyone sees that the intent was that the defendant should have all the while stock sufficient to answer to the plaintiff £20,000 stock pledged by the plaintiff and that he never had sold or disposed of any part of this stock.

But, by his second answer, the contrary appears, for, then, he confesses that he had sold the plaintiff's stock immediately after the transfer to him and that he had no stock of his own, only £340 19s. 8d., which he immediately disposed of, and had no proper stock for a long time. But then, by his third answer, he makes his refuge to the annuity stock, for he says that he had subscribed in South Sea stock on the 28th of April his annuities, for which he was allowed in the South Sea Company £20,448 11s. 5d., which, with the Midsummer dividend, was augmented to £22,493 8s. 6d. and that he had also other stock in his own name to the value of £20,885 1s. 3d., but, upon examination, it appeared that the annuity stock was not transferrable until the 5th of October and that his other stock was for the most part in trust for others and that, for the residue, he had made contracts for sale of that to others, so that he had no stock, or only a very small quantity of stock, upon the 25th of September, with which the plaintiff could be satisfied. And this matter being manifest, he, by his fourth and fifth answers, would resort to the Act of Parliament, by which he says that the annuity stock was in its nature transferrable from the time it was transcribed to the South Sea Company by force of the Statute 6 Geo.

As to the other defendant, it was urged by the Attorney General [*Yorke*] and others of counsel with the plaintiff that it was a plain case that Franks, who had received £70,000 for the use of the plaintiff, as be himself admits, should be accountable to the plaintiff for that sum.

And his pretence, that he had given the plaintiff an account each day in writing to him delivered, that does not amount to a stated account. And an account current never was allowed to be a bar to a bill exhibited in equity against any person to have an account.

And his excuse, that he had lost his books and papers by the fire *anno* [*blank*], is a mere subterfuge, for, although his first answer was sworn to after such fire, yet he makes no mention of his books then lost until his second answer. And, if it were true, yet it is no bar to the account, only it shall be an argument for a special direction of the court for the manner in which his account shall be taken.

But by Mr. *Reeves* and others, of counsel for the defendant Hart, it was insisted that the defendant Hart was not accountable to the plaintiff for the monies raised by the sale of this stock pledged and transferred to him by the plaintiff. But the bill of the plaintiff to such intent ought to be dismissed, for the arguments deduced from the canon and civil law are not material, to which stocks could not be known. But, by the common law, which is the most proper guide in this case, the pawnee has a special property in the goods pledged to him and may sell them if it be without prejudice to the pawner. 2 Salkeld 522.[1] And if he be robbed, he shall have an action against the pawner for the monies lent to him, for he is not bound to take more care than of his own goods, [as] in the case of Coggs v. Bernard, 2 Ann., King's Bench, 2 Salkeld 523.[2]

And, therefore, this case cannot be like a mortgage of lands, which naturally produce profits, which are intended for the satisfaction of the mortgagee. But stock is only an equitable interest, out of which no profits arise, only the dividends or interest. The casual advance of the price is the effect of fancy, for it has no intrinsic value. And, therefore, the plaintiff, who is not party or privy to the transaction in the traffic by sale of the stock, as he will not be charged with any damage that Hart might thereby sustain, therefore, he shall not answer to him for the benefit or gain.

---

[1] *Anonymous* (1693), 2 Salkeld 522, 91 E.R. 445.

[2] *Coggs v. Bernard* (1703), 1 Salkeld 26, 91 E.R. 25, 2 Salkeld 735, 91 E.R. 613, 3 Salkeld 11, 268, 91 E.R. 660, 817, 2 Lord Raymond 909, 92 E.R. 107, 3 Lord Raymond 163, 92 E.R. 622, 1 Comyns 133, 92 E.R. 999, Holt K.B. 13, 131, 528, 90 E.R. 905, 971, 1190.

In the case of Mercer v. Tutt, the second subscription No. 194, and the second subscription No. 195 were both sold; but No. 195 was sold for a great sum; and the defendant would have given him the monies obtained by the sale of the No. 194 and placed his defence upon this, that this number was the subscription pledged to him by the plaintiff and that being found by verdict to the contrary, the defendant was decreed to answer for the No. 195.

The cause of Merrick v. Spark was a mortgage made of land and does not come up to the present case. Nor can any case be shown in which the court has ordered an account of the disposition of stock that was allowed to be disposable in its nature.

As to the contract in this case, it does not appear to be the intent of the parties that Hart should be restrained from the disposal of the stock of the plaintiff transferred to him, for, although stress is laid upon the words of the agreement, yet the words are not to be regarded, for it appears to be a printed form, and not drawn to answer the particular intent of the parties at this time. But, by the words of the agreement, it cannot be collected that the same numerical stock should be transferred to the plaintiff upon the 25th of September, which was transferred by him on the 25th of May without variation. The same in quantity and quality satisfies the words, the same shall remain and be as and for a collateral and further security of the said £30,000 and that, upon payment etc., he shall transfer the said stock to the plaintiff etc. And, by the same argument, it may be said that the same numerical money shall be repaid, for the words are for the repayment of the said sum of £30,000 and, although Hart covenanted to answer for all the dividends etc., it imports only that he shall answer for the stock given in pledge with all augmentation of the value, for the dividends etc. are equally allotted to all the stock in that company and makes each share so much more in value. And, although liberty was given to sell the stock when the price should be diminished to £350 percent, the intent was that the defendant then might make an absolute disposition of all the stock which the plaintiff ought to have upon the 25th of September and that, then, he shall account for the monies which such sale produced, not that the defendant should be restrained from negotiation with the stock of the plaintiff in the interim.

And it cannot be collected that the plaintiff intended to restrain the defendant from negotiation with the stock to him transferred by any part of the transaction between them, for the plaintiff himself on the 25th of May transferred £5000 stock, part of the £10,000 made security for the £30,000, to Collier, Sawbridge, and Wolfe, to whom Hart had sold some stock before, and the plaintiff himself signed the receipt to them for the monies paid by them for the £5000 so sold. And, in the same manner, the plaintiff himself on the 10th of June transferred £3000, part of the second £10,000 stock, to Mann, Count Nassau, and Mark, to whom the defendant Hart had before sold so much stock. And the plaintiff himself signed the receipt for the monies by them paid for such stock to them respectively sold, which shows that the plaintiff knew well that his stock transferred was not to be kept by Hart in his own name. And, although it be then pretended that the plaintiff conceived those persons to whom the plaintiff transferred his stock to be trustees for Hart, yet it seems impossible to be conceived when the stock was not only transferred to them, but they paid also for it, and the payment was made to the plaintiff himself, who gave to them his receipt for the monies. And it all amounts to a demonstration that those persons could not be taken for trustees for Hart. And if it be considered at what time the loan of this great sum was made to the plaintiff without any premium, only the interest at £5 percent, it cannot be imagined that the stock was intended to be useless for so long a time. The plaintiff did not expect his stock until the 25th of September, and it was indifferent to him in what hands it was during that time, if he had so much stock on such a day.

And the words are stronger, for it does not say 'on or before the 25th of September', but 'on the 25th of September'. And, therefore, if the plaintiff had so much stock transferred to him at such a time, it suffices. And, although it be objected that the agreement in writing cannot be explained by words in evidence, yet it is always allowed to take into consideration the circumstances of the case by the exposition of a fact. Between Wilkins and Elkin, an agreement was made to take a lease for nine years and that the lessee should pay £9 for rent; a trial was directed to know the value of the land and, upon that, it was decreed that the lessee should pay £9 a year, and not £9 for the whole term, though the words are so in Lord Cheyne's Case, 5 Co. 68,[1] where a man having two sons named John, devised land to his son John, proof may be admitted to show which son was intended. So if a fine be levied of the manor of D. and there be two manors of the same name. 2 Rolle, *Abridgment*, 676.[2]

Then, if Hart, by the intent of the agreement, was not prohibited the sale of the stock so that he had sufficient [stock] to reassign to Harrison upon the 25th of September, here, it appears plainly that he had sufficient at that time, for he had annuity stock sufficient without doubt. And, though, by order of the South Sea Company, the stock allowed for annuities etc. subscribed to the company was not to be transferred until the 5th of October, yet it was in its nature transferrable. And, then, the order of the Company cannot control. The South Sea Company was erected by the Statute 9 Ann., c. 21,[3] and every proprietor of any share in the joint stock of the Company had power to transfer his share to another. Then, by the Statute 6 Geo., when proprietors of annuities have subscribed, the same proprietors were to have and enjoy such shares as were allowed them by the Company in lieu of money for the annuities etc. by them subscribed and, in respect of such shares, were to be taken as members of the Company and shall

[1] *Lord Cheyney's Case* (1591), 5 Coke Rep. 68, 77 E.R. 158, also Moore K.B. 727, 72 E.R. 867.

[2] 2 Rolle, Abr., *Triall*, 'Evidence', pl. 11, p. 676.

[3] Stat. 9 Ann., c. 15 (*SR*, IX, 428–447).

in proportion to the same shares be entitled to the same benefits, powers, privileges, and advantages as other members of that Company ought to enjoy in respect of their shares of the capital stock. And all such proprietors, from the time of their agreeing by contract, subscription, or otherwise to accept such stock in lieu of their annuities etc. shall have credit in the books of the Company for their proportion or share in the stock of the corporation and in all dividends and advantages to attend the same.

And, therefore, the annuity stock, being subscribed in the time limited by the Act, ought to have all the advantages allowed by the Act which the original South Sea stock had and, by consequence, was sufficient to answer to the plaintiff for the stock pledged by him to the defendant.

But if this annuity stock was not sufficient for such purpose, yet he had other stock in his own name to the value of £20,885 1s. 7d., out of which he could satisfy to the plaintiff the £20,000 by him pledged upon the 25th of September 1720. And, although he was under contracts with others and had purchased part of this stock with an intent to transfer it to the South Sea Company and it was transferred accordingly, yet, upon the 25th of September, all was at his disposal. And, if he had transferred it to the plaintiff, no other had any demand upon it against the plaintiff, nor could he pursue his remedy against the plaintiff in law or equity to recover any part of the stock so transferred to the plaintiff. And it is not to be omitted that it appears by several depositions that the plaintiff himself always declared that he should be content with annuity stock.

And there is one circumstance considerable in a court of equity, that the defendant Hart had persuaded the plaintiff to sell his stock when the price was at £900 percent and had offered him to furnish all the £20,000 stock at such a time and that the defendant Hart was offered £950 percent for all his stock, but refused to take that price, in regard that he was obliged to retain £20,000 for the demand of the plaintiff until the 25th of September 1720.

As to the defendant Franks, it was insisted by Mr. *Lee*, Serjeant *Sheppard*, and others of counsel with him, that, as to the charge that he was confederate with the defendant Hart, it was denied by the defendant, and not proved by the plaintiff; and for all the rest upon the second charge against him, that he ought to account for the several sums which he admits to have received for the plaintiff, *viz.* the £30,000 and £40,000, as to that, the defendant, by his answer, says that he had disbursed all those sums for the use of the plaintiff and had given to the plaintiff from time to time an account in writing how the defendant had disbursed those sums, which the plaintiff had inspected and approved and, afterwards, declares that a balance of £56 remained due to the defendant Franks upon this account, for which sum he, the plaintiff, acknowledged himself indebted to the defendant Franks and promised to pay that balance to him.

And such general answer suffices where the charge by the bill is so general, for the bill charges that the defendant had received those monies and had disbursed several large sums in the purchase of South Sea stock and subscriptions, but some part remained not disbursed, by which the plaintiff admits that the defendant had discharged part of those sums, and yet he demands an account of the whole, and he does not specify for what part he had accounted and for what part he had given no account.

And especially when the defendant acts as servant or agent for the plaintiff and if the plaintiff employ his servant in the purchase of several particular things, who immediately gives an account of his expenses to his master, he shall not, afterwards, demand an account of such particulars. And the bill in this case was not originally exhibited against the defendant Franks, but against the defendant Hart only. But, afterwards, when Franks was to be examined as a witness for Hart, to prevent his testimony, the bill was amended and Franks added as a defendant. And, after his papers were lost by fire, it would be very hard to require a particular account how those sums were disbursed without charging any error or misprision in the particulars of the account before delivered to the plaintiff.

The court delivered no opinion, but directed an issue to be tried.

And afterwards, upon an appeal to the House of Peers, this order was repealed. And the Lords directed an account for all the monies received by Hart upon the sale of the stock pledged by Harrison, and, if the principal and interest were satisfied, the residue of the monies to be paid and that the residue of the stock not sold should be transferred to Harrison.

Harvard Law School MS. 1082, vol. 2, p. 9

Michaelmas term 1726. About a South Sea Contract.

Chief Baron [Pengelly]: It cannot be expected that the court should give their opinion. But I will open the case. This bill is a general demand founded upon the general supposition that every pawnee of stock is to keep it. And this does not depend on the mere right only. And whether a court of equity will establish such a rule notwithstanding circumstances of equity may intervene and whether this will not be of great consequence to all the transactions in the year 1720.[1] Courts of equity have followed the rules of law. And I do not find that, on the plaintiff's part, there is any fraud proved against the defendants.

The defendant Harrison had advanced to him £23,000, and more was advanced than the intrinsic value of the [South Sea Company] stock. And the defendant himself runs the hazard. No fraud or circumvention ought to be presumed. And Harrison himself appoints the defendant Franks his agent. This was a fair contract at five percent. Tutt v. Mercer; Merrick v. Sparks.

If the pawnee transfers the stock, shall he be accountable or obliged to return the specific stock? Stock is a credit for money made transferable by Act of Parliament. And so the contributors are said to have shares and proportions. This being a transferable credit, twenty shares of one man are as good as twenty shares

[1] The year of the burst of the South Sea bubble.

of another. The name of the proprietor is the distinguishing mark, and that is altered on each transfer.

There is a difficulty in the nature of the agreement. Mr. Harrison by it is on the 25th September to transfer so much stock, but not the identical stock. And such stock cannot retain the same quality, as a jewel or a watch, because the latter always remains the same.

The difficulty with me is in relation to £8000 stock directly sold to several persons and the money paid to Harrison as 4640 (3140). It appears that Harrison did not receive the £8000.

The bill is proper for an injunction, and one ought to grant a perpetual one. Hart did this at his own peril. And Hart had annuity stock to answer this demand.

They adjourned for judgment.

Harvard Law School MS. 1082, vol. 2, p. 14, pl. 1

Hilary term 1726/27.

The Chief Baron [Pengelly] delivered the opinion of the court.

Chief Baron: We are of the opinion that this cause cannot be determined without issues directed [to a jury]. The original bill is only to have an account of the sale of stock and to have an injunction. But the amended bill filed a year afterwards prays general relief.

The instances cited of the civil law books in relation to pawns and pledges do not come up to this case because those cases turned on the foot of usury, nor do the cases of pledges of particular things that can be returned in specie agree with this case, for South Sea stock must be considered as money and stock must be considered on a different foot than where the things is to be returned in specie. And, therefore, we cannot give the particular relief prayed by the bill to make the defendant Hart account as a trustee generally or as a tortious doer.

By the books of the South Sea Company, it appears that Mr. Hart had sufficient stock to have performed his part of the agreement on 25 September 1720 if the plaintiff had demanded stock. There was no lien or trust to disable Hart from transferring the stock to the complainant, either in annuity stock or capital stock.

I am not for dismissing the plaintiff's bill because, then, the injunction would fall, for there are circumstances of equity so as not to permit Mr. Hart to sue the complainant on his bond until it is seen or tried what Mr. Hart has received. Therefore, to adjust the demands of Mr. Hart, the court is willing to direct the following issue: whether Mr. Hart is damnified any and what sum by the complainant's not complying with this contract on the 25 September 1720 so the jury may have the whole under their consideration. And we shall allow Mr. Hart the liberty to try this issue if he thinks fit.

Note that this decree was reversed in the House of Lords. See Cases.

[Later proceedings *sub nom.* Hart v. Harrison (1731), 2 Barnardiston K.B. 105, 94 E.R. 385.]

650

Attorney General v. Breedon

(Ex. 1726)

The only kind of clay that cannot be exported is fuller's earth.

Taussig MS. 311, vol. 2, p. 1004

Michaelmas term 1726.

An information [was brought] upon 9 & 10 Will., ca. 40,[1] for exporting 22,000 pounds weight of scouring clay. And the evidence was that this clay was Stourbridge clay. And five several witnesses swore that this clay would scour.

Chief Baron [PENGELLY]: It does not seem to me that the words of this Statute carry the prohibition as to the sorts of clay to be exported further than the former Act, for, in the title of the first Act of 12 Car. II, ca. 32,[2] there is mention of scouring clay. And the said Statute of Car. II was certainly intended only of such clay as was used in the woolen manufacture, for the words are 'any fuller's earth or fulling clay whatsoever'.

This seemed to him to be the difficulty, for both the acts were plainly made for the benefit of the woolen manufacture.

The verdict was for the defendant.

651

Mason v. Hine

(Ex. 1726)

In pleading a modus decimandi *in lieu of tithes in kind, there must be an allegation of a proportionably lesser sum for a lesser quantity.*

Taussig MS. 311, vol. 2, p. 1006, pl. 1

Michaelmas term 1726.

A *modus* of 6s. 8d. for a yardland [alleged] without saying proportionably for a lesser quantity was held ill.

[Further litigation in this case is reported at 3 Gwillim 951, 2 Eagle & Younge 6.]

---

[1] Stat. 9 Will. III, c. 40 (*SR*, VII, 421–423).

[2] Stat. 12 Car. II, c. 32 (*SR*, V, 293–296).

652

Cotes v. Powys

(Ex. 1726)

A landlord has priority for one year's rent over debts due upon an outlawry on behalf of a private debtor.

Taussig MS. 311, vol. 2, p. 1011

Michaelmas term 1726.

N.B. It has been several times determined here that by the Landlords' Act[1] that the landlord shall be satisfied his year's rent out of an execution upon an outlawry for the benefit of the party before the party prosecuting his outlawry shall be entitled to his execution.

653

Piper v. Thompson

(Ex. 1727)

A record cannot be amended unless there is something in the record to show how the correction should be made.

In this case, the court held that in fact no amendment was necessary.

Harvard Law School MS. 1082, vol. 2, p. 16, pl. 2

Hilary term 1726/27.

Mr. *Philip Ward*: He said that a *scire facias* grounded on a recognizance ought not to be amended for that it is a judicial writ. Cro. Jac., Weedon v. Strong; 1 Salkeld 62,[2] Holt said that it was going further than they ought to have done. It was objected Rolle, *Abridgment*, 797, Barnes v. Wolrich.[3] The reason of that amendment was because there was a [writ of] *capias ad satisfaciendum* to amend by. But this case differs from all the cases above mentioned, for this is a *scire facias* against a bail so that the *scire facias* is the only foundation. And it would have altered the case if it had been a *scire facias* against the principal because that is grounded on the judgment, so there was something to amend by. [For] writs original or judicial in

---

[1] Stat. 8 Ann., c. 18, s. 1 (*SR*, IX, 247).

[2] *Wheadon v. Sugg* (1615), Croke Jac. 372, 79 E.R. 318; *Bucksom v. Hoskins* (1704), 1 Salkeld 52, 91 E.R. 51, also 2 Lord Raymond 1057, 92 E.R. 201, 6 Modern 263, 310, 87 E.R. 1010, 1050, Holt K.B. 58, 762, 90 E.R. 930, 1319, *sub nom. Williams v. Hoskins*, 3 Salkeld 32, 91 E.R. 674.

[3] *Barnes v. Worlich* (1605), 1 Rolle, Abr., *Error*, pl. I, 2, p. 797.

the nature of an original, [see] 8 Rep., Blackmoore's Case.[1] This is not amendable because there is nothing to amend by. And the Statute of Jeofails[2] will not help it. 1 Salkeld 61, 62.[3] We have taken advantage of it by a demurrer.

Bootle [argued] for amending the writ. The reason of the case in Salkeld is with me. In a case of impropriety of writing or a mistake in the clerk, it is amendable. It is within the provision of the Stat. Hen. VI.

Chief Baron [PENGELLY]: The amendment desired is an amendment of a record after advantage taken of it by a demurrer. And there is nothing to amend by. And I cannot help the blunder of the clerk, but this is a want of skill in the clerk, and not a mere mistake, which differs much. I admit the difference between a *scire facias* against the principal and that against the bail. Holt takes the distinction. Salkeld 599; Buxsom v. Hoskins.[4] If the defendant had not taken advantage by a demurrer, it might be amendable. Brewster v. Wells, Michaelmas 3 Anne.[5]

HALE: *Hac* and *ea parte*, it might be amended by common sense.

CARTER was against the amendment.

COMYNS: There is no power in the court to amend but an by Act of Parliament. And if it is not within the acts of amendments, it is not amendable. 8 Hen. VI, of jeofails. It is considered as only a mistake of the clerk, not the want of skill. But then there must be always something to amend by. And the case in Rolle's *Abridgment* is the strongest instance of an amendment. Where there is something to amend by, there it is amendable, as 2 Cro. 372; Shower 61.[6]

So the whole court agreed not to amend this *scire facias*, against Baron Hale.

Bunbury 228, 145 E.R. 656

27 January 1726[/27].

There was a *scire facias* upon a recognizance against the bail, the *scire facias* reciting the record was *in hac parte*, whereas, against the bail, it should have been *in ea parte*. It was moved to amend upon these authorities: 1 Salkeld 51, 52; 1 Rolle, *Abridgment*, 797; Stat. 8 Hen. VI, c. 15.[7]

---

[1] *Blackamore's Case* (1610), 8 Coke Rep. 156, 77 E.R. 710.

[2] Stat. 8 Hen. VI, cc. 12, 15 (*SR*, II, 248–249, 252).

[3] *Regina v. Tushin* (1704), 1 Salkeld 51, 91 E.R. 50, also 2 Lord Raymond 1061, 92 E.R. 204, Holt K.B. 424, 90 E.R. 1133, 6 Modern 268, 87 E.R. 1014.

[4] *Lugg v. Goodwin* (1698), 2 Salkeld 599, 91 E.R. 508, also 1 Lord Raymond 393, 91 E.R. 1161; *Bucksom v. Hoskins* (1704), *ut supra*.

[5] Perhaps *Brewster v. Weld* (1704), 6 Modern 229, 87 E.R. 980, or *Attorney General, ex rel. Wells v. Brewster* (1703–1705), Eq. Cases Exch. 476, *sub nom. Attorney General, ex rel. Wells v. Kennett* (1704), Dodd 202.

[6] *Wheadon v. Sugg* (1615), Croke Jac. 372, 79 E.R. 318; *Hammond v. Pursell* (1689), 1 Shower K.B. 61, 89 E.R. 448, also Carthew 70, 90 E.R. 645.

[7] *Parsons v. Gill* (1703), 1 Salkeld 50, 51, 88, 91 E.R. 50, 83, also 1 Lord Raymond

But it was denied *per* TOTAM CURIAM. 2 Salkeld 599; Hilary 3 Ann., in the King's Bench, Brewster v. Wells.

Taussig MS. 311, vol. 2, p. 1013, pl. 1

Hilary term 1726/27.

There was a motion by *Bootle* to amend a *scire facias* against manucaptors after a demurrer. The cause of the demurrer was that the *scire facias* recited the damages in the former suit and the expenses and costs *in hac parte* instead of *in ea parte*.

But by PENGELLY and the other barons, though a *scire facias* is amendable where there is proper matter antecedent to amend by, yet this is *vitium clerici* (if it be a fault) and, therefore, it cannot be amended. And so the motion was refused.

See the cases cited on both sides in a paper folded up in a paper book of this cause.

Taussig MS. 311, vol. 2, p. 1033, pl. 1

Easter term 1727. Piper v. Thompson and Featherstonhaugh, *manucaptores Caroli Baley*.

Scire facias [was brought] against the defendants reciting the judgment or recovery as well of damages in the suit recited as of the expenses and costs *in hac parte*. The defendant demurs and shows this specially for cause and demands judgment of the writ *et quod brevem cassetur*. The plaintiff joins in demurrer and prays judgment and execution. And the questions were whether the writ was not wrong in form, the words *in hac parte* being incongruous; secondly, whether the demurrer to the writ being in abatement and the joinder in demurrer praying his execution was not a discontinuance.

But the court was against the defendant in both points. See the paper book of this term.

Harvard Law School MS. 1082, vol. 2, p. 22

Easter term 1727.

Upon a *scire facias* against the bail, which recites the judgment, the defendant demands oyer of the *scire facias* and return and demurs because of the words *in hac parte* instead of *ea parte*.

Ward, for the demurrer: Upon a return to the *scire facias*, it becomes a new suit. *In hac parte* is the suit now, and not the former suit, against the bail. It is improper in point of grammar and a contradiction.

Bootle, for the plaintiff: The case cited was only a plea in abatement. This may be good either way, by *ea* or *hac parte*. The judgment is the foundation of the

---

695, 91 E.R. 1363, 2 Lord Raymond 895, 92 E.R. 98, 1 Comyns 117, 92 E.R. 991; *Regina v. Tushin* (1704), *ut supra*; *Bucksom v. Hoskins* (1704), *ut supra*; *Barnes v. Worlich* (1605), *ut supra*; Stat. 8 Hen. VI, c. 15 (*SR*, II, 252).

whole. Michaelmas 10 Will. III, Atwood v. Bury, reported in Salkeld.[1] And that was upon a judgment against the principal.

Chief Baron [PENGELLY]: Lord Chief Justice Holt gave way to precedents, *hac parte*, though, in his opinion, it was more right to have it *ea parte*. The precedents are both ways.

Ward replies: It is no plea in abatement. And there might be as well a demurrer in abatement as a plea to the writ. And it will quash it. And so was Burgh v. Atwood in Salkeld.

CHIEF BARON: There are several cases both ways. The difference is, where judgment is given for the defendant, it is not final. The demurrer is wrong because it should only be *quod breve cessetur*, and not an award of execution. Chief Justice Holt thought there could be no demurrer in abatement. This is no discontinuance. Cross v. Bilson, in Salkeld.[2] It is proper for the court to go to the right. A *scire facias* against the principal is as much a new suit, as against the bail. And a letter of attorney for the first original suit will not hold to proceed on the *scire facias*.

We ought to go as far as we can to help this. And we may take it in a reasonable sense; *huiusmodi* is always used and is a much the present tense as *hac parte*. And if the words *hac parte* had been out, it had been a complete recognizance. And so it is surplusage and no hurt. Sir Oliver Butler, 2 Ventris, 3 Levinz.[3]

HALE agreed.

CARTER agreed. And Lilly's *Entries* are so.

COMYNS agreed. It is good either way.

1 Comyns 418, 92 E.R. 1138

A *scire facias* upon a recognizance by the bail after judgment against the principal recited the judgment in the manner following, *viz*. 'Whereas Thomas Piper, lately, that is to say, in Michaelmas term last past, recovered against [*blank*] as well a certain debt upon bond, as also a sum of [*blank*] shillings for his costs etc. *in hac parte*' etc. And upon this, there was a demurrer, and it was shown for cause for that the defendant in the judgment ought not to be condemned for costs *in hac parte*, but it should have been *in ea parte* etc.

And now, it was moved that it might be amended, being only the misprision of the clerk, which was amendable by the Statute of Jeofails in a writ original or judicial, and a *scire facias* was a judicial writ, and, therefore, 1 Rolle, *Abridgment*,

---

[1] *Attwood v. Burr* (1697–1706), 1 Salkeld 89, 402, 91 E.R. 83, 347, 2 Salkeld 603, 91 E.R. 511, 3 Salkeld 369, 91 E.R. 879, also 1 Lord Raymond 328, 553, 91 E.R. 1114, 1269, 2 Lord Raymond 821, 1252, 92 E.R. 48, 325, 5 Modern 397, 87 E.R. 728, 7 Modern 3, 87 E.R. 1057, Carthew 447, 90 E.R. 858.

[2] *Cross v. Bilson* (1704), 1 Salkeld 3, 91 E.R. 3, also 2 Lord Raymond 1016, 92 E.R. 176, 6 Modern 102, 87 E.R. 858, Holt K.B. 627, 90 E.R. 1247.

[3] *Butler's Case* (1680), 2 Ventris 344, 86 E.R. 477, 3 Levinz 220, 83 E.R. 659.

797, S, 2,[1] where the bail sued an *audita querela* and a *scire facias* upon it, which recited the *audita querela*, the [writ of] *capias* against the principal in the time of Queen Elizabeth, and the return upon it, but recited the *capias* to be by writ of 'our lady the queen of England to our sheriff, greeting, directed', which imports the writ should be directed to the king's sheriff, was held to be error in common law, but then amendable. So a writ of inquiry is amendable, being a judicial writ. Cro. Eliz. 761; 2 Cro. 372.[2] And though in 1 Salkeld 52, in the case of Buckskin v. Hoskins,[3] where a *scire facias* upon a writ of error in the King's Bench upon judgment in the Common Pleas *ad assignandum errores quare executionis non etc.* in ejectment of two messuages etc., where judgment was in ejectment of one messuage etc. it was held that it was not amendable, for the writ was good although improper in this case, and [where a] plea of *nul tiel record* is true, the court by amendment ought not to make the plea false; so Vavasor v. Baile, in the same book and folio,[4] where, in a *scire facias* upon judgment, the name of the plaintiff omitted by the defendant was not amended, for there might be such judgment, but the reason of these cases showed that, in other circumstances, a *scire facias* might be amended.

Sed non allocatur, for it seems to me that all which by the Statute 8 Hen. VI, c. 12 and 15,[5] the judges are empowered to amend in a writ original and judicial is what seems to them the misprision of the clerk in affirmance of judgments. If it is not done in affirmance of a judgment, it is not amendable. So a writ of error could not be amended until the Statute 5 Geo., c. 13, as appears from 5 Modern 16, 69,[6] etc. And what is not a misprision of the clerk is not now amendable. And I know of nothing which was taken as a misprision of the clerk only words of form, which ought to be added of course without information of a party, which is the description of the matter of form given by Lord Coke, 5 Co. 35b,[7] where words which are not pursuant to that which ought to be the direction or instruction of the clerk. And, therefore, in a writ of inquiry, a misprision which is not pursuant to the award of the writ upon the roll can be amended, for the roll is the warrant for a writ of inquiry, which the clerk ought to pursue, as appears in the cases cited, Cro. Eliz. 761; 2 Cro. 372; so 3 Modern 112,[8] where the words *per*

---

1 *Barnes v. Worlich* (1605), *ut supra.*

2 *Wolley v. Mosely* (1600), Croke Eliz. 760, 78 E.R. 992, also Moore K.B. 711, 72 E.R. 857; *Wheadon v. Sugg* (1615), *ut supra.*

3 *Bucksom v. Hoskins* (1704), *ut supra.*

4 *Vavisor v. Baile* (1708), 1 Salkeld 52, 91 E.R. 51, also Holt K.B. 59, 90 E.R. 931.

5 Stat. 8 Hen. VI, cc. 12, 15 (*SR*, II, 248–249, 252).

6 *Walker v. Slackoe* (1695), 5 Modern 16, 69, 87 E.R. 492, 524, also Carthew 367, 90 E.R. 814, Comberbach 354, 90 E.R. 524, 1 Lord Raymond 71, 91 E.R. 944, Holt K.B. 54, 90 E.R. 928.

7 *Playter v. Warne* (1583), 5 Coke Rep. 34, 77 E.R. 105.

8 *Wolley v. Mosely* (1600), *ut supra*; *Wheadon v. Sugg* (1615), *ut supra*; *Anonymous*

sacramentum proborum et legalium hominem were omitted in a writ of inquiry. But if the roll does not warrant an amendment, no misprision shall be amended, as if the roll awarded a writ returnable on Friday, *proxime post crastinum Ascensionis*, a writ of inquiry of such return, although after term, was refused by the court to be amended. 1 Shower 61.[1]

So in the case 1 Rolle, *Abridgment*, 797,[2] the *capias* upon the roll being *tempore Elizabethae* and directed 'to our sheriff, greeting', was directed to the queen's sheriff, therefore, a recital of the *capias* in a *scire facias* upon *audita querela tempore Jacobi* might be amended by the roll, for the *capias* recited was not by writ of Queen Elizabeth to our sheriff, *viz.* directed to the king's sheriff, but to the queen's sheriff, and this appears in the same book. 1 Rolle, *Abridgment*, 797, s. 1.[3] If there be a [writ of] *habeas corpora* to summon a jury summoned in a court late the queen's, and a [writ of] *distringas* was for the jury summoned in our court, judgment was reversed there by 3 Jac.;[4] so s. 3,[5] in dower, for the third part of one messuage, one stable, one granary, etc. a [writ of] petit cape, omitting one stable was held not amendable. An original writ, if it varies from the instructions, may nevertheless be amended, but not otherwise. And, therefore, it was answered by the court that the writ was not amendable.

But, afterwards, it was agreed by the court that there needed no amendment in this case, for, though *in ea parte* seemed proper by way of recital, yet, when it is said *in hac parte*, that suffices, for it had relation to the judgment mentioned in this same writ, and, therefore, it might well be said that the plaintiff recovered his debt by judgment and also his costs appointed in the judgment here mentioned. And there are precedents both ways.

654

Attorney General v. Flower

(Ex. 1727)

A person who was not actually present when wines were smuggled is not liable to the statutory penalty therefor.

Bunbury 227, 145 E.R. 656

Tried at Westminster before Lord Chief Baron Pengelly, 14 February 1726[/27].

(1686), 3 Modern 112, 87 E.R. 71.

1 *Hammond v. Pursell* (1689), *ut supra.*

2 *Barnes v. Worlich* (1605), *ut supra.*

3 *Knowles v. Burtenshawe* (1605), 1 Rolle, Abr., *Error*, pl. I, 1, p. 797.

4 Stat. 3 Jac. I, c. 8 (*SR*, IV, 1084).

5 *Rex v. Tashe and Haynes* (1634), 1 Rolle, Abr., *Error*, pl. I, 3, p. 797.

An information was brought by the Attorney General on the Stat. 8 Ann., c. 7, s. 30, for assisting etc. in unshipping of wines, whereby the treble value is forfeited. The defendant pleads not guilty.

Note: The information was that the defendant *tempore exonerationis fuit opitulator vel aliter particeps, Anglice*, otherwise concerned, *in exonerationem praedictum etc.*[1] The words of the Statute are 'The persons who are assisting or otherwise concerned in the unshipping' etc.

Upon the evidence, it appeared that the defendant had been present and assisting in unshipping two parcels of wine, but that he, afterwards, went away. And before he went, he commanded his servant Neve, the witness, to stay and assist in getting other parcels of wine into the cellar, which afterwards came in. And the servant Neve did accordingly assist etc., but the master, the defendant, was then at Andover, about forty miles distant from Pitts Deep in Hampshire, the place where the wine was run.

Mr. Attorney General [*Yorke*] insisted this was sufficient evidence to bring the defendant within the Act as to the two last parcels, and he was within the words 'otherwise concerned' or else those words would amount to no more than the word assisting.

But we, for the defendant, insisted that the Act extended only to those who were actually present at the very act of unshipping and never intended to punish any persons but those with so severe a penalty. And the words 'otherwise concerned' related to such who were present giving orders and directions, but did not actually assist. And the construction contended for by the Attorney General would render the subsequent words, 'or to whose hands they shall knowingly come', totally useless.

And of this opinion was the Lord Chief Baron [PENGELLY], especially as it was laid in the information. And upon the Chief Baron's declaring his opinion only as it was laid in the information, *viz. tempore exonerationis* etc., the Attorney General agreed the defendant should be acquitted as to the two last parcels.

655

Weedon v. Randal

(Ex. 1727)

A writ of prohibition to an ecclesiastical court as to repairs to a church cannot be granted before that court has made a decree.

Harvard Law School MS. 1082, vol. 2, p. 16, pl. 1

Hilary term 1726/27.

---

[1] at the time of unloading, he was an abetter or other participant, *Anglice* otherwise concerned, in the aforesaid unloading etc.

Dr. *Andrews* shows cause against a [writ of] prohibition. And this did arise on the validity of a rate made for repairing a pulpit and candlestick. A custom was alleged for the churchwarden to give notice in the church to meet in order to settle repairs. Randal offers his account of expenses, 14s. for the candlestick, 24s. for the pulpit. The poor's rate was admitted as not proper for repairing the church, but a church rate ought to be made. And the only matter in controversy is whether these sums were necessary or not.

Chief Baron [PENGELLY]: If these matters are or are not proper to be allowed, the ecclesiastical court has given no determination. And the plaintiff on prohibition comes too soon.

656

Stanton v. Russell

(Ex. 1727)

The question in this case was whether a widow of a copyholder has a right against an estate that was mortgaged before the marriage.

Harvard Law School MS. 1082, vol. 2, p. 20

Sittings after Hilary term 1726/27.

This was a bill by the plaintiff to have her free bench of an estate that was in mortgage before her intermarriage. 3 Levinz 385, Benson v. Scot. Query Bodmin v. Vanderbendy, in Vernon.[1]

657

Ralph v. Lady Petre

(Ex. 1727)

The question in this case was whether a general issue will be directed to an advisory jury to try whether there is any modus decimandi *in lieu of tithes in kind and, if so, what it is.*

[1] *Benson v. Scot* (1694), 3 Levinz 385, 83 E.R. 742, also 4 Modern 251, 87 E.R. 377, 1 Salkeld 185, 91 E.R. 168, Comberbach 233, 90 E.R. 448, Carthew 275, 90 E.R. 763, Holt K.B. 160, 90 E.R. 986, 12 Modern 49, 88 E.R. 1157, Skinner 406, 90 E.R. 180; *Lady Bodmin v. Vandenbendy* (1683–1685), 1 Vernon 179, 356, 23 E.R. 399, 520, also Chancery Cases 172, 22 E.R. 899, 1 Eq. Cas. Abr. 219, 21 E.R. 1002, *sub nom. Lady Radnor v. Rotherham* (1696), 2 Freeman 211, 22 E.R. 1165, Precedents in Chancery 65, 24 E.R. 32, *sub nom. Countess of Radnor v. Vandebendy* (1697), Shower P.C. 69, 1 E.R. 48, 2 Eq. Cas. Abr. 383, 22 E.R. 326.

Taussig MS. 311, vol. 2, p. 1014

Hilary term 1726/27.

N.B. In this cause, the court directed two issues to try the two several *modus*es set forth and insisted upon by the answer and the cross-bill of the defendants. And they would not direct the issues general to try whether any and what *modus*es.

Sed quaere per me, for, in a [writ of] prohibition, if issue is joined on a *modus* and the jury finds a different *modus*, no [writ of] consultation [lies] and, therefore, many issues were formerly directed out of this court to try whether there were any and what *modus*es, as by many decrees of this court [show].

658

Rainstorpe v. Dyer

(Ex. 1727)

A modus decimandi *in lieu of tithes in kind that is unintelligible is void.*

Taussig MS. 311, vol. 2, p. 1015

Hilary term 1726/27.

The defendant insisted on a *modus* of 2d. per acre for ridge ground when mowed or not mowed for all rectorial and vicarial tithes and 2d. for flat meadow, both unintelligible and insensible *modus*es. But no day being fixed for payment, the plaintiff first insisted on that objection.

And the court seemed to slight it, Carter more particularly. And so they determined against the defendant on the absurdity of the *modus*es.

659

Crump v. Burke

(Ex. 1727)

A defendant cannot plead a denial and a justification at the same time.

A distress can only be taken at the leased premises.

After goods taken by distress have been given up, they cannot be distrained again.

Taussig MS. 311, vol. 2, p. [1016]

Wednesday, 8 February [1726/27].

Draper opens the case for the plaintiff. [An action of] trespass [was brought] for several particulars. The justification for distress under the new Act justified the taking of corn in a barn, whereas the trespass is laid generally. He pleads not guilty and justifies for the same trespass. 1 Rolle's Rep. 49; 2 Lutw. 1381; one justifies *abduxione averiorum*, but yet does not own that he took them away, but only distrained; 1 Salk. 179; Yelv. 225 (or 235); 2 Lutw. 1247; 1 Lev. 16.[1] As to the main point, a bailiff's power is a delegated power; he cannot outgo the license. 1 Mod. 210; Bro., License, 14; Fitzherbert, *Abr.*, Tresp., 139; he ought to have justified the second entry in his own right. Six Carpenter's Case; Bro., License, 17; the bailiff quitted his distress and could not justify, Cartwright and Comer, latter end of Queen Anne, that, if a bailiff quits the distress, he cannot take to it again before 17 Car. II; Moor's Case, 26 Cro. Eliz., a second distress could not be taken.[2]

Bootle: As to the first, the trespass is laid to be done at Hornden. The distress must be upon the place demised; so, if the barn is on the premises, it is well. [As to the] second objection, he pleads not guilty and justified for the same thing. Either you plead not guilty as to all the trespass *praeter* such and such enumerated or you enumerate the trespasses you plead not guilty to and then you justify *quoad* the residue. But here, as to the third objection, caption and abduction are the same thing. So the fourth, the principal objection as to the bailiff's entering a second time, [is], if there is no agreement between the plaintiff and the bailiff, the thing had been unjustifiable, but here is an agreement between the plaintiff and the defendant which justifies this. It is set forth the plaintiff desired the defendant to leave the goods for five days and, if not paid or replevied within that time, the bailiff might come and take them away as distress. It is alleged that this leaving the goods was at the special request of the plaintiff so that the general

---

[1] *Allen v. Browne* (1614), 1 Rolle Rep. 49, 81 E.R. 319; *Rodoway v. Lowder* (1688), 2 Lutwyche 1381, 125 E.R. 763; *Weeks v. Peach* (1701), 1 Salkeld 179, 91 E.R. 164, also 1 Lord Raymond 679, 91 E.R. 1352, Holt K.B. 561, 90 E.R. 1210, 2 Lutwyche 1218, 125 E.R. 676; *Newhall v. Barnard* (1612), Yelverton 225, 80 E.R. 147; *Simpson v. Telwright* (1700), 2 Lutwyche 1241, 1247, 125 E.R. 688, 692; *Tompson v. Noel* (1661), 1 Levinz 16, 83 E.R. 274.

[2] *Bringloe v. Morrice* (1676), 1 Modern 210, 86 E.R. 834, also 3 Salkeld 271, 91 E.R. 819; YB Hil. 18 Edw. IV, f. 25, pl. 14 (1479), Brooke, Abr., *Licenses grauntes de va*, pl. 14; YB Hil. 21 Edw. IV, f. 19, pl. 22 (1482), Fitzherbert, Abr., *Trespas*, pl. 139; *Vaux v. Newman* (1610), 8 Coke Rep. 146, 77 E.R. 695; YB Hil. 21 Edw. IV, f. 75, pl. 9 (1482), Brooke, Abr., *Licenses grauntes de va*, pl. 17; *Cartwright v. Comber* (1710 x 1718), cited in *Griffith v. Scott* (1726), 2 Lord Raymond 1424, 1426, 92 E.R. 426, 428; *More's Case* (1584), Croke Eliz. 26, 78 E.R. 291.

authority of a bailiff is not in question, but only the special authority of the bailiff under the special agreement of the plaintiff himself.

Draper replies: He has pleaded *quoad* the taking in the barn. A prisoner's consent to be retaken will not justify a retaking; so the consent of the plaintiff to let his debtor go out for a day. 2 Mod. 136.[1]

Chief Baron [Pengelly]: As to the first objection, which is the cause of the demurrer, I should think the plea is good, for it does not show the trespass to be a different trespass from what is complained of and the rather because loose corn was not formerly distrainable. As to the second objection, it is a good objection. If the pleader admit it, leading away is generally implied in a taking. Besides, the word *reduxit* implies and admits an *abduxit*. Secondly, he admits a fugitive *et chasiavit*. As to the third objection, that one cannot plead *non culpabilis* and justify, and that I think is a material objection, for the rule before is certainly right, *que est eadem*. Fourth, as to the main objection, he thought the consent is surplusage, for there does not seem to be a desertion, for it is said he detained and locked up. The lessor for years may keep the distress on the premises; it is otherwise, perhaps, of a lessor at will. But here, since the Statute, it is a plainer case, for the Statute says one cannot remove loose things to the prejudice of the tenant, though indeed he may remove them at his own peril. And, therefore, if the bailiff has done no more than the law admits, then the consent is surplusage. In the next place, the plaintiff might have made by a replication a new assignment of a tortious act to make the defendant a trespasser *ab initio*.

Hale: Upon the whole, I do not see how the defendant can be a trespasser against the plaintiff where the plaintiff has consented.

Carter: The declaration is a charge for keeping him out for a month, and here is only a justification for five days.

Comyns gives the same answer to the first objection as the Chief Baron. Secondly, it is true one cannot plead *non culpabilis* and justify, but I do not think he has done so, for the defendant has pleaded two entries, for the trespass in the declaration is on such a day so that he did not tread down the grass and corn in the declaration, though perhaps he did other grass etc. Thirdly, as to not showing an abduction, I think he has done it. He thinks that forking up the corn is an abduction, as pulling up *spinas* is a removal or asportation. The case in Ventr. Fourth, he agrees that, after a desertion, one cannot take again. And he thinks that the license would justify a second entry. '*Quousque foenem fecit*' is not necessary to be answered as it is only a matter of aggravation. Nash v. Wadman, in the King's Bench, Rolle's Rep.; 2 Ventris is to the same point.

Query whether, as to the showing of taking the money, if the time of five days and a month do agree. *Ulterius concilium*.

---

[1] *Basset v. Salter* (1676), 2 Modern 136, 86 E.R. 985, also 1 Freeman 213, 89 E.R. 150.

660

James v. Nelley

(Ex. 1727)

In this case, the condition of a bond was found to have been broken and that the wages of a mariner were sued for before the entire freight was paid for.

Taussig MS. 311, vol. 2, p. 1020

Thursday, 9 February 1726[/27].

The plaintiff's wife [Susanna James] was executrix of Anthony Chrisday, who entered himself as a midshipman on board the *Hartford*, bound on an East India voyage, whereof the defendant Nelly was master. And, upon his being hired a midshipman, he entered into a bond with the captain, in the condition of which bond, it was recited that Chrisday had received £3 for two months wages and was to have 23s. per month for his wages and that it was agreed between Chrisday and Nelley that Chrisday should not demand or sue for his wages until the whole money was received for the freight; therefore, if Chrisday should perform all and every the premises and be obedient etc. and should not bring over any goods etc. but on the Company's account, then the bond to be void.

Chrisday sails the voyage. And, in his return to England, he died, whereupon his goods were sold for £1 0s. 6d. before the mast. And £7 6s. 3d. [was due] for wages. But before his death, he made the plaintiff, Susanna, his executrix and gave her all his effects.

Susanna was the surety with Chrisday in the bond to Captain Nelley. And a considerable time afterwards, she came to the East India House and demanded her wages, at which time, the goods were delivered in to the Company's warehouse and the Captain had received £2300 for the payment of wages, but the whole wages of the sailors came to £2900. But the defendant Nelley not paying, at last, she brought her action of case against Nelley of *indebitatus assumpsit* for the wages of her testator and for money received to her use for the clothes. And Nelley suffered judgment by default. A writ of inquiry was executed, and £8 6s. 9d. was found. And the judgment was final and a writ of error etc. After all this, the defendant brought an action of debt upon the bond given to the captain. And upon oyer of the condition, the present plaintiff pleaded that, at the time of the suing of the action, the whole freight was not received. And the defendant replied in the negative. And upon the trial, after long evidence, there was a verdict for the defendant. And so there was judgment for the present defendant for the penalty, against which this bill was brought to be relieved and for a perpetual injunction against the bond.

The pleadings upon the bond were thus. To the plaintiff's performance of the condition in general, the defendant replies and assigns the breach, *viz.* that the present plaintiff sued him before the whole freight was paid, and the present plaintiff rejoined that she did not sue before the whole freight was paid. There was an issue thereupon. And the verdict was that the suit was commenced before the whole freight was paid.

661

Attorney General v. Hoskyns

(Ex. 1727)

A charge of smuggling can by brought only against the person who took possession of the goods.

Taussig MS. 311, vol. 2, p. 1022

14 February 1726[/27].

In a *devenerunt* for eight hogsheads of wine, the evidence was that two men went out in two several boats to the sloop; four hogsheads of wine were delivered into the boat where Hoskyns was, and four into the boat where Pollard was, and they separately carried them to shore. And there was no evidence that the four hogshead in Pollard's came to Hoskyns' possession, though Hoskins bought them all aboard.

And the Chief Baron [PENGELLY] held that, upon this evidence, Hoskins was only chargeable with the four he carried ashore, the point of the information being that the goods came to the possession of the defendant.

662

Reynell v. Perrot

(Ex. 1727)

A court of equity has jurisdiction to set aside an arbitral award.

Taussig MS. 311, vol. 2, p. 1033, pl. 2

Easter term 1727.

In a bill to set aside an award, it was thought that 9 & 10 Will., ca. 15,[1] does not absolutely preclude a court of equity from intermeddling.

663

Juggins v. Cardell

(Ex. 1727)

A court of equity has jurisdiction to enforce a right of contribution.

---

[1] Stat. 9 Will. III, c. 15 (*SR*, VII, 369–370).

The Court of Exchequer has no minimum jurisdiction as to the amount of the claim.

Harvard Law School MS. 1082, vol. 2, p. 21, pl. 2

Easter term 1727.

This was a bill to be relieved against the defendant, who, together with the plaintiff, entered into a joint note together with Lawson for £8 17s. 9d. to Johnson. And the money so lent was on account of Lawson only. And Johnson having sued the plaintiff on this note, the plaintiff was obliged to pay the same with costs amounting to £12. And, therefore, the bill prayed that the defendant should reimburse the plaintiff the whole money according to his engagement, which was suggested in the bill to have a moiety of the money paid, being £6, by way of contribution.

And to this bill, the defendant answered as to part and demurred as to the relief. And he assigned two causes of demurrer. One was that, it being for contribution, then the bill was only for £6, which was below the dignity of the court. And another was that it was triable at law.

But the court held that, in regard that here was a proper subject of equity, *viz.* to have contribution, and that the same could not be had at law, that, therefore, this was no cause of demurrer.

The counsel for the plaintiff cited Parsons v. Meredith, Michaelmas 1721,[1] which was for a note of £6 1s. 0d.

And so, in the principal case, the court overruled the demurrer. And there is no stated sum fixed to the jurisdiction of this court.

Taussig MS. 311, vol. 2, p. 1039 [bis], pl. 2

13 May 1727.

There was a demurrer to a bill for that it appears upon the face of the bill that the plaintiff's demand is under £10, *viz.* £8 15s. 9d.

Browne, for the plaintiff, cited the case of Parsons and Meredith, Michaelmas 1721, where a bill was to be relieved against a note for £6 10s. and there was a demurrer thereto because it was under the value, but the demurrer was overruled.

Newman cited the case of Bassett and Parsons, 1723,[2] where a demurrer of this nature was allowed.

Query of Mr. *Browne*, what became of this demurrer.

---

[1] *Parsons v. Meredith* (Ex. 1722), see above, Case No. 356.

[2] *Bassett v. Parsons* (Ex. 1723), see above, Case No. 407.

664

Lloyd v. Jones

(Ex. 1727)

It is not a departure to allege a new tort in point of time in a replication because the time of the tort is not material in an action sounding in tort.

Harvard Law School MS. 1082, vol. 2, p. 21, pl. 3

Easter term 1727.

[To an] action of trespass and false imprisonment, the defendant pleads and justifies. And the plaintiff replies and sets forth a new trespass in point of time. And to this, the defendant demurs.

Bootle, for the demurrer, cited Cro. Car. 228, 559.[1]

Serjeant *Hawkins*, for the plaintiff: I allow that the plaintiff is to pursue his writ, and, so long as the substance of the writ is pursued, a replication, as long as it is consistent with the writ, it is no departure. The matter in evidence and in the pleading is the same. And though the time is varied as to the trespass, as in a case of *quare clausum fregit*, generally, I am at liberty to assign any new close. But he cannot if he ties it down by a particular name of the close. And wherever a plaintiff confesses and avoids, that is sufficient, and the place and time is immaterial. Co. Litt. 282b; Cole v. Hankins, Trinity 13 Queen Anne, King's Bench; 1 Siderfin 228.[2] The substance is that the defendant was a trespasser before the action. Cro. Car. 245, 254; Salkeld 222.[3]

Though the defendant has a warrant to arrest the party, it must be by a *molliter manus imposuit*. And he cannot justify a beating but upon a rescue. 2 Lutwyche 129, 3 Levinz.[4]

Bootle, for the demurrer: Lutwyche and Levinz differ in this report. The arrest will justify the beating of the party without a *molliter manus imposuit*. My argument is *ab inconvenienti*. And pleading will go further than a surrebutter. The traversing of places does not come up to the traversing of time. And though it may be immaterial in point of evidence, yet it is not so in pleading.

---

[1] *Tyler v. Wall* (1631), Croke Car. 228, 79 E.R. 799; *Thornton v. Lyster* (1638), Croke Car. 514, 515, 79 E.R. 1044.

[2] E. Coke, *First Institute* (1628), ff. 282–283; *Cole v. Hawkins* (1714), 10 Modern 251, 348, 88 E.R. 714, 759, Gilbert Cases 279, 93 E.R. 328, 1 Strange 21, 93 E.R. 359; *Bevin v. Chapman* (1664), 1 Siderfin 228, 82 E.R. 1074, also *sub nom. Bevin v. Clapham*, 1 Keble 794, 799, 904, 83 E.R. 1247, 1250, 1311, 1 Levinz 143, 83 E.R. 339.

[3] *Swayn v. Stephens* (1632), Croke Car. 245, 333, 79 E.R. 815, 892, also W. Jones 252, 82 E.R. 132; *Rhemes v. Humphreys* (1632), Croke Car. 254, 79 E.R. 821; *Webly v. Palmer* (1695), 1 Salkeld 222, 91 E.R. 197.

[4] *Patrick v. Johnson* (1694), 2 Lutwyche 925, 125 E.R. 517, 3 Levinz 403, 83 E.R. 752.

Chief Baron [PENGELLY]: I must overrule the demurrer, for time and place are immaterial and you cannot traverse the particular time laid in the declaration, but you must traverse a trespass at any time before the action was brought. The case of Tiler v. Wall that is objected is a sudden opinion. See Hobart 104; 2 Saunders 294, 295.[1]

Where it is an action upon the note or bond or a specialty, there the day is material. But in trespass or *assumpsit*, the time is immaterial unless the defendant makes it necessary. And where the defendant assigns another time and place, the plaintiff is at liberty to assign another time and place, and it is no departure. Salkeld 223, Howard v. Jeanison; Salkeld 222, Webly v. Palmer; Rolle, *Abridgment*, 680.[2]

The CHIEF BARON [gave] judgment for the plaintiff.

HALE and CARTER agreed.

COMYNS agreed and cited Lutwyche 1435.[3]

Judgment [was given] for the plaintiff.

Taussig MS. 311, vol. 2, p. 1038

10th May 1727.

Bootle, for the defendant: The new assignment is a departure. 1 Inst. 304; 1 Syd. 10.[4] The day is not material in evidence, but it is in the pleading, for, if it was not, there might be an infinite production of the pleadings between the parties. Cro. Car. 228. A case in point is Cro. Car. 515.[5]

Per CURIAM: This case has been constantly denied to be the law and the two cases in Rolle's *Abr.*, 680.

Serjeant *Hawkins*, *contra*, admits the principle of maintaining the declaration. But here, the substance of the declaration is pursued though there is a variance between the declaration in matter of form. There is no difference between the evidence and the pleading as to varying from the day. As to varying from the time assigned in the replication, wherever you confess and avoid, it is good. You must traverse all other places that the traverse may be traversed. Co. Lit. 282b. Time is immaterial. And no trick in pleading shall make it material. Cole and

---

[1] *Digby v. Fitzharbert* (1615), Hobart 101, 104, 80 E.R. 251, 253, also Moore K.B. 869, 72 E.R. 962; *White v. Stubbs* (1671), 2 Williams Saunders 294, 85 E.R. 1085, also 1 Levinz 307, 83 E.R. 421, 2 Keble 712, 735, 84 E.R. 449, 464, Lincoln's Inn MS. Misc. 500, f. 142 (Edward Ward's reports).

[2] *Howard v. Jennison* (1696), 1 Salkeld 223, 91 E.R. 197, also Comberbach 361, 90 E.R. 528; *Webly v. Palmer* (1695), *ut supra*; 2 Rolle, Abr., *Triall*, pl. C, 3, p. 680.

[3] *Searle v. Darford* (1696), 2 Lutwyche 1435, 125 E.R. 792, also 1 Lord Raymond 120, 91 E.R. 977, 3 Lord Raymond 110, 92 E.R. 592.

[4] E. Coke, *First Institute* (1628), f. 304; *Weston v. Carter* (1660), 1 Siderfin 9, 10, 82 E.R. 939, or *Butcher v. Whiting* (1660), 1 Siderfin 10, 82 E.R. 939.

[5] *Tyler v. Wall* (1631), *ut supra*; *Thornton v. Lyster* (1638), Croke Car. 514, 515, 79 E.R. 1044.

Hawkins, in the King's Bench, Trinity 1712, is expressly in point. 1 Syd. 228, Bevill and Chapman, matter unforeseen is pleaded; 5 Hen. VII, 19, 20, 21, the plaintiff may depart; Cro. 245; Jones; Salk. 222, as to the plea, one cannot justify a beating but by a *molliter manus imposuit*; 2 Edw. IV, 6;[1] 2 Lutw. 999. But Patrick and Johnson;[2] *cepit et accrestavit* is no justification of a battery.

Chief Baron [Pengelly]: The day is not material in [an action of] trespass for an assault or the like. They traverse all the time after in the case of a release if, by process, you must traverse all the time not included in the process. And, therefore, this is the constant way of traversing. [He] shows Cro. Car. 228. An *obiter* opinion in Hob. 104, it is in nature of joining issue on the defendant's traverse. 2 Saunders 294, it is issuable. It is otherwise where a day is part of a note or a bond, for, then, the day is material as being part of his description. Salk. 222, Medley and Palmer;[3] a judgment for the plaintiff was unanimous; Lutw. 1435, as to place.

Query, if there be three trespasses [and the] plaintiff brings an action for one, the defendant justified [and] the plaintiff assigns a second, whether he may justify this or must plead not guilty.

665

Binstead v. Collins

(Ex. 1727)

A bishop does not have jurisdiction over a trespass to a parish church unless it causes an interruption to a church service.

The right of the freehold of a parish church is in the rector, and not in the bishop.

A writ of prohibition can be granted after a final judgment in an ecclesiastical court where the proceedings in that court were coram non judice.

Harvard Law School MS. 1082, vol. 2, p. 25

Easter term 1727.

Dr. *Henchman* shows cause against a [writ of] prohibition for that there was a libel in the ecclesiastical court against Collins, the churchwarden of Hanulton, for he, without the license of the bishop, broke a hole in the wall and took down a window of painted glass, and a sentence was given against the defendant 8 July 1726.

Articles against a churchwarden as an ecclesiastical officer for any neglect of his duty are punishable in an ecclesiastical court. And the ordinary is obliged to see the churchwarden do his duty so that the ecclesiastical court is a proper court,

---

1 YB Pas. 2 Edw. IV, f. 6, pl. 15 (1462).

2 *Patrick v. Johnson* (1694), *ut supra*.

3 *Webly v. Palmer* (1695), 1 Salkeld 222, 91 E.R. 197.

and [it is] against a proper person. And the question is whether it is *vi et armis*, for then, there might be an action of trespass, as urged on the other side where the freehold of the church is in a vicar or rector. And it does not appear that there was a license from the minister, and the parson has only a freehold under a condition for the use of the parishioners.

If an action of trespass was brought, it will only be [for] damages and those cannot be applied to the repairs of the church. And, therefore, [it is] proper in the ecclesiastical court to put things *in statu quo*. This is only for the repair of a church. And the Statute of Uniformity[1] gives a double punishment reserved to the ecclesiastical court by the Statute of *Circumspecte Agatis.*[2]

Formerly, parsons ought to repair their churches. And now, they are done by the parishioners. By the Statute alone, the exercise of jurisdiction is left to the ecclesiastical court. So *pro [. . .]tero non clau[. . .]* repairing the hedges of a churchyard. This comes under the Canon received according to Lord Hobart, and the cognizance of them belongs to the ecclesiastical court, as by Lord Coke.

[To the] objection that the libel is for cutting yew trees, [he] responded, though the parson has the timber in the churchyard, that is only for the repairs of the church.

The sentence is for breaking down the wall without a faculty and proper authority. The costs [were] £25 *praeter feoda admonitionis.*

Chief Baron [PENGELLY]: Here is no allegation that these deeds interrupted the parishioners in the service of the church.

Serjeant *Belfield*, against a prohibition: The spiritual court has a jurisdiction. A person may commit an act which may subject him to [an action of] trespass and likewise, for the same deed, to the sentence of the ecclesiastical court *pro reformatione morum et salute animae*. Churchwardens are spiritual officers.

[To the] objection of Salkeld 547,[3] [he] responded with 1 Siderfin 281, Welcome v. Lake.[4] The thing in specie is to be restored in the ecclesiastical court. Goldsborough 113; Godbolt 259; 1 Bulstrode 279; 1 Rolle 255.[5]

Philip Ward: The ordinary has only jurisdiction of the church and the ornaments of it. Noy 104;[6] Rushworth, *Collections*, 2 vol., 153.

Bootle, for the prohibition: Collins is sued as a trespasser. Canon 1683, [no.] 89.[7]

---

[1] Stat. 14 Car. II, c. 4 (*SR*, V, 364–370).

[2] Stat. 13 Edw. I, *Circumspecte Agatis* (*SR*, I, 101–102).

[3] *Starky v. Churchwardens of Watlington* (1692), 2 Salkeld 547, 91 E.R. 463.

[4] *Welcome v. Lake* (1666), 1 Siderfin 281, 82 E.R. 1106, also 2 Keble 6, 22, 84 E.R. 4, 14.

[5] *Brown v. Lother* (1597), Gouldsborough 113, 75 E.R. 1031; *Bishop of Salisbury's Case* (1614), Godbolt 259, 78 E.R. 151; Note (1614), 2 Bulstrode 279, 80 E.R. 1121; *Bellamie v. Anonymous* (1615), 2 Rolle Rep. 255, 81 E.R. 471.

[6] *Day v. Beddingfield*, Noy 104, 74 E.R. 1070.

[7] Canons of 1603, no. 89, G. Bray, ed., *The Anglican Canons 1529–1947* (1998), p. 385.

[To the] objection of a remedy in both places, [he] responded this particular sentence is a condemnation in cost and not *pro salute animae*. And the sentence is not for putting the thing *in statu quo*, for this is for £25 *pro expensis*. 2 Cro. 367.[1]

The parson ought to have sued for breaking the church wall. And it is a trespass on the face of the sentence. And where it appears so, a [writ of] prohibition is to be granted after such a sentence. Noy 137; Cro. Eliz. 178; Hetley 94.[2]

Chief Baron [Pengelly]: This is a suit *pro reformatione morum*, and nothing here is given as damages. If the court had jurisdiction in the original cause, then costs follow of course as incident.

This does not seem to be a proceeding for the benefit of the parishioners. And though the ordinary has a jurisdiction over the fabric, yet that is with respect only to divine service, and the ordinary cannot punish for a single trespass to the church without an interruption in the church in the time of divine service. The bishop may proceed against a vicar to compel him to do right by repairing. This suit is for a single trespass, and it was not laid as an interruption to the church or persons going to church. And the right of the freehold is in the rector, and not the ordinary. Michaelmas 12 Will. III [1700], Rayner v. Tufton.

The ordinary has no power to open church doors. And a prohibition was granted in that case. And the whole right is in the parson.

So the rule for a [writ of] prohibition was made absolute.

Bunbury 229, 145 E.R. 656

6 May 1727.

A libel was brought in the spiritual court against Binsted, churchwarden, but it did not appear he was so in the proceedings, for breaking a hole in the church wall and cutting down the boughs of a large yew tree in the churchyard.

Note: There was a decree in the spiritual court for £26 costs, *praeter feodum monitionis et executionem eiusdem monitionis*.

Now, upon showing cause why a [writ of] prohibition should not go, it was insisted against a prohibition that this was a matter proper for the jurisdiction of the spiritual court and that a man may be punished for the same fact in different respects. And he cited Salkeld 547; 1 Siderfin 281; Goldsborough 113; Godbolt 259, that the parson had a freehold in the churchyard for the benefit of the church; 2 Bulstrode 279; 1 Rolle Rep. 255; Noy 104.[3]

---

1 *Frances v. Ley* (1615), Croke Jac. 366, 79 E.R. 314.

2 *Anonymous*, Noy 137, 74 E.R. 1100; *Transam's Case* (1590), Croke Eliz. 178, 78 E.R. 434; *Eaton v. Ayliffe* (1628), Hetley 94, 124 E.R. 370, also Croke Car. 111, 79 E.R. 697.

3 *Starky v. Churchwardens of Watlington* (1692), 2 Salkeld 547, 91 E.R. 463; *Welcome v. Lake* (1666), 1 Siderfin 281, 82 E.R. 1106, also 2 Keble 6, 22, 84 E.R. 4, 14; *Brown v. Lother* (1597), Gouldsborough 113, 75 E.R. 1031; *Bishop of Salisbury's Case* (1614), Godbolt 259, 78 E.R. 151; Note (1614), 2 Bulstrode 279, 80 E.R. 1121; *Bellamie v.*

For the prohibition, it was said that the parson has the right or remedy as well as the freehold and, consequently, might have an action, 2 Cro. 367; Bro. [*Abridgment*] Trespass, 210, that it was not too late for a prohibition, even after sentence, if the proceedings are *coram non judice*; Noy 137; Cro. Eliz. 178; Hetley 94.[1]

Per CURIAM: The ordinary cannot punish a single trespass committed on the body of the church which does not hinder the service, which is the case the Statute of *Circumspecte Agatis de Ecclesia Discooperta* extends to and which is not alleged in the libel. The rector, who has the freehold in him, has a right to bring his action, and, therefore, it would be hard to subject this man to a double prosecution. And the expense here, though properly costs, are in the nature of damages. But the plaintiff might, if he thought fit, declare in prohibition.

Taussig MS. 311, vol. 2, p. 1034

6 May 1727. Barlow et al. v. Collins and Tremearne.

This [case] came now before the court upon a rule made the last term that Barlow etc. should show cause why there should not be a [writ of] prohibition to their suit against Collins and Tremerne in the ecclesiastical court of Winchester for pulling down part of the wall of the parish church of Hambledon in the County of Southampton. The defendant Collins was churchwarden of the parish aforesaid in the year 1723, and Tremerne was a carpenter. Collins, in the said year, employed the said Tremerne to make some alterations in the church, *viz.* to take down part of the wall of the tower of the church and to make a window in it, to cut down or rather lop off the boughs of an yew tree in the churchyard, and he also took down the painted glass in the window and put up new square glass in its stead. This he did without any order of the vestry for that purpose. And, for this, he was sued in the ecclesiastical court *praesertim pro dirimendo partem ecclesiae* whereby it was alleged that the tower and church was much weakened. And this was alleged to be done by him without any faculty or lawful authority and contrary to his duty. And the suit in the ecclesiastical court was not for damages, but *pro salute animae et reformatione morum et excessum*. And upon his appearance and pleadings, he was condemned in costs and, just as he was ready to be excommunicated, he appealed to the [Court of] Arches, and then he deserted his appeal so that the cause was remitted.

And now, he moved the court for a [writ of] prohibition. And the suggestion was that what he had done was a mere trespass and not punishable by the ordinary, who had nothing to do with the freehold of the church, for that was in the

---

Anonymous (1615), 1 Rolle Rep. 255, 81 E.R. 471; *Day v. Beddingfield*, Noy 104, 74 E.R. 1070.

[1] *Frances v. Ley* (1615), Croke Jac. 366, 79 E.R. 314; YB Pas. 21 Hen. VII, f. 21, pl. 11, Brooke, Abr., *Trespas*, pl. 210 (1506); *Anonymous*, Noy 137, 74 E.R. 1100; *Transam's Case* (1590), Croke Eliz. 178, 78 E.R. 434; *Eaton v. Ayliffe* (1628), Hetley 94, 124 E.R. 370, also Croke Car. 111, 79 E.R. 697.

vicar, who was a friend and, indeed, the principal abetter and director of Collins. And therefore, this suit in the ecclesiastical court and all the proceedings upon it was null *et coram non judice*.

And of this opinion was the Chief Baron Pengelly. And he said that, if it had been alleged that the alterations and innovations made in the church had rendered it unfit for divine service, the bishop might interpose, but not otherwise.

See the cases cited *ex utraque parte* on the [*blank*].

Note: I was of counsel with the defendant in the prohibition.

The writ of prohibition was granted.

666

Cuthbert v. Lawrence

(Ex. 1727)

In this case, a modus decimandi *in lieu of tithes in kind and a* non decimando *were proved.*

Harvard Law School MS. 1082, vol. 2, p. 26

Easter term 1727.

So much was to be paid according to the land's rent. A *non decimando* as to tithe lambs was uncertain. And there was a *non decimando* as to agistment and so if the sheep do not go forty days. See the composition itself in the Ma[. . .].

But the court decreed this composition to be established though it did not seem to be made by a proper authority and though such objections were made as above, *quod mirum est*.

667

Thrustout, ex dem. Manwaring v. Baker

(Ex. 1727)

An action of ejectment does not abate upon the death of the lessor because the plaintiff is a nominal lessee.

Taussig MS. 311, vol. 2, p. 1036

Easter term 1727. Thrustout, lessee of Sir Thomas Manwaring v. Baker, in [an action of] ejectment.

Sir Thomas dies before the day appointed for the view. However, the view went on, but the defendant did not attend. And the cause was brought on to trial at the last assizes. But the defendant did not appear to confess the lease, entry, and ouster etc. so a nonsuit was recorded.

Kettleby: Proceedings in ejectment now are fictitious. Farresly's Reports 150.[1] Everything must be fairly done; the ejectment is by a fictitious person. By the rule of court, the lessor is to pay the costs for this reason, but, if there is a real man, then he must pay them. And, therefore, if he dies, the defendant has no remedy for costs. The lessor may bring the action of trespass for the mesne profits. 1 Syd. 24, the name may be altered; 317, a lessor may bring a writ of error, and so may a lessee if he is a real person; 3 Keble 772, the death of the lessee does not abate the suit if it is only a nominal person; 1 Salk. 260.[2] The plaintiff in ejectment was a mere nominal person. And, therefore, he moved that the judgment should be set aside for the irregularity of going on to trial after the death of the plaintiff's lessor.

Wilbraham, contra: [This is an action in] ejectment for ten closes. And the question is no judgment against the casual ejector [where] two terms intervened between the death of the lessor and the trial. The rule of confessing etc. is shorter in this court than in the King's Bench or the Common Bench. Jackson v. Philips, a rule to make a good lessee and several of this sort, Michaelmas 7 Will.; Bishop of Meath and Jones, to name a good lessee; Harrison and Otway, in Keble 772.[3] In the case of 1 Mod. 252, there is a particular agreement, but the lessee's death will certainly abate and for that reason, they make nominal persons lessees; 2 Lev. 66; 6 Mod. 309; Hob. 5, 1 Rolle, *Abr.*, 768, 1.[4] Sir Thomas Manwaring was no party to the action. The plaintiff must recover by his own strength.

Reply: In this case, the court could not have made a rule that the lessor should name a new lessee, for the lessor was dead.

Chief Baron [Pengelly]: Perhaps it may be too hard to change the possession because the defendant might by the advice of his counsel insist upon this, as

[1] *Anonymous* (1703), 7 Modern 150, 87 E.R. 1157.

[2] *Anonymous* (1661), 1 Siderfin 24, 82 E.R. 948; *Cole v. Terre Tenants of Skinner* (1667), 1 Siderfin 317, 82 E.R. 1130, also 2 Keble 143, 84 E.R. 90; *Addison v. Otway* (1677), 3 Keble 771, 84 E.R. 1003, also 1 Modern 250, 86 E.R. 861, 2 Modern 233, 86 E.R. 1044, 2 Ventris 31, 86 E.R. 291, 1 Freeman 227, 240, 89 E.R. 162, 171; *Anonymous* (1705), 1 Salkeld 260, 91 E.R. 228.

[3] *Addison v. Otway* (1677), *ut supra*.

[4] *Henloe v. Peters* (1672), 2 Levinz 66, 83 E.R. 452; *Anonymous* (1704), 6 Modern 309, 87 E.R. 1049; *Wilkes v. Jorden* (1613), Hobart 5, 80 E.R. 155, also Croke Jac. 332, 79 E.R. 283, 1 Rolle, Abr., *Error*, pl. A, 1, p. 768.

if you cannot assign it for error that the lessor died, so neither can you move it in arrest of judgment. But, perhaps, the court may interpose *ex gratia*. It is certain this is no irregularity. And the defendant might have had his aim and every advantage by applying to the court. As Wilbraham has said, the care of the court is that the nominal person shall do no injury to the lessor, and, therefore, he shall not release. Therefore, the plaintiffs are strictly regular, and so the defendant shall pay costs and there shall be a new [action of] ejectment.

Per CURIAM: On the payment of costs to be taxed by the Master, a new [action of] ejectment is to be delivered.

668

Barnes v. Otway

(Ex. 1727)

A writ of execution can be granted where a plaintiff in error does not file a transcription of the record in a timely manner.

Taussig MS. 311, vol. 2, p. 1039 [bis], pl. 1

Easter Term 1727.

Per CURIAM, one cannot move for liberty to take out execution unless the plaintiff in error transcribes the record within eight days until after the fourteen days for receiving errors is elapsed. Order of the House of Lords 13 July 1678.

669

Attorney General, *ex rel.* Anonymous v. Whepdale

(Ex. 1727)

The question in this case was whether relators are competent to testify as witnesses.

Taussig MS. 311, vol. 2, p. 1040

Easter term 1727.

A motion was made by *Foley* to examine the relators, saving just exceptions. He cited the precedents of Nash v. Windowes, Easter 1718, an order to examine a guardian of the plaintiff, saving just exceptions, [and] Arthur v. Thomas, Michaelmas 1722, a like order.

Quaere quid inde veniebat.

670

Benson v. Olliffe

(Ex. 1727)

Non-payment of tithes is strong evidence of a discharge, but it must be in a case where there can be a legal discharge.

The Court of Exchequer has an original jurisdiction as to tithes.

Harvard Law School MS. 1082, vol. 2, p. 27

Easter term 1727.

This was a bill brought by the plaintiff as a lay impropriator of the rectory of Bromley in the County of Middlesex. The defendant Ollyffe insisted his lands were part of a greater monastery called [*blank*] and that they came to the crown by the dissolution of the monasteries and by the Statute 31 Hen. VIII[1] were discharged from the payment of tithes. The defendant Fawden [said] his lands were part of the monastery of the Graces, but he did not properly insist upon the legal discharge of 31 Hen. VIII, but he only said that no tithes had ever been paid for these lands. This had been heard one day and was now upon the second day.

Bunbury, for the defendant Fawden: In this case, there was no instance of any payment of tithes to the plaintiff.

[To the] objection that the defendant has not properly insisted upon a sufficient defense in his answer, [he] responded it is said to be part of the monastery of Graces. And we are proper to insist upon a double defense, as part of a monastery and likewise non-payment against a lay impropriator. There arc several defenses in Fisher v. Croke.[2] Stevens, 2 vol., 48. This may be of the Cistercian order. [W.] Dugdale [*Monasticon Anglicanum*] 546; [John] Speed 602; Weaver [?] 425, new 1 vol., 466.

This is a circumstance coupled with a non-payment, and non-payment is an evidence of a discharge so that it puts the plaintiff upon showing some possession. Before the Dissolution, a layman was not capable of tithes in pernancy. The Stat. 32 Hen. VIII[3] does prescribe a method for a layman to recover. Statute of Limitations, 32 Hen. VIII;[4] you must allege seisin within sixty years to recover tithes, which are a hereditament. Parson and patron and ordinary must concur in the case of an ecclesiastical person, and, therefore, the presumption is much easier in the case of a lay impropriator, where a release will totally extinguish the tithes.

Entries of a parson's books are evidence, but entries of a lord of the manor's books are no evidence.

---

1 Stat. 31 Hen. VIII, c. 13, s. 17 (*SR*, III, 738).

2 *Fisher v. Crooke* (Ex. 1725), see above, Case No. 555.

3 Stat. 32 Hen. VIII, c. 7 (*SR*, III, 751–752).

4 Stat. 32 Hen. VIII, c. 2 (*SR*, III, 747–748).

[To the] objection that tithes of the rectory are incident to the rectory, [he] responded it may be incident, but not an incident inseparable.

The cases I before cited are very strong in this case, *viz.* Carrington v. Mashall, where an issue was directed, and Medley v. Talmley.[1]

Wills, for the defendant Ollyffe, compared this case to that of a lord of a manor, as, where non-payment has been, the possession is nothing, being only from 1700. The ministers' accounts are sufficient evidence that it is one of the greater monasteries and [was] dissolved by Stat. 31 Hen. VIII. And the exhibit shows it came into the crown the 25th [year of] Hen. VIII. And the word 'privilege' will carry tithes, as in Raymond 225, and Hanson v. Fielding, in this court.[2]

[To the] objection of the decree of Seymayne v. [*blank*], 24 Car. II,[3] [he] responded it does not appear to be the same lands.

An action at law is proper between lay persons and whether it passes by the patent; it is not a personal privilege discharged by the Statute of Dissolutions, Stat. 25 Hen. VIII.[4]

Ward, for Ollyff: The words 'liberties' and 'privileges' discharge tithes, so in this Stat. 25 Hen. VIII, and Panill v. Sir John Bendon, 6 June 1687; Hanson v. Fielding, tithes *in prender*; 4 Rept., Bozoun's Case.[5] [There was] no payment of tithes before 1700, and that was only the concession of the tenant. And this is part [. . .] of a manor. 30 April 1722, Bateman v. Nunn; Mayor of Warwick v. Lucas;[6] Corpus Christi College v. Coke.

Whenever there is a possibility of a discharge, non-payment is an evidence of such discharge. Nash v. Molins, Cro. Eliz. 206.[7] The Cistercian order might prescribe in *non decimando.* Monpesson v. Ellis, 28 Feb. 1684; Greenwood v. Granger, 1684; Hawkins v. Kettle.[8] These cases are become lay inheritances and subject to such rules, and usage is the strongest evidence and will supply a bylaw

---

[1] *Medly v. Talmy* (1696), Dodd 164, 347, 1 Rayner 81, 2 Gwillim 559, 1 Eagle & Younge 620, Public Record Office, E.126/16, f. 360.

[2] *Fosset v. Francklin* (1673), T. Raymond 225, 83 E.R. 117, also 3 Keble 208, 217, 84 E.R. 679, 684, 1 Eagle & Younge 501; *Hanson v. Fielding* (Ex. 1726), see above, Case No. 604.

[3] *Jacob v. Semayne* (1672), 1 Wood 125.

[4] Stat. 27 Hen. VIII, c. 28 (*SR*, III, 575–578).

[5] Stat. 27 Hen. VIII, c. 28 (*SR*, III, 575–578); *Hanson v. Fielding* (Ex. 1726), see above, Case No. 604; *Bozoun's Case* (1584), 4 Coke Rep. 34, 76 E.R. 970, also *sub nom. Futter v. Boorome*, Godbolt 35, 78 E.R. 22, 1 Eagle & Younge 86.

[6] *Bateman v. Nunn* (Ex. 1722), see above, Case No. 312; *see Corporation of Warwick v. Lucas* (1711), Eq. Cases Exch. 671, Public Record Office, E.126/19, ff. 191, 221.

[7] *Nash v. Molins* (1590), Croke Eliz. 206, 78 E.R. 462, also 1 Leonard 240, 74 E.R. 220, 1 Gwillim 162, 1 Eagle & Younge 100.

[8] *Greenwood v. Grainger* (Ex. 1684), Eq. Cases Exch. 209; *Hawkins v. Chittle* (Ex. 1696), Eq. Cases Exch. 358, Dodd 156, 1 Eagle & Younge 616, 1 Rayner 77, Public Record Office, E.126/16, ff. 316v, 322v, 1 Wood 356.

and likewise suppose another endowment. And usage controverts an endowment. A term is presumed to be surrendered. Lord Landsdown's Case.

Reeves, for the plaintiff: We have given sufficient proof that this was discharged by the Stat. 27 Hen. VIII and, therefore, subject to the payment of tithes.

[To the] objection that tithes will pass by the word 'privileges', [he] responded but that cannot make it stronger than the Stat. 27 Hen. VIII. It is only to rest this in the crown. But there are no words to exempt the grantee; there is no clause of exemption. 1 Cro. 422, 1 Jones 368; 2 Cro. 607.[1] And it is only a personal exemption. By the Stat. 37 Hen. VIII, chantries are not discharged.

Chief Baron [PENGELLY]: I give no opinion as to the right of an ecclesiastical person, and I must confine myself to the demand of a lay impropriator, who is the present plaintiff. And I do think that a lay impropriator is to make out a title to his demand. And the force of the evidence should be stronger than on the part of the defendant. I own that I thought upon the first hearing to decree tithes against the defendant Ollyff. And the evidence of payment then seemed stronger than the defendant's discharge, the decree of 23 Car. II.

But upon the subsequent evidence, I am doubtful because of the Statute of 25 Hen. VIII, where the word 'privileges' is mentioned. And it must be admitted that it was in the power of the crown to grant it. The words are general. And I am not satisfied that '*tot et talia*' will be sufficient to carry tithes against the crown. If the tithes remain in the crown and the Statute of 25 Hen. VIII was not laid before the court when the decree was pronounced in 23 Car. II, I think that the plaintiff ought to make out his title under the Statute of Edw. VI.[2] And I am under a greater difficulty for that there does not appear to have been any payment until after the purchase by Sir William Benson in 1700. And though there is the word 'privileges', yet proof of payment takes away such a presumption.

As to Fawden, the Statute of 32 Hen. VIII has made these impropriations lay inheritances though they belong to a clergyman and has annexed the same manner of conveyances to them, as by fines and recoveries, and subject to the same rules of law, as any lay inheritance is. 1 Inst. 159[3] confirms it.

All presumptions are to be taken strongly in favor of non-payment. It was intended to sever these inheritances from the clergy. And it was political to do it. And even in Queen Mary's time, there was an express saving of the right of nobles [?] and any other person's right to these lay inheritances so granted as aforesaid. [. . .]er v. Tryon. Length of time is an evidence of a discharge. Bishop

---

[1] *Sydowne v. Holme* (1635), Croke Car. 422, 79 E.R. 967, W. Jones 368, 82 E.R. 193, 2 Gwillim 479, 1 Eagle & Younge 383; *Gerrard v. Wright* (1621), Croke Jac. 607, 79 E.R. 518, also Hobart 306, 80 E.R. 449, W. Jones 2, 82 E.R. 2, 1 Gwillim 375, 1 Eagle & Younge 289.

[2] Stat. 2 & 3 Edw. VI, c. 13 (*SR*, IV, 55–58).

[3] E. Coke, *First Institute* (1628), f. 159a.

of Winchester's Case, 2 Rept.; Yelverton 2.[1] And non-payment will operate by way of an extinguishment of the right, as a grant or release may be presumed. If the plaintiff brought his action on the Statute of Edw. VI and *nil debet* is pleaded, the evidence of non-payment would influence the jury. The non-payment is so far an evidence as to turn the proof of the possession in the plaintiff. Slade v. Drake, Hobart 300.[2] Discharge in abbots must be *a posteriori*. Cro. Eliz., Nash v. Molines, 1 Leonard 240; Archbishop of Canterbury, 48.[3]

The general way of pleading such a defense is good, for they might be discharged within forty or fifty years. A lay person might release, for it is 190 years since Edward VI's time. There is sufficient [matter] to put payment in issue. Hardres 322, Page's Case;[4] Carrington v. Mashal, 4 Jac., an issue was directed. Town of Warwick v. Lucas, 1710; Fisher v. Croke, the answer was uncertain; Medley v. Talmley, 9 Will. III.

And I think that this opinion is agreeable to the common law with the authority in this court. And I must construe it as to lay inheritances.

And as to the defendant Fawden, the bill must be dismissed, but as to the defendant Ollyffe, an action ought to be brought on the Statute of Edw. VI. But I would retain the bill until that is tried.

Baron Hale: I should not be averse to the plaintiff's trying this cause as to the defendant Ollyffe. And as to Fawdon, I am doubtful, for the court has not thought fit to let non-payment alone to be a discharge. I do allow non-payment [to be] very strong evidence against the plaintiff's claim. And there does not seem to be any conscience in the complainant's bill to demand tithes where the impropriator never received any. If this was *res integra*, I should incline to dismiss the bill. But I think that a *non decimando* has never yet been allowed.

Carter: I cannot see that the plaintiff has any right whatsoever to demand these tithes from Ollyffe or Fawdon. And this case differs from that of an ecclesiastical person. The plaintiff or his father never purchased these tithes. And the plaintiff does not want the assistance of this court, or, if he did, I should not assist him. The decree read is doubtful. I will not hinder the plaintiff's trying his right.

Baron Comyns: It appeared on the first day strong proof in favor of Ollyffe. And this could not come to the crown by 27 Hen. VIII, for that Statute commences from 4 February 27 Hen. VIII, and this was surrendered 23 Hen. VIII. I do not see that this case materially differs from the Hospitalers of St. John of

---

1 *Wright v. Wright* (1596), 2 Coke Rep. 38, 76 E.R. 501, also Moore K.B. 425, 72 E.R. 672, Croke Eliz. 475, 511, 78 E.R. 726, 760, 1 Gwillim 167, 1 Eagle & Younge 119.

2 *Slade v. Drake* (1617), Hobart 295, 80 E.R. 439, also Noy 97, 74 E.R. 1063, W. Jones 6, 82 E.R. 5, 2 Rolle Rep. 250, 81 E.R. 780, 1 Gwillim 385, 1 Eagle & Younge 314.

3 *Nash v. Molins* (1590), *ut supra*; *Green v. Balser* (1596), 2 Coke Rep. 46, 76 E.R. 519, 1 Gwillim 189, 1 Eagle & Younge 113.

4 *Page's Case* (1663), Hardres 322, 145 E.R. 478, 2 Gwillim 513, 1 Eagle & Younge 438.

Jerusalem under the Statute of 32 Hen. VIII. And I shall concur with My Lord Chief Baron to have it tried. And so I should incline as to Fawdon.

As to the argument of non-payment, I allow it to be strong evidence of a discharge. But it must be in cases where there can be a legal discharge. Cro. Eliz. and Leonard agree in this.

But upon the Stat. 27 Hen. VIII, there could be no legal discharge. Non-payment is insufficient under an abbey dissolved by 27 Hen. VIII because there can be no legal discharge under that Statute. By the dissolution of the body, the privilege is sunk and ceased.

[To the] objection as to the distinction between a layman and a spiritual person, [he] answered it requires great consideration, but I do not at present see any great difference between a layman and an ecclesiastical person, for, where tithes are granted to a layman, he stands in the same place as a spiritual person.

I concur that they are become lay inheritances, but that is a *non sequitur* that the lay impropriator is to show a better title to the tithes than the ecclesiastical person ought to do.

If a spiritual person may prescribe *in non decimando* but a layman cannot but whether political, I cannot determine, for the presumption is the same. A lay person may alone release. A parson, patron, and ordinary may join. But the discharge before the Dissolution must be [by] spiritual persons, for no presumption can run since the Statute of Dissolutions. Why can one prescribe antecedent to the Statute?

Several things are not capable of a presumption, for, though the king may prescribe, yet his patentee cannot. Hardres 315;[1] 1 Rolle, *Abridgment*, 566.

As to pleading an uncertain way, and [in] general, it has been allowed in this court. There is no difference between the right in equity and at law. This court has an original jurisdiction as to tithes. And I would have both tried.

Chief Baron [PENGELLY]: I am willing to give the plaintiff an opportunity of trying it. The case as to Carrington was an issue. Thorngate v. Wallop, 26 August 12 Will. III.[2] Let the plaintiff bring his action against Ollyffe and Fawdon.

[For later proceedings in this case, see Benton v. Olive (1730), Bunbury 284, 145 E.R. 675, 2 Gwillim 701, 2 Eagle & Younge 24.]

---

[1] *Campost v. Anonymous* (1662), Hardres 315, 145 E.R. 475, 2 Gwillim 514, 1 Eagle & Younge 437.

[2] *Thorngate v. Wallop* (1700), Dodd 192, 1 Rayner 93, 1 Eagle & Younge 636, Public Record Office, E.126/17, f. 167, 1 Wood 396.

671

Cross v. Fursman

(Ex. 1727)

An ecclesiastical court will be prohibited from trying an issue that has been already finally determined in a common law court, such as bigamy.

Harvard Law School MS. 1082, vol. 2, p. 31, pl. 1

Trinity term 1727. Cross v. Sarah Fursman.

Serjeant *Chapple* [moved] for [a writ of] prohibition. The prosecution below is against Sarah Collins for taking upon her the name of Cross. 3 Modern 164, Lloyd v. Lloyd.[1] He produced an affidavit whereby it appeared that Frevel Cross was indicted for marrying Sarah Fursman, his first wife Sarah Collins being alive. And upon that verdict, he was acquitted.

Chief Baron [PENGELLY] said that, if the defendant was to be permitted to prosecute below, it would be to falsify the verdict.

CARTER: The indictment was against Frevel Cross for marrying Sarah, his first wife being alive.

COMYNS: I am doubtful, for there might be an acquittal for want of proof at that time.

CHIEF BARON: The libel admits that Frevel Cross and Sarah Collins lived together as man and wife.

COMYNS: If it was in the case of a conviction, it would be stronger than in this case.

CHIEF BARON: Cohabitation is *prima facie* a proof of a marriage. And he still insisted that, if this matter was to be drawn in question below, it might impeach the verdict. And nothing is doing below to endeavor to trip up this verdict. And, therefore, if this is to be suffered, it will control the temporal courts and so, at last, come to construe acts of Parliament.

COMYNS: Whenever I differ from My Lord Chief Baron, I am diffident in my judgment. But the question is whether this acquittal determines the point in the spiritual court. And I think that it does not determine the question at law because Collins might not prove the first marriage or the second. Therefore, there is no conclusion to be drawn upon it either one way or another.

Chief Baron [PENGELLY] insisted on the first opinion, and if the ecclesiastical court should determine this point contrary to the determination on the indictment and, though there might be a defect of evidence, yet the man being in jeopardy of his life once, that ought to be final. Boyle v. Boyle is a case in point.

---

[1] *Boyle v. Boyle* (1688), 3 Modern 164, 87 E.R. 106, also Comberbach 72, 90 E.R. 350.

Creuys [?], for the plaintiff, cited Cro. Jac. 535, 625; 2 Rolle, *Abridgment*, 304, pl. 5, Bary's Case.[1] If they proceed in the ecclesiastical court for drunkenness where the matters have been determined by the justices of the peace, the court will grant a [writ of] prohibition. Serle v. Williams; Salkeld 552.[2]

[They] ordered a prohibition *nisi*.

[Later proceedings in this case are reported at Harvard Law School MS. 1082, vol. 2, p. 38.]

672

Idle, *qui tam* v. Vanheck

(Ex. 1727)

Where goods are imported illegally, the ship is forfeited to the crown whether the master of the vessel has knowledge of the smuggling or not.

Bunbury 230, 145 E.R. 657

16 May 1727.

An information was brought upon the Stat. 12 Car. II, c. 8, s. 4,[3] for a ship forfeited by bringing over goods from Rotterdam, not being the place of their growth.

Upon the trial, the defence was that these goods were brought either by the passengers or the mariners without the knowledge or privity of the master. And, therefore, it would be hard to subject this ship to a forfeiture by an act he could not help, and much harder upon the defendant, who was the owner, that he should lose the ship. And he cited the Stat. 27 Edw., c. 19; 38 Edw. III, c. 8.[4]

But Lord Chief Baron Pengelly said that his (then) present thoughts were that knowledge in the master was not necessary, for the Act is an express prohibition without any limitation or restriction. And the fact proved comes directly within the description of the Act. The forfeiture is upon the goods themselves and upon the person. The intention of the law was the support of trade, and, therefore, we may presume it was that all persons should take the utmost care that trade should be carried on without any fraud. The owner is to take care what master he employs; the master what mariners and what passengers he takes in. And being *exercitor navis* and having the entire control of the ship, he may search and examine where and when he will. And no damage accrues to the owner, for he may recover against the master of the ship forfeited by his default. And, as he

[1] *Webb v. Cook* (1619), Croke Jac. 535, 626, 79 E.R. 459, 538; *Berrie's Case* (1612), 2 Rolle, Abr., *Prohibition*, pl. R, 5, p. 304.

[2] *Searle v. Williams* (1620), Hobart 288, 80 E.R. 433; *Galizard v. Rigault* (1702), 2 Salkeld 552, 91 E.R. 467, also 2 Lord Raymond 809, 92 E.R. 40, 7 Modern 78, 87 E.R. 1106, Holt K.B. 50, 597, 90 E.R. 926, 1230.

[3] Stat. 12 Car. II, c. 18, s. 4 (*SR*, V, 247).

[4] Stat. 27 Edw. III, stat. 2, c. 19 (*SR*, I, 340); Stat. 38 Edw. III, stat. 1, c. 8 (*SR*, I, 384).

then thought, the master might, against a passenger who created a forfeiture by his act. And there is the more reason he should suffer by this because he has the benefit of the freight of these very goods which occasioned the forfeiture. The master is to report, and, therefore, he is obliged to see what he does report.

There was a case cited, Foster, *qui tam* v. Phillips, in an information on the same Statute, Trinity 1722, where it was said the then Lord Chief Baron [Montagu] was of the same opinion.

Note: Afterwards, it appeared it was not necessary to determine this point, which the Chief Baron would have reserved to the defendant for the opinion of the court, for the jury found the defendant had actual knowledge of the goods.

Note: A new trial was moved for in this cause 11 June 1727, and, upon the motion, all the four barons were of opinion that notice in the master was not necessary to create a forfeiture upon this Act of Parliament, though, for a small matter, they thought it would be hard that a ship should be condemned.

There was cited by Baron Comyns, Malines' *Lex Mercatoria*, edit. Jac. I; Statute Staple, 27 Edw. III, c. 19;[1] and by the Chief Baron [Pengelly], Molloy, 204, 209, 10, 11, 12, 23, 24; 1 Siderfin 298, Husey v. Pusey.[2]

Harvard Law School MS. 1082, vol. 2, p. 33

Trinity term 1727.

This was an information for importing goods whereby the ship was forfeited on the Stat. 12 Car. II. And there was a verdict for the king, but with a liberty to move for a new trial.

Serjeant *Belfield* moved for a new trial for this ship called the *Mary and Johanna*. And he insists in this case that there was no proof that the defendant, the master [Vanneck], had any notice of these goods being concealed or imported. And it must be intended that the master had notice or it would destroy the building of ships or the being concerned in any. 38 Edw. III, cap. 8. There was no actual proof of the privity of the master, but only Fisher, the evidence, said that the defendant declared he was undone 166 pounds of tea [and] 68 pieces of silk.

Bootle, for the defendant: These goods were never imported. And the act of the sailor ought not to affect the owner of the ship.

Attorney General [*Yorke*]: There must be frequent interpretations upon this Act of Navigation in relation to the knowledge of the master. And it is objected that it was a verdict without evidence. But there was no occasion for precise proof of the knowledge of the master. And the presumption is that he did know of it. This Act is a full prohibition for the benefit of navigation. And if the fact is

---

1 G. Malynes, *Consuetudo vel Lex Mercatoria* (1622); Stat. 27 Edw. III, stat. 2, c. 19 (*SR*, I, 340).

2 C. Molloy, *De Jure Maritimo et Navali*; *Hussey v. Pusy* (1666), 1 Siderfin 298, 82 E.R. 1117, also 1 Levinz 188, 83 E.R. 362, 2 Keble 88, 84 E.R. 55.

proved, the forfeiture is incurred. The master has the general care of the ship, and he is answerable for the whole.

Bunbury, for the king, cited 2 Salkeld 460; Ford v. Tilly.[1]

Chief Baron [PENGELLY]: This is a case of great consequence with respect to the crown and the subject. It seemed to me that actual proof of the knowledge of the master was not required. The property of the owner is bound by the act of the master, for the owner has his remedy. I have no doubt that, if passengers' goods were brought, that were prohibited because the owner has a benefit by the freight of such goods, that, therefore, that incurs a forfeiture. As to prohibited goods imported or brought in by seamen, I had some doubt whether the ship should be forfeited. The evidence was only for goods of passengers. And this verdict was given by a jury of gentlemen, and there were circumstances and a reasonable evidence for the verdict given. And yet perhaps it may be proper for a re-examination because it may be too hard to bind the property of the subject forever.

The affidavit that you had other evidence is not of itself sufficient for granting a new trial. This is an information *in rem*. And, therefore, I am not against a re-examination. I should be glad to have the opinion whether this was sufficient evidence as to the knowledge of the master. And the question is whether this does not turn the proof onto the defendant to protect his goods. But there was a defective evidence on the part of the defendant.

Small parcels ought not to affect the master. And I should be glad to know whether, upon the state of the affidavit, a new trial will be of any benefit.

HALE: There is no occasion for a new trial, either upon the affidavit or the point of law. The affidavit is fallacious. And mariners cannot bring such a quantity of goods as these without the privity of the master. And it is not incumbent on the crown to prove notice.

CARTER: The want of a witness is no reason for a new trial. And the affidavit is fallacious. The goods appear to be concealed. And if notice is required, the Act of Parliament will be of no effect. So I am not for a new trial.

COMYNS agrees that there should be no new trial. If the Attorney General proves the offense in the information, that is sufficient. And there is no occasion to prove anything more. 27 Edw. III, 19, Statute Staple. If the verdict was not against the evidence, there ought not to be any new trial.

CHIEF BARON: If the question of notice is not material, then nothing remains for a foundation for a new trial; though I would not conclude the defendant, yet where the information sets forth the whole case, I cannot go out of it. The Act intended to grant a prohibition in the strongest terms. And though the defendant has the misfortune to lose his ship, yet, for the sake of government and the nation and to avoid the eluding of the Act of Parliament, it is best to put this construction on it. And, therefore, I cannot grant a new trial.

[1] *Regina v. Wigg* (1705), 2 Salkeld 460, 91 E.R. 397, also 2 Lord Raymond 1163, 92 E.R. 269; *Ford v. Tilly*, 2 Salkeld 653, 91 E.R. 556.

Molloy agrees with this. And an owner is liable for the default of the master and so shall a master be for the default of his seamen. Molloy 204, 9, 10, 11, 12, 23, 24; Morse v. Slice, in Ventris and Levinz; 1 Siderfin 298, Halsey v. [*blank*].[1] The law has provided a proper remedy.

673

Rex v. Bulley

(Ex. 1727)

An inquisition on a writ of extent will be quashed where the owners of the property being levied upon are not allowed to prove their ownership.

Bunbury 233, 145 E.R. 657, Conroy 120

3 June 1727.

Henry Bulley was indebted in £395 7s. 6d. to Blommart before April 1727. And Blommart was also bound with him to the crown to the value of £300, in consideration whereof Bulley, by two bills of sale of the 8th and 24th of April 1727, assigned to him sixty hogsheads of tobacco, which was to pay him for the £395 7s. 6d. lent by Blommart; the remainder to continue in his hands to secure him against the bond wherein he was security for Bulley.

Upon the 27th of April, a [writ of] extent issued against Bulley, upon which, by warrant from the sheriff, the officer broke open the door of the cellar where Blommart had lodged forty of the hogsheads of tobacco and seized them for the crown.

Blommart was advised to make the best inquiry he could when the inquisition would be taken on the extent, and, accordingly, he did in order to give evidence that these tobaccos were not now the property of Bulley, but, before the extent, were conveyed to him for a valuable consideration. As it appeared by the affidavits, the Secondary of the Compter in Wood Street and his clerk and other officers had been guilty of great shuffling and evasions to prevent Blommart from knowing the time and place of executing the inquisition. And this was not contradicted by any affidavit on the other side.

Therefore, upon this fact, we moved to set aside the inquisition so irregularly taken that we might have an opportunity to assert our property and not be put to the expense, difficulty, and hazard of pleading our property. And we insisted on the statutes 34 Edw. III, c. 13; 36 Edw. III, c. 13; 1 Hen. VIII, c. 8; 2 & 3 Edw. VI, c. 8,[2] all which statutes, though they related to freeholds and chattels real, show the

[1] *Morse v. Slue* (1672–1673), 1 Ventris 190, 238, 86 E.R. 129, 159, 2 Levinz 69, 83 E.R. 453, also Sir T. Raymond 220, 83 E.R. 115, 2 Keble 866, 84 E.R. 548, 3 Keble 72, 112, 135, 84 E.R. 601, 624, 638, 1 Modern 85, 86 E.R. 752, Lincoln's Inn MS. Misc. 500, ff. 207v, 215 (Edward Ward's reports); *Hussey v. Pusy* (1666), *ut supra.*

[2] Stat. 34 Edw. III, c. 13 (*SR*, I, 368); Stat. 36 Edw. III, c. 13 (*SR*, I, 374); Stat. 1

care of the legislature as to the property of the subject and that inquisitions ought to be taken openly, and not privily. And the Statute of Edw. VI implied, at least, that the subject had a right to have his property found on an inquisition. And we also insisted much on the form of the writ of extent, that the sheriff was to inquire *per sacramentum etc. et omnibus aliis viis, mediis, et modis etc.*

Mr. Attorney General [*Yorke*], in answer, admitted the facts as alleged in the affidavit, but he insisted that the party had no right of being permitted to give evidence in this case, but ought to resort to a plea of his property, first, because this has not been the practice; secondly, nor usual to give notice of executing these inquisitions, this being only in the nature of an office; thirdly, admitting it to be irregular, yet that is not a sufficient reason to set aside the inquisition.

But *per* TOTAM CURIAM, the extent and inquisition ought to be superseded, the return of the extent being out, with liberty to take a new extent of the same date as the first. And they laid great stress upon the statutes cited, though they related only to freeholds and chattels real, and also upon the mandatory part in the writ of extent. And it is not enough to say it has not been the practice, unless it can be shown that the practice has been to the contrary. And notice in this case cannot be given because everybody may be concerned, and, therefore, there is nobody particularly to give notice to. But, if a party is there and offers witnesses to prove his property, they ought by law to be admitted; otherwise, the difficulty would be very great upon the subject, for, first, before a plea, he must give security; secondly, he can have no remedy by action against the sheriff because the inquisition has found the goods to be Bulley's, which would screen him against Blommart or other person or any other way; thirdly, he can have no costs or damages if he succeeds in his plea. And it was observed the Statute mentioned might take no notice of mere personals at that time because they were of little value, but have, since, been much increased.

Note that, in a commission of lunacy, there are the very same words in the writ of inquiry, as in this case, and, now, it is usual to give notice there. And the Lord Chief Baron [PENGELLY] thought they should go as far as they could in this case, for this is a right the king had not at common law, but by the Stat. 33 Hen. VIII.[1] And he said he himself had attended on inquisitions on outlawries and on *elegit*s.

Harvard Law School MS. 1082, vol. 2, p. 32

Trinity term 1727.

Bunbury moved to set aside an inquisition because the Secondary trifled with the defendant and would not permit the defendant to show his property before the jury. 1 Hen. VIII, cap. 8; 34 Edw. III, cap. 13; 36 Edw. III, 13; 2 & 3 of Edw. VI.

Hen. VIII, c. 8 (*SR*, III, 4–5); Stat. 2 & 3 Edw. VI, c. 8 (*SR*, IV, 47–78).

[1] Stat. 33 Hen. VIII, c. 39, s. 37 (*SR*, III, 886–887).

Chief Baron [Pengelly]: The former and all the acts extend to all officers in the same degree, and so it extends to the sheriff who acts by virtue of a commission. By the acts, the officers were obliged to hear everything openly and to prevent vexation and hardship. And when an inquisition is taken, all parties are to be heard, as well those on the part of the crown as the subject. And it is of great consequence to the crown that all the subject's property should be taken care of. It appears by the facts in this case that there is a malfeasance in the officer and that the Secondary has acted contrary to his duty. And the inquisition is not well taken unless all parties are heard that desire it. And the entering the claim does not alter the case.

The crown has a proper remedy by commission or otherwise to find these goods the property of Bully. And there may be a particular commission [. . .] endorsed another commission, and it was granted in Lord Chief Justice Glynne's time [1655–1659]. It is stronger in this case because the goods were in the possession of Blomart. And this was a shift and evasion in Benson, the Secondary. And though this does not try the property finally, yet the officer ought to hear everything and all persons. The officers of the crown are contributory to the misbehavior of this officer.

Traverses are given by the statutes as to the realty, but not at common law. And the subject was entitled to it only in the personalty. The party defendant has no remedy for his costs or anything for the delay from the crown. This is only a lien from the date of the inquisition. So he concluded for quashing it.

Hale: I am a friend to notice and think that the inquisition should be quashed.

Carter agreed. It seems to be a fraud and a contrivance in the officers.

Comyns: There appears to be a shuffle in the undersheriff. It is necessary to hear all parties. But I am doubtful whether the sheriff is obliged to hear everything. If the course of the court was consistent with the practice of hearing all parties upon an inquisition, I agree that, in cases of personalty, the party might always traverse, but not in the realty until the statutes before mentioned. But I think that the crown has a remedy by an information. So, at last, though unwillingly, he concluded for quashing the inquisition.

Chief Baron: Counsel attend upon inquisitions *de lunatico*, outlawries, and *elegit*s.

The information was quashed.

674

Harman v. Immings

(Ex. 1727)

An arbitral award that is substantially correct will not be set aside.

Taussig MS. 311, vol. 2, p. 1050

Friday, 9th June 1727.

Chief Baron [PENGELLY]: Little nice objections against an award are not to be received, but, if the award is grossly void, My Lord Chief Justice Holt used to say it would be very hard for a court to grant an attachment against a man for not performing an award, the performance of which could never have been compelled by an action and which would be notoriously unjust.

675

Porter v. Hatfield

(Ex. 1727)

Appearing by an attorney does not waive a defendant's right to object to the jurisdiction of the court.

Harvard Law School MS. 1082, vol. 2, p. 31, pl. 2

Trinity term 1727.

Bootle, for the plaintiff: The defendant pleads in abatement that he is clerk to Edward Ventris, Esq. The plaintiff replies and prays that the appearance may be recorded and Mr. Owen appeared for the defendant and the plaintiff demurs and the defendant joins in demurrer, that, by the appearance of Owen for the defendant, the jurisdiction of the court is admitted, as much as if the defendant had imparled or put in bail, see Dyer 33; Moore 34; 1 Ventris 154; 2 Rolle Rept. 50, 88; Lutwyche 22, 24; 1 Salkeld 277, Kempe v. Goodal; Hobart 206.[1]

Kettleby, for the defendant: The plea in abatement is good notwithstanding the appearance, for the defendant is forced to appear, and he cannot appear but by attorney. And it is not like the case in 3 Levinz 343, Dashwood v. [*blank*].[2] The putting in of bail does not give a jurisdiction. Griffith v. Landen, in Jones. But I do admit that it would be too late after a plea is pleaded.

---

[1] *Anonymous* (1537), 1 Dyer 33, 73 E.R. 74; *Anonymous* (1561), Moore K.B. [33], 72 E.R. 422; *Anonymous v. Hicks* (1671), 1 Ventris 154, 86 E.R. 105, also 2 Keble 824, 84 E.R. 521; *Anonymous v. Fortescue* (1618), 2 Rolle Rep. 50, 88, 81 E.R. 652, 677; *Bartelot v. Burton* (1687), 1 Lutwyche 22, 125 E.R. 12; *Kemp v. Goodal* (1705), 1 Salkeld 277, 91 E.R. 242, also 2 Lord Raymond 1154, 92 E.R. 263; *Speake v. Richards* (1617), Hobart 206, 80 E.R. 353, also Moore K.B. 886, 72 E.R. 974, 2 Shower K.B. 281, 89 E.R. 940, Hutton 11, 123 E.R. 1065, 1 Brownlow & Goldesborough 51, 123 E.R. 659, Noy 22, 74 E.R. 992.

[2] *Dashwood v. Folks* (1692), 3 Levinz 340, 83 E.R. 719, also Fortescue 342, 92 E.R. 882.

Bootle replies: The defendant was not under any necessity to appear by an attorney, but he ought to do it in person. In 3 Levinz 343, there was a necessity, but it is no answer to the case cited by me in Dyer.

Chief Baron [PENGELLY]: The case in Dyer is not in point. And all the cases since are against what has been alleged by Mr. Bootle, for I do not think that the defendant by his appearance is excluded from the benefit of his plea of privilege. And the party cannot plead it until he is in court. And, therefore, it is not inconsistent or contradictory. Salkeld 1, 2.[1]

There is a difference between this appearance and asking for an imparlance, for the first is of necessity, but the last is the grace of the court. So the plea in abatement was allowed, and the demurrer was overruled.

CARTER cited [the Case of] the Company of Ironmongers in Chester.[2] And there is a necessity to plead in this manner. And the putting in of bail does not take away this privilege.

COMYNS agreed and cited Salkeld, Stroud v. Gerrard.

Taussig MS. 311, vol. 2, p. 1048

Friday, 9th June 1727.

An [action of] case [was brought] by the plaintiff against the defendant, who appears by Owen, an attorney of the Exchequer. And he pleads the privilege of the King's Bench, as one of Ventris's clerks. Dier 33.

Per Bootle: Appearing by an attorney of this court, he has affirmed the jurisdiction of this court. And it is equivalent to an imparlance. And to this purpose is the case in Dier; Moor 34; 1 Ventr. 154, Sir William Hicks' Case; 2 Rolle's Rep. 50, 88; Bro., Estop., 24; 1 Lutw. 24,[3] no plea after an imparlance; 1 Lutw. 22, it is proper by way of demurrer; 1 Salkeld 277; Hob. 206.

Kettleby: If we cannot appear but by one of the attorneys of this court, then appearing by an attorney is no admission. 3 Lev. 343, Dashwood v. Folkes. Putting in special bail is not admitting the jurisdiction because one is not in court before bail. Griffith v. Landen Jones. In this court, we plead our privilege and annex our writ *sub pede sigilli* in aid of our plea.

Bootle: He may appear in person; so he is under no necessity of appearing by Owen. And this distinguishes this case from the case in Levinz; Griffith and Jones is not upon this point.

---

[1] *Stroud v. Gerrard* (1707), 1 Salkeld 8, 91 E.R. 7, 2 Salkeld 710, 91 E.R. 598.

[2] *Company of Chester Mercers and Ironmongers v. Bowker* (1725), 1 Strange 639, 93 E.R. 751.

[3] *Anonymous* (1537), 1 Dyer 33, 73 E.R. 74; *Anonymous* (1561), Moore K.B. [33], 72 E.R. 422; *Anonymous v. Hicks* (1671), *ut supra*; *Anonymous v. Fortescue* (1618), *ut supra*; YB Mich. 35 Hen. VI, f. 35, pl. 44 (1456), Brooke, Abr., *Estoppell*, pl. 24; *Bartelot v. Burton* (1687), 1 Lutwyche 22, 24, 125 E.R. 12, 13.

Chief Baron [Pengelly]: There is nothing contradictory between his appearing by an attorney and being an attorney himself. But if a man appears by such a name, he then shall never deny it afterwards. 1 Salk. 1 & 1 & 2. And there is a great difference between an imparlance and an appearance, for an imparlance is by the grace of the court, which, when a man has desired it, he shall not deny the jurisdiction of that court. So judgment must be that the bill abate.

Ceteri barones aggreaverunt.

Comyns: It has been doubted formerly whether the privilege shall be allowed but only by a writ of privilege, but he might always have pleaded it. Salkeld 8, Stroud v. Lady Gerrard, putting in bail by the name of Elizabeth.

Manuscripts And Printed Reports Included

[References are to case numbers, not page numbers.]

British Library MS. Add. 35997, 569
British Library MS. Add. 36651, 43, 44, 59, 89, 384
British Library MS. Hargrave 70, 13, 157, 473, 629
British Library MS. Hargrave 367, 52
Columbia Law School MS. Singleton 4a, 33
Harvard Law School MS. 1082, *passim*
Harvard Law School MS. 1105, 569
Harvard Law School MS. 1162, 13, 157, 473, 629
Indiana Univ. Lilly Library MS. 'Cases in the Exch., vol. 5' (Robert Price's reports), 4, 7
Inner Temple MS. Mitford 32, 5, 14
Lincoln's Inn MS. Misc. 12, 262, 602
Lincoln's Inn MS. Misc. 123, 160
Lincoln's Inn MS. Misc. 177, 564
Lincoln's Inn MS. Misc. 506, 192, 569
Public Record Office E.126, 285, 537, 579
Taussig MS. 311, *passim*

Ambler, C., *Reports*, 582
Bunbury, W., *Reports, passim*
Comyns, J., *Reports*, 31, 602, 631, 633, 643, 648, 649, 653
Equity Cases Abridged, 63, 104, 160, 193, 602, 610
Fortescue, J., *Reports*, 34, 38
Gilbert, J., *Reports*, 307, 403, 413, 515, 567, 568, 569, 603, 604, 605, 606, 610, 614
Gwillim, H., *Tithe Cases, passim*
Modern Reports, vol. 8, 340, 413, 475, 493
Modern Reports, vol. 9, 441
Modern Reports, vol. 11, 381
Parker, T., *Reports*, 32
Peere Williams, W., *Reports*, 602
Rayner, J., *Tithe Cases, passim*
Strange, J., *Reports*, 38, 92, 403, 564, 569, 611
Swanston, C. T., *Reports*, 582
Viner, C., *Abridgment*, 4, 104, 160, 193, 620
Wightwick, J., *Reports*, 41

Index of Names of Persons and Places

[References are to case numbers, not page numbers.
This index does not include judges' and lawyers' names.]

Subject Index

[These references are to case numbers, not page numbers.]

REPORTS OF CASES IN THE COURT OF EXCHEQUER IN THE TIME OF KING GEORGE I

(1714 TO 1727)

MEDIEVAL AND RENAISSANCE TEXTS AND STUDIES

VOLUME 452

CENTER FOR LAW REPORTING

VOLUME 4

REPORTS OF CASES IN THE COURT OF EXCHEQUER IN THE TIME OF KING GEORGE I (1714 TO 1727)

Volume I:
Cases 1 to 402

EDITED BY

W. H. BRYSON

ARIZONA CENTER FOR MEDIEVAL
ACMRS
AND RENAISSANCE STUDIES

Tempe, Arizona
2014

THE ARIZONA CENTER FOR
MEDIEVAL & RENAISSANCE
STUDIES

Published by ACMRS (Arizona Center for Medieval and Renaissance Studies)
Tempe, Arizona

Library of Congress Cataloging-in-Publication Data

Great Britain. Court of Exchequer.
Reports of cases in the Court of Exchequer in the time of King George I (1714 to 1727) / edited by W.H. Bryson.
pages cm. -- (Medieval and renaissance texts and studies ; volume 452) (Center for law reporting ; volume 4)
Includes index.
ISBN 978-0-86698-503-1 (alk. paper)
1. Law reports, digests, etc.--England--History--18th century. 2. Finance, Public--Law and legislation--England--History--18th century--Cases. I. Bryson, William Hamilton, 1941- editor. II. Title.
KD208 1714 .R47 A2 2014
346.42'00409033--dc23

2014026829

∞
This book is made to last. It is set in Adobe Caslon Pro,
smyth-sewn and printed on acid-free paper to library specifications.
Printed in the United States of America

This book
is dedicated to the memory of

WILLIAM WALLER HENING
(1767–1828)

a member of the bar of Richmond, Virginia,
a law reporter, editor of statutes,
and legal scholar.

Preface

This book publishes all of the known law reports from the Court of Exchequer from the reign of King George I, 1714 to 1726, including those in manuscript and those already in print. Most of the ones in print are the short and not very informative reports by William Bunbury. The much more substantial Exchequer reports of Philip Ward and Thomas Browne, which were heretofore unpublished manuscripts, have been conflated with Bunbury's reports and some other miscellaneous case reports.

Philip Ward's reports are published here with the kind permission of Mr. Anthony Taussig, the owner of the single surviving manuscript copy. The reports of Thomas Browne are published here with the kind permission of the Harvard University Law School, the owner of the sole manuscript. We are much in their debt for acquiring these manuscript books, carefully preserving them, and then for making them available to the public in this book.

I would also like to thank the special collection librarians and their staffs at Lincoln's Inn, Harvard University Law School, the University of Virginia Law School, and the University of Richmond Law School for their unfailing courtesies and assistance. I would also like to acknowledge the kind assistance of Rebecca Campbell Cape of the Lilly Library at Indiana University and of Whitney S. Bagnall of the Columbia University Law School library.

Introduction

This volume is an edition of all of the cases from the Court of Exchequer during the reign of King George I, 1714 to 1727, which have been found to date. It includes a new edition of the reports already in print as well as those found only in manuscript. The three major sources of reports are those of William Bunbury, Thomas Browne, and Philip Ward. Although Bunbury's Exchequer reports have been in print since 1755, they are somewhat brief, and the manuscript reports of the same cases add considerable information to them.

The Court of Exchequer

The high court of exchequer evolved within the exchequer department of the English government, the royal treasury, in the middle ages in order to determine legal disputes over the royal revenue.[1] With the rise in international commerce by the English after the defeat of the Spanish Armada in 1588 and the Dutch navy in the middle of the seventeenth century and with the enactment of numerous excise and import taxes, the revenue side of the court became much more important in the time of King George I than it ever had been in the middle ages. Later in the middle ages, the court of exchequer began to hear common law disputes between private persons on the theory that this would assist in the collection of the royal revenue because the plaintiff was a debtor to the crown and, if he could collect his debts, he could then pay his own obligations to the king.[2] In the middle of the sixteenth century, the court of exchequer developed an equity side of its jurisdiction so that it could grant equitable remedies as long as there was some connection to the crown and its revenue.[3] In 1649, by means of fictitious allegations of jurisdiction that could not be challenged in court, the

---

[1] See generally J. Manning, *Practice of the Court of Exchequer, Revenue Branch* (2nd ed. 1827).

[2] See generally H. Wurzel, 'The Origin and Development of Quo Minus', *Yale Law Journal*, vol. 49, pp. 39–64 (1939); P. Burton, *Practice of the Office of Pleas in the Court of Exchequer* (1791).

[3] See generally W. H. Bryson, *The Equity Side of the Exchequer* (1975); H. Horwitz, *Exchequer Equity Records and Proceedings 1649–1841* (2001); D. B. Fowler, *Practice of the Court of Exchequer upon Proceedings in Equity* (2nd ed. 1817).

exchequer extended its jurisdiction to all civil cases of common law and equity without limitation.[4]

The court of exchequer was presided over by the chief baron and three puisne barons. When the court sat to hear equity cases, the four barons were joined on the bench by the lord treasurer of England and by the chancellor of the exchequer. However, by the time of George I, the treasury was always in commission and so there was no lord treasurer. In practice, the chancellor of the exchequer never sat, that office being held by Sir Robert Walpole (1676–1745), who was much too busy with the general affairs of the kingdom.[5]

The court of exchequer had concurrent equity jurisdiction with the court of chancery. However, the exchequer was a collegial court of four to six judges, but the lord chancellor decided cases as a single judge. Although the court of exchequer heard revenue, common law, and equity cases, these three jurisdictions were kept separate procedurally and clerically. The barons heard common law cases one day and equity cases another, as did the court of chancery. The court of common pleas and the court of king's bench had no equity jurisdiction.

The judges of the Court of Exchequer during the reign of King George I were generally very good, the most notable being Sir Jeffrey Gilbert (1674–1726). It is interesting to note that there were six chief barons during the short, twelve-year reign of George I. Whereas the chief baron immediately preceding the accession of George I in 1714 was Edward Ward (1638–1714), who held the office for nineteen years, the office was quickly fatal to five of King George's chief barons, the sixth being quickly promoted to the office of Chief Justice of the Court of Common Pleas.[6] Thus, the average tenure was only a bit more than a brief two years. In truth, this is a mere statistical trifle having no bearing on the Court of Exchequer in any way. The business of the court continued in its usual and ancient course regardless of who was sitting on the bench at any particular time.[7]

William Bunbury

William Bunbury was the second son of Sir Henry Bunbury of Bunbury, Cheshire. He was admitted to St. Catharine's College, Cambridge, on 4 November 1695 and matriculated the next year. He was admitted at the Inner Temple in 1697 and called to the bar of the Inner Temple on 22 June 1702. He was elected a bencher in 1725, reader in 1734, and treasurer in 1737. His legal abilities were also recognized by his appointment as Attorney General of the County

[4] W. H. Bryson, *The Equity Side of the Exchequer* (1975), pp. 25–27.

[5] W. H. Bryson, *The Equity Side of the Exchequer* (1975), pp. 34–63, 170–186.

[6] J. Sainty, *The Judges of England 1272–1990* (1993), p. 97.

[7] For information on the individual judges, see the relevant entries in the *Oxford Dictionary of National Biography* and E. Foss, *The Judges of England*, vol. 8, pp. 8–62 (1864).

Palatine of Cheshire. He retired from the practice of law in 1743 and died on 12 September 1748.[8]

Bunbury regularly practiced in the Court of Exchequer. Upon the death of Sir Constantine Phipps in the Long Vacation 1723, he became the postman of the Court of Exchequer, Mr. Lloyd, who was actually the senior barrister in the Exchequer, not regularly attending the Court.[9] As postman, Bunbury had pre-audience of the Attorney General, the Solicitor General, and all other barristers in the Court in common law cases.[10]

Bunbury's Reports

The majority of the printed cases here come from the reports of William Bunbury, which were first published by his son-in-law, Serjeant George Wilson (d. 1778),[11] in 1755.[12] Bunbury's printed reports date from 1706 to 1741. Lord Mansfield was dismissive of Bunbury's reports.[13] It is true that they are not particularly good; however, they are, in fact, not worse than many other printed reports from the same period. Baron Platt and Baron Parke expressly disputed Lord Mansfield's disparagement of them.[14] Indeed, a comparison with the reports by Thomas Browne and Philip Ward affirms that Bunbury's reports are accurate, though somewhat terse. These reports by Bunbury are important as they were the only collection of printed Exchequer cases from his period of time to the date of this publication. The first editor says that they circulated widely in manuscript and were frequently cited after Bunbury's death before he published them. A few of these manuscripts have survived to the present day:

---

[8] J. Venn and J. A. Venn, *Alumni Cantabrigienses* (1922), part 1, vol. 1, p. 254; F. A. Inderwick, *Calendar of the Inner Temple Records* (1901), vol. 3, p. 367; *Masters of the Bench . . . of the Inner Temple* (1883), p. 67.

[9] Taussig MS. 311, vol. 1, p. 543.

[10] W. H. Bryson, *The Equity Side of the Exchequer* (1975), pp. 5–6; W. Bunbury, *Reports* (1755), preface, p. vii.

[11] Wilson was a prolific reporter and editor of law reports. In addition to the first edition of Bunbury's reports (1755), he edited three volumes of his own reports (1770–1775), the fifth edition of William Salkeld's reports (1773), the third edition of Lord Raymond's reports (1765), and an edition of Sir Edward Coke's reports (1776–1777).

[12] R. W. Bridgman, *A Short View of Legal Bibliography* (1807), p. 42; W. S. Holdsworth, *History of English Law* (1938), vol. 12, pp. 137–138.

[13] *Tinkler v. Poole* (1770), 5 Burrow 2657 at 2658, 98 E.R. 396 ('they are very loose notes' never meant to be published) (*per* Lord Mansfield); see also *Nash v. Nash* (1817), 2 Maddock 133 at 140, 56 E.R. 284 at 287 (a book 'of no great authority') (per Plumer); J. G. Marvin, *Legal Bibliography* (1847), p. 159.

[14] *Regina v. Edwards* (1853), 9 Exchequer 32, at 51–53, 156 E.R. 14 at 22–23; see also J. W. Wallace, *The Reporters* (4th ed. 1882), pp. 419–420.

British Library MS. Hargrave 70, ff. 8–85;
Harvard Law School MS. 1162 [formerly MS. 1216 and Phillipps No. 9959];
Indiana University Lilly Library MS 'Cases in the Exchequer', vols. 5, 6;
Indiana University Lilly Library MS 'Process, pleadings', pp. 300–319.

There were several printed editions:
Reports of cases in the Court of Exchequer, from the beginning of the reign of King George the First, until the fourteenth year of the reign of King George the Second. By William Bunbury Esq. Late of the Inner Temple. Taken in court by himself, and published from his own manuscript by his son in law, George Wilson. [London] In the Savoy, Printed by Henry Lintot, for D. Browne, J. Worrall; and Thomas Gamul, 1755.

viii, 348, [48] p. 33 cm.

Wilson states in his preface that he did not use any of Bunbury's notes which were not reports of cases. These unpublished notes are in British Library MS. Hargrave 70 and Harvard Law School MS. 1162, and four of them are printed here, i.e. Case Nos. 13, 157, 473, 629.

Reports of cases in the Court of Exchequer, from the beginning of the reign of King George the First, until the fourteenth year of the reign of King George the Second. By William Bunbury, Esq. Late of the Inner Temple. Taken in court by himself, and published from his own manuscript by his son in law, George Wilson Serjeant at Law. Dublin: Printed for Sarah Cotter, 1756.

viii, 348, [48] p. 33 cm.

Reports of cases in the Court of Exchequer, from the beginning of the reign of King George the First, until the fourteenth year of the reign of King George the Second. By William Bunbury, Esq. Late of the Inner Temple Taken in court by himself, and published from his own manuscript by his son in law, George Wilson, serjeant at law. The second edition, revised and corrected, with the addition of many references. Dublin, Printed for John Rice, 1793.

viii, 348 (i.e. 198), [37] p. 21 cm. Paging irregular, following starred paging of the first edition inset in the margin of the text.

Reports of cases in the Court of Exchequer, from the beginning of the reign of King George I, until the fourteenth year of the reign of King George II. By William Bunbury Esq. Late of the Inner Temple Taken in court by himself and published from his own manuscript by his son-in-law, George Wilson. The second edition, revised and corrected, with the addition of many references. London, W. Clarke and sons, 1802.

viii, 348 (i.e. 198), [37] p. 22 cm. Starred paging of the first edition inset in the margin of the text.

English Reports, vol. 145, pp. 574–695 (Edinburgh 1914).

Thomas Browne

Browne is identified as the reporter of a set of law reports that is now in the Harvard Law School Library. In several cases, where he refers to himself, Bunbury and Ward refer to Browne but without giving any first name; these cases are:

Attorney General, *ex rel.* Duchess of Buccleuch v. Ayre (1720), Case No. 161;
Sewell, *qui tam* v. Johnson (1721), Case No. 202;
Cuthbert v. Adean (1721), Case No. 229;
Dupuis v. Clarke (1722–1724), Case No. 329;
Goole v. Jordan (1724), Case No. 450;
Torrent v. Burley (1726), Case No. 611.

There is a reference to 'Mr. Brown's notes' in the case of Wallis v. Pain (1738),[15] but the case being quoted is not to be found in the Harvard Law School manuscript. Perhaps it is a reference to a case in the now lost earlier volume.

A Thomas Browne and Sir Constantine Phipps (1656–1723) were counsel in the Exchequer case of Bennet v. Treppass (26 April 1722), 2 Wood 199, see also below, Case No. 307. This is the only evidence so far as to Browne's first name. The most likely candidate as author of these reports is Thomas Browne, son and heir of Francis Browne, Esq. This Thomas Browne was born circa 1687 and was admitted as a student at the Inner Temple on 9 December 1702. He then matriculated at Brasenose College, Oxford, 23 July 1703 at the age of sixteen. He was called to the bar on 8 July 1709, and made a bencher on 3 February 1737/38. He died in November 1743.[16]

Browne's Reports

Harvard Law School MS. 1082 [formerly MS. 1109], in two volumes, is a collection of cases from the Court of Exchequer. The cases in volume one, pages 1–275, date from Easter term 1720 to Easter term 1726 and those in volume two, pages 1–61, from Trinity term 1726 to Easter term 1729. We know from internal

---

15 *Wallis v. Pain* (1738), 2 Comyns 633, 635, 640, 92 E.R. 1245, 1248.

16 F. A. Inderwick, ed., *Calendar of the Inner Temple Records* (1901), vol. 3, p. 414; R. A. Roberts, ed., *Calendar of the Inner Temple Records* (1933), vol. 4, pp. 371, 468; J. Foster, *Alumni Oxonienses* (1891), vol. 1, p. 198.

references that there was an earlier volume. Also, on the flyleaf of the first volume is written 'Notes of the practice of [the] Court of Exchequer commencing Pasch. 1720 where the other folio ends.' However, this was lost before what we now have was acquired by Sir Thomas Phillipps (1792–1872).[17] These volumes were once owned by Craven Ord (1755–1832), the Exchequer official and antiquary. Sometime between 1829 and 1832, they were sold to Sir Thomas Phillipps and catalogued as Phillipps No. 4095. They were sold by Sotheby & Co. on 22 March 1895 to Arthur Reader, a London bookseller, and then sold to the Harvard Law School on 20 May 1901.[18]

Philip Ward

Philip Ward was the fourth son of Sir Edward Ward (1638–1714), who was Chief Baron of the Exchequer from 1695 to 1714.[19] His mother was Elizabeth Papillon Ward (1658–1723), the daughter of Thomas Papillon (1623–1702), a London merchant and politician.[20] Philip Ward was admitted to the Inner Temple on 6 November 1693 and called to the bar on 26 June 1710.[21] He was elected to be a bencher on 3 February 1742/43,[22] but it appears that he declined the honor.

Ward had chambers in the Inner Temple in the King's Bench Building from 1722 to 1726, then in Sir Thomas Robinson's Buildings from 1727 to 1739, and afterwards in Serjeant Hampson's Buildings from 1739 until his death.[23] He became the owner of the manor of Stoke Doyle in Northamptonshire in 1734 upon the death of his older brother, Edward Ward, Jr., and he resided there until his death.[24] He was a close friend of Sir Clement Wearg (c. 1686–1726), the Solicitor General from 1724 until his untimely death in 1726. Wearg left his books and manuscripts to Ward and made him his co-executor. Ward recorded in his reports: 'The solicitor's [Sir Clement Wearg's] will was all of his own handwriting and signed by him 3 October 1723. By his will, he devised to me his manuscripts and books and made me and his wife and brothers executors. "I give all

[17] We would like to thank Sir John Baker for this information.

[18] J. H. Baker, *English Legal Manuscripts in the U.S.A.* (1990), vol. 2, p. 132, nos. 603, 604; Sir John Baker, *The English Legal Manuscripts of Sir Thomas Phillipps* (2008), p. 15.

[19] Many of Chief Baron Ward's reports are printed in W. H. Bryson, ed., *Equity Cases in the Court of Exchequer 1660 to 1714* (2007).

[20] S. P. Menefee and S. Handley, 'Ward, Sir Edward (1638–1714)', *Oxford Dictionary of National Biography*, vol. 57, p. 286. Philip Ward was absent from court the first twelve days of Easter term 1723 because of his mother's death. Taussig MS. 311, vol. 1, p. 481.

[21] F. A. Inderwick, *Calendar of the Inner Temple Records* (1901), vol. 3, pp. 296, 421.

[22] R. A. Roberts, *Calendar of the Inner Temple Records* (1933), vol. 4, p. 456.

[23] R. A. Roberts, *Calendar of the Inner Temple Records* (1933), vol. 4, pp. 84, 141, 165, 171, 398, 559.

[24] *Victoria County Histories—Northamptonshire* (1930), vol. 3, p. 133.

my manuscripts and such of my books as he has not already the same to my friend Philip Ward of the Inner Temple" etc.'[25] He was also a personal friend of Philip Yorke, Earl of Hardwicke, (1690–1764); they visited each other's country homes,[26] and Ward had the occasion to send to Lord Hardwicke some cases from his father's manuscript Exchequer reports.[27] Philip Ward died at Stoke Doyle on 7 April 1752.[28]

Ward's Reports

Philip Ward's Exchequer reports are in Taussig MS. 311, which comprises two books. In addition to the self-identification of Philip Ward as the reporter of these cases in his reference to Wearg's will, he is also identified in the cases of Robinson, *qui tam* v. The African Company (1725), Case No. 542; Spong, *qui tam* v. Fasting (1725–1726), Case No. 565; and Binstead v. Collins (1727), Case No. 665. Taussig MS. 311 is a professional copy made in the eighteenth century. Volume one, pp. 1–641, contains cases dating from Easter term 1720 to Hilary term 1723/24; volume two, pp. 642–1222 (continuous pagination with volume one), contains cases dating from Easter term 1724 to Hilary term 1728/29. These two volumes were purchased by Mr. Anthony Taussig on 21 June 2001 at the Bloomsbury Book Auctions.[29] From internal references, we know that there was an earlier volume.[30]

The following cases in these volumes have not been transcribed here:

Peachy v. Duke of Somerset (Ch. 1721), Taussig MS. 311, vol. 1, pp. 53–54;
Some earlier Exchequer orders, vol. 1, pp. 173–190;
Child v. Sands (K.B. 1693), vol. 1, p. 295;

---

[25] Taussig MS. 311, vol. 2, p. 872.

[26] Some correspondence has been preserved in the Hardwicke papers: British Library MSS. Add. 36136, f. 249; Add. 35584, f. 180; Add. 35587, ff. 147, 164, 192; Add. 35589, ff. 202, 208, 311, 336, 342; Add. 35590, ff. 281, 309, 385, 399, 414; Add. 35591, ff. 118–121, 130, 260, 273; see also G. Harris, *The Life of Lord Chancellor Hardwicke* (1847), vol. 1, pp. 88, 475, vol. 2, pp. 54, 344, 416, vol. 3, p. 530.

[27] See *Chapman v. Smith* (1754), 2 Vesey Sen. 506, 515, 28 E.R. 324, 329; letters from Philip Ward to Lord Hardwicke, 30 November 1751, 4 January 1752: British Library MS. Add. 35591, ff. 260v, 273.

[28] G. J. Armytage, ed., *Musgrave's Obituary*, Harleian Soc., vol. 49, p. 202 (1901).

[29] J. H. Baker and A. Taussig, *A Catalogue of the Legal Manuscripts of Anthony Taussig* (2007), p. 122, no. 311.

[30] E.g., in the case of *Payne v. Attorney General* (1721–1722), Case No. 217, Ward refers to "my prior book", and, at the end of *Leslie, qui tam v. Gray* (1724), Case No. 479, there is a cross-reference to book 3.

Anonymous (K.B. 1723) (affirming an Irish judgment in trover), vol. 1, p. 402;
Some earlier London cases, vol. 1, pp. 424–480;
Cornelius v. Cornelius (Ch. 1723), vol. 1, p. 565;
Whitchurch v. Whitchurch (Ch. 1725), vol. 2, p. 775, pl. 1;
Some records of nonsuits upon trials on informations, vol. 2, pp. 882–885;
Keilway v. Keilway (Ch. 1726), vol. 2, p. 904;
Lord Nottingham v. Inhabitants of Daventry (Duchy 1726), vol. 2, p. 945.

Although Bunbury, Browne, and Ward were working independently in the reporting of Exchequer cases, they were in communication with one another in this endeavor. It is interesting to note that the reports by Bunbury and Browne of the cases of Minnett v. Robinson (Ex. 1722), Case No. 360, and Gold v. Freame (Ex. 1723–1724), Case No. 376, are exactly the same, and Browne appears to have copied Bunbury's report of Pearce v. Penrose (Ex. 1722), Case No. 321. Also Bunbury read Ward's report of the case of Farwell v. Medcalfe (Ex. 1723), Case No. 418, and offered a comment which was included in Ward's report. The Exchequer bar at this time was very small, and it must have been quite collegial. These lawyers were daily together in the courtroom, sometimes on the opposite side of a case and sometimes on the same side as co-counsel. Moreover, all three were members of the Inner Temple.

Table of Cases Reported

[These references are to case numbers, not page numbers. Note that both plaintiffs' and defendants' names are listed first.]

1

Mason v. Watson

(Ex. 1714)

Where a defendant admits partial liability and tenders payment and at the trial prevails as to the rest of the plaintiff's claim, the defendant will be awarded his costs incurred subsequent to his partial admission.

2 Gwillim 611, 1 Eagle & Younge 709

In a bill for tithes, as to part of the demand, the defendant, by answer, tendered £10 with costs to the time of the answer. At the hearing, the court decreed a trial at law as to the other part and reserved further directions. After the trial, the court dismissed the whole bill,[1] except as to the £10, which they decreed the defendant to pay to the time of the answer (inclusive) and no further and that, from the time of the tender, the plaintiff should pay to the defendant the subsequent costs of suit, which subsequent costs were to be allowed to and deducted by the defendant out of the costs which should be taxed and allowed the plaintiff, so far as the same would extend, and the residue of the defendant's costs were to be paid by the plaintiff.

2

Shapter v. Mitchell

(Ex. 1715)

An uncertain modus decimandi *in lieu of tithes in kind is void.*

1 Rayner 126

Shapter, vicar of Saint Goram, in Cornwall, against Mitchell.

The decree in Bean's case[2] was now cited and allowed of for this reason, that the *modus* in question exposes the parson to be greatly imposed on, who cannot know what rent is reserved nor what fine is taken, and, as to the value of the land, that is still more uncertain.

[Order of 15 July 1715: 2 Wood 13, 1 Eagle & Younge 713.]

---

[1] *Mason v. Watson* (Ex. 10 February 1714), 1 Wood 540.

[2] *Bean v. Lee* (Ex. 1713), Dodd 231, 1 Rayner 120, 2 Gwillim 609, 1 Eagle & Younge 703, 1 Wood 537.

3

Hodgson v. Smith

(Ex. 1715)

The tithe of tares, whether green or ripe, are a great tithe, and, in this case, belonged to the rector, not the vicar.

1 Rayner 128, 1 Eagle & Younge 716

John Hodgson, lessee of the Governors of Sir John Hopkins's Hospital, against Smith.

The plaintiff, as impropriator, demands tithes of corn, grain, hay, fodder, etc. in Welling, in the County of Kent.

The defendant sowed tares and cut them green and used them as fodder or hay amongst his cattle. And he insisted that the tithe of hay, clover, and such fodder grass did belong of right to the vicar.

On June 23, the cause was heard, when it was adjourned over to the sittings, and that, in the meantime, the court would consider whether the tithes of tares cut green for fodder did belong unto the plaintiff or to the vicar.

On July 14, the court declared their opinion that the tithes of the defendant's tares cut green and used for fodder did belong unto the plaintiff, who was entitled to the corn tithes, and not unto the vicar, who was entitled to the hay tithe. And, accordingly, they directed an account, which was afterwards taken, the report confirmed, and payment decreed.

It was resolved by three barons, against Price, that tares, whether green or ripe, are a great tithe and belonged to the rector.

[Order of 14 July 1715: Inner Temple MS. Mitford 46, f. 173, 2 Wood 21, 2 Gwillim 743, 1 Eagle & Younge 715.]

4

Nicholas v. Austen

(Ex. 1715–1718)

A prescriptive custom as to tithes is not altered when the method of cultivation is changed.

A decree between other parties may be read as a precedent, though not as evidence.

1 Rayner 129, 2 Gwillim 615, 1 Eagle & Younge 734

19 May 1715. Matthew Nicholas, clerk, vicar of Shalford, plaintiff; Robert Austen, esquire, and Elizabeth Austen, widow, impropriators of the rectory of Shalford, in the County of Surrey, with the chapelry of Bramley, and Thomas

Eames, John Wilkins, and Edward Elkins, tenants of the said impropriators, defendants.

In 1703, the plaintiff was inducted into the vicarage of Shalford and chapelry of Bramley, and thereby became entitled to all tithes, duties, and profits belonging to the same.

The defendants, Robert and Elizabeth Austen, were seised in fee of the impropriation and the great tithes of corn, grain, and hay. And the other defendants were their tenants.

The plaintiff, as vicar, was endowed of all the small tithes and had for a long time received a composition of 3s. 4d. an acre in lieu of the tithes of beans and pease set and planted in rows and ranks that had been hoed and weeded with the hand where the ground had been turned up with the spade, although in the open fields. But where the beans and pease had been set in rows and ranks and hoed and weeded with the hand, where the ground had been turned up only with the plow, the tithes of such beans and pease had been gathered in kind by the impropriator or his farmers.

Until about thirty years before the commencement of this suit, the ground in the parish was usually prepared for beans, pease, and roots, with plow and spade together. And, while this method continued, the impropriator never set up any right to these tithes, so that the same were enjoyed by the vicar. But the farmers and occupiers of some small parcels of land, not considerable about twenty years ago, having contrived a tin or iron plate to be annexed to the plow, the use of the spade was omitted. And, thereupon, the impropriators or their tenants first set up a pretence that thereby the tithes of beans and pease became great tithes and took the same accordingly.

The plaintiff, soon after, brought another bill in the same court, against the defendants for the small tithes arising from the glebe land and to confirm the former decree, but, pending this suit, Elliot brought his action of trover against the plaintiff for taking tithes of pease which were set in rows and ranks and weeded and hoed upon ground turned up with the plow. And upon the trial of that action, wherein the value of the tithes being agreed on, the only question was whether the tithes belonged to the impropriator or the vicar, the plaintiff in the action obtained a verdict.

After this verdict, the cause against the defendants came on to be heard, on the 19th of May 1715, when the barons having admitted their decree against Elliot to be read, though he was not a party to this suit, nor were the defendants parties to that, and rejected the evidence, verdict, and judgment in the action of trover, affirmed their former decree, and ordered the defendants to account with the plaintiff for the said small tithes.

Indiana University, Lilly Library,
MS. 'Cases in the Exch., vol. 5,' p. 58 (Price's reports)

Easter, 2 George [1716].

The plaintiff demands by a bill tithe wool and, by local prescription, tithes of all peas and beans set, drilled, and sowed in rows and ranks between the carrots between the rows, which are hoed and weeded with the hand in a garden-like manner in the common fields and elsewhere in the parish and tithable places there. [He alleges] that, thirty years ago and before, the ground was used to be prepared with plow and spade together and the impropriator never then pretended a right to the tithes, but they were enjoyed by the vicar. But the farmers have within twenty years contrived a fin or an iron plate to be annexed to the plow to supply the use of the spade and so left off the use of the spade. And, thereupon, the impropriator set up a right to the tithes because the farmers varied from the prescriptive right. And now, others are come to that way of garden-like husbandry [so] that the vicar's tithe, formerly worth £30 *per annum*, is not worth £5 *per annum.*

The common difference and distinction between garden husbandry and others in setting, sowing, and drilling peas and beans in rows and ranks and in hoeing and hand weeding after plow or spade separately or jointly used to turn the ground in gardens or fields being in the garden-like manner or garden-like husbandry and took its original from the garden culture of such crops. And the impropriator is not hurt, for it is a great improvement of the crop for corn.

[In margin:] If omitting an instrument in husbandry or changing it can alter a prescription, the right will be soon at an end.

28 of June 1711, there was a decree in the Exchequer at the suit of the same plaintiff against Elliot and others upon the like case,[1] and [it was] decreed by the unanimous opinion of all the court for the plaintiff in the same case as this.

3 Rayner 1093,
C. Viner, Abridgment, vol. 9, p. 22, pl. 3

23 January 1717/18.

There was a custom was for the vicar to have tithes for all pease and beans set, drilled, or sowed in rows in gardens or like manner. Afterwards, a new improvement was found out to use a plow instead of a spade, yet such pease and beans shall pay tithes.

A decree between other parties may be read as a precedent, though not as evidence.

An inquisition is not admitted to be read as evidence, there being no commission to warrant it.

[Order of 19 May 1715: 2 Wood 10.]

[Affirmed on appeal: 7 Brown P.C. 9, 3 E.R. 7, 2 Gwillim 615, 616, 1 Rayner 136, 1 Eagle & Younge 734.]

[1] *Nicholas v. Elliot* (1711), Dodd 227, 4 Gwillim 1581, 1 Eagle & Younge 698, 1 Rayner 119, 1 Wood 523, Bunbury 19, 145 E.R. 580.

5
Cooke v. Lord Montgomery

(Ex. 1715)

The court will enforce a parol testamentary trust that is admitted by the executor of the will.

Inner Temple MS. Mitford 32, p. 354

Trinity term 1 Geo. 1715. Cooke and Cooke v. Lord Montgomery and Frances Fox.

The plaintiffs, who are next of kin to Peter Cooke, deceased, brought their bill against the Lord Montgomery, as executor to the said Peter Cooke, to have a discovery of the personal estate of the testator and to compel him to make distribution etc. Upon the pleadings, the case was that Peter Cooke, the testator, being possessed of a personal estate to the value of £6000 and being at Brussels in Flanders, made his will and made the Lord Montgomery his executor and residuary legatee of all his personal estate, but he declared to the Lord Montgomery that he intended it in trust for Mrs. Fox, as by the Lord Montgomery's answer was confessed. He confessed likewise by his answer that the said testator did deliver to him a proper writing, but he did not remember the contents thereof, save only that the testator thereby desired the Lord Montgomery to accept of a legacy of £100.

This coming to a hearing on the Deputy [Remembrancer]'s report, Mr. *Ward*, for the plaintiffs, insisted that the Lord Montgomery having the legal interest as executor and residuary legatee, having disclaimed all property, and there being no writing declaring the trusts, therefore, the residuum ought to go to the plaintiffs in the course of administration or as a resulting trust, and it being confessed that the residuum was devised to the Lord Montgomery upon trust, he shall not have it, especially since there is a legacy given to him by the testator, which will exclude him as to the residuum.

But the residuum was decreed to Mrs. Fox by the opinion of the whole court for, being devised expressly to the Lord Montgomery etc., no trust expressed in the will, he, by concealing the parol trust, might have retained the whole, both as against the plaintiffs and Mrs. Fox also. But he having disclaimed all interest and it appearing that it was left to his honor to dispose of to Mrs. Fox, we, as by his consent, do decree it so.

And by Montagu, Baron, the practice that had obtained in courts of equity in ordering executors to distribute is now with great reason exploded. Therefore, the Case of Dr. Coppleston[1] is of no authority.

---

[1] *Scamell v. Coppleston* (1705), Dodd 206, Eq. Cases Exch. 510.

6

Keddington v. Bridgman

(Ex. 1716)

A parol contract for retaining tithes upon the payment of a sum of money is valid.

Bunbury 2, 145 E.R. 574,
1 Rayner 132, 1 Eagle & Younge 709

At Serjeants' Inn, 26 February 1715[/16].

It was held by Bury and Price, barons, that a composition by way of retainer by parol can be good only for one year, being by way of contract, but a lease of tithes, even for one year, by parol would be void.

Montagu, baron, seemed to be of opinion that an agreement between the parson and his parishioner for years by parol would be good, though not for life, being only an agreement that he will not sue the parishioner for so many years for tithes.

2 Gwillim 611

14 June 1716. Keddington v. Adamson.

To a bill by the lessee of the rector of Stradishall in Suffolk for tithes in kind, two of the defendants pleaded in bar an agreement made between them and the plaintiff's lessor, the rector, in June 1711 that they should retain their tithes for three years, paying so much. A question was made whether the above agreement by parol, being for three years, were good in law so as to bind the rector and the plaintiff. And, upon debating thereof, many reported cases relating to the same were cited. And the cause was ordered to stand over to the next day, on which day, counsel on both sides were again heard.

And, after many arguments thereupon, it was ordered to stand further over, the court not being ready to give their opinion thereon. And, on the cause coming on again, the court declared that the agreement made with the above defendants for their tithes for three years is good and valid in law and ordered them to pay accordingly.

[Order of 14 June 1716: 2 Wood 47.]

7

Underwood v. Gibbon

(Ex. 1716)

Saddle horses which are worked and have no annual increase are exempt from paying agistment tithes.

The tithes for pasturing unprofitable cattle ought to be paid by the occupier of the land.

Indiana University, Lilly Library,
MS. 'Cases in the Exch., vol. 5,' p. 19 (Price's reports)

31 January 1716. Buxton Underwood against Lawrence Gibbon *et al.*

A bill [was brought] for [tithes for] agistment of saddle horses kept by the defendant in King's Marsh and Portman Croft on the common in the parish of St. Gregory in Sudbury in the County of Suffolk [by] the plaintiff, as lessee to the impropriator. The defendant insists that those grounds were granted to the burgesses and community of Sudbury and the tithes thereof.

The question is [whether] tithes for the agistment of saddle horses in the said ground are due by the defendants.

Chief Baron Bury and Price were of opinion that saddle horses which are worked and have no annual increase are exempt from paying agistment tithes as much as cattle for plow or pail or cattle fatted for the use of the family, being it [is] assisted toward the management of the estate, not like horses hired to carry for carriage. 1 Bulstrode 171, Polhill; Popham 126, Larkin v. Wright; Godolphin, *Repertorium*, 425; Hardres 35, Gilbert v. Eversley; Hardres 184, Perry v. Wright; 2 Croke 430, Hauton v. Wild; Popham 242, Richardson v. Cobb.[1]

The second [question is] that, if agistment tithe was due, yet whether [it is] against the owner of the horse or the occupier of the land.

Bury and Price were of opinion that most of the books were to have it against the occupier. The corporation, in this case, were the owners and occupiers, for the defendants paid them a certain rate for each horse, which they paid to the poor. And yet some of the books, as the case of Perry v. Wright, [by] Chief Baron Hale, said the occupier might pay, but the owner must pay, so that there seemed to be an election. But more incline to believe that it did not lie against the defendant, the owner of the horses, but rather against the corporation, who were owners and occupiers.

Baron Montagu was of opinion that a saddle horse was barren cattle and ought to pay and that the tithe is due from him who has the profit of the land, which was the occupier. But he agreed the bill was ill brought against the defendant as owner of the horse, but it ought to be against the corporation, who were owners and occupiers of the land.

And all three agreed to dismiss the plaintiff's bill with costs.

---

[1] *Pothill v. May* (1611), 1 Bulstrode 171, 80 E.R. 862, 4 Gwillim 1571, 1 Eagle & Younge 199; *Laurking v. Wilde* (1617), Popham 126, 79 E.R. 1229; J. Godolphin, *Repertorium Canonicum*; *Guilbert v. Eversly* (1656), Hardres 35, 145 E.R. 367, 2 Gwillim 502, 1 Eagle & Younge 414; *Pory v. Wright* (1661), Hardres 184, 145 E.R. 442, also 1 Eq. Cas. Abr. 367, 21 E.R. 1107, 1 Eagle & Younge 434; *Hampton v. Wild* (1617), Croke Jac. 430, 79 E.R. 367, 1 Eagle & Younge 262; *Richardson v. Cabell* (1617), Popham 142, 79 E.R. 1243, 1 Eagle & Younge 296.

Bunbury 3, 145 E.R. 574, 1 Rayner 132

31 January 1715[/16].

It was resolved by Bury, Price, and Montagu, barons, that the tithes for depasturing unprofitable cattle ought to be paid by the occupier of the ground, and not the agistor.

And it was said by Lord Chief Baron Bury and Price, *contra* Montagu, that saddle horses shall pay no tithes, no more than cattle for the plow and pail or cattle killed for the use of a man's own family, in respect of the profit that otherwise accrues to the parson from these.

[Order of 31 January 1716: 2 Wood 58, 1 Eagle & Younge 727.]

8

Turner v. Wray

(Ex. 1716)

The right of tithes belonging formerly to an abbey can be granted by the crown to a layman.

3 Rayner 1092

21 March 1716.

An abbot was seised in the right of his abbey of a rectory with all tithes etc. The abbey is dissolved, and the crown grants the tithes etc. The parson disputes the tithes with the patentee, but the bill was dismissed.

9

Rex v. Albert

(Ex. 1716)

A surety is not liable to pay interest or court costs to the crown.

Bunbury 4, 145 E.R. 575

18 April 1716.

A [writ of] extent issued against Albert. Knight puts in his claim to the goods seized and pleads to the extent. Hook and Scanderet were security to the pleader according to the course of the court. Knight, afterwards, withdrew his plea, upon which an order was made for the payment of the money, which accordingly was paid.

Mr. Attorney General [*Northey*] moved that the security should pay costs and interest from the time the recognizance was forfeited.

But Mr. *Turner* and Mr. *Ward* objected that they, having paid the sum mentioned in the recognizance and the condition being only to abide such order as the court shall make and the order that was made by the court being only for the principal sum, neither the principal nor the security ought to be any further charged, though, where a man is bound in a bond to the crown, there, interest shall be allowed in respect of the penalty of the bond. But this recognizance is only a security for a collateral matter.

It was said by Baron PRICE, if there had been judgment for or against the king on this plea, there could have been no costs of either side. And it is against the method of this court to pay costs upon extents, though it is allowed upon writs of *scire facias* by the new Act of Parliament.[1]

Per CURIAM: Neither interest nor costs ought to be allowed against the security, no more than against the principal; so the Attorney General took nothing by his motion.

10

Rex v. Southerby

(Ex. 1716)

Where the crown is the only party in interest in a seizure upon an outlawry, the defendant's landlord has no remedy for unpaid rent.

Bunbury 5, 145 E.R. 575

Southerby was outlawed, and a [writ of] extent issued, and an inquisition was taken thereupon, and his house and goods were seized by virtue thereof. Etchins, the landlord, moved upon the Stat. 8 Ann.[2] to have the goods delivered to him, suggesting that they had been distrained by him for rent three days before the extent.

Per CURIAM: Not the party, but the king only is concerned in the outlawry, and we cannot relieve the landlord upon this motion.

11

Mullins v. Pratt

(Ex. 1716)

An ecclesiastical court does not have jurisdiction over a will that devises real property.

---

[1] Stat. 8 & 9 Will. III, c. 11 (*SR*, VII, 201–203).

[2] Stat. 8 Ann., c. 18 (*SR*, IX, 247–248).

Bunbury 6, 145 E.R. 575

At Serjeants' Inn in Chancery Lane. 28 June 1716.

In a bill for a legacy, the plaintiff set forth the substance of the will and referred to it when produced. The defendant in his answer says he believes there is such a will. When the plaintiff came to make out his proof, he offered to produce the probate, which was not admitted because it was in the case of a real estate, of which the spiritual court has no cognizance, and, besides, the defendant has admitted only that there might be such a will, but does not know that it was executed according to the Statute;[1] otherwise, if the admission of the defendant in his answer had been full, it might have been read.

12

Rex v. Peck

(Ex. 1716)

A sheriff can amend his return of a writ of execution.

Bunbury 8, 145 E.R. 576

4 July 1716.

A [writ of] *fieri facias* issued out of the Court of Common Pleas at the suit of Roberts against Peck, which *fieri facias* was tested 3 April, by virtue of which the sheriff levied the goods, etc. But, before the sale thereof or the return of the writ, a [writ of] extent came to the sheriff at the suit of the crown to levy the goods etc. of Peck tested 2 May. The sheriff returned this special matter on the *fieri facias* and likewise upon the extent into the Court of Exchequer, in which it was said that Peck *fuit possessionatus* of the goods the 30th of April, upon which Mr. A. moved to quash the inquisition, and Mr. F. moved that the sheriff might amend his return.

Baron Price was for quashing the inquisition, which being found by a jury, he did not see how the sheriff could amend it.

Lord Chief Baron Bury and Baron Montagu were of opinion the sheriff might amend his return. And an order was made for that purpose, which was what the counsel for the sheriff wanted [in order] to indemnify him[self] in case anything had been moved against him in the Common Pleas upon the return of the *fieri facias*.

N.B. It was taken for granted that, though the goods were levied by virtue of the *fieri facias* three days before the *teste* of the extent, yet that was no bar to the crown, but query if they had been sold, for, then, execution had been executed.

[1] Stat. 29 Car. II, c. 3, s. 5 (*SR*, V, 840).

13

Hankin v. Massey

(Ex. 1716)

Land that was recovered from the sea by embanking is not exempt from the payment of tithes as improved barren land.

British Library MS. Hargrave 70, f. 8v, pl. 5,
Harvard Law School MS. 1162, p. 20, pl. 151

6 July 1716.

Upon a bill for tithes, the defendant insists that part of the lands are embanked and recovered at a very great expense from the sea and, therefore, within the equity of the Stat. 2 Edw. VI,[1] which exempts barren land improved for seven years.

But it was overruled *per* TOTAM CURIAM.

Beardmore v. Gilbert, February 21, 1723.[2]

[Related cases: Hankin v. Shaffey (Ex. 1721), see below, Case No. 225.]

14

Calvervill v. Hoskins

(Ex. 1716)

Where an ecclesiastical court has proper jurisdiction of a type of action, a writ of prohibition will not be granted after a final judgment in the ecclesiastical court.

Inner Temple MS. Mitford 32, p. 293

Trinity term 2 Geo. 1716.

A libel [was filed] in the Consistory Court of Bristol for calling the plaintiff's wife a whore. After the sentence, the defendant prayed a [writ of] prohibition suggesting that, by the custom of the City of Bristol, whoredom was punishable by corporal punishment, also that, by custom there, an action did lie in the City court for calling a woman a whore. They likewise produced an affidavit to verify their suggestion, as above.

Raby urged that it was not too late to pray for a prohibition after a sentence in this case, it appearing that an action lay for it at common law in the court in Bristol and, therefore, the spiritual court have no jurisdiction of it.

BURY, Chief Baron, said, if the libel had been for a matter actionable at common law and of which the spiritual court had no jurisdiction, a prohibition

---

1 Stat. 2 & 3 Edw. VI, c. 13, s. 5 (*SR*, IV, 56).

2 *Beardmore v. Gilbert* (1724), Bunbury 159, 145 E.R. 632.

might be granted after a sentence. But this is a matter properly of ecclesiastical cognizance. And we cannot take notice of the custom, especially since it was not pleaded in the spiritual court.

PRICE: Where two courts have equal jurisdiction, there, priority of suit must take place, so we never prohibit the spiritual court in a suit for tithes when they proceed properly though this court holds pleas of tithes by English bill.

So the rule for a prohibition *nisi* was discharged.

See 12 Rep. 77[1] [for] reasons for granting a prohibition after a sentence.

15

Hucks v. Phelps

(Ex. 1716)

Where a modus decimandi *in lieu of tithes in kind is denied in an ecclesiastical court, a common law court can remove the case out of the ecclesiastical court.*

Bunbury 8, 145 E.R. 576, 1 Eagle & Younge 724

It was said in the case of Hucks v. Phelps that, if a man libels in the spiritual court for tithes in kind and the defendant in that court pleads a *modus* and the spiritual court refuses that plea, a [writ of] prohibition shall go. A man may libel below for a *modus* or for tithes due by custom, but, if the *modus* or custom be denied, the spiritual court cannot proceed.

16

Powell v. Robinson

(Ex. 1716)

An action for a seizure of a ship in the Court of Admiralty can be prohibited before the filing of the libel there.

Bunbury 9, 145 E.R. 576

The Admiralty granted a warrant according to the course of their court to seize a ship, and, before a libel was exhibited, a [writ of] prohibition was moved for, which was alleged to be too soon, the warrant being only in the nature of process to bring them into court and it not yet appearing that the Admiralty had no jurisdiction.

But it being insisted upon of the other side that it was the constant practice not to exhibit any libel on such warrant, but to proceed only on the warrant and

[1] Note (1610), 12 Coke Rep. 76, 77 E.R. 1354.

precedents being cited of prohibitions granted in like case, a prohibition was awarded by the Lord Chief Baron Bury and Price, *contra* Montagu.

17

Adams v. Carter
Olive v. Carter

(Ex. 1716)

Where two actions are filed for the same matter against the same defendant on the same day, the doctrine of priority of suit will not be applied, but both actions will be dismissed.

Bunbury 9, 145 E.R. 577

[If] two informations [be] exhibited the same day for the same matter, both shall be set aside.

18

Ayde v. Flower

(Ex. 1716–1717)

In this case, a parishioner was ordered to pay tithes and to account for the arrears for the agistment tithes of barren cattle.

Bunbury 7, 145 E.R. 576,
1 Rayner 133, 142, 1 Eagle & Younge 722

28 June 1716.

A vicar preferred his bill for tithe herbage and small tithes. It was objected for the defendant that tithe for the depasturing of barren and unprofitable cattle may be due of common right, but not to the vicar; therefore, it lies upon him to show that he was endowed of it or, at least, that it has been usually received by the vicar, which would be an evidence of an endowment. As to the tithe of meadow ground that has been mowed, of which the vicar has had the tithe and after it is depastured by unprofitable cattle, there is no tithe due for that.

Note: The copy of the *Valor Beneficiorum*,[1] which was taken by commission in the reign of Henry VIII, was produced. And it did not appear that this demand of the plaintiff was mentioned there among the other small tithes.

The Lord Chief Baron Bury and Montagu, *contra* Price, held that the bill should be dismissed.

---

[1] *Valor Beneficiorum: or, A Valuation of All Ecclesiastical Preferments in England and Wales.* London: M. Gillyflower, 1695.

N.B. It was objected to an evidence that he had the inheritance of lands within the parish, though he was not an inhabitant and the lands were in the hands of a tenant, and, therefore, his evidence would be to discharge the inheritance of the lands of the tithes, which would be such an advantage to him as to render him not indifferent. But, notwithstanding this objection, which goes only to the credit of a witness, he was admitted to be read.

Mr. Fortescue Aland being made a baron, this cause was reheard 17 July 1717. And, then, the plaintiff produced the endowment of the vicar by the dean and chapter of York, whereby the vicar is endowed *de omnibus et omnimodis minutis decimis quibuscunque*. And, as to the *Valor Beneficiorum*, it was said, that there were other tithes not mentioned in that book, which the defendants themselves admit belonged to the vicar. And, by the opinion of the four barons, the defendants were decreed to account with costs.

2 Gwillim 613

27 July 1717.

A bill was brought by the vicar of Sturton in Nottinghamshire for the agistment tithes on lands called the Cow Pasture and the Horse Pasture and on eighty cattle gates in the Upper Ing and Lower Ing. The defendant said that the vicar had a sufficient maintenance by an augmentation reserved and made payable to him by the dean and chapter of York's lease of parsonage; that no agistment tithe had ever been paid until within the last three years, that the Cattle Pasture and the Horse Pasture are commons without stint, that the tithe in wool and lamb etc. had been usually paid to the vicar in full satisfaction of all tithes, and that the Upper Ing and Lower Ing were every year mowed and the tithe hay paid to the impropriator, and that, therefore, no tithe was due for the depasturing of cattle on the after-moath thereof.

The plaintiff replied; the defendant rejoined; and witnesses were examined on both sides. And, on reading the answer and the counterpart of the lease from the dean and chapter of York, impropriators of Sturton dated 2nd of December in the thirty-second year of Charles II, also an ancient book from the register of the dean and chapter of York of the first presentation and endowment to the vicarage of Sturton in the Clay, in which presentation and endowment the said town of Sturton is called by the name of Straton, otherwise Stretton in the Clay, and which is dated the 30th of June 1460, also a book from the First Fruits Office, entitled *Valor Beneficiorum*, and also on reading several depositions taken in the cause, and on full debate of the matter, it was ordered by the court, that the defendant should account with and pay to the plaintiff all the tithes due and in arrear for his dry, barren, and unprofitable cattle bred, fed, or depastured upon any grounds within the parish, other than in the after-moath or after-grass of such grounds which he had annually meadowed there and whereof tithe hay had or ought to have been paid in kind to the impropriators or their tenants for the time demanded by the bill. And it was referred to the Deputy Remembrancer to take the said account. And it was further ordered that the defendant should pay to the plaintiff his costs of this suit to be taxed by the said Deputy Remembrancer.

[Order of 27 July 1717: 2 Wood 76.]

19

Benson v. Watkins

(Ex. 1717)

A modus decimandi *in lieu of tithes in kind that is too large is void.*

Tithes are due for all turnips though they be sown and harvested at several times in a single year.

Bunbury 10, 145 E.R. 577,
1 Rayner 135, 2 Gwillim 612, 1 Eagle & Younge 721

20 February 1716[/17].

Upon a bill by an impropriate rector for tithes, the defendant insists upon several *modus*es, *viz.* 5s. per acre for wheat and rye, 4s. per acre for summer corn, 3s. per acre for meadow, etc.

The court disallowed these *modus*es and decreed the defendant to account, they being too rank and too near the value of the land, especially when these *modus*es were supposed to commence when the land was at a much less value and the money at a much greater. It was said in this case that the only difference between a *modus* and a composition is that the first is time out of mind and the last only a late agreement. All the garden ground in England shall pay tithes for different crops. Turnips, when they are pulled, ought to pay tithes, though never so often sowed and though upon the same land. Tithes of after-moath shall be paid, but not tithes of after-pasture, unless by custom. But query of the last points.

3 Rayner 1092

Benson, impropriator of Bromley St. Leonard, Middlesex, against Watkins and others.

The court declared the tithe of turnips to be due, though sowed never so often in the same year and though upon the same land.

The following *modus*es, *viz.* 5s. an acre for the tithe of winter corn, 4s. an acre for summer corn, 2s. 6d. an acre for upland meadow, and 3s. an acre for low land, were set aside as too big.

[Order of 27 February 1717: 2 Wood 56.]

20

Lamb v. Bowes

(Ex. 1717)

A preliminary injunction will not be granted merely because the defendant has demurred for the sole purpose of creating a delay.

Bunbury 11, 145 E.R. 577

17 May 1717.

Sir Constantine Phipps moved for an injunction because the defendant had only demurred to the bill without pleading or answering, which, he alleged, was only in delay. The court refused to grant an injunction upon this reason, but ordered the demurrer to be set down to be argued at a short day.

21

Pierce v. Johns

(Ex. 1717)

A judgment at common law in an action of account is not res judicata *in equity.*

Bunbury 11, 145 E.R. 577

18 May 1717.

To a bill for an account of several sums of money, the defendant pleads a verdict and judgment at law for the money demanded by the bill.

Per CURIAM: The plaintiff cannot be estopped by this verdict, for there is no such thing as an estoppel in a court of equity. It is only a term of art at law. If a bill is preferred where there has been a stated account and the plaintiff sets forth particularly one or more items that are wrong charged, though the defendant may plead the stated account, yet he must answer to those items particularly set forth by the plaintiff. And, in that case, we often open the account. Here, the defendant has answered to what he had pleaded, and that must overrule his plea.

22

Ridge v. Hudson

(Ex. 1717)

Where a will devises land to a trustee to sell the land for the benefit of a child in fee tail, a court of equity can order the trustee to sell the land and pay the proceeds to the child.

Bunbury 12, 145 E.R. 577

23 May 1717.

A., by his will, devises that trustees shall sell his real estate and what arises by such sale shall go to his daughter and her issue and, if she die without issue, then to two other daughters. The plaintiffs preferred their bill to have the real estate sold and to have the money arising by such sale. But the two daughters defendants opposed it because of the contingent interest they had by the will in case the plaintiff died without issue. But the plaintiff insisted there could be no such limitation of a chattel, as this would be, if the land was sold.

And the court, accordingly, did decree a sale to be made, for it would be preposterous to oblige the trustees to sell lands in order to lay the money arising out again on lands and, being the plaintiff was of age, she could bar her two sisters by a recovery, which this court might save the trouble and expense of by decreeing this sale and converting the land into money.

23

Jenkins, *qui tam* v. Larwood

(Ex. 1717)

The Court of Exchequer can grant a commission to examine witnesses who are outside of the court's jurisdiction.

Bunbury 13, 145 E.R. 578

31 May 1717.

Sir Robert Raymond moved upon the Stat. 13 & 14 Car. II, c. 11, s. 29,[1] for a commission to examine witnesses abroad in order to make use of the depositions at the trial of the cause, though the words of the Act are 'a commission out of the High Court of Chancery'. But he insisted, this being a remedial law and though it mentions only one instance, yet it shall extend to others within the same equity, as the Act which says *justiciarii* shall grant a bill of exceptions has been extended to the Chancellor in the Petty Bag and the barons of the Exchequer and the Statute of *Circumspecte Agatis*[2] says, '*circumspecte agatis circa res tangentes episcopum Norviciensem*', which Lord Coke says[3] is put only for an instance and it extends to other bishops. The Statute of Westminster[4] gives an action of debt upon an escape against the Warden of the Fleet, and this has been construed to extend to sheriffs, jailers, etc., though only the Warden of the Fleet is named.

---

[1] Stat. 14 Car. II, c. 11, s. 27 (*SR*, V, 399).

[2] Stat. 13 Edw. I, *Circumspecte Agatis* (*SR*, I, 101–102).

[3] E. Coke, *Second Institute* (1642), p. 487.

[4] Stat. 13 Edw. I, Westminster II, c. 11 (*SR*, I, 80–81).

The Lord Chief Baron BURY and Baron PRICE were of opinion that such commission should go, not upon the Act of Parliament, but by virtue of their original jurisdiction.

Baron FORTESCUE ALAND said that it might go even upon the Statute.

Baron MONTAGU dissented in both.

24

Rex v. Oliver

(Ex. 1717)

An action of replevin does not lie for a distress for any duty owing to the crown.

Bunbury 14, 145 E.R. 578

21 June 1717.

If there be a distress for any duty to the crown, the person distrained cannot replevy, no more than in the case of a fee farm. And, if he does, an attachment shall be granted for this contempt. Oliver, a constable, who was fined by the commissioners of the land tax and distrained upon, replevied.

But note he was discharged of this contempt by the Act of Pardon.[1]

25

Rex v. Tenants of Lord Derwentwater

(Ex. 1717)

A writ of scire facias *must be grounded on a judgment and cannot be used to enforce a forfeiture.*

Bunbury 14, 145 E.R. 578

10 July 1717.

Mr. Solicitor General [*Thompson*] moved upon the Statute[2] for appointing commissioners to inquire into forfeited estates of persons in the rebellion, the commissioners having certified to this court that the defendants were possessed of several lands forfeited, that they did not disclose them according to the direction, and, within the time limited by the Statute, there was an affidavit of the commissioners signing the certificate, and, likewise, a copy of the attainder of

[1] Stat. 3 Geo. I, c. 19.

[2] Stat. 1 Geo. I, stat. 2, c. 50.

lord Derwentwater,[1] and, therefore, he now moved for Exchequer process against them, *viz.* a *scire facias*.

But *per* CURIAM, the clause relating to the certificate is applicable only where the tenants commit waste etc. but, by the clause of not disclosing etc., the forfeiture vests in the crown without an office, and you may take the same method as for lands forfeited for treason.

Baron FORTESCUE ALAND: A *scire facias* is always grounded upon a judgment, and, if we should allow it on this certificate, it would be giving judgment that the tenants had forfeited two years value. And the more proper method would be by information. And they would not permit the certificate to be enrolled.

26

Reynolds v. Rogers

(Ex. 1717)

A composition for tithes in lieu of tithes in kind cannot be revoked as to some but not as to all tithes.

Bunbury 15, 145 E.R. 579,
1 Rayner 141, 1 Eagle & Younge 729

17 July 1717.

Reynel preferred his bill against Rogers for tithe of hops. The defendant insists upon a composition. The plaintiff says he gave notice to determine the composition. But being that the composition appeared to be for all small tithes and the notice to determine only as to hops, the bill was dismissed because you cannot determine a composition as to part and let it continue as to the rest.

2 Gwillim 612

18 July 1717.

Upon a bill by the vicar of Horsham in Sussex for tithes in kind from Michaelmas 1714, the defendant said that the vicar, in 1709, entered into a composition with his parishioners in consideration of being exempted from the poor's rate and that he, the defendant, had paid his proportion of such composition to August 1715, about which time, which was about three weeks before hop picking, the vicar gave notice that he would take tithe in kind, which notice, he submitted, was not binding upon him.

The plaintiff amended his bill and stated that there was no such agreement. And the defendant put in his answer and insisted there was such.

---

[1] See 6 State Trials 1 (Hargrave, ed., 1777); note also *Lord Derwentwater's Case* (1719), 9 Modern 172, 88 E.R. 382, 2 Eq. Cas. Abr. 621, 22 E.R. 520.

The plaintiff replied; the defendant rejoined; and witnesses were examined on both sides. And the cause came on to be heard on the 1st of December last, when, on regarding several depositions taken on both sides and the said agreement dated the 20th of July 1709 for three years and on the defendant's counsel's insisting that the plaintiff had continued the said agreement after the expiration thereof until and for the said year 1715 and that the plaintiff had not given the defendant sufficient notice that he would take his tithe hops in kind for that year, it was then ordered by the court that the plaintiff's bill should stand dismissed. But upon petition, it was ordered on the 6th day of December that the cause should be reheard as to tithe hops upon payment of £5 costs, which costs being paid, and upon reading the answer to the amended bill, it was ordered by the court that the said bill be, and the same was, thereby dismissed with costs to be taxed.

[Order of 18 July 1717: 2 Wood 75, 1 Eagle & Younge 729.]

27

Pettifer v. James

(Ex. 1717)

A woman who was divorced from bed and board on the grounds of adultery is not entitled to a widow's share of her deceased husband's estate by the custom of the City of London.

Bunbury 16, 145 E.R. 579

19 July 1717.

A bill was preferred by a widow for her moiety and widow's chamber, according to the custom of the City of London. The defendant insists in his answer that she was divorced by a sentence in the spiritual court *a mensa et thoro* for adultery and, therefore, that she ought not to be entitled to her customary part.

The Lord Chief Baron Bury was for the plaintiff.

But by the opinion of Price, Montagu, and Fortescue, barons, the bill was dismissed.

And Price said she comes with a very ill grace into a court of conscience to be relieved, in this case, that the civilians were all of opinion that Mrs. Sayer[1] had forfeited her right to the administration by living in adultery with the murderer of her husband, and, *pari ratione*, the widow here should forfeit her right to the distribution.

[1] Note *Sayer v. Sayer* (Ch. 1715), British Library MS. Hargrave 80, p. 426.

28

Offley v. Whitehall

(Ex. 1717)

An ecclesiastical court does not have the jurisdiction to adjudicate a modus decimandi *in lieu of tithes in kind. However, this objection is waived by proceeding to a final judgment in the ecclesiastical court.*

Bunbury 17, 145 E.R. 579, 1 Eagle & Younge 732

This distinction was taken that, if a man libels in the spiritual court for tithes in kind and the defendant below suggests and insists upon a *modus*, there, the spiritual court has no jurisdiction to try the *modus*, their method of trial of prescription being different from ours. But, if a man libels for a *modus* and the defendant admits the *modus*, the spiritual court may proceed in that cause. But, even in the first case, if they permit them to proceed to sentence, they come, then, too late for a writ of prohibition, being it is *pro defectu triationis* only. But you are never too late where it is *pro defectu jurisdictionis*.

29

Note

(Ex. 1717)

A bill for a matter below the jurisdictional amount of the court can be dismissed upon a simple motion.

Bunbury 17, 145 E.R. 579, 1 Eagle & Younge 733

If a bill be preferred for a matter or sum beneath the dignity of the court, it may be dismissed as well upon motion as by demurrer, *per* PRICE, baron, 15 November 1717.

30

Sloane v. Heatfield

(Ex. 1717)

A bill in equity for discovery and common law relief is improper.

Bunbury 18, 145 E.R. 579

15 December 1717.

The plaintiff, [Doctor Sloane,] brought his bill for treasure trove within his manor and to discover what was found.

The court said the bill was proper enough as to the discovery, but he could have no relief because he might bring an action of trover. And the bill was dismissed with costs.

31

St. Amand v. Countess Dowager of Jersey

(Ex. 1717)

A voluntary conveyance can be declared void as to prior and subsequent creditors.

1 Comyns 255, 92 E.R. 1059

James St. Amand v. Barbara, countess dowager of Jersey, administratrix of Edward, earl of Jersey, *et al.*

A bill in the Exchequer was brought by the plaintiff on behalf of himself and other bond creditors of Edward, earl of Jersey, against the defendants, his administratrix, William, earl of Jersey, his son, Henry Villiers, Esq., his younger son, an infant, by his guardian, and other trustees for the said infant, setting forth that Edward, earl of Jersey, was indebted by bond dated the 30th of May 1707 to the plaintiff in the penalty of £7000 for payment of £3500 and interest and to Elizabeth Harris by bond dated the 20th of May 1709 in £400 for payment of £200 and interest, and, being (or one Richard Topham in trust for him) seised in fee of two fee farm rents, one of £40 3s. 4d., the other of £2 5s. 8d., subject to a £40 annuity to Rachel Mason for her life, he and his trustees by lease and release dated the 1st and 2d of June 1710, for natural love to the said Henry Villiers, conveyed the said fee farm rents to his eldest son, lord Dartmouth, and lord Bathurst, and their heirs, in trust, after the death of Elizabeth Mason, to sell, and the money raised by the sale to dispose of in an annuity or place for the said Henry Villiers for his life and, if he died before any sale could be, in trust for himself and his heirs.

After this settlement, Edward, earl of Jersey, becomes indebted to others on bond. And he died in September 1711 without personal assets sufficient for creditors. And the scope of the bill was to subject the said fee farm rents to the bond creditors in like manner as if they had descended to the heir.

Mr. *Vernon*, by his opinion dated the 9th of February 1716, had declared that the conveyance being voluntary and for the benefit of a child will be deemed fraudulent as against bond creditors, and the Statute[1] made for the relief of the bond creditors against fraudulent devises goes upon the supposition that a voluntary conveyance made would have been fraudulent at law, that, if there had been no bond creditors at the time of the conveyance, it might have created a doubt

[1] Stat. 3 Will. & Mar., c. 14 (*SR*, VI, 320–321); made perpetual by Stat. 6 & 7 Will. III, c. 14, s. 2 (*SR*, VI, 595).

whether it had been done to defeat bond creditors, but, there being debts then owing by bond, he thought it would be void, even against bond debts contracted after, or that, if it were otherwise, it would come to the same thing, since the estate in question is not to answer the bond debts prior to the conveyance, and, if necessary, the later bond creditors would be admitted to stand in the place of the prior bond creditors and the assets so marshalled that all might receive a satisfaction as far as the assets will extend.

And agreeable to this opinion, on the 22d of February 1716, the court decreed that the fee farm rents should be sold for the benefit of the bond creditors and that the trustees should all join in any conveyance to be made for that purpose.

32

Rex v. Bowdage

(Ex. 1717)

The crown has priority where there was an earlier seizure for a private creditor and the sheriff has not delivered the goods to the creditor.

An inquisition upon a writ of immediate extent should find the goods previously found upon a writ of extent in aid.

Parker 282, 145 E.R. 780

An extent issued in aid, and goods were found and seized. And upon a *venditioni exponas*, the sheriff returned that he had the money. Then came an immediate extent for the crown, which also found the goods first extended. The king shall have them, but not if they had been delivered.

In this case, there were two immediate extents for the crown. The first found goods, but not what were found on the extent in aid, nor was any evidence offered as to those goods, nor was it insisted that they should be found. Then came another immediate extent. And the person prosecuting it offered to find what was seized in aid. And it was refused. The court ordered a new extent of the like *teste* as the second immediate extent was and refused it to the first immediate extent. And this was held to be the law and course of the Exchequer.

33

Walsh v. Lane

(Ex. 1717)

An abbreviation should be understood according to the intention of the writer.

A rent reserved descends to the heir unless it is express that the rent is not reserved for the entire term.

Columbia Univ. Law Sch. MS. Singleton 4a

Michaelmas term 1717. Hunt Walsh, son etc. of Oliver Walsh v. William Lane.

This is an action of covenant upon articles between Oliver Walsh, the plaintiff's father, and the defendant dated 20 March 1694 on a demise for twenty-one years from the 25th day of March *proxime sequent. data articulorum praedictorum*, in which there is a covenant from the defendant to the said Oliver, his executors, and administrators that the said defendant shall keep up and maintain all such buildings and *emendationes*, *anglice* improvements, as he the said William Lane shall make, build, or erect on the premises in the said term in good and sufficient repair. And he assigns the breach that the defendant did not keep up and maintain the improvements which he made on the premises in good and sufficient repair according to the form and effect of the said articles. But, after the death of the said Oliver, 115 ashes, one oak, 35 beeches and young alderwood, all which the said William Lane during the said term planted on the premises or copied up on the premises until they came to their full growth the said William Lane cut down or permitted to be cut down on the premises.

Upon oyer of the articles, they appear to be dated 20 March 1694 and the term to commence the 25th 'of this instant March'. There is a covenant likewise that the defendant is to have free liberty of cutting and carrying away timber that grows on the said lands as also the hedgebote and ploughbote for fencing and building upon the premises.

The defendant demurs specially and sets forth the variance between the count and articles, *viz.* that the articles are dated 20 March 1694 and the premises are thereby demised for twenty-one years from 25th of March then instant and by the count that the premises are by the articles demised for twenty-one years from the 25 March *proxime sequent.* the date of the articles, *item* that the plaintiff assigns for breach that the defendant cut or suffered to be cut on the premises 115 ashes and other timber trees and yet it appears by the said articles that it was lawful for him to cut and carry away timber growing and *germinandum* on the premises.

As to the first objection, that the articles on oyer are different from those set out in the declaration because in the words *a vicesimo quinto die Martii proxime sequent. data articulorum* they would refer the *proxime sequent.* to the month which would make the term begin a year afterwards. This objection is of no weight, for it is not to be taken as a relative to refer to his next antecedent, as the objectors would have it, but as an adjective, which, being written with an abbreviation, may be either *sequentis* or *sequente*, in the genitive or ablative case, as the parties intended it. And by reading it *sequente*, as it very well may, it exactly agrees with the date of the articles, for the abbreviation, being indifferent, may be read according to the intent of the parties, which appears by the oyer of the deed. And this reconciles the books. And it is a distinction taken [in] 1 Modern 112.[1] And all the cases quoted are hereby reconciled, *viz.* 2 Rolle's *Abridgment*, 251; 2 Cro. 646, 677; 2 Rolle's Reports 394, 398, 414; Cro. Eliz. 420.[2]

As to the word *emendationes*, there is no proper Roman word for improvements in our sense, for *melioratio* is but a barbarous word and not used in the Roman times. And Du Frene[3] mentions *emendare* very near this sense, as *emendata beneficia*, which signifies that the benefice was restored and augmented, though in the old Roman Latin, the word *emendare* signified only to correct. And, since records are made up in Latin that they may be preserved in a language which never changes, the rule is that, where the Roman word is wanting, they may make a word to express their own sense. 2 Cro. 307; *idem* 129; Styles 199.[4]

The next objection is that they have not mentioned in the assignment of the breach that the timber and wood cut was not for the tenant's boots and there was a covenant that he should have them and they would have this shown by way of exception in the assignment of the breach. But this is no objection, for, where the covenants are mutual, the plaintiff, in the assignment of the breach, need not take notice of them. To prove this is the case in the 2d Mod. 34, 35, Hays v. Bickerstaff,[5] wherein Hays brings [an action of] covenant against Bickerstaff on a covenant that, paying the rent and performing the covenants, he should quietly enjoy during the term, the plaintiff need not show the rent paid nor covenants performed because there is a mutual remedy. That is a much stronger case than this. And here, certainly, the plaintiff need not show that this was not cut for the defendant's boots. But, if it was cut for that purpose, it ought to come upon the defendant's side.

But it is objected that this action does not lie because the word heir is not mentioned in the covenant. And there are several cases that might have been quoted, as, if a man makes a lease reserving rent to himself, this shall not go to the heir. 2 Rolle's *Abridgment*, 250; Co. Lit. 47.[6]

---

[1] *Lister v. Stanley* (1674), 1 Modern 112, 86 E.R. 771, also 3 Keble 291, 84 E.R. 727.

[2] *Prescot v. Gwinn* (1623), 2 Rolle, Abr., *Parolls*, pl. E, 4, p. 251; *Prescot v. Anonymous* (1622), Croke Jac. 646, 79 E.R. 558; *Buckley v. Guildbank* (1623), Croke Jac. 678, 79 E.R. 587, 2 Rolle Rep. 398, 414, 81 E.R. 876, 887, also Benloe 142, 73 E.R. 997; *Sharplus v. Hankinson* (1595), Croke Eliz. 420, 78 E.R. 661, also Gouldsborough 187, 75 E.R. 1083.

[3] [In margin:] Du Frene 2 vol., 238 [i.e. C. Dufresne, sieur Du Cange, *Glossarium*].

[4] *Clison v. Proctor* (1612), Croke Jac. 307, 79 E.R. 262; *Wood v. Smith* (1606), Croke Jac. 129, 79 E.R. 112, also Noy 115, 74 E.R. 1080; *Graves v. Drake* (1649), Style 199, 82 E.R. 643.

[5] *Hays v. Bickerstaffe* (1675), 2 Modern 34, 86 E.R. 926, also 1 Freeman 194, 89 E.R. 138, Vaughan 118, 124 E.R. 997.

[6] E. Coke, *First Institute* (1628), f. 47.

So, if a man makes a lease for years reserving a rent to him and his assigns or to him and his executors, this shall not go to the heir. And this is the case of Surry v. Cole, Noy 36, and, likewise, the case of Richmond v. Butcher, reported in Cro. Eliz. 217, 12 Co. 36, 1 And. 261; 1 Cro. 290, Jones 306; Latch 275.[1] And it is the same reason why a covenant should go to the heir unless he would be named.

But as to this, the distinctions concerning reservations are thus, that where a rent *reservando inde annuatim* is reserved generally, it shall go to the lessor and his heirs because the reservation is during the whole term and the rent is a tenure during the whole term and incident to the reversion and commensurate to the term itself.

But if the reservation be to a man for life or to a man and his executors or his assigns, which is only during life, there the tenure and reservation are not commensurate to the whole term by the express words of the party. And, therefore, it cannot descend to the heir, but the lessee shall hold of him by fealty only. But the case of Sacheverell v. Frogale, 1 Ventris 140, 161, 162,[2] if the rent be reserved to a man and his assigns during the term, it shall go to the heir because the reservation is during the whole term. And, therefore, it is plainly the intention of the parties that it should be incident to the reversion and in lieu of it during the whole term. And it is much stronger in this case of a covenant where the party covenants that he shall maintain all the improvements he should make in the premises during the term and, at the end of the said term, should deliver up the peaceable possession of the premises to the said Oliver Walsh, his executors, or assigns. This plainly is a covenant commensurate to the term itself, for it is to hold to the very end of the term. And there is less need of the word heir in a covenant because it does not create an estate, but only to defend the inheritance that goes to the heir. And this is the case of Lougher v. Williams, 2 Levinz 92,[3] where the covenant was with the lessor, his executors, or his administrators that the defendant should repair the premises and leave them in repair at the end of the term; this covenant appeared by the sense of it to be commensurate to the term itself and, therefore, was construed to go to the heir. So here, this covenant

[1] *Sury v. Cole* (1624), Noy 96, 74 E.R. 1062, also Latch, 44, 255, 264, 82 E.R. 266, 373, 378, *sub nom. Coles v. Shury* (1626), Paynell K.B. 80, 198, Benloe 182, 188, 73 E.R. 1041, 1046, Palmer 481, 81 E.R. 1181; *Richmond v. Butcher* (1591), Croke Eliz. 217, 78 E.R. 473, 12 Coke Rep. 36, 77 E.R. 1318, 1 Anderson 261, 123 E.R. 462, also 2 Leonard 214, 74 E.R. 488, Owen 9, 74 E.R. 861, 2 Rolle, Abr., *Reservation*, pl. N, 3, p. 450; *Bland v. Inman* (1632), Croke Car. 288, 79 E.R. 853, W. Jones 308, 82 E.R. 163; *Wotton v. Edwin* (1607), Latch 274, 82 E.R. 383, also 12 Coke Rep. 36, 77 E.R. 1317.

[2] *Sacheverell v. Frogate* (1671), 1 Ventris 148, 161, 86 E.R. 101, 109, also 2 Williams Saunders 361, 85 E.R. 1150, 2 Levinz 13, 83 E.R. 430, T. Raymond 213, 83 E.R. 112, 2 Keble 798, 819, 833, 839, 84 E.R. 504, 517, 527, 531, Hetley 105, 124 E.R. 378.

[3] *Lougher v. Williams* (1673), 2 Levinz 92, 83 E.R. 465.

is with the executors and administrators, and they relied upon it, that the words executors and administrators showed the intention of the parties that the action should continue after the lessor's death and, consequently, must go to the heir, for it cannot go to the executors, for he cannot assign a breach and he cannot have damages for an act done since the death of his testator.

34

Horseman, *qui tam* v. Gibson

(Ex. 1717)

Penal laws must be construed according to the plain meaning of the words used by the legislature.

A statute that is beneficial to many persons and punishes only a few will be construed liberally.

There cannot be two remedies and recoveries for the same offense in a qui tam *action.*

In this case, the master of a ship was found guilty of mooring his ship at the king's mooring contrary to a statute even though he was not on board when the ship was moored.

Fortescue 32, 92 E.R. 749

This was an information against the defendant, as master of a ship, upon the Statute 10th of Queen Anne[1] for the penalty in that Statute for mooring his ship, being a merchantman, at the king's moorings.

There was a verdict for the plaintiff. And the defendant moved in arrest of judgment that the information was naught, for that it avers that, at the time of the mooring, the defendant, the master, had the care of the ship, but does not aver that the master was on board at the time of mooring the said ship. It was urged that this is required by the words of the Statute, and so this case is not brought either within the words or meaning of the Statute, which must be, that he should be then in the actual exercise of his duty as master by his presence on board. And he cited 1 Sanders 49; Hardres 217.[2] That was an information on the Act of Navigation,[3] and it was not averred that the goods were not of the growth of Holland, and it was held ill. And it was further said that the Act did not intend to punish anyone who was not on board and who, perhaps, knew nothing of the matter. And here, he could not, for he went ashore before the ship was moored. And it was further urged that this was a penal law and ought to be expounded

1 Stat. 10 Ann., c. 27, s. 23 (*SR*, IX, 693).

2 *Pitcher v. Jones* (1661), Hardres 217, 145 E.R. 461.

3 Stat. 12 Car. II, c. 18, s. 4 (*SR*, V, 247).

favorably. And it was hard for him to answer for the fault and offence of another. And if this was the true construction, then the mate, or any other person who had the actual command of the ship, would be answerable, as well as the master and so two persons would be answerable for the same crime and offence, which would be unreasonable.

The Attorney General, *Sir Edward Northey*, and others argued to the contrary that the averments in the information were proper and sufficient, that it was laid in the information that the master had the care and government of the ship, that is, the immediate care, for there cannot be two persons that have the immediate care, but they must be in subordination. And the master will be answerable though not on board, for the words of the Statute are in the disjunctive, 'captain, master . . . or person having the care or command of such . . . ship . . . that shall be then on board'.

And the whole court, on taking time to consider of this matter, was unanimously of opinion that it was a good information and that the averments were sufficient to bring it within the Statute. They held that it was both within the words and meaning of the Statute, for that the words in the Statute, 'that shall be then on board', must, in a grammatical construction, as well as in good sense, be referred to the words, 'person having the command of the ship', and not to 'captain' or 'master', for that the particle 'or' plainly disjoins the substantives 'captain' and 'master' from 'person having care and command at the time of mooring' and cannot relate to the captain or master because he has always the command of the ship, as well when he is ashore as on board. And, therefore, this sentence must be read with the word 'other' or other person having care or command, i.e. the actual care and command of the ship at the mooring. The words are 'If any merchant's ship shall fasten to any of the king's moorings or fix themselves to any of the king's ships or hulls, the captain, master, commander, or person having the care or command of such ship, that shall be then on board, to forfeit', etc. This construction is proper from the preamble, which recites the mischief, that the king's ships were subject to fire and the moorings were worn out, that, by this means, there was an opportunity of running goods and embezzling the king's stores and who is the cause of all this? Why, the master and the person left on board, for it is recited this happens through the carelessness of the person left on board. Therefore, there ought to be a remedy adequate to the mischief, which is to give the king an election to punish the master or servant, the master for not putting in a more careful servant and for leaving the ship before she was moored and the servant for his actual breach of duty, doing the mischief. The contrary construction would excuse the master quite and release him from part of his duty which the law creates, that is, to see to his moorings and her bed and lying and put the king to take his remedy perhaps from a cabin boy or common sailor who is actually on board. The master is answerable at common law for the negligence of his servant. The whole care and charge of the ship is committed to the master, who is *exercitor navis*. He engages against everything, except *damnum fatale*, i.e.

pirates and storms. As the master may hypothecate for necessity, so *e contra*, he is answerable if she perish or be injured by his own or the seamen's negligence. Hobart 12.[1]

Suppose this ship had got away from her moorings and fell foul of any other ship or broke her back. Though the master were not on board at the mooring, he would have been answerable. Nay, he is answerable though there be no apparent neglect either in him or his servants and the seamen because of his express engagement to take care of and conduct the ship, and he has wages for it. And so is the case of Morse v. Slue, 1 Ventris 238.[2]

But it was objected it is a penal law and shall be taken by equity. But though this be a law in some sort penal, yet it is a remedial law and beneficial for the public and, therefore, it shall have a free and benign construction, as is Plowden 36b.[3] If a statute be beneficial to very many and punish but a few, those are called gracious and beneficial laws.

The action is given in the alternative to one or other, but not against both, as the case of Morse v. Slue, where it was held that an action of case for goods lost out of a ship would lie either against the master of the ship or against the owners. So escape will lie against the jailer, and yet the sheriff is liable, for *respondeat superior*, 1 Ventris 239,[4] but not against both. And a recovery against one may be pleaded by the other, for a double satisfaction no man ought to have for the same thing.

But then, there was an objection to the finding of the verdict that the jury had found more than was averred in the information or that was in the issue, for the information does not aver that the defendant moored the ship, but the verdict finds it so. But it was overruled by the court, for the information is laid in the words of the Statute, that the ship was moored; so the defendant being master, by necessary implication, the master then did it, who had the care and command of the ship. And if the mooring is supposed to be done by him, then, it is part of the issue. They find *quoad* the mooring of the said ship by the defendant Gibson and lying there five tides, the defendant is guilty. This had been all one and as good sense, as if *per Carolum Gibson* had been left out, for it is not material who the ship was moored by, since the captain is liable. If he is guilty as to mooring and continuing five tides, then, he moored the ship. Morse v. Slue is a stronger case than this; the declaration was that the master received wages of the merchant, and the verdict was according to the truth that the master received wages of the

---

1 *Williams v. Bridgeman*, Hobart 11, 80 E.R. 162.

2 *Morse v. Slue* (1672–1673), 1 Ventris 190, 238, 86 E.R. 129, 159, also 2 Levinz 69, 83 E.R. 453, Sir T. Raymond 220, 83 E.R. 115, 2 Keble 866, 84 E.R. 548, 3 Keble 72, 112, 135, 84 E.R. 601, 624, 638, 1 Modern 85, 86 E.R. 752.

3 *Platt v. Lock* (1550), 1 Plowden 35, 36, 75 E.R. 57, 59.

4 *Morse v. Slue* (1673), *ut supra*.

owner of the ship, but it was held not material, for the merchants pay the owners, and the owners pay it over to the master.

But this is not a construction according to the equity of the Statute only, but it is a case within the words and meaning of this law, according to the most natural and proper construction. And penal laws must be so construed as well as others.

And Baron FORTESCUE ALAND remembered a case between Alymer and Morris, Easter 1 Geo. I, determined by Lord Parker, Chief Justice of the King's Bench, at *nisi prius* in Middlesex, which was an *indebitatus assumpsit* for £220 money received to the plaintiff's use, as his share of a prize taken by the defendant, the plaintiff being admiral and flag officer, given by the Statute 6 Ann., fol. 277,[1] which says, 'If any ship . . . be taken [and condemned] as prize . . . the flag officer . . . or commanders and other officers, seamen, and others, who shall be actually on board such ship . . . which shall so take such prize . . . shall have the sole interest . . . of such prize' in such proportion, as the queen by her proclamation shall think fit; and by the queen's proclamation, the flag officer is to have one-third of the captain's share, who has for his share three-eighths. The Lord Parker, now earl of Macclesfield, held that the prize being taken under the command of Admiral Aylmer and under his direction, though he was not actually on board nor in sight, yet he should have his share. This is a stronger case than ours, for those words are all in the conjunctive, 'flag officer and other officers who shall be on board'; and yet the 'and' was construed 'or' to make it agreeable to good sense and the true meaning of the law makers and within the reason of the common law.

Then, it was objected they may have two remedies and recover two penalties for one and the same offence. The answer is that cannot be and is a mistake, for, when the recovery is against the master, the election is determined. So, judgment as before was finally given.

35

Smith v. Roocliff

(Ex. 1718)

In this case, the court found a modus decimandi *in lieu of tithes in kind to be void.*

Bunbury 20, 145 E.R. 580,
1 Rayner 140, 1 Eagle & Younge 734

The barons were of opinion that a *modus* of 1s. in the pound for pasture according to the value of the land was a void *modus*, as is also a *modus* of 1s. in the pound according to the value of the rent.

---

[1] Stat. 6 Ann., c. 65, s. 6 (*SR*, VIII, 811–812).

[Order of 6 February 1718: 2 Wood 88.]

36

Attorney General v. Mellish

(Ex. 1718)

Where goods are seized for non-payment of customs duties, the owner can claim them without making an oath of ownership.

Bunbury 21, 145 E.R. 580

At Serjeants' Inn, 24 February 1717[/18].

Upon a seizure of bullion in a ship at Portsmouth, the defendant claimed property to the value of £10,000. Mr. Attorney General [*Northey*] moved that the defendant might be put to swear to his property.

But *per* CURIAM, though before the Pepper Act, 8 Ann., s. 76,[1] it was usual to make them swear, yet since, there has been no instance of it but where there were two claimers, and, then, the second was to swear. Therefore, they would not oblige the defendant in this case, though the Attorney General produced an affidavit that the defendant was in mean circumstances, which was some reason for suspecting a fraud.

37

Bate v. Sprackling

(Ex. 1718)

Tithes are not due for hop poles.

Tithe milk is paid by every tenth meal.

Bunbury 20, 145 E.R. 580,
1 Rayner 139, 2 Gwillim 618, 1 Eagle & Younge 736

18 February 1717[/18].

It was decreed by the court that no tithe should be paid of hop poles, that tithe milk ought to be every tenth meal, and that, in all cases, where you do not make out some custom, you must pay according to the canon.

Mr. *Ward* quoted the case of Chitty v. Reeves, *in Scaccario, termino* Trinity 3 Jac. 1687,[2] wherein it was resolved that tithes of hops are not to be paid until after they are picked and before they are dried, every tenth measure.

---

[1] Stat. 8 Ann., s. 12 (*SR*, IX, 218–220).

[2] *Chitty v. Reeve* (Ex. 1687), Eq. Cases Exch. 274, 1 Rayner 67, 1 Wood 251, 1 Eagle & Younge 552.

[Order of 18 February 1718: 2 Wood 86.]

38

Haughton v. Starkey

(Ex. 1718)

A successful plaintiff upon a suggestion for a prohibition is entitled to court costs from the time of the first motion.

1 Strange 82, 93 E.R. 398, 1 Eagle & Younge 734

After a judgment for the plaintiff in prohibition, the question was what costs ought to be allowed, the Statute of 8 & 9 Will. III, c. 11,[1] giving costs in suits upon prohibitions. And whether they should be computed from the first motion or only from the declaration was the doubt. Upon search, it was found to be the course of all the courts to tax only from the time of declaring, except in two instances, Eads v. Jackson, King's Bench, 2 Geo., and Brown v. Turner *et al.*, in the Common Bench,[2] where they were allowed from the first motion. And of this opinion were all the judges, as Baron Fortescue informed me. And all the officers were directed for the future to allow the costs of the first motion.

And afterwards, in Hilary 12 Geo., King's Bench, between Swetnam v. Archer,[3] it was stated in the same manner and agreed to be the uniform practice ever since. And Easter 1 Geo. II, between Sir Thomas Bury and Cross,[4] the same doubt was raised by a new Master, and the court ordered costs from the first motion.

Fortescue 348, 92 E.R. 885

A [writ of] prohibition was brought concerning a seat in a church. And the question was if the plaintiff should have costs in prohibition and from what time. By the late Act which gives costs, 8 & 9 Will. III, cap. 11, if the rule be discharged for a prohibition, it was agreed there could be no costs. The commencement of the suit is the suggestion the counsel urged, and, therefore, costs must be taxed from the motion for a prohibition. They compared it to *habeas corpus* and *certiorari* and *recordare*. The expense of those writs is always allowed, as also of ejectment. Here is a new declaration. The words of the Act are 'in all suits upon prohibition'.

---

[1] Stat. 8 & 9 Will. III, c. 11 (*SR*, VII, 201–203).

[2] *Ead v. Jackson* (1715), Fortescue 345, 92 E.R. 883, Randolph K.B. 58; *Wills v. Turner* (1716), Cooke C.P. 11, 123 E.R. 926.

[3] *Swetnam v. Archer* (1724), 8 Modern 338, 88 E.R. 241, Fortescue 346, 92 E.R. 884.

[4] *Berry v. Cross* (1728), 1 Barnardiston K.B. 47, 93 E.R. 33.

In this case, which was after a verdict, they would have the costs limited from the declaration. And they cited a case in the Common Pleas, Willis and Brown, plaintiffs, and Turner *et al.*, defendants, where they gave costs in prohibition from the motion. But in the King's Bench, they gave costs only from the declaration. But this case was never moved there.

All the judges being met on another occasion, this case was put, and they were all of opinion that costs should be taxed from the motion and suggestion for a prohibition. Lord PARKER, then Chief Justice, said this was like a petition, which formerly was exhibited for an original; it all concerns the prohibition, and it is part of the suit, and, indeed, an original is rather a commission for the court to issue other process.

And the Court of Exchequer, pursuant to this resolution, ordered costs to be taxed from the motion and suggestion in this prohibition. 8 & 9 Will. III, cap. 10, sect. 3. *Vide* Ede and Jackson, if damages in prohibition.

39

Parker, *qui tam* v. Aston

(Ex. 1718)

Where perishable goods are seized for non-payment of customs duties, the court will not release them (upon a forthcoming bond) where it is suspected that they will be taken out of the jurisdiction of the court.

Bunbury 21, 145 E.R. 581

24 February 1718.

The court was moved for a writ of appraisement and delivery for a ship loaded with salt that was seized but ten days before, for, though it was not within one reason for granting writs of delivery, *viz.* delay of prosecution, yet it was within another, that the goods were perishable.

But *per* CURIAM: We will not grant a writ of delivery, which is discretionary in the court, and there is reason to suspect this ship was going to Gothenburg.

40

Anonymous

(Ex. 1718)

Where a person sues for tithes in general terms and then gives notice that he will proceed only as to specific items, this will limit the original demand to those specific items only.

Bunbury 22, 145 E.R. 581,
1 Rayner 140, 2 Gwillim 618, 1 Eagle & Younge 736

If there be a general demand for tithes and a general replication put in, if the plaintiff, upon the commission, gives notice that he will proceed only as to such and such particular matters, it is as well as if the demand had been abridged in the replication. (*Sed quaere.*)

41

Attorney General v. Webber

(Ex. 1718)

In exchange for the payment of a debt to the crown by a private person, the debt to the crown can be assigned to him and he can be given a writ of extent to collect it for himself from the debtor.

Wightwick 3, 145 E.R. 1152

16th May 1718.

Webber was Collector of the Customs at Minehead, and he entered into a bond to the king for the due execution of the office. After having incurred a considerable debt, an information was filed against him by the Attorney General, praying an account of what was due to the king. Webber admitted that a considerable sum was due from him. And, at the hearing, the court decreed an account to be taken. And there being a considerable balance found due, Dr. Coney and Mr. Morgan, who do not appear to stand in the relationship of sureties, apply to the court that, upon their paying the debt reported due to the crown, they might have the aid of its prerogative process to prosecute Webber upon his bond to reimburse themselves.

And, accordingly, the court ordered it and directed the bond given by Webber to the king to be delivered to the attorney of Dr. Coney and Mr. Morgan and to have a [writ of] extent thereon to recover the debt they had paid for Webber, together with all their costs and charges attending the same.

It appears from the order of the 16th of May 1718 that Dr. Coney and Mr. Morgan had, together with Webber, entered into a bond for £1,000 conditioned for the due execution of his office, and 'that a writ of *scire facias* had been awarded upon the aforesaid bond against the said F. Webber and his said security for them to show cause why His Majesty should not have execution against them for the said sum of £1,000'. This case seems to have been much considered by the court, as a second order, ratifying and confirming the first, was made upon the 30th of May following after hearing counsel on behalf of the mortgagee of the estate of F. Webber and upon reading the Deputy Remembrancer's report certifying the sum due from F. Webber and the receipt for the same signed by the Cashiers of His Majesty's Customs.

42

Anonymous

(Ex. 1718)

Where depositions have been taken and the plaintiff fails to proceed, the defendant cannot have the case dismissed unless he has the depositions suppressed.

Bunbury 23, 145 E.R. 581

14 June 1718.

If a replication is put in to an answer and a commission is taken out and the depositions returned, so long as those depositions are in being, the defendant cannot move to dismiss, whatever delay the plaintiff is afterwards guilty of, but he must set the cause down to be heard *ad requisitionem defendentis*. But if he suppresses the depositions upon the delay of the plaintiff, afterward, the defendant may move to dismiss for want of prosecution.

43

Hampton v. Hampton

(Ex. 1718)

By the custom of London, when a widower dies, one half of his estate is divided among his children and one half is available to pay legacies.

A bond made to a child contemporaneously with the making of a will cannot defeat the testamentary custom of London.

British Library MS. Add. 36651, f. 88v, pl. 2

Trinity 4 Geo., 1718. Francis Hampton v. Barbara Hampton.

The bill was to have a child's part of the estate of Adam Hampton, who was the father of the plaintiff and defendant and a freeman of London. The case was that Adam Hampton, having no wife but having two children, about ten days before his death, made his will reciting that, whereas he was indebted to his daughter Barbara £120 by a bond of such a date etc., he first willed that the said debt and funerals should be paid and discharged and then he devised a legacy of £5 to his son Francis, the plaintiff, and devised all the residue of his estate to his said daughter Barbara and made her sole executrix and died.

It appeared by the proofs that the said bond was executed at the same time with the will, but antedated but that the testator, several times before his death, owned that his daughter had laid out several sums of money for him. And, in her answer, she swears that she had lent him £66 at several times, but she made no proof of it.

The court looked upon the bond to be only contrived to defeat the custom [of London] and, therefore, should not affect the orphanage part. But they decreed that the estate should be divided into two equal parts, one part, which is the orphanage part, to be equally divided between the plaintiff and defendant and, as to the other part, which is the testamentary part, that the same should, in the first place, be subject to the payment of the said £120 to the defendant, as being devised to her by the will, and, if anything remain, then the plaintiff is to have his legacy of £5 out of the testamentary part.

44

Elliot v. Davis

(Ex. 1718)

In this case, a court of equity ordered the plaintiff to pay interest upon a bond although it exceeded the penalty of the bond in order to be put into possession of certain land.

Bunbury 23, 145 E.R. 581

16 June 1718.

Interest upon a bond was decreed to be paid, although it exceeded the penalty of the bond.

British Library MS. Add. 36651, f. 89

John Elliot, son and heir of John Elliot, Jr., and grandson and heir of John Elliot, Sr., plaintiff; J. Davis and M., his wife, who is the granddaughter and administratrix of F. Gough and also administratrix of Jane, her mother.

The bill was to be let into the possession of two estates which the plaintiff claims as heir at law and to have satisfaction entered upon the record of two judgments obtained *anno* 1664 upon two bonds entered into by the plaintiff's grandfather, who was seised in fee of the said estates, the one in the penalty of £200 for payment of £100, the other in £100 for the payment of £50, the plaintiff insisting that the said debt was satisfied by perception of profits.

There was a decree to account before the Deputy [Remembrancer] with a special direction that, if he found the sum due to exceed the penalty of the said bonds, to report that specially. And it coming now before the court upon his report, it appeared by the report that there was due to the defendants for principal and interest from the year 1664 to 1717 the sum of £660 8s. 0d.

The query now was whether the plaintiff, as heir at law to his grandfather, the obligor, shall be obliged to pay the whole sum reported due or only so far as the penal sums mentioned in the said bonds will extend before the court will decree him the possession.

The case, as it stood upon the pleadings, was that John Elliot, the plaintiff's grandfather, was seised in fee of these two estates, one £100 *per annum*, the other

£150 *per annum*. And *anno* 1663, he gave a bond to one Windham in £200 for payment of £100 and interest and, in 1664, he gave another bond to one Yates for £100 for payment of £50 and interest and the same year judgments were obtained on both these bonds. Afterward, *viz*. in 1669, the said John Elliot, the grandfather, upon the marriage of his son John Elliot with Jane, the daughter of F. Gough, in consideration of a marriage portion, made a settlement of one of the said estates, *viz*. that of £150 *per annum*, which was to John, his son, for life, remainder to Jane, the intended wife for life, with remainders in tail to the issue of the marriage, and he covenanted that the estate was clear of encumbrances. The marriage took effect. And, afterwards, *anno* 1672, John Elliot, the son, died, leaving issue the plaintiff John Elliot, soon after whose death, the said Windham and Yates, the obligees, threatening to sue execution upon the said estate, which Jane, the wife, then held in jointure, and John, the grandfather, being an incumbered person and not able to pay off the debt, Gough, the father of Jane, the jointress, paid off the money due on the said judgments and took an assignment of them in order to protect his daughter's jointure. Gough and Jane, his daughter, afterwards dying, the defendants Davis and his wife became entitled to the benefit of the said judgments, she being the granddaughter and administratrix of F. Gough and likewise daughter and administratrix of Jane, the jointress. It appeared that John Elliot, the grandfather, died *anno* 1682 and that Jane, his wife, then became entitled to a rent charge of £60 *per annum* out of the estate that was not settled upon the marriage of John, the son, for her jointure, which jointure was prior and not liable to the said judgment and that she lived until the year 1700. *Anno* 1708, the judgments were revived by the defendants and the lands in question were extended.

After long arguments at the bar by *Sir Constantine Phipps et aliis* for the plaintiff and Serjeant *Chesshyre*, Serjeant *Stevens*, and Mr. *Foley* for the defendant, the court delivered their opinions.

The Lord Chief Baron Bury was of opinion that the plaintiff should not be let into possession without paying all that is reported due and not the penalties of the bonds only, for that Gough, after the death of John Elliot, the younger, being under a necessity of paying off the debt to protect his daughter's jointure, it appearing that old John could not do it, being an incumbered man, and he, Gough, having taken the assignment of the judgments in trust for his daughter and to protect her jointure, which it was the duty of old John Elliot and those that claim under him to protect by reason of the covenant against encumbrances, therefore, the plaintiff, as heir of old John Elliot and standing in his place, ought not to be let in upon easier terms than he should have been and the court need not put the defendants to take their remedy at law upon the covenant. He said it was agreed on all hands that they might in some cases upon circumstances extend the debt beyond the penalty. And he thought the circumstances in this case were such as would be sufficient grounds for such a judgment, especially the covenant against encumbrances.

Baron Price said he could not extend it beyond the penalty of the bonds, which is the utmost the law will do, for, if the judgment be extended or [an action of] debt brought upon them, they could have no more and, now, they would have interest for thirty-six years, more than the penalty will reach. He said that equity will go no farther than the law unless something of fraud appears or some apparent willful obstruction by the party, as in the case cited out of Shower's Parliamentary Cases by insisting upon the privilege of Parliament. They might have received satisfaction without all the delay. It appears that old John died in 1682. His estate was £100 *per annum*; his wife had a jointure of £60 out of it, so there remained £40 *per annum* subject to this debt. In 1700, the wife died, and then all that estate was open, and yet no execution was taken out until 1708, which, if it had been taken out in 1682, when old John died, that £40 *per annum*, which was then open and able, would have cleared the whole debt, which then was but small.

Baron Montagu: If the plaintiff will have the possession decreed to him, he must do equity and pay all that is reported due. If I lend £100 upon a note and bring an action upon the note and, upon [a plea of] the general issue, it appears that it has been owing fifty years and no interest was paid but constant demands were made, the jury ought to give me interest for all that time; so in the case of a single bill. But it is objected that, in the case of a bond with a penalty, the party has fixed upon a sum certain for his security. The response [is], as a court of equity will lower the penalty where the debt and interest does not amount to so much, so may a court of equity, upon circumstances, enlarge, as it were, the penalty. And though an execution at law cannot exceed the sum contained in the judgment, yet a court of equity may hold the parties to terms and compel them to do more than, by the strict rules of law, they are obliged to do and oblige them to do equity before the court will decree them what they are not by law entitled to. And, in this case, we may say to the plaintiff, if you will be let into possession, to which you are not by law entitled, you shall pay what we think in conscience to be due to the defendant.

Baron Page: There may be circumstances to carry it beyond the penalty. Anything of fraud or contrivance or other obstructions to the suing of execution, which could not be prevented will do it. But without some such circumstances, equity must follow the law. In this case, the only doubt with me is upon the covenant against encumbrances, for, as to the debt itself, the circumstances are not very material because it is a debt against an heir, who is not bound farther than is expressed. And if he had not been named in the bond, he would not have been bound at all nor the estate in his hands liable, though it came from his ancestor. Therefore, the lien upon the heir extends no farther than the penalty of the bond. But the doubt with me is upon the covenant. If an action of covenant had been brought against the ancestor and judgment [given] for the damages, that would have been a certain lien as well as this penalty. But there was no such judgment, which, if there had, this court would have obliged him to pay both, as, in the case of an heir of a mortgagor who comes to redeem and there is also a bond debt owing, he must pay both. So if the deed of settlement made on the marriage had mentioned this incumbrance and covenanted to discharge it, they must have paid it to the utmost.

It was decreed that the plaintiff should not be let into possession unless he paid all that is reported due, by Bury and Montagu, *contra* Price. Page *dubitavit* and would not give his opinion positively, having been of counsel in the cause.

45

Dudds v. Billings

(Ex. 1718)

Witnesses who have given their depositions cannot be re-examined without leave of court.

Bunbury 24, 145 E.R. 581

17 June 1718.

It was said by Baron Price in this case that witnesses who have been examined upon the first commission cannot be examined upon a second to the same matter without leave of the court.

46

Harrison's Case

(Ex. 1718)

The high officers of the Exchequer are exempt from service as a constable.

Bunbury 24, 145 E.R. 581

17 June 1718.

This day Harrison, who was deputy to Mr. Masham, the Foreign Apposer, was allowed his writ of privilege to exempt him from serving in the office of constable.

47

Rex v. Gibbons

(Ex. 1718)

A writ of immediate extent will be issued against the debtor of a debtor of the crown who has executed a writ of extent in aid if the money is in danger of being lost.

Bunbury 24, 145 E.R. 581

21 June 1718.

It was said in this case that, if a [writ of] extent issues against A., who is indebted to the crown, and B., upon the inquisition, is found indebted to A., upon the return of that inquisition and upon affidavit made that the money in B.'s hands is in danger of being lost, an immediate extent shall issue against B.

48

Rex v. Archbishop of Canterbury

(Ex. 1718)

A fine sent into the Exchequer for collection can be amended only if there is matter of record upon which to base the amendment.

Bunbury 24, 145 E.R. 582

26 June 1718.

A man who lived within the liberty of the archbishop of Canterbury was fined by the judges of oyer and terminer in Southwark for a misdemeanor in court, which fine was estreated, but no notice was taken in the estreat of what place the man was.

Therefore, *Sir Constantine Phipps* moved that the estreat might be amended by adding the place where the man lived so that the archbishop, who had the grant of the fines *tam integre tenentium quam non integre tenentium infra* etc., might come before the Foreign Apposer and claim this fine by virtue of his grant. And he said that a man had been indicted and fined in Essex, which fine was estreated here and such an amendment was made upon application.

But to this, it was said there was an addition in the indictment, which was a guide to the court, being a record to amend the estreat by. But here is a record for the king and nothing but an affidavit of the other side.

And the court refused to do anything in it upon the motion.

49

Woodcock v. Smith

(Ex. 1718)

In equity, a clergyman is presumed to be rightfully in possession of his church.

Bunbury 25, 145 E.R. 582

26 June 1718.

Although, at law, they hold a parson or vicar to the proof of his admission, institution, and induction and reading the Articles, yet *per* TOTAM CURIAM, we never do in equity.

50

Rex v. Barlow

(Ex. 1718)

Where a landowner traverses an inquisition, he must post a bond in the value of two years' income from the land.

Bunbury 25, 145 E.R. 582, Conroy 116

Per Baron MONTAGU: If a man traverses an inquisition, the usual course of the court is to take security to the value of two years' profits of the land because, in that time, it is intended the right of the crown and party will be determined.

51

Bailey v. Peastly

(Ex. 1718)

In a suit for tithes, if the defendant is in default, the plaintiff must prove the value of the tithes due by his own testimony under oath.

Bunbury 26, 145 E.R. 582,
1 Rayner 144, 2 Gwillim 623, 1 Eagle & Younge 739

8 July 1718.

A bill was brought for tithes. The defendant stood out until a sequestration, and the bill was taken *pro confesso*. It was moved for the defendant that, upon paying the costs, the value of the tithes might be ascertained and reduced, either by the taxation of the Master or by the oath of the plaintiff himself, as was done in the case of Crosman v. Goodrick, Hilary term, 2 & 3 Jac. II.[1]

But note: There was a consent in that case.

And the court now would make no other rule but that the plaintiff should show cause why he should not consent to give his oath to the value.

[1] *Crossman v. Goodrich* (1688), 1 Rayner 66, 1 Eagle & Younge 554, 1 Wood 254.

52

Witherington v. Sherecroft

(Ex. 1718)

Sedge is not tithable unless it is sold.

British Library MS. Hargrave 367, f. 26v, pl. 3

Trinity term 4 Geo. 1718. Whitterington v. Shereright.

This was a bill in the Exchequer to discover what quantity and profit the defendants had made of coarse grass called sedge. It was shown that stubble shall not pay tithes. Yelverton 86.[1]

Sir Constantine Phipps said wood spent in the house is tithable unless there is a special custom to the contrary and it has been often adjudged and determined so. The person ought to give notice to the parson or impropriator of his setting out of tithes, but not that morning that he carries his own part away, but he should give longer notice.

It was said on the other side that sedge is of so inconsiderable a value that no tithes are paid for it and it is like stubble.

Lord Chief Baron Bury: If rushes or sedge or fern is fit for nothing but to lay under cattle to make dung of, tithe shall not be paid of it. But he doubted whether wood burned in a house is tithable.

Baron Price: I do not know that the law has gone so far as for the owner of a common in gross to give notice of the setting out of tithes. But the owner must set it out at his peril and if he sets it out by fraud, it is no setting out at all. As the sedge is of a yearly increase, it is tithable, though but of small value if it is not wholly for compost or dung. But, if a year happen that it is of no value, yet it is tithable if, in other years, it has been paid. They, as to wood burned at home, ought to set forth that the wood was burned in the dairy, for wood burned for the use of the same is not tithable, but wood burned in the hall or parlor is tithable.

Baron Montagu said custom may make wood not tithable. But, of common right, it is. A man must have fire for the providing of food to eat and to keep him warm as well as in the dairy. If the sedge was sold for dung, it must pay tithe. But if kept on the farm for dung only, it is not tithable. Brakes are tithable as well as other things if sold or employed to a use or profit.

[Order of 16 July 1717: 2 Wood 74.]

[1] *Grene v. Austen* (1606), Yelverton 86, 80 E.R. 59, also Croke Jac. 116, 79 E.R. 100, 1 Eagle & Younge 164.

53

Benning v. Dowce

(Ex. 1718)

Lands owned by the bishopric of London are exempt from the payment of tithes.

Bunbury 26, 145 E.R. 582,
1 Rayner 143, 2 Gwillim 622, 1 Eagle & Younge 739

This was a bill for tithes. The defendant insisted that the lands where etc. were part of the homestall, which is part of the bishop of London's palace, and, therefore, exempt from payment of tithes. But he did not lay it personally in the bishop.

And this was allowed by Lord Chief Baron Bury and Baron Price, against Page, to be well enough because this exemption goes along with the lands, although it would have been better laid by way of formal prescription as at law that the bishop for himself and his tenants have time out of mind, etc. And, as to lands belonging to a monastery, they must set forth how the prescription is. But, where the land itself is exempt, it is discharged in whatever hands it comes. And, by the opinion of two barons against one (*absente* Montagu), the bill was dismissed.

54

Scott, *qui tam* v. Caswell

(Ex. 1718)

In the case of a seizure of perishable goods for non-payment of customs duties, writs of appraisement and delivery can be issued in vacation time before the information is filed.

Bunbury 27, 145 E.R. 582

23 October 1718.

A seizure of a ship with sugars was in July last after the term. The goods being perishable, the prosecutor consented that a writ of appraisement and delivery should go out in vacation time, the defendant giving security. This term, the information came in. And the court was moved for a new writ of appraisement and delivery and that the old appraised value should be returned upon the new writ of appraisement, which, being by consent, was granted, although regularly the writ of appraisement and delivery cannot issue until the information is in.

55

Abthorp v. Jennings

(Ex. 1718)

The question in this case was whether an ecclesiastical court has the jurisdiction to determine a modus decimandi *in lieu of tithes in kind.*

Bunbury 27, 145 E.R. 583, 1 Eagle & Younge 739

25 October 1718.

Mr. *Bootle* moved for an injunction on a *dedimus* and that it should extend to stay proceedings in the bishop of Ely's court until answer, where the defendant, as rector of Gambliga in Cambridgeshire, libelled against the plaintiffs, his parishioners for all sorts of tithes. And upon alleging that there were several *moduses*, the proof of which would arise out of the answer, the motion was granted. (*Quod nota.*) But the rule was discharged 28 November following.

56

Anonymous

(Ex. 1718)

In a suit for tithes, the defendant must make an account of the tithes that are due.

If the tithes are tendered before the litigation was begun, the parishioner will not be liable to pay court costs.

Bunbury 28, 145 E.R. 583,
1 Rayner 144, 2 Gwillim 618, 1 Eagle & Younge 739

If, to a bill for tithes, the defendant does not show a tender before or make it in the answer, the plaintiff is entitled to an account, although the value be never so small. If there has been a tender before and a tender is also made by the answer, the defendant saves his costs. If the tender is only by the answer, he must account with costs.

57

Seymour v. Rapier

(Ex. 1718)

Stock in trade includes the shop goods and the utensils in trade.

Bunbury 28, 145 E.R. 583

17 November 1718.

A bill was brought for an account of the testator's personal estate. The defendants, in their answer, insisted that the testator had devised to them all his stock in trade and that his book debts, cash, bills, and money in goldsmiths' hands, which was applied to the carrying on of his trade, should be included in those words.

But by the opinion of three barons against the Lord Chief Baron Bury, nothing shall be deemed stock in trade but the shop goods and utensils in trade, though Baron Price thought the ready money in the till might come within that construction, but no farther.

N.B. It was strongly insisted on for the defendants that they should be permitted to prove what directions the testator gave to the person who drew the will and what he intended should be comprehended in these words in his will. This was provisionally read, but no stress was laid upon this evidence by the court.

58

Sheregold v. Brewster

(Ex. 1718)

The question in this case was whether a sum due for court costs could be satisfied by a making a deduction from a judgment debt in another court.

Bunbury 29, 145 E.R. 583

21 November 1718.

The plaintiff obtained a verdict in the Common Pleas for £30 against the defendant, and the defendant had £13 costs taxed against the plaintiff in this court upon the dismission of his bill. The defendant prosecuting the plaintiff in this court for the costs, it was moved that the court would lay their hands on these costs and that so much as they come to should be deducted out of what was due to the plaintiff upon the judgment in the Common Pleas.

The court made an order to stay process of contempt for not paying the costs until further order, though Baron Price thought the proper method would be to prefer a short bill.

59

Thomas v. Williams

(Ex. 1718)

A court of equity can grant common law relief in a suit for discovery.

Bunbury 29, 145 E.R. 583

26 November 1718.

If a bill is preferred against an executor to discover assets, which likewise prays relief, this court will grant relief upon such bill, by the opinion of three barons against PRICE, as was done in the case of Depuis v. Duke of Kingston, 16 June last, and in the present case.

But note: In both these cases, the defendant had joined in a commission. But, if he had demurred to the relief, it seems the demurrer would have been good.

British Library MS. Add. 36651, f. 94v

The bill was for a discovery of assets and for a satisfaction of a debt of £20, which the plaintiff insisted was due to him from the intestate [Rice Williams] for wages as his servant.

The defendant [Williams, administrator of Rice Williams], by his answer, confessed assets, but insisted that the plaintiff had received several sums of money of the intestate in his lifetime and denied the retainer and insisted that nothing was duc to him.

At the hearing, the court were of opinion that the defendant having by his answer confessed assets, the plaintiff might take his remedy for satisfaction at law, for, now, it was become a mere action at law, and, therefore, they would not decree relief and satisfaction for the debt though witnesses were examined on both sides as to that matter.

Now, the plaintiff petitioned for a rehearing for that the court should have decreed relief and not have sent the plaintiff to law to prove his debt.

Baron PRICE said the decree was right and agreeable to the practice of this court and, though the Court of Chancery do usually give relief upon bills of discovery where relief is prayed, yet that has been very much complained of, for, by that means, everything though merely matter at law may be drawn into equity. Therefore, he thought that, in such cases, after a discovery had, they ought to be sent to law unless equitable assets or some other equitable ingredients do appear in the case.

Lord Chief Baron BURY, MONTAGU, and PAGE, *contra*, said it would be very injurious to send the plaintiff to law in this case after a discovery of assets, which discovery is at his own charge, for it is a rule that he that will light his candle must do it at his own cost, and, in this case, those costs may amount to more than his debt. The defendant has by his answer not only discovered assets but has insisted upon several matters which are proper for an account and he has put the plaintiff upon a necessity of replying to the answer and proving his retainer, for, if the plaintiff had gone to law and given the answer in evidence to prove assets, the whole must have been taken for true. If the plaintiff had not replied to it and then his discovery would have been to no purpose and might as well have been [. . .][1]

[1] The next page with the rest of this case is now missing from the manuscript.

60

Walter v. Russell

(Ex. 1718)

Where there was a decree nisi *and the defendant made default and the decree was made absolute, if the court, afterward, grants the defendant a rehearing, the defendant will be ordered to pay £10 court costs.*

Bunbury 30, 145 E.R. 584

28 November 1718.

In this case, it was settled as a rule that, if there is a decree *nisi* and, at the day, the defendant makes default and the decree thereupon be made absolute, if the court, afterward, upon the petition of the defendant, grants a rehearing, the defendant shall pay £10 costs.

And note, in the same case 10 December, that, if exceptions, which are put in only to continue an injunction, are overruled, the injunction is dissolved of course without a motion.

61

Johnson, *qui tam* v. Sowers

(Ex. 1718)

If a seizer of forfeited goods delays filing an information or does not sue out a writ of appraisement, the defendant, upon entering his claim, may move for a writ of delivery.

Bunbury 30, 145 E.R. 584

7 December 1718.

After a seizure of goods, the regular steps are to file an information and then take out a writ of appraisement, upon the return of which the defendant is to enter his claim. And then, he may move for a writ of delivery. If the prosecutor delays filing an information or does not sue out a writ of appraisement, the defendant, upon entering his claim in the book in the office, may move for a writ of delivery. It was very much debated in the case of Allen, *qui tam* v. Cowper, what should be called delay, but no certain rule laid down. So also, the same thing was debated this day in the present case. What was most generally agreed to was that, where a seizure was in the vacation time and there is no information filed the term following, if they could have tried it that term, this would be a delay to ground a writ of delivery upon.

62

Anonymous

(Ex. 1718)

Where a judgment debtor dies, a writ of sequestration will not be discharged before the sequestrators have made a return.

Bunbury 31, 145 E.R. 584

9 December 1718.

A [writ of] sequestration issued against J. for not performing a decree. Lands being seized by the sequestrators, J. died; whereupon, it was moved that the sequestration should be discharged.

But the court refused it because the sequestration was not returned, for the sequestrators are answerable for what profits they have received of the lands and they have nothing to indemnify them but the authority given them by the sequestration. But the sequestration being returned, the court discharged it, as to the lands, from the death of J.

63

Tendring v. London

(Ex. 1718)

A seller of land who does not have the absolute ownership of it at the time of the sale cannot have the remedy of specific performance against the buyer.

2 Eq. Cas. Abr. 680, 22 E.R. 571

Michaelmas term 5 Geo. I, 1718.

If A. contracts for the purchase of an estate and is not absolute owner of it, nor has it in his power by the ordinary course of [common] law or equity to make himself so, though the owner offers to make the seller a title, yet equity will not force the buyer to take it, for every seller that will have such a bargain executed must be *bona fide* a contractor. And it must be such a reasonable title as every purchaser would expect.

64

Cotterell v. Chamberlain

(Ex. 1719)

Monetary legacies are liable to be abated in order to pay the decedent's debts before any specific legacies are.

Bunbury 32, 145 E.R. 584

9 February 1718[/19].

F. Cotterell, senior, by his will, devises his farm at Bristow Causeway, and the stock upon it to his eldest son, whom he made executor. And he devised his stock and farm at Mitcham to his second son, upon condition that he should pay £150 within a year to his executor, the better to enable him to pay the money legacies, which amounted to £120. F., the executor, preferred his bill for this £150, and a legatee preferred his cross-bill to have his legacy of £100 paid to him. And upon all the pleadings, the Master's report, etc., it appeared that the plaintiff had paid above £400 and that, therefore, his legacy of Bristow Causeway farm and stock being a specific legacy and there not being assets sufficient besides, the money legacies ought first to be swallowed up and the specific legacies not broken into until after. And, upon this point, the whole debate was.

And, at last, the whole court agreed that there ought not to be a proportionable deduction between specific and money legacies, but that these ought first to be applied to the payment of debts. And upon this foot, there was a decree for the plaintiff in the original bill, though the Chief Baron [BURY] seemed to think that this legacy of £150 being devised out of Mitcham farm, which was a specific legacy, was as much a specific legacy as that. But *caeteri barones contra*.

65

Lloyd v. Small

(Ex. 1719)

In this case, the court held the alleged payments as moduses *in lieu of tithes in kind were not good or legal.*

2 Gwillim 619, 1 Eagle & Younge 746

23 February 1718.

A bill was brought by the vicar of Epping in the County of Essex for an account of all tithes and duties arising in the parish, except the tithes of corn and grain.

The defendants confessed that the plaintiff was the lawful vicar, but they denied that he or his predecessors were entitled to any tithes or dues, other than those set forth in their answers.

The defendant Small confessed that, during the said year, he had held the farm called Bury Farm, consisting of several quantities of arable, meadow, and pasture ground, and he insisted that there is a *modus* of £8 a year payable in lieu of the tithes thereof. He also confessed that he held the farm called Cobb's Fields, consisting of arable, pasture, and meadow ground, and he insisted that there is a yearly *modus* of £1 10s. payable in lieu of the tithes thereof.

The defendant Chandler confessed that he held a farm called Parvell's Farm, consisting of arable, pasture, and meadow lands, for which there is a yearly *modus* of £4 payable.

The defendant Parry confessed that, in the said year, he held a farm in the said parish called Redsdale Farm, consisting of the same land, for which there is a *modus* of £1 6s. payable yearly.

And all the defendants set forth what tithable matters and things they had in the said year and admitted that they had not set forth their tithes in kind, but they insisted that the plaintiff was not entitled thereto, but only to the several sums of money, which they said were time out of mind paid to the former vicars, and no other, in full [satisfaction] of all vicarial tithes and which sums they averred the vicar had received.

The plaintiff replied; the defendant rejoined; and witnesses were examined on both sides.

And, on debate of the matter, the court was of opinion that the said several sums of money insisted on by the several defendants to be paid by them respectively as *modus*es for the vicarial tithes of their respective farms are not good and legal *modus*es.

3 Rayner 1093

The defendants insisted on several *modus*es for all small tithes arising out of their respective farms. But it appearing by their answer that the small tithes in kind demanded by the bill did not amount to more in that year than the pretended *modus*es, the *modus*es were set aside.

[Order of 23 February 1718: 2 Wood 110.]

66

Lord Arundel's Case

(Ex. 1719)

Account books of a predecessor vicar may be used as evidence by his successor in a suit for tithes.

3 Rayner 1094, 2 Gwillim 620, 1 Eagle & Younge 774

Books of account, memorandums, etc. of a preceding vicar may be made use of as evidence for his successor to support his demands in case of tithes etc. [it was held] by Bury, Chief Baron, and Baron Price.

67

Gregory v. Lutterell

(Ex. 1719)

In this case, the evidence was too vague and uncertain to be sufficient proof of a composition for tithes.

3 Rayner 1094, 2 Gwillim 620, 1 Eagle & Younge 774

A paper dated 1639, signed, etc. to prove a composition for [the tithe of] rabbits on Brampton burrows by the predecessor of the present vicar etc. was read by the barons (PAGE *haesitante*), though there was no direct proof that the defendant claimed under the person that signed it, the warren (that is burrows) etc., it appearing that it was of an ancient date, that the estates mentioned in it were as the defendant now had, and there being proof of the handwriting of one of the witnesses etc. But afterwards, they held, that it was not sufficient to support the plaintiff's demand for the uncertainty, as that there might be a warren at another place or a piece of ground so called or the composition might be for other tithes arising out of the warren.

[Order of 23 February 1718: 2 Wood 114.]

68

Rex v. Earl

(Ex. 1719)

A writ of execution for the debts of the crown has priority over an assignment to commissioners of bankruptcy made the same day.

Bunbury 33, 145 E.R. 585

At Serjeants' Inn, 25 February 1718[/19].

Earl became a bankrupt upon the 26th of January 1718. Upon the 31st of January, a commission of bankruptcy was awarded against him. And an assignment was made by the commissioners the same day, by virtue of which the assignees seized part of his goods etc. Earl being indebted to the crown by several bonds given as a merchant, some of which were forfeited and others not, an immediate extent issued against him tested the 31st of January, by virtue of which the sheriff took the goods out of the hands of the assignees, which they had seized.

Note: The messenger under the commission took possession of the goods before the extent. But it was given up and admitted that the extent bearing equal date with the commission of bankruptcy and assignment, that the extent should undoubtedly have the precedence. But it was moved in regard the extent was only for what was due to the crown at the time of the extent that it should be referred to the Deputy Remembrancer to state what was due at that time, for which the assignees (who now moved) offered to make the crown safe. But there being other bonds not yet forfeited and the extent not returned, the Attorney General [*Lechmere*] opposed it because this could not appear to the court until after the return and never was done without the consent of the Attorney General. And [it was] said the assignees might be relieved either by bill or by pleading properly upon the Statute of Equity,[1] but not upon motion.

So the defendant, *per* CURIAM, took nothing by his motion.

69

Brotherton v. Chancey

(Ex. 1719)

A defendant who puts in a second answer is liable for the court costs occasioned thereby.

Bunbury 34, 145 E.R. 585

31 January 1718[/19].

If a man puts in his second answer, costs are thereupon due to the plaintiff. And though the plaintiff accepts a third answer from the defendant, he does not thereby waive his title to his costs on the second answer, but he may take out a subpoena for them.

70

Bereholt v. Candy

(Ex. 1719–1721)

Officers of the revenue should be sued in the Court of Exchequer for what they do in the execution of their offices, rather than in any other court.

Bunbury 34, 145 E.R. 585

31 January 1718[/19].

Candy, an officer, seized coffee on board a ship, as if it was intended to be re-landed contrary to the condition of the owner's bond. He also seized the ship and carried her to a place where he could conveniently search her in the presence of witnesses. The owner of the coffee brought an action against him in the King's Bench for this seizure, but this action was removed upon motion, as usual, because an information was actually filed for the coffee. But an action being brought in the Common Bench against Candy by the owner of the ship, it was

[1] Stat. 33 Hen. VIII, c. 39, s. 55 (*SR*, III, 891).

also moved to remove this action. But it was opposed by the plaintiff because there was no information for the ship and, therefore, not within the rule.

But, by the opinion of the court, officers belonging to the revenue ought to be sued here for what they do in the execution of their offices. And, although no information for the ship be filed, yet a seizure is not examinable in another court. And, in the action below, the stopping and seizing must be given in evidence. And, therefore, we will remove the action.

An information was tried, and there was a verdict for the defendant. The informer moved for a new trial, which was denied. An action was commenced in the Common Pleas against the officer for the seizure. And the court was moved that it might be removed here. But it was denied because the officer was now out of court and could have no protection here. Easter term, 3 May 1721.

71

Ker v. Duchess of Munster

(Ex. 1719)

A foreign plaintiff, in this case a Scot, may be required to put up security for court costs.

Bunbury 35, 145 E.R. 586

4 February 1718[/19].

A bill of discovery was brought against the defendant, who moved that the plaintiff being a Scotsman, might give security as a foreigner, which was allowed. And the plaintiff, not being able to get security, offered to deposit money, *viz.* £40, which is the usual security, to stand instead of security. But the court refused it.

72

Bennet v. Loggan

(Ex. 1719)

A motion for a preliminary injunction must be supported by an affidavit of the truth of the bill of complaint.

Bunbury 35, 145 E.R. 586

Eodem die et termino [4 February 1719].

In order to get an injunction, Mr. *Ward* produced an affidavit verifying the allegations of the bill, which was admitted to be read.

73

Eddowes v. Deane

(Ex. 1719)

An administrator of a decedent's estate must be appointed before an executor de son tort *can be sued.*

Bunbury 36, 145 E.R. 586

5 February 1718[/19].

Per CURIAM: There is no precedent in a court of equity of a decree against an executor *de son tort*, without setting up an administrator, for, if there should [not] be an administrator and the defendant pay the money, he would be again liable to the administrator.

74

Tanner, *qui tam* v. Allfriend

(Ex. 1719)

The question in this case was whether a seizer of forfeited goods who could not prove the seizure can re-seize and continue the condemnation process on the second seizure.

Bunbury 36, 145 E.R. 586

7 February 1718[/19].

A seizure was made of some snuff in September 1718, but no information was filed. The defendant brought an action against the officer in Michaelmas term following.

On February 6th following, Mr. Attorney General [*Lechmere*] moved, though there was an information then filed, that the defendant might admit the seizure or that the officer might be at liberty to re-seize upon an affidavit the goods were run and that, when the officer seized, he had nobody with him to prove the seizure. After the motion, they filed their information.

And Mr. *Ward* came the next day and showed for cause against it that it was the officer's own fault to seize in such manner as not to be capable of proving it. But here, he might have had the evidence of the coachman who carried away the snuff or of the people of the house where it was carried, and, besides, they had slept two terms and filed no information.

But notwithstanding these reasons, because he would not admit the seizure and upon the circumstances of fraud, which ran high about this time, they stopped the action, Baron PRICE *totis viribus contra*. But as to admitting the officer to re-seize, the court were divided.

75

Attorney General v. Paul

(Ex. 1719)

The court will not grant equitable relief against a bond to export where the goods were stolen out of the ship.

Bunbury 37, 145 E.R. 586

10 February 1718[/19].

This was a *scire facias* upon a bond to export several goods to parts beyond the seas and not to re-land them and to produce a certificate of such exportation. Upon oyer of the condition, the defendant pleaded the Statute of Equity[1] and that the goods were put on board and that they were not re-landed, but that certain persons unknown, by force in the night time, came and carried them away. To this the Attorney General demurred.

And judgment was given by the whole court against the defendant, as in the case of the Attorney General v. King, the Statute extending only to two cases, *viz.* first, to taking by enemies; second, to loss by sea.

76

Hankin v. Gay

(Ex. 1719)

In this case, the defendant failed to allege and prove sufficiently that his lands were discharged from the payment of tithes.

Bunbury 37, 145 E.R. 587,
1 Rayner 145, 2 Gwillim 619, 1 Eagle & Younge 744

At Serjeants' Inn, 20 February 1718[/19].

Upon a bill for tithes, the defendants in their answer insisted that the lands where etc. were formerly belonging to the abbot of Crowland and, therefore, exempt. But they do not say that they were discharged when parcel of the abbey lands, though not one of the orders which was discharged.

(Note: This was one of the greater monasteries dissolved by the Stat. 31 Hen. VIII.[2])

And the defendants insisted that constant nonpayment was a sufficient evidence of an exemption, especially being coupled with being parcel of one of the

[1] Stat. 33 Hen. VIII, c. 39, s. 55 (*SR*, III, 891).

[2] Stat. 31 Hen. VIII, c. 13 (*SR*, III, 733–739).

greater monasteries. And in the case of Collard v. Newton, Hilary term 1681,[1] the defendant there insisted that the lands etc. were discharged by bull, order, prescription, or some other way and it was allowed to be good.

But the court unanimously decreed for the plaintiff in the present case, for that the proof was not full as to non-payment and also, though the defendant says the lands were in the abbot's hands, yet he does not say they were discharged in his hands, and the Stat. 31 Hen. VIII, extends only to such.

[Order of 4 December 1718: 2 Wood 94.]

77

Rex v. Fowler

(Ex. 1719)

Where a writ of levari facias *is executed, upon a writ of* extendi facias, *the proceeds belong to the crown unless a lease had been taken out.*

Bunbury 38, 145 E.R. 587, Conroy 109

Eodem die et anno, [20 February 1719].

Fowler was outlawed in a civil action at the suit of Peck. A [writ of] extent issued out against him. And there was an inquisition and a [writ of] *levari facias* thereon. By virtue of the *levari*, the sheriff levied £50. And it was moved that it might be paid to Peck, which would put an end to all disputes between them.

Although Fowler consented by his counsel, yet the court would not do it because nobody consented for the crown and the king is entitled to the £50, unless a lease had been taken out.

78

Rex v. Wynn

(Ex. 1719)

The lien of a writ of extent attaches as of the date the extent was issued.

Bunbury 39, 145 E.R. 587

Mr. Wynn distrained corn etc. for rent due the first of November 1718. A [writ of] extent issued the 14th of November, by virtue of which the same corn etc. was seized by the sheriff. But Wynn detained so much as would satisfy him his rent, upon which Lloyd, at whose suit the extent issued, moved for an

[1] *Collard v. Newton* (1682), Eq. Cases Exch. 143, 1 Rayner 58, 2 Gwillim 530, 1 Eagle & Younge 526.

attachment against Wynn, being the extent, though executed the 14th of November, was tested the 10th of October. And, upon this motion, it was taken for granted and admitted *per* TOTAM CURIAM that the extent binds from the *teste*, as was resolved in the case of the King v. Tanner Arnold.[1]

79

Geale v. Winter

(Ex. 1719)

When a cause comes on after the postea *returned upon the equity reserved, the decree is never* nisi, *but always absolute.*

Bunbury 40, 145 E.R. 587, 1 Eagle & Younge 744

It was said in this case that, when a cause comes on after the *postea* returned upon the equity reserved, the decree is never *nisi*, but always absolute.

[Order of 20 November 1718: 2 Wood 103, 1 Eagle & Younge 743.]

80

Rex v. Carr

(Ex. 1719)

Where a fine to the crown has been sent into the Exchequer for collection, a discharge can be made only by the Attorney General in person, and not by a mere certificate from the Clerk of Assize.

Bunbury 40, 145 E.R. 587

Carr was indicted at the Kingston assizes for an assault and fined £50, which fine was estreated. It was moved to discharge this fine upon a suggestion that the king had signified his pleasure to the Attorney General that he was willing to remit the same and that satisfaction should be acknowledged upon record, that, in pursuance of this, the Attorney General had issued his warrant to the Clerk of Assize of Surrey to acknowledge satisfaction upon record, which the Clerk did accordingly, and of this a certificate was produced.

But the court took a distinction where the estreat is upon a recognizance forfeited and where upon a judgment and said the Attorney General should come and acknowledge satisfaction here, and they must apply to him for that purpose before the court could grant the motion.

---

[1] *Regina v. Arnold* (1710), Dodd 356, Indiana Univ. Lilly Library MS. Parker 'Cases in the Exchequer', vol. 5, p. 173, Harvard Law School MS. 537, part 2, p. 147.

81

Watson v. Lindsel

(Ex. 1719)

A parishioner is not allowed to testify in a suit for a modus decimandi *in lieu of tithes in kind in his own parish because he has an interest in the outcome of the case.*

Bunbury 40, 145 E.R. 588,
1 Rayner 147, 1 Eagle & Younge 747

This *modus* was insisted upon by the defendant for tithe milk, that he paid the tenth meal from the first of May, inclusive, twice every tenth day at the church porch until the first of August, exclusive. But this cause going off upon another point, no opinion was given as to the validity of the *modus*.

It was said in this cause that it is a good objection to a witness that he is an inhabitant of the parish where the *modus* is insisted upon, and, if he is not in the occupation of any lands tithable, it lies upon the other side to show it.

82

Disney v. Robertson

(Ex. 1719)

A bill in equity does not lie for tolls.

Bunbury 41, 145 E.R. 588

A bill [was] preferred by the plaintiff, as owner of the manor of Kirkshed in the County of Lincoln, for several tolls payable for the landing of goods etc.

But *per* TOTAM CURIAM, the bill was dismissed, being a matter proper at law, and a decree in this case could be of no use, for it could not conclude anybody but the defendants, and it is not like a bill of peace, which binds all parties, as against the inhabitants of a parish or the tenants of a manor, in which cases a bill shall be retained to prevent a multiplicity of suits.

A bill of the same nature was dismissed in Hilary term, 1718, between Bond and the City of Exeter.

83

Anonymous

(Ex. 1719)

If, upon an assignment of a mortgage, the debtor refuses to redeem or to consent to the assignment, the assignee shall have interest on both the principal and the interest due from the debtor.

Bunbury 41, 145 E.R. 588

If a considerable sum be due for interest on a mortgage and the mortgagee assigns over for the consideration of so much as the principal and interest come to, if this assignment be without the privity of the mortgagor, then the interest shall be carried on only upon the principal. But if the mortgagee had applied to the mortgagor before and demanded his money and required him to join in the assignment, if the mortgagor refuses either to pay or join, the assignee shall carry interest both on the principal and interest.

84

Reed, *qui tam* v. Francia

(Ex. 1719)

The question in this case was whether the failure of an information for not paying import duties to allege properly the date of the importation was a fatal defect or not.

Bunbury 42, 145 E.R. 588

An information was exhibited against Francia for importing brandies and landing the same, the duty not being paid etc. There was a verdict for the informer.

And now *Sir Constantine Phipps* moved in arrest of judgment that the offence was not laid to be between such a day and *ante exhibitionem huius informationis*, according to the usual way, but only before the exhibiting etc., though this seemed a fatal objection, says the reporter himself [Bunbury], yet the court were all of opinion for the informer and gave judgment accordingly.

85

Rex v. Packington

(Ex. 1719)

An inquisition upon a writ of extent in aid cannot return a simple debt to the debtor, but, upon a motion in court, it can.

Bunbury 42, 145 E.R. 588

Upon a [writ of] extent in aid, they cannot find debts without a specialty. But upon a motion in court, if in term time, [they can].

86

Rex v. Dale

(Ex. 1719)

Pursuant to the Statute, in order to divest a tenant of ownership, goods distrained for non-payment of the rent due must be sold within five days.

Bunbury 42, 145 E.R. 589,
Parker 141, 145 E.R. 738

A [writ of] extent bearing *teste* the 4th of November issued against Dale, by virtue of which, corn and hay were seized. But Mitchell, the landlord, having distrained the same for rent the 29th of October before, refused to let it go, upon which a [writ of] attachment was moved for against Mitchell, the goods not having been sold within five days, pursuant to the Statute 2 Will. & Mar.,[1] no property was divested by the distress, and they were in the landlord's hands only by way of pledge. But this being a point of law, which Mitchell was not supposed to understand and being the sheriff was negligent in executing his [writ of] *venditioni exponas*, the Court refused to grant an attachment.

87

Earl of Scarborough v. Hunter

(Ex. 1719)

In this case, the court directed an issue to be tried by a jury as to an alleged modus decimandi *in lieu of tithes in kind and if it was not found to be as pleaded, then what it was.*

In this case, the witnesses were in disagreement, and the court proposed a compromise, which the parties accepted.

Bunbury 43, 145 E.R. 589,
1 Rayner 146, 1 Eagle & Younge 747

A bill was preferred by the earl of Scarborough for the tithe of fish due by custom, which custom was laid for all fish taken at sea and brought to land and sold within the parish of Hart, of which the plaintiff was the impropriate rector; secondly, for all fish sold at sea and the vessel came back to the parish; thirdly, for fish taken by the inhabitants and sold at another port.

Although the plaintiff did not prove his custom as laid in the bill, yet by three barons against the Chief Baron [Bury], an issue was directed to try whether there was such a custom as laid in the bill or whether any and what custom, though it was said there never was any instance where either the plaintiff or de-

[1] Stat. 2 Will. & Mar., sess. 1, c. 5 (*SR*, VI, 169–170).

fendant insisted upon a *modus* or custom and did not prove it that ever it went to a trial at law, it being essential to a *modus* or custom that it be certain.

It was also objected that the custom was illegal as it was laid, for, if it is a personal tithe, as insisted upon (and as the court seemed to think), then a double tithe may be payable, not only in another port where the fish is sold, but also where the fisher inhabits, to which three barons against the Lord Chief Baron said it was a good custom, for one tithe may be paid by custom and one of common right.

2 Gwillim 621

4 May 1719.

A bill was brought by the plaintiff, as impropriator of the parish of Hart in the County of Durham, claiming 12d. in the pound for all fish caught in the sea and brought into the port of Hartlepoole and there sold, and the twentieth part of all fish so caught by the fishermen of the parish and sold elsewhere, all reasonable charges being first deducted.

The defendants admitted the plaintiff's title and submitted the customs to the judgment of the court, whether they were good or not.

The plaintiffs replied; the defendants rejoined; and witnesses were examined on both sides. And on reading the depositions of several witnesses and hearing what was insisted on by the plaintiff's counsel and it being admitted by the answer of the defendants that, by custom, the inhabitants of Hartlepoole, who were owners of boats employed in the fishing trade, had usually paid to the rector or impropriator of the said rectory of Hart a customary payment of one twentieth part or 12d. in the pound, after charges deducted, in lieu of tithe fish, and of all other tithes and sums of money which became due for and in lieu of tithe fish and all other ecclesiastical duties and payments, by reason of the profits arising to the owners of such boats, but that such customary payments were not clearly appearing to the court, the witnesses of both sides disagreeing therein, it was by the court proposed to the plaintiffs to accept of 12d. in the pound or a twentieth part of the clear gain, after all charges deducted, for the tithe of the fish taken by the defendants, without costs on either side.

Whereupon, the plaintiffs declaring their consent to accept of 12d. in the pound clear gain, after all charges deducted, for the tithe of the said fish and the defendants also consenting to pay the same without costs on either side and without prejudice, it was thereupon ordered and decreed by the court, by and with the consent of all parties, that the defendants should severally account with and satisfy the plaintiffs for the tithes of the fish by them respectively taken during the time in the bill mentioned after the rate of 12d. in the pound for the clear gain arising by such fish after all charges deducted.

[Order of 4 May 1719: 2 Wood 116.]

88

Doe, *qui tam* v. Cooper

(Ex. 1719)

Where brandy is adjudged to have been imported in casks of unlawful size, the order is for the duty to be paid, rather than for a forfeiture of the goods.

Bunbury 44, 145 E.R. 589

An information was exhibited against Cooper for importing brandy in unsizeable casks. And the question was upon the Stat. 8 Ann., c. 7,[1] whether they should be forfeited or pay duty. And, though the Stat. 4 & 5 Will. & Mar., c. 5,[2] says they shall be forfeited or the value, yet three barons against Montagu gave judgment that they should pay the duty.

89

Ealam v. Freak

(Ex. 1719)

The widower of a deceased legatee has no title to the property bequeathed unless he takes out administration to his late wife.

A bill of complaint cannot be amended to add a completely new title to the property in issue.

British Library MS. Add. 36651, f. 95v

The bill was for a discovery of assets and satisfaction of a legacy devised by J. Freak to Ann, the wife of J.S. And the bill charges that J.S. survived his said wife and afterwards devised the said legacy by will to the plaintiff.

The defendant demurred to the bill and showed for cause that, it not appearing by the bill that J.S. ever took administration to his wife, he was not entitled to the said legacy and, if so, then the plaintiff can have no title.

Mr. *Browne*, upon arguing the demurrer, cited 1 Danvers, *Abridgment*, 700,[3] that a statute or bond given to a husband and wife will survive, therefore, they are joint tenants, also 1 Rolle's, *Abridgment*, 342,[4] if a legacy devised to the wife is received by virtue of a letter of attorney and she die before the husband receives it, yet he shall have it as survivor.

---

[1] Stat. 8 Ann., c. 7 (*SR*, IX, 197–198).

[2] Stat. 4 Will. & Mar., c. 5, s. 6 (*SR*, VI, 384).

[3] YB Pas. 48 Edw. III, f. 12, pl. 4 (1374), 1 D'Anvers, Abr., *Baron and Feme*, pl. C, 1, p. 700.

[4] *Huntley v. Griffith* (1597), 1 Rolle, Abr., *Baron & Feme*, pl. D, 7, p. 342.

Per CURIAM: The cases cited are nothing to the purpose, for this legacy was a mere chose in action and did not survive no more than a bond or other specialty given to the wife, to which the husband is not entitled unless he take administration to her. Therefore, as no good title appeared by the bill, the demurrer was allowed.

Then, Mr. *Browne* prayed leave to amend on payment of costs. And he said his client would take out administration.

Sed negatur [because] the amendment must be by adding a new title, which the court will not suffer.

90

Knight v. Duchess of Hamilton

(Ex. 1719)

A plaintiff suing as an executor does not pay court costs when he or she receives a judgment after the defendant has paid into court the amount of money recovered by the judgment.

Bunbury 44, 145 E.R. 589

In an action upon the case upon an *indebitatus assumpsit*, the defendant brought £16 into court with the usual motion that the plaintiff, who was an executrix, should proceed at the peril of costs. At the trial, the plaintiff proved, and had a verdict for, only £13. And it was now moved that the plaintiff should pay costs and that the £3 overplus paid into court should be restored to the defendant, which last part was granted. But the court would not make the plaintiff, being an executrix, pay costs. But query if the plaintiff should not have costs until the time of the rule.

91

Delaval v. Blackett

(Ex. 1719)

A bill of revivor for court costs does not lie against an executor; however, if the bill of revivor is for the duty, the executor must pay the court costs as well.

Bunbury 45, 145 E.R. 589, 1 Eagle & Younge 748

The plaintiff [Sir Edward Delaval] preferred his bill against the defendant [Sir Edward Blackett] for tithes, and he had a decree for an account. But, before the costs were ascertained, Sir Edward Blackett died. Sir Edward Delaval revived against the executor. And, upon the question whether the defendant should pay costs, this distinction was taken, that, if the revivor against the defendant had been only for costs, which had not been ascertained in the lifetime of the testator, then the defendant should not have paid costs, but, here, the revivor was for the duty as well as the costs, and, therefore, the defendant, though an executor, should pay costs.

[Order of 16 July 1717: 2 Wood 79.]

92

Attorney General v. Elliston

(Ex. 1719)

A reply that denies the allegations of an excuse in a plea is sufficient to produce an issue for the jury to determine.

1 Strange 191, 93 E.R. 466

Scire facias was brought on a bond conditioned to transport coffee and not re-land it. The defendant, as to part, pleaded the Statute of Equity of Hen. VIII,[1] that he did not transport the coffee because, when it was in the ship, one of the officers of the customs came on board and seized the coffee and carried it back to London, that, when it was cleared, he continued the voyage, until he met with a tempest, in which both ship and coffee were lost. And, as to the residue of the coffee, he pleaded it was never re-landed. The Attorney General replied that the seizure was because the coffee was unshipped with an intent to be re-landed. And, on a traverse of this, they are at issue, and it is found with the king.

It was moved in arrest of judgment that here was an immaterial issue, for the bond being only not to re-land, the replication only discloses evidence of an intent to re-land, which is not sufficient to subject him to the penalty.

On the other side, it was said that the plea had admitted a non-performance by offering an excuse and, then, it was sufficient to meet the plea and falsify the excuse in all cases, that of an award only excepted, for, there indeed, if the defendant pleads *nul agard fait*, the plaintiff must not only show an award, but he must go farther and assign a breach. Salkeld 138.[2] But in no other case, is he obliged to do more than falsify the defendant's plea.

And of this opinion was the Court, and judgment was given for the plaintiff.

93

Rex v. Reeves

(Ex. 1719)

No writ of venditioni exponas *can issue except by an order of the court.*

---

[1] Stat. 33 Hen. VIII, c. 39, s. 55 (*SR*, III, 891).

[2] *Meredith v. Alleyn* (1690), 1 Salkeld 138, 91 E.R. 129.

Bunbury 45, 145 E.R. 590

It was said by Baron PRICE in this case that no *venditioni exponas* ought to issue without motion in court, and he ordered the rules [of] 15 Car. II to be inspected.

94

Boning v. Sprott

(Ex. 1719)

The court may allow a witness to be examined as to the credibility of another witness before the publication of the evidence.

Bunbury 46, 145 E.R. 590

Upon motion, you may have an order to examine to the credit of a witness, even before publication passes.

95

Anonymous

(Ex. 1719)

An account book of a plaintiff's predecessor in title is admissible in evidence.

Bunbury 46, 145 E.R. 590, 1 Eagle & Younge 748

Upon a bill by an impropriate rector for a mortuary, the book of some of the predecessors impropriators was offered to be read as evidence, wherein were entries of payments of mortuaries. But it was objected that, although a parson's book (who is only tenant for life, and, therefore, not supposed to enter anything with partiality to his successor) may be read, yet the book of a lay impropriator, who has the inheritance, ought not to be read; to this, it was answered that the book of a lord of a manor who has the fee is admitted an evidence of quit rents.

(*Sed quaere*, if the bare entry of the lord of a manor in his book be evidence, though a bailiff's accounts, where it appears the rents have been paid and allowed in the account, are admitted as evidence.)

Per CURIAM: Let the book be read.

96

Johnson v. Elleker

(Ex. 1719)

Where a person sues for discovery of deeds, he must file an affidavit that he does not have them himself, but, in a bill for discovery of deeds and relief, there is no need for an affidavit.

Bunbury 46, 145 E.R. 590

Where a man prefers his bill to have discovery only of deeds and, having the counterpart, to have the deeds established, there he ought to annex an affidavit to his bill that he has not the original deeds, nor any other person in trust for him, or else it is cause of demurrer. But, if there is relief prayed as well as a discovery, as where the heir prefers a bill against a mortgagee to have a mortgage deed delivered up, suggesting the same has been satisfied and that he has lost the counterpart, there is no need of an affidavit.

97

Duchess of Hamilton v. Fleetwood

(Ex. 1719)

Exceptions to an answer will not be allowed where the court is equally divided.

Bunbury 47, 145 E.R. 590

Where, upon exceptions to an answer, the court are equally divided, the exceptions are overruled of course.

98

Bishop of Exeter v. Trenchard

(Ex. 1719)

In a bill for tithes, the defendant parishioner must tender the tithes that are due or be liable to pay court costs.

Bunbury 47, 145 E.R. 590,
1 Rayner 147, 2 Gwillim 626, 1 Eagle & Younge 749

In a bill for tithes, the defendant, as to some of them, insisted upon a *modus*, but admitted others, which he had not paid, and, having omitted to make a tender of them by his answer, he, upon motion, obtained an order that he might be at liberty to pay so much money in lieu and satisfaction of all his tithes not covered by the *modus*, together with the plaintiff's costs to that time, and the plaintiff to proceed at the peril of costs.

(But I believe this was by consent.)

99

Peploe v. Swinburn

(Ex. 1719)

Creditors by a decree in equity are treated equally with creditors by a judgment at common law.

Bunbury 48, 145 E.R. 591

26 October 1719.

In this case, the question was who should have the preference to be paid by an executor, a creditor by judgment at law or a creditor by decree in a court of equity.

Sir Edward Northey, who was counsel for the judgment creditor, said that it was never taken in the Court of Chancery that a decree should be upon an equal foot with a judgment at law, though it should with a pocket record, as a recognizance etc.

The barons were divided in their opinion, and no judgment was given in the point at this day. But in Hilary term following, it was decreed that the judgment and decree creditors should come in and be paid equally.

See 2 Chan. Rep. 193; 1 Chan. Rep. 194; 1 Levinz 155; Joseph and Mott, *in Cancellario coram* Lord Keeper Wright; 1 Leonard 155.[1]

100

Baldwin, *qui tam* v. Anonymous

(Ex. 1719)

The law does not recognize fractions of days.

Bunbury 49, 145 E.R. 591

Baldwin made a seizure of tea upon the 11th of November. And he exhibited his information the same day, in which it was alleged that, between such a day and the day of exhibiting his information, the tea was imported etc. This would have been bad, for the day of the seizure would have been excluded, there being no fraction of days. But, upon motion, the court gave them leave to amend and to make it the 12th.

---

[1] *Elvard v. Warren* (1680–1681), 2 Chancery Reports 192, 21 E.R. 654; *Cornel v. Sykes* (1660–1661), 1 Chancery Reports 193, 194, 21 E.R. 547; *Joseph v. Mott* (1697), Precedents in Chancery 79, 24 E.R. 38, 2 Eq. Cas. Abr. 459, 22 E.R. 391.

101

Evans, *qui tam* v. Anonymous

(Ex. 1719)

The Court of Exchequer can order a new appraisal of goods seized for the non-payment of customs duties where the first appraisal was too high.

Bunbury 49, 145 E.R. 591

Upon a seizure of a parcel of snuff, there issued a writ of appraisement. The appraisers appraised it at 2s. 6d. per pound, which was 1s. per pound more than it was worth. Therefore, the officer now moved for a new writ of appraisement, for, if it was not really worth so much as appraised at, it would undo the officer, for he must pay the king's moiety according to the appraised value.

And the court ordered the appraisers to show cause.

102

Bill v. Robinson

(Ex. 1719)

In an action for a wrongful seizure of goods, the defendant can prove that there was probable cause for the seizure even though the verdict was to the contrary.

Bunbury 49, 145 E.R. 591

An information was exhibited upon a seizure. And, upon the trial, there was a verdict for the defendant. Therefore, the defendant brought an action against the informer for this seizure *sine aliqua probabili causa*.

Upon the trial of this cause before Baron Price at Winchester, he would not permit the defendant to go into the evidence given upon the trial of the information to prove the *probabilis causa* because, he said, it would be arraigning that verdict.

But, upon a motion for a new trial, the Lord Chief Baron Bury and Baron Page (*absente* Montagu) were clearly of opinion that that evidence should have been admitted, and it made no difference, which was much insisted on, where the action was tried before the information and where after. And it would not be arraigning the verdict on the information, for that there was a wide difference between a strict legal cause and a probable cause. And a new trial was granted.

103

Jones v. Clement

(Ex. 1719)

Where a defendant is arrested by commissioners of rebellion to appear and answer, they may allow the defendant to remain at large upon putting up bail, but they may not allow bail where the arrest is for a contempt of court.

Bunbury 50, 145 E.R. 591

Upon a motion for an attachment, it was said by the court that commissioners of rebellion not only might, but ought to, take a bond as a security from the defendant to appear, where it is upon the ordinary process of the court, though a serjeant at arms could not in that case. But, where it is upon an attachment or contempt of an order of the court etc., there, they ought not to take any security, but to have the body in court at the day of the return of the commission of rebellion.

104

Duchess of Hamilton v. Incledon

(Ex. 1719–1720)

A court of equity will not forbid an action at common law to be continued where the parties at common law have sued an action sounding in common law and have had a fair trial on the merits.

Where an executor hires the decedent's attorney to continue work for on-going litigation, the executor is liable for the amount due for the work done before the decedent's death whether there are sufficient assets in the decedent's estate to pay for it or not.

2 Eq. Cas. Abr. 524, 22 E.R. 442,
C. Viner, Abridgment, vol. 4, p. 103, pl. 20

[Michaelmas term 1719.]

The plaintiff prayed for an injunction to stay the defendant's proceedings at law upon this case. The duke of Hamilton brought an [an action of] ejectment in his own and his wife's name for certain lands that descended to the duchess during the coverture. And he employed the now defendant as his attorney. The duke died pending the suit, and the duchess continued Mr. Incledon, as attorney, to prosecute the suit. And now, he has brought his action for all the money expended in that suit, as well in the duke's time as in the duchess's, against the duchess, and he has recovered a verdict at law.

It was argued, first, that it is a matter of account; secondly, that he has by his answer submitted to the judgment of the court whether the duchess ought not to pay it, and, therefore, he ought to stay until the court has determined it. He insists that the suit did not abate and, therefore, that it is still the same retainer. But the retainer is personally to the duke and cannot affect the duchess, but it is a charge upon the administrator. He admits money received from the duchess, but he would apply that to discharge what was due in the duke's time. But it is a maxim that what money is paid shall be applied according to the intent of the payer.

It was argued *e contra* that there was no admission of a new retainer, but he only says he proceeded upon her request. He denies that he was ordered to keep a separate account. Secondly, they admit that there are no assets of the duke to pay it. As to the objection whether the duchess or the administrator be chargeable, it is a proper defense at law, and so was that matter how the payments were to be applied.

They moved for a new trial, and these matters were insisted upon. And it was denied by the whole Court of Common Pleas.[1] It is objected that this is a matter of account, and the same may be said of every attorney's bill, but the law has provided another remedy, *viz.* to have it taxed. As to submitting to the judgment of the court, that is only whether the duchess is chargeable, which is more proper for a court of law than equity, and it has been determined in the Common Pleas. This verdict cannot be set aside upon this bill, and then there is no use of an injunction.

Lord Chief Baron [Bury] said that this is not brought to be relieved against the verdict, but against the action. In actions that sound in damages, if the party makes a defense at law, he cannot afterwards have relief in equity. The only question is whether, at law, he can recover this against the duchess? This is proper to be determined at law, and it has been there debated and determined. If the judge who tried the cause had been mistaken in his opinion, you would have had a new trial. The duchess has the benefit of what was done before the duke's death. We are not now determining the cause, but only whether we shall stop their proceedings, and I think we ought not to stop them. All attorneys' bills are matters of account, and the proper method is to have them taxed, and he does not submit to an account.

Baron Price went away before the court gave their opinions, but he told his brethren, he was of opinion against an injunction.

Baron Montagu said that, if this was the case of a common tradesman, who delivered goods after the husband's death, he could not recover what was due before. Or suppose the duchess had never employed Mr. Incledon after the duke's death, then, he could not have recovered against her. And desiring him to go on is a separate contract. This is a charge all in her own right, and he having recovered more than is confessed to be due in her time, he has recovered so much wrongfully. And, therefore, in conscience, he ought to stay execution.

[1] Note *Duchess of Hamilton v. Incledon* (1719), 1 Strange 225, 93 E.R. 486.

Baron Page thought there ought not to be an injunction. It is often a good rule that, when more is recovered than ought to be, this court will stay the proceedings at law. If there have been dealings which cannot be discovered at the trial, it is proper for them to be examined in a court of equity. But here is nothing in this case but what was proper for a defense at law. But here is no dispute whether paid or received, but only who is chargeable. And this has been determined by the Chief Justice of the Common Pleas and agreed to by the whole court, for otherwise a new trial would have been granted. And shall we condemn their judgment upon a motion? As to the question whether she is chargeable, suppose it had been a suit upon a bond made to the duchess before marriage. Would not that survive to her and she have the benefit? Then, ought not she in conscience to pay the charges? She by her act has made it her debt. It was commenced for their joint benefit. Suppose the duke had bought a piece of silk for a gown for the duchess and sent it to the makers. Must not she pay for the making before she can have it? Yet, it was originally the duke's debt. He has submitted only to the stating of it in his answer.

No injunction was granted.

2 Eq. Cas. Abr. 456, 22 E.R. 388,
C. Viner, Abridgment, vol. 11, p. 279, pl. 53

January 27th, 1719[/20].

An attorney having delivered up deeds to an executor, which he was not obliged to do until his bill was paid, which deeds would be of great use to the executor in several suits that were then carrying on, the executor having changed his attorney, this is a sufficient consideration to make the executor liable for the full demand, whether assets or not.

[Affirmed on appeal: 4 Brown P.C. 4, 2 E.R. 3.]

105

Johns v. Stafford

(Ex. 1719)

Depositions taken in a former suit between other parties are not admissible as evidence in a later suit.

Bunbury 50, 145 E.R. 592, 1 Eagle & Younge 750

14 November 1719.

Johns exhibited his bill against Stafford to establish a decree relating to a dispute about the right to mills and the water running to them. And, in his bill, *inter alia*, he sets forth that, in King Charles II's time, the City of Exeter preferred their bill against the now defendant's father, to which the then defendant put in his answer, and there were depositions taken, to which he refers. That cause abated by the death of one of the parties before the hearing. And the defendant moved that these depositions might now be published to be made use of in this cause. And he insisted that, though the cause abated by the death and was consequently out of court, yet that the plaintiff, by referring to them in his now bill, had in effect revived the suit.

But Lord Chief Baron Bury, Price, and Page (*absente* Montagu) were against the order for granting publication. And the defendant took nothing by his motion.

106

Namink v. Farwell

(Ex. 1719)

The question in this case was whether there can be a new trial after a special verdict that was signed by both parties.

Bunbury 51, 145 E.R. 592

17 November 1719.

Upon an action brought against an officer for a seizure *absque probabili causa*, there was a special verdict signed by the counsel on both sides.

But the Attorney General [*Lechmere*], notwithstanding, moved for a new trial, and obtained it, although it was said by the counsel on the other side that there never was any instance that a new trial was granted after a special verdict which is signed by counsel.

107

Mellish v. Arnold

(Ex. 1719)

A chance verdict is improper, and it will be set aside and a new trial will be granted.

Bunbury 51, 145 E.R. 592

20 November 1719.

In an action brought against an officer for a seizure *absque probabili causa*, a new trial was granted because the jury threw up cross or pile whether they should give the plaintiff £300 or £500 damages and the chance of £500 came up. And note, the court now made a rule that Middlesex juries at *nisi prius* shall be paid in court.

Note: The affidavits moved upon were made by persons who heard the jurymen talk of the matter, and the jurymen did not think fit to make any affidavit to clear themselves. So a new trial was granted.

108

Carter v. Saywell

(Ex. 1719)

The question in this case was whether a prior condemnation of goods seized should be pleaded or introduced in evidence at the trial.

Bunbury 52, 145 E.R. 592

24 November 1719.

Carter bought a parcel of goods that were condemned in this court, and these goods were afterwards seized. And, upon the trial of the information of seizure of these goods, Carter, who was then defendant, gave in evidence a condemnation in the Exchequer Court, which Mr. Attorney General [*Lechmere*] said ought to have been pleaded. And upon this, a case was stated for the opinion of the court.

109

Crow v. Stoddart

(Ex. 1719)

Tithes are due for turnips sowed in fields after the corn was harvested and though the turnips were eaten by barren cattle.

3 Rayner 1095

Crow, tenant under the church of Rochester of the tithes in the hamlet of Modingham in the parish of Chippinghurst in Kent, against Stoddart.

The court declared the tithe of turnips sowed after corn and eaten by unprofitable cattle to be due, though it was urged to be an improvement of the land and that the parson has the benefit of it the next year.

110

Duppa v. Briddley

(Ex. 1719)

In this case, the parties correctly followed the statutory procedure for affirming an infant's contract.

Bunbury 52, 145 E.R. 592

The method in the Court of Exchequer is, where an infant is to assign pursuant to the Statute 7 Ann., c. 19,[1] a petition is drawn in the name of him who craves the benefit of the Act, and, upon that, it is moved by counsel on his behalf that the infant may assign and counsel is to consent for the infant. But the court refers it to the Deputy [Remembrancer] to state all matters, and, upon his report, they make an absolute order. And so it was done in this case.

111

Whistler v. Webb

(Ex. 1719–1720)

In a suit to redeem a mortgage, the beneficial owner of the mortgage should be a party defendant.

A subpoena to hear judgment is not needed in an adjourned case, but only a notice of the hearing is necessary.

In this case, depositions against the trustee were not allowed in evidence against the beneficiary.

Bunbury 53, 145 E.R. 592

Upon a bill for a redemption, the defendant in his answer sets forth he was only a trustee for A. This was objected to the plaintiff at the hearing that the *cestui que trust* should have been made a party, and he might have amended, this being disclosed in the answer. And for this reason, the bill was dismissed.

Harvard Law School MS. 1082, vol. 1, p. 35

Michaelmas term 1720. Whistler *et al.* v. Webb, Withers, Whistler, *et al.*

This was a bill to have an account of the office of Hall Keeper of the Guildhall of the City of London, which office was mortgaged by the defendant Whistler to the defendant Webb. But Webb in his first answer discovered that his name was only used in trust for the defendant Withers. The cause came on about a year ago without making Withers a party, but only against the defendant Webb. But the cause stood adjourned over for want of parties, paying the costs of the day. And the plaintiffs afterwards made Withers a party and, having replied to Withers' answer but, afterwards, that replication was withdrawn and the cause came on this day to be heard on the former proofs taken against the defendant Webb, who was not now served with a subpoena, but only notice given by the clerk in court on the other side. Thereupon, we that were counsel for the defendant Webb

[1] Stat. 7 Ann., c. 19 (*SR*, IX, 89).

insisted that Webb, not being served with a subpoena again for the hearing this day, that Webb was not obliged to appear.

But the court said that, it being an adjourned cause and Webb appearing before, there was no occasion of any subpoena to hear judgment, and so was the practice in the Court of Chancery.

After which, I opened the defendant Webb's answer. And then, the plaintiffs were going to read the proofs taken against Webb only to prove that this office was fraudulently sold by the defendant Webb. But we insisted that matter would affect Mr. Withers, whose answer was to be taken as true, since the cause as to him was heard upon the bill and answer and this evidence would contradict it and that the *cestui que trust*, who was Withers, and he was the principal defendant and the substance and not the trustee, who was the shadow.

PAGE was for the reading of the depositions because he would distinguish between the trustee and the *cestui que trust*.

Chief Baron [BURY], PRICE, and MONTAGU [were] against it. And so the bill was dismissed.

112

Anonymous

(Ex. 1719)

A reversioner can be estopped to terminate a deceased life tenant's lease where he allowed the lessee to make improvements on the land in reliance on the life tenant's lease and the reversioner's knowing silence.

Bunbury 53, 145 E.R. 593

This was cited by the court as the course of the Court of Chancery, *viz.* that, where a tenant for life makes a lease for years, the lessees, apprehending that the lessor had a power to make such a lease certain, lay out great sums in improvements and he in reversion stands by and lets them go on, without giving notice, that the lessor was only a tenant for life, that the Court of Chancery has, in such case, decreed to the lessees the remainder of the term after the death of the tenant for life.

113

Jones v. Langham

(Ex. 1719)

After a defendant has answered, it is too late for him to except to the bill of complaint on the ground of scandal.

Bunbury 53, 145 E.R. 593

12 December 1719.

Baron PRICE: It is not regular to refer the bill for scandal after the answer is come in.

114

Frazer v. Moor

(Ex. 1719–1720)

A bill to redeem a mortgage can be barred by the plaintiff's laches.

In this case, the defense of laches was allowed to be pleaded by a demurrer.

Court costs can be awarded against an administrator of a decedent's estate.

Bunbury 54, 145 E.R. 593

At Serjeants' Inn, 14 December 1719.

Upon a bill to redeem, it appeared by the plaintiff's own showing that the defendant had been in uninterrupted possession above thirty-four years and no incapacity was pretended, for which reason the defendant demurred. And the demurrer was allowed by PRICE and PAGE, barons, *contra* Lord Chief Baron BURY.

Bunbury 63, 145 E.R. 596

27 May 1720.

A bill was brought by an administrator. The defendant demurs, and the demurrer is allowed, and the bill is dismissed with costs. And so it was said to be the constant course in equity *per* TOTAM CURIAM.

Harvard Law School MS. 1082, vol. 1, p. 3, pl. 1

Easter term 1720. Fraser, administratrix of Harner v. Moon.

This was a bill brought to redeem after thirty-six years, to which a demurrer was put in and allowed. And now, it was moved by Mr. *Ward* and Mr. *Aris* that the plaintiff being an administratrix that she should pay no costs for that the Statute of 4 Jac., cap. 3,[1] was general and so took in matters in law as well as equity. And they cited Hardres 365, Twisleton v. Lady Thelwell.[2]

See Statute 8 & 9 Will. III and 3 Levinz, Mason v. Jackson.[3]

---

[1] Stat. 4 Jac. I, c. 3 (*SR*, IV, 1141).

[2] *Twisleton v. Thelwel* (1659), Hardres 165, 145 E.R. 433.

[3] Stat. 8 & 9 Will. III, c. 11, s. 5 (*SR*, VII, 202); *Mason v. Jackson* (1682), 3 Levinz 60, 83 E.R. 576.

I was of counsel for the defendant and insisted that a plaintiff administratrix in equity was not considered any otherwise than another plaintiff and that the Statute did not affect plaintiffs in equity and cited Cro. Car. 219; 1 Ventris 109, 110.[1]

The court agreed that costs must be paid though the plaintiff was an administratrix and not affected by the Statute and so the constant practice was.

115

Smith v. Watson

(Ex. 1720)

Where the equities are equal, a court of equity will follow the common law.

Bunbury 55, 145 E.R. 593

1 February 1719[/20].

T. Clogie, being indebted to Watson by a judgment, agrees to assign over a lease which he had to Watson as a security for his debt. And Watson, thereupon, agreed to give T. Clogie a defeasance for twelve months. T. Clogie sent his lease to Watson and a letter specifying this agreement to a scrivener with directions to draw an assignment and defeasance pursuant to this agreement. But, before the same was executed, T. Clogie dies, having made his will and Ph. Lassels his executrix, who before any notice of this agreement assigns over the interest of the said lease to Jenkins and King in trust for herself and then for them, who were all likewise judgment creditors. Watson preferred his bill against Lassels, Jenkins, and King to carry this agreement into execution.

Baron Price was of opinion this was a writing within the Statute of Frauds and Perjuries[2] and such a lien upon T. Clogie that, as if he had lived and refused to perfect the said agreement, a court of equity would have obliged him to do it; so they ought likewise to oblige the executrix and her assignees to execute the same.

But Chief Baron Bury and Baron Page (*absente* Montagu), though they thought this letter a writing within the Statute and that it would be a good lien upon T. Clogie himself and even upon his executrix, yet Jenkins and King, the assignees, had not only as good a title in equity as the plaintiff, but they had also by the assignment a title at law too, so they could not decree them to execute the said agreement.

Note: Upon Smith's original bill, the question was only whether Watson should deliver up the writings.

---

[1] *Atkey v. Heard* (1631), Croke Car. 219, 79 E.R. 791; *Anonymous* (1671), 1 Ventris 109, 110, 86 E.R. 76.

[2] Stat. 29 Car. II, c. 3 (*SR*, V, 839–842).

116

Holden, *qui tam* v. Broad

(Ex. 1720)

Where an informer dies pendente lite, *the court will allow the good to be re-seized.*

Bunbury 56, 145 E.R. 593

The informer Holden died pending the information. And, upon motion, the court gave leave to make a re-seizure.

117

Lady Granville v. Ramsden

(Ex. 1720)

An erroneous decree should be corrected by a bill of review, not by a new original bill.

Bunbury 56, 145 E.R. 594

Lady Granville *et al.*, commoners of Epworth v. Ramsden *et al.* 25 January 1720.

A bill was preferred to establish the plaintiffs' right to a common and to set aside several former decrees. The defendant demurred to the whole bill, for, if there was any error in the former decrees, they ought to have a bill of review and not do it in this method. And the demurrer was allowed.

118

Delver v. Hunter

(Ex. 1720)

Where a man died not seised, his widow is not entitled to mesne profits.

Bunbury 57, 145 E.R. 594

A woman recovered in dower and brought a bill for the mesne profits.

Serjeant *Bridges*, for the plaintiff, cited a case of Dean v. Wade, in 1 Chan. Rep. large octavo, and 2 Chan. Rep., Coventry v. Thynn.[1]

But *per* TOTAM CURIAM the bill was dismissed, for, even where the husband dies seised, there shall be no mesne profits until a demand, as by the Statute of

[1] *Dean v. Wade* (1641), 1 Chancery Reports 48, 21 E.R. 505; *Coventry v. Thinn* (1681), 2 Chancery Cases 71, 22 E.R. 851.

Merton.[1] Coke Lit. 32, 33.[2] But if the husband does not die seised, as he did not in this case, the wife can have no mesne profits. And besides, it is admitted that the plaintiff is in possession, so she may have a remedy at law if she has any right to mesne profits.

119

Roe v. Bishop of Exeter

(Ex. 1720)

In this case, the court established various moduses *in lieu of tithes in kind.*

Bunbury 57, 145 E.R. 594,
1 Rayner 148, 1 Eagle & Younge 751

In a bill to establish *modus*es, these were insisted upon and allowed: first, for every cow having a calf, for the tithe of the milk and the calf, 17d.; secondly, for every milk cow milked without a calf, 11d. for the tithe of the milk; thirdly, for every heifer the first year she has a calf, 13d. for the milk and calf – these payable at Michaelmas – for every hogshead of cider made of apples grown in the parish, 8d.; for hoard apples, 1d.; for firewood spent on the farm, an hearth penny; for fruit, herbs, roots, and other garden stuff, a garden penny; for a colt 1d. – these payable at Easter.

[Order of 22 February 1720: 2 Wood 136, 1 Eagle & Younge 751.]

120

Bishop of Exeter's Case

(Ex. 1720)

A contract to pay a modus decimandi *in lieu of tithes in kind affirms the* modus *and does not supersede it.*

3 Rayner 1096

Every composition is an evidence of the right and duty of the tithes for which the composition is made, yet, in the Bishop of Exeter's Case, it was held that a general composition may include a *modus* as well as a tithe in kind, where the *modus*es were for several matters, for some years they may be more, in some years less, and so may be compounded for, and, though this composition continues forty years, yet the *modus* shall continue.

---

1 Stat. 20 Hen. III, Merton (*SR*, I, 1–4).

2 E. Coke, *First Institute* (1628), ff. 32–33.

121

Rex v. Yale

(Ex. 1720–1721)

In this case, the bond to the crown that was in issue was found to be valid and enforceable, and the defendant as surety for the obligor was held liable.

Bunbury 58, 145 E.R. 594

Mr. Pauncefoot was appointed Cashier of the Excise by constitution from the Commissioners of the Excise. He employed Sir Matthew Kirwood to pay the money he should return into his hands to the crown, and he took a bond from Sir Matthew and Mr. [Elihu] Yale, as his security, in the penalty of £40,000 for the payment of the money to the crown and on his own private account. Kirwood broke, and a [writ of] extent issued against him. And a *scire facias* was brought against Yale on his bond.

(Note: If Yale's bond had been for the payment of money, an immediate extent might have gone against him.)

Upon the pleadings to this *scire facias*, there was a demurrer. And it was argued on the behalf of Yale that the bond taken by Pauncefoot was void in law because, first, he was not a commission officer, only constituted cashier without express authority, which he ought to have had, to take such bond; secondly, it is against the rule that any tradesman should be appointed cashier to any farmer etc.; thirdly, this bond is an oppression to the subject, for, by the Stat. 33 Hen. VIII,[1] body, lands, and goods are liable.

But note: 23 November 1720, *per opinionem* TOTIUS CURIAE, this bond was adjudged to be good.

Harvard Law School MS. 1082, vol. 1, p. 29

Michaelmas term 1720.

This was an argument and did arise on this case. Mr. Charlton and Mr. Pauncefort were appointed by warrant from the Commissioners of the Excise joint cashiers of the excise and that Mr. Pauncefort having agreed to employ Sir Matthew Kirwood of London, goldsmith, for receiving for him the said Mr. Pauncefort, his clerks, or agents the money arising by the revenues of the excise and bill or bills of exchange, notes, bonds, and other papers as the said Edward Pauncefort should pay or deliver to him or upon the said Mr. Pauncefort's own particular account, he, the said Mr. Pauncefort took a bond in His Majesty's name in the penalty of £40,000 pay[able] to His Majesty, his heirs, or successors dated 25 April 1718 entered into by the said Sir Matthew Kirwood together with Elihu Yale, Esq., as his security, conditioned that the said Sir Matthew Kirwood

[1] Stat. 33 Hen. VIII, c. 39, s. 37 (*SR*, III, 886–887).

should true account make with the said Mr. Pauncefort, his agents, executors, or assigns of and concerning all sums of money, bills and bills of exchange, notes, bonds, and other papers as he the said Matthew Kirwood or any other person or persons by his order, privity, or consent should receive or collect or that should come to his or their or any of their hands by virtue of the trust reposed in him and should at all times render an account thereof of all matters relating to His Majesty's revenue or unto the said Mr. Pauncefort on his own particular account and how upon the affidavit of Henry Metcalf, clerk to the said Mr. Pauncefort, that he had by the direction of the said Mr. Pauncefort stated an account with Sir Matthew Kirwood of and concerning such sums of money as had been received and paid by the said Sir Matthew Kirwood and that, on the balance of that account, there remained due to the said Mr. Pauncefort from the said Sir Matthew Kirwood £12,153 0s. 8d. which being in danger of being lost and that Sir Matthew Kirwood absconding from his creditors. And upon this affidavit, there was a warrant granted for an immediate extent signed by the Chief Baron dated 2 September 1719 and several extents issued against Sir Matthew Kirwood into London, Essex, and Middlesex and his estate was seized. And likewise, there was a *scire facias* issued against Elihu Yale upon the said bond, and that Mr. Yale procured an extent in aid to be issued against himself upon the aforesaid bond and by an inquisition taken thereupon at the Guildhall, London, it is found that Sir Matthew Kirwood, Robert Jeuts, and William Wallis became bound to the said Yale in £40,000 which the sheriffs seize into His Majesty's hands and that a *scire facias* issued against Wallis to the sheriff of Hertford to summons Wallis to show cause why the king should not have execution against him for the said £40,000, to which said bond the said Mr. Wallis appeared and prayed oyer.

Upon the whole case, there was an argument upon the case of the King and Yale last term or Easter term. And the defendant pleaded performance of covenants. The Attorney General replies. And Yale rejoins that he paid £13,000 to Conrade de Gols for the use of Pauncefort and demurs as to the other part.

Mr. *Bootle* for Yale: The said bond might be good, yet, as the Attorney General has pleaded, judgment ought to be given for the defendant for the replication is wrong, which is the foundation of everything, 2 Cro. 339, 220,[1] '*virtute inde*', is an inducement and not traversable. And it is not distinguished whether it is upon the public or private account. And replications ought to be certain. Plowden, Commentaries, 26, Holter and [*blank*]; 2 Croke 170, Hancock; 2 Saunders 124, Webber v. Tivis.[2] If this matter was well pleaded, yet this bond is void and the

[1] *Freeman v. Sheen* (1614), Croke Jac. 339, 79 E.R. 290, also 1 Rolle Rep. 7, 81 E.R. 288, 2 Bulstrode 93, 80 E.R. 986; *Barret v. Fletcher* (1609), Croke Jac. 220, 79 E.R. 192, also Yelverton 152, 80 E.R. 102, 1 Brownlow & Goldesborough 105, 123 E.R. 694.

[2] *Hancock v. Field* (1607), Croke Jac. 170, 79 E.R. 149; *Webber v. Tivill* (1670), 2 Williams Saunders 121, 124, 85 E.R. 840, 843, also 2 Keble 622, 634, 84 E.R. 391, 399, 1 Levinz 287, 83 E.R. 410.

taking such a bond as this in the name of the crown is unjustifiable. Mr. Paunce-fort is only an agent or servant to the Commissioners of the Excise, and he is to render a true account to the Exchequer. But Mr. Pauncefort is not authorized to employ Sir Matthew Kirwood whereby great hazard is run contrary to the duty of his office and tends to the injury of the crown. And the Statute of 33 Hen. VIII takes away body, goods, and lands, and it destroys purchasers even for a valuable consideration after the date of the extent. In the case of the receiver of the hearth money in [the time of] King Charles II, they had a particular clause in their patent to take a bond in the name of the crown which shows that, without such a power, it could not be done upon the following principles in the cases hereinafter mentioned: Raymond 225, 227, Bishop of Exeter v. Stall, Ventris 166; Moore 864, Hobart 83, Slanney v. [*blank*], Rex v. Porter, in this court.[1]

Sir Edward Northey for the king: I think that Mr. Bootle is not in earnest as to the replication because it is multifarious. If the replication is not good, yet if the plea is bad, judgment ought to be given for the king. As to the bond, it may be good in part, though not in the whole. And I wonder that this bond should be questioned at this time for the crown's money, for a bond to the crown is good, though it may not be according to the Statute of 33 Hen. VIII. You have several bonds in this court to the king and his successors and not to his executors. It is out of the record, and you cannot take notice of the cashier and how he is appointed. The cashier may take such a bond as servant to the Commissioners of the Excise and why not their agents on that behalf as well as receivers general of counties, who always take such bonds to secure the crown's money. I rely upon it that this bond is taken by a person as accountable to the crown for the crown's money, and, as mortgagees or tenants, the court would lay their hands on them. Moore 342; 1 Anderson 129, Scroggs v. Gresham;[2] 3 Leonard 195.

[To the] objection of Attorney [General] v. Porter, in this court, for that such bonds are *colore officiis*, [he] answered there is no inconvenience as to the crown's money and being so is not within any of the rules of this court of 15 Car. I, for this is good for the crown's money, and the bond may be good in part, though not for the whole. Cro. Eliz. 705, Dobson v. Crew; Moore 316, Molineux's Case.[3] And the breach is only assigned for the king's money. Commissioners of the Excise are commissioners and receivers.

---

[1] *Bishop of Exeter v. Star* (1673), T. Raymond 225, 83 E.R. 117, 1 Ventris 166, 86 E.R. 113, also 2 Keble 814, 836, 848, 873, 84 E.R. 514, 529, 537, 552, 3 Keble 219, 285, 84 E.R. 686, 723, 2 Levinz 36, 83 E.R. 441; *Slawny v. Elbridge* (1616), Moore K.B. 864, 72 E.R. 958, Hobart 83, 80 E.R. 233.

[2] *Cholmeley v. Hamner* (1597), Moore K.B. 342, 72 E.R. 617, also 2 Coke Rep. 50, 76 E.R. 527; *Skrogs v. Gresham* (1584), 1 Anderson 129, 123 E.R. 391, also Moore K.B. 193, 72 E.R. 525.

[3] *Dobson v. Crew* (1599), Croke Eliz. 705, 78 E.R. 940; *Mullineux's Case* (1581–1582), Moore K.B. 178, 72 E.R. 516.

Mr. Bootle replies: The replication is wrong and so settled. If it was the king's money only, it might be good. But the bond goes further and, therefore, [is] not good. No such bond was ever taken, though a condition may be good in part and bad in part.

[It was] adjourned for another argument, which was this term between Sir Constantine Phipps for Yale and Solicitor General Yorke for the king. But I was not then in court.

Note that this term [Michaelmas 1720] the court gave judgment in the case above, which was delivered by the Chief Baron on the part of the whole court, which was unanimous for the king, as hereinafter set forth.

Chief Baron [Bury]: He stated the case as came before them and said that the objections to the pleading were of no weight but the chief questions were, first, whether this bond is good by 33 Hen. VIII; secondly, if it appears that this is the king's money.

[To the] objection that it is not a good bond because [it is] not in the words of the Statute, viz. executors, [he] answered such bonds with such a solvendum have been frequent in this court and allowed to be good. The intent of the Statute of 33 Hen. VIII was to expedite the recovery of the king's debts and not to impede it and, therefore, intended as more beneficial to the crown and to be taken as statute staples. The Statute does not say that the bond is void for want of these words [. . .][1] is in [the] statute and case cited in Moore.

[To the] objection that this bond was taken by Mr. Pauncefort, who had no authority to take such bonds, [he] answered I think that any receiver general may take such a bond for the crown's money. If the Lord Treasurer appoints any such person to receive money, he may take such bonds for the better security of his debt. I see no objection to this bond, for this was the king's money. And what Pauncefort has done is the same thing as if the Commissioners of the Excise had taken such bond. And there is no restraint in the Statute.

[To the] objection of the Rules of 15 Car. I, [he] answered those Rules are only to extents in aid and not for the king's money, which ought to be taken care of in the best manner. And this is the king's money and an original extent, so [it is] not within those Rules, which only extend to extents in aid. And I see no ill consequence in taking such bonds.

As to the exceptions to the pleading that it does not appear to be the king's money, [he] answered Yale has pleaded performance of covenants generally, and it appears in the breach assigned to be *tangens reventionum*.

As to the objection that the bond is void because in Mr. Pauncefort's private account, [he] answered the bond may be vicious in that part and yet good as to the rest.

So judgment [was given] for the king *per* TOTAM CURIAM.

---

[1] v. par. *MS*.

Harvard Law School MS. 1082, vol. 1, p. 72, pl. 1

Trinity term 1721.

Judgment in the [Court of] Exchequer Chamber [was] pronounced by Chief Justice PRATT as the opinion of him and Lord Chief Justice KING that the judgment of the Exchequer ought to be affirmed. And then Yale obtained a writ of error returnable in Parliament, after which Yale died, and, thereupon, the writ of error determined. But query how renewed.

[Affirmed on appeal: 6 Brown P.C. 27, 2 E.R. 910.]

122

Kennet, *qui tam* v. Lloyd

(Ex. 1720)

The documents relating to a seizure for non-payment of customs can be corrected after a verdict.

Bunbury 58, 145 E.R. 594

12 February.

An information was brought upon a seizure of a quantity of tobacco; there was a verdict for the plaintiff. It was objected in arrest of judgment that the information was the 16th of June, the writ of appraisement the 17th, returnable the 17th, and the indenture of appraisement the 15th, which was before they had any authority. And writs of appraisements are a necessary part of the information upon a seizure. And, if this be void, there is no value at all set upon the goods, and the course of the court has made it necessary, besides the Act of Tonnage and Poundage[1] directs the moiety of the rate to be answered to the king, which shows there is a necessity for a valuation. There is a distinction indeed between a seizure and a *devenerunt*. Upon a seizure, the general words are sufficient because the return of the appraisement makes a sufficient certainty. (But it is wanting in this case.) But in a *devenerunt*, which is the crown's action of trover, there must be greater certainty, having nothing else to help it.

Note: The court seemed to think this was amendable.

123

Carter v. Salt

(Ex. 1720)

In this case, a jury found that certain alleged mortuaries were not due.

[1] Stat. 12 Car. II, c. 4 (*SR*, V, 181–205).

Harvard Law School MS. 1082, vol. 1, p. 1, pl. 3

Easter term 1720.

This came upon a *postea* on an issue directed whether mortuaries were due or not. And a verdict found for the defendant against the mortuaries.

Mr. *Ward*, for the plaintiff, moved for a new trial, for, in this case, there was a proof of payment by the former minister's books and some living witnesses and the mortuaries are due only by custom, yet some payment will justify that demand and here was a proof of payment for thirty-two years.

Serjeant *Pengelly*, *Northey*, and *Bootle*, for the defendant [argued] that, though the minister's book was admitted as evidence, yet that was contradictory and thirty years will not prove a custom and when it first began was only by the minister's imposition on some poor persons.

Montagu reported Chief Justice King's opinion of the verdict and his notes taken upon the trial to the following effect that the *onus probandi* laid upon the plaintiff and several payments were proved in 1621 and the minister's book admitted in evidence, which was from 1633 to 1638 and several leases were granted and mortuaries [were] therein mentioned. But [there were] not mortuaries in the original lease granted by the dean and chapter. Several witnesses were produced for the defendant. And the son of that minister whose book was produced for the plaintiff said that he never heard of mortuaries. The Chief Justice did not find fault with the verdict.

So this court agreed with it and dismissed the bill as to mortuaries.

[Order of 19 June 1719: 2 Wood 120.]

124

Attorney General v. Allen

(Ex. 1720)

The word 'import' means brought in for the purpose of re-selling.

Harvard Law School MS. 1082, vol. 1, p. 2, pl. 1

Easter term 1720.

This was an information and verdict found for the king. And *Sir Constantine Phipps* moved in arrest of judgment for that it is not laid *per viam merchantizandi*, which he took to be a fatal exception.

Montagu [held] that there was no occasion for it for the word 'importing' signifies by way of merchandise. And he cited Paul v. Shaw, in this court.[1] So the court overruled the exception and gave judgment for the king.

---

[1] *Paul v. Shaw* (1710), 2 Salkeld 617, 91 E.R. 523, 8 Brown P.C. 288, 3 E.R. 588.

125

Bromhill v. Mason

(Ex. 1720)

The question in this case was whether an ecclesiastical court has the jurisdiction to decide the defense to a suit for tithes that the tithes sought are extra-parochial.

Harvard Law School MS. 1082, vol. 1, p. 2, pl. 2

Easter term 1720.

Mr. *Ward* showed cause against a [writ of] prohibition for that it ought to appear by affidavit that the plea was refused which is suggested and the refusal is traversable and, here, it is suggested that it was extra-parochial, which ought to be verified by an affidavit. 2 Rep., Bishop of Winchester's Case.[1]

Page said that there was no occasion to plead it below for then it is a prohibition. In the case of a *modus*, it must be verified by an affidavit and the refusal of the plea [is] not traversable by 2 Lutwyche.[2]

Bootle, for the plaintiff, [said] that by the 5 Rept., Jeffery's Case,[3] the ecclesiastical court cannot try the boundaries of the parish.

Adjornatur.

126

Dean and Chapter of Westminster v. Cross

(Ex. 1720)

The Statute of Limitations will not bar a bill for discovery in equity.

Bunbury 60, 145 E.R. 595

14 May 1720.

The Statute of Limitations[4] was pleaded to a bill of discovery, but it was overruled.

Harvard Law School MS. 1082, vol. 1, p. 3, pl. 2

Easter term 1720.

---

[1] *Wright v. Wright* (1596), 2 Coke Rep. 38, 76 E.R. 501, also Moore K.B. 425, 72 E.R. 672, Croke Eliz. 475, 511, 78 E.R. 726, 760, 1 Gwillim 167, 1 Eagle & Younge 119.

[2] *Morton v. Briggs* (1704), 2 Lutwyche 1043, 125 E.R. 580, 1 Lord Raymond 242, 91 E.R. 1058, 2 Gwillim 561, 1 Eagle & Younge 624.

[3] *Jeffrey v. Kenshley* (1589), 5 Coke Rep. 64, 77 E.R. 153.

[4] Stat. 21 Jac. I, c. 16 (*SR*, IV, 1222–1223).

This was a bill brought by the plaintiffs who were seised of the manor of Westminster and of a parcel of ground as set forth and that the defendants [Railton *et al.*] had built a chapel thereon and insisted upon a title to it and to a nomination of a minister there, which was now the question. So the bill was only for the discovery of the writings and of the defendants' title thereto, to which discovery the defendants pleaded the Statute of 32 Hen. VIII, entitled an act of limitation,[1] with a proviso and also the Statute 21 of King James in bar.

It was argued by *Chesshyre, Comyns, Stevens, Phipps,* [and] myself, for the plaintiffs that this plea ought not to stand in our way for that, as to the length of possession, the discovery would give the reason for the length of possession and, in the cases of a trust or mortgage, the Statute of Limitation can be a bar. Hardres 325; 1 Siderfin 415; 2 Saunders 120; 1 Levinz 273; 2 Can. Cases 26; 1 Chancery Cases 20; 2 Ventris 345; Littleton's Reports 341; 3 Keble 645, 2 Levinz 166; 2 Modern 212.[2]

Serjeant *Pengelly*, for the defendants, [argued] that a fine and non-claim was a bar even to an ecclesiastical body. Hardres 511, 512; Sir William Jones 416; 2 Modern 56, 57; Hobart 240.[3] And this demand is against right and conscience. 1 Ventris 311; Plowden 538.[4]

Chief Baron [Bury]: I think that, since the disabling statutes of 1 and 13 Eliz.,[5] that a fine and non-claim ought to be no bar to an ecclesiastical body. A

[1] Stat. 32 Hen. VIII, c. 2 (*SR*, III, 747–748).

[2] *Hodsden v. Harridge* (1669), 1 Siderfin 415, 82 E.R. 1189, 1 Levinz 273, 83 E.R. 403, 2 Keble 462, 497, 533, 536, 84 E.R. 290, 312, 334, 337, also 2 Williams Saunders 61, 64, 85 E.R. 672, 693; *Chandler v. Vilett* (1670), 2 Williams Saunders 120, 85 E.R. 836, also 1 Siderfin 453, 82 E.R. 1213, 2 Keble 646, 84 E.R. 407; *Ebrand v. Dancer* (1680), 2 Chancery Cases 26, 22 E.R. 829, also 1 Eq. Cas. Abr. 382, 21 E.R. 1118, 79 Selden Soc. 815; *Heath v. Henley* (1663), 1 Chancery Cases 20, 22 E.R. 673, also 3 Chancery Reports 8, 21 E.R. 712, Nelson 75, 21 E.R. 793, 1 Eq. Cas. Abr. 303, 21 E.R. 1062; *Lord Hollis's Case* (1680), 2 Ventris 345, 86 E.R. 477; *Sherwin v. Ex'rs of Sherwin* (1630), Littleton 341, 124 E.R. 276; *Coply v. Dugmying* (1676), 3 Keble 625, 645, 84 E.R. 917, 929, also 2 Levinz 166, 83 E.R. 501; *Cochram v. Welby* (1677), 2 Modern 212, 86 E.R. 1031, also 1 Modern 245, 86 E.R. 858, 2 Shower K.B. 79, 89 E.R. 806, 1 Freeman 236, 89 E.R. 169.

[3] *Wolstan v. Aston* (1669), Hardres 511, 145 E.R. 573; *Thynne v. Cary* (1639), W. Jones 416, 82 E.R. 218; *Chapter of Southwell v. Bishop of Lincoln* (1675), 2 Modern 56, 86 E.R. 938, also 1 Modern 204, 86 E.R. 830; *Threadneedle v. Lynam* (1675), 2 Modern 57, 86 E.R. 939, also 1 Modern 203, 86 E.R. 829, Pollexfen 176, 86 E.R. 551, 1 Freeman 92, 119, 165, 179, 89 E.R. 67, 87, 119, 128, 3 Keble 192, 372, 583, 595, 84 E.R. 670, 773, 892, 898; *Stanhop v. Bishop of Lincoln* (1618), Hobart 237, 80 E.R. 383, also 2 Anderson 23, 123 E.R. 525.

[4] *Howlet v. Carpenter* (1677), 1 Ventris 311, 86 E.R. 201, also 3 Keble 775, 84 E.R. 1005; *Croft v. Howel* (1578), 2 Plowden 530, 75 E.R. 783.

[5] Stat. 1 Eliz. I, c. 19 (*SR*, IV, 381–382); Stat. 13 Eliz. I, c. 10 (*SR*, IV, 544–545).

plea of the Statute of Limitations [was] never allowed in bar of discovery of writings. So he overruled the plea.

Montagu: The plea is not right in form, for it is only belief so that fact is not put in issue. Bills of discovery ought to receive a favorable construction, and the plea must be overruled.

Page agreed. So the plea was overruled.

127

Gumley v. Fontleroy

(Ex. 1720–1721)

In a suit for tithes, the defendant parishioner must answer as to what tithes are due regardless of his defense.

Bunbury 60, 145 E.R. 595,
1 Rayner 149, 2 Gwillim 628, 1 Eagle & Younge 754

Eodem die [14 May 1720].

A bill was brought by a vicar for tithes. The defendant pleads that the plaintiff employed a person to collect the tithes and that he the defendant paid the collector £5. And he does not set forth quantities and values; so the plea was overruled with costs, for this court never admits a plea, even of a *modus*, to cover the discovery of quantities and values because the defendant may die before they go to examination, and, then, tithes lying only in the personal knowledge of the party, there would be no way of coming to the knowledge of the particulars. And the case in Hardres[1] was denied, and it was said it had often been so.

Harvard Law School MS. 1082, vol. 1, p. 1, pl. 1

Easter term 1720.

This was a tithe bill, and the defendant pleads a composition and agreement without setting forth quantities and values, and this was upon arguing the plea.

The Chief Baron [Bury] insisted that it was the rule in the Exchequer to set forth the quantities and values though the agreement was insisted on and pleaded, as in the case of a *modus*.

Montagu doubted.

Ward, for the plaintiff, cited Hardres' reports where a *modus* was pleaded and the quantities and values [were] not set forth.

Montagu, at last, being told by *Sir Constantine Phipps*, counsel for the plaintiff, that the plea might be false and, before it comes to hearing, the defendant might die and then the plaintiff loses the benefit of his discovery.

---

[1] *Randal v. Head* (1661), Hardres 188, 145 E.R. 444, 1 Eq. Cas. Abr. 35, 21 E.R. 854, 1 Eagle & Younge 434.

And, thereupon, Montagu agreed with the Chief Baron [Bury]. And the plea was overruled with costs.

Harvard Law School MS. 1082, vol. 1, p. 49, pl. 2

Hilary term 1721.

Serjeant *Glyde*, for the defendant, moved that it might be referred to the Deputy [Remembrancer] to examine when the bill was filed for that the defendant had insisted on a tender made before Hilary term and the bill did not come in until that term though marked as of Michaelmas term preceding and that this bill was so marked to avoid the tender. And [he] urged the Statute of 4 Queen, for Amendment of the Law,[1] that no subpoena shall issue until the bill is filed unless an injunction bill, and this motion was made as above after an appearance and issue joined in the cause, and therefore [etc.].

Chief Baron [Bury] and Price resolved that they came too late, for they ought to have moved for costs for not filing the bill and that ought to have been before any appearance and, therefore, it is too late to be examined now.

Montagu differed and [said] that it was a manifest breach of an Act of Parliament and that it might be examined at any time.

Page thought it was too late for a motion after an appearance, *a fortiori* after such a proceeding. He thought it was an injustice and, if the defendant had come in a proper time, it might have been remedied without the assistance of the Act of Parliament.

No order [was made].

[See also below, Gumley v. Burt (1724), Case No. 486.]

128

Dodson v. Oliver

(Ex. 1720–1724)

The main question in this case was whether tithes were due for an ancient water corn mill.

Tithe milk is to be paid by the tenth meal.

Easter offerings by parishioners are due by common right.

A decree in the Court of Exchequer is not complete until it is signed and entered.

A plaintiff may revive a lawsuit for the duty and the court costs, but not for the court costs only.

[1] Stat. 4 & 5 Ann., c. 3, s. 22 (*SR*, VIII, 460).

2 Gwillim 623, 1 Eagle & Younge 754

16 May 1720.

The plaintiff, as rector of Husterpoint in the County of Sussex, filed his bill, *inter alia*, for a discovery, account, and payment of the tithes of a water corn mill and for the great and small tithes of the farm and lands occupied by the defendant, according to the following rates, *viz.* every tenth toll dish or pint of corn received by the defendant for corn ground at the said mill and the tithes in kind of corn, grain, hay, milk, and calves.

The defendant admitted that he was occupier of the mill and farm in the bill mentioned. But he insisted that the mill, having been built beyond memory, was an ancient mill and ought not to pay tithes and that, for the other tithable matters, the plaintiff had for the time demanded by the bill received the tithes of his corn, grain, and hay in kind, that he had, according to agreement, paid him tithes for the calves he had and that, as to the tithes of his milk, he had set out the tenth part of such manner as is stated in the answer. He confessed that he had five persons in his family above sixteen years of age. But he said that he knew not whether any Easter offerings were due for them.

The plaintiff, by a special replication to the defendant's answer, admitted that the defendant had paid the great tithes of corn, grain, and hay, and he, therefore, waived his right thereto and discharged the defendant from the examination of witnesses concerning the same.

The cause being at issue on both sides and witnesses having been examined by both parties, it came on to be heard on the 23d day of February last, when, upon reading several depositions in the cause, the court directed it to stand over for further hearing. And it came on to be further heard this day, when the plaintiff relinquished his demands of tithes of calves.

The court, after reading several proofs, ordered the defendant to account for tithes in kind of his milk for the time demanded by the bill, unless he could prove before the Deputy Remembrancer the time when the plaintiff sent a note to him in writing, signifying therein that, for the future, he, the plaintiff, expected the defendant to set out the tithes of his milk upon every tenth meal and that the plaintiff would fetch it away. And, in such case, the Deputy Remembrancer was ordered to take the account only from the time of the delivery of the said note. But, as to the demand for the tithes of corn and grain ground at the corn mill, the cause was ordered to stand over for counsel on both sides to be heard on the point and for the court to give their final opinion therein.

The cause accordingly stood in the paper the 4th of May 1721. And, after hearing counsel on both side, the court was divided in their opinions, which they gave *seriatim*, touching the tithes of the said mill. And neither party afterwards made any application to the Chancellor [of the Exchequer] for a rehearing before him and the barons. But, on the 29th day of November 1721, the plaintiff, by his counsel, consenting in court to waive his further prosecution for the tithes of the said mill, it was ordered that the defendant should show cause why the Deputy Remembrancer should not be at liberty to proceed to take and state an account of the tithes of milk and Easter offerings, which order was made absolute on the 9th of December following.

Harvard Law School MS. 1082, vol. 1, p. 1, pl. 2

Easter term 1720.

This cause came again to be heard. And as to tithe milk, the court agreed that the tithe thereof ought to be paid by the tenth meal.

Montagu said that the tenth day would be best to avoid fraud because the cows might be so milked at one meal that they might be almost dry when it was the parson's meal and, therefore, to avoid fraud, he would have had it the tenth day. But that it might be settled forever, he agreed with the court as to the tenth meal.

[It was] resolved also in this case that offerings were due *de communi jure* and that the Statute of Edw. VI[1] was only as to the regulation of payment.

As to tithe [of] mills, whether due *de communi jure* or whether a personal tithe, [this was] to be spoken to next term.

Harvard Law School MS. 1082, vol. 1, p. 16

Sittings after Trinity 1720.

This was a bill brought by the plaintiff as rector of Hersperpoint in the County of Sussex. And the decree before was for tithes and Easter offerings. And now, the question arises on the tithe of a corn mill and how due.

Mr. Serjeant *Stevens*, for the plaintiff, [argued] that this tithe is either a mixed or praedial tithe. Coke upon [the Statute] of *Articuli Cleri*; Rolle, *Abridgment*, 656; 2 Croke 490; Linwood, *De Decimis*, 194, 195.[2]

The practice of this court is consistent with the common law. 2 Rolle Rept. 84. Tithes are either due *de communi jure* or by custom, and this [was] never set forth to be due by custom in the form of pleading and in the bills in this court. Shower Reports 281; Watson 461.[3]

Sir Constantine Phipps, for the plaintiff: The question is what tithes shall be paid for these corn mills and whether the tithe is personal, praedial, or mixed. I take it that a personal tithe is only by the labor of the person. And I do not know any decree in this court for the clear profit. And until the case of Knute

[1] Stat. 2 & 3 Edw. VI, c. 13 (*SR*, IV, 55–58).

[2] E. Coke, *Second Institute* (1642), pp. 599–638; Stat. 9 Edw. II, stat. 1 (*SR*, I, 171–174); 1 Rolle, Abr., *Dismes*, pl. M, 4, p. 656; E. Coke, *Second Institute* (1642), p. 490; W. Lyndwood, *Provinciale* (1929), title 16 'Tithes', pp. 71–79.

[3] *Gumley v. Falkingham* (1691), 1 Shower K.B. 281, 89 E.R. 574, also 4 Modern 45, 87 E.R. 253, Carthew 215, 90 E.R. 729, 1 Eagle & Younge 571; W. Watson, *Clergy-Man's Law*.

v. Chamberlain,[1] the tithes of mills were taken to be praedial. And though the decree in this court was for the tenth toll dish, even as to those quern mills, yet the House of Lords reversed that decree, and there, it was adjudged only the tenth toll dish, deducting expenses. This tithe in question is mixed with labor, yet such mixture does not make it a personal tithe. the cutting of corn is by the labor of the farmer, yet that does not make it personal. And the case above in 2 Croke shows that it is in respect of the land. Rolle, *Abridgment*, 651, 652; Rolle Reports 84.[2]

A personal tithe must run through the whole parish and not be for any particular person. And I think that the first question is whether tithes are payable *de communi jure*; secondly, whether it is a praedial or personal tithe.

Mr. *Edlin*, for the plaintiff, [argued] that the tithe of mills was due *de communi jure*. Linwood 201; Shower Reports 281; Lambert, *Leges Edwardi Confessoris* 139; Register 48, for there, *duae quartieria bladi* shows that it is not *deductis expensis* and, therefore, [it is] not a personal tithe.

The Statute of *Articuli Cleri*[3] does not mention old mills. And therefore, it is to be inferred that the tithes of such old mills were due *de communi jure*. See Lord Coke's comment on that Statute. If the common law is silent, then the canon law ought to prevail. Paper mills [and] fulling mills seem only to be lately erected, and so [tithes are] only due by custom by the Statute of Edw. VI.

There may be a *modus* for a park, but that is only in respect of the herbage. He cited Crispe v. Theobald, 30 June 1716, where the tenth toll dish of a grist mill was decreed.

Mr. *Wheat*, for the plaintiff, [argued] that tithe is due for everything that is yearly renewing. Watson 384; 2 Inst. 652.[4] Tithes shall be paid for new mills, and a *modus* may be insisted on in bar of tithes. 1 Rolle [*Abr.*], 652; Watson 460.[5]

Mr. *Ward*, for the defendant: This demand is for tithes of an ancient mill. And the question is whether this tithe is praedial or personal. I think that tithes are not due for an ancient mill for a *non decimando* may be insisted on in bar of it, which shows that the tithe is not due *de communi jure*. 2 Inst. 621; King's Bench, Pas. 26 Car. II, Hughes v. Lord Hereford.[6]

---

[1] *Newte v. Chamberlaine* (1705), Dodd 208, Eq. Cases Exch. 552, 1 Eagle & Younge 679, 7 Brown P.C. 3, 3 E.R. 2, 1 Eq. Cas. Abr. 366, 21 E.R. 1107, 2 Eq. Cas. Abr. 731, 22 E.R. 617, 1 Rayner 101, 106, 3 Rayner 1087, 1090, 2 Gwillim 596, Public Record Office, E.126/18, f. 580v, 1 Wood 482.

[2] *Hooper v. Andrews* (1615), 1 Rolle, Abr., *Dismes*, pl. E, 5, p. 651; *Anonymous* (1619), 2 Rolle Rep. 84, 81 E.R. 674.

[3] Stat. 9 Edw. II, stat. 1 (*SR*, I, 171–174).

[4] W. Watson, *Clergy-Man's Law*; E. Coke, *Second Institute* (1642), p. 651.

[5] 1 Rolle, Abr., *Dismes*, pl. F, 2–4, p. 652; W. Watson, *Clergy-Man's Law*.

[6] E. Coke, *Second Institute* (1642), p. 621; *Hughes v. Viscount Hereford* (K.B. 1674), Lincoln's Inn MS. Misc. 500, f. 232, pl. 1.

It cannot be called a praedial tithe because tithe corn has [been] paid already and the tithes are only personal. The canon law is not received as to personal tithes. Degge 257, 343; 2 Inst. 621; Pas. 17 Car. II [1665], King's Bench.

Non decimando [was] never allowed to be insisted on where tithes are due *de communi jure*. And it may be insisted on in this case. And therefore, tithe of mills is not due of common right. Tithes of this kind only subsist by custom as tithe of conies, fish, and quarries of stones. Degge 256; 2 Inst. 622; Cro. Jac. 523.[1]

A mill takes no increase from the land, and, therefore, [it is] not a praedial tithe. So [he] relies on the case in Degge, for a praedial tithe ought to be paid in specie and the tithe of mills cannot be so paid. Watson 460 (Montagu called it a plager's book); 2 Codex Juris Ecclesiastici 713; Newt v. Chamberlain, Exchequer, where, by the authority of the House of Lords, it is adjudged only a personal tithe; see the other book, Ross v. Windsor, 210.[2] All the judges, except Judge Powell, agreed it to be a personal tithe, so the court decreed the account. 17 February 1706. [To the] objection of Lambert 139, [he] answered Selden, [History of Tithes], 8th chapter.

[He said] that, if the Laws of Edward the Confessor were to be regarded at this time of day, then fish, parks, coneys, and everything else is tithable. And I think that no inference ought to be drawn from the canon law, which makes everything tithable, but that the canon law, which was never received by the common law, is not binding.

I admit a specious objection is made that a *modus decimandi* may be insisted on in bar of tith[able] mills, and, therefore, the inference is made that tithes are due *de communi jure*. [In] answer, I take that to be only as to the manner and method of payment, as in the case of fish, the manner of tithing may be insisted on in bar of tithes in kind and yet tithe fish is only due by custom. March, f. 15, pl. 36.[3]

Mr. *Aris*, for the defendant: If the statutes are silent, then the inference is with us that old mills ought not to pay any tithes. 3 Bulstrode 212, 1 Rolle Reports 415; Cro. Jac. 523, Dandridge v. Johnson.[4]

Serjeant *Stevens* said that there was a difference between this case and Knute v. Chamberlain for that was a horse malt mill and it only did arise by labor, but not so here.

---

[1] S. Degge, *Parson's Counsellor*; E. Coke, *Second Institute* (1642), p. 622; *Danderidge v. Johnson* (1619), Croke Jac. 523, 79 E.R. 448, 2 Rolle Rep. 84, 81 E.R. 674, 1 Gwillim 354, 1 Eagle & Younge 304.

[2] W. Watson, *Clergy-Man's Law*; E. Gibson, *Codex Juris Ecclesiastici Anglicani* (1713); *Newte v. Chamberlaine* (1705), *ut supra*; *Ross v. Windsor* (1704), Dodd 203, 1 Eagle & Younge 661, Public Record Office, E.126/18, f. 452.

[3] *Anonymous* (1639), March 15, 82 E.R. 391, 1 Eagle & Younge 398.

[4] *Jakes v. Anonymous* (1616), 3 Bulstrode 212, 81 E.R. 178, 1 Rolle Rep. 405, 81 E.R. 568, 1 Eagle & Younge 257; *Danderidge v. Johnson* (1619), *ut supra*.

Sir Constantine Phipps replies: If a miller lived in a different parish, yet the tithe ought to be paid where the mill is, which shows that it is not a personal tithe. As to tithe fish, it was only a customary method of tithing and no money was ever insisted on in bar.

PRICE said that he thought that the tithe of mills was due of common right.

MONTAGU [was] of the same opinion. And [he] said that the case cited by Aris in 3 Bulstrode was against him.

Sir Constantine Phipps said that wood burned in a house is tithable unless there is a hearth penny to discharge it. Tithe of ewes' milk is due of common right, and yet a *non decimando* may be insisted on in bar of it. Rolle, Abridgment, 642.

[It was] adjourned to the next term for the opinion of the court.

Bunbury 73, 145 E.R. 599,
1 Rayner 155, 1 Eagle & Younge 754

11 May 1721.

The single question adjourned until this day for the solemn judgment of the court was whether tithe of an ancient corn mill that had never paid tithes was payable or due of common right.

Baron PRICE and Baron MONTAGU were of opinion that an ancient mill ought to pay the tenth toll dish, which being a tenth part of the thing itself, was a praedial tithe and due of common right.

But Lord Chief Baron BURY and PAGE [held] that it is a personal tithe and not due of common right, and, not having been paid, is now exempt by the Stat. 2 Edw. VI.[1]

So the court being divided, the plaintiff had no decree as to this matter of the mill.

Note: If there be any custom in a parish for the manner of tithing milk, as to carry it to the church porch or parsonage house, that must be observed by the parishioner. But, if there be no particular custom or usage, the parishioner is obliged *de jure* to pay every tenth meal, to milk the cows at the usual place of milking into his own pail, and the parson is obliged to fetch it away from the milking place in his own pails in a reasonable time. And, if he does not fetch it before the next milking time, the parishioner may justify the pouring the milk upon the ground because he then has occasion for his own pails. And it was determined by the whole Court of Exchequer in this cause of Dodson v. Oliver, at a former day, that the milk ought not to be carried either to the church porch or to the parson's house and that it ought to be fetched by the parson.

Harvard Law School MS. 1082, vol. 1, p. 63

Easter term 1721.

---

[1] Stat. 2 & 3 Edw. VI, c. 13 (*SR*, IV, 55–58).

Page: This was a bill for the tithes of a corn mill. And the defendant insists that no tithes had been paid and, therefore, [it is] not tithable. But I think that there is no pretense that any tithes had been paid for this mill. And I think that the only question is whether an ancient mill be tithable *de communi jure*. But I think that such a mill is not tithable. By the canon law, everything is tithable but all the canons were not received, and, therefore, [they are] not otherwise binding here than as received. Linwood 195; Statute *de Articuli* [*Cleri*]; 2 Inst. 621.

Tithes of new mills are to be paid without doubt. But it is not distinguished what sort of tithe the tithe of mills is. But at the close of the chapter above, it looks as if My Lord Coke took it to be a personal tithe. I shall mention two or three cases not mentioned at the bar. Hundred of Huntspill, Salkeld's Reports, Hicks v. Woodson, Michaelmas 1694, King's Bench.[1]

Though tithe wood had never been paid, yet one could not prescribe in a *non decimando* nor of tithe of agistment of cattle *de communi jure*. Easter 1969, Chief Justice Holt's opinion was that the tithe of mills was not due *de communi jure*. Anonymous case, King's Bench, Easter 1699. That it is not sufficient to suggest that the mill was an ancient mill, but that it had never paid tithe. [In] Lord Hale's time, Hughes v. Bishop of Hereford, Easter 17 Car. II; Linwood 195; Statute of 9 Edw. II, *Articuli Cleri*, which was to restrain the canon.[2]

It does not complain of the payment of tithes for an old mill. But the cases differ whether this is a personal or praedial or mixed tithe.

[As to the] objection of 1 Rolle 405, it cannot be a praedial tithe, for that is from *praedio*, in Linwood, from the soil. A mill does not partake of the soil anymore than a house. A cider mill and a perry mill may as well be tithable after the apples are paid. Fulling mills and wool are mixed tithes. An oil mill, after rape[seed] is paid, may as well be tithable as this. I take this tithe to be neither praedial nor mixed, and, therefore, it must be personal. Shower's Reports. Tithe arose from the increase of the corn.

[As to the] objection that it is not a personal tithe because it is paid where the mill is and not where the party lives, [he] answered I take it to be due where the labor is to be performed; that is where the mill is.

Tithe fish [are] brought into Yarmouth and the men do not live there, yet it is there payable, and it is a personal tithe.

---

[1] *Hicks v. Woodeson* (1694), 2 Salkeld 655, 91 E.R. 558, also 4 Modern 324, 336, 87 E.R. 422, 429, 1 Eagle & Younge 592, 2 Gwillim 550, 3 Lord Raymond 116, 92 E.R. 595, 1 Lord Raymond 137, 91 E.R. 987, 12 Modern 111, 88 E.R. 1200, Skinner 560, 90 E.R. 252, Comberbach 403, 90 E.R. 555, Carthew 392, 90 E.R. 827, Holt K.B. 671, 90 E.R. 1271, Dodd 171.

[2] *Hughes v. Viscount Hereford* (K.B. 1674), Lincoln's Inn MS. Misc. 500, f. 232, pl. 1; W. Lyndwood, *Provinciale* (1929), title 16 'Tithes', pp. 71–79; Stat. 9 Edw. II, stat. 1 (*SR*, I, 171–174).

Non decimando will lie for a mill, and, therefore, [tithes are] not due *de communi jure*.

I do not know why lead, lime kilns, coal, and salt are not yearly renewing and tithe wood, though yearly increasing, is not yearly renewing. A fulling mill is a personal tithe.

[As to the] objection, because there may be a *modus* in discharge of the tithe, therefore, [they are] due of common right, [he] answered it is only called a *modus* because there is some manner of payment in lieu of it. Dr. Grant's Case, in Coke's Reports.[1] In that case, [it was] there called a *modus* for houses, yet the tithe of houses cannot be due *de communi jure*.

[It was] objected Rolle, Abridgment, 656,[2] where Lord Coke says that this tithe is either praedial or mixed, but My Lord gives no reason for it.

[He] concluded that old mills are not tithable and that this was only a personal tithe.

The late determination in the House of Lords, of Knute v. Chamberlain, from a decree in this court, has settled that tithe of quern mills is only personal.

Montagu: When this case was first heard, I was of opinion to decree the plaintiff the tenth toll dish, and, the more I look into this matter, I am the more confirmed in my former opinion that the tithe of an old mill is due of common right and that, therefore, an account ought to be directed. My brother Page has admitted the canon very full in this case, and I allow that canons and provincial constitutions cannot bind without some usage. And the common custom of the realm has made this demandable.

The right of repairing the church is of common right because it is universal; so customs are good for tithe of fish and lead. Time out of mind, fish has been brought to Yarmouth. Littleton's reports[3] says it. Tithe of grist mill for grist has been used time out of mind, but oil and fulling mills have been always so used. [Tithe of] fulling mills [are] only due by custom. 2 Edw. VI. All the cases are since the Statute of Edw. VI. And, therefore, grist mills have been taken to be a personal tithe, which is grounded on the mistake of the Statute of Edw. VI. But I take this tithe to be a praedial tithe. 2 Inst. 642; Statute of 27 Hen. VIII.[4] Tithes [are] to be paid according to ecclesiastical customs.

I think that this canon is received. And then, my brother Page will admit it. And the Statute of 27 Hen. VIII has established it not only by the canon law but by divers laws made since these are received.

The laws of Edward the Confessor are material and ought to be preserved. Lambert 139; Hen. I, c. 11, is Lambert 182. The greatest part of the laws [were]

[1] *Graunt's Case* (1613), 11 Coke Rep. 15, 77 E.R. 1165, 1 Gwillim 259, 1 Eagle & Younge 222.

[2] 1 Rolle, Abr., *Dismes*, pl. M, 4, p. 656.

[3] *Stile's Case* (1629), Littleton 147, 124 E.R. 180, 1 Eagle & Younge 361.

[4] E. Coke, *Second Institute* (1642), p. 642; Stat. 27 Hen. VIII, c. 20 (*SR*, III, 551–552).

introduced in Henry II's time. And so [is] Madox, History; Selwyn 228, Tithes, cap. 8. The Council of Lateran [is] allowed to be authentic here. 2 Inst. 641; 7 Edw. III, fo. 5, yearbook;[1] Selden, [History of Tithes], 232; Close Roll 11 Hen. III; 30 Hen. III, a fine is levied *de decimis molendinorum*; 33 Edw. I; Close Roll 7 Edw. II; 2 Inst. 621, 640.

[A writ of] consultation could not have been granted above if tithes were not due of common right.

I come now to the Statute of *Articuli Cleri*, 9 Edw. And I think that it is an authority with me, though [it was] objected against this opinion. The king said in the Statute above I never ordered a prohibition and new mills ought to pay as old mills paid, and therefore, no prohibition shall go. The contrary construction tends to a *non decimando*.

I take it that these authorities say that these are *decimae delitae* and, if Lindwood did understand it, it must be by the tenth toll dish. Rolle, *Abridgment*, 656.

The division of tithes as to mixed is a new invention, for the old division was praedial or personal, or a better distinction mediate and immediate. I cannot help thinking that, since a *modus* may be insisted on in discharge of this tithe, that it shows that tithes are due *de communi jure*. Rolle Reports 405; 1 Rolle, Abridgment, 651.

[As to the] objection that it ought not to pay twice and that tithe of the corn has been paid already, [he] answered I think that the man does not pay the tithes twice, for the farmer paid before and the miller now.

[As to the] objection [of] Hicks v. Woodson, 1699, [he] answered that reporter takes down what he pleases and perhaps what the court did not say and there is nothing judicially concerning tithe of mill. Chief Justice Holt used to say that it was very difficult to show a *non decimando* as to anything but as to tithe of wood. 4 Modern 344; Salkeld 655; Shower's Reports 281, Gumley v. Falkland.

My Lord Coke does not say that this canon was never received, and I cannot allow it to be a personal tithe, but a praedial tithe. Hilary 16 Jac., Dodderidge v. Johnson, March's Reports 15,[2] [a writ of] prohibition [was] granted. Godolphin [*Repertorium Canonicum*] and Watson go upon the mistake in March's Report.

A general conclusion cannot be drawn from a particular thing [. . .]ed and so the Statute is only that no [writ of] prohibition shall go for a new mill, but it is a *non sequitur* as to an old mill.

[As to the] objection [of the case of] Easter 1699, [he] answered [that], even in that case, it was not sufficient to say it was an old mill, but non-payment must be alleged, and so [was] Chief Justice Holt's opinion.

I think it is fit that this case should be settled. And I am of opinion that the tithe of this mill is due *de communi jure* and that the defendant ought to account.

---

[1] *Abbot of Newnham v. Dean and Chapter of York* (1333), YB Hil. 7 Edw. III, ff, 4, 5, pl. 7.

[2] *Danderidge v. Johnson* (1619), *ut supra*; *Anonymous* (1635), *ut supra*.

Baron Price: It is a case of great consequence. And I must agree with my brother Montagu that an ancient corn mill shall pay tithes, that it is due of common right, and that it is a praedial tithe, and that the defendant ought to account according to the tenth toll dish.

It has been doubted whether it is a praedial, personal, or mixed tithe. I admit my brother Montagu's distinction was only formerly praedial and personal, mediate and immediate. I take it to be a praedial tithe because the tenth toll dish is due and likewise that it is payable where the mill stands as to the tenth toll dish. [He] cited 2 Inst. 816; Lynwood, *De Decimis*, 195, *tanquam praedialis*; Rolle, *Abridgment*, 655; 4 Modern 45, Gumley and [*blank*].

I do not take an old corn mill to be exempt, and [there was] not one Saxon Christian king but enjoins payment. Edward the Confessor's time, 1050. Those laws of Edward the Confessor [were] confirmed in William the Conqueror's time. Bishop Wake, 163, 165, late book of Dr. Wilkins, 198; Spelman, 1 vol., 610, 621; Selden 284; Dr. Comber's *Right of Tithes*, 196; Madox, Coll. Compositions Real, fo. 28; Magna Charter, 9 Hen. III. *Jura sua integra* before the Statute of *Circumspecte Agatis*, 13 Edw. I; and 33 Edw. I; Spellman's second vol., 97, 290; Selden 232.

Canons not repugnant to the laws of the land and received are part of the ecclesiastical and common law, but this was a new notion started upon *Articuli Cleri* as to new mills only. But no inference can be made as to an old mill because that no postulation shall go for a new one. Register 48.

Tithe of corn mill [was] intended due before the Statute. Fitzherbert, *Natura Brevium*, 51; *Reformatio Legum* 115; 2 of Edw. VI, praedial tithes; *non decimando* [is] odious, 2 Inst. 651. My Lord Coke says it was never judicially determined concerning the tithe of mills. 2 Inst. 622.

A *modus decimandi* in bar of tithe of mills has been always allowed, which shows it to be due *de communi jure*. 2 Inst. 490; [1] Rolle, *Abridgment*, 652; 3 Bulstrode 412, 1 Rolle Rep. 405; 2 Cro. 429; best report [is] in a [case in] 2 Rolle Rep. 84, 7 Jac., and the [case of] 5 Jac. there cited, Aly v. Luce, and a consultation was granted; Rolle, *Abridgment*, 641, 652, Johnson v. Dadderidge, very differently reported.[1]

Modus continued: 4 Modern and Shower's Reports 281; Hughes v. Bishop of Hereford; 15 July 1704, Rosse v. Windsor, Exchequer; 30 June 1716, Crispe v. Theobold, Exchequer.

[To the] objection that it is a double tithe, [it was] answered by Brother Montagu.

---

[1] E. Coke, *Second Institute* (1642), p. 490; *Jakes v. Anonymous* (1616), *ut supra*; *Anonymous* (1617), Croke Jac. 429, 79 E.R. 367, 1 Gwillim 286, 1 Eagle & Younge 262; *Anonymous* (1619), 2 Rolle Rep. 84, 81 E.R. 674; *Johnson v. Dandridge* (1635), 1 Rolle Abr., *Dismes*, pl. Q, 18, pl. R, 1, pl. F, 1, 2, pp. 641, 652.

[To the] objection [that it is a] personal tithe, [he] answered such is personal in respect of labor only, not so here.

[As to] quern mills; Knute v. Chamberlain; this court decreed it as a praedial tithe, but the Lords decreed it a personal tithe.

I think that the defendant ought to account for the tenth toll dish.

Chief Baron [Bury]: I own that we have decreed tithe of mill for the tenth toll dish, yet, in those cases, [it was] not insisted on that it was an old mill and that it never had paid tithes. But the question is whether such a mill is not exempt, and I think that such a mill is. I own that the great question does depend on the construction of *Articuli Cleri*. It has been taken that an old mill is exempt because no [writ of] prohibition shall go for new mills. And I do not think it such an unreasonable and foreign construction as my brothers would interpret it, but I think that the Statute is an implication that a [writ of] prohibition shall go for an old mill. And I think that my Lord Coke was of opinion that this tithe of mill was a personal tithe. Miller is an art and faculty, and the tithe [is] due in respect of labor. And paying the tenth toll dish does not make it a praedial tithe. But this ought to be esteemed a personal tithe. Mixed is not to be taken between personal and praedial, but a praedial tithe is such a thing that is fed from the ground and pays tithes, as cattle, wool, etc.

This tithe is a personal tithe. And [it was] so decreed in Knute v. Chamberlain in the House of Lords.

[There is] no difference between quern mills or corn mills. Watson's Clergymen; Lutwyche 460; Jacque's Case, 405.[1]

Canons, if not received, are not to be followed. I cannot have much regard for the Saxon laws or Edward the Confessor's laws. I have read them, but I do not think that there is much in them.

Cider, perry, [and] rape[seed] mills may as well be called praedial mills as the mills in question. And I think this tithe is a personal tithe and so only paid as accustomed according to the Statute of Edw. VI.

I take it that the Lords have called these personal tithes and that the defendant ought not to account because this mill is an old mill and tithe was never paid for it.

Note: The court being equally divided, it must stand for the opinion of the Chancellor of the Exchequer for judgment.

Taussig MS. 311, vol. 1, p. 26, pl. 2

Easter term 1721.

The plaintiff, as rector of Husperpoint in the County of Sussex, brought his bill, *inter alia*, for tithes of a water corn mill. And he insisted on the tenth toll

[1] W. Watson, *Clergy-Man's Law*; *Jakes v. Anonymous* (1616), *ut supra*.

dish as tithes thereof and alleged that he left a sack at the mill with a request to the defendant to put his tithes into it.

The defendant, by answer, said his mill was an ancient water corn mill and that he took the usual toll for grinding there. But as to the quantities ground there, he could not set them forth having kept no account because he took it that no tithes were due. And he hoped to prove the mill was built beyond the memory of man and that no tithe had ever been paid for the mill or multure thereof.

This cause was heard on the 23rd April 1719. And now, the barons gave their opinions *seriatim*.

PAGE, Baron: Tithes of new mills are to be paid, and they are personal tithes. 2 Inst. 621. Hicks v. Woodson, 4 Modern 336, in the King's Bench, in matters due of common right, you cannot prescribe in *non decimando*, except in cases of old mills. Easter 1696, by Holt; there is no tithe of any mill of common right. Easter 1699, in the King's Bench, by Holt, you must not only suggest the mill to be an ancient mill, but also that it never paid tithe. Easter 17 Car. II, Hughes v. Bishop of Hereford agrees.

The Statute of *Articuli Cleri* was made upon a difference between the laity and clergy upon this subject, as by Linwood 195. The Statute does not complain that [writs of] prohibition went for old mills, but only for new mills.

Whether these tithes are personal, praedial, or mixed, some books say that they are praedial, 1 Inst. 621; some praedial or mixed; some personal, 1 Inst. 621. 1 Rolle 405 [says they are] personal and shall not pay tithe unless due. Second, it is not a praedial tithe because praedial is *a praedio*. And in this notion, it is absurd to say that this is a praedial tithe any more than all other houses. Corn indeed is praedial, but that is nothing to the purpose, for the corn has already paid tithe.

Why does not a cider mill pay tithes? If the subject upon which a mill operates denominates the tithe it pays, then a fulling mill is a mixed tithe because wool is a mixed tithe.

A divisione, it must be a personal tithe. Sir Thomas Powis, who was a very good arguer, is puzzled to find a reason for the payment of tithe and gives this, to wit, that it is a new increase. But this is very absurd, for division of matter is no increase of matter. Shower's Reports 281.

[It was] objected it cannot be a personal tithe because it is payable where the mill is, but a personal tithe is paid where the person lives. The solution is it is not necessary that every personal tithe should be paid at the place where the person lives, as, in the case of the fishermen who fish at Yarmouth, they never pay tithe at the places where they live, but where they fish.

All vegetables and minerals grow and increase, though they do not renew. A fulling mill is agreed to be a personal tithe, yet it is paid at the mill.

[It was] objected this must be a tithe of common right or else there could not be a *modus* against it. In Dr. Grant's Case, Lord Coke calls it a *modus*. And *modus* may signify a manner of endowment. In some places, there is 4d. or 6d. for an oven, and yet no tithes are due for an oven of common right, and yet this may be called perhaps a *modus*. Rolle 656 says it is a praedial or mixed tithe; he does not know which.

And so, by him, no tithes are due for old mills. And the House of Lords have lately determined that it is a personal tithe. And there is not one instance since the Stat. 9 Edw. II, *Articuli Cleri*, where tithes have been paid of an ancient mill.

MONTAGU: I am confirmed in my former opinion that tithes are due of common right for mills. Canon law is full in this point, and that is admitted. But it appears throughout all our history that there has been a great unwillingness in the laity to admit the clergy into a share of their profits.

[It was] objected but canon law binds not *vigore suo proprio*, but custom must cooperate. The difference between common right and custom is this that first extends generally, the other only to particular places. The payment of tithes of lead is only by custom because lead is only in particular places.

There is a custom of payment of tithes of fish brought to Yarmouth. Grist mills are as ancient as bread and are general throughout the kingdom. The other mills are of late times. I admit fulling mills [pay] a personal tithe.

No one case is so old as the Stat. Edw. VI. The oldest case is 14 Jac. I, and there is no case upon this point but out of the King's Bench.

The reasons for his opinion [were] 2 Inst. 642; 27 Hen. VIII, ca. [*blank*]; one shall pay his tithes according to the ecclesiastical laws and laudable usage. This Act authenticates all canons then received. This canon law was established at that time, but this point was not only settled by the ecclesiastical laws but also by the temporal laws in the reigns of the old kings. *Laws of Edward Confessor*, fo. 139, is express as to mills, *concessa rege et baronibus.*[1] *Laws of Henry I* [*blank*]; *vide* Wilkins, *Saxon Laws*; and Lambard, fol. 182, edit. 1644. Henry II was the great Justinian and, as Mr. Madox observes, was the founder of our laws. Selden's *History of Tithes* 228; 7 Edw. III, by Parning, fo. 5; Selden, *History of Tithes*, 231.

Hen. III was an old book seen by Selden. *Potissime de molendinis.* 11 Hen. III in Close Roll, *pars prima*, membrane 9 *in dorso*: *dominus rex concessit.* Magna Charta is a *concessit*, and so there is no objection to the phrase of *concessit.* In 30 Hen. III, a fine is levied *de decimis molendinorum in parochia suis existente.* 33 Edw. I, Constitution of the Archbishop, *de proventibus molendinorum.* Close Roll 7 Edw. II and 2 Inst. 621, 640, which cites this close roll. Register Ancient Book, fo. 48: a consultation was granted *de decimatione* of a grist mill.

Now, I come to the Statute *de Articuli Cleri* made upon a complaint of the clergy, and the Statute recites this cause of complaint, and the prohibition was grounded upon this way of reasoning in the laity, *viz.* that the new mills were not capable of custom, therefore, no tithe was due for them. But the answer of

---

[1] B. R. O'Brien, *God's Peace and King's Peace: The Laws of Edward the Confessor* (1999), s. 8.3, pp. 164, 165.

the king was no prohibition was ever granted by him in such cases. Lindwood, *Decima Mensura.*

The division of tithes into personal, praedial, or mixed is not the ancient division, for the ancient division is personal or praedial. But then, there is praedial mediate and immediate, and this is the sense, for there is nothing personal in wood.

Rolle says the custom is the common custom of the realm. And, by him, he ought to pay the tenth toll dish.

Lord Coke says this matter has never been judicially determined. A *modus* is always an endowment. Jaque's Case, 1 Rolle's Rep. 405; 1 Rolle's, Abridgment, 655.

[To the] objection that the corn has already paid tithe, [he] answered the miller pays out of new profits. It is not the farmer or owner of the corn who pays this sort of tithe.

As to the charge, the farmer is at the charge of husbandry as well as the miller, so there is no difference as to this point. And, by him, the word *renovans* does not only signify to renew or grow again, but to arise or become due.

Second, it is a praedial tithe. Michaelmas 1694. My Brother is chiefly governed by the two cases in the King's Bench. And as to the case of Hicks v. Woodson, nothing in that case was judicially before the court as to mills, but that case only related to agistment tithe. And I have taken Lord Holt's words thus, that it is very hard to maintain a *non decimando* unless in a case of wood. 4 Modern 344; Salkeld 655. Shower's Report of the case of Gumley v. Falkingham, 281, Holt, there, was of opinion that it is a praedial tithe.

Lord Coke does not say that the canon was never received; Hilary 16 Jac., Dandridge v. Johnson, and yet this case is only of a fulling mill.

And, by Montagu, there is much more labor required in a fulling mill than a corn mill. March Rep. 15. Not one authority is older than 14 Jac. I. Lord Holt was only a counsel in the case of Hughes v. Bishop of Hereford. A cider mill is not kept for profits, as is a corn mill. But an oven, where the parishioners bake there, must pay tithe. And so he concludes that the mill ought to pay the tithe. And, by Holt, that it is an ancient mill is not sufficient without a prescription that it never paid tithe; therefore, an ancient mill is not discharged from tithes.

Price [held he] ought to pay tithe and that also praedial tithes are due of common right. The old distinction is only between personal and praedial. One tenth toll dish is an argument that it is a praedial tithe *non deductis expensis* and at the place where the mill is. Lindwood 195, *tamquam praediales*; Rolle, *Dismes*, 656, tenth toll dish; 4 Modern 45, praedial tithe; so that Coke, Rolle, and Holt rather seem to think it praedial than personal.

Whether, being an old corn mill, it is discharged, not one Christian Saxon king but has made laws concerning tithes. *Edward Confessor's Laws, vide.* And these laws of former kings were confirmed in 4 Will. *Conquestor* [1069 x 1070] by a Parliamentary sanction. Statute of Church and Clergy by Wake; 163, 165,

Wilkins' *Saxon Laws*; Lambard; Spelman, 1 vol., *Concilia*, 610, 621; Selden, *History of Tithes*. All agree tithes are due of mills.

Decimas garbarum signifies tithe; *aliter, decimas garba*. Selden 284; *Garba* is a tenth part, and not an ecclesiastical portion. Dr. Chambers, *Of the Right of Tithes*, 196, in 1136 in Henry II's time; 6 Hen. III, Madox, *Formulare Anglicanum*, 28, a composition between two religious houses; Acts of Parliament, Magna Charta: *Habeat ecclesia omnia jura etc.*; 13 Edw., *Circumspecte agatis decimas debitas et consuetas*. 2 [*blank*] 97, 290, Councils; 33 Edw. III, Archbishop of Canterbury Winchelsea's Canon; Linwood 195, *decima mensura*; Selden 232; these canons are part of the ecclesiastical common law.

Consider the method and manner of this law of *Articuli Cleri*. Old mills were not then in question, only new mills, and, to this, the answer is given and asserts that new mills shall pay tithes.

Was there any law then in being to distinguish between new and old mills in this case, for, if a mill does not pay tithe *de jure communi*, how come new mills are to pay? [He] supposes the writ in the Register to be about Edward III's time. [He] insists on the antiquity and authority of the Register. Fitzherbert, *Natura Brevium*, 51; *Reformatio Legum* 115 expresses *de decimis molendinorum*.

By Coke, some tithe or other is due for mills, and, then, no *non decimando* is to be allowed. 2 Inst. 622; Lord Coke says he never knew it judicially determined, and this destroys all the contrary authorities in his time. 26 Eliz.; 2 Inst. 4; Mand's Case; 2 Rolle's *Abridgment*, 652; 3 Bulstrode 212; tithes of mill are personal, by Lord Coke; 1 Rolle's Rep. 405; but this is an *obiter* opinion; 2 Cro. 429; 2 Rolle 84; tithes are due for grist mills and not fulling mills. [. . .] and Lux seems to be the very case before us. Rolle, *Abridgment*, 641, 652, Grim; 4 Modern; Shower 281; 15 June 1714, in this court; 13 June 1716, Crisp v. Tibold. Double tithe is no argument, for then it could not be due for any new mills.

As to the case in the House of Lords, it went upon a difference between the sort of mills; in that case, it was a horse mill for malt.

Bury, Chief Baron: The defendant insists that the mill is an ancient mill and had never paid any tithes. Some say that this Statute *De Articuli Cleri* gave tithes of new mills. He thinks himself that the Statute implies a negative for old mills. The Statute makes no distinction between mills of any sort. Lord Coke says plainly that the tithes of corn mills are personal. The miller's profit is for his labor, and he may be paid in money as well as in corn. And, therefore, he sees no reason to call this praedial anymore than the wages of a miller who has a fulling mill. And that is agreed on all hands to be personal. But the case in the House of Lords has determined this point, *viz.* that it is a personal tithe. *Clergyman's Law* 450; old mills, which had never paid tithes, shall be supposed to be built before the Statute.

The canons are, it is true, for the payment of all sorts of tithes. But surely, the canons were never received in this latitude. If it is a personal tithe, then they are not to be paid but by customs and the non-payment of tithes for these mills is an argument that they have been esteemed personal tithes.

So the court being divided, no judgment was given.

Harvard Law School MS. 1082, vol. 1, p. 198, pl. 1

Sittings after Hilary term 1723/24.

The former defendant, John Oliver, was by a report made by the Deputy [Remembrancer] found indebted to the plaintiff in £3 8s. 8d., and John Oliver dies. And the defendants Elizabeth and John Oliver were his administrators. And the bill is revived against the defendants for the duty and costs.

Edlin, for the plaintiff, insisted that the revivor for the duty and costs was proper.

Ward, for the defendants, said that a bill of revivor is a novelty in this case, for you cannot revive for costs. 2 Can. Rept., Temple v. Rouse; 5 Rept., Hall's Case.[1] And by motion, the decree might have been drawn up for the duty, and, without consent, no costs could be paid if the party dies. Town of Warwick v. Lucas.[2] If there had been no decree pronounced, then a revivor had been proper, but not afterwards. Lamplugh v. Chetham.[3]

Edlin replies: There can be no *subpoena scire facias* because that must be relatory to the decree, which was never passed.

PRICE: I think that the bill is right, and there is no other remedy and it is not a complete decree until signed. But I agree that reviving for costs only is going too far, but yet, since the decree was not drawn up, I think the bill is proper.

PAGE: It is no complete decree until it is signed and enrolled. If the suit is depending, the revivor is proper, and where the duty was not paid.

GILBERT: I allow the rule that for reviving for costs only is not right. Costs are *ex maleficio* and die with the party. The duty is the principal, and costs are the accessory. And, therefore, I think that the bill is proper, and the defendant ought to account for the duty and costs.

Taussig MS. 311, vol. 1, p. 640

Hilary term 1723/24.

The single question in this cause was whether a bill of revivor might be allowed for a duty remaining due upon the former decree and for the costs also. It is acknowledged that, for costs only, no bill of revivor shall be allowed.

Et pro defendente: The plaintiff might have had the duty of entering the decree by a motion after the death of the defendant.

---

1 *Temple v. Rowse* (1679), 2 Chancery Cases 7, 22 E.R. 820; *Hall v. Cooke* (1604), 5 Coke Rep. 51, 77 E.R. 132.

2 *Corporation of Warwick v. Lucas* (1711), Eq. Cases Exch. 671.

3 *Chetham v. Lamplugh* (1705), Eq. Cases Exch. 514.

PRICE and PAGE: He may revive for the duty and the costs, though not only for the costs. And this is very reasonable.

GILBERT was of the same opinion. Costs are for vexation, which is a debt *ex maleficio*. And that is by the constant rule of the canon law, by which the Court of Chancery was originally formed and canonists were the judges. A debt *ex maleficio moritur cum persona*. But here is a debt *ex contractu* as well as *ex maleficio*.

And the court decreed accordingly.

Bunbury 160, 145 E.R. 632

24 February 1723[/24].

A bill of revivor was brought both for the duty, which was £3 6s. 8d. for tithe milk and Easter offerings, and costs, against the defendants as executors to the defendant, who died after the decree but before the costs were taxed. And, therefore, it was objected for the defendant that, the costs not being ascertained in the lifetime of the party by taxation, there could be no revivor for them now.

But, *per* CURIAM, although there can be no revivor for costs alone, yet there may be for the duty and costs. And it was decreed accordingly.

Note: In the Exchequer, all the enrollment there is the entry.

Note: There can be no *subpoena scire facias* until the decree be entered.

[Order of 16 May 1720: 2 Wood 143.]

129

Rex v. Bishop

(Ex. 1720)

The Court of Exchequer can order commissioners of sewers to show that they had jurisdiction when they imposed a particular fine.

Bunbury 61, 145 E.R. 595

20 May.

It was moved to discharge issues set by commissioners of sewers, alleging they had no jurisdiction by the Stat. 33 Hen. VIII, c. 5,[1] because this was only a bank thrown up by the sea. And it was ordered for them to show cause on notice to the clerk of the sewers, though it was doubted whether this could be done by motion because it was a judgment of the commissioners and no [writ of] *certiorari* would lie originally to remove their order.

Harvard Law School MS. 1082, vol. 1, p. 2, pl. 3

Easter term 1720.

---

[1] Stat. 23 Hen. VIII, c. 5 (*SR*, III, 368–372).

Sir Constantine Phipps moved to set aside fines set by the commissioners of sewers for that these banks in question were flung up by the sea, over which, by the Statute of 23 Hen. VIII, the commissioners of sewers have no jurisdiction.

The Chief Baron [BURY] said that this place was no arm of the sea, but I do not know why the commissioners should not show cause.

MONTAGU and PAGE [held] against the commissioners' showing cause. But at last, they agreed to a show cause [order] against the first day of the next term and process to stay [and] notice to be given to the clerk of the commissioners of sewers.

130

Jordan v. Colley

(Ex. 1720)

Where tithes of wood are claimed, the burden of proof to show that they are not due lies upon the parishioner.

A parish cannot prescribe in non decimando *for wood.*

Bunbury 61, 145 E.R. 595,
1 Rayner 150, 2 Gwillim 625, 1 Eagle & Younge 754

23 May 1720.

A bill was brought by a rector for tithe wood in the parish of Little Wenlock in the County of Salop as it had been time out of mind paid in that parish against the defendants as vendees of Sir William Forrester. The defendants, in their answer, say that no tithe had been paid for this coppice wood called Holebrook Coppice when felled before and that they never heard that any tithe or *modus* had been paid for wood in the parish. It was insisted upon for the defendants that tithe wood was not due *de communi jure* and, therefore, that the proof lay upon the plaintiff and that it was only founded upon a canon in Bishop Stratford's time, *anno* 17 Edw. III,[1] and, therefore, the defendants need not allege any prescription or custom by way of exemption. But it was answered for the plaintiff that occupiers must always set forth an exemption.

And it was held *per* CURIAM that the defendants ought to have shown some exemption. And there is no instance that a parish can prescribe in *non decimando* for tithe wood. Wilds and hundreds are upon another consideration.

But note, says the reporter [Bunbury] himself, though the defendants were decreed to account, I do not find that it is yet certainly determined that tithe wood is due *de communi jure*.

---

[1] W. Lyndwood, *Provinciale* (1929), p. 162.

Harvard Law School MS. 1082, vol. 1, p. 4

Easter term 1720.

The plaintiff, as rector of Little Wenlock in the County of Salop, brings his bill against the defendant for tithe wood of the defendant, who purchased the same and was to cut it down. The defendant in his answer says that he believes the wood in question or any other wood [. . .] did never pay tithes and that it was used for an iron furnace and insists it to be oak and ash above twenty years growth and not liable to pay tithes.

Mr. *Ward*, for the plaintiff: This is a bill for the tithe of coppice wood, and, in the answer, he insisted on that no tithe wood was paid within the parish, and a *non decimando* will not lie for a parish. I shall not enter upon the old question whether tithe wood is due *de communi jure* or by custom for I think that it is now settled by the decrees of this court that tithe wood is due *de communi jure* and that, in a demand for tithe wood in bar of it, you must insist upon something in lieu of it, as a hearth penny etc. and by the form of bills used in this court, it is never demanded by custom only, as the tithe of fish, coneys, and mortuaries are. And he cited Bate v. Sprackling, Hilary 1717/18,[1] other book, fo. 378, where an account for tithe wood was directed because no discharge was showed or that it was on account of husbandry. The complaint against the Statute of *Sylva Caedua*[2] was only upon the account of timber. See 17 Edw. III.

Serjeant *Pengelly*, for the defendant, [said] that there is no pretense for this demand and the defendant Colley was only an agent for Lord Torrington and Boycot, so the bill must be dismissed. I insist upon it that tithe of underwood is only due by custom and so is the law below stairs and, therefore, the proof lies on the plaintiff that tithe wood had been paid. Tithe wood only subsists by Archbishop Stratford's canon, Linwood 190, and only subsists by custom.

Wood is not annually renewing, and it cannot come to perfection within the year. So it can be no subsistence to the parson. And the commons complained of this canon. And it was answered it should be only paid as formerly. Cotton, *Records*, 40, to which book Montagu objected as a foolish book.

Hicks v. Woodson, Michaelmas 6 Will. & Mar., King's Bench, 4 Modern 34, Salkeld 665, 666.[3]

---

[1] *Bate v. Sprackling* (Ex. 1718), see above, Case No. 37.

[2] Stat. 45 Edw. III, c. 3 (*SR*, I, 393).

[3] *Hicks v. Woodeson*, 4 Modern 324, 336, 87 E.R. 422, 429, 2 Salkeld 655, 91 E.R. 558, also 1 Eagle & Younge 592, 2 Gwillim 550, 3 Lord Raymond 116, 92 E.R. 595, 1 Lord Raymond 137, 91 E.R. 987, 12 Modern 111, 88 E.R. 1200, Skinner 560, 90 E.R. 252, Comberbach 403, 90 E.R. 555, Carthew 392, 90 E.R. 827, Holt K.B. 671, 90 E.R. 1271, Dodd 171.

There is no difference between a hundred and a parish, for a parish may as well prescribe as a hundred. 1 Saunders 141, 143; Coke, *Entries*, 460.[1]

Northey, for the defendant: Tithe wood is not due of common right. Selden 246.[2] This bill ought to be dismissed because there is no proof that tithes had been paid. I do admit that it is not necessary to set it forth in the bill that he is entitled by custom because he has liberty to make it out at the hearing.

MONTAGU mentioned what Lord Chief Justice Holt said in the case cited in Salkeld concerning 27 Hen. VIII.[3]

Northey answered that Statute only extends to canons put in use.

PAGE said that Statute ought to operate no further for that personal tithes were ordered by the canons yet were not established by that Statute.

Sir Constantine Phipps, for the defendant: The plaintiff has failed because he has laid it by custom and not supported it by proof. Prescription in *non decimando* may be in a weald or in a hundred. And why not in a parish, which may include the hundred? No prescription in *non decimando* could be allowed if wood was due of common right. Rolle, *Abridgment*, 654.[4]

Mr. *Ward* replies for the plaintiff: This demand is well made. And if this doctrine laid down by the defendants[5] is to be allowed, it will destroy all the decrees in this court for fifty years last past. The reason, as I take it, why a prescription is allowed in a hundred and not a parish is because a parish may conspire to defeat the parson of his tithes, but not of a hundred which consists of many parishes, and such a combination cannot be presumed. Greenway v. Earl of Kent, 1709.[6] An occupier is obliged to set forth some discharge. Cro. Car., Norton v. Palmer,[7] *per legem terrae*, tithes are due. A *modus decimandi* is allowed in a parish, and a *modus decimando* shows that it is due of common right. Rolle Reports 175; Jones v. Calvert 1709. Tithe pigeons sold is due of common right.

Chief Baron [BURY]: The defendant pleading that he never knew tithes were paid is not insisting on a prescription, and the reason in *Doctor and Student*[8] between a parish and a hundred is right and it was so always held. It is never put

---

1 *Croucher v. Collins* (1668), 1 Williams Saunders 141, 85 E.R. 151, also 2 Keble 319, 84 E.R. 199, 4 Gwillim 1576, 1 Eagle & Younge 469; *Bartlett v. Long* (1607), E. Coke, *A Booke of Entries* (1614), 'Prohibition', pl. 8, f. 460.

2 J. Selden, *History of Tithes*.

3 Stat. 27 Hen. VIII, c. 20 (*SR*, III, 551–552).

4 1 Rolle, Abr., *Dismes*, pl. H, 11, p. 654.

5 Plaintiffs *MS*.

6 *Greenway v. Earl of Kent* (Ex. 1706), Bunbury 98, 145 E.R. 609, 1 Rayner 161, 1 Wood 479, 1 Eagle & Younge 677, Eq. Cases Exch. 546, 644.

7 *Norton v. Fermer* (1628), Croke Car. 113, 79 E.R. 699, also *sub nom. Norton v. Harmer*, Hetley 88, 110, 117, 124 E.R. 365, 382, 387, Littleton 5, 152, 124 E.R. 108, 182, 1 Eagle & Younge 363.

8 C. St. German, *Doctor and Student* (T. F. T. Plucknett and J. L. Barton, edd., 1974), 91 Selden Soc. 303–304.

upon the plaintiff to prove that coppice wood has been paid and there is no occasion to set forth for the plaintiff in his bill that such tithes were due by custom. So [he] decreed for the plaintiff.

MONTAGU: The first law about tithe wood was in Archbishop Stratford's time. Lambert 139; Dr. Prideaux's book about tithes.[1] And there have been several bills to this effect and by the law of Edward the Confessor[2] and so it is in Lambert. And I shall regard the canon and think that tithe wood ought to be paid.

PAGE: I think that tithe wood is not due of common right and that rule is manifested by the allowance of a prescription in *non decimando*. I think that the common law has concurred so far with the ecclesiastical court as to the canon so as to make the defendant prove a discharge and, therefore, the defendant ought to prove his discharge. A parish cannot prescribe in *non decimando*, for it might happen in a parish that there was no wood and it would be too hard to put the parson upon proof of it. So he agreed to decree an account *pro omnes*.

The Chief Baron [BURY] answered the case of yearly renewing by the case of a nursery [?], which was in the same manner, yet tithes shall be paid.

[Order sub nom. Jordan v. Jenkins, 23 May 1720: 2 Wood 145.]

131

Yarroth v. Seys

(Ex. 1720)

Sequestered property will not be ordered to be sold until after there has been a return filed on the writ of sequestration.

Bunbury 62, 145 E.R. 595

24 May 1720.

Upon a commission of sequestration, the commissioners sequestered some live cattle, which not being sufficient to answer the debt, it was moved for leave to sell these cattle. But it was denied because the commissioners had not returned the commission. But, when that was done and it appeared what they had sequestered and the value as so much in part of the debt, then, for the remainder, a new sequestration should issue and a *venditioni exponas* to sell the goods sequestered upon the first.

---

[1] H. Prideaux, *Original and Right of Tithes* (1710).

[2] B. R. O'Brien, *God's Peace and King's Peace: The Laws of Edward the Confessor* (1999), s. 8.1, pp. 164, 165.

132

Rex v. Robinson

(Ex. 1720)

No writ of execution may be issued on a dormant writ of extent without a court order.

Bunbury 62, 145 E.R. 596

25 May 1720.

A [writ of] extent issued against the defendant so long ago as 3 Will. III [1691–1692], and an inquisition was taken thereupon, but no process issued against him because there was a former extent against him. But that being now satisfied, Mr. *Foley* moved that process might issue upon this last inquisition, for it was settled in Chief Baron Ward's time that, upon dormant extents, no process should go without a motion in court. And it was now granted, unless cause [be shown to the contrary].

133

Anonymous, *qui tam* v. Jackson

(Ex. 1720)

Where only small amounts of forfeited goods are seized, several seizers can join in a single writ of appraisement and information.

Bunbury 63, 145 E.R. 596

30 May 1720.

Where there are several seizures by several persons and the whole does not amount to £100, it is allowed that all may be put into one writ of appraisement and one information only may be exhibited in the names of all the persons seizing for the several matters seized. *Quaere.*

134

Attorney General v. Pocock

(Ex. 1720)

Court costs and sheriff's fees are not payable out of the money that is refunded to a judgment debtor where there was an excessive levy.

Harvard Law School MS. 1082, vol. 1, p. 6

Easter term 1720.

Serjeant *Stevens*, for the defendant, moved to have the residue of the money levied on a [writ of] extent without costs or poundage because the debt was only due by a simple contract.

Raymond, Attorney General, and *Ward*, for the king, cited Attorney General v. Quash and Rex v. Bowdage,[1] where costs were paid. And in the case of an outlawry, poundage must be paid to the sheriff.

Serjeant *Stevens* said that no costs were due on an extent in aid and the sheriff ought to be paid out of the money due to the crown and not out of the residue of the money.

Sir Constantine Phipps, for the defendant: I agree [with] the case of Attorney General v. Quash and Attorney General v. Bowdage so far where there are bonds and penalties. There the costs shall be paid out of the penalties, but not where the debt was upon a simple contract.

The Chief Baron [BURY] said that this case differed from the Attorney General v. Quash and Bowdage's Case. I think that no costs are to be paid and, if the sheriff has levied more than the debt, the money ought not to be paid to the sheriff out of the surplus.

PRICE said that this case differed from Quash's [Case] and Bowdage's Case. He never observed that in a case of aid that costs were paid. In the case of the crown, costs are never paid to or from the crown and, where there is no penalty, the sheriff shall have his money out of the money that is due. And he cannot justify levying more than is due.

PAGE agreed that the poundage to the sheriff ought not to be paid out of the surplus, but out of the money due.

The court agreed that the residue of the money shall be paid to Pocock, but, before he parts with the money to Flower, the sheriff shall deduct the poundage, but not out of the residue of the money due to Pocock.

135

Gibson v. Nayres

(Ex. 1720)

Time of performance is not of the essence of a contract in a court of equity.

Taussig MS. 311, vol. 1, p. 1

Easter term 1720, 6 Geo. I.

---

[1] *Regina v. Quash* (1713), Parker 281, 145 E.R. 780, Dodd 365; *Rex v. Bowdage* (Ex. 1717), see above, Case No. 32, note also *Attorney General v. Bowdage* (1709), Parker 277, 145 E.R. 779, Dodd 218, Lincoln's Inn MS. Misc. 535, f. [214], Georgetown Univ. Law Sch. MS. B88–9, f. 340v (Ward's Reports), Public Record Office, E.127/26, f. 70, E.127/27, f. 33, E.126/19, ff. 166, 192v.

The plaintiff, as eldest son of James Gibson, Town Clerk of London, exhibited his bill against Nayres to compel a specific performance of an agreement between Nayres and him, by which agreement the plaintiff Gibson covenanted that, before 25 March ensuing the date of the agreement, he would convey and assure or cause to be conveyed etc. unto the said Nayres a good, perfect, absolute, and indefeasible estate of inheritance free from all manner of entails as by counsel shall be advised and the defendant Nayres promised, on such conveyance, to pay Mr. Robinson £511 upon the execution of such conveyance having already paid Gibson £32 in hand. Gibson's title, when he made this agreement, stood thus. His father, the Town Clerk, by his will devised that John Elsington and John Jacob, who were seised of the premises in trust for him should stand seised thereof in trust to raise £500 with interest for Robinson's wife, who was the devisor's daughter, and this was to be raised by them either by sale or mortgage and, after payment thereof, that they should convey the premises or such parts as should not be sold to the use of the plaintiff for life without power to commit waste and then to the use of the plaintiff's sons.

The trustees by their answer said that they were not privy or consenting to this contract at the time of making it. And the defendants insisted that, though they had entered into such agreement, yet that, inasmuch as the plaintiff had not conveyed nor could make a title by the 25th March, as was owned by the plaintiff's own counsel, for the estate was in the trustees and they could no ways be compelled to join but by a bill in equity and inasmuch as the premises by them contracted for, which were mills, were now since the agreement diminished in value by Mr. Duncomb's erecting another mill thereabouts, which took off from the business and profits of their mills, therefore, they should not be obliged to a specific performance.

But the court decreed the performance of the contract, time being only a circumstance and not material in equity.

136

Wynn v. Hughes

(Ex. 1720)

A writ of prohibition does not lie from the Court of Exchequer to the Court of Great Sessions of Wales.

Harvard Law School MS. 1082, vol. 1, p. 7

Easter term 1720.

Mr. *Bootle*, for the plaintiff, [moved] to have a [writ of] prohibition to the Grand Sessions of the County of Caernarvon, where the defendant below and plaintiff here pleaded that he was not resident or had any goods or estate within the county.

First, [he said] that the proceeding below is irregular because the person is not residing within the county so that no process can go.

Second, there could be no benefit by the execution because no goods or lands [were there].

It was formerly objected that this should have been pleaded below and that writs of error lie there.

[It was] objected further that no [writ of] prohibition will lie to the principality of Wales for that the Grand Sessions is a superior court never conquered, only by consent, and that the judges can write to the bishops there, as the judges in Westminster Hall can to the judges[1] here.

He answered a mandatory writ will lie to the principality of Wales and that Wales is different from any inferior jurisdictions, for process there might lie, yet not into Wales. Wales owed allegiance to England before Edward I's time, though [they were] governed by their own laws. Writs of safe conduct, protection, etc. would lie into Gascony, Guernsey, and Jersey. And so writs of error would lie, yet no private writ will issue, though public writs *pro re publicae*. See Stat. 34 Hen. VIII; Godbolt 214,[2] how remedial writs would go, whatever writs have gone, yet that matter subsists by statute, and not by common law. See Lord Vaughan 417; Cro. Car. 34, 341.[3]

[To the] objection that judges can write the bishops there, [he] answered [there is] no express resolution and [it] proves nothing that there is any remedy by any process out of Wales. And there is a difference between lordships, manors, and shires [?], for, in the first, they are subject to the laws in Westminster Hall, but not to the latter. Bishops in Wales are on the foundation of the princes of Wales and, by the union, the same power remains so that they may write to their own bishops, but there is no consequence from that that their process will run out of Wales.

Prohibitions have gone to the [Court of the] Marches of Wales and to the ancient shires: 1 Rolle Reports 54, 83; 2 Rolle Reports 312. Prohibitions to the principality: 1 Rolle Report 301, 246; 3 Bulstrode 116; 1 Rolle Report 368; Hilary 9, Tranter v. Fitzgerald.[4]

---

[1] Sic in MS.

[2] Stat. 34 & 35 Hen. VIII, c. 26, ss. 53, 55 (*SR*, III, 935); *Anonymous* (1613), Godbolt 214, 78 E.R. 130.

[3] 'Concerning Process . . . into Wales', Vaughan 395, 417, 124 E.R. 1130, 1140; Memorandum (1626), Croke Car. 34, 79 E.R. 633; *Cort v. Bishop of St. David's* (1634), Croke Car. 341, 348, 79 E.R. 899, 905, also W. Jones 330, 82 E.R. 174.

[4] *Anonymous* (1614), 1 Rolle Rep. 54, 81 E.R. 323; *Gibbs v. Cann* (1614), 1 Rolle Rep. 83, 81 E.R. 344; *Anonymous* (1623), 2 Rolle Rep. 312, 81 E.R. 821; *Vawdrey v. Pannell* (1615), 1 Rolle Rep. 246, 331, 81 E.R. 464, 522, also 3 Bulstrode 116, 81 E.R. 99 (Chancery Court of Chester); *Bromage v. Genning* (1616), 1 Rolle Rep. 368, 81 E.R. 540;

Mr. *Morris*, for the defendant: [There can be] no prohibition. [He said] that it is not sufficient to oust the jurisdiction of Wales without maintaining the truth of the fact by affidavits, for we cannot traverse the plea below. 1 Siderfin 464; 1 Ventris 181; 3 Keble 742.[1] And no writs can go to an acquired dominion. This writ is *breve remediale mandatorum*, and the statutes do not lessen the jurisdiction. 12 Edw. I; 27 Hen. VIII.[2]

Though prohibitions may go to the Marches [of Wales], yet it is not from thence to be inferred that it will go to the principality of Wales. Ireland is part of England, yet it is not to be inferred that writs here will run there. See Stat. 34 Hen. VIII.

This court cannot prohibit the Court of Common Pleas. Plowden 267. The words in the Stat. 34 Hen. VIII exclude this court. Fines have been levied in the Court of the Marches, but never in the principality.

[To the] objection of Cro. Jac., Wheatly v. Price, [he] answered Lutwyche 1026, Turner v. Weston.[3]

MONTAGU said that, in the case of Tranter v. Fitzgerald, prohibition was ordered, but he doubted the case.

PRICE was against a prohibition, especially after ten years standing and no end of controversy.

The court ordered the rule for a prohibition to be discharged.

137

Hart v. King

(Ex. 1720)

A person may sue to have a distribution of an intestate's estate within a year after his death.

Harvard Law School MS. 1082, vol. 1, p. 9

Trinity term 1720.

This came upon the defendant's plea to a bill for to have distribution of an intestate's estate, to which bill the defendant pleaded the Stat. of 22 & 23 of Car. II, para. 8,[4] that no distribution should be within the year and that the intestate died so lately that the year was not expired.

Tranter v. Duggan (1698), Comberbach 468, 90 E.R. 595, 12 Modern 138, 172, 88 E.R. 1219, 1243.

[1] *Waineman v. Smith* (1670), 1 Siderfin 464, 82 E.R. 1219; *St. Aubin v. Cox* (1672), 1 Ventris 180, 181, 86 E.R. 122; *Anonymous* (1677), 3 Keble 742, 84 E.R. 985.

[2] Stat. 12 Edw. I, of Wales (*SR*, I, 55-70); Stat. 27 Hen. VIII, c. 26 (*SR*, III, 563-569).

[3] *Turner v. Weston* (1688), 2 Lutwyche 1023, 125 E.R. 570.

[4] Stat. 22 & 23 Car. II, c. 10, s. 5 (*SR*, V, 720).

Chief Baron [Bury]: I think that, before the Act of Parliament, that the ordinary could not distribute. But I take it that a court of equity had always power to compel a distribution. And the clause is that the court shall not make distribution within the year, but it does not say that a bill may not be brought and the court does not make a distribution upon bringing the bill. I am for overruling the plea.

Price: I never heard of this plea before. If it shall be allowed, it would occasion two suits, *viz.* a bill of discovery and another for relief. The Act was not designed to prohibit a bill from being brought. So I am for overruling the plea as such, but it is to stand for an answer with liberty to except.

Montagu: I think that the bill points at the distribution chiefly and it is not brought for a discovery, but a distribution. And I think that the plea is a just plea. And I cannot make myself wiser than the law. And I think that the bill is brought too soon and that such a bill is prohibited by the Act. And I am for allowing the plea.

Page: If this plea was not allowed, it would overturn all justice. I do not take the Act to be prohibitory on the party, for an administrator may make a distribution the next day. The Act only operates on the ecclesiastical court, and not any other. And the Act is only to prohibit an actual distribution if an executor is going beyond the sea, not staying him but by a bill. If an administrator dies within the year, may not there be a bill of discovery before a reversioner may bring a bill? And it is a present duty, and this Act does not operate on the means. The plea must be overruled, but [the defendant] ordered to stand for an answer without costs.

Bunbury 64, 145 E.R. 596

28 June 1720.

A bill was brought for the discovery of a personal estate against an administrator and for a distribution. The defendant, in his answer, sets forth the personal estate. But, as to the distribution, he pleads that the intestate died but in March last and, therefore, by the Stat. 22 Car. II, cap., he was not obliged to a distribution until the year was expired.

But by the opinion of the Lord Chief Baron [Bury], Price and Page, barons, the plea was overruled, and it was ordered to stand for an answer with liberty to except, in which case there were no costs; Montagu, baron, *dissentiente.*

138

Mills v. Harrison

(Ex. 1720)

A sheriff's return can be challenged upon an affidavit.

Harvard Law School MS. 1082, vol. 1, p. 10, pl. 1

Trinity term 1720.

The sheriff returns a rescue. The persons so returned would have falsified the return by an affidavit.

MONTAGU was against it, for you ought not to falsify the return by affidavits, but you ought to bring an action against the sheriff for a false return. And he cited Hargrave v. Johnson, where the affidavits were refused to be read.

BURY and PRICE were for reading the affidavits because an attachment was to be granted on this return and, in the King's Bench, an attachment goes upon an affidavit without showing cause, but the rule is otherwise here.

[It was] adjourned until the first day of next term, and, then, affidavits on both sides are to be read.

139

Williams v. Small

(Ex. 1720)

The answer to a bill of complaint for tithes of mills must set forth the values and quantities of the mills even though the answer denies that any tithes are payable.

Harvard Law School MS. 1082, vol. 1, p. 10, pl. 2

Trinity term 1720.

[To a] bill for tithes of mills, the defendant says that they never paid tithes, but he sets forth no value, but, if the court should be of opinion that they were tithable, he submits to be examined on interrogatories. So this came upon exceptions to the defendant's answer as to quantities and values.

Mr. *Ward*, for the plaintiff, insisted that it was not a good answer, and he cited Gumley v. Fontleroy, in this court, and Dodson v. Oliver.[1]

PAGE and PRICE, at first, thought the answer sufficient for that these tithes were not due of common right.

BURY and MONTAGU were of the contrary opinion.

And the court, at last, ordered the defendant to answer with costs.

See Gumley v. Fontleroy and Dodson v. Oliver in this book and Cradock v. Allen in the other book.

[1] *Gumley v. Fontleroy* (1720-1721), see above, Case No. 127; *Dodson v. Oliver* (1720-1724), see above, Case No. 128.

140

White v. Roberts

(Ex. 1720)

The question in this case was whether a writ of error filed in the House of Lords when it is not sitting is a supersedeas *if the record is not transcribed.*

Harvard Law School MS. 1082, vol. 1, p. 14

Trinity term 1720.

The Attorney General *Raymond* [argued] that a writ of error returnable in Parliament is a *supersedeas* though the Parliament is not sitting. 2 Levinz 43, Roberts v. Sedgwick, 3 Keble 231.

Mr. *Fazakerly*, for the same [side], cited Raymond 383, 384.[1] This writ of error is a *supersedeas*, and so is the constant practice. And when a writ of error is depending in Parliament, no court will intermeddle. And it is the common case of a writ of error depending in the Exchequer Chamber. 5 Modern 338; 1 Salkeld 261; see the case Delanoire v. Brice.[2]

Serjeant *Chesshyre*, for the defendant in error: By the standing order of the House of Lords, if the record is not transcribed, it is of no effect. See Rules of 13 July 1678. See Statute of Hen. VIII, of appeals. If this method should prevail, nothing can be done here or in the House of Lords, for, if the record is not transcribed, the House of Lords cannot meddle with it, and yet, according to the gentlemen on the other side, the writ of error is a *supersedeas* and, therefore, this court cannot intermeddle, which is an absurd interpretation and a failure of justice.

Mr. *Bootle*, for the defendant in error: I believe the usual practice is that, if a writ of error is brought and transcribed and the Parliament rises, it is usual to take out execution. And so the Master certified.

Mr. *Fazakerly* replies: You may get rid of this writ of error, for, when there is a rule, you may *non pros* it.

Chief Baron [Bury]: I think that the writ of error is gone and that is no *supersedeas* of itself. And I will not grant a *supersedeas*.

Price: I cannot answer the case in Levinz. And there is much reason in the case of a writ of error as in the case of appeals. But the mischief is unanswer-

---

[1] *Rex v. Earl of Castlemain* (1680), T. Raymond 379, 383-384, 83 E.R. 198, 200.

[2] *Brace v. Pennoyer* (1697), 5 Modern 338, 87 E.R. 692; *Howard v. Pitt* (1692), 1 Salkeld 261, 91 E.R. 230, also 1 Shower K.B. 402, 89 E.R. 667, Carthew 236, 90 E.R. 741, Holt K.B. 1, 90 E.R. 898; *Penoyer v. Brace* (1722), Carthew 404, 90 E.R. 834, Holt K.B. 640, 90 E.R. 1254, 1 Lord Raymond 244, 91 E.R. 1059, 1 Salkeld 319, 91 E.R. 282, 8 Modern 108, 88 E.R. 85, Comberbach 441, 90 E.R. 579, 12 Modern 130, 88 E.R. 1214.

able. I do not think that it is a *supersedeas ex debito justitiae* and, therefore, will not grant it.

MONTAGU dissented. If the taking out of execution is irregular, then we ought to set it aside. And it is now settled that a writ of error is a *supersedeas* of itself. Perhaps there may be no opportunity of trying it in a shut sessions. And I am for allowing it to be a *supersedeas*. And he cited Pennoire v. Brace.

PAGE: I think that this writ of error is not to be understood a *supersedeas*. I allow that a rule may be given by the defendant in error to *non pros* it. But I take the rule in 1678 to be a standing order of the House of Lords. It must have a reasonable construction that the sessions has twenty-four days. I do not think that this matter is depending because the writ of error was not returned, and a writ of *excommunicatem capiendum* is not depending until it is returned. I think that it is a *supersedeas* if the writ of error is allowed and that a dissolution of Parliament will not determine a writ of error. The writ of error is gone and, therefore, I am against a *supersedeas*. And it is agreeable to the standing rule of the House of Lords. And so [he] agreed [it to be] no *supersedeas*, against the opinion of Montagu.

Bunbury 64, 145 E.R. 596

6 July 1720.

A writ of error was brought in the House of Lords upon a judgment in the Exchequer. The Parliament was prorogued, and, then, execution was taken out upon the judgment here, and the money was levied.

The Attorney General [*Raymond*] and Mr. *Fazakerly* moved to set this execution aside, for, though the Parliament was prorogued, yet the writ of error continued in force, and, consequently, it is a *supersedeas* to the execution.

But upon hearing Serjeant *Chesshyre* on the other side and inspecting the orders of the House of Lords, whereby it appeared that the writ of error should have been transcribed within fourteen days, which was not done in this case, the court thought it not reasonable to hang up the party, but that he ought to have the benefit of his execution, Baron MONTAGU, *dissentiente*.

And the case of Hood v. Godfrey, in Hilary term, 1710, was cited, in which case, there was a judgment in an action of *assumpsit* in Trinity term before and a *fieri facias* issued and then a writ of error was brought in Parliament; the Parliament was dissolved in September following; then, a *testatum fieri facias* issued and was executed, which was set aside because the *testatum fieri facias* was grounded upon the *fieri facias*, which was certainly superseded by the writ of error.

But note this proves that an original execution might well be taken out after the dissolution of the Parliament.

141

Binstead v. Coleman

(Ex. 1720)

An oral contract that has been partly performed will be enforced in equity, but a written contract cannot be varied by contrary evidence.

Bunbury 65, 145 E.R. 597

12 July 1720.

This distinction was laid down upon the Statute of Frauds and Perjuries[1] that, where there is a whole agreement by parol and part of it is executed, a court of equity will decree a specific execution of the whole, for the Statute of Frauds, says the Chief Baron [Bury], does not extend to that, but, where there is an agreement by writing executed, you cannot come by evidence to supply any defect in that agreement, which was intended to be part of that agreement, but not inserted in it, for that would be to evade the Statute of Frauds and introduce more perjury. The whole court were of the same opinion.

142

Clark v. Dashwood

(Ex. 1720)

An occupier of land claiming a discharge of tithes must prove that the land in question was owned by one of the greater monasteries.

Bunbury 66, 145 E.R. 597,
1 Rayner 151, 1 Eagle & Younge 756

13 July 1720.

A bill was brought for the tithes of the rectory of Carsington in the County of Oxford, particularly of the coppice wood called Burleighwood. And the plaintiff derives his title from the lessee of the dean and chapter of Christchurch. The defendant insists, that no tithe of this wood was ever paid but once, being terrified, for that it was exempt as part of the possessions of Eynsham Abbey, which was one of the greater abbeys and, consequently, capable of an exemption by the Stat. 31 Hen. VIII.[2]

And it was insisted by Mr. *Ward*, for the defendant, that constant non-payment was an evidence of exemption in the case of a lay impropriator.

---

[1] Stat. 29 Car. II, c. 3 (*SR*, V, 839-842).

[2] Stat. 31 Hen. VIII, c. 13 (*SR*, III, 733-739).

But note the proof was only belief and hearsay, and the defendant was decreed to account.

Harvard Law School MS. 1082, vol. 1, p. 20, pl. 1

Trinity term 1720.

The plaintiff, as lessee of the dean and chapter of Christchurch, claimed the tithe of coppice wood arising in [*blank*] near Oxford. The defendant insisted on it that this wood was part of the Abbey of Eynsham and, therefore, ought not to pay any tithes.

And the plaintiff had no proof that tithes were ever paid, except once to the vicar, which was a wrong payment, and a very strong proof by the defendant that this wood in question was reputed part of the Abbey of Eynsham and that no tithes were ever paid.

And, because the defendant did not prove further that it was part of the abbey by some record or minister's accounts in the Augmentations Office, the court ordered the defendant to account for tithes in kind.

143

Loveday v. Moorer

(Ex. 1720)

A modus decimandi *in lieu of tithes in kind that is too large is invalid.*

2 Gwillim 626

13 July 1720.

A bill was brought by the rector of Hedsor in Buckinghamshire for tithes in kind of the defendant's farm. The defendant insisted on a *modus* of 24s. a year payable in lieu of the tithes of the said farm.

The court declared that the *modus* was too great a *modus* for the said premises and, thereupon, ordered the defendant to account for the value of his titles in kind.

[Order of 13 July 1720: 2 Wood 151, 1 Eagle & Younge 760.]

144

Bliss v. Chandler

(Ex. 1720)

The tithes of hops are measured and payable after they have been picked, and not before.

1 Rayner 152

The defendant Chandler, a planter of hops at Maidstone in Kent, having set forth the tithe of his hops by the tenth pole unpicked, the plaintiff Bliss, the impropriator, brought this matter before the Court of Exchequer, where, after long debate of counsel on both sides and reading three former decrees, the court again declared this method of setting forth to be illegal.

2 Gwillim 625

15 July 1720.

A bill was brought by the lessee of the rectory of Maidstone for the tithe of hops in kind. The defendant said that he paid the tithes of early hops by the bushel after they were picked and the remainder by stripping the bines from every tenth pole or hill and leaving them on the ground for the plaintiff to pick and that this is as equal a mode of tithing as setting them out when picked by the tenth bushel.

The court declared that hops are not tithable until they are picked and that the tithes thereof ought to be paid in kind by the bushel, viz. every tenth bushel of the whole after picking. And they ordered the defendant to account accordingly.

Harvard Law School MS. 1082, vol. 1, p. 22

Michaelmas term 1720.

The plaintiff, as lessee of the rectory of Maidstone, brings his bill against the defendant for tithes of hops, who, for the first three days, paid the tenth bushel, but now he insists that he set out the tenth pole, which he thinks as good as the tenth bushel. And if hops were to be measured, it would be worse for the parson, for, by the measuring, the hops might be damnified and, thereby, the rector would likewise be deprived of the bines which were growing on the poles and were valuable. And a bill might be brought even for the bines.

Sir Constantine Phipps, for the plaintiff: No custom is pretended to be insisted on; so the question now depends upon common right, which is now settled in this court to be by the tenth measure, and so are the cases here, *viz.* Pearch v. Gee, Michaelmas 1698; Gee v. Pearch, 1704; Chitty v. Read, 3 King James, 1687, Trinity; 1 Siderfin 442.[1]

---

1 *Perch v. Gee* (1699), Dodd 184, 1 Eagle & Younge 633, 1 Rayner 87, Public Record Office, E.126/17, f. 67v, 1 Wood 386, 2 Gwillim 563; *Gee v. Perch* (1704), Dodd 202, 1

It was formerly doubted in the cases of Rolle, *Abridgment*, 644;[1] but [it is] now settled in this court to the contrary, as in the cases above.

Mr. *Edlin*, for the plaintiff: Corn and wheat must be set out by the tenth sheaf or shock and so grass by the tenth cock. And a custom to the contrary is void, so was Witherington v. Harris, Michaelmas 3 Queen, Exchequer. The tenth stick is not regular to set out, but the tenth faggot, 4 King William. [As to] turnips, the tenth turnip is irregular; so was Crispe v. Rayman [?], 12 King William; so the tenth meal of milk, and not the tenth pint, as in Dodson v. Oliver, last term [in the] Exchequer.[2] Tithe of young are not to be taken until it can live without its dam. 34 Car. II, Crofts v. Black.[3] And the tenth pole is as unequal and as inconvenient as in the several cases above.

Serjeant *Chesshyre*, for the defendant, answered the cases in this court by saying that every case must stand on its own bottom and that usage might govern those cases for what appeared. I take it that this tithe is due on severance. And, if so, then the tenth pole is proper. And I do insist that a bill might be brought for the bines, and it could not be insisted on in bar that the defendant had set out the tenth measure and had no regard to the bines. And in this case, there is more labor required than the occupier is obliged to do. And it may be as well insisted that he should thresh the corn.

Mr. *Ward*, for the defendant: The defendant in this case has done everything that could be expected from a kind parishioner and more, for he gave the plaintiff notice, which he is not by law obliged to do. The law requires no more than the tenth part. I think that tithes become due on the severance. As to the case mentioned of corn, the tenth sheaf may be unequal and yet setting out the tenth sheaf is sufficient without the tenth shock, which is only by custom. Hobart 250.

The tenth measure is deceitful. And it was Justice Twisden's opinion in that the tenth pole was sufficient, and so is 1 Siderfin 443, 282; 2 Keble 36, Langley v. [*blank*]; Hutton 77; 1 Rolle, *Abridgment*, 644.[4]

Mr. *Ward* answered the cases of Gee v. Pearch, for that the defendant insisted on a *modus* of 10s. per acre, and so it is an extrajudicial opinion. As to the

---

Eagle & Younge 660, 1 Rayner 97, 2 Gwillim 581, Public Record Office, E.126/18, f. 424v; *Chitty v. Reeve* (1687), Eq. Cases Exch. 274, 1 Rayner 67, 1 Wood 251, 1 Eagle & Younge 552; *Crouch v. Risden* (1670), 1 Siderfin 443, 82 E.R. 1207, also 1 Ventris 61, 86 E.R. 43, 2 Keble 612, 84 E.R. 385, 1 Eagle & Younge 481.

[1] *Barham v. Goose* (1617), 1 Rolle, Abr., *Dismes*, pl. Y, 2, 3, p. 644.

[2] *Dodson v. Oliver* (1720–1724), see above, Case No. 128.

[3] *Crofts v. Blake* (1680), 2 Gwillim 530, 1 Eagle & Younge 527.

[4] *Crouch v. Risden* (1670), *ut supra*; *Legard v. Elcocke and Langley* (1666), 2 Keble 25, 36, 84 E.R. 16, 23, also 1 Siderfin 283, 82 E.R. 1107, 1 Eagle & Younge 448, Lincoln's Inn MS. Misc. 499, f. 196, pl. 2; *Uvedall v. Tindall* (1626), Hutton 77, 123 E.R. 1112, also Croke Car. 28, 79 E.R. 629, Benloe 159, 73 E.R. 1024, 1 Eagle & Younge 339; *Barham v. Goose* (1617), *ut supra*.

case of Chitty v. Read, there it is said that it was a good custom to set out by the tenth row or pole with the bines uncut. But he admitted the case of Gee v. Pearch in 1704 to be full against him. Turnips and wool are due upon severance.

The several precedents were read, *viz.* Chitty v. Read, 3 June 1687, there the tenth row hill [?] or tenth bushel was decreed after picking where there was no custom to the contrary. Gee v. Pearch, 17 September 1698, was read; a *modus* of 10s. per acre was insisted on, but that was declared void, and [it was] decreed the tenth part of the hops by measure after picking, and so the precedent of Gee v. Pearch, 11 May 1704, was so decreed after picking.

Chief Baron [Bury]: I think that tithe hops ought to be paid according to the tenth measure after they are picked and so [it is] agreeable to the former resolutions.

Price, Montagu, and Page agreed, and so [it was] decreed for the plaintiff.

[Order of 15 July 1720: 2 Wood 146, 1 Eagle & Younge 757.]

145

Smith v. Leach

(Ex. 1720)

The goods of a judgment debtor that are subject to distress for rent cannot be seized upon a writ of sequestration.

Harvard Law School MS. 1082, vol. 1, p. 13

Trinity term 1720.

Mr. *Ward* [argued] for Lightfoot, the landlord, to have half a year's rent according to the Statute of 8 Queen[1] for goods seized on a sequestration. If this was an execution for a just debt, the landlord by the Statute was entitled to his year's rent; *a fortiori*, in the case of a sequestration, which is only to bring the party into a contempt.

Mr. *Bootle* [argued] against it and said that they were not proper in their application for that it ought to be before execution was executed and then the landlord was entitled and not afterwards. It does not appear by the affidavit that he was a tenant. Outlawry is not allowed to be within this Statute, as is the case of the Attorney General v. Ekins, in this court, and so in this case.

Mr. *Ward* replies for the landlord: The landlord cannot have notice until execution is executed, and so, until the sequestration comes, the landlord is not injured. Upon a *distringas* or in the case of a seizure on a commission of bankrupt, the landlord's right is always allowed, for it is antecedent to any other.

[1] Stat. 8 Ann., c. 18 (*SR*, IX, 247–248).

MONTAGU doubted as to the point of time in making application to the court, for the landlord might follow the distress for five days and why did he not take them then and not come so late.

PAGE: The landlord does not want the aid of the court before execution is executed, for the landlord knows nothing of his tenant's circumstances until that time, and then is the only proper time for the landlord to apply to the court. I admit that a sequestration after a decree is an execution. Perhaps I might make a doubt in the case of an outlawry where it was at the suit of the party whether it was within the Statute of 8th of the Queen or not.

PRICE says that the landlord cannot have notice until the execution was executed and it would destroy the intent of the Act of Parliament if this application was not allowed.

MONTAGU still insisted that he ought to have had notice first.

PAGE entirely differed as to notice.

Chief Baron [BURY]: These goods were not liable to be taken by the sequestrators, for there was an antecedent right in the landlord, and so it was a tort to take them away. And it is reasonable to apply to the court in this manner. I am for examining it by the Deputy [Remembrancer] whether such rent was due or not and whether there was any collusion between the landlord and tenant.

And [it was] so agreed to.

146

Graves v. Richardson

(Ex. 1720)

Where there was a defect in a trial in an ecclesiastical court, a writ of prohibition may be issued at any time.

Harvard Law School MS. 1082, vol. 1, p. 15

Trinity term 1720.

Mr. *Ward*, for the defendant, showed cause against a prohibition that it was too late, [being] after the sentence. 2 Rolle, *Abridgment*, 290, 310; Robert Chapel of Castlebromidge. The ecclesiastical court may have jurisdiction of the cause though a prescription or *modus* may be insisted on. 2 Ven. 239; 1 Ven. 5.[1]

Mr. *Fazakerly*, for the plaintiff: Where the matter appears on the face of the libel, it is never too late to come for a [writ of] prohibition, even after an appeal. Sir Henry Haughton v. Starkey.[2]

[1] *Williams v. Bond* (1690), 2 Ventris 238, 86 E.R. 415; *Philips v. Clever* (1669), 1 Ventris 5, 86 E.R. 5, also 2 Keble 452, 84 E.R. 284, 1 Eagle & Younge 479.

[2] *Haughton v. Starkey* (Ex. 1718), see above, Case No. 38.

Mr. *Bootle*, for the plaintiff: A suit may be for tithes or a pension. But when a *modus* is put in issue, the ecclesiastical court has no jurisdiction.

The court said that, when it appears that there is a defect of trial in the ecclesiastical court, a prohibition may go at any time.

147

Rebow v. Bickerton

(Ex. 1720–1721)

The owners of a franchise of a lighthouse cannot be required to contribute to the repair and maintenance of the local parish church.

A case can be removed out of an ecclesiastical court after a final judgment there where the ecclesiastical court did not have jurisdiction in the original matter.

Harvard Law School MS. 1082, vol. 1, p. 10, pl. 3

Trinity term 1720.

Mr. *Bootle*, for the plaintiff, [moved] in prohibition that the plaintiff was entitled to the lighthouse in question by virtue of letters patent and so received the tolls and duties from all ships. And the question was whether these lighthouses were subject to a parish rate. The defendant has pleaded that, as to that part of the declaration about the letters patent, that the judges below admitted the plaintiff's proofs and accepted that plea and took issue on the refusal. I admit that the question is whether Sir Isaack Rebow, in respect of these rates and tolls, is chargeable to the repair of the chapel of Harwich and, in the next place, whether, coming after the sentence, it is too late to come for a [writ of] prohibition. I think that the traverse of the refusal of the plea below is idle and nugatory. And he cited 2 Lutwyche 1070.[1] It appears upon the face of the proceeding that the ecclesiastical court has no jurisdiction or cognizance of this matter, and, therefore, it is not too late after the sentence. The plaintiff is no inhabitant or parishioner and, therefore, it is plain that this rate is only in respect of these lighthouses. Rates for repairing a church only sound in the realty, and lands are chiefly liable for repairs of a church. And it is so settled by canon and common law. An occupier in respect of lands is chargeable. Linwood 354; Coke 5 Reports, Jeffry's Case; 3 Modern 211.[2] Such tolls and duties do not sound in the realty and are not issuing out of land or in respect of land. And these tolls are only payable by virtue of the letters patent, and it was so tacitly admitted by the plea. These tolls only arise by

[1] *Johnson v. Wrightson* (1701), 2 Lutwyche 1066, 1070, 125 E.R. 593, 595.

[2] *Jeffrey v. Kenshley* (1589), 5 Coke Rep. 64, 77 E.R. 153; *Woodward v. Mackpeth* (1688), 3 Modern 211, 87 E.R. 136, also Comberbach 132, 90 E.R. 387, 1 Salkeld 164, 91 E.R. 152.

the king's grant. 4 Inst. 148.[1] This rate is not for ships coming to Harwich, but only for such as are passing and repassing on the high sea. If these lighthouses were chargeable, then a distress might be taken at the lighthouses, which cannot be, for you can only stop the ship, which is the only thing liable. And, therefore, it is not like the case of a mill or a house. There, the remedy is at the place, and the profits are not received at the lighthouses.

The lighthouses belonging to Trinity House were never rated, and these lighthouses in question depend upon the same foot. The letters patent were made at Westminster, and Sir Isaak Rebow resides at Colchester. As to a stall [in a market], the weekly profits of it make an inhabitancy more than lighthouses. 2 Rolle, *Abridgment*, 285, Follence v. Church Wardens of Kettering.[2]

[He said] that, in this case, [it is] proper to come after sentence because it appears on the face of the libel that this demand is not of spiritual cognizance.

As to the first point, [see] 2 Inst. 602; *Articuli Cleri*, 619; 2 Modern 273; Noy 137; Gardiner v. Booth in Salkeld's reports; 2 Rolle, *Abridgment*, 318.[3]

A lighthouse is a term appropriated to the structure and so taken notice of by the common law, for private persons cannot erect lighthouses. 4 Inst. 149; 10 Edw. III; 28 Hen. VI; Stat. 8 Eliz., cap. 13.[4]

[He said] that a lighthouse is well known at common law and the ecclesiastical court has no jurisdiction of it and to plead it would be nugatory because the libel shows it. 1 Siderfin 100, Parker v. Williams; 13 Rept. 44.[5]

And it has been objected that this is after an appeal. [It is] answered by the cases 2 Rolle Reports 24; 2 Rolle, *Abridgment*, 318, 319, James's Case; 2 Levinz 102, 186, Wise v. Creech.[6]

So he prayed judgment for the plaintiff.

Sir Constantine Phipps, for the defendant, [said] that a [writ of] prohibition ought not to go, but a [writ of] consultation ought to be awarded. And so he speaks to Mr. Bootle's second point first, that the plaintiff in this case comes too late for a

---

[1] E. Coke, *Fourth Institute* (1644), p. 148.

[2] *Hollynes v. Kettering Churchwardens* (1622), 2 Rolle, Abr., *Prohibition*, p. 289, pl. H, 5.

[3] E. Coke, *Second Institute* (1642), pp. 602, 619; Stat. 9 Edw. II, stat. 1 (*SR*, I, 171–174); *Mendyke v. Stint* (1677), 2 Modern 271, 86 E.R. 1067; Note, Noy 137, 74 E.R. 1100; *Gardner v. Booth* (1698), 2 Salkeld 548, 91 E.R. 464, also 12 Modern 196, 88 E.R. 1259; 2 Rolle, Abr., *Prohibition*, p. 318, pl. L, 1–3.

[4] E. Coke, *Fourth Institute* (1644), p. 148; Stat. 8 Eliz. I, c. 13 (*SR*, IV, 496–497).

[5] *Parker v. Williams* (1663), 1 Siderfin 100, 82 E.R. 995, also 1 Keble 433, 83 E.R. 1037, 1 Eagle & Younge 438; *Case of Modus Decimandi* (1609), 13 Coke Rep. 37, 44, 77 E.R. 1448, 1454; 1 Eagle & Younge 183.

[6] *Brabin v. Trediman* (1618), 2 Rolle Rep. 24, 81 E.R. 634, also Popham 140, 79 E.R. 1241; *James's Case* (1610), 2 Rolle, Abr., *Prohibition*, p. 318, pl. L, 3; *Brown v. Palfry* (1674), 2 Levinz 102, 83 E.R. 470, also 3 Keble 286, 325, 84 E.R. 724, 746; *Wife v. Creeke* (1677), 2 Levinz 186, 83 E.R. 510, also *sub nom. Wise v. Creek*, 3 Keble 727, 791, 809, 84 E.R. 976, 1014, 1025.

prohibition after sentence and an appeal. Cro. Eliz. 595.[1] I admit all the cases put by Mr. Bootle where the ecclesiastical court had not original jurisdiction. Cro. Car. 97; Dowson v. Nichols, 27 June 1710;[2] that case in 2d Rolle, *Abridgment*, 319, cited by Mr. Bootle is with me. Suits for the repair of a church are originally of spiritual cognizance. 2 Inst. 487; 5 Rept. 8, 9, 67; Yelverton 173.[3]

The rate is only for the lighthouses themselves, and, surely, they are rateable. And so the suggestion makes it out. And is not a lighthouse a house or place of residence? And tolls and duties are only taken notice of as to quantity and greatness of the rate, of which the ecclesiastical court has certainly jurisdiction. A corn mill is rateable, and there is no difference between mills and lighthouses. And if the tolls had been rated, it had not been bad. Town of Wicomb, Dalton 148; Statute 43 Eliz.

If tolls are rateable to the poor, so they are to the church, though not mentioned in the words of the [Stat.] 43 of Eliz. And tolls arising out of a tenement are rateable, and this matter is only incident to the original cause. And so the ecclesiastical court has jurisdiction of this matter. Sir Robert Lee, 2 Rolle, *Abridgment*, 289;[4] Godbolt Reports 152.

I do not know but that anybody may erect a lighthouse. These letters patent are only alleged as accessory to the original cause, of which the ecclesiastical court has jurisdiction and so as of consequence of the construction of letters patent. Reg. 57, 58; 1 Leonard 10; 2 Rolle Reports 42; 2 Rolle, *Abridgment*, 306, 307; 1 Rolle Reports 56, 12; 2 Bulstrode 227; 12 Rept. 66, 67, Cro. Jac. 269, 270, Roberts' Case; 1 Siderfin 89; 2 Brownlow 215; Yelverton 172; Jenkins, *Centuries*, 184; Keilway 39; Hardres 502; Levinz 64, Sir William Juxon v. Lord Byron.[5]

---

1 *Somerset v. Markham* (1597), Croke Eliz. 595, 78 E.R. 838.

2 *Smith v. Ex'rs of Poyndreill* (1627), Croke Car. 97, 79 E.R. 686.

3 E. Coke, *Second Institute* (1642), p. 487; *Caudrey v. Atton* (1591), 5 Coke Rep. 1, 9, 77 E.R. 1, 11, also Popham 59, 79 E.R. 1175; *Jeffrey v. Kenshley* (1589), *ut supra*; *Starkey v. Barton* (1610), Yelverton 172, 80 E.R. 115, also Croke Jac. 234, 79 E.R. 202.

4 *Lee's Case* (1607), 2 Rolle, Abr., *Prohibition*, p. 289, pl. H, 6.

5 *Registrum Brevium*; *Sutton v. Dowse* (1583), 1 Leonard 10, 74 E.R. 10; *Barnewell v. Tracy* (1618), 2 Rolle Rep. 42, 81 E.R. 647, 1 Eagle & Younge 295; *Reynolds v. Hayes* (1614), 1 Rolle Rep. 55, 81 E.R. 324, 1 Eagle & Younge 233; *Anonymous* (1614), 1 Rolle Rep. 12, 81 E.R. 291, 1 Eagle & Younge 223; *Parker v. Kemp* (1614), 2 Bulstrode 227, 80 E.R. 1081, 1 Eagle & Younge 223; *Roberts' Case* (1610), 12 Coke Rep. 65, 77 E.R. 1344, Croke Jac. 269, 79 E.R. 231, 1 Gwillim 230, 1 Eagle & Younge 193; *Butler v. Yateman* (1662), 1 Siderfin 89, 82 E.R. 988, also 1 Keble 354, 369, 83 E.R. 990, 999, 1 Levinz 78, 83 E.R. 306, 1 Eagle & Younge 437; *Barton's Case* (1609), 2 Brownlow & Goldesborough 215, 123 E.R. 905; *Starkey v. Barton* (1610), *ut supra*; Case 76, Jenkins 184, 145 E.R. 123; *Anonymous* (1498), Keilwey 39, 72 E.R. 197, 115 Selden Soc. 382; *Berkeley v. Morrice* (1668), Hardres 502, 145 E.R. 569; *Juxon v. Lord Byron* (1672), 2 Levinz 64, 83 E.R. 451.

Mr. *Bootle*'s reply: I agree with the rule laid down by Sir Constantine Phipps. But I think that the ecclesiastical court has no original jurisdiction in this case. Rates for the repair of a church with respect to proportion belong to the ecclesiastical court. And there is no foundation for a prohibition. But that case does not come up to this because the original matter was there cognizable. But the ecclesiastical court in this case has not jurisdiction of the original matter.

This differs from the case of a mill, which may be erected without license or letters patent. But I insist, if these lighthouses are chargeable, it is in respect of these duties, which are not due and paid at the lighthouses, but upon the high sea.

The ecclesiastical court cannot be a judge of these letters patent. [To the] objection [of] Dalton 148, that book is of no authority but was denied by the judges.

MONTAGU said that it was of better authority than the Modern Reports.

Bootle: The Statute of 43 Eliz. is concerning personal estates only so chargeable to the poor, but differs from a church rate, which is only chargeable in the realty. And so it is in the Register, 57, 58. And the cases cited by Sir Constantine are either for tithes, legacies, and rates generally, but this falls on neither of them. And no case can be cited where there was no original jurisdiction that coming after sentence was too late.

MONTAGU put some cases and desired to know whether waterhouses, glasshouses, or such kind were rateable to the church. And he agreed that the ecclesiastical court might have cognizance of the letters patent.

PRICE inclined that the ecclesiastical court had original jurisdiction of this matter and so of the letters patent as incident to it.

[It was] adjourned for further argument.

Harvard Law School MS. 1082, vol. 1, p. 23

Michaelmas term 1720.

Serjeant *Pengelly*, for the plaintiff, [moved] in prohibition, first, that lighthouses were not chargeable; secondly, that the ecclesiastical court has no jurisdiction. First, that no rate ought to be in respect of lighthouses for they are not taken notice of at common law, 4 Inst. 148;[1] 3 Inst. 150, lighthouses are a trust in the crown and may be granted with a toll appertaining. Moore 474.[2] The receipt of this toll will not subject Sir Isaac Rebow no more than in the case of the Lord High Admiral or the king himself, for this is a royal franchise. The toll is merely incorporeal and not settled at any particular place, neither does it arise within the parish, but it is payable by all ships passing and repassing on the sea. About repairing of bridges, what is called an inhabitant, [see] 2 Inst. 702, 703. Lands and tenements so described are corporeal and not incorporeal. And this toll would not pass by the word tenement. Jeffry's Case, 5 Rept. 66.

---

[1] E. Coke, *Fourth Institute* (1644), p. 148.

[2] *Heddey v. Welhouse* (1597), Moore K.B. 474, 72 E.R. 705, also Croke Eliz. 558, 591, 78 E.R. 803, 834.

There is no residence to make the plaintiff a parishioner, and there is no manurance, as in the case above. And next to the church, this lighthouse is as meritorious in saving people's lives.

The ecclesiastical court has no jurisdiction, or, if so, yet it proceeded wrongly in giving judgment against Sir Isaac Rebow. He compared it to the case of a stall in a market. 2 Rolle Reports 238; 2 Rolle, *Abridgment*, 289, pl. 3; 291, pl. 42; Coke, *Entries*, 463, 464; 4 Modern 148.[1]

It is a gravamen in giving sentence against Sir Isaac, and the [writ of] prohibition ought to go to the whole. Goddard v. Haldray, Michaelmas, 13 King William, King's Bench, Michaelmas, 1 Queen, King's Bench; and Prouse, 5 Modern 447, 448.[2] Prohibition lies after sentence though the letters patent are not pleaded, for the libel shows that the rate is for these lighthouses, and so it appears on the face of the libel and the court is obliged to take notice of this lighthouse as a trust from the crown because no other person can erect it. And here is a defect of jurisdiction. And this matter is controllable by the temporal courts after sentence. 1 Modern 236, 237; Lutwyche 1019, 1023; 5 Modern 447;[3] Salkeld 163, 165; 2 Rolle, *Abridgment*, 319.

This matter concerns the king, so [the writ is] grantable after sentence. 2 Inst. 602, 603; 2 Rolle, *Abridgment*, 318.[4]

The whole matter is brought before the court because this prohibition was moved for when this matter was depending in the Court of Arches by the appeal brought. And if this suit in the ecclesiastical court was not well instituted, a [writ of] consultation will never be awarded. Lutwyche 1070;[5] Cro. Eliz. 511, 665; Hobart 192, 300, 301; Yelverton 129; 1 Ventris 32.

So he prayed judgment for the plaintiff.

Serjeant *Chesshyre*: I may admit what my brother has said that, where it appears on the face of the libel, that a prohibition may be granted at any time. But I insist that the ecclesiastical court has jurisdiction of this matter, but I agree that a landlord in respect of the rent is not chargeable and the tenant must pay. And a rate of a church is of ecclesiastical cognizance, though Jeffry's Case was said to be the first where it was settled, yet the case of 44 Edw. III, 19, was so.[6]

---

[1] *Hollege's Case* (1622), 2 Rolle Rep. 238, 81 E.R. 771; *Hollynes v. Kettering Churchwardens* (1622), *ut supra*; *Anonymous* (1692), 4 Modern 148, 87 E.R. 315.

[2] *Anonymous* (1699), 5 Modern 447, 448, 87 E.R. 756.

[3] *Rogers v. Davenant* (1672–1677), 1 Modern 79, 194, 236, 86 E.R. 747, 823, 852, also 2 Modern 8, 86 E.R. 910; *Watkins v. Seaman* (1685), 2 Lutwyche 1019, 125 E.R. 567; *Anonymous* (1699), 5 Modern 447, 87 E.R. 756.

[4] E. Coke, *Second Institute* (1642), pp. 602, 603; 2 Rolle, Abr., *Prohibition*, p. 318, pl. L, 1–3.

[5] *Johnson v. Wrightson* (1701), *ut supra*.

[6] YB Trin. 44 Edw. III, f. 18, pl. 13 (1370).

Where it appears that the chancel is rateable, there the prohibition shall go, for, in England, it belongs to the parson. This rate is made for the repairs of the church only, and it is a charge as well on the person as the thing. And as to the quantum of the charge, the ecclesiastical court has certainly jurisdiction, and so is Robert Lee's Case, 2 Rolle, *Abridgment*, 289, 290, sec. 10. Jeffry's Case mentions it. 3 Cro. 659, Paget's Case; 1 Ventris 308; 3 Keble 742.[1]

The court must judge of the case as it was at first and not upon the appeal. And, therefore, it is now on the first case as it stood before Dr. Newton. And there, Sir Isaac insisted on the want of notice. 1 Jones 273; 6 Modern; 1 Ventris 331.[2]

I may admit that these lighthouses cannot be erected without lawful authority. The Cinque Ports have a right to erect beacons to defend their coasts. And they make rates to maintain the beacons. Raymond 448.[3]

By a lighthouse being erected, the benefit arising to the church may be diminished and may the church not receive benefit from it and the making it a lighthouse will not alter the case, for the place on which it stands is rateable. The king may exempt persons from tolls, yet the king must pay a toll traverse if he goes over other persons' lands. Plowden, *Commentaries*, 236, 246;[4] 46 Edw. III, pl. 50. The king's lands are subject to commissioners of sewers. 11 Rept. 70; Style 13.[5] The king cannot discharge a person from contributing to the repair of a bridge. I insist that malt houses, glass houses, smelting houses, [and] wych houses are so chargeable in Cheshire and so dove houses and so in Durham way[. . .] es, and so are locks and weirs in a river. Bedford Level, Ashley's Case. *Est onus reale*. Linwood, lib. 3, fo. 254, 28; Godolphin, Appendix, 19.

A play house, though by license from the crown, is rateable. An iron house and a market place are likewise rateable. And yet the argument is the same. Derelict lands within a parish are rateable, and so is the South Sea House, the Bank of England, all the halls in the City are rateable, and so is the Royal Society.

Serjeant *Pengelly* was to reply. But I left the argument.

Harvard Law School MS. 1082, vol. 1, p. 84

Trinity term 1721.

---

[1] *Lee's Case* (1607), *ut supra*; *Anonymous* (1633), 2 Rolle, Abr., *Prohibition*, p. 290, pl. H, 10; *Jeffrey v. Kenshley* (1589), *ut supra*; *Paget v. Crumpton* (1599), Croke Eliz. 659, 78 E.R. 898; *Anonymous* (1677), 1 Ventris 308, 86 E.R. 198; *Anonymous* (1677), 3 Keble 742, 84 E.R. 985.

[2] *Rex v. Halstead* (1632), W. Jones 273, 82 E.R. 143; *Rex v. Fanshaw* (1678), 1 Ventris 331, 86 E.R. 214, also 3 Keble 855, 84 E.R. 1051.

[3] *Town of Winchelsea's Case* (1681), T. Raymond 448, 83 E.R. 234, also 1 Freeman 99, 89 E.R. 73, 3 Keble 154, 324, 84 E.R. 648, 745, 2 Levinz 86, 83 E.R. 462.

[4] *Willion v. Berkley* (1561), 1 Plowden 223, 236, 75 E.R. 339, 359.

[5] *Whitley v. Fawsett* (1647), Style 12, 82 E.R. 492.

Page began and opened the case. And the question is whether lighthouses erected by virtue of letters patent for the term of sixty years whether the duty arising by ships passing and repassing on the sea is rateable to the church. The defendants as chapel wardens of the Chapel of St. Nicholas in Harwich having made a pound rate for the repair of the church at 5s. 6d. in the pound and that, upon a suit commenced by the said chapel wardens below, sentence was pronounced against the plaintiff, which was afterwards affirmed by the Court of Arches. The plaintiff declared in this prohibition. And as to part, an issue was tendered, to which the plaintiff demurred.

I think there are two points in this case: first, whether a [suit for a] prohibition is too late after such proceedings; second, whether these rates or duties thus arising are chargeable or not.

If these proceedings are out of the jurisdiction of the spiritual court, then all are *coram non judice*. And I think they are in two respects: first, for the cause; secondly, for the thing sued for.

If a rate was made for repair of the highways, the court Christian cannot take notice of it, nay, if the cause is rightly instituted as to repairs of a church, but if they carry even the consequential matter contrary to the common law, it is void. If a court Christian had rated a man of another parish, that would have been void.

These lighthouses or the duties arising by them are not rateable. And the court below has exceeded their jurisdiction. Cro. Car. 394.[1] In cases of Taunton and Cambridge, the putting in of a plea does not give jurisdiction to the court. Hetley 61, Roberts' Case.[2]

I think the point will turn on this, whether these duties are rateable, and, if they are not, Sir Isaac Rebow comes soon enough. Rectors formerly did repair the church and chancel for charity and so [. . .] the inferior clergy and ornaments are only rateable as personal. Linwood 254; 2 Rolle, *Abridgment*, 262, 270.

It cannot be a personal charge because [he is] not resident. If [it be] real, then it is within the words 'tenements or hereditaments' or if it lie within the parish, these duties thus arising cannot be called tenements or hereditaments, neither can they be said to lie within a parish. And it can be only personal in respect of the expense and labor of the patentee. These duties are erected by letters patent and are in the nature of tolls or a franchise.

You may as well charge for making [. . .] or lighting lamps in the streets or for erecting beacons as well as in this case. A stall in a market is not rateable; so in this case. 2 Rolle, *Abridgment*, 288.

If it was a tenement, by what construction can it be said to lie within a parish? If these duties are tenements, then they are alienable and can be separated.

---

1 *Nichols v. Walker* (1635), Croke Car. 394, 79 E.R. 944, also W. Jones 355, 82 E.R. 187.

2 *Roberts' Case* (temp. Car. I), Hetley 61, 124 E.R. 343.

And can it be urged that Sir Isaac Rebow can separate these duties from the lighthouses?

Here can be no locality, for the duty is paid by ships passing and repassing. I take this matter to be out of the jurisdiction of the court below so that the plaintiff comes soon enough. And I think that, in respect of these duties, he is not rateable. And it is so admitted by the demurrer. And the prohibition ought to stand.

MONTAGU: I think that there is sufficient reason for establishing this prohibition, for, generally speaking, the church ought to be repaired by the inhabitants and whether chargeable in respect of the duties of these lighthouses and whether too late after a plea pleaded, sentence, and affirmation of it upon an appeal to the [Court of] Arches. As, to argue syllogistically, lighthouses being houses, I think that lighthouses are not houses, so they are not taxable.

Consider the definition of a lighthouse, *quod vide* in 4 Inst., and there it is a [. . .]ial, in Latin *pharos* or *domus luminans*, and not a house. The duty is the subsidy for the tonnage of ships.

[To the] objection that the soil is taxable, [he] answered it is not to continue forever, but according to the letters patent.

A house is local; this is not. This rate is not rightly laid, for, if anything, it is *onus reale*, as in Linwood, for it is not pretending that Sir Isaac is a parishioner, either in respect of residence or occupier of lands. And so is 4 Rept., Jefry's Case. So I think he is not chargeable in respect of the duty of these lighthouses. But [to the] objection that this matter is incident to the original jurisdiction and where a court Christian has an original jurisdiction and so of the consequential part, I answer that must be where they have such a jurisdiction which is not so in this case. Rates laid for churches are properly within the jurisdiction of a court Christian, but then, if they rate what is not rateable by law, such consequential proceeding is *coram non judice*. Terry v. Huntingdon, in Hardres,[1] supposes three things, *viz.* parishioner, thing liable, [and] thirdly locality. And this case has failed in all. And though all these proceedings have been, yet, being *coram non judice*, the plaintiff is not come too late. Michaelmas 10 Will., Cook v. Gardiner, stall in a market; in 2 Rolle, *Abridgment*, prohibition upon the same reason; Latch Rept., Davis's Case; Salkeld, Gardiner; and Brooke, [*Abridgment*], tit. Prohibition, the same case mentioned before. The prohibition ought to stand.

And so he agreed with Page.

PRICE: I differ from my brothers whether the demurrer of the plaintiff as to the plea of the defendant is not immaterial. Cases cited [were] 2 Rept., Bishop of Winchester's Case, Cro. Eliz. 511, Wright v. Wright, refusal of a plea is frequently traversable, by Lord Coke.[2] And I do not think but that it is still so.

[1] *Terry v. Huntington* (1668), Hardres 480, 145 E.R. 557.

[2] *Wright v. Wright* (1596), 2 Coke Rep. 38, 76 E.R. 501, Croke Eliz. 475, 511, 78 E.R. 726, 760, also Moore K.B. 425, 72 E.R. 672.

Though those cases are against me, I think that the plaintiff ought to have come earlier, before sentence and appeal. And I think that the court Christian has jurisdiction of the original cause. And rates are always allowed except in the cases of Bowen, Davys, and [. . .]est; 2 Rolle, *Abridgment*, 319; 2 Lutwyche 1022, Watkins v. Seamour; Michaelmas 1710, Dawson v. Nicholson, Exchequer; 2 Rolle Rept. 42, Burwell.[1]

I agree that there are opinions both ways and, though the court Christian exceeds their jurisdiction, yet to avoid expense, you have admitted that court to hold it. Everybody was originally rateable to the church. Dr. Prideaux 929.[2] What was the common acceptation as to a parishioner: Yelverton 173, Slatter's Case; Godbolt's Reports, fo. 10. In Lindwood, *numerus animalium* is to be considered, not barely lighthouses, but the profits of it.

This charge is not personal, but it is *onus reale* and the personality may be extinguished by the realty. The lighthouse is chargeable in respect of the toll. And though of a public nature, yet I do not take the patentee to be exempt. If the lighthouse falls, I admit the duty is expired and that it is not severable. A house with a lantern [?] upon it is inhabitable, and £5 was paid for the land upon which the lighthouse was erected. Raymond 448.[3] And as to the quantum, whether too much or too little, that is proper for the spiritual court.

And so he concluded for a [writ of] consultation.

Chief Baron [Bury]: I agree with my brothers Montagu and Page and that Sir Isaac is not chargeable in respect of this toll or duty. 4 Inst. 143; 8 Eliz., cap. 3. Tolls are not within the court Christian's jurisdiction. If the king grants a fair or market and as to pickage and stallage, and this is not so much in the nature of land as pickage and stallage, and such is not chargeable and the keeping of a lighthouse is but the keeping of a regal office, so it is not within their jurisdiction and either proper before or after sentence. And a stall in a market [is a] very strong case in favor of this opinion. Rolle, *Abridgment*, 284; Moore 474, 425.[4]

Judgment was given for the plaintiff in prohibition against the opinion of Baron Price.

Taussig MS. 311, vol. 1, p. 82

Friday, June 23, Trinity term 1721. In prohibition.

Page, baron: A [writ of] prohibition is a proper remedy whenever the ecclesiastical court exceeds its jurisdiction. Now, a court may exceed its proper jurisdiction with respect to the nature of the cause or with respect to the nature of the thing, as for instance, if they should compel a rate to be made for the repair of the

1 *Watkins v. Seaman* (1685), *ut supra*; *Barnewell v. Tracy* (1618), *ut supra*.

2 H. Prideaux, *Directions to Churchwardens*.

3 *Town of Winchelsea's Case* (1681), *ut supra*.

4 *Hollynes v. Kettering Churchwardens* (1622), *ut supra*.

highways or if they should tax a parishioner of A. with the repair of the church in the parish of B., this would be void. 12 Car. 394.

Now, the question is whether the lighthouses or Sir Isaac Rebow in respect of them or in respect of the toll arising from them be chargeable by the common law, for, if he is not, then their proceedings are void. Prohibitions are grantable in all cases where they proceed contrary to law, though they have jurisdiction, unless in a case of citing out of the diocese. Hetley 61, Roberts' Case.

So then, the true question is whether these duties are taxable. The rector formerly repaired the church as well as the chancel in England as well as abroad, but the canons have altered this. As to the repair of the body of the church, it is a real tax *onus reale secundum* [*blank*]. For ornaments, it is a personal tax. Linwood 254; Rolle, *Abridgment*, 264, 270.

Sir Isaac Rebow does not live in the parish, so, then, this must be a real charge. And the question is then whether these duties are for lands, tenements, or hereditaments.

Lands they are not, nor tenements or hereditaments, but only a reasonable consideration for the labor and expense of the owner of the lighthouse, and, therefore, if the duty is unreasonable, the king's patent is void; so of tolls in fairs, markets, ferries, etc.

This is indeed a franchise, but that does not alter its nature. It subsists by a sort of contract, as suppose one man should make a contract with another to give him so much money for making a bonfire yearly, this is no tenement or hereditament, but only a personal contract.

2 Rolle, *Abridgment*, 288, is a stronger case than this. It is there said that a stall in a fair is not rateable and yet that seems to be local, but all that is to be done here is only keeping up the lights, which is an expense and trouble.

But supposing the duties could be laid to tenements or hereditaments, yet they do not lie within the parish, for the duties are not paid in respect to the house but in respect of the lights. And, these duties arise at Sunderland, London, and other ports. If they are tenements or hereditaments, they are alienable to others, and, then, they will be real inheritances in any other place.

Montagu, baron: Sir Isaac Rebow pleaded below a trifling plea, but, upon his appeal to the Court of Arches, he alleged this matter, *viz.* the grant of the king, and this plea was disallowed. And, therefore, the true questions upon this record are: first, whether lighthouses are taxable or Sir Isaac chargeable in respect of them; second, whether prohibition is the proper remedy for Sir Isaac; third, whether he is not come too late after another plea was pleaded and a sentence [given] against him.

The arguments maintain the other side of the question reducible to this syllogism. All houses are taxable, lighthouses are houses, therefore, they are taxable. This is the argument of the defendant's counsel. But this is a mistake for want of due attendance to the nature of the thing spoken of, for a lighthouse is, in my apprehension,[1] only a lantern pharos and has no affinity with a house or a place of habitation for men and the duty is the toll given for the benefit of this light.

It is the office of the crown to take care of navigation and to fix lights etc. The king licenses A. to light, and the king lays a duty on ships for the purpose of maintaining it.

If a man has land, he may erect an habitation and pull it down again at pleasure. But no man may erect a lighthouse nor pull it down without the license of the crown, nor can it be converted to any other use.

If a man lets a house, rent is demandable at the house. It is otherwise in this case, for the duty is not leviable here, but at other ports.

He who lives in his house receives the benefit of the house. It is otherwise of the lighthouse, for Sir Isaac nor anyone else receive any such benefit.

The repairs of the church are an *onus reale.* Jeffry's Case says that a man may be a parishioner in respect of his occupying land in a parish, but that is a favorable construction. But Sir Isaac is no parishioner. So I am of opinion Sir Isaac is not chargeable.

The second point is whether a prohibition is proper. The spiritual courts have jurisdiction of rates and power to compel payment by the Statute of *Circumspecte Agatis.*[2] But this is a limited jurisdiction and implies a negative, as by the observation of the Lord Chief Baron Hale in the case of Terry v. Huntingdon.

Jurisdiction is circumscribed in respect of place, subject, and person. There is a threefold restriction as to the person: first, he must be a parishioner; second, the things for which the tax is charged must be chargeable; and, thirdly, it must be taxed or charged in the proper place and be within the parish in order to be rateable to the church of the parish.

It is true indeed that, if a tax be illegal, one may have an action against the collector, but remedies preventive are the best. And it is more agreeable to justice to stop them than to let them go on in order to bring an action against them afterwards.

Third, whether pleading other matters has stopped his pleading the truth and barred him of this present defense, I think not, for, whenever it appears from the libel or *ex visceribus causae* that the matter is not within the jurisdiction, then it cannot be too late, except in the case of suing *extra-diocesim.* Salkeld, title 'prohibition', Michaelmas 10 William, Poole v. Gardiner.

Price, baron: Here are two demurrers before the court. The defendant has demurred to the plaintiff's plea, which plea was the patent, and the plaintiff has demurred to the defendant's traverse of this allegation of refusal of his plea.

A traverse of a matter of form is not material. But the question is whether this traverse is material. A refusal of a plea where material is traversable. Bishop of Winchester's Case, 2 Rep.; Cro. Eliz. 511. Authorities are to be submitted to,

[1] approbation *MS.*

[2] Stat. 13 Edw. I, *Circumspecte Agatis* (*SR*, I, 101–102).

but not when the reason given for the judgment destroys the authority. And in that case, the plea was admitted, and so the reason is against the very fact.

A refusal is traversable in some cases, as in the two cases cited there. Whether it is proper after a sentence and appeal, I think not. And yet I agree that, where the principle is that, where no jurisdiction appears, it is a cause of prohibition. 2 Rolle's *Abridgment*, 319; 2 Lutwyche 1022, Trinity 1710, Dawson v. [*blank*]; 2 Rolle Rep. 42. The reason of the books is the great expense and trouble.

Whether a lighthouse is rateable, Sir Isaac is first charged in the libel as a proprietor, but, in the other part of the libel, it is charged that the lighthouse was occupied, possessed, and enjoyed by Sir Isaac.

Dr. Prideaux, *Office of Church Warden*, 929, is contrary to the notion that the rector ought originally to repair. [*blank*] that is Yelverton 173. It is agreed that rates for repairs of churches are of ecclesiastical jurisdiction. Originally, the limits of parishes were of spiritual cognizance and direction. The consent of the majority binds all in the making of rates.

Godolphin, *Repertorium Canonicum*, in 'Appell' 10. *Numerus animalium* is only an evidence of the value of the land. The toll here is not rated, but the person in respect of the toll.

The public use of lighthouses does not exempt the king or his patentee from the charge towards the church. One cannot suppose the toll to be severed from the lighthouse; the grant shows the contrary.

It appears the £5 *per annum* was payable to the corporation for the ground on which the lighthouses stood. And will the making of a lighthouse discharge the land which was before chargeable? Surely not.

If a house is turned into an iron mill, the rate shall rise in proportion to the greater advantage which is made of it. The toll is so annexed to the lighthouse that it cannot be severed. Raymond 448.

The reason of my opinion is that the ecclesiastical courts seem to me both by common and statute law to have jurisdiction and that the lighthouses are rateable and the toll as annexed to them.

Lord Chief Baron [Bury]: The only question is whether Sir Isaac Rebow in respect of this lighthouse or the tolls belonging to it is taxable. Lighthouses are public things. 4 Inst. 148; 8 Eliz., ca. 13. If it was in the power of the ecclesiastical court to tax them, they might destroy the very end of erecting these lighthouses and to such degree as to prevent the possibility of maintaining the lights.

Tolls are not part of the land, nor do they relate to it, only by things. The grant and the erecting of a lighthouse is an execution of the regal office only. Jeffry's Case is that the owner is not taxable in respect of rent if he lets his land. So, Sir Isaac is not chargeable in respect of the toll, it being no ways the produce of the land.

The case in Moore is that stallage and pickage shall go to the heir in borough English, but the toll goes to the heir at the common law. Moore 474.

I never knew that any tolls were taxable, much less tolls on shipping. And I think the tolls may be severed upon this condition, that the lighthouses are kept up, and, on this foot, the patentee's grantee may enjoy the rent under his grant.

As to the traverse, whether the ecclesiastical court rejects or receives the plea signifies nothing if the court has no jurisdiction. Moore 425. So here, whether they admit or reject the plaintiff's plea signifies nothing. Allowing a plea in My Lord Coke's sense is allowing the effect of the plea. Receiving a plea and determining according to the plea are very different propositions.

Bunbury 81, 145 E.R. 602

23 June 1721.

This was a prohibition to the spiritual court of the bishop of London, where a libel was exhibited against Sir Isaac to oblige him to contribute towards the repairs of the church, in respect of a lighthouse erected for the benefit of navigation at Harwich, which received a toll and duty from ships passing etc.

Upon a demurrer to the declaration, the court, this day, gave their opinion. And two points were made: first, whether they were not too late to come for a prohibition after the sentence below and an appeal to the [Court of] Delegates; second, whether the thing in its own nature was rateable towards the repairs of the church.

And, in both points, Lord Chief Baron Bury, Montagu, and Page were of opinion for the plaintiff in prohibition; Baron Price held contrary in both points, and he cited in support of his opinion lib. 2, Bishop of Winchester; Cro. Eliz. 571; 2 Rolle, *Abridgment*, 319; Cresswell; 2 Lutwyche 1022; Dawson v. Nicholson, in the Exchequer, Mich. 1710; 2 Rolle Rep. 42; Dr. Prideaux's *Office of Churchwardens*; Yelverton 173.[1]

148

Clarke v. Cutler

(Ex. 1720)

Parol evidence is not admissible to show a discharge of a bond.

Harvard Law School MS. 1082, vol. 1, p. 19, pl. 1

Sittings after Trinity 1720.

This was a bill to have satisfaction for a bond from lands subject to the payment of debts. And this was against an executrix. And it was proved that the plaintiff had declared that this bond should never hurt the defendant and, if the defendant was to be chargeable, she would be guilty of a *devastavit*.

1 *Wright v. Wright* (1596), *ut supra*; *Watkins v. Seaman* (1685), *ut supra*; *Barnewell v. Tracy* (1618), *ut supra*; H. Prideaux, *Directions to Churchwardens*.

PRICE thought that, upon this whole matter, it was hard to charge the defendant with a *devastavit*.

The Chief Baron [BURY], MONTAGU, [and] PAGE differed from him and said that such evidence as this might be of very bad consequence and that something in writing should be showed to discharge this bond or it would be a great introduction to perjury. So they decreed for the plaintiff.

149

Thompson v. Field

(Ex. 1720)

In this case, the defendant was ordered to pay tithes in kind.

Harvard Law School MS. 1082, vol. 1, p. 19, pl. 2

Sittings after Trinity 1720.

This was a bill for tithes. And the custom was laid exactly as it was in the case of Lord Scarborough v. Hunter, *quod vide.*[1]

Chesshyre, for the defendant, [said] that this custom was too extensive to be good and might be the occasion of a double tithe. Cro. Car. 164, 339; Noy 108; 2 Rolle, *Abridgment*, 636; 1 Siderfin 278.[2]

A decree in this court in 1654 wherein Audley, lessee of the crown v. Fiddy[3] was read in this court as to this very point.

And so the court decreed for the plaintiff without further trouble.

[Order of 16 July 1720: 2 Wood 154.]

150

Baldwin v. Coppin

(Ex. 1720)

The issue in this case was whether, in a bill of discovery, the court would retain the case and grant common law relief.

---

[1] *Earl of Scarborough v. Hunter* (Ex. 1719), see above, Case No. 87.

[2] *Anonymous* (1632), Croke Car. 264, 79 E.R. 830, 1 Eagle & Younge 376; *Dawes v. Huddleston* (1634), Croke Car. 339, 79 E.R. 897, 1 Eagle & Younge 382; *Holland v. Heale* (1603), Noy 108, 74 E.R. 1073, 1 Eagle & Younge 156; *Sheppard v. Penrows* (1666), 1 Siderfin 278, 82 E.R. 1104, also 2 Keble 2, 73, 84 E.R. 2, 47, 1 Levinz 179, 83 E.R. 357, 1 Eagle & Younge 448.

[3] *Audley v. Fiddy* (1654), 1 Wood 5.

Harvard Law School MS. 1082, vol. 1, p. 19, pl. 3

Sittings after Trinity 1720.

This was a bill brought by the plaintiff, who was rector of Telford [?] in Suffolk, against the defendant, who was lessee, for the tithes by virtue of an agreement made between the plaintiff and defendant and pursuant to a counterpart of a lease made with a former lessee. And the bill was also to have that counterpart delivered up and to have the rent in arrear.

The defendant, by his answer, insisted that this was a matter triable at law and that an action was more proper than a bill, it being for rent, though, by his answer, it also appeared that there was rent due to the plaintiff.

Mr. *Ward* and I, counsel for the plaintiff, [said that] we were proper to have relief and that our bill for a discovery and for the delivering up the counterpart was well instituted and that a discovery ought to draw relief in this case because it appears out of the defendant's own answer that there was rent due to the plaintiff and it would be too hard to put the plaintiff to law and especially since he himself had in his two answers [admitt]ed the agreement. And it would be too hard [. . .] special action on the case. Thomas v. Williams; Dupuis v. Duke of Kingston.

Sir Constantine Phipps, counsel for the defendant, insisted that this was a bill for rent and, if triable anywhere, it must be at law and, since the plaintiff has his discovery, he ought to pay for it, but he could have no relief here.

PRICE thought it was proper at law and that the bill ought to be dismissed.

MONTAGU and PAGE [held] to the contrary and that it would be too hard to put the plaintiff to law when it appeared that there was money due to the plaintiff.

MONTAGU said that he believed it would puzzle all the counsel at the bar to frame a special action on the case upon this matter.

At last [he] agreed to take the money due to the plaintiff without costs on either side, *quod mirum est*, it being only triable at law.

151

Jones v. Denston

(Ex. 1720)

Where a modus decimandi *in lieu of tithes in kind was not proved in a former case, the parishioners can prove it in a subsequent case.*

Harvard Law School MS. 1082, vol. 1, p. 20, pl. 2

Sittings after Trinity 1720.

The plaintiff, as rector of Downham, brought his bill for tithe of milk against the defendants, who insisted upon a *modus* of a 1½ and 12d. and the whole morning milk on Whitsun Monday to run through the whole month in bar of tithes in kind. A bill had formerly been brought by the same parson against the same defendants and, for want of duly setting forth the *modus*, the plaintiff in the former suit obtained a decree for tithe milk in kind. It came upon the proofs of some of the same witnesses that were examined in the former cause that swore to a different *modus* yet now swore to this as now laid and that, by their testimony and others, that this *modus* ran through the whole parish, except the Frith and Park, which was part of the parish.

And so the counsel for the plaintiff insisted that the defendants were totally irregular and that the method now pursued would introduce the greatest perjury for persons to lay at first a *modus* one way and then, when that would not do, to lay the *modus* another [way] and then to examine the same witnesses over again to another *modus* who prove it exactly as the former. And as to the second point, that this *modus* and the proofs differed for that the *modus* is laid through the whole parish and the Frith and Park are excepted by the defendant's own witnesses and, therefore, this *modus* cannot run through the whole parish.

To which it was answered by *Selby, Stevens, Phipps*, and myself, for the defendants, that, as to the first point, it would be the hardest case in the world that the defendant should be forever debarred of his right because the *modus* was once laid wrong[ly]. And there is no inconsistency in the evidence but what a country fellow might easily mistake without incurring willful perjury. And as to the second point, we said that a court of equity was not so nicely tied up when an issue was to be directed, which was all we desired. And since there was no proof that tithes in kind were ever paid, we hoped that we had given such satisfaction on behalf of the defendants as to direct an issue.

And I cited the case of Lord Scarborough v. Hunter,[1] where the court directed whether there was such a prescriptive manner of tithing as in the bill or any and what other. *Quod vide* other book, f. 434.

The court declared that, as to the first point, it would be the hardest case to say that the defendant should mistake his *modus* and forever to be deprived of the benefit of it. And, therefore, all the judges overruled the first objection.

But, as to the second, MONTAGU declared that the *modus* laid and the *modus* proved was different, so he would not direct an issue, but decree for the plaintiff.

The other three judges were for directing an issue and agreed with the case cited by me; so an issue was directed.

But afterwards, the plaintiff acquiesced and submitted to the *modus*.

[Order, sub nom. Jones v. Cawthorne, 15 July 1720: 2 Wood 149.]

[1] *Earl of Scarborough v. Hunter* (Ex. 1719), see above, Case No. 87.

152

Thomas v. Thomas

(Ex. 1720)

Wills are to be construed according to the intention of the testator.

In this case, a legacy to two persons went to the survivor of them rather than to the heir at law.

Harvard Law School MS. 1082, vol. 1, p. 26

Michaelmas term 1720.

Thomas, the devisor, devised to Griffith Thomas, who died before him, and to the plaintiff Lewis Thomas and their heirs.

Mr. *Wills*, for the defendant, who claimed as heir at law, insisted for the heir at law that it ought to be considered what estate passed from the devisor for, the devisee dying before the devisor, nothing passed to him and no construction in a will ought to tend to the disherison of the heir. And, if, by anything, it must be by survivorship, but there being no joint tenancy in this case, therefore, [there is] no survivorship because no interest could pass to Griffith Thomas. Littleton 278.[1]

The intention of the testator will signify nothing to the disherison of the heir. Where the words are doubtful, it shall be construed for the benefit of the heir at law. Vaughan 262, Gardiner v. Shelden; Cro. Car., Sturton v. Bence; Cro. Jac. 75, Horton v. Horton; Sir Thomas Jones 98.[2]

Mr. *Probyn*, for the plaintiff: I will agree [with] the cases laid down by Mr. Wills. But surely, all wills are to be construed according to the intention of the testator.

[To the] objection [there are] no joint tenants, and, therefore, [they] can take nothing, [he] answered the intention was to the whole, and it shall go by survivorship. 1 Rept., Shelley's Case; Carter Rept., fo. 2, Davies v. Kemp; Plowden, *Commentaries*, Wright v. Rigden.[3]

Barons Price and Montagu agreed [with] the case in Carter to be as cited by Probyn. [It is] also in 2 Siderfin.

---

[1] T. Littleton, *Tenures*, s. 278.

[2] *Gardner v. Sheldon* (1671), Vaughan 259, 262, 124 E.R. 1064, 1066, also 1 Freeman 11, 89 E.R. 9, 2 Keble 781, 84 E.R. 495, 1 Eq. Cas. Abr. 197, 21 E.R. 986; *Horton v. Horton* (1605), Croke Jac. 74, 79 E.R. 63; *Smartle v. Scholer* (1677), T. Jones 98, 84 E.R. 1165, also 1 Ventris 323, 86 E.R. 209, 1 Freeman 458, 89 E.R. 342, 2 Levinz 207, 83 E.R. 521, 3 Keble 816, 832, 84 E.R. 1029, 1039.

[3] *Wolfe v. Shelley* (1581), 1 Coke Rep. 88, 76 E.R. 199, also 1 Anderson 69, 123 E.R. 358, Moore K.B. 136, 72 E.R. 490, Jenkins 249, 145 E.R. 176, 3 Dyer 373, 73 E.R. 838; *Davies v. Kempe* (1664), Carter 2, 124 E.R. 789, also O. Bridgman 384, 124 E.R. 647; 1 Eq. Cas. Abr. 216, 21 E.R. 1000; *Brett v. Rigden* (1568), 1 Plowden 340, 345, 75 E.R. 516, 524.

PRICE agreed.

Judgment [was given] for the plaintiff, Chief Baron [BURY] doubting.

This was a cause tried before the Chief Baron last assizes in Oxford Circuit. And he decreed a case might be made of it and the matter might be argued before the whole court, as this was.

153

Yale v. Wallis

(Ex. 1720)

A writ of extent in aid cannot be granted without an affidavit of a debt to the crown.

Harvard Law School MS. 1082, vol. 1, p. 33

Michaelmas term 1720.

Last term or Easter term, on the above case, we that were counsel for Wallis moved to stay the proceedings on [Elihu] Yale's [writ of] extent. And the reasons against the original bond were much the same as before mentioned;[1] yet, if that bond was not good, the extent in aid on behalf of Yale was void, for that this was a bond for performance of covenants which, by the rules of the court, ought not to be found. See 5 Rule, 15 Car. I.

And agreeable to this, when several merchants petitioned the king in council, concerning extents, which was referred to the barons of the exchequer, the minutes were taken 24 June 1687, *non constat* what money was due on this bond, so [there was] no sufficient certainty to be found by inquisition. Hardres 227, Attorney General v. Sparrow; Hardres 322, Mildmay's Case; 377, Howard and St. John; Savile 45;[2] Attorney General v. Hind, 6 December 1694, Exchequer.

No oath [was] made by Yale according to the Second Rule, 15 Car. I. And he could not make this oath. See Child v. Arnold, Michaelmas 1703, Exchequer.

If it should be enquired who are the immediate debtors to the crown in this case, it must be the Commissioners of the Excise. And Pauncefort is debtor to them. Yale is indebted to Pauncefort, and Wallis [is] indebted to Yale, and that is carrying it in the fourth degree, which was further than was ever known. Mr. Yale is neither farmer, receiver, nor accountant and so not entitled to the aid of the court. This was what I chiefly insisted on, being counsel for Wallis.

Serjeant *Chesshyre*, for Wallis, cited Rex v. Porter, 10 November 1693, Exchequer; that was upon a *scire facias* on a bond taken in the name of the crown;

---

[1] See *Rex v. Yale* (Ex. 1720–1721), above, Case No. 121.

[2] *Attorney General v. Sparrow* (1662), Hardres 227, 145 E.R. 465; *Mildmay's Case* (1663), Hardres 322, 145 E.R. 478; *Howard v. Lenthall* (1664), Hardres 376, 145 E.R. 505; Note (1583), Savile 45, 123 E.R. 1003.

the defendant pleaded the Statute of 33 Hen. VIII[1] and that the officer would not let him proceed on his voyage until he had given such a bond, which was void, and the Attorney General, after argument, would proceed no further; the officer, though for the public good, cannot take such a bond, for, if so, any landlord may take such a bond from his tenant. Here is no oath made or any account stated, so there is no sufficient certainty to ground an extent.

Mr. *Ward*, for Wallis: Yale is not entitled to the aid of this court. Receivers are appointed by warrant from the Treasury, but it was not so in Mr. Pauncefort's case. And the bond is not taken according to the Statute of 33 Hen. VIII, 'his heirs and successors', [but] upon a private purpose. 4 Inst. 115; 18 Car. II, Bruen's Case.[2] Nothing was stated. Hardres 226;[3] Attorney General v. Stickey.

Sir Constantine Phipps, for Yale: There have been several objections, first, as to the bond and the want of an affidavit. Here is an affidavit of Metcalf, a book-keeper. Mr. Yale is bound to the crown and has paid £5000 or £6000 and so becomes an original debtor.

Mr. *Bootle*, for Yale: An extent to find debts is proper. 5 Coke, Broughton's Case; 1 Ventris 36, 78.[4]

Mr. *Fenwick, pro eodem*: The objection of Savile 45, is answered by 7 Coke, Sir Thomas Cecil's Case; Hardres 366.[5]

Chief Baron [Bury]: I am for taking time to consider of it. If it appears that the bond is forfeited, I shall incline for Yale.

Price: I think that this proceeding by Yale against Wallis is irregular. And I think that we might determine that without vacating the original bond entered into by Kirwood and Yale to the crown, for I think that there is no foundation for an extent against Wallis, for this is a debt found for himself at his own instance. And here is no proper affidavit according to the Rules of 15 Car. I. Neither could Yale make such an affidavit as therein required. And I cannot break those Rules. And Hardres' report is so as cited. And Wallis cannot have notice until the *scire facias* comes, for the inquisition is taken behind Wallis's back.

Montagu: I shall break the case, but not be concluded by my opinion now. He, Pauncefort, is cashier to the Commissioners. Kirwood and Yale [are] cashiers to Pauncefort. And Wallis [is] indebted to Yale. I shall consider of it.

---

1 Stat. 33 Hen. VIII, c. 39, s. 36 (*SR*, III, 886).

2 E. Coke, *Fourth Institute* (1644), p. 115; perhaps *Brewen v. Rowe* (1665), 1 Keble 894, 920, 83 E.R. 1305, 1321, 1 Siderfin 264, 82 E.R. 1095.

3 *Rex v. Williamson* (1662), Hardres 226, 145 E.R. 465.

4 *Broughton v. Pretty* (1600), 5 Coke Rep. 24, 77 E.R. 86; *Rex v. Atkins* (1669), 1 Ventris 35, 78, 86 E.R. 25, 54, also 1 Siderfin 442, 82 E.R. 1206, 2 Keble 529, 596, 609, 642, 739, 747, 84 E.R. 331, 375, 383, 404, 467, 472..

5 *Cecil's Case* (1597), 7 Coke Rep. 18, 77 E.R. 440; *Attorney General v. Waring* (1664), Hardres 366, 145 E.R. 500.

PAGE: The extent is irregular, as I take it, and that may be determined without vacating the bond. Here is no proper affidavit made, which ought to be in the case of an extent in aid. And the Rules of the court are full in this case. So [he] concluded for Wallis.

The CHIEF BARON cited Rex v. Templeman, 1683, [and] ordered all proceedings against Wallis to stay until further order.

Note that, after judgment [was] given in the case of the King v. Yale[1] against Yale, *Sir Constantine Phipps* and Mr. *Bootle*, counsel for Yale, attended the Attorney General in order to have a writ of error allowed, which he, at first, denied, but he, afterwards with difficulty granted, *quod vide*.

154

Bryer v. Lord Lansdowne

(Ex. 1720)

Process can be served on a defendant at his usual place of abode though he is actually out of the jurisdiction.

Harvard Law School MS. 1082, vol. 1, p. 36

Michaelmas term 1720.

Sir Constantine Phipps, for the defendant, moved that the defendant being served with a [writ of] *venire* at his house when he was out of the kingdom, *viz.* in France, which was returned and a [writ of] *distringas* issued that, it being all irregular, it might be set aside. An affidavit of the defendant's being in France was read.

Serjeant *Chesshyre*, for the plaintiff: The affidavit shows that the attorney has a correspondence with the defendant. And service of a subpoena at the house where the family is, though he is out of the kingdom, is sufficient. A summons at the house is good, and the *distringas* also [is] good to bring the party in, and that is only to compel the return of good issues. And if the party is at Lichfield and he has a house in town, the notice at his house here is sufficient. And why should not the notice be as good here as in the case of an outlawry?

Mr. *Bootle*: There is no occasion in this case of personal service, for leaving a copy at the house is sufficient. The first process is a *venire*, upon that there is a return *quod nil habet per quod summonire potest* and, after that, a *distringas*, which is *in rem* and not personal.

[It was] objected that the defendant cannot have notice; [he] answered that his servants will give him notice.

If this is not a right service, it would be of greater inconvenience. And it is not so mischievous as in the case of outlawry or a real action. And if a lord goes out of

[1] *Rex v. Yale* (Ex. 1720–1721), see above, Case No. 121.

the kingdom, there will be an entire impediment to justice. I must refer myself to the custom of the office, and the Master of the Office of Pleas reported that he never knew such a motion made, but there was no stay of process in the case of Lord Peterborough and the Duke of Marlborough when both were abroad.

Sir Constantine Phipps replied: If the defendant was in England, then this notice would be sufficient. This may be the case of all persons abroad who may be totally undone by this method. There never has been any precedent contested so that precedents *sub silentio* will be of no weight. And he mentioned Sir John Whitaway's Case in the King's Bench.

Chief Baron [BURY]: Consider the case of an outlawry. And is not that the same as in this case? And if this notice is good there in a real action, why not in this case at bar?

PRICE: I take this method against the defendant to be contrary to the practice of the court. If it was in the case of a common sailor, it would not be good. And why may not a nobleman have as great a liberty as a sailor? I allow the old process was a *venire*, which was before a *quo minus*. Attachment will not lie against a commoner. But why will [it] not stop the *distringas*, which is only for issues for the case of the crown? If a person is beyond the sea, he is not amenable. And does not the law regard such persons in the Statute of Limitations and the Statute of Fines and Non-claim?[1]

MONTAGU: I think that there is no difference between a peer and a commoner. I allow the case of a subpoena on the equity side because the service is personal there. But it is not so in this case. And I think that this proceeding is regular.

PAGE: I see no inconvenience in proceeding this way and no difference between this and an outlawry or any real action and the case of a subpoena and an attachment. That process is personal. If it was a distress for rent, could that distress be discharged because the party was out of the kingdom? On whose behalf does Sir Constantine move, for nobody is in court? The case cited by Sir Constantine of Sir John Whitaway was upon notice of trial, which must be personal and so not like this case.

So the court, against Price, agreed the proceeding against the defendant to be regular.

Bunbury 67, 145 E.R. 597

25 November.

It was moved by *Sir Constantine Phipps* to set aside a *venire facias*, which was the old process of this court on the plea side, and a *distringas* thereupon, upon

[1] Stat. 21 Jac. I, c. 16, ss. 2, 7 (*SR*, IV, 1222–1223); Stat. 4 Hen. VII, c. 24 (*SR*, II, 547–548).

an affidavit that the defendant was in France when the *venire facias* was left at his house.

But upon hearing Serjeant *Chesshyre* and Mr. *Bootle*, on the other side, the process was adjudged to be good by three barons against PRICE, baron.

155

Saywell, *qui tam* v. Carter

(Ex. 1720–1722)

The question in this case was whether a condemnation of goods may be given in evidence upon an information of seizure of the same goods as being imported without payment of duties where the defendant has pleaded the general issue.

If goods be not liable to import duties, anything which proves that may be given in evidence.

A writ of delivery will not be granted where there was a great delay in requesting it.

Harvard Law School MS. 1082, vol. 1, p. 40

Michaelmas term 1720.

This was an information of seizure of goods, which were imported, the duties not being paid, to which the defendant pleaded the general issue, *viz.* that they were not so imported. And now, the question is whether the condemnation of goods in this court can be given in evidence on this general issue or whether it ought not to have been pleaded specially. And a case was made of it.[1] And now it came to be argued on that case.

Attorney General *Raymond*, for the informer: It plainly appears by the issue joined that judgment ought to be given for the informer for the defendant has pleaded that the goods were not so imported, whereas now, by the condemnation which the defendant would insist on, it does appear that they were so imported. This cannot be given in evidence no more than anything that goes by way of excuse, as a lease etc., which must be pleaded. In the common case of an action of trespass, you cannot give in evidence a license to enter on the land. 14 Hen. VIII, 51; 2 Rolle, *Abridgment*, 676; 1 Brownlow 24.[2] And this matter of a condemnation is by way of excuse to the information. Dyer 196, Barker v. Hungerford.[3]

Special pleading ought to be encouraged to prepare the opposite party to controvert it. And this matter is like to an acquittance, which is in the nature of

[1] *Carter v. Saywell* (1719), see above, Case No. 108.

[2] *Bishop of London v. Nevell* (1522), YB Mich. 14 Hen. VIII, f. 1, pl. 1, 119 Selden Soc. 88, 2 Rolle, Abr., *Triall*, pl. 28, p. 677; *Willoughby v. Small*, 1 Brownlow & Goldesborough 24, 123 E.R. 642.

[3] *Speake v. Hungerford* (1561), 2 Dyer 196, 73 E.R. 434.

a discharge, which must be pleaded specially. How was it possible in this case for us to controvert this point unless we knew by something in the pleading that the defendant would insist upon it?

Solicitor General *Yorke* was going to speak to it, but it was said by Mr. *Ward*, counsel for the defendant, that is was expected only one counsel of a side [was] to speak to it. But the court said, as it was a case only for the opinion of the court, more counsel might speak to it, and [it is] not like the case of a special verdict. But the Solicitor [General] did not proceed.

Mr. *Ward*, for the defendant, [said] that this condemnation ought to be received in evidence and [it was] no damage to the crown but a great inconvenience to the party and this, by the case, is admitted to be a just defense. I insist that everything may be given in evidence that goes in bar of the demand. And it is laid in the information that these goods being liable to payment of duties, it is incumbent on the Attorney General to show that these goods were liable, and the cause assigned is non-payment of duties and the defendant is at liberty to show that these goods were not liable. In an action of debt for rent, eviction may be given in evidence on [a plea of] the general issue, so, in [a plea of] *non detinet*, a gift may be given in evidence. This court is a market overt for all goods seized, and it has been esteemed a benefit to the revenue to encourage bidders. Condemnation does discharge all precedent duties and forfeitures. Syms, *qui tam* v. Reynardson, Michaelmas 1709, Exchequer; Miles v. Clarke, Easter 1712, Exchequer.

When goods are seized and condemned, all prior duties are discharged and a property is vested in the buyer of those goods and the court is the guaranty of the sale. Pidgeon v. Slater, 1679, Exchequer.

The case above shows that, when this information was brought, that these goods were not liable to the payment of duties.

I may admit the cases put by the Attorney General where they go in excuse of the action, but this is in bar of the cause of action. And I wonder that this should be a doubt now, since the condemnation was always given in evidence in Sir Edward Northey and Lechmere's time, when they were attorneys general. Payment of duties may be given in evidence and so may stress of weather. It would be impracticable to plead it, for then the whole record must be pleaded and all that the Attorney General could say that the goods were not the same, which must be likewise in the evidence given in this point. And the *onus probandi* is upon the defendant. I do not know that it is necessary for the crown to know what the defendant will insist upon, for the Attorney General is only to show the seizure, and the *onus probandi* as to all the rest is on the defendant. If this matter is pleaded, it only amounts to the general issue, and the court has discouraged such pleading because of the prolixity of the record. In a [plea of] *plene administravit*, a retainer may be given in evidence.

And with respect to the hardship and charge it would be to a poor defendant, he had better submit for small seizures than be at the expense of it. And so [he] prayed judgment for the defendant.

The *Attorney General* replies: [To the] objection that it has been settled, [he] answered it never was. I must admit what is mentioned by Mr. Ward so far that a condemnation does discharge all prior duties but it is not to be inferred that, therefore, that condemnation might be given in evidence. Mr. Ward would make a difference where the cause of action is admitted. There, the special matter must be pleaded, but not where the cause of action is denied. And what he says of the *onus probandi* on the defendant, I must answer so it is in all cases where the excuse is pleaded, which I insist this to be, and that it is proper to be pleaded specially that the crown may be prepared to answer it.

[To the] objection of the inconvenience and charge of such pleading, [he] answered it is as well for the party to be at the inconvenience and charge as the crown.

[It was] to be spoken to again at the beginning of next term, but the judges opened the case as hereafter, *viz.*

Montagu thought it would be too hard to put the crown to the trouble of it and he never did. In the case of Syms v. Reynardson, there, the cause of action was totally denied. But it is not so in this case, for it is admitted that these goods were so imported.

Price asked the Attorney General if he would make any difference between the crown and party and party. What think you of an action of trover? And he cited Hardres 131 and said that the Chief Justice Holt was very angry for removing actions here by prerogative process because the officer might plead the special matter in the court below, but the answer that was given [was] that we would not put the officer to the trouble.

Page mentioned the case of bankruptcy. Before the Statute, you may have pleaded it specially. See Stat. 21 King James, cap. 4;[1] Lord Coke.

Adjourned.

Taussig MS. 311, vol. 1, p. 45

Easter term 1721.

The single question is whether a condemnation of goods in this court may be given in evidence on [a plea of] the general issue of *non importata contra formam statuti*.

Mr. Solicitor General [*Yorke*], for the king, said that it may not. The charge in the information is that, between 1 November 1717 and 27 October 1718, the goods were imported and landed, customs not being paid. The issue is that the goods were not imported and laid on land *contra formam statuti*. This evidence in question admits the very point of the information charged. A condemnation upon another information is a confession [and] avoidance, which certainly is not to be given in evidence on [a plea of] not guilty. 2 Rolle's *Abridgment*, 682, pl. 1,

[1] Stat. 21 Jac. I, c. 4 (*SR*, IV, 1214–1215).

pl. 3; 5 Rep., Whelpdale's Case.[1] If indicted of an offense whereof one was before convicted, one must plead *auterfois convict*.

The rule that the defendant may give in evidence anything which proves that the plaintiff has no cause of action must be restrained thus, *viz.* that proves no right of action did ever accrue, as on *nil debit* an eviction, on *non detinet* a gift, on *non assumpsit* infancy or coverture. Syms v. Reynaldson, 1709, in this court. Brandy in unsizeable casks was never chargeable with duties, and, therefore, that case comes under the same rule with the others.

The condemnation is a discharge, for the goods were certainly originally liable to duties. Payment of duties goes to the very gist of the information, and, therefore, is good evidence. This point contended for will put matter of law and fact in issue to the jury.

Sir Constantine Phipps, on the other side: Not permitting this to be given in evidence would be too great a discouragement to bidders. This court is a market overt. Hilary 1 Will. & Mar., Jones, *qui tam* v. [*blank*], upon the Statute 20 Car. II, ca. 17.[2] The goods, having been once fairly seized and condemned, are ever after free and disposable as other goods.

[In an action of] debt against an executor, the revocation of a will may be given in evidence upon the issue of *ne unques executor* or that there were *bona notabilia* where administration is committed or the will proved in a particular diocese. 1 Siderfin 359.[3]

[In an action of] trespass for taking goods, one may plead *non culpabilis* and give evidence that he was a collector of a subsidy or fifteenth or by virtue of office for avoiding prolixity or captiousness of pleading. 1 Inst. 283.[4] Whatever may be given in evidence on [a plea of] not guilty may be given in evidence on this issue. Dyer 234, 193.[5] Condemnation is the act of the court and prior to the defendant's title. Rolle, *Abridgment*, 676. A license cannot be given in evidence on *non culpabilis* in [an action of] trespass. 2 Rolle's *Abridgment*, 684, pl. 7, 8; 5 Rep., fo. 60, Gouge's Case; Dyer 31, pl. 15; Dyer 122;[6] 6 George, pp. 414, 415, 416, for preventing frauds; 21 Jac. I, ca. 4, § 4; 3 Inst. 193; 4 Inst. 173; 4 Inst. 174; [for] the practice of this court, [see] Michaelmas 2 Will. & Mar., the case of Polson v. Clarke; Jones, *qui tam* v. W.

---

[1] 2 Rolle, Abr., *Triall*, pl. 1, 3, p. 682; *Whelpdale v. Whelpdale* (1604), 5 Coke Rep. 119, 77 E.R. 239.

[2] Stat. 19 & 20 Car. II, c. 7 (*SR*, V, 636).

[3] *Noell v. Wells* (1668), 1 Siderfin 359, 82 E.R. 1156, also 1 Levinz 235, 83 E.R. 385, 2 Keble 337, 343, 641, 84 E.R. 210, 214, 403.

[4] E. Coke, *First Institute* (1628), f. 283.

[5] *Bonner's Case* (1564), 2 Dyer 234, 73 E.R. 517, also Jenkins 228, 145 E.R. 158, 109 Selden Soc. 103.

[6] *Rous v. Gooch* (1590), 5 Coke Rep. 60, 77 E.R. 146; *Anonymous* (1537), 1 Dyer 31, 73 E.R. 69, *Martaine v. Hardy* (1556), 2 Dyer 122, 73 E.R. 268.

The court here has determined that the king may bring an information for duties of brandies imported in unsizeable casks; so that answers Mr. Solicitor's objection.

Reply by Solicitor General [*Yorke*]: There is scarce anything that can be pleaded in trover that admits a conversion. And, therefore, it must be naught as a plea, and, consequently, it must be given in evidence. The goods were chargeable with duties during the time charged in the information, so that the giving in evidence that they were bought in a lawful way of trade is the same as payment. It is constructive payment.

The Statute of King George meddles not with any distinction between pleading and giving in evidence, but only relates in general to the *onus probandi* and says it shall lie on the defendant.

The proviso in the Statute of 21 Jac., ca. [*blank*], perfectly exempts this case from the enacting part thereof. As to inconvenience, it is none because special pleading is allowed in some cases. And why not in this as well as others? The defendant might as well come to the knowledge of the condemnation in order to plead it as to give it in evidence. To the contrary, there is a great inconvenience in suffering it to be given in evidence because the Attorney General might perhaps have replied [with] fraud or covin in the condemnation or might have replied *nul tiel record* or taken issue upon the identity of the goods, which he is now by this method prevented from doing.

Adjornatur.

Taussig MS. 311, vol. 1, p. 149

Michaelmas 1721.

The barons now delivered their opinion *seriatim*.

PAGE: The question is whether a condemnation of goods in this court may be given in evidence upon an information of seizure of the same goods as being imported without payment of duties and *non importata contra formam statuti* pleaded. I am of opinion it cannot. And in giving my opinion, I shall consider how the law stands, first, in similar cases; secondly, what would be the inconveniences if this were to be admitted; thirdly, I shall speak to the Statute of [*blank*].

The similar cases are [actions of] trover, case, and debt. But the reason on which the judges have gone so for in these cases is not applicable to the present.

*Assumpsit*s are founded on the authority of Slade's Case, 4 Rep. 92.[1] But the reason inducing the judges to come into that resolution was to prevent wager of law. And in lieu of this privilege taken from the defendant, all other advantages which the defendant had in [an action of] debt and, therefore, *non assumpsit*,

[1] *Slade v. Morley* (1602), 4 Coke Rep. 91, 76 E.R. 1072, also Moore K.B. 433, 667, 72 E.R. 677, 827, Yelverton 20, 80 E.R. 15.

though the plea runs in the preter-perfect tense, it is the same as *nil debet* which runs in the present tense.

Infancy and coverture go to the validity of contracts; so [in actions] in debt for rent, entry and expulsion.

The rule of not pleading what amounts to the general issue must be restrained to simple facts only and not facts mixed in law.

In trover, conversion is the gist of the action, and, therefore, everything may be given in evidence which proves [. . .] alteration of property, and this is not confessing and avoiding.

But in this place, here is a plea of a direct contradiction, for the plea is *non importata contra formam statuti* and, to maintain this plea, you give in evidence that they were so imported and condemned afterwards.

Rolle *Abr.*, 682, 683; *son assault demesne* is a bar and proves that the beating was not tortious, but yet it must be pleaded.

In detinue, *non cepit*; you cannot give in evidence that they were delivered as a pledge.

I do not know any case where you may give evidence of such matter which matter might be traversed in pleading. And an issue might be taken upon the Statute of Engrossers, Edw. VI.[1]

Replevin, *non cepit*; you cannot give property in evidence, but you must plead it. 1 Ventr. 249.[2]

In an indictment for not repairing a highway, *non culpabilis*; you can give nothing in evidence but that this way is in repair, and you are not allowed to give in evidence that another parish was to repair.

And, if the law was otherwise, the plaintiff would not know what to depend upon.

In this case, the officer did his duty in seizing. If the plaintiff claimer had pleaded the condemnation, perhaps the officer would have gone no farther or, if he did, perhaps, he might have shown that the goods were not the same goods or, thirdly, he might have replied that the goods were reshipped and relanded again.

The case indeed says these were the same goods, and yet how could that be, for it is tea. They may prove the identity of the canisters. But how is it possible to prove the identity of tea?

[To the] objection this would prevent buyers, [he] answered I do not see how.

But I think it would put an end to all seizures, for it would put a great many tricks into the merchant's head to trick the officer.

We that go the circuit find that persons very often counterfeit as if goods were landed in order to invite a seizure that they may punish an officer. As to the Stat. of 21 Jac. I, ca. 4, this Act does not extend at all to proceed[ings] *in rem*. The

---

[1] Stat. 5 & 6 Edw. VI, c. 14 (*SR*, IV, 148–150).

[2] *Wildman v. Norton* (1673), 1 Ventris 249, 86 E.R. 167, 2 Levinz 92, 83 E.R. 465, 3 Keble 219, 232, 84 E.R. 686, 693.

Act says in all informations against any person or persons, but an information *in rem* is not against any person and the information is so far against a person that no person is mentioned until proclamations. And the claimer is not in the nature of a defendant, but like the party in replevin. Here is no personal information, but where *nil debet* or *non culpabilis* is the general issue.

The preamble of the Act, *viz.* to prevent multiplicity of actions recites malicious informations to put to special pleading. But, in this case, here is a seizure previous to the information. The general issue is not *non importata contra formam statuti.*

In replevin, *non cepit* is the general issue. On this Act, *non culpabilis* is the general issue. And this was my Lord Hale's opinion, as reported [in] 2 Keble 859.[1]

You may give everything in evidence which destroys the original forfeiture, as composition etc. And perhaps, if the plea had gone further that the goods *non importata fuerunt sine solutione* of the duties, perhaps, it would have been better, but here, by this evidence, you confess and avoid.

It has been said that it has been practiced here to give this matter in evidence, but use makes not law. And I do not find it was ever solemnly determined even in this court.

MONTAGU: This way of giving evidence is making a very false way of reasoning, for the evidence does not maintain the assertion of the plea, that is to say, either confess [and] avoid or traverse and deny. And all pleadings are reducible to these two sorts.

Wherever an assertion or argument is reducible to an absurdity, it is certainly wrong. But it is sometimes difficult to find out the ways or mediums by which the absurdity is to be discovered.

Upon a [plea of] *non devenerunt* of these goods to the claimer's hands *contra formam statuti*, this sort of evidence which is now contended for might perhaps be good evidence, for there it is no contradiction or absurdity between this evidence and that plea, though there is between the evidence and the present plea.

Towards the latter end of Hen. VII, nothing was to be left for juries, the [Court of] Star Chamber determining everything, and when that was taken away, they ran into the other extreme.

This certainly, if it came in on a reply or rejoinder, would have been a departure in pleading. Whenever you confess and avoid, you must plead, and you cannot give it in evidence. This is a settled rule.

An *assumpsit* may be given in evidence on an *assumpsit* which upon the very face of the declaration appears to have been beyond the time of limitation, and, upon this principle, it is that the Statute of Limitations[2] is to be pleaded. And can any man say that the Attorney General ought not to have an opportunity of replying to this if it had been pleaded?

---

[1] *Burleigh v. Child* (1672), 2 Keble 859, 84 E.R. 544.

[2] Stat. 21 Jac. I, c. 16 (*SR*, IV, 1222–1223).

Secondly, it is a matter to be left to a jury whether a condemnation discharges the duty or no. It was held a great debate even among us whether forfeited goods were liable to custom.

[It was] objected this is the common practice, but yet no instances were cited except one cited, *viz.* Syms v. Reynoldson.

[To the] objection it would discourage bidders, [he] answered there is nothing in this, for it may be put into Latin as well as English.

[To the] objection [it is] more easy to give in evidence than to plead, the solution is that ease is the mother of ignorance.

He cited Savil's reports, the Case of Fleetwood, Recorder of London, coming into court. I believe the law or the course of the court is now altered, but I question whether it be altered for the better.

[To the] objection query these goods were bought in the market, [he] answered but that is not to be given in evidence in any case but in trover; in all other actions, it must be pleaded.

[To the] objection of a release in evidence upon *non assumpsit,* [he] answered that is only to an *assumpsit* in law; it is otherwise in the case of an *assumpsit* in fact.

[To the] objection of Dyer 234, the offense was that Bonner had refused the oaths tendered by the bishop, therefore, that the party tendering was not a bishop was evidence to the gist of the offense charged.

To say *ne granta pas,* no attornment [is] evidence; *causa patet quia* no grant if no attornment.[1]

In this case, if the plea had been that these goods were not liable to pay duties, the evidence contended for had been good evidence.

Gooche's Case, 5 Rep., fo. 60; 4 Inst. 172.[2] This is nothing but a recital of the Statute of 21 Jac. I, ca. 4, and the reason is because the justices' clerks in the country do not understand pleading.

20 Hen. VII, fo. 2;[3] three justices there were against the Chief Justice, though indeed I think that the Chief Justice was in the right and that this was only answering the plaintiff's argument to disprove the defendant's plea.

I take it there would have been a great difference between an information against this man for having such goods in his custody and in the information before us.

[To the] objection that entry and eviction may be given in evidence, [he] answered this comes up to my rule.

The case of Syms v. Reynoldson, 6 Anne 423, was grounded on a statute not in force. That is not a case to the present point.

---

1 Sic in MS.

2 *Rous v. Gooch* (1590), 5 Coke Rep. 60, 77 E.R. 146; E. Coke, *Fourth Institute* (1644), p. 172.

3 YB Mich. 20 Hen. VII, f. 2, pl. 5 (1504).

The *onus probandi* always lies on the owners. If a proviso be in the same statute, it may be given in evidence.

[He was] of the same opinion with Page that the Stat. 21 of Jac. I does not extend to any informations but to personal ones or any general issues except the issues of *non culpabilis* or *nil debet*. It is the duty of the officers to exhibit informations whenever they seize; therefore, the information is not malicious.

In the case of The Queen v. [*blank*],[1] where a seizure of property was claimed for the queen, the wine being brought in for her own use and this was given in evidence upon *non importata contra formam statuti* and it was agreed to be good because this evidence showed that the duties never did attach upon the wines. Graves v. Rumsey was an information for importing thrown silk; upon [an issue of *non*] *importata contra formam statuti*, [that it was] taken by prize was given in evidence and it was well. But in both these cases, the evidence goes to the disowning of any duties at all. The case of Reiniger v. Fogassa[2] was on the pleading, and that is the safest and best way. Our opinions do not bind my Lord Chief Baron, it being only a case, but it is my opinion that the evidence is not allowable.

PRICE: Do not conclude my Lord Chief Baron. This sort of evidence has been commonly admitted, and [there is] not one record to the contrary. The methods of this court as a [court] of revenue are distinct from the proceedings of any other court. The condemnation of goods here is the most solemn judgment, and no such sort of judgment is given anywhere else. On proceedings *in rem*, the judgment is for the things and the rules of proceeding at trial may be as different. A condemnation discharges entirely from any seizure. And it is not seizable because it is not now any longer liable to [pay] duty.

It is agreed by my brothers that, if goods be not liable to duties, anything which proves that may be given in evidence. A condemnation in the Admiralty Court [is] evidence; so a decree in the Consistory Court has been given in evidence upon *non culpabilis* upon 6 Edw.[3] In an assize for [*blank*], *nul tort* was pleaded. Bro., *Abr.*, 46.

This case is within the Stat. 21 Jac. I. The Statute is to be construed beneficially. Besides, the claimer is a person defendant when he is made party to the record. The proviso shows that the Statute extends to the cases of customs. And *non culpabilis* and *nil debet* cannot be pleaded in any cases of concealing customs.

In the Stat. 21 Hen. VII, ca. [*blank*], *non tenet seu tenuit contra formam statuti* is the general issue. A general issue is such an issue as answers the charge in general. 6 Geo. 416.

Lord Chief Baron [BURY]: I made the case for my brothers' opinion. And two of my brothers are for the plaintiff and one for the defendant, and, for my own part, I see no reason to think the evidence may not be admitted.

---

1 *Bruse, qui tam v. Attorney General* (1709), Parker 274, 145 E.R. 778, Dodd 355.

2 *Reniger v. Fogossa* (1550), 1 Plowden 1, 74 E.R. 1.

3 Stat. 5 & 6 Edw. VI, c. 4 (*SR*, IV, 133–134).

And so the court was divided.

Harvard Law School MS. 1082, vol. 1, p. 125, pl. 1

25 April 1722.

This day the Lord Chief Baron [Bury] gave his opinion in this case that the condemnation ought not to be pleaded, but it may be given in evidence. Query upon what reasons.

Taussig MS. 311, vol. 1, p. 257

Easter term 1722.

The Chief Baron [Bury] gave his opinion in this cause that the condemnation might be given in evidence, for, in his opinion, the proof of identity of the goods was the same as when it was pleaded and it was never used to be pleaded heretofore. And it is a record of the same court. And in his opinion, it was for the advantage of the crown that it should be given in evidence because, otherwise, it would very much discourage bidders.

Per Montagu and Page: We went upon this ground that this was not the general issue. And we admit it may be given in evidence in [actions of] trespass and trover.

And so the court was divided.

Bury and Price [held] that it might be given in evidence; Montagu and Page *contra. Vide* Hardres 421.

Taussig MS. 311, vol. 1, p. 388, pl. 2

December 1722.

Several writs of delivery were granted by the court upon seizures made in August last. And no writs of appraisement were returned until the last day of Michaelmas term, which the court thinking a very great neglect and delay of the officers, [they] granted writs of delivery.

But Mr. *Bootle* moved between Sawell and Carter for a writ of delivery upon a seizure in August. And it appearing that the defendant made no claim until the last day of the term, on which day the writ of appraisement was returnable, as in other cases, the court thought this was as great laches in the claimer as in the officer inasmuch as the claimer might have entered it in the Master's book, though no appraisement was returned. And for this reason, the court refused to grant a writ of delivery in this particular case.

156

Attorney General v. Pecks

(Ex. 1720)

To give a false destination of goods to be exported is a fraud as to a refund of duties paid.

Harvard Law School MS. 1082, vol. 1, p. 42

Michaelmas term 1720.

This was an information in the nature of an action of debt for that the defendant had received the sum of [*blank*] to the use of the crown for that the defendant, by the several statutes of the 5 Queen Anne [and] 2 Queen Anne, was entitled to a drawback upon landing the salt at such places and the party gives a bond for that purpose and he pretends that he had landed it accordingly and gets up his bond and debenture. The defendant makes an entry for to land his salt in Barbados but, instead of that, lands it in Ireland. Bonds [were] given, but no money [was] paid. A case was made of this. And the defendant would have been entitled to the same drawback if he had landed it in Ireland as if he had landed it in Barbados. So the question was whether this was an evidence of money had and received to the use of the king. And it was insisted on by the Attorney General that the obtaining his bond to be delivered up which was forfeited that it was the same as if so much money had been paid and that the delivering up the bond was a fraud on the crown.

The Attorney General [*Raymond*] cited as cases in point Rex v. Cadman, Hilary 2 Queen, Exchequer; Queen v. Tildesley, Trinity 4 Queen, Exchequer; Queen v. Hodgkinson, Trinity 5 Queen, Exchequer; Ward v. Evans, Michaelmas 2 Queen, reported in 2 Salkeld 442.[1] No money [was] paid in this case, yet an *indebitatus assumpsit* will lie.

Justice and law is with the crown. So he prayed judgment for it.

Mr. *Ward*, for the defendant: This is a severe prosecution, and the crown receives no damage. The merchant is not confined to any particular entry. See the statutes 5, 6, 9, 10 Will. III. But by the Statute of 1 Queen Anne, it does restrain, and 5 Queen carries it further.

It must be understood of a debenture only of salt landed in Ireland. If salt is entered for Ireland and afterwards carried to Barbados, would not the party be entitled to the drawback? And the debenture being made out, it discharges the duty. I do insist upon it that the Attorney General could not have maintained an action of debt for this duty. And then, how can he maintain this information for Jenings *propriis dominis regis*?

The defendant is a considerable dealer in salt at Droitwich and sends it to his correspondent at Bristol and makes the entry, which he mistakes, but [there is] no fraud in it, no imposition on the officer, or suggestion of fraud or suppression of truth. And the oath is only that it is not relanded in Great Britain, which is true. And it would have been as easy to have landed it at the place where the en-

[1] *Ward v. Evans* (1704), 2 Salkeld 442, 91 E.R. 382, also 2 Lord Raymond 928, 92 E.R. 120, 1 Comyns 138, 92 E.R. 1002, 2 Salkeld 442, 91 E.R. 383, 3 Salkeld 118, 91 E.R. 726, 6 Modern 36, 87 E.R. 799, 12 Modern 521, 88 E.R. 1492, Holt K.B. 120, 90 E.R. 965.

try was made. I do admit that, if there was any fraud, that an information would have lain. And so are those cases cited by the Attorney General. Rex v. Consett, where there was bribery in the officer. The case in Salkeld 22 makes for me. *Indebitatus assumpsit* will not lie on an usurious contract.

[To the] objection that there is a receipt on the debenture, [he] answered that the officer is not entitled to act.

[To the] objection of the case [in] Salkeld cited by the Attorney General, [he] answered the giving of the note is not money itself and that is not the case before you.

The *Attorney General* replies: If the Act of Parliament had not made this law, then something might have right as has been urged by Mr. Ward. But the Act has made the destruction because Ireland is too near to you as to the fraud of relanding.

MONTAGU: I did mention the case of Rex v. Consett to Mr. Ward, and the receipt shows it to be for so much money.

PRICE thought the receipt was as so much money. And it does not differ from the case cited by the Attorney General out of Salkeld.

Judgment [was given] for the king.

157

Rex v. Edwards

(Ex. 1720)

A surety of a receiver of the crown cannot have a writ of extent against his own debtors.

Harvard Law School MS. 1082, vol. 1, p. 37

Michaelmas term 1720.

John Cowper was bound to the crown as receiver general of the County of [*blank*]. And Thomas Cowper, his brother, and others were bound in the bond to the crown as sureties for John Cowper. And the said Thomas Cowper, the surety, sold some shares in stocks to one Edwards, a trader, upon credit, who, afterwards, failed and became a bankrupt. And now, the said Thomas Cowper, the surety, takes out an extent against Edwards and seizes the effects of Edwards without any original extent taken out against the receiver.

Sir Constantine Phipps, for the creditors of Edwards, moved to set aside the extent for that Thomas Cowper was no more than a surety for his brother John and no proper oath [was] taken as to the Second Rule of 15 Car. I. And a surety for a receiver cannot have an extent without first an extent issuing against the receiver himself. And it does not appear that Thomas Cowper was indebted to the receiver. He cited Rex v. Yale and Wallis.[1]

[1] *Rex v. Yale* (Ex. 1720–1721), see above, Case No. 121.

The affidavit is defective for it is not sworn that he was indebted to John Cowper, but Thomas has negotiated this money in stocks instead of paying it into the Exchequer. But it would be too hard to say that then it ought to be followed as the king's money, for I may admit that money due to the crown may be followed into any hands. But *non constat* when this money has so returned, for it might be a year or two ago, and then, if such person trades with it in stocks, shall such person be entitled to an extent, though, in the case of exigency, there might be an original extent against John Cowper, the receiver, see 6th Rule, 15 Car. I, *non constat* that any debt is due to the crown.

Serjeant *Stevens, pro eodem*: [There is] no proper affidavit. And if this method should prevail, it would be rather advantageous than otherwise to be a surety for a receiver.

Mr. *Ward*, for the extent: A surety, where he is bound in the bond, is looked upon as the principal. And so Thomas Cowper must be taken to be a debtor to the crown. Where the money is the crown's money, you will follow it into whose hands soever it comes. And the crown, in this case, must lose the money if it cannot be recovered this way, for Edwards is become a bankrupt.

It appears on the face of the bond that Thomas Cowper is bound, and so he becomes as principal, for they are all in the nature of principals to the crown. And an immediate extent may issue against any of them. That rule as to taking out extents is only meant as to extents taken in term time and open court and not meant as to vacation time. It is a case of extremity, and [it is] not sufficient to controvert this by a motion on an affidavit.

Serjeant *Stevens* replies: [There is] no pretense that this money urged to be the crown's money was returned to Thomas Cowper within a year before this happened.

Sir Constantine Phipps replies: [To the] objection that this money is the king's money, [he] answered that is where the money is immediately returned. I allow what is laid down, but, then, it must be recent. And such person is not to trade in stocks with such money and then prostrate the prerogative of the crown to help him to his money won at play.

[To the] objection that, as surety and bound in the bond, he becomes a principal, [he] answered he is not a debtor until there is an extent against the principal though there is an order for an extent, yet the proper and first method was by a commission to find debts.

Chief Baron [Bury]: The affidavit is not proper, for it is not sworn that Thomas is indebted to his brother, though it is sworn that this is the king's money and was returned to be paid into the Exchequer. But it is not sworn that the crown debt is not paid.

Price: What is the practice in this case? I believe it is that, if a receiver or surety is bound, that is sufficient for an extent. But I think it hard, though the practice is so. So I must take it that there is no difference between John and Thomas Cowper. And it is as strong for Thomas to have the extent as John. The rules vary between the practice in term time and vacation time. And I think that is no ingredient in this case that this was the king's money returned to Thomas, who gamed with it. But yet, I think the extent [is] regular.

Note that the extent was granted by himself.

Baron MONTAGU: I think that the case ought to be stated by the Deputy [Remembrancer] though I now think the extent ill grounded and that we cannot act contrary to the established rules at our chambers. Sureties are not entitled to any extent. So said by Chief Baron Atkyns in Trinity 1687, Rex v. Huntley. And there [it was] agreed to be an abuse of the prerogative process, and the extent [was] discharged. John Cowper ought to swear that he was indebted to the crown. Easter 1683, Rex v. Templeman; that the course of all the precedents is that the king's debtor's debtor is not immediately taken to be a debtor to the crown. And my brother Price even thinks that it being the crown's money is no ingredient in this case. I must own that Cowper did apply to me for an extent. But I think that the affidavit is not good for the surety according to the rule in the case of 1687 before mentioned and that this extent ought to be set aside.

PAGE: I once though it hazardous for a person to be a surety for the crown. But if this rule as now laid down is true, I would advise all merchants and traders to be bound to the crown and, by this method, this court would be the handle to all imaginable oppression to traders. I cannot take the surety in this case to be a principal. And it is not the bond. For who is to do the act? John is to pay the money, and not Thomas. Let the case be stated though I think that the extent is ill grounded and that, if the practice, if to it, is an ill practice.[1] But let there be no *venditioni exponas*, and all further proceedings [are] to stay.

And so [it was] agreed by the CHIEF BARON, MONTAGU, and PAGE against Baron PRICE.

British Library MS. Hargrave 70, f. 45v, pl. 250,
Harvard Law School MS. 1162, p. 73, pl. 396

12 November 1720.

John Cooper was made a receiver to the crown. Thomas Cooper was his security. Before it appeared that John was indebted to the crown or any [writ of] extent [was issued] against him, Thomas takes out an extent against himself and finds Edwards indebted to himself.

Upon motion, the court inclined to discharge the extent.

And Baron MONTAGU cited a case in 1687, Rex v. Huntley; A. was indebted by a bond to the crown; B. and C. are bound with him; D. is indebted to C., who takes out an extent.

It was said by Baron ATKYNS that this is an abuse of the prerogative process and that the extent ought not to go in such case.

---

[1] Sic in MS.

158

Isaakson v. Busby

(Ex. 1720)

A written lease is enforceable against the lessor by an action of ejectment.

Harvard Law School MS. 1082, vol. 1, p. 48, pl. 2

Michaelmas term 1720.

This was a bill to have a specific performance of an agreement, which was reduced into writing, for the term of forty-seven years. And, when the memorandum was produced, it was an agreement to lease and to farm let the said premisses. So, we insisted upon it that, if it was anything, that it was a lease itself and so not proper in this court by way of a specific performance, but only proper by way of [an action of] ejectment, to which the court agreed and dismissed the bill.

159

Israel v. Etheridge

(Ex. 1720–1721)

An action of trover does not lie against an officer for a wrongful seizure of imported goods because there is no conversion.

An action of trespass or trespass upon the case does not lie against an officer for a wrongful seizure of imported goods where there was probable cause for the seizure of the goods.

Harvard Law School MS. 1082, vol. 1, p. 47

Michaelmas term 1720.

This was action of trover and conversion brought by the plaintiff against the defendants [Custom House officers] for seizing a parcel of lace and converting it to their own use and that there had been an information exhibited against the now plaintiff and upon trial before the present Chief Baron [BURY], a verdict [was] found for the now plaintiff, and then defendant.

Attorney General [*Raymond*] and Solicitor General [*Yorke*], for the defendants, [argued] that this was not a proper action and there is no conversion in the officer but the seizure only puts it *in custodia legis*. And the now plaintiff might have had his writ of delivery. But the proper action is an action of trespass for seizing the goods without a reasonable cause. And, therefore, the reasonable cause is [the] matter, to be deprived of which defense,[1] the present defendants have proceeded by this new invented action. And, therefore, it is like an indictment for a malicious

[1] Sic in MS.

prosecution where the malice is the jet of the indictment, and so it is in the action. And, therefore, an action of trespass is the only proper action.

Sir Constantine Phipps, for the plaintiff: It is a seizure for the use of the king and the informer. And it is a tortious taking, which is a conversion. And this was an action commenced in the Court of Common Pleas and removed by a prerogative order, so that the first action was well instituted.

The *Attorney General* replies for the defendants: This is an action of the first instance and contrived on purpose to take away the officers' proper defense. This will be an encouragement to all fraudulent running of goods. And therefore, if the gentleman for the plaintiff think there is anything in it, I will have a special verdict found.

Then, the counsel for the plaintiff desired a case might be made of it, but the *Attorney General* said that he would have a special verdict. And rather than that, the counsel for the plaintiff submitted to be nonsuited.

Note that Sir Constantine told me that there was such an action formerly brought, but the court overruled it and would not suffer it.

Bunbury 67, 145 E.R. 597

At the Guildhall sittings 1720. Etriche v. Anonymous.

Upon an information of seizure of goods, there was a verdict for the defendant, who, afterwards, brought [an action of] trover against the officer for these goods, which was tried before the Lord Chief Baron Bury at the sittings after this term.

And the Attorney General [*Raymond*], for the defendant, objected that trover did not lie for these goods, for that the seizure of the goods and putting them into the Custom House warehouse could not be said to be any conversion to his own use, but [an action of] trespass or trespass upon the case [lay]. And Mr. *Attorney General* insisting upon a special verdict and the Chief Baron inclining to be of that opinion, that trover would not lie, the plaintiff chose to be nonsuited.

Harvard Law School MS. 1082, vol. 1, p. 89, pl. 4

Sittings after Trinity term 1721.

This was an action of trespass against a custom house officer for the taking of goods, [and the words] '*absque probabili causa*' [were] omitted. And a verdict was obtained upon it. And it was now moved in arrest of judgment by Solicitor General [*Yorke*] that, by the omitting of these words, it was an improper action. And so there is a case in Hardres of Hale's opinion. And likewise [it is] proper for a new trial on the excessive damages.

The Chief Baron [Bury] declared that this was an improper action for '*absque probabili causa*' is the jet of the action, for, if there was a probably cause, the defendant ought not to have been found guilty. The lace was valued only at £25, and only the lace ought to be given in damages.

Price: I think that the officer is without excuse. And the measure of the damages is in the breast of the jury. And I always thought than an action of trespass was a proper action against an officer or any wrongdoer and also an action of trover, for, if the officer exceeds this duty, it is a tort and a conversion in the officer. And I think that the defendant in the information has his election either to have a writ of delivery or resort to his action of trespass, for, after the writ of delivery, you may come for consequential damages. And so I am for no new trial.

Montagu: I do not apprehend that anything has been irregularly done by this officer. Surely, an action of trover is not proper. And a common action of trespass is no more than trover, but only a special action of the case lies. And the words '*absque probabili causa*' ought to be inserted. It cannot conclude as a common action of trespass does, *viz. contra pacem*, which an officer cannot be guilty of. I think that you deprive the officer of his defense if these words are omitted. Therefore, I am for a new trial.

Page: An action of trespass will lie if there is no probable cause. Lord Coke takes notice what a probable cause is. And the law will not give a general liberty to an officer. And it is an aggravation where an officer exceeds his duty for an action of the case will lie for consequential damages and a special action of trespass will lie. And, in this case, the officer having intelligence that lace was brought in late at night, that was a probably cause, which is put in opposition to a malicious cause. And it is a sufficient defense if there is a probable cause. Trespass may lie for taking the goods. But after the goods are in the king's warehouse, they are *in custodia legis*. And he is no trespasser then, for the goods are not in the hands of the officer, but the crown. He is entitled to a writ of restitution by warrant from the judge *ex debito justitiae*. And the probably cause, for what I know, may be given in evidence, *quod vide*.

So a new trial was granted on payment of costs, against the opinion of Price.

Taussig MS. 311, vol. 1, p. 71

20 June 1721.

Etheridge seizes lace. A claim is put in, and, upon an information, it is tried for the claimer. Israel brings [an action of] trespass. He had formerly brought [an action of] trover and was nonsuited in that action because that sort of action does not lie. And the jury find a verdict for the plaintiff Israel and £170 damages.

And Mr. Solicitor General [*Yorke*] now moved for a new trial upon two points: first, because this sort of action is not proper inasmuch as the plaintiff might have had a writ of delivery and, therefore, should not bring trespass, and, again, there was a probable cause for the seizure; second, the damages were excessive, the goods seized being not worth more than £25.

E contra, it was said for the plaintiff that he might either have a writ of delivery or his action, and it would be very hard to oblige him to take his goods again when they were damaged. And, as to the probable cause, that was before the jury. As to the excessive damages, it was proved that the plaintiff had actually contracted to sell them for £170 to another person before the seizure and they were bought at £150 of the merchant, and so there was but four percent profit even by the second contract.

By the *Solicitor General*: The judgment upon the record is *quod bona restituantur*, which is a judgment *in rem*, and yet he will not have them but he brings the action *in personam*. There may be an action of trespass in this case if laid specially without probable cause, but not a general action of trespass. Trover does not lie because there is no conversion.

By Chief Baron [Bury], against the officer, the action should be laid without probable cause. And he said that he directed the jury that, if they thought there was probable cause, they should find the defendant not guilty. So, says he, this point was left to the jury, as also the value of the lace, upon the whole evidence given upon this point. It is true the jury when they came in they did say that, if the officer would let the plaintiff have the lace again, then they would give but £50, but the officer would not consent to it.

Per Price: The jury have found there was not probable cause. And I do not find there was probable cause.

As to value, I think it is sufficiently proved and the jury are judges *inde* it was contracted for to be sold at £173.

I think trespass does lie. And I see no reason why trover does not lie, for, if he does not do his duty, he converts the goods to his own use in the sense of the law. By him, the claimer is at his election to take the goods or the value of them, so his action is well brought. If he had taken the goods, then he could not have had this general action, but a special action.

He sees no reason for a new trial.

Per Montagu: By the report of the Chief Baron, there seems to be no irregularity in the officer. The goods were brought in at an unseasonable time of night, so that, if the officer had a just cause of suspicion, he had been inexcusable if he had not seized. Trespass *vi et armis* does not lie any more than trespass. Trespass does not lie for imprisoning a man for felony if there is cause of suspicion, if there is distress and the party claims the property. In trespass, it must always be proved *contra pacem*.

A special action on the case does lie, and not trespass. And special actions on the case have been brought on such occasions, for probable cause is the very gist of the action.

He takes these damages to be consequential damages and such ought not to be given.

Page: Trespass lies in all the cases put by my Brother Montagu, but probable cause for taking excuses. *Colore officii* aggravates the trespass. So, by him, he is a trespasser *ab initio*. Trespass will lie *vi et armis*. And an action on the case will lie too for consequential damages, which are not recoverable in trespass.

Probable cause stands in opposition to malice. He thinks here was probable cause for the seizure. And, in this case, I do not apprehend that the damages given for them divest the property as in the case of a common trespass where a recovery in the action divests the property and vests it in the trespasser. But here, I do not see but the party may have execution, *viz.* a writ of restitution, for the goods themselves. And, therefore, if the party may have the goods again, the damages are excessive.

And so, MONTAGU, PAGE, and Chief Baron [BURY] thinking there was probable cause and that damages were excessive, a new trial was granted.

Bunbury 80, 145 E.R. 602

20 June 1721.

Upon an information of seizure, there was a verdict for the claimer, who did not move for a writ of delivery, but brought an action of trespass for the goods against the officers that seized.

Upon a motion for a new trial, there being a verdict for the plaintiff in this action, PRICE, Baron, said that it was now allowed and taken for law that trover did not lie against an officer for seizing *absque probabili causa*, but trespass would, and, if the claimer had moved for a writ of delivery, he seemed to think he could not have this action because, then, he would have a double remedy.

Baron MONTAGU was of opinion that neither trover nor trespass would lie because the seizure is not *contra pacem*, but that trespass upon the case setting forth that the seizure was *absque probabili causa* would lie, as was done in the case of King v. Mellish.[1]

Baron PAGE was of opinion that trespass or case for the consequential damages will lie. But now, the verdict was set aside, for that they thought here was *probabilis causa*.

Note: BURY and PAGE seemed of opinion that, in trespass, the party shall not recover the value of the goods, but only the damages for the unlawful seizing.

160

Fisher v. Leaman

(Ex. 1720)

Agistment tithes are payable by the occupier of the land and not by the owner of the cattle.

Harvard Law School MS. 1082, vol. 1, p. 27

Michaelmas term 1720.

---

[1] *King v. Melling* (1672), 1 Ventris 225, 86 E.R. 151, 1 Ventris 214, 86 E.R. 144, Pollexfen 101, 86 E.R. 526, 3 Keble 42, 52, 95, 84 E.R. 584, 589, 614, 2 Levinz 58, 83 E.R. 448, 3 Salkeld 296, 91 E.R. 835, 1 Eq. Cas. Abr. 181, 21 E.R. 973.

A bill was brought against the defendant [Robert Leaman], owner of the cattle that fed and agisted on his father Thomas Leaman's land, and Thomas Leaman was not brought to hearing though he was at first made a party.

The present defendant was a butcher and fed his cattle as he brought them to market.

Serjeant *Stevens*, for the plaintiff: The defendant as an agistor was an occupier, and the plaintiff has an election, as in the case of wood against the vendor or vendee.

Mr. *Ward*, for the plaintiff: The owner of the cattle is as well chargeable as the occupier of the land. Hardres 184, Corey v. Wright; Sir William Jones 254, Facey v. Long.[1] This is a contrivance between the father and son.

Mr. *Cox*, for the plaintiff: In the case of commoners, the agistor is liable.

Sir Constantine Phipps, for the defendant: I am surprised that this should be made a question now, for the only doubt is whether the owner of the land or the agistor shall pay tithes. And it has been settled several times in this court that the owner of the land shall pay. In the case of wood cut, if the vendor fells and sells it, he shall pay tithes and not the vendee. I admit the case as cited in the case of commoners, for that is grounded on the Statute of Edw. VI.[2] Watson 355; 2 Rolle Reports, Johnson v. Parker; Sir William Jones 191, 254; Underwood v. Gibbon, in this court, 1716, where the bill brought against the owner of the horse was dismissed.[3]

Mr. *Foley*, for the defendant, cited Godolphin 384; 2 Cro. 42; Cro. Car. 273, 559; Sir Williams Jones 254.

Mr. *Bootle*, for the defendant: This case may be compared to the case of agistors, travelers, and an innholder. The son is only a butcher or boarder, and he brings his cattle only for some nights to market. Hardres 35, Gilbert v. Eversly, 7 King Charles II.[4] Mr. Ward admits that there is an election; if the owner has accepted satisfaction, he has determined his election.

---

[1] *Pory v. Wright* (1661), Hardres 184, 145 E.R. 442, also 1 Eq. Cas. Abr. 367, 21 E.R. 1107, 1 Eagle & Younge 434; *Facy v. Longe* (1632), W. Jones 254, 82 E.R. 133, also Croke Car. 237, 79 E.R. 807, 1 Eagle & Younge 376.

[2] Stat. 2 & 3 Edw. VI, c. 13 (*SR*, IV, 55–58).

[3] W. Watson, *Clergy-Man's Law*; *Johnson v. Parker* (1620), 2 Rolle Rep. 191, 81 E.R. 743; *Whitton v. Weston* (1627), W. Jones 182, 82 E.R. 96, also Godbolt 392, 78 E.R. 231, Latch 89, 82 E.R. 289, Benloe 168, 185, 73 E.R. 1031, 1043, J. Bridgman 32, 123 E.R. 1179, 1 Gwillim 410, 1 Eagle & Younge 340, Paynell K.B. 35, 44, 258, 342; *Facy v. Longe* (1632), *ut supra*; *Underwood v. Gibbon* (Ex. 1716), see above, Case No. 7.

[4] *Guilbert v. Eversly* (1656), Hardres 35, 145 E.R. 367, 2 Gwillim 502, 1 Eagle & Younge 414.

Serjeant *Stevens* replies for the plaintiff: Tithe is due on severance. 2 Bulstrode 183.[1]

Mr. *Ward* replies for the plaintiff: As to the case in Godolphin, the other cases cited are not in affirmance of Godolphin's opinion so that Godolphin is mistaken. I admit the case of Hardres 35, and, there, it is said that the owner is liable, but, if the agistor is to be found and continues some time, he is liable. The case of Underwood v. Gibbon did not turn on the case of owner or agistor, but the only question there was whether a saddle horse was liable. There is an election either against the occupier or the owner of the land. And so was Chief Baron Dodd's opinion.

Chief Baron [Bury]: I think that it was very hard for this parson to sue this defendant. And I take this case to be only as cattle that rested on the road, by which it is plain that the occupier of the land is liable and not the owner of the cattle and that herbage tithe is already paid by the owner of the land, who is the only person liable. And, therefore, I am for dismissing the bill.

Price: I am of the same opinion. And I think that the plaintiff has taken the wrong defendant. And the son here is only like the case of a traveler, and there is no difference between weeks or days or a month, for, if cattle are taken in by agistment, the occupier of the land is liable. If the father rented the land but put no cattle on and the son put the cattle, then I take the son to be the occupier. But if part one and part the other, then the occupier of the land shall pay. In the case of a common, it cannot be doubted, and every commoner is an occupier, for the owner of the horse was liable in the case of Underwood v. Gibbon. As to the election whether agistor or occupier, though I value Chief Baron Hale's opinion, yet I cannot agree to it as reported by Hardres 184. The bill should be dismissed.

Montagu: This bill was against the agistor, and the question was whether a saddle horse was liable in Underwood and Gibbon's Case, and the bill was there brought against the owner of the horse, and the bill was there dismissed because a saddle horse was not liable. Larkin's Case, in Popham's reports, and in Hardres 184, is a strong case; Hardres 35. The owner of the land is the parishioner. And he is liable and best known to the parson and not the traveler. If the after-moath is let out, then such person that lets it is the occupier. The bill ought to be dismissed.

Page: I am of the same opinion that the occupier of the land is liable. And it would be a hardship on the parson to put him to seek out the traveler. It is a contradiction that a duty shall arise from two persons *simul et semel*. I cannot come into the notion of an election, but I take it that [in] all events, the occupier of the lands is liable. If the occupier of land was poor and takes in strangers' horses, there would be a fraud. But I take it that the agistor cannot be liable from the

[1] *Moyle v. Ewer* (K.B. 1614), 2 Bulstrode 183, 80 E.R. 1053, also Croke Jac. 361, 79 E.R. 309, 1 Gwillim 276, 1 Eagle & Younge 204, related case, *Moyle v. Ewer* (Ex. 1608–1610), 117 Selden Soc. 355, Lane 83, 145 E.R. 318.

inconvenience that would ensue and the multiplicity of suits. The bill ought to be dismissed, which was done, with costs.

Lincoln's Inn MS. Misc. 123, f. 11

The plaintiff, being rector of the parish of Henyobe in Devonshire, brought a bill for agistment tithes against the agistor. The case appeared to be thus. The defendant's father lived in the parish and rented a farm there. The defendant lived with him, and he, being a butcher and renting a farm in an adjacent parish, frequently brought cattle and put them in his father's ground for two or three nights and sometimes killed some of them off, but generally he sent them to his own farm. The question was whether the owner of the land or the owner of the cattle should pay agistment tithes.

Mr. *Ward*, for the plaintiff: The parson may demand it against either owner or occupier. Hardres 184; Sir W. Jones 254.

Sir Constantine Phipps, for the defendant: The parson may demand tithe wood against the vendor only. It is true a commoner must pay, but that is grounded upon the Statute Edw. VI. Watson 455; 2 Rolle Reports 191; 1716, Underwood v. Gibbon, Exchequer case of the Corporation of Sudbury in Suffolk, a demand of tithe against the owner of a horse, being a commoner, and it was held it would not lie because it was a saddle horse; Godolphin 384; and 2 Croke 42 and 3 Croke 237, 539. The defendant's having a farm in another parish and only resting the cattle here a night or two makes it exactly the same as the case of a traveler and innkeeper. Hardres 35.

He replied: 2 Bulstrode 138. As to praedial tithes, he that takes the profit by the beasts ought to pay them.

The Chief Baron [Bury] and the other barons agreed that the demand ought to have been against the occupier of the land for the agistment tithes if any had been due, but they thought in this case nothing appeared due.

And Baron Page said that, as to what had been said that the demand might be against either occupier or agistor, that could not be, for the same duty could not arise in two different persons at the same time.

2 Eq. Cas. Abr. 732, 22 E.R. 619,
C. Viner, Abridgment, vol. 9, p. 38, pl. 7

J.S., being rector of the parish of Hemyoke in Devon, brought a bill for agistment tithes against the agistor. The case appeared to be thus. The defendant's father lived in the parish and rented a farm there. The defendant lived with him, and he, being a butcher and renting a farm in an adjacent parish, frequently brought cattle and put them in his father's grounds for two or three nights and sometimes killed some of them off. But, generally, he sent them to his own farm. The question was whether the owner of the land or the owner of the cattle should pay agistment tithes.

The Chief Baron [Bury] and the other barons agreed that the demand ought to have been against the occupier of the land for the agistment tithes if any had been due. But they thought in this case nothing appeared due.

And Baron Page said that, as to what had been said that the demand might be either against the occupier or agistor, that could not be, for the same duty could not arise in two different persons at the same time.

Lincoln's Inn MS. Hill 29, p. 48

Michaelmas 7 Geo. I.

The defendant's father rents a farm in the parish of A. The defendant, who is a butcher, lives with his father but rents a farm in the parish of B. The defendant frequently bought cattle and sometimes put them into his father's grounds for five or six days and nights together and sometimes killed them off his father's farm, sometimes off his own.

The parson of the parish of A. brings his bill against the defendant only for agistment tithes. The question was whether the bill should not be dismissed and whether the parson should not have his election either to sue the agistor or the occupier for tithes at his pleasure.

In the resolution of this case, I did not hear the Chief Baron and Baron Price give their opinions, which were as [I was] informed the same in substance with those of Montagu and Page.

Montagu: I think it always best to reduce things to a certainty. The landowner is always known and it would be unreasonable to oblige the parson to go to every man who perhaps puts in his cattle for ten or twelve days to receive his tithes. Where a man indeed lets out land for depasturing a horse for half a year, he becomes by that a tenant, and the parson may recover of him. In the case of Gilbert v. Haversham, [it was] there adjudged that the landowner should pay tithes for depasture. As to the case in Hardr. 184, since the landowner was exempt, the occupier must be so.

(N.B. Baron Price answered this case in Hardres by saying that was a common and, therefore, out of doubt but the owner of the horses must pay.)

In the case of Underwood v. [*blank*], which was lately determined in this court, it was the Lord A. gave a piece of ground to the Corporation of Sudbury; the members of the corporation only used to put in their horses; it was held that it was well brought against the agistor because there was no occupier of the land, but [it was] dismissed as to the defendant because [it was] brought for his putting in a saddle horse. And that case was grounded on a case in Popham.[1]

Page: If the duty of the tithes arises from the profits, the occupier is to pay the tithes. Where land is let out for some time for pasture, the renter is the occupier and must pay. But, in the case of mixed pasturage, sometimes one person's

[1] *Laurking v. Wilde* (1617), Popham 126, 79 E.R. 1229.

cattle, sometimes another's are let in. It is unjust to say the parson has his election, for at that rate, a drover, coming to town puts in his cattle for a night or two, must he stay to go to the parson and give him 1d. for tithes.

Per totam curiam, the bill was dismissed with costs, for it should have been brought against the father, the occupier, and not the defendant, the agistor.

2 Gwillim 626

16 November 1720.

A bill was brought by the rector of Hemyock in Devonshire, *inter alia*, for agistment tithe of lands called Cley Park.

The defendant Leaman said that his father, for three years, had held and enjoyed Cley Park. But he insisted that he had fully paid and compounded with the plaintiff for the tithes of the same. He denied that he had ever rented, occupied, or enjoyed as tenant any messuage or lands in the parish, or in the tithable places thereof or that he had ever bred up, fed, depastured, or agisted on the said farm any horses or other cattle, as in the bill is alleged. And he said that he was a butcher and boarded with his father, but that he rented lands in Clehydon parish and did sometimes bring home cattle from a fair late at night and put them upon the said farm called Cley Park, but that he drove them away the next morning home to his said parish, and that he had satisfied his father for the same before this suit was commenced, and, therefore, he is advised that no tithe is due from him to the plaintiff. He confessed that he had used the trade of a butcher ever since the expiration of his apprenticeship with his father and had bought all sorts of cattle in the way of his trade, but had never depastured any of them in the parish of Hemyock, other than as aforesaid. And he denied that any tithes were due from him, as in the bill is alleged.

The plaintiff replied; the defendant rejoined; and witnesses were examined on both sides. And, upon reading the proofs taken in the cause and hearing counsel fully on the matter, it is ordered and adjudged by the court that the bill is dismissed with costs to be taxed by the Deputy Remembrancer.

[Order of 16 November 1720: 2 Wood 158, 1 Eagle & Younge 762.]

161

Attorney General, ex rel. Duchess of Buccleuch v. Ayre

(Ex. 1720)

In this case, a claim of a toll through by prescription was not proved.

Harvard Law School MS. 1082, vol. 1, p. 44

Michaelmas term 1720.

This was a bill brought against the defendants [Ayre, Williamson, and Nelson], who were persons that carried goods through the manor of Spalding, in order to have satisfaction by way of a toll through for such goods, setting forth that the manor of Spalding with the appurtenances within the parts of Holland in the County of Lincoln is a very ancient lordship or manor and has been so long before the Norman Conquest and comprehends and extends itself unto all the extreme parts of the towns of Spalding, Pinchbeck, Moulton, and Weston with several hamlets and granges within its jurisdiction and the demesnes thereof and do likewise extend into the several parishes of Sarfleet, Gosberton, Whapload, Holbeach, and divers others adjacent towns and villages and that for the time whereof the memory of man is not to the contrary,[1] there has been of right due and payable and usually paid and ought still to be paid unto the lords of the said manor of Spalding *cum membris* or their farmers or tenants a certain toll or duty called a through toll by all persons whatsoever, except only by the tenants within the said manor, leading, driving, or carrying their goods, cattle, chattels, and carriages unto or through the said manor as also divers or other duties and tolls for passing or leave or license to pass or come unto, through, or out of the said manor or any of the demesnes or wastes thereof or any part thereof with carts, wagons, pack horses, or other horses laden or other cattle unladen and all other carriages and manner of carriage goods or chattels, wares, merchandises, or other things whatsoever, either by land or water, for which every person, except as aforesaid, time out of mind ought to pay and usually has paid to the lords and owners of the said manor for the time being or to the farmers and tenants the rates following, *viz.* for every wagon passing through the said manor 6d., for every cart 4d., every score of sheep 4d. etc. and sets forth that William the Conqueror was seised of this manor and granted the same and that, afterwards, it vested in King Charles II, who granted the same to several persons in tail reserving the rents of £1 6s. 8d. and £1 payable at Michaelmas and Lady Day and that the reversion was still in the crown and that the plaintiffs entitled themselves to the said manor and premises by virtue of the grants aforesaid and are, therefore, entitled to the tolls aforesaid and that the defendants did carry goods through the said manor and ought to have paid the said tolls, which they have refused, and that they might discover the premises and be relieved and His Majesty righted therein.

The defendants insisted that they never knew of any toll paid in such manner as in the bill. And so, upon the examination of several witnesses, it came to be heard this term and, afterwards, at the setting down of causes, for it lasted three days, on the objections made by us that were of counsel for the defendants against the bill itself and the toll as it was prescribed to.

Serjeant *Stevens*, Mr. *Gilby*, Mr. *Foley*, and *Fazakerly* were for Aire and Williamson; Mr. *Cox*, Jr., and [. . .] were for Nelson: And we objected, first, that, as

[1] This is the verbal formula used to allege a prescriptive right.

it was laid to be a toll through, there was no consideration alleged, as reparation etc. And for that purpose was cited 1 Siderfin 454, Hesford v. Wills, 1 Modern 47; Moore 887, 576; Hobart 189, about the uncertainty of the custom, Hardinge; Coke 2 Inst. 219, 220, tolls are destructive to trade;[1] 2 Modern 243; 4 Modern 423; 3 Levinz 85; 1 Jones 162.

And secondly, [it was] objected that the custom was too uncertain as to coming 'unto' the manor so that, if any person came towards it, he was to pay.

Thirdly, [it was] objected that this was a bill proper for discovery only and not for relief, for any decree in this case would not be binding to other travelers, and, therefore, it would be more proper at law than in this court. And they cited City of Exeter v. Bond, Hilary 1718, Exchequer; Disney v. Robertson, Easter 1719;[2] Harding v. Ainge, sittings after Trinity 1719.

As to the first, we were answered by Serjeant *Chesshyre, Sir Constantine Phipps, Ward, Sawyer*, and *Johnson*, for the plaintiffs, that this was a toll traverse and not a toll through. But in the case of a toll through, it is not always necessary to allege a consideration for that, in such prescriptive usage, a consideration will be implied. And they cited Cro. Eliz. 710; 1 Modern 231; 3 Levinz 424; 2 Rolle, *Abridgment*, 222; Keilwey 152.[3]

[They argued] that, as to the second objection, the custom was laid as formerly in the very same cases in this court and that, as to the third objection, that this case was not like those because here is a fee farm rent reserved and a reversion still in the crown and the Attorney General is a party to this suit and prays an establishment of these customs, neither of which was in the cases cited above.

Upon this matter as heard in term, the court delivered their opinions as follows, *viz.*:

Chief Baron [Bury]: It is a strange bill to establish this right against strangers. And I think it was better to have gone to law first. I never remember a decree in this court until the right was first established at law. You have had the discovery, and that is sufficient. And I think that it is a bill of great oppression and ought to be dismissed. If a right was to be established, it must be against all the people of England that travel that way.

---

1 *Heshord v. Wills* (1670), 1 Siderfin 454, 82 E.R. 1214, 1 Modern 47, 86 E.R. 722, also Lincoln's Inn MS. Misc. 500, f. 96, pl. 2; *Harbin v. Green* (1616), Moore K.B. 887, 72 E.R. 975, Hobart 189, 80 E.R. 336, also 1 Brownlow & Goldesborough 18, 123 E.R. 638; *Davenant v. Hurdis* (1599), Moore K.B. 576, 72 E.R. 769; E. Coke, *Second Institute* (1642), pp. 219–220.

2 *Disney v. Robertson* (1719), see above, Case No. 82.

3 *Smith v. Shepherd* (1599), Croke Eliz. 710, 78 E.R. 945, also Moore K.B. 574, 72 E.R. 768; *James v. Johnson* (1677), 1 Modern 231, 86 E.R. 849, also 2 Modern 143, 86 E.R. 989; *Crispe v. Belwood* (1695), 3 Levinz 420, 83 E.R. 760; *Anonymous* (temp. Edw. III), Keilwey 152, 72 E.R. 325.

PRICE: It is much to me that no precedent has been showed on the part of the plaintiffs for this proceeding. And since none is produced, I shall not suppose any. I think that this bill is more properly a bill of discovery than to establish the right, for it only prays a discovery and an injunction to stay actions at law. Perhaps, if it was the king's own case, it might make a difference. But in the case of the king's farmer, I think there is no privilege in this case. But if it was the king's own case, he might choose this court to proceed in, but the king's farmer cannot. But if this matter was a matter of right, yet it is not proper to establish this against all the persons of England and against strangers. And this decree, if made for the plaintiffs, will not bind them.

In the case of a toll through, I took it that a consideration must be alleged. I think that the cases of the City of Exeter v. Bond, Disney v. Robertson, [and] Harding v. Ainge do agree with this, and, as the bills there were dismissed, so I am for dismissing this bill.

MONTAGU: I am not for determining this matter without further consideration. We sit here as a court of revenue. And in Madox and Glanvill and other books, [they] say that the separation was to take care of the king's revenue, and so is the speech of Lord Shaftesbury to a baron in this court. The Attorney General may exhibit his bill for waifs and strays, and so is Coke's *Entries.* [In] that case cited of the City of Exeter v. Bond, the inheritance is out of the crown. And I think that this present case before the court does concern the crown. And I do not know any difference between the king and his farmer, but that the farmer has the same privilege. I must own that I think that the bill is set forth very loosely. And I desire to consider of toll through and toll traverse and upon the whole case. And I think that [it is like] the bill against the brewers where a demurrer was overruled, and therefore, I am against dismissing the bill at present.

PAGE: I think that it is a cause of consequence and that the cases cited do not come up to it because, here, the inheritance is in the crown though it is not in the pleading said on behalf of His Majesty. But I think that a decree in this cause would not tend to any benefit for the crown. If this had been once determined at law, I should have gone further. The king's tenant or farmer has not the same privilege as the king. And I think that this custom [as] to the manor is bad. And, therefore the bill should be dismissed. But, at last, [he] agreed with Montagu to consider further of it and to search for precedents in this court if there ever were such bills and decrees made thereon, to which the other barons agreed.

And so, at another day in term, several precedents were read in court, *viz.* Halford and Baines' Case, 4 Will. & Mar., for the manor in question; Dr. Edisbury's Case, 22 October 14 Car. II, Exchequer; Sir Edmund Sawyer's Case, 22 Car. II, Exchequer.

Sir Constantine Phipps and Mr. *Ward*, for the plaintiffs, [argued] that this case at law was much stronger than those where, in some of them, the inheritance was out of the crown.

We that were counsel for the defendants insisted that those cases did not turn upon this point, but upon particular exemptions. But note that we could not answer the precedents unless that by saying that they passed *sub silentio.* And then we insisted that there was a difference between the king and his farmer and that the latter should not have the same privilege as the king. And I cited Marshal v. Ball and Radland, Hilary 1717, where a fee farmer had put several into a bill and there was a demurrer to [it] on that account, and the demurrer was allowed. Hardres 177, White v. Potter.[1]

Upon the whole, Chief Baron [Bury], Montagu, and Page, at the sittings after this term [Michaelmas 1720], agreed to read the proofs, but saved the objections to us. But, upon reading them, there was no proof of the prescription, and the bill was dismissed on the merits.

Bunbury 68, 145 E.R. 598

At Serjeants' Inn, 6 December 1720.

This was a bill brought for establishing a right to tolls in the manor of Spalding etc. in the County of Lincoln. And it was laid that, time out of mind, there has been a duty payable to the lord of the manor for all carts etc. coming to the manor etc.

Note: In this case, there was a fee farm rent reserved, which, it was said by *Sir Constantine Phipps*, for the plaintiff, distinguished it from the case at pl. 64, *ante.*[2]

But it was insisted by Mr. *Browne* and Mr. *Toller*, for the defendant, *inter alia*, that this was a toll thorough and, consequently, void without alleging a consideration.

And the court, except Montagu, who thought the fee farm rent reserved gave the court jurisdiction, inclined to dismiss the bill.

But they, afterwards, went into proofs, and the bill was dismissed, it not appearing that the place where the toll bars were erected was within the manor of Spalding.

162

Fox v. Rutty

(Ex. 1720–1721)

Where tithes have not been paid in recent times but the vicar has an endowment of tithes, tithes will be ordered to be paid.

Harvard Law School MS. 1082, vol. 1, p. 48, pl. 1

Michaelmas term 1720.

---

[1] *White v. Porter* (1661), Hardres 177, 145 E.R. 439.

[2] *Disney v. Robertson* (1719), see above, Case No. 82.

The defendant insisted on a current composition of 9d. in the pound in bar of tithes in kind demanded by the plaintiff as vicar of Melsham and that he had no notice to the contrary. Query.

Harvard Law School MS. 1082, vol. 1, p. 101, pl. 2

Michaelmas term 1721.

The plaintiff, as vicar of Melsham in Wiltshire, exhibits his bill for the tithes of lands called Iley. The defendant insists that these lands called Iley were lying within the tithable places of Whaddon and that no tithes were ever paid to the vicar of Melsham. And upon the hearing, an issue was directed whether this piece of ground called Iley did lie within the parish of Whaddon or within the parish of Melsham. The second issue was whether tithes were usually paid to or received by the rector of Whaddon or the vicar of Melsham.

The cause was tried, and a verdict was given that this ground called Iley [lies] in the parish of Melsham and not in the parish of Whaddon, but that the tithes were not usually received either by the vicar of Melsham or the rector of Whaddon. So this cause came upon the equity reserved.

Serjeant *Pengelly et alii*, counsel for the defendants, insisted that there was not sufficient [matter] found to satisfy the conscience of the court, for it does not appear that the vicar of Melsham ever received these tithes [and] so is not entitled. And it was the intention of the court to try the usage, which not being satisfactorily found, there ought to be a new trial.

Chief Baron [Bury] thought that the issue was sufficiently found to decree the defendant to account. If there is an express endowment, as there was in this case, that will entitle the vicar without usage, but where the endowment is doubtful, there the usage ought to explain it.

Baron Price: I am of the same opinion. And it is well found against an occupier. The essential part is found. And I take an endowment to be equal with common right. Perhaps, if the payment for tithes had always been made to the rector of Whaddon, there, something might be said against the plaintiff, but that is found against the defendant. It is a *non decimando* in the defendant, and I think that he ought to account.

Montagu: It is hard to be told that, when issues are directed, that they are not proper. The vicar with such an endowment is entitled to tithes of common right. And the verdict gives me satisfaction.

Page agrees.

So the defendant was decreed to account according to the yearly value.

Taussig MS. 311, vol. 1, p. 126

Thursday, 16 November 1721.

The plaintiff, as vicar of Melcham and endowed of all small tithes *infra parochia de* Melcham, exhibits his bill against the defendant as tenant of a close called

Iley for pasturage tithe. The defendant says, first, that Iley was not within the parish of Melcham and, secondly, though it was, that the tithes of this close were payable to the rector of Whaddon. And upon this, the court directed two issues to try, first, whether the close called Iley lay within Melcham or Whaddon. And as to this, the verdict was that it did lie within Melcham.

The second issue was whether tithes of the close were usually paid to the rector of Whaddon or to the plaintiff, the vicar of Melcham. And as to this, the verdict finds that they were not usually paid either to the vicar, the plaintiff, or to the rector of Whaddon.

Upon the return of the *postea*, it was moved that the plaintiff ought to have a decree, the verdict finding the issues for him, the first expressly, the second a full bar to the rector of Whaddon.

E contra per Pengelly: The court cannot properly decree because, here, the court is to determine the right of the rector of Whaddon, who is no party to this bill, and the right of the rector of Melcham, who is likewise no party.

Second, the plaintiff in every bill is to make out his title to his demand or else the court cannot decree for him. And the jury having found that the plaintiff had not received tithes, therefore, though they found that the tithes were not usually paid to the rector of Whaddon, still there is no title for the plaintiff.

As to the endowment, *per Stevens* and *Phipps*: It being not supported by usage, it may leave room to think that there is a new endowment. That the impropriator of the tithes of one parish may receive a portion of the tithes in another parish is certain and admitted on all hands.

Per Serjeant *Pengelly*: We could have proved at the assizes that the impropriator of Whaddon had received a *modus* for tithes of this close, but it was doubted whether the issue being tied up to receiving tithes, the *modus* could be given in evidence upon it.

Per Chief Baron [Bury], Price, Montagu, and Page: The verdict is found for the vicar as to both points. If the defendant had pleaded that he had paid tithes to the impropriator of Whaddon, perhaps, it would have been proper to have made him a party to the bill. But all that he says is that there is some composition or *modus* without saying what is payable to the impropriator of Whaddon. And the reason of the second issue was that, if it had fallen out that there had been a perpetual usage to pay to the impropriator of Whaddon, it would have caused doubt in us whether the impropriator of Whaddon had not a portion and, if so found, it would have shaken the endowment as to this close.

And so the court decreed that the defendant should account for the tithes of this close with costs at law and in equity.

Bunbury 87, 145 E.R. 604,
1 Rayner 159, 2 Gwillim 627, 1 Eagle & Younge 763

16 November 1721.

A bill was brought by the vicar of Melsham against a parishioner for tithes; an issue was directed to try whether a parcel of lands, called Islay, usually paid tithes to the vicar of Melsham or to the rector of Whaddon, who was not before the court. The jury find that it had paid tithes to neither. And, upon the *postea* returned, it was insisted for the defendant that, by this finding, the court could make no decree, for that they had no satisfaction by it.

But *per* CURIAM: The vicar is endowed *de omnibus minutis decimis infra parochiam etc.*, and the defendant's defence, both in law and equity, is falsified. And though tithes have never been paid, yet the vicar has the same right to all within his endowment, even without usage, unless an usage to the contrary is shown, as the rector has of common right, in which last case, a man cannot insist that tithes have never been paid, which is a *non decimando*. And they decreed for the vicar accordingly.

Serjeant *Glyde* and Mr. *Ward* [were] for the plaintiff; Serjeant *Pengelly*, Serjeant *Stevens*, *Sir Constantine Phipps*, and Mr. *Bootle* [were] for the defendant.

[Order of 7 December 1720: 2 Wood 160, 1 Eagle & Younge 763.]

163

Bull v. Allen

(Ex. 1721)

Where a bill of complaint is brought against different defendants for different claims, this is a misjoinder of parties and a misjoinder of claims.

Bunbury 69, 145 E.R. 598

12 February.

A bill was brought to be relieved against several contracts entered into by the plaintiff with the defendants relating to shares in a bubble called the Pennsylvania bubble and to have his money repaid, which he had paid to the defendants for shares sold by them respectively. And it charges that the defendants had formed themselves into a society to carry on the fraud. The defendants demurred because the bill contained several and distinct charges against several and distinct defendants. And the demurrer was allowed.

Note: They denied a combination, as is necessary upon such a demurrer as this.

164

Asgill v. Dawson

(Ex. 1721)

The defense of usury cannot be pleaded to a pure bill of discovery.

A plea of usury must allege an illegal agreement.

Bunbury 70, 145 E.R. 598

13 February.

A plea to the discovery and relief in a bill, when the bill prayed only a discovery, was overruled.

Harvard Law School MS. 1082, vol. 1, p. 51, pl. 1

Hilary term 1721.

This was a bill of discovery of a certain agreement between the plaintiff [Asgill] and the defendants [Dawson and Dell] concerning the sum of £4200 lent by the plaintiff to the defendant Dawson on £400 South Sea stock, to which bill the defendant pleads the Statute of Usury setting forth that £150 was the loan of this £4200 for three weeks, but he does not set forth that it was *corrupte aggreatum*.

Serjeant *Chesshyre*, for the defendant, [argued] that this was a good plea at law and so in equity and that it makes the whole contract void and might be as well pleaded to the discovery as to the relief.

Mr. *Reeves*, for the defendant: This contract is totally void on the Statute of 29 Car. II and 12 of Queen Anne. And though it does not appear on the face of the contract, yet the plea of a usurious contract is good at law and so in equity.

Sir Constantine Phipps, for the plaintiff: This plea is neither good in substance or in form, first, because the plea is a discovery and, therefore, cannot be in bar of it. And as to form, it is not averred in the plea to be a corrupt agreement and no relief is prayed by this bill, but it is only purely a bill of discovery.

Chief Baron [Bury] thought that this bill was not in order for relief and that the plea was good as to that and it is a good plea *in toto*.

Price: I take this to be purely a bill of discovery, and the plea is not good. Dean and Chapter of Westminster v. Herbert.[1] And it is wrong in form. And the rules of pleading ought to be strict. And it ought to be alleged to be a corrupt agreement, which is not. And therefore, the plea ought to be overruled.

Montagu: It is a bill of discovery only. And, therefore, the plea is not good.

Page: No relief is prayed. And this plea cannot be allowed in bar to a bill of discovery. And no decree can be made if you reply to this plea. And it is wrong in form, for it is not averred to be a corrupt agreement.

And the plea was overruled.

---

[1] *Dean and Chapter of Westminster v. Cross* (Ex. 1720), see above, Case No. 126.

165

Rhodes v. Lovit

(Ex. 1721)

Where a seller contracts to deliver, the buyer need not accept a delivery from a third party.

Pleadings cannot be amended after a verdict has been set aside and a new trial ordered.

Bunbury 70, 145 E.R. 598

Eodem die [13 February 1721].

In an action upon a contract for the sale of stock, the plaintiff averred in his declaration *quod paratus fuit* at the day to transfer. Upon the evidence, it appeared that the plaintiff had another person ready to transfer. And [there was] a verdict for the plaintiff, for which reason a new trial was moved for and granted because the defendant was not obliged to accept this stock from a third person.

Harvard Law School MS. 1082, vol. 1, p. 56, pl. 3

Hilary term 1721.

[In an] action upon the contract for 1000 London Assurance and the plaintiff avowed that he was ready to deliver at the time of opening the books for that he had a trustee ready to transfer and the verdict was for the plaintiff [. . .] a new trial [was] ordered because [there was] no privity with the defendant and such trustee.

Taussig MS. 311, vol. 1, p. 16, pl. 1

Easter term 1721. Lovell v. Rhodes.

A motion was made to amend the declaration and to add in the declaration according to the truth of the contract, 'transfer or cause to be transferred'. This was after a trial had, but a new trial being granted, and this motion was made for amending the declaration before the new trial, and it was said that the record must be a new record and so [it would be] no inconvenience, all other things being in paper as if no trial had been had.

But the court refused to admit any such amendment after a trial.

166

Glanvill v. Trelawney

(Ex. 1721)

The owner of an impropriation must be made a party to a suit to establish a modus decimandi *in lieu of tithes in kind.*

Bunbury 70, 145 E.R. 598,
1 Rayner 154, 2 Gwillim 622, 1 Eagle & Younge 753

24 February 1721.

Where a man prefers a bill to establish a *modus* against the lessee of the impropriation, he must make the owner of the impropriation a party, for this court will not bind the inheritance of any person unless he is before the court.

[Order of 1 June 1719: 2 Wood 126.]

167

Frost v. Dawes

(Ex. 1721)

If a plaintiff in error does not transcribe the record and assign errors, the plaintiff below can get execution of his judgment.

Harvard Law School MS. 1082, vol. 1, p. 49, pl. 1

Hilary term 1721.

Sir Constantine Phipps and *Bootle*, for the defendant in error, moved that the plaintiff might transcribe the record or that the defendant might be at liberty to take out an execution. And this was a writ of error in Parliament after a *non prosequitur* of a writ of error in the [Court of] Exchequer Chamber. And they cited Perry v. Johnson, in this court, to the same purpose.

Montagu doubted because the writ of error was not transcribed in the Exchequer Chamber so that there was nothing to take notice of, but after the manner of entering up the *non prosequitur* was read and, thereby, it appearing to be a formal judgment, he changed his opinion and, with the rest of the court, allowed the motion.

Bunbury 69, 145 E.R. 598

23 January 1720/21.

A writ of error was non prossed in the Exchequer Chamber for want of assigning errors. And upon that, a writ of error was brought in the House of Lords, but the second was not transcribed according to the order within fourteen days. Therefore, upon motion on the behalf of the defendant in error, it was ordered that the record should be transcribed in eight days and certified into Parliament or the defendant in error to be at liberty to take out execution.

168
Hicks v. Goulding
(Ex. 1721)

Removing cattle to a place where no tithes in kind are due shortly before they give birth is a fraud on the rector.

A question in this case was whether, upon a general allegation of a non decimando, *the parishioner can give in evidence a* modus decimandi *in lieu of tithes in kind.*

Taussig MS. 311, vol. 1, p. 5

Monday, February the 6th, 1720[/21].

The plaintiff, as rector of Broughton Gifford, exhibited his bill for tithes of calves and tithes of hay. And he complained that, in such a year, the defendant had cows, which he kept upon his own lands *in parochia praedicta*, that, just before the time of calving, he removed the said cows into other lands of the same parish, which other lands paid a composition to the plaintiff for all tithes therefrom arising. And this, the plaintiff complains, was done by the defendant in order to defraud him of his tithes of calves.

The defendant confesses he removed the cows and that they calved in the lands under the composition. But he insists that this was no fraud, but that he had the right so to do. And, as to the tithes of hay, he says that the place where was exempt and free from payment of tithes, without showing how.

Upon the hearing, it appeared by the depositions that the removal of the cows was in order to let the calves drop in the lands which were under the composition and that the defendant had gone about the parish to inquire for land under such composition for the purpose aforesaid and the lands where the calves were dropped were two acres of stubble.

Et per CURIAM: This is a plain fraud. And they decreed an account of the tithe calves.

As to the tithe hay, the defendant would have been let in to prove that the place where was four acres of meadow and that the meadow was divided into several parts and one part was allotted to the parson in lieu of tithes.

Sed non allocatur, for [it was said] by the court that is not in issue. The defendant should have showed this in his answer, for his defense now amounts to no more than a *non decimando* and he shall not be admitted to help it by evidence.

The Chief Baron [BURY] hesitated a little because, in cases where the defendant does show a particular discharge, there are added general words or by some other lawful ways or means, which, by him, is altogether as uncertain as the present defense.

Sed per alios barones: Evidence in such cases can only be applied to the discharge particularly pleaded.

Et per Baron Page: The use of the general words is to prevent the parties' being concluded by that suit in case he should hereafter find out another lawful discharge though he was not now capable of proving the particular discharge pleaded.

Et per totam curiam, an account was decreed according to the demand of the bill.

Harvard Law School MS. 1082, vol. 1, p. 50, pl. 1

Hilary term 1721.

This was a bill for tithes and a fraud particularly charged for removing the cows just before calving into two acres of stubble and other lands, for which the defendant was under a composition with the complainant. And for some part of the lands and tithes, the defendant generally insists upon a tender for [an]other part that it was free generally but does not particularly set forth how and in what manner exempt.

Mr. *Ward*, for the plaintiff: As to the first, concerning the fraud, it is plainly proved; as to the second, there is no tender in the answer and, therefore, [it is] not good; and as to the third, saying it is tithe free without showing how or in what manner was never allowed in pleading, and, therefore, a general account ought to be directed for all these matters.

Mr. *Edlin*, for the plaintiff: As to the last point, concerning tithe free generally, that it was never allowed, he cited Bridge v. Wall, in this court, sittings after Trinity 1717.

Sir Constantine Phipps, for the defendant, insisted as to the fraud that it was only removing from one part of the parish to another part in the same parish, which ought not to be construed fraud. [He said] that saying it was tithe free or exempt generally that was sufficient to entitle the defendant to read his depositions. But [he] gave up the point as to the tender.

Chief Baron [Bury]: As to the last point, saying it was tithe free, [he] thought it sufficient to read the depositions as saying that it was belonging to some religious house or discharged by virtue of that or 'other lawful ways and means', which are general words.

Price, Montagu, [and] Page [were] against it and that the defendant ought not to be suffered to read upon pleading so generally.

But Page said that, upon those general words of 'lawful way and means', the defendant can only read as to the first discharge as belonging to a religious house and to no other.

Note: I take this to be a mistake, for a defendant is at liberty to set up any other exemption by virtue of those words.

[Order of 6 February 1720[/21]: 2 Wood 165.]

169

Whittingham v. Chaldron

(Ex. 1721)

Different receivers for the revenue of the crown can be separately appointed for different parts of a county without being liable for the receipts from the whole county.

Taussig MS. 311, vol. 1, p. 4, pl. 1

Hilary term 1720[/21]. Whittingham v. Chaldron, executor of [*blank*], receiver of the County of Devon.

Two receivers were appointed for the County of Devon and for separate parts of the said county, and they gave separate security. It was moved that each of them may pass their accounts separately. And a precedent was showed where this was granted upon a former motion.

But the court doubted and directed [them] to give notice to the Attorney General and ordered the conditions to be brought before the court.

By the Chief Baron [Bury]: It is but one account for the whole county.

Taussig MS. 311, vol. 1, p. 13, pl. 2

Hilary term 1720[/21].

Mr. Attorney General [*Raymond*] appeared and admitted that the commissioners were several and the duplicates were several. The commissions were for part of the County of Lincoln, *viz.* naming such places.

The court now thought, the Attorney not opposing it and the certificate of the auditor asserting that it had been done before, that these persons might pass their accounts severally. And they made an order accordingly.

170

Lightbound v. Russell

(Ex. 1721)

A privilege to be sued in another court must be formally pleaded.

A question in this case was when can a defendant plead a privilege to be sued in another court.

A bail bond for lack of a timely appearance will not be set aside so that the defendant can plead in abatement.

Harvard Law School MS. 1082, vol. 1, p. 52

Hilary term 1720/21.

Mr. *Raby* moved, for the defendant, that proceedings might be stayed on a [writ of] *distringas* against the defendant, who had his writ of privilege as an attorney of the [Court of] King's Bench, and that the plaintiff's privilege as *debitor domini regis* was a common suggestion and nothing in it. 2 Bulstrode 36; Hardres 316, 365; Dyer 287.[1]

The court said that they could do nothing with it but by way of plea and so denied the motion.

Upon the former motion, the court having told the defendant that he ought to plead his privilege, which the defendant did accordingly and so insisted upon for the defendant that the privilege of this court being allowed in other courts, as the Court of Chancery in Harvey v. Hatton, and so the same regard will be paid by this court to other courts. And, therefore, he moved that this plea should be received.

Mr. *Bootle*, for the plaintiff, [argued] that the defendant comes too late to have this plea received, for the writ was returnable *octabis Hilarii*, though not actually returned until the third instant. And, therefore, the plea of privilege ought to have come in within four days of the term, which are mentioned in the writ, though the same is not actually returned. The proceedings upon the bail bond are regular. And the same being assigned, it is too late to receive a plea in abatement. And the writ of privilege ought to be annexed to the plea.

Sir Constantine Phipps, for the defendant: I admit that the privilege ought to be pleaded, but I hope the court will not think that this bail bond is regularly assigned pending the application to this court. And he insisted that the plea of privilege was proper within four days after the actual return of the writ. In Hardres' and Lutwyche's reports, it is said that a plea of privilege may be received so far as after an imparlance, but that is not contended for here.

Mr. *Ward*, for the defendant, insisted on a difference between the return in the writ and the return of the writ, which last is the actual return. Hardres 265, 316.

Chief Baron [Bury]: The plaintiff's proceedings are regular. But I do not know but that we may stay proceedings and receive the plea of privilege if you will take notice of trial.

Price: I think that it is hard upon the defendant. And I think we ought not to permit the plaintiff to proceed upon the bail bond and [it was] never denied on payment of costs. I think within four days after the actual return is time enough for a writ of privilege.

Montagu: All the plaintiff's proceedings are regular. And it is too late to receive a dilatory plea. And where a man has his privilege, he ought to have always his writ of privilege ready. And it is too late after an appearance. Browning's

[1] *Anonymous* (1612), 2 Bulstrode 36, 80 E.R. 939; *Carterett v. Massam* (1662), Hardres 316, 145 E.R. 475; *Clapham v. Lenthall* (1664), Hardres 365, 145 E.R. 499, also British Library MS. Hargrave 62, f. 4v, pl. 2; *Anonymous* (1570), 3 Dyer 287, 73 E.R. 643.

Case, King's Bench; 9 Edw. IV, Young's Case; Dyer, Lassell's Case.[1] If the privilege is [pleaded] before bail, then it ought to be received.

PAGE: It is not sufficient to bring the writ tested the first day of the term, but it ought to be actually brought within the four days. And so it was in the case of the University of Cambridge. This plea must be pleaded within four days on the writ, and the actual return of the writ is not material, for sometimes the writ is never returned so that the defendant is out of time and the plea ought not to be received.

If the bail bond is regularly assigned, it is too late to receive a dilatory plea, which a writ of privilege is. If the defendant will plead in chief and go to trial, I will stay proceedings on the bail bond. See Brooke, [*Abr.*], tit. Privilege; Salkeld, [Reports], tit. Privilege, [pp. 543–546].

Note that Mr. *Marriot*, the Master, next day, reported the practice to be that the defendant must appear within four days after the return day in the writ though the writ is not returned and that proceedings on a bail bond are never stayed in order to receive a dilatory plea. So nothing was granted on the former motion. But the next day the subject matter being a South Sea contract upon an affidavit that the books were in great confusion and not be come at, the trial was put off until next term.

Taussig MS. 311, vol. 1, p. 4, pl. 2

Hilary term 1720[/21].

A *quo minus* issued out of this court against the defendant. And he sued out a *supersedeas* to the sheriff alleging himself to be an attorney of the King's Bench. The sheriff, not returning the *quo minus*, was several times amerced.

And Mr. *Raby* now moved the court in behalf, as he pretended, of the sheriff to stop the amercements. And he cited Hardres 316, 365,[2] that the privilege of [*blank*] being the king's debtor will not hold against the special privilege of the officer of any other court. He also cited 2 Bulstrode 36; Dyer 287; *Thesaurus Brevium* 145.[3]

The court would not make any rule, for the sheriff ought to return the *supersedeas* as a cause for his not returning his writ of *quo minus* if he thinks that the *supersedeas* is an excuse.

After this motion in the Exchequer, Mr. *Raby* went in the King's Bench and there moved the same motion. But the court declared it as their opinion, which they had also done a year before, that no notice was to be taken of such a writ of

---

[1] *Yong v. Clerk of the Hamper* (1470), YB Hil. 9 Edw. IV, f. 53, pl. 18, also Jenkins 131, 145 E.R. 92; *Lord Dacres v. Lassells* (1561), 2 Dyer 196, 73 E.R. 435.

[2] *Carterett v. Massam* (1662), *ut supra*; *Clapham v. Lenthall* (1664), *ut supra*.

[3] *Anonymous* (1612), 2 Bulstrode 36, 80 E.R. 939; *Anonymous* (1570), 3 Dyer 287, 73 E.R. 643; *Thesaurus Brevium*.

privilege, but that the party insisting on a privilege should plead it, and, therefore, they denied his motion.

Ex relatione Fazakerly.

Taussig MS. 311, vol. 1, p. 8, pl. 2

Hilary term 1720[/21].

This case was again moved, but now upon a different foot, for the sheriff having actually returned the writ of *quo minus*, the plaintiff went and obtained an assignment of the bail bond and proceeded thereupon and the defendant, having put in bail, gave notice that he would move the court to set aside the proceedings upon the bail bond and to supersede the original action, by which last expression, as he explained it by his counsel, he intended no more than to obtain that the plaintiff should proceed against him in the original action and that he might have liberty to plead his privilege thereto. And he now produced to the court a writ under the seal of the King's Bench directed to the barons to supersede the suit here, whereas the former writ was only a writ to the sheriff to supersede his arresting him. And this writ directed to the barons was tested the 23 January and was now produced to the court.

N.B. The *quo minus* was a special *quo minus* and returnable at the first return of the term. And the question was whether the court would set aside these proceedings upon the bail bond and let the party in to plead his privilege.

Bury, Chief Baron, and Price inclined to do it; Montagu and Page *contra*.

As to the first part of the motion, the Chief Baron and Price said that the court had certainly a power over these proceedings upon the bail bond and had often set them aside in order to come at the merits of the cause, that though it is true that the bail bond was forfeited by the defendant's non-appearance on the *quarto die post* and the assignment of the bond was strictly regular, yet on the other side, it was a very hasty proceeding, especially in this case where the sheriff had applied to the court for their direction in the point of returning the writ in virtue whereof this bond had been taken and, therefore, the defendant having been under these doubts and difficulties, it was hard to preclude him from a legal defense and privilege by such proceedings, that the defendant has had no opportunity of pleading his privilege, for, to them, it seemed doubtful whether the defendant was obliged to appear and put in bail within four days after the return mentioned in the writ or within four days after the actual return of the writ, then the defendant was to be admitted to his plea, for he applied to the court for the allowance of his privilege before the actual return *inde*.

But Montagu and Page [were] *contra* and said that, where a privilege was claimed as an attorney or officer of another court than that where he was sued, he ought not to appear to the writ, but bring his writ of privilege to the court and pray an allowance of it. And for this MONTAGU cited Justice Younge's Case in the 9th of Edw. IV, fol. 53, pl. 18.[1]

But the points of that case are two, *scil.* that, where the Justice sued the Clerk of the Hamper in the Exchequer by a bill and the Clerk imparled to Hilary term and then brought a *supersedeas* upon this reason, that he ought to be sued in the Chancery only, that the *supersedeas* ought not to be allowed because the Clerk, by imparlance, had affirmed the jurisdiction. Secondly, they held that the Clerk of the Hamper might be sued in the Exchequer, being an accountant, as well as in the Chancery. And this case was determined by all the justices in the Exchequer Chamber, the case being put to them by Illingworth, then Chief Baron, *et ibidem dicitur* that no *supersedeas* lies to the King's Bench *propter dignitatem* where an officer of the Exchequer is sued there, but the record of his account is to be sent there, but a *supersedeas* lies to the Common Bench in such cases.

Taussig MS. 311, vol. 1, p. 13, pl. 1

Hilary term 1720[/21].

A special *quo minus* was returned the first return of the term, 10 or 11 January; he was arrested and gave a bail bond. The bail bond was assigned 4th February. The constant practice is that a bail bond, if bail is not put in within four days after the return of the writ, is forfeited. Secondly, the court never give way to setting aside a bail bond in order to plead a dilatory [plea]. This was the master's report.

171

Attorney General v. Payman

(Ex. 1721)

An estate tail can be found by implication in a will.

Harvard Law School MS. 1082, vol. 1, p. 54

Hilary term 1721.

The court was unanimous in their opinion, and the Chief Baron [BURY] delivered the opinion of the whole court upon the clause of the will which was, after the death of Thomas, the nephew, without issue male, then to trustees for a charity. So the question [was] whether Thomas was a tenant in tail by implication. And it seems to be the will of the testator that Thomas should have an estate tail. And the words in the will are sufficient to carry it. And in a will, it will be construed by implication as much as by explicit words in a conveyance. The devise [was] to Thomas and his first and second son; there can be no estate tail, but

[1] *Yong v. Clerk of the Hamper* (1470), *ut supra.*

it is afterwards by implication. 9 Rept. 128, Sunday's Case; 2 Levinz 28, King v. Mellish; 1 Ventris 225, 232; Lisle v. Gray in Raymond and Levinz reports, Sir Thomas Jones 115; 11 Rept. 79.[1]

[To the] objection of Cro. Eliz., Arden's Case, [he] answered 2 Saunders 386.[2]

I do think Langley v. Baldwin, in the Common Pleas in 1708,[3] is a very strong case in favor of our opinion. So he pronounced judgment for the defendant that Thomas, the nephew, had an estate tail.

Taussig MS. 311, vol. 1, p. 11

Hilary term 1720[/21]. Attorney General v. Sutton and Paman.

Chief Baron [Bury] delivered the opinion of the court. So long as J.S. had issue of his body, the remainderman was to have nothing. In this case, there are no more remainders than to the first and second son and their issue male so that he might have other sons to whom he had not expressly provided, and, therefore, he provided for them in general inclusively by this clause, for issue male cannot take but in his ancestor. 9 Rep. 218, Sunday's Case, which case proves that if an estate be given to A. and if he dies without issue male of his body, this is an entail. 2 Levinz 58, 61; 1 Ventris 232, 225, Melling's Case.

[To the] objection of express estate for life, [he] answered, in Melling's Case, the estate is expressly limited for life, so that objection is answered, for it was there held an entail. Pollexfen 582, Lisle's Case, T. Jones 115, Raymond's Reports; 1 Rolle's *Abridgment*, 77; Lewis Bowles' Case, 11 Rep.[4]

[To the] objection that here are contingent remainders intermediate between the issue male and the estate for life, as in the case in Cro. Eliz. 315, [he] answered this case is exploded. 2 Saunders 286 denies it to be [good] law. And so this objection is answered. Langley and Baldwin's case was referred to the justices of the Common Bench out of the Chancery, and they give their opinions under their hands, which exactly agrees with our opinion (Trevor, Tracy, Blencowe, and Dormer).

---

[1] *Sonday's Case* (1611), 9 Coke Rep. 127, 77 E.R. 915; *King v. Melling* (1672), 1 Ventris 225, 86 E.R. 151, also 1 Ventris 214, 86 E.R. 144, Pollexfen 101, 86 E.R. 526, 3 Keble 42, 52, 95, 84 E.R. 584, 589, 614, 2 Levinz 58, 83 E.R. 448, 3 Salkeld 296, 91 E.R. 835, 1 Eq. Cas. Abr. 181, 21 E.R. 973; *Lisle v. Gray* (1680), T. Raymond 278, 302, 315, 83 E.R. 143, 156, 163, 2 Levinz 223, 83 E.R. 529, T. Jones 114, 84 E.R. 1174, also 1 Freeman 462, 89 E.R. 345, 2 Shower K.B. 6, 89 E.R. 758, Pollexfen 582, 86 E.R. 653, Dodd 34; *Bowles v. Bury* (1615), 11 Coke Rep. 79, 77 E.R. 1253, also 1 Rolle Rep. 177, 81 E.R. 413.

[2] *Purefoy v. Rogers* (1671), 2 Williams Saunders 380, 85 E.R. 1181, also 2 Levinz 39, 83 E.R. 443, 3 Keble 11, 84 E.R. 566, 1 Eq. Cas. Abr. 189, 21 E.R. 980, Lincoln's Inn MS. Misc. 500, ff. 192, 194b (Edward Ward's Reports).

[3] *Langley v. Baldwin* (1707), 1 Eq. Cas. Abr. 185, 21 E.R. 976.

[4] *Lisle v. Gray* (1680), *ut supra*; *Bowles v. Bury* (1615), *ut supra*.

And so judgment was against the Attorney General.

[On appeal: 1 Peere Williams 754, 24 E.R. 600, 3 Brown P.C. 75, 1 E.R. 1187, 2 Eq. Cas. Abr. 314, 22 E.R. 266.]

172

Powell v. Powell

(Ex. 1721)

In this case, the defendant parishioner proved a modus decimandi *in lieu of tithes in kind and the plaintiff vicar failed to prove a right to tithes by an endowment or by prescription.*

Harvard Law School MS. 1082, vol. 1, p. 55

Hilary term 1721.

The plaintiff, as vicar of Landino in the County of Monmouth, brings his bill for tithes. The defendant insists, as to part, upon 2d. for every day moath payable to the vicar and, as to the other part, that tithes in kind were never paid and that, though, in this case, it was clover that was the question, yet that it was of the same species with hay and, therefore, included in the same *modus*.

And so [it was] insisted on by Mr. *Ward*, counsel for the defendants, that clover is of the same species and included in the same *modus*, and [it was] so settled several times in this court and likewise in Lutwyche 1071, Durrant v. Bottle.[1] And it does not appear in this case that the plaintiff ever received coleseed. And a vicar being only entitled by usage or endowment and he not showing that he is entitled by either, Your Lordship cannot make a decree in favor of the plaintiff. And so it was adjudged in this court in December 1710, Wright, vicar of Stepney v. Elderton,[2] where the summer crop of turnips had always been received by the vicar, but the question was on a winter crop of turnips, which is a second crop and new increase, but [there was] no proof that the vicar ever received the winter crop, for which reason, it was decreed against the vicar.

As to the other part of the defense, it appears no tithes were ever paid and, therefore, the vicar not showing usage or endowment, he cannot be entitled. Town of Warwick v. Lucas, 1710,[3] where, in the case of a lay impropriator, a real discharge is supposed.

[1] *Durrant v. Booty* (1701), 2 Lutwyche 1071, 125 E.R. 595, 2 Gwillim 578, 1 Eagle & Younge 639.

[2] *Wright v. Elderton* (Ex. 1710), Dodd 224, Eq. Cases Exch. 659, 1 Rayner 119, 1 Eagle & Younge 694, 2 Gwillim 607, Public Record Office, E.126/19, ff. 149, 250, 1 Wood 518.

[3] *Corporation of Warwick v. Lucas* (1711), Eq. Cases Exch. 671, Public Record Office, E.126/19, ff. 191, 221.

And as to the 2d. for a day moath, that is certain enough, for a day moath is as much as a man can mow in a day and well known in the country. 2 Cro. 116, Green v. Austen.[1]

Clover, though a late invention, falls under the same genus as hay. [To the] objection that it is seed but that arises from the separation, [he] answered the court turned the plaintiff to prove that these tithes had been received by the vicar.

To which, Mr. *Cox*, Sr., counsel for the plaintiff, answered what the court said for that the defendants insist on a *modus* payable to the vicar for tithe hay, which shows that the vicar is entitled to hay and, therefore, there was no occasion to show any tithes paid for hay, since something is payable in lieu of it. [He said] that day moath is uncertain and that foyne is a new increase.

Mr. *Edlin*, for the plaintiff, insisted that 2d. for a day moath is too uncertain, and so [is] 1 Keble 612, Took v. Ledgeerd,[2] for what can be more uncertain than a man's strength, for one man may mow as much again as another.

But the court said that the *modus* was certain enough and dismissed the bill because there was no proof, either by endowment or prescription, for the plaintiff's demand.

Note *quod mirum est* for that the defendants had insisted on a *modus* payable to the vicar in lieu of tithe hay, which shows that the vicar is entitled. And, therefore, [there was] no occasion to show any further payment.

[Order of 23 February 1720[/21]: 2 Wood 166.]

173

Morrison v. Allgood

(Ex. 1721)

The Register of the Court of Exchequer can practice as a solicitor and clerk in the Exchequer, and he can sue there a bill in equity for his fees as such.

Harvard Law School MS. 1082, vol. 1, p. 56, pl. 1

Hilary term 1720/21.

This bill [was] brought by the plaintiff, who was Register of the Court of Exchequer, for fees as a solicitor and clerk in the office, to which it was objected that it was a matter properly triable at law. And another objection [was] that, as Register, he could not practice as an attorney or solicitor and, therefore, that the bill ought to be dismissed.

But the court overruled both objections and decreed the defendant to account, *quod vide.*

---

1 *Green v. Austen* (1606), Croke Jac. 116, 79 E.R. 100, also Yelverton 86, 80 E.R. 59, 1 Eagle & Younge 164.

2 *Took v. Ledgierd* (1663), 1 Keble 612, 83 E.R. 1142, 1 Eagle & Younge 440.

174

Bodwell v. Bishop of Meath

(Ex. 1721)

The Statute of Limitations does not bar an action for a current account.

Harvard Law School MS. 1082, vol. 1, p. 57, pl. 1

Hilary term 1720/21.

[There was a] bill of discovery and account, and so [it] prayed relief against the defendant, who pleads the Statute of Limitations[1] in bar, *viz.* that six years had elapsed before any suit [was] commenced or subpoena served, to which last words there was great exception because [there can be] no occasion for the service of the subpoena, which cannot be until after the bill is filed.

Chief Baron [Bury] thought that it appeared on the face of the bill and the proceedings to be an account current and, therefore, the Statute ought not to interpose, but the plea ought to be overruled.

Price: This is a bill of discovery as well as relief, and this plea goes to both and, therefore, ought to be overruled and likewise upon the same reason with the Chief Baron because it is an account current.

Montagu: I think that you cannot compel a discovery where the discovery is the jet of the thing. But in the case where a bill of discovery is for writings only, as in the case of the Dean and Chapter of Westminster v. Herbert,[2] there, such a plea was and ought to be overruled. But I think that this plea is not good in form for the promise is not denied to be within the six years, which [it] ought to be, the rather because the bill charges promises in subsequent years.

And so the plea was overruled, *quod vide.*

175

Anonymous

(Ex. 1721)

In this case, the plaintiff was allowed to amend an information qui tam.

Taussig MS. 311, vol. 1, p. 7

Hilary term 1720[/21].

Mr. *Bunbury* moved to amend an information *qui tam* grounded upon 8 Anne, ca. 9,[3] which charges 6d. per pound on every sum under £50 and 12d. per

[1] Stat. 21 Jac. I, c. 16 (*SR*, IV, 1222–1223).

[2] *Dean and Chapter of Westminster v. Cross* (Ex. 1720), see above, Case No. 126.

[3] Stat. 8 Ann., c. 5, s. 40 (*SR*, IX, 193).

pound on every sum exceeding £50, which shall 'be given, paid, contracted, or agreed for with . . . every apprentice'. The amendment desired was that, instead of charging the money as paid, he might alter it and make it contracted to be paid.

Mr. *Bootle* opposed the motion and said this was vitiating instead of amending the information. But he said this not knowing the words of the Statute were, as above, paid or contracted to be paid.

The Chief Baron [Bury] said it was not proper to allow an amendment which destroyed the declaration.

By the other barons: This is at the discretion of the plaintiff. And, therefore, they thought the plaintiff ought to have his motion however the words of the Act were.

And thus the plaintiff had his motion upon payment of costs, all being yet in the paper.

176

Note

(Ex. 1721)

A defendant must sign his answer when he swears to it.

Taussig MS. 311, vol. 1, p. 8, pl. 1

Hilary term 1720[/21].

The court made a rule that the defendant should sign his answer when he came to swear it. And this is to prevent the answers being sworn by a supposititious person.

177

Rex v. Rawlins

(Ex. 1721)

The crown can take possession of land leased by its debtor and evict a sub-lessee.

Bunbury 71, 145 E.R. 599

27 February 1721

Upon a [writ of] extent, an inquisition was taken, which found a term of so much value. The defendant pleaded to the inquisition, and it was found for the crown. And this day, it was insisted for the defendant that the court should order a [writ of] *venditioni exponas*, for, if the crown was to be put into possession, the defendant, who was to have the residue of the term after the crown is satisfied, would be without a remedy. But afterwards, 20 May 1721, *per opinionem* totius curiae, an injunction was awarded to put the crown into possession.

Harvard Law School MS. 1082, vol. 1, p. 56, pl. 2

Hilary term 1721.

Mr. *Bootle*, for the king, moved for the injunction of this court to put the crown into possession where [it was] upon a plea put in to an extent and inquisition and a verdict found for the king. And this was a lease for years in a house in Covent Garden.

And it was said by the court that, in an information of intrusion, there, it is proper to grant an injunction to put the crown into possession, for, there, the crown is entitled to the whole. But, upon an extent for a debt due to the crown, the only proper thing for the crown to pray for is to have a *venditioni exponas* to sell the term, for, after the crown is satisfied, the party is entitled to the remainder. So, in this case, a *venditioni exponas* was ordered, but not an injunction.

Harvard Law School MS. 1082, vol. 1, p. 58

Easter term 1721.

The Attorney General [*Raymond*] moved for an injunction to put the crown into possession of a house, which was held for a term of years, which term was found by inquisition and after a plea was pleaded, verdict, and judgment for the crown. It was said that this was a seizure in law and that the crown might sell this term and why may it not put the crown into possession and the crown may have a *venditioni exponas*. But suppose that the term is valued at too little. [He] cited Bouden v. Receiver of Salop.

Sir Constantine Phipps, for the defendant: This was moved the 23 of February last and denied, and there is no reason to grant it, and so it is void not having found the term certain. I admit precedents where lands or houses are actually seized and where the term for years is only seized *quod valet ad vendendum* and a *venditioni exponas* ought to issue and no other proceeding. And there is another inconvenience that the law will not suffer, which is that the king would be tenant to the ground landlord and it is below the dignity of the crown so to be.

The Attorney General [*Raymond*] replies, as to the objection of the uncertainty in the inquisition, that is now over, for here is a judgment, and so that is over.

[As to the] objection [of] no seizure of the term itself, [he] answered *terminus annorum* includes the house.

[As to the] objection that the king cannot be a tenant, [he] answered are not all the leases in cases of high treason forfeited and would not there be the same objection? Where is the prejudice and why may not the crown proceed this way?

Mr. *Bootle* replies for the king: The term ought to be seized in the king's hands.

[As to the] objection of finding the term and the house, [he] answered surely that house is included in the term and the constant form of pleading is *de interesse termini* and that he was possessed of the house and so the *terminus* includes it. And if the term is sold, must not the house be sold if this had been found generally of a term of such a yearly value and because of the words '*valet ad vendendum*'? Therefore, now, it would be urged that the crown should be deprived of the benefit of being put into possession and [there is] no difference between the seizure whether it was of a freehold or a term. And where it is a freehold, it is not doubted but an injunction may be awarded.

[These] precedents were read in court, 21 February 1703, George Hories' Case.

Sir Constantine Phipps: The precedents are nothing to the purpose, for the lands there were of a seisin in fee. And as in the case of leases cited by Mr. Attorney General in cases of treason, there, the lands themselves are seized, and nothing but the term, in this case, is found by inquisition.

The Chief Baron [Bury] thought it would be hard to turn the under-lessee out of possession.

Price: I think that it is a paradox that the crown may have an election to sell or to have an injunction to put the crown into possession. If a term in a house and the house are not the same, then the distinction is proper, but I see no difference and, though a *venditioni exponas* is proper, yet [it is] not debarred by the other. And I know of no difference between selling and putting the party into possession. And if there is any distinction, it is without a difference.

Page: I think that the king has an election for selling or to be put into possession. And if the king cannot be a tenant, then leases for years cannot be forfeited, as in cases of high treason. This is an interest and authority vested together. And I think an injunction is very proper to turn the seisin in law into a seisin in fact.

And so [it was] granted unless a cause [be shown to the contrary on] Monday. And there being no cause showed, the order for an injunction to put the crown into possession was [made] absolute.

Taussig MS. 311, vol. 1, p. 49

Easter term 1721.

Mr. Attorney General [*Raymond*] moved the court that the crown might be put into possession of a house, which was seized into the king's hands upon an extent and inquisition that found that A. was possessed *de termino annorum de et in uno messuagio adtunc durante et nemine expirato* without saying for what number of years. And, to this inquisition, B. comes in and pleads a title, *viz.* an assignment of this very term. And the Attorney General replied that the assignment was by fraud. And, upon the trial, a verdict was for the king and judgment. And now, the crown moved for an injunction to be put into possession of the house. And it was said there were many precedents of this in the Office.

Sir Constantine Phipps, to the contrary: The inquisition is void, for the term is not described. Secondly, the crown cannot be put into possession of the house when a term of years only is seized because the term seized does not necessarily include the possession of the house. Thirdly, the reason why the crown is never put into possession of terms is because it is not decent for him to become a tenant to another landlord. 21 February 1703, George Hosier's Case. This was a case where the king was put into possession of a fee simple by an injunction.

Per Baron PRICE: The king has certainly an election either to have the things seized or the value of them. And, therefore, if he is entitled to sell the house, he may have the house. And by him and the other barons, *possessionatus de et in uno messuagio pro termino annorum* and *possessionatus de et in termino annorum de et in uno messuagio* is the same.

Sed quaere per me [Philip Ward], for, if A. is lessee for twenty years of a house and enters and is possessed and makes an under-lease to C. for five years, A., in this case, is not possessed of the house, but he is possessed of a term of years in the house, *viz. de et in termino 20 annorum de et in messuagio.*

N.B. Sir Gerrard Fleetwood's Case, 8 Rep. 17.[1] It is in the election of the sheriff to extend or sell a lease. In this case, the court granted an injunction *nisi.*

178

Pye v. Rea

(Ex. 1721)

Where a vicar sues for tithes and the defendant pleads an exemption from paying tithes, the burden of proof lies on the defendant.

Bunbury 72, 145 E.R. 599,
1 Rayner 155, 2 Gwillim 628, 1 Eagle & Younge 755

27 April 1721.

A bill was brought by a vicar for tithes. The defendant admitted in his answer that the plaintiff was entitled to all sorts of tithes, but he insisted upon a special exemption. Upon this admission, the plaintiff was not obliged to show any special title, either by endowment or prescription, which, otherwise, he ought to have done.

Harvard Law School MS. 1082, vol. 1, p. 61, pl. 1

Easter term 1721.

[To a] bill as vicar, the defendant insisted on a discharge of the tithe wood because it was belonging to a priory called the Priory Wood.

Mr. *Edlin*, for the defendant, [said] that the vicar ought to show that he was entitled by endowment or prescription. And so [he] cited Powell v. Powell, last term.[2]

Sir Constantine Phipps and *Ward*, for the plaintiff, answered the objection by saying that the defendant had insisted on a special discharge, which the defendant ought to prove.

[1] *Fleetwood's Case* (1610), 8 Coke Rep. 171, 77 E.R. 731.

[2] *Powell v. Powell* (Ex. 1721), see above, Case No. 172.

Note: It was said in this case that the lesser monasteries might be continued by letters patent to 31 Hen. VIII, and, if then discharged, that then the lands are as well discharged from tithes as the greater monasteries.

[Order of 27 April 1721: 2 Wood 170.]

179

Lock, *qui tam* v. Williford

(Ex. 1721)

An information upon a seizure of goods imported unlawfully can be dismissed and a new information upon a different ground can be brought upon the same seizure.

Bunbury 72, 145 E.R. 599

3 May 1721.

Linen was seized and an information was filed for being brought from a wrong port. The officer, finding himself mistaken upon this first information, brings a second for that it was imported, the duty not being paid. And he moved that the second information might be received, which was granted upon these terms, *viz.* that the Attorney General should enter a *non prosequitur* upon the first and the officer should pay the costs. And the second was permitted to bear *teste* as the first did to make it agree with the writ of appraisement and to save the informer's time.

Taussig MS. 311, vol. 1, p. 16, pl. 2

Easter term 1721.

There were two questions: first, whether the officer seizing is obliged to declare the cause of the forfeiture. It was agreed by all that he was not.

Second, supposing an information for one cause of forfeiture and the information is discharged, whether this discharges the seizure or else a new information may be exhibited upon the same seizure for another cause of forfeiture of the same goods. Before trial, it is usual for the Attorney General to *non prosequitur* and then the officer is to exhibit a new one.

But whether, after a judgment upon an information, a new information may be exhibited or no is the difficulty. The difficulty on one side is the loss to the crown by the mistake of the officer. *Ex altera parte* is the perpetual or continual vexation of the subject who will never know an end of his business nor when his goods are discharged from a seizure.

By Price: We never allow an amendment *in casu regis* so as to make a new or different information any more than in the case of a subject. And it is reasonable to discharge one information before you file another.

But here, the motion was to exhibit a new information pending the other information. And the rule of the court was that, upon discharging the first information by *non prosequitur* and paying costs, they might exhibit a new information. In this case, there had been no trial had.

Harvard Law School MS. 1082, vol. 1, p. 57, pl. 2

Easter term 1721.

After a seizure and a former information exhibited and then another information is exhibited for another cause of forfeiture without *non prosequitur* of the first, MONTAGU thought that the crown had an election to lay any cause of forfeiture, but, if not, the Attorney General may exhibit a new information.

PAGE: I think that it is too hard to exhibit a new information, especially for £5, and you cannot plead the former information depending because it is not for the same offense.

PRICE thought it consistent with reason to exhibit a new information. The Attorney General may grant a *nolle prosequi*, and you may file a new information.

BURY: I think that it is too hard to have two informations at the same time.

The court ordered, upon *non prosequitur* [to] the first information and on payment of costs, for liberty to exhibit a new information.

180

Phillips v. Winter

(Ex. 1721)

Where a defendant is given permission to file a late answer or a commission to answer without more, he cannot thereafter demur.

Bunbury 74, 145 E.R. 599

17 May 1721.

Where time is given or a commission is granted to answer without more, the defendant cannot demur or plead and answer.

Taussig MS. 311, vol. 1, p. 43, pl. 1

Easter term 1721. Phillips v. Wentworth.

The defendant had time to answer. And he answered and also demurred, but the demurrer was only to the relief. And the question was whether this was regular.

Per PAGE, Chief Baron [BURY], and MONTAGU: He ought not to demur because this is the same delay as if he had not answered, for he cannot except to an answer until a demurrer is determined.

Per PRICE: You may pray a commission to answer and return a demurrer, *quod fuit negatur per alios* barons and [*blank*]; so if you pray time to answer and demur because this is altering the motion which was granted.

And the court, in this case, set aside the demurrer though it was only to the relief of the bill.

181

Rex v. Blundell

(Ex. 1721)

The crown can collect its debts by either a scire facias *or an* extendi facias.

A question in this case was whether a writ of extent can be granted based on the minutes of a lost record.

Bunbury 74, 145 E.R. 600

Eodem die [17 May 1721].

A *scire facias* was brought against a general receiver upon his bond. And, afterwards, a [writ of] immediate extent was moved for against him upon an affidavit that one of his bail was become bankrupt and he was decayed in his credit. And it was granted, for the king may be at liberty to proceed either by *scire facias* or extent, which is the speedier method, or by both.

Taussig MS. 311, vol. 1, p. 44

Easter term 1721. The King v. Blundell, Receiver General of Leicestershire and Receiver of the Tax on Houses.

Mr. Solicitor General [*Yorke*] moved the court for an immediate extent upon an affidavit which set forth that one of Blundell's securities was failed and absconded, that he had inquired and was informed that he was in arrear in such and such sums that were due all of them half a year ago. And the affidavit was further that he was informed that he had misapplied money so by him received.

And the barons said that a *caveat* did not bind them not to make a warrant for an immediate extent, but only not to grant it without hearing counsel.

An extent was granted.

Mr. Baron Montagu observed that the court was now urged by arguments for granting extents, which, if the rules of their predecessors had been observed, they never could have heard of, for, by the rules of the court, no man liable to a statute of bankruptcy should be a receiver general.

Bunbury 88, 145 E.R. 605

18 November 1721.

The Attorney General [*Raymond*] moved, that the clerk in court might have liberty to newly engross an extent and inquisition thereon, which were lost.

Note: The sheriff had the minutes of what was found by the jury signed by the jury. And this was compared to the case where a person had, in a false name, taken a record from Pickering, the associate in the Oxford circuit; they permitted a new *postea* to be made from the minutes in his book; there had been made out a [writ of] *venditioni exponas* upon the copy of the extent and inquisition that were lost. And there being a consent for Blundell, a new extent etc. was ordered to be engrossed, *dissentiente* MONTAGU.

Harvard Law School MS. 1082, vol. 1, p. 105, pl. 1

Michaelmas term 1721.

The Attorney General [*Raymond*] moved to be at liberty to impose a new extent by a copy, for that the old one was lost among Mr. Butler's papers.

And *Bootle*, for the defendant, consented.

MONTAGU said that it was entirely irregular to grant the motion and you cannot make out a record by a copy and there ought to be another inquisition and the same is not returned so he could not agree to make up such a record.

It was answered that, in the case of Pickering, a new *postea* was ordered where the other was taken away by deceit.

MONTAGU said, in that case, the *postea* was afterwards brought in.

PRICE and PAGE were for granting the motion.

Chief Baron [BURY] and MONTAGU ordered it to be moved again.

182

Gatehouse, *qui tam* v. Reith

(Ex. 1721)

Where perishable goods have been seized, the court will grant possession pendente lite *upon giving security for their value.*

Bunbury 74, 145 E.R. 600

25 May 1721.

Mr. *Ward* moved for a writ of delivery, which was granted, for a parcel of gold watches upon giving security, the springs and steel work being perishable goods and liable to receive damage by lying in a damp warehouse.

183

Smith v. Nottingham

(Ex. 1721)

A court of equity will enjoin execution of a common law judgment for the payment of a harsh bargain.

Bunbury 75, 145 E.R. 600

25 May 1721.

Upon a contract to assign to Smith a £300 [in] the third subscription in the South Sea [Company], on the 28th of August, Smith did covenant upon assigning to pay £1050, for which he gave a bond. And judgment was obtained thereupon in the Common Pleas. Now, Smith prefers his bill for an injunction, and he obtains it because the money the bond was given for was the consideration of the contract. And, this being a mutual agreement, we will not put them to cross-actions at law.

184

Goddard v. Keble

(Ex. 1721–1722)

In order for a modus decimandi *in lieu of tithes in kind to be valid, it must be payable at a fixed time.*

3 Rayner 1097

Goddard, rector of Castle Eaton in Wiltshire, against Kable.

The defendant insisted upon several *modus*es, *viz.* 3d. for a milk cow, 3d. for a lamb, 3d. for a colt, 1d. for a garden, and the like. But they were all set aside in regard that no time for the payment thereof was ascertained by the defendant.

Taussig MS. 311, vol. 1, p. 247, pl. 2

19 April 1722.

The plaintiff, as rector of Castle Eaton in the County of Wiltshire, brings his bill for great and small tithes. The defendant sets up several *modus*es, *viz.* 3d. for milk of every milk cow; 3 for lamb yeaned in the parish; 12 for each dry cow or ox; 1d. for a garden; 1d. for each dry sheep not shorn there; 3d. [for the] fall of every colt; 1s. in 10s. for wool when fed half the year and 1 in 20 when fed the whole year.

Sir Constantine Phipps, for the plaintiff: The defendants are defenseless as to beans and pease, which they admit they had in the garden and which, by him, being great tithes, cannot be covered by the garden penny.

For the defendant: There is a yearly payment alleged in the answer, but the answer sets not forth what day it is payable, but this is not required in English proceedings.

Sed per CURIAM: This is as necessary in a case of English proceedings as in a case of Latin proceedings. And the court decreed an account and would not split costs for the demands which were well answered, nor would they direct any issue because no *modus* was sufficiently set forth whereon to ground an issue.

Bunbury 105, 145 E.R. 611,
1 Rayner 163, 2 Gwillim 631, 1 Eagle & Younge 777

19 April 1722.
A bill was brought by the rector of Castle Eaton in the County of Wilts for tithe.
The defendant insists upon several *modus*es: first, 3d. for every milk cow in lieu of tithe milk; secondly, 3d. for every lamb yeaned in the parish, but this was given up as too rank, for ten three pences amount to the present value of a lamb; thirdly, 1s. for a dry cow and ox depastured etc.; fourthly, one penny for each dry sheep not shorn in the parish; fifthly, 3d. for every colt fallen. It not being alleged at what time these *modus*es were payable, the defendant was decreed to account.
Note: I believe this is the first instance in a court of equity that *modus*es were disallowed upon this reason.

Harvard Law School MS. 1082, vol. 1, p. 123

19th April 1722.

A bill was brought by the plaintiff as rector of Castle Eaton in the County of Wilts for tithes.

The defendant insists upon these *modus*es: first, 3d. for every milk cow in lieu of tithe milk; secondly, 3d. for every lamb yeaned in the parish to be given up to the defendant; thirdly, 1d. for dry cows depastured and ox; fourthly, 1d. for each dry sheep not shorn in the parish; fifthly, 3d. for every colt foaled.

Note: These *modus*es were set forth without alleging at what time the same was payable. If there be a garden penny payable for an ancient garden, if the garden be enlarged, the penny shall not cover that part so enlarged.

Baron Price: There is no certainty in these *modus*es, no time being fixed for the payment of these *modus*es.

Barons Montagu and Page were of the same opinion and thought that 3d. per lamb was a void *modus*.

The defendant was decreed to account, *per* TOTAM CURIAM.

[Order of 19 April 1722: 2 Wood 189.]

185

Woodford v. Crosse

(Ex. 1721)

In pleading a modus decimandi *in lieu of tithes in kind, the date on which the payment is due must be alleged.*

3 Rayner 1097

Woodford, vicar of Ebeshame, *alias* Ensom, in Surrey, against Crosse.

A *modus* was alleged of 4d. a cow for milk and calf, 2d. for a dry beast, 3d. for a lamb, and so on. But no day of payment was set forth by the defendant. It was set aside for that reason.

186

Pemberton v. Sparrow

(Ex. 1721–1722)

In order for a modus decimandi *in lieu of tithes in kind to be valid, it must be payable at a fixed time.*

3 Rayner 1098

Pemberton, vicar of Belchamp St. Paul's in Essex, against Sparrow and others.

Several *moduses* were set aside because no time for the payment of them was ascertained by the defendant's answer.

Harvard Law School MS. 1082, vol. 1, p. 144, pl. 2

7 June 1722.

In a bill for tithes, *moduses* were insisted upon without setting forth the day of payment. Lutwyche 152.

Mr. *Ward*, notwithstanding the resolution in the case of Goddard v. Keeble,[1] insisted upon it that that was the first resolution unless Offley v. Whitehall[2] and that all the precedents both in law and equity before then were otherwise. Hicks v. Woodson, 2 Salkeld; Cooper v. Andrews, Hobart.[3]

The Chief Baron [Montagu] continued of the same opinion as did the other judges, so this point seems established.

Taussig MS. 311, vol. 1, p. 328

7 June 1722.

In this cause, the defendants, by answer, insisted on a *modus* of 7s. 6d. in lieu and satisfaction of vicarial tithes arising on a farm. And they set it forth without assigning any time for the payment of the *modus* and though several precedents

---

[1] *Goddard v. Keble* (Ex. 1721–1722), see above, Case No. 184.

[2] See also *Offley v. Whitehall* (Ex. 1717), above, Case No. 28.

[3] *Hicks v. Woodson* (1697), 2 Salkeld 655, 91 E.R. 558, also Dodd 171, 4 Modern 324, 336, 87 E.R. 422, 429, 1 Eagle & Younge 592, 2 Gwillim 550, 3 Lord Raymond 116, 92 E.R. 595, 1 Lord Raymond 137, 91 E.R. 987, 12 Modern 111, 88 E.R. 1200, Skinner 560, 90 E.R. 252, Comberbach 403, 90 E.R. 555, Carthew 392, 90 E.R. 827, Holt K.B. 671, 90 E.R. 1271; *Cowper v. Andrews* (1614), Hobart 39, 80 E.R. 189, also Moore K.B. 863, 72 E.R. 957, Godbolt 237, 78 E.R. 138, *sub nom. Hooper v. Andrews*, 1 Rolle Rep. 120, 81 E.R. 372, 1 Gwillim 275, 1 Eagle & Younge 240.

of Latin entries, *viz*. Hobart, Cooper v. Andrews, Lutwitch, were cited to prove that this was not requisite, yet the court, *scil.* Chief Baron MONTAGU and PRICE, stuck close to their former resolution and told to the counsel, who asserted that there had never been above two resolutions that the time was necessary [and] that they would now add to the number and make a third.

187

Rex v. Burgold

(Ex. 1721)

The question in this case was whether permission to challenge a writ of extent should be granted after two defaults were returned.

Harvard Law School MS. 1082, vol. 1, p. 59, pl. 1

Easter term 1721. Rex v. Burgold and Salkeld.

Sir Constantine Phipps [moved] for liberty to plead to a [writ of] extent after two nichils returned, which were contrived to overreach a commission of bankruptcy.

Bootle, for the king: It might have been pleaded at first, but it is too late after a judgment, for, after two nichils, the court does award an execution, as an extent.

Sir Constantine Phipps: [There was] no judgment on the two nichils on the *scire facias*, for it is only an order for an extent. If the note was endorsed to Rowclift before the extent, it would be good.

I think that liberty was given to plead.

188

Dean v. North

(Ex. 1721)

A party may orally assign at the hearing additional causes for a demurrer.

In this suit to redeem a mortgage, the plaintiffs did not plead sufficiently, but the court allowed them to amend their bill of complaint.

Harvard Law School MS. 1082, vol. 1, p. 60

Easter term 1721.

A bill to redeem was brought setting forth that John Drury was seised of this estate and that, [on] 4 March 1683, £5600 was lent and a mortgage was made, that Drury died in 1688 and Christopher Dean purchased the equity of redemption and made his will and codicil. And the plaintiff, by his bill, suggests coverture and infancy, that he could not sooner bring his bill, to which the defendant demurs.

First cause: The plaintiff makes no title for John or George Drury and does not set forth that George Drury was entitled to an equity of redemption and no consideration of the release of the equity of redemption.

Second: As to length of time, ever since 1683, the mortgage and no excuse for it.

Third: [He is] not entitled to an account for want of parties.

Sir Constantine Phipps [argued] for the demurrer that Eleanor was the surviving trustee of Christopher Dean and left three children, infants, and it is not said that the children, the plaintiffs, were heirs at law to Eleanor.

Second: [There was] uninterrupted possession ever since 1683.

Third: Account of the profits from 1688, to which the executors of John Drury are entitled, one of which was George Drury, and he is no party.

Mr. *Wilkinson*, for the plaintiff: It is sufficiently alleged in the bill, for the yearly value is said £600, and that is sufficient where only £5600 was lent. The interest was paid until 1688. And for want of further payment, the defendant entered. Now, if the plaintiffs were but three years old so there was infancy until 1705, that is a sufficient excuse as to length of time and the loss of the defeasance which the defendant gave.

Mr. *Bootle* for the plaintiff: As to want of consideration of the release of the equity of redemption, there is no occasion for a consideration, and, if it was voluntary, it is sufficient. A mortgagee is only a trustee for the mortgagor.

Aris, for the defendant, cited Frasier v. Moor[1] as to length of time, in this court.

Price thought forty years possession to be sufficient and a good objection. And in Lord Nottingham's time, twenty years possession was thought sufficient and agreeable to the Statute of Limitations. But they go further for, in Chancery, there was a disability. And I cannot get over the first objection.

Montagu: The cause of demurrer is only as to John and George Drury, and not for want of heirs of Eleanor. And the *cestui que trust* is here, and that is sufficient.

Page: Perhaps a *cestui que trust* may bring a bill without the trustee, but it does not appear that he is a *cestui que trust*. But I think that a trustee cannot sue without a *cestui que trust*. But I think that is not mentioned in the demurrer. I have known very little take away the objection as to length of time, and infancy is always allowed. And, where deeds were mislaid, that is sufficient.

The demurrer was allowed without costs because for want of parties not mentioned in the demurrer but only on the general words.

[1] *Frazer v. Moor* (Ex. 1719–1720), see above, Case No. 114.

Taussig MS. 311, vol. 1, p. 20

Easter term 1721.

Upon a demurrer to an English bill, there were three causes of demurrer: first, that the plaintiffs do not show any title in themselves by the bill; second, that the defendant's title commenced in 1683 and so, by the rules of equity, the plaintiff, after this length of time, ought not to be admitted to a redemption; third, there is want of parties.

John Drury, seised, conveys absolutely to North. In 1683 was the defeasance. North enters in the life of John Drury. George Drury, in 1693, conveys the equity of redemption to Christopher Dean and devises to his wife Eleanor and French and their heirs, and she dies leaving three children, but survived French.

There is no title because they do not say the plaintiffs are heir at law to Eleanor Dean, who was the surviving trustee of the mortgage in 1683.

In 1688, North entered in Drury's life. Drury's son in 1693 conveys to Dean. The devise by Christopher Dean was of the equity of redemption for the benefit of his three children, one son and two daughters, and he makes his wife and French and their heirs trustees.

By Baron Price: It is certain that you have not sufficiently asserted that the children of Dean are heirs at law to Eleanor Dean and this certainly ought to be showed.

But by Baron Montagu: This is not the cause of a demurrer alleged, for the objection in the demurrer is that title is not showed to George Drury and the general conclusion that the plaintiff has not showed title must be understood with relation to the particulars before set forth.

By Baron Page: Perhaps a *cestui que trust* may bring a bill to redeem, *quod* Price *dubitavit*. But then, it must appear that the *cestui que trust* has a valuable trust. But it does not appear here that there is a valuable trust, for the estate devised to Eleanor was to be sold to pay debts and the residue [went] to the children and whether any residue or surplus would be coming to the *cestui que trust*, by him, here is a good account enough of the reason why the plaintiffs did not come sooner. The want or mislaying of deeds is a good excuse.

But it was agreed by all the court that, though the party had not assigned this particular defect of title as a cause of his demurrer, yet he might assign it *ore tenus* at the bar, it being material and a matter of substance. But the plaintiff should not pay costs for an amendment of his bill in this particular because it was not assigned as a cause of his demurrer. And the court gave the plaintiff leave to amend without paying costs.

189

Dixy v. Gosham

(Ex. 1721)

A final decree cannot be set aside to relieve a meritorious person who has relied on the bad advice of his lawyer.

It is better that a private hardship happen than that a public evil be created.

Taussig MS. 311, vol. 1, p. 22

Easter term 1721.

The court refused to suffer an affidavit to be read in order to set aside a decree signed, which decree charged the defendant with £200. The defendant insisted upon surprise, and the affidavit was to that purpose. And also it appeared [*blank*] that the defendant was a trustee for only one particular purpose, *viz.* a bond, which bond was specifically devised and, therefore, no part of the estate subject to the plaintiff's demands. But, however, the bond was actually in court. And as to other parts of the personal estate, the executors were before the court. The decree, upon hearing the cause, was, according to custom, that all the defendants should account. And the solicitor in the country, being the same for this defendant, who was one Mr. Mason, a clergyman, as for the other defendants, told this defendant that he might safely acquiesce in the matter, for that the decree could not affect him, nay, he would be entitled to costs, being only a trustee. This defendant, therefore, sat still and never heard one word more of the cause until they served him with a writ of execution in the decree, which was to pay £200, whereas he never had a penny in his hands liable to the demand in the bill, but not appearing before the Master, [who] proceeded to settle the accounts *ex parte* and charged him with this sum.

He now applied by motion to the court to set aside the decree as to him and that he might have an opportunity of going before the Master and being heard before him, which, by the neglect or contrivance of his solicitor, he had never yet had an opportunity of. And all this he offered to make out by an affidavit. And the counsel insisted for him that were there any other way of being helped, they would not have applied in this way. But they could not have a bill of review because a bill of review is only for errors apparent in the decree, whereas, here, the decree was just and the only gravamen was the adjusting of the accounts subsequent to the first decree. And the court did certainly right in confirming the Master's report and thereupon pronouncing the final decree grounded on those reports, no objection having been made to the court against it. But this happened by the party's being misinformed by his solicitor. But, however, for the reason above, no bill of review lay nor could he have a rehearing because the decree had been signed and, when a decree is signed, it is too late to have a rehearing.

But the court would not suffer the affidavit to be read and said, if the party had been deceived by his solicitor, he must take his remedy against him, for however compassionate his case was as to the merits, they must observe the rules of the court and not suffer men to lie by and neglect all the usual and proper methods and, then, when all things are settled, come to the court and expect they should unsettle them again. This would be to overturn all methods of proceeding. And a private hardship is better to be borne than a public inconvenience introduced.

190

Anonymous

(Ex. 1721)

An exception to an insufficient answer must be for a material cause.

Taussig MS. 311, vol. 1, p. 26, pl. 1

Easter term 1721.

N.B. Filing exceptions to an answer for insufficiency is not sufficient to maintain an injunction, but one must show a material exception to the answer or else the court will not grant an injunction upon the motion.

And Mr. *Bunbury* opened an exception, and *Sir Constantine* [*Phipps*] was ready to argue it. And a doubt arose whether the exception was to be argued or no.

And Mr. Baron PRICE questioned.

But the Chief Baron [BURY] and PAGE thought it was to no purpose to oblige them to open an exception unless they might also enter into the materiality of it. And, therefore, they ordered the exception to be argued as soon as the plaintiff pleased and nothing to be stayed in the meantime.

191

Tipping v. Morecraft

(Ex. 1721)

The common understanding of a word is sufficient to ground an action for defamation without any averment of its meaning.

Harvard Law School MS. 1082, vol. 1, p. 61, pl. 2

Easter term 1721.

[This was an] action for words, *viz.* 'that Husband stole all the nails from the Excise Office that did Mr. Heather's work and all the candles he used in his family'. [There was a] verdict for the plaintiff.

Sir Constantine Phipps [moved] in arrest of judgment that it ought to be averred that Heather used nails and that candles were used in his family and, for want of such averment, the declaration was naught. There are several similitudinary cases. Love v. Playter, Cro. Car. 40;[1] Walter v. Browne, Popham.

Mr. *Bootle*, for the plaintiff, admitted that several of the old books were as cited by Sir Constantine, but those cases have been altered by the later resolutions, and the common import of the words is the only thing necessary.

The whole court agreed that the common parlance was sufficient to ground an action without any averment. And so they agreed with Bootle's rule.

Taussig MS. 311, vol. 1, p. 15, pl. 1

Easter term 1721.

An action was brought for slander that A.B. did steal all the nails from the Excise Office which did Mr. A.'s work. It was moved in arrest of judgment that there is no averment of work done or that the nails were used in the work.

But the plaintiff had his judgment notwithstanding.

192

Josseline v. Brewet

(Ex. 1721–1722)

Where a testator devises all of his estate to his executrix-widow for life, without more, the residuum passes by the rules of intestate succession.

A devise of personalty for life will be construed according to the intent and meaning of the testator.

A person can die testate as to some of his property and intestate as to other property.

Harvard Law School MS. 1082, vol. 1, p. 59, pl. 2

Easter term 1721.

This was a devise of an estate to his executrix for life. And the question was what was become of the residue, the bill being to have a distribution.

The Chief Baron [Bury] and Montagu thought it now settled that an executrix should take the whole as executrix and that Foster and Mont's Case[2] and Sir William Bassett's Case was now altered and settled in the Duchess of Beaufort's Case,[3] that an executrix should take the whole.

---

1 *Love v. Playter* (1626), Croke Car. 40, 79 E.R. 639.

2 *Foster v. Munt* (1689), 1 Vernon 473, 23 E.R. 598, 1 Eq. Cas. Abr. 243, 21 E.R. 1020, 2 Eq. Cas. Abr. 433, 443, 22 E.R. 368, 378, Dodd 78.

3 *Duchess of Beaufort v. Lady Granville* (1710), 3 Brown P.C. 37, 1 E.R. 1161, 2 Vernon 648, 23 E.R. 1023, 1 Peere Williams 114, 24 E.R. 317, 1 Eq. Cas. Abr. 245,

PRICE and PAGE: That opinion [was] too large where there was such an express devise, as in this case, to the executrix for life. They admitted the cases above cited. But whether it was to be held against an express devise was doubted.

PAGE doubted whether an executrix should take the whole. Hughes v. Hughes, in Modern reports.

[It was] adjourned for a case [to be made] and to be further spoken to.

Taussig MS. 311, vol. 1, p. 18

Easter term 1721.

A., upon the marriage of his daughter and after she was married, promises to her husband that he would give all his children alike and all his personal estate should be divided among them after the death of his wife. He dies and gives £20 apiece to all his children and all the residue of his personal estate to his wife for life and makes her executrix. Afterwards, she dies and makes her will and gives all to one of her children. And this bill was exhibited to have an equal distribution of the residue of this estate, inasmuch as the mother had the estate only for life and so had no power to dispose of this residue.

By Baron MONTAGU: The decree of the House of Lords has reestablished the common law, and so making an executor is a gift of all. But here, he only gives to his wife for life. But still, he thought that no distribution ought to be made, and so did the Chief Baron [BURY].

But PRICE and PAGE thought there was a great difference between this case and Foster v. Munn.

The court took time to consider of it and did not care to make a case of it, it being only of small value, the whole surplus being not above £200 or thereabouts.

N.B. As to the promise, the court thought there was no color to insist upon it because it was after the marriage and not in writing and so not good within the Statute of Frauds and Perjuries.[1]

Taussig MS. 311, vol. 1, p. 40, pl. 3

Easter term 1721.

Sir Constantine [*Phipps*] moved for hearing counsel.

And MONTAGU said he should be glad to hear counsel, for it was a difficult case, and, by him, query whether if a man dies intestate only as to part of his estate, the distribution must be made according to the Statute or as the common law would have divided it before that Statute. This is upon a supposition that the residue is not by law disposed of to the executor as executor and by virtue of naming him as executor only. And I doubt both these points.

---

21 E.R. 1022, 2 Eq. Cas. Abr. 415, 22 E.R. 352.

[1] Stat. 29 Car. II, c. 3 (*SR*, V, 839–842).

Per Baron PAGE: It is to be governed by the intent upon the whole of the will, and, if all can stand together, then, I think we ought to make that construction.

Harvard Law School MS. 1082, vol. 1, p. 72, pl. 3

Trinity term 1721.

This came again to be mentioned by the court, Hilary 1712, Barley v. Barley; Lady Gainsborough's Case,[1] in the last where the attorney was admitted to give evidence to explain the testator's intention. Knightley v. Farrington, in Chancery last term, 10 June 1721, upon Judge Upton's will;[2] the executor was obliged to distribute, he having £50 given him. Against this [was cited] Ball v. Smith in Chancery, 17 June 1712,[3] [and the] Duchess of Beaufort's Case in 1710.

Harvard Law School MS. 1082, vol. 1, p. 114, pl. 2

Hilary term 1721/22.

This was a bill to have a distribution of the personal estate of Thomas Brewet, who gave it to Frances, his wife, during her life and, likewise, a legacy, and he appointed, likewise, the defendant his executrix.

It was insisted on by the defendant that, though the use of the personal estate was only for life, yet, as executrix, she takes the whole as executrix and no distribution ought to be made. In the case of a stranger, if a legacy had been given to the executrix, there [would be] a[4] distribution. But here was a relation, and, therefore, she should take the whole.

But in this case, it was said by *Comyns* and *Bootle*, counsel for the plaintiff, that, though at law, an executrix as executrix takes the whole, but here, the intent of the testator is manifest that the wife should only have it for life. And in the case of Foster v. Munts, in Chancery 1686, where there was only a specific legacy of £10 and the party was made executor, yet, in that case, [he was] only declared a trustee. 3 Levinz 71; the intent of the testator will carry things against the rules of law. 3 Leonard 24. In several cases, the executor is only declared a trustee. Baily v. Power, Lord Somers's time, 1698; Sir Cirill Wych v. Parrot, Exchequer; Kersdale v. Bookey, 1698, Chancery; Morley v. Morley, Michaelmas 1702, Lord Keeper Wright; Farrington v. Knightley, about J. Repton's will, 1721, Lord Parker; Cook v. Walker, December 1704, Lord Cowper; Lord

[1] *Countess of Gainsborough v. Earl of Gainsborough* (1692), 2 Vernon 252, 23 E.R. 764, 2 Freeman 188, 22 E.R. 1152, 1 Eq. Cas. Abr. 230, 21 E.R. 1010.

[2] *Farrington v. Knightly* (1719–1721), 1 Peere Williams 544, 24 E.R. 509, Precedents in Chancery 566, 24 E.R. 254, 10 Modern 442, 88 E.R. 801, 2 Eq. Cas. Abr. 245, 421, 424, 440, 22 E.R. 208, 358, 360, 375.

[3] *Ball v. Smith* (1698–1711), 2 Vernon 633, 675, 23 E.R. 1014, 1039, 2 Freeman 230, 22 E.R. 1179, 1 Eq. Cas. Abr. 245, 21 E.R. 1022, 2 Eq. Cas. Abr. 133, 434, 22 E.R. 114, 369.

[4] no *MS.*

Cowper v. Duchess of Beaufort, Trinity 1709; use of the plate given in the Court of Chancery ordered to distribute reversed in the House of Lords; Earl of Bristol v. Hungerford, 9 King William in Bassett's will; Randall v. Boohey, 18 January 13 King William; Wood v. Lane, 30 October, Lord Harcourt's time; Westcomb v. Jones; Batchellour v. Searle, Lord Harcourt's time; Edwards v. Ives, the use of the whole personal estate.[1]

There are cases determined in Chancery in favor of executors to take the whole. Ball v. Smith; Littlebury v. Buckley; Coatesworth v. Brangnin, in Lord Harcourt's time; Cauthen v. Noden, to the contrary.[2]

It is admitted where no legacy is given, the executor takes the whole. Wingfield v. Atkinson,[3] both had legacies, Sir John Trevor; Sir John Packington's Case [in] Lord Keeper Wright's time.

Notwithstanding these cases, yet the present Lord Chancellor [Lord Macclesfield] decreed the distribution in the Case of Farington v. Knightley upon Judge Upton's will. Since the Statute of Distributions,[4] it has been settled in a court of equity that an executor is no more than a trustee who is ordered to sell a real estate.

Mr. *Bootle, pro eodem*, for a distribution: I take it to be settled that, where a particular legacy is given to the executor, it is a bar of the residue and a person may die intestate as to part of his estate and testate as to another part.

It is plain by the words of this will that it is only designed to Frances Brewet for life. And so the testator intended no more as if the use of the personal estate had been given only for years. A personal estate may be given in the same manner to limit it as long as a real estate, so [long as] it does not go too far towards

---

[1] *Parker v. Thacker* (1682), 3 Levinz 70, 83 E.R. 582, also 1 Eq. Cas. Abr. 180, 21 E.R. 973; *Bayly v. Powell* (1698), 2 Freeman 225, 22 E.R. 1175, 2 Vernon 361, 23 E.R. 827, Precedents in Chancery 92, 24 E.R. 44, 1 Eq. Cas. Abr. 244, 21 E.R. 1020; *Packington v. Wyche* (Ex. 1707–1709), Eq. Cases Exch. 619, *Wych v. Packington* (H.L. 1712), 3 Brown P.C. 44, 1 E.R. 1166, 2 Eq. Cas. Abr. 507, 744, 22 E.R. 429, 632; *Pawlett v. Morley* (1702), 2 Freeman 263, 22 E.R. 1199; *Farrington v. Knightly* (1719–1721), *ut supra*; *Cook v. Walker* (1704–1708), 2 Freeman 276, 22 E.R. 1207, 1 Eq. Cas. Abr. 244, 21 E.R. 1021; *Earl of Bristol v. Hungerford* (1697), 2 Vernon 524, 645, 23 E.R. 938, 1021, Precedents in Chancery 81, 24 E.R. 39, 1 Eq. Cas. Abr. 44, 142, 245, 272, 21 E.R. 862, 944, 1021, 1040; *Randall v. Bookey* (1701), 2 Vernon 425, 23 E.R. 872, Precedents in Chancery 162, 24 E.R. 78, 1 Eq. Cas. Abr. 272, 21 E.R. 1040; *Batchellor v. Searle* (1716), 2 Vernon 736, 23 E.R. 1081, Gilbert Rep. 125, 25 E.R. 88, 1 Eq. Cas. Abr. 246, 21 E.R. 1022.

[2] *Ball v. Smith* (1698–1711), *ut supra*; *Buckley v. Littlebury* (1711), 3 Brown P.C. 43, 1 E.R. 1165, 1 Eq. Cas. Abr. 245, 21 E.R. 1021; *Colesworth v. Brangwin* (Ch. 1712), Precedents in Chancery 323, 24 E.R. 153, Gilbert Rep. 79, 25 E.R. 56, 2 Eq. Cas. Abr. 438, 22 E.R. 373; *Cordell v. Noden* (1690), 2 Vernon 148, 23 E.R. 702, Precedents in Chancery 12, 24 E.R. 6, 1 Eq. Cas. Abr. 244, 21 E.R. 1021.

[3] *Wingfield v. Atkinson* (1711), 2 Vernon 673, 23 E.R. 1038.

[4] Stat. 22 & 23 Car. II, c. 10 (*SR*, V, 719–720).

a perpetuity. And this being for life only given to Frances Brewet, it implies a negative, as in the case of the Statute of Hen. VI, for fees.

I thought that this case was settled in Farrington and Knightley's case [and] the Duchess of Beaufort's Case, where Lord Cowper, for the use of the plate being given, ordered a distribution, but [it was] reversed in the House of Lords because they did not take this use to be such a legacy as would bar her. Barley v. Barley, Hilary 1712, Master of the Rolls; Trott v. Lady Tyrrell; Scattergood v. Edge, reported in Salkeld, that chattels might be entailed as well as a real estate.[1]

Montagu doubted and cited Henneage v. Lady Peters that chattels could not be entailed.

Page thought that it might be done and cited Sir Godfrey Copley's Case.[2] [. . .] by way of use of a chattel is good.

Montagu denied it any further than where the use is; then there may be a remainder. And he cited Lady Gainsborough's Case to support the right of an executrix or executor, parol evidence has been admitted, but not to take away the right of an executor. I take it that the executor at law is not a trustee, but takes the whole. [He] cited Littlebury v. Buckley; the Duchess of Beaufort's Case.

I take these two to be the last cases in the House of Lords, which are against obliging the executor to distribute. Lord Harcourt had found a new figary and distinction, *viz.* when the executor was a stranger, there, he should not be entitled to the residue. And so was the case of Foster and Munts, where Foster was an attorney and so a fraud appeared. And if this distinction should hold, it would [be] difficult to fix how near a relation it ought to be to entitle him to the residue.

The intent of the testator, as it should be argued at the bar and the bench, gives so great a latitude that new wills have been made for the testator which he never intended. And, therefore, I am for going according to the express rules of law and to let the executrix, according to that, take the whole.

Price: I do not take it that the Duchess of Beaufort's Case will influence this before us, for, there, the use of the plate was only an ornament and heirloom, but [there was] no profit. And if the duke, her husband, had given her the plate absolutely, I believe that the Lords would have been of another opinion. There, the personal estate is only given for life. And I think that there ought to be a distribution. I think that the case of Foster v. Munts is right because Foster was an attorney. And I think that the distinction is right between a relation and a stranger. And I do not know that there was any fraud proved in Foster and Munt's Case. Lord Guernsey said that there was no fraud; the Master of the Rolls said that there was a fraud.

---

[1] *Scatterwood v. Edge* (1697), 1 Salkeld 229, 91 E.R. 203, also 12 Modern 278, 88 E.R. 1320, 1 Eq. Cas. Abr. 189, 21 E.R. 980, 2 Eq. Cas. Abr. 337, 22 E.R. 287.

[2] *Copley v. Copley* (1711), 1 Peere Williams 147, 24 E.R. 333, 2 Eq. Cas. Abr. 639, 22 E.R. 536, British Library MS. Hargrave 80, p. 89.

Taussig MS. 311, vol. 1, p. 278

Easter term 1722.

Per Sir Constantine Phipps: The wife is entitled to the whole. The executor is entitled to the estate as executor. The giving a legacy was first found out in Foster and Munt's Case. [There was] no administration as to the residuum during the lifetime of the executor. The case of a will made is entirely out of the Statute of Car. II. It is very hard to imply a trust against an express rule of the common law. This doctrine is entirely founded on the doctrine of intention, that the testator intended the wife to have nothing more, but yet the wife is certainly entitled to part of the residue. And this is the opposite. And giving a chattel for life without a devise over is giving the whole. Whatever is not taken from the executor remains in the executor.

It is reasonable to give a legacy to an executor, especially if he designs her an equal favor with other legatees. In this case, there was no legacy but the residue. And [it would be] strange to say a devise of the residue is an exclusion from the residue. From the time of the Duchess of Beauford's Case, the old law revived.

Shepherd, on same side: [There is] no resolution like this case because here is no legacy at all and an express devise of the residue, 'the residue to my wife after debts and legacies paid.' Here is no use, but she has a property absolute. So there is no part of the testator's estate whereof he could be said to die intestate.

For the difference between real chattels and personal chattels, [see] Rolle, *Abr.*, 610. A remainder of a chattel personal is void. Bulstr. 191; 34 & 35 Hen. VI; Bro., title Devise, pl. 13; March's Rep. 106,[1] the difference between a use and the goods themselves. And that case allows that the use of goods is different from the property; it is otherwise in the case of lands, as Matthew Manning's Case.[2] Supposing the executor had sold them all, how could there be any remainder of them?

Whether it passes to her as executrix, whatever does not pass to her by express devise passes to her as executrix.

Comyns, by way of reply: [There is the] same power of disposing of personal estate [as] of real estate. A trust is implied. And yet the replication is there against the rule of law. Restraining the gift to her for life is surely not giving her the absolute property. Giving a chattel for life is not giving it forever. Plowd. 516; 8 Rep. 89; 1 Lev. 11, intent.[3] An express demise is stronger than any of the cases in Chancery. Cro. Jac. 559; Palmer [*blank*]; Coke, in Lampett's Case, chattel's

---

[1] *Anonymous* (1607), 1 Rolle, Abr., *Devise*, pl. K, 4, p. 610; *Price v. Atmore* (1612), 1 Bulstrode 191, 80 E.R. 879, also 4 Leonard 246, 74 E.R. 850; Brooke, Abr., *Devise*, pl. 13; *Anonymous* (1641), March 106, 82 E.R. 432.

[2] *Clark v. Manning* (1609), 8 Coke Rep. 94, 77 E.R. 618.

[3] *Welcden v. Elkington* (1578), 2 Plowden 516, 523, 75 E.R. 763, 772; *Milner v. Fraunces* (1609), 8 Coke Rep. 89, 77 E.R. 609, also 2 Brownlow & Goldesborough 940; *Plunket v. Holmes* (1661), 1 Levinz 11, 83 E.R. 271, also 1 Siderfin 47, 82 E.R. 961, 1 Keble 29, 119, 83 E.R. 792, 848, T. Raymond 28, 83 E.R. 15.

personal;[1] Cro. Eliz. 387, residue of personal estate for life. There it was held she should have an election. Moor 315; Cro. Eliz. 223, Lain's, 10 Rep. 41; Rolle's *Abr.*, title Devise; Dyer 277; 3 Leon. 3. She has never done anything to show her intent to take as executrix. 1 Lev. 25; Plowd. 525.[2] And therefore, she takes as legatee. Pinberry and Elking, in Chancery,[3] the decree was it was a devise of money. And that is a stronger case than any other chattel.

Per MONTAGU: How shall the value be computed? Whether the value at the time of the death of the testator or at the time of the executrix?

Bootle insists on the case of Farrington and Knightly as the last determination. [There is] no difference between personal and real chattels, for an executor has the same power of disposing and selling in both cases. There is no repugnancy in being testate and intestate as to different interests in the same goods anymore than as to different goods.

[We will] take time to give our opinions to the second day of the next term appointed for that purpose.

Harvard Law School MS. 1082, vol. 1, p. 132

Easter term 1722.

Sir Constantine Phipps, for defendant, the wife, [said] that she ought to have the residuum and no distribution is to be made. The first instance of the distinction where there was a specific legacy was Foster and Munt's Case. The Statute of Distributions takes effect only where the party dies intestate. The Lords Commissioners reversed that decree of Lord Jeffreys. Foster v. Mont.

As to the residuum, the executor is trustee for the children, [he] responded there was no express trust and it would be hard to imply it.

[To the] objection that, by giving a legacy to the wife, it shows the intention she should have no more, [he] responded there are legacies given to the children and that reason might extend to them.

[To the] objection the residuum was devised to her for life and the distribution should be after, [he] responded but it is not devised over and, being a personalty, it vests entirely in her. Here is no legacy given her, but the residuum for life, which distinguishes this from the cases cited before.

Note: The Lords Commissioners' decree was reversed in the House of Lords.

Mr. *Sheppard*, for the defendant: At law, the executrix is certainly entitled. This case differs from the cases cited which all went upon a supposition that the residue was not disposed of. Here, the executrix has two legacies, as all the resi-

---

[1] *Lampet's Case* (1612), 10 Coke Rep. 46b, 77 E.R. 994, *sub nom. Lampit v. Starkey*, 2 Brownlow & Goldesborough 172, 123 E.R. 880.

[2] *Garrett v. Lister* (1661), 1 Levinz 25, 83 E.R. 279, also 1 Keble 15, 83 E.R. 782; *Bransby v. Grantham* (1578), 2 Plowden 525, 75 E.R. 776.

[3] *Pinbury v. Elkin* (1717–1719), 2 Vernon 758, 766, 23 E.R. 1095, 1099, Precedents in Chancery 483, 24 E.R. 217, 1 Peere Williams 563, 24 E.R. 518.

due is expressly disposed of. 'I give the residue after debts and legacies paid to my wife for life.' There is no limitation of the residue over after the wife's death to anybody mentioned. There is a distinction between the use and the property. If it had been limited over, being a chattel personal, yet it would be void. 1 Rolle 610; Bulstrode 191; Dyer, page 8; Br., *Ab.*, 275, p. 13; and March 106.[1] There is a difference between the [. . .] of goods and the use of goods.

The specific legacy here, *viz.* the residuum, is the very thing in controversy. All rights of administration must commence from the intestate's death. But that cannot be here, for that which they contend for should go in the course of administration is devised to the executrix for life.

Mr. *Comyns* replies: [To the] objection, at law, by being appointed executor, the whole is given to him, [he] responded that I admit all [to be] law, but the testator may give with what limitations he will.

[To the] objection that no trust was expressed, [he] responded it is sufficient that it is implied and, in such case, an executor is no more than a trustee.

[To the] objection the children have legacies and why should they not be barred as well as the wife, [he] responded the whole is given for life.

[To the] objection, if it is given for life, then, in consequence, forever, [he] responded, if she had been appointed generally executrix, it would be so, but not with this limitation.

[To the] objection absolute property was given, [he] responded that, by giving it for life, it shows the intention to be only the use.

Mr. *Bootle* replies: Rolle's *Abridgment*, 207; Dyer 277; 3 Leonard 36.[2] If the usufructory part only is given to the executor, then the property is vested in her in trust for those who are entitled by virtue of the Statute of Distribution.

[To the] objection a person cannot be said to die testate and intestate, [he] responded a man may die testate as to one part and intestate to another part.

Query, if a man possessed of money and goods makes his will and devises his money reciting that he has money and goods and names his executor and says that he shall have nothing to do with his goods, then he may be said a testator as to the money and intestate as to the goods, but note this is not as to the same thing.

Note: The bill here was against the executor of the wife's executrix. [It was] adjourned, for the opinion of the court, to the second day of next term.

Harvard Law School MS. 1082, vol. 1, p. 141, pl. 2

30 May 1722. *Judicium curiae.*

---

[1] *Anonymous* (1607), 1 Rolle, Abr., *Devise*, pl. K, 4, p. 610; *Price v. Atmore* (1612), *ut supra*; *Abbot of Bury v. Bokenham* (1536), 1 Dyer 7, 73 E.R. 19; Brooke, Abr., *Devise*, pl. 13; *Anonymous* (1641), March 106, 82 E.R. 432.

[2] *Platt v. Goldsmith* (1614), 1 Rolle, Abr., *Amendment*, pl. 18, p. 207; *Barrett v. Barrett* (1568), 3 Dyer 277, 73 E.R. 620; *Lord Windsor's Case* (1573), 3 Leonard 35, 74 E.R. 524.

Baron Page: All the residue etc. was given to the wife during her life. She makes her will and devises to the defendant and dies. The defendant possesses himself of her personal estate and also the residue of the husband's personal estate. The bill is for a distribution. I am of opinion the plaintiff is well entitled to a distribution in this case.

1. [The question is] whether an executor has, as executor, as full a power and interest in his testator's estate as he has in his own. And I am of opinion he has not. If an executor dies intestate, [his] next of kin is not entitled to the administration, but the next of kin to the first testator, which shows being named executor is not an absolute gift of the testator's goods too. Michaelmas Term 1699, Nicholson v. Sykes; 1 Ventris 217.[1]

2. To what purpose has the executor the power over the testator's goods to perform the testator's will as a faithful trustee [where] the whole is not disposed of? [For] what power the executor has, see Archbishop Stratford's Constitution, Linwood, *Concilia*, fo. 46; *Codex Juris Ecc.*, 558; Stat. 31 Eliz.; 4 Hen. VIII, cap. 5; Slanie's Case, Hobart 83; 22 & 23 Car. II.[2]

[To the] objection of the making of an executor is an implied gift of the residue, [he] responded, carry that as far as you will, that cannot influence this case, for there can be no implication against express words. Now here, it is expressed to her for life and his intendment cannot be carried farther than his own expression. Though it may not at law, yet, in a court of equity, he may be said to die intestate as to the residue after her life.

[To] objection one, that a devise of personalty for life is a devise forever, [he] responded, by a deed, it would be forever, but, in a will, the construction is to be made by the intent and meaning of the party. A devise of an horse for a time etc. is not a devise of property, but of the use only. Sir Geofrey Copley's case.[3]

[To] objection two, that there was no devise over and so there was nobody [who] was to take, [he] responded a man may make his will as to one part of his estate, as in Middlesex, and die intestate [as] to his estate in Surrey. An executor is a trustee for the remainder of the residue. After the wife's life, then that will make no difference whether there is a devise over or no. It is an inconsistency to say he has given it for her life and forever.

Baron Price was of the same opinion. The difference is where you give by will the use to one and the property to another. In this case, the wife is to have the occupation for life, but the property is to be distributed. [One] being named

---

[1] *Thomas v. Butler* (1672), 1 Ventris 217, 86 E.R. 146, also 2 Levinz 55, 83 E.R. 447, 3 Keble 23, 27, 34, 55, 84 E.R. 573, 575, 579, 591.

[2] W. Lyndwood, *Provinciale* (J. V. Bullard and H. C. Bell, edd., 1929), pp. 65–67; E. Gibson, *Codex Juris Ecclesiastici Anglicani* (1713); *Slawney v. Elbridge* (1616–1621), Hobart 83, 80 E.R. 233, also Moore K.B. 864, 72 E.R. 958; Stat. 22 & 23 Car. II, c. 10 (*SR*, V, 719–720).

[3] *Copley v. Copley* (1711), *ut supra*.

executor is but a bare trustee (but this I give no conclusive opinion in) by the civil and common law. Calvin's *Lexicon*, executors are of three sorts; see Swinburn, *Of Wills*, executors, *viz. executores legitimi, dativi, et testamentariis*. The first were the ordinary; the second were by virtue of the Stat. 31 Edw. III, being the administrators; the third were the executors named in the will. And he cannot convert the residue to his own use without direction from the testator. See Sir John Nisbit's *Scotch Laws or Decisions*; Swinburn.[1]

Where an executor has the residue given him, he is an interested executor, otherwise only *nudus*. By the common law, an executor could not have an account; his actions are in the *detinet*; the judgments against him are *de bonis testatoris*. An executor cannot devise the estate of the testator, but it must go to the administrator *de bonis non*. If an executor makes an executor, he is not an executor to the executor, but to the first testator by relation. The reason of this seems to be grounded upon the Stat. 25 Edw. III.[2] If a man is named executor and there is no disposition of the estate, he is a trustee for the payments of debts. Foster v. Munt, 1684; Morley v. Morley, 1702.[3] These cases go to show, where a specific legacy is given to the executor, the residuum shall be distributed. Barrington v. Knightley, upon Mr. Upton's will, *coram* Parker, Lord Chancellor; the will was imperfect. Swinburn 424.

The ground he went upon was that an executor without an express direction has not an interest, but only a trust. If it had been a new thing, I should be for making an executor a trustee as much as an administrator, but that would be going too far at this time of day.

Lord Chief Baron MONTAGU: I cannot think an executor can by law be made only a bare trustee. It is not forty years since Foster v. Munt, and that is the first instance that ever a distribution was prayed against an executor. The common law will not let the ecclesiastical courts order a distribution when there is an executor. Why then should a court of equity do it, for the ecclesiastical courts had original jurisdiction.

Hughes v. Hughes, 18 Car. II, was of another opinion. A legatee cannot take even a specific legacy without the consent of the executor, which shows he has the right to it before, for he may bring an action for it. Magna Charta, cap. 18, *residuum relinquatur executoribus*; Bracton, lib. 2, fo. 61.[4]

[To the] objection, if an executor dies intestate, an administration must be taken out *de bonis non*, [he] responded that is true for this reason, because the first testator dies intestate as to the goods not administered.

---

[1] J. Nisbet, *Some Doubts and Questions in the Law Especially of Scotland*; H. Swinburne, *Brief Treatise of Testaments and Last Wills*.

[2] Stat. 25 Edw. III, stat. 5, c. 5 (*SR*, I, 321).

[3] *Pawlett v. Morley* (1702), *ut supra*.

[4] Stat. 25 Edw. I, Magna Carta, c. 18 (*SR*, I, 116); *Bracton on the Laws and Customs of England* (S. E. Thorne, trans., 1968), vol. 2, pp. 180–181.

[To the] objection the executor has to perform the will, [he] responded, where there is express direction, he must pursue it, and, if there are debts, he must stand in the place of the testator. *Breve de rationabili parte bonorum.*

[To the] objection that, by the ecclesiastical laws, an executor has no benefit to himself, I admit there has long been a struggle between the common and ecclesiastical courts about this jurisdiction, but, by the Stat. 31 Edw. III, the administrator is to stand in the place of the executor, by [Croke] Car. 62, executor, and he is to have the absolute interest. Hobart 191.[1]

By the Stat. 22 Car. II,[2] the administrator is made a trustee, but he was not so before. But this Statute does not affect an executor.

[To the] objection there can be no implication against the express words of the will, [he] responded, though this is true, yet given the residuum for life, she takes it only so long as she is a legatee, but, though there is no gift further, yet, being undisposed of, it comes to the executors. If a man seised in fee devises his estate to his eldest son for life and he does not devise over, this does not exclude him from nothing, taking the reversion in fee if he will take by the will. It is inconsistent that a man should die testate and intestate *quoad* the same thing. '*Instituo Titium executorem*' is a good will, according to Justinian's *Institutes*.[3] A devise of a chattel, 1 Rolle, *Abridgment*, 610,[4] an interest for life, a remainder afterwards is void where the matter devised for life is not determined. In its nature, a stock of a farm, I should not be, after an express devise for life, be for construing that to be capable of being devised over, either of a certain thing, as plate. 1680, Cases [*tempore*] Lord Nottingham, in Zouch v. Lord Anglesey.[5]

[To the] objection this devise ought to be taken as a sufficient satisfaction and she ought to expect nothing further, [he] responded nothing further as an express legatee, but, as an executrix, she ought. The plaintiff himself is an express legatee of £20, and, by that way of reasoning, he ought to expect nothing more.

[To the] objection there is a difference between a devise of the thing and the occupation, [he] responded, here, the very thing is devised. There was fraud in the case of Foster v. Munt; two attorneys enticed that man to a tavern and persuaded him to make his will. The reason of the cases cited where, when a legacy is given, the executor is excluded of the residue proves he is not a trustee, for they say, by that legacy, he is excluded of what is not the trust, but the right to the legacy. It is admitted here he is *heres mobilibus*. Then he is not a trustee. He is as much heir to the *mobilibus* as the heir at law is to the real estate. A man is not more an executor after the residue is given to him than he was before. Plowden's

---

1 *Fotherby's Case* (1627), Croke Car. 62, 79 E.R. 657, also Littleton 21, 124 E.R. 116; *Tooker v. Loane*, Hobart 191, 80 E.R. 338.

2 Stat. 22 & 23 Car. II, c. 10 (*SR*, V, 719–720).

3 Justinian, *Institutes*, 2. 16. pr.

4 *Anonymous* (1607), 1 Rolle, Abr., *Devise*, pl. K, 4, p. 610.

5 *Zouch v. Turner* (1680), 79 Selden Soc. 836.

Commentaries, Grantham's Case.[1] In the case of Littlebury v. Buckley,[2] the Lords admitted proof *dehors* of the intention of the testator, which sometimes has been admitted to fortify a will, never to invalidate it. He thought it would be breaking into the rule of the common law and introductory of great uncertainty to make such a construction as was contended for on the other side. And, therefore, he concluded for the defendant.

Bunbury 112, 145 E.R. 614

30 May 1722.

A man makes his will and, after several legacies, devises the rest and residue to his wife during her life and dies. She makes her will and devises to the defendant and dies. He possesses himself of her personal estate and also of the residue of the husband's personal estate. The plaintiff, as next of kin, prefers his bill for a distribution of the residue of the husband's personal estate, which was only devised to her for life, and, upon this, the long controverted question arose, whether a legacy, being given to an executor specifically, did not exclude him from the residuum.

And this case having been several times argued, this day judgment was given by PAGE and PRICE, barons, for the plaintiff, that he ought to have a distribution, the Lord Chief Baron MONTAGU being of a contrary opinion.

Mr. *Comyns* [was] for the plaintiff.

Lincoln's Inn MS. Misc. 506, p. 44

Easter 8 Geo. [1722].

T. Bruet, having made his will 27 October 1716, died in the year 1718. By that will, he gives £20 apiece to his children and all the rest of his goods, chattel, stock on the farm, and all his personal estate whatsoever he gives to his wife Frances Bruet for her natural life, but he leaves her no other legacy, and he makes her sole executrix. The question was whether the wife, as executrix, be not entitled to the whole undevised residue absolutely or, after her death, it shall be subject to the distribution of the Statute.

It was insisted on by *Sir Constantine Phipps* etc., on behalf of the plaintiff, who was the universal legatee and executor of the wife, that, by common law, the executor, of course, is entitled to the residue and the Statute makes a distribution only where the party dies intestate, which cannot be where there is an executor, for then there ought to be an administration. It would be hard to imply a trust in the executor when there is none expressed. As to the testator's intention, why should it be intended that the particular legacy should exclude the wife any more than the legacies to the children should exclude the children? But here is

[1] *Bransby v. Grantham* (1578), 2 Plowden 525, 75 E.R. 776.

[2] *Buckley v. Littlebury* (1711), *ut supra*.

an express bequest to the wife of the residue, and, though it be only [for] life, yet, being personal chattels, it is gone forever. Besides it is the thing that is given, not the use of it, and, she being executrix, what was not given away goes to her as much as land to the heir. 1 Rol., *Abr.*, 610; Bul. 191; Dyer 106.[1] The intent of the legacy given to the wife might be that, if there should be a deficiency, she might have her share as well as the other legatees. And he cited a case of Hall and Smith,[2] where Lord Harcourt refused to decree away the residue from the executor though he had a legacy, and the like in the case of the Lady Granville and the Duchess of Beaufort, 2 Vern. 648.

On the other side, it was insisted that it appeared plainly to be the testator's intent that the wife should have the use during her life, which is the same as for life only and implies a negative as to anything not bequeathed, that it cannot be intended to secure the wife something at all adventures in this case, for nothing is given here but after debts and legacies paid, and, if he intended to have given her more than for life, he would have made her executor generally. And, therefore, this is a stronger case than where there is no mention made of the residue, that, as to what was objected, that there never was an administration where there was an executor, was not universally true, as, where the executor renounces, there is an administration *cum testamento annexo* or, where the executor dies before he has fully administered, there is an administration *de bonis non*. The Statute of Distributions takes place as well where there is a will as where there is not *quoad* what is not bequeathed, that an executor is not in the same case as an heir would be, for that an heir takes by descent though there were no will, whereas an executor can claim only under the will and, therefore, can claim no more to his own use than what the will gives, that a chattel may vest and re-vest at the testator's pleasure. 1 Lev. 11, Plunkett and Holmes.[3] The use may pass when the thing itself does not. Plow. 526; 8 Co. 95, Manning's Case; 10 Co. 47, Lambert's Case; Cr. Jac. 459, Palm. 333, that personal chattels as well as real may be devised for life. Cr. Eliz. 387, Portman and Willis; Mo. 350, Cr. Eliz. 223; Dyer 277b; 3 Leon. 36; 1 Lev. 25, and the case of Pinbury v. Elkin, Chancery 1720,[4] a legacy of money to a wife and, if she die without issue, then £40 of it to A. It was

---

[1] *Goffe v. Haywood* (1615), 1 Rolle, Abr., *Devise*, pl. 8, p. 610; *Price v. Atmore* (1612), 1 Bulstrode 191, 80 E.R. 879, also 4 Leonard 246, 74 E.R. 850; *Townsend's Case* (1554), 1 Dyer 106, 73 E.R. 233, also 1 Plowden 111, 75 E.R. 173.

[2] *Ball v. Smith* (1698–1711), *ut supra*.

[3] *Plunket v. Holmes* (1661), *ut supra*.

[4] *Bransby v. Grantham* (1578), *ut supra*; *Clark v. Manning* (1609), *ut supra*; *Lampet's Case* (1612), *ut supra*; *Child v. Bayly* (1618), Croke Jac. 459, 79 E.R. 393, Palmer 48, 333, 81 E.R. 972, 1109, also W. Jones 15, 82 E.R. 9, 1 Eq. Cas. Abr. 192, 21 E.R. 982, 2 Rolle Rep. 129, 81 E.R. 704; *Portman v. Willis* (1595), Croke Eliz. 386, 78 E.R. 632, also Moore K.B. 352, 72 E.R. 326; *Pannel v. Fen* (1594), Moore K.B. 350, 72 E.R. 622, also Croke Eliz. 347, 78 E.R. 595, Gouldsborough 185, 75 E.R. 1082; *Barrett v. Barrett*

construed if she die without issue at the time of her death, and the £40 was decreed to A. As to the objection that she might sell the goods, the objection might lie to a term devised which is confessed may be devised for life only. But she cannot do everything by her will that she might have done in her life, for, upon her death, it is that the right of distribution commences, that all cases, especially the last of Farringdon and Knightley, were express that the executor is only a trustee for the next of kin.

The next term, being Trinity 8 George [1722], the court gave their opinion *seriatim*.

Baron PAGE: By the canon law, as may appear from Stratford's Constitution, 16 Edw. III, 1342,[1] the executor was not entitled to the residue unless it was expressly given, but he was only to have what the ordinary thought fit to allow him for his expense and trouble. Linwood, f. 46; Gibson, *Codex*, 558. Before the [Stat.] 31 Edw. III,[2] the ordinary stood in the place of an executor where there was a will; by that Act, he is bound to give administration to a relation of the intestate, who, in all respects, was to be instead of an executor. If there were a surplus, that was still under the power of the ordinary, as being the person who had the care of the intestate's soul when living and so the ordinaries usually took bonds for the due administration and rightly distributing the surplus. The [Stat.] 21 Hen. VIII, c. 5,[3] gives express directions to whom administration should be granted. But still, the bonds continued in the same form. 11 Jac. I, Slawney's Case, Hob. 83;[4] the court were of opinion that the administration being to be granted to the next of kin should be looked on as a gift of the residue. The [Stat.] 22d of Car. II makes the distribution, but taking it for granted that the making him executor is an implied gift of the residue. Yet that cannot be in this case, for there cannot be an implication against express words. Here the testator gives the residue for life, which to me is the same as if he said for life only, for what need had he to give it to her for life if he intended, as executrix, she should have it absolutely?

It has been objected that a devise for life of a chattel personal is an absolute devise, but there cannot be much weight in that. It has always been a rule to construe wills according to the intent of the party. And as a devise of the thing itself cannot by law be for life, therefore, when the testator devises it for life, it has always been construed not to be a devise of the property, but of the use. As in Sir John Cropley's Case, he devised all his goods to his wife for life; that was construed to be a devise only of the use of them.

(1568), *ut supra*; *Lord Windsor's Case* (1573), *ut supra*; *Garrett v. Lister* (1661), *ut supra*; *Pinbury v. Elkin* (1717–1719), *ut supra*.

[1] W. Lyndwood, *Provinciale* (J. V. Bullard and H. C. Bell, edd., 1929), pp. 65–67.

[2] Stat. 31 Edw. III, stat. 1, c. 11 (*SR*, I, 351).

[3] Stat. 21 Hen. VIII, c. 5, s. 2 (*SR*, III, 286–287).

[4] *Slawney v. Elbridge* (1616–1621), *ut supra*.

But it is objected that there is no devise over. The consequence of that can only be that, as that he is dead intestate. It was never a doubt but a man may make a will as to part and die intestate as to the rest, and then, as to the undisposed part, the executor is a trustee just as an administrator would be and must apply it in the same manner. If he has declared his intention to dispose of it only for life, there needs no devise over, but, as to that, he dies intestate. By the construction contended for, the devise is taken away. The cases in equity have been upon particular legacies, which is a different case, because no man can tell what his estate may be when he shall die and he may be willing to secure to his executor something at all events and to put him upon a par with other legatees. But here is no benefit to the wife by this devise, which she would not have otherwise, for her legacy is only out of the residue. But I take the meaning to be to restrain, not to enlarge, what she would have as executrix. I am, therefore, of opinion that the wife has no title further than for life and that the plaintiff, as one of the children of the testator, is entitled to distribution.

Baron Price: The question is whether the defendant's testatrix be entitled to the residue or whether the devise has overthrown it. I think it has. It is such a declaration of the testator's intent as shows that he meant the wife [to have] no more than an estate for life. The gift of the residue is as much a legacy as a specific legacy and such a legacy as is inconsistent with her taking as executrix. I think that an executor, both by civil and common law, is no more in creation than a trustee. Calvin, *Lexicon*; Swinburne *of Wills*.

The statute law makes administrators and gives them power to pay debts and to dispose of the residue only for the good of the intestate's soul, which has been construed to distribute in charity among his relations. The Act seems to make no distinction between an executor and an administrator. Sir John Nesbit, of the Scotch Laws, says an executor is to execute the will of the testator and the will of the law.

By the acts of Parliament, an executor is but a trustee. Before the Statute of 13 Edw. I, an executor had not an account. 1 Inst. 404.[1] If a man make a deed of gift of all his goods, the goods he has as executor do not pass, nor can an executor devise what he has as executor; it is a void devise. If an executor dies intestate, administration must be to the first testator. If an executor die before probate, his executor cannot prove the first will. The law says that an executor of the first executor is the executor to the first testator by relation. The [Stat.] 25 Edw. III gives the action to the executor of the executor as executor to the first testator. Foster and Munt, 1687, before Chancellor Jeffreys; a wealthy man is taken up by an attorney, carried to a tavern where a will was made for him, and the attorney and another were made executors and £10 apiece given them for a legacy; it was decreed that the legacy barred them of the residue. The Lords Commissioners

[1] E. Coke, *First Institute* (1628), f. 246b.

reversed that decree, but the House of Lords reversed theirs. Randall and Booky; Mordley and Mordley, 1702; Edwards and Eyles; and Farringdon and Knightley, 1721, where one Upton makes a will and devises several legacies and makes one of the legatees executor; it was decreed by the now Lord Chancellor that the executor was but a trustee of the residue for the next of kin; [in] Colesworth and Bragg, where there were two executors and one had a legacy and the other not, they were decreed to be but trustees of the residue, which does indeed show that, as executors, they had an implied interest. Lady Gainsborough's Case. If it were the first instance, I should make all the executors trustees, but, perhaps, now that might be going too far. But where there is a legacy given to be sure it was intended, that should be all the benefit the executor should have by the will. I, therefore, think the plaintiff is entitled to a distribution.

Chief Baron Montagu: Though with respect to this particular case, the question may be of small consequence, yet, as a precedent, it is of universal consequence. Foster v. Munt is the oldest case wherever distribution was prayed against an executor. There have been attempts in the spiritual courts to compel distributions, but the temporal courts always prohibited them, which they would never have done if they thought they proceeded by law. Lewis and Lewis, 18 Car. II. This is law still and cannot be altered but by act of Parliament. An executor has the absolute interest of the personal estate, for a legatee cannot take but by his assent. Magna Charta, c. 18, is an express authority, '*residuum relinquatur executoribus*'. The English Statute has it 'to the use of the dead', that is, says Coke, to the executor who represents the dead. Br., L. 2, f. 61. The writ *de rationabili parte* lies not at common law, but by custom. There has for many years been a struggle about this matter between the ecclesiastical courts and the temporal. Cr. Car. 62; Hob. 191. But will it follow that, because the Parliament has subjected administrations to the Statute of Distributions, therefore, a court of equity by parity of reason may do so with an executor? In the case of Zouch and Lord Anglesey, 1680,[1] Lord Nottingham said that a devise to an executor is a devise of nothing but what he has by law and, therefore, it shall go to exonerate the land the same as if there had been no devise, for he takes not as devisee, but as executor. Lord Cowper's decree in Littlebury and Buckley was set aside by the House of Lords. What is now prayed was refused in the case of the Duchess of Beaufort and Lady Granvil. As to the case of Farringdon and Knightley, the will was not quite finished, and so there might be room to suppose that, if he had finished it, he would have disposed of the residuum from his executor, so that I think the bill ought to be dismissed.

There being two against one, there was a decree for the plaintiff to have distribution.

---

[1] *Zouch v. Turner* (1680), 79 Selden Soc. 836.

Taussig MS. 311, vol. 1, p. 307

Trinity term 1722.

PAGE, baron: I am of opinion the plaintiff is well entitled to a discovery and distribution.

[1.] Whether an executor as such has as full a right in his testator's estate as of his own, I think not because he is only entitled *sub modo*, for, if an executor dies intestate without selling or disposing of the testator's estate, the next of kin to the testator, and not the next of kin to the executor, shall have the administration. Richardson and Sykes, in the King's Bench, 1699; 1 Ventr. 217.

2. To what intents he has the power of the estate and that is only to perform the testator's will. Where the whole is disposed of by the will, there can be no doubt, but the question is, where the whole is not disposed of, by the canon law, the executor had not the power of the undisposed part of the testator's estate. Constitution of Stratford in 1342, Linwood 46; [Gibson,] Bishop of Lincoln, *Codex*, 558.

By the Statute, an ordinary shall grant administration to a friend, who, in all respects, shall be in the place of an executor, and, after that Act, the surplus under the power of the ordinary. And so the bonds run. 21 Hen. VIII, ca. 5.[1] This takes away the discretionary power to whom administration [may be granted]. But still the bonds continued in the former form until 12 Car. I [1636 x 1637]. Hob. 83.[2] And from thence, the form of the bond was altered. 22 & 23 Car. II.

I do not think the Chancery cases will govern this, for taking it for granted that making an executor is an implied gift, yet it is a rule that implications cannot be admitted against express words. And here are express words that she should have it for life. And we cannot intend he designed to give her the whole interest when he gives it to her only for life. In this case, the testator cannot be said to die intestate in law, but in equity he may.

[To the] objection a devise for life is a devise forever of chattels, [he] answered it is so in a deed, but not in a will. A devise for a term or a horse for a limited time is now settled. Sir Godfrey Copley's Case in Chancery.

[To the] objection [there is] no devise over, therefore, nobody can take the remainder, no doubt, but a man may die testate and intestate as to several parts of his estate, as a will of an estate in the County of Middlesex and an executor thereof and yet he may die intestate as to an estate in Oxford. And then the executor will be only a trustee for the undisposed estate as an administrator, and then [there is] no objection from want of a devise over because the Statute directs who shall have it.

And in the construction of wills, it is a just rule that all the words of a will shall stand if possible. To give for life and forever is giving all and some. This is

---

[1] Stat. 21 Hen. VIII, c. 5, s. 2 (*SR*, III, 286–287).

[2] *Slawney v. Elbridge* (1616–1621), *ut supra*.

a much stronger case than the cases in Chancery of a specific legacy, for a specific legacy to an executor does not exclude an intent that he should not have a surplus, but, here, the words do manifestly restrain the gift of the law to her as executrix, as if he had said, 'I will not trust my executor with the whole interest, but only for life'. So in equity and conscience, he dies intestate as to the residue after her death.

PRICE was of the same opinion. The testator never intended any more than for life.

[To the] objection [that the] residuum is no specific legacy, the solution is the residuum is reducible to a certainty and so stands upon the same foot as a specific legacy.

[To the] objection a personal chattel is not devisable for life, Bro., title *Executor*, shows that the use of a personal thing may be given for life. Otherwise it is in the case of a deed. Besides, this objection lies not in the mouth of the defendant.

What does naming executors import? I am loath to say executors are now no more than trustees. Calvin's *Lexicon*, *verbo* executor; Swinburne, *Of Wills*. Executors [are] *legitimi*, the ordinary, and he is only a trustee, 31 Edw. III; *dativi*, administrators; *testarii*, an executor cannot convert the residuum to his own use. Sir John Nisbett's case; the executor is to execute the will of the testator or the will of the law.

The goods of executors are not simply the executors', but only for the payment of debts, legacies, and for the next of kin. This is by the civil law. By the common law, the executor is only a trustee. An executor could not have an [action of] account or trespass.

Second, his estate is only *in auter droit* and an action lies against him only in the *detinet*. A gift of all goods passes not the goods as executor, and an executor cannot devise his testator's estate. If an executor dies before probate, his executor is not the executor to the first testator, but there must be an administrator to the first testator. And this is by the construction of 25 Edw. III.

So an executor is a trustee in law and in equity. And [it is] no great stretch in courts of equity to make the construction that the executor should be a trustee for the next of kin as to the distribution. Foster and Munt's Case; Morley and Morley, 1702; Farrington and Knightly, in that case, the will was imperfect.

And the Lord Chancellor went upon the same reasons we go, *scil.* that the executor was a trustee. Swinburne 424; the Duchess of Beauford's Case [is] not contrary to Foster and Munt's, but only explanatory.

MONTAGU, Chief Baron: This case is of small consequence as to value, but great as to extent. Foster and Munt's Case is the oldest case that was ever adjudged to the purpose for which this bill is designed. The courts of common law always prohibited the ecclesiastical law in the suits for distribution. Case of Hughes and Hughes, 18 Car. II. And this is the foundation of the Statute of Distributions.

Brother Page thinks that an executor has not the absolute power of the estate of the testator. And if he means that he must pay debts etc., I agree to his proposition in that sense. But yet, if even a particular legatee takes a legacy without the assent of the executor, he is a trespasser. 18 ca. of Magna Charta and Lord Coke's exposition thereof; the ancient law books; Bracton, lib. 2, fol. 61.

And as to Brother Page's argument, it makes nothing, for it is plain the only reason is that there is no continuation of authority. The executor stands *in loco testatoris*. The writ *de rationabili parte bonorum* only lay by custom and not at common law.

[To the] objection, by the ancient ecclesiastical law, an executor is only a trustee, I admit this.

The Statute makes the ordinary grant administration in spite of his teeth. And the Statute puts an administrator upon the same foot with an executor. Cro. Car. 62, 101, Fotherby's Case; Hobart 191. These authorities prove that an administrator has an absolute right in the residuum.

I agree the Stat. 22 Car. II was made to alter the law and make the administrator a trustee. But I do not see any consequence that can be drawn from thence to the case of an executor. The Chancery never thought they had the power to compel an administrator to distribute before 22 Car. II. How comes the Chancery to have the power now to do it with respect to executors since 22 Car. II only extends to administrators?

I admit that, in this case, the wife takes only for life as a legatee and that no implication can be admitted against it, but the giving it to her for life as legatee does not exclude her taking in another sense, *scil.*, as executor, as in the case of an heir at law, and I think an executor is the same with respect to the personal as the heir to the real estate.

Testate and intestate seems an absurdity. And equity no more admits absurdities than [common] law. The distinction of an estate in different counties does not in anywise reach this case.

Justinian, *Instituo Titium executorem*; Doddridge, *Executors, ad idem*. To this, Sir Godfrey Copley's Case is opposed.

I agree that, in the case of particular things, there may be such a distinction, but I am not satisfied it can be done in this case, which is of a stock on a farm. Plowden, in Grantham's Case, says that, in the case [where] an executor has a term which he does not alter in his lifetime, he cannot devise it by his will, but the same case allows that he may assign or alien it by a deed. There is no authority that the law of the land will execute this trust.

[To the] objection it must destroy the estate for life if you construe it that she takes as executrix, [he] answered, by Lord Nottingham in the case of Zouch and Lord Anglesey, 1680, a devise to an executor *nihil operatur*, the plaintiff is an express devisee, and, therefore, the case is stronger against him. Why am I not at liberty to say that a devise for £20 is a devise for £20 and no more as well as that an estate for life is an estate for life and no more?

By the words of the will, the thing itself is devised. And my Brother Price has no ground to say the use is devised any otherwise than as it is necessary to support the distribution he would have made. This case shows the reason of the certainty of law forms. I think Foster and Munt's Case is a right determination with respect to the fraud. *Haeres mobilibus.* Sir John seems to me to contradict himself when he makes an heir to be a trustee.

And so he was for dismissing the plaintiff's bill. But the other two were for a distribution.

193

Strong v. Duke of Marlborough

(Ex. 1721)

A person is bound by contracts made by his agents.

A decree cannot be amended after an appeal has been perfected.

2 Eq. Cas. Abr. 19, 22 E.R. 15,
C. Viner, Abridgment, vol. 5, p. 533, pl. 36

8 May 1721.

Earl Godolphin agrees with builders before the Act[1] made for building Blenheim at the expense of the crown. And [the contract] recites that he made such agreements at the instance and desire of the duke of Marlborough. The duke is bound by such agreement, and [he is] as well liable to pay for the work done after the Statute as before.

Taussig MS. 311, vol. 1, p. 15, pl. 2

Easter term 1721.

A motion was made by *Ward* to alter a recital entered in the decree in this cause, from which the duke had appealed to the Lords. And the recital was of an interlocutory order relating to a time to which the hearing of the cause had been put off. The objection was that it was immaterial and not to the purpose.

Sed per CURIAM: You ought to have settled the decretal orders and agreed upon it before you appealed. And, therefore, we will not meddle with it.

[Later proceedings sub nom. Strong v. Duchess of Marlborough (Ex. 1723), see below, Case No. 405.]

[On appeal: 1 Brown P.C. 175, 1 E.R. 496, 4 Brown P.C. 539, 2 E.R. 367, 2 Eq. Cas. Abr. 531, 22 E.R. 448.]

---

[1] Stat. 3 & 4 Ann., c. 4 (*SR*, VIII, 336–339); Stat. 1 Geo. I, stat. 2, c. 12, s. 34.

194

Rex v. Flanders

(Ex. 1721)

A fine sent into the Exchequer for collection cannot be challenged in the Exchequer, even where the fine was conditional.

Taussig MS. 311, vol. 1, p. 38

Easter term 1721.

Sir Constantine Phipps moved to discharge issues estreated that were set upon his clients by the Commissioners of Sewers. The amercements were levied and in the hands of the sheriff. And he offered affidavits contradicting the facts for which the amercements were set.

But the reading of the affidavits was opposed because the commissioners had certainly jurisdiction and the court must presume that they have done right and, therefore, the court will not now go into the merits, the process having gone out from the Pipe [Office]. There is no dispute of the regularity of the commissioners' proceedings. The commissioners have a right to proceed this way or else to grant a warrant to discharge.

By *Sir Constantine*: The amercements, that is to say three of them, were set conditionally that, if they did not repair within such a time, then the amercements. Now, it is certain we have had no opportunity to controvert these, though, in fact, we have and did repair before the amercements estreated.

By PAGE: The record says that they presented you and gave you notice to traverse the presentment and you have neglected to do it. You might also have removed the orders by a [writ of] *certiorari* into the King's Bench. And you have neither done this nor traversed before the commissioners, but have stayed until the issues estreated and then come to us to relieve you.

And the court refused to read the affidavits, so Sir Constantine took nothing by his motion.

Harvard Law School MS. 1082, vol. 1, p. 61, pl. 3

Easter term 1721.

Sir Constantine Phipps moved for the defendant for liberty to try the fact concerning amercements set by commissioners of sewers, which fines were estreated here.

Serjeant *Whitaker*, for the king, opposed the reading [of an] affidavit, and [the amercements] ought not to be annulled by it. And [there was] no pretense of want of notice.

Sir Constantine Phipps answered the objection by saying that the amercements were only set *nisi* repaired by such a day.

The whole court said the motion should be denied and, if the notice was regular, you cannot controvert it, and, here, the money was levied.

195

Rex v. Chapman

(Ex. 1721)

A receiver of the revenue of the crown can have a writ of immediate extent to collect it, but a deputy receiver cannot.

Harvard Law School MS. 1082, vol. 1, p. 62, pl. 1

Easter term 1721.

Hutchinson was a deputy receiver, and Mr. *Bootle* moved for him to have the aid of the court.

Baron Price said that a deputy receiver was not entitled to the aid of the court and so are the Rules of 5 Car. I. But, in this case, the deputy receiver [was] bound in the bond with the principal receiver, and, therefore, [he was] entitled, and not otherwise.

Taussig MS. 311, vol. 1, p. 40, pl. 1

Easter term 1721.

Mr. *Bootle* moved for a [writ of] immediate extent in behalf of a deputy receiver.

By Mr. Baron Price: A deputy receiver is not entitled to an immediate extent. But here, the receiver[1] being also bound in the original bond, therefore, upon this, the court grants the motion.

196

Anonymous

(Ex. 1721)

A defendant who appears pursuant to a writ of capias *cannot plead or demur, but he must file an answer to the entire bill of complaint.*

Taussig MS. 311, vol. 1, p. 40, pl. 2

Easter term 1721.

If, after an attachment is taken out for want of an answer, a proclamation issues, the party against whom it issues is not then admitted to plead or demur, but he must answer. In this case, they had proceeded so far as to a commission of rebellion.

[1] deputy receiver *MS.*

197

Note

(Ex. 1721)

Sundays are included in the number of days allowed by a deadline.

Taussig MS. 311, vol. 1, p. 41

Easter term 1721.

In all other causes and for trials and for writs of inquiry in the country, eight days notice exclusive is sufficient, and a Sunday shall be accounted for one of the days.

In all special rules given with the Secondary to plead in bar or reply or rejoin, sur-rejoin, etc., each party shall have a copy of the said rule given him and shall have four days exclusive after notice and copy of such rule given to plead, reply, etc., and Sundays and holidays, if days in court, shall be reckoned as days within this rule.

198

Rhodes v. Reynolds

(Ex. 1721)

The question in this case was whether a proposed amendment to the declaration should be allowed.

Taussig MS. 311, vol. 1, p. 42

Easter term 1721.

Mr. *Bootle* moved to amend his declaration.

Mr. Baron Montagu asked what he would amend.

Mr. *Bootle* replied it is a motion of course, all things being in the paper.

The cause stood thus. The declaration was delivered in before the essoin day in Hilary term, a plea was pleaded then, and issue was joined in that term. The thing moved to be amended was this, *viz.* upon a stock contract to insert *causavit transferri.* And the question was whether it should be amended paying costs.

Mr. *Fazakerly* objected to the court's refusal to amend in the former case in this term,[1] but, to this, it was answered that that denial was grounded on its being after trial and the new trial must certainly be on the same record.

---

[1] *Rhodes v. Lovit* (Ex. 1721), see above, Case No. 165.

199

Note

(Ex. 1721)

At a hearing for a continuance because of the absence of a material witness, no affidavits in contradiction of former affidavits are admissible.

Taussig MS. 311, vol. 1, p. 43, pl. 2

Easter term 1721.

If a motion be to put off the trial upon affidavits of want of a material witness and a day [is given] to show cause, at the day, one may offer other affidavits in confirmation only of the former affidavits.

200

Jeffreys v. Jeffreys

(Ex. 1721)

A technical averment omitted from a declaration will not cause a verdict for the plaintiff to be set aside.

A small consideration will be sufficient to raise a consideration for a promise.

Harvard Law School MS. 1082, vol. 1, p. 62, pl. 2

Easter term 1721.

Mr. *Bootle* [moved] in arrest of judgment, there being four counts and entire damages given, if one of the counts is bad, it must all be set aside, and one of the counts is in consideration that, [if] the plaintiff would permit the defendant to do such a thing, the defendant promised to pay so much and it is not averred that the plaintiff did permit. [He] cited Plowdens's Commentaries, Browning's Case;[1] Dyer.

Mr. *Wills*, for the plaintiff, agreed [with] the rule laid down of four counts where one is bad and entire damages given that will vitiate the whole. But surely, in this case, after a verdict, it will be presumed that the plaintiff did permit.

PRICE, MONTAGU, and PAGE agreed and a little consideration will be sufficient to raise a consideration for a promise. And the judgment [was] affirmed.

---

1 *Browning v. Beston* (1555), 1 Plowden 131, 75 E.R. 202.

201

Rex v. Anonymous

(Ex. 1721)

Where a person is fined and imprisoned for assaulting a Custom House official and pays the fine, the term of imprisonment remains discretionary with the Court of Exchequer.

Harvard Law School MS. 1082, vol. 1, p. 63, pl. 3

Easter term 1721.

A fine [was] set for beating a Custom House officer, and the fine [was] paid for it. But the Act says that the Court of Exchequer must discharge him.

MONTAGU thought that, on payment of the fine, that the party must be discharged and that the party was not at liberty either to pay or discover.

PRICE and PAGE were of opinion that it was discretionary in the court whether he ought to be discharged or not and that notice ought to be given to the Solicitor of the Customs.

Chief Baron [BURY]: I think that it is discretionary in the court whether the party shall be discharged or not.

MONTAGU said that the judgment was *quod imprisonetur donec* the fine was paid.

But the majority of the court was for giving notice to the Solicitor of the Customs.

Taussig MS. 311, vol. 1, p. 51

Easter term 1721.

A man beats a Custom House officer, for which he is fined £5 and imprisoned.

And Mr. *Bootle* moved upon a certificate from the sessions of the fine paid to discharge him.

And the question which seemed to be doubted among the barons was whether they were obliged to discharge him upon payment of the fine.

The Chief Baron [BURY], PRICE, and PAGE thought that they had a discretionary power to discharge, and, therefore, they were for having notice given to the Commissioners of the Custom House etc., for the commitment upon the whole is a commitment during the pleasure of the Court of Exchequer.

MONTAGU said with warmth that the court refused doing justice if they did not discharge him upon payment of the fine.

202

Sewell, *qui tam* v. Johnson

(Ex. 1721)

A person who buys forfeited goods must pay the full price bid for them even though the goods have sunk in value after the bidding.

Harvard Law School MS. 1082, vol. 1, p. 79, pl. 2

Trinity term 1721.

I moved for Mr. Mayhew, the bidder, that he might be discharged, who bid for the goods the 17th of May, and a rule given which is seven days within the Port of London and fourteen days in other ports and this being in the Port of London, the seventh day the claim was entered so the bidder could not have the goods and since that the goods, being tea, have sunk 3s. in the pound, for which reason, I moved to discharge it, which was denied because the bidder bids on the contingency and he must take it in all events. This was moved before the verdict.

Harvard Law School MS. 1082, vol. 1, p. 88, pl. 1

Trinity term 1721.

I moved for Mr. Mayhew, the bidder of some tea in this court. A rule was given 17 May and expired 24th of May, and then a claim was put in which prevents the bidder from having the goods but must stay until the trial was over. And, before that time, the goods were sunk the third part in value. So I moved that he might be discharged.

And the court denied the motion, for, if a bidder bids, he does it with his eyes open and he must take all incidents and contingencies with it. And if they had risen as much, the bidder would have had the advantage. And besides, the record is made up with the bidder, and, if judgment goes for the king, the judgment is entered that the bidder *oneretur* with the goods. And the same case was denied in the cause of Leaper, *qui tam* v. Combs.[1]

Taussig MS. 311, vol. 1, p. 55

Wednesday, 14 June 1721. Mayhew v. Johnson.

Mr. *Browne* moved to discharge the bidding by Mr. Mayhew, who had bid upon a parcel of tea, but a claim was put in and the value of the goods very much sunk since that time, whereof an affidavit was made by the party and notice was given to the Solicitor of the Customs, who did not oppose.

[1] *Leaper, qui tam v. Combs* (1721), see below, Case No. 206.

Sed per CURIAM and [*blank*] by MONTAGU: The bidder knows that he bids upon a contingency, *scil.* that the goods may grow worse. Therefore, he is supposed to bid within compass.

To the contrary, it is very hard to keep the bidder to his bargain where he cannot have the benefit of it, *viz.* the goods within the eight days after the bidding.

Query, for the court could not agree about it.

Taussig MS. 311, vol. 1, p. 75, pl. 1

Trinity term 1721.

Goods were proclaimed in court 17th May. A claim was put in so that we could not have the goods at the seven days end by the court.

Per CURIAM: He bids knowing that the goods are liable to be claimed.

The claim was put in 24 May last. A motion to be discharged was made at the beginning of this term, and now the court refused to discharge him.

Bunbury 76, 145 E.R. 600

14 June 1721.

Mayhew bids in court for a parcel of tea. After his bidding, there is a claim put in, whereby the goods could not be delivered until the claim was tried. In the meantime, a great quantity of tea is imported, whereby the value of the tea, since the time of bidding, sunk £70. Therefore, Mayhew moved to have his bidding discharged, which, as was alleged, is frequently done where goods are perishable and a claim is put in after the bidding and there is delay in the prosecution.

But *per* CURIAM, by this method, if a man thinks he has outbid himself, he may set up a claimer and make that a pretence for a discharge. And it is by no means a rule that a bidder shall be discharged when a claim is put in afterwards.

And upon further motion, June 20, the bidder was held to his bidding.

And in Michaelmas term, 10 November 1721, Leaper, *qui tam* v. Bound, Bound had bidden in the same manner and paid £160, and, the claim being tried, there was a verdict for the crown; and Mr. Attorney General then moved that Bound might take the goods and pay his bidding pursuant to the order of court in 1715, 'That if bidders do not within fourteen days after the goods are legally condemned take out a *debet* and pay the king's and officer's moieties, the bidding money shall be forfeited to the officer that seized the goods', which, note, Bound was willing to do, but the court would not discharge him. The court had some doubt what execution to order against Bound, this being an information of seizure, upon which, regularly, process of the Pipe [Office] should issue, but that being long and tedious, they, at last, ordered a *fieri facias* against Bound, as, in the case of a personal information, is usual.

After trial, if there is a verdict for the crown, the judgment is that the bidder shall be charged one moiety to the king, the other to the seizor.

Where there is a condemnation without a trial, the bidder must stand to all hazards; but if, after trial, the bidder suffers by delay, the court often discharges the bidder.

(*Sed quaere*, says the reporter [Bunbury] himself.)

A bidder has a right to have his goods delivered eight days after the bidding if they are then condemned.

203

Bradley, *qui tam* v. Long

(Ex. 1721–1723)

The word brandy implies foreign brandy.

In this case, brandy that was imported unlawfully was forfeited even though the pleading omitted to state that the brandy was of foreign origin.

Harvard Law School MS. 1082, vol. 1, p. 78

Trinity term 1721.

An information was brought on the Statute of 5 Geo. 241[1] for taking brandies on board at high sea, and it is not alleged it to be foreign brandies.

Mr. *Ward* and *Bootle*, for that reason, moved in arrest of judgment and though this does conclude '*contra formam statuti*', yet that will not help in material cases. Hardres 217, Pitcher v. Jones; Hardres 105; 1 Saunders 49; 11 Rept. 58; Cro. Car. 464; Dyer 363.[2] It was no offense, the taking of brandy on board at high sea, before this Statute.

It was adjourned to be further spoken to, which was the last day of this term, but I did not attend.

Taussig MS. 311, vol. 1, p. 56

Trinity term 1721. In arrest of judgment. Gilbert Bradley, *qui tam* v. Isaac Long.

[It was] objected it is nowhere alleged in the information that the brandies taken in were foreign goods. And the prohibition of the Act extends to foreign goods only. Therefore, he ought to have alleged that the goods were foreign. '*Contra formam statuti*' does not aid. Hardres 217, Pitcher v. Jones. And the same

---

[1] Stat. 5 Geo. I, c. 11.

[2] *Pitcher v. Jones* (1661), Hardres 217, 145 E.R. 461; *Morbye v. Urlin* (1657), Hardres 105, 145 E.R. 403; *Barker v. Thorold* (1667), 1 Williams Saunders 40, 85 E.R. 53, also 2 Keble 145, 84 E.R. 91; *Shoyle v. Foster* (1614), 11 Coke Rep. 56, 77 E.R. 1222, also 2 Bulstrode 324, 80 E.R. 1158, 1 Rolle Rep. 88, 81 E.R. 349; *Rex v. Cholmley* (1636), Croke Car. 464, 79 E.R. 1002; *Regina v. Tregeon* (1578), 3 Dyer 363, 73 E.R. 815, also 110 Selden Soc. 368, Jenkins 243, 145 E.R. 171.

case proves that a verdict does not aid. Hardres 20; Hardres 105. [The words] '*contra formam statuti*' do but make the conclusion of the premises and are no part of the case itself. And. 49, 1st part;[1] 11 Rep. 58, in Dr. Foster's Case, penal statutes are strictly to be pursued in informations according to the words of the Act of Parliament. Cro. Car. 464; Dyer 363.

Adjourned.

Bunbury 78, 145 E.R. 601

14 June 1721.

This was an information upon the Statute 4 Geo., c. [*blank*],[2] for importing brandy in a collier; [there was a] verdict for the king.

Mr. *Ward* moved in arrest of judgment that it is not alleged in the information that the goods alleged to be taken in this collier were foreign goods, which the Statute expressly requires. To this, it was observed for the informer that the information concludes '*contra formam statuti*' and the verdict supposes everything necessary was proved.

On the other side, it was replied that these words only make the conclusion of the case, not the case itself. Mr. Attorney General being absent, no judgment [was] yet given.

Taussig MS. 311, vol. 1, p. 101

Trinity term 1721.

[It was moved] in arrest of judgment upon an information on the Act 5 George, an act against clandestine running uncustomed goods, fo. 241. It enacts 'if any foreign goods'.

First objection: The information here leaves out the word 'foreign'.

Second objection: The ship is not described into which the goods were taken, for the Statute is in the disjunctive, yet the information ought to have set it forth with certainty. Michaelmas 7 William, Rex v. Stocker in the King's Bench; *fabricavit vel fabricari causavit* was a naught indictment by the opinion of Holt and Rokeby.[3] Easter 11 William, in the King's Bench, Rex v. Fox; for not serving an apprenticeship *infra regnum Angliae aut Walliae*, the indictment was naught *quia Wallia non est regnum sed dominium.*[4]

If the information had been some ship in general, this had been too uncertain and this is much the same. The information does not say that the goods were foreign. And brandy may be made at home as well as abroad.

---

[1] *Emmot v. Fulwood* (1575), 1 Anderson 49, 123 E.R. 347.

[2] Stat. 5 Geo. I, c. 11.

[3] *Rex v. Stocker* (1695), 5 Modern 137, 87 E.R. 568, 1 Salkeld 342, 371, 91 E.R. 300, 323.

[4] *Rex v. Fox* (1699), 1 Salkeld 67, 91 E.R. 62, 12 Modern 251, 88 E.R. 1300.

Contra formam statuti is only an inference, otherwise there is no need of the description of any offense. [There is] no intendment but where there is an allegation of facts. But here is no facts alleged, which was in issue. We could not have nonsuited them upon the trial though not foreign because it was not alleged in the information to be foreign. Hardres 217. A verdict aids not.

Per Sir Constantine [*Phipps*]: We have laid the very name of the ship averring it to be either one or other of the species in the Act mentioned. Raymond 487; the rule there laid down is that whatsoever is necessary to maintain the issue must be presumed to have been given in evidence. 3 Keble 354; no day laid for an *assumpsit* is good after a verdict. Horsman, *qui tam* v. Gibson, in this court, Hilary 2 George; Read v. Francia, 11 May 1719, after a verdict is good.[1] Wine in common understanding is foreign wine, and the like of brandies. Sir William Jones 156; Dyer 212; Cro. Eliz. 743; 1 Siderfin 344.[2]

Reply: Trinity term 1706, in this court, Anderson v. Allen; Hardres 105.[3]

Price, baron: Brandies, I believe, are never called by any other term than that of *vinum adustum*.

Montagu, baron: Supposing this be not a good information, query whether the non-payment of customs is not a forfeiture and so the crown may be entitled to judgment upon that account, though it should not upon the other account?

Bunbury 119, 145 E.R. 617

22 November 1722.

In an information for importing brandy, *vinum adustum*, upon the Stat. 5 Geo.,[4] it was not alleged that it was foreign brandy, but concluded '*contra formam statuti*'. In arrest of judgment, *per* curiam, the conclusion '*contra formam statuti*' will not aid, but the question is whether *vinum adustum* does not *ex vi termini* import the brandy to be foreign. And now, it was adjourned to be considered and precedents to be searched.

Note: Afterwards, in Michaelmas term 1723, it was held *per* Price, Page, and Gilbert, barons, judgment ought not to be arrested upon this objection.

---

[1] *Hitchins v. Stevens* (1683), T. Raymond 487, 83 E.R. 254, also T. Jones 232, 84 E.R. 1233, 2 Shower K.B. 233, 89 E.R. 909; *Sorrel v. Lewin* (1674), 3 Keble 354, 84 E.R. 762; *Horseman, qui tam v. Gibson* (Ex. 1717), see above, Case No. 34; *Reed, qui tam v. Francia* (Ex. 1719), see above, Case No. 84.

[2] *Bedoe v. Alpe* (1627), W. Jones 156, 82 E.R. 83; *Anonymous* (1562), 2 Dyer 212, 73 E.R. 468; *Baldry v. Johnson* (1600), Croke Eliz. 743, 78 E.R. 976; *Jemott v. Cowley* (1667), 1 Siderfin 344, 82 E.R. 1147. [These cases do not appear to be relevant; perhaps the copyist misread Ward's original manuscript.]

[3] *Morbye v. Urlin* (1657), *ut supra*.

[4] Stat. 5 Geo. I, c. 11.

Harvard Law School MS. 1082, vol. 1, p. 153, pl. 2

Michaelmas term 1722.

In an information for importing brandy, *vinum adustum*, upon the Stat. 5th Geo., it was not alleged in the information that it was foreign brandy, but it concluded '*contra formam statuti*'. The doubt that now stuck with the court was whether '*vinum adustum*' does not *ex vi termini* import foreign brandy, it being but lately that brandies were made in England. It was admitted that the [words] '*contra formam statuti*' would not aid at all in this case. Before the Revolution, there was no such thing as English brandy. Precedents [were ordered] to be searched.

Taussig MS. 311, vol. 1, p. 375, pl. 2

Michaelmas term 1722.

5 *Georgii* [1718 x 1719]; that in case any foreign goods etc.

Per Chief Baron [Montagu]: *Vini adusti*; query whether this does not imply foreign brandy, for, if it does, then there is no need of the word *forinsecum*. Therefore, he desired to know how the precedents are, *viz*. whether the informations do mention *vinum adustum forinsecum* or only *vinum adustum* without more. We desire this may be looked into, and we will not determine this point until then.

Per Page: Until after the Revolution, there was no such thing as English brandy, but it is since Revolution mentioned in our statutes.

Per Montagu: I have seen several precedents. Some '*vinum adustum Anglice* foreign brandy', some '*vinum adustum a partibus transmarinis*', some '*vinum adustum forinsecum*'.

All the court seemed clear of opinion that the [words] '*contra formam statuti*' could not help unless the words '*vinum adustum*' implied foreign brandy.

Adjornatur.

Harvard Law School MS. 1082, vol. 1, p. 184, pl. 1

Michaelmas term 1723. Judgment of the court. Long, *qui tam* v. Bradley.

This arose on the words of the Statute that directed that no foreign brandy should be taken on board a ship at high sea. Upon this Statute, an information was grounded, and a verdict was given for the king. And it was called in the information *vinum adustum*, and the word *forinsecum* was omitted. And it having been several times argued upon motions in arrest of judgment, the court was of opinion that the plaintiff should have his judgment for that *vinum adustum vi termini* imports foreign brandy for that no brandy was known but what was foreign. So judgment was [given] for the informer.

Note that *Sir Constantine Phipps*, that drew the information, told me that he drew the information and that it was an error, though the court gave judgment as above.

Taussig MS. 311, vol. 1, p. 558

Trinity term 1723.

All the court, *viz*. PRICE, PAGE, and GILBERT, gave their opinions that *vinum adustum* must be understood *ex vi termini* to mean foreign brandy. And, therefore, they would not arrest the judgment.

204

Franklyn v. Jenkins

(Ex. 1721)

A modus decimandi *in lieu of tithes in kind that is too large is void.*

The parishioners have a duty to supply the sacramental wine and bread regardless of the vicar's endowment.

An endowment of a vicar with small tithes includes the tithes of hops.

Harvard Law School MS. 1082, vol. 1, p. 74

Trinity term 1721.

This was a bill, brought by the inhabitants of Fareham in the County of Southampton against the vicar to establish several *modus*es and manner of tithing and to be exempt from payment of tithe wood and to compel the minister to find bread and wine for the Sacrament. This seemed to be in the nature of a bill of interpleader for the impropriator of Fareham was a defendant, and he claimed the tithes of cinque foine clover and hops as a new increase and so not belonging to the vicar by endowment, and usage or custom cannot be to a new increase. The *modus* was for 12d. for a cow in lieu of tithe milk, 1½ for a calf penned or sold, and 1d. in lieu of all fruit, and so for all sheep brought in after Lady Day [25 March], 1d. or half the tithe wool.

[It was] insisted by counsel for the plaintiff that tithe wood is not due *de communi jure*. And they cited Hicks v. Woodson, 4 Modern; 1 Rolle, *Abridgment*, 641; 2 Cro. 42; *Clergyman's Law* 456.[1]

---

[1] *Hicks v. Woodeson*, 4 Modern 324, 336, 87 E.R. 422, 429, 1 Eagle & Younge 592, 2 Gwillim 550, also 3 Lord Raymond 116, 92 E.R. 595, 1 Lord Raymond 137, 91 E.R. 987, 12 Modern 111, 88 E.R. 1200, Skinner 560, 90 E.R. 252, Comberbach 403, 90 E.R. 555, Carthew 392, 90 E.R. 827, Holt K.B. 671, 90 E.R. 1271, 2 Salkeld 655, 91 E.R. 558, Dodd 171; 1 Rolle, Abr., *Dismes*, pl. R, 3, p. 641; *Hall v. Fettyplace* (1604), Croke Jac. 42, 79 E.R. 34, 1 Eagle & Younge 157, also 1 Gwillim 222, Moore K.B. 758, 72 E.R. 887; W. Watson, *Clergy-Man's Law*.

Bootle, as to wood, cited Palmer 38, 2 Rolle Reports 132.[1] Though the endowment is produced in this case, which mentions wood due to the vicar, which was in 1440, yet that will not destroy the inhabitants' right, who are no party to the endowment if Penly's Croft was given in satisfaction.

Sir Constantine Phipps, Mr. *Ward*, and myself were counsel for the defendant Jenkins only. We insisted that tithe wood was due *de communi jure* unless a hearth penny or something was given in satisfaction. And we answered the cases cited above by a late case in this court, Jordan v. Colley, Easter 1720, Exchequer.[2] The endowment mentions wood due to the vicar. [We insisted] that the *modus* of 12d. for a cow is too high and too large. And we cited Jones v. Cawthorne, lately in this court,[3] where 6d. for a calf was esteemed too high. Tithes of clover cinque foyne follow the tithes of hay to which the defendant Jenkins is entitled without doubt. And we cited 3 Keble 479, Darrell v. Withers; Hall v. Babb, Trinity 1683; Pomfret v. Parson of Luton in Bedfordshire, 1680, that a *modus* for hay may extend to clover; Lutwyche 1071, Darrant v. Booty.[4]

There is no proof of the other *modus* except 1½ for a colt. As to the *modus* for 1d. or half the wool in lieu of tithe wool, there can be no pretense for it. As to hops, there have been none raised there until within these twenty years and, ever since, the vicar has enjoyed them, but they are not mentioned in the endowment, which was produced, in 1440. But that endowment mentions that the bread and wine shall be provided by the vicar. But we insisted that, by the 20th Canon in 1603,[5] that the church wardens of every parish against the time of the Communion shall at the charge of the parish provide a sufficient quantity of wine and bread for the communicants.

One pence for a garden I do admit as fair, ancient gardens, but not if they are increased. Jescomb *et al.*, parishioners of Widmore in the County of Somerset v. Honaton, Easter 1704, in this court.

The Chief Baron [Bury] and Page were of opinion that a vicar could only be entitled by endowment or usage and, since hops were planted within the twenty years, such usage of twenty years will not establish a custom to the vicar. And they are not mentioned in the endowment.

Price thought hops ought to be paid to the vicar and that there were words in the endowment of 1440 that would carry tithe hops; the word '*alteragium*' has

---

[1] *Earl of Clanrickard v. Lady Denton* (1619), Palmer 37, 38, 81 E.R. 967, 2 Rolle Rep. 122, 81 E.R. 699, 1 Gwillim 360, 1 Eagle & Younge 306.

[2] *Jordan v. Colley* (Ex. 1720), see above, Case No. 130.

[3] *Sub nom. Jones v. Denston* (Ex. 1720), see above, Case No. 151.

[4] *Darrel v. Withers* (1675), 3 Keble 479, 514, 535, 728, 84 E.R. 833, 852, 864, 977, 1 Eagle & Younge 505; *Hall v. Babb* (1683), 1 Wood 220, 1 Eagle & Younge 541; *Pomfret v. Lander* (1680), 2 Gwillim 530, 1 Eagle & Younge 527; *Durrant v. Booty* (1701), 2 Lutwyche 1071, 125 E.R. 595, 2 Gwillim 578, 1 Eagle & Younge 639.

[5] G. Bray, ed., *The Anglican Canons 1529–1947* (1998), p. 289.

carried all small tithes. I shall interpret the words as extensive as I can for the benefit of the person that officiates at the altar. And the word 'gardens' may carry it, for hops were at first used in gardens.

But they agreed [for] a case to be made of it to be further spoken to as to tithe hops only. Court [. . .].

But, as to the rest of the matters of the bill, they agreed that tithes of cinque foyne clover and all new grass shall go to the vicar, as he is entitled to tithes of hay, that 1s. for each cow for milk was too high. And so they dismissed the bill as to that and as to wood.

They decreed no tithes to be due for after-pasture or feeding on the stubble.

They dismissed the bill as to establishing the *modus* of wool, eggs, fowls, offerings, and as to providing bread and wine for the Sacrament, for that, by the Canon, ought to be provided by the church wardens. But they declared nothing due for burying in the church and churchyard of any of the inhabitants without prejudice. And they only established a *modus* of 1d. for an ancient garden and 1½ for a colt, which, being so small, the plaintiffs were ordered to pay the defendants' costs.

Taussig MS. 311, vol. 1, p. 57

15 June 1721. Franklin *et al.*, parishioners of Faram in the County of Southampton v. Jenkins, vicar of the same parish, the Master and Brothers of St. Cross, impropriators of the rectory, and Bennet, their lessee.

The bill was brought by the parishioners to establish several *modus*es for diverse kinds of tithes and dues and to state and adjust the several rights of the impropriator and vicar as to others. And there was an endowment of the vicarage in the year 1440, by which endowment, it was provided expressly that the vicar should furnish the sacramental materials. The endowment was not general of all small tithes, but by particulars. *Sed quaere* the words of the endowment.

The *modus*es set up by the parishioners were 12d. for the milk of every milk cow, 6d. for every calf killed and sold before weaning, 1½d. for every calf weaned, 1½d. for every colt, 1d. for tithe wool of a sheep brought into the parish after Lady Day or else half the wool of such sheep, 1d. for the tithe of eggs of poultry, 1d. for herbs and fruit of every garden, 4d. for the offerings of all persons before sixteen years old, marriage fee 6s. 8d. for a burial fee. I suppose these [last] were insisted on by the vicar.

The parishioners also insisted that no tithe wood had been paid in the parish and that, if any was due, there was a close called Compound Close, which was held and enjoyed by the vicar in lieu of tithes of wood, and also that nothing was due for pasturage of after-grass and stubbles.

The matters in dispute between the vicar and the impropriator were the tithes of clover and ever grass, which was sowed in very great quantities in the parish, and the tithes of hops, which tithes of hops had been for thirty years received by the vicar. And it did not appear that any hops had been planted in the parish above that space of time.

For the parishioners, it was said:

First, that wood, not being due *de communi jure*, there might be a prescription against it in *non decimando*. Palmer 38, *per* Henden; 2 Rolle's Rep. 122; 4 Modern 344.[1]

Secondly, that Compound Close should be intended for wood, none having been paid in kind. Moore 911, Austin v. Pigot.[2]

Thirdly, no tithes are due for pasturage of after-grass or stubbles. 1 Rolle's *Abridgment*, 641; 13 Rep. 16; 2 Cro. 42; *Compleat Incumbent*, 456.[3]

Fourthly, as to the vicar's demand of 6s. and 8d. for breaking ground, it could not be maintained *de jure*. 1 Ventris 274; *Compleat Incumbent*, 295.[4]

Sir Constantine Phipps, for the vicar:

1. Wood is due of common right, [and it was] so held in this court a year and a half ago in the case of Jones v. Cawthorne and in the case of Jordan v. Parson of the Wenlock Parva, 1720.[5]

2. [There is] no manner of proof to apply Compound Close as in lieu of tithe wood, and the court could not intend it.

3. If the vicar be entitled to tithes of natural grass, he would be so of course to seed grass. 3 Keble 479; Lutwyche 1071.[6]

4. As to hops, the vicar only has received them, and, therefore, on the circumstances aforesaid, it is good evidence of his right to them.

5. Though it is expressed in the endowment that the vicar shall furnish sacramentals, yet that is as between him and the impropriator and shall not be construed to discharge the parishioners, on whom this charge is laid by the Canon.

6. As to the *modus* for a cow of 1s., it is too large; ditto for a calf, and it has been overruled in this court for that very reason.

Serjeants *Pengelly* and *Belfield*, for the impropriator: The impropriator is entitled to all tithes not expressly given to the vicar. 2 Rolle, *Abridgment*, 335, pl. 4, 334, pl. 1.[7] And, by this rule, he is entitled to hops.

---

[1] *Earl of Clanrickard v. Lady Denton* (1619), *ut supra*; *Hicks v. Woodeson, ut supra*.

[2] *Austin v. Pigot* (1600), Moore K.B. 911, 72 E.R. 991, also Croke Eliz. 736, 78 E.R. 968, 1 Eagle & Younge 151.

[3] 1 Rolle, Abr., *Dismes*, pl. Q, 13–15, p. 641; *Case of Modus Decimandi* (1608), 13 Coke Rep. 12, 77 E.R. 1424; *Hall v. Fettyplace* (1604), *ut supra*; W. Watson, *Clergy-Man's Law*.

[4] *Anonymous* (1675), 1 Ventris 274, 86 E.R. 183; W. Watson, *Clergy-Man's Law*.

[5] *Sub nom. Jones v. Denston* (Ex. 1720), see above, Case No. 151; *Jordan v. Colley* (Ex. 1720), see above, Case No. 130.

[6] *Darrel v. Withers* (1675), *ut supra*; *Durrant v. Booty* (1701), *ut supra*.

[7] *Anonymous* (1609), 2 Rolle, Abr., *Parson, Patron*, pl. 4, p. 335; *Anonymous* (1609), 2 Rolle, Abr., *Parson, Patron*, pl. 7, p. 334.

Secondly, seed grass is now so generally sowed in the parish and in so great quantities that it ought to be allowed to the impropriator. Wharton and Lisle's case, *per* Holt.[1]

As to hops, the court had some doubt, for Baron PRICE thought that the vicar might claim them under his endowment of garden herbs. But the Chief Baron [BURY] and PAGE were *contra*, so a case was made as to hops.

But as to the 12d. for a cow, 6d. for a calf, 1d. for wool, 1d. for eggs, 4d. for offerings, and as to sacramentals and Compound Close, the court dismissed the plaintiffs' bill, but declared that no tithes were due for pasturage of after-grass or stubbles and allowed the *modus*es for a colt and gardens. The plaintiff is to pay costs.

Bunbury 78, 145 E.R. 601,
1 Rayner 157, 2 Gwillim 629, 1 Eagle & Younge 768

15 June 1721. Franklyn et al., parishioners v. Master and Brethren of St. Cross, as impropriators, Bennet, their lessee, and Jenkins, the vicar of the parish of Fareham in the County of Southampton.

This was a bill brought by the plaintiffs, the parishioners, against the defendants to establish certain *modus*es in the parish of Fareham. The first *modus* insisted upon was 12d. for a milk cow and the second was 6d. for every calf killed and sold. These were both of them adjudged to be void *modus*es, being too rank, the first being above half the value of the milk at the time the *modus* was supposed to commence and the second, if ten calves were sold, 5s. must be paid, which is in effect for one calf, for the tithe is one in ten. A penny for gardens and orchards was allowed to be good.

(But note: This can be only for ancient gardens and orchards, as was adjudged between Perret and Markwick, 5 July 1716.[2])

The vicar being endowed of small tithes and hay, it was decreed that he was thereby entitled to hops, being a small tithe though of growth since the endowment, and also to clover, saint-foin, and rye grass, which are species of hay, that is the genus. No tithes were due for after-pasture or cattle fed on stubble. Although, by the endowment, the vicar was to find the sacrament wine, yet the court were of opinion it should be found by the parishioners, according to the direction of the Canon.

Note: Where *altaragium* is mentioned in the old endowments and supported by usage, it will extend to small tithes, but not else.

---

[1] *Wharton v. Lisle* (1693), 4 Modern 183, 87 E.R. 337, 3 Levinz 365, 83 E.R. 733, Comberbach 201, 209, 90 E.R. 428, 433, Carthew 263, 90 E.R. 756, Skinner 341, 356, 90 E.R. 152, 158, 3 Salkeld 349, 91 E.R. 865, 12 Modern 41, 88 E.R. 1152, 1 Eagle & Younge 579.

[2] *Perrot v. Markwick* (Ex. 1721), see below, Case No. 224.

3 Rayner 1096

The bill was brought by the parishioners of Fareham in Hampshire against the vicar and tenant of the impropriator there under the Hospital of St. Cross to establish several *modus*es, some of which were set aside as too big, and among the rest, a pretended *modus* of 6d. for the tithe of a calf.

[Order of 15 June 1721: 2 Wood 185, 1 Eagle & Younge 768.]

205

Leaper, *qui tam* v. Smith

(Ex. 1721)

In this case, the court found there to be an importation into a port even though the goods had not been unloaded.

The master of a ship who claims an interest in the ship is not competent as a witness as to an importation in the ship.

Where a judgment is given against a successful bidder for forfeited goods, the court will not make a special order for payment, but the judgment will be enforced by the usual process of execution.

Harvard Law School MS. 1082, vol. 1, p. 68

Easter term 1721, at *nisi prius*.

An information of seizure was brought of a parcel of tea that the goods were imported. And these goods were seized twenty miles below The Hope. And several merchants gave evidence that they never accounted a ship imported until she came above The Hope and that frequently orders were sent down to their ships to sail to some other port from The Hope and that they land there for fresh orders from their respective merchants.

Sir Constantine Phipps, for the defendants [Smith and Elliot], insisted on it and cited the Coffee Cause to that effect.

Mr. *Fazakerly* objected that the information was not maintained for that the seizure was not in the name of Leaper, but it now appears that Googe and Leaper seized, and so [it is] not the same. But that was overruled.

Andrews, the master of the vessel, was produced as a witness for the defendant, but [he was] objected to by the Attorney General [*Raymond*] as a party concerned and the rather for that there was an information for the ship, which Andrews claimed.

Chief Baron [Bury]: Since Andrews had claimed the ship, his evidence ought not to be allowed.

Upon the principal case, a verdict was found for the king, though the ship was seized twenty miles below The Hope, this tea being seized in the ship called the *Dove*, which is a notorious smuggler and the carrying of tea being [. . .] a great discouragement to the East India trade.

Bunbury 79, 145 E.R. 601

17 June 1721.

Upon a motion for a new trial after an information of seizure of goods in a ship that was twenty miles below The Hope, but within the limits of the port of London, the question was whether it could be said to be an importation before the ship comes above The Hope. But a new trial was denied *per* TOTAM CURIAM; so that it seems it shall be deemed an importation if within the limits of the port, though below The Hope.

Taussig MS. 311, vol. 1, p. 121

Michaelmas term 1721.

One Bourne being a bidder and judgment given for him by which judgment he is charged with the whole sum, both in the appraisement and the bidding, the Attorney General [*Raymond*] moved for an order to make him pay the money.

But the court made no order. However, they said it was their opinion that a *fieri facias* might go out for the whole money at the suit of the king. By 33 Hen. VIII, ca. [*blank*],[1] the barons of the Exchequer have power to frame new process in order to get in the king's debts. *Vide* the Statute.

Query whether an extent could go in this case, for it was affirmed by *Bootle* that it might, it now being made a debt upon record against the bidder. And wherever there is a debt upon a record, an extent may be granted.

N.B. The reason of Mr. Attorney's motion was this. It was doubted what process to take out in this case, for, by the clerks in the office, the usual method to execute this judgment is by a summons of the Pipe, then, by the long writ out of the same Pipe [Office], but this would require a year's time, and, therefore, this motion was made for an order to pay the money, and, if the court had thought fit to come into it, then the next step was to pray an attachment for non-observance of that order.

And Mr. Baron PRICE was inclinable to come into this.

But BURY, Chief Baron, doubting, the court made no order and intimated their opinions as before.

Query as to the order of 7 or 8 November 1715 concerning bidders.

[1] Stat. 33 Hen. VIII, c. 39, s. 37 (*SR*, III, 886–887).

206

Leaper, *qui tam* v. Combs

(Ex. 1721)

In this case, the court found there to be an importation into a port even though the goods had not been unloaded.

Harvard Law School MS. 1082, vol. 1, p. 79, pl. 1, 3

Trinity term 1721.

Sir Constantine Phipps moved for a new trial for that this was a seizure of tea below The Hope and so not within the Port of London. And he mentioned the cases Jenkins, *qui tam* v. Harwood; Bowen, *qui tam* v. [. . .]oriden; Smith and Elliot.[1] The Act of 5 Geo.[2] shows that a ship might come within the limits of a port by appointing a bond to be now given.

Attorney General [*Raymond*]: [There is] no necessity to prove an actual importation. The intention is sufficient, and, if that appears, [there is] no further occasion. And this was a notorious smuggler in smuggling ship called the *Dove*. And this is a growing mischief. And the East India trade will be destroyed if this practice prevails. The Statute of 5 Geo. was intended to enlarge for the benefit of the crown, not to take away the benefit of former acts.

[It was held] by the whole court no new trial.

For Bourne, the bidder, the same case [as Rex v. Johnson[3]], the bidding [was] not discharged, only this was after the verdict and the record cannot be altered.

Taussig MS. 311, vol. 1, p. 64

Trinity term 1721.

In a motion for a new trial, *Sir Constantine Phipps*, for the defendant, asserted that it had been often determined in this court that, if a ship does not come to or above The Hope, it was not reckoned to be an importation.

The tea in this case was from Ostend, but there were also 1500 guineas aboard, which money was to be landed here, *viz.* twenty miles below The Hope, but the tea and all the rest of the goods were bound for Middelburg.

By 5 George, ca. 2, it appears that a ship may be within a port and yet there be no importation, and, therefore, that Act obliges such ships to give security not to run the goods.

Attorney General [*Raymond*] *contra*: Importing is bringing within a port, but, then, there has been a reasonable construction made upon the Act, *viz.* that, where a ship was brought within the limits of a port by stress of weather, it has

---

1 *Leaper, qui tam v. Smith* (Ex. 1721), see above, Case No. 205.

2 Stat. 5 Geo. I, c. 11.

3 Perhaps *Sewell, qui tam v. Johnson* (Ex. 1721), see above, Case No. 202.

not been construed to be within the meaning of the Act. But, where there is a coming within the limits of the port with a plain design to land or run goods, this always has been construed to be an importation within the meaning of the Act.

Solicitor General [*Yorke*], *ad idem*: If it is within the limits of the port, then it is incumbent to show some particular reason for such coming within the port or, otherwise, the coming within the limits of the port must be intended to be with a design to land, and, consequently, it is an importation.

Per Sir Constantine: In this case, there was no breaking of bulk. And the received opinion has been that there is no importation unless the ship was above The Hope.

By Lord Chief Baron [Bury], a report [was given] of the trial, which I could not hear, his speaking so very low.

The court was fully satisfied that the ship came in in order to run and for no other purpose, nor was there any probable reason assigned or given in evidence for her coming in, unless that only. So no new trial [was granted].

207

Anonymous

(Ex. 1721)

A ship suspected of being used for smuggling will not be released upon security for its later surrender.

Taussig MS. 311, vol. 1, p. 65

Trinity term 1721.

Mr. *Foley* moved for a writ of delivery of a ship called the *Dove* upon giving security, but it appearing the ship was built and chiefly fitted for the running trade and used for such, as by the Chief Baron [Bury]'s report in the case immediately preceding,[1] which was an importation in this very ship, moreover, the trial upon the seizure of the ship being to be had this very term, the court would not grant the motion but *nisi causa* at the setting down of causes after term. And it was said that the delivery of a ship was never denied upon security, unless for the *Thomas* of Calais, which I suppose was a famous runner.

208

Bourne's Case

(Ex. 1721)

[1] *Leaper, qui tam v. Combs* (Ex. 1721), see above, Case No. 206.

A person who buys forfeited goods must pay the full price bid for them even though the goods have sunk in value after the bidding.

Taussig MS. 311, vol. 1, p. 61

Trinity term 1721.

Sir Constantine Phipps moved in behalf of one Bourne, who had bid upon a parcel of tea, and, a claim being entered to the goods, a trial was afterwards had and a verdict was for the crown, but between the bidding and the trial, tea sunk 3s. in the pound in its value.

The seizure of the ship and the tea was on 30 March 1721. The appraisement of the whole and the claim was entered and the goods were proclaimed on the 27th, which was the same day the claim was entered and, thereupon, the bidding by Bourne. Two informations were exhibited, one for the tea, the other for the ship. The last was not yet tried, and, therefore, here is a delay.

Secondly, there is but one bidding for the whole. By the rules of the court, fourteen days after the proclamation are allowed for the owner to enter his claim where the goods are not in the Port of London; eight days after the proclamation where the goods are in the Port of London.

Mr. Attorney General [*Raymond*] *contra*: The party bidding knows that a time is allowed for claims and that, if a claim is allowed, it will necessarily delay the goods, so he buys upon a contingency. The first proclamation is to show cause why the goods should not be forfeited, then, upon nobody's coming in, a writ of appraisement is awarded and, upon the return of an appraisement by indenture, then, the second proclamation, upon which the bidding is had.

Per Sir Constantine: A bidding cannot be severed, either for the benefit of the crown or the benefit of the bidder, but one must take all together.

Chief Baron [Bury]: It is certain that bidders have often been discharged. The question is whether here is a reason or no. Here has been a great glut of tea from Ostend. And I see no harm if the bidder is discharged. Nobody can say that the bare putting in a claim will discharge. The counsel do not insist upon that. And, therefore, if there is no affected delay, as there has not been in this case, then there is nothing said in this case for discharging but what may be said in every case, that the goods are fallen in value after the bidding.

Mr. Baron Montagu declared that, since he had sat in the court, which was now seven years, he could not recollect that such a motion had been before made. It sets forth the form and method of proceeding upon these seizures as they appear upon the record. By the record, it appears that Mr. Bourne is bound to the crown to answer for the money bid. And if we set aside this bidding, it is overturning the whole record, so that, by him, it is a much stronger case after a verdict by which the goods are condemned because, by the record, it appears that he undertook to pay the money in case the goods should happen to be condemned. And, by the record, it appears now that they are condemned.

As to the point whether we shall discharge before trial in case a claim is entered, I will declare no opinion.

But PAGE thought it was the same before the trial.

And so the court refused to discharge Bourne.

Sir Constantine Phipps, Fazakerly, Foley, and *Browne* [were] for Bourne; Attorney General [*Raymond*], Solicitor General [*Yorke*], *Ward*, and *Bootle* [were] *contra.*

209

Note

(Ex. 1721)

This note gives the form of a record of a bidding for forfeited goods where no claim was ever entered.

Taussig MS. 311, vol. 1, p. 80

Trinity term 1721.

See before the cases of Mahew v. Johnson and Bourn's Case.[1] Here follows the manner of entering seizures made for non-payment of customs and the bidding thereupon in court upon record as the same is abridged from the record.

The record begins thus, *viz.* A. and B. came before the barons on such a day *et [. . .] pro domino rege quam etc. [. . .] curiam intelligi et informari* that they, between such a day and the exhibiting of this information, seized such a parcel of goods, the goods of a merchant unknown *pro eo quod* the goods being such as were liable to pay duties were brought from foreign parts into port and unshipped customs not paid or agreed for, *et unde* the seizers *petunt advisamentum curiae ad quod bona et merchandiza praedicta ob causa praedicta remanent forisfacta* and they, the seizers, may have the moiety of them *super quo facta proclamatione pro dicto domino rege pro ut moris est* that, if any would inform the court why the goods should not remain forfeited, he should come and be heard, *et nullus ad hoc faciendum comperuit concordatum est* that appraisers named should appraise the goods and return their appraisement *per indenturem*, which indenture of appraisement the record sets forth *in haec verba super quo facta iterum proclamatur* that, if any would come and inform why the goods *ob causas praedictas* should not *tanquam forisfacta remanere quod veniret et audiretur et super hoc venit hic quidem* (the bidder) *in propria persona sua et obtulit sedare pro bona praedicta summa* £84 3s. 11d., being the sum of £10 more than the goods are above appraised at *et nullo curia informante quare bona praedicta ob causa praedicta tamquam forisfacta remanere non debent consideratum est per eosdem baronum quod praecit. in informatione praedicta specificata ob causa praedicta reman. forisfacta et quod* the bidder *de summa* £42 etc.

[1] *Sub nom. Sewell, qui tam v. Johnson* (Ex. 1721), see above, Case No. 202; *Bourne's Case* (Ex. 1721), see above, Case No. 208.

a moiety of the price or value of the said goods *secundum ratam oblacionem praedictam* the bidder *ergo denarius dominum regem nunc in oneretur et ei inde satisfaciatur et quod* the bidder *de alia summa £42 etc. pro altera medietatur erga A. at B. inde, scil. satisfaciatur ac quod bona praedicta in informatione praedicta spectante praefatur* the bidder *deliberentur praetextu statuti praedictis et ceterorum praemissorum.*

This is a record of a bidding where no claim was ever entered.

210

Bisset v. Brent

(Ex. 1721)

The question in this case was whether or when a defendant can demur to only a part of the bill of complaint.

Taussig MS. 311, vol. 1, p. 66

Trinity term 1721.

It was denied by the court that a man cannot answer to the whole bill and demur to any part thereof.

But MONTAGU and PRICE [said], where a man answers to all the facts in the bill, this is not within the rule because the prayer of the relief is to the court only. *Et in eadem causa*, if a party will waive costs, he may assign other causes of demurrer *ore tenus*.

As to a demurrer for want of sufficient value, Mr. Baron PRICE said that he thought there was a distinction, *viz.*, where a suit was originally commenced in equity for a demand under the value of £10, there, the court will disallow the bill for this cause. But, where the bill is brought for relief against a trial at law, which suit at law is under the value, he thought it not reasonable to disallow the suit for that cause because relief in equity ought to be granted against an unconscionable proceeding at law where it was for a small demand as well as where for a great.

The other barons spoke not as to this. And the demurrer was allowed upon another reason without costs.

211

Turton v. Clayton

(Ex. 1721)

A modus decimandi *in lieu of tithes in kind that is uncertain as to the total sum payable is invalid.*

Taussig MS. 311, vol. 1, p. 75, pl. 2

22 June 1721.

The plaintiff [William Turton], as rector of Standish in Lancashire, exhibited his bill for tithes of hay, agistment for barren and unprofitable cattle, and potatoes.

The defendants, by their answer, say that, within the said parish, there is and time out of mind has been by ancient usage or custom a certain *modus* or customary payment of 3d. and no more yearly paid by all and every parishioner of the said parish to the rector or incumbent of the said parish church in lieu or full satisfaction of all and all manner of tithes arising, growing, renewing, or becoming due or payable in, upon, or for all and every his, her, and their house and houses, yard, and yards within the said parish and for all his, her, and their hay arising and growing and all and every hen and hens kept by him or them within the said parish, that is to say, for the tithe of every house within the said parish, 1d.; for the tithe of all hay of every parishioner growing and arising within the said parish, 1d.; for the tithe of all the hens of every parishioner kept within the said parish, an half-penny; and for all the tithes of fruit and other tithable matters arising, growing, or renewing in, upon, or from every yard within the said parish, an half-penny, which all and every parishioners and parishioner have held, enjoyed, and kept within the said parish, which *modus* or customary payment is described and is vulgarly styled for house, hay, hen, and yard 3d.

And the defendants brought a cross-bill to establish this *modus*. And, by the rector's answer thereto, he denied that the *modus* extended to hay.

By the cross-bill, the *modus* was subdivided, as in the answer to the original bill. And the counsel for the defendant insisted on the *modus*es as separate *modus*es for all the things mentioned. But the witnesses, in their depositions, could not come up to the distribution of the 3d., as by the answer and cross-bill. And several of the witnesses for the rector swore that it did not extend to hay, as the rector by his cross-bill insisted.

Upon the hearing of the cause, it was insisted for the rector, plaintiff in the original cause, that this *modus* was naught: first, upon account of the inequality because he that has one acre of meadow pays as much as he that has twenty; secondly, it is naught because it is liable to fraud, for, by this *modus* as laid, if one parishioner should have all the hay ground in the parish, he would pay but 1d. penny for it and it is a *non decimando* to all hay in the hands of tenants not living within the parish. And the cases of Barker v. Cocker, Hobart 329; 1 Keble 602; Startup v. Doddridge; and Bean v. Lee were cited for that purpose.[1]

---

[1] *Barker v. Cocker* (1620), Hobart 329, 80 E.R. 471, 1 Gwillim 385, 1 Eagle & Younge 321; *Baudink v. Bushel* (1663), 1 Keble 602, 83 E.R. 1136, also 1 Levinz 116, 83 E.R. 325, 1 Eagle & Younge 440; *Startup v. Dodderidge* (1705), 2 Lord Raymond 1158, 92 E.R. 266, 2 Salkeld 657, 91 E.R. 559, 11 Modern 60, 88 E.R. 885, 1 Eagle & Younge 666, note also *Doddridge v. Startop* (1690), Dodd 91, 1 Wood 283, 1 Eagle & Younge 566; *Bean v. Lee* (1713), Dodd 231, 1 Rayner 120, 1 Eagle & Younge 703, 2 Gwillim 609, 1 Wood 537.

On the other side, it was said that all uncertainties and inequalities do not destroy a *modus*, for, in the case of a pecuniary *modus* for milk, he that has one cow must pay as much as he that has 100. And the case in Hetley 94 was cited, Cornhill's Case,[1] towards the end of which case, it is said that a *modus* for a garden should extend to so much only as was ancient garden, and not to any enlargement of it.

N.B. It appeared by the evidence on both sides that no tithe hay had ever been paid in kind.

And, therefore, the Chief Baron [Bury] was inclinable to have the *modus* tried.

But the other barons said that they were not to imagine a *modus* which might be good, but to take it as alleged in the pleadings and proved by the depositions, for, if you lay a naught *modus* and prove it, it signifies no more than if you lay a right *modus* and do not prove it. In both cases, the defendant must account for the tithes in kind. They agreed that this *modus* was neither certain nor equal, and, therefore, it would signify nothing to try any part of it.

Montagu observed that there was a great deal of difference between a certain and customary *modus* for the payment of 3d. for several things and a customary payment of 1d. for one thing, an half-penny for another thing, and 1d. ½ for another thing. If, says he, a close consists of three acres and is let at 3s. *per annum*, the rent is entire and the whole issues out of every part; otherwise, says he, if it be let reserving 1s. for one acre by name and 2s. for the two other acres; in this case, the rents are separate.

And so, upon the whole, the defendant's cross-bill was dismissed and an account was decreed upon the original bill for tithes in kind.

N.B. This was insisted upon by Mr. Serjeant *Chesshyre* and the other counsel as several *moduses*, *scil.* 1d. for house, 1d. for hay, an half-penny for hen, an half-penny for yard, which seems strange to me, for, if there is any color for the *modus* as it was at first laid entire, so it should also have been maintained as entire, for, if the parishioner was not to pay his penny for hay in any year where he had no hay, then, the objection that the parson might have upon the foot of this custom but 2d. or 3d. for all the hay of the parish is obvious, for, if it should all come into three parishioners' hands, then they should pay but each 1d., but, if every parishioner was bound to pay 1d., then, whether all the hay ground in the parish was in one hand or in many, the income of the parson would be exactly the same.

Harvard Law School MS. 1082, vol. 1, p. 73

Trinity term 1721.

This original bill was brought by the plaintiff Turton as rector of Standish in Lancashire for tithes of hay, agistment, and potatoes. The defendants insisted

[1] *Thornhill's Case* (1628), Hetley 93, 124 E.R. 369, 1 Eagle & Younge 362.

on a *non decimando* as to agistment and set forth a custom of 3d. for house, hen, hay, and yard, and they divide it by 1d. for house, ½ for hen, that is for all poultry, and ½ for yard, *viz*. things in the yards and gardens, and 1d. for hay. And he, therefore, insisted on this customary payment in bar of tithe hay. And there was no proof that ever any tithe hay was ever paid or anything in particular in lieu thereof. The cross-bill was to establish customs.

Sir Constantine Phipps, Serjeant *Stevens, Ward*, [and] myself, counsel for the plaintiff in the original cause, insisted that, as a custom was to have a reasonable beginning, this never could, for 1d. was to be paid whether a man had 5000 acres or only one acre and, in respect of the uncertainty, it could not be good, for a *modus* ought to be to some fixed and stated matter, as to an acre or particular farm and lands, and not so uncertain as this is, for, if the house fell down, then nothing was paid for the land and so [it] would be a *non decimando*. One shilling in the pound has been adjudged in this court to be too uncertain and shipping a *modus*.

And Mr. *Ward* cited Startup v. Dodderidge, 4 Queen Anne, Easter [term]; Hobart's reports, Wilson v. Bishop of Carlisle; Bean v. Lee, Exchequer, sittings after Trinity 1713. I cited Smith v. Rowcliff, Hilary [term] 1717/18, to the same effect.[1]

Serjeant *Chesshyre, Bootle*, and *Fazakerly*, for the defendants, [argued] that a *modus* was to be presumed and a non-payment is an evidence of it. They insisted that a general *modus* might include everything, as in the case of gardens and milk, and, in particular, if gardens are enlarged. And so [they] cited Hetley 94.[2] A *modus* for all mills the court will attach [to] new mills as well as old.

But the court denied it.

Chief Baron [Bury]: Here is no proof that ever any payment was made for tithe of hay. And, therefore, a *modus* shall be presumed. I cannot tell what to try because the *modus* is alleged different ways, for a *modus* must be certain. But yet something should be tried.

Baron Price: You must take it as the *modus* is set forth. And the defendants are short in proof. But, if the *modus* was proved, I take it to be void. This modus is insisted on against common right. And one evidence against the defendants' answer goes for nothing. And I cannot send this matter to a trial where there is no doubt, for the *modus* is not good at law as it is too uncertain and not fixed to any particular thing and a man that has 100 or 1000 acres and a person that has a quarter of an acre shall pay the same so that I think the defendants ought to account for the tithes of hay, agistment, and potatoes.

Montagu: The modus is not good. And it is *felo de se* as laid. And if proved, the *modus* would not be good, yet in respect of the uncertainty, if a man has half

---

[1] *Startup v. Dodderidge* (1705), *ut supra*; *Wilson v. Bishop of Carlisle* (1615), Hobart 107, 80 E.R. 256, 1 Gwillim 279, 1 Eagle & Younge 250; *Bean v. Lee* (1713), *ut supra*; *Smith v. Roocliff* (1718), see above, Case No. 35.

[2] *Thornhill's Case* (1628), *ut supra*.

an acre, then 1d. is paid; if 100 acres, only the same. But if let to 100 people, then 100 pennies are paid to the parson, so the *modus* rises and falls, which is against the nature of a *modus*, which must be always certain and determined. And so [he] decreed for tithes of hay, agistment, and potatoes.

PAGE: I cannot help thinking that it is dark, but I cannot intend a *modus* but, as it is laid, it is a joint *modus*. And the *videlicet* must explain it, for it cannot be repugnant to the premises. It is agreed that agistment was never paid for the same reason. Tithe hay might be never paid. If the *modus* is joint, then you have severed it, and, if several, then you have alleged it entire. A *modus* must be certain and determinable and cannot vary. One penny for a garden may be good, but that must be for an ancient garden and not if it is enlarged or made new if [. . .].

The defendants were decreed to account for tithes of hay, agistment, and potatoes, and the cross-bill was dismissed.

Bunbury 80, 145 E.R. 602,
1 Rayner 157, 2 Gwillim 628, 1 Eagle & Younge 771

A bill was brought for tithes by the rector for Standish in the County of Lancaster. The defendant insisted on a *modus* of 3d. for house, hay, hen, and yard, *viz.* for hay 1d., for an house 1d., for a hen an half-penny, and for yard an half-penny.

Per opinionem TOTIUS CURIAE, this is a void *modus*, taking it either distributively or entirely, for, as to the hay, 1d. is unreasonable, for, if a man has sixty acres of hay, he pays only 1d., and if he lets them to sixty several persons, they shall pay 1d. apiece. If a man should declare in debt for one entire rent of 6d., *viz.* 2d. for Black Acre, 2d. for White Acre, and 2d. for Green Acre, this would be bad, *per* PAGE, Baron.

The defendant was decreed to account.

[Order of 22 June 1721: 2 Wood 180.]

212

Rex v. Ashby

(Ex. 1721–1722)

The lien of a writ of fieri facias *attaches when the writ is issued.*

The question in this case was whether a writ of execution can be antedated so as to defeat the priorities of the creditors of a bankrupt.

Harvard Law School MS. 1082, vol. 1, p. 69

Trinity term 1721.

At first, a [writ of] extent was tested 16 May and a warrant the same day. But finding an assignment of the commissioners of bankruptcy is made the 15th of May proceeding, then, in order to overreach that commission of bankruptcy, they take out another extent tested 26 April and this by virtue of the same warrant of the 16th of May, as aforesaid.

The Attorney General [*Raymond*] insisted that this is a contrivance in order to defraud the crown, for that the assignment was made the same day as the commission was taken out.

Now, the *teste* being prior to the assignment and all such extents binding from the *teste* and agreed not to be within the Statute of Frauds,[1] therefore, the crown ought to have the preference.

All executions before the Statute of Frauds bind from the *teste*, Cro. Eliz., and the crown is not bound by the Statute of Frauds. Queen v. Arnold, in court;[2] Dr. Woodward's Case and the Duke of Salisbury, that the execution was good though taken after the death of the party.

This Act of Parliament ought not to bind the crown, and the *teste* of this extent is prior to the assignment and, in the case of the crown, if an execution came the same day, the crown ought to have the preference.

Sir Constantine Phipps, for the assignees of the commissioner of bankrupts: The reasons, as I take it, is that a [writ of] *fieri facias* will not lie out of term, but an extent may be granted in vacation time, and therefore, shall not by this new method and contrivance overreach a commission of bankruptcy. In Rex v. Quash,[3] the extent, for that reason, [was] set aside. Rex v. Mann, now depending.[4] If this practice shall prevail, it would be so great an inconvenience that there would be no dealing between merchants, and all commissions of bankrupts would be of no effect.

Baron PRICE said that there was a great difference between Quash's Case and this. Nothing has taken away the king's prerogative. At common law, the writ of *fieri facias* binds from the *teste*. And I think that the king ought to have the priority.

There is a great difference between granting such an extent in the case of aid and for an immediate debt due to the crown. Perhaps, in a case of aid only, I should not grant such an extent. But such contrivance in the commissioners of bankrupts will always overreach the king's debt.

The Statute of 33 Hen. VIII[5] gives this court a right to pursue the king's debts. Hardres report, Sir William Bagg's Case,[6] upon a *diem clausit extremum*.

Perhaps the practice of the clerks in court has not gone so far, but that might be grounded on a mistake because the *fiat* must be first from the baron and the

---

1 Stat. 29 Car. II, c. 3 (*SR*, V, 839–842).

2 *Regina v. Arnold* (Ex. 1710), Dodd 356.

3 *Regina v. Quash* (Ex. 1713), Parker 281, 145 E.R. 780, Dodd 365.

4 *Rex v. Mann* (Ex. 1723–1724), see below, Case No. 403.

5 Stat. 33 Hen. VIII, c. 39, s. 37 (*SR*, III, 886–887).

6 *Attorney General, ex rel. Ceely v. Bagg* (1658), Hardres 125, 145 E.R. 413.

clerks go no further than the *fiat*. I granted it *de bene esse*. And the king's revenue is in a worse condition than a private man's if this is not law. And I think that the books in this case ought to be produced to find the debts in order to make a record, but not to take them out of his custody.

Montagu: This antedating of extents is of great consequence. And it makes my ears tingle to take out an extent upon such a warrant. This is not at common law. Bonds on the Statute of 33 of Hen. VIII ought to be sued by *scire facias*, and so was the old method. And there is a clause in that statute to warrant extents to be granted in vacation time.

A *fiat* is not so until it exists. And, therefore, can a *fiat* made the 16th of May be a warrant for an extent 26th of April proceeding? And it was never pretended that such a *teste* might be so antedated until now.

In the case of the Queen v. Tanner Arnold, 8th of the Queen, there, the doubt where the warrant and *teste* was before the assignment whether the extent should take place before that time, it was a question. But now, it is settled that such an extent shall take place.

[To the] objection that there is no offense against the Statute of Bankrupts, [he] answered, because the rules are not pursued which direct that no tradesman or scriveners shall be appointed receivers.

The commission of bankruptcy is grounded on an Act of Parliament and [. . .] extents are only grounded on another Statute, *viz*. 33 Hen. VIII.

Page: I think that this case differs from Northcott's and Mann's Case. I did not know that a person was bound to take out an extent in vacation time, but, if it happens in term time, there, you shall not antedate the extent. And it is agreed that extents are not bound by the Statute of Frauds. I think that, in the case of The King v. Mann, the extent [was] well issued because that was in vacation time and from the necessity of the thing. But can you antedate a writ in term time?

If judgment is in Michaelmas term, can you take out a *fieri facias* after the death of the party tested the first day of that term? I think that it is hard in term time for a writ to have retrospect to another term. For the same reason, it may retrospect seven years. And it might be hard in cases of sales and purchases.

Price said that an extent and inquisition may be good without a *fiat*.

The Chief Baron [Bury] said that he thought the books ought to be produced to enable the crown to find debts.

So the motion was granted for producing the books.

Taussig MS. 311, vol. 1, p. 208

7 February 1722.

The case is now brought to a point by the Master's report whereby it appears that, on the 15th May 1721, a commission of bankruptcy was taken out and that an assignment of the bankrupt's estate was made on the very same day, that, on the 16th May 1721, which was in Easter term, a fiat was signed for a [writ of] extent, and that an extent was accordingly sued out immediately, though the same was made to bear teste on the 26th day of April, which was the first day of the term. And whether this way of testing the extent is warrantable is now the sole question.

Attorney General [*Raymond*]: In the judgment of law, the term is but one day and, at common law, the property of the goods are bound by the *teste* of the [writ of] *fieri facias* and yet the *fieri facias* if taken out in the middle of the term is always tested on the first day of the term. And if this retrospect is permitted in cases of a subject, why not in the case of the crown? There is no case in point for or against us, and, therefore, we must go upon the reason of the law in like or parallel cases. And the inconvenience would be very great, for the crown can never be secure in these cases unless the crown takes out an extent immediately as soon as default is made, which practice would be thought exceeding hard.

Solicitor General [*Yorke*], *ad idem*: We can only argue from similar cases. He insisted on the case of the *fieri facias* which, if taken out in term, must be tested the first day of term. If in vacation time, it must be tested the last day of the term.

The crown is not bound by the Statute of Frauds,[1] and, therefore, the goods are still bound from the *teste in casu regis*.

Take it, for argument's sake, that the warrant is in the nature of a judgment or else only as a point of formality. If in the nature of a judgment, then, being given in term time, it must be referred to the first day of term as well as other judgments are unless we are to make distinctions in order to defeat the crown of a benefit, which it is certain the subject has.

The Statute of Hen. VIII gives the court a discretionary power to issue process and it being a rule in the construction of statutes to bring them as near to the rules of the common law as can be and it will follow from this rule that the warrant must relate to the first day of term. Secondly, the discretion of the court may and should be extended to meet with new practices contrived to defraud the crown. And, by him, the extent, if in vacation, ought to be tested on the last day of the term.

This case is more proper to be settled on the record. If it is possible to be done, it may be by pleading and demurrer.

Raby, ad idem: The precedent in Quash's Case[2] does not come up to this. There is no inconsistency in this case.

The writs sued out which hold to bail are by Act of Parliament to be marked on the day of suing out, and yet, they always bear *teste* in term time.

[A writ of] *certiorari* to the Isle of Ely must be by a *fiat* of a judge, and, if a *fiat* is signed in vacation, yet the *certiorari* is tested in the precedent term. Lutw. 333; the case of Lestrange of Caius College, 1676, in the Common Bench; Trinity 5 George, Bayley and Bunning's Case, 1 Syd. 272; and, in Hilary 8 *Regi-*

---

1 Stat. 29 Car. II, c. 3, s. 15 (*SR*, V, 841).

2 *Regina v. Quash* (Ex. 1713), Parker 281, 145 E.R. 780, Dodd 365.

nae, Arnold's Case, in this court,[1] it was determined that the crown is not bound by the Statute of Frauds and Perjuries.

Sir Constantine Phipps contra: I admit that writs must bear *teste* in the term in other courts. And it must be admitted that an extent may bear *teste* in vacation time. By the practice of this court, there is no one instance since the time of Henry VIII of an extent taken out with an antedate to the warrant. And the practice of a court is the law of the court. Quash's Case is directly in point, and, there, the court set aside the land tax extent only for this reason, that the extent bore date before the warrant. Mr. Solicitor's position that extents cannot be tested in vacation time would set aside above half the extents that have issued out of this court.

Mr. *Ward, ad idem*: Goods and chattels of the subject are only bound from the *teste* of the extent; so is Sir Gerrard Fleetwood's Case.[2] And this distinction between chattels and lands is taken notice of in the very writ of extent.

The reason why writs of common law in the cases of a subject may bear *teste* in the term before is because the judgment is in term. But there is only a bond, and a bond is no more of this than of any other term.

Discretio curiae est discretio sana. And the practice is founded on the rules formerly established by these. An affidavit of danger of debt is necessary previous to granting the extent and here the effect of the affidavit, which was made before the *fiat*, must be this, that on the 16th of May, the party swears the debt was in danger of being lost on the 26th April preceding. An extent on a judgment for the crown may be tested on the last day or the first day of the term; it is otherwise of these extents, for they are not a common law proceeding, but a proceeding on the Statute.

This matter is proper to be settled on a motion. And so it was done in former cases in Trinity and Michaelmas 1712 and many cases in Hardres on motions; see Moor 239.

Bootle, ad idem: That the clause in the Statute relating to the king's suit being to be taken before judgment for the crown shows plainly that the executions cannot be antedated.

Reply: In Moreton's Case, the second extent was tested on the same day on which the first extent was made *teste* so that the court did use a discretionary power in that case. And we only contend for carrying on the *teste* to the term preceding.

If the warrant be a judgment by the barons, then the argument holds as before.

---

1 *Aldworth v. Hutchinson* (1688), 1 Lutwyche 329, 125 E.R. 173; *Baily v. Bunning* (1665), 1 Siderfin 271, 82 E.R. 1100, also 1 Levinz 173, 83 E.R. 355, 1 Keble 638, 930, 932, 83 E.R. 1157, 1326, 1327, 2 Keble 32, 84 E.R. 21; *Regina v. Arnold* (1710), Dodd 356.

2 *Fleetwood's Case* (1610), 8 Coke Rep. 171, 77 E.R. 731.

Query whether this court can sit and give judgment in revenue causes out of term, as in an information of seizure etc.

Per Bootle: It may.

And Page seemed also to assert it.

Per Baron Montagu: There is no instance of awarding a *fieri facias* or a *levari facias* out of term. And as to the conclusion of the extent, it mentions the warrant and the seal is put *per barones*. Before the Statute of 33 Hen. VIII,[1] the crown could not take out executions in vacation.

Price insists that the words of the Statute plainly warrant the use and exercise of the barons' discretion. The Statute makes the bond equivalent to a statute staple, but says nothing of any warrant, but the Rules of 15 Car. I make the affidavit and warrant necessary.

Per Montagu: There must be a *scire facias* in a case of a statute. And, therefore, if the Act had gone no further, the Act would not have avoided the aforesaid inconvenience.

Page: The difficulty with me is that there is no instance of this nature since 33 Hen. VIII. The warrant of the baron does not affect the *teste*, but only legitimates the going forth of the writ, but it does not relate to the *teste* of it.

Nor, by Price, is there anything in the Statute that speaks of the warrant.

Per Page: The process of every court is in the power of the court. And, if we see any inconveniences which did not formerly appear, may we not remedy them by an alteration of our process?

And the court at last left it to the consideration of the parties whether they could not put this point in some method whereby it might come before the court judicially, and then, if the court should err in judgment, it might undergo a further consideration and examination elsewhere.

Taussig MS. 311, vol. 1, p. 227

Hilary term 1722.

Mr. Solicitor [General *Yorke*] moved that the court would appoint a receiver for taking into his custody the goods of Ashby and disposing of them to the best advantage, at least of such goods as are perishable.

This was opposed by *Sir Constantine Phipps et al.* as unreasonable, for, if the crown should have a title to these goods, the crown is helped to it by the diligence of the creditors. And there is no affidavit that the assignee of the commission is either faulty or insolvent.

Reply: There is an order that Mr. Vanderbank shall not get in the debts etc., and, therefore, this motion is for the advantage on both sides.

But the court proposed this to the Solicitor [General], *viz.* that the assignee of the commission of bankrupts should give such security as the Attorney

[1] Stat. 33 Hen. VIII, c. 39, s. 37 (*SR*, III, 886–887).

General should approve. And this was agreed to and said to have been done in the Case of Tanner Arnold.[1]

213

Ferrand v. Bill

(Ex. 1721)

Uninterrupted possession of a mill for twenty years is sufficient proof of the title of the mill for a claim of suit of mill.

Harvard Law School MS. 1082, vol. 1, p. 71

Trinity term 1721.

A bill was brought for suit of mill belonging to the manor of Settle in Yorkshire, this being a mill held in fee farm under a rent of £6 3s. 8d. and granted by Lord Cumberland to Barrow for 6000 years and so vested in the plaintiff. And this bill was likewise to have the other mill destroyed.

The custom in this case was for all inhabitants within that manor to grind all their corn and grain and malt by them spent or used ground <in their respective houses> within the said manor.

Price said that it was not every mill that was a prerogative mill and, if you set forth a particular title, you ought to prove it.

Montagu said that a recital in an old deed with possession will carry a right as to this suit, for possession of itself is sufficient.

The court agreed that possession for twenty years was sufficient without any other title and the rather because the defendant cannot be twice charged.

214

Ferrand v. Batty

(Ex. 1721)

A plaintiff bringing an action for suit of mill need not allege his right to the mill with the same completeness as if he were suing for an ejectment from it.

Taussig MS. 311, vol. 1, p. 93, pl. 1

Trinity term 1721.

The plaintiff exhibits his bill for suit of mill etc. And he sets forth that an ancient lease was made to A. of this mill, which mill by several mesne assignments was come to him. And, in making out the title, the plaintiff had not one of the

[1] *Regina v. Arnold* (1710), Dodd 356.

mesne assignments, but the same was only recited in a subsequent assignment thereof. And the question was whether this was sufficient.

And the court held it was, inasmuch as the plaintiff was not making a title to the mill against the defendants, but only a title to the suit of the mill. And it needs not such precise evidence, as upon an ejectment for the mill. And, therefore, notwithstanding this defect, the court suffered the plaintiff to go on and read the subsequent assignment.

N.B. The assignment missing was 100 years old.

215

Hathaway v. Edwards

(Ex. 1721)

Tithes are not payable for pigeons eaten by the family or for cattle used for plowing.

Harvard Law School MS. 1082, vol. 1, p. 72, pl. 2

Trinity term 1721.

A bill was brought for tithes. And the court would not decree the defendant to account for tithes of pigeons used in the family, and Jones v. Calvert was cited, nor for agistment of young cattle brought up for the plow and pail and so insisted upon generally.

[Order of 26 June 1721: 2 Wood 178.]

216

Young v. Russell

(Ex. 1721)

A plea of the plaintiff's outlawry cannot be made puis darrein continuance.

A question in this case was whether a defendant married woman should file an answer by a guardian ad litem *when her husband is abroad.*

Another question in this case was whether a record that is pleaded must be produced under the seal of the court in which the record is found.

Taussig MS. 311, vol. 1, p. 93, pl. 2

Tuesday, 27th [June] 1721.

The defendant pleaded to an English bill that the plaintiff was outlawed, and he annexed the writ of *capias utlagatum* to the plea. But, by the very plea, it appeared that the outlawry was subsequent to the filing of the bill, though prior to the defendant's putting in his answer.

Mr. *Ward* made two objections: first, that the outlawry was subsequent to the time of filing the bill; second, that the outlawry was ill pleaded, it ought to have been pleaded *sub pede sigilli*, and not with an 'as it appears by the writ of *capias*' *utlagatum* annexed to the plea. And he cited 2 Ventris 282.[1]

Mr. Baron Montagu asked him what he meant by that expression *sub pede sigilli, sed non intellexi responsum.*

Mr. Baron Price said that outlawries were always pleaded as this, but he took an objection to the plea, *viz.* that it being pleaded by a married woman whose husband was abroad and she being only to answer notwithstanding *per ordinem curiae*, it should have been taken notice that she was admitted by a guardian, for married women are always to answer by a guardian.

Mr. Baron Page thought the plea of outlawry came too late, not being pleadable *puis darrein continuance.*

Mr. Baron Montagu thought the plea ill pleaded, as I take it for the reason before.

As to this question, what is meant by the phrase *sub pede sigilli*, in Plowden, it is said by Weston in Newis and [*blank*]'s Case, fo. 411,[2] that, if a man pleads a record in bar, he shall have a day to bring it in under the great seal. And all the justices had a little before said that a man cannot make himself title in any case by a record without showing it under the great seal. The question was in that case concerning a fine and a recovery.

But it seems to me that, when they say of record under the great seal, it ought to be understood of records in Chancery only, and not of records of other courts, or, otherwise, that the expression of great seal does not mean the great seal of England, but the great seal of the particular court where such records remain, for it is certainly that the records of other courts may be exemplified under the great seal of their own court. And the Court of Common Pleas has a great seal for that purpose. And it is a constant practice to exemplify all recoveries under this seal. And, formerly, they very often exemplified fines, though seldom now. And, as they may exemplify fines and recoveries, so they may any other judgments. And this I suppose to hold true of the King's Bench likewise. Then, if the record pleaded in bar be a record of the Common Bench or the King's Bench, what is meant by pleading this *sub pede sigilli* is no more than producing it exemplified under the great seal of these courts. *Sed quaere.* And see Dyer 228, pl. 45,[3] that the defendant brought into the Bench an exemplification under the seal of the King's Bench.

---

1 *Web v. Moore* (1691), 2 Ventris 279, 86 E.R. 440.

2 *Newis v. Lark* (1571), 2 Plowden 403, 411, 75 E.R. 609, 619.

3 *Palmer, qui tam v. Franklin* (1564), 2 Dyer 227, 73 E.R. 503, also Benloe 140, 123 E.R. 107.

But I never yet saw a precedent of an outlawry pleaded *sub pede sigilli.* See Lutwyche, fo. 6.[1] But they are pleaded *prout patet per recordum*, and this is whether the record is in the same court or in another court, but the difference is that, where the record is in another court, there, the party has a day to bring in the record. And he must, in justification of his plea, produce the record *sub pede sigilli.* Where it is in the same court, there is no need of any exemplification of the record under seal, for the justices may read the record itself, it being before them. And for this, see Lutwyche 40, 1514, 1604.[2] And the case of Ventris is of a record of an outlawry in the same court. See also Dyer 228, pl. 45.

But, if an outlawry be pleaded, to verify it by a [writ of] *capias utlagatum*, it seems to me to be exceedingly ridiculous, for there may be no outlawry though there be a *capias utlagatum*. And process upon a judgment is no proof of a judgment. In any case, a man may as well verify the being of a judgment in debt by a [writ of] *fieri facias* as a judgment of the outlawry by a *capias utlagatum*.

Sed quaere, et vide Lutwyche, fo. 6.

N.B. The plea was set aside in the original cause, by the court, though for the aforementioned very different reasons.

Harvard Law School MS. 1082, vol. 1, p. 72, pl. 4

Trinity term 1721.

The plaintiff pleads an outlawry obtained after the bill [was] exhibited. [It was] objected that it was not under seal and that it did not conclude well.

PRICE and PAGE thought that the bill being well instituted that the subsequent outlawry should not bar the plaintiff and the conclusion is whether he shall make any other answer. In this case, the defendant was a terre tenant and this plea [was] put in alone by the order of the court.

PRICE thought the title of the answer of a married woman was not good without a guardian.

PAGE [held] contrary, [there being] no occasion for a guardian.

Note: This plea was overruled chiefly for the reason that the outlawry was subsequent to the filing of the bill.

217

Payne v. Attorney General

(Ex. 1721–1722)

[1] *Gawen v. Surby* (1683), 1 Lutwyche 5, 6, 125 E.R. 3, 4.

[2] *Draycote v. Curzon* (1700), 1 Lutwyche 39, 40, 125 E.R. 21; *Clerke v. Scroggs* (1701), 2 Lutwyche 1510, 1514, 125 E.R. 832, 834; *Powys v. Williams* (1698), 2 Lutwyche 1601, 125 E.R. 880.

In this case for relief against an execution of a common law judgment to which the plaintiff in equity did not plead a defense, the court denied relief primarily because the fraud alleged was not proved.

Harvard Law School MS. 1082, vol. 1, p. 76

Trinity term 1721.

A bill was brought to be relieved against a *scire facias* and extents. And the case was thus. William Crosby was a collector of the excise, and, as such, wanting money to be returned to the excise, he employs Crabb, the younger, and, for Crabb, the younger's, due performance of articles as to the payment of the money, a bond was prepared wherein the plaintiff and Crabb, the elder, were both bound. And the bond was dated in October 1706 and then executed by Crabb, the elder, but not executed by the plaintiff until 9th of May 1707. Crabb became bankrupt, and bills were delivered 7th of May and postdated to the 15th of May in order to make the plaintiff liable. Upon this bond, extents and *scire facias* issued and several sums had been paid by the plaintiff on account of this bond. But he was not then informed of the postdating of these notes.

The Attorney General, in his answer, insisted that the plaintiff never pleaded to these extents and then was the proper time to have insisted on this matter, but, after execution executed, then comes this bill for £1800 delivered 7th of May and filled up the 15th of May 1707.

Mr. *Bootle* insisted for the plaintiff that a bond was only a lien from the execution of the bond.

Mr. Attorney General [*Raymond*], for the defendant: This was proper by way of plea, *viz. primo deliberatione* such a time *sigillatum* such a time and this is proper by way of plea and not to unravel this matter by this bill and the rather since part of this money is actually paid and now it is ten years ago since this matter was transacted. And I must submit to the court whether, after all these transactions, this bill ought to have relief and since everything was proper at law but not here *vigilantibus et non dormientibus*, which is now slipped by omitting to plead it.

Solicitor General [*Yorke*]: The plaintiff has nothing of equity in this matter, for this pretense set up by the complaint is contrary to the intention of the parties, for it was intended that the plaintiff should be bound in October 1706 and the bond ought to have been entered into according to the articles.

Sir Constantine Phipps, for the plaintiff, answered the length of time by proceedings at the Treasury. And as to the objection that there was a defense at law, he answered the plaintiff was not privy to these transactions between Crabb and Crosby until afterwards. And the plaintiff was security before; that will not influence this case.

Mr. *Bootle*, for the plaintiff: It could not be pleaded at law because it was complicated with several things so it is only pleadable by the Statute of Equity[1] and whether ever that Statute is proper to be pleaded, it is likewise proper by way of bill. 2 Saunders, Ferrell, Lord Arlington's Case.[2]

Page objected a thing very material, there is no breach of the bond until there is a default in payment which is not until twenty-four days afterwards, which is without doubt after the bond was executed by the plaintiff of his own showing.

Bootle endeavored to answer it by saying the bond is relative to the articles and such bills are relative proper in equity. Sir Thomas Cecil's Case, 7 Rept.[3]

Montagu compared this case to a policy of insurance where the party signs after the ship is lost. There, such party shall not be bound.

Sir Constantine Phipps: The breach arises from the articles to which the plaintiff is no party. It is in the future tense, and the breach is committed before the 9th of May.

Chief Baron [Bury]: I think that it is a strange case in equity after judgment by default, and the intention was to be executed before.

Price: This bill would have [been] better founded on a fraud between Crosby and Crabb. And the postdating is not so well proved.

The rule that has been laid down that, after judgment on a *scire facias*, no bill is proper. I take that rule to be a mistake. And I think wherever you can plead the Statute of 33 Hen. VIII, a bill in equity is proper. But here was no surprise in the plaintiff, neither could he be a stranger to it. At first, I thought it a hardship on the plaintiff as to a breach of the articles. But I now think that the breach is sufficiently grounded according to my brother Page's observation, for the breach is not until after default of payment, which is twenty-four days afterwards.

Montagu: After a transaction of fourteen years, I cannot relieve the plaintiff against this bond and especially since he himself had an extent on this very bond against Crabb, the younger, which extent recites this very bond [and] it was produced in court. And I do not approve of the complainant's proceeding.

Page: It would be very hard when he drops a word in a debate that he should be tied by it. This was a lien on the plaintiff from the articles. Crabb was the undertaker until the 9th of May. And then, the plaintiff was bound. If this was a fraud, then a court of equity is proper for relief. But none being proved in this case, he and the whole court agreed to dismiss the bill.

Taussig MS. 311, vol. 1, p. 67

19th June 1721.

---

[1] Stat. 33 Hen. VIII, c. 39, s. 55 (*SR*, III, 891).

[2] *Lord Arlington v. Merricke* (1672), 2 Williams Saunders 403, 85 E.R. 1215, also 3 Keble 45, 59, 84 E.R. 586, 593.

[3] *Cecil's Case* (1597), 7 Coke Rep. 18, 77 E.R. 440.

The plaintiff brought his bill to be relieved against a *scire facias* and proceedings thereupon. This *scire facias* was grounded upon a bond entered into by the plaintiff and Thomas Crabb and [*blank*] Crabb. And the case was this. One Crosby was made Collector of the Excise in South Wales, and he agreed to take Thomas Crabb as a sub-collector and to return the money for him. And upon the 1st October 1706, articles were entered into between Crosby and Thomas Crabb, by which Crabb covenants to attend to receive the money from time to time and, after the receipt thereof, to draw bills on sufficient persons, payable within twenty-four days, that the persons on whom the bills should be so drawn should accept the same and pay the money thereupon within the twenty-four days. And a bond was drawn bearing date on the same day with the articles in which [*blank*] Crabb and Pain, the plaintiff, who was son-in-law to Thomas Crabb, were named as obligors. And the condition of the bond was generally for the performance of articles, *viz.* that Thomas Crabb should perform all and singular covenants, conditions, articles, clauses, which, on the part and behalf of the said Thomas Crabb, were and ought to be performed and observed, referring to the aforesaid articles. This bond was signed by [*blank*] Crabb at the time it bore date, but it was not signed and executed by Pain until the 9th of May 1707, seven months after the date.

Before the 7th May, Thomas Crabb received £1875, for which he drew three several bills payable in twenty-four days after date. And, on 17th May, he failed, and the bills were not paid. Extents were issued out against Crabb, and, amongst the rest, an extent was taken out in aid of the plaintiff Pain upon this very bond. And he, thereupon, seized part of Crabb's estate, Crabb being indebted to him. But Crabb's estate not being sufficient to pay the crown, an extent issued out on the behalf of the crown, and, upon an inquisition thereupon, the articles entered into by Crabb and Crosby and the bond entered into by [*blank*] Crabb and the plaintiff were found and that Crabb had received the aforesaid money and drawn bills for the same which were not paid. And, thereupon, a *scire facias* issued against Pain upon the bond, and judgment was obtained against him by default.

And now, Pain exhibited this bill to be relieved against the proceedings on the *scire facias*, and he suggested for equity that the money received by Thomas Crabb was received by him before Pain had executed the bond and that Crabb never received any money for Cosby after Pain had executed the bond, and, therefore, though it was true that this money was not paid according to the articles within twenty-four days after the bills were drawn, yet, inasmuch as the money for which the bills were drawn was received before Pain executed the bond, it could not be within the condition of that bond.

And, for the plaintiff, they relied upon the case of Lord Arlington in 2 Saunders Rep., fo. [*blank*].

But the court were of opinion that the plaintiff had no equity because the money not being paid within the twenty-four days after Pain had executed the bond, it was a forfeiture of the bond, though the money for which the bills were drawn was received before the plaintiff actually executed the bond. And the court said that, if the bond was not forfeited on this account in strictness of law, that then the plaintiff should have taken advantage of it by pleading to the *scire facias*. But, in equity, there was no foundation for relief inasmuch as it was plain that Pain did intend to be security for all moneys that he received after the articles and his signing of the bond afterwards showed this and did in effect carry back the lien and obligation to the time of the date of the bond. And it appears upon the whole that Pain has already made some advantage of his being bound in this bond by having an extent in aid of himself against Crabb and having got in part of Crabb's estate for his own benefit. Therefore, the bill was dismissed by the unanimous consent of all the barons.

Taussig MS. 311, vol. 1, p. 249

Easter term 1722. See my prior book.

This cause came on now upon a rehearing. And the plaintiffs amended their case by showing that the non-payment of the supposed bills of exchange which was insisted on before to be a breach of the condition made after entry into the bonds by the plaintiff and so chargeable on the plaintiff was not true, for, in reality, there were no bills of exchange but only promissory notes and so were a breach of the articles before the plaintiff entered into the bond, for, by the articles, Crabb was to give bills of exchange and not promissory notes, and so the very giving of these notes are a breach of the articles before the plaintiff signed the bond.

Attorney General [*Raymond*], for the king:

1. The plaintiff had an opportunity of pleading to the *scire facias*. Therefore, how a party who has willfully neglected to plead shall be relived afterwards in equity is to be considered.

2. [There is] no equity nor proper consideration for a court of equity to enter into because it is only a legal defense.

3. The condition of the bonds is to perform articles, and the articles are to draw bills on some responsible persons. But the substance is to secure the crown money. And, therefore, whether by bills drawn on others or by promissory notes is no circumstance of equity, for, in equity, it is equal if the notes are sufficient, whether promissory notes or bills of exchange.

4. A man may certainly be bound with a retrospect. And there is good reason for this, for Paine's name being in the bond, the supposition of his intention of signing it was an inducement to the Commissioners to admit Crabb to the office.

5. The plaintiff has not fully made out the fact as to the post-dating of the notes.

Mr. *Bootle*, *contra*: As to slipping the time of pleading, it is self-evident that Mr. Pain was not cognizant or apprised of this sort of defense. If he had, he would never have suffered his estate to be stripped from him in the manner he did. This is contradictory to common sense to imagine.

As to its not being a proper subject of equity, the answer here is fraud, *viz.*, the post-dating of the bills, second, surprise, *viz.* non-acquaintance with these circumstances, third, he insists on the Statute of Equity and, therefore, that the plaintiff is relievable upon this bond. And in Sir Thomas Cecil's Case, he did not plead to the recognizances, though he might have done it, but he took advantage by English bill.

Lord Chief Baron [Bury]: I retain my former opinion and think the bill ought to be dismissed. Mr. Pain's general intention was to answer for the default of this receiver, and, therefore, though it was signed by him after the time of the breach, yet there is no relief in equity.

Price: The plaintiff's bill is to be relieved against all his own acts, *viz.* his bond, his judgment, and his mortgage. If this might have been pleaded at law, then it is not equity nor any particular foundation for an English proceeding on the Statute. He thinks that the articles warrant either notes or bills upon others. There is no evidence of post-dating the notes.

Montagu: This rehearing is grounded on a reason given by some of the court *ex abundanti*. But, for my own part, I cannot believe a word of this evidence at this distance of time. And this bill would set aside the Statute of Frauds and Perjuries.[1] And *cui bono* was the post-dating of the bills? Crabb could have no advantage thereby, and, therefore, the post-dating of these bills is a fraud; if a fraud, it was for the benefit of this plaintiff.

Page: There is no difference in this case in point of equity between a bill or a promissory note. In equity, the undertaking and not the particular time of undertaking is the thing. And Pain's executing the bond which was executed before by the others without making any objection thereto is evidence of his original agreeing to become surety for Crabb from the time of his entering into the office.

And so, by the opinion of the whole court, the bill was dismissed.

The articles were that Thomas Crabb or some other person to be by him appointed shall and will from time to time for the space of one year receive money etc. and shall immediately from time to time after receipt of the same draw and deliver to the said Crosby or the person who shall pay the same a bill or bills a note or notes for the same upon some sufficient person in London payable to the Commissioners of the Excise within twenty-four days after the date of each respective note or bill, which bill shall express of whom value was received, that the party on whom bills directed or notes directed shall accept of such bills and pay the same etc.

[1] Stat. 29 Car. II, c. 3 (*SR*, V, 839–842).

218

Leslie, *qui tam* v. Brandon

(Ex. 1721)

A plaintiff in a qui tam *action can inspect and sample the goods to be forfeited.*

Harvard Law School MS. 1082, vol. 1, p. 80, pl. 1

Trinity term 1721.

Mr. *Bootle* moved for inspecting the goods, being linen, and to have samples.

MONTAGU [was] strenuously against it.

But the court granted the motion.

219

Brittle v. Bradbourne

(Ex. 1721)

The possession of a tenant of the crown is the possession of the crown.

An action of ejectment does not lie against the crown.

The question in this case was whether the crown was in possession of this land in this case.

Harvard Law School MS. 1082, vol. 1, p. 80, pl. 2

Trinity term 1721.

Mr. *Fazakerly*, [argued] for the plaintiff, upon the special verdict, which finds that Henry Eccleston was seised of lands etc. and that Thomas, his son and heir, entered until Richard Norris, the sheriff, ejected him. It finds the Stat. 1 Geo.,[1] concerning the commissioners of enquiry, who made an adjudication that the premises were settled to popish uses and afterwards a warrant was made by the said commissioners to the sheriff to take possession of the premises and that, *praetextu warranti*, the sheriff seized and the defendant, under him, entered, and the plaintiff brought an [action of] ejectment.

The question is whether an [action of] ejectment will lie or whether the party is put to his petition.

And I hope to make it appear that the lands thus given to superstitious uses are vested in the crown yet that, in this case before you, an ejectment will lie. The power that is given to the commissioners as to this point is only in relation to lands given to superstitious uses; therefore, unless it appears by the adjudication of the commissioners that these lands were given to superstitious uses, then

[1] Stat. 1 Geo. I, stat. 2, c. 50.

it is *coram non judice*. And the contrary appears by the special verdict, for it finds that Thomas was in the peaceable possession until ejected by the sheriff. And, if these lands were given to the crown, then Thomas could not be in peaceable possession.

Where there is a special jurisdiction, as in this case, it ought to be set forth how entitled, for, by this adjudication, *non constat* that it was given to superstitious uses, I cannot say that this seizure *virtute warranti* was an actual possession in the king. And Magna Charta[1] says that nobody shall be disseised but by due course of law, and the king cannot be a possessor. [C. St. German], *Doctor and Student*, 84, and, if what the commissioners have done is wrong, then it is a disseisin in them and not in the king, who cannot be a possessor, as above.

The commissioners have only a limited authority. And when they exceed that authority, it is *coram non judice*. Cro. Car. 394, Nichols v. Walker; Marshalsea, 10 Rept.; Lutwyche 1565, Wynn v. Williams; Hardres 480, Perry v. Huntingdon; Annesley v. Michenson, Hilary 5 Anne [1707],[2] lands seized not forfeited and an ejectment was brought for these lands, and it was determined by three judges that the commissioners had no power to enquire into it and that an ejectment would lie. If commissioners of hackney coaches should execute their authority over a gentleman's coach, it would be *coram non judice*.

I should be glad to know whether the king is in possession by virtue of this act of the commissioners of enquiry or by his prerogative. I think him to be in possession by virtue of this act or not at all, for it was not in the power of the said commissioners to put the king out of possession.

And if the question above was against me, which I do not admit, yet the second question is whether, upon these loose proceedings, the party shall be turned out of possession. In the cases of inquisitions, where they are returned, the party aggrieved is at liberty to move to quash them. But this inquisition is nowhere returned so that you cannot apply to rectify it, as in the case of an escheator. And it cannot be traversed, neither can the party have a *monstrans de droit*.

The power by this Act is given to the commissioners only. And it cannot be delegated to another, as in this case, for the adjudication takes notice of their foundation for it, *viz.* the report of their master of the references. And that is no foundation for the commissioners to go by.

---

[1] Stat. 25 Edw. I, Magna Carta, c. 29 (*SR*, I, 117).

[2] *Nichols v. Walker* (1635), Croke Car. 394, 79 E.R. 944; *Hall v. Stanley* (1612), 10 Coke Rep. 68, 77 E.R. 1027, also 1 Brownlow & Goldesborough 199, 123 E.R. 753, 2 Brownlow & Goldesborough 124, 123 E.R. 851; *Gwinne v. Poole* (1692), 2 Lutwyche 935, 1560, 125 E.R. 522, 858; *Terry v. Huntington* (1668), Hardres 480, 145 E.R. 557, also Lincoln's Inn MS. Misc. 499, p. 462, Lincoln's Inn MS. Misc. 500, f. 12v.

In the common cases of justices of the peace, 4 Rept. 47,[1] this is as much void as one commoner joining with another. By this adjudication, it is not found when these lands were thus given to superstitious uses, where or what such lands were, or in whose occupation, or in any manner described.

Can this be called, according to Magna Charta, to be turned out by due course of law? The Act requires that commissioners should make entries upon their books. If a letter had been sent, would that have been sufficient to turn the party out of possession? And such letter would have been as authentic as this adjudication. It is not so much as averred that these lands so seized were the lands thus given to popish uses. In informations of intrusion in this court, it ought to be shown by some record. Coke, *Entries*, 372, 387.[2]

If an escheator or officer had found some minutes or memoranda, could that have been sufficient? And these were only minutes, not being entered in their books, and no power [was] given to the commissioners to seize. And the king is not in possession until a seizure and entry. Stat. *Parco Regis*, 54, 55.

The sheriff, in this case, let these lands to other tenants; that is not good. These commissioners cannot carry this case further than an escheator. And any office so uncertainly found as this would have been void. Fitzherbert, *Abridgment*, tit. Office, pl. 2; Brooke, *Abridgment*, 42; 2 Hen. IV, fo. 5, pl. 17; Bro. 130, tit. Pet., pl. 2.[3]

An action of trespass is a possessory action and shows that the king was not in possession. About the power of escheators, see 4 Inst. 225, 226.[4] And so he prayed judgment for the plaintiff.

Mr. *Bootle*, for the defendant: The first question, I admit, is whether an [action of] ejectment will lie to oust the king of his possession. [For] several hundred years, it has been agreed that it would not. And it does sufficiently appear by the verdict that the king was in possession. But I had nothing to do with the drawing it up.

[To the] objection [of] *praetextu warranti*, [he] answered that must take the whole proceedings.

These lands are so far vested in the crown as to bar an [action of] ejectment. I allow all the cases, and they are all enumerated in 2 Lutwyche 1565, and that

---

[1] *Wrote v. Wigges* (1591), 4 Coke Rep. 45, 76 E.R. 994, also Croke Eliz. 276, 78 E.R. 531.

[2] *Attorney General v. Heydon* (1578), E. Coke, *A Booke of Entries* (1614), 'Information', pl. 10, f. 372, also 3 Coke Rep. 7, 76 E.R. 637, Moore K.B. 128, 72 E.R. 485; *Attorney General v. Arundel* (1595), E. Coke, *A Booke of Entries* (1614), 'Information', pl. 15, f. 387.

[3] YB Mich. 5 Edw. IV, f. 7, pl. 15, Fitzherbert, Abr., *Office*, pl. 2 (1465); YB Mich. 7 Edw. IV, f. 16, pl. 11, f. 22, pl. 25, Brooke, Abr., *Office devant escheator*, pl. 42 (1467); *Bromeflete's Case* (1400), YB Mich. 2 Hen. IV, f. 5, pl. 17; YB Trin. 9 Hen. VI, ff. 20, 21, pl. 15, Brooke, Abr., *Peticion et monstrans de droit*, pl. 2 (1431).

[4] E. Coke, *Fourth Institute* (1644), pp. 225–226.

principal case will make for me, for everything that the commissioners have done in this case is within their jurisdiction. And though the inquisition is not so strictly drawn up, yet I do contend for the former part.

The king is in possession either upon these proceedings of the commissioners or the other operations of the Statute. And, if either way, it is sufficient to bar an ejectment. This power of the commissioners is lodged in them by the Statute to proceed in a summary way. And, therefore, the report of the master of the references, which has given such offense, is out of the case, for the commissioners are not tied down according to the rules of law or equity. But the legislature has given this uncontrollable power to the said commissioners, and it cannot now be objected. In this case, there is an actual possession in the crown, for, when an estate is let and a rent is reserved to the crown, that gives possession to the crown. And so it is in the case of a subject. This proceeding was only to make an actual seizure, and the sheriff only acts ministerially.

The verdict has made this matter certain. And as to the objection of the forms of the jurisdiction in time, place, and description of the lands, I answer as before that the commissioners are not so tied down.

I insist that all lands given to superstitious uses vested in the crown without an inquisition by the Act of Parliament. And to show that it was given to superstitious uses is the adjudication of the commissioners. And he cited 4 Rept., Sadlers' Case; 33 Hen. VIII, cap. 14; 36 Edw. III, cap. 13; 2 Edw. VI, cap. 8.[1]

Terre tenants may traverse. 5 Coke 105, Haldane's Case.[2]

The dignity of the crown cannot be affected by the judgment in ejectment and the *damna* that are to be received cannot be against the crown. Dyer 258 (octavo).

I agree with the difference in the case of an escheator *virtute brevis* and *virtute officii*.

Montagu doubted it, for, if the crown is entitled by the warrant or the adjudication of the commissioners or by the Act of Parliament, an [action of] ejectment will not lie.

Mr. *Fazakerly* replies: I think that Mr. Bootle fails in his foundation, for I cannot agree that the crown is in possession. Seisin is found in Eccleston, and the use is found in Thomas. And it should be found that these lands were given to superstitious uses. I admit that, if the crown is in possession either way, that an ejectment will not lie. But Mr. Bootle ought to show which way, which he has not. *Monstrans de droit* is not proper because that is admitting the party [to be] out of possession, which I cannot do.

---

1 *Warden and Commonalty of Sadlers' Case* (1588), 4 Coke Rep. 54, 76 E.R. 1012, also 1 Anderson 180, 123 E.R. 418; Stat. 31 Hen. VIII, c. 14 (*SR*, III, 739–743); Stat. 36 Edw. III, stat. 1, c. 13 (*SR*, I, 374–375); Stat. 2 & 3 Edw. VI, c. 8 (*SR*, IV, 47–48).

2 *Smith v. Alden* (1601), 5 Coke Rep. 105, 77 E.R. 217, also Croke Eliz. 826, 78 E.R. 1053, 2 Anderson 178, 123 E.R. 609.

I believe the word 'otherwise' is in the Act, but then *secundum sanam discretionem* is not so here.

Mr. Bootle has given no answer whether the proceedings ought not to be entered in books. And the master of the references is not authorized by Act of Parliament and not answered.

It is not in the power of the verdict to make the warrant good.

[To the] objection that the king is an actual possessor by the rent reserved, [he] answered this does not put the crown into possession, but the reservation must be from the party reserving. And so is *Coke upon Littleton*.

There is a difference between a general jurisdiction and a limited one, which last I take this to be. And the commissioners may be called inquisitors, but not judges.

Escheator *virtute brevis* and *virtute officii*, and the difference is this, the first is by order of the court, the latter by the limited authority. It is said that an escheator is by common law and that this case is upon the Act of Parliament; that by common law is as valid as by Act of Parliament.

Montagu: You seem to admit that an escheator *virtute officii* might return into the Exchequer and, if he turns him out, an assize will lie. You agree then it vested in the crown [and] that an office might go, and we could have done it in this court. 7 Hen. IV, fo. 46; Fitzherbert, *Abridgment*, 12; 24 Edw. III, fo. 54.[1]

The Act of Parliament has given this power, and we cannot help it. The sheriff formerly used to let the crown lands, and [he] so answered in the first accounts. Norris, the sheriff, acted right by the authority of the commissioners. Possession of the tenant of the crown is the possession of the crown. And you cannot bring an [action of] ejectment.

As to the case cited of Annesley v. Nickerson, that was an estate sold and an [action of] ejectment brought against the bargainee, but the contest there was not immediately with the crown. Stat. 1 Hen. IV, cap. 8.[2] And here, these lands remain in the hands of the crown.

Price: This is an actual possession if these lands were given to superstitious uses. But it does not appear that these lands were so given. And I cannot call this script of paper of the commissioners an inquisition or adjudication. It might be proper to ground an information of intrusion on this finding, but not to give possession, and it gives no possession by this Act.

Page: I incline to my brother Price's opinion that nothing is given by this Act but what was given to superstitious uses. And how does that appear? But if it was so, I doubt whether it was such a possession in the crown as would bar an ejectment. But, as this case is, it is no finding at all.

Montagu: This Act was to supply the former deficiency.

---

[1] *Earl of Suffolk v. Countess Marshal* (1406), YB Trin. 7 Hen. IV, f. 46, pl. 5; YB Trin. 24 Edw. III, f. 55, pl. 40 (1350).

[2] Stat. 1 Hen. IV, c. 8 (*SR*, II, 114).

Price: I know of no statute that vest the lands given to superstitious uses in the crown.

[They] adjourned for further argument.

220

Doe, *qui tam* v. Misor

(Ex. 1721)

In a qui tam *action, the Attorney General cannot withdraw a juror and the informer can be nonsuited.*

Harvard Law School MS. 1082, vol. 1, p. 88, pl. 2

Trinity term 1721. At *nisi prius*.

It was insisted by the counsel for the defendant that the Attorney General could not withdraw a juror and the plaintiff may be nonsuited. Farewell, *qui tam* v. Brutt was cited.

The Attorney General [*Raymond*] insisted that, if the prosecution is in the name of the king, that the Attorney General might withdraw a juror though an informer is named and, in all such cases, the Attorney General joins issue.

Solicitor General [*Yorke*]: The [writ of] *distringas* is *inter nos*. And it is the king's writ of *nisi prius* etc.

Chief Baron [Bury]: I am at present of opinion that, in such case as above, that a juror cannot be withdrawn by the Attorney General and that the informer in such case may be nonsuited. And as it is a matter of consequence, I will have a verdict given for the defendant subject to the opinion that shall be given in a case to be made of it.

221

Anonymous

(Ex. 1721)

It is unlawful to pay money in exchange for an appointment to a public office, even where the office is held only during pleasure.

Taussig MS. 311, vol. 1, p. 97

Wednesday, 26 [June] 1721.

A bill was exhibited to be relieved against two bonds given by A. to B. in consideration that B. should procure the office of a watchman at the Custom House for the plaintiff. The bonds were not given previous to procuring the office, but in pursuance of a parol promise then made that, if B. should surrender that office, which he then enjoyed, and procure the office to be conferred on the plaintiff, then, he was to pay. The office was only during pleasure, and the facts above are confessed by the answer.

And *Sir Constantine* [*Phipps*] moved for an injunction on the merits because this is plainly a void bond by the Stat. Edw. VI, ca. [*blank*].[1]

Sed per PRICE and PAGE: I doubt that, it being only an office during pleasure.

Secondly, by PAGE: These bonds were no part of the original contract. *Ideo quaere.*

But both thought that, though these sort of contracts were not within the words of the Statute, yet they are within the equity. And, as to the discovery of the consideration of these bonds, it was proper for a bill, so, when such a consideration is discovered, it is very proper for relief in equity, though not pleadable at law. And *per* CURIAM, the injunction was continued.

222

Dormer v. Anonymous

(Ex. 1721)

The amending of a bill of complaint after the filing of exceptions to the answer is a waiver of the exceptions.

Taussig MS. 311, vol. 1, p. 99, pl. 1

Trinity term 1721.

In a cause between Sir William Dormer, a *non compos* [*mentis*], by the Judge,[2] his guardian, against several copyhold and freehold tenants of the manor of [*blank*], and the defendants put in their answer, to which he excepted, and, after exceptions were filed, the plaintiff moved and had leave to add parties to his bill and also to amend the same, which he accordingly did, and he would now have argued the exceptions.

Sed per CURIAM: The amending of the bill after filing exceptions is a waiver of the exceptions, and you must serve the defendants with new process to answer the amended bills.

But the court would not give the defendants costs because, by PRICE, the exceptions are overruled by construction of law.

223

Anonymous

(Ex. 1721)

[1] Stat. 5 & 6 Edw. VI, c. 16 (*SR*, IV, 151–152).

[2] Sic in MS.

Where a defendant who is sued for tithes in an ecclesiastical court offers to pay the tithes claimed, the Court of Exchequer will enjoin the proceedings in the ecclesiastical court.

Taussig MS. 311, vol. 1, p. 99, pl. 2

Trinity term 1721.

Mr. Bunbury moved for an injunction on a *dedimus* and that the injunction might also be extended to stop the proceedings in the ecclesiastical court, where the defendant in this court had exhibited his libel for some tithes. And by the bill, the plaintiff offered to account and pay for all the tithes. And the injunction was granted accordingly.

224

Perrot v. Markwick

(Ex. 1721)

The question in this case was whether a modus decimandi *in lieu of tithes in kind for orchards and gardens extends to new ones.*

Taussig MS. 311, vol. 1, p. 104

Trinity term 1721. Perrot et al. v. Markwith, parson of East Brent in the County of Somerset.

A bill was brought by the plaintiffs as parishioners of East Brent to establish certain *modus*es, *viz.* 2d. for every orchard within the parish, 2d. for Easter offerings, 6s. 8d. if seven calves, 1d. for eggs, 2s. for milk of every cow, 1s. 6d. for a heifer, 2d. for an acre of meadow mowed, 4d. for every acre of meadow plowed.

And for the plaintiff, Woolmerston's Case in Hetley, fo. 85,[1] was cited, where it is said that, if the custom be that a parishioner shall pay 4d. for every orchard, this will extend to new orchards as well as old orchards. *Compleat Incumbent*, fo. 447.[2]

But the court was of another opinion. And this being the principal point insisted upon by the plaintiffs, they dismissed their bill without prejudice to the rest of the *modus*es. See Hetley 94, *per* Hutton;[3] if a man has an ancient garden for which he paid 1d. and it is enlarged, of that enlargement, tithe ought to be paid in kind.

Harvard Law School MS. 1082, vol. 1, p. 89, pl. 1

Sittings after Trinity term 1721.

---

[1] *Woolmerston's Case* (1628), Hetley 85, 124 E.R. 362, 1 Eagle & Younge 362.

[2] W. Watson, *Clergy-Man's Law.*

[3] *Thornhil's Case* (1628), Hetley 93, 94, 124 E.R. 369, 1 Eagle & Younge 362.

This was a bill to establish *modus*es and 1d. for every garden, whether old or new, and [. . .] 2d. for an orchard, whether old or new. And the cases cited for the custom were Hetley 89; Durrant v. Booty, Lutwyche 1071; Watson 447; Lutterell's Case, 4 Rept., where the custom was re[. . .]ed.[1]

But notwithstanding these authorities, the bill for establishing these *modus*es was dismissed.

225

Hankin v. Shaffey

(Ex. 1721)

Land newly cultivated following an embankment pays tithes, and the statute exempting barren land newly cultivated does not apply.

Harvard Law School MS. 1082, vol. 1, p. 89, pl. 2

Sittings after Trinity term 1721.

This was a bill for tithes. The defendants insist that the lands in their occupation were barren lands and yielded no profit until they were embanked and that they lost £2000 embanking. And if tithes were to be paid, they would exceed the rent reserved. And so they insisted upon the equitable construction of the Statute of 2 & 3 Edw. VI.[2]

But the whole court decreed for the plaintiff and said that there were several cases in opposition to that insisted on by the defendants.

Taussig MS. 311, vol. 1, p. 105, pl. 1

Trinity term 1721. Hankin v. Massey.

The plaintiff was lessee of the tithes of Holbatch in the County of Lincoln, and he brought his bill for tithes of corn arising upon lands which were newly embanked.

It appeared by the answer of the defendant [Massey], who insisted that his lands ought not to pay tithes of corn, that the lands were lately embanked, that never any tithes had been paid before nor ever any rent paid for them. [*blank*] Case, in Dyer, fo. 171, was cited; Godolphin, *Reports Can.*, fo. 387; 3 Bulstrode 167.[3]

---

1 *Norton v. Harmer* (1628), Hetley 88, 110, 117, 124 E.R. 365, 382, 387, also Littleton 5, 152, 124 E.R. 108, 182, Croke Car. 113, 79 E.R. 699, 1 Eagle & Younge 363; *Durrant v. Booty* (1701), 2 Lutwyche 1071, 125 E.R. 595, 2 Gwillim 578, 1 Eagle & Younge 639; W. Watson, *Clergy-Man's Law*; *Cottel v. Luttrel* (1601), 4 Coke Rep. 84, 76 E.R. 1063.

2 Stat. 2 & 3 Edw. VI, c. 13, s. 5 (*SR*, IV, 56).

3 *Pelles v. Saunderson* (1559), 2 Dyer 170, 73 E.R. 374, also Jenkins 218, 145 E.R. 150, 1 Gwillim 130, 1 Eagle & Younge 57; J. Godolphin, *Repertorium Canonicum*.

And the court thought it a clear case and decreed that the defendant should account for his tithes.

[Order, sub nom. Hankin v. Fotheringham, 6 July 1721: 2 Wood 184, 1 Eagle & Younge 772.]

[Related cases: Hankin v. Massey (Ex. 1716), see above, Case No. 13.]

226

Ashton v. Brooke

(Ex. 1721)

Where a third mortgagee purchases the first mortgage with notice of the second mortgage, he must pay off the second mortgagee upon a foreclosure.

Taussig MS. 311, vol. 1, p. 105, pl. 2

Trinity term 1721.

Brook contracted for the purchase of an estate of one Moorcroft, upon which estate Ashton had a mortgage bearing date 24 December 1708 for the sum of £70. And also Ashton had lent £20 more upon a bond in the year 1712. Brook, after the contract, applied to Ashton to deliver up the deed of mortgage and said he would take an assignment of it, but, some short time afterwards, he told Ashton that he would not, for that he had discovered a former mortgage made by Moorcroft to one Davis which bore date 6 September 1708 and so was prior to Mrs. Ashton's encumbrance. Of this mortgage, he got an assignment and now refused to pay off Mrs. Ashton, whereupon she brought her bill to compel him to pay off her mortgage and also the bond.

And for the plaintiff, it was insisted that Brook having notice before his contract for the purchase should not avail himself by a subsequent assignment of a prior title to hers. And for this, the case of Moor v. Mayhow, first Can. Cases, fo. 34, and the case of Churchill v. Grove, fo. 36, were cited.[1]

And of this opinion was the court. And they decreed him to pay the plaintiff her money upon the mortgage, but not upon the bond.

Harvard Law School MS. 1082, vol. 1 p. 89, pl. 3

Sittings after Trinity term 1721.

The third mortgagee purchases in the first mortgage with notice of the second. And I think the opinion of the court was that he might cover it in that manner. *Sed quaere.*

---

[1] *More v. Mayhow* (1663), 1 Chancery Cases 34, 22 E.R. 680, also 2 Freeman 175, 22 E.R. 1141, 1 Eq. Cas. Abr. 38, 334, 21 E.R. 857, 1084; *Churchill v. Grove* (1663), 1 Chancery Cases 35, 22 E.R. 681, also 2 Freeman 176, 22 E.R. 1142, Nelson 89, 21 E.R. 797.

227

Attorney General v. Powell

(Ex. 1721)

A writ of extent can be amended with leave of court.

Harvard Law School MS. 1082, vol. 1, p. 91, pl. 1

Michaelmas term 1721.

Serjeant *Comyns* [moved] to discharge a [writ of] extent upon an estate purchased by the duke of Chandos upon the account of Burton that took a bond in the crown's name. And my objection to the extent is that there is no *teste* to it, for it is *undecimo die nostri septimo* and no month is mentioned. And if a *teste* is wanting, it is null. And he cited 2 Jones 83; 11 Edw. III; 1 Levinz 20; Cro. Eliz. 592.[1] A *teste* out of term is void. 1 Siderfin 304; Latch 11; Salkeld 700.[2]

Mr. *Bootle*, for the same: The extent binds from the *teste*, which is the foundation. And the property is bound from that term, for an impossible *teste* or no *teste* cannot bind. Shower 80, Simplon v. [*blank*].[3] Here is nothing to amend it by, for as the court inclined in the case of Northcott and Mann[4] that an extent might have relation prior to the warrant, then there is no foundation for an alteration, for the warrant signifies nothing.

Montagu said that there was a difference between judicial writs and original writs. And I do not know why it may not be amended by my brother Price's warrant. Let there be notice to the Attorney General.

I [the reporter] was afterwards informed, though not in court, that the extent was permitted to be amended by Baron Price's warrant against the opinion of Montagu, who declared that he could not amend it.

Harvard Law School MS. 1082, vol. 1, p. 107, pl. 1

Michaelmas term 1721. Rex v. Fletcher Powell.

Sir Constantine Phipps and *Bootle* moved to set aside an extent, there being no month mentioned therein, but only *undecimo die* [*blank*] in the year 1721. This is

1 *Wynne v. Wynne* (1677), T. Jones 83, 84 E.R. 1158, also 3 Keble 781, 806, 84 E.R. 1008, 1023; *Heath v. Paget* (1660), 1 Levinz 1, 2, 83 E.R. 266, also 1 Keble 3, 13, 19, 24, 25, 60, 83 E.R. 774, 781, 785, 788, 789, 811, 1 Siderfin 40, 82 E.R. 957; *Grondy v. Ischarn* (1597), Croke Eliz. 592, 78 E.R. 835.

2 *Sterling v. Moniers* (1666), 1 Siderfin 304, 82 E.R. 1121; *Ramsey v. Michel*, Latch 11, 82 E.R. 249; *Shirley v. Wright* (1702), 2 Salkeld 700, 91 E.R. 592, also 2 Lord Raymond 775, 92 E.R. 17, Holt K.B. 761, 90 E.R. 1319, 7 Modern 29, 87 E.R. 1075, 1 Salkeld 273, 91 E.R. 239.

3 *Sympson v. Inhabitants of Penryth* (1689), 1 Shower K.B. 80, 89 E.R. 463.

4 *Rex v. Mann* (Ex. 1727), see below, Case No. 403.

no *teste*; so it is not amendable, for, though there may be a regular warrant or *fiat*, yet it does not follow that the extent must be at the same time.

And it has been doubted, as in the case of The King v. Mann etc. whether the extent might not bear *teste* before.

This was answered by the counsel for the king that it was amendable and that a warrant was a ground for it, as in the case of an original writ, as if there is any defect therein, it is amendable by the directions given to the cursitor.

Chief Baron [Bury], Price, Page agreed that it was amendable, for the *fiat* was a proper ground for it.

Montagu was against it and that there was nothing to amend it by.

But by the opinion of the other three judges, it was amended.

Taussig MS. 311, vol. 1, p. 110

Saturday, November 4th, 1721.

Mr. Serjeant *Comyns* moved to quash an extent and set aside the inquisition and [writ of] *levari* [*facias*] thereupon grounded and that the sheriff might show cause why an attachment should not go against him for his misbehavior in executing the *levari*.

The objection to the extent was that it had no date, for the *teste* ran thus, *teste undecimo anno regni nostri septimo*, so no day or month was mentioned. And that the writ was null for this default, he cited T. Jones 83, where, upon [a writ of] error to reverse a fine, it was objected that there was no *teste* to the original writ of covenant and the objection was allowed. 1 Levinz 2, where, in an assize, the writ was '*teste duodecno*' instead of *duodecimo* and it was abated for that reason. Cro. Eliz. 592; where in error to reverse an outlawry, the error assigned was the [writ of] *capias* was *este Edmundo Anderson* instead of *teste* and the outlawry was reversed because the *teste* is the warrant of the writ, and the book adds 'and so it is of judicial writs'.

And Mr. *Bootle* cited Shower's 80, where it is said that the *teste* of an original is not amendable because it is not form, but is a mistake in the law and not a bare misinstruction from the client.

Mr. Serjeant [*Comyns*] further said that it was a known rule that writs tested out of term were void. And he cited Latch 11 that judicial [writs] cannot bear *teste* out of term; it is otherwise of writs original because Chancery is always open. 1 Siderfin 304, where it is also said that no *capias* or other writ issuing out of the King's Bench can be tested out of term; the original case there was of a *mandamus*. And Salkeld 700, Shirley v. Wright, where Holt says that a writ of execution that bears *teste* out of term is a void writ.

It seemed to me that, as to this last argument, it was not pertinent to the matter before the court, for I have often heard it affirmed that extents may bear *teste* out of term and that is the reason that they shall not be antedated, for the chattels of the debtor are bound from the *teste* of the extent.

The court ordered that the party at whose instance it was pursued and the Attorney General should have notice and the matter moved again, for, as to the question concerning the validity of the brief, they would not hear anything further without such notice *ut supra*. But, as to the misbehavior of the sheriff, upon an affidavit read, they granted a rule that he should [show] cause *quare non* attachment [should go] against him.

As to the *teste* of the writ, Mr. Baron Montagu said that original writs were not perhaps amendable because there is nothing to amend by; it is otherwise of judicial writs because they may perhaps be amended by the award of the court and, in this particular case, by the warrant of the baron.

Taussig MS. 311, vol. 1, p. 139

Michaelmas 1721.

Attorney General [*Raymond*] moves to amend the writ of extent in this case. He admits that an original cannot be amended as to the *teste*; it is otherwise of judicial writs. As *scire facias* upon patents or judgments, there may be an amendment and the like in this present case because there is somewhat to amend by, *scil.* the *fiat*, for that is the time on which the extent ought to bear date. And this a judicial writ and, therefore, amendable.

Serjeant *Chesshyre*: Originals may be amended by the instructions of the cursitors and this is *actum clerici*. In a case of a judicial process, it is hard to put a case where an amendment has been divided[1] as in a jury process. A *fiat* of the baron is quasi an award of judgment *secundum cursu Scaccarii*. Therefore, an extent is a judicial process. Smith v. Harwood, in Sir Thomas Jones's Reports 4, Michaelmas 27 Car. II.[2]

Ward, ad idem: The *fiat* is dated 11 February. But *die Februarii* is omitted in the extent. The extent is 7 *Regis* returnable 15 *Pasch.* Hardres 126;[3] Rex v. Arch; a recognizance to abide the decree of this court. The recognizance is 18 May, and the extent finds a seisin 28 May, and that was afterwards amended by the minutes of the inquisition and made 18 instead of 28. 33 Hen. VIII; process founded upon this Statute. Therefore, the *fiat* is the authority. No extent can go out without an affidavit and a *fiat* from a baron.

Sir Constantine Phipps [argued] against the amendment. A writ without a *teste* is void. [There is] nothing to amend by, for the *fiat* does not say when the extent shall issue. If it is tested before the *fiat*, [it would be] of very strange consequence.

Secondly, if the *teste* is *post fiat* and not taken then there may be a great injury by [*blank*] mesne heirs on the personal estate, and it is not necessary that

---

[1] Sic in MS.

[2] *Smith v. Harward* (1675), T. Jones 41, 84 E.R. 1137.

[3] *Attorney General, ex rel. Ceely v. Bagg* (1658), Hardres 125, 145 E.R. 413.

the extent should bear *teste* the same day as the *fiat*. And so there is nothing to warrant an amendment by.

Bootle, ad idem: 14 Edw. III, ca. 6, letter or syllable. 9 Hen. V, ca. 4, confined; 8 Hen. VI, ca. 12, misprision of clerks amendable; 8 Rep. 156, it extends only to misprision of clerks; 5 Rep. 42, a misnomer in a *venire* is not amendable, though a *venire distringas* may [be]. 8 Hen. VI, ca. 15; 32 Hen. VIII etc. [It is] not amendable at common law.[1]

He denies Mr. Attorney's position as too general, for, in some cases, where there is matter to amend by, yet there is no amendment. This is a void writ. And, therefore, it is distinguishable from the case in Jones.

And a writ with no *teste* is void, whether judicial or original. 1 Levinz fo. 1; T. Jones 83; Salkeld 700.[2] In Blackmore's Case, the misprision of the clerks was not amendable in another term. And here are two terms intervening.

This mistake was in the legal form and is not amendable. There was a *teste* in the case of Smith v. Harwood. And, secondly, there was a substantial circumstance to amend by.

If the *teste* may be after the *fiat*, it may be tested at any day subsequent. Goods and chattels are only bound from the *teste*, though lands are from the time of the bond.

If the *teste* is now added according to the *fiat*, it may defeat mesne conveyances of a personal estate. Cro. Eliz. 820, *venire*; 2 Siderfin 7, 12; a *capias ad satisfaciendum* returnable out of term was amendable.[3] Rex v. Tutchin;[4] Holt declared that whatever was amendable at common law in civil cases might be amended in criminal cases. [It was] not amendable in that case, being a mistake of a clerk in skill.

Reply: The extent is by the warrant of Baron Price 11th.

Original writs are amendable by the instructions of the Cursitor, as in Cro. Car. 54 or 74; Hobart 118, 249.[5] [There were] no instructions to amend by in the

---

[1] Stat. 14 Edw. III, stat. 1, c. 6 (*SR*, I, 283); Stat. 9 Hen. V, stat. 1, c. 4 (*SR*, II, 205–206); Stat. 8 Hen. VI, c. 12 (*SR*, II, 248–249); *Blackamore's Case* (1610), 8 Coke Rep. 156, 77 E.R. 710; *Codwell v. Parker* (1593), 5 Coke Rep. 42, 77 E.R. 120, also Croke Eliz. 320, 78 E.R. 569; Stat. 8 Hen. VI, c. 15 (*SR*, II, 252).

[2] *Heath v. Paget* (1660), *ut supra*; *Wynne v. Wynne* (1677), *ut supra*; *Shirley v. Wright* (1702), *ut supra*.

[3] *Carew v. Merler* (1601), Croke Eliz. 820, 78 E.R. 1047; *Smithsby v. Lentil* (1657), 2 Siderfin 7, 12, 82 E.R. 1226, 1229.

[4] *Regina v. Tuchin* (1704), 2 Lord Raymond 1061, 92 E.R. 204, 1 Salkeld 51, 91 E.R. 50, 6 Modern 164, 268, 87 E.R. 922, 1014, Holt K.B. 424, 90 E.R. 1133, 5 State Trials 527 (Hargrave, ed., 1777).

[5] *Davie v. Hawkins* (1626), Croke Car. 53, 54, 79 E.R. 650; *Turner v. Palmer* (1627), Croke Car. 74, 79 E.R. 665; *Brickhead v. Bishop of York*, Hobart 118, 80 E.R. 267; *Marsh v. Sparrey* (1617), Hobart 249, 80 E.R. 395, also 1 Brownlow & Goldesborough 130, 123 E.R. 710.

case of 2nd Siderfin. The case of Scott v. Pygran, 7 Anne, 1708, was a resolution in this court directly contrary to Lord Holt's notion in the case of the King v. Tutchin, and it was subsequent to that case. At common law, goods are bound by the *teste* of the *fieri facias*.

Chesshyre: [It is] no consequence to the party because the lands are bound by the bond whether this writ is set aside or no. Many cases in the books are contrary to Cro. Eliz. 820.

Chief Baron [BURY]: I think it ought to be amended because it is a plain mistake of the writer and the *fiat* is a sufficient warrant for it.

PRICE: We ought to amend it. And the case of Scott and Pigram is a full authority, and so is the case of Sir Thomas Jones 41.

MONTAGU: The warrant is no justification to take out an extent before the date of the *fiat*, but the extent in this case has no date at all. In this case of the King and Quash,[1] you will find extents of a subsequent date to the fiats. Therefore, I find no certain rule to amend by.

In the case of a [writ of] *fieri facias*, it must bear *teste* after the judgment so that there is a necessity in that case. Scott and Pigram's Case is different from Tutchin's case. And both of them are good law. The process was amendable there because the subsequent process must bear *teste* on the return of the former process, and, therefore, the return of the precedent process is a certain rule to amend by.

But if there is no necessity that the extent should bear *teste* on the same day with the warrant, then this case is not like those cases because there is then no certain rule to amend by, as there was in those cases.

PAGE: I do not lay it down as a rule that all extents must bear *teste* the same day with the *fiat*, but I think they always ought unless contrary directions are given. An immediate extent is an extent to be taken out immediately so that the warrant seems to be in plain English 'let the extent go out this day'. And, if this be the meaning, then it would be a sufficient warrant to amend by. If there had been no aim to a *teste* at all, then it would have been hard to amend it because that might have been indeed the ignorance of the clerk, but here is only a mistake. So he is for amending.

And the writ was amended, the three barons being for the amendment, but MONTAGU *contra*, at least until he could see whether all extents were tested on the same day as the warrants were signed by the baron.

Bunbury 83, 145 E.R. 603

4 November 1721.

A purchase was made of lands lying in Radnorshire of Powell by the duke of Chandos. While the purchase was depending, Burton, the receiver general

[1] *Regina v. Quash* (1713), Parker 281, 145 E.R. 780, Dodd 365.

of that county, paid Powell £300 and took a bond in the name of the crown, upon which, an extent issued against Powell. The extent was tested *undecimo anno Georgii Regis septimo*, omitting the month, for which reason, it was moved by Mr. Serjeant *Comyns* and Mr. *Bootle* to discharge it. And the cases in the margin[1] were cited to prove that writs without a *teste* shall abate.

Baron MONTAGU said that the distinction is between original and judicial writs, which last only are amendable, because there is a record to amend them by.

But query (says the reporter [Bunbury] himself) if an extent is not an execution and may not be amended by the *fiat*?

And afterward, November 22nd following, this was amended by three barons *contra* MONTAGU.

228

Scawen's Case

(Ex. 1721)

An affidavit cannot be used to contradict a record.

The question in this case was whether the Court of Exchequer would discharge a debt to the crown or would make the alleged debtor defend against an execution.

Taussig MS. 311, vol. 1, p. 114

Michaelmas term 1721.

Mr. *Bootle* and *Fazakerly* moved in behalf of Sir William Scawen and Mr. [*blank*] that it might be referred to the Auditor to examine and then to report to the court the state of the case as it appeared to him with relation to the sum of [*blank*], set in super upon the aforesaid persons in the accounts of Sir Charles Harbord and Lord Conningsby, who were paymasters of the forces in Ireland, upon which in supers, several *distringas*es has issued and did from time to time issue against the said persons *ad computandum pro summa praedicta*.

They stated the case thus, that, so long ago as 1690, these persons were contractors for clothing some regiments in Ireland, that the moneys set in super upon them in the aforesaid accounts were paid to them as money due to them for clothes, which, according to their contract, they had furnished for those regiments, and, therefore, they were not accountable to the crown for those moneys, the said moneys being paid to them as a debt due to them from the crown for the said clothes. And though it was true that they might plead this to the *distringas*,

[1] *Ramsey v. Michel, ut supra*; *Sterling v. Moniers* (1666), *ut supra*; *Wynne v. Wynne* (1677), *ut supra*; *Heath v. Paget* (1660), *ut supra*; *Grondy v. Ischarn* (1597), *ut supra*; *Sympson v. Inhabitants of Penryth* (1689), *ut supra*; *Regina v. Tuchin* (1704), *ut supra*; *Smith v. Harward* (1675), *ut supra*.

yet there were many precedents where the court has dispensed with pleading and had discharged upon motion. And they particularly cited the Case of Mr. Dorrington who had been helped by this way of motion upon a report from the Auditor. And these in supers being of so long standing, *viz.* thirty years, they hoped the court would indulge them so far as to refer the fact to the Auditor and to discharge them upon his report.

Mr. Baron Montagu objected to them that the court had nothing to ground a rule upon, to which they answered that they had an affidavit. By him, this is not sufficient, for the court cannot proceed upon an affidavit where the matter is of record.

Then, they produced the original account passed and allowed by the Auditor, which was signed by Conningsby etc. and in which account the in supers were set.

By him, neither is this sufficient, for this account is of record, the same being entered and registered in the office. And from thence, says he, those supers are transcribed and sent down to the Pipe [Office] in order for the making out of process thereupon. Therefore, you should produce a *constat* or certificate from this Office of the supers and show to the court, likewise the *distringas*es returned, before we can take proper notice of this matter.

And the court made no rule but ordered that they should give notice to the Attorney General and should move it again having first obtained a certificate from the proper officer and brought with them the *distringas*es and then, upon Mr. Attorney General's consent, the court might give way to a reference to the Auditor and, upon his report, relieve them without putting them to plead.

Et sic fuit adjornatur.

And by me, as to the nature of these supers, for I should think it much more reasonable that, in the same account wherein they are mentioned, there should be mentioned at the same time that the moneys were paid for things delivered to the use of the crown where the fact so is than that the parties who have so delivered them should by the method aforesaid be brought in *ad computandum cum rege* whereas, in truth, they received the money only in payment of a debt due to them from the crown. And the persons only to whom the crown moneys are imprested are the proper accountants to the crown.

229

Cuthbert v. Adean

(Ex. 1721)

A messenger can be sent to arrest a defendant who is legally in the custody of a sheriff but is at large having put up a bail bond.

Bunbury 82, 145 E.R. 602

24 October 1721.

The defendant was taken upon an attachment for want of an appearance. And the sheriff returns a *cepi corpus* and assigns the bail bond to the plaintiff, who moves for a messenger to bring in the body of the defendant and offers to waive all proceedings upon the bail bond, according to the sixth rule, which see. And the motion was granted.

But Baron MONTAGU opposed this because, if there was any delay in the party, it should appear by an affidavit and, because this method would be so great an expense to the party.

Note (by the reporter [Bunbury] himself): As I apprehend, there had been proceedings upon the bail bond, which may distinguish it from the sixth rule.

Taussig MS. 311, vol. 1, p. 107

Monday, 25 October 1721; Tuesday, 24 October 1722.

Mr. *Browne* moved for a messenger to bring the defendant [Deane] upon a return of a *cepi corpus* upon an attachment for want of appearance. The plaintiff had taken an assignment of the bail bond but was willing to waive that and had given a rule to bring in the body four days since, and, therefore, he insisted that, according to the rules of the court, he might have a messenger.

But by MONTAGU: It is absurd to have a messenger to bring in a body when, by the return of the sheriff, it appears that he is in the sheriff's custody. The use of a messenger is to bring in those who are at large and not those who are in custody.

To this, it was answered that the course was to and it was different from the course at common law because here is a personal answer required which may be lost in case of death.

N.B. The court did not take notice that the party had taken an assignment of the bail bond, which seemed to me to be the most material objection to Mr. Browne's motion.

Harvard Law School MS. 1082, vol. 1, p. 101, pl. 1

Michaelmas term 1721.

After the return of a *cepi* and the rule for four days given, I moved for a messenger. This was a return two years ago; a bail bond was given and assigned, and the order of court was read that directs a messenger.

MONTAGU was against the motion unless you have an affidavit.

PAGE: It is a standing order for this rule.

PRICE: Upon a *cepi* returned at Bristol, a messenger goes of course.

So I obtained my motion for a messenger.

230

Rex v. Tomkins

(Ex. 1721)

A person convicted of exporting wool unlawfully can be transported if he does not pay the statutory fine.

Harvard Law School MS. 1082, vol. 1, p. 108, pl. 1

Michaelmas term 1721.

Sir Constantine Phipps showed cause why the defendant should not be transported on a judgment for exporting wool according to the late Act of Parliament, *viz.* 4 Geo.[1] And the order was to commit him to the Fleet [Prison] in order to be transported. And [it was] said not to be within the Act, but [it] only relates to such person as was committed for want of bail. The defendant was in custody 7 January, but there acquitted and not committed for want of putting in bail. And the information ought to have been delivered to the jailer and [it was] not so here.

If an information is filed and not delivered, the defendant is not bound to plead, and judgment must relate to such a person as was before mentioned in the Act. And this Act was only intended to take away the obstinacy of such as refused to plead.

Attorney General [*Raymond*], for the king: 'Such person' is not to be construed as Sir Constantine Phipps contends for, but, if any person is committed upon account of exporting wool and it is not meant such only where judgment has been given by default, but there are the words 'or otherwise', which include everything.

Sir Constantine Phipps: If the defendant pleads [and] the judgment is against him, the words 'or otherwise' are answered; if the defendant demurs and there is judgment upon it, he shall be transported.

MONTAGU thought it to be taken 'if any person' and he is so liable to be transported.

PRICE differed and thought 'such person' only related to such person that was in custody 20 January and did not put in bail.

PAGE: Before this Act, judgment could not be given if the defendant did not plead and the remedy is chalked out if the defendant does not plead. Such person that has judgment against him, let it be in what manner it will, the intention of the law was that he should be transported. And so he agreed for transportation.

Chief Baron [BURY] agreed.

So, against the opinion of Price, the defendant was ordered to be transported.

---

[1] Stat. 4 Geo. I, c. 11.

Taussig MS. 311, vol. 1, p. 108

Friday, 27 October 1721.

Sir Constantine Phipps showed cause why Tompkins should not be transported according to the Stat. of 4 of the present king, he having been committed to the Fleet [Prison]. And Tompkins appeared at the bar. The words of the Act are [*blank*].

No man can be transported upon this Act unless imprisoned for want of bail. Tompkins was in custody 7th January, and this Act refers to 20th January. An information must be delivered to him or to the turnkey. [There was] no pretense that he was in custody for want of bail, nor was ever any information delivered to him or to the turnkey. Therefore, no judgment can be given against him by virtue of this Statute because he was not imprisoned for want of bail nor was any information delivered to him or the turnkey, this Statute being made only to prevent the obstinacy of such as would not plead.

Mr. Attorney General [*Raymond*] *contra*: The Act must not be construed so strictly as to tie up the word 'such' to persons only who were imprisoned etc.

PRICE, baron, was of opinion that the word 'such' must be tied up to the 'imprisoned for want of bail'.

But the Chief Baron [BURY] and MONTAGU and PAGE being of opinion that the Act plainly extended to every person against whom judgment was given if he did not pay the money within the time prescribed, therefore, they gave judgment that Tomkin should be transported.

Bunbury 83, 145 E.R. 603

27 October 1721.

There was a judgment upon an information against Tomkins for running wool. And he not having paid the sum in the Act mentioned, the Solicitor General [*Yorke*] moved upon the Stat. 4 Geo., c. 11, for preventing burglaries etc., that he might be transported.

Note: Tomkins had been committed to the Fleet Prison, charged with the said judgment.

It was objected by *Sir Constantine Phipps*, for Tomkins, that he was not within the words or meaning of the Act, for, first, he must have been committed for want of sufficient bail, but he was in custody before the day mentioned in the Act; secondly, an information must have been delivered to him or the turnkey; and, this being a penal statute, no equitable or liberal construction ought to be made upon it.

But notwithstanding these reasons (which I thought not answered), the man was transported *per* CURIAM, *dissentiente* Baron PRICE.

231

Awbrey v. Fitzhugh

(Ex. 1721)

A court of equity will set aside a harsh contract that has not been fully performed.

Harvard Law School MS. 1082, vol. 1, p. 91, pl. 2

Michaelmas term 1721.

The plaintiff agreed with Garbrand for £500 South Sea stock at 530 percent in the month of September 1720 to be accepted by the plaintiff in October following, that Garbrand after[wards] offered this bargain to the defendant who accepted it and Garbrand informed the plaintiff that the defendant was his man and, at the time appointed, the defendant tendered the stock to the plaintiff, and he declared that he could not pay for it and would give him a bond for £500 for the difference of £200 part of the said £500 stock pay[able] at [. . .], which he did, and for the remaining £300 stock he would give his bond for the whole money contracted for at 530 percent, which came to £1590, for which the plaintiff gave his bond in the penalty of £3180 for payment aforesaid. Judgment was obtained on this bond so that we who were counsel for the plaintiff came for a judgment setting forth the last Act of Parliament and that we could not plead anything at law but *non est factum*. Therefore, [it is] proper in a court of equity to stop execution and the rather because the stock still remains in the defendant's name so he would recover the penalty of the bond and have the stock in his own hands. And, therefore, [it is] proper for an account and deduction for the value of that stock. And we cited Smith v. Nottingham, in this court,[1] on a bond for payment of so much money absolutely, yet it being for a South Sea contract, the court granted an injunction.

[. . .] the counsel for the defendant, answered that this was not within the Act of Parliament for that it was a contract made up by giving the bond, which is payment of so much money and, as for the stock, the plaintiff has his proper remedy.

Chief Baron [Bury] [was] against an injunction for that the giving the bond was making up the contract so the plaintiff [was] not within the benefit of the Act of Parliament.

Price: I am for an injunction. And it is proper for an account of the stock in the defendant's hands whether sold or not.

Montagu: The defendant keeps his own stock. And I am for an injunction because I take everything done according to this pernicious scheme was a fraud and so all contracts about it ought to be esteemed fraudulent.

[1] *Smith v. Nottingham* (Ex. 1721), see above, Case No. 183.

Page: I think that this is a contract within the Act of Parliament and that there was no defense at law and, though bonds are given, yet they are still contracts for stock and not executed and this is a subsisting contract and here is a penalty and the defendant has likewise the stock for which he ought to account, and, in both respects, [it is] proper for an injunction, which was granted against the opinion of the Chief Baron.

Bunbury 84, 145 E.R. 603

7 November 1721.

Awbrey contracts upon the 17th September 1720 with Fitzhught for the purchase of £500 South Sea stock at £530 *per centum* to be delivered in October following. Awbrey not being able to pay the money then, a new agreement was entered into, that upon Awbrey's giving a bond for the payment of £1060, being the difference of £200, part of the £500 stock, and entering into another bond for £1590 for the other £300 stock, the time of acceptance should be enlarged until the 14th of May following. Accordingly, Awbrey entered into a bond on the 4th of November 1720, for the payment of the said £1590 in the penalty of £3180 on the 4th of May following. And an indenture of defeasance of the same date was executed between the plaintiff and defendant, reciting the said bond and that the £300 stock was to remain in the defendant Fitzhught's hands as a collateral security. Fitzhught thereby covenanted that, in case Awbrey paid the £1590 due by the bond, to transfer the £300 stock, but, if the £1590 was not paid, then the defendant Fitzhught was to be at liberty to sell the £300 stock towards payment of the £1590. The money was not paid pursuant to the bond, and Fitzhught put the bond in suit. And the plaintiff Awbrey preferred his bill, setting forth this matter and that the defendant had not transferred nor tendered and also setting forth the clauses in the bill of credit, 7 Geo. relating to contracts, that this was a contract unperformed, and that, by the Act, execution ought not to go, and therefore prayed an injunction.

The defendant, in his answer, admitted the fact, as before set forth, and that he did not tender nor transfer, but he gave the plaintiff notice that he was ready to do it; but it was upon the plaintiffs request that he did not do it, and he insists that this was not a contract within the Act of Parliament.

Now, upon motion for an injunction upon the merits, the defendant's counsel insisted that the parol contract was merged in the bond and that, if the plaintiff had any remedy, he had it as much at law as he could have had it in this court.

But it was answered that the plaintiff could have no remedy below now. If it had remained upon the parol contract, in an action upon that contract the plaintiff there must have averred and proved a tender, according to the course of the South Sea [Company]. But, upon this bond, he will have nothing to do but to prove the bond, and the defendant cannot either by special pleading or upon the general issue at law show what the consideration of the bond was or that there was no tender, but that it was proper for a court of equity, before whom all this matter appeared, to take cognisance of the whole matter. And, though the parol contract is admitted to be merged by the bond, yet, in a court of equity, it will be considered as part of the contract unperformed, since the consideration of the bond is the same as the consideration of the parol contract. And, if they should obtain judgment upon the bond, we could not come by affidavit to stop execution and set forth all this matter, since nothing appeared upon the record to prevent the common method of taking out execution.

And an injunction was granted upon these grounds by three barons *contra* Lord Chief Baron BURY.

And Baron PRICE said the last clause of the Act extended to all contracts whatsoever, as well as those mentioned in the preceding clauses.

232

Tarent v. Trewit

(Ex. 1721)

Court costs are not taxable for not moving upon three notices, but there can be no motion after the fourth notice without paying court costs for the first three notices.

Bunbury 86, 145 E.R. 604

15 November 1721.

Upon a motion that T. might pay costs for not moving according to notice, which was denied by the whole court, it was said by one of the barons that, if there are three notices of motion given, and, after a fourth notice given, they shall not move upon the fourth without paying costs of the three first.

233

Winch v. Page

(Ex. 1721)

In this case, an injunction was granted to stay an action at common law on a bond payable to a married woman where the plaintiff-obligor paid the money due into the court of equity so that the court could order it to be settled on the married woman.

Harvard Law School MS. 1082, vol. 1, p. 95

Michaelmas term 1721.

The plaintiff, who was the father of defendant's wife, [gave] a bond in the penalty of £300 for the payment of £150 to the defendant's wife that the defendant Page afterwards married the daughter without the consent of the father. And the defendants sue the plaintiff on this bond. And the plaintiff brings his bill suggesting the want of consent and that the defendant was in low circumstances.

And, as this £150 was intended for a provision, he prays that the money might be brought into court. And so he moved for an injunction.

The Chief Baron [Bury] and Price were of opinion that an injunction was proper upon bringing the money into court for that it was not reasonable for the husband to run away with this money and let the defendant, his wife, starve.

Page said that he had never known a court of equity go so far, for he was desirous that children should marry with their parents' consent. And he could wish that it had been so practiced. But, since it had not, he could not go any further. But he said that, if the plaintiff, the husband, wants to sue in equity for the fortune, there, a court of equity will hold it and order it to be settled [on the wife].

But the other two judges ordered an injunction on bringing the money into court, against the opinion of Page, who was right in denying the motion.

Taussig MS. 311, vol. 1, p. 125, pl. 2

Michaelmas term 1721.

A father exhibits a bill for an injunction against a suit on a bond given to his daughter for her portion, who marries without [his] consent. And the plaintiff suggests that the husband was an indigent man and desires proceedings at law to be stayed and that the court would take care to settle it to the daughter so that the whole might not be spent extravagantly.

And the court continued the injunctions upon the father's bringing the money into court within a week and speeding the cause to a hearing, which, by Page, is carrying things farther than ever I knew it, for I thought the distinction was that the court of equity had no jurisdiction to interfere in such cases but where the party seeking the fortune was obliged to have the assistance of a court of equity. And then, the rule is, if you would have equity, you must do equity.

Bunbury 86, 145 E.R. 604

15 November 1721.

A father gives a bond to his daughter for the payment of a sum of money, being her portion, at the age of twenty-one or marriage. He deposits this bond in another person's hands. She, afterwards, marries without his consent. The person who had the bond delivers it up to the husband, who puts it in suit.

The father prefers his bill for an injunction and sets forth that he is willing to pay the money, but he insists that the court should lay their hands on it and secure it for his daughter and her children.

And the injunction was granted upon bringing the money into court. But this was going a great length, and, I believe, beyond what has been done in Chancery, for the obligee is defendant here. Indeed, if the husband in these circumstances comes in a court of equity to have the wife's portion paid, then they will put terms upon him, for he that comes for equity must do equity. But the person who was to have the money is defendant here, and he asks nothing of the court.

Note: It did not appear in this case whether the daughter was under age; but query what alteration that would make in this case.

234

Steward v. Hammond

(Ex. 1721)

A court of equity will not set aside a harsh contract that has been fully performed on both sides.

Harvard Law School MS. 1082, vol. 1, p. 93

Michaelmas term 1721.

This was a bill to be relieved against a bond in the penalty of £6000 for payment of £3000, being part of money due on a South Sea contract for £500 South Sea stock at 695 percent, and the defendant was to transfer the stock, but the stock was not transferred. And the plaintiff, who was the defendant at law, had there pleaded the Act of the last sessions [of Parliament]. And for the plaintiff were cited the cases in this court of Smith v. Nottingham; Aubrey v. Fitzhugh, above.[1]

[It was] insisted upon by the plaintiff's counsel that, though this was a parol agreement, yet the bond being given for the same thing, in a court of equity, they will be taken together and, though at law you cannot controvert or enquire into the consideration of a bond, yet in equity you may. Counterbonds, though mutual, you cannot plead one against the other, and, in this case, no stock was transferred. And the intention of the Act was that the party was to continue possessed of the same stock.

For the defendant, it was insisted on that this was a contract executed and that the defendant had pleaded the Act at law, to which the plaintiff there replied so the whole matter is at law. And the case of Aubrey v. Fitzhugh differs, for the reason there given was that the defendant had taken no advantage at law. But [it is] otherwise in this case, where the whole comes in issue at law. The Act does not prohibit any person from proceeding to judgment though it stops execution, and other intermediate debts may get in and deprive the plaintiff at law of his judgment. And this case was compared to the pleading of the Statute of Usury.[2] And the case of Aubrey v. Fitzhugh was after judgment, and so it differs from this case. This contract, in construction of law, is extinguished, so it only depends upon the bond, which is a new contract.

The counsel for the plaintiff reply and denied that it was after judgment in Aubrey v. Fitzhugh, and, there, the plaintiff desired the defendant to keep the

---

1 *Smith v. Nottingham* (Ex. 1721), see above, Case No. 183; *Awbrey v. Fitzhugh* (Ex. 1721), see above, Case No. 231.

2 Stat. 13 Ann., c. 15 (*SR*, IX, 928).

stock. And though a parol agreement at law is merged in the written agreement, yet, in a court of equity, it will be construed together. If the contract is within the Statute, then he ought to have the benefit here; if [it is] not within the Statute, then the defendant should have demurred at law.

Chief Baron [Bury]: I am of the same opinion as in the case of Aubrey v. Fitzhugh and that there ought to be no injunction, for the construction of the Act of Parliament is at law and it is properly set forth in the pleading at law.

Baron Price: I think that this case varies, though I am of opinion to grant an injunction to stay execution and there may be reason to return a suit in equity, though it may be tried at law. And [it was] always thought proper in a court of equity where penalties are.

These are mutual contracts and bargains and so multiply any suits, to prevent which a court of equity is certainly proper. In this case, the stock is to be transferred. And upon the decree, the court will take in the whole. The intention of the Act was to assist unfortunate contractors and, though the parol agreement may be extinguished at law by the bond, yet it is not extinguished equity.

In Aubrey v. Fitzhugh, there was no special pleading there, for, if the Act had been pleaded, I would have permitted them to have gone on to trial. But, in that case, it was an executory agreement for £300 stock which remained unperformed in the defendant's hands.

Page: I would not be thought to be inconsistent with myself. I take contracts for South Sea [stock] to be the same and as valid as for hops etc. And I was not governed by the penalty in the case of Aubrey v. Fitzhugh. And if the stock there had been sold and it was to have been deducted out of the money due to the defendant and to remain in the vendor's hands and, likewise, when that stock was proper to be sold, it was fit for a decree. But there is nothing of it in this case. And the plaintiff's bill is improper, for it is not brought to be relieved against the penalty, for the bill is to impeach the whole bond. If the bill had been only on account of the penalty, then the plaintiff ought to have proffered payment of principal, interest, and costs.

So, no injunction [was] granted against the opinion of Price.

235

Appletree v. Strut

(Ex. 1721)

An estate tail can be barred by a fine and recovery.

Taussig MS. 311, vol. 1, p. 118, pl. 2

9th November 1721.

Philip Appletree and Mary, his wife, who was the daughter of William Rookes, exhibit their bill against Anne Strut, spinster, devisee of all the real and personal estate of Robert Strut, her uncle, and also his executrix. And the intent of the bill was to oblige the said Strut to pay unto the plaintiff the remainder of a £100 legacy devised to the plaintiff Mary by the will of her great uncle William Rookes, the elder. And the case was this. William Rookes, the elder, devises his estate to the plaintiff's father, William Rookes, the younger, to hold to him for and during the term of his natural life and from and after his decease, then, to and for the use and behoof of the heirs male of the said William Rookes his body lawfully begotten and to and for the use and behoof of the heirs and assigns of such heirs male forever, but, if the said William Rookes should die without heirs male, then from and after his death to and for the use and behoof of Thomas Rookes, who was a younger brother of William Rookes, his heirs, and assigns forever, provided and on condition that Thomas Rookes should pay £100 to the daughter of William Rookes, supposing he should have a daughter. William Rookes had only one daughter, the plaintiff Mary, and no issue male, and he died in the year 1711. But in the year, William Rookes, by lease and release, conveys to Jenkins in order to make him tenant to the *praecipe*, and, by the release, the uses of the recovery are declared to Robert Strut in fee, subject to a proviso for redemption by William Rookes, senior, on payment of £500. And afterwards, Strut agreed for the absolute purchase of the lands and, thereupon, by lease and release to [. . .] uses of a fine, in which fine both William and Thomas Rookes joined. The lands were conveyed by Rookes to one halfpenny for 500 years to secure £500 and after that are limited to Robert Strutt in fee. £700 was paid by Strut for the absolute purchase, and Thomas had £100 thereof for joining in the fine.

Robert Strut, after his purchase, paid about £14 to the plaintiff Mary towards and in discharge of the legacy afore[said]. But the defendant insisted it was in his own wrong and that he was not obliged to pay any of it because the remainder out of which it issued was barred by the recovery and so there was no lien on the estate nor any obligation on him or her to pay it, though they had notice of the will and purchased under it. And of this opinion was the court, the cause coming to be heard on the bill and answer.

In the argument of this case, it was contended on behalf of the plaintiffs that this was an executory devise to Thomas Strut. And for this purpose, the cases of Plunket and Holmes; Cro. Jac. 592, Pell and Brown's Case; Carter 52,[1] were cited for the plaintiffs.

[1] *Plunket v. Holmes* (1661), T. Raymond 28, 83 E.R. 15, 1 Levinz 11, 83 E.R. 271, 1 Siderfin 47, 82 E.R. 961, 1 Keble 29, 119, 83 E.R. 792, 848; *Pell v. Brown* (1620), Croke Jac. 590, 79 E.R. 504, also Palmer 131, 81 E.R. 1012, 2 Rolle Rep. 196, 216, 81 E.R. 746, 760, Godbolt 282, 78 E.R. 165, J. Bridgman 1, 123 E.R. 1157; *Smith v. Farnaby* (1666), Carter 52, 124 E.R. 819, also 1 Siderfin 285, 82 E.R. 1108, 1 Levinz 144, 83 E.R. 340, 2 Keble 29, 55, 84, 84 E.R. 19, 35, 54.

E contra were cited 2 Salkeld 570, 571; 1 Modern 108; Raymond 127; Lloyd and Cary's Case.[1]

And the plaintiffs' bill was dismissed.

Harvard Law School MS. 1082, vol. 1, p. 96

Michaelmas term 1721.

William Rook, the elder, being seised of Driver's End Farm, 22 October 1697, devises to his son,[2] William Rook, the younger, to hold to him for and during his natural life and, after his decease, then, to and for the use of the heirs male of him the said William Rook, the younger, of his body lawfully begotten and to R. for the use and behoof of the heirs and assigns of such heirs male forever, and, if the said William Rook, the younger, dies without heirs male, then, from and after his death to and for the use of Thomas Rook, brother of the said William Rook, the younger, his heirs, and assigns forever, provided always and upon condition that said Thomas Rook, his heirs, and assigns did and should pay among such of the daughters of the said William Rook, the younger, as should live to the age of twenty-one or be married £200 within six months after such age or marriage and, if one daughter, upon the same contingency, £200. William Rook, the testator, dies. William Rook, the younger, enters and marries and dies without issue male and left only the plaintiff, Mary, his child. But the said William Rook levies a fine and suffers a recovery, under which the defendant claims. And the plaintiffs, being married, bring their bill for this legacy.

It was insisted on by us that it was an executory devise and not barred by the recovery and that the reason of a common recovery is because of the intended recompense and that this was a mere possibility and could not be barred because it was not *in esse*. And they cited 1 Modern 108, Benson v. Hodson; Carter 52; Raymond 28; Palmer 135; Calthrop 232; 1 Levinz 11, Plunket and Hicher's Case; 1 Rept. 3; Levinz 431, Ludington; 10 Rept. 53, Lampet's Case; 1 Coke Inst. 9; 2 Cro. 591, Pell v. Browne; Vaughan's Reports 260, Gardiner v. Sheldon.[3]

---

[1] *Page v. Haywood* (1704), 2 Salkeld 570, 91 E.R. 481, also 11 Modern 61, 88 E.R. 886, Holt K.B. 618, 90 E.R. 1242, 3 Salkeld 96, 135, 91 E.R. 714, 736, 2 Eq. Cas. Abr. 362, 22 E.R. 308; *Benson v. Hodson* (1674), 1 Modern 108, 86 E.R. 768, also T. Raymond 236, 83 E.R. 123, 1 Freeman 362, 89 E.R. 269, 3 Keble 274, 287, 292, 84 E.R. 717, 724, 727, 2 Levinz 28, 83 E.R. 438; *Loyd v. Carew* (1697), Precedents in Chancery 72, 24 E.R. 35, Shower P.C. 137, 1 E.R. 93, 1 Comyns 20, 92 E.R. 938.

[2] Sic in MS.; according to Taussig MS. 311, he is a nephew.

[3] *Benson v. Hodson* (1674), *ut supra*; *Smith v. Farnaby* (1666), *ut supra*; *Plunket v. Holmes* (1661), *ut supra*; *Pell v. Brown* (1620), *ut supra*; *Page, ex dem. Bowes v. Griffin* (1588–1590), 1 Coke Rep. 3, 76 E.R. 8, also 2 Leonard 60, 74 E.R. 358, 4 Leonard 123, 74 E.R. 772, Moore K.B. 271, 72 E.R. 574, 1 Anderson 227, 123 E.R. 444; *Loddington v. Kime* (1695), 3 Levinz 431, 83 E.R. 766, also 1 Lord Raymond 203, 91 E.R. 1031, 1 Salkeld 224, 91 E.R. 198, 2 Eq. Cas. Abr. 331, 22 E.R. 282; Lampet's Case (1612),

Mr. *Bunbury* and *Bootle*, for the defendant: In this case, Thomas Rook never took, and this fine and recovery is a paramount collateral charge and exactly Capel's Case, 1 Rept.; Attorney General v. Payman, in this court; 2 Levinz 28, 1 Modern 108, and that this was an estate tail executed, 2 Cro. 189; Wild's Case, 7 Rept.[1] It cannot be called an executory devise after a limitation to heirs male. And so is Salkeld, Scattergood v. Edge;[2] Raymond 127.

Chief Baron [Bury]: I think that the only question is whether William Rook, the devisee, had an estate tail; if he had, the fine and recovery will bar. And Sutton and Payman, in this court,[3] is the same. And I think that William had an estate tail.

Price: I am of the same opinion. Whether the recovery operates or not, yet it is under William Rook that the defendant claims. And I think nothing [is] plainer but that William Rook had an estate tail executed. 1 Inst.; Shelley's Case.[4] The recovery bars everything. I know of no difference between this case and Capel's Case. How can an executory devise be raised on a contingent remainder so that it is not an executory devise or an estate tail by implication? And this case [is] the same with Attorney General v. Payman, in this court.

Page: I am of the same opinion. If [it is] an estate tail, it is gone. If it is an executory devise, Lloyd v. Cary, in the Chancery,[5] it was too remote. Sir Thomas Howard's Case; Manning's Case, 8 Rept.; Archer's Case is altered.[6]

And so the bill was dismissed.

---

10 Coke Rep. 46b, 77 E.R. 994, *sub nom. Lampit v. Starkey*, 2 Brownlow & Goldesborough 172, 123 E.R. 880; E. Coke, First Institute (1628), f. 9; *Gardner v. Sheldon* (1671), Vaughan 259, 124 E.R. 1064, also 1 Freeman 11, 89 E.R. 9, 2 Keble 781, 84 E.R. 494, 1 Eq. Cas. Abr. 197, 21 E.R. 986.

[1] *Hunt v. Gateley* (1581–1593), 1 Coke Rep. 54, 76 E.R. 121, also Popham 5, 79 E.R. 1129, Jenkins 250, 145 E.R. 177, 4 Leonard 150, 74 E.R. 788, Moore K.B. 154, 72 E.R. 501, 1 Anderson 282, 123 E.R. 473, Gouldsborough 5, 75 E.R. 958; *Attorney General v. Payman* (Ex. 1721), see above, Case No. 171; *Hudson v. Benson* (1671), 2 Levinz 28, 83 E.R. 438, 1 Modern 108, 86 E.R. 768, also T. Raymond 236, 83 E.R. 123, 3 Keble 273, 287, 292, 84 E.R. 717, 724, 742, 1 Freeman 362, 89 E.R. 269; *Beaudely v. Brook* (1607), Croke Jac. 189, 79 E.R. 165.

[2] *Scattergood v. Edge* (1697), 1 Salkeld 229, 91 E.R. 203, also 12 Modern 278, 88 E.R. 1320, 1 Eq. Cas. Abr. 189, 21 E.R. 980, 2 Eq. Cas. Abr. 337, 22 E.R. 287.

[3] *Attorney General v. Payman* (Ex. 1721), see above, Case No. 171.

[4] E. Coke, *First Institute* (1628); *Wolfe v. Shelley* (1581), 1 Coke Rep. 88, 76 E.R. 199, also 1 Anderson 69, 123 E.R. 358, Moore K.B. 136, 72 E.R. 490, Jenkins 249, 145 E.R. 176, 3 Dyer 373, 73 E.R. 838.

[5] *Loyd v. Carew* (1697), *ut supra*.

[6] *Clark v. Manning* (1609), 8 Coke Rep. 94, 77 E.R. 618; *Baldwin v. Smith* (1597), 1 Coke Rep. 63, 76 E.R. 139, also Croke Eliz. 453, 78 E.R. 692, 2 Anderson 37, 123 E.R. 533.

236

Harcourt v. Thompson

(Ex. 1721–1723)

A court of equity will set aside a harsh contract that has not been fully performed.

Objections to a master's report must be first argued to the master before being brought to the court.

Where depositions in a cross-cause are read in the original cause, the court costs of those depositions cannot be taxed in the original cause.

Harvard Law School MS. 1082, vol. 1, p. 99

Michaelmas term 1721. Bill for an injunction on a South Sea contract.

Serjeant *Chesshyre*: In this case, it is part equity and part law and, therefore, proper for a court of equity.

Mr. *Reeves*: The first agreement [was] of 18 June and, if an action is brought on the second agreement of 5 October, then we could have no advantage of the agreement of 18 June. £700 was sold; £200 only remaining.

[To the] objection that annuity stock would make up this, [he] answered Mr. Moult could not be obliged; so, if it were a beneficial contract to Mr. Harcourt, yet he could not oblige Mr. Moult to perform it.

The proviso is that, under hand and seal, Mr. Moult, if he thought proper, might sell. The said agreement was entered into on the misrepresentation of Mr. Thompson. The deposits are matters of account, and they have not answered the matters as to the penalty. And they may declare [at common law] so as to recover the whole contract. The defendant in this case had not the stock at the time of the delivery.

And *Sir Constantine Phipps* cited Rodes v. Lovel,[1] and here must be a specific performance for the defendant to transfer, which cannot be done at law.

Chief Baron [Bury]: As it stood on the first contract before the Act of Parliament and whether the contract is void or not in part or in whole, I think that it is all matter of law. As for the fraud, I see no manner of it. And, therefore, I am not for an injunction.

Price: This cannot be determined at law. And the first contract cannot be taken notice of. Where the case is so complicated as this is, I think it is proper for an injunction. And I do not see the party is delayed in this case. And I doubt that it would be too hard to plead this at law, where entire contracts must be performed.

Upon the first contract, Mr. Thompson ought to have transferred this stock, and, then, he had no more than £200. But whether Mr. Moult would do it or

[1] *Rhodes v. Lovit* (Ex. 1721), see above, Case No. 165.

not, it was in Mr. Moult's power. What was in Mr. Moult's hands is nothing to the purpose, and a court of equity can settle this whole affair. I take Mr. Baynes to be a trustee, and so is Mr. Moult. And there is one thread of equity through and, therefore, proper for an injunction.

PAGE: I am of the same opinion. Here are several things intermixed. One trial cannot determine this, and the first contract cannot be given in evidence at law.

The defendant says in this answer that he will go on the second contract. If £6000 is the measure of the damages he insists on, then the defendant had but £200 stock, or at most but £700 and then could recover for £1000 stock, but the proportion must be two tenths or seven tenths. And I think that Aubrey v. Fitzhugh[1] is this very case, for Mr. Baynes is to sell and, if so, the plaintiff is entitled to have an account. I think in this case that Mr. Moult is worse than a stranger for Mr. Moult could not have made it his own.

Moult was not a trustee only for Thompson for life and so for his wife and so for the children. And if this had been trust money and [he] had notice, I believe that a court of equity might take hold of it from Mr. Harcourt if it had been a beneficial contract and he had notice of this trust. Here are so many difficulties and complicated [issues] that it is proper for a court of equity to have cognizance of this matter.

So an injunction was granted contrary to the opinion of the Chief Baron.

Taussig MS. 311, vol. 1, p. 486

Friday, the 17th [May 1723].

The depositions taken and read at the hearing of this cause were all taken in the cross-cause and were read by virtue of an order for that purpose. And the decree was that Mr. Harcourt should pay the costs of the original bill and Mr. Thompson's cross-bill should be dismissed without costs. And the Master, in his taxing of costs, did not allow costs for the examinations taken by Thompson in the cross-cause, and he had no examinations in the original cause.

And now, it was moved to explain this decree and for the court's direction to the Master in relation to the costs, as also with respect to the interest for the money, which Thompson said ought to be carried on to the time of payment, and, thirdly, with respect to the £290 stock to be transferred by Thompson. And the words of the decree were '£290 stock with the dividends and profits'. And the Master was of opinion that the £33 6s. 8d. percent addition[2] should be added.

For Thompson, it was said that the cost of suit must exclude the costs of the examinations read in the suit, whether taken in the first cause originally or read therein by orders of the court. The words of the decree are 'dividends and profits received by Mr. Harcourt since the first of May' which can never exclude the £33

[1] *Awbrey v. Fitzhugh* (Ex. 1721), see above, Case No. 231.

[2] Sic in *MS*. for dividend.

6s. 8d. dividend which Mr. Thompson never had, in fact having sold his stock before it was added.

Per Chief Baron [MONTAGU]: The motion is not regular. The proper method is to object before the Master and, if he does wrong, then you must appeal from him by way of exceptions. But the Master has not yet determined one way or other.

Per CURIAM: Though you cannot except to the question of costs as to the particulars which the Master has considered, yet, if the Master does not take the particulars into his consideration, which he ought, you may take exceptions with respect to them. And so the court made no order, but bid them attend the Master and make their objection there and then take exceptions to his report if they thought he did not do them justice.

Taussig MS. 311, vol. 1, p. 544

Monday, [October] 28, 1723.

Per PAGE and GILBERT, upon the hearing of Thompson's exceptions to the Master's report, the order for reading the depositions in the original cause, which were taken in the cross-cause, does not make them part of the original cause, but they still continue part of the cross-cause only. And, therefore, the decree of the court which directs the Master to tax the costs of the original cause will not warrant his meddling with the costs of the depositions in the cross-cause.

237

Leaper, *qui tam* v. Andrews

(Ex. 1721)

A successful bidder for forfeited goods is liable for the full amount contracted for and cannot break his contract and merely forfeit the deposit.

Harvard Law School MS. 1082, vol. 1, p. 103

Michaelmas term 1721.

Attorney General [*Raymond*] moved that Bourne, the bidder, might take the goods, for that his bidding was refused to be discharged, or that an attachment should go.

Sir Constantine Phipps, for the bidder: The judgment is that the bidder *exoneretur* and, then, you have a proper remedy upon it. The Rule of November 1715 was read, which was *viz.* that, if the bidder does not take the goods, then he forfeits the bidding money only and judgment shall be entered up for the officer.

Mr. *Ward*, for the Attorney General: The bidder is not permitted to come off by losing his bidding money only after judgment, especially for that is so made up that the bidder cannot be discharged. The bidding is such a contract with the court, which is a market overt for this particular purpose, that the bidder cannot be discharged.

Bootle, pro eodem: It is too late after judgment, for, by it, the bidder is charged. The order read was not made for the benefit of the bidder. And the consequence of this is that it will fall on the officer, which is too hard. The judgment is *quod Johannes Bourne oneretur* with the whole money and that a moiety should be paid to the crown and the other to the informer.

PRICE: This order was not designed in favor of the bidder, and, if this interpretation is put upon it, it will destroy the judgment.

PAGE said that, by this judgment, the bidder is a debtor to the crown. And I do not know but that an extent might go. But Mr. Attorney General only prays for an order for payment and, if not, I shall consent for an attachment.

Eyles, the Clerk, said that, if so, you must let it go into the Pipe [Office], and the summons from thence goes but twice a year.

PRICE: I think that it is well warranted by the Stat. 33 Hen. VIII,[1] if any new rule may be made for expediting the getting in of the king's debts.

Bootle said that it was a debt upon record and it is mandatory on the bidder to pay and that an extent might go or a *fieri facias ad compertandum* or *ad satisfaciendum*.

The *Attorney General* said that it was like a judgment on an information of debt.

PAGE said that a *fieri facias* was proper and might issue as to both.

The court did not order a *fieri facias* but declared that it might issue on this judgment.

But Bourne, the bidder, submitted to pay the money.

238

Crofts' Case

(Ex. 1721)

A custom of paying tithes of lambs in kind before they are old enough to live on their own is void.

Rayner 160, 2 Gwillim 630, 1 Eagle & Younge 776

Crofts, Rector of Upper Clatford in Hampshire.

The defendant insisted on a custom in that parish to set forth tithe lambs at Saint Mark's Day [25 April]. The court declared it to be a void custom and that the time for setting forth tithe lambs is when they are fit to live without their

[1] Stat. 33 Hen. VIII, c. 39, s. 37 (*SR*, III, 886–887).

dams and thrive on the same food which their dam lives on and when the owner weans his own.

[Note also Croft v. Blake (1680), 2 Gwillim 530, 1 Eagle & Younge 527.]

239

Rex v. Spencer

(Ex. 1721)

The Act of General Pardon pardoned the offense of assaulting a customs officer.

Bunbury 88, 145 E.R. 605

17 November 1721.

Sir Constantine Phipps moved to discharge the recognizance of a person who was indicted for beating a Custom House officer in the execution of his office *in diminutionem reventionum domini regis.*

And this was opposed by Mr. *Raby*, for the crown, upon these words, the Act of Pardon 7 Geo., c. [*blank*],[1] excepting that offence.

But the recognizance was discharged *per* TOTAM CURIAM; and, if the fine was levied and still in the sheriff's hands, it must be restored by an express clause in the Act, which gives the fines to the party.

And the Lord Chief Baron BURY said that the words *in diminutionem* etc. were only pepper and salt.

Baron MONTAGU quoted a case upon the Act of Pardon in 1709,[2] The Queen v. Hinton, where an information for carrying salt without a permit etc. was pardoned, being only consequential defrauding.

Harvard Law School MS. 1082, vol. 1, p. 104, pl. 2

Michaelmas term 1721.

Mr. *Raby*, for the king, showed cause against discharging the recognizance of the defendant for that he was bound over for beating a Custom House officer and whether this offense was within exception of the Act of Pardon touching the public revenue and that this did concern the revenue, Rex v. Bartlet, 1709;[3] Rex v. Honton, and if it is laid *ad diminutionem reventionum.*

And the court agreed it to be pardoned.

And the Chief Baron [BURY] said that laying it *ad diminutionem reventionum* was no more than pepper and salt and not material and that it could not be

[1] Stat. 7 Geo. I, stat. 1, c. 29.

[2] Stat. 7 Ann., c. 22 (*SR*, IX, 95–101).

[3] See *Bartlett v. Attorney General* (1707–1709), Eq. Cases Exch. 561, Parker 277, 145 E.R. 779.

called within the exception touching the revenue. So the recognizance was discharged.

240

Harwood v. Faulke

(Ex. 1721)

An irregular condemnation of goods seized for the non-payment of duties can be set aside by the court.

Bunbury 89, 145 E.R. 605

18 November 1721.

Faulke and Rawley seized a parcel of goods in the hands of Harwood, the Cambridge carrier. The seizure was made in September 1720. Part of the goods were appraised in Michaelmas term in the name of Faulke only and condemned the last day of that term. And the other part was returned in the writ of appraisement in Hilary term following, in the name of Rawley and condemned the last day of that term. Harwood entered his claim in the book of appraisement before condemnations and, afterwards, searched the writs of appraisement, but found no writ in the names of Faulke and Rawley nor any such goods as seized described in any writ of appraisement. By the order of 1st November 1715, which see, they should have returned but one writ of appraisement, and the species of goods should have been particularly described, which was not done in this case.

And, therefore, it was now moved by *Sir Constantine Phipps* to set this condemnation aside, all this fact appearing upon the Master's report.

Note: Before a writ of appraisement is returned, the claim after a seizure must be entered in the book in the office, but, after the writ is returned, it must be indorsed on the back of the writ. But Harwood could never be able to do this because no such writ could ever be found. Upon a seizure, there ought to be an information, which in itself is a sufficient notice. But here was no information, and, consequently, there could be no condemnation on the roll. In this case, the goods were condemned and sold, and one moiety was paid to the crown and the other to the officer.

But, however, upon the circumstances of this case, the court thought that Harwood ought not to be without a remedy. And, therefore, they ordered the appraisers to show cause why the condemnation should not be set aside and why there should not go an attachment against them.

Mr. Attorney General [*Raymond*] was of counsel for Faulke and Rawley.

Taussig MS. 311, vol. 1, p. 129

Saturday, 17 November 1721.

Foulke and Royall seize several goods from the Cambridge carrier in September. Harwood enters a claim in the claim book the first day of Michaelmas term following, no writ of appraisement being returned. And by the standing order of the court in 1715, the seizers are to describe the goods.

One part of these goods are returned in one writ of appraisement in Michaelmas term, but not described, and another part of them in a writ of appraisement in Hilary term following. And both parcels were severally condemned on the last days of Michaelmas and Hilary terms. And it having been formerly referred to the Master to examine and report the matter, it was now moved that the condemnation might be set aside for irregularity.

The court made a rule that the appraisers should show cause why an attachment should not go against them for an irregular appraisement. See the Order of Court of 1 November 1715.

241

Clarke v. Clarke

(Ex. 1721)

A specific legacy will be abated to pay a decedent's debts before real estate will be sold.

A decedent's real estate is liable for the payment of bonds.

Where mortgaged land is devised, the devisee takes subject to the mortgage and the decedent's estate is not liable to pay off the mortgage.

Harvard Law School MS. 1082, vol. 1, p. 51, pl. 2

Hilary term 1720/21.

The question was whether the real estate given to an heir at law shall be subject to the payment of debts, for the testator at the close of the will appoints the heir at law to be executor paying his debts and legacies. And there was a mortgage of £500 on an estate given to the younger son. And whether the real estate should come in aid to pay this mortgage and other debts [was a question].

The second question was whether a copyhold estate not surrendered to the use of the testator's will should be sold for the payment of debts.

Chief Baron [Bury]: I think that the real estate is as well charged as the personal estate with the payment of debts, as well the mortgage as simple contracts.

As to the second point, I think that a court of equity will supply the want of a surrender for the payment of debts or provision for younger children. See Peck v. Elmes, in this court, see the other book.

Price: I think that the Master's report does not fully state the matter to us for our opinion, for we should have a more particular account of the personal estate and the certainty of the value of the copyhold estate. But I shall make no doubt of supplying the want of a surrender for the payment of debts or for provision for younger children.

The common acceptation is of an estate *cum onere*, and if so, the younger son must take the estate with the mortgage. But I shall not determine the point.

It ought to be enquired what debts are due upon bonds and what upon simple contracts, for the bonds in a court of equity will be a lien on the land and, if the person estate falls short, the real estate ought to go in aid and [be] subject to the payment of the mortgage of £500 on the land given to the younger children.

Montagu: I should think it too hard to charge the eldest son's estate with the mortgage due on the younger son's estate. I must admit that the copyhold estate is given by the will to be sold for payment of debts, but as I took the surrender of a copyhold estate to be a certain method of going, yet, if a court of equity is to interpose and supply such surrenders, it will reduce copyhold estates to the same uncertainty as other estates. And, therefore, I am against supplying such defect. And I believe that I remember the first case of that kind.

Page said that it was often done to supply the want of a surrender in a court of equity.

[The case was] to be further spoken to upon a further report from the Deputy [Remembrancer].

Harvard Law School MS. 1082, vol. 1, p. 105, pl. 2

Michaelmas term 1721.

John Clerke, the testator, had two sons and a daughter: John, the eldest, Edward, the second, and Mary Clerke. This man dies seised of an estate settled, and some real estate descended to the heir. And how far it was liable to the payment of debts [was a question], for the farm called Coster's Farm was given to Edward, the younger son, but there was a mortgage of £500 upon it. And one question was whether it should be taken *cum onere* or whether the estate descending shall go to discharge that and other debts.

Mr. *Hungerford*, for Edward and Mary, [said] that the fee simple should be subject to all debts and that Coster's Farm should be declared to the defendant Edward free from incumbrance and that this £500 mortgage shall be decreed a lien on the fee simple estate, and in this case, rather because £400 *per annum* is settled and the elder son has besides £300 *per annum* that descended unsettled.

And he said that the testator seemed to point out that the son should be the same as the daughter, which, if Coster's Farm is decreed to Edward free from encumbrances with his legacy of £500 more, it will be worth about £2000, which is the same as Mary has. And the testator, by his will, makes John, his eldest son, his executor paying all his debts and legacies whatsoever. And if [it] had been all his real estate paying his debts and legacies, that would have subject[ed] him so to have done. And, though put in a different place, yet a will must be taken altogether. Not v. Vernon, 31 January 1715, in Chancery, Lord Cowper; Sir Oliver Ascomb's Case.[1]

Another question was concerning a copyhold estate given to the younger son where there was no surrender.

Mr. *Hungerford* said that a court of equity had always supplied the want of a surrender in the case of payment of debts or for a provision for younger children.

As to the debt upon Coster's Farm, the mortgage upon it is included in the general words.

Mr. *Aris*, for John, the eldest son, cited Puleston v. Puleston.[2]

Chief Baron [Bury]: I know no reason [for the words] 'paying all debts whatsoever'. I think that the personal estate ought first to go in aid, but then the estate in fee simple unsettled should discharge the mortgage, but not to be liable to specific legacies.

Price: The legacies must be paid first. By the Statute of King William,[3] a purchaser or devisee shall be liable to debts upon specialties. The personal estate must go as far [as] it can first, and legacies cannot be paid out of land. The words 'paying all his debts whatsoever' only relates as to making him executor.

Where there is a defect of assets, no specific legacy can be paid. And, therefore, the jewels, though specifically devised, must go into the personal estate to pay debts. I think that the youngest son must take the estate *cum onere* of the mortgage and the giving him £500 besides looks like such was the intention of the testator.

Montagu: The personal estate must go first for the payment of debts. And so was Puleston v. Puleston and so Trot v. Tirwet,[4] and though by Lord Chief Baron Montagu's will, it was directed that a term should be raised for the payment of debts and legacies, yet the Court of Chancery declared the specific legacies to go for nothing, but this judgment was reversed in the House of Lords.

I cannot go so far as to fancy an equality between son and daughter. If the real estate had been given and paying debts etc. had been annexed, I should have ordered it, but it is not so.

I think the funeral charges due are too great where the testator dies indebted. I do not know why the debts on specialties may not be turned upon the land. The younger son must take the estate *cum onere*. I never can supply the want of a surrender.

---

[1] *Trott v. Vernon* (1715), Gilbert Rep. 111, 25 E.R. 77, Precedents in Chancery 430, 24 E.R. 192, 2 Vernon 708, 23 E.R. 1065, 1 Eq. Cas. Abr. 198, 21 E.R. 987, 2 Eq. Cas. Abr. 291, 22 E.R. 244; *Ashcomb's Case*, 2 Eq. Cas. Abr. 291, 22 E.R. 244.

[2] *Puleston v. Puleston* (1677), Reports *tempore* Finch 312, 23 E.R. 171, 73 Selden Soc. 295.

[3] Stat. 3 Will. & Mar., c. 14 (*SR*, VI, 320–321).

[4] *Tyrwhitt v. Trotman* (1714), 3 Brown P.C. 52, 1 E.R. 1171.

PAGE: I am inclined that the £500 in Coster's Farm should be paid by the eldest son, for he gave it to him when it was free from encumbrances. Jewels must be liable to debts.

I shall always supply the want of a surrender for a copyhold.

In the Court of Chancery, as to the expenses of the funeral for the honor of the deceased, though there has been a defect of assets, [it] directed that the trustees should be reimbursed out of the heir's estate.

PRICE never knew them go so far.

[It was] adjourned to be considered of again.

Taussig MS. 311, vol. 1, p. 131

19th November 1721.

'I make my son John executor, paying all my debts whatsoever.' In the first part of his will, he gives all his real estate to his son John.

Now, *per Hungerford*, if the words 'paying all his debts' had been annexed to the devise of the real estate, it had been plain. Trot and Beard, 31 January 1715, Chancery, *coram* Cowper, Lord Chancellor, upon the devise of Sir Harry Boothby.[1]

And by him, the inserting these words after the clause of executorship does not alter because these words *nihil operatur* unless they are construed to charge the real estate. The testator gave part of his real estate called Coster's Farm of £60 *per annum* to his younger son, but this farm was charged with a mortgage. None but specialty debts do bind the lands; in this case, the testator does by the mortgage bind his heirs, executors, etc. Nowis and Mordaunt, *coram* Cowper,[2] and reheard before Harcourt 1712; fee simple estate to his eldest daughter, all entailed lands to his second, and part entailed and part freehold to his third daughter; the court decreed that the eldest daughter should be looked upon as a trustee.

I query whether the daughter shall have the jewels not charged with debts.

3 Cro. 161[3] [is] that, where a devise is to an heir at law paying debts, it prevents a descent.

Clarke was seised of two estates, one entailed of £396 *per annum* and another freehold, debts by specialty £1600 and debts by simple contract only, £1300 personal estate.

A will must be taken entire, and, therefore, in this case, the words 'paying his debts' must be applied to the devise of the real estate.

Mr. *Aris*: An infant heir must be favored.

---

[1] *Trott v. Vernon* (1715), *ut supra*.

[2] *Noyes v. Mordaunt* (1706), Gilbert Rep. 2, 25 E.R. 2, Precedents in Chancery 265, 24 E.R. 128, 2 Vernon 581, 23 E.R. 978, 1 Eq. Cas. Abr. 273, 21 E.R. 1041.

[3] *Gilpin's Case* (1625), Croke Car. 161, 79 E.R. 740.

First question: Whether the testator's real estate of £396 *per annum*, which is subject to two several annuities of £30 is not by the words of the will subject to the payment of the testator's debts by specialty and simple contract debts.

Second question: Whether the mortgage of Coster's Farm shall be discharged by the heir at law. Puleston and Puleston, *coram* Lord Somers in Chancery. Personal estate, even specifically devised, was in that case decreed to go and be applied to the discharge of debts by simple contract before the real estate shall be affected.

Lord Chief Baron [Bury]: It seems to me that the heir's estate is subject to all the testator's debts and that the jewels must go towards payment of the debts.

Per Price: We must not make wills, but only expound them. Debts upon a specialty are fixed upon the land – this is by the Statute of William – were £1600; debts upon a simple contract were £1200, the funeral was £240, and the personal estate was but £1300, including the value of the jewels. So there is a deficiency. Legacies cannot be turned upon the land nor, by him, can we charge so great a sum as £240 for funeral expenses.

Paying all his debts whatsoever, by him, is to be tied up to the executorship only.

By him, a debtor cannot have jewels.

As to the copyhold, which is expressly devised to the eldest with liberty to sell or otherwise as the executors shall think proper, and, by him, I think it is proper to sell it in aid of the personal estate.

As to £500 upon Coster's Farm, *terra transit cum onere*, and the son must take it with the charge. And the rather because here is a legacy of £500, but this is not payable until twenty-one, but yet it might pay the interest in the meantime.

Per Montagu: I do not know how to understand a man's will but by his words. Personal estate must be always applied in discharge of real estate. Therefore, we must see what there is to pay with. He cited the Case of Lord Chief Baron Montagu's will, where the Lords reversed the Master of the Rolls's estate. Whether, [by] the last words 'paying debts whatsoever' the daughter's portion is expressly charged on the freehold, 'I make such a one my executor paying all my debts whatsoever', this is common form; 'I give him my plate [. . .] if he pays'; there is no doubt but the testator intended to give the jewels. But yet it is very plain that the jewels must be taken into the personal estate. Special debts [lie] on lands by the Statute of William. The personal estate is £1322 so that is £153 short to pay the simple contract debts. I think the funeral expenses are too large.

Whether copyhold must be sold, I think we cannot do it, for we must go according to the rules of law. This is overturning the rules of certainty, which is the rule of law.

As to the £500 mortgage, *terra transit cum onere*. We ought to take further time to consider.

Page: Paying is annexed to the executorship on whom the £500 should lie. He devises the estate of £60 *per annum*, which he bought, for it was not incumbered when bought.

Secondly, a mortgagor binds himself and heirs. Query how he can be discharged from encumbrances in the case of an action brought.

Jewels must go into the personal estate.

As to the copyhold, he disagrees with Montagu, for there is no uncertainty. There must be a surrender and admittance in this case as well as in any other case.

'With liberty to sell', this liberty is given to the heir at law. We never do decree to sell, but only do decree the parties shall hold. And, therefore, we cannot go so far for want of sufficient power.

As to funerals, in this case, both the executor and heir at law are defendants, though in equity the excess of the funeral charges have been allowed as against creditors.

Bunbury 90, 145 E.R. 606

20 November 1721.

Where jewels are devised as a specific legacy, yet they shall be applied to payment of debts upon simple contracts if the rest of the personal estate falls short in ease of the real estate.

Mr. *Hungerford* [was] for the plaintiffs; Mr. *Aris* [was] for the defendant.

242

Baker v. Sweet

(Ex. 1721)

Depositions taken where the parties have not pleaded to an issue are not admissible in evidence.

Depositions taken in a prior case are admissible in evidence only where the parties are the same and the matters in issue are the same.

After a great length of time, a deponent will be presumed to be dead without any proof of death.

An interested witness may be allowed to prove a handwriting.

Bunbury 90, 145 E.R. 606,
1 Rayner 160, 2 Gwillim 629, 1 Eagle & Younge 776

Eodem die [20 November 1721].

In this case, it seemed to be admitted that wool of lambs shall pay tithes, though the lambs had paid tithes two months before and that there ought to be paid tithe for the agistment of yearlings, being a new increase.

Sir Constantine Phipps and Mr. *Bootle* [were] for the plaintiff; Mr. *Ward* [was] for the defendant.

Bunbury 91, 145 E.R. 606

27 November 1721.

Depositions were taken in a cause in Chancery in 1675, relating to *modus*es now in dispute, to establish these *modus*es wherein the occupiers of land in this parish were plaintiffs and the impropriator, who was the Provost and College of Eton, and the vicar were defendants but the impropriator had never answered and there was no replication to the vicar. And, therefore, it was objected that these depositions could not be read, for that *modus*es being to affect the inheritance, the act of the former shall not bind, unless the impropriator or landlord be made a party and issue be joined as to them.

And *per* CURIAM: They cannot be read. And the bill and answer upon these occasions must be produced to make the depositions evidence in another cause to show that it is between the same parties or those under whom they claim, and, secondly, that it is the same matter that is now in issue. (*Absentibus* Price and Montagu.)

Sir Constantine Phipps [was] for the plaintiff; Mr. *Ward* [was] for the defendant.

Harvard Law School MS. 1082, vol. 1, p. 97

Michaelmas term 1721.

A bill was brought by the impropriator and vicar of Modbury, the impropriator being entitled to the two thirds of all great and small tithes and the vicar to the other third part.

The defendant insisted on several *modus*es, which were laid to be in full for several small tithes and it likewise included some *modus*es and other tithes in kind, and, by reason of the compositions for forty years that included both, it was difficult to prove by any living witnesses the several *modus*es, upon which, we who were counsel for the defendant offered an exemplification of a bill, answer, and depositions under the great seal in the Court of Chancery wherein Hele *et al.*, parishioners of the said parish, were plaintiffs and the lessee of the rectory were defendants, and this bill was to perpetuate testimony, but the Provost and Fellows of Eton, that were the lessors and impropriators of the rectory, were not parties. But we insisted that this being between the same parties or their representatives, that this evidence ought to be read.

But it was opposed by the plaintiffs for the following reason, *viz.*, first, that the lessors were not parties; secondly, that there was no replication to the vicar's answer and so no proper issue [was] joined; thirdly, the witnesses were not proved to be dead.

To which last reason, we answered that it would be presumed after fifty years and, as to the other reasons, we said that there was no occasion because the vicar had admitted the case as set forth in the bill, so [there was] no occasion for a replication.

But Chief Baron [BURY] and PAGE, being the only persons in court, agreed that, for the two first reasons, that they would not allow the exemplification to be read.

It was objected in this case that a parishioner to prove the hand of the vicar ought not to be admitted because that would tend to prove *modus*es. But that objection was overruled because a parishioner may be admitted in some cases, as to prove payment.

But for want of proving the *modus*es, the defendant was decreed to account.

Taussig MS. 311, vol. 1, p. 160

27 November 1721. Baker, Rhodes, etc. v. Sweet *et al.*, parishioners of Modbury.

The case came on to be heard on Monday last, but stood over to this day on account of the defendants' not having the order for producing the exemplification.

Rhodes *et al.* were joint-tenants of the rectory of Modbury, and Baker was the vicar there. And the rectory is divided by thirds, two-thirds to the impropriators and one-third to the vicar.

The bill was exhibited against the parishioners for all sorts of tithes, both great and small. And the defendants, by their answer, insisted on a great many *modus*es. And to prove them, they offered to read an exemplification of a bill, answer, and depositions in Chancery. The bill was brought in Chancery *anno* 1676 and was brought by several parishioners and occupiers of land in the parish against the then lessees of the impropriation, the provost and fellows of Eton College, impropriators, and the then vicar to perpetuate the testimony of the witnesses concerning the *modus*es now insisted on by the defendants. And upon opening the exemplification, it appeared that the provost never answered, that though the vicar did answer, yet there was no replication to his answer, and the replication to the answer of the lessees of the impropriation was upon a double 6d. stamp, which could not be at that time and so must have been supplied since.

And therefore, *Sir Constantine Phipps*, for the defendants, objected to reading the exemplification on several accounts:

First, because the exemplification is irregular, part of the proceedings being wanting, *viz.* the replication to the defendants' answer, for this replication on a double 6d. stamp could not be the real replication and the defendants are now applying to the Court of Chancery to examine into the regularity of the exemplification.

Second, the provost, who is impropriator, never answered; so he was no party to the suit. And, therefore, the depositions cannot be evidence against him or any claiming under him.

Thirdly, there was no replication to the vicar's answer, so there was no issue as to him.

Fourthly, it does not appear that the witnesses then examined are now dead, and, if not, their depositions cannot be read as evidence.

Fifthly, the bill is not brought by all the parishioners and occupiers of the land within the parish, but by some of them only and perhaps against the knowledge and consent of the others.

But the Court, that is the Chief Baron [Bury] and Page, said that, as to all exceptions relating to the irregularity of the exemplification, they could take no notice of them, for the exemplification before them was under the seal and whether the parts of and from which the exemplification was made were right and formal, the Court of Chancery could only examine into that; they must take the exemplification for a good record.

Secondly, as to the witnesses being dead, they made no scruple about that, for the depositions were above forty years standing and it was every day's practice to read deeds of forty years standing without proof because, in such a length of time, witnesses may be reasonably supposed to be dead.

But they thought that the provost having never answered and so being no party to this suit, the exemplification could not now be given in evidence against his lessees or any claiming under him. And so they rejected it.

But Serjeant *Pengelly*, seeing their opinion, moved the cause might stand over until the court be full, *quod fuit negatur.*

Another piece of evidence offered by the plaintiff was several records signed by the former vicar for some of the *modus*es, and these the plaintiffs had liberty to prove *viva voce* at the hearing of the cause. And to prove them, they called the parish clerk, and his testimony was objected against, as a parishioner.

Sed per Chief Baron [Bury] and Page: He may be a good witness to prove the vicar's handwriting. And he was accordingly admitted though he was no subscribing witness to the receipts and it is possible that they might have been proved by some other person.

Upon the whole, the court decreed an account, [there] not being evidence enough to support and prove the *modus*es.

N.B. The court thought that the lessees of the impropriator and vicar might well join in this bill since it was admitted that two-thirds of the tithes belonged to the impropriator and one-third to the vicar.

243

Shipton, *qui tam* v. Newman

(Ex. 1721)

An owner of goods who successfully defends them from a seizure for an alleged customs violation is entitled to receive court costs, and a collateral lawsuit in another court is not material to this issue.

Taussig MS. 311, vol. 1, p. 100

Trinity term 1721.

Chief Baron [BURY]: After judgment on an information for the party claiming, he brings his action of trespass against the officer for the goods seized, *viz.* cocoa nuts and bags. And the action was tried in the Common Pleas, and there was a verdict for the plaintiff and 2s. 6d. damages. But Lord Chief Justice King said that, as to the cocoa nuts, which were contained in the information, the claimer is not entitled to damages, for, by the Act of Parliament of 6 King [George], pa. 415, 416,[1] the claimer is to have costs upon the information, which costs are to be a full satisfaction to the claimant for the taking and detaining his goods.

And now *Sir Constantine Phipps* moved for costs upon the information. The damages were only for the bags upon the trial in the action, which bags were not contained in the information, for the bags were certainly the claimant's own. And the officer took the cocoa nuts and poured the nuts into these bags and took them away all together so that, as to the bags, it was certainly a trespass.

Per MONTAGU: The action of the Common Pleas is not before us, but only the information. And we must pursue the Act of Parliament notwithstanding.

But by the other barons: We think it proper since the action in the Common Bench is mentioned to see what the action was for. Perhaps it may not be material, but we ought to see it before we determine. Therefore, move this again next term and produce the *postea*.

Taussig MS. 311, vol. 1, p. 146

Friday, 24 November 1721.

A motion was made by *Sir Constantine Phipps* for costs for the defendant upon the information. And the motion was grounded on the Stat. 6 George, ca. 21, §§ 39, 40, 41.

The verdict was obtained upon an action of trespass for bags and cocoa nuts, but the damages was only of 2s. 6d. for the bags. And, as to the rest of the trespass, it was found for the defendant, the Chief Justice of the Common Bench being of opinion that the plaintiff could not be recompensed by damages in this action of trespass for the cocoa nuts, which were contained in the information. See the words of the Act [*blank*].

These costs are given *in toto* of all damages for the seizure and detention of the goods seized.

Mr. Attorney [General *Raymond*] and Solicitor General [*Yorke*] *contra*: The party should not have traveled the officer into another court by an action of trespass and put him to all these expenses and then resort back again to this court for costs upon an information as if he had never sought another remedy, for the Statute must receive this construction that the defendant in the information may have his costs, *scil.* if he will come here for them, but not if he goes another way

[1] Stat. 6 Geo. I, c. 21.

for *quilibet potest renunciare juri* etc., and, therefore, the party having taken his remedy by an action of trespass cannot resort hither.

Secondly, the *postea* is rased in this case, and so are the notes which were taken upon the back of the [writ of] *distringas* by the associate so that the record has been altered. But taking it for granted that the *postea* is conclusive, still the party ought not to have damages, for the trespass is for the bags. Now, an officer cannot seize goods but in bags; therefore, the damages for the bags are damages occasioned by the seizure.

Per Sir Constantine Phipps: The *postea* has been set right by the order of King, Chief Justice, because it was drawn up contrary to his rule.

The bags were never put into the information, nor were the goods in the bags when seized, but were, in fact, in tubs, and the officer took the bags that lay loose in the warehouse to carry away the goods.

There is no election or pretense of election in the Act, but the words are very positively otherwise.

There is no inconvenience, for if a man cannot now recover upon an action at law, he must pay costs for bringing such action.

The taking the bags was collateral to the seizure and not properly a damage occasioned by the seizure, no more than firing the house would have been. As to costs, the acts giving costs where no costs were before, it seems plainly to show that the party had another way to recover what was equivalent to the costs before the Act, though he could not have costs.

PRICE: We must give costs or else the party is without a remedy; he thought the Act was plainly intended to relieve him.

PAGE was of the same opinion. And upon a verdict on an information, we ought to give judgment for the costs upon this Statute. And this Act is for the benefit of the officer and not for the merchant because the merchant must now take his costs in lieu of all damages for the seizure. And Mr. Attorney [General] will not allow that the merchant has an election, for it certainly was not the intent of the Act that he should.

Chief Baron [BURY] assented. And the party had his costs.

Bunbury 90, 145 E.R. 606

24 November 1721.

An information was brought upon a seizure of a parcel of cocoa nuts and tried. And there was a verdict for the defendant, who brought his action against the officer for this seizure of the nuts and also some bags, which the officer took to carry away the nuts in. This action was tried in the Court of Common Pleas, and there was a verdict for the plaintiff. And Lord Chief Justice King was of opinion he might have his costs and damages below for the bags, but, for the nuts, the officer was acquitted, being included in the information. And the defendant in the information having a verdict thereon for him, his proper remedy was to move this court for his costs on the Stat. 6 Geo., c. [*blank*], which he now did by his counsel, *Sir Constantine Phipps*.

But it was opposed by the Attorney [General, *Raymond*], and the Solicitor General, [*Yorke*], who insisted that the Act never designed the party a double remedy, but only gave him his election to bring his action or have his costs, but not both.

But [it was held by the] CURIA *contra*, for, though he has joined the nuts in his action, when he might have brought it for the bags alone, that shall not preclude him of the satisfaction the Act gives him.

And Baron PAGE said that, if the action had been brought for the nuts alone and damages had been recovered, this court would have allowed costs on the information because we ought to do right, though another court does wrong, and the party could not, in that case, have had judgment.

(Query; *absente* Montagu.)

Harvard Law School MS. 1082, vol. 1, p. 102

Michaelmas term 1721.

Sir Constantine Phipps moved costs [pursuant to] 6 Geo. in respect of the damage of detaining goods by a seizure, these being cocoa nuts, and an action was brought, and only half a crown was given for the bags.

Attorney General [*Raymond*], for the plaintiff, [said] that there ought to be no costs because damage was given for the bags and he proceeded on his action and had £16 costs taxed, so the officer is doubly vexed and charged.

[It was] adjourned to be moved again until the *postea* was brought in.

244

Attorney General v. Gradyll

(Ex. 1721)

A power of attorney to appoint trustees to make leases is a personal right which does not pass to the crown as forfeited by high treason.

Harvard Law School MS. 1082, vol. 1, p. 50, pl. 2

Hilary term 1720/21.

The question was whether a power that was to let leases for twenty-one years was forfeited by high treason, which was insisted on not to be forfeited, as Combe's Case [and] Gresham's Case, 9th Reports.[1] [And it was] to be further spoken to.

[1] *Atlee v. Banks* (1613), 9 Coke Rep. 75, 77 E.R. 843.

Harvard Law School MS. 1082, vol. 1, p. 98

Michaelmas term 1721.

Dickenson was tenant for life with a power to make leases for three lives or twenty-one years and that he might by letter of attorney appoint trustees for that purpose. [*blank*] Dickenson, brother and heir of [*blank*] Dickenson, deceased, commits treason. The question is now how this power shall be executed and whether the trustees shall be obliged to nominate such persons to have such leases as the crown shall appoint.

Attorney General [*Raymond*]: This power is vested in the trustees and ought to be executed by the direction of the crown. Sir Thomas Jones 110, Witfield's Case; Moore 612; Rolle, *Abridgment*, 642, 842; 1 Ventris 338.[1]

Sir Constantine Phipps, of the same side: The crown can have no benefit until the debts are paid.

Serjeant *Stevens*, for the trustees: This is a forfeiture under a marriage settlement.

Serjeant *Reynolds*, for the trustees, cited Comb's Case, 9 Rept.; 1 Rolle, *Abridgment*, 330; Hardres 410.[2] In the case of How v. Whitfield, it was annexed to the estate for life.

Mr. *Fazakerly*, for the same [side], [cited] 1 Rept. 176; 2 Rolle 260; 9 Rept. 75; 8 Rept. 71.[3]

Mr. *Bootle*, for the trustees: Here is a term for ninety-nine years still subsisting. And it is a collateral and cannot be executed so as to let the crown into possession. Dame Gresham's Case, 9 Rept. 76. It cannot be executed by an attorney, which is personal, and, where an authority is given by a person attainted, there, that authority is gone. King v. Melling, 1 Ventris.[4] A common recovery will discharge all collateral matters; so in this case of treason.

The *Attorney General* replies: This power ought to be executed by the trustees. It is said by one of the counsel that it was a power annexed to the estate and

---

[1] *How v. Whitfield* (1678), T. Jones 110, 84 E.R. 1171, 1 Ventris 338, 339, 86 E.R. 218, 219, also 2 Shower K.B. 57, 89 E.R. 791; *Anonymous*, Moore K.B. 608, 612, 72 E.R. 790, 792.

[2] *Atlee v. Banks* (1613), *ut supra*; *Comb's Case* (1613), 1 Rolle, Abr., *Authoritie*, p. 330, also 9 Coke Rep. 75, 77 E.R. 843; *Edwards v. Sleater* (1665), Hardres 410, 145 E.R. 522, also Lincoln's Inn MS. Misc. 499, pp. 250, 292.

[3] *Kingsmill v. Sharington* (1582–1584), 1 Coke Rep. 175, 76 E.R. 379, also Croke Eliz. 34, 78 E.R. 300, Moore K.B. 144, 72 E.R. 495, Jenkins 247, 145 E.R. 174; [see generally] 2 Rolle, Abr., *Powers*, p. 260; *Atlee v. Banks* (1613), *ut supra*; *Chappel v. Whitlock* (1609), 8 Coke Rep. 69, 77 E.R. 580, also 1 Brownlow & Goldesborough 169, 123 E.R. 734.

[4] *King v. Melling* (1672), 1 Ventris 214, 225, 86 E.R. 144, 151, also 2 Levinz 58, 83 E.R. 448, 3 Keble 42, 52, 95, 84 E.R. 584, 589, 614, Pollexfen 101, 86 E.R. 526, 3 Salkeld 296, 91 E.R. 835, 1 Eq. Cas. Abr. 181, 21 E.R. 973.

by other counsel that it is a collateral power. The power is transferred to others in their own name, but, where by letter of attorney, and I admit Dame Gresham's Case to be [good] law, the power is not gone by the attainder, as the Duke of Norfolk and Englesfield's Case, 10 Rept.[1] The reason of Mildmay's Case[2] is mistaken, for that was upon a covenant to stand seised.

PRICE: I am at present of opinion that the Attorney General's motion cannot be granted, but it is a personal power and likewise collateral and it looks flagrant. But if it is a personal power, it cannot go with the land.

PAGE: I am of the same opinion.

And so the Attorney General's motion <was denied> for the trustees to nominate such persons for leases as the crown.

Bunbury 92, 145 E.R. 607

28 November 1721.

In a marriage settlement, there was a power for William Dickenson, who was thereby made tenant for life, to make leases for three lives or twenty-one years. William Dickenson makes a lease to trustees for ninety-nine years, if he should so long live, in order for the payment of his debts.

(Note this was not by virtue of his power.)

And in the same deed, he constitutes the trustees his attorneys to make leases for three lives or twenty-one years, pursuant to the power in the settlement. William Dickenson is outlawed for high treason. And the Attorney General now comes into the court to compel the trustees to execute this power vested in them by making leases for twenty-one years or three lives to such nominees as the crown shall appoint. And he insisted upon it that this was a power transferable and, since the forfeiture, ought to be executed for the benefit of the crown. And he cited Moore 612; 1 Ventris 338; Sir Thomas Jones 110; and lib. 7, Englefield's Case.

But to this, it was answered that, where a power is collateral to an estate, there, the alteration of the estate does not affect it; but, where the power arises out of the estate, any alteration of the estate will suspend it for so much; and, if the alteration be total, it will totally extinguish it. Hardres 410.[3]

But note the counsel for the defendants seemed to differ whether this was a personal or a collateral power. But they all insisted that the authority given to the trustees to act as attorneys was destroyed by the attainder of William Dickenson.

---

1 *Regina v. Englefield* (1591), 7 Coke Rep. 11, 13, 77 E.R. 428, 431, also Moore K.B. 303, 72 E.R. 595, 4 Leonard 135, 169, 74 E.R. 779, 800, Popham 18, 79 E.R. 1139, 1 Anderson 293, 123 E.R. 480.

2 *Hethersall v. Mildmay* (1605), 6 Coke Rep. 40, 77 E.R. 311, also Moore K.B. 632, 72 E.R. 805.

3 *Edwards v. Sleater* (1665), Hardres 410, 145 E.R. 522.

PRICE and PAGE, barons, were clearly of opinion that, by making the lease of ninety-nine years, the power was suspended and William Dickenson had nothing left in him, but a reversion during his life after ninety-nine years, and the power of attorney can subsist no longer than the power of William Dickenson himself, which is gone by the attainder.

And the Attorney General took nothing by his motion (*hesitante* Lord Chief Baron BURY; *absente* Montagu).

Mr. Attorney General [*Raymond*] and *Sir Constantine Phipps* [were] *pro rege*; Serjeant *Stevens*, Serjeant *Reynolds*, Mr. *Fazakerly*, and Mr. *Bootle* [were] for the defendants.

Taussig MS. 311, vol. 1, p. 164

Michaelmas 1721.

The question in this case was concerning a power to make leases for twenty-one years or three lives and whether a court of equity could compel trustees to execute this power for the benefit of the crown, the person to whom or for whose benefit this power was reserved being attainted and having forfeited his estate to the crown. And the court was of opinion they could not. *Sed quaere statu casus.* Authorities [were] cited *ex parte* the Attorney General, Sir T. Jones Rep. 110, Ventr. 338; Moor 612; Rolle, *Abr.*, 844; *e contra* 1 Rep. 176; 2 Rolle, *Abr.*, 260, pl. 1; 9 Rep. 76; 2 Rolle, *Abr.*, 393; Palmer's Rep. 426; Hardres 410; 8 Rep. 71.[1]

245

Caswall v. Godfrey

(Ex. 1721)

A court of equity has jurisdiction over matters of accounts and matters of trusts.

Harvard Law School MS. 1082, vol. 1, p. 104, pl. 1

Michaelmas term 1721.

The plaintiff [Sir George Caswall] brings his bill for an injunction for that the defendant desired him to buy £500 [South Sea] stock at 768 percent, which was transferred to Sir George Caswall and so declared by him to the defendant's son and so it was entered in Sir George Caswall's books and partners and on the account of the defendant. And instead of the defendant's paying £2343, [he] demands £1500 which was sent by the defendant towards payment.

[1] *How v. Whitfield* (1678), *ut supra*; *Anonymous*, Moore K.B. 608, 612, 72 E.R. 790, 792; *Kingsmill v. Sharington* (1582–1584), *ut supra*; *Crosse v. Barse* (1607), 2 Rolle, Abr., *Powers*, pl. A, 1, p. 260; *Atlee v. Banks* (1613), *ut supra*; 2 Rolle, Abr., *Recoverie common*, pl. A, 1, p. 393; *Edwards v. Sleater* (1665), *ut supra*; *Chappel v. Whitlock* (1609), *ut supra*.

The defendant, in his answer, admits that he did desire the plaintiff to buy the stock and that he paid £1500 in the subscription [and] £2340 was lent at five percent. But the defendant insisted that he bought this stock to sell again and that he could not get it from Sir George Caswall. It is a matter of account and so proper for an injunction, as Aubery v. Fitzhugh.[1]

Sir Constantine Phipps, for the defendant, said that this defense was at law.

Wills, for the plaintiff, said that there was no laches in the plaintiff, for the defendant never desired to have it transferred and there can be no defense at law and the contract must be taken *in toto*. And, though he might make a defense at law as to part, yet not to the whole.

Ward, for the plaintiff: It is an entire agreement and to split this matter is the province of a court of equity. Though the plaintiff purchased by the direction of the defendant, yet it was transferred to the plaintiff in trust to the defendant, yet such an authority could not be given in evidence at law and, then, the plaintiff is defenseless at law.

No note was given by Mr. Godfrey to the plaintiff to that purpose and the loan of the money is a matter of account and settling principal, interest, and costs.

Chief Baron [Bury]: I am for granting an injunction. And the defendant would split an agreement which is entire. And whether he is a trustee or not for the defendant is a question in equity.

Baron Price agrees, for here are all the ingredients for a court of equity, *viz.* matter of account [for an] entire agreement and a trust. [There is] no pretense that this stock was demanded whilst the books were open. And notice to the son is admitted of the stock in trust and the entry of this trust in the plaintiff and the partners' books, which are of a public nature, is material.

Montagu: I agree, but not that it is a South Sea contract, but because the plaintiff is defenseless at law. It is agreed by all that £1500 is laid out. What is become of the other? Whether this stock was bought in trust is the single question. Such a purchase is no bar at law.

Page agreed for an injunction. At first, I thought it proper at law and the book may be evidence of a matter at the time of the entry. And so [he] agreed for an injunction, which was granted *per* totam curiam.

246

Thompson v. Coombes

(Ex. 1721)

The question in this case was whether an attorney of the Court of King's Bench has a privilege to be sued only in that court.

[1] *Awbrey v. Fitzhugh* (Ex. 1721), see above, Case No. 231.

Taussig MS. 311, vol. 1, p. 117

Michaelmas term 1721.

Thompson brings an action against Coombs upon a bond in this court. Coombs pleads that he is an attorney of the King's Bench and ought not to be sued here.

Per Bootle: He ought to show a writ of privilege, as *per* 9 Edw. IV, Justice Young's Case; Dyer 287.[1]

Per Raby: Salkeld, title Privilege,[2] [holds] that it is a good plea, if pleaded with a writ, it is not traversable; if without a writ, it may be replied to.

Per Montagu: You have here pleaded that you are an attorney of the Court of King's Bench, but I do not apprehend that there are any attorneys there but only as clerks. Holt and Ventris.

Per Raby: There is a roll of attorneys in the King's Bench, but, however, if the plea is not good, let the plaintiff demur.

247

Loving v. Barney

(Ex. 1721)

A defendant can plead double even though one of the defenses lies within the knowledge of the defendant.

Taussig MS. 311, vol. 1, p. 118, pl. 1

Michaelmas term 1721.

[Upon an action of] debt upon a bond, the defendant moved to plead double, *viz. plene administravit* and a usurious contract.

The motion was opposed by Mr. *Ward* because the fact of *plene administravit* was entirely in the cognizance of the defendant.

But the motion was granted notwithstanding.

248

Sheriff of Middlesex v. Lords of the Franchises

(Ex. 1721)

The question in this case was whether grantees of crown revenues can be taxed thereon.

---

[1] *Yong v. Clerk of the Hamper* (1470), YB Hil. 9 Edw. IV, f. 53, pl. 18, also Jenkins 131, 145 E.R. 92; *Anonymous* (1570), 3 Dyer 287, 73 E.R. 643.

[2] *Dillon v. Harper* (1703), 2 Salkeld 545, 91 E.R. 461, also 1 Salkeld 328, 91 E.R. 290, 2 Lord Raymond 898, 92 E.R. 99, Holt K.B. 589, 90 E.R. 1226.

Taussig MS. 311, vol. 1, p. 122

Michaelmas term 1721.

12 Ric. II, ca. 10,[1] appoints six justices and 14 Ric., ca. 11,[2] eight justices. Query whether if the king makes more justices. There was a warrant made by the Lords of the Treasury upon the Restoration that the Lords of the Franchises shall be contributory to eighteen justices in Middlesex and twelve in other counties. And another warrant or order was made in 1691 to allow for twenty-four justices.

Sir Constantine Phipps moved for a direction to the Foreign Apposer to allow no more out of the Lords of the Franchises' fines and amercements than for eight justices.

Per PRICE: Where the crown grants fines and amercements, the grantee has as absolute a property in the fines etc. as in other things. And I do not know that the Lords of the Treasury can bind the property of the Lords of the Franchises. And, if the Lords of the Franchises cannot be helped or aided elsewhere, I think we ought to help them here.

Per PAGE: I think this matter ought to be settled in full court. (Note Montagu was absent.) I doubt whether we can say that the Lords of the Franchises shall be excused in a case where there may follow a defect of justice. Move it again when the court is full, and give notice to the barons.

249

Anonymous

(Ex. 1721)

A plaintiff need not give notice of a deed mentioned in the bill of complaint unless he must prove it.

Taussig MS. 311, vol. 1, p. 124, pl. 1

Michaelmas term 1721.

Per CURIAM: A man need never give notice of a deed which he has pointed out in his bill unless it needs proof.

N.B. The deed in this case was above thirty years old.

Sed quaere per PRICE where such deed is denied in the defendant's answer.

Per PAGE: By the Statute of Frauds and Perjuries,[3] supposing there is a resulting use to the grandfather *pur auter vie*, this will be subject to the debts of the grandfather.

---

[1] Stat. 12 Ric. II, c. 10 (*SR*, II, 58–59).

[2] Stat. 14 Ric. II, c. 11 (*SR*, II, 77).

[3] Stat. 29 Car. II, c. 3 (*SR*, V, 839–842).

250

Young v. Slave

(Ex. 1721)

Where an ecclesiastical court refuses to acknowledge the testimony of a single witness but requires more, the case will be removed into one of the common law courts.

Taussig MS. 311, vol. 1, p. 124, pl. 2

15th November 1721.

[Upon a] suggestion for [a writ of] prohibition that the party defendant had proved his plea by one witness, which the ecclesiastical judge had refused, [he] produced the libel, answer thereto, the suggestion, and an affidavit that the judge refused the single testimony. Shotter and Friend, Shower's Report,[1] that the refusal of a plea is traversable; it is otherwise of a refusal of testimony.

A prohibition [was awarded] *nisi.*

251

Rex v. Masters

(Ex. 1721)

Property in the possession of a trustee cannot be levied upon for the debts of the trustee.

Taussig MS. 311, vol. 1, p. 125, pl. 1

Michaelmas term 1721.

Sir Harcourt Masters, being a debtor to the crown and a [writ of] extent having issued, an inquisition finds him possessed of so much stock. And part of this stock being in trust for a private person, it was moved on behalf of Mrs. Owen that Sir Harcourt might have liberty to transfer this stock to the *cestui qui trusts.* And Mr. Attorney General [*Raymond*] appeared and consented to the motion, being satisfied that he was only entitled to this stock in trust for Mrs. Owen.

---

[1] *Shatter v. Friend* (1691), 1 Shower K.B. 158, 172, 89 E.R. 510, 518, 3 Modern 283, 87 E.R. 188, also Carthew 142, 90 E.R. 687, Holt K.B. 752, 90 E.R. 1313, 2 Salkeld 547, 91 E.R. 462, Comberbach 160, 90 E.R. 404.

252

Somers v. Somers

(Ex. 1721)

Wherever an oath is required, if the party is a Quaker, an affirmation may be taken in lieu thereof.

Taussig MS. 311, vol. 1, p. 130

Michaelmas term 1721.

[Upon a] motion to suppress the defendant's answer as taken irregularly because taken upon a *dedimus* of the common form, which is *super juramentum*, the answer is returned *super solemne affirmatione*, therefore, he ought to have had a special *dedimus* or else he ought to have shown in the return that he is a Quaker, which is not done here.

Sed per CURIAM: It is well enough, for, by the Act,[1] wherever an oath is required, if the party is a Quaker, an affirmation may be taken in lieu thereof. Therefore, unless the plaintiff will produce an affidavit that the defendant is not Quaker, we shall take it he was because he has taken the solemn affirmation.

253

Baker v. Davis

(Ex. 1721)

Proceeding to trial on an improper issue is cured by the verdict.

Taussig MS. 311, vol. 1, p. 136

22 November 1721.

The plaintiff brings [an action of] case and sets forth that A. was in the custody of C. and D., bailiffs, at the plaintiff's suit by virtue of a *quo minus*. And the defendant, in consideration that the plaintiff at the request of the defendant would suffer the party arrested to be discharged and go at large to such a day, which was before the return of the writ, promised that he would pay the money or render him again into the custody of the same bailiffs. The defendant pleads that he *paratus fuit et obtulit* to render the party on the day. And, on this, issue is joined and found for the plaintiff.

Per Serjeant *Reynolds* in [a motion of] arrest of judgment: This is an immaterial issue because he could never be returned into the same custody under that writ. Therefore, the only issue should have been whether he had paid the money.

---

[1] Stat. 1 Geo. I, stat. 2, c. 6.

Per Branthwait: I admit the issue to be immaterial. But it being found for the plaintiff, you shall not object, Cro. Car. 25, 78,[1] to it, as in the Case of Nicholls, 5 Rep. 43,[2] and the cases before in Cro. Car.; Salkeld 623;[3] *paratus fuit et obtulit* to transfer stock is not sufficient without saying that the other who was to accept was not there or else that he refused to accept. *Sed ibidem tenetur* that [upon] a verdict, this may be well enough.[4]

The second [question] in this case was a promise to the bailiffs that if the bailiffs would let him go at large, which, by Serjeant *Reynolds*, is a void promise as being without consideration. Yelverton 197; Siderfin 132; 1 Levinz 183, Walsingham v. Combe.[5] The difference is between an informal and immaterial issue. And, by him, the case in Coke is only an informal issue, i.e. defect of circumstance. But here, an issue is taken upon an immaterial part of the declaration and, therefore, it is an immaterial issue. 1 Levinz 98, same case as Siderfin 132.

If the plaintiff consents that the bailiffs shall discharge the party arrested, he can never arrest him again.

Page for the defendant: [There is] no notion of escape without a wrong to the party and the consent of the plaintiff makes the escape worse.

Per Price: I take this to be an informal issue and not material.

Judgment was given afterward for the plaintiff.

254

Rex v. Whittingham

(Ex. 1721)

Where a tally and the foil do not match up, the Court of Exchequer will not grant relief without a report from the Chamberlain of the Exchequer.

---

1 *Knight v. Harvy* (1625), Croke Car. 25, 79 E.R. 627; *Purcase v. Jegon* (1627), Croke Car. 78, 79 E.R. 669, also Noy 85, 74 E.R. 1052, W. Jones 140, 82 E.R. 75, Latch 158, 82 E.R. 324.

2 *Chamberlain v. Nichols* (1595), 5 Coke Rep. 43, 77 E.R. 121, also Moore K.B. 692, 72 E.R. 844, Croke Eliz. 455, 78 E.R. 694, Jenkins 257, 145 E.R. 183.

3 *Lancashire v. Killingworth* (1701), 2 Salkeld 623, 91 E.R. 527, also 3 Salkeld 342, 91 E.R. 862, 1 Comyns 116, 92 E.R. 991, 12 Modern 529, 88 E.R. 1498, 1 Lord Raymond 686, 91 E.R. 1357.

4 Sic in MS.

5 *Martin v. Blithman* (1611), Yelverton 197, 80 E.R. 130, also 2 Bulstrode 213, 80 E.R. 1076, Godbolt 250, 78 E.R. 146; *Benson v. French* (1663), 1 Siderfin 132, 82 E.R. 1013, also 1 Levinz 98, 83 E.R. 316, 1 Keble 483, 83 E.R. 1066; *Walsingham v. Comb* (1666), 1 Levinz 183, 83 E.R. 359, also 1 Siderfin 289, 82 E.R. 1111, 2 Keble 10, 13, 48, 51, 84 E.R. 7, 9, 31, 32.

Taussig MS. 311, vol. 1, p. 145

Michaelmas 1721.

It was moved that a new foil of a tally of sol might be made to fit and join with the tally delivered out to Whittingham, whose executors, when they came to pass his accounts as one of the receivers in the County of Lincoln, brought in a tally of sol, which was for such a sum and of such a date. But when it came to be compared with the foil, it agreed in sum and date, yet it did not tally with it by any means, and, upon this, it was refused in the Pipe [Office]. And this application was now made to the court for a new foil to be made.

But the court would do nothing in it before the matter was examined. And, therefore, they referred it to the Chamberlain [of the Exchequer] to examine how it happened that the tally and the foil did not join and agree with one another in this case. And upon his report, the court was to be moved again.

N.B. When money is paid in, a tally is struck, and the tally is delivered out to the person paying in the money and the foil or counterpart thereof is filed and kept in the Tally Joiners' Office. When the party who has the tally comes to pass his account and to produce his tally as the voucher of his having paid so much money, the tally must be first examined in the Tally Joiner's Office or else it cannot be allowed in the Pipe [Office].

255

Perkin v. Parris

(Ex. 1721)

The court will set aside a verdict for a plaintiff in an action on a contract where the consideration was illegal and thus the issue was immaterial.

Harvard Law School MS. 1082, vol. 1, p. 107, pl. 2

Michaelmas term, 1721.

Serjeant *Reynolds* moved in arrest of judgment for that the consideration laid is that the defendant promised to render or remand James Davies but did not do it and laid to damage of £50. The serjeant said that this was an illegal consideration to let him escape, that he would remand him to the bailiffs. If the plaintiff discharges him, then it is a total discharge. Therefore, the second issue is immaterial as to the render.

[They] ordered the *postea* to stay.

256

Moore v. Walter

(Ex. 1721)

The question in this case whether the heir of mortgaged land was entitled to the profits of the land while the title was in abeyance.

Harvard Law School MS. 1082, vol. 1, p. 109

Michaelmas term 1721.

The plaintiff was heir and administrator of William Moore, which William Moore was the son and heir of William Moore by Sarah, his wife, and that there was a settlement dated 4 & 5 July 35 Car. II [1683] made between William Moore, the plaintiff's grandfather, and Anne, his wife, of the first part, Thomas Shoper and John Lewis, the trustees, of the second part, and the plaintiff's father and mother of the third part, in consideration of that marriage and £700 as a portion, [which] did grant the premises in question to the trustees, their heirs, and assigns to the use of the plaintiff's father during his natural life without impeachment of waste and, after his decease, one annuity of £10 to the plaintiff's mother during her natural life and, after the death of the plaintiff's father and mother, to the use of the son and sons of the body of the said William on the body of Sarah in tail male and for want of such issue to the heirs of the body of the plaintiff's father and remainder to his right heirs. But the plaintiff's father and mother mortgaged the premises to those under whom the defendant claims. And the plaintiff had proved his title at law by [an action of] ejectment and now brought his bill for an account of the rents and profits. And the single question was concerning the account of the premises during the life of Sarah because she survived William and, during that time, the estate was in abeyance. And who was entitled thereto was the question.

Mr. *Eyre*, counsel for the defendant, said that, if the plaintiff was entitled to it, it was under his father. And, therefore, in equity, he ought to take it subject to his father's mortgage.

Sir Constantine Phipps, for the plaintiff, said that the plaintiff does not take this under his father, but he claims it by title paramount by virtue of a settlement under the grandfather. And so he is a purchaser for a valuable consideration. And the plaintiff is administrator to his brother and father and, likewise, heir.

Chief Baron [Bury] was of opinion that, during the life of Sarah, that it was a resulting trust to the grandfather, who was the donor and to whom the plaintiff is heir. And, therefore, he is entitled to have an account.

Price thought that it was a contingency and might be a resulting trust for the donor, *viz.* the grandfather, and so vest in the plaintiff. But I will allow a case to be made of it out of compassion to the defendant, who is an honest mortgagee.

PAGE thought that this was not a contingency, but a remainder vested, and that the heir of the grandfather was only tenant during *auter vie, viz.* Sarah, and the profits would be assets in the hands of the plaintiff to answer the mortgage.

But they ordered a case to be made of it.

It was afterwards agreed [out of court] but [he] allowed the plaintiff very well.

257

City of London v. Rich

(Ex. 1721)

A suit in equity lies to compel an accounting for tolls due and payable to a municipality.

Harvard Law School MS. 1082, vol. 1, p. 110, pl. 1

Michaelmas term 1721.

This was a bill setting forth that the plaintiffs and their predecessors have been always entitled to the tronage or sole weighing of butter and cheese and that all persons that bring the same by water up the River Thames eastward of London Bridge to the Port of London ought to pay 8d. per tun for cheese and a farthing a firkin for butter and that the plaintiffs brought an action against one Garret and had a verdict upon this very point. And, therefore, the bill prayed the defendants to account.

The defendants answered and denied everything. But the plaintiffs proved their case very fully, so we that were of counsel for the defendants objected to the bill that it was only proper for a discovery, which they had, and the remedy for the toll was proper at law. And so I cited City of Exeter v. Bond; Disney v. Robertson;[1] Harding v. Ainge.

[It was] answered by the plaintiffs that the reason of those cases was because the title had not been ascertained at law and it had [been] ruled to be proper for an establishment in this very case. City of London v. Gascoigne; City of London v. Garret.

PRICE said that he believed decrees had been obtained in this court by the plaintiffs for these matters, but he could not distinguish between this and the City of Exeter v. Bond, but yet the City of London v. Gascoigne is express in point.

MONTAGU: Wherever there has been a right ascertained at law, it is proper for an establishment in equity. And the reason of the City of Exeter v. Bond was because there was no recovery at law. And the City of London v. Gascoigne and many cases to the same effect have been decreed in this court.

So the defendants were decreed to account notwithstanding the cases we before cited.

---

[1] *Disney v. Robertson* (Ex. 1719), see above, Case No. 82.

258

Price and Crompton v. Bulkeley

(Ex. 1721)

In this case, an arbitral award was enforced although the authority of the arbitrators to act was questioned.

Harvard Law School MS. 1082, vol. 1, p. 110, pl. 2

Michaelmas term 1721.

Mr. *Fazakerly* [moved] in arrest of judgment for the declaration on the award and reference was [. . .] for there was neither consideration or anything mutually to be done, which ought to be in all awards and Brinley, whose goods were the subject matter, was no party, and awards ought to be mutual. Baspole's Case, 8 Rept., 1 Rolle, *Abridgment*, 94, 253; 1 Rolle, *Abridgment*, 252.[1] And the authority is exceeded, for the debt of another man cannot be submitted.

Mr. *Bootle*, for the plaintiff: Brinley is not concerned in this affair. I admit that awards ought to be mutual. And here, in this case, it is so, as far as the parties submitting and that the arbitrators had done properly and not exceeded their authority.

Chief Baron [Bury] thought that the judgment ought to stand.

Price [said] that the plaintiff ought to have his judgment and the award is mutual and Brinley is not concerned in this case.

Montagu: I differ, and this brings to my memory the partition treaty concerning the disposing of the king of Spain's dominions; so I take this to be disposing of Brinley's goods with which the parties submitting or the arbitrators had [not] anything to do. And, therefore, the authority and submission must fall to the ground.

Page: As it appears, the declaration is not right, for the arbitrators exceeded their jurisdiction. The award is void, for the goods of Brinley are awarded *ad usum proprium* of the defendant. And this cannot discharge the debt due from Brinley. And this first dispute arises on taking Brinley's goods in execution.

Awards must be final, though they may be good in part and void in part. And the defendant is not to pay the money until he could have the use of the goods, which he could not have.

Judgment was entered *nisi* in the book, so the court was equally divided, yet judgment was given for the plaintiff.

[1] *Freeman v. Baspole* (1610), 8 Coke Rep. 97, 77 E.R. 624, also 2 Brownlow & Goldesborough 309, 123 E.R. 959, Croke Jac. 285, 79 E.R. 244, 1 Bulstrode 144, 80 E.R. 837, 1 Rolle, Abr., *Arbitrement*, pl. K, 1, 2, 5, p. 253; 1 Rolle, Abr., *Arbitrement*, pl. I, p. 252.

259

Huse v. Lawes

(Ex. 1721)

The court will only consider objections to a master's report that were previously made to the master.

Bunbury 93, 145 E.R. 607

5 December 1721.

Upon exceptions to the Master's report, the court would not permit them to go into any exceptions as to any matter not objected to before the Master.

260

Taylor v. Crampton

(Ex. 1721)

Where a defendant is an executor, a court of equity will grant relief as well as discovery as to a trespass to land.

Bunbury 95, 145 E.R. 608

5 December 1721.

This was a bill brought by the vicar of Madely in the County of Salop, who was endowed of the glebe, to have an account against the defendants of what quantity of coals were dug and got by them by a work carried by them through a foot way under his glebe and also to have satisfaction for the coal. And he also prayed an injunction to stay the works.

The defendants answered. But at the hearing, they insisted that this was a bare action of trespass, and, though the plaintiff might be entitled to a discovery, yet he ought not to have relief, for that the quantum of the coals might be ascertained by a jury or, if discovered by the answer, they could ascertain the damages more properly than this court.

And of this opinion, the court were at first. But, afterwards, they would not dismiss the bill absolutely, but retained it until the plaintiff had ascertained his title at law. The reason seemed to be because there were several defendants copartners in these works, some of them executors and some administrators, and the plaintiff would be under great difficulty in proceeding entirely at law for the damages.

Harvard Law School MS. 1082, vol. 1, p. 113, pl. 1

Sittings after Michaelmas term 1721.

A bill was brought against several defendants, some of whom were executors and others who had been concerned in the digging of coals in ground belonging to the plaintiff as parson, being part of his glebe, and to have a discovery and account of what coals were so dug and, though it was objected that this was a matter at law only and a common action of trespass, yet being proper for a discovery and to have an account of assets from some of the defendants as executors that thereupon the court retained the bill until the matter was tried at law.

And so they retained the bill for that purpose.

261

Ashby v. Aleyn

(Ex. 1721)

A plaintiff in a suit to enforce a contract must be ready, willing, and able to perform it.

In this case, the court found that the plaintiff himself had abandoned the contract in issue and thus could not enforce it.

Harvard Law School MS. 1082, vol. 1, p. 111

Sittings after Michaelmas term 1721.

A bill was brought by the plaintiffs to have a specific performance of an agreement which was in the manner following, *viz.* 19 June 1720 [it was] agreed between the defendant Aleyn and plaintiff Ashby that the defendant Aleyn should give plaintiff Ashby £6250 for the residue of the term of twenty-one years and that the term should be assigned to such person as the defendant should appoint.

The defendant admitted the agreement, but insisted that, by letters and otherwise, that the plaintiff had waived the agreement and that it would be too hard in a court of equity to be obliged to perform an agreement in these circumstances after the rate of above forty years' purchase and that the plaintiff never demanded this matter until after the fall of stocks.[1] And in some of the letters, the plaintiff wrote 'Depend upon it you shall never have it.'

Chief Baron [Bury] [said] that the plaintiff ought not to have a specific performance, for the plaintiff Ashby refused to give security. And I think that it is a waiver of the agreement and that the words in the letters manifest the same.

Price: I am of the same opinion. And I think that the design of this agreement was to be free from encumbrances. The agreement is in writing, and, though it is a mutual agreement, I think that it may be waived on one side and that is sufficient where the plaintiff has waived it, who comes for a specific performance of it, which he can never do in a court of equity. And the times are material. The letters of July and September 1720 and the letter of the 4th of September [are] very material. [In] the case in Chancery of Herbert v. Lord Winchelsea,[2] a letter

[1] The burst of the South Sea bubble in 1720.

[2] Perhaps *Herbert v. Earl of Winchelsea* (1714), 1 Brown P.C. 145, 1 E.R. 475.

on one part set aside the agreement and, at the meeting at Slough, the defendant desired the plaintiff to settle it. And I do not know but that a fine *sur concessit* was necessary. And I think that the women that had encumbrances on this estate ought to have been made parties. And I think that the plaintiff ought to have tendered the conveyance, and it is a fatal objection. And it ought to have been set forth in the bill that the plaintiff had tendered a conveyance. I cannot decree a specific performance on these circumstances, but will leave the plaintiff where I found him and dismiss his bill.

PAGE: I differ, for I do not think that Ashby ever waived this agreement, though I admit it might have been done and that it would have been a waiver without being mutual, though I deny that a letter would have discharged this agreement. And I think that the defendant is like a dog in the manger that would neither take it himself or suffer anybody else to have it[1] and that the obstruction has been in Aleyn, the defendant, and not in the plaintiff.

Where the purchaser can draw the writings, then I think the purchaser should do the first act. And, in this case, he could, for the defendant had the reversion and so the writings of the estate, but that is but a ceremony which a court of equity does not regard, though I think that the women ought to have been made parties.

The court dismissed the bill against Page's opinion, and the contract was burned in court.

Taussig MS. 311, vol. 1, p. 169, pl. 2

Michaelmas term 1721.

Memorandum whereas it has been agreed by Mr. Eyre that Mr. Thomas Allen shall pay £6000 for the purchase of a lease which was formerly granted by John Allen to Ashby free from the encumbrances of the jointure therein named, Mr. Thomas Allen agrees to take Mr. Ashby's security for the same after the determination of the lease. On 19 July 1720, this was signed by Thomas Allen and by Ashby.

In this case, Ashby brought a bill to compel Allen to a specific performance of the contract. But it appeared that the plaintiff's mother and sisters, who had charges on the lease, had in the interim refused to comply so as to enable Ashby to assign this lease free from all encumbrances. And, by several letters, Mr. Ashby did positively inform Mr. Alleyn that he should never have the lease, for that the women, says he, will never consent.

But it did not appear that the defendant had ever assented to waive the agreement. And, therefore, for the plaintiff, it was insisted that the agreement was not vacated, but Allen had still a power to compel an execution of the agreement and, therefore, so has the plaintiff.

[1] Aesop, *Fables*.

Bury, Chief Baron: We ought not to decree a specific performance, being the plaintiffs have refused to perform the agreement on their part.

Price: The agreement may be waived on one side, and he that waives it on his part shall never afterwards compel specific performance, though, perhaps, the other may. In this agreement, the time is very material, for it would be very hard the plaintiff should keep off and waive the performance of the agreement until it becomes more for the disadvantage of the defendant and then insist afterwards on the specific performance.

It is very plain by the evidence in this cause that the plaintiff waived the agreement, for, after the signing of the agreement, it appears that the plaintiff contracted with a stranger, one Garden, for the purchase of the self same lease.

And *per* Price: The women should have been made parties, for we could not decree the conveyance of this lease without taking in their interests, and, therefore, they ought to have been parties. The plaintiff ought to have shown a tender of an assignment of this lease in order to compel an execution *in specie*.

Page: Ashby might have done enough to discharge his right to compel a specific performance though Allen's right did still remain to compel an execution thereof, but he thought that, upon the evidence, he had done enough to show this waiver of the judgment, for Alleyn was the first person who refused to comply with the agreement because he insisted upon another sort of title and conveyance than was stipulated for by the agreement.

The plaintiff's entering into another agreement with another purchaser was not a discharge of his agreement with Alleyn, for Alleyn then interposed to prevent Garden's purchase.

Ashby could not after his signing this agreement discharge the same by a letter disaffirming it, though it had been written the next day.

As to the women being parties, that is the great objection, but it seems it is not necessary, for Ashby has undertaken for them and so I do not think it necessary they should be joined.

The bill was dismissed and the cross-bill also without costs on both sides.

262

Borrett v. Gomeserra

(Ex. 1721–1723)

A court of equity will order specific performance of an oral contract for the sale of land that has been partially performed.

Time is not of the essence of a contract in a court of equity unless it is expressly stated to be.

Specific performance of a contract for the sale of land can be granted to the seller to recover the purchase price.

Bunbury 94, 145 E.R. 607

7 December 1721.

A bill was brought to have a discovery of a parol agreement for the sale of copyhold lands and whether the defendant did not pay £200 part of £2300, being the purchase money, and if the plaintiff did not give the defendant a note, acknowledging the receipt of the said £200 in part etc. and thereby also promising to make a good title etc. and whether the plaintiff did not bring his writings before the defendant's counsel, who approved of the title, and to have a specific performance.

The defendant pleads the Statute of Frauds and Perjuries[1] to the whole bill, it being a parol agreement.

But it was overruled *per* TOTAM CURIAM.

This cause afterwards, 31 May 1722, came to a hearing. And, though it was objected for the defendant that this was within the Statute of Frauds etc. that it was an hard bargain and not to be carried into execution in equity, being, as they pretended, £1300 more than it was worth, yet, upon proof of the plaintiff's side that there was no fraud, that it was worth £2335, that the defendant had done several acts of ownership, as ordering in bricks, fishing in ponds, etc. and had made frequent promises etc., there was a decree for the plaintiff *per* TOTAM CURIAM, *viz.* Lord Chief Baron [BURY], MONTAGU, Barons PRICE and PAGE.

Harvard Law School MS. 1082, vol. 1, p. 112

Sittings after Michaelmas term 1721.

This was a bill for to discover an agreement made with the plaintiff for his house and, some money being paid in part, to oblige the defendant to a specific performance of the said agreement, to which bill the defendant pleads the Statute of Frauds and Perjuries, *viz.* 29 Car. II, without putting in any answer.

But I insisted upon, for the plaintiff, that, though this was a parol agreement, that it was in part executed and, therefore, the Statute could not be pleaded and cited Sir John James v. Killegrew in 1680; Hatton v. Gray in Can. Rept.[2] Besides, this plea was never allowed alone without answering, so it could not be pleaded in bar to the discovery, no more than the Statute of Limitations,[3] as in the case of the Dean and Chapter of Westminster v. Herbert,[4] in this court.

The court overruled the plea.

[1] Stat. 29 Car. II, c. 3 (*SR*, V, 839–842).

[2] *James v. Killigrew* (1680), Eq. Cases Exch. 118; *Hatton v. Gray* (1684), 2 Chancery Cases 164, 22 E.R. 895, 1 Eq. Cas. Abr. 21, 21 E.R. 843.

[3] Stat. 21 Jac. I, c. 16 (*SR*, IV, 1222–1223).

[4] *Dean and Chapter of Westminster v. Cross* (Ex. 1720), see above, Case No. 126.

Taussig MS. 311, vol. 1, p. 315

31 June 1722.

The plaintiff exhibits his bill in this court setting forth an agreement between him and the defendant for the plaintiff's sale of a house etc. to the defendant for the sum of £2300. And £200 was paid in part. And a receipt was given for it as follows, *viz.* '15 December 1720 received of Gomersera £200 in part of £2300 for the purchase of our house at Epsom, the remainder to be paid on and before 25 March next following. And I do promise to make good the title to Gomersera and to do all such things as his counsel should advise.'

Trinity 1680, Sir John Killigrew and Sir John James was a case in point as to the retaining a bill for specific performance of an agreement on the part and at the suit of the vendor.

N.B. Before going into the evidence, the defendant objected *ut supra* that this was a bill for the money, and this objection was founded on the distinction above in Armiger and Clarke's Case.[1]

And it was answered by the case above. And it was further said that there was a difference between the cases, *viz.* here, it was a parol agreement, there, articles in writing, so there was no remedy in this case upon this agreement at law, it not being within the Statute of Fraud and Perjuries. But it has always been allowed that execution in part brings the parol agreement out of the Statute. And so it was determined by the court in this case when they overruled the demurrer in this very case. Besides, the distinction in the case of Armiger and Clarke was no judicial determination of the court.

Per Chief Baron [Montagu]: The objection is that the bill is brought for damages and, of consequence, if no damages can be recovered in an action at law, the objection is answered. I think it is plain. No action at law can succeed because the agreement is by parol. But then, how can equity interpose? I answer the Statute does not say no remedy, but no action, and the courts of equity have taken upon them, and that very rightly, to execute agreements by parol where they are already executed in part. And as to the other point, I will never declare against executing a [*blank*] bargain, for I do not understand that we are here arbitrarily, but we are bound to do justice.

And Price and Page being of same opinion, the plaintiff went on.

For the plaintiff: The defendant confesses the agreement and, therefore, the court executes it because there is no danger of perjury where the defendant confesses the agreement. 2 Canc. Rep. 164.[2] And this is a constant rule of courts of equity. Lady Russell and Kingsford, Michaelmas term 1711, in Chancery.

Second, the agreement here is executed in part. Bourne v. Bourne, in Lord Keeper Wright's time.

---

[1] *Armiger v. Clarke* (Ex. 1722), see below, Case No. 323.

[2] *Hatton v. Gray* (1684), *ut supra*.

As to the objection for want of title, we have done everything the defendant's counsel directed. Hook v. Brocket; Lister v. Foxcroft, Cases in Chancery,[1] upon the partial execution of the agreement.

Bunbury cited the case of Gibson v. Nairne[2] to prove there was no difference between a bill for a vendor and a vendee.

Chesshyre, for the defendant: If the case was such as an action at law might have been grounded, still the jury would have considered and mitigated the damages, *a fortiori* in equity, where there is no room for an action at law.

As to the value, the house new cost £650, the ground itself £350, the goods £70, about £50 *per annum*, so that, if the court does think itself bound to execute this agreement, yet you will execute it with regard to a reasonable price. The defendant swears he made the agreement with Mr. Borret, the father. And the receipt is for our house. And then, the bill is not proper, for the son is the plaintiff here and not the father.

Mr. *Melmoth*, for the defendant:

[1.] The agreement confessed is the agreement with the father.

2. The agreement confessed implies that the plaintiff ought to have made out a title before 25 March, whereas, by the plaintiff's own showing, he had no title until a recovery was suffered by one Bourne. And it appears upon the evidence that this recovery was not suffered until after 25 March.

3. Where a party comes for a specific performance, the plaintiff must show his execution of his part and his execution of it in such a manner as that he cannot be put into the same condition again and, therefore, has a right to compel the other party to execute it.

4. If the execution in part is put out of the case, then there is no color for a court of equity to compel an execution of this agreement, for, if the defendant only confesses such an agreement as the Statute says is void, then it is no more than if he had been at law.

Bootle insists rather more largely [that] the plaintiff is not proper on account of his not having made out his title before the 25th of March. The answer to the time of the recovery was that there was a recovery suffered before 25 March and a recovery suffered by the direction of the defendant's own counsel and, though it is true that the person who did suffer the first recovery was a wrong person, yet that was the defendant's own fault and the recovery suffered after 25th March was only to aid and supply the defect of the former recovery.

Per Chief Baron [Montagu]: My own opinion is that every man is in point of honor and conscience obliged to perform his agreement. And here is an agreement confessed and confessed it is not performed.

2. [There is] no objection to the agreement on account of fairness.

3. [There is] no proof of any value set upon the house to be leased.

---

[1] *Lester v. Foxcroft* (1700), Colles 108, 1 E.R. 205.

[2] *Gibson v. Nayres* (Ex. 1720), see above, Case No. 135.

In the defendant's computation, the gardens are not taken in nor the finishing on the inside so that it does not appear upon the proofs that it is a hard bargain. And the South Sea [bubble] is out of case, for it was after the South Sea time.

CHIEF BARON: The point of time is no objection in a court of equity, but it is necessary at law. And this is a reason why there was no action at law as well as the other reason that there was no writing.

The Act of Parliament does not extend but to actions [at common law], and we in equity are obliged to have our eyes upon the mere right. Besides, this agreement does in great measure subsist by writing, *viz*, accepting the receipt.

So he was for decreeing a specific performance. And PRICE and PAGE agreed. And there was a decree accordingly.

Lincoln's Inn MS. Misc. 12, p. 70

Trinity 1723.

In December 1720, the defendant agreed to purchase of the plaintiff a house in Epsom for £2300. The agreement was not reduced into writing, but the defendant paid the plaintiff £200 in part of the purchase money. And thereupon, the plaintiff gave the defendant a receipt in the words following, *viz*.:

15 December 1720, Received then of Mr. Jacob Gomeserra the sum of £200 in part of the purchase money being £2300 for our mansion house and the premises in Clay Hill in Epsom the remainder being to be paid by Mr. Gomeserra on and before the 25th day of March next, and I do hereby promise to make good the title to the premises to said Mr. Gomeserra and do all such things as his counsel shall advise. /s/ *W. Borrett*.

The plaintiff laid his writings before counsel. And some difficulties arising about the title and the defendant not proceeding, the plaintiff brought his bill and alleged that the title had been approved by the defendant's counsel and the plaintiff had ordered a bricklayer to lay in bricks to raise the roof of the house and to make a drain and called the house his own and had fish in the pond and the agreement being so far executed, the plaintiff prayed a specific performance.

The defendant pleaded the Statute of Frauds etc., which was overruled. And, upon the hearing, it appeared by the proofs that, after the agreement, 150 bricks were laid in and some small drains in the garden were made therewith by the defendant's order, that the defendant once brought some gentlemen and fished in the ponds with nets and carried the fish away with him and that the defendant several times called the house his own and that, in May or June 1721, the defendant said he had received a letter acquainting him the title was approved of and the plaintiff said he was as glad as if anybody had given him £300.

The defendant insisted on the extravagance of the price and the defect of the title. And it was proved for the defendant by three persons that the premises were worth to be let but £50 a year and to be sold £950, as one said, and £970, as the other said. And by two other workmen that the premises, about seven years ago, cost £350 and that the house had been since built and cost £700, as one said, and £650, as the other said.

On the other hand, it was proved by two workmen that the premises were worth £2335.

Upon the whole matter, the court decreed the defendant to perform the agreement and sent it to the Deputy Remembrancer to look into the title and make his report to the court.

263

Doe, *qui tam* v. Butland

(Ex. 1721)

The question in this case was whether one smuggler can be charged with the goods smuggled by another person who took them ashore from the same ship at the same time independently.

Taussig MS. 311, vol. 1, p. 165

Charles Doe, *qui tam* v. John Butland; *coram* Bury, Chief Baron, at *nisi prius* in the Exchequer, Tuesday, 29 November 1721.

Upon an information in the nature of a *devenerunt* for 24 half anchors of brandy, which came to the defendant's hands knowing them to be run, the evidence proved the brandy was run and laid on the shore and that the defendant came down with several other persons and took away 4½ anchors, loading them on his own horse, and that the other persons took away the rest. But it did not appear that the other persons were under the directions of the defendant or carried away the rest either by his order or on his account. And the question was whether this was sufficient evidence to charge the defendant with the whole.

Mr. Attorney General [*Raymond*] said it was and that it was at the crown's election to charge any one of the persons with the whole or else to charge every of them with that particular quantity only which he respectively carried off and that, in case the crown charged any one of them with the whole, that would be a bar to an information against the others. And he said it was like the case of trover wherein it had been adjudged that any of the persons concerned might be charged *pro toto*.

The Chief Baron [Bury] seemed to come into this notion. And the jury found against the defendant for the whole. But whether upon this notion or else because they believed that it was all carried away on the defendant's account I did not understand; therefore, I query this point.

264

Conway v. Pennant

(Ex. 1721)

A plaintiff's laches will bar a bill to redeem a mortgage.

Taussig MS. 311, vol. 1, p. 166

At Serjeants' Inn in Chancery Lane, Chief Baron [Bury], Price, Montagu, and Page *praesentibus*, 5 December 1721.

The plaintiff exhibited his bill to redeem a rent charge of 48s. *per annum* granted by his ancestor to the defendant's ancestors in the year 1627 with a proviso of redemption within thirty years. The rent was granted with a *nomine poenae* distrainable as well as the rent. There was a proviso that, if the grantor give notice to redeem the said rent at any time within thirty years next and do pay the said £30 and all arrears and the *nomine poenae*, then the rent was to cease etc.

Per Serjeant *Chesshyre*: This 48s. is by way of interest and is 8 percent for the £30 original sum lent and, though it is now 94 years past, yet the rent having been paid until within three or four years past, this receipt affirms the mortgage.

E contra: In the deed, there is no word of interest mentioned. And here is so great a length of time since the mortgage was made, and the rent was the thing mortgaged. It has been admitted that, if the mortgagee has been a very long time in possession uninterrupted, then it is not redeemable. That is our very case. We have been in possession of this rent 64 years since the end of the thirty years

And the bill was dismissed, the court being unanimous not to relieve on these circumstances.

265

Rex v. Barnfield

(Ex. 1721–1722)

An inquisition upon an outlawry is only an office of instruction and not an office of entitling.

A terre tenant can plead as such to an inquisition upon an outlawry without alleging a title.

Taussig MS. 311, vol. 1, p. 169, pl. 1

Michaelmas term 1721.

Barnesfield was outlawed. And a [writ of] extent, inquisition, and [writ of] *levari* [*facias*] issued thereupon. Barnesfield died, and his wife comes and applies to the court showing his death and that he was seised in her right, as it appeared on the face of the inquisition, and, therefore, she prayed to have the king's hands removed.

The Attorney General [*Raymond*] being unwilling to confess the fact of Barnesfield's death, the court directed that fact should be tried. And it was tried and found for Barnesfield.

But *Probyn* now objected that the woman, having made no title, consequently could not have judgment, this action on which the death of her husband was found being entirely collateral to the outlawry. See the case in Lutwyche.[1]

Harvard Law School MS. 1082, vol. 1, p. 108, pl. 2

Michaelmas term 1721.

In arrest of judgment on an outlawry, the defendant pleads that the testator died before such a day and it was found for the defendant Mary that pleaded. She was not entitled to restitution and the defendant should have showed how she was entitled as well as putting in the plea or else an *amoveas manus* cannot be awarded.

Adjourned. Query what [was] done at the sittings after this term.

Bunbury 102, 145 E.R. 611, Conroy 110

22 February 1721[/22].

Upon an outlawry against the defendant's husband, there issued an extent, and an inquisition was taken thereupon, which finds that the husband was seised of the lands in right of his wife and *in jure suo*. The estate was seized into the king's hands. The defendant pleads as terre tenant that her husband died the [*blank*] day of October and prays that the king's hands may be amoved and she restored to the possession and perception of the profits, without setting forth any title.

It was insisted by Mr. *Probyn, pro rege*, that it ought to appear upon record that the defendant has a title before the king's hands can be removed. Before the Stat. 2 & 3 Edw. VI, c. 8,[2] when the king's title was found, there was no way but by petition, but that Statute gave a traverse. Now, this matter being traversable, the party ought to set forth a title that such title might be traversed.

But it was answered by Mr. *Foley*, for the defendant, that, where the crown is entitled only to the profits, to plead as terre tenant is sufficient without setting forth a special title and an inquisition upon an outlawry is not an office of entitling, but of instruction only.

And *per* TOTAM CURIAM, the plea was allowed, it being the usual method of pleading the death of the party outlawed. And, upon affidavit of the fact, the Attorney General usually allows the plea, which is the most summary method, there being after the party's death no title subsisting in the crown.

---

[1] *Rex v. Hungerford* (1698), 2 Lutwyche 996, 125 E.R. 555.

[2] Stat. 2 & 3 Edw. VI, c. 8 (*SR*, IV, 47–48).

Harvard Law School MS. 1082, vol. 1, p. 119, pl. 2

Mr. *Foley*, for the defendant: See the case in 37. Where the crown is entitled only to the profits, to plead as terre tenant, it is sufficient without setting forth a special title. An outlawry, 4 Inst. 215,[1] without two *capias*es is actually void. See the precedents. [They] are only before the Attorney General, not before the court.

Mr. *Probyn, contra*: The defendant pleads that the person outlawed is dead and prays the king's hands may be removed. If the king be entitled either to the lands, as upon a forfeiture, or to the profits, as upon a contempt, yet the pleader in both cases must show some title to take it out of the crown. Being this matter is traversable, the party ought to set forth a title that the said title might be traversed. Rex v. Hungerford, Lutwyche.[2]

Baron Montagu [cited] Hardres 58, 59, 422; see Brockham, 1, 75, 101, 191, *vide.*[3] An inquisition upon an outlawry is not an office of entitling but instruction only. 9 Hen. VI, fo. 20, was cited by Montagu; 1 Levinz 33.[4] And he was of opinion the plea was good.

Baron Price: This is the usual method of pleading, and the most of the person outlawed, and it is usual for the Attorney General, upon affidavit of the fact, to admit the plea, which is the most summary method. And I think we ought to allow this plea.

Per totam curiam: The plea is well as to the terre tenant without setting forth a special title in this case, there being no subsisting title in the crown.

Taussig MS. 311, vol. 1, p. 237

At Serjeants' Inn in Chancery Lane. 22 February 1722.

Mr. *Wills* and *Foley* showed to the court further reasons for removing the king's hands notwithstanding the defendant in this case had not showed her title to the lands in the plea, *viz.* that, upon an outlawry, the king is only entitled to the profits and that it was not therefore to be compared to a case where the party traversed the king's title. And Mr. *Foley* cited 4 Inst. 215; and they showed five precedents of the like nature with the present case, *viz.* Cornwall, Hilary 9 Anne, Bywest v. Fresodden; Somerset, Michaelmas 10 Anne, Richard Sanderwick v. Thomas Chappell; Glamorgan, Michaelmas 3 Geo., Elizabeth Tomb v. David Lewis, gent.; Berkshire, Easter 4 Geo., David Allen v. Edmund Clerke.

E contra, Mr. *Probyn* cited the case of Rex v. Hungerford, Lutwyche.

---

[1] E. Coke, *Fourth Institute* (1644), p. 215.

[2] *Rex v. Hungerford* (1698), 2 Lutwyche 996, 125 E.R. 555.

[3] *Attorney General v. Fox* (1665), Hardres 422, 145 E.R. 528; *Protector v. Cutterel* (1656), Hardres 58, 145 E.R. 379; *Attorney General v. Brockman* (1628), Paynell Exch. 189, 201, 226, 439.

[4] YB Trin. 9 Hen. VI, f. 20, pl. 15 (1431); *Windsor v. Saywell* (1661), 1 Levinz 33, 83 E.R. 283, also T. Raymond 17, 83 E.R. 10, 1 Keble 57, 74, 76, 83 E.R. 809, 820, 821.

Mr. Baron Montagu, to [op]pose the counsel, cited Hardres 58, Protector v. Cutterel; Hardres 101, Attorney General v. Sir Ralph Freeman;[1] Hardres 422, the Attorney General v. Fox, Baynard, etc. But he then declared his opinion to be that the king's hands should be removed, though the party had shown no title, but only pleaded as a terre tenant because, by him, the difference between these cases upon the outlawry and all the other cases is this, that an inquisition upon an outlawry is only an office of instruction and not an office of entitling. For this, he cited 9 Hen. VI, fo. 20; Hardres 191.[2] And so he agreed with the precedents produced.

And all the rest of the barons [agreed] with him. And the king's hands were removed.

And note that, by Hardres 230, by Hale,[3] the terre tenant, though he do not make a title, may plead by way of exoneration and discharge of the land; so may any occupant or disseisor.

266

Heaton v. Regal

(Ex. 1721)

Tithes in kind of lambs are payable on the first of August after their birth.

A custom of paying tithes of lambs in kind in the April following their birth is void.

1 Rayner 160, 2 Gwillim 630, 1 Eagle & Younge 776

Heaton, Impropriator of Garnthorp in Lincolnshire, against Regal.

The defendant insisted on a custom in that parish to set forth tithe lambs on the first of May. But the court disallowed of it, for that they were not fit to live without their dams, as appeared by the depositions in the cause. And it was referred to three neighboring justices of the peace to inquire what was a fit time for setting forth tithe lambs in that country, who certified the first of August, in their judgment, to be a proper time. And the court approved of it.

267

Thompson v. Greaves

(Ex. 1721)

The question in this case was whether a testator's debt secured by a mortgage should be paid out of his personal estate where it would defeat the legacies.

---

[1] *Attorney General v. Freeman* (1657), Hardres 101, 145 E.R. 402.

[2] *Wilford v. Greaves* (1661), Hardres 191, 145 E.R. 446.

[3] *Attorney General v. Stonehouse* (1662), Hardres 229, 230, 145 E.R. 466.

Taussig MS. 311, vol. 1, p. 167

Michaelmas term 1721.

If a man mortgages his land and devises several legacies and his personal estate is not sufficient to pay his legacies nor sufficient to pay off the mortgage, query whether the heir shall have the benefit of the personal estate to discharge his land and to defeat all the legacies or whether the debt shall lie on the land on which it is now charged.

2 Chancery Cases, fo. 5;[1] Coke and Gwavas, in this court, 34 Car. II [1682], was cited by MONTAGU.

A court of equity will marshal assets so as to do the best for all.

N.B. In the case before, the testator devised all his real estate for the payment of debts and legacies and, after the payment of debts and legacies, then he devised the same to the plaintiff. And this will was not executed in the presence of three witnesses according to the Statute of Frauds and Perjuries[2] so that the land could not pass thereby.

Sed per PAGE: It seems a good intimation to a court of equity to marshal the testator's assets according to his intent in aid of the personal estate so as to apply it to the payment of other debts and legacies to which the real estate is not subject and to let the charge of the mortgage lie upon the land mortgaged.

Harvard Law School MS. 1082, vol. 1, p. 113, pl. 2

A bill was brought to have the personal estate go in and to pay off a mortgage, which, by the will, was charged.

And it was said by Baron MONTAGU that in the case of Chief Baron Montagu, in Chancery,[3] upon his will, though he had ordered terms to be raised for the payment of debts and legacies, yet the court, in opposition to an express direction of the will, declared that the personal estate must be first applied that way, but Baron Montagu appealed to the House of Lords, who reversed that decree and there being terms expressed to be raised was the judgment of the House of Lords, but without that in all cases the personal estate must first be applied.

Sir Constantine Phipps, for the defendant, said that an account could not be denied, but legacies should be paid first.

Mr. *Biddulph*, for the defendant, cited Clifton v. Bird, in Chancery, 7 Geo.; Meredith v. Wynn.[4]

---

[1] *Anonymous* (1679), 2 Chancery Cases 4, 22 E.R. 819.

[2] Stat. 29 Car. II, c. 3, s. 18 (*SR*, V, 841–842).

[3] *Tyrwhitt v. Trotman* (1714), 3 Brown P.C. 52, 1 E.R. 1171.

[4] *Clifton v. Burt* (1720), 1 Peere Williams 678, 24 E.R. 566, 2 Eq. Cas. Abr. 555, 22 E.R. 467; *Meredith v. Wynn* (1711), Precedents in Chancery 312, 24 E.R. 147, Gilbert Rep. 70, 25 E.R. 49, 1 Eq. Cas. Abr. 70, 21 E.R. 883, 2 Eq. Cas. Abr. 352, 22 E.R. 299, British Library MS. Hargrave 80, p. 50.

Mr. *Ward* said that legacies cannot take place of debts.

MONTAGU said that it was the intention of the parties that legacies should be paid as well as debts.

PAGE: The heir shall not take contrary to the direction of the testator.

Mr. *Ward* said that the Statute of Frauds would not allow the intention of the testator to be explained.

MONTAGU: I agree with Mr. Ward that, if the will is not executed according to that Statute, I think that his declaration will not affect this matter. And this will was only executed by two witnesses.

PAGE: I think that Mr. Ward is right, and let the defendant go to account and let the Deputy [Remembrancer] state anything specially.

268

Anonymous

(Ex. 1722)

A defendant who has not been served with process cannot voluntarily appear and answer.

Taussig MS. 311, vol. 1, p. 191, pl. 1

24 January 1721/22.

Per PAGE: If the plaintiff makes several defendants and does not serve some of them, those who are not served cannot answer, *quod alii concesserunt*. And by him, though the plaintiff does serve some of them, yet notwithstanding he may carry on the cause against the others who have answered if he will and, if he will carry on the cause without an answer of those others whom he has served and examines witnesses in the cause, those other defendants cannot insist upon putting their answers and make themselves parties to the cause because the plaintiff may move at any time to dismiss his bill against any of the defendants.

269

Note

(Ex. 1722)

A final decree can be drawn up at any time, but a interlocutory order should be drawn up within a term after it is made.

Taussig MS. 311, vol. 1, p. 191, pl. 2

Hilary term 1721/22.

Per PAGE: The minutes of a decree are not to be discharged because they are not drawn up within a term's time, for the party may draw up the decree at any time by them. But as to interlocutory orders, it is usual to discharge them if they are not drawn up within the space of a term after such order is made.

270

Jones v. Traherne

(Ex. 1722)

An ecclesiastical court has jurisdiction over tithes of water mills.

Taussig MS. 311, vol. 1, p. 192

Hilary term 1721/22.

A suggestion for a [writ of] prohibition [was made] that suits for tithes and all sums of money payable for and in lieu of tithes for water mills do belong to the king's temporal courts and not to the ecclesiastical courts.

Against the prohibition, *Ward* shows *viz.* that there is no controversy but that the ecclesiastical courts have jurisdiction of tithes as by the statutes of *Circumspecte Agatis, Articuli Cleri*, 2 Edw. VI, etc.[1] And yet this is the only suggestion for the prohibition.

Squibb, contra: A custom is not triable in an ecclesiastical court. And by Linwood, last edition, fo. 192, tithe of mills is a predial tithe, 195,[2] *decima mensura; ergo*, this must be a customary payment and, therefore, not suable in the ecclesiastical court and the libel should have been for the tenth part of the toll dishes. And, by him, the parson cannot sue but for tithes in kind in the ecclesiastical court.

Bootle, of the same side: Pensions are only suable for in the ecclesiastical court because they are only between spiritual persons. Lord Coke's comment on *Articuli Cleri*, 2 Inst. 621; 1 Keble 602;[3] an ecclesiastical court cannot hold suits for tithes for rabbits because they are not due of common right, otherwise for a *modus* for things which are due of common right, 2 Keble 452;[4] and by Lord Coke, 2 Inst. 621, tithes of mills are only a customary payment.

Bury, Chief Baron: [There is] no cause for a prohibition.

Page was of the same opinion, for want of form in a libel is no cause of prohibition, but the libel is good. And, by him, if you come into a spiritual court and sue for rabbits as due for common right, prohibition lies, otherwise if you sue for

---

[1] Stat. 13 Edw. I, *Circumspecte Agatis* (*SR*, I, 101–102); Stat. 9 Edw. II, stat. 1 (*SR*, I, 171–174); Stat. 2 & 3 Edw. VI, c. 13 (*SR*, IV, 55–58).

[2] W. Lyndwood, *Provinciale* (1929), pp. 71–79.

[3] E. Coke, *Second Institute* (1642), p. 621; *Towerson v. Winget* (1663), 1 Keble 602, 83 E.R. 1136, 1 Eagle & Younge 440.

[4] *Philips v. Clever* (1669), 2 Keble 452, 84 E.R. 284, also 1 Ventris 5, 86 E.R. 5, 1 Eagle & Younge 479.

rabbits as due by custom. Old mills is a matter of discharge and ought to come on the other side.

Query whether one may sue for a composition in an ecclesiastical court.

And the rule for a prohibition was discharged.

271

Mills v. Willcox

(Ex. 1722)

In this case, the court ordered an account to be made pursuant to a contract.

Taussig MS. 311, vol. 1, p. 194, pl. 2

Thursday, 25 January 1722.

The [English] bill was exhibited against Willcox, High Bailiff of Westminster, to have an account of the post fines belonging to the office of High Bailiff of Westminster collected and also of the leet fines there, according to an agreement made upon the sale of the office of High Bailiff of Westminster, by Mills, who was the father and testator, to Willcox. And the bill set forth the agreement whereby Mills was to have the fines of both sorts then due and uncollected and Wilcox, who came into the office, was not to interrupt him in the collection of the same. The bill suggested an interruption as to the collecting of the leet fines. But the same was not made out by the evidence. And also the bill prayed an execution of the agreement and satisfaction for the aforesaid interruption.

The defendant, as to the post fines, submitted to account. As to leet fines, he denied the receipt of any of them and also any interruption given to Mills in the collecting of them.

After the cause was set down to be heard, Willcox died and Mills revived the cause as against his widow, who was also his executrix, who answered that she had not assets.

Upon the hearing, the court, *viz.* Bury and Page, the other barons being absent, dismissed the bill *quoad* the leet fines, no interruption being proved, and dismissed it with costs. And as to the post fines, they sent it to an account and reserved costs upon the account until after the account be taken.

As to costs upon the dismission of the bill *quoad* the leet fines, it was thought very hard because, had Willcox been alive at the time of the hearing, Mills was certainly entitled to a decree against him to perform the agreement. As to this part, that he had failed in his proof of an interruption and all these examinations being had in the lifetime of Willcox and being set down to be heard before his death, though it was true the court could not decree a performance of the agreement against an executrix, the office being now determined by death, yet it is no reason that she should have costs for this part of the bill which would have been proper against her husband. But Mr. Baron Page was peremptory as to these costs. And so the decree was made.

272

Attorney General v. Snow

(Ex. 1722)

A defendant, with leave of court, can plead two inconsistent defenses.

Taussig MS. 311, vol. 1, p. 194, pl. 1

Friday, 26 January 1722.

Mr. *Bootle* moved on behalf of the defendant that he might have liberty to plead double to an information of debt upon a bond, *viz. non est factum* and performance of covenants.

But, by Page, the pleas are inconsistent and we cannot give you leave to plead them.

But the court said that he might move it again, Bury and Page *praesentibus.*

Taussig MS. 311, vol. 1, p. 196

Saturday, 27 January 1722.

Mr. *Bootle* now produced an affidavit of Mr. Snow that he, upon the view of the bond, did believe that it was not his deed nor executed by him, and he [renewed] his motion to plead double as before.

And, by Bury, Montagu, and Page, liberty was given to plead these pleas.

Per Page, *non cepit* and justification has been allowed; so to justify as tenant at will and as tenant for years.

Bunbury 96, 145 E.R. 608

27 January 1721[/22].

Snow was surety for one of the clerks of Mr. Pauncefoot, Cashier of the Excise. And he entered into a bond for that purpose. Now, upon an information of debt upon this bond, it was moved by Mr. *Bootle*, on the behalf of the defendant, upon the Statute for the Amendment of the Law, 4 & 5 Ann.,[1] for leave to plead double, that is to say, *non est factum* and conditions performed, which was granted.

Quod nota, for query, first, if the Statute extends to this case of the crown and, secondly, the pleas seem contradictory.

[1] Stat. 4 & 5 Ann., c. 3, s. 4 (*SR*, VIII, 458).

273

Warwick, *qui tam* v. Rawlins

(Ex. 1722)

The questions in this case were whether there were two separate seizures of goods or only a single seizure and, secondly, whether court costs should be awarded in this case against the seizer for not going on to trial.

Taussig MS. 311, vol. 1, p. 197

Wednesday, 31 January 1722.

A Custom House officer comes to Rawlins' warehouse and makes a seizure of tea and, finding one parcel of tea in canisters, seizes it and, as to another parcel of tea, which stood in tubs, he doubted whether he should venture to seize the same, whereupon he only sealed up the tubs. And all this was done on the Saturday. And on the Monday following, the officer, having in the meantime conferred with the Commissioners of the Custom House, came again and seized the other parcel of tea, which he had only before sealed up in the tubs.

Two separate informations are given of these seizures and two separate writs of appraisement. And then comes in the owner and claims the property.

And upon affidavit of the fact *ut supra*, he moved the court by *Sir Constantine Phipps* and Mr. *Bootle* that the officer should be obliged to put both these seizures, which, as they insisted, were in truth or ought to be looked upon only as one, into one information and one writ of appraisement, and so one security would then serve for the whole, whereas, by this method of splitting a seizure, as they called it, the owner was put to unreasonable charges, double of what he ought to sustain or be put unto for contesting his property.

And Bury, Chief Baron, and Price though the practice above irregular, and they were for setting aside the aforesaid proceedings and granting the motion. But Montagu and Page were contrary, for, by them, this is determining the very point in controversy upon a motion, for it seemed to them very doubtful whether there were not two different seizures and, if they were, then, to be sure, the officer ought to give different informations and the proceedings thereupon of consequence ought to be separate and it might be very inconvenient to oblige the officer to rely on this as one and the same seizure. And so they were against the motion.

It was objected against the motion by Mr. *Ward* on behalf of a bidder that, by reversing the aforesaid proceedings and ordering new writs of appraisement, he would lose the benefit of his bidding. But this was not much regarded.

Bunbury 96, 145 E.R. 608

1 February 1721[/22].

A seizure was made of 1700 pounds weight of tea on the 16th of December last. The officer took away part of the tea at that time and sealed down the rest of the canisters and came another day and took away the sealed canisters. Upon this, two writs of appraisement issued, and two informations were filed upon this seizure.

And it was moved by *Sir Constantine Phipps* that, the seizure being but one in point of law, there ought to have been but one information and one writ of appraisement, and, therefore, the former ought to be set aside.

And of this opinion were Lord Chief Baron Bury and Price. Otherwise, the defendant would be doubly grieved, obliged to give double security, and liable to double costs. But this being opposed by a bidder, Montagu and Page, barons, were of another opinion. So no rule was made.

Note: On 23 February, it was moved for costs against the seizer for not going on to trial, in which the court were divided, being on an information of seizure, though they said it was usual in a case of a *devenerunt*.

Harvard Law School MS. 1082, vol. 1, p. 121, pl. 2

23 February 1722.

The information upon this seizure being tried and a verdict [being found] for the defendant, it was now moved for a writ of delivery; secondly, for costs for not going on to trial on the second information upon the Statute 6 Geo.; thirdly, for an attachment against the officer, the tea being seized amounting to 800 pounds weight, as appears by affidavit, but, in the writ of appraisement, there was no more than 400 pounds weight, so that it is an injury to the claimer and a fraud upon the crown.

Note the words of the Act are 'or shall forbear prosecution'.

[It was] objected by Mr. Attorney General [*Raymond*], first, that they ought not to have an attachment because they may have an action of trespass against the officer and the court will not try that matter upon affidavits; second, as to the costs, the course of the court is the law of the court and there is no precedent of costs given upon prosecutions of this nature and Mr. Solicitor [General *Yorke*] said the word forbearance in the Act must be intended a desertion of the prosecution, query what is meant by that; third, they were willing to consent to a writ of delivery giving security, which the defendants could not have had without. By consent, the defendant had a writ of delivery without security as to the goods in the first information which was tried. As to the others, upon the second, they were to give security.

Note: the clerks of the court certified that it had been usual upon these prosecutions of seizure even before the Act of Parliament to grant costs for not going on to trial.

Chief Baron Bury: (Query of what opinion.)

Baron Price always took it that, upon an information of seizure, no costs were [given] for not going on; upon a *devenerunt*, they always had costs. The reason of the difference is, before the Act, the party claimer might upon the first have an action; the defendant in the second could not.

This Act certainly intended that costs should be allowed in this case. The Act was made for the benefit of the officer, for, by allowing costs in full satisfaction, the claimer is deprived of his action, and the costs for not going on etc. shall be taken to be in full satisfaction etc. He was for costs. And, as to the attachment, he was for referring it to the Deputy [Remembrancer] to report the fact.

Baron Montagu: I think the defendant cannot [well], nor in point of prudence, insist upon costs in this case, for, if he has his costs by the Act, it must be in full satisfaction for his damages. He thought it a thing of such consequence as to the costs that he would not determine his opinion upon it until he had seen precedents. As to the attachment, it is not the officers who put the goods in the writ of appraisement, but the appraisers. And in the case of Harwood, *qui tam* v. Foulte (*vide* [*blank*]), the attachment was granted against the officers and [. . .] against the attachment.

Taussig MS. 311, vol. 1, p. 240

Friday, 23 February 1722.

Per Price: Before the late Statute, I take it there was a distinction between an information upon a seizure and an information in the nature of a *devenerunt*. In the first place, the informer was not to pay costs for not going on to trial, as in case a verdict was against him and the costs for not going on to trial must be looked upon as a satisfaction for and a discharge of damages as well as where there is a verdict.

Montagu: As to the course of the court before the Statute and, secondly, upon the Statute, as to the Statute, I think it would be dangerous to ask for costs, for the costs are certainly to be in satisfaction. Before the Statute, I never knew costs against the Attorney General for not going on to trial. The Attorney General may waive a demurrer and go to issue or waive an issue and demur. And he may refuse to ask for a *tales*. And my Brother Price, he never knew of costs in a case of a seizure. Therefore, I will not determine hastily, but will see what has been done before. In this case, I do not understand the difference between an information in the nature of a *devenerunt* and an information of seizure. Therefore, I suspend my opinion as to this point, whether he shall have costs or not.

274

Wallis v. Combs

(Ex. 1722)

A defendant must justify his bail before filing a dilatory plea.

Taussig MS. 311, vol. 1, p. 199

31 January 1722.

A special [writ of] *quo minus* issued against the defendant Combes returnable *tres Michaelis*. On this, Combes was arrested and he put in bail to the sheriff. But the plaintiff excepting to his bail, the defendant, instead of justifying his bail, gave in a dilatory plea that he was an Attorney of the King's Bench, whereupon the plaintiff took an assignment of the bail bond.

Now Mr. *Raby* came to set aside the proceedings on the said bail bond and offered to justify his bail and to plead the former plea.

But the court would do nothing in it, for, by not justifying his bail in time, he had deprived the plaintiff of the benefit he had of trying his cause last term, for the writ being a special writ, the defendant ought to have pleaded to it so that the plaintiff might have had time enough to have given notice of trial in the term.

275

Hawkins v. Joyce

(Ex. 1722)

Tithe of wood is due by common right.

Harvard Law School MS. 1082, vol. 1, p. 114, pl. 1

Hilary term 1721/22.

The plaintiff, as rector of Higham Gobion in the County of Bedford, brought his bill for tithe wood and milk. And the defendant insisted on a *non decimando* as to tithe wood within the parish. And as to tithe milk, he fed them in one parish and milked them in another. And as to tithe wood being due of common right, for the plaintiff, [*blank*] cited Jordan v. Colley in this court.[1] And tithe wood is due of common right because wood is not annually renewing. Therefore, a prescription [of] *non decimando* in a parish is not allowed, but in a hundred it is.

And Serjeant *Stevens*, in relation to depasturing, cited, as to depasturing of horses, which was a question in this case, that the innkeeper is accountable and not he that depastures. Hardres 35, 184.[2]

The court decreed tithe wood of common right [to be] due.

---

[1] *Jordan v. Colley* (Ex. 1720), see above, Case No. 130.

[2] *Guilbert v. Eversly* (1656), Hardres 35, 145 E.R. 367, 2 Gwillim 502, 1 Eagle & Younge 414; *Pory v. Wright* (1661), Hardres 184, 145 E.R. 442, also 1 Eq. Cas. Abr. 367, 21 E.R. 1107, 1 Eagle & Younge 434.

276

Attorney General v. Stranyforth

(Ex. 1722)

The crown cannot sue a bankrupt's assignee or any of the distributees of the bankrupt's estate for the bankrupt's debt to the crown after his estate has been finally settled and distributed.

As to a partnership debt, each partner is liable for the whole debt.

Bunbury 97, 145 E.R. 608

1 February 1721[/22].

An English information was brought by the Attorney General setting forth that Nicholas Skinner in the year 1710, for himself and company, imported 117 tuns and thirteen gallons of Galicia wine and, upon application to the Custom House, obtained a sight, in pursuance of which, the officers appointed to view certified by indorsement on the order of sight that thirty-three tuns were so damaged as to be only fit to make spirits or vinegar and sunk one third in value. The agent of Skinner entered the said wines for Skinner and Company in the Custom House. And, by a mistake of the clerk in the office, the whole thirty-three tuns was allowed for damage, though no more than one third of the thirty-three tuns was intended to be allowed by the commissioners so that the crown was by this mistake defrauded in its duties £535. And the discovery being made about the year 1715, this information was not brought until [*blank*] term, which prayed that the defendants, being five, might make good this deficiency.

And the court decreed accordingly that, though the importation and entry was only by Skinner, yet all the partners, who were so at the time of importation, were liable in the whole to the crown. And the decree was drawn up that the defendant should pay the said sum to the crown as Mr. Attorney General should think fit.

Note: Skinner became a bankrupt in 1715, and Richards, one of the defendants, was assignee. And he insisted in his answer that he had long ago made a distribution of all the effects of Skinner to the creditors so that he had nothing left in his hands. And, as to him, the court were in some doubt and took time to consider whether the sum of £535 occasioned by this mistake was a debt so vested in the crown that the assignee could come upon the effects so distributed or whether the king is bound by the Statute of Bankrupts.[1]

Taussig MS. 311, vol. 1, p. 200

1 February 1722.

---

[1] Stat. 4 & 5 Ann., c. 4, s. 8 (*SR*, VIII, 463).

This was an English information in the name of the Attorney General to have satisfaction for an over allowance made by the officers of the customs to the defendants for damaged wine. And the information was brought against Pauncefort, Dowman, Stanyford, Maccarell, Welsh, and one Richards, who was an assignee of a commission of bankruptcy taken out against Skinner, who became a bankrupt in the year 1715 and of whose estate one or more dividends had been made to the creditors by the said assignee.

The information set forth that Nicholas Skinner, in August 1710, imported so many casks of Galicia wines containing such quantity and imported the same for himself and company that, afterwards, upon suspicion that a great part of the wines was damaged, Skinner, in the name of himself and company, presented a memorial to the Commissioners of the Custom House for a sight, which was granted on the 11th of August 1710. And, thereupon, a report was made by the officer of the quantity damaged, and an allowance was directed to be made. But by the mistake of the officer, £536 was allowed for the damage more than, by according to the rule and direction of the Commissioners of the Customs, ought to have been made, which mistake appeared plainly upon the comparing of the sight report of the officer and the allowance that had in fact been made thereupon. But though apparent upon the face of the proceedings, it had been but lately discovered and taken notice of. And, therefore, for the satisfaction of this over allowance of £536, the information was brought. And the information charged that Pauncefort and Dowman, Maccarel, Welsh, Stanyford, and Richards were concerned as partners in the wines at the time of the importation, *viz.* Pauncefort and Dowman one-fifth, Maccarel one-fifth, Welsh one-fifth, and Richards one-fifth.

The defendants severally answered. And Stanyford, who chiefly opposed this demand, put in an evasive answer, avoiding as much as he could, answering how far he was concerned in the wines at the time of the importation. However, he did not directly deny his part-ownership in the wines, but he said that, to the best of his recollection and belief, he was not to be at any risk of them in the voyage. And as to Richards, he, by his answer, said he had no notice of this demand of the crown until after the dividends were made upon Skinner's estate.

It was said by the Attorney [General, *Raymond*] and Solicitor General [*Yorke*], on behalf of the crown, that a mistake of the officer of the crown should not bar the crown of its right, that the mistake was apparent upon the face of the proceedings, and was an error in computation, and, therefore, as apparent now as when it was first made, and that bills in equity were frequent for rectifying mistakes of this kind, even in the case of subjects, and, therefore, held stronger in the case of the crown. And they insisted that, as all the defendants were part-owners at the time of the importation, the crown had a right for the satisfaction of the whole money against any one of them, and he should take his remedy over against the other for his contribution.

On the other side, it was said by *Sir Constantine Phipps* and Mr. *Bootle*, for the defendants, that this was an unreasonable demand after such a length of time and that it was much better and more reasonable that the crown should be obliged to take its remedy against the officer who made the mistake than to come against the merchants at such a distance of time, especially in this case where one of the parties interested had become a bankrupt and his estate had been divided so that the rest of them could have no remedy against him.

There was some doubt among the barons whether, upon the whole evidence in the case, it did appear sufficiently to them that Stanyford was a partner or jointly concerned in the wines at the time of their importation. And, therefore, at last, they decreed a trial as to that point against Stanyford, Stanyford agreeing to produce his books before the Deputy [Remembrancer] to be inspected on behalf of the crown. There was also some diversity of opinion among them concerning the crown's demand as against Richard, the assignee of the commission, against Skinner and how far the crown was bound by the assignment and whether, if the whole estate of Skinner was exhausted, the crown would come in for what remained and in what proportion.

Price, baron, seemed to be of opinion that the crown ought to be preferred before the rest of the creditors as to such part of Skinner's estate as remained undivided among the creditors, but he thought it a clear case that this debt could not be looked upon as relying on Skinner's personal estate, which had been divided. And as to this last point, all the rest of the barons were of the same opinion.

As to the first, the Chief Baron [Bury] and Montagu doubted.

But Page declared himself to be clear in opinion that the assignment under the commission of bankruptcy bound the crown and that the crown could not come in as a common creditor for the residue of the bankrupt's estate.

And they seemed to be doubtful whether they could decree for the whole demand against any of the defendants. But at last, they ordered a trial, as aforesaid, against Stanyford and made a general decree against the rest.

Taussig MS. 311, vol. 1, p. 232

Tuesday, 13 February 1722.

This cause came on again as against Pauncefort and Dowman, against whom there was formerly pronounced a decree. And the money being paid for the default, the cause was heard as between them and the Attorney General. These two defendants admitted a fifth part of the wines came to their hands, but it did not appear that they were interested in this fifth part at the time of the importation. And they might become partners after the importation and then, by the former opinion of the court, they are not chargeable. Second, there is no color to charge these defendants with the whole, for there is no fraud charged nor any privity between them in procuring this over-allowance. If there had, perhaps it might be reasonable to charge these defendants with the whole, but there is no pretence of this nature. It is a pure mistake of the officer. And the bill says that the crown is defrauded, yet the word defrauded is only intended as deprived, and, besides, the Attorney General only charges them with a fifth and does not pretend that there is more than a fifth part of the benefit arising by this mistake. Therefore, you shall [not] pay the whole.

E contra: The crown is not bound to take notice of the partnership, i.e. of the proportion of the partnership, but may come against anyone. And he must have his remedy against the rest for their proportions. And as to the answer of the defendants, it appears they were concerned in freight, prime, costs, and insurance, and all these are previous to the actual importation.

Chief Baron [Bury]: I am satisfied these persons were concerned from the beginning by the circumstance of their paying the said proportion of freight, prime, costs, etc.

Price: It is too hard to decree against these defendants *pro toto*, for these defendants swear that they knew not by whose order the wines were imported. And they swear positively they were not to be at the risk of the wine. And you must take the answer altogether. So I think these defendants were not the original importers nor was here any fraud. And, therefore, they only ought to make up the fifth part of their proportions of the allowance.

Montagu: First, these defendants are, in my opinion, original importers. And if I thought they were not, I should be of opinion that they ought not to be charged with any part of this allowance. But now, I think they ought to be charged with the whole, for all merchant importers are liable to the whole customs. And it is the same case as if the king had a fee farm rent out of land belonging to the five several persons. The crown may take all from one. So in an action against the hundred, the whole may be levied upon one. So, if several are bound by a recognizance to the crown, the crown may have the whole against one of them. So it is very clear that the former decree ought to stand against these defendants *pro toto*.

Price: I am clear that, if these were partners *tempore importationis*, then, no doubt, they must pay the whole.

The Chief Baron and Montagu differing from Price, the decree formerly pronounced stood confirmed.

Taussig MS. 311, vol. 1, p. 253

21 April 1722.

The defendants exhibited their petition for a rehearing and insisted, first, the petition, that it did not sufficiently appear that these defendants were partners *tempore importationis*, second, that they are only chargeable *pro rata*.

As to the first, the court directed an issue as to Stanyford and so the point insisted upon in the information is *adhuc sub judice*.

As to the second point, first, there is no fraud; secondly, they had only the benefit of a fifth and should be only answerable for a fifth; third, a long delay and a remedy over is prevented. He cited the case of the Attorney General and the East India Company.

Chief Baron [Bury] admits it to be a hard case.

PRICE was doubtful, as before, whether the evidence is sufficient of the partners' trespass *tempore importationis*. The partners are not guilty of fraud. But, if the partners shall answer *per my et per tout*, there will be a great hardship in point of time. He is for a rehearing in order to send the point to a trial at law.

MONTAGU: If there is a difficulty in the cause, there is reason to rehear. But hardship only is not a cause to rehear. If the matter is otherwise plain, length of time is an objection because it darkens, but if it is clear notwithstanding the length of time, then the maxim *quod nullum tempus occurrit regi*[1] takes place. As to the point of partners, if it is so, all are chargeable as in the case of a rent charge.

PAGE: The length of time did stick a little with me because there is no remedy over. I looked upon the sight and find that all these persons were privy to this mistake, and, if so, all are answerable for this mistake.

But notwithstanding, all the court inclined and gave way for a rehearing.

Per MONTAGU: A mis-computation in an account is as plain twenty years afterwards as in the next year.

277

Stukely v. Cain

(Ex. 1722)

A defendant cannot plead his own delay in order to defeat his contractual obligation.

Taussig MS. 311, vol. 1, p. 216, pl. 2

Thursday, 8th February 1722.

Articles of agreement [were made] dated 20th July 1720 for the purchase of a house and land of the value of £20 *per annum* in Lincolnshire at forty years purchase, the title to be approved by the defendant's counsel, and conveyances to be made by 29th September following.

The defendant's counsel was Mr. Ward, who, soon after the writings were laid before him, went into the country. And, for this reason, the conveyances were not made in time and, therefore, the non-executing or preparing the conveyances by the time limited by the articles, *scil.* 29th September, was the defendant's fault and not any neglect of the plaintiff.

Serjeant *Stevens*, for the plaintiff: This is an unreasonable contract, being made at an excessive price, and, therefore, this court will not assist in carrying it into execution. And he cited Young and Clarke in Chancery, which was heard on 18 November 1720.[2]

---

[1] That no time [limits] run against the king.

[2] *Young v. Clerk* (1720), Precedents in Chancery 538, 24 E.R. 241, 2 Eq. Cas. Abr. 18, 22 E.R. 15.

Bunbury, ad idem: (1) A court will regard the nature of the time when this agreement was made and not pin down an unreasonable agreement on the defendant. (2) The defendant has not made a title as by the agreement was to be done. And, therefore, he proposed that it might be referred to the Master to state the title because, if the title be not good, the court will not compel the agreement, though the counsel should have approved it.

But the court was all unanimous that they must decree a performance of this agreement as well as of any other, there appearing no fraud or surprise or any default in the plaintiff in the making out of his title, but this happening by the defendant's counsel's going into the country. And they knew no difference between this and other agreements. And, therefore, they decreed a performance without hesitation and directed the deeds to be carried before the Deputy [Remembrancer] and that he should inspect the title and report it, and, if there were any reasonable objections to it, then the court would consider them.

Harvard Law School MS. 1082, vol. 1 p. 116

Hilary term 1721/22. Stukeley v. Lien.

This was a bill to have a specific performance of an agreement [for] an estate of £20 *per annum* in Lincolnshire at forty years' purchase, *viz.* £800. And articles were accordingly drawn and £120 paid in part [payment]. The defendant says that he would have performed it if he could have had the estate before the fall of stocks happened.[1] But since they have fallen [in value], he has been made incapable of performing it. And the articles were dated in the mad time, *viz.* July 1720. And the conveyances [were] to be executed at Michaelmas following and the writings delivered in August last.

Serjeant *Stevens*, for the defendant: [It is] too hard for a court of equity to compel the execution of an agreement at forty years' purchase.

Bunbury, for the defendant, cited Clarke v. Young, in Chancery 1720, about an agreement for a hop ground at [. . .] per acre, and the court would not decree an execution. There was no fraud in this case or [any] pretended.

Page said that he could not think any fraud since it was proved that the plaintiff could have sold it to another person at as high a price.

So the court decreed an execution of the said agreement.

But an appeal is lodged in this cause. Query the event.

(This decree was reversed in the House of Lords.)[2]

[Reversed in Keen v. Stuckely (1722), Gilbert Rep. 155, 25 E.R. 109, 2 Eq. Cas. Abr. 19, 22 E.R. 16, 1 Brown P.C. 191, 1 E.R. 506.]

---

[1] I.e. the bursting of the South Sea bubble in 1720.

[2] This note was written at the beginning of the report in a different hand.

278

Paisley v. Potter

(Ex. 1722)

A court of equity has jurisdiction to decree an account of the proceeds of a bond owned by the plaintiff, which proceeds were received by the defendant in whose hands the bond was deposited.

Harvard Law School MS. 1082, vol. 1, p. 117, pl. 1

Hilary term 1721/22.

A bill was exhibited for a bond given by Firebrass to Sarah Waterworth, to whom the plaintiff's wife was executrix, which was deposited in the defendant's hands by Sarah Waterworth. And the defendant has received the money due thereby.

It was objected by counsel for the defendant, and I thought right, that this was an action of trover turned into a bill in equity, and, though proper for a discovery, yet not for relief.

But the court overruled the objection and said the action of trover would only be for the paper and wax. And so the court decreed for the plaintiffs for the principal and interest, the defendant having received it.

Bunbury and *Bootle* [were] for the defendant; *Sir Constantine Phipps* and myself [were] for the plaintiff.

Taussig MS. 311, vol. 1, p. 218

Hilary term 1722.

A bill [was exhibited] by the plaintiff to have a bond delivered up to him and an account of the money received by Potter by way of interest and the principal also if received. The plaintiff was executrix of the person to whom the bond was given.

First, it was objected by *Bootle* and *Bunbury* that this was a plain action at law, for it had been often resolved that it was not necessary to insert the date of a bond in an action of *detinue* or trover for a bond. See Cro. Car. 262[1] to this purpose. And, therefore, a bill is not necessary to discover that.

Sed per CURIAM: Here is an account prayed. And, therefore, the bill is proper.

And the defendant then proceeded to show a gift of the bond to him.

But upon reading his evidence, the same not being sufficient to prove a gift, but only that it was deposited with him to receive the interest, the court decreed payment of the principal and the interest.

279

Mead v. Wyndham

[1] *Wilson v. Chambers* (1632), Croke Car. 262, 79 E.R. 828.

(Ex. 1722)

Where a defendant pays money into court in part payment of the plaintiff's claim, he cannot thereafter plead the defense of the Statute of Limitations.

Bunbury 100, 145 E.R. 609

9 February 1721[/22].

An action of *indebitatus assumpsit* was brought for goods sold and delivered. The defendant moved that, upon bringing £6 into court, it might be struck out of the declaration etc. And, afterwards, he pleaded *non assumpsit infra sex annos.*[1]

It was now moved by *Sir Constantine Phipps* that the plea might be set aside and the defendant be obliged to plead the general issue, which the court ordered accordingly, the bringing the money into court being a sort of an admission that the promise was within six years.

Then, Mr. *Bootle*, for the defendant, moved to withdraw his money out of court, it being in the Master's hands and in the power of the court. But that they would not permit.

Harvard Law School MS. 1082, vol. 1, p. 117, pl. 2

Hilary term 1721/22.

After the defendant had been allowed by rule of court to bring £6 into court, now, it was moved by Mr. *Bootle* that he might plead double.

But [it was] said that in the [Court of] Common Pleas, after money [is] brought into court, the defendant is not suffered to plead anything but the general issue. And so [it was] ruled here, and the motion [was] denied. But Mr. *Bootle* would have had the money also out of court [so] that he might plead to [it], which was refused.

Taussig MS. 311, vol. 1, p. 219

Friday, 9 February 1722.

An action of case upon an *indebitatus assumpsit* for butcher's meat [was brought] by an executor. And in this term, the defendant came and moved to bring £6 into court and to strike it out of the declaration, which was granted. And then, the defendant pleaded *non assumpsit infra sex annos.*

And now *Sir Constantine Phipps* moved that this should not be admitted after such an indulgence, but the party should be obliged to plead the general issue. And the plaintiff further produced an affidavit that the defendant had promised not to take advantage of the Statute of Limitation.

N.B. It is agreed that neither in the Common Pleas nor the King's Bench the declaration is altered, though the striking out is the general phrase of the motion. But there is a difference between these two courts, for, in the Common

[1] Statute of Limitations, Stat. 21 Jac. I, c. 16, s. 3 (*SR*, IV, 1222).

Pleas, the rule is never given in evidence, but, in the King's Bench, the rule is given in evidence.

Per CURIAM: In this case, it would be unreasonable, for, if we should give you leave to plead the Statute, this would be a very great inconvenience on the plaintiff, for you would apply the £6 for the meat delivered since the six years, and, as to the rest, you plead the Statute, whereas continuing the delivery of the meat is a continuing of the account.

N.B. As to the rule for bringing in money into court where an executor is plaintiff *quod querens admittatur custagium.*

In this case, the defendant had actually brought the money into court. And the court would neither let him plead the Statute nor let him take back the money and plead the Statute; so he was forced to plead *non assumpsit quoad* the residuum.

280

Crawford, *qui tam* v. Hyam

(Ex. 1722)

A seizure of forfeited goods can only be settled out of court with the approval of the Chief Baron and the Attorney General, and they must take into account the interest of any bidder.

Taussig MS. 311, vol. 1, p. 222

Hilary term 1721/22.

[There was a] seizure by an officer, and the goods were appraised at £75. And [there was] a bidding thereupon; then, a claim is put in. And the claimer takes out a license to compound. And the officer compounds for £25, and, then, the claimer would have rated the fine at £25 for the crown, but the bidder opposed it. And, therefore, *Foley* moved the court to have the fine rated.

Per MONTAGU, baron: A composition must not be under a third, *quod fuit concessum.* And query by him whether the composition does not admit the forfeiture.

It was objected on behalf of the bidder that he had been at charges and yet, by this composition, he was to be ousted of his bidding.

The court bid Mr. Foley look into precedents and move it again.

Taussig MS. 311, vol. 1, p. 242

Hilary term 1721/22.

The single question was whether, after a bidding, the officer may have a license to compound because this is defeating the bidder and the composition admits a forfeiture and, therefore, it would be very unreasonable to admit such a composition, for that would be to defeat both the bidder, who is bound at all adventures, and the crown too of the price advanced by the bidder.

And the court ordered that the composition should not be rated, i.e. they would not allow a composition after a bidding.

Bunbury 100, 145 E.R. 610

20 February 1721[/22].

Crawford seized a parcel of hippocociana upon the 23d day of September. In Michaelmas term following, Crawford took a writ of appraisement, and Hyam put in his claim and gave security. A letter of licence was granted to enable Crawford to compound with Hyam. And, upon an affidavit made by Crawford that the composition was made, it was moved by Mr. *Foley* that the fine might be rated, there being no collusion between the officer and the claimer and composition having been at one third according to the rule.

But this motion was opposed by Mr. *Ward* on behalf of the bidder, who had been at some expense.

And the motion was denied *per* CURIAM.

Bunbury 116, 145 E.R. 616

25 June 1722.

Per Lord Chief Baron MONTAGU, the power of compounding was only by virtue of their privy seal. The Statute of Frauds[1] says it shall not be less than one third by the privy seal so as they shall not rate any fine at less than one half of what the seizer is to have. See the Rules of 1697.

Note: No fine by the privy seal can be rated without the leave of the Lord Chief Baron and the Attorney General.

The court now determined that, when anybody applies to rate a fine, they will inquire first whether there was any bidder and, if there was, the court would in rating the fine take his interest into consideration.

Harvard Law School MS. 1082, vol. 1, p. 147, pl. 2

25 June 1722.

Upon an information upon a seizure of a parcel of hyppocomacia, Chief Baron MONTAGU, in speaking to this matter, said that the power of compounding was only in virtue of their privy seal. The Statute of Frauds says it shall not be less than one-third by the privy seal so and they shall not rate any fines less than at one-half what the officer is to have.

The Rules made in 1697 were read. Query where they are to be found.

Note: No fine can be rated without leave of the Chief Baron and the Attorney General. When anybody comes to apply to rate a fine, the court resolved to inquire first whether there was any bidder, and, if there was, they would, in rating the fine, take his interest into consideration.

---

[1] Stat. 14 Car. II, c. 11, s. 18 (*SR*, V, 398).

Taussig MS. 311, vol. 1, p. 324, pl. 2

Trinity term 1722.

Mr. *Browne* moved for a writ of delivery. And the reason he gave for the writ of delivery was that the officer had delayed prosecution upon his seizure. The seizure was 23 September 1721. The claim was entered [*blank*], and no information is hitherto exhibited.

But this was opposed.

And the court made a rule that the Commissioners of the Customs should be acquainted with this matter and that the officer who made the seizure should attend.

And Lord Chief Baron [Montagu] said he would examine him why he did not go on. My Lord also ordered that the claimer should also attend.

And the reason [for] this opposition to the writ of delivery was that, hereby, the bidder would be of the benefit of his bidding and it would greatly discourage bidders if they are to be held to their bargains, as Bourne[1] was, in case the [value of the] commodity falls and to have the commodity taken out of their hands in case it rises. And it was also said that, if the court would oblige the officer to prove the seizure, the bidder would carry on the prosecution as it was alleged he might do being made a party to the record by his bidding.

281

Monkhouse v. Hutchison

(Ex. 1722)

The question in this case was whether the names Elizabeth and Isabel are the same for the purposes of the pleadings.

Bunbury 101, 145 E.R. 610

10 February 1721[/22].

A bond was entered into to the plaintiff by her name of Elizabeth, in which name the action was brought. The defendant pleaded in abatement that the plaintiff's name was Isabel, and not Elizabeth.

But upon motion, this was set aside as a sham plea, *per* TOTAM CURIAM.

Query the difference as to the time allowed for pleading in abatement upon a special *quo minus*.

Taussig MS. 311, vol. 1, p. 223

Saturday, 10 February 1722.

[1] *Bourne's Case* (Ex. 1721), see above, Case No. 208.

[An action of] debt [was brought] on a bond given to the plaintiff and others by the name of Elizabeth. And the defendant comes and pleads that the plaintiff's name was Isabell and pleads this in abatement.

[There was a] motion to set aside this plea as a sham plea.

Fazakerly: It is a very good plea and sworn to be true. And, if they join issue on it and go to trial on it and it is found for the plaintiff, they must have judgment in chief.

But the court overruled the plea because the affidavit was short and imperfect in verifying the plea.

282

Mayor of Boston v. Jackson

(Ex. 1722)

A court of equity does not have jurisdiction to adjudicate rights of beaconage.

Bunbury 101, 145 E.R. 610

10 February 1721[/22].

A bill was brought for beaconage, i.e. a duty for setting up lights for the benefit of navigation, which the plaintiff claimed by letters patent. The defendants admit they had paid this duty, but insist they had paid it in their own wrong.

It was objected by *Sir Constantine Phipps*, for the defendants, that this [case] was [more] proper at [common] law. And the cases underneath were cited.[1]

On the other side was cited by Serjeant *Chesshyre* the case of The City of London v. Pallister, Michaelmas 1721, to which it was answered that the court retained their bill because there had been precedents of such bills by the City of London and their usages and customs are confirmed by Act of Parliament,[2] and they had also ascertained their title at [common] law.

And the bill in the present case was dismissed by three barons against Montagu, who thought that, where a matter extended to several persons and was of little value, a court of equity ought to take cognizance of the matter to save trouble and expense.

Harvard Law School MS. 1082, vol. 1, p. 117, pl. 3

A bill was brought for the payment of beaconage, i.e. duties for setting out lights for the benefit of navigation, against the defendants, owners of several ships. The defendants admit they had several vessels and offered to pay 1s. for each vessel upon sailing from [*blank*] to [*blank*] for beaconage.

---

[1] *Disney v. Robertson* (1719), see above, Case No. 82; *Harding v. Ange* (1719); *City of Exeter v. Bond* (1718).

[2] Stat. 27 Hen. VIII, c. 24, ss. 11, 17 (*SR*, III, 557).

It was objected for the defendant that this is a matter at law and proper for an action there. And a bill of the same kind was dismissed in the cases of the City of Exeter v. Bond, Hilary 1718, toll for petty customers; Easter 1719, Disney v. Robinson, a bill for toll for passage of boats on the water; sittings after Trinity 1719, Harding v. Ange, a bill for payment for weighing of cheese. In the City of Exeter v. Bond, there was a fee farm rent reserved.

Serjeant *Chesshyre, contra*, [cited] The City of London v. Pallister, Michaelmas 1721, and ditto v. Gascoigne.

Sir Constantine Phipps replied: The reason of the distinction in those cases was because there had been precedents of such bills by the City of London and their usages and customs being confirmed by Act of Parliament was the reason why the court retained the bill and also the plaintiff had before asserted their title at law.

Note: The plaintiffs in this cause claim by virtue of letters patent.

Baron PRICE admitted that to be the reason they went upon in the case of the City of London, which does not extend to this or the other cases mentioned by the defendant. And he was for dismissing the bill.

Baron MONTAGU thought, where a matter extended to a whole parish and was of little value, a court of equity ought, to save trouble and expense, to take cognizance of the matter. Where the right is litigated, as in the cases mentioned by the defendant, we will not in equity take upon us to determine that right. But, here, they admit that this duty has been paid.

But query, for they say it was paid but in their own wrong.

But, by the opinion of the other three barons, the bill was dismissed.

Taussig MS. 311, vol. 1, p. 235

Wednesday, the 21st February 1722.

A bill was brought to establish the right of the Town of Boston to a payment of 4s. of every Scotchman's vessel and 5s. for every other foreigner's. And it is for the maintenance of sea marks in a certain place called the Norman Deeps.

It was dismissed because the title was not affirmed at law.

283

Bouchier v. Duke

(Ex. 1722)

The question in this case was whether there was a modus decimandi *in lieu of tithes in kind.*

Taussig MS. 311, vol. 1, p. 205

Hilary term 1721/22.

A bill for tithes [was exhibited] by the plaintiff, as vicar of Amport in the County of Southampton, *viz.* of pigeons, calves, gardens, and Easter offerings.

The defendant, by his answer, insists on a *modus* for his farm, *viz.* a *modus* of 15s. *per annum* in lieu of all small tithes arising on the farm called Sarston's Farm, except wool and lamb.

Sir Constantine Phipps, for the plaintiff, [made] two objections to the *modus* as laid in the answer.

1. New lands were added to this farm within twenty years so that the *modus* for them extends to this as well as the old farm.

2. The value of the tithes set forth in the answer for the time demanded in the bill, *viz.* two years only, amounts to £3 so that 15s. cannot be esteemed as a *modus* for it, but only as a composition. And the plaintiff's witnesses swear that the small tithes of the farm do not amount one year with another to 30s. *per annum.*

Jones and Calvert, 1714, in Easter term, [tithe] pigeons are not due but by custom.

284

Butler v. Pearce

(Ex. 1722)

A defendant's answer must respond sufficiently to the plaintiff's bill of complaint.

Taussig MS. 311, vol. 1, p. 206

Hilary term 1721/22.

The plaintiff had deposited £10,000 in Ram Insurance upon borrowing or taking up £7000 from the defendant here in equity, who was the plaintiff at law and had recovered against him a judgment for the whole £7000. And, thereupon, the plaintiff exhibited his bill wherein he charged that he deposited the £10,000 Ram Insurance as a full equivalent for the £7000 and that the defendant took it as such and the rather, for that the defendant did not request the plaintiff to give any other security, nor did the plaintiff give any.

In the interrogatory part of the bill, the plaintiff only asks whether he did give the defendant any bond or other security. The defendant answers that the plaintiff did never give any other security and says that, at the time of depositing the £7000 of the Ram, he, the defendant, looked upon it as a sufficient security, but he never took it as an entire or absolute satisfaction for the money.

The plaintiff excepted that the defendant had not answered fully, for he had not answered whether the defendant did request him to give further security and this was material, for, if he never did request any other security, it is a strong evidence that he took this as the only security.

Sed per Bury, Price, and Montagu: The answer is sufficient.

But PRICE and MONTAGU thought the charge of the bill coming in under the rather,[1] for that was not so full and particular as it ought to have been and, therefore, the plaintiff should not have insisted on this more particularly in the interrogatory part of the bill.

But PAGE thought the answer was defective for that the charge was good and full enough and the answer that no other security was given is no manner of answer to this, whether any other security was requested.

Per CURIAM: If a bill requires you to set forth whether you have any papers whereby such a matter in certain may appear and you answer that you have no papers whereby such a matter in certain may appear, this is not a direct and full answer, for, by this, you take upon yourself to judge of the efficacy of those papers, whereas the court, and not you, are to judge of these things.

285

Swallow v. Fenn

(Ex. 1722)

The Court of Exchequer can approve the binding out of an infant as an apprentice.

Public Record Office E.126/22, f. 172, pl. 1

22 February 1721[/22]. Norfolk.

Whereas by order of this court made upon the hearing of this cause on Wednesday the 5th day of July last, it was, *inter alia*, ordered, adjudged, and decreed by the court that it should be referred to the Deputy Remembrancer of this court to examine into the fitness of a person for the binding out of the defendant John Fenn an apprentice and what sum was required for that purpose and, in the meantime, the said cause was continued in the paper of causes to be further heard, upon the coming in of the said Deputy's report pursuant to which said order on hearing, John Harding, Esq., Deputy Remembrancer, made his report to this court bearing date the 6th day of this instant February and thereby certified that, in obedience to an order of this court made on the hearing of this cause the 5th day of July 1721, he had in the presence of the clerk and solicitor on both sides considered of the matters thereby to him referred and did find that Mr. William Barwick of the City of Norwich, apothecary, was a fit person and who offered to take the infant, John Fenn, an apprentice for the term of seven years and insisted upon having £80, which sum he thought reasonable for that purpose, and submitted to the court for their approbation, which cause coming this day to be further heard upon the said report at Serjeants' Inn Hall in Chancery Lane before the Rt. Hon. Sir Thomas Bury, Kt., Lord Chief Baron, and the rest of the barons of this court, upon reading the said order on hearing and the

[1] Sic in MS.

Deputy's said report and upon hearing of Mr. Browne, of counsel with the plaintiff, and Mr. Bunbury, of the defendants' counsel, praying that the said report may be confirmed by the authority of this court, it is thereupon this day ordered, adjudged, and decreed by the court that the said Deputy's report be and is hereby ratified and confirmed and that the said infant, John Fenn, be put an apprentice for seven years to the said William Barwick and that the plaintiff Robert Swallow do pay to the said William Barwick the sum of £80 upon binding him, the said John Fenn, apprentice as aforesaid and the plaintiff shall be and is hereby indemnified for his so doing.

286

Rhodes v. Barrett

(Ex. 1722)

When a married woman sues as the agent for her husband, she must sue in her husband's name.

Taussig MS. 311, vol. 1, p. 216, pl. 1

Hilary term 1721/22.

The plaintiff was a *feme covert*. And it appeared that her husband was alive, but her husband had given her a letter to receive a banker's annuity, which letter of attorney was got into the defendant's hands. And the bill was dismissed for not being brought in the husband's name.

287

Anonymous

(Ex. 1722)

The court will order a corporation to make its records available to a party only after the party, upon a request, has been refused access.

Taussig MS. 311, vol. 1, p. 221, pl. 1

Hilary term 1721/22.

A motion [was made] by *Sir Constantine Phipps* that the South Sea Company should produce the third subscription book at a trial. But it not appearing that the party had applied to the Company and in the case the Company refused, then, perhaps, the court would assist them. But though it was [not] convenient, they should first apply to the Company.

288

Anonymous

(Ex. 1722)

The court will order a corporation to make its records available to a party only after the party, upon a request, has been refused access.

Taussig MS. 311, vol. 1, p. 231

Hilary term 1722.

Mr. *Fazakerly* moved this day on behalf of a plaintiff that he might have liberty to inspect and take copies of such part of the South Sea books as they should think convenient at their own charges in order to give the same in evidence on a trial about a fourth subscription.

But the court refused the motion, he never having made any previous application to the Company for that purpose, though Mr. *Fazakerly* said that this was a motion of course in the King's Bench and that court never insisted upon the party's making any such previous application to the Company. But the court told him that the rule here was otherwise. And he took nothing by his motion.

289

Wakefield, *qui tam* v. Platt

(Ex. 1722)

A condemnation of goods must be proved by the record of the condemnation; the tally is not sufficient evidence.

Taussig MS. 311, vol. 1, p. 221, pl. 2

Hilary term 1721/22.

Upon an importation [and] seizure of wines for not paying customs, *non importata* was pleaded. And, at the trial, the defendant gave in evidence that the wines seized were part of a parcel of wines which the defendant had bought under a condemnation in this court. And, for this, he produced the tally of sol. And then, he would have gone on to prove the wines were the same.

But by the Chief Baron [Bury], the tally of sol is not sufficient. You must produce the record of the judgment of condemnation.

290

Philpott, *qui tam* v. Rotchell

(Ex. 1722)

A plea in abatement auter action pendant *must be supported by an affidavit.*

A plea in abatement cannot be amended.

Taussig MS. 311, vol. 1, p. 224, pl. 1

Hilary term 1721/22.

An action was brought for £436 16s., the treble value of money won at play. And the action was brought by the person losing the money.

The defendant pleads a suit for this money brought in the Common Pleas by one Anne Plaiderley, *qui tam*. But the suit there was for £406 16s. And it was moved to set aside the plea because, if the plaintiff should reply *nul tiel record*, they would make up such a record.

And the court set aside the plea because there was no affidavit to support the truth of the plea, and, therefore, there was no occasion to look any farther.

Taussig MS. 311, vol. 1, p. 230

Hilary term 1721/22.

See the case before.

Mr. *Kettleby* now came and moved to set aside the order made in this cause on Saturday last, which was for rejecting the plea of a former suit depending for the same penalty. And he showed that the omission of £30 in the plea of pendency of the former information on the action *qui tam* in the Common Bench was a pure mistake of counsel, that the instructions to the counsel for drawing the plea were right, that the original in the Common Pleas was right. And he offered to produce a copy thereof.

Sed per CURIAM: We shall not reverse[1] our former order for setting aside the plea, for, as the plea stood, it was certainly wrong and we never give way to the amending of a plea in abatement, for dilatories are to be discouraged as much as may be.

Mr. *Kettleby* then moved that the defendant might have four days time to plead.

Sed per CURIAM: We will not allow you one.

Kettleby: We shall then be in a very hard case indeed for, instead of paying the treble value of the money, we must now pay six times the value. The action *qui tam* will be tried in the Common Pleas on Wednesday next, and, there, the plaintiff will recover against us and, in this court, another plaintiff will have a judgment against us for want of a plea for the selfsame penalty. And, besides, it was the plaintiff's fault to suffer this plea in abatement to stand until the last day but one of the term and then to come and set it aside without notice, whereas, had he moved earlier in the term to set it aside, as he might and ought to have done, we might have had time enough to have pleaded another plea.

But notwithstanding this, the court would not allow him any time to plead.

[1] reserve *MS.*

291

Lutwyche v. Broham

(Ex. 1722)

A claim on a seizure of goods for not paying customs duties cannot be settled by arbitration.

Taussig MS. 311, vol. 1, p. 224, pl. 2

12 February 1722.

An information of seizure [was brought] by Broham *et al.* Lutwyche claims, and the information goes down to trial at Carlyle and the officers there submit to an arbitration and that is made a rule of the Common Pleas.

And Lutwyche now brings a bill for discovery of several facts relating to the award and for the relief against it. And the bill particularly charged that this award was not within the Statute 9 Will., ca. [*blank*].[1]

The defendants, as to the award and all matters concerning the same, demur.

But the court overruled the demurrer.

Per MONTAGU: None but an officer can seize. Secondly, an officer cannot make up or cease his prosecution upon a seizure, for, if he does, we will lay him by the heels. Third, they all agreed that this submission and award was not within the Statute of 9 William. Fourthly, if it is only a submission *in pais*, we shall certainly take notice of it where it appears that the crown is prejudiced in its interest and is defrauded by such a submission etc.

And, therefore, the court overruled the demurrer.

292

Abbotson v. Dawson

(Ex. 1722)

A claim of a modus decimandi *in lieu of tithes in kind will not be removed out of an ecclesiastical court after there has been a final judgment there.*

Taussig MS. 311, vol. 1, p. 226

Hilary term 1722.

A suit [was brought] in an ecclesiastical court for tithes. And the party suggests a prescriptive sum of £21 for the land in lieu of tithes in kind and suggests that the prescription is not triable in the spiritual court and, therefore, moves for [a writ of] prohibition. But this was after the sentence.

---

[1] Stat. 9 Will. III, c. 15 (*SR*, VII, 369–370).

And against the prohibition, it was alleged that the party not only pleaded in the ecclesiastical court (Rolle's *Abr.*, 319)[1] this prescriptive right, but also further that he had paid this sum of £21 (Rolle, *Abr.*, 290),[2] whereas he ought only to have relied upon the prescriptive right and so have excepted to their jurisdiction *propter defectum triationis*, whereas here is a sentence against him in the ecclesiastical court and, perhaps, for the non-payment of the sum prescribed for. Here is, therefore, an admission of jurisdiction and a sentence against him. And it is now too late to move for a prohibition, as by the authorities before [cited] and 1 Ventr. 5.[3]

Bootle: The suggestion of a *modus* certainly ousts a spiritual court of its jurisdiction. And payment of the money prescribed for does not alter this. The decree in the spiritual court is for £1 10s. for the value of the tithes so that they have disallowed this prescription and decreed for tithes in kind. One cannot come too late where there is a want of jurisdiction.

PRICE: The court may try it if you submit to a trial, and no prohibition lies.

MONTAGU was of the same opinion and discharged the rule for a prohibition. But MONTAGU seemed to found himself upon this allegation that the party had paid the prescription money.

293

Tyler v. Newton

(Ex. 1722)

The defense of the Statute of Limitations must be asserted by a plea and not by a demurrer.

Taussig MS. 311, vol. 1, p. 228

Hilary term 1722.

A bill [was exhibited] to have an account of rents and profits of an estate, to discover the deeds, and to be let in to redeem the premises.

The defendant demurs because, by the plaintiff's own showing, neither he nor any under whom he claims have been in possession or have had or demanded any account of the rents, issues, or profits out of or from the same for above thirty years, and, therefore, etc.

E contra, the plaintiff has given a good reason for this non-possession or want of demand, his father being in prison and he being a soldier abroad in the wars and he did not return until 1713. Besides, this is not proper for a demurrer, but for a plea, because, by a demurrer, you cut off the plaintiff from any advantage

---

1 *Frizewell v. Anonymous* (1634), 2 Rolle, Abr., *Prohibition*, pl. M, 2, p. 319.

2 *Penneland v. Toye* (1635), 2 Rolle, Abr., *Prohibition*, pl. I, 2, p. 290.

3 *Philipps v. Clever* (1669), 1 Ventris 5, 86 E.R. 5, also 2 Keble 452, 84 E.R. 284, 1 Eagle & Younge 479.

of replying with any proper excuse by way of bar to the fact, and, therefore, in this very case, the plaintiff is forced to supply them by way of affidavits, which is not proper. And this is the reason why a man cannot demur on account of the Statute of Limitations,[1] but he must plead.

And of this opinion was Baron MONTAGU, though Mr. *Browne* insisted that, in the case of Frazier and [*blank*],[2] it was a demurrer, and, by him, a demurrer is proper where the fact is apparent on the face of a bill.

294

Pocock v. Titmarsh

(Ex. 1722)

In this case, the court found that tithes of a house were due.

Taussig MS. 311, vol. 1, p. 236

21 February 1722. Pocock v. Titchmarsh.

The plaintiff, as lessee of the tithes of the rectory of Saint Olave, Southwark, exhibits his bill for the tithe of a house, *viz.* 12s., being, as charged, the customary payment for the house wherein the defendant lived.

For the plaintiff: There is no judicial determination that houses may not pay tithes. Dr. Grant's Case, 11 Rep., and Dr. Leyfield's Case, in Hob. 11 and 12, are that a *modus* may be for a house.[3] And the Statute of Hen. VIII[4] recites that tithes were payable for houses in London precedent to that Act. And so the recital of the Act establishes our first position, *viz.* that there may be tithes for houses. And, if there could not, there would be no maintenance for the rector of several parishes. Evidence was given of fifty years payment of 12s.

Sir Constantine Phipps, contra: [There is] no pretence or suggestion in the bill that there is a custom in the parish that houses pay tithe there, nor does the bill lay such custom in the parish in general, but it only laid a customary payment with respect to the defendant's house and one other house in particular and several other houses in general, which the court thought sufficient. And so the party went into proofs.

N.B. The plaintiff's proof went to certain and fixed sums for houses without any variation for according to the alteration of the rent. And he produced books, by which tithes in this parish had been collected, made in the time of Dr. Maggot.

---

1 Stat. 21 Jac. I, c. 16 (*SR*, IV, 1222–1223).

2 *Frazer v. Moor* (Ex. 1719–1720), see above, Case No. 114.

3 *Graunt's Case* (1613), 11 Coke Rep. 15, 77 E.R. 1165, 1 Gwillim 259, 1 Eagle & Younge 222; *Leifield v. Tysdale*, Hobart 10, 80 E.R. 161.

4 Stat. 27 Hen. VIII, c. 21 (*SR*, III, 552).

Sir Constantine Phipps objected to the evidence that there was not one proof of payment by the tenant of this house. And yet it is not usual to fix down a customary payment or *modus* before a trial at law.

The court decreed an account without the least hesitation.

Bunbury 102, 145 E.R. 610,
1 Rayner 162, 2 Gwillim 630, 1 Eagle & Younge 776

21 February 1721[/22].

A bill was brought for tithe of houses not within the City of London and so not within the Statute 27 Hen. VIII.[1] It was admitted by the plaintiff that this demand was against common right, and he did not allege this payment to be either by custom or prescription, but that this was the only provision for St. Saviour's, Southwark, in right of which church, the plaintiff claimed. It was proved that the houses in the parish had, since the year 1653, generally paid 12s. *per annum*. But there was no proof that the defendant's house had paid for twenty-five years, but by one single witness. Yet the court decreed an account without directing an issue.

Harvard Law School MS. 1082, vol. 1, p. 118

A bill was brought for tithes of houses.

Mr. *Ward*, for the plaintiff, cited Dr. Grant's Case, Lib. 11; Hobart, Dr. Layfield's Case, 10 or 11.

Note: These houses are not within the City of London and so are not within the Statute 37 Hen. VIII. It was alleged for the plaintiff that this payment for houses was the only provision for the rector of St Saviour's, Southwark, under whom the plaintiff claimed. It was admitted this is a demand against common right and the plaintiff had not alleged this payment either to be by custom or prescription. It was proved that the houses in the parish had generally paid for a long time, since 1653, 12s. *per annum*, but there was no proof as to this house of the defendant's having paid within twenty-five years, only by one witness.

Though the proof was so short, the court decreed an account without sending them to an issue.

295

Wilson v. Phillips

(Ex. 1722–1725)

If a London freeman devises more than his testamentary part, his children who claim legacies under the will can take both the legacies and their customary shares. But where he devises his whole estate, the children must make an election to take either one or the other.

[1] Stat. 27 Hen. VIII, c. 21 (*SR*, III, 552).

Making a child a business partner is not an advancement.

Harvard Law School MS. 1082, vol. 1, p. 119, pl. 1

22 February 1722.

A freeman of the City of London, seised of several houses in freehold and possessed of a considerable personal estate, makes his will and devises to the defendant, Rachel Philips, who was wife to the testator, more than the testamentary part. And the plaintiffs, who were the testator's children, by their bill, pray to have their customary part.

Note that two or three of the houses were assigned by the testator in trust for his wife. Note: This cannot be taken to be part of the customary estate. Note: There were several legacies left in the will, and Rachel, in her answer, submits whether she must pay the legacies in the will or distribute according to the custom of the City. Note: The houses were in lease under the parish and the plaintiff insisted that the assignment was fraudulent.

The whole matter was referred to be stated by the Deputy [Remembrancer].

Harvard Law School MS. 1082, vol. 1, p. 231

Easter term 1725.

This came upon the Master's report touching a freeman's will.

GILBERT said that, if it appears on the complexion of the will that the whole estate was devised, then the orphan is to make his election, but, where the third part seems to be devised, which is the testamentary part, and a legacy is given to an orphan, there, the child shall have his share and the legacy over and above the share by the City out of the dead man's part.

Foley, for the defendant: (First point) It does plainly appear by the will that there is an entire disposition of the whole estate. And, therefore, the children ought to be put to their election. And they have offered by their answer to make their election.

(Second point) Whether a son having received his share in his lifetime being raised by being taken in as partner with the testator, whether that being worth £100, that should not be esteemed an advancement.

(Third point) Two houses as to make it part of his estate, which were given by the aunt to the use of the wife, and though not given to the separate use of the wife, if the husband does not dispose of it, *Foley* said it went to the wife by survivorship; so does a devise of any real chattel to a wife.

(Fourth point) Five houses in St. Giles, which the father renewed in trust for the son who paid the fine.

Hungerford, for the plaintiff: John, the son, was sufficiently provided for; so Robert is taken in as a partner, which is a provision. But it may be flung into hotchpot and £100 is proved to be the value of it. [As to the] third point, [what] vested in the wife as a residuary legatee and of consequence vests in the husband so that it ought to be esteemed part of the husband's estate.

Chief Baron EYRE: I do not think that the taking in of son Robert as a partner is an advancement, for the son paid for half the stock, being £13 0s. 0d. Neither do I think the right of renewal [to be] any advancement, not [being] worth anything. This estate so devised by the aunt to the wife of the testator, in all cases at law, it will survive to the wife; if the husband had altered it, it might have been made part of the personal estate. There can be no fraud because, if he had not altered it, then, it would have gone to the wife of course; so it is no part of the husband's present estate. The first consideration as to making the election ought to be further considered.

PRICE agreed.

PAGE: I agree in all except about Robert's renewing the estate, for whatever a stranger would give, that ought to be reckoned part of his estate.

GILBERT agreed. The surrender of a tenant's right of a bishop's lease may be some advantage. But this being a lease just expired, no fine paid for it can be any advantage.

Bunbury 195, 145 E.R. 645

22 April 1725.

A freeman of London makes a will of his whole estate. And now, the plaintiffs, who were his children, come to have the legacies devised to them by the will and also their shares of the customary part. And a debate arising whether the plaintiffs ought not to make their election either to have one or the other, Baron GILBERT informed the court that this point had come before the Lords Commissioners in the Court of Chancery the day before and that Commissioner Jekyll laid this down as a rule observed in equity, that, if a freeman of London devises more than his testamentary part, his children who claim legacies by virtue of such will shall be entitled to both the legacies and the customary share. But where he takes upon him to devise his whole estate, there, they shall make their election to take either one or the other.

296

East India Company v. Hughes

(Ex. 1722)

The court can grant a defendant permission to file a late answer.

Taussig MS. 311, vol. 1, p. 239

Hilary term 1721/22.

A bill was brought for discovery etc. of goods sunk, which the defendant had taken up from the bottom of the sea by a new engine, for which he had a patent.

The [defendant], upon motion, had six weeks time [to answer, and], upon a second motion, further time. And he now moved for a fortnight's further time, and he brought into court a draught of an answer.

And, notwithstanding a strenuous opposition, the court gave way to it without hesitation.

297

Balshen v. Eldridge

(Ex. 1722)

Court costs are lost by the death of the party who is to pay them.

Taussig MS. 311, vol. 1, p. 241

Hilary term 1721/22.

Costs are always lost by the death of the party who is to pay them.

But Mr. *Ward* cited two cases where, upon the death of the party to whom costs are payable, his representative has been admitted to claim the costs, especially where the party to pay the costs consented to the dismission of his bill.

Sed quaere [whether] the executor is not entitled where the party does not consent.

298

Gregory v. Busey

(Ex. 1722)

A commission cannot be granted to demur only, but the defendant may answer, plead, and demur.

Taussig MS. 311, vol. 1, p. 243

Wednesday 11th April 1722. Gregory, administrator of Lambert v. Busey *et ux.*

Mr. *Browne* moved for a commission to take an answer, plea, or demurrer.

Sed per CURIAM: You cannot demur alone, for there is no need of a commission for that, but you may plead, answer, and demur.

299

Blackbourne v. Abbot

(Ex. 1722)

In a suit for a distribution of a decedent's estate, the letters of administration should be pleaded, but, if they are not, it is sufficient for them to be produced to the Master upon the taking of the evidence.

Taussig MS. 311, vol. 1, p. 245

Monday, 16 April 1722.

This cause came on to a hearing upon the bill and answer. And the bill was by the plaintiffs for a distribution of the estate of Dr. Blackbourne. Some of the plaintiffs were brothers and sisters and the representatives of the brothers and sisters of the whole and some of the half blood. And when the plaintiff opened his cause, it was objected that one of the plaintiffs had not shown his [letters of] administration to his principal and, therefore, was not entitled to an account, especially the defendant having laid in his answer that he did not know that he was an administrator.

Sed per CURIAM: You ought to have shown us your administration regularly, but, if they produce it before the Master, it will be more for the advantage of the plaintiffs and defendants than to put the plaintiff to a replication. And so they decreed an account, the plaintiff producing his administration before the Master at the time when he went upon the account.

300

Willett v. Dunmore

(Ex. 1722)

A modus decimandi *in lieu of tithes in kind that is too large in amount is invalid.*

Taussig MS. 311, vol. 1, p. 246

Easter term 1722.

In this case, it was said for the defendant that, in the case of Bishop v. Arundell, Easter 1706,[1] £26 *per annum* was suggested as a *modus* for a farm of £400, and the court sent it to a trial whether there was such a *modus*. The farm here, called Russell's Farm, as the plaintiff says, is only worth £20 *per annum* and 16s. is set up as a *modus* for it. We say the farm is really worth £35 *per annum*, and, therefore, the *modus* of 16s. does not exceed the *modus* before directed to be tried.

But the court decreed an account [for the tithes in kind] without hesitation on the rankness of the *modus*.

---

[1] *Bishop v. Arundel* (1704), Dodd 205, 1 Rayner 98, 1 Eagle & Younge 664, 2 Gwillim 585, 1 Wood 459.

301

Morris v. Marlow

(Ex. 1722)

The court can allow a defendant to file a double plea.

Taussig MS. 311, vol. 1, p. 247, pl. 1

17th April 1722.

The court gave leave to plead *non assumpsit* and a release. The case was an *indebitatus assumpsit* for goods sold and delivered.

And Mr. *Agar* moved it, as above, and the same was granted. And this was not the case of an executor.

302

White v. Hildersley

(Ex. 1722)

A verdict for excessive damages can be set aside and a new trial will be ordered.

Taussig MS. 311, vol. 1, p. 258

Easter term 1722.

A motion was made for a new trial in [an action of] battery for excessive damages, *viz.* £100.

And the Lord Chief Baron [Bury] declaring he thought the damages excessive, the court unanimously agreed to a new trial, though, *per* Baron Montagu, were I to give my opinion upon the circumstances of the case, I think it a very heinous matter. The plaintiff was a seaman and pressed by the Captain [White] and beaten after he was pressed, for which the action was brought.

303

Rex v. Blunt

(Ex. 1722)

A writ of venditioni exponas *does not lie upon an outlawry.*

Where a debt is not in default, the mortgagee not in possession has priority over a subsequent purchaser of the mortgaged land at a sheriff's sale upon a writ of venditioni exponas *upon an outlawry.*

Taussig MS. 311, vol. 1, p. 244

Easter term 1722.

Sir Constantine Phipps moved that Atfield etc. might have liberty to plead to an inquisition on an outlawry against Sarah Blunt, by which inquisition Sarah Blunt was found possessed of a term which was afterwards sold upon a [writ of] *venditioni exponas* and Atfield was a mortgagee of this term under Blunt previous to the outlawry. And, therefore, the motion was that the mortgagee might have liberty to plead to the inquisition after the *venditioni exponas* was executed.

Mr. *Ward*, on the same side, cited Sir Thomas Cecil's Case, [Coke's] Report.[1]

Bootle, *contra*: The inquisition was taken in December, was twelve months [ago]. The *venditioni exponas* was executed in Michaelmas vacation. And everybody is supposed to have cognizance of what is done upon the land. And, therefore, the inquisition is notice itself. The proceedings are regular, and, if the court breaks through them, no purchaser can be quiet and safe.

Reply: The seizure is to those on the land, but not to a mortgagee, for we have had interest paid us by the mortgagor.

Per Montagu: While an inquisition is depending, any person may come in and plead.

Per Chief Baron [Bury]: A sheriff cannot deliver possession upon a *venditioni exponas*.

Per Price: I do not know we ever gave leave to plead after a *venditioni*. As to the notice, records are public and everybody is bound to take notice of them, especially in this case, for a *venditioni exponas* is not like other process, for it cannot be taken out but in term time and upon motion. Move it again on Wednesday next.

Bunbury 104, 145 E.R. 611, Conroy 112

14 April 1722.

Blunt made a mortgage for years to Atfield for £50, of which eight years were to come. Blunt was waived, and a [writ of] *capias utlagatum* issued, and an inquisition was taken thereupon in December 1720, and this term for years was found and sold by virtue of a [writ of] *venditioni exponas*, which issued in November 1721 and was returnable *in octabis Sancti Hilarii*. But no notice was given to the mortgagee, who was not in possession, the interest being regularly paid.

It was, therefore, now moved by *Sir Constantine Phipps* and Mr. *Ward*, on the behalf of Atfield, the mortgagee, that she might be at liberty to plead to the inquisition, not having had any notice, and for that, if she was to bring an [action of] ejectment, in that action, they could not try the validity of the inquisition, for the term is bound by the inquisition and seized into the hands of the crown and the king's title shall not be contested in an ejectment and, therefore, Atfield will be without remedy, unless she be permitted to plead.

---

[1] *Cecil's Case* (1597), 7 Coke Rep. 18, 77 E.R. 440.

In answer to this, it was said by Mr. *Bootle*, that the inquisition itself was notice in law and this method proposed would tend to defeat purchasers for a valuable consideration, who have title by virtue of the sale by the sheriff.

(But note here the mortgagee never was in possession and so could not take notice of the proceedings upon the inquisition.)

And it was also farther objected on the behalf of Atfield, that the *venditioni exponas* was void, for, by the outlawry, the profits only are forfeited to the king, but the sheriff has sold the term itself. And this was a doubt with the court, whether the sheriff can sell a term upon an outlawry, as he may a chattel personal, and as he also may a chattel real upon a [writ of] extent or a judgment. The court seemed inclined to permit Atfield to plead, but they referred it to the Deputy [Remembrancer] to state the fact, that they might more fully consider the matter.

Harvard Law School MS. 1082, vol. 1, p. 122

14 April 1722.

Blunt made a mortgage for [*blank*] years of some houses to Atfield for £50, of which eight years were to come. Blunt was waived, and a [writ of] *capias utlagatum* issued and an inquisition was taken thereon. And this term for years was found and sold upon a *venditioni exponas* without any notice, either of the outlawry, inquisition, or *venditioni exponas* to Atfield, the mortgagee, who was not in possession, the interest being regularly paid.

It was, therefore, now moved on the behalf of Atfield, the mortgagee, that she may now, having discovered these proceedings, be admitted to plead to the inquisitions.

Mr. *Booth* of the other side: The inquisition was taken December 1720.

[To the] objection of notice to be given upon an inquisition taken on an outlawry or extent, [he] responded whoever has an interest in land is supposed in law to have notice of everything done upon the land that affects the land. It is the inquisition they are to plead to, which is above a twelvemonth ago, and they ought not now to be let in to defeat a purchaser for a valuable consideration. By the same rule, the mortgagor would be concluded; in this case, the mortgagee ought to be.

[To the] objection of the Stat. 33 Hen. VIII,[1] [he] responded it does not extend to this case, for this is a proceeding at law upon an outlawry to which the Statute does not extend. See Sir Thomas Cecil's Case, Lib. 7.[2]

Sir *Constantine Phipps* replied: [To the] objection that a seizure of the land is notice, [he] responded it is to those that are in possession, but not to strangers, though the inquisition was a year ago, yet the *venditioni exponas* was but in

[1] Stat. 33 Hen. VIII, c. 39, s. 37 (*SR*, III, 886–887).

[2] *Cecil's Case* (1597), 7 Coke Rep. 18, 77 E.R. 440.

January last, and interest was paid regularly in the meantime. We cannot upon an ejectment try the validity of the inquisition, and, therefore, we have no remedy but this.

Mr. *Ward, pro eodem*: [To the] objection of a rule given in Michaelmas term for a *venditioni exponas*, [he] responded we were strangers to that and could have no notice of it. And interest being regularly paid to the mortgagee, an ejectment will not lie. And you cannot try this matter in that method, for the term is bound by the inquisition and seized into the hands of the crown and the king's title shall not be contested in an [action of] ejectment. The inquisition is not an actual but only a seizure in law. And, by the bill of sale, the buyer is not put into actual possession. Though the *venditioni exponas* be executed, yet the sheriff cannot give possession without an order of this court. Query Hardres' report.

Baron Price: I do not remember. After a *venditioni exponas* and sale made, a party has been admitted to plead. Upon a *venditioni exponas*, they may sell a term. This you cannot have without a motion in court in term time, which is notice of itself.

Baron Montagu: After two nichils returned to a *scire facias*, we have admitted the party to plead.

[It was] adjourned for further consideration.

Harvard Law School MS. 1082, vol. 1, p. 134, pl. 2

5 May 1722.

There was an order that Horten, at whose suit the outlawry was, should show cause why the defendants Atfield [and Blunt] should not be at liberty to plead their matter to the inquisition.

Serjeant *Chesshyre* and Mr. *Bootle* now moved to discharge this order.

Mr. *Bootle*: A purchaser under an outlawry can never be safe if this is to be allowed. The inquisition executed is notice of itself from the notoriety of the proceedings in it. A *venditioni exponas* has issued, and the lands [have been] sold accordingly, and the purchaser has a bill of sale from the sheriff. Now, all this is to be overturned, which is regular and upon record if the mortgagee may be at liberty after so long a time to plead.

[To the] objection they had not notice, [he] responded the sheriff is not to give notice; it is impossible for him to know who is a mortgagee. And where can he give notice?

Sir Constantine Phipps, contra: [To the] objection of hardship to purchasers, [he] responded the court will consider where the greatest inconvenience is. Here is no purchaser for a valuable consideration. We are a mortgagee not in possession, which varies this case, for, if we had been in possession, we should have had notice, which, in our own case, we could not possibly have. He who is the pretender purchaser is the party at whose suit the outlawry was. We can prove they had notice of our mortgage before the *venditioni exponas*. We brought an [action of] ejectment, but before we knew anything of the inquisition or *venditioni exponas*.

Mr. *Ward*: By the outlawry, the crown is only entitled to the profits by the *venditioni exponas*. The term itself is sold. All purchasers for a valuable consideration may be defeated in this method by a matter *ex post facto*. The sheriff can only sell subject to the charge, and, while it remains in the king's hands, it is subject to the charge.

In the Case of Bradnell, 1684, a lease taken by the prosecutor of the second outlawry shall govern the process of this court and have the preference of the first outlawry. This case differs from that where there is an original debt due to the crown. By pleading, we do not put the purchaser in a worse condition than he would have been before. The mortgagees constantly received their interest and could, therefore, have no notice. Lib. 7, Sir Thomas Cecil's Case; David Poole, Michaelmas 1710, in the Exchequer.[1]

Serjeant *Chesshyre* replies: [To the] objection of inconvenience if a party be excluded from pleading as soon as notice, [he] responded the inquisition was December 1720; in Hilary 1721[/22], they had notice of the *venditioni exponas*, which issued November 1721. The *venditioni exponas* was returnable *octabis Hilarii*, and they had notice before that. The sale was 19 January. In the case of an inheritance, where the profits only are forfeited, they cannot be sold, but a [writ of] *levari facias* must issue. But where it is a chattel, a *venditioni exponas* may go as much in the case of a term as a case of personal chattels. And if the outlawry is reversed, there must be a restitution as much as in the case of a [writ of] *fieri facias*.

Mr. *Bootle*: This would overturn all the proceedings that have been upon this extent. Note this is an outlawry upon mesne process.

Baron Price: First, whether when a chattel real is found upon an outlawry upon mesne process, a *venditioni exponas* issues; I think at present it does not lie in this case. There is no distinction where, when it is seized into the king's hands, whether it is a term and when an inheritance. By an exchequer lease of a term, he has only the profits. In a case of a personal chattel, a *venditioni exponas* is very proper. There is great difference between an extent and an outlawry. In the last case, only the profits, in the first, the thing is forfeited. Two nichils upon a *scire facias* is a [*blank*] judgment, and yet the party may be admitted to plead, which is stronger than this case. This is only an interlocutory judgment. He seemed of opinion that the mortgagee ought to be permitted to plead.

Baron Montagu: The difficulties are great, both on the mortgagee and also the purchaser. If we grant liberty to plead, it must tend to overthrow all the proceedings that have been had upon the extent. I had some doubt how this term could be sold upon an outlawry. There is no precedent or authority produced in this case. All that have been are in cases of extents or judgments, but none of a

[1] *Cecil's Case* (1597), 7 Coke Rep. 18, 77 E.R. 440; *Poole v. Attorney General* (1709), Parker 272, 145 E.R. 777, Dodd 217.

venditioni exponas upon an outlawry. The precedents are that no *venditioni exponas* issues until three proclamations have been made in this court. As to the king's interest, outlawry before judgment and after judgment is the same. A *venditioni exponas* was very improper in this case. A *venditioni exponas* is to sell the thing itself, whereas the profits only are forfeited by the outlawry. If this had been upon an extent, I should not have come in to have admitted the party to plead if proclamations had been regularly made. But this case differs, being upon an outlawry. And, therefore, the question will be in this case whether a *venditioni exponas* can issue in this case. And they should have moved for setting aside the *venditioni exponas* for irregularity. But they are not proper for this motion. And he was for having it referred to be examined.

Baron Page: As long as this *venditioni exponas* stands, no [action of] ejectment will lie. If the sheriff had notice of these mortgages, he ought to have found them. It appears now that here is a wrong done to the mortgagee without any fault of his. And, therefore, we ought to give him an opportunity to redress this. He concurred in having it referred to be stated and considered, and he so ordered. But he seemed of opinion that they ought to be admitted to plead.

Taussig MS. 311, vol. 1, p. 290

5th May 1722.

The [writ of] *venditioni exponas* was returned by the sheriff that he had sold the leases for £130 and had the money *paratus*.

The inquisition remained on the record for a whole year before a *venditioni exponas* was issued, the bill of sale from the sheriff, and the money was paid, and the purchaser is in possession. The policy of the law is to quiet possessions. The sheriff cannot take notice of or give notice to mortgagees.

This is a new case, and there is no precedent as I can find.

The inquisition was December 10th and the *venditioni exponas* November 1721. Atfield has received the interest during all this time, even since the inquisition, and so had no notice of this inquisition or the subsequent proceedings.

Second, we can give evidence that the vendee under the *venditioni exponas* had notice of our mortgage though we had no notice of their mortgage. The prosecutor of the outlawry has gone out of the way; he ought not to have taken out a *venditioni exponas* upon an outlawry, for, upon an outlawry, the king is only entitled to the profits and to nothing else. And there is no instance of a *venditioni exponas* upon an outlawry. And the crown is only entitled *quamdiu in nostris manibus*. The prosecutor ought to have taken a lease from the crown.

The mortgagee is not to search for after encumbrances. 1684, in Brudenell's Case and Dewy and Paine's Case, cited in Brudenell's Case.

The lease governs the process of this court. There was no notice to us, for we were not mortgagees in possession. Sir Thomas Cecil's Case, in Sir William Herbert's Case. The government of process is entirely under the direction of the court. David Pool's Case, 1710. This process issues from time to time to levy profits.

Per Serjeant *Chesshyre*: They admit they had notice in Hilary term last, which was when the *venditioni exponas* issued. It is a principle in law that, where no one is bound to give notice, everybody must take notice *quorum* interest.

The *venditioni exponas* issued by the advice of Sir Constantine Phipps. And so I presume this is no novelty. They brought [an action of] ejectment instead of coming in to plead, and they took judgment in ejectment after the time they acknowledge they had notice.

The difference is between a freehold and a chattel interest. In the case of a freehold, the estate is not forfeited, but in the case of chattels, they are *ipso facto* forfeited. In the case of an outlawry, if reversed, everybody knows there is restitution; it is otherwise where there is a sale upon a *scire facias*. And as to inconveniences, there can be no greater inconvenience in the sale of this term than there is in the case of any other chattels.

And if there is any objection to a sale upon a *venditioni exponas*, it must be drawn from the practice of the Exchequer, for there is no principle in law to contradict it. And if this be so, then the only true question is whether the mortgagees have not delayed themselves by not coming in to plead in time before the *venditioni exponas* issued, or at least was executed.

The inquisition is that the party outlawed was possessed *ut de bonis suis propriis* of the lease. Offley's Case, in Hilary and Easter term [*blank*] may.

N.B. This was an outlawry upon mesne process.

The question is whether a *venditioni exponas* is usual on an outlawry.

Second, whether first process of *venditioni exponas* ought not to go, the outlawry does not distinguish between the different interests or estates in law. There is no right to the land in the case of an outlawry. As to an extent and outlawry, they are alike as to mere chattels. This I apprehend is only a pledge, as in the case of a grand or petit cape.

So he was of opinion that the court ought to admit them to plead.

Montagu: The inconveniences, or rather absurdities, are great on both sides. For us to admit them in to plead would be to contradict our own proceedings. It seems to me that a *venditioni exponas* is a very improper process upon an outlawry, both before and after judgment too, because, in truth, the king seizes in this case as upon a contempt to compel the party *ad stand' juris*, which in the case of an outlawry before judgment is to appear; after judgment, it is to pay the debt. And there is a great difference between a horse etc. and leases.

Secondly, there is a difference between process for the king's debt and process for a party, and this is for the party.

And in cases where a *venditioni exponas* is proper, in all the precedents, I can find there ought to be three proclamations; [there was] here only one. One was in hopes to hear cases from the bar, for the true question in this case is certainly whether this process was proper. And that must be made out either by precedents or cases to this purpose in our lawbooks. There is no law or precedent that I can find to authorize such a process as a *venditioni exponas* upon an outlawry. And as I at present am advised, it is wrong. And, therefore, I would have the motion changed and have it turned this way, *viz.* a motion to set aside the sale, etc., but to let them in to plead is to contradict ourselves. And, therefore, I think that the motion is improper. Precedents *sub silentio* are of little value. He would have the precedents looked into and stated.

304

Talamy v. Vivian

(Ex. 1722)

The objection that a bill of complaint calls for a discovery of penalties should be pleaded by a demurrer and not by an answer.

Harvard Law School MS. 1082, vol. 1, p. 120

A bill was brought for the discovering of a quantity of tobacco, where and to what part it was exported, in order that the plaintiffs might have the drawback upon the tobacco according to an agreement. An exception was taken to the defendant's answer, that he does not discover where and what quantity of tobacco was exported and in what ship and whether it was really exported or no. In the answer, the defendant insists that, by this discovery, he may subject himself to penalties. 13 & 14 Car. II, cap. 11.[1]

Note: The penalty in the Act is not waived by the bill.

Mr. *Ward*, for the exception: Knowing or believing that the tobacco was landed etc. does not subject any man to a penalty. But if he was, he should have demurred.

The exception was allowed.

305

Taylor, *qui tam* v. Weeks

(Ex. 1722)

The question in this case was the propriety of the method of granting licenses to settle out of court qui tam *actions for forfeitures.*

Harvard Law School MS. 1082, vol. 1, p. 121, pl. 1

An information was exhibited by A. against Weeks, and, afterwards, a second information was exhibited against the same defendant.

(Note: They were both personal informations for the treble value.)

Before the rules for pleadings to the second information were out, there was a composition on the first information and the fine was rated.

---

[1] Stat. 14 Car. II, c. 11 (*SR*, V, 393–400).

Now, Mr. Attorney General [*Raymond*] moved that this, being a fraudulent practice, might be referred to the Deputy [Remembrancer] to examine and report.

But note he had no affidavit.

This method was objected to, for this is a new extrajudicial and unnecessary method, for, first, here are no affidavits; second, here is no necessity, for there is another method, for the first information is pleaded to the second information and the Attorney General may reply *per fraudem*, which will bring all this matter in issue.

Chief Baron [BURY] and PRICE were for having it examined by the court; MONTAGU, by the Deputy [Remembrancer]. And so Mrs. Page [was]. At last, Mrs. Eyres being examined as a foundation, the court ordered it to be by the Deputy [Remembrancer].

Now the court designs to alter the usual method of granting licenses for compositions, which are as yet taken to be of course and not so much as an affidavit that there is no collusion between the parties and the officer.

306

Warwick, *qui tam* v. White

(Ex. 1722)

The question in this case was whether the Court of Exchequer can grant a writ of execution upon a seizure and information in another court.

Harvard Law School MS. 1082, vol. 1, p. 124

21 April 1722.

Serjeant *Stevens* [moved] for a writ of delivery of a parcel of brandy, value £1200. An information was before the Commissioners of the Excise, who have jurisdiction by the Stat. 6 Geo., to prevent frauds and abuses, fo. 401.[1] There are no negative words to take away the jurisdiction of this court.

Sir Constantine Phipps: The seizure was by one of the officers of the Excise. The goods were carried to the warehouse, and they were seized by the very officers who gave leave to carry the goods there. There are no exclusive words in the Act. They are to be tied up strictly to the words in the Act. They have no power to determine by a jury, which, by common law, is the proper trial of property. There was no bidding [and] no proclamation. There can be no motion in arrest if judgment be there. Though there be a fault in this information, we have no method of getting at it there.

Mr. *Ward*: This case is not within either the words or meaning of the Act and, consequently, is not within the jurisdiction of the commissioners, for there was both notice and permit, as appears by affidavit.

[1] Stat. 6 Geo. I, c. 21.

Mr. *Browne*: We have entered our claim and given security. If [there was] any offense, it is an importation, duties not being paid, which is excepted out of the Act.

Mr. Attorney General [*Raymond*], *contra*: Here is express jurisdiction given to the Commissioners and you shall not come and take that away by denying the fact. But if that is so, that it is not within their jurisdiction, they will determine accordingly. Nothing is depending before this court. If the officer has made a wrong seizure, you may bring an action.

Solicitor General [*Yorke*]: Here is nothing in court to be a foundation for a writ of delivery.

Sir Constantine Phipps answers to this objection, if there be no prosecution, after a seizure, the party comes, though there is nothing before the court, and properly moves for a writ of delivery. It appears in their information that they have not jurisdiction, for it is for removing from one port to another without a permit, which is an unlawful importation.

The court granted a writ of delivery upon giving security.

Taussig MS. 311, vol. 1, p. 255

Easter term 1722.

A motion was made for a writ of delivery for 300 gallons of brandy seized by an officer of the excise, upon which seizure, an information was exhibited before the Commissioners of the Excise. And the information before the Commissioners of the Excise set forth that the goods were carried to a warehouse without notice and were sent up without a certificate. On behalf of the motion, it was said that the seizure is pretended to be by virtue of § 21 of 6 Geo., ca. 21.[1]

1. Proceedings before the Commissioners are not by jury.

2. There was no bidding.

3. There was no motion in arrest of judgment.

4. The Statute has no negative words on the jurisdiction of the Exchequer, but this practice would effectually disappoint this jurisdiction.

Per Baron Montagu: The preamble of the clause seems to be a libel against the Court of Exchequer and its proceedings, and we never saw it before, so that here is one set of the king's servants libeling others of them.

5. All cases of importation without payment of duties are expressly excepted.

6. We have entered our claim and given security, and so we are proper to move for a writ of delivery.

These goods were brought from Portsmouth and landed here in London.

Mr. Attorney [General *Raymond*]: It is impossible to elude the jurisdiction of a court by denying the fact. One may as well deny that any tithes are due and so prohibit. I do not justify the Act, but, while it stands, it must be obeyed. Writs

[1] Stat. 6 Geo. I, c. 21, s. 21.

of delivery are granted here, but then the writs are founded on an information in this court. But, in this case, there is no information in this court. By this Act of Parliament, a new offense is created and a summary jurisdiction is erected thereupon. And it seems to exclude the jurisdiction of this court.

Reply: The judges of Westminster Hall have the undoubted right to construe Acts of Parliament.

This motion is grounded on the same foundation as where a seizure is made. And no information is thereupon filed etc. A defect appears in this jurisdiction of their own showing.

If goods are carried from one port to another without a certificate, this is a cause of forfeiture. And, if there is a cause of forfeiture precedent to the cause of forfeiture here supposed, then this court has the jurisdiction.

Per Chief Baron [Bury]: We ought to see the proceedings.

Per Price: I desire the case may be stated.

Per Montagu: All bringing into port is an importation.

The court made a rule to show cause why a writ of delivery should not be granted and all things to stay in the meantime.

Taussig MS. 311, vol. 1, p. 270, pl. 1

Easter term 1722.

The officer of the Excise now submitted to waive the information *coram* Commissioners of the Excise and to consent to a writ of delivery and to exhibit their information in this court, and so the question of jurisdiction was quieted.

Bunbury 106, 145 E.R. 612

21 April 1722.

Upon the Stat. 6 Geo. *regis*, cap. [*blank*], which gives jurisdiction to the Commissioners of Excise to condemn forfeited goods therein mentioned, this court will hold them very strictly to the letter of the Act, since it breaks in upon the ancient jurisdiction of this court. And, in this case, a writ of delivery was granted for goods seized by their officer, upon giving security, it appearing in the information before them, that the goods were removed from one port to another without a permit, which is an unlawful importation and, therefore, not within their jurisdiction.

Serjeant *Stevens, Sir Constantine Phipps, Ward*, and Mr. *Browne* [were] for the writ of delivery; Mr. Attorney [General *Raymond*] and Solicitor General [*Yorke*] [were] *contra*.

307

Bennet v. Treppass

(Ex. 1722–1726)

In this case, customary payments in lieu of the statutory tithes for houses in the City of London were found to be due.

The account books of a vicar's predecessor in office are admissible in evidence.

Taussig MS. 311, vol. 1, p. 259

Thursday, 26 April 1722.

The plaintiff, as vicar of Cripplegate, brings his bill for 2s. 9d. upon the Statute.[1] Four several *modus*es were insisted upon by the defendants. And the case stated by the counsel[2] was as follows: that the plaintiff, having been vicar of the parish church of St. Giles without Cripplegate at London ever since 4 April 1717, did in Trinity term 5 Geo. [1719] exhibit his bill in this court against the defendants for tithes in London after the rate of 2s. 9d. per pound for the yearly rent of their houses by virtue of the Statute and Decree of 37 Hen. VIII; that the defendant Treppass was on the said 4th of April and has ever since continued an occupier of a house within that part of the parish which lies within London or the liberties thereof of the yearly value £12, Brocket of 16, and Whitchell was occupier of two houses from April the 4th aforesaid until midsummer 1719 at £22 *per annum*.

There is no proof in this cause whether these houses were or any of them was in lease at the time of making the Act or not, nor that the sum of 2s. 9d. per pound was at any time paid according to the value of the houses according to the Statute and Decree of Hen. VIII. It is proved by some of the plaintiff's witnesses in their cross-examinations on the part of the defendants that, until the time of the present vicar, they never heard of any such demand as 2s. 9d. per pound for tithes within the said parish; that, in two ancient tithe books, there appears charged for tithes against the names of the then occupiers of Treppass' house the several sums of 5s. and 3s. 4d. and, in another ancient tithe book, the several sums of 5s. and 3s. 4d. and 2s. 6d. so charged, which last mentioned sums of 3s. 4d. and 2s. 6d. are proved to be the collector's handwriting, and, in another book, the several sums of 3s. 4d. and 2s. 6d. so charged and proved to be the collector's handwriting, but no customary sum, *modus*, or certain sum annually was proved to have been ever paid otherwise than as aforesaid; that, in a book commencing in the year 1708 and ending in the year 1713, Beskett's house is charged 1s. 6d. and Whitchell's houses 1s. each.

It is proved by one Sureties that, for nine years during the time of Bishop Fowler, he lived in Treppass' house and, during that time, never paid more to the vicar than 10s. *per annum* or 2s. 6d. per quarter.

---

[1] Stat. 37 Hen. VIII, c. 12 (*SR*, III, 998–1000).

[2] *Bennet v. Treppass* (26 April 1722), 2 Wood 199.

The question is if 2s. 9d. per pound of the yearly rents of the said defendants' respective houses be due for tithes by virtue of the said Statute and Decree of 37 Hen. VIII or not.

For the plaintiff: If the *modus*es are not proved, then we suppose the decree must be for 2s. 9d. according to the Statute and Decree. 2 Inst. 660; Degg 351; Watson 387; Hard. 116; Littleton's Report, 102, 141; Cro. Car. 596, Anonymous; Hob. 11.[1] In these cases are two questions: first, whether the spiritual court had jurisdiction; second, whether this court had. 7th July 1705, Townly against Wilson, a decree for 2s. 9d.; upon an appeal to the Lords, the case was referred; Sawyer and Muntford, Michaelmas 1694, there was a decree and it was confirmed upon a rehearing; St. Lawrence Jewry, this was settled by Baron Lechmere and Powell; Grant and Cannon, Michaelmas 5 William & Mary, a decree against Cannon; Sheffield v. Serjeant, 1657, St. Swithin's Parish; Humphrevil and Plumsted, in 2 Car. II, St. Botolph without Aldgate.[2] If lands were never let, then it is a *casus omissus*.

Ward, ditto: I cannot apprehend what the question in this case is unless it be a question of the jurisdiction of this court, for, as to the *modus*es, they are out of the case and not proved. And, therefore, in this, as in all other cases, we resort to tithe in kind, which in London is 2s. 9d., for an Act of Parliament may certainly give a right as well as the common law. 16 Jac. I, Ivot and Warren, fol. 408, this is as to jurisdiction; Scudamore and Lambert, 1676.[3]

As to Treppass, his payments are various, and so there is no *modus*.

Edlin, on same side: The Statute is positive. Yelv. 31;[4] unity of possession in an abbey founded within memory does not discharge. He understands the clause of exception to mean a customary payment of a less sum in the pound. And Doctor Bennett could not have had a decree for the customary payment because it is various.

Secondly, whether they were not leased *tempore actus*, the Statute extends to houses to be let afterwards; [there is] a clause for an additional rent. Grant and

---

[1] E. Coke, *Second Institute* (1642), p. 660; S. Degge, *Parson's Counsellor*; W. Watson, *Clergy-Man's Law*; *Langham v. Baker* (1658), Hardres 116, 145 E.R. 408, 2 Gwillim 511, 1 Eagle & Younge 428; *Burgess v. Symons* (1628), Littleton 102, 141, 124 E.R. 158, 177, 1 Rayner 13, 16, 2 Gwillim 433, 434, 1 Eagle & Younge 365, 118 Selden Soc. 565, Paynell Exch. 198, 246; *Anonymous* (1640), Croke Car. 596, 79 E.R. 1113, 1 Eagle & Younge 400; *Leifield v. Tysdale*, Hobart 10, 80 E.R. 161.

[2] *Townley v. Wilson* (1705), Eq. Cases Exch. 517, Western 117, 2 Gwillim 635, Public Record Office, E.126/18, ff. 490, 514; *Sayer v. Mumford* (1694), 1 Wood 324, 1 Eagle & Younge 587; *Grant v. Cannon* (1693), 1 Wood 313, 1 Eagle & Younge 582; *Sheffield v. Serjeant* (1657), Hardres 102, 145 E.R. 402, 2 Gwillim 503, 1 Eagle & Younge 419.

[3] *Ivatt v. Warren* (1618), Western 88, 3 Gwillim 1054, 3 Eagle & Younge 1203; *Scudamore v. Lambert* (1676), Eq. Cases Exch. 81, Public Record Office, E.126/12, ff. 203, 327v.

[4] *Gibson v. Holcraft* (1603), Yelverton 31, 80 E.R. 23, 1 Gwillim 222, 1 Eagle & Younge 156.

Cannon in St. Dunstan's in the West; this case is full in point that newly erected houses in London must pay tithe. Sir Patience Ward and Kidder, 5 William & Mary, St. Lawrence Poultney,[1] the court said the defendant must either prove the customary payment to be immemorial or else must pay 2s. 9d. in the pound. The City of Coventry pays 2s. by the Act in [4 & 5] Phil. & Mary. The City of Canterbury, by an ancient usage, pays 2s. 3d.

It is impracticable to prove that houses now in being were let *tempore statuti*, and, therefore, these words must be understood of the last letting before the demand of tithes.

Chesshyre for the defendant: 2s. 9d. was never demanded nor ever paid. And this is a good argument as evidence of some contrary payments.

As to jurisdiction, I do not think we are at liberty to dispute it.

As to the houses being not leased, that is not fit for us to argue because we have admitted something to be and, if there had not, then it proves that nothing ought to be paid.

But we are under the exception that a lesser sum has been paid; 10s. *per annum* for Trepass; 6 *per annum* for Bockets; 4 *per annum* for each of Whitchell's houses.

There is no contrary proof of these payments. The vicar's own book puts it down at 5s. half yearly. The book charges it. The demand must be the rule and not the sum entered to be actually paid.

And by Serjeant *Chesshyre*: The Act does not require a prescription. There is a great difference between a customary payment and a prescriptive payment.

Fazakerly: It appears by the case that 2s. 9d. has never been paid.

Browne: [Money] never paid is an evidence of a discharge. Town of Warwick and Lucas, Easter 1710.[2] In that case, the court determined non-payment to be an evidence of discharge. Brewster and Arnold, 1713.

Mr. *Wheat* takes notice that the sums entered in the book do not at all interfere with the sums charged, for 3s. 4d. is a third part; 2s. 6d. is half of the sum charged.

Reply: It must be an immemorial custom. We who are plaintiffs are not to prove anything at all. A *non decimando* may be admitted against a lay impropriator, but not against a spiritual person. And the case of Warwick cited by Mr. Browne was the case of a lay impropriator.

By *Sir Constantine Phipps*: No houses in London can be discharged as being part of a monastery because this Statute is subsequent to the Statute for the Dissolution of Monasteries.[3] Whether leased or not leased signifies nothing.

---

[1] *Ward v. Hilder* (1693), Eq. Cases Exch. 336, 1 Wood 305, 2 Gwillim 538, 1 Eagle & Younge 576, Western 103, Public Record Office, E.126/16, ff. 98v, 106.

[2] See *Corporation of Warwick v. Lucas* (1711), Eq. Cases Exch. 671, Public Record Office, E.126/19, ff. 191, 221.

[3] Stat. 27 Hen. VIII, c. 28 (*SR*, III, 575–578); Stat. 31 Hen. VIII, c. 13 (*SR*, III, 733–739).

And this is proved by the exception of noblemen's houses, which are not to pay at all unless leased. It is wholly unusual to ask for an issue after a case is made. The case in Lord Coke is where a house is not nor ever was let. Thirteen or fourteen years are not sufficient to put the plaintiff to a counter-proof.

Per MONTAGU: Suppose, before the Statute, 6d. per pound was payable, it must alter yearly as well as since the Statute because the rent may alter yearly.

Chief Baron [BURY]: 6d. per pound rent is a naughty custom.

Per MONTAGU: The houses were not let at all. The second exception is of a lesser sum. Tithes for houses is only a customary payment and so is not to be governed by the rule before, as is laid down by the [*blank*]. The sum is in gross. It cannot be, by MONTAGU and PRICE.

Per PAGE: It might be 5s. in gross. But it seemed to me that the judges were not at all agreed amongst themselves. The case stated admits variable payments, and the court must go upon it as stated. We must make some decree, but, if not of the statutory payment, then of some other certain rate. But we have no foundation to decree any other rate. Therefore, we must decree according to the Statute. The defendants insist upon 10s., a certain sum, and the court, therefore, can never presume any other.

Per MONTAGU: The objection from the defendants is that they have constantly paid less. And, for my part, I do not understand the case stated. If I did, I would be bound by it.

This he said in relation to what was intimated by the Chief Baron and Price as to the court's being bound by the case.

The court gave no rule, but said they would consider of it.

PAGE: I do not understand the case.

Per PRICE: It is not to be doubted but, if the plaintiff had not produced his books, the plaintiff must have had a decree according to the Decree of Hen. VIII. The Act of Hen. VIII was intended for the benefit of the clergy.

Per PRICE: I was always against *modus*es unless they were very certainly and precisely proved.

Per MONTAGU: We must set all the parishioners upon the same foot.

Bunbury 106, 145 E.R. 612, 1 Eagle & Younge 782

26 April 1722.

A bill was brought by the vicar of Cripplegate for 2s. 9d. per pound, according to the rent of the houses, pursuant to the Decree and Stat. 37 Hen. VIII. And to support the jurisdiction of this court, the Statute giving power to the Lord Mayor of London to determine etc., the cases in the margin were cited: several instances were given, where the 2s. 9d. per pound had been decreed, as the Case of St. Brides, Townley v. Wilson, Michaelmas 1705; Sawyer v. Montford, 1694; Grant v. Cannon, Michaelmas 5 Will. & Mar.; Sheffield v. Serjeant, 1658; St. Swithin's, Humfreville v. Plumsted, Aldgate Parish, 21 Car. II. But the difficulty in this case was that here appeared to have been paid from time to time several payments, at 10s. for Treppass's house, 6s. for Bockett's, and 4s. for Whichett's, and the charges in the vicar's books appeared to be the same, though, in some of them, the payments sometimes varied and the right of the vicar cannot be destroyed but by an uniform, constant payment. See the Statute. This being a thing of great consequence, the court took time to consider of this decree.

In Michaelmas term, 26 October 1722, the court gave judgment.

Baron PRICE [held] that there ought to be a general decree for the plaintiff.

MONTAGU, PAGE, and GILBERT directed an issue to try whether there had been such customary payments as was set up by the defendants [Treppass, Bocket, and Whitehall]. And a verdict was for the defendants.

From this decree Doctor Bennett appealed, and the decree was confirmed.[1]

Sir Constantine Phipps, Mr. *Ward*, Mr. *Edlin*, and Mr. *Bootle* [were] for the plaintiff; Serjeant *Chesshyre*, Mr. *Fazakerly*, Mr. *Browne*, and Mr. *Bunbury* [were] for the defendants.

Harvard Law School MS. 1082, vol. 1, p. 125, pl. 2

26 April 1722.

A bill was brought by the plaintiff as vicar of Cripplegate for 2s. and 9d. in the pound according to the Stat. of 37 Hen. VIII. The defendants insisted upon several *modus*es of 8s. 6d. Upon a case stated, it was admitted that there was a variation as to the *modus* of defendant Trepass of 8s. *per annum*.

Sir Constantine Phipps for the plaintiff: Admitting the *modus*es are not supported, the question is, in what proportion the tithe shall be paid. As to that, it must be paid as the Statute of Hen. VIII directs. The jurisdiction of this court [is] not excluded, there being no negative words in the Decree or Statute. Hardres 116; 2 Inst. 660; Litt. Rep. 102; Degge 351; [*blank*] 141; Watson 387; Cro. Car. 596; Hobart 11.

Instances of a decree for the 2s. 9d. per pound [are] the case of St. Bride's, Townsley v. Wilson, Michaelmas July 1705; Sawyer v. Mountford, 1694; Rector of St. Lawrence Jewry; Grant v. Cannon, Michaelmas 5 Will. & Mar.; Sheffield v. Serjeant, 1657, St. Swithen; Humfield v. Plumstead, Aldgate parish, 4th Car. II.

If the land was always in the hands of the owner, never let, it is a *casus omissus* out of the Act of Parliament. But that is not the case here.

Mr. *Ward*: The *modus*es are void upon the stating in the case. The Statute gives as much a common right to the vicar as the common law gives in other cases to a rector.

[To the] objection that jurisdiction is given by the Statute to the Lord Mayor, [he] responded this objection has often been overruled and the jurisdiction of

[1] *Bennet v. Treppass* (H.L. 1722), 4 Brown P.C. 650, 2 E.R. 442, 1 Rayner 182, 2 Gwillim 633, 1 Eagle & Younge 782.

this court established. Easter 16 Jac. I. J. Wall v. Warren, fo. 408 of the decree book; Scudamore v. Lambert, November 1676 in the Exchequer.[1]

Since various payments have been made by the parishioners, the court will not presume a *modus* decree is in the 37 Hen. VIII.

Mr. *Edlin*: They must either pay according to the Statute or to be at liberty to pay what they shall think fit. Gibson v. Holcroft, Gilbert 31.[2] See the clause in the Act where a less sum has been customarily paid. But that must be an uniform, constant payment, but not various, as in this case.

[To the] objection of no proof that these houses were in lease at the time of the Act, [he] responded it is not at all material, if it after comes to be let, then there is a standard for to go by. Where there is an improved rent, there shall be an additional tithe in proportion to the additions of the rent. Grant v. Cannon, St. Dunstan's; Sir Patience Ward v. Kidder; St. Lawrence Poultney, 5 Will. & M.

Bootle: The Statute refers to another Statute made in the 27th year of Hen. VIII. Noy 130.[3]

Serjeant *Chesshyre*, for the defendant: 2s. 9d. per pound was never demanded [and] never paid. And that will be an argument against the right. The case in Cro. Car. is against the jurisdiction of this court, but the court being in possession, he waived that point of the jurisdiction. If no sums had ever been paid, it would have been an evidence that it never was let, and, then, it would have been exempted by the clause in the Statute. But the case does state several sums were paid for each of the defendants and [there were] no variations but 10s. *per annum* for Trepass, 6s. for Bockett, and 4s. for Whichetts.

He appealed to the entries in the vicar's books where the charge is always the same, but the payment may be different. And he proposed to try the point, whether there ever had been any variations in the charge.

Mr. *Fazakerly*: There is an uniform usage of payment of less sums than given by the Statute. The charge has been always the same. And though there may have been different payments, yet they might be by design. As to Bockett, there was no variation in the payments as well as the charge. By the Act, it is payable quarterly by the charge. Against Trepass, it is only half yearly, which shows they went according to some customary payment and had no eye to the Act. He proposed an issue.

Mr. Browne: It never being paid is an evidence of a discharge. Town of Warwick v. Lucas, Easter Term 1710.

---

[1] *Ivatt v. Warren* (1618), *ut supra*; *Scudamore v. Lambert* (1676), *ut supra*.

[2] *Gibson v. Holcraft* (1603), Yelverton 31, 80 E.R. 23, 1 Gwillim 222, 1 Eagle & Younge 156.

[3] *Meadhouse v. Taylor* (1607), Noy 130, 74 E.R. 1094, 1 Eagle & Younge 172.

These houses were never let. Schidmore v. Bell;[1] Brewster v. Arnold, Michaelmas 1713, no decree. There was no variation as to the payments.

Mr. *Wheat*: These payments cannot be compositions because they admit in the case that 2s. and 9d. was never paid in the parish. The entry of the 3s. 4d. is a third of the 10s. payable by Trepass. Not one of the cases mentioned go upon a customary payment.

Sir Constantine Phipps replies: [To the] objection [he] ought not because [he] never paid, [he] responded the right of the vicar cannot be destroyed but by an uniform constant payment before the Statute [. . .] should be tried. It is no *modus* to try; there was no constant payment by Trepass.

[To the] objection that Bockett and Whichett [were] uniform in payment, [he] responded only for eight or nine years at most and it can be only taken to be a composition.

[To the] objection you do not prove any other payment, [he] responded a plaintiff is never put upon the proof in this court, but the defendant is to make out his *modus*es.

[To the] objection of the Town of Warwick v. Lucas, [he] responded that was in the case of a lay impropriator.

Mr. *Ward*: [To the] objection it does not appear that these houses were in lease at the time of the Statute, the proof lies upon them to show they were not in lease if the fact was so. Besides, the Act must be understood let at the time of the demand made.

[To the] objection of being not paid, the court shall presume a legal discharge. This Statute is since the Act for Dissolution etc., but, if there was any discharge, they should have shown and insisted upon it in their answer.

Mr. *Edlin*: After a case stated, it is usual to go to an issue.

[To the] objection of always 5s. the charge, it is not stated in the case.

[It was] objected by Montagu, if there had been 6d. per pound according to the rent, that may show the reason of the variation insisted upon, according to the rent [which] must be paid according to the rise or fall of the rent, to which Price said it would be material to show that the payment varied as the rent did and also variation of the rent.

Mr. *Edlin*: There is nothing in the clause that lies to the customary payment down to the proportion of the rent; nothing could be intended by this Act but a certain sum.

Price: The customary payment must be before the Stat. 37 Hen. VIII.

Curia advisare vult.

---

[1] *Skidmore v. Bell* (1607), 3 Eagle & Younge 1202, E. Coke, *Second Institute* (1642), p. 659.

Harvard Law School MS. 1082, vol. 1, p. 150, pl. 2

Michaelmas term 1722. Judicium curiae.

Lord Chief Baron MONTAGU: At present, my opinion is, first, the bill is well because it appears that the defendants are inhabitants within the City; second, this demand upon the Statute stands upon an equal foot with a rector's demand at law.

[To the] objection of no compliance with the Act, which has been made above 150 years ago, [he] responded why there has been no practice pursuant to the many decrees that have been produced, but that does not prove that the decrees are of no force. And so is it in the case of the Statute. A practice against a statute can never take away the force of it. What should hinder this Act from taking effect? These houses might have been uninhabited or they might have paid some customary payment. If the defendants could make it appear that there has been a constant payment for each particular house, they say something. But I can never come in to take away the tithes, which is a certain right, without they show something certain in lieu of it.

[To the] objection that lesser sums than the 2s. 9d. per pound have been paid, [he] responded but there was a variation as to the lesser sums and there is not also any fixed time for the payment of those sums.

Baron GILBERT: Customary payments have been equal in the City. This is not a common right of tithing, but it was introduced only by custom. Before the Statute of Dissolutions, the service of the Church was carried on principally by the monasteries, but, after the Dissolutions, the legislature thought fit to provide for the seculars, but not to break in upon the accustomed payments. The custom was to prevail where it had obtained, and the 2s. 9d. was introduced only where it had not obtained. And, therefore, I cannot put it upon the same foot with *moduses* set up in bar of a common right. If there is any doubt as to the custom, the defendant has a right to try it. And he thought there ought to be an issue directed.

Baron PAGE: This customary payment is not in bar to common right. The same Act that gives the 2s. 9d. in the pound saves also the customary right.

[To the] objection the sums are not certain, [he] responded, though in the books, the payments vary, yet the sum in gross amounts to the same, yet at least the payments are so certain as to induce the court to direct an issue to try the custom.

[To the] objection, if you allege this payment as a *modus*, you have not shown at what time it shall be payable, [he] responded this is not strictly a *modus*. The word 'accustomed', I think, is no more than 'usual'. The Act of the Parliament seems to direct the time of payment, and, therefore, it need not be set forth in the answer. The Act says the tithes shall be paid quarterly.

The defendant cannot have any witnesses in the parish because they are all equally concerned. It is not probable that, in so long a time, the several rectors of this parish, who were learned and knowing men, would have waived their advantage the Act has given them if they did not know there was some reason why it should not be paid. How can a rent of a house be a rent beyond the memory of man since it is a thing liable to decay? And perhaps the best rent in the first year of Richard I[1] was not above 5s. He was of opinion that an issue should be directed.

Baron Price: Note the defendants do not so much as offer in their answer to pay the customary payments. The words of this Act are general, and so of the Decree, that all citizens shall pay forever. Calthrop Rep. 63;[2] Linwood [*Provinciale*], 146; Stow's *Annals*, 2d vol. If the defendants cannot show something of their side, why then should not the plaintiff have a decree for his right?

[To the] objection of less than 2s. 9d. per pound has been accustomarily paid, [he] responded I see no difference between this and a *modus*. A *modus* is a customary payment and both must be set forth in certain as to the sum and the time of payment. The defendant does not set forth that he pays a less rate than 2s. 9d. per pound. He only says he pays 10s. *per annum*, but he does not show what the rent is and what proportion the 10s. bears to the rent. If there had been proof of payment of a certain rate eight years before the Act and continued since, I should have taken it to have been an accustomed payment within the Act.

[To the] objection it is proper for a trial, [he] responded can you try a thing not well set forth and what no certainty can be fixed? You do not say it is a customary rate nor when it is to be paid. If it was upon a bill and answer only, there could be no foundation for a decree for the defendants.

He was of opinion against the issue and that the defendants ought to be decreed to pay the 2s. and 9d. per pound.

One defense only was material that they have set forth, *viz.* that they have usually paid less than the 2s. 9d. per pound. The Act used the words 'customary payment' because there could be no *modus* as to houses, for which tithe was not due of common right. I think, since it is doubtful whether there have been these payments, it will be proper that this should be tried by a jury.

Taussig MS. 311, vol. 1, p. 350

Michaelmas term 1722.

Sir Constantine Phipps, for the plaintiff: There are three defendants. No certain sum was paid; there is no proof of any immemorial payments; and so the *modus*es fail.

The books take notice of the Statute. 2 Inst. 660; Noy 130; Degge 351; Hardres 116; Watson 394; Cro. Car. 596. He cites these cases to prove that 2s. 9d. in the pound is demandable. He cites also the several decrees in this court *ut ante* just in the same manner.

---

1 I.e. the time of legal memory.

2 *Dunn v. Burrell* (1617), Calthrop 54, 80 E.R. 672, 1 Gwillim 299, 1 Eagle & Younge 270.

Ward: Though the plaintiff is a vicar, yet he is in this case equal to a rector, the right being established in both by the words of the Act. 'Accustomably paid' in the Statute must be construed immemorial payment, for that is the legal import of the phrase. And here is no proof of any certain payment. Ivot and Warren, 16 Jac. I. And so he insists upon the decrees in this court as a refutation of the argument of disuser of the Act in case that could be admitted to be any argument.

Edlin: Doctor Bennett's predecessors' remissues is no bar against him, and, therefore, the first pretense of non-payment is trifling. Yelv. 31 is like this case. The case of a deed and an Act of Parliament is very different because a deed may be forged.

A customary payment is not proved, and, therefore, this second pretense is void. And this further, the defendants do not allege any certain day of payment and, if that is faulty in a case of country tithes, so it is here, for the Statute vests this sort of tithes in the London clergy as firmly as common right does tithes in specie. Doctor Bennet could not have a decree for any of the customary payments pretended because they are various and uncertain. Sir Patience Ward and Kidder.

As to the third defense, *viz*. that they suppose their houses were not let at the time of the Statute, but, by him, the Statute does not only look towards the then present state of things, but provides for futurity and, therefore, though the house was not let at the time of the Statute, yet if let afterwards or if newly built after the Statute, according to the authority of Grant and Cannon's Case, it shall then pay tithes. And so he concludes that all these defenses are idle.

Bootle, of the same side: The answer was read, and, by the same, it was only insisted upon as a yearly payment without saying payable quarterly or half-yearly. *Lunae*, 11 May 16 Jac. I, Ivot v. Warren *et al.*

Pengelly, pro defendente: I admit jurisdiction. I admit tithes have been demanded under the Statute. But there is not one parish in the City that pays according to the Statute, notwithstanding the several decrees. The case is not like the case at common law, for all the books agree that tithes are not due of common right. And the proviso is coeval with the right of demand. And the proviso must not be understood of a strict *modus*, but only of an usual payment. And the word 'accustomably' is of promiscuous use and must have the same construction as the same word in the Statutes enabling the clergy to let leases.[1] We do not use the evidence as a *non decimando*, but as evidence of payment of a lesser sum.

If, in prohibition, the plaintiff proves any *modus*, no [writ of] consultation can go. So here, if there is any payment of a lesser sum, it destroys the demand of 2s. 9d. Throughout the whole book, 5s. is charged upon Trepass's house. The vicar's acquiescence is so strong an evidence that any, the least, proof will serve. And if this will not serve, it will introduce an infinite confusion in London.

[1] Stat. 32 Hen. VIII, c. 28 (*SR*, III, 784–786); Stat. 13 Eliz. I, c. 10, s. 2 (*SR*, IV, 544–545); Stat. 14 Eliz. I, c. 11, ss. 3, 4 (*SR*, IV, 602).

As to Bocket's case, the book indeed is a new book, but it must be supposed to be made up from an old book.

If the Statute intended a *modus* strictly so called, it would have made use of that term.

Browne: The Statute does not require a *modus* strictly so-called, and, if so, then all the plaintiff's arguments fail. Variation in rent would perhaps vary the payment of tithes, and yet a parochial rate would be a payment within the Statute. In the book, the charge is always uniform. But if it had been various, it is answered before. And non-payment is an evidence against the statutory right.

Fazakerly: A weak evidence is better than none, and they have none. The inhabitants in London are fluctuating and changing habitations. And no man knows anything of it but the party himself who pays it, which occasions difficulty of proof. I do not know that the Act of Parliament has ever been extended to houses on a new foundation. He doubts whether the Statute and Decree extend to this parish, which is partly within the City and partly without.

Sir Constantine Phipps: The court cannot take notice of any non-observance of former decrees, for the church may accept of other payments. If no tithe is due at common law, that is an argument for us, for, then, we can have no tithe if not the Statute tithe. Custom is a term of art. The Serjeants' Case, of prohibition, may be law, but it would be otherwise in the case of an English bill here if the verdict should find another *modus* than that insisted upon by the answer. Aldgate is part in London and part out of London. And there is a decree in point against Mr. Fazakerly's last notion.

The Court adjourned the rest of the reply to the next day.

Friday 26.

Ward, in reply, insists the word 'accustomed' as applied to tithes signifies *modus* and so it is to be understood in the Statute of *Circumspecte Agatis*. Moor 912.[1] The charge in the book is not the evidence of a customary payment, but the payment that is made in pursuance of the charge that is the proper evidence of the customary payment. He insists that the defendants have not set forth their payment to be a customary payment nor how and when payable.

Edlin: The words in the Statute of Leases are 'most accustomably reserved', which word 'most' shows that the word 'accustomably' must not be understood of immemorial custom.

Bootle [argued] to the same purpose.

Chief Baron Montagu: We are only to regard the right without considering the consequences. I do not design finally to give my opinion, but I desire to have the assistance of my brothers' thoughts.

The Act extends to all citizens. This bill stands as fairly before us as if it were founded on a canon law right. And the plaintiff's being a vicar is no objection.

---

[1] Stat. 13 Edw. I, *Circumspecte Agatis* (*SR*, I, 101–102); *Green v. Piper* (1592), Moore K.B. 912, 72 E.R. 992, Croke Eliz. 276, 78 E.R. 531, 1 Gwillim 164, 1 Eagle & Younge 105.

The Act of Parliament was made so many years ago, and yet it was never put in use. But non-practice on the Statute or non-pursuance of decrees in this court are no argument against the validity of the Act. But yet total neglect gives some suspicion of a latent reason. And the proviso in the Statute seems to be the reason. Whether a lesser sum goes through[out] the parish or only extends to the particular houses is not material. I am of Hobart's opinion never to destroy the Act without setting up the certainty of something else. And that is the point, whether the defendants have set up any certain payments.

He thinks the evidence of the several sums squares well with the 10s. set up.

Mr. Baron Gilbert: I believe customary payments have been usually paid in London. This appears by the Act itself. And, by our law books, houses pay no tithes but by custom. Before the dissolution of the monasteries, the service of the church was carried on by monastics. The Statute was never designed to destroy the old payments, and, therefore, the 2s. 9d. does not affect any houses which were affected by the customary payments. And as the Statute separates the houses, so I must keep the [*blank*]. And, therefore, I cannot think this is like the common case of a *modus*, for, here, the right of usual payment is previous to the Statute. And, therefore, I think the defendant has a right to try whether his case stands upon the old foot before the Statute or whether he must be tied down by the Statute. So he was for a trial.

Page: The defendant has insisted upon the right point of defense. If here was an established customary payment, then the Act gives him no right to 2s. 9d., for, then, the Act does not extend to this case. I think the books are certain enough to prove a certain payment. If not, I think it ought to be tried. The demands in the books seem entirely agreeing with the sums insisted on by the defendants. The 3s. 4d. and 2s. 6d. in the books are of the receiver's hand and so does not break the uniformity of demand.

As to the time of demand, the Act of Parliament [*blank*]. The word 'accustomably', I think, cannot be understood as usually; nor do I think it means immemorially neither, but that the word must be construed by the rule of the spiritual [law] or by reference to the rule of that court.

The Act of Parliament enacts that the old payments shall continue so that this does not only come in by way of the proviso. I think that the Act of Parliament fixes the time of customary payments as well as of the 2s. 9d.

I think it doubtful whether any inhabitant of the parish can be a witness in this case, though Sir Constantine thinks otherwise.

Houses change tenants. And this makes proof difficult. And, therefore, I think non-payment of 2s. 9d. is considerable evidence in this case. And, accompanied with a small proof on the other side, it will be sufficient. If nothing had been paid, that had been another case. But here, the vicar has received something, and that is not what the Act requires, but lesser payments.

No instance of 2s. 9d. is charged in the book. And I cannot think the Doctor's predecessor's charity extended so far as to give up his right to the rich as well as the poor. Accustomed rent is mentioned in the Act, but surely no one can understand this of immemorial rent to the time of Richard I.

Accustomed rent I understand as rent acquiesced in. However, if this payment be doubtful, I think we must direct a trial and we cannot tie down the inheritance without a trial.

Price: The defendants do not offer the lesser sums which they insist upon in their answer. The intent of the Act is to appease and quiet dissention, and it is in favor of the clergy. Lindwood [*Provinciale*], 146; Stow's *Chronicle*, 2 vol.; Chamberlain of London's Book.

The ancient customary payments did not amount to less than 2s. 6d. Coventry and Canterbury have customary payments as well as London. He looks upon the Act as common right and decrees according to it.

Customary payments are not well set forth as a customary payment. I do not see any difference between a *modus* and a customary payment. There is no time certain when they are to be paid.

In the next place, he does not say according to what rate he pays. And the Statute extends only to a pound rate. But he only says 10s. without applying it to any rate, only a lump.

The Act says, 'if any parish or place', and, therefore, it does not seem to me that the Act relates to every particular house. I do not put it upon an immemorial custom, for the Statute speaks of eight years before the Statute. And, therefore, I understand 'accustomed' to mean ancient and usual. The question is whether you are within the Act or no. And what we must send to a trial here is nothing certain set up.

Lord Chief Baron Montagu: All agree the Stat. of Hen. VIII is a subsisting law. All agree that the allegation of a lesser sum is the only defense. And all agree that something must be paid, either a lesser sum or 2s. 9d. Two of my brothers are satisfied that there has been payment and that is not possible to be controverted, but whether the payments are certain and this case is like a *modus*. In a *modus*, the pleader confesses and avoids. The Act of Parliament could never mean a *modus* because a *modus* could never be of tithes of houses from the eight years before the Statute. If the defendant makes out a lesser payment, he rebuts the Act of Parliament; the law affects him not.

I agree with my brothers that something has been paid. And I think it ought to be ascertained by a jury what. I think a lump, as my brother calls it, is within the Statute as well as rates. And, therefore, I think we should direct an issue to try, in the words of the Act, whether and what less than 2s. 9d. in the pound has been accustomably paid.

Bunbury 143, 145 E.R. 626,
1 Rayner 181, 1 Eagle & Younge 787

31 January [1724].

An issue was directed in this cause to try whether there had been any variation in the payment of tithes, or sums of money in lieu of them, for houses in London, according to the Stat. 37 Hen. VIII.

It was now moved that the plaintiff should produce at the trial the books of the former rectors. And, although it was objected that these were properly private books and the plaintiff's own evidence, yet, as they had before been produced at the hearing of the cause and as the issue to be tried is to inform the conscience of the court, the jury ought to have all the light the court can give them.

So, *per* CURIAM, the plaintiff was ordered to produce these books at the trial.

Harvard Law School MS. 1082, vol. 1, p. 195, pl. 3

Hilary term 1723/24.

A motion was made by the defendants to have books produced upon an issue directed out of this court, which said books were used at the hearing of the cause and were the former parsons' books of the parish of Cripplegate.

Chief Baron [EYRE] was for the motion.

PRICE doubted because they seemed to him to be private books.

PAGE: I am for granting the motion because this was concerning facts before the hearing and, this issue being to satisfy the conscience of the court, all things ought to be produced. And he said that he did not call these private books.

GILBERT agreed.

So the court ordered these books to be produced at the trial.

Taussig MS. 311, vol. 1, p. 590

Hilary term 1723/24.

A motion was made *per Pengelly* upon notice that the Doctor should produce on oath all books that came to his hands since he was the vicar of the parish, that the books should be produced at trial, and the defendants should have liberty to inspect the books four days beforehand.

Per Lord Chief Baron [EYRE]: The difference is between public and private books.

And by him and PAGE and GILBERT: A book kept by the parson only for regulating his own collection is a private book. But a book which is kept for entries between him and the parishioners is in the nature of a public book. But whether the books here are public or private, they having been produced at the trial and the defendants' ought to inspect beforehand and so, as to these books, they were ordered to be put into the hands of the plaintiff's clerk in court and the defendants to have access to them and the books to be produced at the trial.

Taussig MS. 311, vol. 1, p. 622

Thursday, 13 February 1723[/24], *coram* EYRE, Chief Baron, at *nisi prius*.

The issue was directed in this cause now to be tried, and it was this, *qu[. . .] aliqua denaria [. . .] quam duo solidi et novem denarii per libram pro qualibet libra de annualo reddito sive ann[ual]o valore separatum messuagiorum praedictorum respective customarie solute fuit pro decimis cujuslibet messuagiorum illorum.*[1]

The defendants, as to the house of Trepass, proved the payment of 2s. 6d. per quarter for that house of the yearly value to be let £12 about forty years ago, by a living witness who knew the house in the possession of one Captain Buggins and that it then paid the sum of 2s. 6d. per quarter for tithes to the vicar. And this 2s. 6d. per quarter had been paid for the same house for twelve or thirteen years last. It was also proved by a living witness who had collected it for Doctor Fowler, who was the bishop of Gloucester and the vicar of that parish. And it stood charged at 2s. 6d. in the later books, by which the vicar's collector gathered tithes.

And the *modus* of 6s. for Bocket's house was also proved to be paid, *viz.* 1s. 6d. per quarter for about twenty-three years last past, by a living witness. And it stood charged in the same book at that sum of 1s. 6d. per quarter. This house was let at £22 *per annum.*

The *modus* of 4s. *per annum* was also proved to have been paid, by a living witness, for each of Witchell's houses for about sixteen years past. And they likewise stood charged in the said books at 1s. per quarter.

Sed nota none of these books were older than 1700.

E contra, the Doctor proved by other books of the same nature, but beginning in 1673, that, as to Trepass' house, when in Buggins' possession, there was a charge of 5s. and under it 3s. and 4d., both which he would have understood to have been quarterly charges and so a variation from the *modus.* But all the books were so unintelligible that scarce anything certain could be collected from them. And there was no pretense to prove by any living witness that any other sum had been actually paid for any of the houses than what the defendants insisted upon.

And so *per* Chief Baron [Eyre], the jury shall take out all the books and consider them. But I do not see anything directly proved by them contrary to the testimony of living witnesses. As to Witchell's two houses, the Doctor would have proved them lately built on new foundations, but his own witness, who was called for this purpose, said there were old sheds and workhouses belonging to the houses which stood on the ground whereon they were built. And so he failed in this point.

And after a trial of five hours, the jury found the several *modus*es insisted on by the defendants.

Et nota it was agreed on all hands by the witnesses that there had been no payment or even a demand of 2s. 9d. per pound.

[1] . . . as 2s. 9d. per pound for any pounds of annual rent or ann[ual] value of the several messuages aforesaid respectively customarily was paid for the tithes of any of their messuages.

And by the CHIEF BARON, this sort of evidence is the only evidence that can be expected at this time of day to prove that the houses paid less than 2s. 9d. per pound at the time of the Statute, as in the case of bishops' leases, which, by the Stat. Hen. VIII,[1] must have such a rent reserved as they had been accustomably let for the greatest part of twenty years last past. We never expect they should give evidence of the rent reserved before the Statute.

Gilbert Rep. 191, 25 E.R. 133,
1 Eagle & Younge 784, Western 125

[1726]

The case is that the plaintiff having been vicar of the Parish Church of St. Giles's without Cripplegate, London, ever since the 4th of April 1717, did, in Trinity Term 5 Geo. I [1718], exhibit his bill in this court against the defendants for tithes in London, after the rate of 2s. 9d. per pound, according to the yearly rent of their houses by virtue of the Statute and Decree 37 Hen. VIII. The defendant Trespass was on the said 4th of April and has ever since continued an occupier of an house within that part of the said parish which lies within London or the liberties thereof of the yearly value of £12, Bockett of another of £16 *per annum*, and Whitehall of two houses from April the 4th aforesaid until Midsummer 1715 at £22 *per annum*.

There was no proof in this case whether these houses were, or any of them was, in lease at the time of making the Act or not, nor that the sum of 2s. 9d. in the pound was at any time paid according to the value of the houses according to the Statute and Decree of Hen. VIII. But, it is proved by some of the plaintiff's witnesses in their cross-examinations on the part of the defendants that, until the time of the present vicar, they never heard of any such demand as 2s. 9d. per pound for tithes within the said parish, that, in two ancient tithe books, there appears charged for tithes against the names of the then occupiers of Trespass's house the several sums of 5s. and 4s. 4d. and 2s. 6d. so charged, which said sums of 4s. 4d. and 2s. 6d. are proved to be the collector's handwriting, but the 5s. is of another handwriting, and, in another book, the several sums of 4s. 4d. and 2s. 6d. so charged and proved to be the collector's handwriting. But no customary sum, *modus*, or other certain sum was proved to have been ever paid than as aforesaid. [It was proved] that, in a book commencing in 1708 and ending in the year 1713, Bockett's house is charged 1s. 6d. and Whitehall's houses 1s. each.

It is proved by one Sureties that, for nine years during the time of Bishop Fowler, he lived in Trespass's house and, during that time, he never paid more to the vicar than 10s. *per annum, viz.* 2s. 6d. per quarter.

The question is if 2s. 9d. per pound of the yearly value of the said defendants' respective houses be due for tithes by virtue of the said Statute and Decree of 37 Hen. VIII or not.

[1] Stat. 32 Hen. VIII, c. 28, s. 2 (*SR*, III, 785).

For the plaintiff, it was argued that the sum of 2s. 9d. in the pound ought to be paid by the Decree on the Statute of 37 Hen. VIII, c. 12, and they looked upon that Statute to be the general law of tithing in the City, and that, if the defendants could not set up a *modus* or composition whereby it appeared that they paid less, that this rule of tithing ought to take place. And they made several objections to this *modus* set up by the defendants, as:

First, that it was not proved to be time out of mind, and nothing less than an immemorial custom ought to be a bar against a common right;

Secondly, it was not set out that the *modus* was paid annually or half-yearly, and, if the particular time of the payment of a *modus* be not set out, that *modus* is not well pleaded nor is it a good bar. And the reason is because the original agreement must be certain [so] that the person may know when and what to demand. But here, there was no time set forth in this *modus*, and, therefore, it could be no good bar, nor was the *modus* tendered to the plaintiff.

In this case, they quoted for the plaintiff a decree in the 16 Jac. I [1618–1619], wherein the court had decreed 2s. 9d. in the pound; and likewise the case of Sheffield v. Sergeant, in Michaelmas 1657; and likewise the case of Humfrevill v. Plumstead, Trinity 26 Car. II [1684–1685]; Grant v. Cannon, Michaelmas 5 Will. & Mar. [1693]; Sir Patience Ward and others v. Kidder, 5 Will. & Mar. [1693–1694]; Sayer v. Munford, Michaelmas 6 Will. & Mar. [1694]; and the case of Townly v. Wilson, 7 July 1705, in all which cases, the court had decreed the sum of 2s. 9d. per pound according to the said Statute and Decree.

And Mr. Baron Price, who was of opinion for the plaintiff, said the Statute was thought to be in derogation of the rights of the clergy, for it appears by Linwood, 201, and by Stow that the laity used to pay ½d. in the pound to the clergy upon every Sunday and Holiday, which came to a greater sum than 2s. 9d., *viz.* 3s. 5d. per pound.

But it was resolved by the other three judges that the case upon this Statute was not like a *modus*, for the decree in the Statute is that all houses within the City of London and liberties shall pay 2s. 9d. for every 20s. rent; and then comes the provision in the 18th Section, 'Provided also and it is agreed that, where any less sum than 2s. 9d. in 20s. rent has been accustomed to be paid for tithes, that then in such places the said citizens and inhabitants shall pay only after such rate as has been accustomed.'

Now, they said it was plain by the Statute itself and by the citation before mentioned in Linwood that, in many places in the City, there had been a custom to pay tithes according to the pound rate and these the Statute never intended to alter or enlarge, but to establish, for the Statute was not designed in destruction of any settled right. Nay, they took it farther that, if there had been a payment of lesser sums by agreement between the parson and parishioners, they were confirmed by the Statute because it was the design of the Statute to settle such customary payments. And it was their design that they should not be unravelled on either side, and, accordingly, such customary payments and agreements have been complied with ever since the Statute, and that lesser sums have been paid by almost every parishioner to the parson and therewith they have been content. And although several decrees have been made in this court for the payment of 2s. 9d. in the pound, yet no customary payments in any parish have been set aside or broken through, but these matters have been compounded between the parties, and the manner of tithing has continued the same in each parish, except in such parishes as are otherwise regulated by the Statute 22 Car. II, c. 15.[1]

They said that the 18th Proviso was a perfect exception of all those that had paid lesser sums out of the Decree and, therefore, this could not be urged as a *modus* or set up in bar of tithes, for tithes were originally due, and, therefore, the bar must be complete. But there are no tithes of houses due of common right, for they are none of those things that *renovare in annum*, and, therefore, the common law, which followed the Levitical[2] pattern, did not make them tithable. And, therefore, they are tithable only by custom or agreement where there have been such customs and agreements.

The new rate of 2s. 9d. per pound was super-induced by the Decree. And it is a strange thing to say that the Decree was in prejudice of the clergy when it appears that less sums are now constantly paid for houses in the City than what would be paid if they were rated under the Decree.

And note it appears the ancient payments in lieu of tithes of houses in London were somewhat less than 2s. 6d. per pound.

But it plainly appears that, before the dissolution of monasteries, a great deal of service in London was performed by the regular priests, who not only said their masses, but visited the sick and performed offices of devotion in many parts of the City. And when they were extirpated, this duty fell upon the parochial clergy. And then, it was necessary that their maintenance should be increased, and, therefore, this Decree was made that all persons should pay the received rents from houses, that is, where there had been accustomed payments, the tithes were to continue payable according to that custom, and, where there was no immemorial custom, yet, if there had been by agreement etc. a payment for eight years past, this, according to the frame of the Statute, is to be looked upon as a customary payment, for the divisions and severances of the houses, wharfs, and warehouses were to be as they had been for eight years past, so that the construction seems to be that, if there had been an agreement to pay tithes for eight years past, they were accustomed payments within the Statute. And this will form an uniform notion that, if there were tithes, by custom or by agreement, for eight years past, they are within the 18th Proviso of that Statute. But where there were no such accustomed payments, there, the Statute is introductive of a new law and lays the charge upon all others to pay 2s. 9d. in the pound.

---

[1] Stat. 22 & 23 Car. II, c. 15 (*SR*, V, 725–727).

[2] Leviticus, chap. 27, verses 30–33.

As to the objection that there was no particular time of payment alleged, Baron Page said that the Statute, by the 11th Proviso, had appointed the payment of tithes quarterly and, therefore, it need not be set out in the bill as the authorized payment.

But it seems doubtful whether that Proviso extends any farther than to the 2s. 9d. mentioned in the Decree, and not to the accustomed payments mentioned in the 18th Section of the Act.

But in this, all the three judges agreed that they were not obliged to set up these customary payments as *modus*es in bar of tithes, for these customary payments are exemptions out of the decree, and, therefore, in what manner soever they have been paid, if there has been a customary payment since the Statute of a lesser sum, they cannot be bound by the Decree to pay 2s. 9d. per pound.

Now, if all that pay less sums be exempt from payment under the Decree and are not within the Decree nor within the obligation of the Statute, we ought to try whether there be such accustomed payments or not, especially since, in this case, it appeared by the books of the parson that less sums were collected and it could not have been presumed that they would have collected in that manner if they had not been the old accustomed payments, for how could those sums have come into the parson's books if they had not been the old accustomed dues. And the difference of the payments in the books may be reconciled by supposing some of the to be quarterly, some half-yearly payments.

This case relates to the inheritance, and the inheritance is to be bound by our decree. And where the inheritance is charged merely by custom, it is usual and just, if the parties desire it, to try such custom at law.

Therefore, the court directed an issue at law to try whether any less sum than after the rate of 2s. 9d. in the 20s. rent had been accustomed to be paid by the defendants for tithes and what such sum was.

In this case were quoted 2 Inst. 660; Noy 130; Hardres 116; Watson 387 to 399; Cro. Car. 596; Yelverton 31; Moore 912; Coke 15, Grant's Case.[1]

From this decree, the plaintiff appealed to the House of Lords, where the decree was (*dissentiente clero*) justly affirmed.[2]

[Order of 26 October 1722: 2 Wood 197.]

---

[1] *Graunt's Case* (1613), 11 Coke Rep. 15, 77 E.R. 1165, 1 Gwillim 259, 1 Eagle & Younge 222.

[2] *Bennet v. Treppass* (H.L. 1722), 4 Brown P.C. 650, 2 E.R. 442, 1 Rayner 182, 2 Gwillim 633, 1 Eagle & Younge 782.

308

Lady Carrington v. Cantillon

(Ex. 1722)

Service of process on an agent who is a business partner is valid service on the principal.

Bunbury 107, 145 E.R. 612

Eodem die [26 April 1722].
Cantillon, senior, and Hughes were partners in France. Cantillon, senior, withdrew and put in his nephew, a child of eight years old, into the partnership. A bill was preferred against the two Cantillons, Hughes, and Lady Herbert to have an account of ninety-three actions and eighty primes deposited in Cantillon's and Hughes's hands, as a security for Lady Herbert.
The defendant Cantillon, senior, in his answer, admits that he is agent for Hughes.
And it was now moved by Serjeant *Pengelly*, on the behalf of the plaintiff, that service of the subpoena upon the Cantillons or their clerk in court may be deemed good service as to Hughes, who was then abroad in France,
And *per* TOTAM CURIAM, the service was allowed, as was done in the case of Furnes v. Lawes, the service on the brother here being allowed, Mr. John Lawes being in France.
Serjeant *Chesshyre* [was] for the defendants.

Harvard Law School MS. 1082, vol. 1, p. 128

Serjeant *Pengelly* moved that service of a subpoena upon Cantillon, senior, [one] of the defendants (or his clerk in court) may be good service as to Hughes, the other defendant. Cantillon, the elder, and Hughes were partners in France. Cantillon, senior, withdrew and put in his nephew, a child of nine years old into the partnership. The bill was to have an account for primes and actions deposited in their hands as a security for £25,000 for Lady Mary Herbert. Cantillon, senior, admits he is an agent for Hughes. See Furnes v. Laws. Hughes and Cantillon had orders to dispose of these primes and actions as soon as ever they were deposited. The words of the answer were 'was to be accountable for the said bills as agent or correspondent only and not as partner'.

Serjeant *Chesshyre, contra*: It appears that Lady Carrington is proceeding against Cantillon for these primes and actions in France.

Per TOTAM CURIAM, such service was allowed.

309

Attorney General, ex rel. v. Starkey

(Ex. 1722)

An injunction lies to an ecclesiastical court to stay proceedings there in a case where that court has no jurisdiction in a matter involving the crown's title.

Harvard Law School MS. 1082, vol. 1, p. 127

27 April 1722.

Mr. Attorney [General *Raymond*], at the relation, moved for an injunction and that it may extend to stay proceedings in the spiritual court of Richmond in the County of York. The question will be first upon the constructions of deeds, the construction of which properly belongs to the common law; second, the relator is only a lessee, the inheritance is in the crown; third, whether the lands are extra-parochial, which the spiritual court cannot try; and fourth, whether they are forest lands, which they cannot try.

Mr. *Bootle*, *contra*: He distinguished between an injunction and a [writ of] prohibition, that by this method the question will amount to a prohibition which inverts the order of proceeding. See the former book, Jennings v. Althrop; Lib. 5, Jeffrey's Case.[1] They ought to have taken the proper method (if the spiritual court cannot try it), which is by prohibition which will bring the matters properly in issue by a trial by jury.

Sir Constantine Phipps replies: [To the] objection of Althrop v. Jennings, [he] responded we are here in the case of the revenue, which the other case had no relation to.

[To the] objection that it is proper for a prohibition, [he] responded perhaps we may have a decree without directing any issue.

Chief Baron Bury and Baron Price were for an injunction.

Baron Montagu: Mr. Starkie must make his title in the court where he is suing for the tithes. If the bounds of the parish are denied below, it must be tried in the courts of common law. The question is whether they are proper here to move for an injunction. And he thought not.

Baron Page: The occupiers are parties below, but they are not parties in the information here. And if we should grant an injunction, it would stay proceedings as to parties that are mere strangers. He thought a prohibition the more regular way.

The court were divided, and, therefore, no injunction could go, it being a matter doubtful.

---

[1] *Abthorp v. Jennings* (Ex. 1718), see above, Case No. 55; *Jeffrey v. Kenshley* (1589), 5 Coke Rep. 64, 77 E.R. 153.

Montagu and Page, upon their agreeing to speed the cause, came in to grant the injunction.

What seemed to have great weight was that the revenue of the crown was concerned.

Taussig MS. 311, vol. 1, p. 267

27th April 1722.

[There was a] grant to Starkie and his heirs of the wapentake of Longsdale and the priory and parish of Lancaster. And he exhibits his suit in the ecclesiastical court of Richmond for the tithes of Quarmore Town and Quarmore Park. And the defendants below, as lessees of the crown, exhibit their bill here setting forth their lease and title under the crown and suggesting the places where to be a part of Quarmore Forest and extra-parochial. And upon this bill, they obtain an injunction here *pro defectu responsum*.

And the Attorney [General, *Raymond*] now moved for a continuance of the injunction upon these reasons, *viz.* because:

1. The question is parochial or extra-parochial, which is a question not triable in an ecclesiastical court;

2. The title upon both sides depends upon the construction of patents and deeds, which the spiritual court is no judge of;

3. The title of the crown is concerned, the crown being in reversion after the lease of the plaintiffs in this court, and they are obliged by an express covenant in their lease to defend the crown's title.

Per Bootle, contra: This is an English bill instead of a prohibition.

He admits that [the issue of] parochial or extra-parochial is not triable by the ecclesiastical court, but that is not the true question here.

Secondly, no prohibition lies for the second reason, for the ecclesiastical court may determine of deeds, but they must construe them by the rules of the common law and it is time enough to apply for [a writ of] prohibition when they act contrary.

Third, the injunction is new and ought not to be granted because it is an innovation.

Starkie: The ecclesiastical court may maintain their jurisdiction in a case where the crown is a party, as in other cases. Secondly, where lands are disafforested and granted to a subject, they are liable to tithes.

By the Attorney [General *Raymond*]: A prohibition is certainly very proper to restrain excess of jurisdiction, and an injunction [lies] to stay them when there is a suit exhibited in another court which is more proper to try it in, as the Court of Chancery grants injunctions in cases of suits for legacies and distribution of estates among creditors, etc.

Per Sir Constantine Phipps: The crown, in a case of a question of its own revenue, may certainly enjoin and is not bound to proceed by a prohibition. The suit against the ecclesiastical court is against the relators and against the occupiers also of those tithes.

Chief Baron [Bury] was for an injunction. (The reasons *non audivi.*)

Price, ditto: This is the common case of a bill for tithes, for that is the end of the bill, and the right of tithes goes along with the title *et e converso.*

Per Montagu: Mr. Starkie is already in a very proper court which has jurisdiction. The relators here say that the tithes demanded are not within Starkie's parish, and it is true. If this comes there to be suggested, then a prohibition must go *causa triationis*, but it seems to me that the relators here upon their present bill be only entitled to a discovery of Starkie's title.

Per Price: The crown may choose its own court.

Sed per Page: I do not know whether the crown can on behalf of lessees take away the right of another to sue them in a proper court.

Montagu and Page, though they seemed against the injunction at first, at last consented.

And an injunction was granted to stay the suit until the hearing of the cause.

310

Shaw v. Maxey

(Ex. 1722)

A court of equity can relieve against a contract and a bond where the other party has failed to perform his obligation.

Harvard Law School MS. 1082, vol. 1, p. 129

28 April 1722.

A bill was brought to be relieved against a South Sea contract. A contract was made for £2000 stock at £700 on 13 June 1720 to be paid upon transferring. The transfer was to be at the next opening of the books, which happened the 22nd August. The defendants had no stock then, but had long annuities subscribed, which were not then transferable. And it was insisted for the plaintiff [Joseph Shaw], for that reason that, by the Act of Parliament, it was a void contract. Upon the 5th of October, when the stock was at £270, the defendants [Hunt Maxey *et al.*] had stock to transfer, but, on 22nd August, it was at about £900 percent.

Note: The plaintiff gave bonds for the money he was to pay the defendants.

But it was insisted by *Sir Constantine Phipps* that this was not performance of the contract, but keeping the old contract afoot and a farther security for the performance of it. The defendants had not transferred the stock but had received the dividends ever since upon it. By the Act, thus, one cannot take advantage of his contract not having registered it, for it is neither performed nor compounded.

This was the case. And this matter the plaintiff insisted upon for obtaining an injunction. And it was affirmed by the counsel that the bonds were but a continuance of the original contract. The defendants admit that they had received all the dividends, by which the plaintiff would make it a matter of account.

[To the] objection that it was a contract compounded, that cannot be, for it is the same sum payable by the contract. See f. 4, Aubrey v. Fitzhugh.[1] The words 'contract for the sale' etc. extend to all agreements by writing, bond or otherwise, relating to the sale of stock, and land and defeasance make but one security in a court of equity.

[It was] objected by Mr. *Reeves*, for the plaintiff, that the defendant has a remedy at law for the money due by the bonds, but the plaintiff has no remedy at law for the stock and, therefore, a court of equity ought to take cognisance of the whole where the remedy may be mutual.

Serjeant *Chesshyre*, for the defendant: The plaintiff was the broker for the defendant [and] has been taken into custody of the House of Commons. The defendants had no stock but what the plaintiff knew of, and it was wholly negotiated by him. And he knew whether the annuity would be made stock by the 22nd of August. On 5th October, £1500 of the stock was actually transferred to the plaintiff; on 30th November, £1000 more.

Note: At the first, the plaintiff pleaded to the action at law that these contracts were not registered, but upon application to the court, they had leave to withdraw their plea.

[To the] objection of the bond of great penalty, [he] responded that does not alter the law; they might have brought a bill to be relieved against the penalty, but that is not the case here.

[To the] objection the contract was not registered, [he] responded the first contract was discharged before the time for registering was out. The old agreement was canceled and delivered up by the parties.

[To the] objection that you should have registered the bonds, the bond is no contract either for us to sell or buy stock.

The court broke in here and said they need [not] press this, for not registering they may take advantage of at law as well as here. The matter of offering to account seemed to have most weight with the court. Without entering further into the matter, the plaintiff agreed to give security to abide the order of [the court].

An injunction was awarded.

311

Baker v. Planner

(Ex. 1722)

[1] *Awbrey v. Fitzhugh* (Ex. 1721), see above, Case No. 231.

The question in this case was whether the defendant's answer to a bill for tithes was sufficiently specific.

Bunbury 108, 145 E.R. 613,
1 Rayner 164, 2 Gwillim 631, 1 Eagle & Younge 777

28 April 1722.

To a bill for tithes, an exception was taken to the answer that the defendant does not set forth quantities and values. The defendant sets forth what tithable matters he had and says he had no other tithable matters whatsoever.

Barons Price and Page thought this insufficient and that he should set forth particularly that he had not such and such things as charged in the bill. And upon their opinion, the exception was allowed.

(But note this seems very extraordinary and contrary to the constant method of drawing answers.)

Baron Montagu thought it would be well enough if the defendant says he has no other tithable matters in the bill mentioned.

But note: Then it might be thought insufficient if there were, as is usual, a charge in general in the bill that the defendant had divers other tithable matters.

Taussig MS. 311, vol. 1, p. 270, pl. 2

Easter term 1722.

N.B. In the case of Barker v. Planner *et al. per* Price, Montagu, and Page, if a defendant denies generally that he had no other tithable matters, that is not sufficient, for this is making himself a judge whether any other of the tithable matters expressly mentioned in the plaintiff's bill other than he has particularly answered to are tithable or no. But by them, if too many things are expressly demanded, the defendant answers expressly and then says that he had no other tithable matters demanded in the bill, this is a good answer.

Per eosdem: If Easter offerings are demanded in general and there is no particular charge or demand in the bill that the defendant should discover the number of his family, it is not necessary for the defendant so to do where he denies in general that Easter offerings are due.

Per Price: The parson is not entitled to any such [tithe] for one colt only, and, therefore, the exception that the defendant had not set forth the value of the colt was overruled.

Sed multa dubito and believe that the court, having seen by many former exceptions that the plaintiff had given unnecessary trouble, gave ear less willingly to those exceptions which perhaps, if they had been single, would have prevailed.

N.B. The colt in the answer was said to have fallen from a cart mare which he used in husbandry, and, therefore, he conceived no tithes were payable. But surely, this is no discharge unless it had been alleged more particularly that the mare was used in the husbandry work of that parish. But the court overruled all the plaintiff's exceptions, *ut dixi*.

Harvard Law School MS. 1082, vol. 1, p. 130, pl. 1

A bill was brought for tithes. An exception was taken for that the defendant does not set forth quantities and values. The defendant sets forth what tithable matters he had and says he had no other tithable matters whatsoever.

This, PRICE and PAGE thought the answer insufficient and that he should have set forth particularly that he had not such and such things as charged.

MONTAGU thought it well enough if he says no other tithable matters in the bill mentioned.

312

Bateman v. Nunn

(Ex. 1722)

One question in this case was whether a lay impropriator suing for tithes must allege his title thereto.

Another question was whether, in a plea of non decimando *to a suit for tithes, the defendant must allege the former monastery that was discharged or merely allege non-payment for a long period of time.*

Another question was whether the Statute of Limitations runs against a lay impropriator or against the Church.

Harvard Law School MS. 1082, vol. 1, p. 130, pl. 2

30 April 1722.

A bill was brought by the impropriate rector of Erith in the County of Kent for the great tithes. Chapman was the lessee of these tithes to Bateman. The defendants [Nunn and Bodle] insist in their answer that the lands of which they are occupiers, and that they were tenants of Christ Church Hospital, to whom they belonged for these 100 years, that these lands formerly belonged to some greater abbey, whether to the Abbey of Lisney or what other they cannot tell, but that they believe they came to the crown by the Stat. 31 Hen. VIII[1] and thence derived to Christ Church Hospital, and that these lands never paid any tithes in kind.

Mr. *Ward*, for the plaintiff: The defendant should have shown that he was capable of a discharge by being dissolved by the Stat. 31 Hen. VIII or should have shown which of the greater monasteries. See in the first book, Clark v. Dashead.[2]

---

1 Stat. 31 Hen. VIII, c. 13 (*SR*, III, 733–739).

2 *Clark v. Dashwood* (Ex. 1720), see above, Case No. 142.

Serjeant *Stevens*, for the defendant: We insist that no tithes have ever been paid and that it is exempt by some legal means or other, which is sufficient against a lay impropriator and, after such a length of time, non-payment is an evidence of an exemption, though this would not be good against the spiritual rector. Town of Warwick v. Lucas.[1]

Sir Constantine Phipps: [To the] objection that we do not say what abbey they belonged to, [he] responded we are in a case of a lay impropriator and need not show how it is discharged, but constant non-payment is an evidence of a discharge, for the court will presume that the impropriator had released or otherwise parted with the tithes. See the cases in Hankin v. Gay, 1718.[2]

Mr. *Foley*: Powell v. Powell, Hilary 1720.[3]

Note: This was in the case of a vicar.

Serjeant *Chesshyre*, for the plaintiff: [To the] objection of a lay impropriator, [he] responded that, before the disabling statutes, the parson, patron, and the ordinary might have released the tithes.

[To the] objection that a *non decimando* may be insisted in the case of a lay impropriator, [he] responded the common right is with us, and, at law, we are never put to prove the payment of tithes. The defendant has put nothing in issue that we could be let into the proof of. If there be a discharge by an order, that will hold only *quamdiu propriis manibus*.

Mr. *Ward*: The rule laid down is that a layman cannot prescribe in a *non decimando*. The incapacity is in the person presenting, and not against whom you prescribe.

[To the] objection that a lay impropriator might alien the tithes, [he] responded so might the parson *ut supra* before the disabling statute. The Town of Warwick v. Lucas is the only instance where this distinction was taken, but it appeared in the answer there that it was parcel of one of the greater monasteries.

Mr. *Browne*: By this defense, the plaintiff is debarred of all opportunity of proof.

Lord Chief Baron Bury thought the defense was too loose without naming the monastery and that the plaintiff ought to account.

Baron Price: It is not a good discharge as set forth by the defendant, being too loose without setting forth the monastery, nor have they proved it. But the plaintiff has not made out a right, for there is a greater deal in the distinction between an impropriate rector and a spiritual person. I do not think a lay impropriator has the common right as a spiritual rector. Now, there is no possession or right proved by the plaintiff. By receiving rents at law in an action, he must show some possession. In the case of a spiritual person, *nullum tempus occurrit ecclesiae*, but a layman purchases with his eyes open, In Town of Warwick v. Lucas, no

[1] See *Corporation of Warwick v. Lucas* (1711), Eq. Cases Exch. 671, Public Record Office, E.126/19, ff. 191, 221.

[2] *Hankin v. Gay* (Ex. 1719), see above, Case No. 76.

[3] *Powell v. Powell* (Ex. 1721), see above, Case No. 172.

possession was shown in the plaintiff. And, for this reason, no right being proved by the plaintiff, he was for dismissing the bill.

Baron MONTAGU: The answer does not insist that that plaintiff is only a lay impropriator. There is an absurdity in the answer. He says he does not know to what monastery it belongs and yet doubts not to prove that it belongs to some of the greater monasteries. The answer is too uncertain and loose.

[To the] objection by Baron Price that the plaintiff has made out no title, [he] responded he has made out a title to the rectory, which is the principal, and the tithe is of consequence. A rectory is the same inheritance whether it be in a layman or clergyman, and, in both cases, the right of tithes is the same. And he was of opinion the defendant should be decreed to account.

If a spiritual rector brings an [action of] ejectment for a glebe, he will be bound by the Statute of Limitations[1] as well as a lay impropriator.

Baron PAGE: I think the defendant has made a good defense and has put the plaintiff upon the proof of his right. The distinction is very right between a lay impropriator and a spiritual person.

[To the] objection that the spiritual rector could alien the tithes before the disabling statute, [he] responded that could not be without the concurrence of parson, patron, [and] ordinary.

[To the objection] of twenty years possession against a spiritual ruler in ejectment for a glebe, [he] responded that I deny, for the church is always in its infancy. It may bind the parson himself, but not his successor because [he] is a stranger [who] comes in not [as] from father to son. But, in lay hands, it is become a lay fee and [has] the same incidents as any other inheritance. If a man is in possession of a glebe for twenty years, it is a bar to a lay impropriator. If a portion of tithes had been paid for 100 years, it would be a bar in this court to a lay impropriator. He was for dismissing the bill.

The court being divided, no decree [was made, and the case] is to stand over.

Taussig MS. 311, vol. 1, p. 271

30th April 1722. Bateman and Chapman v. Nunn and Boodle.

The plaintiffs, one as impropriator of the rectory of Erith in Kent and the other as his lessee of the tithes etc., exhibit their bill for tithes against the defendants. The defendants, by their answer, deny the plaintiffs' title to the rectory or the lease. And they further say they kept no account of the tithable matters because they apprehended no tithes were due because no tithes were ever paid for these lands [and] that they hold the lands as tenants of Christ's Church Hospital. They have heard that the lands did belong to some of the greater monasteries or abbeys, but to what they do not know, and that the abbey was discharged *tempore dissolutionis*, came afterwards to the crown, and was then granted out from the

[1] Stat. 21 Jac. I, c. 16 (*SR*, IV, 1222–1223).

crown. And so they convey the title to Christ's Church Hospital. And the defendants say that their lessors, *scil.* the Mayor and Citizens of London as governors of that hospital can prove that the lands were tithe free as belonging to some greater monastery, but which greater monastery they do not know.

For the plaintiffs: The defendants must show to what greater monastery the lands belonged or else there is no issue, nor can the plaintiffs examine to any monastery in particular.

Serjeant *Stevens*: These lands never paid tithe in the memory of man. And the plaintiff is a lay impropriator. We have set forth that, either as belonging to a greater [monastery] or else by some other lawful ways or means, we are exempt.

A release from a lay impropriator may be presumed where there were never any tithes paid or demanded, but, against a spiritual person, there is no such presumption because a spiritual person cannot alienate the inheritance of the church. 22 June 1696, Medley and Tanley[1] [and] Hankin and Day, 1718, proves that a *non decimando* may be admitted against a lay impropriator. Warwick v. Lucas, Easter 1710. And the case of Hankin and Gay was determined at Serjeants' Inn in the sittings after Hilary 1718.

Besides, a discharge may be supposed upon some other account. Powell and Powell, sittings after Hilary term 1720. The Case of Powell was the case of a vicar where the defendant set up a *non decimando* as to hay, and it was held well because per curiam a vicar has no title but by endowment or usage.

Reply *per Chesshyre*: Before the disabling statutes, the parson, patron, and ordinary might have released or extinguished. And, therefore, I do not understand the difference between a lay impropriator and a spiritual one. [There is] not one case of an exemption pleaded, as this is, and this is a bare non-payment. And I do not know any such distinction between a lay and a spiritual impropriator.

Per CURIAM: In the case of Warwick and Lucas, there was a defense as being parcel of the Priory of Warwick, and, in that of Hankin and Gay, there was a pretense of a discharge as being parcel of the Abbey of Crowland. There is not one book, case, or authority which lays down the doctrine that, against a lay impropriator, a *non decimando* may be admitted, but not against a spiritual one. And the reason is the same, for the prescription of *non decimando* is grounded on the incapacity of the person alleging such prescription and so *non refert* against whom such prescription is alleged.

If the monastery had been set forth, we might have proved it [to have been] one of the lesser monasteries. [There is] no proof in this case about its being any monastery at all.

The defense in this case is inconsistent with the notion on which they support a *non decimando* because they insist in this case that a release may be supposed

---

[1] *Medley v. Talmy* (1696), Dodd 164, 347, 1 Rayner 81, 23 Gwillim 559, 1 Eagle & Younge 620.

from a lay impropriator, whereas the defense in the answer is that tithes are not due, the lands having been parcel of one of the great monasteries.

Chief Baron [Bury]: I think this defense is naught and the defendants ought to have shown what monastery.

Price: The defendants' discharge is not good, for the allegation is a great deal too loose. But the plaintiff has not made out his title. And the distinction between a lay impropriator and a spiritual one is a good distinction, for a lay impropriator has not a common right, but a spiritual one has.

As *nullum tempus [occurrit] regi*, so *nullum tempus occurrit ecclesiastico.*

A lay impropriator is a purchaser and must claim by conveyance or by possession. And here, no possession is in the plaintiff, and, therefore, no decree can be for him, and the bill ought to be dismissed. *Vide* Hobart 196.

Montagu: The answer does not all insist upon the weakness of the plaintiffs' title, but it makes a defense by way of discharge *ut supra.* This sort of pleading carries a very great absurdity with it, for he admits he knows not what monastery, and yet, in the same answer, he says he hopes to prove that such monastery never paid tithes *infra temporem memoriae.* There might have been good evidence of what monastery if in truth there were any, for, in [John] Strype's *Annals*, mention is made of this grant to the Spittalls.

Second, the plaintiff has made a title to the rectory, and making a title to the principal is making a title to the accessory.

We must not found our judgments upon the distinction of persons – and yet this would be so doing – but upon things. And surely, the thing, i.e. the rectory, is the same in the hands of a layman as of a clergyman.

And as to my Brother Price's case of an ejectment for a glebe, it is certainly the same in the case of a clergyman; he must prove possession of his glebe, as a lay rector must do in the same case.

I never heard of the maxim of *nullum tempus occurrit ecclesiastico.*

Page: A spiritual rector and a lay impropriator differ much. It is true there might have been an alienation of tithes before the disabling statutes. But then, the church is in its infancy *et nullum tempus occurrit ecclesiastico.* And, therefore, the Statute of Limitations would not bar the successor in an [action of] ejectment, though the predecessor had suffered a possession of twenty years against him as to his glebe.

But now, a rectory in lay hands is a mere lay fee, and he has the same right to this as to any other lands. And, therefore, the Statute runs against a lay impropriator.

Landholders purchase tithes of lay impropriators. And, therefore, the lay impropriator can no more maintain his title without showing it as to the tithes than as to any other part of his estate.

The answer is that he does not know that the plaintiff or his lessee has been or is at any time entitled to tithes so that this puts the plaintiff upon proving his title. I would suppose, [if he] buys an impropriation, he is to enjoy as much as the person of whom he purchased, but, if the person he bought of had no tithes, there is no reason his purchaser should have any. And the chief reason of the difference between a lay impropriator and a spiritual one is drawn from the difference between the solemnity of a church alienation and the alienation either of the whole or of part of the tithes by a lay impropriation, which may be done privately by a deed *in pais*, but the other required great formality and was usually registered, which is *quasi* a record.

Per MONTAGU: Was it ever required by the court that, in a bill by a lay impropriator, the lay impropriator should lay any other or different title to his tithes than a spiritual person should do? If not, where is the foundation for such a difference?

But the court was equally divided, and so no judgment could be given.

313

Town of Cambridge v. University of Cambridge

(Ex. 1722)

The question in this case was whether a tax deficiency should be charged against one joint taxpayer for the default of the other.

Taussig MS. 311, vol. 1, p. 281

1 May 1722.

The land tax charges so much upon the Town and University. But the duplicates of the land have ever since the year 1693 been separate and distinct, *viz.* such a proportion on the University and such a proportion on the Town, but, of late days, the University have failed of their proportion. And, there being an arrear, the receiver returns this. And, in his account before the Auditor, a super is set upon the Town and University. And the Town now applied to the court to alter this super and set it only on the University, who had been deficient.

And the Chief Baron [BURY] and PRICE were of opinion that the super should be altered and set only upon the University.

MONTAGU doubted and inclined to think they could not alter the super because, the Act charging the University and Town together and jointly, we cannot alter it and make it otherwise.

Sed per PAGE: Then there can be no supers but upon a county at large, for the Act only charges the county and the county is to pay. But everybody knows that supers must be set upon the parish and no parish can pay more or less than according to the proportion it paid in 1693. Every distinct assessment must pay its distinct proportion, and, if it does not, a super must be set upon it and not upon the hundred or other larger division.

Per MONTAGU: These supers are actually allowed and passed, and process is gone out against both. And can we alter the process, which must go out according to the foundation on which it is grounded and that is joint? Therefore, the process must be so. If we discharge one, we cannot charge another. By the Auditor, we must set the super upon the whole county in general and so we always do in *quo quidem comitatu* etc. But we take it every parish pays just the same money as it did in 1693.

And the court bid the counsel move it again.

Query how the process goes against the deficient parish.

Harvard Law School MS. 1082, vol. 1, p. 134, pl. 1

1 May 1722.

Sir Constantine Phipps, for the plaintiff, [moved] that the super may be set upon the University only for the arrear of the land tax [in] 1719, 1720. Act 4 Will. & Mar.[1] See the land tax: the University's proportion [is] £266; the Town's proportion, £257.

Harvard Law School MS. 1082, vol. 1, p. 137, pl. 2

26 May 1722.

The Town moved that a super set upon them jointly by the Commissioners of the Land Tax should be taken off and set only upon the University.

But the court was unwilling so to do it until some precedents were produced where a super has been taken off one and set upon another upon motion.

Note: The charge was joint, and the super was set pursuant to the charge. Note: Process goes against the Commissioners who signed the duplicate. No party is to be charged with no more than what they were charged within the year 1693, expressly by the Act of Parliament.

Lord Chief Baron Montagu thought they could not alter this, it being a matter of record, upon a motion, though it perhaps might be done in equity. He said they were not regular in this motion without producing a *constat* of the *distringas*. (*Quaere* of this.)

The court would do nothing at present but enlarge the rule.

Mr. *Ward* says in the case of Mr. Doddington, 1712, no *constat* was produced of the *distringas* that issued.

Taussig MS. 311, vol. 1, p. 300

Trinity term 1722.

Per Montagu, Chief Baron: I thought you would have shown some precedents of an alteration of a super upon a motion, but you have not. And, as I said before, the super is set according to the charge in the Act. And I do not know [that] we can alter this upon a motion any more than in Sir Thomas Cecil's Case,[2]

[1] Stat. 4 Will. & Mar., c. 1 (*SR*, VI, 323–372).

[2] *Cecil's Case* (1597), 7 Coke Rep. 18, 77 E.R. 440.

though, perhaps, in this as well as in that case, you may be relieved by an English bill.

It was now universally admitted that the process goes against the acting commissioners of that district or place which is in arrear and deficient, and so is the express direction of the Act of Parliament.

Until 1718, the distinct and several taxations have been constantly answered. Here, the return of the super is wrong, for the *viz.* is as large as the charge, whereas the precedent from Essex is right. There, the charge is *super residentes comitatu* so much, *viz.* such part thereof on several townships. He ought to produce a *constat* of the *distringas.*

Adjourned.

Bunbury 117, 145 E.R. 616

27 June 1722.

A motion was made by the Town of Cambridge that a super, which was set upon them jointly with the University, might be taken off and put only upon the University for the arrear of the land tax. But the court was unwilling to do this without producing precedents, and, at last, one was produced of Sir William Fleming in 1709. But, in that case, the super was not altered, but the process was directed to issue against the persons who were chargeable, who were the commissioners that were in default, and not against all the commissioners.

At last, it was, by compromise, agreed that the super should stand and the *distringas* issue against those commissioners only of the Town and University, who signed the deficient duplicates.

Mr. *Reeves* [was] for the University.

Taussig MS. 311, vol. 1, p. 347

Trinity term 1722.

Westmoreland is divided into four wards, *viz.* Kendal Ward and Lonsdale Ward, East Ward and West Ward, but the receiver in 1709 set a super on the whole county. Sir William Fleming's [Case]. But the East Ward and West Ward only were in arrear for the year 1706. And process issued upon this super to the sheriff against all of the commissioners of the county. And Sir William Fleming, one of the commissioners for the two other wards,[1] made a complaint to this court. And, thereupon, this court discharged that process and ordered new process against the two other wards which were deficient. *Martis 26 die Julii* 1709 is the date of Sir William Fleming's order. It is ordered that the sheriff should execute the process against the commissioners of East and West Ward and not against the commissioners for the other two divisions.

[1] counties *MS.*

Per Reeves, e contra: The commissioners of the Town and University join and do not subdivide, as in the case of Westmoreland, and their precedent does not go so far as to alter the super, but only to restrain the process.

And the court made an order that the process should not be executed against all the commissioners, but only against such as signed the deficient duplicates, which happened to be some of the Town and some of the University commissioners.

Harvard Law School MS. 1082, vol. 1, p. 147, pl. 3

27 June 1722.

This case was now moved again. And a precedent was produced of Sir Thomas Fleming, where the like had been done; upon a motion in 1709, the super was set by order of the court upon the person liable to be charged.

Note: In the case of Sir William Fleming, the super was not altered, but the process was directed to issue against the persons who were chargeable. The order was issued in 1709; the last order was 26 July 1709. In this case of Fleming, the court did not alter the super, but they only ordered the process to go against those commissioners only who had been in default and not upon all the commissioners.

Mr. *Reeves*, for the University, objected that the commissioners for the Town had been in default by not levying the arrears for 1717, which might have been levied upon Stourbridge Fair.

It was agreed by compromise at last that the super should stand and the *distringas* should go against those commissioners of the Town and University only who signed the deficient duplicates.

314

Little v. Darcey

(Ex. 1722)

Statutes to prevent frauds are to be construed liberally.

Equity looks more upon the substance of the thing than the form.

In this case, the defendant's plea was not sufficiently certain.

Taussig MS. 311, vol. 1, p. 284

Easter term 1722.

The plaintiff, as devisee, brings her bill to redeem. The defendant pleads the Statute of 4 & 5 Will. and Mar., against fraudulent mortgages.[1] And he says that the testator mortgaged to A. in consideration of £100 and then mortgaged to B., who assigned to the defendant. [It was] objected to the plea it does not aver that

[1] Stat. 4 & 5 Will. & Mar., c. 16 (*SR*, VI, 404–405).

the money was paid or that it was made for a valuable consideration; secondly, it does not aver that the plaintiff's devisor did not give notice in writing, but only says that the mortgagor did not discover the first mortgage; thirdly, he does not aver the lands to be the same; fourthly, the Statute does not extend to assigns, but only excludes heirs, executors, and administrators.

Per Bootle: He ought not only to aver that the first mortgage was made for a valuable consideration, but to show what the lawsuit was in particular.

Secondly, the plea is defective in this, that it was not discovered to Vinor, the second mortgagee, at the time of its making that there was a prior mortgagor, whereas it ought also to have shown that the assignee had not notice of the first mortgage at the time of the second mortgage.

Thirdly, the Act does not tie up the giving of notice to the very particular time of making the second mortgage, for he might have notice thereof before the making of the second mortgage.

Testatum existit is good in [an action of] covenant; it is otherwise in debt or avowry. By the indenture mentioned to be made between A. and B. for and in consideration of £100, A. did convey.

Per Chief Baron [Bury]: It ought expressly to aver that there was good consideration and what it was. The plea is not good.

Price: The plea is not good. This law is calculated for a court of equity, as Lord Somers said in the Case of Henning and Pitt, in Chancery, and, therefore, says he, 'I will make you aver everything, *viz.* that there was a valuable consideration, and you shall name the sum itself and shall also aver that there was no notice in writing.'

Montagu: The plaintiff stands in the place of the mortgagor. The defendant stands in the place of the second mortgagee. The Act is made to prevent fraud. The Statute to prevent frauds must be taken liberally, especially in a court of equity. And the distinction between a court of law and equity is that the latter of them looks more upon the substance of the thing than of form.

Things necessary to be averred are, first, that a prior mortgage was made upon a valuable consideration; second, he made a second mortgage upon a valuable consideration; third, that the discovery of the first mortgage must be in writing.

I agree that *testatum existit* that there was a mortgage is not good, but, by the indenture mentioned to be etc., he did grant, but the words mentioned do not at all take off from the certainty and positiveness of the proposition or affirmation.

I agree it is not enough to say 'for a valuable consideration', but, if I say 'for £85', I show the certainty of the sum which is apparently valuable consideration. And the Act does not, as I apprehend, restrain to any particular sum.

Secondly, the averment as to notice is that the first mortgage was not discovered to the second mortgagee. The objection is that this averment should be not discovered in writing, the first includes the second. And it does, therefore, in my apprehension, plainly appear.

PAGE: No advantage can be taken of this law but in equity. And it is a good law to prevent fraud, and it must not be made a handle to commit fraud. A plea must be certain at all events. And it is doubtful to what part of the deed the words mentioned to be made between A. and B. for consideration, and, if only doubtful, it is not sufficient. The averment is that he made the deed for £80 or other valuable consideration. These words do take off from the certainty of £80, but I take it that the value of the consideration is to be left to the judgment of the court, and the party must not take upon himself to judge thereof. And I think the money ought to be averred to be paid. And so I think the plea is not good.

And it was accordingly disallowed, MONTAGU only dissenting.

315

Lewis v. Jones

(Ex. 1722)

A bond to perform an arbitral award is enforceable where the award was not performed.

Taussig MS. 311, vol. 1, p. 287

Easter term 1722.

[An action of] debt [was brought] upon a bond *oyer inde* condition to perform an award. And he pleads that the arbitrators made no award. The reply was that the umpire did, and it sets it forth and assigns the breach.

And the defendant demurs.

[1.] The award is totally uncertain, *viz.* that Jones shall sign under his hand a solemn recantation of the scandolary words and these words are uncertain and import nothing.

2. He is to sign it and deliver it before four clergymen. Now, the defendant has no power to compel these clergymen to come.

3. The arbitrators have left the nomination of these clergymen to the plaintiff's own wife, but he ought to have nominated them himself. See Salkeld, [Reports], title Award.[1]

4. As to the cause in the Exchequer, the award is that both should equally pay the costs. Now, if any of the costs accrued after the time of the submission, the award is naught, Hardres 45.[2]

---

[1] 1 Salkeld 69–73, 91 E.R. 64–73; note *Glover v. Barrie* (1698), 1 Salkeld 71, 91 E.R. 67, also 2 Lutwyche 1597, 125 E.R. 878.

[2] *Hunter v. Bennison* (1655), Hardres 43, 145 E.R. 371.

5. The award ought to be final and the awarding releases between Morgan Lewis and Jones is not sufficient, for the wife may sue in the spiritual court for this defamation notwithstanding her husband's release. Salkeld 115.[1]

Price, Baron: The award is sufficient. If there were costs after the submission, it should be shown by way of replication.

Montagu was of the same opinion, a breach being assigned in non-payment of £4 whatever uncertainty [there be] in the other parts. As to this respect, it is certain.

Page: The award is made *de et super praemissis.*

Judgment [was given] for the plaintiff.

316

Coke's Case

(Ex. 1722)

The Court of Exchequer does not have jurisdiction over a criminal imprisonment and a fine that was not sent to the Exchequer for collection.

Taussig MS. 311, vol. 1, p. 289

Easter term 1722.

Sir Constantine Phipps moved for the discharge of Coke, who was committed to prison for a fine of £50, being convicted upon the clause in the Statute of Frauds[2] for the punishment of those who beat Custom House officers. And the objection was made to the indictment. But the court would do nothing, the fine not having been estreated here nor [was there] anything before the court whereon to ground any motion.

Query of the method of bringing such a person before the court, for this court said they could not order the estreat to be sent up hither. Query of *habeas corpus* to remove the person and a *certiorari* for the fine. Query also of Sir Constantine's objection to the indictment, *viz.* that the indictment did not set forth that the party was armed, which the Statute, by him, expressly requires.

---

[1] *Chamberlain v. Hewson* (1696), 1 Salkeld 115, 91 E.R. 107, also 5 Modern 69, 87 E.R. 524, 12 Modern 89, 88 E.R. 1184, Holt K.B. 99, 90 E.R. 953, 1 Lord Raymond 73, 91 E.R. 945.

[2] Stat. 14 Car. II, c. 11, s. 6 (*SR*, V, 395).

317

Foster v. Thompson

(Ex. 1722)

In this case, a writ of prohibition to the Court of Admiralty was granted.

Taussig MS. 311, vol. 1, p. 295, pl. 2

7th May 1722, last day of the term.

I moved on Saturday last for a [writ of] prohibition to the Admiralty Court, out of which a warrant was directed to arrest 5/8ths of the *Elizabeth and John* lying at anchor at Wapping and directing my client, one Foster to show cause why, the plaintiff there *in possessione* 5/8ths, *defendi fuerit seu saltem mitti non debent.* And a rule was made that the plaintiff in the Admiralty Court should show cause on this day. Accordingly by counsel, he moved to enlarge the time of showing cause until next term, which was opposed because [it would be] a hindrance to a voyage, the ship being ready freighted to sail. And with very much difficulty, we had the rule made absolute, MONTAGU and PAGE opposing us chiefly.

PRICE was clear in his opinion for the prohibition, and the others afterwards assented, we undertaking to declare.

In the case of Transer and Watson, the warrant was to arrest goods landed *in causa salvagii*, and a prohibition was denied before the libel because the salvage might be at sea. Salkeld 35.[1] The process was in that case by the Master against the owners, and a prohibition was denied. 1 Mod. 63, 81, is a general suggestion of a cause of action arising out of the jurisdiction, the first to the Court of Bristol; 81 to London.[2]

Note *per* MONTAGU and PAGE: The rule and practice of this court has been to grant prohibitions without a libel on such warrants. But by them, other courts do not. And, upon the strength of this practice of the Exchequer, we prevailed to have the rule made absolute, *ut supra.*

318

Anonymous

(Ex. 1722)

[1] *Transer v. Watson* (1703), 1 Salkeld 35, 91 E.R. 36, also 2 Lord Raymond 931, 92 E.R. 122, 6 Modern 11, 87 E.R. 776.

[2] *Wayman v. Smith* (1670), 1 Modern 63, 86 E.R. 733, also 2 Keble 673, 84 E.R. 423, 1 Siderfin 464, 82 E.R. 1219, 1 Ventris 88, 86 E.R. 61; *Cox v. St. Albans* (1672), 1 Modern 81, 86 E.R. 748, also 2 Keble 853, 854, 84 E.R. 540, 1 Ventris 180, 333, 86 E.R. 122, 216.

The question in this case was whether an ecclesiastical court has the jurisdiction to determine whether land is barren or not for the purposes of tithes.

Taussig MS. 311, vol. 1, p. 297

Easter term 1722.

[There was a] suit in an ecclesiastical court for tithes. And the defendant suggests that the lands are barren and discharged by the Act of Parliament.[1] And he produced an affidavit that the defendant had offered this plea to the court and the court had not thereupon surceased the suit.

Et per MONTAGU: I see no reason for a [writ of] prohibition, for the spiritual court may certainly try whether the lands are sterile or no. Indeed, in the case of a *modus*, it is otherwise.

And of the same opinion was PAGE, baron.

But, however, PRICE seeming of the contrary opinion, there was a rule to show cause why a prohibition [should] not [be granted].

319

Diggs v. Colebrook

(Ex. 1722)

A court will not enforce a contract that is not within the requirements of the Statute of Frauds.

Harvard Law School MS. 1082, vol. 1, p. 136, pl. 1

7 May 1722.

The points insisted upon for an injunction were:

1. It was a usurious contract, being 100 percent for time;

2. It was not ended or compounded and, therefore, it ought to be registered;

3. A pardon was obtained by Colebrook;

4. Current account; response: not as to this matter;

5. The stock was in trustees' names, but not in the defendant's own name, and the defendant is not entitled;

6. He did not make the first payment at the time of sale [. . .];

7. Whilst the House of Lords was examining about the South Sea Company, the defendant took out a writ;

8. It is within the Statute of Frauds.[2]

Mr. *Bootle* for the defendant: To the fourth, the defendant swears the balance was remitted for consideration of the bond mortgage defeasance etc.; to

---

[1] Stat. 2 & 3 Edw. VI, c. 13, s. 5 (*SR*, IV, 56).

[2] Stat. 29 Car. II, c. 3 (*SR*, V, 839–842).

the fifth and sixth, by the Act of Parliament, he is entitled or possessed and, in a court of equity, an equitable title is sufficient. The defendant applied to the cashier and was ready to pay, but Mr. Knight, by reason of the hurry, desired him to put it off. So the defendant had done everything of his part for payment. There was no occasion to register, for the contract was actually compounded by the bond of £9000. To the eighth, if this is within the Statute of Frauds, either it must be because there was no writing or no money was paid. Here is a deposit and a bond with endorsement executed. Barrett v. Gomesierra.[1] This is to answer its being a contract of only one side. To the first, if it was usury, the plaintiff had no occasion to compound, but the plaintiff might have pleaded the usury to the first bond; where it was for time, it was according to the usual market price.

[To the] objection of forbearance, [he] responded there can be no forbearance but where there is a debt contracted.

Mr. *Reeves* for the plaintiff: If a second contract is built upon the first that is usurious or unconscionable, a court of equity will enter into the consideration of it. The endorsement on the first bond was signed by the defendant, and it could not be evidence against him. Though he paid in the money on account of his trustees, yet it does not appear that they knew anything of it. Interest of the £30,000 was made part of the consideration of the second bond within the Statute of Usury.

[It being] a thing within the Statute of Frauds, the court were against an injunction.

320

Fotheringham v. Mozata

(Ex. 1722)

A harsh contract that has been agreed and settled out of court will not be set aside by a court of equity.

Bunbury 108, 145 E.R. 613

10 May 1722.

Upon a motion for an injunction upon a South Sea contract, the case was that the plaintiff had given three notes for the payment of the money. It was insisted that this was a contract neither performed nor compounded within the Stat. 7 Geo.[2] and, therefore, ought to have been registered.

And Mr. *Bootle*, who moved it, endeavoured to distinguish this case upon a note from that of a bond, which had often been resolved to be a performance or

[1] *Borrett v. Gomeserra* (Ex. 1721–1722), see above, Case No. 262.

[2] Stat. 7 Geo. I, stat. 2.

composition, for that the bond was a specialty which extinguished the contract, but a note is to be taken as part of the subsisting contract.

But the court, upon the first opening, were clearly of opinion that these notes, being for a less sum, were a composition, and they denied an injunction.

Harvard Law School MS. 1082, vol. 1, p. 136, pl. 2

10 May 1722.

Upon a motion for an injunction upon a South Sea contract where three notes were given for payment, the plaintiff insisted that this was a contract not compounded within the Statute and, therefore, ought to be registered.

And Mr. *Bootle*, who moved it, endeavored to distinguish this case upon a note from the case of a bond, which being special, extinguished the contract, but this being only a note, it is to be taken as part of the subsisting contract.

But upon the first opening, these notes being given pursuant to a reference, they were clearly of opinion this was a composition and denied an injunction.

321

Pearce v. Penrose

(Ex. 1722)

Upon an allegation of a disturbance, a plaintiff in possession of land may have ex parte *an interlocutory injunction to quiet possession before service of process.*

Bunbury 110, 145 E.R. 613

25 May 1722.

It was said by Baron Price, and so admitted *per* curiam, that, if a bill be filed to quiet the plaintiff in possession etc. upon an affidavit of disturbance and the bill being filed, the plaintiff may come before service of the subpoena to answer and move for an injunction to quiet him in such possession as he had at the time of filing the bill.

Harvard Law School MS. 1082, vol. 1, p. 137, pl. 1

It was said by Price and it was so admitted *per* curiam, if a bill be filed to quiet the plaintiff in possession etc. upon an affidavit of disturbance and the bill being filed, he may, even before service of the subpoena to answer, move for an injunction to quiet him in possession.

322

Bishop of Lincoln v. Ellis

(Ex. 1722)

The question in this case was whether an earlier decree against a lessee of the plaintiff's predecessor was admissible in evidence against him.

Taussig MS. 311, vol. 1, p. 301

Trinity term 1722.

A bill was exhibited by the bishop as entitled in virtue of his corporation to the rectory impropriate of Bardney in the County of Lincoln under a rent by a grant from the crown in Edward VI's time. And he exhibits his bill for the tithes of Bardney, except only for the demesne lands of the manor of Bardney, so that, here, the bishop is in the nature of a lay impropriator.

Some of the defendants insisted upon a dismission of a bill formerly brought in this court founded upon a nonsuit on an issue directed to try whether these lands were exempt from tithes. And this bill was exhibited by the lessee of the bishop, Sir Thomas Shipworth, who was lessee for three lives.[1] And it was made a question whether this dismission was evidence and could be read because a trial between the lessee of a bishop and the parishioners will not bind the bishop.

Per Chief Baron [MONTAGU]: Before a jury, I should scarce admit this to be evidence, but I think we may trust ourselves with it.

Per PRICE: We ought to read it. And I think there is a difference between evidence in equity and before a jury.

Per PAGE: I think it cannot be read. It would have been evidence for the bishop, but it is not evidence against him. And, therefore, I think it so far from being conclusive evidence that it is no evidence at all.

But by the CHIEF BARON: All evidence is reciprocal.

And it was read. And, upon the reading of it, it appeared that this trial had been upon a general issue whether the land was tithable and, secondly, the trial was against a tenant for years then and not against the owner of the inheritance, who was now the party claiming the discharge. And so it was objected that this record was no color of defense for the present defendant because it was not evidence of the right this defendant insists upon, which is that these lands were parcel of the demesnes of the manor of Bardney.

So the court decreed the vicar to account for the horse pasture etc., which I think was very hard because of the decree reciting the lands were not tithable and this upon a trial at law and no evidence of any tithes ever since paid. I think the court ought not to have decreed an account, but at least to have directed an issue.

---

[1] *Skipwith v. Pickering* (1688), 1 Wood 265.

If the reason why this dismission upon a nonsuit should not be some sort of evidence of a discharge for the benefit of the present defendant was because it does not appear that the point now insisted on as a defense was then tried, this will be a reason against all sorts of general verdicts that they should never be admitted to be read as evidence but against the very parties themselves between whom the trial was had.

(1) Non-payment; (2) reputation; these are not sufficient to decree an issue upon, nor [is] (3) being near the site.

But in my apprehension, in this case, the question was parcel or not parcel.

And the court decreed an account against the several defendants.

Bunbury 110, 145 E.R. 613,
1 Rayner 165, 2 Gwillim 632, 1 Eagle & Younge 777

28 May 1722.

Upon a bill for tithes as rector of Barney in the County of Lincoln, the defendants insisted that the lands were parcel of one of the greater monasteries dissolved by the Stat. 31 Hen. VIII.[1] A decree was offered to be read in evidence, wherein Sir Thomas Skipwith, lessee of the then bishop of Lincoln, was plaintiff against the then tenants of the land. But it was objected to the reading of this, for that no admission of the lessee shall bind him that has the inheritance and who was no party to the decree.

But by the opinion of the Lord Chief Baron Montagu and Baron Price, it was read, who said they should have made no doubt of reading it if the lessee had prevailed, and, therefore, they saw no reason why it should not since he did not prevail.

But Baron Page was of another opinion, and his reasons seemed to be the better.

Mr. *Ward* [was] for the plaintiff; Serjeant *Chesshyre* [was] for the defendants.

Harvard Law School MS. 1082, vol. 1, p. 140

28 May 1722.

A bill was brought for tithes as rector of Barney in the County of Lincoln. The defendants insisted that the lands were parcel of one of the greater monasteries dissolved by 31 Hen. VIII and, therefore, discharged. For the plaintiff, it was said that this greater monastery was not dissolved by the Stat. of 31 but by 33 Hen. VIII.[2]

And to the objection that tithes had not been paid for many years, they [showed] that there had been an unity of possession.

[1] Stat. 31 Hen. VIII, c. 13 (*SR*, III, 733–739).

[2] Stat. 37 Hen. VIII, c. 4 (*SR*, III, 988–993).

Mr. *Ward* for the plaintiff: It is not said that these lands come to the crown freed and discharged from the payment of tithes, as it should have been. They have not one witness to show that these lands were part of the demesnes of the abbey.

Serjeant *Chesshyre*, for the defendant Vyner and his tenants. [To the] objection [it was] parcel of the demesnes or other possessions of the abbey, [he] responded we say they were held discharged at that time, also that they came to the crown after the Stat. 27 Hen. VIII[1] but before the Stat. 31 Hen. VIII [and] partake of the discharge of the last Act. The decree was offered to be read in evidence wherein Sir Thomas Skipwith, lessee of the Bishop of Lincoln, was plaintiff against the then tenants of this land, but [it was] objected to the reading of this, for no admission of the tenants should bind him that has the inheritance and who was no party to the said decree.

Lord Chief Baron [Montagu]: If the lessee had prevailed, I should be for reading this decree, and I see no reason why we should not since he did not prevail.

And he and Baron Price were for the reading of it, against the opinion of Baron Page, who seemed to have the better reason on his side.

[Order of 26 May 1722: 2 Wood 193.]

323

Armiger v. Clarke

(Ex. 1722)

A court of equity will not decree specific performance of a contract to order payment of the purchase price.

Whether a bargain is harsh depends on the circumstances at the time the bargain was made, and not at a subsequent time.

Taussig MS. 311, vol. 1, p. 304

Trinity term 1722.

Mr. Armiger, by articles on 27 July 1720, covenants to convey his lands in Norfolk to Mr. Clarke free from encumbrances with the usual covenants. Mr. Clarke covenants, upon the execution of proper conveyances, to pay to the said Mr. Armiger the sum of [*blank*], being thirty years purchase for the lands, on the first day of October then following in case the conveyances could be got ready in that time. These articles were under the hand and seal of both parties. And £500 was paid down by Clarke. And there was a receipt thereof endorsed on the articles whereby Armiger acknowledges the receipt thereof as so much in part [payment] of the purchase money. And he promises to repay the same with interest in case he did not convey by the time in the articles mentioned. At the time of

[1] Stat. 27 Hen. VIII, c. 28 (*SR*, III, 575–578).

executing these articles, Armiger was only a tenant for life; there was a tail to his son of some part, and another part was settled on his present wife.

Within three or four days afterward, Armiger writes a letter to Mr. Clarke wherein he informs him that he had not duly considered of what he had done, for that he could not possibly make a title for the reasons before, begs pardon, and promises repayment of the money, and he desires Clarke would not give himself the trouble of going down to view the premises. But the letter not coming to Clarke's hands soon enough, he went down and viewed and came up again and then received the letter. Upon the third of August, Armiger died. And now, his son, as heir in tail and executor of his father, exhibits his bill for a specific performance of the articles. And he insisted upon these two points:

1. That though the plaintiff's father had by a letter subsequent to the articles seemed to waive them, yet that was not in his power to do, for, by a letter, a man cannot discharge his deed, and, therefore, notwithstanding the letter, the articles continued obligatory on old Armiger and, of consequence, also on Mr. Clarke;

2. It was said that it appeared by a positive witness that Clarke, that the defendant Clarke had insisted upon these articles long after the writing of that letter and he said he would spend any money rather than lose the purchase, so that, hereby, he plainly showed his intention of going on with it.

And now, all the objections for want of title being answered by the widow and the heirs offering to convey, the court [should] compel a specific performance, as they had done in the case of Stukely and Cain, which see before.[1]

E contra, pro defendente, it was insisted that old Armiger's letter was full evidence of his not being able on his part specifically to perform the articles for want of title and, consequently, as he could never have been entitled to have had a specific performance against Clarke, so neither shall his heir or executor or the remainderman.

2. This is a hard bargain, and courts of equity do not think themselves bound to execute hard bargains. This bargain of thirty years purchase in Norfolk, where lands generally sell for seventeen, is very extravagant.

But to this way of reasoning, MONTAGU, Chief Baron, *et al.* did not agree, for they said it could not be looked upon as a hard bargain at the time it was made and that was the time by which the court was to regulate themselves in judging of the bargain.

3. [There is] no need of coming into equity to compel a specific performance of the bargain on the side of the vendor because he may recover the quantum of money in damages at law, but a vendee cannot recover the land itself at law, and, therefore, he must come into a court of equity or else he can never come on the land.

And with this way of reasoning, the Chief Baron [MONTAGU] seemed to agree.

---

[1] *Stukely v. Cain* (Ex. 1722), see above, Case No. 277.

And all the court was clear that there was no color for this suit and, accordingly, dismissed the bill.

Bunbury 111, 145 E.R. 614

28 May 1722.

A bill was brought for the specific performance of articles for the purchase of lands at thirty years value, whereupon £500 had been paid by the defendant in part. There was a memorandum endorsed on the articles that the £500 should be repaid in case the plaintiff did not make out a good title by the time agreed upon and fixed for that purpose. It appeared in the proofs that the plaintiff's father, who was the person contracting for the sale of the lands, had written the defendant a letter, intimating that he could not make out any title, the same being in settlement upon his wife etc. And so it appeared in the proofs that the plaintiff's father was only tenant for life and, consequently, the son, who was now plaintiff, would not be concluded by his father's covenant and, since the lien is not reciprocal, it ought not to conclude in a court of equity, where also a writing under hand has the same consideration as a writing under hand and seal, and, therefore, the letter shall be taken to be a waiver of the articles. It was also insisted upon for the defendant that this was an hard bargain and a court of equity will relieve not only against fraud and circumvention in an agreement, but also against an hardship. In the first case, they will set the agreement aside; in the second, they will only not carry it into execution.

The bill was dismissed *per* TOTAM CURIAM chiefly upon this principle that the remedy was not mutual.

The Lord Chief Baron [MONTAGU] took this difference, if a man comes for a specific performance as to the land itself, a court of equity ought to carry it into execution because there is no remedy at law. But, if it is to have a performance in payment of the money, they may have a remedy for that at law.

Sir Constantine Phipps [was] for the plaintiff; Serjeant *Chesshyre* and Mr. *Ward* [were] for the defendant.

Harvard Law School MS. 1082, vol. 1, p. 141, pl. 1

A bill was brought for the specific performance of articles for the purchase of land at thirty years purchase whereupon £500 had been paid by the defendant in part. The defendant insisted that the plaintiff's father himself had written him word that he could not make any title, the same being in settlement, upon which the defendant never thought there would be [. . .] [in]tention afterwards of going on with the said purchase.

[It was] insisted for the plaintiff that, after this letter, yet the defendant persevered [?] and was determined to compel Mr. Armiger to go on with the purchase.

Note: There was a memorandum endorsed that Armiger would repay the £500 in case he did not make out a title by the time therein mentioned.

Serjeant *Chesshyre*, for the defendant: Where there is fraud in an agreement, a court of equity will set it aside; where there is only hardship, they will only not carry it into execution, but will not set it aside.

Note: The father was only a tenant for life, and, consequently, his son would not be concluded by his father's covenant, and, since the lien was reciprocal, it cannot conclude in a court of equity. In a court of equity, a writing under hand has the same consideration as a writing under hand and seal, and, therefore, the latter should be taken to be a waiver of the articles.

Mr. *Ward*: A specific performance can be had only in a court of equity. And if there be any fraud, circumvention, or hardship, that court will not carry it into execution.

Per TOTAM CURIAM, the bill was dismissed.

Lord Chief Baron [MONTAGU]: If a man comes for a specific performance of the land itself, a court of equity ought to relieve because they have no remedy at law. But if [he comes for] performance of money, they may have a remedy at law for that.

Sir Constantine Phipps: This was not a hard bargain at the time of the agreement, but became so by a subsequent accident.

324

Prosser v. Winston

(Ex. 1722)

As to time limits, Sundays are not included in matters in court, but they are in matters in pais.

Harvard Law School MS. 1082, vol. 1, p. 144, pl. 1

1 June 1722.

The question was whether, [as to] the four days that a defendant has to plead in, Sunday shall be taken to be one of the days or whether he shall have four days exclusive of a Sunday.

Note: This was an action of trespass, and the defendant would have pleaded the place where was ancient demesne.

Lord Chief Baron [MONTAGU]: [As to the] eight days for notice of trial, Sunday is one of the days. He distinguished between matters *in pais* and matters transacted in court. In that last case, Sunday is not to be computed a day. And, in this case, he thought the plea came in soon enough and Sunday is not to be one of the days.

Baron PRICE was for referring it to the Master to know how the practice had been.

Baron PAGE was of the same opinion with the Chief Baron.

The plea was received.

Bunbury 113, 145 E.R. 614

1 June 1722.

The question was whether Sunday shall be taken to be one of the days a defendant has to plead in.

Note: Sunday is included in the eight days for notice of trial, but the distinction is between matters *in pais* and matters transacted in court. And, therefore, in this case, the plea was received.

Note: This was an action of trespass, and the defendant pleaded the *locus in quo etc.* was ancient demesne.

Taussig MS. 311, vol. 1, p. 322, pl. 1

Trinity term 1722.

The question was whether a plea in abatement delivered on the fifth day of term should be received or no because Sunday was one of the days, though neither the first nor the last.

Chief Baron [MONTAGU]: In the case of persons indicted for treason, there must be five days exclusive of Sunday. And by him and PAGE, we think Sunday is not a day.

PRICE was for referring it.

But the other two were for receiving the plea, and it was accordingly received.

325

Upton v. Coward

(Ex. 1722)

A plea of the privilege to be sued only in the Court of King's Bench can be asserted by an affidavit without a writ of privilege.

Such a plea can be asserted after a general appearance.

Taussig MS. 311, vol. 1, p. 322, pl. 2

Trinity term 1722.

316, 365 in Hardres.[1]

To an action of the case, the defendant pleads that he is one of the attorneys of the King's Bench.

Bootle moved to set aside the plea because the writ of privilege was not annexed to the writ. Lutw. 639, 196, 1665; 3 Lev. 340.[2]

---

[1] *Carterett v. Massam* (1662), Hardres 316, 145 E.R. 475; *Clapham v. Lenthall* (1664), Hardres 365, 145 E.R. 499, also British Library MS. Hargrave 62, f. 4v, pl. 2.

[2] *Camfield v. Warren* (1701), 1 Lutwyche 639, 125 E.R. 335; *Baker, qui tam v. Duncalfe* (1694), 1 Lutwyche 193, 125 E.R. 101, also 3 Levinz 398, 83 E.R. 749, *sub nom.*

Chief Baron [Montagu]: The late Statute[1] directs an affidavit, but I think, in this case, we ought to have had the writ because that is the best evidence.

Price: I do not know any instance of a writ annexed.

Et sic per Page: And an affidavit is the method chalked out by the Statute. And, yesterday, ancient demesne was pleaded and nothing but an affidavit was produced; so in this case.

The case was adjourned.

Taussig MS. 311, vol. 1, p. 330

Trinity term 1722.

Sir Constantine Phipps [argued] that the plea should not be received. Dyer 33, pl. 18;[2] after an appearance, one cannot plead a privilege. Dyer 287, pl. 48.[3] Producing the writ of privilege is necessary. 2 Rolle's *Abr.*, 275, pl. 40, 276.[4] One shall not have the privilege after bail.

Bootle: This case is distinguishable because, in this case, the plaintiff is privileged as a debtor. Therefore, the defendant must show his privilege by a writ, though perhaps, where there is no privilege to the plaintiff, there, such a privilege may be pleaded without a writ of privilege. He admits there are many precedents of pleading without producing his writ. 3 Lev. 340.[5] I admit the case to be as cited, but I believe there was a *salvo* at the time of putting in bail by affidavit or other probable matter. But the affidavit is not proper here. And the Statute must be taken *reddendo singula singulis*.

E contra: The case in Levinz is expressly for us. Levinz is not single. Salkeld 545, Dillon and Harpur; 445, Scawen and Garret, one may plead without [a writ of] privilege; 1 Salkeld 1, Jones and Bodimore.[6]

Chief Baron [Montagu]: There are three objections: (1) affidavit; (2) bail; (3) want of a writ. The solution is the affidavit being direct, I think it had been

---

Baker v. Duncomb, Skinner 549, 90 E.R. 247; *Routh v. Weddell* (1704), 2 Lutwyche 1664, 125 E.R. 915; *Dashwood v. Folks* (1692), 3 Levinz 340, 343, 83 E.R. 719, 721, also Fortescue 342, 92 E.R. 882.

[1] Stat. 4 & 5 Ann., c. 3, s. 11 (*SR*, VIII, 459).

[2] *Anonymous* (1537), 1 Dyer 33, 73 E.R. 74.

[3] *Anonymous* (1570), 3 Dyer 287, 73 E.R. 643.

[4] YB Trin. 11 Hen. IV, f. 68, pl. 1 (1410), 2 Rolle, Abr., *Privilege*, pl. I, 1, p. 275; YB Pas. 20 Hen. VI, f. 26, pl. 14 (1442), 2 Rolle, Abr., *Privilege*, pl. I, 11, p. 276.

[5] *Dashwood v. Folks* (1692), *ut supra.*

[6] *Dillon v. Harper* (1703), 2 Salkeld 545, 91 E.R. 461, also 2 Lord Raymond 898, 92 E.R. 99, 1 Salkeld 328, 91 E.R. 290, Holt K.B. 589, 90 E.R. 1226; *Scawen v. Garret* (1705), 2 Salkeld 545, 91 E.R. 461, also 2 Lord Raymond 1172, 92 E.R. 275, Holt K.B. 587, 90 E.R. 1225; *Jones v. Bodinner* (1697), 1 Salkeld 1, 173, 91 E.R. 2, 159, also 5 Modern 225, 310, 87 E.R. 623, 674, 1 Lord Raymond 90, 135, 91 E.R. 956, 986, 1 Comyns 8, 92 E.R. 931, Comberbach 379, 90 E.R. 540, Carthew 370, 90 E.R. 816, Holt K.B. 149, 90 E.R. 980.

good. Three cases are that the writ may be produced or not, as by the cases in Salkeld.

The plea was accordingly received.

Harvard Law School MS. 1082, vol. 1, p. 144, pl. 3

The question was a plea of privilege as an attorney of the King's Bench after bail put in and an appearance by the defendant. The cases cited for the plaintiff were Dyer 33, 287; Hardres 316, 365; 2 Rolle, *Abridgment*, 276, 5. Cited for admitting the plea were 3 Levinz, Sir George Dashwood's Case; Salkeld 545, Dillon; 445, Jones v. Scudamore.

[It was ruled] *per* TOTAM CURIAM that the plea should be received.

Bunbury 113, 145 E.R. 614

9 June 1722.

The defendant's plea of privilege as an attorney of the Court of King's Bench was received *per* TOTAM CURIAM after an appearance by the defendant and bail put in.

These cases were cited against it: Dyer 33, 287; Hardres 316, 365; 2 Rolle, *Abridgment*, 276, 5.

These [were] cited for it: 3 Levinz, Sir George Dashwood; Salkeld 445, 545.

326

Note

(Ex. 1722)

The party who obtains a show cause order has the right to reply to the respondent's answer.

Taussig MS. 311, vol. 1, p. 321

Friday, 1 June 1722.

N.B. If, upon a motion, a rule be made that the counsel shall show cause and they come another day and show cause, the reply belongs to the counsel who obtained the rule, for it is the same as if cause had been showed the same day and then, to be sure, the reply had been on the side of those who make the motion and the hearing on a subsequent day is *nunc pro tunc*.

327

Moslyn v. Lloyd

(Ex. 1722)

A writ of inquiry can be sent out of the Court of Exchequer to an English justice of assize, but not to the Court of Great Sessions of Wales even though the cause of action arose in Wales.

Taussig MS. 311, vol. 1, p. 323

Tuesday [*blank*] June 1722.

An action of trespass by Moslyn was laid in Denbighshire, and the judgment went by default, and a writ of inquiry was awarded.

Mr. *Bunbury* moved that the inquiry might be executed before the Judge of the Grand Sessions, which by Chief Baron [MONTAGU] and PRICE, we cannot do, but we can order it to be executed before the Judge of Assize in Shropshire if you think it worth your while.

And the court made such rule *nisi causa* the last day of the term.

328

Morgan v. Husband

(Ex. 1722)

The question in this case was whether a defendant must answer as to misrepresentations made by himself.

Taussig MS. 311, vol. 1, p. 324, pl. 1

Trinity term 1722. Exceptions.

The question was whether the plaintiff[1] was not prevailed upon by the suggestions and pretenses of the defendant to do such things.

Per MONTAGU: The defendant cannot answer to this because whether these pretenses did prevail.[2]

Per PAGE: He may and ought to answer whether he made such pretenses or no. This is in his own knowledge.

But MONTAGU was *contra*.

329

Dupuis v. Clarke

(Ex. 1722–1724)

In this case, the court held that the plaintiff did not have a right to renew the lease that was in issue.

---

[1] defendant *MS.*

[2] Sic in MS.

After a case has been dismissed upon a plea in abatement, it is out of court and it cannot thereafter be dismissed for lack of prosecution.

Taussig MS. 311, vol. 1, p. 325

7 June 1722.

The King Charles II grants two terms, one of twenty-nine years ending in 1720, a subsequent term of twenty years which ends in 1740. 2 Chancery Cases 291. These terms were granted to Lord St. Albans and by mesne assignments to Lord Dover, who in consideration of a fine grants to Dupuis the whole interest except five days only, which five days excepted by the lease thereof were excepted for the sake of enabling Lord Dover to come at his rent. And notwithstanding this exception, the Lord Dover declares that the said Dupuis should have the right and benefit of renewal. 2 Rep. 246. Lord Dover's surviving trustee conveys and grants the reversion of the five days to Doctor Clarke who renewed, fol. 112, 2 Chancery Cases 274, from the crown.

And the plaintiff exhibits his bill to have the execution of the covenant or agreement in Lord Dover's lease. The defendant admits he renewed with the crown and admits he had notice of Dupuis's lease, but he denies he had notice of the covenant or declaration in the lease to Dupuis, which *per Chesshyre et al.*, of counsel with the defendant, is notice of the whole, as by the cases above.

N.B. The houses are in Pall Mall Field.

Sir Constantine Phipps: Lord Dover had no right to renew himself, and, therefore, it could never be conveyed by Lord Dover to Dupuis.

Secondly, Doctor Clarke does not claim under Dupuis, so there was no notice. And there is the difference, for a man must take notice of clauses of a deed under which he claims, but not in the clauses of a lease under which he does not claim.

Third, it appears in this case that Doctor Clarke's ancestors had the first interest in these houses, for Clarke made the first lease to Dupuis for six years [and] odd days and then Dupuis goes to Lord Dover and gets the lease to himself over Clarke's head so that Clarke has only got from the crown over Dupuis's head what Dupuis got from Lord Dover over Clarke's head.

Fourth, the defendant only had notice of Dupuis's lease from Lord Dover's trustees by what he heard from Sir Robert Dover, who told him upon his application to him that he had granted the lease to Dupuis, but he never saw the lease. And he swears in his answer he never saw the clause in the Lord Dover's lease for the right of renewal.

N.B. The Attorney General was a defendant in this case. And he answered that the crown was not at all concerned nor did any ways interpose in this contest.

The interest of Mr. Clarke was purchased under a decree of the Court of Chancery.

Per Chief Baron [Montagu]: I think the recital of the lease is not notice of the declaration therein. Dupuis never acquainted Mr. Clarke, at least as it appears in the cause, that he intended to renew, which I think was in point of honesty and equity as much incumbent on him as it was for Clarke to give him notice of his application to the crown, for, upon the lease of Clarke, Clarke reserved five days as well as Lord Dover reserved five days on the subsequent lease to Dupuis.

And all the court was unanimous that the plaintiff's bill should be dismissed. And so, accordingly, it was.

Taussig MS. 311, vol. 1, p. 522

Saturday, June 22, 1723.

The plea between Dupuis and Clarke was argued by *Stevens*, Brother [*Edward Ward, Jr.*], myself [*Philip Ward*], and *Bootle, pro querente; Sir Constantine Phipps* and *Browne, pro defendente.*

PRICE and PAGE [held] that it was a good plea, both in substance and form.

MONTAGU was *contra* as to both points, and so the plea was allowed.

Harvard Law School MS. 1082, vol. 1, p. 197, pl. 1

Hilary term 1723/24.

The defendant pleaded a former suit depending. And upon argument, the plea was allowed and 3s. costs [were] allowed.

And now, I came and moved to dismiss the bill for want of prosecution the third term in order to have full costs. And I mentioned the Statute of 4 & 5 of Queen,[1] for Amendment of the Law, but the Rule of the court saying that 3s. costs should be allowed and though the Statute was made since that Rule, yet the court denied my motion. And by allowance of the plea, the court said that the bill was out of court.

But see, for, if this doctrine is to prevail, then, upon allowance of a plea and demurrer, it is an injury to the defendant to plead or demur because, at the end of the suit, the defendant will have full costs.

Taussig MS. 311, vol. 1, p. 606

Hilary term 1723[/24].

It was agreed *per* CURIAM that, after a plea put in to a bill has been argued and allowed by the court, the defendant cannot move to dismiss the plaintiff's bill for want of prosecution because the bill is already dismissed by the allowance of the plea.

Nota this was attempted by *Browne* for two reasons: first, because the costs upon the allowance of the plea is but 30s. which, by him, is no manner of satisfaction for the charge, and, by the new Statute, the defendant, upon a dismission of the plaintiff's bill, either by himself or by the defendants for want of prosecution, is allowed costs to be taxed.

---

[1] Stat. 4 & 5 Ann., c. 3, s. 4 (*SR*, VIII, 458).

Sed per CURIAM: The Statute extends not to any case where a bill is dismissed by the judgment of the court. And we will not make a new rule in this case.

Sed nota the true intention of gaining a rule to dismiss the bill for want of prosecution, as I believe, was not so much for the sake of costs as thereby to have prevented an appeal to the Lords on the plea, which, in my opinion, ought not to have been allowed, being an insufficient plea.

330

Cotes v. Casswell

(Ex. 1722)

A new trial will not be granted for an inadequate verdict though one may have a new trial for an excessive verdict.

Taussig MS. 311, vol. 1, p. 329

Trinity term 1722.

The plaintiff brought [an action of] trover for four South Sea subscription receipts which he had pawned to the South Sea Company for £4000 and which the Company afterwards pawned for £8800. And upon the trial, the jury gave £700 damages. And the plaintiff, thinking he ought to have had £2700 damages, moved for a new trial.

But the court was unanimous not to grant it for this reason, that new trials had never been granted to a plaintiff where he had a verdict for him. They had often been for excessive damages. But none of the barons attempted to give any reason for the difference.

331

Morgan v. Skinner

(Ex. 1722)

In pleading a toll, the amount of the toll due need not be stated.

Bunbury 114, 145 E.R. 615

9 June 1722.

In an action of trespass for taking *duos boves*, the defendant justifies for a toll. Upon a demurrer, this exception was taken to the defendant's plea, that he had not given notice how much the toll was.

But to this, it was answered by Serjeant *Comyns, pro defendente*, and held *per* TOTAM CURIAM, that laying a demand was sufficient notice of itself. And the plea was held to be good.

Harvard Law School MS. 1082, vol. 1, p. 145, pl. 1

In an action of trespass for taking *duos boves*, the defendant [Schudmore] justifies for a toll. The exception to the plea was that he had not given notice how much the toll was, but it was only demanded. 3 Levinz 224; Lutwyche 377 [were] precedents.[1]

Serjeant *Comyns* in answer: The demand is notice itself.

[To the] objection the prescription was laid to be *infra manerium de Langharden* [and] the demise is alleged to be *in parochia de Lamunden*, [he] responded this demise is laid to be of the fair belonging to the manor.

Chief Baron MONTAGU and PRICE were of opinion the demand was well enough without notice. And all the court were of opinion the plea was good.

Taussig MS. 311, vol. 1, p. 331

Trinity term 1722. Morgan v. Skirwood.

2 Cro. 372.

There were three exceptions to the plea. [1] It ought to have said that the plaintiff had notice how much the toll came to. 3 Lev. 224; Lutw. 377. But here, the defendant has not mentioned how much the toll came to. (2) The defendant has shown no title to the fair, for he shows a lease to a fair in the parish, but the prescription is for a fair *infra villam*. (3) The traverse is not good because it is too large.

As to the replication, the time is as certain in the declaration as in the replication.

As to the plea: [1] The demand of a toll is notice of the toll; (2) The demise is of a fair *manerio spectanto*; (3) At any time during the fair, we may seize, and it cannot be supposed before a sale, for we say we seized for the refusal of the toll.

Chief Baron [MONTAGU]: The replication is naught. And the plea is good.

PRICE: The replication is naught. The plea is good.

PAGE was of the same opinion.

And GILBERT agreed.

And the plaintiff had judgment.

332

Waterman v. Bank

(Ex. 1722)

A vicar can join in one lawsuit several parishioners as defendants for separate claims.

Taussig MS. 311, vol. 1, p. 332

---

[1] *Bodle v. Williams* (1685), 3 Levinz 224, 227, 83 E.R. 661, 663; *Ange v. Patterson* (1684), 1 Lutwyche 374, 125 E.R. 196.

Trinity term 1722.

The plaintiff, as vicar of Olvaston and Alveston, brings his bill against two persons, one, a parishioner of Olvaston and one of Alveston. And the plea was that the plaintiff ought not to have joined both the parishioners in one bill.

But the court overruled the plea.

N.B. There was one institution and induction to both vicarages.

333

Birchall v. Smethurst

(Ex. 1722)

In this case, a proviso in a contract was construed to be a condition and not a covenant.

Harvard Law School MS. 1082, vol. 1, p. 145, pl. 2

12 June 1722.

An action of covenant was brought upon an indenture of lease for cutting down five oaks contrary to the words of the deeds, 'proviso that, if the tenant shall commit willful waste, then, the lease shall determine and cease'.

Upon a demurrer, the question is whether these shall be words of condition or covenant. Mr. *Bootle*, who demurred for the defendant, [said] that they are words of condition and not of covenant and, therefore, the breach was improperly assigned. 1 Rolle, *Abridgment*, 518, C.2.[1]

Mr. *Fazakerly*, for the plaintiff: It does not appear that the case of Rolle was by deed poll or indenture, as this case is. Whenever a man [who] is bound to do a thing whereby he is disabled to deliver up in the same plight as it was at the time of the binding, Fitzherbert, *Natura Brevium*, covenant himself, it is an immediate breach of the covenant. That which immediately proceeds must be construed as a covenant, which is one reason why this should be taken as a covenant. That [an action of] covenant lies upon a proviso, [see] Dyer 150, p. 83; 1 Leonard 277.[2]

[To the] objection it properly inures by way of condition, [he] responded, if it does, it may operate by way of covenant, *demissi enury*,[3] of a grant of an estate, and as a covenant, so *reddi et concessi* the same. Covenant will lie upon an indenture against the lessee on these words, though they are strictly the words of the

[1] *Holder v. Tayloe* (1614), 1 Rolle, Abr., *Covenant*, pl. C, 2, 3, p. 518.

[2] *Parker v. Gravenor* (1557), 2 Dyer 150, 73 E.R. 326, also 1 Anderson 19, 123 E.R. 331, 109 Selden Soc. 20; *Bishop v. Redman* (1584), 1 Leonard 277, 74 E.R. 252.

[3] Sic in MS.; i.e. to lease to farm.

lessor. 2 Levinz 116, Tomles; 40 Edw. III, fo. 5; 1 Rolle, *Abridgment*, 518, p. 5, 6; 1 Levinz 274, Pordage v. Cole, Raymond.[1]

Mr. *Bootle* replies: Where the word 'proviso' is so inserted as to explain the meaning of the parties, as in many cases it does, I do not contend but that it may be construed [as a] covenant. But there is no necessity in this case that the proviso should operate by way of covenant, for there is sufficient provision in the other part of the deed to prevent detriment accruing to the lessor.

[To the] objection of Tomlys v. Chandler, [he] responded there was a proviso there, but no covenant to pay the money. Yelverton 206, 2 Cro. 281, Brestow v. Knight.[2]

Chief Baron Montagu: A covenant is only the undertaking of the party. The deed testifies to that undertaking; the proviso shows that he has undertaken that there shall be no waste. After the proviso, there is an express covenant to do such a thing etc., which would have been unnecessary if the word 'proviso' had amounted to a covenant. He was of opinion for the defendant that it does not amount to a covenant.

Baron Price: There is a covenant that the lessee should pay the taxes. The proviso comes after and says that, if you cut down trees, the lease shall be void. This cannot be a covenant, but must be taken to be a condition.

Baron Page was of the same opinion. A proviso may amount either to a condition or a covenant, that must be when the intent of the parties leads to take the construction respectively. But there is no intention here that it should be a covenant. The lessor is not without a remedy here, for he may [sue] upon the Statute of Gloucester[3] to recover the place wasted.

[To the] objection of the case in 2 Levinz, [he] responded the deed appears to be only a mortgage, which is, upon the payment of the money, the man shall have his lands again, which, in its own nature, is a mutual agreement.

Baron Gilbert: The clause closes with this, that the lease shall cease, determine, and be void. The proviso is intended only as a further remedy for the lessor for what he had a remedy for before. This cannot be construed a covenant when the intention of the proviso is so odd a penalty to the rest of the covenants.

Judgment [was given] for the defendant *nisi per* TOTAM CURIAM.

---

[1] *Tomles v. Chandler* (1674), 2 Levinz 116, 83 E.R. 476; YB Hil. 40 Edw. III, f. 5, pl. 11 (1366), 1 Rolle, Abr., *Covenant*, pl. C, 5, p. 518; *Pordage v. Cole* (1669), 1 Levinz 274, 83 E.R. 403, T. Raymond 183, 83 E.R. 96, also 1 Williams Saunders 319, 85 E.R. 449, 2 Keble 542, 84 E.R. 339, 1 Siderfin 423, 82 E.R. 1194.

[2] *Bristoe v. Knipe* (1611), Yelverton 206, 80 E.R. 135, *sub nom. Briscoe v. King*, Croke Jac. 281, 79 E.R. 241, also 1 Bulstrode 156, 80 E.R. 848, 1 Brownlow & Goldesborough 113, 123 E.R. 699.

[3] Stat. 6 Edw. I, c. 5 (*SR*, I, 48).

Taussig MS. 311, vol. 1, p. 333

12 June 1722.

[Upon a] covenant, the plaintiff, as assignee of the reversion, brings his action against the defendant, the lessee of Leach. And he assigns for breach that he cut down oak trees. And the words of the lease upon which the breach was assigned were these, *viz.* 'provided that, if the lessee should commit willful waste or should not perform the other covenants on his part to be performed, then the lease is to be void'.

Per Bootle: The words of the lease are words of condition and not words of covenant. 1 Rolle's *Abr.*, 518, lre. C, pl. 2.[1] Therefore, this action is misconceived, and he should have taken his advantage by an entry.

Fazakerly, contra: The case in Rolle's *Abr.* does not appear to have been upon an indenture, and so it might perhaps be on a deed poll *sustentur ut praefertur*, which is contained in a subsequent covenant. And so this refers to the clause against willful waste. F.N.B., title Covenant.[2]

Second, a proviso in an indenture will amount to a covenant. [An action of] covenant will lie on a proviso. Dyer 150, pl. 3; 1 Leonard 277. So the words *absque denegatione* amounts to a covenant not to hinder or deny.

[An action of] debt or covenant will lie on a *reddendum*; so *demisi* will support [an action of] covenant; so *dedi et concessi* will support this action, for the same words will serve for different purposes.

And I make this further use of these cases, *viz.* though these are the words of the lessor, the lessee may have an action upon them. 2 Levinz 116; 40 Edw. III, fol. 5; 1 Rolle's *Abr.*, 518, A, *et ibidem*, pl. 6; Pordage and Cole, 1 Levinz 274; Raymond etc.

Bootle replies: The *sic ut perfertur sustentur* does not relate to the proviso because there is an intermediate covenant to sustain.

Secondly, a proviso will maintain [an action of] covenant where it appears to be the intent of the party it should so inure. But here is an express covenant to sustain and repair. And *expressum cessare facit tacitum.*[3]

2. The plaintiff may have [an action of] waste upon the Statute of Gloucester. And, therefore, this case is not like the cases cited where the words were construed to sound in covenant for necessity's sake lest the party should be remediless. 2 Croke 281; Yelverton 206, Bristow and [*blank*].

Per Fazakerly: This case was upon a deed poll.

Per Chief Baron [Montagu]: It is plain that covenant would not lie if this proviso was not in the deed, for there is no mention of cutting down trees in any other part of the deed. And, by him, the proviso, at the same time it prohibits,

[1] *Holder v. Tayloe* (1614), *ut supra.*

[2] A. Fitzherbert, *Natura Brevium.*

[3] That which is expressed makes that which is implied cease.

it also taxes and points out the penalty for a breach of the prohibition, i.e. to be void. And so he thinks the proviso is not a covenant.

PRICE: The intention is plain to avoid the lease and not to inure as a covenant. But he cannot answer the case in Levinz.

PAGE was of the same opinion. The case in Levinz about a mortgage is good law, for the notion of a mortgage is security for money.

GILBERT, ditto, for the same reason as the Lord Chief Baron, *viz.* this [way] of avoiding is an additional remedy to an action of waste. The intent of the case in Siderfin was to induce a personal lien which is the mortgage.

Judgment [was given] *nisi causa* the last day of this term.

Bunbury 114, 145 E.R. 615

12 June 1722.

This was an action of covenant upon an indenture of lease, for cutting down five oaks etc. The question arose upon these words, 'proviso that, if the lessee shall commit willful waste, then the lease shall determine and cease'. Upon a demurrer, the only question was whether these words, 'proviso' etc., shall be construed to be words of condition or covenant, for, if it shall be taken to be a condition, then a breach of covenant is improperly assigned and judgment ought to be for the defendant, of which opinion was the whole court, for, though a proviso may amount either to a condition or covenant, yet that must be when the intent of the parties leads to such construction respectively. But there is no such intention, nor any necessity here to construe it a covenant, for there were other provisions in the lease by way of covenant for the benefit of the lessor.

Mr. *Bootle*, who demurred, [was] for the defendant; Mr. *Fazakerly* [was] for the plaintiff.

334

Earl of Carlisle v. Wymondsel

(Ex. 1722)

A motion for a preliminary injunction should not be heard without reasonable notice of the hearing to the other parties.

Taussig MS. 311, vol. 1, p. 336

Trinity term 1722.

The plaintiff exhibited his bill for relief against a bond on which the defendant sued him. The defendant put in his answer last night, and the plaintiff drew exceptions to it and put them in this morning between 10 and 11. And, now, about 1, the plaintiff moved for an injunction upon opening a material exception.

And it was opposed because they should have filed their exceptions before the very day they move upon exceptions.

But for the plaintiff, it was insisted that the standing rule of the court was with the plaintiff and it is the constant practice thereupon.

Per Chief Baron [MONTAGU]: The rule is that no injunction be granted or day given to show cause why etc. without a motion in court. We, therefore, must hear counsel on both sides, but we cannot hear counsel on the other side because the defendant's counsel is not instructed. Where there are exceptions put in, I think this must be understood of exceptions put in before the day on which the plaintiff moves upon them or, otherwise, the defendant cannot instruct counsel.

PRICE: There is no certain rule for time, but I cannot understand but that thereby the exceptions shall have been so long put in as that the defendant's counsel should be instructed. But since the practice has been otherwise, I am for hearing the exceptions now.

PAGE: I think the rule has been always to allow such a motion where exceptions are actually filed. This has been the practice hitherto. And I am not for making a new rule in this case, though, perhaps, it would be convenient for the future to ascertain the time. So he was for hearing the exceptions.

GILBERT: The defendant's proceeding at law after an insufficient answer is contrary to conscience. And an insufficient answer is no answer. And, therefore, I think we ought to hear the exception. But, as to the practice, my late sitting here will discharge me from speaking to the practice.

Per Chief Baron [MONTAGU]: Let us make this rule for the future, *viz.* that no injunction shall be obtained for the future upon opening a material exception unless the exceptions have been filed two days before and notice of the motion given of the same exceptions filed to move for an injunction on the exceptions.

And this the rest of the barons agreed to as a standing rule for the future.

Harvard Law School MS. 1082, vol. 1, p. 146, pl. 1

Upon a motion for an injunction, a question arose whether, when you come to move originally for an injunction, it be sufficient to say that exceptions are filed and offer to open and argue a material exception or whether there should be a reasonable time of filing them before so that the other party might have time to inspect them.

PRICE and PAGE thought it reasonable that exceptions should be filed sometime before, but, being there had been no certain rule before for this, they were for going into the exceptions now, but that a time ought to be ascertained for the future.

Baron GILBERT: If a defendant puts it in an insufficient answer and is at liberty to proceed after, he proceeds against conscience.

The court settled this rule for the future. Upon an original motion for an injunction, the exceptions shall be filed two days before and notice is to be given two days before of filing the exceptions and motion.

Bunbury 116, 145 E.R. 616

12 June 1722.

Upon a motion originally for an injunction, it was settled in this case that, where you show for cause that you have filed exceptions, they must be filed and notice given at least two days before the motion or the injunction, upon that reason, is not to be granted.

335

Lord Strafford v. Farmer of the Duchy

(Ex. 1722–1725)

All lands are presumed to be in the Gildable that are not in the Duchy of Lancaster.

There may be a tenure in capite *of the king as duke of Lancaster.*

If the king grants manorial lands in the Duchy of Lancaster to be held in capite, *those lands are severed from the manor.*

Taussig MS. 311, vol. 1, p. 338

Trinity term 1722. Lord Strafford, Farmer of the Fines of Gildable v. the Farmer of the Duchy Liberty.

If lands be contained in a fine, part lying in the liberty and part in the Duchy, the post fine wholly belongs to the Farmer of the Gildable. Fines belonging to the Farmer of the Duchy do belong to him as the fines of *integre tenentes*. Lands held *in capite* must be understood tenants *in capite* of the crown, and not of the Duchy. 22 Edw. III.[1] The *Nomina Villarum* is very faulty. The bailiffs of the Duchy formerly were sworn upon their apposal, but not so now, but his oath now is omitted, which may be another cause of mistakes. It is proper to revive the giving in the *Nomina Villarum* upon oath. And we further move that the fines hitherto wrongly set forth may be set forth.

E contra: Both one and the other farmers [are] tenants to the crown [and] equally lessees to the crown. And this makes a difference between the Lords of the Liberties and the Farmers of the Duchy. The *Nomina Villarum* is *prima facie* evidence. And it is incumbent on the other side to show the faults. He knows no rule in law but that lands may be held *in capite* in the right of the Duchy, as well as in the right of the crown. A bill was brought by Sir Charles Inglefield to establish and settle this matter between the Farmers of the Gildable and the Farmers of the Duchy. And secondly, an action of law will lie for the fines received if they are unduly set over and received. Unless the titles of the lands are examined, the court most probably may do wrong.

---

[1] *Prince of Wales v. Basset* (1347), YB Mich. 21 Edw. III, f. 41, pl. 46.

Attorney General [*Raymond*]: When lands are said to be held *in capite*, they must be understood to be held of him *in jura coronae*, and the contrary must come on the other side. With respect to the crown, the Duchy is only a liberty, as all other liberties.

Chief Baron [Montagu]: I think the method by motion is good and proper, for the subject matter is a complaint of our officers. And the precedents produced justify this method.

Secondly, all lands are supposed to be in the Gildable that are not in the Duchy, and so the proof is to come from the Farmer of the Duchy.

The *Nomina Villarum* is nothing but an *inspeximus* of a record of the Duchy Court. And it was made at the request of Colepepper, Farmer of the Duchy. Lands held *in capite* are such as are held in gross and cannot be held [*blank*] *de manerio* etc. 1 Edw. VI, ca. [*blank*].[1] And, therefore, for this reason at this very time to prevent a tenure *in capite*, when the kings grant lands, there is always inserted a clause that the lands shall be held of his Manor of East Greenwich or Castle of Windsor etc.

As to *indebitatus assumpsit*, I think this would be a matter too long for a jury and more proper for examination of our officers, which, if they cannot do it in one day, they may in two or three. And as to a bill, it would only probably end in a direction for a trial.

The Duchy liberty with regard to the crown is only to be considered as other liberties.

This motion is of two parts: first, for direction, second, for judgments. First, for direction, and this I think proper, for the Foreign Apposer is our officer and, if he tells us that he goes by a faulty rule, we may correct his method. He tells us he goes by the *Nomina Villarum*; that, we see has been often impeached, as by the former orders in this court, and, therefore, we will certainly order that the *Nomina Villarum* shall be delivered in upon oath. And I think the Foreign Apposer must consider whether the lands are *integre tenenta*.

As to tenure *in capite*, Price cited [T.] Madox, 1 *History of the Exchequer*, but he was doubtful as to the nature of it. I think we ought to have copies of this report and to consider of this matter in the vacation.

Page thinks the old order ought to be revived. As to what passed, I think it ought to be further considered, for, otherwise, it may be a considerable surprise to the Farmers of the Duchy.

Gilbert: There is no doubt but this may be determined by a motion. A tenant[cy] *in capite* is immemorial and Duchy.[2] There may be a tenure *in capite* of the king as duke of Lancaster, but then this must appear, for all these sort of tenures must have been created within time of memory and will appear by the several grants.

---

[1] Stat. 1 Edw. VI, c. 4 (*SR*, IV, 9).

[2] Sic in MS.

The court ordered copies of the report to consider of.

Harvard Law School MS. 1082, vol. 1, p. 174, pl. 2

5 June 1723. Between the grantee of post fines in the Duchy of land and the grantee of the post fines in the Gildable.

Attorney General [*Raymond*] moved in behalf of the Gildables that a sum of money in the hands of [*blank*] raised by the post fines may be paid to Lord Strafford, who was grantee of the Gildable. He insisted that fines levied of lands of the Gildable, though within the Duchy, yet, if not Duchy lands, 2 Rolle, *Abridgment*, 193,[1] ought to go to the grantee of the Gildable. Bro., Pat., 139.[2]

Note: Some of the lands were held *in capite* of the king, and it was laid down as a rule these should belong to the Gildable. Note: Though a place is in the *Nomina Villarum*, yet that does not consequently follow that all that [*blank*]. Query, shall the *Nomina Villarum* be understood to be all liberty lands unless Gildable be shown? [It was] said, if one acre in a vill be shown to be Gildable, that shall bring in all the vill. Query, if they are *in capite* lands, they are not Duchy lands. Note: The *Nomina Villarum* is a survey taken upon oath in King Charles II's time of the Duchy lands. The question will be whether the Duchy fines ought not to be claimed upon oath as well as other liberty [ones] are.

Taussig MS. 311, vol. 1, p. 523

Trinity term 1723.

[Upon the] report of 11 February last, £203 are the fines in difference between the Duchy and Gildable farmers arising upon fines levied upon lands etc.

Page: It would be very hard to say that, because a fine contains one acre of the Gildable and £100 *per annum* in the Duchy, that the Farmer of the Gildable shall have the whole post fine.

But the other barons said that this practice of levying fines of many different persons' lands would not alter the law and, if the old authorities are so that when one person levies a fine of £100 *per annum* of Gildable lands and one acre of land *extra*, the whole post fine will go to the crown. It will be the same where a fine is levied between several different proprietors of different lands.

Gilbert: The *Nomina Villarum* is of no use whatsoever if every piece of land contained in the *Nomina Villarum* must be claimed by oath.

In Lord Chief Baron Turner's time,[3] the *Nomina Villarum* was given in by the Duchy officers on oath.

---

1 2 Rolle, Abr., *Prerogative le Roy*, pp. 193–194.

2 YB Mich. 2 Hen. VII, f. 6, pl. 20 (1486), Brooke, Abr., *Patentes*, pl. 109.

3 Sir Edward Turnor was Chief Baron of the Exchequer from 1671 to 1676.

GILBERT: The question is now reduced to this, whether the Duchy liberties are not to be claimed by the same methods as all other liberties are to be claimed, that is by oath.

It was adjourned to the next term.

Bunbury 132, 145 E.R. 622

Between the grantee of the post fines in the Duchy of Lancaster and the grantee of the Gildable, it was insisted on behalf of the latter that the fines of lands levied of the Gildable, though within the Duchy, ought to go to the grantee of the Gildable.

Note: First, if they are lands held *in capite*, they belong to the Gildable; secondly, though a place is in the *Nomina Villarum*, yet it does not follow that the whole town is Duchy lands.

Harvard Law School MS. 1082, vol. 1, p. 241

Trinity term 1725.

Mr. *Bunbury*, for the Farmer of the Gildables, cited Co. Litt. 108; Davis rept. 49,[1] that such persons as held *in capite* are *integri tenentes*. Fitzherbert, *Natura Brevium*, 5; Brooke, *Abridgment*, tit. Patent, 109; 2 Rolle, *Abridgment*, 193, letter B. And I may assert that everything held *in capite* is of the crown. 18 Hen. IV.

In all the reports made by the officers to this court in relation to these matters that some part of the things in question is held *in capite*, if so, the Duchy [of Lancaster] ought to ascertain and make their particular claim. But it is objected that the book entitled *Nomina Villarum* has been the direction to the Foreign Apposer to set over the fines to the Duchy, but there are several mistakes in that book, and the survey [was] taken in Charles II's time.

[To the] objection of a decree in the Duchy Court, [he] answered that cannot be of any weight because the Duchy Court would endeavor to enlarge their jurisdiction.

Reeves, for the Duchy of Lancaster: The Duchy lease is expired so that now this is as well vested in the crown and the fines belong to the crown. And I am informed that the *Nomina Villarum* has been the only test and the constant course of the Foreign Apposer's setting over the fines. And there must be almost in every place some lands held *in capite*. But it would be hard, therefore, to carry all that into the Farmer of the Gildables.

Chief Baron [GILBERT] and PRICE declared that, before the Statute of Edw. I,[2] lands held *in capite* might likewise be held of others.

[It was] adjourned. Query what became of it.

[1] E. Coke, *First Institute* (1628), f. 108; Resolution (1606), Davis 49, 80 E.R. 535.

[2] Stat. 18 Edw. I, *Quia emptores*, c. 1 (*SR*, I, 106).

Taussig MS. 311, vol. 2, p. 802, pl. 2

Trinity term 1725.

Co. Lit. 108a; Davis 49; F.N.B. 5; Bro. *Abr.*, Patent, 109; 2 Rolle's *Abr.*, 193. The *Nomina Villarum* is of little authority. The bailiff does not swear the certificate which he makes of the lands of his bailiwick.

Mr. *Reeves* said that, if the rule is to be understood as generally as it is laid down, *viz.* that wherever there are *capite* lands in any village which is contained in the *Nomina Villarum*, there, such lands must be Gildable. We think the rule is long and too large because lands may be held of the king *qua in capite.*

It is objected that there is no difference between lands held *in capite* of the king as of his crown and lands held *in capite* of the king as of his Duchy of Lancaster. Whereas there are many records in the Duchy of Lancaster where lands are expressly said to be held of the king as duke of Lancaster *in capite* so that, though we do not dispute the principle that the post fines are due to the Farmer of the Gildable, yet we dispute the evidence on which the Master grounds his report, *viz.* because [they are] *capite* lands there without saying any more, therefore, they are Gildable, which is a *non sequitur.*

Chief Baron [Gilbert]: If a manor be Duchy [lands], the king may grant those lands to be held *in capite* and then those lands will be severed from the manor. And he also said that the reason why the lands of the Duchy of Lancaster were disannexed from the crown was not the reason given by Plowden[1] to prevent a forfeiture, but because he would not subject his tenants to services to the king as such and to oblige them to come to the Exchequer and make them take out licenses to make deputies to do homage, which they must have done in the case of lands held *in capite* of the crown though they might do homage for lands held of a subject *in capite* by an attorney.

This case came on before the court upon the Master's report, e.g. the report [*blank*].

The court ordered the money to be paid over to the Farmer of the Gildable, but [there were] no directions as to the future.

336

Penny v. Hopper

(Ex. 1722–1724)

A lessee of tithes must prove the title of the impropriator lessor to the tithes.

Harvard Law School MS. 1082, vol. 1, p. 146, pl. 2

21 June 1722.

---

[1] *Duchy of Lancaster's Case* (1562), 1 Plowden 212, 75 E.R. 325.

A bill was brought for tithes in Lucton in the County of Hereford. The plaintiff [Penny, executor of William Penny] sets out his title to the tithes thus, that Sir Herbert Croft was possessed of a long term of years of the great and small tithes in Lucton [and] demised to the testator the said tithes. At the hearing, the defendant [Richard Hooper] objected that they had made out no title, for, first of all, they had not proved Sir Herbert Croft's lease and, secondly, if they had, that a lease would not be sufficient, for they ought to have shown in whom the fee rested and derived the title down.

The court seemed of this opinion and that the bill ought to be dismissed. But they let the cause stand over, the plaintiff paying the costs of the day, and he was to be at liberty to prove Sir Herbert Croft's lease to make out his title.

Cro. Ja., Arnold;[1] this was grounded upon a wrong, but, if it was a matter of right, it would not be sufficient.

Bunbury 115, 145 E.R. 615,

1 Rayner 166, 1 Eagle & Younge 777

21 June 1722.

In a bill for tithes in Lucton in the County of Hereford, the plaintiff sets out his title that Sir Herbert Croft, being possessed of a long term of years unexpired of the great and small tithes, demised to the plaintiff's testator. It was objected at the hearing that the plaintiff had made no sufficient title, for, first, they had not proved Sir Herbert Croft's lease so that it might appear whether his term was subsisting or not, and, if they had, that alone would not be sufficient, for they ought to have shown, it being a lay impropriation, in whom the fee is vested and derived the title from thence.

And the court seemed of this opinion, but they let the cause stand over with liberty to amend.

Taussig MS. 311, vol. 1, p. 388, pl. 1

Monday, 10th December 1722.

Per CURIAM: The lessee of a lay impropriator must set forth his title in a tithe bill because the defendants have a right to object to any part of his title. In this case, the plaintiff, by his bill, set forth that Sir Herbert Croft, being possessed of a long term for years yet unexpired of the tithes of all the Township of Lupton in the County of [*blank*], demised to the plaintiff. And this was held ill. And the court ordered that the plaintiff should amend his bill and then bring his cause to a hearing next term.

---

[1] *Arnold v. Bidgood* (1613), Croke Jac. 318, 79 E.R. 272, also 2 Bulstrode 65, 80 E.R. 963, 1 Gwillim 249, 1 Eagle & Younge 202.

Harvard Law School MS. 1082, vol. 1, p. 214, pl. 1

Sittings after Trinity term 1724.

This was a bill for tithes brought by a lay impropriator. And [it was] insisted for the defendant that the title should be shown and deduced down from the original grant.

Gilbert: Before the Council of Lateran, persons gave their tithes to whom they would, but, since that, the Canon[1] does direct that there shall be a vicar appointed unless there should be a dispensation from the pope. I cannot say how far a person may prescribe in *non decimando* against lay impropriators, for though it was wrong in the pope to dispense, yet when an inheritance was obtained in such tithes, then, they might be granted away. And it must be agreed that [there was] no possession of hay, hops, or small tithes in this case.

Price: My opinion is well known as to a lay impropriator that has not received tithes. And he put the case of a glebe, which cannot be recovered unless there is a possession within twenty years.

[It was] adjourned to next term.

337

Baily v. Worrall

(Ex. 1722)

In a suit to partition tithes, the vicar must be a party to the litigation.

Bunbury 115, 145 E.R. 615,
1 Rayner 167, 2 Gwillim 632, 1 Eagle & Younge 778

22 June 1722.

A bill was brought by the plaintiffs, as lessees of the rector of Winterbourn, for a portion of great and small tithes in Stoke Gifford, being a neighboring parish. The tenants and the lay impropriator, who claimed the great tithes in Stoke Gifford, were made parties. But, because the vicar of Stoke Gifford, who might be entitled to the small tithes, was not made a party, the bill was ordered to be dismissed. But, upon application, it stood over with liberty to amend.

Harvard Law School MS. 1082, vol. 1, p. 147, pl. 1

24 June 1722.

A bill was brought as lessees of the rector of Winterborn for a partition of tithes in Stoke Gifford, a neighboring parish. The defendants admit that part of the tithes had been paid, but they insisted that this had been paid in consideration only that they had the liberty of burying in Winterborn churchyard, their

[1] X, 3. 30. 18 and 20.

own not being consecrated until 1710. And, thereupon, having no further occasion to bury, they ought to pay tithes no longer. One of the defendants claimed the great tithes of Stoke Gifford as impropriator.

It was objected that the vicar of Stoke Gifford, who might be entitled to the small tithes, ought to have been made a party, of which opinion the court was. And the bill was dismissed, but they ordered the cause, at last, to stand over with liberty to amend.

Taussig MS. 311, vol. 1, p. 345, pl. 3

Trinity term 1722.

Baily, rector of Winterbourn, demanded a portion of the tithes out of Stoke Gifford, both in the County of Gloucester, which parish of Stoke Gifford was an impropriation. And the impropriator and his lessee were made defendants, but not the vicar, so the cause stood over to make the vicar a party.

338

Bettison v. Long

(Ex. 1722–1723)

A plaintiff need not join as co-plaintiffs all of the persons who have the same right against the defendant.

A defendant cannot answer by claiming a lack of memory, but must affirm or deny.

The Court of Exchequer cannot issue a writ of ne exeat regno.

Taussig MS. 311, vol. 1, p. 341

Trinity term 1722.

A bill was brought by the plaintiffs [Sir Edward Bettison *et al.*], who were about 92 proprietors in [*blank*] shares of Jamaica Gold in behalf of themselves and other proprietors of [*blank*] against the patentees of the Jamaica gold mines to have an account of what shares the patentees had disposed of.

And Long, who was one of the defendants, demurred because the plaintiffs had not made all the proprietors parties. There were 2000 shares at £75 a share. 250 shares were reserved to the patentees, [and] 506 shares to Shuckbrough were in trust for the patentees.

The court overruled the demurrer notwithstanding the Case of Temple Mills, cited out of Chancery.[1]

[1] *Chancey v. May* (1722), Precedents in Chancery 592, 24 E.R. 265.

Taussig MS. 311, vol. 1, p. 416

Tuesday, 12th February 1723, Long v. Bettison.

If a man is asked by a bill whether he does not know that he promised such or such a thing to be done, it is not a sufficient answer to say that he does not remember, for *per* Baron Gilbert, if a man does not remember the contrary, he ought to admit the thing charged.

And an exception was allowed upon this account.

Taussig MS. 311, vol. 1, p. 540, pl. 1

Trinity term 1723. Long v. Bettison.

Query whether this court can grant a *ne exeat regno* or whether it is only grantable in Chancery.

Per Lord Chief Baron [Montagu]: I think we cannot grant a *ne exeat regno* because the Lord Chancellor does not grant such writ as judge of a court of equity or of Chancery, but only as having the Great Seal, under which the writ issues.

339

Penrice v. Dugard

(Ex. 1722)

A modus decimandi *in lieu of tithes in kind must be paid on a specific day, and the date must be alleged in the pleadings.*

3 Rayner 1098, 2 Gwillim 632, 1 Eagle & Younge 778
Penrice, vicar of Dodderhill in Worcestershire v. Dugard.

A *modus* of £4 10s. for all small tithes arising on an estate called Impney was set aside because no day of payment was set forth by the defendant in the answer.

Taussig MS. 311, vol. 1, p. 342

Trinity term 1722.

*Modus*es were pleaded of 3d. a calf etc., but no day of payment of the *modus*es. And the defendant's counsel insisted on the objection of no time. Parish of Dodderell in the County of Worcester. [There was a] decree to account.

340

Lord Coningsby's Case

(Ex. 1722)

As to the time limits within which a defendant has to plead, Sundays are not counted.

8 Modern 46, 88 E.R. 36

Trinity term, 8 Geo. I, 1722.

By a rule of court made on a Thursday in the said term [Trinity term 8 Geo. I], it was ordered that the defendant should plead in four days after, and the plea came into the office on Tuesday after, and not before, which the attorney for the now plaintiffs refused.

It was insisted by their counsel that it ought not to be received, for, though, by the course of the court, the defendant has four days exclusive to plead, yet such custom will not warrant five days exclusive, which was this case, because Sunday shall be reckoned as one of the days, as well as it is one of the fourteen days where notice is given of a trial. It is true pleas have been received on the fifth day, but never where the matter was contested.

The Court answered that the pleas which are now put into the respective offices of the several courts were originally pleaded in court and that the defendant may as well plead on the first as on the second day or the fourth day but that, now, by the course of the court, if the defendant do not plead within four days, the plaintiff may sign a judgment for want of a plea. But these four days must always be reckoned such days wherein the defendants may plead and when the offices are open. And, therefore, Sunday is never reckoned one of those days because neither courts nor offices are then open. And this is not like the case mentioned on the other side, where Sunday is reckoned one of the fourteen days for giving notice of trial because a man may prepare for his journey or come up to London on that day, as well as on any other day of the week. And for this reason it was resolved that the plea should be received.

341

Read v. Woolaston

(Ex. 1722)

A modus decimandi *in lieu of tithes in kind that consists of access to a park for cattle is not destroyed if the park is partially disparked.*

Taussig MS. 311, vol. 1, p. 343

Trinity term 1722.

The plaintiff, as vicar of Tenbury with the chapelry of Rotchford in the County of Hereford, brings his bill for tithes of part of Sutton Park lying within the chapelry of Rotchford. The defendant pleads that the vicar has his election to have the running of a horse, two milk [cows], or three two-year-old beasts in the said park in lieu and satisfaction of all tithes arising upon that part of the lands lying within the said chapelry.

For the plaintiff: This can only be understood of a satisfaction for pasturage tithe. Second, it is in proof the defendant has disparked 300 acres of his park and turned the ground to arable. 28 Car. II Trinity term, Case of Hartlebury Park.[1] Wherefore, upon this point, the defendant must only be decreed to account for tithes in kind notwithstanding this pretended *modus*, for it is the same thing as if he had totally converted the whole park into tillage, for a man can no more abridge a [*blank*] any more than enlarge it. Rolle's *Abr.*, 651; 1718, Jones and Corthorne, in this court.[2]

Sir Constantine Phipps: This park is still continuing, and 300 acres of pasture ground. [There is] no park but sometimes it is plowed even for the benefit of the deer. An interruption of a *modus* is no destruction of it, nor does it revive[3] tithes in kind any more than a refusal to pay a *modus* will revive tithes in kind.

Second, the plaintiff is vicar, and, as such, he has no right but by usage or endowment. Powell v. Powell, sittings after Hilary term 1720.[4] And, therefore, if this was (Wright and Elderton, 1710[5]) to be looked upon as a disparkation, still it is no consideration that the plaintiff is entitled. And we do not admit he is entitled any otherwise than his predecessors, and, therefore, the plaintiff must prove his title.

And the court put the plaintiff to read his evidence of title, which he did by one witness.

And then the court put the defendant to prove his *modus*, but the defendant's witnesses could not prove the *modus*.

And so there was a decree to account [for the tithes in kind].

N.B. The *modus* was laid for the park and not for lands in the park.

342

Goddard v. Parker

(Ex. 1722)

A modus decimandi *in lieu of tithes in kind must be paid on a specific day, and the date must be alleged in the pleadings.*

---

1 *Skinner v. Smith* (1676), 1 Eagle & Younge 510, 1 Wood 161.

2 *Spurdam's Case* (1609), 1 Rolle, Abr., *Dismes*, pl. E, 3 and 4, p. 651; *Jones v. Denston* (Ex. 1720), see above, Case No. 151.

3 receive *MS.*

4 *Powell v. Powell* (Ex. 1721), see above, Case No. 172.

5 *Wright v. Elderton* (Ex. 1710), Dodd 224, Eq. Cases Exch. 659, 1 Rayner 119, 1 Eagle & Younge 694, 2 Gwillim 607, Public Record Office, E.126/19, ff. 149, 250, 1 Wood 518.

Taussig MS. 311, vol. 1, p. 345, pl. 1

Trinity term 1722.

A *modus* [was pleaded] without laying any time of payment. And an account [for the tithes] was decreed.

343

Hawkins v. Barker

(Ex. 1722)

A lessee of tithes must allege and prove his right to receive the tithes.

Taussig MS. 311, vol. 1, p. 345, pl. 2

Saturday, 21 [blank] Trinity term 1722.

Per CURIAM: If tithes be demanded by a lessee or under-lessee of tithes, unless the defendant admits title, the plaintiff must prove it.

And, by MONTAGU, Chief Baron, the plaintiff ought to set forth his title in the pleadings.

344

Anonymous

(Ex. 1722)

A composition for a fine to the crown must be signed by the Chief Baron of the Exchequer and the Attorney General. Motions in court for compounding fines to the crown are not proper.

Taussig MS. 311, vol. 1, p. 346, pl. 1

Trinity term 1722.

MONTAGU, Chief Baron, the Attorney General [*Raymond*], being present, said that he did not think motions for compounding or rating fines were proper because this liberty of compounding was *ex gratia regis* by virtue of a privy seal and the Chief Baron and Attorney General must sign the composition.

345

Emerson v. Danke
Woodford v. Gorse

(Ex. 1722)

A modus decimandi *in lieu of tithes in kind must be paid on a specific day, and the date must be alleged in the pleadings.*

Taussig MS. 311, vol. 1, p. 346, pl. 2

Trinity term 1722.

In both of these cases, the defendants' *modus*es were set aside and an account was decreed for want of setting forth the time of payment.

346

Mason v. Holton

(Ex. 1722)

A modus decimandi *in lieu of tithes in kind that is unreasonable will not be enforced.*

3 Rayner 1099

Mason, rector of Luggershall in Buckinghamshire, against Holton.

The defendant insisted that a small meadow had always been enjoyed by the rector in lieu of the tithe hay of another very large one. It appeared that the first bore, one year with another, about four loads of hay, the other about one hundred and fifty.

The court said it could never be supposed that any men in their wits would agree to take four loads instead of fifteen, and the *modus* was set aside as unreasonable.

347

Corpus Christi College v. Vincent

(Ex. 1722)

A modus decimandi *in lieu of tithes in kind must be paid on a specific day, and the date must be alleged in the pleadings.*

3 Rayner 1099

A *modus* of three half-pennies for a young milk cow and 2d. for an old milk cow was set aside because no time for payment of them was ascertained or set forth by the defendant in his answer.

348

Harwood v. Railston

(Ex. 1722–1723)

Agistment tithes are due for sheep and cattle fed on turnips sowed after a harvest of corn.

3 Rayner 1099

Harwood, vicar of Erith in Kent, against Railston.

The court declared tithe to be due of turnips sowed after corn in the same year and fed upon the land by barren cattle.

Taussig MS. 311, vol. 1, p. 539

Tuesday, 16 July 1723.

A bill was brought by the vicar for the agistment tithe of sheep fed on turnips in his parish.

And it seemed to the court that, though the sheep had ewes and lamb, of both which tithes were paid in the adjacent parish, yet the vicar has a right to demand agistment tithe of the turnips on which they are fed in his parish.

349

Mackay v. Kirn

(Ex. 1722)

Whether the defendant should move immediately for court costs against the plaintiff for delaying the trial is discretionary with the court.

Harvard Law School MS. 1082, vol. 1, p. 148

23 October 1722.

Mr. *Bootle* showed cause against the rule for costs for not going on to trial because an assize was slipped. Michaelmas 1722, Lloyd v. Price.

Chief Baron [Montagu]: It is discretionary in the court, and the subject matter may be considered. And this was an action against a Custom House officer. There is no stated time, and this application is too late.

Page: It is proper, and the Master and I will not say whether it is too late. In the King's Bench, you may come at any time. In the Common Pleas, it is otherwise. And the defendant laid dormant in this case.

Taussig MS. 311, vol. 1, p. 364, pl. 2

Michaelmas term 1722. Mackay v. Keen.

Upon a motion of Mr. *Bootle* against a rule for the payment of costs for not going on to trial in this cause, he insisted upon it that it appeared by the rule that the defendant did not apply to the court for costs until after an assize intervening and that is too late.

E contra: Costs are in the discretion of the court. And if the plaintiff can show any particular reason for not going on to trial, then the court will spare the cost. But only to say that an assize is past is not sufficient. And there are many instances in this court of the contrary. And it is well known to be the rule of the

Court of King's Bench that they do not continue the party to any precise time, though it is said the Common Bench does.

Per MONTAGU: I do not know that there is any precise time, and so PAGE, but then, if they do not come before a subsequent assize, they should show the reason why they did not apply sooner.

And in this case, they ordered that the rule should be discharged.

But the Chief Baron [MONTAGU] chiefly founded himself on the insufficiency of the affidavit whereon the original rule was made.

350

Rex v. Michener

(Ex. 1722–1723)

An objection to a writ may be made by a simple motion, but an objection to an inquisition must be pleaded.

Wherever a writ of extent might have issued against a person in his lifetime, a diem clausit extremum *may issue against his estate after his death.*

Whoever seeks an amoveas manus *must plead a better title in himself than is in the crown.*

Harvard Law School MS. 1082, vol. 1, p. 149

24 October 1722.

Thomas Newsham was receiver general of County of Warwick. And William and two other of his sons were his security to the crown for what money they should receive. They became indebted to the crown. John Michener, who was one of the sureties to Thomas Newsham, dies, Thomas Newsham being indebted to the crown. After John Michener's death, a *diem clausit extremum* issued against his estate whereby two houses etc. were seized. Robert Michener, the defendant, now moved to set aside this writ upon a suggestion that he was a mortgagee and purchaser for a valuable consideration without notice. It was objected too that the order for the *diem clausit extremum* was for that John Michener was surety for Thomas and William Newsham as receivers etc., whereas Thomas only was receiver and William only surety.

[To the] second objection that that one surety ought not to have an extent against another co-surety without that it appears that he had paid all the money, *Sir Constantine Phipps, contra,* [said], first, the writ issued regularly. The court will not upon motion grant this, but put them on pleading. Notice is not necessary in cases of issuing extents, for, otherwise, the party would convey away all his effects. The purchase was subsequent to the bond. The mortgagee, they may plead.

Mr. *Ward*: Whenever an extent might have issued against a man in his lifetime, a *diem clausit extremum* may issue against his estate after his death.

[To the] objection he is the only principal in the bond, [he] responded then they may plead or demur, but, as to the crown, they are all principals.

Mr. *Williams* replies: Of the writ issued or [. . .], it is admitted it may be set aside upon motion now. The bond upon which the writ issued shows that Thomas only was the receiver.

Baron PRICE: Where writs issued irregularly, we do set them aside without a plea to ease the subject. But this writ of *diem* etc. did not issue irregularly. They are all jointly bound by the bond, and the condition only shows that Thomas was principal. You may plead to the inquisition.

Baron PAGE: The affidavit is, I think, a sufficient warrant for issuing out this writ. This small variance between the affidavit and the bond is not material. He was of the same opinion that the defendant ought to plead.

Baron GILBERT was of the same opinion. If there had been a variance in the obligation, then, it would have issued irregularly, but the variance is only in the condition, and that I do not think material and that the defendant ought to plead to the inquisition.

Taussig MS. 311, vol. 1, p. 349

Michaelmas term 1722.

[There was a] motion to set aside a *diem clausit extremum* and an inquisition thereupon *quia erronice*. And the objection was that, in the affidavit to warrant the issuing of the writ, the party making the affidavit had been mistaken in the recital of the condition of the bond on which the writ issued. The bond itself was rightly described only in setting forth the condition, and there was a small mistake in the transcribing thereof.

The court refused the motion.

Query whether, if A. is bound to the crown in 1720 and has land mortgaged to B. in 1719 and then A. sells the lands to C. and C. takes in the mortgage from B., whether the crown can overreach this purchase.

Bunbury 118, 145 E.R. 616

24 October 1722.

Thomas Newsham was receiver general of the County of Warwick. William and two others of his sons and others were his security. Thomas Newsham became indebted to the crown. John Michener, one of his sureties, dies, against whose estate a *diem clausit extremum* issued, and two houses etc. were seized.

Robert Michener moved by his counsel, Mr. *Williams*, to set aside this writ, the order for it being that John Michener was surety for Thomas and William Newsham, whereas William was only surety for Thomas. And it was also suggested that Robert Michener was a mortgagee and purchaser of these houses for a valuable consideration without notice.

To the first, it was answered by *Sir Constantine Phipps* that they were all jointly bound by the obligation to the crown and it was the condition only that showed that Thomas was the principal, and this small variance between the affidavit, upon which the order for the *diem clausit extremum* was made, and the bond is not material. And the other matter the defendant may take advantage of by pleading to the inquisition.

Per CURIAM: We will do nothing in it upon motion.

Note: It was laid down as a rule in this case that, wherever an extent might have issued against a man in his lifetime, a *diem clausit extremum* may issue against his estate after his death.

Harvard Law School MS. 1082, vol. 1, p. 174, pl. 1

21 June 1723. Rex v. Hampe and Michener, *vide ante* 149, that matter now pleaded and a demurrer.

Sir Constantine Phipps, for the king: It appears that a term for years is standing out and the title [in] the lessee for years, and, therefore, the defendant can have no title.

Mr. *Williams*, for the defendant: The lessee for years is a trustee for the defendant Hampe, who is the assignee of Robert Michener, who had the inheritance. Hampe is a purchaser for a valuable consideration without notice. Though we show a legal title in a third person, yet [it is] showing it in oneself,[1] but, if this is not good at common law, yet it will be so by the Stat. 33 Hen. VIII, cap. 39.[2] This is a general law. Lib. 07, 19, of which the court will take notice; Hardres 304, 27.[3] [The court will] judicially take notice. If a man seised in fee voluntarily grants a term of 500 years to A. and afterwards enters into a judgment or a statute in consideration of money to B. and then sells the inheritance for a valuable consideration to C. without notice, if C. afterwards takes in this term, then B. and C. have equal equity, yet C. having the legal term, Plowden, Dame Hales,[4] as well as equity, shall protect his inheritance against B.'s judgment.

[It was] objected Attorney General v. Baden, Sir B. Shower's Parliament Cases.[5]

Sir Constantine Phipps replies: [To the] objection that a trustee is trustee for them, [he] responded they might have pleaded in his name.

[To the] objection of the Statute of Equity, [he] responded, then, they should have pleaded it.

---

1 one selve [?] *MS.*

2 Stat. 33 Hen. VIII, c. 39, s. 55 (*SR*, III, 891).

3 *Cecil's Case* (1597), 7 Coke Rep. 18, 77 E.R. 440; *Waller v. Travers* (1662), Hardres 301, 304, 145 E.R. 467, 469; *Attorney General v. Andrew* (1655), Hardres 23, 27, 145 E.R. 360, 363.

4 *Hales v. Petit* (1562), 1 Plowden 253, 75 E.R. 387.

5 *Rex v. Baden* (1693), Shower P.C. 72, 1 E.R. 50, Lords' Journal, vol. 15, p. 501, also Dodd 129, 133, 332, 2 Salkeld 495, 91 E.R. 424.

[To the] objection of a purchaser for a valuable consideration without notice, [he] responded that it is never a sufficient bar to the king's debt found by the inquisition.

[To the] objection that it is a mortgage term and we could have no more than the mortgage money, [he] responded yet still it would be a title against the king, being prior to his debt.

Lord Chief Baron MONTAGU: The debt of the crown is admitted by the plea, and the plea should have been founded upon the Statute of Equity. Here is no prior title shown in the defendant, but in the trustee.

Et per TOTAM CURIAM (*absente* Gilbert): The plea is bad in form and substance.

Taussig MS. 311, vol. 1, p. 520

Trinity term 1723. Rex v. Kemp.

A *diem clausit extremum* inquisition finds one Mitchmor was seised in fee and that he entered into the bond. The defendant comes in and pleads that, long before, A. conveyed to B. for a term of years and then pleads a purchase of the reversion under Mitchmor for a valuable consideration and shows the term of years to be in B. in trust for him to attend the inheritance.

Peere Williams: Showing a title in the party's trustee is the same as showing it [in] himself, especially since the Stat. 33 Hen. VIII, which is a public act. 7 Reports 19; Hardres 304; *ibidem* 27. If this was in the case of a subject, there would be no color to say that the prior term should not protect the purchaser without notice. And there is no difference between king and subject and subject and subject since all pleas of equity and good conscience are made good and available against the king by the Statute. Plo., Dame Hale's Case, allows it. Attorney General v. Baden, in Sir Bartholomew Shower's Parliamentary Cases.

Sir Constantine Phipps, contra: A title at law is shown in another person, and it is between subject and subject. Secondly, [there is] no assistance from the Statute of Equity without pleading it expressly. Thirdly, a purchase without notice is no bar to the crown.

Chief Baron [MONTAGU]: Whoever comes for an *amoveas manus* must show a better title in himself than is in the crown. This is common law. The next question is then whether this is matter of equity and aidable by the intent of that Statute; so reads the clause [*blank*]. You do not here plead against the debt, as this clause speaks, but you admit it to be just and subsisting, but you only object against his charging the debt on the land.

PRICE: The Statute of Equity must be pleaded expressly. And we cannot admit any plea but what is a good plea in law or conscience in discharge of a debt or in discharge of an extent.

PAGE: The Statute does not enable any man to plead any such plea who is not entitled to plead at law.

Judgment [was given] for the king.

351

Vernon v. Cholmondeley

(Ex. 1722)

In an action for a sale of goods, the verdict of the jury cannot include interest as a part of the damages.

Harvard Law School MS. 1082, vol. 1, p. 150, pl. 1

26 October 1722.

Upon a motion to set aside a writ of inquiry for that, in an *indebitatus assumpsit* for goods sold and delivered, the jury had given interest for the money, the Chief Baron [MONTAGU] seemed of opinion they might do it as well as upon a promissory note, bill of exchange, or for money lent.

Barons PAGE and GILBERT thought it could not be done upon an *indebitatus assumpsit* for goods sold, though, in the other cases, it might. And of the same opinion was PRICE.

Taussig MS. 311, vol. 1, p. 361

Friday, 26 October 1722.

Mr. *Bunbury* moved to set aside a writ of inquiry because the jury gave interest by way of damages and the action was *indebitatus assumpsit* for goods sold, which, by him, ought not to have been done in this action.

PRICE doubted it.

Sed per MONTAGU: It is usually done.

PAGE thought it is not generally done for goods sold, though always done in promissory notes. But, by him, it is certain the jury may do it. It is in their discretion, and it does not appear to us that the damages are excessive.

Bunbury 119, 145 E.R. 617

26 October 1722.

Per CURIAM: The jury upon a writ of inquiry of damages may give interest upon a promissory note, bill of exchange, and money lent, and, *per* MONTAGU, Chief Baron, upon an *indebitatus assumpsit* for goods sold and delivered. But PAGE, PRICE, and GILBERT, barons, thought it could not be upon an *indebitatus assumpsit* for goods sold, though, in the other cases, they were of opinion it might.

352

Harrison v. Gough

(Ex. 1722)

The question in this case was the sufficiency of the defendant's answer to a bill of complaint to set aside a contract to buy stock in the South Sea Company.

Harvard Law School MS. 1082, vol. 1, p. 151, pl. 1

27 October 1722.

Upon a motion for an injunction upon a South Sea contract, it was objected for the plaintiff that the defendant [Sir Richard Gough] says only in his answer that he was possessed of or entitled unto the stock to be sold, whereas he should have set forth how much and in what manner he was entitled to or possessed of and he should have said. And there seems to be nothing in this objection. In the answer, it was positive that he was possessed.

Mr. *Bootle*: Even in courts of law, there have been a mitigation of damages notwithstanding the contract, as in a case of buying a horse for so much of each nail to be doubled.

No injunction was granted.

353

Cardonel, *qui tam* v. White

(Ex. 1722)

The question in this case was whether justices of the peace have jurisdiction over the forfeiture of horses used to carry wine that was unlawfully imported.

Harvard Law School MS. 1082, vol. 1, p. 151, pl. 2

7 November 1722.

Sir Constantine Phipps moved to stop proceedings before two justices of peace upon a seizure of horses for coming away. See Stat. L. 8 Geo., cap. 18.[1]

Where there is a seizure of the goods prohibited or uncustomed, one can proceed before the justices.

Note: The horses were seized because they were carrying away wine which was run. The wine being imported without paying customs, the jurisdiction belongs to this court. And the question is whether we, having jurisdiction of the principal, have not, consequently, jurisdiction as to the horses and cart etc., which is only the company, accessory. Note: By the Statute, the justices have no jurisdiction as to the wine. The goods ought to be first condemned in this court before the justices proceed as to the carts and carriages.

[1] Stat. 8 Geo. I, c. 18, s. 16.

354

Vaughan v. Howell

(Ex. 1722)

To call a justice of the peace a jacobite and a papist is defamation per se.

Taussig MS. 311, vol. 1, p. 369

Michaelmas term 1722.

An action for words was brought that the plaintiff was a justice of peace and candidate for a member of Parliament for Brecknock, but no special damages were laid. The words spoken were that 'he is not an honest man; he is a jacobite.' Whereupon, being asked the sense of those words, he explained himself thus, 'a papist plain'. The second *colloquium* was 'he is no honest man; he suffers some to drink the Pretender's[1] health in his house, and he is a jacobite and keeps a Jesuit of a chaplain in his house'.

Per Probyn, in arrest of judgment: Jesuit, that is a cunning and artful man for his chaplain. Jacobite is of uncertain interpretation [and] can only mean that he was well affected to the late King James. The explanation is contradictory to the words; Jesuit of a chaplain is not Jesuit for a chaplain.

6 *Regis*, Ashton v. Blagrave, in the King's Bench,[2] 'thou art a rascal, villain, and liar' spoken of a justice of peace was held not actionable though spoken of a justice and with reference to the execution of his office. Parliamentary Cases, Duval and Price;[3] 'He is disaffected to the government.' And there, it was held that jacobite was not actionable.

But none of the words in this case do amount to so much as this. 'Suffer' is neutral and does not amount to consent, but rather that he suffered it with pain and uneasiness. 22 Eliz. [*blank*] makes it very penal to keep a Jesuit, and 'Jesuit' has a determinate sense.

Per Chief Baron [Montagu]: 'Jacobite' means a friend to James III, though originally it meant a friend to James II. And such a person must necessarily be an enemy to the present establishment.

Page: 'Papist' is actionable now, though, in Charles II's time, it was held not actionable.

Price: 'Suffers' means permits. How and Prin, in Salkeld.[4]

---

[1] James Stuart (1688–1766), the son of King James II.

[2] *Aston v. Blagrave* (1724), 2 Lord Raymond 1369, 92 E.R. 391, Fortescue 206, 92 E.R. 820, 1 Strange 617, 93 E.R. 736, 8 Modern 270, 88 E.R. 192.

[3] *Duvall v. Price* (1694), Shower P.C. 12, 1 E.R. 8, Lords' Journal, vol. 15, p. 458, Dodd 142.

[4] *How v. Prinn* (1702), 2 Salkeld 694, 91 E.R. 588, also 7 Modern 107, 87 E.R. 1128, Holt K.B. 652, 90 E.R. 1260, 2 Lord Raymond 812, 92 E.R. 42, 1 Brown P.C. 64, 1 E.R. 419.

The court gave judgment *pro querente nisi causa* this day sennight.

Harvard Law School MS. 1082, vol. 1, p. 152, pl. 1

9 November 1722.

An action was brought for Welsh words: 'he is not an honest man; he is a jacobite.' And, upon a *colloquium* of the defendant with one Thomas explaining the word jacobite, the defendant said it was a plain papist and that he keeps a Jesuit as a chaplain in his house.

Mr. *Probyn* [moved] in arrest of judgment that the word jacobite has no certain import or determinate sense. (Note £100 damages were given.) If he had said he had kept a Jesuit as a chaplain, it might be of another consideration. The second words were that he suffers persons to drink the Pretender's health in his house *post Georgii regis*, in the King's Bench, Blagrave v. Ashton. 'Thou art a rascal, villain, and a liar' spoken of a justice of the peace was adjudged not to be actionable. Parliament Cases, Duvall v. Price.

Damages entire being given, where the words are spoken at different times, if one part of the words are not actionable, the judgment ought to be arrested. The first words are plainly actionable. In the second words, he charges him with a fact of keeping a Jesuit as a chaplain, and the whole tenor of the words show it was the defendants' intention to charge him with an offense in law to the keeping of a Jesuit.

Per TOTAM CURIAM, judgment was given for the plaintiff *nisi*.

Taussig MS. 311, vol. 1, p. 382

Wednesday, 28th November 1722, being the last day of Michaelmas term 1722. Vaughan v. Powell.

The case, having been formerly spoken to in this term by Mr. *Probyn* in arrest of judgment, was now again spoken to by Mr. Serjeant *Chesshyre* on the same side. And he cited the cases following in maintenance of his assertion that the words were not actionable, *viz*. the case of Duval and Price, Parliamentary Cases, fo. 12; 3 Cro. 746, 297; 2 Cro. 58; Hardres 501; 3 Bulstrode 167.[1]

E contra per Bootle: [He said] that words must be taken in the sense which is applied to them in the time when spoken, though formerly these were used in a quite different sense. 3 Mod. 26, 3 Lev. 30, Raymond 482; Salkeld 694; 3 Lev. 50; 2 Ventr. 265; 3 Mod. 103.[2]

---

[1] *Duvall v. Price* (1694), *ut supra*; *Hollis v. Briscow* (1605), Croke Jac. 58, 79 E.R. 49, also Yelverton 64, 80 E.R. 45; *Pugh v. Owen* (1668), Hardres 501, 145 E.R. 568, also Lincoln's Inn MS. Misc. 500, f. 13 (Edward Ward's reports); *Crofts v. Brown* (1616), 3 Bulstrode 167, 81 E.R. 141.

[2] *Roe v. Clarges* (1683), 3 Modern 26, 87 E.R. 15, 3 Levinz 30, 83 E.R. 561, T. Raymond 482, 83 E.R. 252, also Skinner 68, 88, 90 E.R. 33, 42, 2 Shower K.B. 250, 89 E.R. 922, 1 Freeman 280, 89 E.R. 201; *How v. Prinn* (1702), *ut supra*; *Stawel v. Caune* (1682),

N.B. *per* MONTAGU, PRICE, and GILBERT: The words in this declaration are certainly actionable and can be understood by a court of justice in no other sense than that of scandal any more than they could be understood by any other person. And it is the duty of the court to lend a quick ear to actions of this sort to prevent the mischiefs of which otherwise would necessarily ensue by frequent breaches of the peace and so, in the end, to the dissolution of all civil government. And they gave judgment immediately for the plaintiff.

355

South Sea Company v. Curzon

(Ex. 1722)

A corporation cannot substitute the delivery of stock for the delivery of a subscription as performance of a contract; this is a non-performance of the contract, and the obligee is entitled to the return of the purchase price.

Harvard Law School MS. 1082, vol. 1, p. 152, pl. 1

17 November 1722.

A bill was brought for an injunction setting forth that they resolved to sell great quantities of stock at 300 and 400 percent, and also it set forth the third subscription and proceedings thereon, that the defendant procured her name to be inserted in the list of subscribers and paid £1000. And, by the entry in Mr. Webster's list, it appeared she had paid in the said £1000, that the defendant's name in the alphabetical list was by mistake in the name of Edward instead of Elinor and so continued. It set forth the reductions of the subscriptions so it does not appear that Edward Curzon [paid] in any money upon the subscription, that the defendant [came] to claim the stock in lieu of the subscription, but finding this mistake, she has brought her action against the plaintiff for the same and has obtained judgment in this court, though they are willing to give her stock in lieu of the subscription and to have an injunction. The defendant demurs for that there is no equity in the bill. Second, it appears by the bill that the defendant has obtained judgment at law and that there is no ground to stay her proceedings there.

Note: In the cash book, the name was Elinor, but, in all the other books, Edward.

[To the] objection that, by Stat. [*blank*] Geo., section [*blank*],[1] the Company may now alter the name and make it Elinor and, therefore, she ought to

3 Levinz 50, 83 E.R. 571; *Walden v. Mitchell* (1691), 2 Ventris 263, 86 E.R. 430; *Peak v. Meker* (1686), 3 Modern 103, 87 E.R. 65.

[1] Stat. 7 Geo. I, stat. 1, c. 5, and stat. 2.

take the stock for the £1000, note the Statute was made after the recovery and, therefore, cannot extend to this case.

It was insisted upon at the trial that, if the stock had risen, Elinor could not have had any benefit by this subscription. Whatsoever equity they have now suggested by the bill, they insisted upon in their defense at law. Mrs. Elinor Curzon never was a proprietor, which is the word of the Act, and, therefore, it does not extend to her. And secondly, this Act was made long after the verdict and judgment, where all the matters now suggested were then insisted on.

It was said for the plaintiff that it was plainly the intention of the defendant to become a subscriber, and, if it appears so by her answer, it is an equitable consideration why the plaintiff should be relieved upon allowing the proportion of stock for the £1000.

[To the] objection by the defendant that this bill being for discovery as well as relief, therefore, the demurrer as to the discovery, at least, is bad, [he] responded that might be a reason if they had come for a discovery of matters that would have been an assistance to them upon a trial at law, but, now, that matter is over, there being both a verdict and a judgment. And if it was a discovery now, it would only tend to defeat the evidence that was given upon the trial. The discovery prayed in the bill is of a matter that lies in their own cognizance.

Lord Chief Baron [Montagu]: Discovery and relief was prayed. By a demurrer, everything in the bill is admitted.

[To the] objection the defendant was a subscriber, [he] responded and yet it was not pretended that she ever put her name to any paper. If she had been in a list, that would not have made her a subscriber.

[To the] objection the defendant has paid in £1000 in order to her being a subscriber, [he] responded that £1000 would not entitle her to be a subscriber and her being in a list would not make her so. If money is deposited upon certain conditions and for a certain use, it cannot be recovered again as to so much had and received to her use.

[To the] objection of the Act of Parliament 7 Geo., [he] responded nothing in the bill charges the defendant as being a proprietor.

[To the] objection that it is proper for a discovery though after judgment, [he] responded that here is nothing in any suggestion of the bill for a discovery, which if discovered, could have altered the verdict etc.

That demurrer ought to be allowed, *per* TOTAM CURIAM.

Taussig MS. 311, vol. 1, p. 374

Michaelmas term 1722.

A bill was brought to stay proceedings on a verdict and judgment obtained by Curzon against the Company. Barwell v. South Sea Company in the Common Bench, *coram* King, in this very term. Barwell pays in £1000, but was told by the clerk to whom he paid the money, that this signified nothing unless he was in some list, but he never was in any list nor entered in any book until 26 October, and, until then, he was always told he was no subscriber and that he should have his money again. And Lord Chief Justice King determined he had a good action against the Company and he was not a subscriber. And the Act did not help this case. This was cited by *Chesshyre*.

Per Chesshyre: There is an equity that arises upon the Act of Parliament, and it was not in being at the time of the trial.

[Affirmed: 2 Brown P.C. 500, 1 E.R. 1092.]

356

Parsons v. Meredith

(Ex. 1722)

The Court of Exchequer will take jurisdiction of a case where equitable relief is proper regardless of the smallness of the amount in controversy.

Harvard Law School MS. 1082, vol. 1, p. 153, pl. 1

20 November 1722.

A bill was brought to be relieved against a note of £6 1s. suggesting that the note was satisfied, but the plaintiff not knowing, paid it over again by giving a new note for £6 1s., and he now prays relief. The defendant answers to the discovery and demurs to the relief for that the relief prayed is only of £6 1s., which is beneath the dignity of the court.

For the plaintiff, [it was said] this is a fraud upon the plaintiff, he not knowing the note had been discharged before. There is no stated rule in this court as to any particular sum.

Note: The defendant denies the fraud.

James v. Bird, Hilary 1718; this was for £2 10s.; Trinity 1721, Bissett v. Brent,[1] an agreement for 9d. per week for lodgings and to be relieved against a judgment for 3s. recovered for lodgings, and a demurrer was allowed in that case.

Lord Chief Baron [Montagu]: This is a complicated matter. And it appears plainly the defendant has received double his money, and, therefore, it would be contrary to conscience to let the defendant proceed at law. If, indeed, a bill comes originally to demand the sum of £6, it might be below the dignity of the court. But, in this case, it cannot. And the demurrer was overruled.

Taussig MS. 311, vol. 1, p. 375, pl. 1

Michaelmas term 1722.

Hilary 1718, James and Bird; Trinity 1721, Bissell v. Brent. Both these cases were cited as precedents of such like demurrers. In this case of Parsons and

[1] *Bisset v. Brent* (Ex. 1721), see above, Case No. 210.

Meredith, there was a demurrer to the relief for want of value. The whole sum demanded was £6 1s.

Per CURIAM: The defendant in this case being now proceeding at law, it is never below the dignity of the court to prevent a vexatious suit at law.

357

Ram v. Dohos

(Ex. 1722)

A payment by means of a note (or a bill of exchange) drawn on an insolvent payor is invalid.

Harvard Law School MS. 1082, vol. 1, p. 154, pl. 1

In this case, upon a motion for an injunction, there was a case cited by Lord Chief Baron [MONTAGU] of Colonel Lancaster v. Colesehin. Selwin sold bank stock to Lancaster, and Lancaster gave him a note on his goldsmith, Sheppard, for the money. Lancaster went with the note to the goldsmith on Saturday and delivered up the note drawn on him and took a new note from the goldsmith on the Tuesday, Monday being a holiday. Lancaster went to receive the money on his note, who broke on that morning, upon which Selwin brought his action against Lancaster for the money he sold his stock for, and he recovered. Query Salkeld Reports.

Baron PAGE: Notes only are not payment in a case of assignees.

Taussig MS. 311, vol. 1, p. 376

Michaelmas term 1722.

The case of Selwin and Lancaster, cited by the Chief Baron [MONTAGU] in giving his opinion in the case of Ram and Dehaizee, was this. Selwin sold to Lancaster bank stock and Lancaster offers to pay him by a £2500 note on Sheppard, and, that being £2000 more than was due, Sheppard takes up this note [and] gives Selwin a note for £500 and Lancaster another for £2000. This was on a Saturday afternoon at four o'clock. Monday being a feast day, Selwin carries the note to Sheppard on Tuesday, when he was failed. And, thereupon, Selwyn recovered against Lancaster.

Per PRICE: I fancy this case depended upon some knowledge in Lancaster that Sheppard was in a failing condition.

358

Lowther v. Whorwood

(Ex. 1722–1723)

Depositions cannot be taken before the parties are at issue.

Taussig MS. 311, vol. 1, p. 377

Michaelmas term 1722.

Lowther was appointed Governor of Barbados, and, by his patent, he is obliged to observe such orders as from time to time he should receive from the Privy Council. And accordingly, he receives orders to secure pirates' goods. The *Royal James*, a piratical ship, comes into the bay of the island *infra praesidia*, upon which he seizes it. And Captain Whorwood contested this matter with Lowther. And, upon this, he imprisoned him. And, thereupon, he brings an action of trespass against him. The Governor brings a bill in this court and sets forth the case as before and prays a commission to examine witnesses and an injunction to the law proceedings. And now, he moved for an injunction or else that depositions taken in Barbados under the seal of the Island might be admitted as evidence at trial or else that it would be impossible for the Governor to make his defense at law.

Whorwood puts in his answer whereby it appeared that he was the captain of the *Rye Galley*, a man of war, that he was appointed to cruise and take pirates and carry them to the next bay. He put into Barbados to mend his ship. And he had notice of a piratical vessel hovering at sea off Carlisle, an Admiralty port, to have them condemned that he took the *Royal James*, but did not carry it into the Bay of Barbados, but it was carried to another island and there condemned.

Per Chesshyre: This is a bill to put off a trial, a new method of proceeding, instead of an affidavit to put off a trial in a court of law where the action is depending.

The true question is whether the captain seized the *Royal James* within the jurisdiction of Barbados or no. By the captain's answer, he swears that the ship when seized was not within the jurisdiction of the Island.

The plea to the action was that the ship was *infra praesidia* in Carlisle Bay within the Governor's jurisdiction. And the plaintiff at law has admitted all this and has joined issue singly on this point, *viz.* that Whorwood did not endeavor to carry the ship away without the consent of the Governor. And this issue puts the proof very cunningly on the Governor.

Per Reeves: This is a particular case, and there is no arguing from this case to others not under the same circumstances. We do not move upon the defendant's answer, for we agree the defendant has denied the facts in the bill and thereby has expressly contradicted our bill and his own plea, too, at law. We only insist on the nature of the case itself. We cannot have our witnesses in person because they are in the service of the crown in the Island, and, then perhaps, their depositions may be read as evidence in a court of law. The affidavit for putting off a trial must show that the witnesses are expected over in some time. The common suggestion in a bill of equity is that the witnesses are abroad. Here, that suggestion is actually true.

Per Montagu: In an action in the King's Bench, they are to try the cause and they must do everything requisite to enable them to do justice. And we must not enjoin another court unless we are better able to do them justice ourselves, which we cannot do because no relief is prayed by the bill. 14 Car. II, ca. [*blank*].[1] See this Act. I apprehend the depositions when taken on this commission will not be evidence. So he was against the commission.

PRICE: No issue was joined in this cause in equity. Therefore, no commission can go. Second, [there can be] no evidence of depositions taken on such commissions because they are not within the Stat. 14 Car. II. So he was against the motion.

PAGE: Defect of justice and defect of trial are both causes of equity, but here no issue is joined. Therefore, a commission can issue; so he should have prayed for relief.

Second, there is no necessity, for the witnesses being abroad is not sufficient of itself. The Governor has not done enough. He should have applied to the crown to fetch over these witnesses.

He cites a case where Lord Chief Justice Holt said he would grant a perpetual imparlance unless a man would admit a deed to which another was a witness whom the party could not procure. And so he doubts whether the court might not grant a perpetual injunction until depositions are admitted. But there being no issue joined, depositions cannot be evidence. Therefore, he was against the motion.

GILBERT: A suggestion of absence of witnesses only is not sufficient for an injunction, but there must be also a further case made for the relief in equity. And in this case, there is no case set forth upon the pleadings for relief. And, therefore, we cannot enjoin. So he was against the motion.

Bunbury 120, 145 E.R. 617

23 November 1722.

A bill [was brought] for an injunction and to stay proceedings at law in an action of false imprisonment and to have a commission to Barbados to examine witnesses there, whose depositions might be made use of in the trial at law, which was now moved for.

But, *per* CURIAM, the application had been proper in the Court of King's Bench, where the action is brought, but no issue is joined here. And the court would not grant a commission.

Note: In this cause, the plaintiff obtained an order to amend his bill, and, afterwards, he amended only by praying relief, it being before only for a discovery. And it was now moved, December 8th, for the defendants, that this order should be set aside because it deprived the defendants of the opportunity of demurring. And they cited Asgill v. Dawson, Trinity 5 Geo.;[2] Hely v. Clarke, 30 May, 5 Geo.

But *per* CURIAM, though you have answered to the original bill, you may still demur to the amended part.

---

1 Stat. 14 Car. II, c. 11, s. 27 (*SR*, V, 399).

2 *Asgill v. Dawson* (Ex. 1721), see above, Case No. 164.

Mr. *Reeves* [was] for the plaintiff; Serjeant *Chesshyre* [was] for the defendant.

Harvard Law School MS. 1082, vol. 1, p. 154, pl. 2

23 November 1722.

A bill was brought for an injunction to stay defendant's proceedings at law in an action of false imprisonment and to have a commission to Barbados to examine witnesses there, whose depositions may be made use of at the trial at law, which they now moved for, and also for an injunction.

Serjeant *Chesshyre* opposed this motion. All the equity in the bill was denied by the answer. They should have applied in the King's Bench, where the action is brought, to have put off the trial, where they might have succeeded or had terms put upon the plaintiff, but it is not proper to apply here. See 14 Car. II, Statute of Frauds.

It was said by Mr. *Reeves* that, if a commission goes out of this court to examine witnesses and depositions are taken upon the commission, those depositions may be read in the action at law between the same parties.

But query as to this point, for it seems they cannot, or at least not until there is an issue joined.

Lord Chief Baron [MONTAGU]: This court can do no justice as to this cause and why should we hinder another court from doing it? He seemed to think, since the Stat. 14 Car. II has tied up commissions to be granted out of Chancery, that this court cannot grant such, though it has been done here. He was against an injunction or commission.

Baron PRICE: The proper application had been in the King's Bench, where the action is commenced, but this court cannot aid the party defendant in that court since here is no issue joined here, and I do not know how we can grant a commission before or even after issue. I doubt the deposition could not be used as evidence at law in cases of the revenue. By the course of [. . .], commissions have been granted.

Baron PAGE: That the depositions should be evidence is not now asked. The courts of law have never allowed depositions as evidence where issue is not joined.

Baron GILBERT: This, upon the pleadings in equity, appears to be a case of great oppression, and, therefore, not a case proper to stop the proceedings at law.

Per TOTAM CURIAM, both injunction and commissions were denied.

Harvard Law School MS. 1082, vol. 1, p. 155, pl. 3

8 December 1722.

The plaintiff obtained an order to amend his bill and afterwards made no other amendment; then, he prayed relief, it being only a bill of discovery before.

It was objected to this, to set aside this order, for the defendants, that this was irregular because it deprives the defendant of the opportunity of demurring. Trinity 5 Geo., Asgill v. Dawson; Kelly v. Clerk, 5 Geo., 30 May. In this case, there was no equity in the bill for relief, and, therefore, if it had been prayed at first, the defendant might have demurred as to so much, which now, after answer, they cannot do.

But *per* CURIAM, the defendant may still demur to the amended part.

Harvard Law School MS. 1082, vol. 1, p. 157, pl. 2

Hilary term 1722/23.

Note: Wherever a bill is for discovery only and the plaintiff has a discovery by the defendant's answer, the plaintiff cannot afterwards reply or proceed, for, by the discovery, he has had the end of his bill. The end of this bill was for a discovery of matters transacted abroad in order to use the same in evidence in an action brought by Whorewood against Lowther in the King's Bench for a false imprisonment, and also it prays an injunction, and the plaintiff afterwards amended his bill and prayed relief.

To this part of the bill that prayed relief, the defendant demurred for that it was a bill for a discovery only and for the aid of this court to enable the complainants to examine witnesses touching matters merely triable at law and which center in damage, which can only be assessed by a jury and, thereby, to make this court subservient to the King's Bench, where the action is brought, and for that there appears no equity in the bill.

Now, the plaintiff suggested that the revenue of the crown was interested, and the Attorney General was made a defendant.

The demurrer was overruled.

Harvard Law School MS. 1082, vol. 1, p. 158, pl. 3

Hilary term 1722/23.

The demurrer to this bill being overruled, it was moved as a matter of course for an injunction, though an injunction had been denied upon the merits before, [*quod*] *vide*. Now, no precedent [was shown] that, upon overruling a demurrer, an injunction is [granted] of course.

Baron PRICE: Since nothing appears in the answer to support an injunction, I do not see any cause to grant it upon overruling the demurrer.

Baron PAGE was of another opinion but was desirous that precedents should be searched and it to be moved when Baron Gilbert came.

359

Long v. Bland

(Ex. 1722)

A discharge of a bankrupt's debts does not discharge a debt that was made before the adjudication of bankruptcy but was not payable until after the date of the discharge.

Bunbury 120, 145 E.R. 617

28 November 1722.

A note was given upon a day, promising payment a year after. The person who gave the note became a bankrupt after the note was given and before the day of payment. And the question was whether, the bankrupt being discharged by the Stat. 5 Ann. and 5 Geo.,[1] this note was discharged.

And it was held by three barons against PRICE it is not.

Harvard Law School MS. 1082, vol. 1, p. 154, pl. 3

28 November 1722.

A note was given one day promising to pay a year after [and] the person you gave the note became a bankrupt after the note was given and before the day of payment. And the question was whether, by the acts of 5 Anne and 5 Geo., the bankrupt being discharged, this note is a debt due and owing at the time of the bankruptcy so as to be discharged. Callowell v. Clutterbuck, King's Bench, Easter 10 Anne.

Note: The words of the act are 'due or owing'. Stat. 4 & 5 Anne; see Stat. 5 Geo., fo. 431. The question is whether this note, which is mentioned to be for value received, is not a debt, though not due, yet owing.

[To the] objection that you have pleaded that the cause of action accrued before the act of bankruptcy, [he] responded we could plead nothing else, and note the very form prescribed in the Act of Parliament. Co. Litt. 76.

Three barons [held] against PRICE that this note was not discharged.

360

Minnett v. Robinson

(Ex. 1722)

Where a ship is forfeited to the crown for illegally importing goods, it is discharged from liability for seamen's wages and any other encumbrances.

Bunbury 121, 145 E.R. 617

Ann Robinson libels in the Admiralty court as administratrix to her husband for his wages due as mariner abroad the *Prince Frederick*. Minnett and Heys move for a [writ of] prohibition upon a suggestion that this ship was seized for importing wines from Holland, not being Rhenish or Hungarian wines, and, therefore, forfeited by the Stat. 12 Car. II.[2] That a claim being put in by Bowen, the master, an information was filed by the seizor, and Bowen pleaded the

[1] Stat. 4 & 5 Ann., c. 4 (*SR*, VIII, 461–465); Stat. 5 Geo. I, c. 24.

[2] Stat. 12 Car. II, c. 25 (*SR*, V, 266–268).

general issue. But, before trial, Bowen submitted and compounded according to the course of the court. And upon payment of £136 to the informer etc., there was judgment *quod vas deliberetur* etc.

It was likewise suggested that the libel was for wages due before the seizure. Upon this motion, I [Bunbury] insisted that the Act of Parliament had so altered the property of the ship that, by the seizure, submission to a fine, and judgment *quod deliberetur* etc. upon it, all precedent encumbrances were discharged.

But the court, upon showing cause, discharged the rule, though they admitted, if there had been a condemnation, that would have been a good ground for a prohibition and a discharge of all precedent encumbrances.

Therefore query, for the fine does imply a condemnation, although not actually given, but prevented by the submission.

Harvard Law School MS. 1082, vol. 1, p. 155, pl. 1

Michaelmas term 1722.

Ann Robinson libels in the Admiralty Court as administratrix to her husband for his wages as a mariner aboard the *Prince Frederick*. Minnett and Hoys move for a [writ of] prohibition. And, upon a suggestion that this was seized for importing wines from Holland not being Rhenish or Hungary wines, being forfeited by Stat. 12 Car. II, by one Smith and a claim being put in by Bowen, the master, an information was filed by Smith, and Bowen pleaded the general issue. But before trial, Bowen submitted and compounded according to the course of the court. And, upon payment of £136 to the informer, there was a judgment.

It was likewise suggested that the libel was for wages due before the seizure. And upon a motion for a [writ of] prohibition, it was insisted that the Act of Parliament so altered the property of the ship that, by the seizure, submission to a fine, and judgment *quod deliberetur* upon it, that all precedent encumbrances were discharged.

But the court, when they came to show cause, discharged the rule, though they admitted, if there had been a condemnation, that would have been a good ground for a prohibition and a discharge of all precedent encumbrances.

Query, therefore, for the fine does imply a condemnation, though it is not actually given but it is prevented by the submission.

Taussig MS. 311, vol. 1, p. 381

Michaelmas term 1722.

A [writ of] prohibition was prayed for to the Admiralty Court to a suit there by seamen for their wages, which suit was against the ship. And the suggestion for the prohibition was that the ship was forfeited and condemned in the Exchequer. But upon looking into the proceedings, it appears that the ship was never actually condemned, but was delivered to the master upon a fine paid by the master.

Et per CURIAM: Had the ship been actually condemned, no doubt, but, by the condemnation, all the prior encumbrances and charges upon the ship are thereby discharged. [It is] otherwise in case the ship is not condemned by a judgment, for, then, the property was never actually out of the master of the ship nor the charge upon it was ever divested. But the court gave a further day to Mr. *Bunbury* to speak on behalf of the master of the ship if he thought fit.

361

Lord v. Turk

(Ex. 1722)

In this case, the court found the land in issue was not discharged from the payment of tithes.

Bunbury 122, 145 E.R. 618,
1 Rayner 178, 1 Eagle & Younge 778

At Serjeants' Inn, 7 December 1722.

A bill was brought by the vicar of Tischurst in the County of Sussex for tithes. The defendant insists the lands were parcel of the monastery of Robertsbridge, which was of the Cistercian Order and, therefore, discharged, being dissolved by the Stat. 31 Hen. VIII,[1] as one of the greater abbeys.

But note lands, though of the Cistercian Order, were not discharged but *quamdiu in propriis manibus*, and even not all those, but only such as were in them before the Council of Lateran, as is expressed in that Council, which was held 5 Hen. II, *anno* 1179.[2] The method of proving whether the lands were purchased before or since the Council of Lateran is only by payment of tithes, which will induce a presumption that they were purchased after.

And *per* CURIAM, the defendant was decreed to account for that it appeared that the lands were in tenants' hands and, consequently, not discharged when they came to Henry VIII.

Sir Constantine Phipps [was] for the plaintiff.

Harvard Law School MS. 1082, vol. 1, p. 155, pl. 2

Serjeants' Inn, 7 December 1722.

A bill was brought by the vicar of Tice in Sussex for tithes. The defendant insists the lands were parcel of the monastery of Robert Bridge, which was of the Cistercian Order and were, therefore, discharged, it being dissolved by the Stat. 31 Hen. VIII, as one of the greater abbeys. 2 Rolle Rep. 142, Cro. Ja. 159;

---

[1] Stat. 31 Hen. VIII, c. 13 (*SR*, III, 733–739).

[2] X, 3. 30. 10.

Lord v. Puck, 25 Car. II.[1] Since [*blank*] the defendant produced a surrender of the Abbey *de Ponte Roberti* being *ordinis Cistertionis* 16 April 29 Hen. VIII to hold to the king, his heirs, and successors *in perpetuum*. Also ministers accounts, 30 Hen. VIII, out of the Augmentation Office, whereby it appears this was one of the larger abbeys and so within 31 Hen. VIII.

Sir Constantine Phipps for the plaintiff: It does not appear that this abbey was dissolved by 31 of Hen. VIII, being surrendered the 29th, but not continued by letters patent until the 31st. There is no evidence that no tithes have been paid and that these lands were in the owner's hands. And they have constantly paid small tithes to the vicar. They admit they are liable to pay tithes in tenant's hands. All the lands in the Cistercian Order were not exempt though *in propriis manibus*, but only such as were in them before the Council of Lateran and not such as were purchased after. The method of proving whether before or after is only by payment of tithes, which will induce a presumption that they were purchased after the Council of Lateran. Hilary 7 Will. III, [*blank*] v. Wilkinson; 13 Will., Pollard v. Penn.[2]

Note: The Council of Lateran itself expresses that lands purchased afterwards by the Cistercian Order shall not be exempt from tithes. The Council of Lateran was in the year 1179, 5 Hen. II. 2 Inst. 611.[3]

Chief Baron [Montagu]: It does not appear that these lands were discharged at the time they came to Henry VIII, and, if so, they will not be discharged. The ministers' accounts show plainly they were not discharged, for that they were let to tenants and rents of assize were reserved and these were freehold tenants.

And the whole court were of the same opinion and decreed the defendant to account.

Taussig MS. 311, vol. 1, p. 384

Setting down of causes after Michaelmas term; Friday, December 7th, 1722.

The plaintiff, as vicar of Tisehurst in the County of Sussex, brought his bill for small tithes against the defendants [Turk and Dupleck] as tenants and occupiers of lands in Maplesden within his parish. And the defendants, by answer, insisted that their lands in Maplesden were parcel of the Abbey of Robert's Bridge, which was one of the greater abbeys and dissolved by the Stat. 31 Hen. VIII, ca. [*blank*], and of the Cistercian Order and so by § 21 of the Statute was discharged from tithes.

---

[1] *Porter v. Bathurst* (1620), 2 Rolle Rep. 142, 81 E.R. 712, Croke Jac. 559, 79 E.R. 479, also Palmer 118, 81 E.R. 1006, 1 Gwillim 373, 1 Eagle & Younge 312; *Lord v. Pooke* (1673), 1 Wood 134.

[2] *Wilkinson v. Newson* (1696), Dodd 158, Eq. Cases Exch. 361, 1 Eagle & Younge 618, Public Record Office, E.126/16, f. 316, 1 Wood 355; *Pollard v. Penn* (1701), 2 Wood 203, note c.

[3] E. Coke, *Second Institute* (1642), p. 641.

And to prove that Maplesdon was parcel of the Abbey, they showed and read in court an *inspeximus* of 11 Edw. III of a grant made by Richard I of Maplesden to the Abbot. And to show that the Abbey was of the Cistercian Order, they read the very surrender of the Abbot in 29 Hen. VIII, which recited it to be of the Cistercian Order. And they also cited the case of Porter and Bathurst, 2 Rolle's Rep. 142, which takes notice that the Abbey was of that Order. And to show that it was of the value of £200 *per annum*, they showed the minister's accounts in 30 Hen. VIII in the Augmentation Office, which proved the same. And they cited a decree in this court 17 April, 25 Car. II, in Lord Chief Baron Turner's time.[1] And they proved by a witness examined in the cause that Maplesden lands were reputed to be parcel of the Abbey of Robert's Bridge. But they produced no witnesses to prove that, in fact, the lands did not use to pay tithes.

E contra pro querente, it was insisted by *Sir Constantine Phipps* and Mr. *Edlin* that the discharge of the Cistercian Order was only *quamdiu propriis manibus excoluntur*, that all the lands of the Cistercians were not privileged, but only such lands as they had in possession before the Council of Lateran. And lands purchased after were forced to pay tithes although *in propriis manibus* and so the grant of Maplesden by Richard I, who began his reign in 1189, being subsequent to the Council of Lateran, which was held in 1179, *prout* 2d Inst. 641,[2] it will follow of consequence that these lands were not discharged. See the Canons of this Council in Gibson's *Codex*, and see Dyer 277b in margin to pl. 60 [*blank*] 18 Jac.; 2 Inst. 652, where it is laid down for law that the discharge only extends to lands purchased before the Council of Lateran.[3]

Secondly, they said that it did not appear that the defendants here were owners of the inheritance. And, if they are only occupiers and tenants, then the privilege did not extend to them, for the privilege was only *quamdiu propriis manibus*.

Third, they said there was not the least syllable of proof that these lands were in the hands of the Abbot *tempore* the dissolution. And, if not, then, the discharge by the Stat. Hen. VIII did not extend to them.

Fourthly, they had strong evidence that they were not, for these lands had paid tithes in former times *prout*, by witnesses examined in the cause and former incumbents' tithe books and by decrees in this court between Wilkinson and Newsam, Hilary 7 Will., *intratur, Jovis, 20 die Februarii*, and Pollard and Penn, 13 Will.

Et per Montagu, Chief Baron: It is certain that, if these lands were not in the hands and actual occupation of the Abbot at the time of the dissolution, then they are not discharged of tithes by the Stat. Hen. VIII. Now, by him, it appears plainly that these lands were not in his hands at that time, for, by the minister's accounts, a rent of assize is answered and accounted for these lands, and a rent

---

[1] *Lord v. Pooke* (1673), 1 Wood 134.

[2] E. Coke, *Second Institute* (1642), p. 641.

[3] E. Gibson, *Codex Juris Ecclesiastici Anglicani* (1713); *Porter v. Bathurst* (1620), *ut supra*; E. Coke, *Second Institute* (1642), p. 652.

of assize is the same as a fee farm rent, which implies the land itself to be in the hands of fee simple tenants, and so the tenants of Maplesdon lands are called in the minister's account *libere tenentes*. And so, by him, the defendants ought to account, *et alii barones concordaverunt*.

But note, by me, if the lands had been only leased to tenants *tempore* the dissolution and the inheritance been in the Abbey, though the tenant was chargeable with tithes during the continuance of his lease, yet the inheritance would have been discharged by virtue of the Statute. And this is the express resolution in the case of Porter and Bathurst, 2 Rolle's Rep. 142, Cro. Jac. 559; and see Hobart 248, 190.[1]

[Order of 7 December 1722: 2 Wood 201.]

362

Hughes v. Billinghurst

(Ex. 1722)

A claim for the tithes of a mill must be proved by some evidence of payment of tithes in the past.

2 Gwillim 644

To a bill by the vicar of Sunning in Berkshire, *inter alia*, for the tithes of corn mills, the defendant insisted that the mills in question were ancient mills and, having been erected before the Statute of 9 Edw. II,[2] ought not to be charged with the payment of any tithes.

The court declared that the bill ought to be dismissed as to the demand of the tithes of the mills, no proof having been made of the payment of tithes at any time for the same. And the bill was accordingly dismissed as to them with costs.

[Order of 10 December 1722: 2 Wood 207, 1 Eagle & Younge 781.]

363

Lavin v. Austin

(Ex. 1722)

The question in this case was whether there was a breach of trust by a trustee's improper investing of the corpus of a trust.

---

[1] *Porter v. Bathurst* (1620), *ut supra*; *Farmer v. Shereman* (1618), Hobart 248, 80 E.R. 394, also Hetley 133, 124 E.R. 401, 1 Eagle & Younge 303.

[2] Stat. 9 Edw. II, stat. 1, *Articuli Cleri*, c. 5 (*SR*, I, 172).

Harvard Law School MS. 1082, vol. 1, p. 156

Michaelmas term 1722.

A trustee of £500 by a will for the mayor and aldermen of Oxford subscribed the £500 without the privity of the mayor and aldermen into the South Sea Company, though he first bought lottery orders and then subscribed these orders into the Company without the consent of the persons interested by the will in this £500.

Note: It was express by the will this £500 was to be laid out in land and the produce of that to be applied to the plaintiff, the testator's widow, for life and, afterwards, to go to the mayor etc. for charitable uses.

See the Act for Empowering the South Sea Company etc., the clause there relating to trustees, 6 Geo., fo. 1722.[1] And it was said for the plaintiff that the defendant should have had first directions of a court of equity. The cause was put off, there being no replication nor any proof in what manner the subscription was made.

364

Merrick v. Spark

(Ex. 1722–1723)

Where a mortgagee (or a pawnee) in possession sells the property mortgaged in violation of the parties' agreement, this is a breach of trust and the mortgagee will be required to pay any profits therefrom to the mortgagor.

Taussig MS. 311, vol. 1, p. 362

Michaelmas term 1722.

Upon a motion for continuing an injunction upon the merits, the case appeared thus. Merrick having £550 South Sea stock conveys the same to Spark by way of a mortgage for £2576. And, by a defeasance, he agrees that Spark should sell the stock in case the stock came down to 520 percent, otherwise not to transfer. And the defeasance thereon from Merrick was on the 20th August 1720 when the stock was at 1000 percent. And Merrick gave a bond for the money. On the 26th of August, Spark mortgages the stock to the company for £2200, according to the usual way of such mortgages at that time, i.e. by an absolute transfer thereof and without any defeasance at all in writing. Spark sues Merrick for the money lent him. And Merrick exhibits his bill in this court for an injunction and relief. By the amended bill, the plaintiff sets forth that he borrowed only £2300 and that £276 was by way of a premium. And this the defendant waived in his answer.

[1] Stat. 6 Geo. I, c. 4.

The court continued the injunction by reason that the defendant had manifestly acted contrary to the defeasance by transferring the stock to the Company without giving Merrick any notice thereof, as, by the express words of the defeasance, he ought to have done.

Taussig MS. 311, vol. 1, p. 570

Michaelmas term 1723.

Merrick borrows £2300 on pawning £550 South Sea stock to Spark while at £850 per cent, and [there was] a defeasance that, when the stock sunk to £520 upon three days notice thereof, the defendant might sell it. This was a defeasance on a bond for £4000 to Spark. Spark transferred it the next day, while the stock was at £800 per cent, to the Company and received £2200 thereon. And the plaintiff brings a bill for a perpetual injunction to prevent the suing of the bond and to have an account for the profits Spark had made of the stock pawned.

The court held that Spark had committed a breach of trust by the transfer of the stock to the Company and decreed that the bond should be given up and that the plaintiff and defendant should give mutual releases. So they gave the plaintiff the £100 overplus which had been lent him more than Sparke borrowed from the Company for his breach of trust. And the court held it was the same thing whether the transfer to the Company be looked on as a mortgage or a sale, for a pawnee has no more power to mortgage than to sell the pawn.

365

Paris v. Reese

(Ex. 1722)

The court can refuse to allow a defendant to plead double.

Taussig MS. 311, vol. 1, p. 363

Michaelmas term 1722.

The court would not give leave to plead *non culpabilis* and *son assault demesne* and this notwithstanding the plaintiff was absent and gone abroad before the declaration was delivered.

N.B. The subpoena in this court does not mention the cause of action.

366

Anonymous

(Ex. 1722)

A plaintiff suing in forma pauperis *will not be allowed to amend his bill of complaint without counsel's assurance to the court of the propriety of the amendment.*

Taussig MS. 311, vol. 1, p. 364, pl. 1

Michaelmas term 1722.

Mr. *Bootle* moved in behalf of a pauper that he might be at liberty to amend his bill by adding parties and proper charges.

But the court asked him whether he knew that the amendments were proper or else they would not do it.

And Chief Baron [MONTAGU], PAGE, and GILBERT agreed that it should be a standing rule of the court that, upon all such motions, the counsel moving it should be able to inform the court that he had considered the amendments to be made and that they were proper, i.e. pertinent to the subject matter for which the bill was exhibited. And the Deputy [Remembrancer] was directed to take the rule accordingly.

367

Brown v. Marsh

(Ex. 1722)

An assignment for value of a note or of a bond cuts off personal defenses thereto.

Taussig MS. 311, vol. 1, p. 365

Michaelmas term 1722.

Whether, upon an *indebitatus assumpsit* on a promissory note for value received, the promisor may give in evidence that there was no consideration given, that it was fraudulent, and by surprise, for PAGE and GILBERT were of opinion that he might.

MONTAGU and PRICE were *contra*. But all agreed that no such thing can be given in evidence against an assignee of such note.

Per GILBERT: I think there is no reason in equity to relieve the original contrivers of bubbles against any disadvantageous contracts; it is otherwise where a remedy is sought against such contrivers.

Per MONTAGU: I have seen great inconvenience by giving infancy and coverture in evidence.

Per MONTAGU: The Statute puts the very gist of the action upon the note itself. And, therefore, I think the case is the same upon a bond. See the Act. Formerly, the action was only brought upon a promise and the note was only an evidence. And I see no difference between a note assigned and the action as conceived against the drawer, for it is a rule *quod initio non valet tractu temporis non convalescit*.

[Query as to] usury and gaming, whether these are not to be given in evidence because other acts of Parliament have avoided such contracts.

PAGE: If a deed be voluntary, it is fraudulent against creditors. But if a security be assigned over for a valuable consideration, it is never reckoned fraudulent, which is contrary to the rule before. It is certain that the money endorsed must be allowed in evidence, but circumvention and fraud do not entirely come up to this.

The name of this case was Brown and Marsh upon a motion for an injunction. The point, which the court said was of very great consequence in this case as affecting all contracts upon bubbles and, therefore, thought it reasonable to consider further of it, was this. Brown contracts for two shares in Essington's Brass and Copper Works at 700 percent and pays down £480, gives a promissory note for £1000 value received, and, afterwards, pays £350 more in part of discharge of the note. Marsh sues the note at law for the rest. And Browne exhibits his bill and suggests Marsh had no title to the two shares and that he had no transfer thereof nor could have, and, therefore, prayed the money again which he had already paid as well as an injunction to the proceedings at law on the promissory note. The defendant, by his answer, sets forth that one Fowler was possessed of two receipts for £1000 each in this bubble, that the same was in one Edwards' hands, that Fowler died and his widow and executrix, having occasion to raise the money, determined to sell these receipts and employed Marsh to do it, who contracted with the plaintiff for the same in the presence of Edwards and knew at the time of the contract that these receipts were in Edwards' hands. And, in truth, he and Edwards were the original contrivers and promoters of this bubble. And, therefore, whether he should be relieved in equity from his contract upon the account, that he could not have a *quid pro quo* for his money, the receipts being now of no value, was the main question of the cause.

And the parties plaintiff took time to consider whether they would give a judgment on the note or security for the residue of the money unpaid to wait the event of the decree of the court on hearing the cause.

368

Thomas v. Godfrey

(Ex. 1722)

A court of equity will not decree specific performance of a contract to convey land where the performance is impossible.

Taussig MS. 311, vol. 1, p. 371

Monday, 12 November 1722.

The bill was to oblige the defendant to execute a further conveyance according to a covenant in the purchase deed. It appeared in the proofs of the cause that the defendant had conveyed three acres as freehold, one whereof was copyhold, and that he himself knew it because he had taken it in exchange from a copyhold tenant thereof. But the lord of the manor and the copyhold tenant were not parties to the bill.

The court said they could not decree a specific performance of the covenant because it appeared to them to be impossible, for, as to the acre which the defendant gave in exchange, it was not conveyed and so, as to that, whether the exchange was good or not, it being not conveyed, no further assurance could be had of that because the tenant and lord were not parties. And, therefore, because the thing desired by the bill was impossible now to be done, they dismissed the plaintiff's bill, but spared his costs because the defendant had been guilty of a notorious fraud.

Sed quaere, for I never knew a court of equity excuse themselves from decreeing specific performance because the plaintiff had rendered it impossible for him to perform his covenant *in specie*. And I take it the plaintiff must either do it or lie in jail, which is the only way the court can ever take to oblige the covenantor to perform his covenant *in specie*. But the court decreed as above, Baron Gilbert *dissentiente*.

369

Hassell v. Price

(Ex. 1722)

An arbitral award between private parties cannot bind the crown.

The Court of Exchequer will not order the payment of a stipend due from the crown where the right to the payment has not been proved by sufficient evidence.

Taussig MS. 311, vol. 1, p. 372

Michaelmas term 1722.

Mr. *Foley* moved on behalf of Mr. Hassell, preacher of the Chapel of Bewdley, that a stipend of £8 *per annum* payable to the curate of Bewdley should be paid him by the crown. And Price, being parson of Rixborough, laid claim to this stipend as parson of Rixborough, to which, he pretended, the curacy of the Chapel of Bewdley was annexed to Rixborough. Hassell, as curate of Bewdley, exhibits his bill against Price concerning this pension and the arrears thereof for ten years. Price answers, and, after the answer, the point is referred to two arbitrators, who award that the stipend shall be paid to Hassell.

And upon a motion that the Auditor should pay him the stipend accordingly, the court directed that the Auditor should be applied to and should certify whether and how the stipend was payable. And, accordingly, the Auditor's certificate was now produced, whereby it appeared that a stipend of £8 was payable to the curate of Bewdley and that ten years thereof was now in arrear.

But *per* MONTAGU: We must take care that the stipend be but once paid by the crown. And it does not judicially appear to us that this Hassell is the curate of Bewdley, for, as to the award, it cannot bind the crown nor us. And, therefore, unless you can give us better satisfaction that Hassell is the curate, we shall not direct the payment to him. As to the proceedings on the bill, to which it seems the Attorney General was not a party, there are no depositions to prove this point. And the admission of the parties, no more than the award, will [not] be sufficient for us to direct such a payment to Hassell.

Per PRICE: We have often directed the payment of pensions to the crown's preachers upon a certificate of Auditors.

But, however, the court directed them to go back to the Auditor and see if he would certify that Hassell was the curate of Bewdley.

N.B. Mr. *Bunbury* on behalf of Price consented to Mr. Foley's motion, but the Chief Baron [MONTAGU] would not grant it notwithstanding, *causa qua supra*.

370

Cotes v. Turner

(Ex. 1722–1723)

A plea must specially respond to each part of the bill of complaint that is not answered to.

Where an incomplete answer is given, the plaintiff can file exceptions to it, but, where no answer at all is given, the plaintiff can get a writ of attachment to compel an answer.

Taussig MS. 311, vol. 1, p. 383

Michaelmas term 1722.

To plead to a bill in this manner, *viz.* to all matters not hereinafter answered, is a naughty way of pleading. And the plea in this case was set aside for that very reason.

Taussig MS. 311, vol. 1, p. 393

Friday, January 25th, 1723. PRICE, PAGE, GILBERT, *praesentibus*.

The defendant pleaded to the plaintiff's bill *prout* before, *viz.* to such part as not answered, and he answered to such part as not pleaded to. And this plea was overruled in Michaelmas term last. And two or three days before the beginning of this term, the plaintiff took out a [writ of] attachment against the defendant supposing that, by the rules of the court, the defendant ought to have put in a new answer. The defendant now moved to discharge this attachment.

And it was discharged by the court for this reason, that the plaintiff ought to have taken exceptions to the defendant's answer, for that there was an answer in being, though perhaps insufficient, and the difference is where the plea or demurrer goes to the whole bill. There, if overruled, the defendant must answer because, in such a case, there is no answer at all; it is otherwise where there is a plea to part and an answer to part.

Harvard Law School MS. 1082, vol. 1, p. 157, pl. 1

26 January 1722[/23].

It was ruled *per* CURIAM that, where a plea or demurrer is, upon a hearing, overruled and the defendant answers also (even only by denying a combination), that, in that case, the defendant is not obliged to put in a farther answer until the plaintiff has put in exceptions for that purpose. But where the plea or demurrer is to the whole bill, there, the defendant must answer according to the rules of the court without exceptions put in by the plaintiff.

Bunbury 123, 145 E.R. 618

26 January 1722[/23].

Per CURIAM: Where a plea or demurrer is overruled upon a hearing and the defendant answers also, even by only denying combination, the defendant is not obliged to put in a farther answer until the plaintiff has put in exceptions for that purpose. But if the demurrer is to the whole bill and is overruled, the defendant must answer according to the rules of the court without exceptions put in by the plaintiff.

371

Anonymous

(Ex. 1723)

Where a claim is made to forfeited goods but no security is put in, the claimer has a right to notice of the hearing on the order of forfeiture by default.

Taussig MS. 311, vol. 1, p. 390, pl. 1

Hilary term 1722[/23]; Wednesday, first day of term, Montagu, Chief Baron, absent.

A claim was made and entered in the middle of the last term, and no security is yet given according to the custom to make good his claim. And so Mr. *Browne* now moved that the claim might be discharged.

But Mr. Baron PRICE would not absolutely discharge the claim, notwithstanding this long delay without hearing the claimer. And so he pronounced the rule of discharge only *nisi causa*.

372

Somers v. Foster

(Ex. 1723)

A mariner cannot sue a forfeited ship for his unpaid wages, but his cause of action in debt therefor remains.

A mariner is a disinterested witness in an action for the forfeiture of a ship in which he sailed.

Taussig MS. 311, vol. 1, p. 390, pl. 2

Thursday, 24th January 1722[/23].

[An English] bill [was exhibited] by the owners of the ship the *Good Intent* of Liverpool and the master and freighters *inde.* And the scope of it was to have satisfaction for the loss of the ship and for the price agreed upon for the freight of it *prout* by the charter party. The ship freighted at £39 per month for ten months certain and for fourteen months after if the voyage should so long last. And the ship was to sail to New England and thence back to England; that the ship, after its departure from the Black Rock, went into Ireland and there took in brandies, pepper, and gloves;[1] that, afterwards, the ship sailed to New York and was condemned there on account of the brandies which were put on board in Ireland, and these were put on board by the defendants, the freighters and master, the freighters themselves being on board and sailing the whole voyage.

The defendants admit their charter party *prout*, but they deny that the ship was ready to sail at the exact time agreed upon by the charter party. They say they had no power over the ship, but that the defendant, the master, had the whole power over it and went into Ireland against their consent and that the brandies were there taken in by the desire of the master and was no more than proper for provision.

Litchfield, the master, by an answer, swears that going into Ireland was only owing to the obstinacy of the defendants, the freighters, and that the defendants, the freighters, proposed the buying of the brandies. And he says, when he came to New York, he made his report of the ship's cargo according to his own cocket, but that there were other goods on board not contained in this cocket, and that, therefore, the ship was forfeited.

N.B. By the charter party, the freight, though computed by £39 per month for ten months certain and fourteen months longer if the voyage so long lasted, was to be paid by the special direction of the charter party in the manner following: one third part upon the discharge of the goods at Liverpool, one other third

[1] Sic in MS. for cloves.

part within six weeks after the discharge, and the other third part six months after the said discharge.

After this charter party was read, the plaintiff would have read the deposition of a mariner. And the objection was that a mariner could not be a witness because he is interested, for, if the freight is not due, then wages are not due.

Per CURIAM: It is of no consequence, for though, if the ship be lost, this is true, yet in case the ship is forfeited, there is no color that the wages are lost, though indeed by the forfeiture of the ship, the mariners cannot go upon the ship itself, for that lien is lost by the forfeiture.

The cause was adjourned until next term [to] settle issues to try by whose default the ship was forfeited, what damages the plaintiff sustained, third, whether anything and what be due for demurrage.

373

Anonymous

(Ex. 1723)

Exceptions do not lie to a master's report that an answer is scandalous or impertinent, but the objections to the report should be made at the hearing on the report.

Taussig MS. 311, vol. 1, p. 394, pl. 1

Hilary term 1723.

Raby moved to confirm the Master's report whereby an answer was reported to be scandalous and impertinent. And he moved further that the scandal and impertinency may be expunged.

By *Aris*: We have put in an exception to the report.

Sed per CURIAM: We do not admit exceptions to such reports in this court, but we will hear you *ore tenus* what you can say in defense of the matter which is reported impertinent. And, upon the hearing, the court determined that the answer was neither scandalous nor impertinent.

374

Locket v. Legreys

(Ex. 1723)

A purchaser of an equity of redemption can sue the mortgagor-seller for specific performance of the contract without joining the mortgagee as a party.

Taussig MS. 311, vol. 1, p. 394, pl. 2

Hilary term 1723.

If a man agrees for the purchase of an equity of redemption, in a bill for [specific] performance of this agreement, a mortgagee need not be made a party and brought before the court. But, if a man makes an agreement for an absolute purchase without encumbrances and then, in his bill, sets forth an incumbrance in B., he must then bring B. to the hearing, for perhaps B. may insist on an absolute purchase. And, therefore, in this case, it is not proper to leave this matter to go before the Master.

And so the court was adjourned.

375

Rex v. Tollett

(Ex. 1723)

A tenant by a statute merchant can plead his priority to an outlawry against the same debtor.

Bunbury 123, 145 E.R. 618, Conroy 115

25 January 1722[/23].

Tollett was outlawed at the suit of Baily, *termino Paschae, 8 Georgii Regis* [1722]. An inquisition was taken thereupon and returned into the Exchequer. A [writ of] *levari facias* issued returnable *octabis Hilarii anno nono Georgii Regis* [1723], by virtue of which the sheriff levied £120. Craddock, who had a statute merchant against Tollett for £1000, *Maii*, 7 Geo. [1721] and was in possession of the land, moved for time to plead to the outlawry and inquisition and that, upon giving security, the money in the sheriff's hands might be repaid to him, which was granted and said to be the constant course of the Court of Exchequer.

376

Gold v. Freame

(Ex. 1723–1724)

Where the right to receive a copyhold fine is in dispute, the defendant cannot pay into court a lesser sum than is demanded.

The tenants of a manor have a right to inspect the court rolls.

The amount of a copyhold fine based on the value of the premises refers to the value settled in the past without regard to later improvements.

Taussig MS. 311, vol. 1, p. 398

Hilary term 1722[/23].

In [an action of] debt for a copyhold fine, Mr. *Bunbury* moved to bring 4s. and 2d. into court and that it might be struck out of the declaration. And he cited instances of bringing money into court on an action of debt for rent.

And *Sir Constantine Phipps* now showed cause that the instances wherein money might be brought into court were only where the plaintiff might recover less than what he declared for. But, in this case, if he did not prove the whole fine due for which he declared, he could recover nothing at all.

Mr. *Bunbury*, on the other side, said the defendant could not safely plead *nil debet* because 4s. 2d. is certainly due and legal, though the fine of £15 is not due.

Et per CURIAM: You ought not in this case to bring the money into court because, in this declaration, if the plaintiff does not prove the legality of this £15 fine, he must be nonsuited, he having insisted on it as an arbitrary fine and declared for it as such, though, in other cases of debt, the plaintiff may recover only part of his demand.

So Mr. Bunbury's motion was denied.

Taussig MS. 311, vol. 1, p. 408

Hilary term 1722/23.

A motion that the trial in this cause might be put off, that the defendants might inspect the court rolls and take copies of them, and that others of the rolls might be produced at trial was granted upon the defendants' having given notice of the motions.

Per PRICE: The tenants have a right to inspect court rolls.

Harvard Law School MS. 1082, vol. 1, p. 157, pl. 6

Hilary term 1722/23.

In an action of debt for £15 set for a fine in the court of the lord of the manor, the court refused the defendant to bring 4s. 2d. into court, as has been done in debt for rent.

Note: The dispute was whether the fine was certain or uncertain.

Bunbury 124, 145 E.R. 619

1 February 1722[/23].

In an action of debt for £15 set for a fine in the court of the lord of a manor, the court refused to let the defendant bring 4s. 2d. into court etc. as had been done in debt for rent, covenant, etc.

Taussig MS. 311, vol. 2, p. 661

Easter term 1724. Gould v. Freame and Ecclestone.

The plaintiff, as lord of the manor of Edmonton, brought an action of debt for £15, being assessed on the defendants as a fine for their admittance to a copyhold house and gardens on Bushill within that manor, to which they pleaded *nil debet*. And the cause came to be tried before the Chief Baron [Eyre] on Friday 22 May.

The plaintiff [was][1] in possession, and the courts were held in his name (though, in truth, he was lessee for a term of years under the crown) and the fine assessed being under the yearly value of the premises to be let, amounting to no more than they were taxed at to the land tax and so very much short of the true value *per annum*.

The Chief Baron thought this was sufficient *prima facie* for the plaintiff, fines of copyhold manors being by presumption of law uncertain and at the will of the lord.

The defendants, therefore, went into their defense, which defense was that the fines in this manor were certain. And to prove this, they produced a decree made 2 June 6 *Jacobi primi* [1608] made by the then Lord Treasurer, Chancellor [of the Exchequer], and Barons of the Exchequer reciting a controversy between the king and the tenants of this manor concerning the certainty of the fines and that the tenants had given up their pretense and submitted to the king's grace; they decreed that the tenants of the manor forever thenafter should pay for admittances upon descents, surrenders, and alienations these fines and no other, *viz.* for every admittance in possession, one whole year's value of the lands and tenements according to a survey taken of the said manor 2 Jac., the yearly quit rents payable for the said lands and tenements being deducted and not above, and for an admittance into an estate for life, reversion, or remainder one-half year's value according to the said survey, the yearly quit rents deducted. Then they showed an Act of Parliament 7 Car. I confirming this decree with a clause therein extending to all such parts of the manor as were not surveyed and valued at that time, but should afterwards be surveyed and valued within two years after the decree.

Then they showed that the place whereon this house and gardens stood and were erected about twenty-two years ago was parcel of three acres of ground and one rood in the possession of one R.H. and valued together in the survey of the 2 Jac. I with two other copyhold parcels held by the said R.H. at £3 12s., quit rent £1 14s. And they deduced the title to these three acres and one rood from this R.H. to the builder of the house etc. in question by several surrenders and admittances, in some of which, mention was made of apportionments of the rent and values, as the tenements were from time to time divided and split into several copies.

And though it was objected *ex parte querente* that the changing of the nature and improving it by building would entitle the lord to a fine according to the improved value at the time of every admittance, yet the Chief Baron [Eyre] was clear of opinion that, by the express words of the decree, the value was tied up

[1] being *MS.*

to the time of the survey and that was to be the rule of all subsequent fines and that the lord could set no other fine than what was agreeable to the then value and that the tenements then valued if they became afterwards divided and split into many and different copies, which was this case and perhaps 100 more in this manor, must be rated in proportion to the old valuation and the quit rent apportioned accordingly. And this he said was agreeable to the plain intent of the decree and Act of Parliament, which was to make the fines certain for the future and thereby encourage improvements, which in all probability would never have been made without this encouragement. And this being his opinion and judgment, it was certain that the fine for which this action was brought, though under the real annual value of the house at present, was greatly above the proportionable value of the place whereon it was built at the time of the survey and the value then set upon it, the plaintiff submitted to be nonsuited.

N.B. I was of counsel with the plaintiff. And I think the Chief Baron was clearly in the right, though my client showed me the opinions of three very great men in the profession in his favor, *viz.* that he had a right to assess fines according to the present yearly value. See 2 Mod. 229, a dispute somewhat of this nature; Cro. Car. 196, that a year [and] one half value according to a rack rent is enough for a fine even where the fines are uncertain at the will of the lord; see the case 2 Leon. 117, 3 Leon 114, feoffment before the Statute of *Quia emptores terrarum solvendi post quilibet vacationem sive alienationem valorem annualem proficiarum [?] terrae.*[1]

Per CURIAM: The value shall be intended to be such value as the land bore *tempore feoffamenti*, and not such value as the land has gained by the succession of time.

377

Tingary v. Bishop of London

(Ex. 1723)

In this case, a vicar proved his right to a portion of the great tithes of the parish and the court granted a commission to set forth the metes and bounds of the vicar's portion of the lands.

Harvard Law School MS. 1082, vol. 1, p. 157, pl. 4

31 January 1722/23.

A bill was brought by [Tingary], the vicar of Brent Pelhem in the County of Hertford, for a portion of the great tithes arising upon three farms within the said parish and to have a commission to set forth the metes and bounds out of

[1] *Trotter v. Blake* (1677), 2 Modern 229, 86 E.R. 1042; *Dow v. Golding* (1630), Croke Car. 196, 79 E.R. 772; *Marsh v. Jones* (1587), 2 Leonard 117, 74 E.R. 406, 3 Leonard 114, 74 E.R. 575; Stat. 18 Edw. I, c. 1 (*SR*, I, 106).

which the portion of the tithes is arising and what part belongs to the vicar and what to the impropriator.

Taussig MS. 311, vol. 1, p. 396

Hilary term 1722[/23]. Tinge, vicar Brent Pelham v. Hill, Hamond, Bishop of London, Dean and Chapter of St. Paul's, and the Treasurer of St. Paul's, defendants.

The vicar exhibited his bill against Hill, who was the lessee of the impropriate rectory of Burnt Pelham, and against Hamond, his under-lessee, for the great tithes arising upon part of three farms called Beeches, Showkes, and Grays, which farms consisted of 300 acres of land. But the vicar only pretended to great tithes of 200 acres of those farms and admitted the impropriator was entitled to the great tithes of the 100 acres residue. And the proof he gave was of a composition of £15 *per annum* yearly paid to him for above sixty years last, which sum of £15 he also proved was three times as much as the value of all small tithes arising upon the whole three farms. There was also some evidence offered of the lands being formerly staked out and distinguished by marks to signify which part of the lands were tithable to the vicar and which to the impropriator. And there was some evidence from the church register.

Et super totam materiam, the court decreed for the vicar, there being no counter-evidence, and they declared that he was entitled to rectorial tithes for part of these farms and decreed a commission to be issued to set out these lands in certain to prevent future controversies.

N.B. A commission was prayed by the bill.

378

Tyrrell v. Kennett

(Ex. 1723–1725)

In this case, the court found that the plaintiff was entitled to the tithes that were in issue.

Harvard Law School MS. 1082, vol. 1, p. 157, pl. 5

1 February 1722/23.

Where a defendant prays a commission to answer, he is obliged to rejoin *gratis*.

Taussig MS. 311, vol. 1, p. 422

Hilary term 1722/23.

Tyrrell, as impropriator of the rectory of Shopland with the Island of Foulness annexed, exhibits his bill against the defendant for tithes arising on lands lying within the Isle of Foulness.

The defendant, by his answer, sets forth that Foulness was an isle recovered from the sea and has been ever since the Reformation a rectory and the rector thereof is entitled to the tithes there.

And the cause was put over on account that the rector of Foulness ought to have been made a party in order to litigate the right to these tithes.

Taussig MS. 311, vol. 2, p. 731

Thursday, 19th November 1724.

The plaintiff, as lay impropriator of the parish of Shopland with the Island of Foulness annexed, brought his bill for great tithes arising upon a farm called Little Borwood within the Island of Foulness.

17 May 6 Eliz. [1564], [there was] a presentation of a parson, *viz.* Christopher Broadwater, *ad rectoriam de ecclesia de Foulness vacata per mortem Johannis Stansworth per presentatione [blank] Richardi, veri patroni dictae ecclesiae.*[1] William Gould was presented in 1586, 28 Eliz., to the said rectory, so that there is a rectory from the Reformation presentable. 43 Eliz., Act for the Relief of the Poor,[2] recites that 'whereas the Island of Foulness' etc. and expressly recites that the Island was no parish, but lay in several parishes.

The court directed an issue to try whether the farm of Little Borwood or any and what part of the same was within the parish of Shopland.

Taussig MS. 311, vol. 2, p. 786

Easter term 1725.

In this last case, though the plaintiff was a lay impropriator and though the defendant insisted that neither he nor any of his predecessor impropriators had ever received any tithes for the lands in question, which lay in the Island of Foulness, yet because he chiefly insisted by his answer that these lands did not lie in the parish of Shopland of the rectory whereof the plaintiff was impropriator and upon that account were not tithable to the plaintiff, for which reason the court directed an issue to try whether it did or no, which issue was found for the plaintiff.

Therefore, the court would not suffer the defendant to go upon the point of non-payment, but they decreed an account of the tithes of the said lands.

And the Chief Baron [Eyre] observed that the defendant had not insisted or controverted his right to the great tithes in the rest of the parish and, it being now found that these lands were in the parish, it shall be presumed that they are tithable unless a particular exemption is shown.

N.B. I was of counsel with the defendant.

[Order of 7 December 1722: 2 Wood 204, 1 Eagle & Younge 779.]

---

[1] to the rectory of the church of Foulness vacated by the death of John Stansworth by the presentation of [blank] Richards, the true patron of the said church.

[2] Stat. 43 Eliz. I, c. 2, s. 17 (*SR*, IV, 965).

379

Gravener v. Clarke

(Ex. 1723)

A defendant can dismiss a commission to answer in the country and get a new commission to plead, answer, and demur.

Harvard Law School MS. 1082, vol. 1, p. 157, pl. 7

Hilary term 1722/23.

The defendant appears and takes out a commission to answer in Michaelmas term as of course, the defendants living at Ipswich. After the setting down of causes, the defendant Clarke brought the bill to counsel, upon inspecting of which it was thought proper to plead, answer, and demur, and he moved for a commission for that purpose the first day of the term and had an order for it.

The plaintiff coming this day to discharge this order, there being a commission before to answer, the court refused to discharge the order for, the first commission being dropped, it was regular to move for the second commission.

380

Calverly v. Parker

(Ex. 1723)

A plaintiff in a bill in equity for discovery must pay the court costs.

Bunbury 124, 145 E.R. 619

1 February 1722[/23].

Wherever a bill is for a discovery only and the plaintiff has a discovery by the defendant's answer, the plaintiff cannot reply or proceed, for, by the discovery, the plaintiff has obtained the end of his bill, and, when he has had the benefit of it in an action brought at law and comes afterwards to dismiss his bill, which he must do or the defendant will, such dismission will be with costs to be taxed, which seems hard, since the defendant was the occasion of this bill by his false plea below and the plaintiff there can be allowed no costs in equity. See Stat. 4 & 5 Ann., c. 16, s. 23.[1]

Harvard Law School MS. 1082, vol. 1, p. 158, pl. 1

Hilary term 1722/23.

---

[1] Stat. 4 & 5 Ann., c. 3, s. 23 (*SR*, VIII, 460–461).

See Lowther v. Whorewood.[1] When the plaintiff has had the benefit of his discovery in equity in an action brought at law and comes afterwards to dismiss his bill, which he must do or the defendant will, such dismission must be with costs to be taxed, which seems hard since the defendant was the occasion of the bill by his false plea and the plaintiff there will be allowed no costs in equity. But see Stat. 4 & 5 Anne, Amendment of Law.

381

Price v. Lord Coningsby

(Ex. 1723)

A letter sent to a peer to appear and answer to a bill in equity is a process, and it will give the plaintiff priority of suit as to a bill filed afterwards by the defendant against him.

A judge who is interested in a lawsuit must recuse himself from hearing it.

If, in a suit on a bond to perform covenants, there be a plea of covenants performed, the plaintiff must show a covenant or condition that was broken in order to show that the condition was suspended.

Taussig MS. 311, vol. 1, p. 395

Hilary term 1722[/23].

Price *et al.* brought a bill against Lord Conningsby in Trinity term, but they took out no process until a letter from the Lord Chief Baron dated on 13 June 1722, which was served on My Lord on the same day.

Per Kettleby: This letter is no process. No subpoena was taken out on this bill until this day against the other co-defendants. My Lord exhibits his bill against the plaintiffs in the original bill in Michaelmas term last and serves process.[2] An order was made in Michaelmas term that the plaintiffs should not answer My Lord's bill until My Lord had answered the original bill. And now My Lord moves to discharge this order upon two suggestions: first, because there was no process on the original bill; second, because My Lord's bill is not in the nature of a cross-bill. The original bill is against My Lord to be confirmed in their copyhold estates. My Lord's bill is to have a discovery of the copy of court rolls of his manor.

The court referred the matters of the two different bills, as also the fact concerning the process, to the Deputy [Remembrancer] to examine and to report.

Per Page and Gilbert: The first process gives the title to priority of answer. *Et per eosdem*: A letter is such a process.

Price being a defendant in the Lord Conningsby's bill, though no plaintiff in the original bill, My Lord insisted he should not sit on the bench while this

[1] *Lowther v. Whorwood* (1722–1723), see above, Case No. 358.

[2] *Lord Coningsby v. Price* (Ex. 1723), see below, Case No. 382.

motion was in the making, and he accordingly quitted the bench and sat down on the side of the court where the king's counsel usually sit.

Harvard Law School MS. 1082, vol. 1, p. 157, pl. 3

28 January 1722/23.

[It was] said upon this motion that the letter sent by the Chief Baron to a peer to answer is no part of the process upon a bill. See the Rules.

But it was denied by PAGE, for it is a matter of right, and not of grace. See Stat. 12 & 13 Will. III, cap. 3.[1]

Baron GILBERT said that it is a process yet not such a process as subjects the party to a contempt.

Note: If a man files his bill and takes out no process upon it, if a cross-bill be filed, the plaintiff in the original cause cannot compel the defendant to answer his bill first, he having taken out no process in his bill.

Bunbury 124, 145 E.R. 618

28 January 1723.

Though a letter sent by the Lord Chief Baron to a peer is not such process as subjects the party to a contempt, yet it is such process as gives the party suing it out, priority of suit. If a man files a bill and takes out no process upon it, if a cross-bill be filed, the plaintiff in the original cause cannot compel the defendant to answer his bill first, he having taken out no process on his bill.

Taussig MS. 311, vol. 1, p. 547, pl. 2

Eodem die [9 November 1723].

If exceptions are regularly set down according to the course of the court, it is to be presumed the answer is not sufficient. And, therefore, in this case, there being an original bill to which Lord Coningsby put in his answer, to which exceptions were filed and set down, and My Lord having filed a cross-bill, the court ordered that the plaintiffs in the original cause should not be obliged to answer this cross-bill until My Lord had fully answered their original bill, his present answer to their bill, being excepted to, not being to be looked upon as an answer.

Taussig MS. 311, vol. 1, p. 574

Michaelmas term 1723.

[To the] plea that one of the children was not of age, [it was] replied that he was of age.

---

[1] Stat. 12 & 13 Will. III, c. 3 (*SR*, VII, 638–639).

Kettleby: The plaintiff should have showed the money was not paid *prout* Sanders, fol. 102, 1 Syd. 340; Cro. Eliz. 889, Yelv. 24, Baily v. Taylor;[1] 2 Cro. 442. Secondly, it does not appear upon the pleadings that James Hely was the youngest of the sons, and, if he was not the youngest of the sons, then nothing is yet due. Thirdly, [if one] shall happen to die before they or either of them shall attain their age [*blank*] so it appearing now that one of them did attain his age.

Comyns, contra, admits he has not paid the last sum. And Lord Chief Justice Holt used to say that the case of a bond to perform an award is an anomalous case. And if the defendant pleads *non submisit* and that is found against him, the plaintiff shall have judgment without showing a breach.

The cases where it is said that the want of showing a breach is helped by the verdict makes for us, for a verdict cannot help the matter if it is necessary to be shown.

Second, if any part of a condition be not performed, the whole penalty is forfeited. And whether James Hely was the eldest or the youngest, if the money was not paid within a month after his attaining his age, then the bond is forfeited.

Third, they or either of them attained their age. This must be understood distributively or respectively. Moor 591;[2] the defendant must show the exact performance. 1 Lev. 303; 1 Syd. 215.[3] And so it was adjudged *coram* Parker, Lord Chancellor, upon a recognizance with a condition entered into by Sir Humphrey Mackworth, who pleaded a bad plea, *scil.* that he had performed all and singular *in conditione ex parte sua performanda*, and, the plea being bad, on a demurrer, the plaintiff had judgment.

Replication *per Kettleby*: There was no defense in the Case of Sir Humphrey Mackworth. He had no counsel to open the demurrer and so judgment [was given].

Gilbert: By a reply of an arbitration, the suspension of the bond is not determined, and this is the particular reason of that case. But if a bond be for the performance of covenants, this is a good plea. Therefore, the plaintiff must reply to a breach. Where there is a particular condition, there the defendant must show the performance or else he does not show the continuance of the suspension. And so he was of opinion that the plaintiff should have judgment.

But they only pronounced the judgment *nisi causa* the first day of the next term.

11 Modern 395, 88 E.R. 1110

Michaelmas term, 10 Geo. I, 1723.

In an action on a bond, on oyer prayed, the bond and condition were set forth *in haec verba*, and, amongst other things, it was that the defendant should

---

[1] *Hayman v. Gerrard* (1667), 1 Williams Saunders 99, 102, 85 E.R. 108, 109, 1 Siderfin 340, 82 E.R. 1144, also 1 Levinz 226, 83 E.R. 381, 2 Keble 258, 275, 84 E.R. 160, 171; *Baily v. Taylor* (1602), Croke Eliz. 899, 78 E.R. 1122, Yelverton 25, 80 E.R. 18.

[2] *Creswel v. Holmes* (1597 x 1598), Moore K.B. 591, 72 E.R. 778.

[3] *Wimbleton v. Holdrip* (1670), 1 Levinz 303, 83 E.R. 419, also 2 Keble 720, 84 E.R. 455; *Woodcock v. Cole* (1664), 1 Siderfin 215, 82 E.R. 1065, also 1 Keble 760, 83 E.R. 1228.

pay such a sum to the plaintiff within two months after he came to age. The plea was that he is not come to age. The reply was that he is. There was a demurrer.

Kettleby: The exception is that the replication should have gone on and averred that the money was paid, for that is the right of action. In the case of Hammon v. Garrett,[1] the condition was to account for all such monies and goods as belonged to A.; it was pleaded that no goods came to his hands; the plaintiff replied that a silver tankard came to his hands; and, on a demurrer, the court *seriatim* were of opinion that there was no cause of action stated, for that they did not show the money was not paid. In the case of an award, you must show a breach of an award if you reply *fecit* to a plea of *nul fecit arbitrium*. In the case of Baily v. Taylor, a bond was conditioned that the defendant should redeem a mortgage; the defendant pleaded 'no mortgage'; the plaintiff replied 'a mortgage'; and, on demurrer, it was held a void replication for not averring that the mortgage was not redeemed. The condition of this bond was for the payment of several sums to the three sons of Chief Justice Kelly in Ireland within two months after they severally came to age.

Serjeant *Comyns, contra*. If the bond is for performance of matters contained in the condition, the defendant must show that he has performed the defeasance or the bond is absolute against him, unlike when the condition is for the performance of covenants. They admit by *nient dedire* that they have not paid the money, and they excuse themselves by saying that James was not of age. An award is the only case in law where the plaintiff need assign any breach. If they plead no submission [and they] reply a submission without more and the submission is found, judgment will be with the plaintiff because the defendant put his defence on that foot. There is no necessity to show more than one branch. Moore 591; 1 Levinz 303.[2]

Baron GILBERT. The rules for pleadings on a bond are thus. A bond *prima facie* appears to be absolute, and every condition is to suspend it. The reply, therefore, must take away the suspension. If '*nul award*' be pleaded and the plaintiff reply 'an award', this shows that the bond is still under suspension, and, therefore, the plaintiff must go further and show a breach, that it may appear to the Court the bond is absolute. If, on a bond to perform covenants, there be a plea of covenants performed, the plaintiff must show one that is broken to show the condition suspended. Where there is a condition which is for the performance of a particular thing there mentioned, the defendant must show a suspension of the condition, which is here done, that James is not at age. The reply that he is at age tenders a proper issue of that matter, to which the defendant has demurred. Therefore, the plaintiff ought to have his judgment.

And of that opinion were the other barons.

But, at the request of Mr. *Kettleby*, it was adjourned.

---

[1] *Hayman v. Gerrard* (1667), *ut supra*.

[2] *Creswel v. Holmes* (1597 x 1598), *ut supra*; *Wimbleton v. Holdrip* (1670), *ut supra*.

382

Lord Coningsby v. Price

(Ex. 1723)

The lord of a manor can file a single bill of discovery against all of the stewards, bailiffs, and tenants of the manor to find out the extent of his rights in the manor.

Taussig MS. 311, vol. 1, p. 402, pl. 2

Tuesday, 5th February 1722[/23].

The plaintiff, as lord of the manor of Marden in the County of Hereford, exhibits his bill against fifteen persons, who were some of them stewards, other bailiffs, other tenants of the said manor, and charges them with a combination to secret his court rolls and thereby to extinguish and destroy his rents and services. And, therefore, he prays that the defendants may set forth and discover what rolls are in their hands [and they] may set forth what titles they claim by, what tenures they hold under, [and] what rents and services are due from them. To this, eight of the defendants demur generally to the bill and show for cause that the plaintiff had joined several defendants in one bill for several distinct and independent matters and thereby put every one of these defendants to the unnecessary charge of taking copies of the bill and other unnecessary charges. And, in the maintenance of this demurrer, it was urged that a man claiming a fee farm might not join several tenants. Michaelmas 1715, Marshall v. Bubb; Dixon v. Dixon.

E contra, it was said that all this matter in the bill relating to the manor and rights of the manor was one entire thing and that this was exactly like the case of a tithe bill brought by the parson.

And *per* Page and Gilbert, the demurrer was overruled.

By Gilbert: This allowing of demurrers in equity was first introduced to prevent the prolixity of proceedings, but if there is a proper foundation for a bill, a court of equity will never dismiss it and send it out of court though, perhaps, there may be some questions or enquiries of the bill are intermixed and confused extending a little further than strictly proper.

Per Price: I do not know that the overruling of a demurrer is a cause for an injunction, whether such demurrer is to discovery or to relief. In this case, it was to relief.

Per Page: I believe that, where a demurrer to discovery is overruled, there, perhaps, an injunction goes; it is otherwise, where the demurrer is to relief.

383

Lord Coningsby v. Witherston

(Ex. 1723)

The lord of a manor can file a single bill of discovery against all of the tenants of the manor to find out the extent of his rights in the manor.

Harvard Law School MS. 1082, vol. 1, p. 158, pl. 2

5 February 1722/23.

A bill was brought for a discovery of the customs of a manor, for the court rolls, and to set forth the title of the several defendants to their copyholds. The defendant demurs for that it contains several and distinct matters against several and distinct persons and, therefore, the defendant will be put to unnecessary expense in taking out a copy of the bill, part whereof has no relation to him. It was objected that the demurrer should not be to the whole bill but to that part only which has no relation to the defendant. [. . .] Query if there ever was an instance.

384

Bate v. Hodges

(Ex. 1723–1724)

In this case, the parishioner was ordered to pay his tithes in kind.

Harvard Law School MS. 1082, vol. 1, p. 158, pl. 4

February 1722/23.

A bill was brought by the rector of Wareham in the County of Kent. The defendant insists upon this *modus*, 1s. per acre for marshland [and] 4d. per acre for upland payable at Michaelmas for hay and all small tithes within the parish, except hops. Now, it was admitted, if this *modus* had been for the tithes of hay only or the tithe on the land, the first had been too weak a *modus*. And were cited to that purpose Cro. Eliz. 139, Bury v. Soames; Grascomb v. Jeffries, 17 November 1687;[1] Gardner v. Wickford, 1704. Cited in support of the *modus* was Smelter v. Bridges *et al.*, Hilary 1694;[2] 4d. per acre of marshland in lieu of all vicarial tithes as well upon marshland as upland.

Note: This was an answer to the objection that the *modus* ought to be annexed to the land and ought not to be extended to matters arising out of the

[1] *Perry v. Soam* (1589), Croke Eliz. 138, 78 E.R. 395, also 2 Leonard 27, 74 E.R. 330, 1 Eagle & Younge 96; *Grascomb v. Jeffreys* (1687–1688), Eq. Cases Exch. 285.

[2] *Smelton v. Bridges* (1695), Dodd 145, 1 Eagle & Younge 590, Public Record Office, E.126/26, f. 247, 1 Wood 337.

lands. It was said in this case it was resolved in Dodson v. Oliver[1] that Easter offerings are due of common right or by Statute.[2]

Baron PRICE: Though there is a variety in evidence, yet here is a sufficient proof, taking it all together, of this *modus*. But the defendant is short as to hops lying within the *modus*. And though that is within time of memory, yet, now, they should prove it as laid, which is fatal to the defendant. I am against sending this to an issue and take this *modus* to be void in itself. And it ought to be construed only as an evidence of a composition.

Note: There was an entry in *Valor Beneficiorum*[3] in Henry VIII's time, where it appears £13 13s. 4d. was due to the parson for twenty acres of marshland and twenty of upland. It was admitted to be too weak if it only had extended to the land, and, now, it extends to all the small tithes in the parish [and] is also void. A sum of money confined to any particular place is not a satisfaction for tithes arising in another place. This may be a fraud upon the rector, for, if a man has never so much small tithes and only three or four acres, that is to cover the whole. And he was of opinion for the plaintiff that the defendant should account.

Baron PAGE: Here is no evidence that ever tithes were paid in kind.

[To the] objection that the custom was not good, except hops, [he] responded this *modus* is good, for the court will take [judicial] notice that there was no such thing as hops at the time of the agreement when the *modus* began, and this exception is no more than what the law makes. It was admitted this would have been too rank for the land itself. Upon the discovery of the West Indies, money began to be of less value. A tithe of one thing cannot be a *modus* for a tithe of another.

[To the] objection that, though this is a sum of money, yet, in reality, it is the same as above, [he] responded this is not paying for the tithe of the land, but is an admeasurement of the tithe to be paid so that there can be no fraud in this case, for the rector must have 12s. and 4d. per acre for all the land lying in the parish.

[To the] objection one man may have a great deal of small tithes and yet no land, [he] responded that it does not appear to be the case now nor is that the *modus* as laid here, for, now, it supposes a man to have lands. This does not differ from a sum certain paid by the year.

[To the] question whether a man that has small tithes and no lands ought to pay tithes at all in this parish, [it was] objected there are three sorts of lands in this parish: marsh, uplands, orchards and gardens, [he] responded whatever is not marshland is upland. And why are orchard and gardens? He thought the case of Smelter v. Bridges to be right.

[To the] objection of Cro. Eliz., Bury v. Soames, 1d. for a calf for tithe calves and all agistment tithes, [he] responded the answer is the same as in the case of

---

[1] *Dodson v. Oliver* (1720–1724), see above, Case No. 128.

[2] Stat. 2 & 3 Edw. VI, c. 13 (*SR*, IV, 55–58).

[3] *Valor Beneficiorum: or, A Valuation of All Ecclesiastical Preferments in England and Wales*. London: M. Gillyflower, 1695.

cider, which is bad because the parishioner may defraud the parson by making no apples at all into cider and so the parishioner here might keep no calves at all, which would be a fraud. But here, the manor has lands which must lie within the parish and, consequently, no fraud can be put upon the parson. And he concluded for the defendant but that he ought to pay for the four acres added to the tender.

Baron GILBERT: As to the *modus* in general, a sum of money may be paid in lieu of tithes, and that was originally the measure of all tithes, and so was the original establishment of all parishes, either in the payment of a *modus* or tithes in kind. *Modus*es are the measure of the payment of tithes, and, if proved for a length of time, they are to be favored. A *modus* according to yearly value of land is bad because it is fluctuating and uncertain, too rank when it exceeds or comes near the value of the tithe itself and there is not a right proportion between the tithe and the *modus*. If this *modus* had been confined to the acre alone, it had been too high and rank. Whensoever there is a possibility of an ancient composition, there may be a good *modus*.

[To the] objection that tithe hops are excepted and, therefore, could not be in the minds of the parties then agreeing since they were not then subsisting, [he] responded, if there be an established *modus* in a parish and a new matter is introduced, that will not destroy the *modus* though the parish submit to a decimation as to the new thing. I do not take this *modus* to be too rank because it is in proportion to the profits of the whole parish. He was of opinion for the defendant, but he referred it to the Deputy [Remembrancer] to consider how far the tender extends. The costs were reserved.

Note: By this decree, the *modus*es were established by two barons, *absente* Montagu, Chief Baron. A rehearing was ordered.

Bunbury 125, 145 E.R. 619,
1 Rayner 179, 2 Gwillim 645, 1 Eagle & Younge 787

February 1722[/23].

A bill was brought by the rector of Wareham in the County of Kent for tithes. The defendant insists upon this *modus*, *viz.* 1s. per acre for marshland, 4d. per acre for upland, payable at Michaelmas, for hay and all small tithes within the parish, except hops.

Note: It was admitted, if this *modus* had been for tithe hay only or the tithe arising on the land, the 1s. had been too rank.

Baron PRICE was of opinion this was, as laid, a void *modus*.

PAGE and GILBERT, barons, thought that it was good and decreed accordingly for the defendant.

Against the *modus* was cited Croke Eliz. 139; Bury v. Grascomb and Jeffreys, 17 November 1687; Gardener v. Wickford, 1704. For the *modus*, Smelter v. Bridges, Hilary 1694.

This cause of Bate v. Hodges was reheard, 23 November 1724, before EYRE, Chief Baron, and PRICE, PAGE, and GILBERT, barons, and the decree, was reversed, *dubitante* GILBERT.

Note: After this, upon a new bill and cross-bill, the several objections to the manner of laying the *modus* were cured, and it was allowed to be good at last.

Taussig MS. 311, vol. 2, p. 709

Trinity term 1724.

The plaintiff, as rector of Wareham in the County of Kent, [sued] for tithes of wood, pasturage tithe, and tithe hay. As to wood, the defendant says he only cut down wood in hedgerows and that the parish is within the Weald of Kent. But this demand was waived by a special replication. 12d. for every acre of marshland and meadow and 4d. for every acre of upland meadow and pasture [was alleged] in satisfaction of hay and all small tithes within the rectory.

Ward, pro querente: The *modus* is not good because it is a certain and infallible rule that tithes of one sort are not satisfaction for tithes of another sort. Cro. Eliz. 466; Moor 911.[1]

Taussig MS. 311, vol. 2, p. 728, pl. 2

On Monday, 16th, 1724, the court directed an issue in this cause which now came on before the court upon a petition to rehear. And the issue directed was to try whether there was any such custom in the parish as was laid in the defendant's answer in the cause, which see before. *Sed non inter fui.*

Taussig MS. 311, vol. 2, p. 733

Michaelmas term 1724.

Pro querente, the first objection is to the manner of alleging the *modus*, for, if this is to be taken as a general *modus* in discharge of all tithes of the parishioners within the rectory, then it amounts to one man's paying tithes for another, which is absurd. And the case in Rolle's *Abr.*, 649 is express against it.

Second, take it as a discharge for the tithes of the parishioners occupying the lands, whether those tithes arise on the particular lands or elsewhere to destroy, and, in this sense, one acre of meadow and one acre of pasture would discharge him of all his small tithes. And so, if the pastureland or meadow be plowed up and sowed with flax or hemp, these tithes being small will be discharged by this *modus*, though of a different nature.

Tithes in kind are those which arise on the land. A custom to reckon all lambs in the parish as one man's lambs has been adjudged a bad custom. Hob. 349.

[1] *Austin v. Pigot* (1600), Moore K.B. 911, 72 E.R. 991, also Croke Eliz. 736, 78 E.R. 968, 1 Eagle & Younge 151.

In Dr. Finche's Case;[1] the *modus* was confined to a farm and, as a farm cannot be enlarged, so that *modus* was certain. But this is not, and it is a most unreasonable *modus*.

Curtis and Brown,[2] a *modus* of 2d. for every cow going upon four closes was void for uncertainty. 1 Keble 602.[3] There is no precedent of a *modus* not confined to any certain parcel of land.

Edlin: It is said that this 12s. and 4d. has been always accepted from every occupier of marshland and upland in lieu and satisfaction of all small tithes for every acre.

Every *modus* must be taken in the literal sense, Cro. Eliz. 475,[4] and there is no injury, for the parishioners are not bound by this suit. They may amend their case as to pleading upon another occasion. The prescription in Cro. [Eliz.] 475 was of 12d. for every milk cow in lieu of tithes of milk kine and beasts agisted.

Per Chief Baron [Eyre]: That is a very different case from the present, for cows are tithable in kind, but acres are not tithable as acres and, therefore, the meaning must be tithes of 1s. by the acre and not for an acre.

Edlin: It is unreasonable to suppose there could be any commencement of such a *modus*. 1 Modern 229;[5] March 79; Moor 454; Lut. 1043. Tithes in kind do revive upon an extinction of a *modus*, as by Lord Hobart, Cowper and Andrews, Moor [*blank*]; Pigot and Hearne, in the Bishop of Winchester's Case, Cro. Eliz. 587.[6] Custom of lords of manors paying tithes for the tenants of his manor. That case [*blank*].

[To the] objection that the parish may have been originally endowed not of tithes, but of money in lieu of them; the solution is this is contrary to the settled maxim and principle of judging of tithes in this court, for it has ever been supposed that tithes are originally due in kind.

Bootle: Taking this to be a rate or admeasurement, then it is in the power of the parishioner to alter the admeasurement and consequently his tithe. Cro. Eliz. 139.[7]

---

1 *Finch v. Masters* (Ex. 1724), see below, Case No. 463.

2 *Curtis v. Browne* (Ex. 1724), see below, Case No. 480.

3 *Baudink v. Bushel* (1663), 1 Keble 602, 83 E.R. 1136, also 1 Levinz 116, 83 E.R. 325, 1 Eagle & Younge 440.

4 *Sherington v. Fleetwood* (1596), Croke Eliz. 475, 78 E.R. 727, also Moore K.B. 430, 599, 909, 72 E.R. 676, 784, 990, Gouldsborough 147, 75 E.R. 1055.

5 *Moor v. Field* (1677), 1 Modern 229, 86 E.R. 848, 1 Eagle & Younge 511.

6 *Cowper v. Andrews* (1614), Hobart 39, 80 E.R. 189, Moore K.B. 863, 72 E.R. 957, also Godbolt 237, 78 E.R. 138, *sub nom. Hooper v. Andrews*, 1 Rolle Rep. 120, 81 E.R. 372, 1 Gwillim 275, 1 Eagle & Younge 240; *Pigot v. Hern* (1597), in *Wright v. Wright* (1596), Croke Eliz. 599, 78 E.R. 841, also 2 Coke Rep. 38, 45, 76 E.R. 501, 518, Moore K.B. 483, 72 E.R. 710, 1 Gwillim 200, 1 Eagle & Younge 135.

7 *Perry v. Soam* (1589), *ut supra*.

Secondly, this 12d. per acre must be paid by every occupier of the acre, and, if so, then it is a *non decimando* in all the other parishioners.

Pengelly: The court will take this upon the whole, and, then, there will be no occasion to account at common law, though it be a different *modus* than what is alleged. No [writ of] consultation [should be granted].

As to the objection that this runs into a *non decimando*, the same might have been objected in the case of 1 Rolle's *Abr.*, 651, pl. 2; Finch and Gerrard.[1] Orchards and gardens are included within the admeasurement.

As to the manner of alleging, it is sufficient to direct an issue to try the substance. Equity proceedings are not to be so strictly taken as at law, for, in fact, he understands that the *modus* only extends to the occupier and to the small tithes arising upon these lands, and the words 'arising within the said rectory' do not carry it further.

Bunbury: This is a general custom laid throughout the whole parish and not a particular prescription to any one single person. If the words are respective and 'their' had been inserted, then it would have been good without controversy.

Per Chief Baron [Eyre]: I thought this case could never be made good unless upon the parity of reason of the case of the lord of a manor. But the cases are widely different, for the lord of a manor may be supposed to have been the occupier of all the lands and so there may be a reasonable account of the commencement of a *modus* for a certain sum in lieu of all the tithes of the manor. But here can be no such supposition, for it is not to be supposed that any one of these occupiers of any marshland of three or four or five acres was possessed of all these lands. The case in Sanders 142[2] shows that every man's discharge must be applied to himself and to himself only.

Price thought the *modus* was naught, [as] in every respect unreasonable and uncertain.

Page was glad that this cause was reheard. As to the main point, he is in doubt because every one of the defendant's counsel have given it up and think it is too hard to maintain it. He thought it might be good for all small tithes of the parish. If not, it is certainly void.

If at the commencement of a *modus*, it might be reasonable, subsequent changes will not alter the right. If the agreement had been that, in consideration of his paying 12d. for pasture, he should be discharged of an orchard etc., the alienation of the orchard afterward will not make the orchard tithable.

It may be supposed that, at the time of this agreement, there were no small tithes but what were in the hands of such occupiers of the meadow or marsh, and so the *modus* may be good yet. And this would have confined the *modus* to the

---

[1] *Sharp v. Coult* (1609), 1 Rolle, Abr., *Dismes*, pl. E, 2, p. 651; *Finch v. Masters* (Ex. 1724), see below, Case No. 463.

[2] *Croucher v. Collins* (1668), 1 Williams Saunders 141, 85 E.R. 151, also 2 Keble 319, 84 E.R. 199, 4 Gwillim 1576, 1 Eagle & Younge 469.

very land considered as meadow and pasture though it was plowed up and sowed because the alteration of the husbandry of the land would otherwise defeat the intention of the parties to the agreement. But if this is to be intended only to the privy tithes of a particular occupier, then I agree it must be bad. So he concurs with the Chief Baron and Price that the *modus* is void.

GILBERT: [I am] doubtful and should desire further time. A *modus* may be supposed to have taken its rise either in the foundation of the parish itself or else by a subsequent agreement between the parson, the patron, and the ordinary subsequent [*blank*].

A criterion to discern between a *modus* and a composition is this, *viz.*, that, if the nature of the agreement be such as may tend to destroy the maintenance of the parson, it is a composition and not a *modus*, for a single parson may be more rationally supposed to be deceived in an agreement than the parson and ordinary. But *modus*es are *leges loci* and ought not to be overturned by critical exceptions. And he thinks the reason to support this *modus* is the same as was mentioned by Baron Page. But he concluded that he would be glad to consider further of it.

Per Chief Baron [EYRE]: It is a very strange supposition that there were no other parishioners but owners of marsh and meadow when this *modus* was agreed upon.

The CHIEF BARON and PRICE thought that it was a void *modus*.

PAGE and GILBERT inclined to have it taken that they did not absolutely determine against the *modus* but that they agreed with the Chief Baron and Price in disallowing it because, as to the 4d. for the upland, there was no day of payment alleged in the answer.

There was a day inserted by Mr. Browne's own hand, who drew the answer.

The *modus* was overruled.

British Library MS. Add. 36651, f. 108

[. . .][1] that as the *modus* is alleged, it makes a *non decimando* for such parishioners as have no meadow or pasture in the parish and a *modus* paid by one parishioner cannot be in discharge of tithes arising on lands in the occupation of another parishioner. And [he] cited 1 Saunders 142,[2] where a parishioner insisted on a custom to pay no tithe of thorns where the same were used in repairing fences within the parish [and it was] held ill, not being confined to fences of lands in his own occupation. But [he] agreed [with] the case of Piggott v. Herne in the Bishop of Winchester's Case,[3] for a lord of a manor to pay a sum in gross in lieu of all tithes within the manor, for it will be intended that, at the time of the commencement of the *modus*, the lord held all in demesne.

[1] The beginning of this case was on the previous page which is now missing from the manuscript.

[2] *Croucher v. Collins* (1668), *ut supra*.

[3] *Pigot v. Hern* (1597), *ut supra*.

The eighth exception [is] that, in the answer, it is not set forth when the 4d. per acre for the uplands is payable. And, upon a view of the record, it was so, which, *per* CURIAM, makes the *modus* ill.

Also, the court, except Baron Gilbert, were of opinion that the *modus* as set forth is ill in itself for the reasons alleged by the plaintiff's counsel in the sixth and seventh objections. As to the other objections, they made no account of them, but they decreed the defendant to account for tithes in kind.

[Order of 7 February 1723: 2 Wood 210.]

385

Shenton v. Jordan

(Ex. 1723)

In this case, the court of equity granted an injunction against a final judgment at common law on the ground that the contract was incorrectly construed by the jury.

Harvard Law School MS. 1082, vol. 1, p. 159

11 February 1722/23. Jordan v. Shenton.

An action was brought upon a contract for the sale of some shares in Welsh Copper. And a verdict was obtained and a judgment in Easter Term before the Act was made concerning the registering of contracts for the sale of stocks and subscriptions etc. And it was now insisted upon [by] the defendant that this contract being merged in the judgment, the subsequent Act cannot extend to this case and can raise no equity to the plaintiff.

Note: The fact was that it was actually registered.

Secondly, how far that will waive the benefit of their former argument.

Note: They refused to admit the copy of the register to be read in evidence, this being only a private charter corporation not established by act of Parliament.

Adjourned.

Taussig MS. 311, vol. 1, p. 399

Hilary term 1722[/23].

[On] 16th August, a contract [was made] for ten shares in the Copper Bubble to be taken at the next opening of the books [at] £83 per share. [On] 20th August, [there was an] advertisement against bubbles. [On] 22nd August, [was] the books opening.

On the contract, it was declared that each party had deposited [*blank*] in the hands of Mr. Long with a note that, if either party does not perform the contract, then the deposits [were] to be forfeited. And this was done all at once, and so it was an entire agreement. Jordan brings an action at law upon this contract and recovers *coram* PRATT, Chief Justice. The plaintiff reads proofs that the defendant had the original contract and [it was] 16th August 1720. 'Memorandum that Patrick Jordan has sold to J.S. ten shares of W[elsh] Copper the next opening of the books at £83 per share, for performance of which each has deposited £200 in Long's hand. Note if either does not perform the above agreement, [they are] to forfeit their deposit.'

The bill suggests that this note was added to show that the forfeiture was the only thing intended to be hazarded. But this was expressly denied by the defendant in his answer.

Joshua Wilson swears that the original contract was produced in court at the trial. [In] the *London Gazette*, Whitehall, August 10, 1720, the advertisement was published [by] Allen Evans. [On] 22nd August 1720, the defendant told Evans of the former contract with the plaintiff.

Sir Constantine Phipps: If the defendant had shares sufficient in his own right, though not in his own name, it is all that is required by the Statute; as to the contract and deposit, it is determined and settled by the verdict.

Fazakerly: The bill here is for no purpose but only to set aside the verdict. And it suggests nothing in equity but what was or might have been given in evidence on the trial. And this would never turn around the law and fix a jurisdiction in equity courts, which will blow up the whole law.

As to the advertisement in the *Gazette*, there is nothing in that because *scire facias* is the only proper way to destroy the charters and, until a *scire facias*, they subsist. The plaintiff, by contracting to purchase, is as much a party to the fraud of blowing up the stock. He knows no authority from the *Gazette* and so [it has] been determined in the law courts. Fraud is not to be intended, but must be proved.

The second point is as to the note, *viz.* the note at the end of the contract.

The third point is as to the charter. A man might be a member of a corporation though he had not taken the oaths. He might be a member *de facto*.

Secondly, the proviso in the charter is void ordaining an oath for no new oath can be framed nor any old oath applied to a new office or case but by the authority of Parliament. [There is] no pretense of surprise at the trial or want of evidence suggested in the bill.

Reply [*blank*].

N.B. The contract did not appear to have been registered. And so the cause was ordered to stand over to the next day of causes.

Per Baron GILBERT: If a corporation be erected to carry on a business with a joint stock and, instead of carrying on the business, they set up a trade for their stock before any carrying on proper business, this is fraud. And I think, though this is a fraud, it will not affect an innocent purchaser, yet I apprehend that such a purchaser should have paid the money or else he shall or may be looked upon as party to the fraud.

Per Baron PRICE: The note seems only to imply that the deposits should be forfeited.

Query whether [there was] any judgment at law.

Taussig MS. 311, vol. 1, p. 410

Monday, the 11th of February 1723.

The case now came on again. And the defendant produced a copy of the register examined, and the plaintiff also produced the book. The court said that, the book being there, the book itself and not the copy shall be read because the book is the better evidence.

And the reason why the plaintiff insisted on producing the book was because, precedent to this entry, there were several other contracts registered before this and, thereby, it proved that the plaintiff had not stock enough to perform this contract with.

And by the defendant's counsel, this is reasonable and nothing but a natural consequence from the court's opinion, for the court has already, by ordering the defendant to produce the register of the contract before the Act, for the judgment was in Easter term and the Act made long after, yet the registering ought to be produced and, if so, then the defendant ought to prove his quantity of stock *tempore contractus* or else the Act will avoid the contract.

And the court so far countenanced this way of reasoning as to adjourn the cause to the next term to give the plaintiff an opportunity to look into this matter.

N.B. The defendant consented to the adjournment upon the plaintiff's paying £5 costs of the day.

Taussig MS. 311, vol. 1, p. 524

Thursday, 27 June 1723.

There was a verdict for £630 and judgment thereupon in Easter term before the Act of Parliament. The cause was tried before Pratt, Chief Justice, and he held upon the trial that the £100 deposit did not detract from the contract.

Per Fazakerly: The judgment was of Easter term, and the Act is of 31 July subsequent. And no contract was subsisting after the judgment *quia transit in rem judicatam*. Michaelmas 8 *Regis*, Baker v. Fidel, in the King's Bench. So in the case of Lady Shirley v. Decosta,[1] judgment having been obtained on a South Sea contract, the South Sea contract was gone and determined. And so, in an action of debt upon that judgment, the King's Bench held the party to special bail, not being within the words of the Statute. The judgment being read, it was signed the first day of June 1721, i.e. of Easter term precedent to the Act of Parliament.

N.B. Long, in whose hands the deposit was made, became bankrupt. And, therefore, the £200 deposit being looked upon as part of the damages sustained by non-performance of the contract and to be Jordan's, the jury gave only £630,

[1] *Shirley v. Dacosta* (Ex. 1723), see below, Case No. 414.

whereas, otherwise, they would have given £830. And Jordan came in and paid his contribution for this £200 as a creditor to Long for so much.

The defendant read evidence to prove himself entitled to the stocks at the time the contract was made.

Carter: The judgment is enquirable into in equity.

Chief Baron [Montagu]: In Curzon's Case,[1] we determined that the Act of Parliament did not extend to her because the verdict was previous to the Act of Parliament.

Ward: The utmost intended by this contract was the forfeiture of the £200. A judgment at law does neither compound nor perform a contract. In the case of Baker and Fidel, the parties themselves compounded. Shirley and Decosta was an eluding of the Act of Parliament. The defendant's registering his contract concludes him from saying that his case is not within the Act of Parliament.

Browne: Judgment neither compounds nor performs, and the Act extends only to the acts of the parties themselves. This would be fraud in equity before the Act of Parliament. Contracting to sell what he had not would be esteemed fraudulent in a court of equity.

Chief Baron: The action at law was for ten shares of stock sold and transferred. And the judgment is upon that count in the declaration. It does not appear that there was any stock sold unless the stock sold by Allen Evans be the stock. Therefore, it was My Lord Chief Justice Pratt's opinion that the transfer of Allen Evans was equivalent to the transfer of Jordan himself, whereas we determined the contrary to this in the case of Rhodes v. Lovell[2] and granted a new trial upon this very point, *scil.* that the vendee is not obliged to accept a transfer from any other person than the vendor himself. The note itself runs thus: '*Memorandum* Patrick Jordan has sold' so that the words of the note imply a sale, and not only a contract to sell. Whereas it appears that, at that time, Jordan had no stock, therefore, he could not sell it. And, therefore, we ought to set aside the verdict. A proclamation makes not law, but only declares what was made law by the Act. This bill is in the nature of an *audita querela*. And the party is now not otherwise relievable.

Price: I am now satisfied that the judgment amounts to a performance and has altered the nature of the contract. But yet the plaintiff here ought to be relieved because the nature of the contract was only to forfeit. But the plaintiff here ought to pay £200 to the defendant, which was the sum deposited and was lost by Long's becoming bankrupt. And upon payment thereof, I think he ought to be relieved against the verdict.

Page: The contract was only to forfeit the £200. And it is so explained by the evidence if it had needed explanation. If this was a forfeiture, then the verdict should have been for £830 and not for £630. In the case of Lovell v. Rhodes,

[1] *South Sea Company v. Curzon* (Ex. 1722), see above, Case No. 355.

[2] *Rhodes v. Lovit* (Ex. 1721), see above, Case No. 165.

Lovell refused to accept, and so we adjudged it a bad tender. But I do not think this note implies a sale, but only a contract to sell. Everybody knows that shares are not actually to be sold but by actual transfer; so this is only a contract to sell.

Abercromie was Jordan's trustee. And perhaps, it would not have been a good tender if Shenton had absolutely refused for this reason to accept the stock. But it appears by two witnesses that Shenton agreed to accept the transfer from Evans, though perhaps but in jest. The difference, therefore, between this case and that of Rhodes and Lovell was that, in that Company, two transfers could not be in one day. But perhaps in this Company, they may be permitted. And, therefore, though I do agree that Jordan's transfer by Evans was not a good transfer, yet Shenton's not actually disagreeing to this transfer was a misleading of Jordan, who, if he had notice of Shenton's not agreeing to the transfer, he might, perhaps, and had all that day to mend it, *viz.* by making Evans transfer to him and they transferring to Shenton.

But I agree with Price as to the decree.

GILBERT: I think the parties upon the contract have agreed only upon the forfeiture and the Statute would have affected this judgment but that Jordan had the stock.

So by three barons, the judgment is to stand for security for Shenton's payment of the £200 deposited in Long's hands, Long being broke. And upon Shenton's payment thereof, the judgment upon the verdict is to be vacated and no costs on either side.

Harvard Law School MS. 1082, vol. 1, p. 175

27 June 1723.

The contract was that Shenton had sold to Jordan ten shares of Welsh Copper for the next opening of the books [at] £97 per share. For the performance of each party, he has deposited £250 in Long's hands. (Note: If either party does not perform the above agreement, to forfeit their deposit.) The bill was to be relieved against a verdict obtained for £600 on this contract. And the principal question was whether the defendant ought to have recovered any more than the £200 deposited.

Note: The defendant does positively deny that it was the intent of the agreement that the damages for non-performance were to be confined to the deposit only.

It was said by *Fazakerly* this is only in the nature of a penalty to enforce the agreement and not like the case of a horse race where it is the express agreement that, upon not running, the party has only the forfeiture. (Query of this distinction.) Now, in the case of the horse race, there can be no rule to ascertain any damages for not running, besides the express forfeiture. It cannot be known which horse would have won, but, in these contracts, there is a rule for damages besides the forfeiture, by computing the value of the stock at the time etc.

Note: The verdict and judgment was in Easter Term 1721; the Act of Parliament was not until July following. Now, by the Act, nothing was to be registered but contracts. Now, in this case, the contract is not subsisting after the judgment, but it is quite merged in the judgment. Baker v. Fiddel; Fazakerly, Michaelmas 8 Geo., South Sea Company v. Curzon.

Bunbury 132, 145 E.R. 622

27 June 1723.

A bill was brought to be relieved against a verdict upon a contract for sale of ten shares in Welsh Copper, the plaintiff at law having recovered £600 more than the deposit. It appeared by the pleadings now that the contract was thus: 'Memorandum, that Jordan has sold to Shenton ten shares in Welsh Copper for next opening of the books, at £87 per share, for the performance of which, each party has deposited £200 in Long's hands. Note, if either party does not perform the above agreement, to forfeit their deposit.'

And *per* TOTAM CURIAM, the plaintiff was relieved on paying the £200, for that the plaintiff at law should have recovered no more than the £200 deposit.

But query, for this seems an extraordinary opinion.

386

Tully v. Kilner

(Ex. 1723)

A modus decimandi *in lieu of tithes in kind must be certain.*

Harvard Law School MS. 1082, vol. 1, p. 160

Hilary term 1722/23.

A bill was brought by the rector of Aldingham in the County of Lancaster for the tithes of ley ground formerly used as arable ground, but since converted into hay ground. The defendant insists in his answer upon this *modus*, that the occupiers of ancient tenements within particular vills or townships in the said parish with their own carts, carriages, and horses led and carried and ought to lead and carry a cartload of peat and turf to the parsonage house for the use of the parson and rector, his farmer, or deputy on such day or within the space of every two years as they have or should require the same in full discharge of all the tithes of hemp and flax and hay grown on the said ancient tenements.

Sir Constantine Phipps, for the plaintiff, objected to the *modus*. First, it should be in discharge only of the fuel, which are the matters to be carried, Waterman v. Jones, 14 June 1705;[1] lot acre. Secondly, who is the deputy of the rector?

[1] *Waterman v. Jones* (1705), 1 Eagle & Younge 671, 1 Wood 463.

Mr. *Ward*, *pro eodem*: First, it is unreasonable. There is no instance to be given of a *modus* to be paid once in two years, whereas every *modus* ought to be yearly payable, as the tithes themselves. If the parson dies in the first year, is his successor to have the carriage for one year only? Secondly, it is uncertain, for it is not confined to any certain place but to all the ley grounds parcel of these ancient tenements. Thirdly, it is unequal; if a man has but one acre of ley ground, he must do the same service as a man that has 1000 acres. For one of the vills, the carriage must be once in every year. There seems to be no reason for this difference.

Mr. *Browne*, of the same side: It is not alleged what particular time this service is to be done, only once in two years, which is totally uncertain. And the late resolutions have made it necessary to fix a certain time. Tithes are annually renewing, and what is set up in bar of tithes ought to be annually due. It is unequal for the reasons alleged by Mr. Ward. Turton v. Clayton, Trinity 1721, in the Exchequer.[1] A cartload with his own horses is totally uncertain. What sort of cart; how many horses, etc.?

(Serjeant *Chesshyre*, for the defendant, [cited] Watson 409; 3 Cro. 276; 1 Rolle 649, 650.[2])

[To the] objection it is unreasonable, [he] responded, admitted it would have been a good discharge as to such and being a service whereby the parson receives a benefit, it may be extended to any other tithable matter.

[To the] objection that it was only once in two years whereas it ought to be annually paid, [he] responded a *modus* that the parson should take the profits of such a close every other year is good. Secondly, and this is liable to the same objections as that now in question. Besides, here it is to be upon request.

[To the] objection suppose the parson let part of his tithes, [he] responded, by agreement of the parties, the parishioners shall not be deprived of their right, but they have nothing to do but to convey their cart to the parsonage house.

[To the] objection of 'a cart' as too uncertain, [he] responded, in a declaration at law, '*carucata*' is a sufficient certainty, and the parishioners are to carry for the parson as they carry for themselves.

[To the] objection that it is unequal, [he] responded that is an objection that should rather come from the defendants than the plaintiff.

[To the] objection no time is alleged, [he] responded it is to be upon request.

[To the] objection of 'or his deputy', [he] responded whether he makes his request by his agent or servant, who is in the nature of a deputy, the service is to be performed.

[To the] objection the *modus* may be exhausted, [he] responded that they have not made it part of the case.

---

1 *Turton v. Clayton* (1721), see above, Case No. 211.

2 W. Watson, *Clergy-Man's Law*; *Favely v. Easton* (1632), Croke Car. 269, 276, 79 E.R. 835, 841, also *sub nom. Eveley v. Eston*, Godbolt 440, 78 E.R. 258, W. Jones 301, 82 E.R. 159; 1 Rolle, Abr., *Dismes*, pp. 649–650.

Baron GILBERT made this objection, what remedy has the parson for this service?

To which Mr. *Fazakerly* said the parson may have an action on the case for the non-performance.

Mr. *Bootle* [cited] 2 Cro. 501, 587; 3 Cro. 736; 1 Rolle, *Abridgment*, 649; 1 Rolle Rep. 2, Brothers, 650; Hutton 58.[1]

[To the] objection this is a *modus* for tithes of a different species, [he] responded the case in Hutton and the rest are an answer. If the defendants do not perform this duty, the parson may prefer his bill in this court to compel them to it or bring an action at law.

It was objected by PAGE, Baron, [that] it does not appear as laid in the answer that the parson either had a right to gather turf and peat in this messuage or the defendants to take it there, and the defendant should have laid a prescription for that purpose.

Note: It was alleged in the answer that, time out of mind, peat and turf had been tied [?] to be conveyed to the parsonage house and used for firing there. Query if the court will presume that they have a right to take etc. after such a length of time.

Baron PRICE: There ought to be a certainty in *modus*es as to time, place, persons, and things. Where it is for the tithe of another nature, it ought to be adequate to the tithe. Being to be performed once in two years, it cannot be so certain as to support this *modus*. I do not think a cart is so certain, for it may be drawn by two or six horses, which may vary the weight.

Baron PAGE: 12d. yearly has been adjudged to be bad; 12d. in two years surely is much worse. I do not think a cartload is certain enough. In [an action of] trover or trespass, you are to recover in damages if it is a small load, but, here, the parson is to be concluded whether it is a great load or a little load. 'A deputy' I think is uncertain. And he insisted upon his objection he had made before, that no prescription was laid of his right of digging turf and peat.

Baron GILBERT insisted principally upon this cart objection, that there was no right of turbary alleged in the parsonage or in the defendant's ancient tenements. But he thought it would be well enough as to the payment in two years and so as to the payment to the farmer or deputy. And so, as to the messuage being exhausted, which, from the nature of it, it is not to be presumed it being inexhaustible. But, upon the former objection, he concurred.

[1] *Moore v. Bullock* (1618), Croke Jac. 501, 79 E.R. 427, 1 Eagle & Younge 297; *Somerton v. Cotton* (1597), Croke Eliz. 587, 78 E.R. 830, 1 Gwillim 199, 1 Eagle & Younge 141; *Austin v. Pigot* (1600), Croke Eliz. 736, 78 E.R. 968, also Moore K.B. 911, 72 E.R. 991, 1 Gwillim 217, 1 Eagle & Younge 151; *Moore v. Bullock* (1618), 1 Rolle, Abr., *Dismes*, pl. D, 6, p. 649; *Boocher v. Rogers* (1614), 1 Rolle Rep. 2, 81 E.R. 284, 1 Eagle & Younge 223; *Poole v. Reynolds* (1622), Hutton 57, 123 E.R. 1098, also Winch 1, 44, 124 E.R. 1, 38, 1 Eagle & Younge 322.

And the defendants were decreed to account.

Taussig MS. 311, vol. 1, p. 411

Hilary term 1722/23.

The rector of Aldringham in the County of Lancaster exhibits his bill against the defendants as occupiers of land within the rectory, formerly arable and now lately laid down for hay.

The defendants plead a *modus* in discharge of hemp, flax, and hay, that every occupier of an ancient tenement with their horses and carts have time out of mind used to carry a cartload of peat and turf from a certain place to the parsonage house for the use of the parson and rector of the said parish, his farmer, or deputy at such a day within two years, as should be required, in lieu of hemp, flax, and hay arising on the grounds parcel of such ancient tenements. Waterman and Jones, 1705, in this court.

Per Sir Constantine Phipps: First, peat can only be in satisfaction of firewood; secondly, it is once in two years; thirdly, it is payable to the parson or his deputy; fourth, 'occupiers of ancient tenements' is uncertain.

Ward: [There is] no instance of a *modus* payable once in two years, for as tithes do *annuatim renovare*, so ought the satisfaction to be annual.

Second objection: It is uncertain to all the ley ground parcel of the said ancient tenement.

Third objection: It is unequal because [it is for] one occupier who has but one acre of ley ground as he who has 100 acres, and so it cannot be supposed to have a reasonable commencement.

Browne: No time for doing the service is fixed. Whitehall v. Offley, Easter 1719.[1] The doing it on request is not sufficiently unequal. Trinity 1721, Turton against Clayton *et al.* And in that case, it was determined that the *modus* was void because he that had one acre paid 1d. as well as he who had 100 acres from Alverston Moss and Cartwell Moss. So it may cease and run into a *non decimando*. And every *modus* ought to carry with it a perdurable satisfaction.

Thirdly, as to 'cartload with his own horses', query what cart and how many horses.

Chesshyre, pro defendente:[2] A *modus* must be taken to be proved, for they dare not appeal to the evidence. Service is as good a satisfaction as enjoyment of lands. A parson having a seat in church strawed with straw or rushes; 3 Cro. 276.[3]

---

[1] *Offley v. Whitehall* (Ex. 1717), see above, Case No. 28.

[2] *querente* MS.

[3] *Favely v. Easton* (1632), *ut supra*.

The smallness of value is no objection to a *modus*. Piggot and Hern's Case; 1 Rolle, *Abr.*, [Dismes, p.] 649, 650; repairing this chancel is a satisfaction for tithes; Watson's, *Clergy*, 408, 409.[1]

[To the] first objection of fuel only, [he] answered it is not of weight because it is not necessary that there should be a relation between satisfaction and the thing for which the satisfaction is given.

Ley hay is ground used three years for arable and then laid down for three or four years for pasture.

[To the] second objection of once in two years, [he] answered, if the parson was to take the profits of a close every other year, it would be a good *modus*.

As to inconvenience, the parsons must take their choice. It is at request and that makes it certain enough.

[As to] 'deputy or farmers', this is still the parson's right if part of the tithes be let, the solution [is it is] no objection because that is the parson's fault.

A 'cartload' if uncertain, it is a sufficient objection against all declarations in trover etc. This must be understood to be such loads as usual.

Parcel of tenements, if tenements be divided, the charge multiplies, as in the case of a heriot [or] a service, if divided into many tenements. As to inequality, that is no objection from the parson; it might be from the poorer parishioners.

In the North, it is a custom for the parson to set out the tithes and the parson insists upon it as his right so to do. And so the request here; if part of the custom, it is incumbent on the parson and it is certain by his own act.

Fazakerly: All lay lands parcel of ancient tenements would be certain enough in the case of a prescription for common for beasts levant and couchant on such ley lands. A cartload of peat is as certain as a wagonload. And both are certain in [actions of] trespass or trover, Therefore, it is certain enough in this case.

Per Baron GILBERT: What remedy has the parson for this service?

Per Bootle: 3 Cro. 587; ditto, 736; Austin and Pigot, 2 Cro. 501; 1 Rolle Rep. 2 [*blank*] v. Rogers; Hutton 58. As to the parson's remedy, it may be either in this court by bill or by action, as in the case of a buck or a part thereof in lieu of park tithes.

PAGE: Turbary does not appear either to lie within the manor or within the parish, and it does not, therefore, answer the end. Perhaps, it cannot by turves at that place or that they have a right of digging turves in that place. So the objection is that they have not shown a prescriptive right to the turf digging.

PRICE: It is a naught *modus*. (1) Once in two years to carry a load and this is not satisfaction for any certain time. (2) A cartload is not certain. One cart may carry a bushel, another ten bushels.

---

[1] *Pigot v. Hern* (1597), in *Wright v. Wright* (1596), Croke Eliz. 599, 78 E.R. 841, 2 Coke Rep. 38, 45, 76 E.R. 501, 518, Moore K.B. 483, 72 E.R. 710, 1 Gwillim 200, 1 Eagle & Younge 135; W. Watson, *Clergy-Man's Law*.

Page: Twelve yearly is bad. Twelve in two years is very bad. It does not appear from what determinate time, either from the last load or from a new parson's coming in. Second, load is certain as to timber because it contains so many feet. And I believe it is never seen that [an action of] trespass was brought for a cartload of bricks. Third, one must lay a prescription in the parson's house for such a quantity of turves.

Gilbert: Not being annual is no objection, and, therefore, I think, if the right of digging of turves was shown to belong to the parsonage, turf grows and renews so it is not to be presumed that the moss will fail and the turves be destroyed.

Bunbury 126, 145 E.R. 619,
1 Rayner 179, 2 Gwillim 644, 1 Eagle & Younge 787

11 February 1722[/23].

A bill was brought by the rector of Aldingham in the County Palatine of Lancaster for the tithes of ley ground formerly used as arable, but since converted into hay ground. The defendant insisted upon this *modus*, that the occupiers of ancient tenements within particular vills or townships (expressed) within the said parish with their own carts, carriages, and horses led and carried, and ought to lead and carry, a cartload of peat and turf from Ulverston Moss to the parsonage house for the use of the parson and rector, his farmer, or deputy, on such a day or within the space of every two years, as they have or should require the same, in full discharge of all the tithe of hemp, flax, and hay growing or arising on the said ancient tenements.

This was held to be a void *modus* by three barons (*absente* Lord Chief Baron Montagu), for a cartload is too uncertain; it may be drawn by two or six horses; and there is no right of turbary alleged in the parsonage house or in the defendant's ancient tenements.

Sir Constantine Phipps, Mr. *Ward*, and Mr. *Browne* [were] of counsel for the plaintiff; Serjeant *Chesshyre*, Mr. *Fazakerly*, and Mr. *Bootle* [were] for the defendant.

[Order of 11 February 1723: 2 Wood 208.]

387

Rex v. Fleming

(Ex. 1723)

An action of replevin does not lie for goods taken by distress for rent due to the crown. However, where a private person is given the right to collect rent due to the crown, he must show to the tenant the warrant to collect the rent before he can have the tenant held in contempt for suing an action of replevin in regards to the rent due to the crown.

Taussig MS. 311, vol. 1, p. 404

Friday, the 8th of February 1723.

Mason being indebted to the crown, his lands were extended thereon. And [writs of] *levari* [*facias*] issued from time to time to levy the rents and profits of his land. Fleming, being a tenant of some land under Mason, paid his rent to the sheriff from time to time, but, after this, the Lords of the Treasury granted a *cessatur processus* to those *levari*s and made a warrant to one Whittington to receive the rent from the tenants as the said rent became due and to distrain for the rents for non-payment of rent to Whittington. Fleming was frequently distrained, and now, upon it, a fresh [writ of] attachment is issued against Fleming and he had time to show cause against the attachment. And this day he came and showed cause against it, *viz*. first, that the Lords of the Treasury could not grant any warrant of this nature and thereby take the receipt of the rents out of the sheriff's hands; second, this warrant being made to a private man and not to a public person, the tenants had a right to demand the sight of such warrant and, if not shown, the tenants had a right to oppose this distress and to replevy the distress, for, by him and *Bunbury*, though no replevy lies in the case of the crown's distress, as the law has been held of later times, that must be where there is plain authority from the crown; it is otherwise, where the distress is by a private person or one not known as a public officer of the crown.

E contra: As to Mr. Fleming's not being cognizant of Whittingham's authority, that is a sham, for it appears by the affidavits on both sides that Fleming had often submitted to pay the rent to Whittingham. Whittingham had good authority by the warrant to distrain:

> Nominate, constitute, and appoint Whittingham to collect, gather, and receive rents of the extended estates, to give acquittances, and to levy the rents by distress and further commands him to pay the money into the Exchequer and to take tallies for the same and further order and declare that this warrant should be in force for two years unless the debt due from Mason be paid before that time.

Signed by the Chancellor and the Lords of the Treasury. The warrant also recited the cesser of the *levari facias*.

And by Mason's counsel: The Lords of the Treasury may grant [writs of] extent in vacation time or such a warrant of this if they please.

Reply: It does not follow because the Chancellor of the Exchequer or the Lords of the Treasury may grant extents in vacation time that, therefore, they may make such a warrant as this, for any person may grant an extent out of term, but no baron ever granted such a warrant and, though a single baron does grant an extent, yet all future applications when an extent is issued are made to the court only.

Per PRICE: [There is] no reason for an attachment against Fleming, for the warrant ought certainly to have been showed to Fleming or else we cannot justify an attachment against him, for, wherever we grant process of contempt against a man for suing a replevin, it must be made positively to appear to us that the party suing it knew that he sued it for the crown's distress. And he held strongly that the warrant of the Lords of the Treasury was naught, unprecedented, and unjustifiable, only signed, not under seal. And I do not know that the Treasury or we can frame any new methods of levying the king's debts and set aside the practice of the court hitherto used and approved for that purpose. The Lords of the Treasury may certainly grant a *cessatur processus*; so may a private baron. But this method of warrant will create infinite confusion and blow up the whole course of proceedings. How must the payment of these rents be pleaded? Suppose new *levari*s should issue against the tenant, surely he has no remedy but in equity, for it is no discharge to the tenant unless he pays his money in the regular way and method.

Ditto PAGE and GILBERT. And all agreed that no [action of] replevin [lies] against the king's debts *quia per recordo* and in the nature of an execution.

And by GILBERT, the king may retain against gages and pledges though private persons cannot detain against pledges. By him also, the Lord Treasurer himself could not receive this debt if he was upon the spot. Therefore, he cannot delegate such power. This warrant if good is, notwithstanding, revocable. And, therefore, if not continued or shown to continue, it is the same thing.

And the order for an attachment was discharged *per omnes*.

388

Mears, *qui tam* v. Hancock

(Ex. 1723)

In this case, the wines in issue were found to have been imported without the payment of duties.

Taussig MS. 311, vol. 1, p. 409

Coram Price and Page at *nisi prius apud* Westminster, Saturday, Hilary term 1722/23.

An information [was brought] against the defendant for the seizure of wines imported not having paid duties. The seizure was proved by a witness. The defense was that the eight hogsheads of wine for which duty was paid by the defendant at Poole and of seven hogsheads more fifteen[1] whereof were bought of the informer sometime before at Southampton and two of another officer at Poole, which had been seized and condemned as forfeited for non-payment of duties. And whether the eight seized were part of the very wines so mixed, as aforesaid,

[1] five *MS.*

was the question of fact. And it seemed somewhat doubtful. And the jury found they were not, for they found a verdict for the king.

An affidavit sworn *coram* justice of the peace and acknowledged to be the defendant's witnesses' hands was read to confront their evidence, seeming to imply the contrary to what they had particularly sworn. But they were not read as affidavits, but as a writing that they had signed.

389

Robinson v. Conibers

(Ex. 1723)

The question in this case was the validity of an arbitration.

Harvard Law School MS. 1082, vol. 1, p. 161, pl. 1

12 February 1722/23.

An action was brought on articles for a horse race and if deposits, to be determined by A. and B. And they did arbitrate that the defendant should pay the plaintiff £15. And for the £15, the action is brought.

Mr. *Philip Ward*, for the defendant, in arrest of judgment, said it does not appear that any difference did arise at all between the plaintiff and the defendant. And, therefore, A. and B. had nothing to do in the matter, being £15 was to be forfeited if they did not start. Being a sum certain, it is not a proper subject matter of an arbitration. 4 Hen. VI, fo. 17, p. 3; 1 Rolle, *Abridgment*, 264, A, 2; Cro. Eliz. 422.[1]

390

Lloyd v. Mackworth

(Ex. 1723)

In a suit for tithes, timber is presumed to be above twenty years growth and not tithable, unless the plaintiff proves the contrary.

One co-defendant can be ordered to pay all of the court costs.

One cannot controvert any part of a master's report unless formal exceptions have been taken thereto.

Taussig MS. 311, vol. 1, p. 419

Hilary term 1722/23.

[1] YB Pas. 4 Hen. VI, f. 17, pl. 3 (1426); 1 Rolle, Abr., *Arbitrement*, sect. R, p. 264; *Sower v. Bradfield* (1595), Croke Eliz. 422, 78 E.R. 663.

To a bill for tithes of wood, the defendants say that the wood was timber, but they do not say they were twenty years old. And it appears by the proofs that the wood cut was used for faggots and cordwood. And, therefore, [it was said] for the plaintiff [Lloyd, rector of Berrington in the County of Salop, there is] no proper defense, first, because no age of the trees [was shown], second, if of age, yet being applied to the use of faggoting and cordwood, it ought to pay tithes according to the case of Greenway and the Duke of Kent's Case.[1]

E contra, for the defendant: We have shown that they were timber trees. And that is enough to let us into the proof that they were *infra crescentiam viginti annorum*.

And of this opinion was the court. And so the plaintiff went into proof to show that the wood was fallen and made into faggots and cordwood was [*blank*].

Per contra: We shall show that all the wood that was cut down and employed in faggoting and cordwood was either made of polls of timber trees about twenty years growth or did arise from the stumps of old timber trees.

Per PRICE: Though Lord Coke says that germins arising from old stools are privileged, yet that does not now pass for current doctrine. And by him and PAGE, most of the coppice wood now in England is of that sort and, therefore, they inclined that it should be tithable.

But it being late in the day, they sent it to the Deputy [Remembrancer] to state the account and to report specially what part of the wood arose from old stools and what was truly coppice or underwood. And so the debate of this point was deferred to the coming in of the report.

Bunbury 126, 145 E.R. 620,
1 Rayner 180, 2 Gwillim 645, 1 Eagle & Younge 788

At Serjeants' Inn. 21 February 1722[/23].

A bill was brought for tithe wood. The defendant insists that it was timber, but he does not say that it was above twenty years' growth.

Per CURIAM: We will presume timber to be above twenty years' growth, unless the plaintiff proves the contrary.

Harvard Law School MS. 1082, vol. 1, p. 161, pl. 2

At Serjeants' Inn. 21 February 1722/23.

A bill was brought for tithe wood. The defendant insists in his answer that it was timber, but he does not say it was above twenty years' growth. It was said for the defendant they cannot be timber if they be not above twenty years' growth.

Per CURIAM: We will presume timber to be above twenty years' growth unless the plaintiff proves the contrary.

So the plaintiff went into proof.

---

[1] *Greenway v. Earl of Kent* (Ex. 1706), Bunbury 98, 145 E.R. 609, Eq. Cases Exch. 546, 644, 1 Rayner 161, 1 Wood 479, 1 Eagle & Younge 677.

Bunbury 138, 145 E.R. 624,
1 Rayner 196, 2 Gwillim 646, 1 Eagle & Younge 792

11 November 1723.

A bill for tithes was brought against two. The defendants answer separately, and there were separate examinations. One defendant made default, and there was now a decree against the other with the whole costs. And the court would not distinguish as to the costs between the two defendants, but left Mackworth to get his contribution from the other as he could.

But note: This, as it seems, can only be by bill.

Harvard Law School MS. 1082, vol. 1, p. 180, pl. 2

Michaelmas term 1723.

This was upon a master's report after a decree, which directed the Deputy [Remembrancer] to state what was due to the plaintiff as rector for tithes of wood, *viz*. what for coppice and what for stubs and roots of old timber trees. And he reported 8s. due for coppice wood and [. . .] for stubs and roots of old timber trees where used for charcoal.

And, for the defendant, we urged that no tithes were due for old timber trees and, therefore, a report being only for 8s., no costs [should be ordered]. But the court ordered costs.

Query whether trunks, roots, toppings, and loppings of old timber trees are tithable.

Taussig MS. 311, vol. 1, p. 548

Trinity term 1723.

This came before the court upon the Master's report whereby the Master reported 8s. was due for tithes of faggots made from underwood and £2 6s. for cordwood cut from the springs of the stools of old trees without saying timber. No exceptions were taken to the report. But the defendant's counsel *ore tenus* objected that no tithes were due for the springs of old trees, which they would understand to be timber trees, and the whole of the other demand amounting but to 8s., the defendant should have costs.

Sed per CURIAM: You cannot be admitted to controvert any part of the report not having taken any exception thereto. And so they confirmed the report with costs to the plaintiff.

391

Harris v. Finlay

(Ex. 1723)

A court of equity will not enforce a harsh contract.

Taussig MS. 311, vol. 1, p. 417

February 21st, setting down of causes, 1723.

Harris applies to Finlay to get a subscription in South Sea [stock]. Finlay gets £500 of the third subscription. And Harris and Finlay borrowed £1000 to pay for it under a notion that £1000 of the subscription should be bought, but £500 of the subscription was only to be gotten, and so £250 of the over-plus of the £500 was paid to Harris and £250 to Finlay, the £500 was paid in for the subscription, and Dr. Finlay was to have half of the benefit of the subscription. The subscription rises. Then, says Finlay, I desire to sell my share. And Harris agreed to become the purchaser of it for £350. The consideration of Finlay's being admitted to one half of this £500 subscription was Finlay's procuring the subscription and the money to pay for it, which was at that [time] reckoned to be a sufficient consideration. And many such bargains were made. Harris gives a note for £600, which was for £250, half part of the over-plus of £500, and the £350 for half of the subscription.

And Harris now exhibits his bill to be relieved against the note.

The note was thus. In consideration that Finlay had made over to Harris his share in £500 of the subscription, which stands in Finlay's name, Harris gives him a note for £600 for his share in the £500 subscription 'when he shall deliver me the said subscription receipt'. And it appeared by the answer that Harris only promised half the profits of the subscription, whereas it was plain that this note was given for a moiety of the subscription itself.

And *per* CURIAM, the note for £600 ought to be delivered up.

GILBERT, baron, now declared that, what he had said of hard bargains being to be executed by a court of equity as well as others, he, upon further consideration, retracted, for he had since that time heard that it had been the constant practice of the courts of equity for thirty years last past not to enforce hard bargains, but to leave them to a jury.

This, I suppose to be with relation to what the baron had said in Harcourt and Thompson's case.[1] And I suppose what he said of the thirty years' practice contrary was what he had been informed by the Chancellor.

392

City of London v. Pricket

(Ex. 1723)

The duty on cheese brought to London is payable by freemen of London as well as by others.

[1] *Harcourt v. Thompson* (Ex. 1721–1723), see above, Case No. 236.

Taussig MS. 311, vol. 1, p. 420

Hilary term 1722/23.

The City of London is entitled to 8d. per tun of all cheese brought to London eastward of the Bridge.

[An English] bill was brought against the owners and masters of the ships who imported the cheese. 3 Lev. 37; tronage.[1]

Defense: The cheese was brought to London from Chester not for immediate sale, but to be delivered at their ships chiefly by freemen, that freemen ought not to pay this duty. And the defendants insisted chiefly on this point, that, though this duty of 8d. per tun was payable by strangers and had been so determined both by the trial at the bar in the King's Bench, 32 Car. II, and by a decree now lately in this court, yet it had never yet been determined that it was payable by freemen, for, by the record of the trial at bar, it does not appear that this point was in question. And, therefore, it was [at the] same time insisted upon for the defendant that it ought not to be read as evidence but overruled, and, for these reasons, they hoped the court would direct an issue to try this point, *scil.* whether freemen were excused from the duty.

But the court was unanimous and decreed an account without directing any issue, the plaintiff's witnesses proving the custom or prescription effectually for sixty years of their own knowledge and by forty years by hearsay from old men and, further, that they never heard of any difference between strangers and freemen, and the defendant's witnesses not denying the payment, but saying that they often paid less than the 8d. and that what they did pay was by compulsion and that they looked upon it as an imposition. And, therefore, the court said they had not the least doubt upon the right and, therefore, it would only be to put the City of London to an unnecessary charge to try an issue concerning a point the court had no doubt about.

Per PAGE: The subject matter of this suit is truly nothing but a plain action of law. But the rights and franchises of the City of London have been at all times looked upon of so great consequence that this court have always countenanced their demands by English bill, though, in other cases, they would have sent the parties to law.

393

Robinson v. Jago

(Ex. 1723)

A court of equity will compel the mortgagee of an advowson to present to the church the nominee of the mortgagor if the mortgagor gives security to redeem the mortgage.

---

[1] *Mayor of London v. Hunt* (1681), 3 Levinz 37, 83 E.R. 565.

Taussig MS. 311, vol. 1, p. 423

Hilary term 1722/23.

A bill was brought by a mortgagor to redeem an estate mortgaged. The mortgagee being in possession and the mortgage including an advowson, the incumbent dies and the mortgagee would take advantage thereof and would present his own son.

And now Mr. *Wilkinson* moved that the mortgagee might be obliged to present such person as the mortgagor should nominate to him for that purpose, the mortgagor being ready to give security to redeem. It was alleged that the mortgagee had appeared and was in contempt for not answering.

And the court said they could not compel the mortgagee to present the mortgagor's nominee, but would grant the mortgagor an injunction against the mortgagee from presenting his own clerk.

Taussig MS. 311, vol. 1, p. 516

Trinity term 1723. Robinson v. Iago and Cowde.

Robert Jago, seised, grants the next presentation to Sabina, his daughter, then mortgages it to Cowde. Then Jago conveys the equity of redemption to Robinson.

The court confirmed the former order that, upon giving security to redeem, the mortgagee should present the mortgagor's nominee.

Harvard Law School MS. 1082, vol. 1, p. 165, pl. 1

22 May 1723.

It was said *per* CURIAM upon a motion by Mr. *Aris* that the mortgagee might present the nominee of the mortgagor though there was only a bill filed to redeem, *inter alia*, a perpetual advowson mortgaged, and, though no answer was yet come in, they made a rule for that purpose and, especially, if the plaintiff gives security to redeem or will bring the money into court, as was offered in this case.

Bunbury 130, 145 E.R. 621

22 May 1723.

There was a bill filed to redeem a perpetual advowson that was mortgaged. And the incumbent dying, the mortgagor moved before the answer came in that the mortgagee might present the nominee of the plaintiff, the mortgagor. And so it was ordered *per* CURIAM, as, it was said, was usual, especially where the plaintiff will give security to redeem or bring the money into court, as was now offered.

Harvard Law School MS. 1082, vol. 1, p. 172, pl. 2

15 June 1723. Robinson v. Goode.

A mortgagee of the next presentation and also of the perpetual advowson, the incumbent being dead, presented his son. The question was whether the mortgagee should present such person as the mortgagor as the plaintiff, who claims under him, should nominate to Goode, the defendant and mortgagee. Now, there was a presentation by the defendant before the motion and a *quare impedit* was brought.

And, therefore, *Sir Constantine Phipps* opposed this motion made on behalf of the plaintiff, that Goode should present according to the plaintiff's nomination.

Note: The assignment of the equity of redemption was made to the plaintiff by one Page.

Mr. *Wilkinson*, for the plaintiff: No answer has yet come in to the plaintiff's bill filed before the death of the incumbent, the plaintiff [being] a purchaser for £1400. Though there has been a presentation, yet, being pending the suit, it may be revoked, and the defendant ought not to take advantage of his own contempt. The plaintiff, at any time before foreclosure, is entitled to the presentation, and he is willing to pay the defendant all his money upon giving security to redeem.

The former order is to stand that the defendant shall present at the nomination of plaintiff.

394

Rex v. Taylor

(Ex. 1723)

A subsequent creditor can enter into a bond to the crown and then get a prerogative writ of extent and thus defeat the priority of other creditors of their common debtor.

Bunbury 127, 145 E.R. 620

8 May 1723.

Newman was indebted to Taylor and others. And Newman committed an act of bankruptcy. Before a commission was taken out, the creditors met in order to settle their shares owing by Newman. Taylor, having executed a bond to the crown, takes out a [writ of] extent against himself. And upon the inquisition taken thereon, Newman was found indebted to Taylor.

It was now moved by Mr. *Bootle* to refer the regularity of entering into this bond by Taylor to the crown and of taking out this extent upon a suggestion that it was done with an intent to strip the rest of the creditors.

But Mr. Attorney General [*Raymond*] opposed it with warmth for the precedent's sake, it never having been done before.

And *per* CURIAM, it was denied.

N.B. The Chief Baron [MONTAGU] doubted whether Newman, who was ignorant of the transactions between the crown and Taylor, shall upon this finding be liable to an immediate extent, but that rather a *scire facias* should first issue against Newman, for there is no plea to this, as there is to a *scire facias*.

Per Baron PRICE: This was the regular way, but, however, that upon an affidavit made that Newman was in a decaying condition and the king's debt likely to be lost, an immediate extent might issue against Newman.

Baron GILBERT thought this last was the right method, for this is more than a debt acknowledged, in which case a *scire facias* might be proper.

Per CURIAM: If a general receiver pays over the money to A. and this is found by inquisition against the receiver, an immediate extent may issue against A., for this is the crown's money. See the Rules of 15 Car. I.

Harvard Law School MS. 1082, vol. 1, p. 162

28 May 1723.

Mr. *Bootle* moved to refer the regularity of entering into a bond to the crown and taking out an extent upon it. Newman was indebted to Taylor and others. And Newman committed an act of bankruptcy. Before a commission was taken out, the creditors met in order to settle their shares owing by Newman. Taylor executed a bond to the crown dated 24th September 1722 and takes out an extent upon that and an inquisition, which finds Newman indebted to Taylor. So, as it was suggested, this was done with an intent to deprive the rest of the creditors of Newman's effects. And, upon this suggestion, he moved as above.

But Attorney General [*Raymond*] opposed it with warmth for the precedent's sake, it never having been done before.

And *per* CURIAM, the motion was denied.

Note: The Chief Baron [MONTAGU] doubted whether, there being an inquisition against Taylor, which inquisition found Newman indebted to Taylor, whether Newman, who was ignorant of the transaction between the crown and Taylor, shall upon this finding be subject to an immediate extent, but that rather that a *scire facias* should issue first against Newman, which PRICE said was the regular way, but, upon an affidavit being made that Newman was in a decaying way and the king's debt likely to be lost, to grant an immediate extent.

Baron GILBERT thought an immediate extent the right process in the case above, for this is more than a debt acknowledged, in which case it might be proper.

The CHIEF BARON was for referring it to the Deputy [Remembrancer] to report the regularity of taking out the extent against Newman, for there is no plea to this as there is to a *scire facias*, and the Deputy is to report whether this method is according to the common course. [. . .] See Rules of 15 Car.

But note, if a general receiver pays over the money to B. and this is found upon an inquisition against the receiver, an immediate extent may issue against B., for this is the crown's own money.

395

Smith v. Green

(Ex. 1723)

Where a judgment debtor is in execution in prison, the judgment creditor must proceed against him within three terms of court.

Harvard Law School MS. 1082, vol. 1, p. 163, pl. 1

10 May 1723.

If a person, against whom, when a judgment is obtained, surrenders himself in discharge of his bail and the plaintiff neglects to proceed against the defendant in two whole terms exclusive of the term wherein the surrender is, the defendant may have in the term following a [writ of] *supersedeas* to the execution upon the judgment so that, if a person surrenders in Michaelmas term, he may have a *supersedeas* in Trinity following if there is no proceeding against him.

But note the practice is different in the Common Bench and the King's Bench.

Bunbury 128, 145 E.R. 620

10 May 1723.

If a person against whom a judgment is obtained surrenders himself in discharge of his bail, as, for instance, in Michaelmas term, and the plaintiff does not proceed against him in the meantime, the defendant may have a *supersedeas* to the execution against him in Trinity term following.

But note the practice is different in the King's Bench and the Common Bench.

396

David v. Jones

(Ex. 1723)

A contract not supported by consideration is not enforceable.

Taussig MS. 311, vol. 1, p. 481

Tuesday, 14 May 1723. Montagu, Price, Page, Gilbert, *praesentibus*.

[To an] action upon the case on a promise to repair a tenement consisting of buildings and land, the defendants plead severally, one that he did repair etc. and one demurs. And it came now to be argued on the demurrer.

[To the] objection it does not appear in the declaration in what respects the premises are out of repair, [he] answered this need not be shown because the plaintiff can only recover damages for what is out of repair. 1 Rolle's *Abr.*, 14.

[To the] objection the assignment of the breach of the promise for not repairing is applied to some things impossible, for the word *praemissa* relates to the whole and so a bill includes the *centum acrae*,[1] [he] answered, as to those things which are incapable of reparation, the breach cannot be applied and, therefore, the word *praemissa* must be taken only to relate to that part of the premises which may be out of repair. The law, to prevent prolixity, does not require you to set forth all the particulars. Moor 806.

[To the] objection that no request to repair is alleged, [he] answered it is set forth that he was requested at B. in the County of Merioneth and this is sufficient, as by Lutw. 115.[2] Second, no request was necessary in this case, as by Lutw. 231; 2 Ventr. 73; Cro. Eliz. 548, 721; 1 Inst. 303.[3]

[To the] objection [there is] no consideration for the promise but it is a lease which might be a lease only at will and so determined before reparation, [he] answered it cannot be taken to be a lease at will, for a demise generally is to be understood of a lease of the freehold and, where there is an actual promise, a consideration will be presumed. Hob. 5; Cro. Eliz. 715;[4] Danvers, *Abr.*, 70. Secondly, a demise at will is sufficient to raise such a promise and [there are] many instances stronger than the present. Hob. 105; Hob. 4, 10; 1 Ventr. 120, 268;[5] Rolle's *Abr.*, 226, 27; Danvers 50. As to the case of Cro. Eliz. 565,[6] cited on the other side, there, it was a consideration executory, but, here, it is executed. Poph. 183;[7] Rolle's *Abr.*, 223, 227, were all cases where it appeared expressly that the demise was at will only, but, in ours, it does not. And, surely, it ought not to be inferred or presumed.

[To the] objection that [no] consideration passed so [it is a] *nudum pactum*, [he] answered the request previous couples the promise to the consideration.

[To the] objection it does not appear when the repairs were to be done and that the defendants have had time to do them, [he] answered this is matter of excuse and ought to be shown on the other side, as by 2 Sanders 419, 219; 6 Coke, Boothie's Case, 31; Inst., 1st part, 208.[8]

---

[1] Sic in MS.

[2] *Reynolds v. Hewett* (1700), 1 Lutwyche 115, 125 E.R. 61.

[3] *Coningsby v. Rodd* (1687), 1 Lutwyche 229, 231, 125 E.R. 120, 121; *Blake v. Clattie* (1689), 2 Ventris 73, 86 E.R. 316; *Capp v. Lancaster* (1597), Croke Eliz. 548, 78 E.R. 794; *Thomson v. Butler* (1599), Croke Eliz. 721, 78 E.R. 955, also Moore K.B. 522, 72 E.R. 733; E. Coke, *First Institute* (1628), f. 303.

[4] *Lane v. Mallory* (1614), Hobart 4, 80 E.R. 154, also 1 Rolle Rep. 26, 81 E.R. 302; *Riggs v. Bullingham* (1599), Croke Eliz. 715, 78 E.R. 949.

[5] *Lampleigh v. Brathwait* (1615), Hobart 105, 80 E.R. 255, also Moore K.B. 866, 72 E.R. 960, 1 Brownlow & Goldesborough 7, 123 E.R. 630; *Lane v. Mallory* (1614), *ut supra*; *Grisley v. Lowther* (1614), Hobart 10, 80 E.R. 161; *Davis v. Wright* (1671), 1 Ventris 120, 86 E.R. 83; *Anonymous* (1675), 1 Ventris 268, 86 E.R. 179.

[6] *Fereby v. Lurkyn* (1597), Croke Eliz. 566, 78 E.R. 810, also Noy 65, 74 E.R. 1033.

[7] *Beven v. Cowling* (1626), Popham 183, 79 E.R. 1277.

[8] *Walton v. Waterhouse* (1672), 2 Williams Saunders 415, 85 E.R. 1226, also 3 Keble 40, 84 E.R. 583; *Bothey v. Smith* (1605), 6 Coke Rep. 30, 77 E.R. 298; E. Coke, *First*

Reply *per Weldon*: Rolle's *Abr.*, 23, § 27,[1] is express that an estate at will is no consideration for a promise; so Cro. Eliz. 565. There are also several cases where *paululum temporis* has been held not to be a good consideration. And as to presuming a consideration or benefit, the court cannot presume any such thing, for the count must always be taken more strongly against the party counting.

Chief Baron [MONTAGU]: I look upon the promise to repair to be too general; secondly, that the lease must be a lease at will, which may be a consideration to raise a promise in some cases though not in other cases. And I think it is not a good consideration in the case before us. Thirdly, no time being set for the repair, it is an objection to the promise itself and takes off from the source of it. And, for these reasons, the demurrer ought to be allowed.

PRICE, ditto: In consideration that he had let is a consideration past. And the case in Croke 565 is a case in point; so there does not appear to be any continuing consideration. Secondly, there ought to have been a request.

PAGE: As it appears by the declaration, the promise is thus. In consideration that A. had let a house to B., by virtue of which B. entered, C. promised to repair. This is plainly a *nudum pactum*.

GILBERT: [There is] no need of any other allegation of the request than is laid here in general, for, wherever a request is of the essence of a promise, there, a request must be expressly laid. In other cases, a *saepius requisitus* is sufficient. But here is no sufficient consideration. And, for that, I depend on the authorities in Cro. Eliz. and Popham. And we cannot intend it a lease for life because there is no livery of seisin. Therefore, it is to be looked upon as a *nudum pactum*.

And judgment was given for the defendant.

Harvard Law School MS. 1082, vol. 1, p. 163, pl. 2

15 May 1723.

[An action was brought in] *assumpsit* in consideration that the plaintiff would make a lease for a certain yearly rent, the defendant promised to put the premises in repair, and that the defendant had not put them in repair though requested. The defendant demurred.

Lord Chief Baron [MONTAGU]: It shall be intended that this is only a lease at will and, therefore, it was not a sufficient consideration unless upon a positive promise to pay rent, but it will not be a good consideration for the payment of twenty or repair because the plaintiff may, Cro. Eliz. 565; Rolle, *Abridgment*, 125 [?],[2] determine his will as soon as the money is paid or repairs done. See the cases above.

Institute (1628), f. 208.

[1] *Kent v. Pratt* (1610), 1 Rolle, Abr., *Action sur Case*, pl. V, 27, p. 23.

[2] *Fereby v. Lurkyn* (1597), *ut supra*; perhaps *Cruse v. Berrie* (1633), 1 Rolle, Abr., *Action sur Case*, pl. V, 35, p. 25.

[To the] objection it was not mentioned what time the defendant had to repair, he was of opinion that this declaration was too uncertain, both as to the consideration and the promise. And so were the rest of the court, and judgment was given for the defendant.

397

Evans v. Newell

(Ex. 1723)

Assart lands are woodlands that were grubbed up and turned into agricultural lands.

In this case, the plaintiffs failed to prove their right to tithes of wood.

Taussig MS. 311, vol. 1, p. 484

Easter term 1723. Evans, vicar of Newland, and the bishop of Llandaff v. Neville *et al.*

The plaintiff, as vicar of Newland, exhibits his bill for tithe wood arising from certain woods within in the Forest of Dean by virtue of a grant of Edward I of assart lands within the forest, which was made to the bishop of Llandaff for the augmentation of the vicarage, and for the tithes of other lands lying within the parish of Newland.

By the answer, the defendants insist that some of the lands lie within the parish of Lindley and so are liable to the vicar of Lindley. And the defendants objected that the Attorney General ought to be a party, as likewise the vicar of Lindley.

Chief Baron [Montagu]: The plaintiffs' demand is of extra-parochial [tithes] and also of tithes within the parish of Newland. If either not extra-parochial or not within Newland, then the plaintiff has no right and it would be very hard to oblige the plaintiff to make the vicar of Lindley a defendant because the defendants say the lands are in another parish.

Secondly, the crown is not interested in this controversy, but only the patentees. And so the objections [should be] overruled.

Anno 33rd Edw. I [1304 x 1305], a grant [was made] to the bishop of Llandaff *omnes decimas de assartis infra forestam de novo assartatis et assartandis dum licit assarta, scil. extra aliquas parochia quascunque.*[1]

N.B. The court suffered the plaintiff to read evidence to explain the meaning and understanding of the word assart land and that woodlands not grubbed up might be assart lands, which seemed strange to me.

[1] all tithes of assarts within a forest new assarted or to be assarted as long as he permits the assart, to wit outside of any parish whatsoever.

Taussig MS. 311, vol. 1, p. 491

Easter term 1723.

The court, now, upon recollection, were perfectly satisfied that assart lands signified woodlands grubbed up. But they said, if there had been usually tithes paid of wood, it would have been some sort of evidence that these lands might have been formerly asserted and then turned to wood again. And there being no proof of that sort, the court thought the bill ought to be dismissed as to the pretense of the assart lands. Blount's *Nomo Lexicon* and Spelman, *verbo* 'assart'.[1]

Sir Constantine Phipps said that Lord Pomfret and Lord Halifax had each of them grants of asserted woods; if so, wood ground and asserted lands cannot be a contradiction.

Chief Baron [Montagu]: I believe it is true that Lord Halifax may have a grant of what the country people call sart woods. But I always understood it in this sense, that the woodlands had in reality been assarted, but, not turning to account, had been again either sowed with acorns or let run into coppice, which the very nature of some sort of soil will produce.

Harvard Law School MS. 1082, vol. 1, p. 163, pl. 3

20 May 1723.

A bill was brought for tithe of wood of all extra-parochial lands within the Forest of Dean by virtue of a grant by Edward I of all tithes issuing *de assartis* within the said Forest *de novo assartatis et assartandis*.

Mr. *Bootle*, for the defendant: According to the legal understanding of the word assart, it is only such lands as have been grubbed up and made fit for tillage. Spelman, *Glossarium*, '*de assartis*'; Manwood, cap. 9.[2]

Mr. *Ward*: [It was] objected for the plaintiff [that] assart lands are only forest lands granted by the crown, [he] responded this is contrary to all the authorities. Stat. 4 Edw. I.[3] This comes either from *exarendo* or *asserendo*; it is still contrary to their construction. Register.

[To the] objection it may be presumed that these lands were once assarted, but are become woodland again, [he] responded all the proof runs that it is and always has been woodlands and there is not the least proof of its ever having been otherwise, nor is there any proof of tithes having ever been paid, and the defendants deny that they were ever called assart lands or were within the description of assart land.

Sir Constantine Phipps replied: The defendants ought not to put it upon us to prove that these lands were once assarted. [For] the definition of assart lands, see

[1] T. Blount, *Law Dictionary*; H. Spelman, *Archaeologus*.

[2] H. Spelman, *Archaeologus*; J. Manwood, *Laws of the Forest*.

[3] Stat. 25 Edw. I, *Carta de Foresta*, c. 4 (*SR*, I, 120).

DuFresne; Blunt, *Law Dictionary*, *verbo 'assart'*,[1] it being to glade or make a glade in a wood. Woods asserted may be and have been granted. Now, if the woods must be grubbed up, then they are not assarted woods. Grants of this kind [were made] to Lord Pomfret and the earl of Halifax in Salcy Forest.

Per CURIAM: It does not appear that these lands were ever assarted. See Manwood. And the bill, as to this demand, was dismissed.

Bunbury 128, 145 E.R. 620,
1 Rayner 187, 2 Gwillim 645, 1 Eagle & Younge 788

20 May 1723.

A bill was brought for the tithe wood of all extra-parochial lands within the Forest of Dean by virtue of a grant from King Edward I of all tithes issuing *de assartis* within the forest *de novo assartatis et assartandis*. But, by the proofs, it appeared that these lands never were grubbed up, but were always woodlands, and no tithes were ever paid.

Note: The debate in this case was principally upon the meaning of the word 'assart'.

And *per* CURIAM, it is only such lands as have been grubbed up and made fit for tillage. And the bill was dismissed.

Sir Constantine Phipps [was] for the plaintiff; Mr. *Bootle* and Mr. *Ward* [were] for the defendant.

[Order of 26 May 1723: 2 Wood 212.]

398

Parish of Stoughton's Case

(Ex. 1723)

Money levied for not repairing a highway is payable to the surveyor of the highways, and not to the sheriff.

Taussig MS. 311, vol. 1, p. 487

[Easter term 1723.]

Mr. Serjeant *Stevens* moved that issues which had been levied by process issuing out of this court upon the parish of Stoughton in Worcestershire for not repairing their ways might be repaid to the parish or else it might be paid into court and the sheriff might be discharged upon his account.

Sed per CURIAM: The Act[2] provides that this money is not to be returned into the Exchequer, but it ought to be paid to the surveyor of the highways. The

[1] C. Dufresne, sieur Du Cange, *Glossarium*; T. Blount, *Law Dictionary*.

[2] Stat. 3 Will. & Mar., c. 12, s. 13 (*SR*, VI, 318).

court said the sheriff need not charge himself with the money in his account, but should pay it over to the surveyor of the highways.

399

Anonymous

(Ex. 1723)

Proceedings on a seizure of a ship can be removed out of the Court of Admiralty into the Court of Exchequer.

Taussig MS. 311, vol. 1, p. 488, pl. 1

[Friday, the 17th of May 1723.]

On the same day, Mr. *Bootle* moved for a [writ of] prohibition to the Admiralty Court on a warrant of theirs to seize five-eighths of a ship.

Per Lord Chief Baron [MONTAGU]: My brothers know my opinion upon this point; so I must leave it to them.

Per PRICE: We have always done it since I sat here. And so, by him and the others, a prohibition was granted.

400

Lord Coningsby v. Churchyard

(Ex. 1723)

A lord of a manor can have a discovery of the court rolls of the manor.

Taussig MS. 311, vol. 1, p. 488, pl. 2

Saturday, 18th [May] 1723. On a demurrer to an English bill.

Lord Coningsby exhibits his bill and sets forth that he is possessed and entitled to the manor of Marden and, as lord thereof, he prays a discovery of deeds and surveys, rent rolls, and court rolls and to have an account of arrears of rents and profits and to have relief. The defendants, by the bill, are suggested to be tenants of the manor or to hold lands belonging to the manor.

Fazakerly for the demurrer: My Lord ought to show he is so entitled as to have a right to the evidences, which, unless he be a tenant of the inheritance, he ought not to have, as by the first case in Coke's report.[1]

And *Foley* cited the case of Penny and Hopper.[2]

---

[1] *Lord Buckhurst v. Fenner* (1598), 1 Coke Rep. 1, 76 E.R. 1, also Moore K.B. 488, 72 E.R. 713, 2 Anderson 118, 123 E.R. 576, Tothill 141, 21 E.R. 148, 117 Selden Soc. 155, 221.

[2] *Penny v. Hopper* (Ex. 1722–1724), see above, Case No. 336.

Chief Baron [Montagu]: I am sorry to see such a demurrer signed by counsel which has no color in it, for My Lord in his bill says he is seised, which must be of a freehold at least. Now, unless you can make it out that a tenant for life is not entitled to the court rolls of his manor, there is nothing at all in the point.

The demurrer, therefore, was overruled.

401

Taylor v. Crayhorne

(Ex. 1723)

Where a court is equally divided upon the hearing of a demurrer, the demurrer will be overruled but without costs awarded.

The question in this case was whether the plaintiff, the lessee of the tithes of an impropriate rectory, had adequately alleged his title to the tithes.

Taussig MS. 311, vol. 1, p. 489

Easter term 1723.

Redman, being seised of a fee or of some other estate of inheritance or possessed for some long term or otherwise entitled either in his own right or in trust for Redman and others particularly named, made him a lease of the impropriation, and so he demands an account of the tithes. And a demurrer was put in to this bill, and cause was shown in the demurrer that the plaintiff had not shown any title.

Bootle insisted that this was uncertain.

Sir Constantine Phipps, contra: *Firmarius* is enough at common law, and this is much more full. In the case of Penny and Hopper,[1] it was not so much as alleged that Sir Herbert Crofts had any estate at all.

Chief Baron [Montagu]: There is a difference between this case and the case of Penny and Hopper, for, in that case, it was only said that Sir Herbert Crofts was possessed of a long term and leased to the plaintiff and there was no title either set forth or indeed proved in Sir Herbert Crofts. If, at trial, this lease in Sir Herbert Crofts had been proved, perhaps it had been well enough. And by him and Gilbert, this will be sufficient.

Page: The title here alleged does not come up to saying that he was seised or possessed and so does not import he was a *firmarius* or *proprietarius* because a man may be entitled who is out of possession.

Price: I think every plaintiff ought to set forth his title certainly if he claims under a rector, much more under a lay impropriator.

---

[1] *Penny v. Hopper* (Ex. 1722–1724), see above, Case No. 336.

CHIEF BARON: [There is] no difference between a lay impropriator and a rector, and there is not one law book that says a rector may not declare as *firmarius* or *proprietarius*.

PRICE: I think there is a difference between a lay and a spiritual person. And he cited the case of Bateman and Nunn.[1]

But the CHIEF BARON said, as the truth was, that, in this case, there is an appeal to the Chancellor.

And the demurrer was overruled without costs by the proposal of PRICE, though he and PAGE were strongly for it.

1 Rayner 189, 1 Eagle & Younge 795

The plaintiff, [William Taylor, Esq.,] exhibited his bill this term in the Court of Exchequer against the defendant, [Ralph Crayhorne, Esq.], stating that William Redman of York, Esquire, being seised in fee or of some other estate of inheritance or possessed for some long term of years or otherwise entitled in his own right or in trust for his children, William Redman, Watkinson Redman, and Alice, the wife of Richard Atkinson, in and to all those the tenths and tithes of corn, grain, hay, and other tithes, as well great as small, of what nature and kind soever, with all and singular the rights, members, and appurtenances yearly arising and growing within the villages, fields, and hamlets of Eastnesse, Crook Holme, and South Holme, within the parish of Hovingham in the County of York, by indenture dated 27th January 1721 made between the said William Redman of the one part and the plaintiff of the other part, the same Redman demised to the plaintiff all and singular the said tithes of corn, grain, and hay with all and singular their rights, members, and appurtenances yearly and from time to time coming, growing, increasing, and renewing within the villages, fields, and hamlets of Eastnesse, Crook Holme, and South Holme, or in any of them within the parish of Hovingham aforesaid and late belonging to the dissolved monastery of Newbrough in the said county and all other the tithes, as well great as small, with their and every of their rights, members, and appurtenances of whatsoever nature, kind, or condition the same were, and all his, the said William Redman's, right, title, interest, claim, and demand whatsoever, as trustee for his said children, of, in, or to the said tithes and premises, or any part thereof, to hold the same to the plaintiff, his executors, administrators, and assigns, from the 25th of March preceding the date of the said indenture for twenty-one years under the yearly rent of £20, that by this lease, the plaintiff became fully and legally entitled to receive or otherwise to have a satisfaction made to him for all the said tithes growing or arising within all or any of the places aforesaid, that the defendant, who was owner and occupier of several lands, pasture, and meadow within Eastnesse aforesaid, refused to pay the plaintiff, or to make

[1] *Bateman v. Nunn* (Ex. 1722), see above, Case No. 312.

him any satisfaction, for the small tithes and herbage arising from the appellant's lands in Eastnesse aforesaid or which did grow or renew in the year 1721 out or upon the said lands and grounds. Wherefore, the bill prayed that the defendant might set forth the particular quantities and values of the said tithes and that the plaintiff might have a satisfaction for the same and be otherwise relieved in the premisses.

To this bill, the defendant demurred. And for the causes of demurrer, he alleged that the plaintiff had not by his bill set forth, as he ought to have done, how William Redman, who thereby appeared to be a layman, became entitled to the tithes demanded by the said bill, whether by grant, prescription, or otherwise, or what estate the said William Redman had in the said tithes, or whether he had power to demise the same, or that any estate in the said tithes did or could pass from the said William Redman to the plaintiff, for which reasons and other defects in the said bill, the defendant prayed the judgment of the court whether he should be compelled to make any further or other answer thereto. And he prayed to be dismissed with costs.

On the 28th of May 1723, this demurrer was argued, when the court were divided in opinion, the Lord Chief Baron MONTAGU, and Mr. Baron GILBERT being for overruling it, and Mr. Baron PRICE and Mr. Baron PAGE for allowing it. Whereupon, according to the course and practice of the court in such cases, the demurrer was ordered to be overruled but without costs and the defendant should put in his answer to the said bill.

[Order of 26 January 1727: 2 Wood 273.]

[Affirmed on appeal: 2 Brown P.C. 512, 1 E.R. 1099, 2 Gwillim 650.]

402

Burwell v. Coates

(Ex. 1723)

In a claim for tithes, the plaintiff can allege his right in general terms.

A modus decimandi *in lieu of tithes in kind that is uncertain in extent is void.*

An issue in this case was whether the clergy are exempt from the Statute of Limitations.

Harvard Law School MS. 1082, vol. 1, p. 164

Easter term 1723.

A bill was brought by an impropriator, *inter alia*, for tithe hay in the parish of Normanby in the County of Lincoln. The defendant insists upon this *modus* for tithe hay, except in Motley Meadow, that there has been time out of mind payable to the impropriators and their lessees 4s. payable at Easter for and in lieu of tithe hay arising on his farm.

Mr. *Ward*, for the defendant, insisted, first, that here was no tithe set forth by the plaintiff, for that he only says that he was possessed of a term of years by demise from the Dean and Chapter of Lincoln. And he cited the case of Penny v. Hooper.[1]

Mr. *Browne*, for the defendant: Even in a case of a vicar, where a *modus* is insisted upon, the vicar must prove his tithe. Powell v. Powell, sittings after Hilary 1720; Town of Warwick v. Lucas.[2]

Lord Chief Baron [MONTAGU] asked whether there are any instances that there is a difference between setting out the tithe of a lay and a spiritual rector.

Baron PRICE: Here is a lessee of a dean and chapter, which I do not look upon as a lay impropriator, for, if a lay impropriator brings an [action of] ejectment, he must prove his possession within twenty years, but a parson need not. And I think there is a great difference between a lay impropriator and a spiritual parson. *Vide ante* Bateman v. [*blank*].[3]

Baron PAGE: A tithe in a lay hand is no more than a fee farm or a quit rent. The estate and interest of a lay impropriator differs very much from that of a spiritual parson. The first might alien his tithes, the other could not. Deans and chapters are restrained by the acts.[4]

[To the] objection the plaintiff, having received the 4s., shall be concluded as to the time he seeks relief in a bill against his own acceptance, he responded, if he suggests any fraud, he shall be admitted notwithstanding his acceptance to demand his tithes in kind. Query, unless he can make it out to be an imposition.

Baron GILBERT: If general allegations are proper in the case of an ecclesiastical person, the same ought to be admitted without any distinction in the case of a lay person. This is as to the issue to be joined, but, as to the *probata*, there is great difference arising from their different interests. And this is the true distinction between the *allegata* and the *probata*. I think general allegations would do in both cases.

The LORD CHIEF BARON thought this was a lay impropriator.

Sir Constantine Phipps, for the plaintiff: Wherever a title is good at law, it surely is good in equity. The title is well enough set forth here.

The LORD CHIEF BARON said there could be no *non decimando* in a case of a lay impropriator anymore than of a spiritual person. He took it that the Dean and Chapter in this case were to be looked upon as a lay impropriator. The only difference between a dean and chapter and a lay impropriator is only that the first

---

[1] *Penny v. Hopper* (Ex. 1722–1724), see above, Case No. 336.

[2] *Powell v. Powell* (Ex. 1721), see above, Case No. 172; see *Corporation of Warwick v. Lucas* (1711), Eq. Cases Exch. 671, Public Record Office, E.126/19, ff. 191, 221.

[3] *Bateman v. Nunn* (Ex. 1722), see above, Case No. 312.

[4] Stat. 13 Eliz. I, c. 10 (*SR*, IV, 544–545).

are restrained by the Stat. 13 Eliz.[1] The Statute of Limitations, 21 [Jac.],[2] does not extend to a spiritual person because the law looks upon him to be always under age.

Sir Constantine Phipps: This is a void *modus* for all the meadow ground, for it can go no further than the ancient meadows. Hetley 94; Hutton 58.[3]

Mr. *Gilly*: This is uncertain because it is for all the lands in the defendant's occupation, which may vary to be sometimes more, sometimes less.

Mr. *Cox*: This *modus* is void because it may introduce a fraud, for, if the farmer should turn all his arable ground into meadow, he would be discharged for the whole for only 4s.

Mr. *Ward* replied for the defendant: We do not confine our *modus* to all the lands etc., but set forth particular lands and, then, confine our *modus* to them. And we do not pretend to cover any other lands than those. And, therefore, the objection as to the old and new gardens does not extend to this case. There are but two sorts of *modus*es, one that goes to the extinguishment of all the tithes or such as goes to the particular species of tithes. Bate v. Hodges.[4]

Mr. *Browne*: A *modus* is good for farms and lands. Bishop v. Arrundle, 1706; a *modus* for the farm and lands of £25 *per annum*.[5]

Lord Chief Baron: *Judicium curiae.* First, the tithe is well set forth, *per* TOTAM CURIAM. Secondly, the defendant has failed in proof that the plaintiff had received the 4s. in discharge of all the tithes, and, therefore, there is no occasion to enter into that proof. The receipt of the lessee shall conclude the right of the lessor. This *modus* is uncertain and void, it not being certain what a farm consists of and it is laid too loose. And, therefore, it ought not to be sent to a trial.

Taussig MS. 311, vol. 1, p. 492

Easter term 1723.

The plaintiff, as lessee of the dean and chapter of Lincoln of the impropriate rectory of Normanby in the County of Lincoln, exhibits his bill for tithes.

[To the] first objection that no title is set forth in the dean and chapter, [he] answered the dean and chapter are spiritual persons, so no title or payment of tithes need be shown. It is otherwise in a case of a lay impropriation.

---

1 Stat. 13 Eliz. I, c. 10 (*SR*, IV, 544–545).

2 Stat. 21 Jac. I, c. 16 (*SR*, IV, 1222–1223).

3 *Thornhill's Case* (1628), Hetley 93, 124 E.R. 369, 1 Eagle & Younge 362; *Poole v. Reynolds* (1622), Hutton 57, 123 E.R. 1098, also Winch 1, 44, 124 E.R. 1, 38, 1 Eagle & Younge 322.

4 *Bate v. Hodges* (Ex. 1723–1724), see above, Case No. 384.

5 *Bishop v. Arundel* (1704), Dodd 205, 1 Rayner 98, 1 Eagle & Younge 664, 2 Gwillim 585, 1 Wood 459.

[To the] second objection, that this bill is for tithes in kind, where the parson has actually accepted of a sum in money in lieu thereof and, therefore, he ought not to demand the tithes in kind for the self-same years.

Chief Baron [MONTAGU]: I think a bill is good without setting forth a title to the tithes any more than in general.

GILBERT [held] to the same effect.

Sed per the CHIEF BARON: If it is not good, then it is not good in a case of a spiritual anymore than in a case of a lay impropriator.

PRICE and PAGE *contra*.

Sir Constantine Phipps: A *modus* for hay can only extend to ancient meadow. Hetley 94; Hutton 58.

N.B. The CHIEF BARON said that the reason why a lay impropriator must prove possession within twenty years and a spiritual person need not is because one is within and the other not within the Statute of Limitations *quia ecclesia tangitur vice minoris* and so is within the exception in the Statute.

But this point of a difference between a lay and a spiritual impropriator was not determined.

As to the acceptance of a sum of money as a *modus*, there was a variety of evidence. And the court thought the evidence against the acceptance was much the stronger and the *modus* is not alleged and applied to all the lands in the defendant's occupation, but is applied to a farm, and that is uncertain.

Bishop v. Arundel is *contra*, that a *modus* applied to a farm is good; Easter 1706.

CHIEF BARON: A farm is uncertain. One year it consists of more and another of a less quantity of ground; much more of a farm and lands in occupation.

And the defendants were decreed to an account for want of proof of their *modus*.

Bunbury 129, 145 E.R. 621,
1 Rayner 188, 2 Gwillim 646, 1 Eagle & Younge 788

10 May 1723.

A bill was brought by the plaintiff, as lessee of the impropriate rectory of Normanby in the County of Lincoln under the Dean and Chapter of Lincoln, for tithe hay. It was insisted upon for the defendant that the plaintiff, being a lay impropriator, had not set forth a sufficient title. And upon that, the long controverted question, whether there was any difference between a lay and a spiritual person, claiming tithes, was revived. But it was not now determined, for, *per* CURIAM, the title was well enough set forth in the present case.

The defendant insisted upon a *modus* of 4s. payable at Easter in lieu of tithe hay arising on his farm and other lands particularly set forth.

But *per* CURIAM, this is a void *modus* because it may introduce a fraud, for, if a farmer should turn all his arable land into meadow, he would be discharged of the whole for 4s. Besides, it is too uncertain, it not being certain what a farm consists of.

Mr. *Ward* and Mr. *Browne* [were] for the defendant; *Sir Constantine Phipps* [was] for the plaintiff.